HEATH BIOLOGY
CONNECTIONS

Douglas J. Yack
Philip G. DeSantis
Garnet J. Dobsky
Ronald E. Phillips
Jean Bullard

HEATH

D.C. Heath Canada Ltd.

To Homer, Doris, Monica, Peter, and Stephanie; Kathleen; Susan and Sarah; Paige, Shannon, Laurel, and Al; and John F. Trant.

Acknowledgements
The authors wish to extend sincere thanks to the following people who worked diligently to make this book a reality:
Design   Jack Steiner Graphic Design
Developmental Editor   Jean Bullard
Stylistic and Copy Editor   Louise M. Oborne
Photo Research   Jane Affleck
Illustration   Celia Godkin/ Jackie Heda/ Jim Loates/ Lisette Mallet/ Joe Stevens, Full Spectrum Art/ Peter Van Gulik/ Jane Whitney
Feature Writers   Julie E. Czerneda/ Kathleen Gibson/ Jo Mrozewski/ Judy Ross
Photography   Birgitte Nielsen
Typesetting   Compeer Typographic Services Ltd.

The authors thank the interview subjects of the science-related careers for their time and effort.

The authors also thank their colleagues John Pettit and Ken Liscombe, who reviewed the manuscript during its development.

Canadian Cataloguing in Publication Data

Main entry under title:

Heath biology connections 11

For use in secondary schools.
Bibliography: p.
Includes index.
ISBN 0-669-95300-8

1. Biology. I. Yack, Douglas J. II. Title: Biology connections 11.

QH308.7.H42 1989   574   C89-093724-9

ISBN 0-669-95300-8

Printed and bound in Canada
    2 3 4 5 6 7 8 9 BP 98 97 96 95 94 93 92 91 90

C O N T E N T S

UNIT I

The Study of Life
I

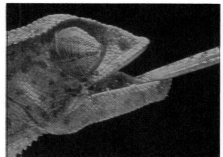

UNIT II

Animals
67

UNIT III

Plants and Fungi 371

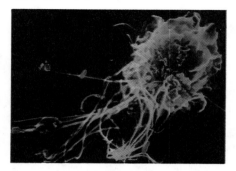

The Study
of Life

CHAPTER

1

A World of Diversity

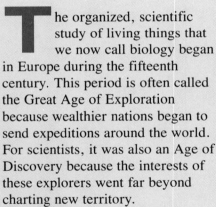

The organized, scientific study of living things that we now call biology began in Europe during the fifteenth century. This period is often called the Great Age of Exploration because wealthier nations began to send expeditions around the world. For scientists, it was also an Age of Discovery because the interests of these explorers went far beyond charting new territory.

In addition to navigators and map makers, most major expeditions also carried a naturalist whose job was to collect samples of new plants or animals. Everywhere they travelled, these naturalists found incredible diversity among living things, and they brought back an amazing variety of specimens — some alive, some preserved, and some in the form of sketches.

In only three centuries, 50 000 new kinds of organisms were collected. At first, scholars were overwhelmed, but soon they began to develop methods to investigate the underlying similarities of these organisms. Their efforts eventually led them to an understanding of the fundamental unity behind the diversity of life.

The organized study of life has changed the world just as the explorers did. When the big ships first set sail, few children survived infancy, and few adults lived beyond their early thirties. Plant diseases caused widespread famine, and nobody understood what caused human diseases. Biological science has solved many of these problems, but the voyage of discovery is far from over. Biological discoveries still have a major impact on the

world you live in, and that makes it a worthwhile study for everyone.

Whether you plan to become a scientist, or not, your life will be affected by biological discoveries. Future lawyers will need to understand the legal implications of genetic engineering. Future engineers will need to understand how to generate power without polluting the environment. And future politicians will need to understand the importance of biological research. In fact, everyone will need a knowledge of biology to help build a better future for all of the living things that share this planet.

Chapter Objectives

When you complete this chapter, you should:

1. Appreciate the historical context of scientific and technological achievements, and the connection between science and technology with specific reference to the development of microscopy.

2. Understand the basic principles of microscopy and appreciate the role played by the microscope in increasing scientific awareness of the diversity of living things.

3. Develop skill in using reference materials from your school's resource centre as well as current journals and telemedia resources to gather information relevant to biological problems.

4. Understand the concept of species, demonstrate skill in using binomial nomenclature, and be able to describe its advantages over the use of common names.

5. Understand the role of organizational techniques such as classification in making biological information more manageable.

6. Use appropriate terms such as autotroph and heterotroph to describe the interaction-based system that ecologists use to classify living things.

7. Appreciate the complex links that exist between organisms and their environments, and relate them to adaptations and diversity.

8. Appreciate that humans and all other simple or complex organisms interact directly or indirectly with all living things.

9. Be able to define taxonomy and be able to describe the challenges faced by taxonomists in their efforts to establish standards for biological classification.

10. Be able to identify the major categories of the five-kingdom classification system, and briefly describe the characteristics of each.

11. Develop a respect for living things, appreciate their complexity, and be able to recognize the importance of biological studies in everyone's education.

Observing Earth from space shows how thin and fragile the biosphere is.

In this textbook, you will find words in **bold** type. These terms appear in the glossary and often in the *Key Words* at the end of each chapter. You should pay special attention to these words. To help you remember key concepts and terms, some **boldface** words appear more than once.

DID YOU KNOW?
Many hunter-gatherer societies named only the parts of their environment that had a significant impact on the life of their group. Organisms were often named in a way that described a characteristic or a use. In the language of some Pacific Coast Indians, the name for rabbit translates as "hops-a-lot" while the name for a certain shellfish means "walks-like-a-dog." One society had 80 names to describe water conditions but only one for red-flowering plants.

Some societies still depend on early technology to make use of their environment. These Penan hunters use blowpipes and poisoned dart quivers to obtain food. But the tropical rain forest in Sarawak in northwest Borneo is being destroyed rapidly, threatening the survival of one of the last hunter-gatherer societies.

1.1 Observing the World of Diversity

The Age of Exploration has never really ended. Wealthy nations are still launching voyages of discovery. But today we send scientists and automatic cameras into orbit around the Earth or toward distant planets. These voyages give us a view early scientists could only dream of, but as yet no other planet shows the remarkable variety of surface features found on Earth.

The visible layer that space travellers see when they return to Earth is often called the **biosphere** — *bios* means life — because it is the only part of Earth where living things can survive. Even from a height of 400 km, it is clear that the biosphere includes many different environments. Within a few hours, an orbiting observer passes over saltwater oceans, freshwater lakes, stagnant swamps, fertile plains, rocky mountains, ice caps, deserts, and rain forests. But the diversity of these environments is more than matched by the variety of organisms that inhabit them.

The first observations of living things were made by early hunter-gatherers. Their knowledge of animal habits, seasonal cycles, and plant properties helped them develop technology to meet their needs for food, shelter, clothing, and safety. **Technology** refers to the knowledge, the tools, and the techniques that enable a society to make use of natural resources. Early societies knew a

1 THE STUDY OF LIFE

great deal about useful, edible, or harmful organisms, but they knew very little about living things that did not have an impact on their daily lives.

By 2500 B.C., ancient Egyptians were keeping extensive environmental records. The resulting body of knowledge about seasons, weather, and flooding patterns of the Nile helped them develop efficient farming technology. They also developed surgical techniques and methods for manufacturing plant products such as paper, dyes, and preservatives. However, despite their technology, ancient Egyptians still had a rudimentary knowledge of the nature of living things.

The study of living things to satisfy intellectual curiosity began in ancient Greece. By 600 B.C., some individuals were spending their lives as full-time thinkers or **philosophers.** Many early philosophers believed they could understand the universe through reasoning alone. Some claimed their thoughts were more real than the universe itself, placing little value on observational skills. This idea was challenged by the philosopher Aristotle (384-322 B.C.).

Aristotle was a skilled observer and collected a great deal of data on many topics. Around 334 B.C., he formally organized a set of observations about the environment in which he and his students attempted to describe all the living things they knew and had observed. Their list soon grew so long — around 1000 organisms — that they reorganized it into two **"kingdoms."** Organisms that grew from the ground were assigned to the vegetable or **plant kingdom.** Those that moved about to hunt or gather food were assigned to the **animal kingdom.**

By 1500 B.C., the agricultural technology of ancient Egypt included wooden ploughs. The ability of ancient Egyptians to tame animals and cultivate plants made them independent of animal migration and free to develop other kinds of technology.

DID YOU KNOW?

The practice of mummifying human remains for burial gave Egyptian physicians the opportunity to gain a great deal of medical knowledge. They understood the significance of the heartbeat and the heart's relation to the rest of the human body.

Aristotle identified about 1000 different kinds of living things within a few kilometres of his Mediterranean home.

Naturalists found thousands of new kinds of organisms in the colder environment of northern Europe.

Aristotle defined natural philosophy as the study of change. He wrote extensively on the nature of change, as well as on many other subjects — psychology, logic, literature, and reality.

There seem to be as many definitions of science as there are textbooks and teachers. In Chapter 2, you will learn about the nature of science in greater detail.

DID YOU KNOW?

Ancient Greece declined as the Roman Empire spread across the Mediterranean and into what is now Europe. The Romans were more interested in putting what they had learned about nature to practical use instead of trying to understand it. As the Roman Empire declined, scholars turned to religion, and philosophers debated matters that could not be tested by experiment such as the number of angels that could dance on the head of a pin. But traces of the old empires remained. The Romans left their language, and the Greeks left their learning.

DID YOU KNOW?

Many modern scientific terms are derived from the languages used by early scholars. European naturalists wrote to each other in Latin, but they used many of Aristotle's Greek terms. This mini dictionary will help you understand the meanings of some scientific terms as you encounter them.

Root	Meaning
logy	study of
makros	great
mikros	small
phileo/philos	love/loving
skopeo/skopeein	look at
sophos	wise
techno/techne	art/craft

Which convex lens magnifies the most? How does it differ from the other?

Aristotle's teachings about the diversity, structure, and nature of plants and animals influenced scientific thought far beyond his lifetime. However, his studies would not meet today's standards for scientific investigation. **Science** is defined as the discovery of how the world works through observation, measurement, and experiment, as well as through reason and thought. Aristotle reached many incorrect conclusions because he did not perform experiments to test his ideas. Nevertheless, his writings were preserved and taught for many centuries because people believed they contained the sum of all human knowledge.

Interest in the study of living things declined after A.D. 400. Its revival, which took place around A.D. 1400, shifted the centre of scholarship from the Mediterranean to northern Europe. Scholars who took an interest in the world around them became known as natural philosophers or **naturalists.** At first, they depended on Greek writings and regarded Aristotle as an authority. But once they began to observe their own environment, most naturalists realized that living things were far more diverse than Aristotle had supposed. By 1600, the number of known living things had increased from 1000 to 10 000.

Technology for Observing the Natural World

Early naturalists were limited to observing **macroscopic** objects. Macroscopic objects are those that can be seen by the unaided eye. Convex lenses were not used to magnify the fine details of objects until Italian monks began to grind eyeglasses around A.D. 1100. Five more centuries passed before lenses were used as **microscopes** to view **microscopic** objects, which are objects too small to be seen by the unaided eye. The use of microscopes to view objects is called **microscopy.**

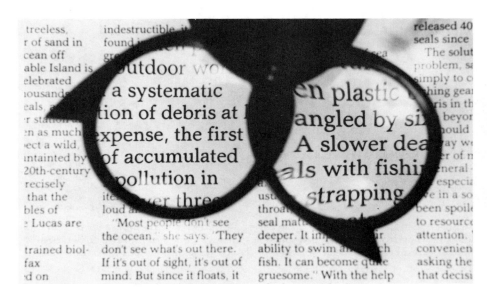

I THE STUDY OF LIFE

LABORATORY EXERCISE 1-1
Investigating the Principles of Microscopy

A microscope is a device that enlarges the image of a small object. Early microscopes were of two kinds: simple (containing one lens) or compound (containing more than one lens). In this exercise, you will investigate the most basic principles of microscopy by building some unusual models of simple and compound microscopes.

The Science-Technology Cycle

Both science and technology rely on investigative techniques such as observation, measurement, and experiment, but there is an important difference between them. (See Figure 1-1.) Science seeks to find out how the world

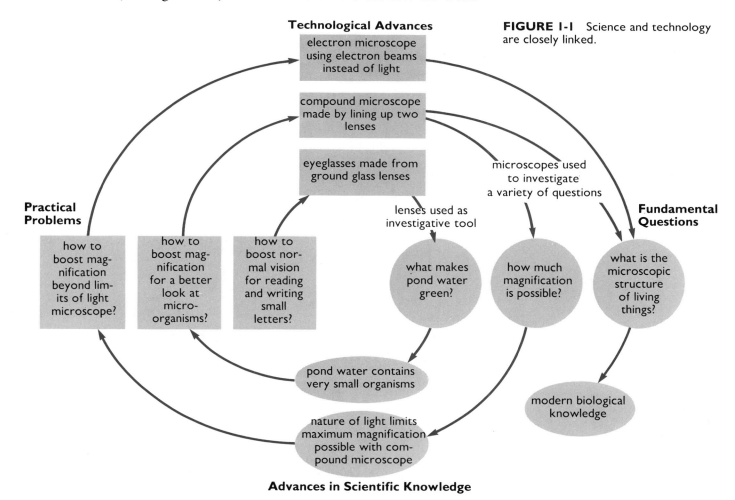

FIGURE 1-1 Science and technology are closely linked.

Technological Advances

electron microscope using electron beams instead of light

compound microscope made by lining up two lenses

eyeglasses made from ground glass lenses

lenses used as investigative tool

microscopes used to investigate a variety of questions

Practical Problems

how to boost magnification beyond limits of light microscope?

how to boost magnification for a better look at microorganisms?

how to boost normal vision for reading and writing small letters?

what makes pond water green?

how much magnification is possible?

Fundamental Questions

what is the microscopic structure of living things?

pond water contains very small organisms

nature of light limits maximum magnification possible with compound microscope

modern biological knowledge

Advances in Scientific Knowledge

The period in European history from A.D. 400 — A.D. 1100 is often called the Dark Ages because so little new learning took place. Very few people were educated, and much of the knowledge acquired during ancient Roman and Greek times was lost or survived only in monasteries.

works while technology seeks to solve practical problems. In ancient times, technology developed through trial and error. Now, however, science and technology are closely linked. Science depends on technology for investigative tools. Technology is often developed through the application of scientific knowledge. And new technology often leads to important advances in scientific knowledge.

For example, convex lenses were originally developed as a solution to the problem of writing or reading very small letters. The use of lenses eventually led to the microscope, which, in turn, led scientists to the discovery of a whole new world, one populated by microscopic organisms and just as diverse as the macroscopic world.

Section Review Questions

1. a) Define technology.
   b) State three examples of technology, each from a different society.
2. a) State a simple definition of science.
   b) Explain why Aristotle's studies are not regarded as truly scientific.
3. a) How does the accumulated knowledge of a hunter-gatherer society resemble science? How does it differ?
   b) How does the accumulated knowledge of ancient Egypt resemble science? How does it differ?
   c) Repeat part (b) for ancient Greece.
4. a) Explain the difference between a macroscopic observation and a microscopic observation.
5. a) Examine the photograph of convex lenses on page 6. How do more powerful convex lenses differ from less powerful ones?
   b) Is the convex lens a technological development or a scientific one? Explain.

1.2 Discovering the Microscopic World

Galileo used a compound microscope to observe biological materials, but he left no record of what he saw. He was primarily interested in making observations with telescopes. These instruments have lenses that are arranged to enlarge the images of distant objects.

The first **compound microscope** was built in 1590 by Hans and Zacharias Janssen, two Dutch eyeglass makers. As Figure 1-2 shows, it contained two lenses: one to enlarge the image of a small object and one to magnify the enlarged image. The Janssen brothers did use their invention to view specimens of once living material, but they left no records of their observations. In fact, another 80 years passed before the world of microscopic organisms was discovered.

I THE STUDY OF LIFE

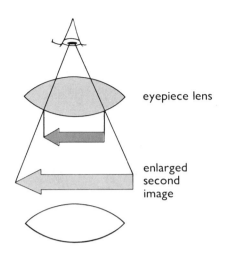

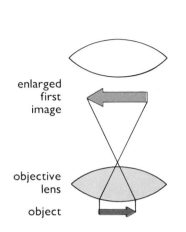

enlarged
first
image

eyepiece lens

objective
lens

enlarged
second
image

object

FIGURE 1-2 How a compound microscope works. For clarity, the two stages of magnification are shown separately. **Left:** The objective lens bends light from the object to produce an enlarged first image. **Right:** The eyepiece lens bends light from the first image so the eye sees an even larger second image.

The main reason for this delay was that early compound microscopes produced dim, distorted images. Of the few naturalists who used them, the first to leave records was the English experimenter, Robert Hooke. In 1665, Hooke used the term "cell" to describe the tiny, compartment-like structures he saw in plant and animal specimens. Hooke did not recognize the significance of these cells, but he did recognize the importance of a letter published by *The Royal Society of London for Improving Natural Knowledge* in 1677. The letter was sent by Anton von Leeuwenhoek announcing the discovery of "cavorting beasties" in pond water.

The Royal Society of London has been continuously active as a kind of clearing house for scientific knowledge since 1660. Hooke saw Leeuwenhoek's letter because he was the secretary at the time. In 1677, the society published the letter in their journal, *Philosophical Transactions*, under the title: "Observations communicated to the publisher by Mr. Anton van Leeuwenhoek in a Dutch letter of the 9th of October, 1676, here English'd: Concerning little animals by him observed in Rain-Well-Sea-and-Snow water, [and] also in water wherein Pepper had lain infused."

Hooke's microscope, 1665

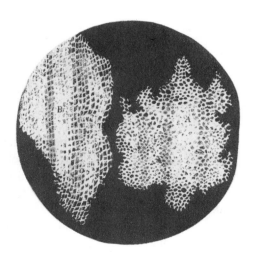

Hooke's drawing of cork cells. The cork slices were dead, and the cell compartments were empty. Look for the letters A and B. What do you think they represent?

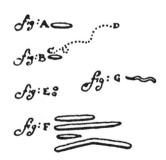

Leeuwenhoek included these sketches with a letter describing his observations of teeth scrapings.

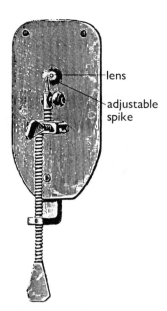

Leeuwenhoek's microscope had an adjustable spike on which a small object or drop of liquid could be placed. The small size of this microscope made it completely portable, a great advantage over the larger compound microscopes of Janssen and Hooke.

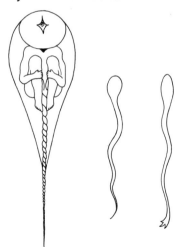

FIGURE I-3 Leeuwenhoek also examined human sperm, which he described as an infinity of animals like tadpoles. His diagrams upset the current belief that each baby grew from a preformed embryo known as a homunculus. Soon other investigators were claiming that they could see the features of a compact but complete human being in the head of a sperm.

Leeuwenhoek and the Simple Microscope

Leeuwenhoek was a Dutch merchant, surveyor, and part-time janitor who built microscopes as a hobby. Both his tools and his investigative methods differed considerably from those of formally trained scientists.

Simple Microscopes
Because compound microscopes require the user to look through two lenses, they double the chance of distortion. Leeuwenhoek reduced distortion by using only **simple microscopes,** instruments that contain a single, extremely curved lens.

Superior Lenses
Although Leeuwenhoek was an amateur lens grinder, his lenses were much better ground than most other lenses. This further reduced distortion. In addition, Leeuwenhoek's lenses were much more powerful.

Better Lighting
Compound microscopes had to be placed on a table or stand with the specimen underneath. This made providing adequate light difficult. Leeuwenhoek's simple microscope was small and had an adjustable spike for holding the specimen near a window or a flame.

Specialized Design
Leeuwenhoek is thought to have built nearly 250 microscopes, each specialized for a different viewing task. As a result, he was able to match the lens to the subject, locate the subject at an ideal distance from the lens, and include specialized holders for each type of specimen. One microscope even had a container for live fish.

Unusual Subject Matter
Hooke and others used their compound microscopes only to view the fine structure of large organisms. Leeuwenhoek used his simple microscopes to search for tiny organisms. He examined every liquid he could think of such as rainwater, sea water, and pond water. (See Figure 1-3.)

Within these liquids, Leeuwenhoek discovered a microscopic world that rivalled the macroscopic world for diversity. Today, biologists refer to most of the things Leeuwenhoek saw as **micro-organisms,** but to him, they were "animalcules." In fact, some *were* little animals, but others were more like plants, and today many would be called yeasts or bacteria.

For decades, Leeuwenhoek continued to write to the Royal Society of London, but naturalists who tried to verify his observations found it to be frustrating work. None had his lens-grinding skills, and few had the patience to build a different microscope for each new situation. Most of these naturalists were skeptical about the importance of things that were so difficult to see.

They were much more excited by the diverse array of plant and animal specimens expeditions were bringing back from around the world.

Although the existence of Leeuwenhoek's "beasties" greatly increased the number and the variety of known living things, naturalists of the time did not pursue further investigation of micro-organisms. It was 1800 before improved glass-making skills turned the compound microscope into a practical, widely used scientific tool. Until then, most naturalists ignored micro-organisms and concentrated on the much more rewarding task of discovering, listing, describing, and naming macroscopic organisms.

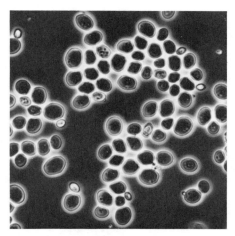

Yeasts photographed through a modern microscope. In which liquid did Leeuwenhoek probably find yeasts?

RESEARCH PROJECT
Investigating Two Naturalists

Few early naturalists specialized in a single field of study. Most had diverse interests, and many wrote books or articles on several subjects. Some naturalists were amateurs, individuals with no formal scientific education, who pursued scientific interests.

This project will give you an opportunity to compare the scientific contributions of an amateur with those of a formally trained scholar. Consult at least three encyclopedias or other reference works, and read the entries listed for Robert Hooke and Anton von Leeuwenhoek. Jot down brief points on each. Use this information as a basis for answering the following questions.

- List the topics studied by Robert Hooke.
- What evidence is there that living things were not Hooke's main interest?
- How do you think Hooke happened to discover cells?
- List the topics studied by Leeuwenhoek.
- Do you think living things were Leeuwenhoek's main interest?
- Was Leeuwenhoek's lack of formal education an advantage or a disadvantage? Discuss.
- Suppose Hooke had been able to make compound microscopes as powerful as Leeuwenhoek's simple microscopes. Do you think he would have learned as much about micro-organisms as Leeuwenhoek did? Discuss.
- One way science differs from technology is that scientists attempt to understand and explain the natural world, and technologists make use of it. Was Hooke a scientist in this sense of the term? Was Leeuwenhoek? Discuss.
- Who do you think had the greater influence on modern science—Hooke or Leeuwenhoek? Support your answer.

Based on your answers to these questions, write a report comparing the scientific contributions of Hooke and Leeuwenhoek. Remember to support your statements based on the information you have gathered.

Leeuwenhoek's most powerful lens magnified objects about $270 \times$. By comparison, the most powerful lens in a standard school microscope is only $100 \times$. It must be combined with a $4 \times$ eyepiece to give a maximum magnification of $400 \times$.

Section Review Questions

1. a) Who invented the compound microscope? When?
   b) Briefly describe how the structure of a compound microscope differs from the structure of a simple microscope.
2. a) Who provided the first records of microscopic observations? When?
   b) Do these records reveal the discovery of micro-organisms? Explain.
3. a) Define the term micro-organism.
   b) Are micro-organisms plants or animals? Explain.
4. a) Who discovered micro-organisms? When?
   b) What role did the compound microscope play in this discovery? Explain.
5. Describe how Leeuwenhoek's microscope differed from Hooke's microscope in at least three ways.
6. What is the most important difference between Leeuwenhoek's investigative methods and the methods used by other naturalists of the time?

1.3 Organizing the World of Diversity

For scientists, the first step in understanding diversity involves **nomenclature,** which means giving each different kind of living thing its own distinctive name. Scientific nomenclature is necessary because common names are misleading. For example, the bird North Americans call a robin is not the same bird the British call a robin. In this case, the same common name is used for two very different birds. In other cases, the same organism may have more than one common name. For example, woodchuck, groundhog, and gopher are used in different places to describe the same burrowing animal. Imagine the confusion that would result if scientists used common names to communicate with each other. Clearly, scientists must use a standardized system of nomenclature.

The first recorded efforts at systematic nomenclature were made by Aristotle and his students around 334 B.C. Their task was not too difficult since they knew only 1000 distinctly different kinds of organisms. But by 1600 that number had grown to 10 000. Around 1650, the English naturalist Jon Ray (1627-1705), decided to catalogue all of the organisms in the world. He began with an extensive journey through Europe, during which he described and named close to 20 000 new plants, birds, and four-footed animals.

Nomenclature of Species

Ray was the first person to describe each different kind of organism as a **species.** A species is a group of organisms so similar that they can mate and

Both of these robins have red breast feathers; otherwise they are quite different. When European settlers moved to North America, they often named the new organisms after the more familiar ones they had left behind. The European robin is in the photograph on the bottom.

I THE STUDY OF LIFE

produce fertile offspring. Ray's catalogue gave each distinct species its own descriptive Latin name. But many other naturalists were doing similar research and often on the same organisms. As a result, some plants and animals had four or five completely different scientific names, each consisting of several words. A typical example is *dianthus floribus solitariis, squamis calycinis subovatis brevimis, corollis crenatis*, which you probably know as the carnation plant!

All scholars of Ray's era understood Latin, but even the most fluent found multi-part names cumbersome. Explorers continued to bring back strange new organisms for European scientists to study. By 1700, both the names and the number of species had become unmanageable, and the need for organizing the data had become obvious.

Methods of organizing information are just as important to scientists as the microscopes and the other instruments they use. Two methods developed during the 1700s established **biology** as the organized, scientific study of living things that we know today. These two methods were binomial nomenclature and classification.

Binomial Nomenclature

The solution to the problem of organizing information about plants and animals was proposed by the Swedish botanist Carolus Linnaeus (1707-1778). In 1753, he published a book called *Species Plantarum*, in which he showed how each species could be described using only two words. Linnaeus's new system was immediately welcomed by naturalists because it allowed them to identify organisms precisely when discussing their findings with other scientists.

Linnaeus's system is called **binomial nomenclature** because it gives each species a two-part name. The first word refers to the organism's **genus,** which is the group of similar species to which it belongs. The second word is based either on some specific characteristic of the organism, or on the name of a person or a place associated with it. (See Table 1-1 on page 14.) The first letter of the genus name is capitalized, and both words are italicized. For example, the human species is *Homo sapiens*. By 1800, 70 000 species had been named using this system. Binomial nomenclature is so efficient and convenient that scientists all over the world still use it for the nearly two million species they know today.

But binomial nomenclature is much more than a simple way to identify species. It is also an organizational technique. Before naturalists used Linnaeus's system to communicate effectively with each other, their individual findings were simply a huge collection of facts. Once they began to use standardized names for plants and animals, these facts could be classified into a distinctive body of knowledge.

The old Latin name for carnation translates as the "pink" that has solitary flowers with scalloped petals and short, egg-shaped calyx scales.

Early naturalists drew detailed diagrams of the new organisms they discovered. Modern biologists often do the same. What advantage do drawings like this have over photographs?

When you write or type the name of a species, you should underline both words to show that they are to be read as italics.

Carolus Linnaeus was born Karl von Linné, but Latinized his name to correspond with the language in which his books were written.

TABLE 1-1 Examples of Binomial Nomenclature

Common Name	Scientific Name	Meaning
Coyote	• *Canis latrans*	• barking dog
Dog	• *C. familiaris*	• family dog
Plum	• *Prunus domestica*	• domestic plum
Peach	• *P. persica*	• Persian plum
Cherry	• *P. avium*	• bird plum
Apricot	• *P. armeniaca*	• Armenian plum
Robin (Britain)	• *Erithacus rubecula*	• red breast
Robin (N.A.)	• *Turdus migratorius*	• migrating thrush
Climbing Rose	• *Rosa setigera*	• bristly rose
Rose of Sharon	• *Hibiscus syriacus*	• Syrian hibiscus

Classification

Classification means sorting large, complex collections of data to make information more manageable. You are classifying when you decide whether to put your biology notes in the same binder as your math notes or in a binder by themselves. With nearly two million known species, scientists studying living things have a special need for classification.

A good classification system must group similar things together and keep different things apart. It must also be clear and practical for the people who use it. If the basis for sorting is carefully chosen, classification may also reveal relationships that would otherwise go unnoticed. (See Figure 1-4.)

The best basis for sorting data depends on how it will be used and who will be using it. In this biology course, you will be investigating living things to find out how they work. If you had to study all two million species to do this, you would run out of time long before you ran out of organisms. Classification reduces an impossibly huge task to manageable size.

In the remainder of this chapter, you will look at two systems of classification that are used extensively in the scientific study of the living world. In Section 1.4, you will consider ecological classification. **Ecologists** study how living things interact with their environments. Understanding ecological relationships will help you appreciate why there is so much diversity among living things. In Section 1.5, you will investigate biological classification. **Biologists** are primarily concerned with the structure and operation of the body parts of a living thing rather than with its environmental interactions. Biological classification will help you appreciate how the living world can be understood, despite its diversity, through the intensive study of a few representative species.

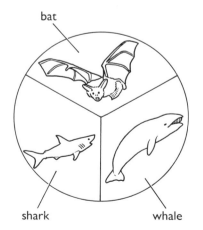

FIGURE 1-4 Classifying by natural environment would group whales and sharks together. Classifying by skeletal structure, however, would show that whales are more closely related to bats.

Fossils are the remains of organisms that lived in the past and have been preserved in rocks. This fossil imprint shows that tree-sized ferns once flourished not far from southern Saskatchewan. Why do you think these species no longer exist?

DID YOU KNOW?
The word ecology is derived from the ancient Greek word *oikos*, which means home. The home referred to is Earth.

Concept Map

A concept map is a diagram that summarizes relationships among ideas. For example, a concept map about schools might look like the one in Figure 1-5. Use this method to construct a concept map for the history of biology up to A.D. 1800. Use as many boxes, arrows, and terms as you need.

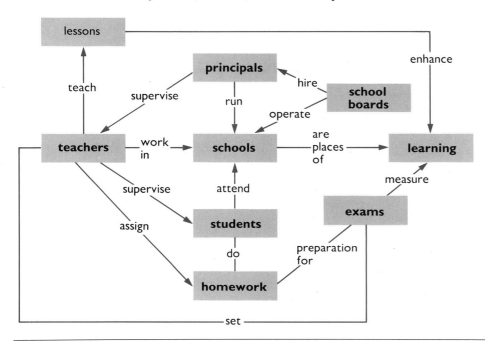

FIGURE 1-5 An example of a concept map

Section Review Questions

1. For each of the following pairs of terms, explain how the two terms are related and how they differ.
   a) common name, scientific name
   b) nomenclature, classification
   c) genus, species
   d) dog, *Canis familiaris*
   e) ecology, biology
2. a) Why do scientists need a standard system for the nomenclature of living things?
   b) What is the system now used for this purpose? Who invented this system and when?
3. a) Explain the meaning of the term species. Who first used the term?
   b) How many different species were known in 1600? In 1700? What factors contributed to this increase?
4. a) Explain what each word in the species name *Canis familiaris* represents.
   b) State the scientific names for the British robin and for the North American robin. (See Table 1-1.) How similar are these birds? How do you know?
5. The scientific name for a carnation is now *Dianthus caryophyllus*.
   a) In what way is the current name an improvement on its old scientific name?
   b) How is the current name less useful than the old scientific name?

1.4 How Ecologists Classify the Natural Environment

In addition to the nearly two million species already identified, scientists estimate that another three to eight million species remain undiscovered. However, some parts of the natural environment are being destroyed by human activities. The resulting loss of living space has already caused the extinction or the endangerment of many known species. Ecologists fear that many unknown species may also become extinct before they are discovered if environmental destruction continues at its present rate.

Adaptation and Diversity

The biosphere includes hundreds of distinct environments, each with its own characteristic organisms. For example, ferns occur naturally on forest floors,

Most organisms are adapted for a particular environment. Humans are an exception. We manage to survive in a wide variety of environments because of one important adaptation: a brain that enables us to construct artificial environments that meet our needs.

Around the world, large tracts of rain forest are being burned to create new land for homes and farms. After a few years, such farms must be abandoned and new ones created because the soil will no longer grow crops. Ecologists say the original plant species will not grow again on the abandoned land.

seaweed in oceans, and cacti in deserts. All of these organisms live by manufacturing their own food from energy and materials in their surroundings, but none of them could survive in the other organisms' environments. This is because each species has **adaptations,** specialized structures or abilities that enable it to live in its usual environment.

A survey of the biosphere would show that there is a life form adapted to suit almost every natural environment on Earth, regardless of its elevation, soil type, water condition, and climate. The resulting diversity among living things is so great that their interactions with each other are innumerable.

Like all ocean dwellers, kelp is able to prevent salts and minerals in the surrounding sea water from entering its body. In large quantities, these materials are harmful to living things. A geranium moved to the same environment would die because freshwater plants lack the adaptations to keep salts and minerals out.

The fern's broad feathery leaves maximize its exposure to sunlight in a shady environment.

Kelp maximizes exposure to sunlight with air-filled bladders that keep its broad streamers floating near the water's surface.

The prickly pear cactus has three adaptations that suit it for its hot, dry environment. Small thorn-like leaves reduce the area from which water can escape. Flat paddle-like stems have a waxy covering that provides protection and helps reduce water loss. And the stems swell up after a rainfall, storing water for months.

A Basis for Ecological Classification

To make sense of the interactions among living things, ecologists classify the biosphere as shown in Figure 1-6. This chart shows that grouping organisms according to their environmental role divides them into two major categories: **autotrophs,** which produce food, and **heterotrophs,** which consume it. For example, deer, whales, and rattlesnakes are heterotrophs, but ferns, kelp, and cacti are autotrophs.

Autotrophs can live in any environment that provides them with enough energy and raw materials for food production. Figure 1-7 only hints at their diversity in size and structure. Some tree-sized producers grow to heights of 100 m or more, but the most important autotrophs are not always the most

Although autotrophs make up only 15% of all living species, they make up 99% of all living material in the biosphere.

Plants and most other producers manufacture food by photosynthesis, a term derived from the Greek word *photo* which means light, and *synthesis* which means make. Although it involves a complex series of chemical reactions, photosynthesis can be summarized as follows:

light + carbon dioxide + water ⟶ sugar + oxygen

Here are the meanings of more Greek and Latin roots that will help you understand any unfamiliar terms.

Root	Meaning
auto	self
carnis	flesh
herba	green crop
heteros	other
omnis	all
trophikos	nourish
vorare	devour

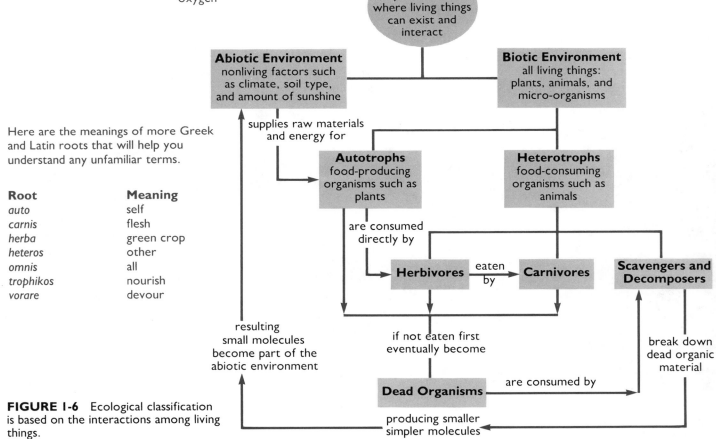

FIGURE 1-6 Ecological classification is based on the interactions among living things.

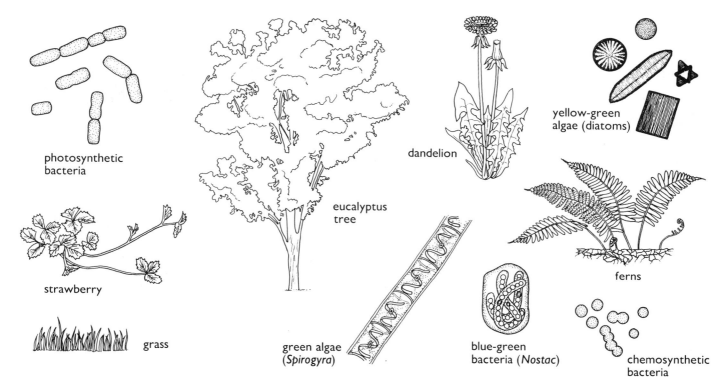

photosynthetic
bacteria

strawberry

grass

eucalyptus
tree

green algae
(*Spirogyra*)

dandelion

yellow-green
algae (diatoms)

ferns

blue-green
bacteria (*Nostac*)

chemosynthetic
bacteria

FIGURE I-7 Diversity among autotrophs. Most autotrophs make food by photosynthesis, using solar energy (sunlight). A very few (mostly bacteria) make food by chemosynthesis, using the energy stored in chemicals such as hydrogen sulphide (also known as "rotten-egg" gas).

visible. Microscopically small algae play a major role in the production of food for ocean dwellers and oxygen for the entire biosphere.

Heterotrophs are grouped according to how directly they interact with autotrophs. For example, all of the consumers in Figure 1-8 are classified as herbivores because they feed directly on producers such as plants. Herbivorous heterotrophs differ greatly in appearance and vary in size from microscopically small aquatic grazers to the tallest land animals on Earth.

The heterotrophs in Figure 1-9, however, are classified as carnivores. Because they eat other heterotrophs, carnivores depend only indirectly on producers. All carnivores share the common problem of finding, catching, and consuming their prey, but their body structures, hunting methods, feeding habits, and environments differ greatly.

There is also great diversity among decomposers and scavengers. Figure 1-10 shows that these organisms have a wide range of adaptations for feeding on dead organisms. Scavengers such as buzzards take the once-living material into their bodies and then break it down by digesting it. Decomposers such as fungi release dissolved chemicals that break down dead material into molecules small enough to be absorbed. Both decomposers and scavengers depend indirectly on food produced by autotrophs.

Bears, pigs, humans, and many other animals are omnivores. They eat either plant or animal matter.

FIGURE 1-8 Diversity among herbivorous heterotrophs. Each herbivore has its own method of obtaining and eating food. Even those that feed on similar plants display structural differences that enable them to eat different plant types and parts.

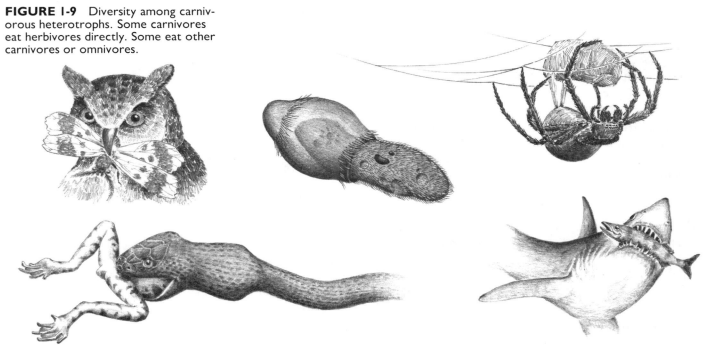

FIGURE 1-9 Diversity among carnivorous heterotrophs. Some carnivores eat herbivores directly. Some eat other carnivores or omnivores.

FIGURE 1-10 Diversity among scavengers and decomposers. These specialized heterotrophs play a vital role in recycling materials to the abiotic environment for use by other organisms.

Ecologists have found interaction-based classification to be extremely useful. This kind of classification system reveals that only a few types of food relationships exist, and supports the conclusion that all living things are part of a worldwide food web, each directly or indirectly dependent on all of the others. But using interactions as a basis for classification results in groups containing species with distinctly different body sizes, patterns, and parts. For this reason, it does not suit the needs of biologists, who study the structure and operation of living things instead of their environmental interactions.

RESEARCH PROJECT
Ecological Awareness

Scan a daily newspaper for a current example of environmental destruction or species endangerment taking place somewhere in the world. These articles may appear on the front page, in the weekly science section, or sometimes under world affairs or current events. Once you have identified a topic, look for two other sources of information about it. You might consider television newscasts, educational programs, or science-oriented magazines. Ask your school librarian for suggestions. Consider the questions on page 23 when you are gathering information and write a brief report on your findings.

Ecologists and biologists would investigate these two species from different viewpoints. An ecologist might conduct a population study to find out how many eucalyptus trees are needed to support the koala. A biologist might study the koala's body structures to find out how it assimilates the nutrients in eucalyptus leaves.

Ecological knowledge has been important to humans since the appearance of the first hunter-gatherers, and scholars have discussed environmental interactions since Aristotle's time. But ecology as we understand it today is a relatively young science. Biology has been a distinct discipline for almost two centuries, but ecology did not become a science until the 1950s.

Because ecology draws heavily on biological knowledge, it is usually regarded as a branch of biology. However, its true nature is multidisciplinary since it draws on geology, chemistry, physics, meteorology, soil science, and mathematics to deal with the multifaceted nature of ecological problems.

The earliest North American use of the term ''oecology'' occurred in the 1890s in connection with the geographical distribution of terrestrial plants. By the 1930s, European ecologists were developing the concept of food chains and including aquatic plants in their studies. It was not until the 1940s that scholars became concerned with the flow of energy from the sun through the biosphere. However, plant ecologists ignored interactions with animals, and animal ecology developed along separate lines for several decades. Eventually, the concept of plants and animals interacting with each other in a community evolved.

Ecology: The Birth of a Science

The major scientific influence on present-day ecology was the International Biological Program (IBP), which was launched in 1960 amid growing concern among scientists about environmental problems they saw developing worldwide. IBP stimulated a great deal of research on photosynthesis, water cycles, and

Rachel Carson

decomposition. But ecology was still a term known only to scientists; the general public did not become aware of environmental issues until the publication of Rachel Carson's best-selling book, *Silent Spring* (1962). Carson was a marine biologist for the United States government, and a science writer with an intense concern for the natural environment. Carson's book was a shocking introduction to the environmental issues that are so widely publicized today. She warned that pesticides poisoned the food consumed by all animals, especially birds and the carnivores that ate birds. Her prediction that pesticides would eventually contaminate human food resulted in substantial reductions in pesticide use and accelerated the passage of many laws governing the manufacture, sale, and application of pesticides.

Carson's book also precipitated greater public awareness and concern about the environment to the extent that ecology is now a household word. Many environmental groups such as Pollution Probe started in the decade that followed the book's publication.

The environmental movement has had an impact on pre-university education. Almost all junior and senior high school science curricula in North America include at least one unit of ecology —quite an achievement for a science that was virtually unheard of three decades ago.

- What kind of environment is being destroyed? In what part of the world?
- What species are endangered? Can the endangered species live in any other environment? Explain why or why not.
- What human purpose is being served by the destructive activity? What alternatives exist that might serve the same purpose? Is it possible that these alternatives will be pursued? Explain why or why not.

Section Review Questions

1. Define and state an example of a) an autotroph and b) a heterotroph.
2. For each of the following pairs of terms explain how the two terms are related and how they differ.
   a) biosphere, environment
   b) adaptation, interaction
   c) producer, consumer
   d) herbivore, carnivore
   e) scavenger, decomposer
3. Classify each of the following as an autotroph or as a heterotroph.
   a) penguin   d) crab grass
   b) maple tree   e) algae
   c) grasshopper   f) frog
4. a) Classify each of the following as a herbivore or as a carnivore: deer, wolf, crow.
   b) Explain why it is difficult to be sure you have classified the crow correctly.
5. a) Explain what is meant by the phrase ''Organisms have adaptations that suit them to the environment in which they live.''
   b) Using the cactus as an example, explain how it is possible to infer something about an organism's environment by examining its structural features.

1.5 A Basis for Biological Classification

Biologists need a classification system that simplifies the study of individual species. A system that groups spiders and lynxes together because both are carnivorous does not do this. Studying a lynx would provide little information about the structures, abilities, or behaviour of a spider. But a system that groups lynxes and house cats with lions, leopards, and tigers would provide much more useful information. More can be learned about the body structures

This leopard and lioness are mates, the parents of hybrid offspring known as leopons.

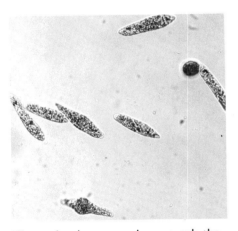

The euglena's green colour reveals the presence of chlorophyll and indicates its ability to manufacture its own food by photosynthesis. During prolonged dark periods, the euglena can absorb the food substances it needs from its surroundings.

Viruses have been a taxonomic question mark ever since they were discovered. They do not fit into any of the five kingdoms, and it is not clear whether they can actually be called living things. Viruses are usually studied with disease-causing organisms such as bacteria, even though they differ greatly in structure, size, and function.

of a less common species by comparing them to those of a familiar animal such as a house cat.

Using structural similarities as a basis for sorting living things has obvious advantages for biologists. However, establishing standardized rules for biological classification has been a difficult, ongoing task. In fact, describing, naming, and classifying organisms requires so much observation and thought that it has become a specialized science called **taxonomy.**

Taxonomy began with Aristotle. His two-kingdom system proved practical for many centuries, and it was used to classify, as plants or as animals, the tiny life forms discovered by investigators using early microscopes. However, the dramatically improved instruments of the 1800s revealed that many microscopic organisms could not be assigned to either kingdom. First, they exhibited characteristics of *both* plants and animals. Second, individual micro-organisms consisted of only a single cell, whereas each plant and animal contained large numbers of cells. For this reason, some taxonomists suggested adding a third kingdom called "protists."

By 1900, as microscopes and other investigative tools improved, scientists observed even more cellular details. Some taxonomists wondered whether tiny life forms such as bacteria really belonged to the same kingdom as protists. There was also disagreement about whether fungi, which cannot manufacture food, should continue to be classified as plants. Many systems were proposed to resolve these disagreements.

The system shown in Figure 1-11 sorts all life forms into one of five kingdoms: Animalia, Plantae, Fungi, Protista, and Monera. In this textbook, you will also use this five-kingdom system, even though taxonomists do not completely agree about certain details, and some still prefer a three- or four-kingdom system (see Figure 1-11 on pages 25 and 26).

You should realize that scientific knowledge is limited. Like other scientists, taxonomists have to accept the limits imposed on their classification systems by the natural world. This means that no system of biological classification is perfect. Efforts to clarify relationships among organisms may make a system harder to use, but simplifying it may obscure relationships.

Taxonomists also have to accept the tentative nature of scientific knowledge. This means that no taxonomic system is ever final. In the past, biological classification was based entirely on external form (morphology) and internal structure (anatomy). These criteria are still important, but modern taxonomists use evidence from other fields to help them classify living things. As new species are discovered and improved tools reveal new facts about known species, the five-kingdom system you will use here may also be modified.

FIGURE 1-11

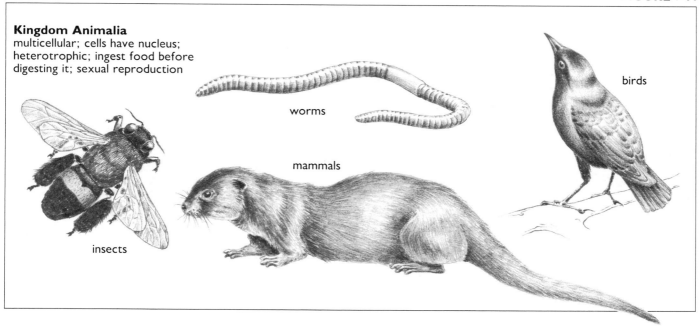

Kingdom Animalia
multicellular; cells have nucleus; heterotrophic; ingest food before digesting it; sexual reproduction

worms

mammals

birds

insects

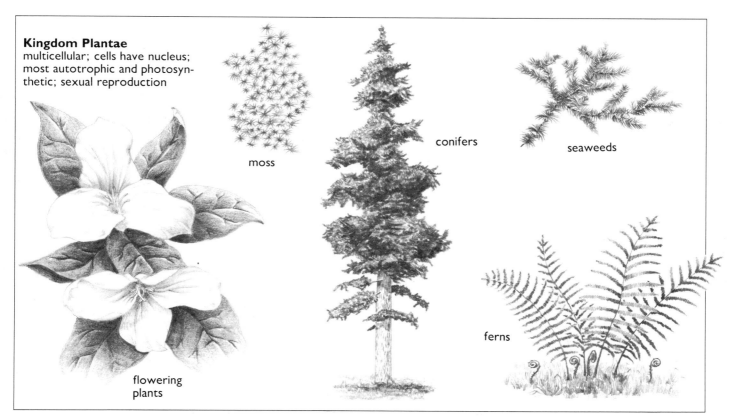

Kingdom Plantae
multicellular; cells have nucleus; most autotrophic and photosynthetic; sexual reproduction

moss

conifers

seaweeds

ferns

flowering plants

Kingdom Fungi

both multicellular and unicellular forms; cells have nucleus; all heterotrophic; absorb food after digesting it; sexual reproduction

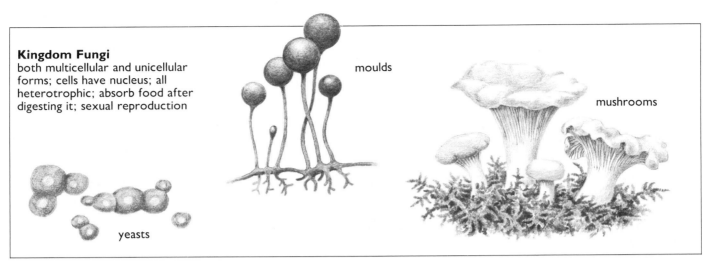

moulds

mushrooms

yeasts

Kingdom Protista

mostly unicellular; cells have nucleus; some heterotrophic, some autotrophic, some both; mostly asexual reproduction

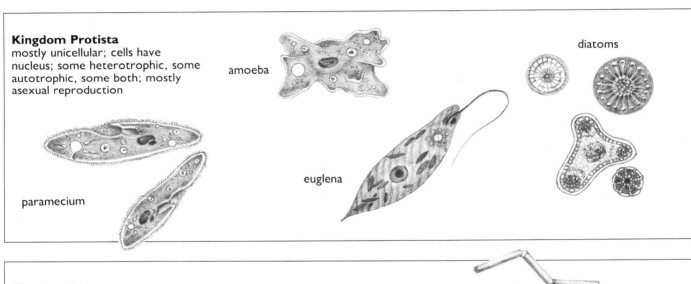

amoeba

diatoms

euglena

paramecium

Kingdom Monera

all unicellular; cells lack nucleus; some heterotrophic, some autotrophic; asexual reproduction

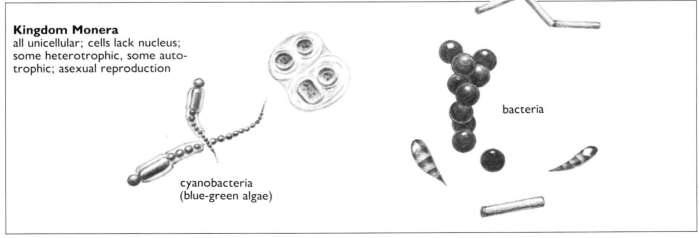

bacteria

cyanobacteria
(blue-green algae)

INQUIRY ACTIVITY
Five-Kingdom Classification

A kingdom is the largest taxonomic grouping used in biological classification. In this activity, you will assign a variety of organisms to their appropriate kingdom. Some examples have already been done for you in the following chart.

Animalia	Plantae	Fungi	Protista	Monera
• Koala (hetero-trophic; eats food)		• Yeast (single-celled; grows on food)	• *Euglena* (single-celled; able to live as either autotroph or hetero-troph)	

Procedure

1. Copy the chart into your notebook.
2. Study Figure 1-11 (see pages 25 and 26) to familiarize yourself with the characteristics for each kingdom.
3. Study the examples shown in the chart. Note that each entry includes the name of an organism and two reasons for assigning it to a particular kingdom. Follow the same format to complete Question 4. (Use the organism's genus name or its binomial if you know it, otherwise use its common name.)
4. a) Reclassify the autotrophs in Figure 1-7.
   b) Reclassify the herbivores in Figure 1-8.
   c) Reclassify the carnivores in Figure 1-9.
   d) Reclassify the scavengers and decomposers in Figure 1-10.

The Importance of Biological Classification

Sorting organisms into kingdoms is only the first step in biological classification. Each kingdom includes numerous species, many of which appear to be quite unlike. For example, both elephants and sponges possess the most basic characteristics of animals, but they have little else in common. Nevertheless, kingdom groupings provide a convenient way to break the study of the living world into more manageable parts.

This course will be conducted as a kingdom-by-kingdom survey of the living world, beginning with your own kingdom, Animalia. Before this survey begins, however, you will have an opportunity in Chapter 2 to refresh the skills and the knowledge you have acquired in earlier studies.

Section Review Questions

1. a) Why is ecological classification unsuitable for biologists?
   b) What is the main basis of biological classification?
2. a) Which science describes, names, and classifies organisms?
   b) Explain why no system of biological classification can ever be perfect or final.
3. a) Describe Aristotle's two-kingdom system of classification. How did discoveries made with the microscope affect the two-kingdom system of classification?
   b) What problems did fungi pose to a two-kingdom system of classification?
4. a) What are the major categories of the five-kingdom system?
   b) Prepare a simple chart to summarize the distinguishing characteristics of the five kingdoms.
5. To which of the five kingdoms do each of the following organisms belong?
   a) daffodil   e) toadstool
   b) clam   f) tuberculosis bacterium
   c) euglena   g) *Homo sapiens*
   d) yeast

Chapter Review

Key Words

adaptations
animal kingdom
autotrophs
binomial nomenclature
biologists
biology
biosphere
classification
compound microscope
ecologists
genus
heterotrophs
kingdom

macroscopic
micro-organisms
microscopic
microscopy
naturalists
nomenclature
philosophers
plant kingdom
science
simple microscope
species
taxonomy
technology

Recall Questions

Multiple Choice

1. Which of the following scholars first attempted to classify living things?
   a) Aristotle
   b) Robert Hooke
   c) Jon Ray
   d) Carolus Linnaeus

2. Which of the following scholars first used the term species as biologists define it today?
   a) Aristotle
   b) Robert Hooke
   c) Jon Ray
   d) Carolus Linnaeus

3. Which of the following scholars first proposed the system of binomial nomenclature used today?
   a) Aristotle
   b) Robert Hooke
   c) Jon Ray
   d) Carolus Linnaeus

4. In which of the following has the species name for lobster been written correctly?
   a) Homarus Americanus
   b) *Homarus americanus*
   c) Homarus americanus
   d) *homarus Americanus*

5. Taxonomists classify living things according to
   a) structural similarities
   b) nutritional patterns
   c) environmental roles
   d) binomial nomenclature

Fill in the Blanks

1. The compound microscope was invented in _____ by _____. Prior to that time, scholars had to depend on _____ observations of the living world. The first scholar to leave records of _____ observations was _____, who used a compound microscope to view thin slices of cork and gave the name _____ to the compartment-like structures he observed. During the late 1600s, an amateur scientist called _____ made numerous detailed observations of _____, using _____ microscopes. Although these observations were reported in the journal of the _____, and read by many scientists, little progress was made in observing the microscopic world until _____ when better _____ technology dramatically improved the quality of compound microscopes.

Short Answers

1. Is the use of convex lenses to magnify small objects an example of science or technology? Explain.

2. How many lenses does a compound microscope have? Briefly describe the function of each.

3. Identify two organizational methods biologists use to simplify the study of living things. State an example of each.

4. Is the use of binomial nomenclature an example of science or technology? Explain.

5. a) Which naturalist initiated the use of binomial nomenclature?
   b) Explain why other scientists adopted this system so quickly.

6. The scientific name for a certain kind of dolphin is *Delphinus delphis*.
   a) What does the term *Delphinus* indicate about this dolphin?
   b) What does the term *delphis* indicate?

7. a) What do ecologists mean by the term biosphere?
   b) How does biosphere differ in meaning from environment?

8. a) On what basis do ecologists classify the biosphere?
   b) Explain why other biologists use a different basis for classification.

9. Identify one term that does not belong with the others and state your reasons.
   a) mushroom, decomposer, heterotroph, herbivore
   b) consumer, herbivore, carnivore, producer

10. a) Define taxonomy.
    b) What special problems do taxonomists face?

11. a) List the categories in the two-kingdom system of classification.
    b) Who originated this system and when?
    c) Why have most biologists stopped using the two-kingdom system?

12. a) List the categories in the five-kingdom system of classification.
    b) Why did this system originate?

13. a) List the characteristics that identify each of the five kingdoms.
    b) Which kingdom do you belong to?

14. a) What is a virus?
    b) Explain why viruses are not included in the five-kingdom system of classification.

15. Match the terms in Column A with the descriptions in Column B.

Column A	Column B
i) adaptation	a) study interactions of biosphere
ii) autotroph	b) specialized structures or abilities
iii) carnivore	c) organism that produces food
iv) decomposer	d) organism that consumes food
v) ecologist	e) consumer that eats producers
vi) herbivore	f) consumer that eats consumers
vii) heterotroph	g) consumer that eats dead heterotrophs
viii) scavenger	h) heterotroph that does not ingest food

Application Questions

1. Briefly describe what the ancient Egyptians contributed to the sum of human knowledge. Was this contribution scientific or technological?

2. Repeat Question 1 for a) Aristotle, b) Hooke, c) Leeuwenhoek, d) Ray, and e) Linnaeus.

3. What requirements must be met for autotrophs to thrive? Explain how the requirements of heterotrophs differ.

4. Consider the following organisms: grass, grasshopper, fox, hawk, mouse, and sparrow.
   a) How would an ecologist classify them?
   b) How would a taxonomist classify them?
   c) Explain why your answers to parts (a) and (b) differ.

5. Which kingdoms can only be studied with a microscope? Could the other kingdoms be studied adequately without a microscope? Support your answer.

6. For each pair of kingdoms listed below, list three ways in which the two kingdoms differ.
   a) Protista and Monera
   b) Fungi and Protista
   c) Plantae and Fungi
   d) Animalia and Plantae

7. Explain why the five-kingdom system of classification was not proposed until the middle of this century.

8. Scientific knowledge is said to be limited and tentative. Explain what is meant by this statement. What implications does this statement have for your own study of biology?

9. Many students complain that it is difficult to learn scientific names such as *Canis familiaris* since "dog" means the same thing, and is both shorter to write and easier to remember. If you were a teacher, what would you say to convince such a student that scientific names are really a shortcut?

Problem Solving

1. Classify the following organisms according to the five-kingdom system. State your reasoning in each case.
   a) *Entamoeba histolytica* (which causes amoebic dysentery)

b) *Rhizopus stolonifer* (which makes bread go mouldy)

c) *Mycobacterium tuberculosis* (which causes tuberculosis)

2. Classify the organisms listed in Question 1 as autotrophs or heterotrophs. State your reasoning.

3. How many different species did Aristotle know? How many were known by 1600? By 1700? How many are known now? Use this information to plan a graph showing how scientific awareness of the diversity of life has increased since Aristotle's time. Sketch the general shape of the graph. Explain why actually drawing the graph would be difficult.

4. Suppose you were reading a new biology textbook in 2020. What would you expect it to say about the total number of different species living on Earth at that time? State reasons for your answer.

5. Some biologists estimate that less than 1% of all species that ever lived are present on Earth today. Use this information to calculate how many species have lived on Earth in total. What do these figures indicate about conditions on Earth in the past?

6. Explain why the classification of living things is a task that will never be finished.

Extensions

1. Obtain a list of the science equipment in your school's laboratory. Develop a classification system that groups this equipment into kingdoms. (Remember that you will have to balance convenience with the need to show relationships.)

2. Compare the system used to classify students in your school with the system for classifying organisms. What school category corresponds to the kingdom level? The genus level? The species level?

3. a) Conduct research to find out about abiotic conditions in your environment. Consider annual precipitation, average temperature, and length of growing season.

   b) What autotrophs can live naturally in this environment? What heterotrophs?

   c) What autotrophs and heterotrophs actually do live in your environment?

   d) Explain any differences between your answers to parts (b) and (c).

4. A food web is a diagram that describes interactions among organisms living in the same area. How would you expect a food web in the Arctic tundra to differ from one in a tropical rain forest? What similarities would you expect between the two food webs?

CHAPTER

2

Biological Science

The scientific body of knowledge we now call biology was built up slowly by thousands of researchers trying to answer questions about living things. Advances in biological knowledge often raise contentious issues. Such issues may centre on methods used to gain the knowledge. For example, European laws forbade human dissections until A.D. 1300. As a result, progress in understanding the human body was slow.

Sometimes biological knowledge itself becomes an issue. In our century, this has happened to biotechnology, a term that refers to using biological methods to produce materials, drugs, vaccines, micro-organisms, plants, and animals for industry, medicine, and agriculture. The potential benefits of biotechnology are great. Its achievements so far include bacteria that produce hormones for humans who cannot produce their own, plants that produce their own pesticides, and tests that link suspects to crimes. But many people worry about potential risks. For example, some fear that "bio-engineered" bacteria might escape and cause widespread disease, or that the ability to predict inherited disorders might lead to unfair treatment of affected individuals.

Occasionally, the lack of biological knowledge becomes an issue. Some of the most vexing issues of this kind are those surrounding life and death. *When does life begin? When does death occur? Is a legal definition desirable? Is it possible?* Questions concerning population growth are also contentious. *Is uncontrolled population growth really a problem? Should steps be taken to control it? If so, how?* Such questions are clearly related to biology, but so is almost every other scientific issue. For example, most questions about the use of nuclear power are really about its safety for living things.

All of these issues involve differences of opinion about what is valid or what should be done. Opinions are often based on deeply held religious or political viewpoints and beliefs. Such

viewpoints are valid, and you should realize that some decisions are outside the realm of biological science. However, "science" is often quoted to support opinions that have no solid scientific basis, but nevertheless influence public or personal decisions. The potential for harm from decisions based on such opinions can only be checked through continued vigilance by a scientifically literate society.

In this chapter, you will explore some of the questions biologists ask and the scientific methods they use to answer these questions. You will also examine some of the answers that have been obtained through scientific research. Before you begin, you may find it interesting to jot down your own views on some of the issues raised here. Review them when you finish this chapter and again when you finish the course. How has what you have learned enabled you to have a more informed opinion? Did anything you learned change your mind about a specific issue?

Chapter Objectives

When you complete this chapter, you should:

1. Recognize that biology is a distinct scientific discipline with a characteristic set of basic assumptions, and be curious about the scientific studies on which this knowledge is based.

2. Be able to demonstrate familiarity with basic biological concepts such as internal

environment, homeostasis, adaptation, diversity, unity, continuity, reproduction, growth, development, and inherited variability.

3. Be aware of the relationship between structure and function in living things.

4. Develop basic skills in deriving the meaning of biological terms through analysis of their Greek or Latin roots.

5. Develop skills in the basic techniques of microscopy, using the compound light microscope.

6. Understand the nature of the scientific method as it applies to biology, and appreciate that scientific knowledge is both limited and tentative.

7. Be able to state the cell theory and describe the history of its development.

8. Be able to describe the basic structure of a living cell and relate a cell's life functions to the structure of its parts and organelles.

9. Be able to describe briefly the outcome of mitosis and meiosis, and explain their roles in cell division, growth, and reproduction.

10. Be able to explain the role of new investigative technologies such as electron microscopy and chromatography in modern biological research.

2.1 What Biologists Study

TABLE 2-1 Summary of Scientific Disciplines

Discipline	Field of Study
Astronomy	• properties of planets, moon, and stars
Biology	• living things
Chemistry	• composition and interactions of matter
Geology	• how Earth was formed and how it changes
Physics	• properties of matter and energy

Few early scientists confined their investigations to one field of study. For example, Robert Hooke's interest in cells arose from his study of the properties of light. He also studied gravity and the elasticity of springs, subjects that are far removed from living things. But during the past two centuries, scientific information has been accumulating at such a rapid rate that no one can hope to keep up with all of it. Most scientists find it necessary to specialize in one of the major scientific disciplines listed in Table 2-1. These divisions organize scientific study and make it more efficient.

Every science discipline has its own viewpoint and its own set of basic assumptions. Chemists assume that all matter is made of atoms. Physicists assume that a moving object will keep moving unless an external force acts to change its motion. Geologists assume that the Great Lakes were created by a glacier. These assumptions are the results of much more than mere speculation or guesswork. Each is supported by evidence from thousands of observations and experiments carried out by hundreds of investigators. Biology, as you will learn, has a characteristic viewpoint and its own set of basic assumptions.

Most early scientists crossed disciplines freely. For example, the Law of Conservation of Energy, which is now considered one of the most important ideas in physics, was first presented by a medical doctor. In this century, however, scientists who cross disciplinary boundaries are regarded with suspicion by other scientists. Linus Pauling, who won a Nobel Prize in chemistry, was later greeted with extreme skepticism when he published his views on the role of vitamin C in nutrition.

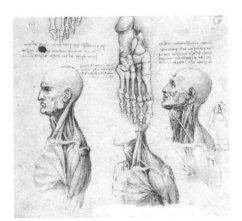

Leonardo da Vinci (1452-1519) was the greatest experimental scientist of his era. His interests included geology, astronomy, engineering, and botany. His interest in anatomy began as research for his painting. Historians think he must have illegally obtained bodies to produce anatomical drawings such as this.

Basic Assumptions of Modern Biology

Philosophers have been asking what it means to be alive since the earliest days of the Greek Empire, and they still disagree. Biologists answer this question in terms of scientific knowledge and observable facts.

Defining **biology** as "the study of life" compresses many major ideas into a very few words. In fact, what is known at present about living things would fill hundreds of books the size of this one. Nevertheless, the basic assumptions listed below provide all the information you will need to begin your own study of living things. Much of this information will be familiar from earlier studies, although it may have been presented differently. As you read, remember that each assumption sums up centuries of effort by biologists to answer one simple question: *What does it mean to be alive?*

34

For most beach dwellers, the conditions required for life cannot be met after an oil spill contaminates their environment. These biologists are looking for birds that might survive if they were cleaned up, and collecting ones that have already died so that they do not poison the food chain.

Living and Nonliving

The characteristic that distinguishes living things from nonliving things is their ability to *organize*, or assemble and manufacture, their own body substances from the materials around them. Anything that has this organizational ability is a living organism. Anything that lacks it is nonliving. For example, a living tree can organize materials from soil, air, and water to manufacture new wood and leaves. A fallen log can no longer do this. Its body parts soon become food for living organisms such as fungi and bacteria. Eventually, the nonliving log fragments become part of the forest floor and provide nourishment for new plants.

Some nonliving things may seem to organize materials. For example, a cloud may grow in size or change its shape. However, the cloud cannot regulate these changes. Its size and shape depend entirely on external winds and temperatures.

A living tree collects materials from the environment and organizes them to maintain its body and further its growth, while the fallen leaves and rotting log shown here gradually become disorganized into separate atoms and molecules as they break down.

Internal and External Environment

An organism's **internal environment** includes everything inside its body. Everything surrounding its body belongs to the **external environment.** To remain alive, an organism must be able to maintain a stable internal state despite any changes in external conditions. To do this, an organism must regulate the chemical composition of its internal environment by controlling what goes in and what goes out of it. An organism must also perform whatever chemical reactions are needed to manufacture materials and produce energy. This complex process is known as **homeostasis.** The activities an organism must carry out to maintain homeostasis are often called its **life functions.** (See Table 2-2.)

Reproduction is often listed as a life function, but individual organisms do not need to reproduce to live out their normal lifespan. They do, however, need to replace worn or damaged body parts.

TABLE 2-2 Summary of Life Functions Necessary for All Organisms

• Collecting, converting, storing, and utilizing energy for all activities
• Obtaining and processing materials needed for body parts or energy
• Organizing materials as required for growth, repair, or reproduction
• Disposing of waste materials produced by chemical reactions
• Responding to stimuli such as moving toward food or away from danger

Maintaining homeostasis despite external conditions requires constant activity on the part of an organism. As a result, these bears have a constant need for energy.

Structure and Function

Structure may refer to either the shape of body parts or to the pattern in which they are arranged. For example, the *structure* of your nervous system is an interconnected network. Each nerve in the system is a long, thin, wire-like *structure*.

Function refers to the abilities of body structures or materials. It is a fundamental principle of biology that structure and function are closely related. For example, the wire-like structure of nerves suits them for their function of transmitting signals throughout the body. (See Figure 2-1.) However, nerve-like structures are not suited for other functions such as keeping internal fluids inside the body. In humans, that function is performed by skin, and the structure of skin is very different from the structure of nerves. (See Figure 2-2.)

FIGURE 2-1   The structure of the human nervous system can be compared to a household wiring system. Both contain numerous long, thin units arranged in a network so that electrical signals can be transmitted to and from every part of the system.

FIGURE 2-2   The structure of human skin can be compared to floor tiling. Both are made of flat, thin units that fit tightly together to form a waterproof covering.

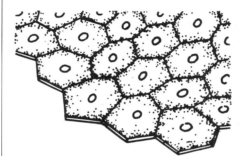

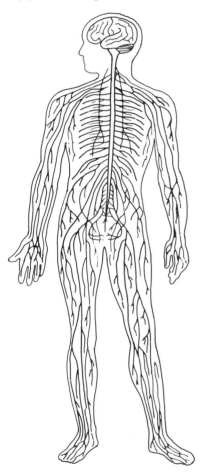

The ears of the desert fox provide a large surface area from which heat can escape.

Adaptations and Environment

Each species has specialized **adaptations** (structures, abilities, or behaviours) that suit it for life in its natural environment. For example, desert foxes have extra large ears that help disperse body heat, minimizing overheating. The

DID YOU KNOW?

Adaptations are most noticeable in extreme environments. For example, the 4000-m level on Mount Kenya in equatorial Africa enjoys plenty of bright sunshine and mild daytime temperatures. At night, however, there is always frost and often snow. Everything that lives there must be adapted to deal with a winter each night, a spring thaw every morning, and summer each day.

kidneys of desert rats conserve fluids so efficiently that they obtain all the liquid they need from their food and never have to drink water. But the desert is just one of many distinctly different environments on Earth. The numerous ways in which organisms have adapted to suit these many environments has resulted in millions of species that differ in size, structure, and complexity.

Diversity and Unity

Diversity refers to the ways in which living things differ. **Unity** refers to the ways in which they are similar. The great diversity of species on Earth reveals that many solutions exist to the problem of maintaining homeostasis. Despite certain dissimilarities, living things are not entirely different from each other. When biologists look for unity among living things, they often find structural and functional similarities. (See Figure 2-3.) Even organisms that appear to have the greatest differences can resemble each other in several ways. They may contain the same chemical substances. They may use energy in the same way to remain alive. And they may respond to stimuli and reproduce in similar ways.

LEFT: FIGURE 2-3 Even the most primitive animals have structures that enable them to respond to stimuli much as you do. The hydra's structures enable it to respond positively to the stimulus of food.

RIGHT: FIGURE 2-4 It is a fundamental assumption of biology that offspring will resemble their parents. Continuity is possible only if each generation passes all of the characteristic features of the species on to the next generation. The hydra is able to do this with only one parent.

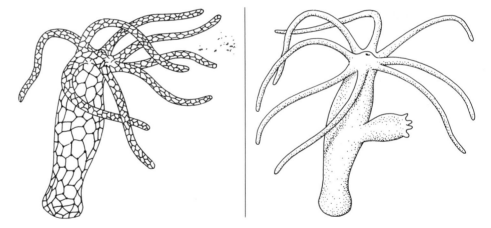

Continuity of Species

Continuity refers to the continued existence of living things. Since all organisms die eventually, continuity depends on their ability to produce offspring. This process is called **reproduction.** A species can only continue to exist if two reproductive conditions are met.

First, the members of a species must reproduce enough offspring to replace individuals that die. Second, each generation must pass the characteristics of the species on to the next generation. (See Figure 2-4.) This principle is usually referred to as "like produces like." You expect that a dog's offspring will be puppies, and that the puppies will grow up to be dogs. This assumption is exactly what you observe in nature, and may seem too self-evident to mention, but biologists did not develop an adequate explanation for the passing of characteristics from one generation to the next until this century.

By 1941, overhunting and loss of natural habitat had caused the world's total whooping crane population to drop to 22. Thanks to the heroic efforts of wildlife biologists in Canada and the United States, that number has now increased to 217.

Successful species maintain or increase their numbers through co-ordinated mating seasons, flowering times, or other reproductive adaptations. These pussywillows are actually the female flowers of the extremely successful species *Salix discolour Muhl*. Both the male and female flowers mature at a time when other trees have not yet come into leaf, thereby increasing the likelihood that the wind will transfer male pollen to the female flowers.

Change and Variability among Individuals

Although like produces like, nearly all new offspring are smaller than their parents, and some must undergo many changes before they resemble adults. These changes include **development** (formation of adult body structures) and **growth** (increase in body size).

If the species requires only one parent for reproduction, the adult offspring will be identical to the parent and to each other. (See Figure 2-5.) But in species that require two parents for reproduction, the offspring will vary somewhat from each other and also from either of their parents. For example, all kittens in a litter inherit all of the characteristics of their species, *Felis domesticus*. However, each one inherits a different combination of parental features. This outcome is called **inherited variability.** It ensures that no two members of the same species will be exactly alike. Even purebred cats and dogs vary somewhat. This is why some become champions and others are family pets.

FIGURE 2-5 Bacterial species normally reproduce by simple cell division — one parent, two identical offspring.

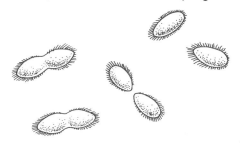

Tadpoles must grow large in size and undergo considerable development before they become adult frogs.

Like human brothers and sisters, these young kittens are clearly young cats, yet they are different from their parents and each other.

Plant and animal breeders take advantage of inherited variability to develop varieties with a desired colour. Apricot-coloured poodles, blue roses, and yellow petunias were all developed by breeding individuals with unusual colouring.

Change and Variability in a Species

Over time, inherited variability may lead to changes in a species. Most of these changes occur far too slowly to be observed in a human lifetime, but colour changes can occur more quickly. A particularly dramatic example is *Biston betularia*, an insect native to England. The species is usually called the peppered moth because of its variegated black and white wing patches. Differing proportions of black and white from one moth to another result in a range of wing colours that vary from light to dark. Before 1850, 99% of the moths had light-coloured wings. By 1900, only 1% did. The rest had dark wings. Biologists link this rapid colour shift to changes in the moths' environment.

Can you spot all four moths? Which form do you think would be the easiest prey in an area where trees were blackened by soot? What environmental change would account for the colour change in this species between 1850 and 1900?

I THE STUDY OF LIFE

The Vocabulary of Biology

Students who are just beginning to study biology often complain that there are too many new words to learn. It is true that some biological terms contain many syllables, and that the syllables reflect their Greek and Latin origins. (See Table 2-3.) Consequently, the words may seem long, foreign, and difficult. But when you use this specialized terminology, you are actually saving time because you will be able to communicate precisely. It is often easier to use a single, specialized word than it is to write out a long phrase in simpler language. Consider the word dermatomyositis. A person who has never heard this word before but who has a knowledge of biological terminology could quickly determine that it means ''a disorder causing both skin and muscle to become inflamed.'' With a little practice, you will also be able to use biological terms as a shortcut.

TABLE 2-3   Roots Derived from Greek and Latin Used in Biological Terms

Root	Meaning	Root	Meaning
-auto-	• self	-lysis	• burst or break apart
cardi-	• of the heart	morph-	• form
carni-	• meat	myo-(e)-	• of muscle(s)
cerebr-	• of the brain	neuro-	• of the nerve(s)
chemo-	• chemical	-ology	• study of
chloro-	• green	-osis	• condition, disease
chromo-	• coloured	osteo-	• of the bone(s)
cyto-, -cyte	• cell, of the cell	ova(i,u)	• egg
-derm-	• layer, skin	peri-	• around, surrounding
-duct-	• tube	-phyte	• plant
endo-	• on or toward inside	-pod-	• of the foot
-epi	• upon, on top	pseudo	• false
erythro-	• red	skeleton	• part left after drying
exo-	• on or toward outside	-some	• body
hypo-	• under	-spino	• of the spine
intra-	• within, inside	-spore	• seed-like structure
-itis	• inflammation, infection	-vore	• feeding
leuko-	• white	xero-	• dry

Building Biological Terminology

Table 2-3 lists several word roots that are used repeatedly in biological terminology. Some are prefixes and some suffixes, but others may appear in either position. For example "derm" is a suffix in epidermis but a prefix in dermatitis.

A. Word Analysis

In science, analysis refers to the process of breaking something complex into smaller units in order to understand how they are related. Word analysis lets you define a word by breaking it down into its roots.

Example: Use word analysis to define the word hypodermic.
Solution: From Table 2-3,
  hypo- means under
  -derm means skin

Therefore, hypodermic refers to something that is placed under the skin. (For example, a hypodermic needle is used to inject medication just under the skin.)

Use the word analysis method to define the following biological terms: autolysis, dermatitis, epidermis, erythrocyte, exoskeleton, leukocyte, morphology, oviduct, periosteum, and pseudopod.

Discussion Questions

1. Check your definitions against the glossary in this textbook or in a science dictionary. (Not all definitions will appear in this textbook.) How closely do the definitions derived by word analysis approximate the formal definitions? Discuss.
2. a) Which body parts are affected by each of the following disorders: appendicitis, dermatitis, gastritis, laryngitis, and osteomyelitis? (Table 2-3 does not list the roots for all of these body parts. Try to work out the meaning from your own knowledge before you consult a dictionary.) Discuss.
   b) How is the body part affected in each case? Discuss.

B. Word Synthesis

In science, synthesis means combining separate elements to form a connected system. Word synthesis allows you to create a word by putting roots together.

Example: Synthesize a word that means meat eater.
Solution: From Table 2-3,
     carni- means meat
     -vore means feeding

So, carnivore means meat eater.

Use the word synthesis method to synthesize words for each of the following definitions.

   a) study of the heart
   b) inside the cell
   c) coloured body or part
   d) membrane around the heart
   e) bone cell
   f) spore-producing plant
   g) inflammation of the nerves
   h) use of chemical energy to produce body substances
   i) transport materials away from a cell
   j) fluid that cushions the brain and the spinal cord against shock

Discussion Questions

1. Exchange word lists with a partner and write definitions for your partner's synthesized words. (Remember to close your textbook while you complete this part of the activity.) How closely do these definitions correspond to the original definitions? Discuss.

2. Check your synthesized words against the glossary in this textbook or in a science dictionary. (Not all of these terms will appear in this textbook.) How closely do the terms created by word synthesis approximate the formal terms? Discuss.

Branches of Biology

Many biologists specialize in one of the branches of biology shown in Table 2-4. The dissection described on page 45 is a contribution from anatomy, one that greatly expanded our understanding of the structure of the human nervous system. However, physiology and biochemistry have also contributed to our present understanding of nerve function. Clearly, some branches of biology are interdependent, and some require a thorough understanding of other science disciplines. Not surprisingly, each branch has its own specialized investigative tools and techniques. Nevertheless, all share the characteristic views and assumptions of biology, and all share the biological approach to scientific research. You will learn more about this approach in Section 2.2.

TABLE 2-4 Branches of Biology

Branch	Topics Studied
Anatomy	• structure of organisms
Biochemistry	• chemical substances and reactions in living things
Botany	• plants
Cytology	• cells
Ecology	• how living things interact with their environment
Embryology	• how living things form and develop into independent organisms
Genetics	• how inherited characteristics pass from one generation to the next
Microbiology	• micro-organisms
Paleontology	• fossils
Pathology	• animal diseases
Physiology	• how living things perform life functions
Taxonomy	• classification of living things
Zoology	• animals

Section Review Questions

1. a) What is a science discipline?
   b) Name a discipline other than biology and identify one of its central assumptions.

2. This section identifies eight major assumptions of biology. Summarize each in a single sentence.

3. a) From what basic question do all biological assumptions arise?
   b) How does the scientific use of the term assumption differ from its use in everyday conversation?

4. For each of the following pairs of terms, explain how the two terms are related and how they differ.
   a) living thing, nonliving thing
   b) internal environment, external environment
   c) structure, function
   d) adaptation, environment
   e) diversity, unity

5. Write a short phrase to explain the meaning of homeostasis.

6. Name two branches of biology. Describe what they have in common and how they differ.

The Gift of Harriet Cole

Rufus J. Weaver (1841-1936) was a trained physician whose interest in human anatomy was so intense that he did not practise medicine in his lifetime. One of his jobs as an anatomy instructor at Hahnemann Medical College in Philadelphia, Pennsylvania, was to provide specimens for teaching and research. He took this duty seriously and stocked the museum with thousands of normal, abnormal, and diseased hearts, lungs, kidneys, bones, and almost every conceivable kind of body tissue except a preserved nervous system. No one had ever done such a dissection and most anatomists believed the task was almost impossible.

Harriet Cole was a janitor. Her job included cleaning the laboratory where Weaver demonstrated human anatomy to medical students. Far from being repulsed by the task of cleaning up after Weaver's dissections, she became fascinated by his learning and dedication, and eventually showed her respect in a practical way. Upon her death at age 36, it was discovered that Harriet Cole had willed her body to Hahnemann for medical research.

Here at last was the anatomically perfect specimen Weaver needed to provide the museum with a nervous system. He immersed the unexpected gift in a large vat of preservative while he considered how best to use it. After eight years of planning, he began the actual dissection, which took him seven months, working 12 h a day.

To get at the nerves without damaging them, Weaver made thousands of incisions to remove

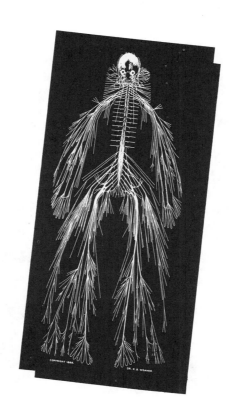

the surrounding flesh in tiny slices. It took four weeks of patient slicing to release the nerves in the skull and spine. To keep the nerves from tangling or drying out, Weaver rolled each one in moist gauze and covered it in rubber cloth.

Finally, Weaver stiffened the nerves with white shellac and mounted the entire system on a board, using nearly 2000 pins. The original dissection was complete, but the mounted version lacks certain components. The soft tissue of the brain was removed, so that only its membranous covering remains. Weaver also sacrificed the intercostal (chest) nerves and the sympathetic nerves (see Chapter 8) when he realized they couldn't be mounted without obscuring the rest of the system.

Weaver went on to a long career of professional accomplishments. And when he died at age 95, his obituaries honoured him most for the enduring patience, unremitting care, and manipulative skill with which he completed what many regard as the greatest dissection ever done.

After Weaver's death, his dissection of Cole's nervous system fell into disrepair and was stored away for years, but a 1960 restoration project has enabled "Harriet" to begin teaching a new generation of medical students.

All of these tools are used to conduct biological research, even the calculator. Biologists use more numerical methods than you might think.

Some people with exceptionally good eyes can see objects as small as 0.1 mm if viewing conditions are perfect. For most people, 0.2 mm is a more realistic limit.

A modern compound microscope. Early models had only two lenses — an eyepiece and an objective. Modern instruments avoid the distortion of early models by using lens sets instead of single lenses for each eyepiece and each objective.

This light micrograph magnifies the grooves of a standard recording disc 10×.

2.2 Tools and Techniques of Biological Research

All biological research has one common goal — to answer questions about living things. Like other scientists, biologists depend on observations to collect data. Consequently, they use a wide variety of scientific tools and techniques. One observational tool, however, has played a very special role in biological research. It is called a **compound microscope**, or a compound-light microscope, because it uses visible light to form an enlarged image of the object being viewed, and because it has several lenses.

Magnification refers to a microscope's ability to enlarge an image. A typical school microscope has an eyepiece magnification of 10× and a choice of three or four objective settings. The total magnification when a 10× eyepiece is combined with a 4× objective is 40×. Most school microscopes can magnify up to around 400× if the most powerful objective is chosen. Some professional-quality compound microscopes magnify up to 1500×, but two factors limit the usefulness of the resulting image: the structure of the human eye and the nature of light.

The structure of the human eye limits your ability to see objects smaller than about 0.2 mm. This limit is a measure of your eye's **resolving power,** or resolution, which is its ability to deliver a clear, sharp image. For example, the photographs on this page appear clear and sharp to your unaided eye. Magnification would show that these pictures are actually made up of separate dots, but your unaided eye cannot see this. Spacing the dots less than 0.1 mm apart makes them seem continuous rather than separate.

The nature of light is a limiting factor because it restricts the microscope's ability to produce a clear, sharp image. A microscope's lens system enlarges images by causing light from the object being observed to spread out. (Recall Figure 1-2 on page 9.) When you look through the eyepiece, you see a circular

field that contains only a fraction of the spread-out light. When you switch to a more powerful lens, the light spreads out even more. This magnifies the image but also causes two problems. First, the image gets dimmer because spread-out light is not as intense. Second, the fraction of the image that appears in the circular field becomes even smaller. For example, the dots in the photograph would appear farther and farther apart as magnifying power increases. At $1500\times$, the field might contain only a part of one dot or no dot at all. The ability of a microscope to deliver a clear, sharp image is almost completely lost at this setting. The $400\times$ setting on your school microscope would actually provide much more detail in this situation.

Any specimen that must be magnified $400\times$ to be seen is too small to measure in millimetres. For this reason, microscopic specimens are often measured in **micrometres (μm).** One micrometre (1 μm) is equal to $\frac{1}{1000}$ of a millimetre (0.001 mm). If you determine your microscope's field diameter in advance, you can easily estimate the size of the objects you view.

LABORATORY EXERCISE 2-1
The Compound Microscope: A Tool for Extending the Senses

Maximum benefit and enjoyment from your study of living things will depend in part on the skillful use of a compound microscope. This exercise is divided into several parts, each reviewing one of the following skills.
- The parts of a microscope
- How to prepare a slide
- How to estimate the size of microscopic specimens
- How to set up and care for a microscope
- How to operate a microscope
- How to report microscopic observations

Biological Research and the Scientific Method

Although biology employs particular methods of observing and gathering data, biologists use the same general research procedure as other scientists. This procedure is often called the **scientific method.** Most scientists and most textbooks would agree that the scientific method is an orderly, logical system for solving problems. However, as Table 2-5 indicates, scientists have not completely agreed on the specific steps that are involved.

Despite these differences of opinion, three terms — problem, hypothesis, and controlled experiment — appear in the same order. Most scientists would agree that these are the key steps, but few would claim that they always follow

TABLE 2-5 The Scientific Method: Three Different Approaches

Textbook A	Textbook B	Textbook C
• define the problem	• observe	• idea or observation
• collect related information	• define the problem	• statement of problem
• form a hypothesis	• form a hypothesis	• hypothesis
• design a controlled experiment to test the hypothesis	• test hypothesis with a controlled experiment	• controlled experiment
• observe and record experimental data	• observe and record results	• collect and analyze data
• draw conclusions	• form conclusions by confirming or modifying the hypothesis	• compare results with hypothesis
	• report results	• perform further experiments for confirmation

FIGURE 2-6 A cyclical view of scientific research shows that the cycle can be entered at any stage. It also shows that a first hypothesis seldom leads directly to an acceptable theory.

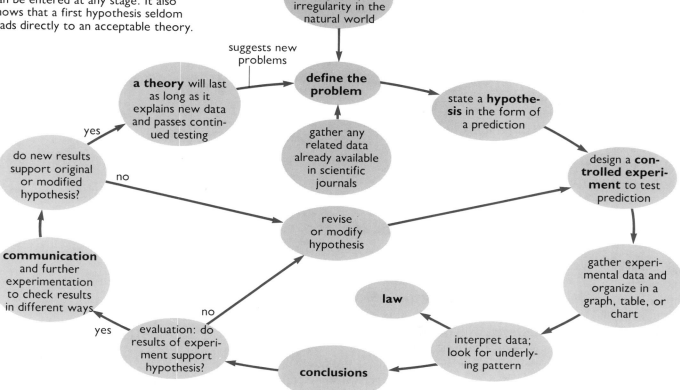

these steps in the order listed. They would point out that science is, after all, a creative activity. Often, a few experiments must be conducted before a problem can be defined clearly. Sometimes a hypothesis may be based on a single observation. In fact, it is simply not possible to list one scientific method that encompasses every example of scientific research. The cyclical model in Figure 2-6 probably describes scientific research more realistically, but understanding this model depends on understanding what scientists mean by the key terms in it. You will learn more about these terms in the remainder of this section.

Facts, Observations, and Laws

Any information gathered through the senses or through an instrument that extends the senses such as a balance or a microscope is an observation. If enough observers agree about an observation, it is regarded as a fact. For example, "cats always give birth to kittens" is a fact. No one has ever observed a cat giving birth to anything else. Scientists often organize facts into graphs or tables to look for regularities, patterns, or relationships. (See Figure 2-7.)

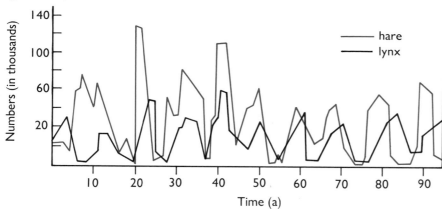

FIGURE 2-7 Reorganizing population data to produce a graph reveals a close relationship between the Canadian lynx and the snowshoe hare.

In some cases, a regular pattern can be stated in the form of a scientific law. The Universal Law of Gravitation, for example, defines the rate at which a ball that has been thrown will fall to Earth, or the rate at which a shuttle must be launched to remain in orbit around the Earth. However, laws do not explain. They can only describe or define relationships. Physicists are still trying to explain gravitation. Scientific laws are more common in chemistry and physics than in biology. However, biologists cannot avoid understanding the laws of physics and chemistry since all living systems are affected by them.

Defining a Problem

In science, a problem usually arises from one of two sources — wondering why a regular pattern exists or wondering why a break in a usual pattern has occurred. For example, a clear spot on a culture plate that should have been covered with bacteria made Alexander Fleming ask himself why the usual bacterial growth pattern did not occur. Defining a problem is actually a very difficult step. Asking big questions is easy. Asking a question in such a way that it can be investigated using current technology is not as easy. Scientists investigate, analyze, and think about a question until the true nature of the problem becomes clear.

Hypothesis

A **hypothesis** is a possible solution to a problem. Most hypotheses begin as educated guesses. Fleming guessed that the culture plate had been contaminated with a spore from some kind of fungal mould. A guess becomes a hypothesis when it is stated in a form that suggests a way to test it. The following "if . . . then" statement is an example. "If the bacteria in my original culture were killed by a mould, then sprinkling mould spores on a new culture should kill some of the bacteria." In effect, a hypothesis is a prediction.

Controlled Experiment

An experiment tests the ability of the hypothesis to make a correct prediction. The only fair way to test a hypothesis is with a **controlled experiment.** A controlled experiment is conducted using two almost identical sets of apparatus

FIGURE 2-8 A controlled experiment to test the hypothesis that mould spores kill bacteria. After three days of incubation, the clear patch in the experimental apparatus reveals that mould spores do inhibit the growth of bacteria. However, the researcher still does not know whether other mould spores have the same property. Further controlled experiments must be conducted to determine whether this is the only kind of mould whose spores kill bacteria.

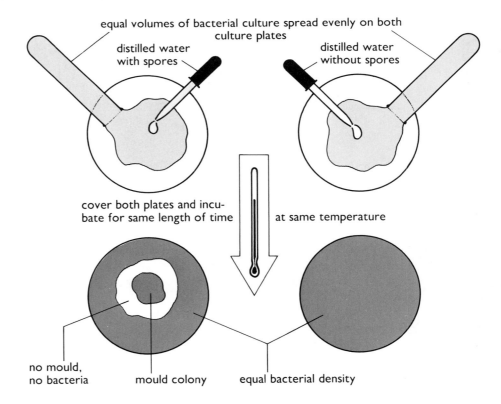

equal volumes of bacterial culture spread evenly on both culture plates

distilled water with spores

distilled water without spores

cover both plates and incubate for same length of time

at same temperature

no mould, no bacteria

mould colony

equal bacterial density

I   THE STUDY OF LIFE

and under almost identical conditions. All factors that could affect the outcome of the experiment are kept exactly the same in both set-ups except for one. The one factor that differs is called the **variable.** The set-up in which the variable is absent is called the **control.**

Figure 2-8 shows how a modern researcher might design a controlled experiment to test the hypothesis that mould spores kill bacteria. In the example shown here, the variable is the presence of the mould spores in the experimental set-up. The control set-up shows how bacteria grow when the variable is not present. By comparing both sets of results, the researcher can tell whether the variable makes a difference. Without a control, it could be argued that the drop of liquid containing the spores had prevented bacterial growth.

Controlled experiments allow scientists to test the effect of one factor at a time. Such experiments are more common in biology than in any other science. Geologists and astronomers, for example, cannot usually conduct controlled experiments to support their hypotheses.

Theories, Communication, and Proof

Because any hypothesis is only one of many possible solutions to a problem, scientists must keep an open mind until enough evidence exists to justify a conclusion. If many scientists test a hypothesis in many different ways, and all of their experiments support it, then the hypothesis may become widely accepted as a valid explanation for the original problem. Over time, if the hypothesis continues to explain new observations, it may eventually be called a **theory.**

Only one of the lists in Table 2-5 mentions reporting results as a part of the scientific method. Yet communication is probably the most consistent feature of all scientific research. All reputable scientists communicate the results of their research by publishing articles in well-respected journals or giving lectures to scientific societies. Once results have been published, other scientists interested in the same topic can test the researcher's hypothesis.

The nature of scientific verification means that no theory can ever be completely "proven." The best it can do is explain all the data collected so far. But theories can be tested by using them to predict the outcome of new experiments. If the results are not as predicted, the theory is refuted (disproved) and will have to be revised or even discarded. But there is no way to "prove" a theory. A theory survives only as long as it continues to account for new evidence.

"It didn't work!" How many times have you or a classmate said this about the results of an experiment? Experiments always work. Unexpected results mean only that the experiment did not work in the way that you predicted. Many important discoveries were made when a researcher kept an open mind about an experiment that did not meet his or her expectations.

Through experiment, Louis Pasteur developed an anti-rabies vaccine, even though he was unable to identify a ''germ'' that might cause the disease.

RESEARCH PROJECT
Examining a Theory

One theory universally accepted by modern scientists is the germ theory of disease. This theory is usually credited to Louis Pasteur, a French biologist. A century ago, it was just a hypothesis. Few other scientists believed that micro-organisms caused disease, and many nonscientists believed that illness was caused by evil spirits, curses, or sin.

In your school library, find out about the early research that led Louis Pasteur to state the germ hypothesis, and the role played by controlled experiments in elevating this hypothesis to the status of a theory. Report your findings in the form of a poster, a concept map, or a short essay as suggested by your teacher.

Limits of Science

Science is a human endeavour, and therefore subject to the same kinds of prejudice, jealousy, and shortcomings as any other human endeavour. But despite human frailties, the framework in which scientists conduct research is inherently honest and fair. By communicating their results, and testing each other's ideas, scientists themselves make scientific research a self-regulating enterprise. Nevertheless, there are limits to scientific knowledge.

All scientific knowledge is tentative and open-ended. Past knowledge and research have provided the basis for today's understanding of biology. Today's knowledge and research will form the basis for tomorrow's understanding of biology. Nothing in science is ever proven, and everything is subject to revision. You should also remember that science is limited to the natural world and is only one way of understanding it. History, philosophy, and religion also contribute greatly to human knowledge and have valid viewpoints.

Despite its limits, however, scientific knowledge and research create issues that necessitate responsible decision making. Suppose in the future biologists learn how to prevent elderly people from dying at a cost of one million dollars per person. Who should benefit from this knowledge? Should anyone? Is this knowledge dangerous? Should it be banned? Who should decide?

The world you live in has many real problems: an ever-increasing human population, widespread pollution, shrinking rain forests, diminishing ozone layers, and malnutrition. Scientific knowledge can help society resolve such issues, but only if citizens understand its limits and recognize that moral, ethical, economic, and political views must also be considered.

I   THE STUDY OF LIFE

Section Review Questions

1. a) What is the goal of all biological research?
   b) Which tool that extends the senses has played a special role in biological research? Explain.

2. a) Define magnification and show how it can be expressed numerically by stating the usual magnification for a microscope eyepiece.
   b) Define resolution and show how it can be expressed numerically by stating the resolving power of the human eye.

3. Suppose you are given a photomicrograph of a specimen that has been magnified 1500×. What factors limit the scientific value of this image? Explain.

4. a) Which unit is used to measure specimens observed with a compound microscope? Explain why.
   b) What is the correct abbreviation for the unit you identified above? Relate this unit to a more familiar metric unit.

5. a) What is the general meaning of the term scientific method?
   b) Explain why it is difficult for scientists and textbooks to agree on the steps involved in this method.

6. List three key terms that appear in most detailed descriptions of the scientific method. Define and state an example of each.

7. Explain the relationship between
   a) an observation and a fact
   b) a law and a theory
   c) a theory and a proof

2.3 Cells and the Cell Theory

Robert Hooke first saw empty, compartment-like cork cells in 1665. Over the next one and a half centuries other investigators also saw cells in biological specimens, but they made little progress in understanding them. Around 1800, however, improvements in glass-making made powerful, distortion-free lenses possible, turning the compound microscope into a reliable investigative tool. As a result, scientists all over Europe were using microscopes to look at plant and animal parts. What they saw soon had them asking questions. What are cells? Where do they come from? What do they do? Do all living things contain cells? The efforts of scientists to answer these questions eventually led to development of the **cell theory.**

Development of the Cell Theory

The cell theory summarizes our current understanding of cells. Like all scientific theories, it is based on the work of many people, each of whom contributed a small part to the puzzle.

☐ **1700s** Some investigators confirm Hooke's observation that the cells of some biological specimens contain liquid.

☐ **1809** Jean Baptiste de Lamarck, a French naturalist, claims that "Every living body is essentially a mass of cellular tissue in which more or less complex fluids move more or less rapidly." This claim is not accepted by other scientists because Lamarck's supporting evidence is inadequate.

☐ **1824** Henri Dutrochet, a French biologist, observes repeatedly that macroscopic organisms are made of many cell units and states a hypothesis. "The cell is truly the fundamental part of the living organism." Dutrochet's evidence convinces many researchers to accept this hypothesis for plants, but few apply it to animals.

☐ **1831** Robert Brown, a Scottish botanist, observes a denser central structure in many kinds of plant cells and calls it the **nucleus.**

☐ **1835** Felix Dujardin, a French biologist, confirms the presence of fluids in many kinds of living cells and proposes the idea that all living cells contain a common "life substance," which is later called "protoplasm."

☐ **1838** Matthias Schleiden, a German botanist, presents convincing evidence to support his conclusion that all plants are made of living cells. He also recognizes that the nucleus is somehow involved in producing new cells.

☐ **1839** Theodor Schwann, a German zoologist, reaches similar conclusions regarding animal cells. His evidence persuades other scientists that no great barrier separates the plant and animal kingdoms; they are united by a common structural unit—the cell.

☐ **1855** Rudolph Virchow, a German biologist, after observing cell division in a variety of organisms, concludes that cells arise only from other cells. Virchow's hypothesis, along with those of Schleiden and Schwann, form the basis of the cell theory.

- All living organisms are made up of cells.
- The cell is the basic structural unit of living organisms.
- The cell is the basic functional unit of living organisms.
- All cells come from pre-existing cells.

More than a century later, the cell theory continues to explain much of what is observed about living things, and is considered to be one of the most important concepts in biology.

DID YOU KNOW?

In earlier times, the plant kingdom was considered to be inferior to the animal kingdom, and most people were unwilling to believe that the two might have anything in common. This belief was so strongly held that wealthier classes refused to eat fruits and vegetables. Some medical historians suggest that Henry VIII died of scurvy, a disorder caused by a lack of vitamin C-containing plants in the diet.

The intellectual climate prevailing in the early 1800s was ideal for the development of the cell theory. In 1808, John Dalton claimed that all kinds of matter were made up of tiny units called atoms. As the atomic theory became more widely accepted, it fostered the idea that living things might also be made up of many small units.

Structure of Living Cells

Because many cells are almost transparent, few details of cellular structure could be observed until chemical discoveries in the 1850s led to the manufacture of synthetic dyes that were much stronger than any previously known. Once biological samples were stained with these dyes, scientists could see that cells were many different sizes and shapes. (See Figure 2-9.)

In addition, dyes enabled microscopists to see why plant and animal cells had appeared to be so different. (See Figure 2-10.) Each plant cell is surrounded by a nonliving **cell wall** made of a tough, but porous, fibre called cellulose. The box-like wall protects and supports individual plant cells and gives them a distinctive shape. Plant cells also contain distinctive structures called **plastids.** The most common plastids are **chloroplasts,** which manufacture food with the help of a green substance called **chlorophyll.** Animal cells do not have walls or plastids. These structures are found only in plants and plant-like organisms.

Apart from these differences, most living cells consist of similar components such as a thin covering called the **cell membrane.** The membrane surrounds **protoplasm,** a complex fluid containing everything a cell needs to survive. In most cells, the protoplasm is organized into two distinct regions, the nucleoplasm and the cytoplasm. The **nucleoplasm** is the fluid inside the

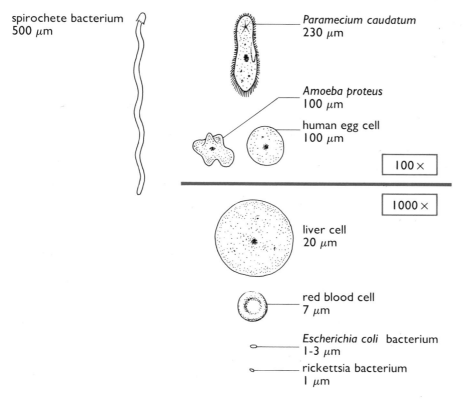

spirochete bacterium
500 μm

Paramecium caudatum
230 μm

Amoeba proteus
100 μm

human egg cell
100 μm

100 ×

1000 ×

liver cell
20 μm

red blood cell
7 μm

Escherichia coli bacterium
1-3 μm

rickettsia bacterium
1 μm

FIGURE 2-9 Cells vary in shape and size. Those above the line have been magnified 100 ×. Those below the line have been magnified 1000 ×.

The shape of a cell may reveal its function. Human nerve cells and skin cells differ greatly in shape from muscle cells. However, muscle cells from dogs, cats, and humans, are similar.

FIGURE 2-10 Cell structures as seen through a compound microscope

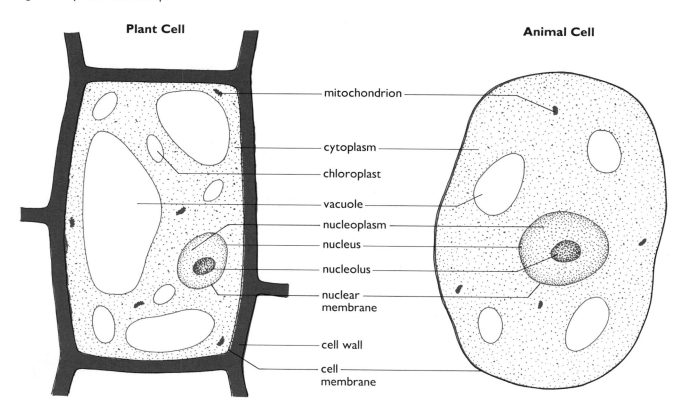

Plant Cell   Animal Cell

mitochondrion
cytoplasm
chloroplast
vacuole
nucleoplasm
nucleus
nucleolus
nuclear membrane
cell wall
cell membrane

cell's nucleus. The nucleus has its own membrane, which separates the nucleoplasm from the rest of the cell. The **cytoplasm** includes everything between the nuclear membrane and the cell membrane. Cytoplasm appears grainy under a microscope, but the suspended ''grains'' are actually internal cell structures called **organelles.** Like the organs in the human body, each kind of organelle performs a specific function. Table 2-6 describes the appearance and function of all cell components that can be seen through a typical school microscope.

LABORATORY EXERCISE 2-2
Comparing Plant and Animal Cells

In this exercise, you will use a staining technique to examine plant and animal cells under a microscope. You will also compare both kinds of cells. Table 2-6 and Figure 2-10 will help you to recognize the cell parts you see.

Natural interactions enable a pond environment to support a diverse array of organisms. Microscopic species may number in the millions, but populations of large species tend to be smaller. An entire lake ecosystem may be needed to support a single family of loons.

Human interactions with the environment frequently focus on altering, controlling, or manipulating it to provide food, living space, or material goods. Such interactions decrease ecosystem diversity by reducing the number of species, but without them Earth could not support such a large human population.

TABLE 2-6 Cell Features Visible through a Compound Microscope

Structure	Identifying Features	Function
Cell Membrane	• thin covering; barely visible when stained; difficult to distinguish from cell wall in plant cells	• separates cell from its external environment; allows necessary materials to enter and wastes to pass out
Nucleus	• large, dark-staining structure near centre of cell	• controls cell and directs its activities
Nucleoplasm	• fluid inside nucleus	• contains materials needed by nucleus
Nucleolus	• darker spherical structure suspended in nucleoplasm	• directs production of essential organelles
Cytoplasm	• grainy fluid between nucleus and cell membrane	• grains are organelles that perform cell functions; fluid contains materials needed for functions
Vacuoles	• clear, fluid-filled membrane-lined sacs (most prominent in plant cells)	• storage areas for water, food, minerals, and wastes; contents exert pressure to keep plant cell walls rigid
Mitochondria	• barely visible, sausage-shaped structures	• release energy for cell's life functions
Plastids (e.g., chloroplasts)	• large green structures, usually oval	• carry out photosynthesis in plants
Plant Cell Wall	• surrounds cell membrane • highly visible when stained	• protects and supports plant cells

The cells of bacteria and other members of the kingdom Monera do not have nuclei. They also lack almost all kinds of cell organelles. These differences help to explain why taxonomists classify them in a separate kingdom.

Life Functions of a Cell

Whether a cell is a unicellular bacterium or a single unit in a multicellular organism such as an elephant, it must perform certain life functions in order to survive. The four main cell functions are the release of energy, the transport of materials, the manufacture of substances, and reproduction. As you progress through Units II-V, you will be able to upgrade your present understanding of these cell functions. Meanwhile, the following subsections will help you review what you have already learned in earlier studies.

Release of Energy

To maintain homeostasis, and to perform other functions and activities, cells need energy. Most cells obtain their energy from food molecules such as glucose. The energy stored in the food is converted to a usable form in the **mitochondria** through a chemical process called **cellular respiration.** This

The glucose most cells use as an energy source is produced by plants and plant-like organisms through photosynthesis. To perform this function, the chloroplasts of plant cells need sunlight and a supply of carbon dioxide and water. The glucose produced is stored in the plant's body. Oxygen, which is also produced, escapes as a waste product. Both glucose and oxygen are used as raw materials in cellular respiration.

process uses oxygen as well as glucose, and produces waste water and carbon dioxide. For continued release of energy, the cell must be able to bring in required materials and dispose of waste products.

Transportation of Materials

All materials that enter or leave a cell's internal environment must move across the cell membrane. The membrane is said to be selectively permeable because its numerous pores admit some substances but not others. Molecules such as water, oxygen, and carbon dioxide are small enough to diffuse in or out of a cell membrane through its pores. **Diffusion** is the natural movement of particles from a region of high concentration to a region of low concentration. (See Figure 2-11.) The diffusion of water is so common and so important to living cells that it has been given its own name — **osmosis.** Diffusion and osmosis are often called **passive transport** because a cell does not have to use its own energy to move the molecules. However, a cell cannot control diffusion directly. The natural direction of diffusion depends entirely on differences in concentration from one region to another.

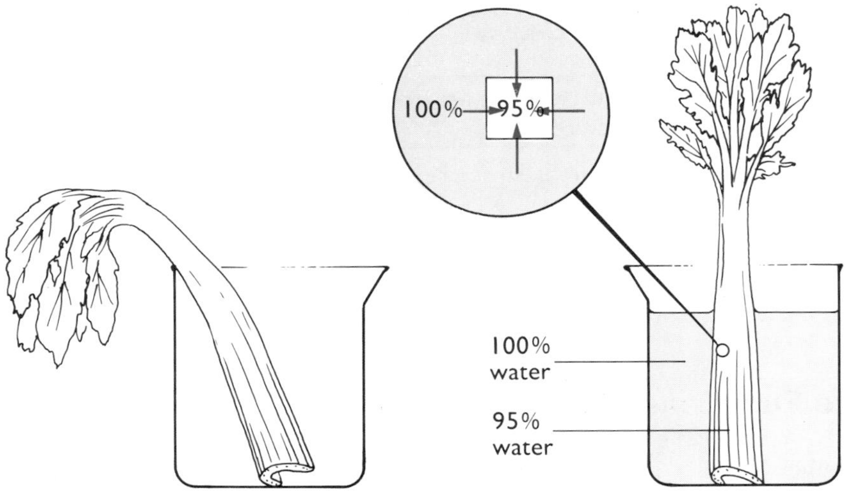

FIGURE 2-11 The celery on the left is limp because it cannot replace the water lost by evaporation. The celery on the right remains rigid because the concentration of water outside its stalk is greater than the concentration of water inside its cells. As a result, water diffuses inward across the cell membranes.

100% →95%

100% water

95% water

FIGURE 2-12 The cells of plant roots keep the concentration of minerals inside the root much higher than that in the surrounding soil.

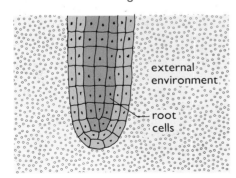

external environment

root cells

Sometimes a cell has to work against the natural direction of diffusion in order to control its internal environment. This process is called **active transport** because the cell must use its own energy to move the molecules. Active transport is also needed to move large particles across the cell membrane. Active transport enables a cell to maintain an internal environment very different from its surroundings. (See Figure 2-12.)

Manufacture of Cell Parts and Products

In addition to releasing energy by cellular respiration, each cell must manufacture all of the substances it needs to make its own structure. Some cells also manufacture substances for use in the external environment. For example, fungal cells release digestive chemicals to decompose the external food supply that the fungus grows on.

Cell parts and products are produced in the cytoplasm, but directions for manufacturing them are stored in the cell's nucleus. Each nucleus contains a hereditary material called **deoxyribonucleic acid,** or **DNA.** The arrangement of atoms in the cell's DNA forms a code that contains all the instructions for the operation of the cell. Each species has its own unique DNA code.

Cell Division and Reproduction

Continued production of cell parts and products results in cell growth. But beyond a certain size, a cell can no longer function efficiently. As a cell grows, the surface area of its membrane does not increase in proportion to the volume of its protoplasm. As a result, the membrane cannot transport substances quickly enough to meet the cell's needs. When this occurs, the cell prepares itself to divide.

Before cell division actually begins, the nucleus manufactures a complete additional set of DNA. Then the nucleus divides, sorting the DNA into two identical sets, one for each new nucleus. (See Figure 2-13.) The duplication of DNA and division of the nucleus is called **mitosis.** Mitosis is the most important part of cell division since the DNA contains all the instructions for cell activity. After mitosis is complete, the cytoplasm is divided into two approximately equal parts, and new cell membranes grow between them. In plant cells, a new cell wall also forms. The division of the cytoplasm is called **cytokinesis.** Each of the two new cells contains exactly the same DNA code as the original cell and therefore will be able to perform all the same functions.

All multicellular organisms grow through repeated mitotic cell divisions. Single-celled species such as the amoeba also reproduce by means of mitotic cell division. The offspring are smaller than the parent cell but identical in structure and function. Because this type of reproduction involves only one parent, it is called asexual reproduction. The characteristics of the species are passed from one generation to the next by the DNA in the duplicated nuclei.

Many multicellular species produce offspring by sexual reproduction, a process in which two sex cells (egg and sperm) unite and then develop into a new individual. Sex cells are produced by a very specialized kind of cell division, one in which the nucleus divides by **meiosis.** During meiosis, the nucleus is first duplicated and then divides twice. The result of meiotic cell division is four sex cells, each with only half of the usual amount of DNA.

Section Review Questions

1. State two examples of nineteenth century technology that expanded scientific understanding of cells and explain how each example contributed.
2. a) State the main points of the cell theory.
   b) Based on this theory, define the term cell in your own words.

Every cell contains the complete DNA code for the entire organism. However, in multicellular organisms, not every cell uses the entire code. Skin cells differ from blood cells because some parts of the DNA are turned off in skin cells, and different parts are turned off in blood cells.

You will learn more about cell division in Chapter 22.

FIGURE 2-13 Mitotic cell division in an animal cell. In plant cells, a new cell wall must be formed as well.

1. Mitosis begins: DNA in nucleus is duplicated.

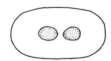

2. Mitosis continues: nucleus divides and new nuclei separate.

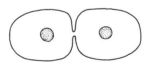

3. Cytokinesis occurs: cytoplasm pinches off; new cell membrane forms.

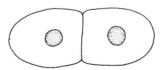

4. Cell division is complete: two new cells have been produced.

3. a) Define protoplasm, nucleoplasm, and cytoplasm. How do these cell components differ?
   b) How does a cell keep its protoplasm separate from the external environment?

4. a) Define the term organelle.
   b) List three organelles found in both plant and animal cells. Briefly describe the function of each.

5. a) List two cell structures found in plants that are not also found in animals.
   b) What function(s) do these structures perform for the plant cell? How do animal cells survive without them?

6. a) List four life functions that must be performed by all cells. Beside each, identify the cell substance, structure, or organelle most closely associated with that function.
   b) Briefly describe why each function in part (a) is needed for a cell's survival.

2.4 Modern Tools and Techniques

For biologists, the most significant tool developed in this century is probably the electron microscope, which overcomes the limitations of compound microscopes by using beams of electrons to form images. The electron microscope has two advantages over the compound microscope: its resolution is 40 times greater, and it can magnify images up to 200 000 × or more. This combination

An electron micrograph of a diamond stylus on a standard turntable

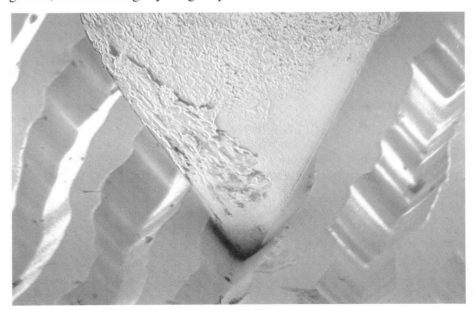

I THE STUDY OF LIFE

enables electron microscopes to produce astonishingly clear images of micro-organisms, individual cells, and even cell organelles. The images can be displayed on a television monitor or photographed to produce an electron micrograph. (You will learn more about electron microscopes and the images they produce in Chapter 20.)

The electron microscope was developed in the 1930s, but it was not commonly used in hospitals, universities, and research laboratories until the 1950s. What the electron microscope revealed about the cell made scientists even more curious, leading to the development of more technology for biological research. Techniques that make it possible to dissect a single cell are now available. It is even possible to "operate" on a cell. But perhaps the most exciting development of this part of the century is the application of chemistry to the study of cell function.

Biochemical Methods of Investigation

Biochemists study the substances organisms are made of. These substances include fats, carbohydrates, and proteins, which are the very substances you find in your food. This is hardly surprising, since most of what you eat was once part of a living thing. Fats and carbohydrates are fairly similar regardless of the organism they come from, but proteins are both varied and distinctive. Your body contains hundreds of different kinds of proteins. Some are used to build body parts such as blood, hair, skin, and muscle. Others are used to control chemical reactions such as cellular respiration.

A full understanding of cell function depends in large part on knowing which substances cells contain. But each living thing and each cell contains

Insulin is a protein that controls the intake of glucose by body cells. Underproduction of insulin leads to a disorder known as diabetes. The insulin most diabetics inject is obtained from beef cattle or pigs. But although animal insulin is similar enough to control the disorder, it is not exactly the same as human insulin and often causes undesirable side-effects.

Balanced meals should include fruit, vegetable, and protein sources.

many different substances. Before the substances can be identified or tested for function, they have to be separated. To be successful, a separation technique must overcome two problems: biological samples are usually very complex, and they are also usually very small. The two most important separation technologies are chromatography and gel electrophoresis.

LABORATORY EXERCISE 2-3
Paper Chromatography

In this laboratory exercise, you will use a technique called paper chromatography to separate the substances in a familiar and seemingly simple material.

Separation Technology: Chromatography

The liquid used in chromatography moves up the paper medium much as water climbs up a cloth left hanging over the edge of a full sink.

Chromatography depends on the fact that some substances are more soluble than others. A dot-sized sample of a mixture is placed on a porous *medium* such as paper. One end of the paper is then lowered carefully into a liquid such as alcohol or water. The liquid begins to climb up the paper. When the liquid reaches the sample, some of the substances in the sample begin to dissolve and climb upward. However, they climb at different rates. The most soluble substances move fastest; the least soluble move more slowly. This effect separates the substances into distinct bands. To study the substances further, biochemists cut out each separate band and remove the separated substance from the paper by soaking.

Separation Technology: Gel Electrophoresis

In addition to fats, carbohydrates, and proteins, all living things contain DNA. Since DNA contains the instructions needed to run an organism, its precise structure differs considerably from one species to another. **Gel electrophoresis** displays these differences. First, the DNA is mixed with a powerful digestive chemical produced by one particular type of bacteria. This substance acts like "chemical scissors," cutting the DNA molecule into fragments. Both the number and the size of the fragments produced differ from one species to the next.

The gel's consistency is similar to that of a gelatin dessert made with one-fourth the usual quantity of hot water.

The mixture of DNA fragments is then placed on a slab made from the same flexible material used to manufacture soft contact lenses. The slab of gel is lowered into a tank of liquid, and an electric current is used to pull the fragments along the surface of the gel. Moving DNA fragments in this way works because they all have a slight charge. The shortest, lightest fragments move the fastest, leaving the longest, heaviest ones behind in a distinctive banding pattern. A dye is added so that the movement can be seen. The resulting pattern is just as distinctive as the familiar striped product code found on most grocery items.

Gel electrophoresis is not limited to distinguishing between different species. It can also be used to identify different individuals and has already been used to link criminals to the scene of violent crimes. For this reason, gel electrophoresis is often called "DNA fingerprinting." It is also useful for diagnosing inherited illnesses and cell abnormalities such as cancer before they do lasting damage.

Chromatography and gel electrophoresis are only two of the many exciting technologies biologists are using to guide them in their ongoing voyage of discovery through the living world. Your own voyage of discovery is now well underway, and will continue with a kingdom by kingdom tour through the living world, beginning with the largest, most familiar organisms: animals (Unit II) and plants (Unit III). You will then explore less familiar and ever smaller micro-organisms until you reach the ambiguous world of the virus (Unit IV). By then, you will know enough about biological diversity to appreciate the commonalities that unite all kingdoms: cell structure, cell processes, and biological continuity. You will also be ready to explore the most exciting field in biology today — human genetics.

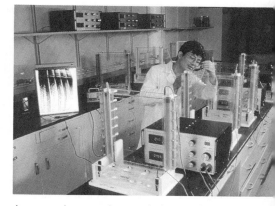

A researcher conducts gel electrophoresis for the DNA of *drosophila* (fruit fly). Several DNA samples can be tested at the same time.

Section Review Questions

1. a) State an example of modern technology that has expanded scientific understanding of cell structures.
   b) Explain briefly how your chosen example improves on earlier technology for the same purpose.

2. a) Which branch of biology studies the substances found in living things?
   b) List four substances found in all living things.

3. a) What can be learned about cells by studying their substances?
   b) What problems must be solved before cell substances can be studied?

4. a) Which separation technology depends on differences in solubility?
   b) Describe briefly how this technology works.

5. a) Which separation technology depends on differences in mass and electrical charge?
   b) Describe briefly how this technology works.

Chapter Review

Key Words

active transport
biology
cell theory
cellular respiration
continuity
control
controlled experiment
deoxyribonucleic
    acid (DNA)
development
diffusion
diversity
external environment
function
growth

internal environment
life functions
meiosis
micrometre (μm)
mitosis
nucleus
osmosis
passive transport
reproduction
scientific method
structure
theory
unity
variable

Recall Questions

Multiple Choice

1. Physiology is
   a) a science discipline
   b) a step in the scientific method
   c) a branch of biology
   d) the study of matter and energy

2. A species can only continue to exist if
   a) enough offspring are reproduced to replace organisms that die
   b) the offspring that are produced closely resemble their parents
   c) (a) but not (b)
   d) both (a) and (b)

3. In a family with four daughters, one has red hair, one has blond hair, one has brown hair, and one has auburn hair. This is an example of
   a) diversity   c) adaptations
   b) continuity   d) variability

4. A kitten's eyes open about three weeks after birth. This is an example of
   a) development   c) homeostasis
   b) growth   d) reproduction

5. Which of the following requires the cell to supply energy?
   a) active transport   c) cellular respiration
   b) passive transport   d) inherited variability

6. Which of the following is not a characteristic of science?
   a) use of technology   c) conclusions
   b) observations   d) proof

7. What do scientists call a trial explanation that must be tested by experiment?
   a) hypothesis   c) theory
   b) problem   d) variable

Fill in the Blanks

1. The characteristic that identifies living things is their ability to _____ body substances from materials in the environment. The process of maintaining normal chemical composition in an organism's _____ environment is called _____.

2. The ability of a microscope to enlarge images is called its _____. Its ability to produce a clear, sharp image is called its _____. A microscope with a $10\times$ eyepiece and a $40\times$ objective lens will enlarge images _____ $\times$. Microscopic specimens are usually measured in _____.

3. The basic structural unit of living organisms is _____. The basic functional unit is _____. Structures or abilities that enable an organism to survive in a particular environment are _____.

Short Answers

1. State and briefly describe two central assumptions of biology.

2. State the procedure that scientists often use to solve problems.

3. For each of the following pairs of terms, explain how the two terms are alike and how they differ.
   a) cytoplasm, protoplasm   c) structure, function
   b) mitosis, meiosis   d) theory, law

4. Briefly explain why communication is an important aspect of science.

5. State the cell theory.

6. The continued existence of any particular species depends on two related factors. Name these two factors, and explain why they are important.

7. List the life functions that must be performed by all living things.

8. State an example that explains the relationship between structure and function in living things.

9. Define the term experiment and identify its role in the scientific method.

10. Define the term controlled experiment and briefly identify its main features.

11. How do organisms obtain the energy they need to carry out their life functions?

Application Questions

1. a) List the four main life functions that must be performed by every cell.
   b) Beside each function, write the cell part(s), organelle(s), or substance(s) that are involved in performing the function.

2. Arrange the following events in the proper historical sequence. Identify the scientists most closely associated with each.
   • Animals are made of cells.
   • A cell contains a fluid.
   • A cell contains a nucleus.
   • The naming of a cell.
   • New cells come from pre-existing cells.
   • The nucleus plays a role in reproduction.
   • Plants are made of cells.

3. a) Copy the following list into your notebook: cell wall, cell membrane, chloroplast, mitochondria, nucleus, protoplasm, vacuole.
   b) Write P beside those structures that are found in the cells of most plants. Write A beside those that are found in the cells of most animals.
   c) List the organelles that are found in both plant and animal cells.

4. Would you expect the single cell of a unicellular organism to be more or less specialized than a single cell from a multicellular organism? Explain.

5. Which of the following is an adaptation and which is not?
   a) an elephant's trunk
   b) a camel's hump
   c) an amoeba's mitochondria

Problem Solving

1. What is the difference between something that is alive, something that is dead, and something that has never been alive? State examples to illustrate your answer.

2. Taxonomists estimate that there are at least one million species as yet undiscovered. How can biologists be sure that the cell theory applies to these undiscovered species as well as to those that are already known?

3. a) Occasionally, albino (white) alligators are born in the Florida everglades, a region which resembles Ontario's marshland. Explain why no white adults have ever been found.
   b) Recently, a white alligator estimated to be about 20 years old was found in Australia. What external environment do you think enabled this animal to reach adulthood?

Extensions

1. Research how biologists take photographs through a microscope. What special equipment is needed for the camera? For the microscope? Prepare a simple diagram to demonstrate this technique.

2. How would you set up a controlled experiment to determine whether a new toothpaste ingredient was effective in reducing dental decay? Identify the variable in your experiment and the control. What difficulties would you anticipate in such an experiment? How would you plan in advance to avoid them?

Animals

3

Diversity in the Animal Kingdom

Regardless of their environment, animals share the fundamental problem of all heterotrophs: they must obtain and use the food produced by autotrophs. Even where abiotic conditions are harsh, and autotrophs scarce, the animal kingdom displays an amazing variety of body types. For example, Antarctic vegetation consists mainly of mosses and lichens that grow in scattered locations along the coast during the brief, cool summer. These few autotrophs support almost 50 species of land animals,

but the population count for each species is quite small, and the animals themselves are mostly microscopic. The largest, an insect similar to a wingless housefly, is only 3 mm long. Clearly, the limited food supply restricts both the numbers and the kinds of land animals.

By contrast, sea life is abundant. Huge numbers of unicellular autotrophs in the Antarctic ocean form the basis of a food chain that supports very large populations of fish and many other marine species. Directly or indirectly, thousands of

whales, millions of seals, and several million penguins all obtain their food from the sea.

Antarctic seals, whales, and penguins share certain features with each other and all cold-climate animals. These include warm blood, a thick layer of fat, and large body size. The ability to maintain a constant body temperature in cold surroundings enables these animals to remain active all year. Fat serves both as an insulator and as a stored food supply. For example, emperor penguins are able to go without food for months while incubating eggs and raising chicks.

Antarctic birds and mammals are also adapted for life in the water, even those that are not fully aquatic. The penguin's streamlined body represents a considerable variation on the usual body type of birds, although slow-motion photography has shown that penguins actually "fly" through the water, moving their wings much the same way as flying birds do.

Seals and whales display variations on the usual pattern for mammals. Their limbs are so adapted for moving through water that seals are extremely awkward on land and whales cannot move on land at all.

Each Antarctic species has its own specialized niche and its own way of catching food. Penguins eat fish near the surface while Weddell seals dive to great depths. Crab-eater seals strain small shrimp-like organisms, and enormous blue whales filter micro-organisms. Similar diversity among birds and mammals can also be found in each of the earth's many environments.

Chapter Objectives

When you complete this chapter, you should:

1. Be able to state the distinguishing characteristics of the kingdom Animalia and recognize the diversity of body patterns included within it.

2. Be able to list the seven taxonomic levels from kingdom to species in order and understand the degree of similarity that each level represents.

3. Be able to describe at least three distinguishing characteristics and state at least one example for each of the following animal phyla: Porifera, Cnidaria, Platyhelminthes, Annelida, Mollusca, Arthropoda, and Chordata.

4. Be able to describe the structural characteristics of and state examples for each of the following arthropod classes: Arachnida, Crustacea, and Insecta.

5. Be able to explain how the terms vertebrate and invertebrate relate to phylum groupings, especially Chordata, and recognize that most animal species are invertebrates.

6. Be able to classify several invertebrates into correct phyla based on their external characteristics, using identification keys as necessary.

7. Be able to classify several vertebrate members of the phylum Chordata into correct classes based on their external characteristics, and be able to describe a complete kingdom-to-species classification for humans.

3.1 Classifying the Animal Kingdom

Members of the kingdom **Animalia** can be found in almost every imaginable environment, from the harsh extremes of the Arctic or the Sahara desert to the warm waters of the Caribbean Ocean. Wherever they live and whatever they look like, all animals are multicellular. Each animal cell contains a membrane-bound nucleus and a variety of membrane-bound organelles, which are all surrounded by a cell membrane but do not have a cell wall. All animals are heterotrophs, and must therefore obtain and ingest living or dead organisms for food. Most animal species are **motile,** which means they are able to move around in their environment. But even **sessile,** or stationary, species such as corals are motile during the earliest part of their lives. Most animals reproduce sexually.

This coral reef is home to a diverse collection of animal species, including some that seem to resemble plants.

From Species to Kingdom: Degrees of Similarity

Members of the same species are so similar that they can mate and produce fertile offspring. Consequently, the degree of similarity within a single species is very high. But almost 1 500 000 species meet the previous description for the kingdom Animalia, from colourful fungus-like sponges and flower-like sea anemones to humans and grasshoppers. So, the degree of similarity within a single kingdom is very low. Clearly, the kingdom grouping is too inclusive and general to help biologists look for the unity underlying animal diversity, and the species grouping is too specific and too small.

To facilitate the study of animals, taxonomists have defined five levels of classification between species and kingdom: genus, family, order, class, and phylum. As Figure 3-1 shows, each level represents a greater degree of similarity than the levels above it, and a greater degree of diversity than the ones

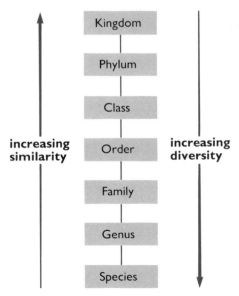

increasing similarity → increasing diversity

Kingdom
Phylum
Class
Order
Family
Genus
Species

FIGURE 3-1 The sequence of classification levels for animals

below it. You will learn more about the five intermediate levels in the following descriptions.

A **genus**, the plural of which is **genera**, is a group of similar species. For example, it would be easy to mistake a coyote for a dog from a distance, and some dogs resemble wolves very closely. The degree of similarity among these three species is reflected in their binomials: *Canis lupus* (wolf), *Canis latrans* (coyote), and *Canis familiaris* (dog). Identical first names indicate that dogs, wolves, and coyotes are placed in the same genus. Mistaking a fox for a dog is less likely, and this degree of difference is reflected in the fox's binomial, *Vulpes vulpes*, which indicates that a fox is placed in a different genus than a dog.

A **family** is a group of similar genera. The family is larger and more inclusive than the genus. For example, the family Canidae includes both the genus *Canis* and the genus *Vulpes*. Family diversity is limited, however. For example, cats are too different from dogs, wolves, and foxes to be placed in the same family. Both the small cats of the genus *Felis* such as house cats and the large cats of the genus *Panthera* such as tigers are grouped together in the family Felidae.

An **order** is a group of similar families. For example, the family Canidae and the family Felidae are considered similar enough to be placed in the same order, Carnivora. (See Table 3-1.) As the name suggests, most members of this order are meat eaters. Features common to the order Carnivora include structures such as a flexible skeleton with strong running muscles, claws, a powerful jaw, and teeth shaped to pierce and tear flesh. These structures help carnivores hunt and capture prey. All members of Carnivora have a highly

You may find it easier to remember the correct sequence of the seven classification levels by memorizing the following mnemonic:
K ing **P** hilo **C** omes **O** ver **F** or **G** olf every **S** unday.

Both parts of a species binomial are italicized. The genus name is also capitalized. Family, order, class, phylum, and kingdom names are capitalized but not italicized.

TABLE 3-1   Major Families of the Order Carnivora

Family	Example
Canidae	• wolf
Felidae	• lion
Hyaenidae	• hyena
Mustelidae	• weasel
Procyonidae	• raccoon
Ursidae	• bear

Efforts to increase deer populations by reducing wolf populations have opened up environments suitable for *Canis latrans*. As the wolf disappears, the coyote has spread into many parts of Canada where the species was previously unknown.

To understand what degree of similarity is represented by the family level, compare this member of the family Felidae with the member of the family Canidae **(left).**

A tight-hinged jaw and sharp pointed teeth are typical of the order Carnivora.

TABLE 3-2 Major Orders of the Class Mammalia

Order	Example
Artiodactyla	• buffalo
Carnivora	• hyena
Cetacea	• dolphin
Chiroptera	• bat
Edentata	• sloth
Hyracoidea	• hryax
Insectivora	• shrew
Lagomorpha	• hare
Marsupalia	• kangaroo
Monotremata	• duck-billed platypus
Pinnipedia	• walrus
Proboscidea	• elephant
Rodentia	• mouse
Perrisodactyla	• rhinoceros
Primates	• gorilla
Sirenia	• manatee

FIGURE 3-2 Tunicates and lancelets are classified in the same phylum — Chordata — as deer and frogs.

Tunicate

Lancelet

developed sense of smell that helps them to hunt. They also have scent glands that play a major role in social interactions. An outstanding feature of animal families placed in Carnivora is their ability to teach and to learn hunting behaviour.

To understand the degree of difference that places a family in a different order, consider the horse. Along with the domestic donkey and the wild ass, the horse is classified in the family Equidae. Members of this family have hooves instead of claws, and their teeth are adapted for grinding rather than tearing. The structures shared by members of the family Equidae are too different from those shared by dogs and cats to place horses in the order Carnivora. Instead, Equidae is placed in a different order, Perrisodactyla.

A **class** is a group of similar orders. As Table 3-2 shows, Carnivora and Perrisodactyla are similar enough that both orders are grouped together in the class Mammalia. Characteristics common to mammals include warm blood and the development of body hair at some stage of the life cycle. Most mammals bear live young, and all females nourish their young with milk from mammary glands. Classes are large, diverse groups. Many dissimilar species fit the criteria for inclusion in the class Mammalia. But birds are so different from mammals that they are grouped in a separate class, Aves.

A **phylum,** the plural of which is **phyla,** is a group of similar classes. All members of the same phylum share certain fundamental similarities in body pattern. But a single phylum often includes organisms that seem quite unlike each other. For example, you may find it difficult to see what the tunicate and the lancelet in Figure 3-2 might have in common with animal classes such as **Mammalia** (*example:* deer), **Aves** (*example:* crow), **Reptilia** (*example:* turtle), **Amphibia** (*example:* frog), and **Osteichthyes** (*example:* perch). But all of these organisms are placed in the phylum **Chordata.**

This hairless mammal is an armadillo. Many closely fitted, small bony plates in the upper layer of its skin protect it from predators. Despite its outward appearance, the armadillo nurses its young and meets all other criteria for classification as a mammal.

If you think about it, you can probably see that warm blood links mammals to birds, that the covering on a bird's feet faintly resembles a reptile's skin, and that tadpoles resemble fish. But which characteristics link the tunicate and the lancelet to the same phylum? The answer is that the phylum is a large, general grouping, and criteria for inclusion in the phylum Chordata are broadly defined. Despite their many differences, all of the chordates mentioned above share the following features at some stage of their development.

- *A hollow nerve cord* lying beneath the animal's dorsal (back) surface
- *A notochord*, or flexible skeleton-like rod, lying beneath the nerve cord
- *Gill slits*, which are openings that lead directly from the animal's throat to the external environment

So far in this discussion, you have considered classification as a process of grouping. Viewed from species to kingdom, repeated groupings result in fewer and fewer shared features at each level. At the phylum level, the groups are larger and more diverse than any classification category except the kingdom itself.

But you can also think of classification as a process of sorting. A kingdom is sorted into phyla, which are further sorted into classes, and so on until the genus and species levels are reached. Viewed from kingdom to species, the organisms that occupy each level become more and more similar.

From either viewpoint, however, chordates make up only 50 000 of the animal kingdom's 1 500 000 species, and the phylum Chordata is only one out of twenty or so phyla associated with the kingdom Animalia. Each of the 20 animal phyla has a distinctive body pattern. The simplest is that of the phylum **Porifera**.

Sponges are grouped in the phylum Porifera because they resemble each other more closely than any other animal. The basic body pattern of a sponge is very simple. It consists of a hollow bag supported by an elastic or glassy skeleton secreted between the cells. The bag is pierced by pores through which water carrying food is drawn into a central cavity.

Even among taxonomists who agree on five-kingdom classification, there is not complete agreement on how the animal kingdom should be divided into phyla. Most high school textbooks list 16-22 of the most common phyla. Unless you go on to specialize in biology, you are not likely to encounter any of the others.

Three Worm Phyla

Most people associate "worm" with the familiar earthworm, but there are seven distinct worm phyla in the kingdom Animalia. You will consider the three phyla with the greatest number of species in the following descriptions.

The phylum **Platyhelminthes** has approximately 6000 species commonly called flatworms. Flatworms that inhabit streams and ponds are said to be free-living. Free-living flatworms have the same basic body pattern: a soft, flattened, unsegmented hollow tube with one opening through which food enters and wastes exit. Many flatworm species are parasitic. They live on or in the body of another animal. The tapeworm is so completely adapted to the parasitic life that it lacks a hollow gut. Because tapeworms live inside the intestine of other animals, they simply absorb the digested food that surrounds them.

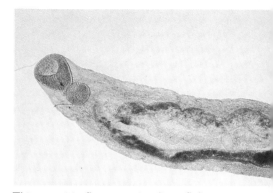

This parasitic flatworm is a liver fluke. Which external features suggest the phylum it should be placed in?

The phylum **Nematoda** contains approximately 10 000 species, which are usually called roundworms. All nematodes have narrow, cylindrical, unsegmented bodies that are tapered at both ends. The smooth outer covering is so tough that it must be shed to permit growth. Some parasitic species can grow to 1 m in length, but most roundworms are 1 mm or less. Free-living roundworms are important decomposers. Some parasitic roundworms cause serious diseases in plants and animals, including humans.

The phylum **Annelida** encompasses about 6500 species commonly called segmented worms. Annelids have much more complex body patterns and structures than other worm phyla. All annelids have a series of ring-shaped segments along their soft, cylindrical bodies. Internally, the segments are separated by thin membranes that divide the animal into numerous compartments. Annelids have a simple system with five tiny, heart-like structures for circulating blood. They also have a simple brain and a solid nerve cord that runs near the ventral (belly) surface. Familiarity with the earthworm might suggest that most annelids are terrestrial and legless. In fact, most are aquatic and have appendages.

A young nematode of the species *Pelodera strongyliodes*

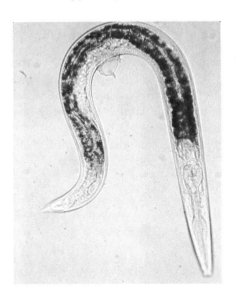

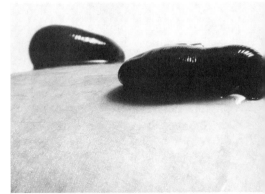

Many annelids are adapted to life as parasites. This leech has suction cups at each end that enable it to cling to its host.

Two Phyla with Radial Symmetry

Earthworms, humans, and most other animals have bilateral, or two-sided, symmetry. They have a distinct head end, and well-defined left and right sides. But some animal phyla display radial symmetry. Their body pattern radiates from a central axis, and has no distinct left side, right side, head, or tail. As a result, several different lines can be drawn to divide the bodies of these animals into two similar parts. You will learn about the two radial phyla with the greatest number of species in the following discussion.

The phylum **Cnidaria** has about 9000 species, including some of the most beautiful marine animals on Earth such as jellyfish, sea anemones, and corals. The nearly microscopic hydra is a freshwater cnidarian. Cnidarians share a bag-like body pattern. The walls of the "bag" have only two cell layers, which are glued together with a jelly-like noncellular material. The bag has a single opening through which the animal takes in food and ejects waste. This dual-purpose "mouth" is surrounded by tentacles with stinging cells that release small poisonous darts to stun prey. The mouth is mainly directed downward in jellyfish and mainly upward in sea anemones.

All cnidarians are motile as juveniles, but the adults of corals, anemones, and many other species are sessile. Adult corals live in colonies that consist of numerous hydra-like individuals, and their mouths can point in almost any direction. Each individual coral secretes its own protective external skeleton. Coral reefs are built up from the skeletons of dead corals.

The phylum **Echinodermata** includes about 5000 species, all of which live in salt water. Examples include starfish, sand dollars, and sea urchins. All echinoderms have five-way radial symmetry. In other words, their body pattern can be divided into five equal parts from the centre. The spines for which the phylum is named are actually extensions of the hard, shell-like endoskeleton that lies just beneath the skin.

The most familiar echinoderms are the several species of starfish that inhabit shallow ocean water everywhere in the world. The starfish has a centrally located mouth on its ventral surface and an anus on its dorsal surface. Each arm has numerous tiny tube feet equipped with suction cups. These help the starfish move and capture prey. A starfish can easily open the tightly closed shell of an oyster by pulling on it with its feet. Starfish have a remarkable ability to regenerate missing body parts. It is common to see a starfish that has one arm much smaller than the other four. But even a single arm can produce a complete, new individual providing enough of the central part of the starfish is still attached.

Humans have bilateral symmetry. One line can be drawn to divide humans into two similar parts.

Older reference books may place corals and their relatives in the phylum Coelenterata. Most taxonomists now group coelenterates into two separate phyla — Cnidaria and Ctenophora. The ctenophores are commonly known as comb jellies. They do have radial symmetry, but they lack stingers.

The hydra's method of locomotion is unique among Cnidarians. To move about, the hydra detaches the basal disk that attaches it to an underwater surface and "stands" briefly on its tentacles. After a quick somersault, it reattaches the basal disk at a new location.

DID YOU KNOW?
Echinos is a Greek word that originally meant hedgehog. Eventually, it came to mean sea urchin.

DID YOU KNOW?
Starfish are predators that feed by eating other animals alive. In the 1950s and 1960s, a population explosion among crown-of-thorns starfish led to the destruction of large stretches of coral reef in the south Pacific.

The jellyfish is not a fish at all. It feeds by pumping itself to the surface and drifting downward, stunning prey with poison from its tentacles.

Starfish are common in shallow ocean waters. Is the starfish really a fish?

A Very Successful Phylum: Animals with Exoskeletons

Including approximately 750 000 living species, the phylum **Arthropoda** is by far the most varied and successful of all animal phyla. The body pattern of the arthropods includes a solid ventral nerve cord, jointed legs, a protective exoskeleton, and usually a segmented body. Worldwide distribution of the arthropod species indicates that the arthropod body pattern has adaptations that suit it to a wide variety of environments.

Two important classes of the phylum Arthropoda are **Arachnida** and **Crustacea**. Spiders, mites, and scorpions are classified in Arachnida. Arachnids have four pairs of legs attached to their abdomen, simple eyes, and no antennae. Lobsters, crabs, and shrimps are classified in Crustacea. Crustaceans have two pairs of antennae and numerous paired appendages. Some of these appendages are attached to the animal's thorax and some to its abdomen. Most crustaceans have several paired mouth parts that grasp, bite, and chew food.

The most familiar arthropods are those of the class **Insecta**. This single class includes 900 000 animal species. Although sizes range from 0.5–300 mm, all insects are characterized by three distinct body regions: an abdomen that may be segmented, a thorax that usually has one or two pairs of wings, and a head with two large compound eyes, three small simple eyes, and a pair of antennae. Adult insects have three pairs of legs, which are all

Arthropoda is derived from the Greek word meaning jointed legs. What other external evidence reveals this crayfish's phylum?

The female mosquito's mouth parts are adapted for sucking blood. Other insects may have mouth parts adapted for biting or chewing.

attached to the thorax. An insect's mouth parts are adapted to its feeding needs. Most insects are terrestrial, although many are aquatic when they first hatch and may not look anything like adults. Insects have a complicated life cycle that enables them to adapt to changing seasons. Although adults die in the autumn, continuity of the species is ensured by the laying of eggs or the construction of cocoons that survive the harsh winter.

A Very Successful Subphylum: Animals with Backbones

The phylum Chordata includes such a wide range of organisms that most taxonomists sort it into three subphyla: Urochordata, Cephalochordata, and Vertebrata. The sessile adult tunicates of Urochordata retain a primitive nervous system but lose the notochord. The motile adult lancelets of Cephalochordata retain the notochord. These two primitive subphyla include fewer than 1000 chordate species. The remaining 45 000 chordates are grouped together in the subphylum Vertebrata.

Vertebrata is so named because the notochord develops into a vertebral column, or backbone, that surrounds and protects the nerve cord and also provides skeletal support. The backbone is flexible enough to allow a wide range of movements because it consists of a series of separate units called vertebrae. The vertebrae are strong because they are made from bone or cartilage. (Cartilage is the rigid material that gives shape to your nose and ears.) The seven classes that taxonomists place in subphylum Vertebrata are summarized in Table 3-3 on page 80.

Animals with backbones are often referred to as **vertebrates,** a name that distinguishes them from other chordates and also from all other animals. Animals without backbones are often called **invertebrates** regardless of their classification. Insects, echinoderms, worms, and cnidarians are all regarded as invertebrates. Clearly, the vertebrates are outnumbered by the invertebrates, especially by insects. Nevertheless, the vertebrates are a very successful group by biological standards. While insects live mainly in terrestrial or freshwater environments, vertebrates also inhabit the oceans. Many land vertebrates remain active throughout the winter, whereas insects must migrate or adopt a dormant form to survive.

What clues enable you to name the phylum and subphylum of the animal from which this skeleton was taken?

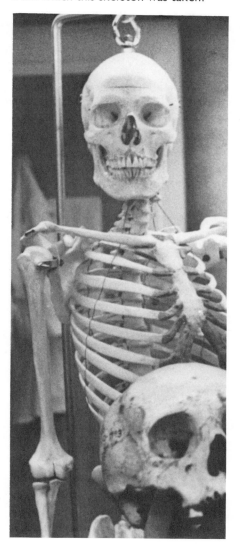

INQUIRY ACTIVITY
Charting the Animal Kingdom

This activity will give you an opportunity to practise the principles of animal classification. The incomplete chart in Figure 3-3 on page 78 includes all of the animal phyla discussed in this chapter. Uncommon phyla, or those with few species, are not included. Refer to the tables in this chapter as you need to.

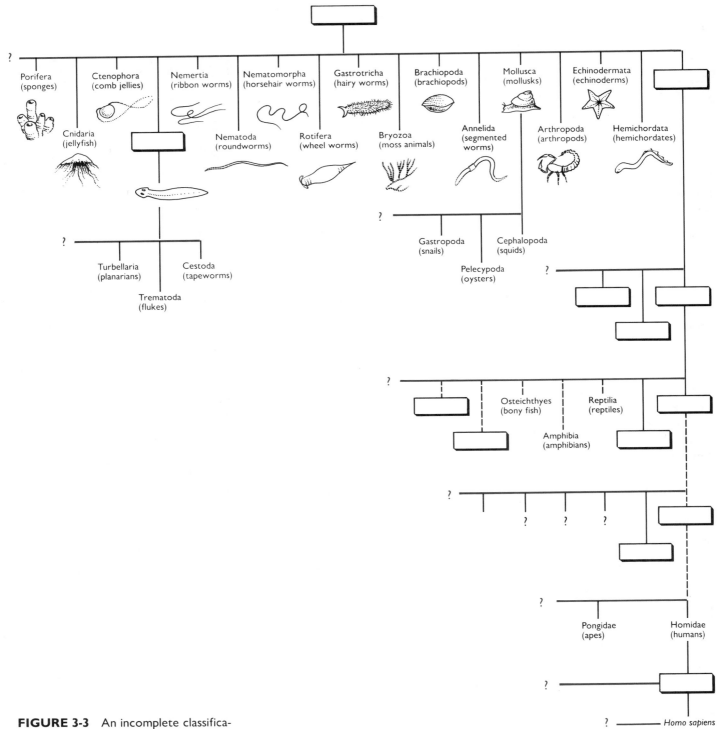

FIGURE 3-3 An incomplete classification chart for the animal kingdom

Procedure

1. Copy Figure 3-3 onto a large piece of paper and study it carefully.

2. Beside each coloured question mark, add a label to indicate the classification level it represents.

3. Fill in the blank boxes with the correct name for the missing phylum, class, order, and so on.

4. Add lines and labelled boxes so that the chart includes a complete classification for a human, a horse, a house cat, and a dog.

5. Add a small simple sketch to show a representative chordate.

6. Use a coloured marker to circle or highlight the names of all invertebrate phyla and/or subphyla.

Discussion Questions

1. List the vertebrate phyla and/or subphyla on your completed chart.

2. a) How many worm phyla are shown?
   b) Do these worms appear to have anything in common? Discuss.

3. a) Which classification level does the group Turbellaria represent?
   b) In which phylum is Turbellaria placed? Discuss how you identified Turbellaria's phylum.

4. a) Which classification level do the black question marks represent? How many of these groups are missing?
   b) To what class, order, and phylum are the above groups assigned?

5. Write out a complete kingdom-to-species classification for a human.

6. a) Based only on the information in Figure 3-3 and what you already know about the phylum Mollusca, write a short phrase that describes all mollusks.
   b) Discuss what this exercise reveals about the degree of similarity within a phylum.

7. Compare your representative chordate with those selected by your classmates. After a class discussion, conduct a vote to select the best possible representative.

8. What problems might arise if the format of Figure 3-3 were used to produce a complete classification of the kingdom Animalia? How might this difficulty be overcome?

The Challenge of Life in the Animal Kingdom

The goal of biological classification is to simplify the study of functioning organisms. This very short survey of the animal kingdom has given you enough background to begin a more detailed exploration of structure and

TABLE 3-3   Classes of the Subphylum Vertebrata

Class	Characteristics	Example
Agnatha (jawless fish) 10 species	• aquatic, gill breathers • poorly developed skeleton • no jaws, suction feeders • adults retain notochord • eggs laid in water, fertilized externally	• lamprey
Chondrichthyes (cartilaginous fish) 600 species	• aquatic, gill breathers, no gill covers • cartilaginous skeleton • no air-filled swim bladder, fish must swim to avoid sinking • tooth-like scales cover skin • internal fertilization, bear live young	• stingray
Osteichthyes (bony fish) 20 000 species	• aquatic, gill breathers, with gill covers • bony skeleton • air-filled swim bladder prevents sinking while fish is stationary • scale-covered skin • eggs laid in water, external fertilization	• perch
Amphibia (amphibians) 2800 species	• aquatic, gill-breathing young • four-legged adults are mainly terrestrial and breathe with lungs • moist, smooth, scale-free skin assists lungs • eggs laid in water, external fertilization	• frog
Reptilia (reptiles) 7000 species	• all breathe air with lungs, most are terrestrial • young and adults four-legged (except snakes) • overlapping scales, waterproof skin • internal fertilization, leathery-shelled eggs laid on land • little or no parental care	• Komodo dragon
Aves (birds) 8600 species	• warm-blooded air-breathers • four-limbed: two legs and two wings • skin covered in feathers • body parts adapted for flight; not all can fly • feet and beaks adapted for food gathering • internal fertilization, hard-shelled eggs laid on land or in dry nest • helpless young receive intensive parental care	• bald eagle
Mammalia (mammals) 5000 species	• warm-blooded, air-breathers • four-limbed: usually all legs for walking • body hair present at some stage of development • internal fertilization, most bear live young • mammary glands secrete fluid to nourish young • helpless young receive intensive parental care	• kangaroo

function in animals. Clearly, animals display great diversity in body pattern and structure. But regardless of how simple or complex it may be, and regardless of how large or small, every animal must perform the same fundamental functions to remain alive.

Expressed as simply as possible, the problem all animals face is that of maintaining a stable internal environment while living in a changeable, often hostile, external environment. For animals, this challenge is even greater than it is for other organisms since, as heterotrophs, animals cannot make their own food. Not surprisingly, this factor has an enormous influence on the structures animals need to perform their life functions. In each of the remaining chapters in Unit II, you will consider one of the major life functions animals must perform and investigate the structures associated with each function.

Review Questions

Key Words

Animalia	invertebrates
Annelida	Mammalia
Arachnida	motile
Arthropoda	Nematoda
Chordata	order
class	phylum (phyla)
Cnidaria	Platyhelminthes
Crustacea	Porifera
Echinodermata	sessile
family	Vertebrata
genus (genera)	vertebrates
Insecta	

Recall Questions

Multiple Choice

1. Which of the following is not the name of a worm phylum?
   a) Annelida
   b) Arthropoda
   c) Nematoda
   d) Platyhelminthes

2. Which of the following worms does not have a body pattern based on a hollow tube?
   a) liver fluke
   b) tapeworm
   c) planaria
   d) roundworm

3. Which of the following worms has a system for circulating blood?
   a) planaria
   b) flatworm
   c) annelid
   d) nematode

4. The protective covering that surrounds a nematode is called the
   a) exoskeleton
   b) skin
   c) echinoderm
   d) cuticle

5. Which of the following terms best describes a major difference between arthropods and echinoderms?
   a) symmetry
   b) exoskeleton
   c) mouth
   d) backbone

Fill in the Blanks

1. *Canis familiaris* and *Felis domesticus* are placed in different _____ but are grouped together in the same _____ .

2. *Paramecium caudatum* and *Paramecium bursaria* are different _____ of the same _____ .

3. Animals of the phylum _____ have a solid nerve cord, but animals of the phylum _____ have a hollow nerve cord.

4. The vertebrate phylum with the fewest species is _____ . The one with the most species is _____ .

Short Answers

1. a) Define the terms species and kingdom. State an example of each.
   b) List the five major classification levels between species and kingdom, beginning with the most diverse and ending with the most similar. Define and state an example of each.

2. a) Which classification level does Chordata represent?
   b) Which structural features are shared by all animals classified as chordates?

3. Repeat Question 2 for a) Vertebrata, b) Mammalia, and c) Carnivora.

4. a) Why do taxonomists divide the phylum Chordata into subphyla?
   b) List the subphyla and explain how they differ.

5. a) Briefly describe the body pattern common to all Cnidarians.
   b) Which two variations of this pattern are seen within the phylum?

6. Match the group names in Column A with the classification level in Column B.

Column A	Column B
i) Animalia	a) Class
ii) Canidae	b) Family
iii) *Canis lupus*	c) Genus
iv) *Felis*	d) Kingdom
v) Carnivora	e) Order
vi) Mammalia	f) Phylum
vii) Platyhelminthes	g) Species

Application Questions

1. a) In which phylum or phyla discussed in this chapter do the members have nerve cords?
   b) In which does the nerve cord run along the animal's ventral surface? In which does it run along the dorsal surface?
   c) How else do the ventral nerve cord(s) differ from the dorsal nerve cord(s)?

2. a) Which term do biologists use to describe a classification group that has many species?
   b) Which worm phylum has the greatest number of species?
   c) Which feature of this phylum do you think accounts for the large number of species? Explain.

3. a) Sketch a rough outline of the body of a starfish viewed from the top.
   b) Do the same for a jellyfish, an earthworm, and a frog.
   c) Show how many lines can be drawn to divide each animal's body in half. State the kind of symmetry involved in each case.

Problem Solving

1. A taxonomist writing an article about the family Canidae discusses *Canis latrans* in detail and later compares this species to *C. lupus* and *C. familiaris*. What does the letter C stand for? Use a similar method to show how a taxonomist might refer to *Paramecium aurelia*, *Paramecium bursaria*, *Paramecium caudatus* when comparing them to *Paramecium caudatum*.

2. Suppose that by conducting a massive co-ordinated effort, biologists manage to discover, describe, and classify every living animal on Earth by 2010. Do you think the work of taxonomists would then be complete? Discuss.

Extensions

1. Try matching the mammalian species listed below to the orders listed in Table 3-3. Use a reference book such as an encyclopedia to learn the orders of any species that do not match.

   - manatees
   - whales
   - rabbits
   - armadillos
   - moles
   - platypuses
   - koalas
   - bats
   - elephants
   - horses
   - camels
   - seals
   - humans

2. Humans often find themselves in competition with starfish for the same edible shellfish species. In the past, some people tried to eliminate these competitors by chopping them up and throwing the pieces back into the sea. What effect do you think this practice might have had on the starfish population? On the shellfish population?

CHAPTER

4

Gas Exchange

I t is difficult to imagine an earthly environment more hostile than Antarctica, even in summer. Yet, many scientists have travelled from North America to study the Weddell seal.

These researchers are interested in the way animals use oxygen. They chose the Weddell seal to study because it copes so well with limited oxygen supplies.

Maintaining homeostasis in a body as big as the Weddell seal's requires a lot of food, especially in a cold climate, and it should require a lot of oxygen as well. But the Weddell seal routinely dives to depths of 1 km for periods up to 2 h. Some large whales can submerge for an hour or so, but no other mammal its size can stay down as long as the Weddell seal.

For biologists, this break in the usual pattern presents an irresistible problem. *What structures or abilities enable the Weddell seal to perform its life functions for such a long time on a limited supply of oxygen?* The answer cannot be obtained through dissection, but controlled experiments with living seals have failed. Since the seal's oxygen-conserving mechanisms do not function unless it dives normally, researchers had to design an experiment they could conduct under natural conditions. This need led them to invent a backpack computer, which, when attached to a seal, monitors the animal's depth, speed, heartbeat, blood pressure, and blood chemistry.

Fortunately for the scientists, the Weddell seal will allow humans to come close enough to attach the backpack to its fur with glue. Later, the glue will be removed with a solvent. If the seal does not return to its usual surfacing hole, the device will fall off when the seal moults, and new fur grows in.

This experiment is an example of what scientists call pure or basic research, but it has practical significance as well. The study of extreme adaptations sheds new light on less extreme systems. Much of what is known about the human body and its functions was learned by studying other animals. Research about Weddell seals may eventually lead to new surgical techniques or to better equipment for space travel.

But perhaps more important than either the practical or intellectual benefits basic research of this kind can provide is the reminder that we are animals, too. Making an effort to understand how other animals solve the most fundamental problems of life may help us appreciate how dependent we are on our environment, and encourage us to do whatever we must to maintain the fragile biosphere on which all animals depend.

Chapter Objectives

When you complete this chapter, you should:

1. Appreciate the diversity of structure and function found in the gas-exchange systems of vertebrates and invertebrates.

2. Be able to define and distinguish between breathing, gas exchange, and cellular respiration.

3. Based on experimental procedures such as dissection, be able to identify the main components of different vertebrate gas-exchange systems, and explain how the structure of each part suits its function.

4. Through microscopic examination, be able to describe the types of tissue found in vertebrate gas-exchange systems, and describe how airborne pollutants affect human respiratory tissue.

5. With reference to the human system, be able to describe the mechanics of breathing, explain how oxygen and carbon dioxide are transported through the internal environment, and how they are exchanged with the external environment.

6. Be able to compare the human gas-exchange system with that of another mammal and a non-mammalian vertebrate.

7. By comparing measured lung volumes and analyzing related data, be able to identify several external and internal factors affecting human lung capacity.

8. Investigate and describe how various external and internal factors, for example, smoking and lung capacity, affect breathing rate in humans.

9. Understand the health benefits of an efficient gas-exchange system, identify factors that interfere with its function, and recognize the personal habits that enhance respiratory health.

10. Be able to describe some of the benefits derived from a knowledge of the human gas-exchange system such as treatment of respiratory disorders, procedures to reverse breathing interruptions, and regulations to limit the detrimental effects of airborne pollutants.

11. Know appropriate first-aid procedures to be used if someone is choking or drowning.

4.1 The Role of Gas Exchange in Animal Cells

DID YOU KNOW?
Large predators such as lions will often not eat for several days after a big kill. Prey such as antelopes spend most of their waking hours eating or searching for food.

All organisms require energy for life functions such as growth, reproduction, and movement. Most living things obtain the energy they need from the chemical reaction described in this word equation.

$$\text{glucose} + \text{oxygen} \longrightarrow \text{carbon dioxide} + \text{water} + \text{usable energy}$$

This process is called **cellular respiration** because it only takes place in living cells. The cells of most plants, fungi, bacteria, protists, and animals obtain energy in this way.

However, before cellular respiration can release any energy, each cell must be supplied with glucose and oxygen. Animals can store glucose in their bodies. Consequently, humans and many other animals can go for days or even weeks without eating. But most animals cannot store oxygen, so each cell requires a constant supply.

Humans obtain the oxygen they need for cellular respiration by **breathing.** When you breathe, you alternately inhale and exhale air. Each inhalation brings in fresh supplies of oxygen from the external environment. Each exhalation disposes of unwanted carbon dioxide from the internal environment. How well the human body can obtain the oxygen it needs and expel unwanted carbon dioxide depends on breathing efficiency.

You may remember from earlier studies that breathing involves muscle action; gas exchange involves the diffusion of dissolved gases; and cellular respiration involves a chemical reaction.

Breathing efficiency can be affected by a variety of factors. For example, if you are sick with a cold, your breathing will probably be shallower, and its rate more rapid. In fact, **breathing rate** is a useful indicator of breathing efficiency because it provides external evidence of internal conditions. Doctors often use breathing rate to help diagnose illness.

Breathing rate can also be affected by conditions in the external environment. For example, mountain climbers breathe more rapidly at high altitudes, where reduced air pressure results in oxygen-deficient air. (See Figure 4-1.) In the following exercise, you will investigate a variety of factors that may affect breathing rate.

LABORATORY EXERCISE 4-1
Factors Affecting Breathing Rate

A knowledge of the structure and function of the human breathing apparatus has led to effective diagnosis and treatment of breathing disorders. This knowledge has also contributed to the development of life-saving procedures and devices such as respirators and resuscitators. This exercise provides a basic background for understanding how some of this present knowledge was acquired.

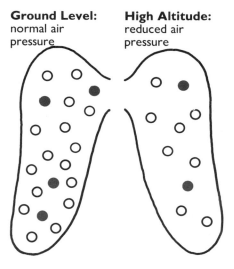

Ground Level: normal air pressure

High Altitude: reduced air pressure

Experienced mountain climbers are very fit, but even they require supplementary oxygen when climbing at very high altitudes.

FIGURE 4-1 Air at high altitudes contains fewer oxygen molecules (shown in blue) per lungful than air inhaled at ground level.

Breathing and Gas Exchange

Breathing and gas exchange are two different processes. The act of breathing simply pushes exhaled air out of your lungs and brings fresh air in. Although the fresh air is inside your body, it has not yet entered your internal environment because your lungs are simply air sacs that connect directly to the outside environment. (See Figure 4-2.) In your lungs, oxygen molecules from inhaled air enter your internal environment and carbon dioxide leaves. This two-way movement of materials between internal and external environments is called

Air with a carbon dioxide content greater than normal always causes an increase in breathing rate, even when the air also contains normal amounts of oxygen. Enriching the air with oxygen does not help because the breathing centre cannot detect oxygen. Only the carbon dioxide content of the blood is involved in determining breathing rate.

Gas exchange does not refer to the water vapour that is released in exhaled breath. Only a small percentage of the water produced by cellular respiration is disposed of in this way.

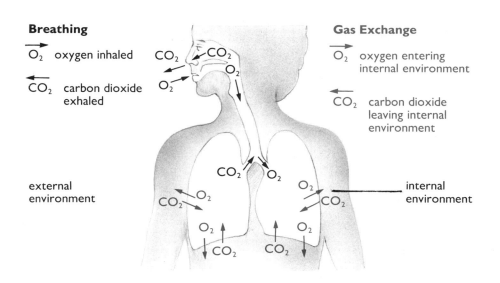

Breathing

O_2 oxygen inhaled

CO_2 carbon dioxide exhaled

external environment

Gas Exchange

O_2 oxygen entering internal environment

CO_2 carbon dioxide leaving internal environment

internal environment

FIGURE 4-2 Breathing and gas exchange

Molecules of water and the dissolved gases are already in motion. They move through the cell membrane by their own kinetic energy. The cell itself does not need to supply energy to make them move.

Normal breathing rate is 10-14 breaths per minute with a total air exchange of around 6 L. The maximum possible breathing rate is about 300 breaths per minute with a total air exchange of 150-200 L.

gas exchange. However, you should realize that the carbon dioxide and oxygen being exchanged are no longer in the gaseous state. Only dissolved molecules can pass through the thin, moist membranes lining the lungs.

In an animal's internal environment, oxygen and carbon dioxide are dissolved in water. The amount of oxygen required by your body varies according to the amount of energy you need for a given activity. For example, you would need much more energy to run 10 km than you would to rest, thereby increasing your need for gas exchange. A more rapid breathing rate will provide more oxygen for working muscles. Muscle cells can then provide the extra energy needed for a physical activity such as running.

Your breathing rate also responds to changes in the external environment by adjusting to compensate for the change. For example, the body obtains enough oxygen by breathing more rapidly in oxygen-deficient air. Similarly, more rapid breathing helps meet the needs of the internal environment when the surrounding air contains more carbon dioxide than usual.

Because breathing rate is so sensitive to internal and external change, the amount of oxygen and carbon dioxide exchanged provides a reliable indicator about the level of cell activity. The total chemical activity of the cells, including cellular respiration, is called **metabolism.** The rate at which energy is released by cellular respiration when you are resting is called **basal metabolic rate.** This rate can be determined by measuring your oxygen intake or your carbon dioxide output. Hospital laboratories usually find it more convenient to measure the amount of carbon dioxide given off in exhaled air. Basal metabolic rate varies with age, sex, and body size. Readings tend to be 7-10% higher for males than females, and basal metabolic rate decreases as a person becomes older.

The Role of Oxygen in Releasing Energy

The aerobic exercise illustrated in the photograph on this page is associated with an increased need for energy, an increased need for gas exchange, and much more rapid breathing. **Aerobic** means "requiring oxygen," and this type of muscular activity can only occur if muscle cells are supplied with an abundance of oxygen molecules.

The energy needed for moving the muscles is released by cellular respiration within the muscle cells. This chemical reaction requires two raw materials: glucose and oxygen. The energy that is finally released is actually stored in the glucose, a simple type of sugar obtained from food and transported to the muscle cells by the blood. The oxygen is not a source of energy, but it is needed to break up the chemical bonds in which the energy of the glucose is stored. (See Figure 4-3.)

Aerobic exercise is a very popular way to maintain physical fitness.

Glucose	+	Oxygen	→	Carbon Dioxide	+	Water

Key

C = carbon atom   H = hydrogen atom   O = oxygen atom

FIGURE 4-3 A model for cellular respiration. Removing the energy stored in a glucose molecule involves converting all of its carbon and hydrogen atoms to carbon dioxide and water. How many extra oxygen atoms does each glucose molecule need to release all its energy?

Obtaining Energy Without Oxygen

In an emergency, energy can be obtained from glucose through **anaerobic respiration,** a completely different chemical reaction that occurs only in the *absence* of oxygen. During anaerobic respiration, glucose is only partially broken down as in the following word equation.

glucose ⟶ lactic acid + usable energy

In humans, anaerobic respiration occurs most often in muscle cells when the muscle is overworked and deprived of oxygen.

Anaerobic respiration differs from ordinary cell respiration in two important ways. First, it is very inefficient. Anaerobic respiration releases only 3% of the energy stored in each glucose molecule. Second, it produces lactic acid instead of carbon dioxide and water. Lactic acid molecules do not take part in gas exchange. They remain in the muscle cells, increasing their acidity so that the muscle loses its ability to contract. This condition is called muscle fatigue.

Strenuous physical activity often results in muscle soreness. Like muscle fatigue, this soreness is due to the buildup of lactic acid, which acts as an irritant. The lactic acid cannot be disposed of until extra oxygen is supplied for new reactions that will convert it to harmless, reusable products. Because the muscle cannot return to normal until this happens, the amount of oxygen needed is referred to as an oxygen debt.

Runners in short-distance races always build up an oxygen debt. The amount of oxygen needed after this kind of exercise is much greater than that required during a rest period, so runners usually gasp for several minutes

A limited amount of oxygen is available for the muscles of this weight lifter.

Exercise Testing

Health is not just absence of disease; fitness is not the concern of athletes only. Health and fitness cannot be separated, and with exercise, both fitness and health may be improved.

One of the many indicators of fitness is the way in which the respiratory system responds to stress. Exercise tests use regularly increasing work levels to stress the respiratory system and measure the response. A calibrated treadmill can set the work level while the subject breathes into a closed system. Physiological changes resulting from the increasing work can be detected in many ways. Kinesiologists are finding that any one kind of testing measurement can occasionally give misleading information about fitness. As a result, modern computerized fitness-testing equipment can measure volumes of inhaled and exhaled gases, analyze exhaled gases, and measure heart rate to provide as complete a picture of fitness as possible.

The process indicated by testing fitness is essentially the same for all people. At low work levels, aerobic respiration provides almost all the energy required. The small amounts of lactic acid produced are easily removed. As work increases, the body reaches the aerobic threshold. At this point, the aerobic system, although still able to increase the amount of energy it contributes, can no longer keep pace with the increasing requirements of the muscles. Anaerobic systems begin to compensate, but lactic acid begins to accumulate. Exercise now becomes difficult, since lactic acid can cause discomfort. If work increases, the anaerobic threshold is reached. The body's ability to remove lactic acid is exhausted. Beyond this point, lactic acid accumulates rapidly, and activity is very difficult to maintain. At a still higher level of work, the capacity of aerobic systems reaches a maximum. The maximum volume of oxygen that can be used by the body is called the Max VO_2.

The relative positions of these thresholds on a testing scale reflect fitness. A distance runner's extraordinary endurance is the result of a high Max VO_2 with an aerobic threshold that is near 90%

of that. The runner can work aerobically at a high rate for a long time. A basketball player exhibits a different kind of fitness. Since intense bursts of energy exceeding the aerobic threshold are required at intervals, the ability to remove lactic acid from muscle between bursts is necessary. This ability is reflected by widely spaced aerobic and anaerobic thresholds in athletes such as basketball players and sprinters. In people who are not physically active, neither sign of fitness is apparent. In inactive people, aerobic thresholds may be as low as 50% of the Max VO_2, and the ability to remove lactic acid is absent.

Your own fitness can be improved through exercise. Continuous rhythmic activity such as jogging or walking at or below the aerobic threshold will improve aerobic performance and raise the aerobic threshold and Max VO_2. Short, intense workloads above the aerobic threshold increase the ability to remove lactic acid and build muscle mass. If you are not as fit as you would like to be, you should begin exercising at or below your aerobic threshold to develop aerobic fitness. As a rule of thumb, if you can talk while you exercise, you are exercising at aerobic levels. This level of exercise is ideal for the beginner because lactic acid is not accumulated, and the exertion is not uncomfortable.

after a race. Runners in long-distance races such as a marathon must regulate their speed so that they do not build up an oxygen debt. Marathon runners cannot stop to rest, thereby repaying the debt.

Obtaining energy from glucose in the absence of oxygen is very inefficient. Most animals, including humans, use anaerobic respiration only during a state of emergency. Some bacteria like the tetanus bacteria actually die if exposed to oxygen. But for most bacteria and all animals, oxygen is the gas they need to live.

Section Review Questions

1. a) Define breathing, gas exchange, and cellular respiration.
   b) Explain what these processes have in common and how they differ.
2. How is breathing rate affected by the following?
   a) increased altitude
   b) a poorly ventilated room
   c) strenuous physical activity
   d) a common cold
3. a) Define metabolism.
   b) How is basal metabolic rate measured? Why is it an important test?
4. a) Write the word equation for cellular respiration and explain how the role of glucose differs from the role of oxygen.
   b) How are cellular respiration and muscle movement related?
5. a) Write the word equation for anaerobic respiration and explain how it differs from cellular respiration.
   b) How are anaerobic respiration and muscle fatigue related?
6. a) What is an oxygen debt?
   b) When does an oxygen debt occur? How is it repaid?

Celia McInnes is helped by medics after completing the National Capital Marathon. Marathon runners suffer from oxygen debt and an accumulation of lactic acid after completing an event.

DID YOU KNOW?
To run 100 m, an athlete needs at least 6 L of oxygen, but the body cannot absorb more than 1 L in such a short time. To pay off the oxygen debt of 5 L, the athlete's breathing rate must increase sharply and remain rapid for several minutes after the race.

4.2 Anatomy of the Human Gas-Exchange System

Anatomy refers to the study of body structures in living things, especially the study of their internal parts. Often such studies involve dissections and investigations using a microscope. Figure 4-4 on page 92 summarizes what has been learned by such methods about the principal structures of the human gas-exchange system. The main features of the human gas-exchange system are internal air sacs called lungs, and a system of tubes connecting the sacs to the external environment. These structures are typical of the gas-exchange systems found in most land-dwelling vertebrates, particularly in mammals.

FIGURE 4-4 The human gas-exchange system

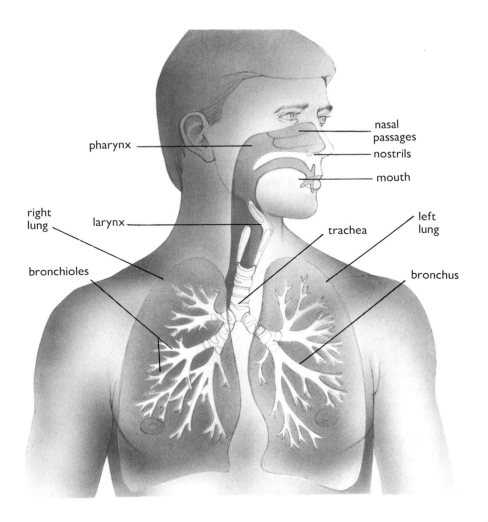

pharynx

nasal passages

nostrils

mouth

right lung

larynx

left lung

trachea

bronchioles

bronchus

There is no general agreement among biologists on how the term respiration should be used. You may consult other biology books that use external respiration for inhaling and exhaling, internal respiration for the movement of gases across the lung lining, and respiration for the chemical reactions within a cell. To avoid confusion, this book will use the terms breathing, gas exchange, and cellular respiration for these three processes.

Because gas-exchange systems deliver and remove materials involved in cellular respiration, they are sometimes referred to as respiratory systems. Regardless of what they are called, such systems have two major functions.

- *Breathing*: Bringing oxygen inside the body and expelling carbon dioxide.
- *Gas exchange*: Transferring oxygen molecules into the blood for transportation throughout the internal environment, and transferring carbon dioxide molecules out.

This section will focus on the structures involved in breathing and gas exchange. You will learn more about how these structures perform such important functions in Section 4.3.

Structure and Function of the Nose and Pharynx

Perhaps you can recall your last cold and the difficulty you may have had breathing through your mouth all the time. Mouth-breathing feels awkward because most of your breathing is done through your nose. (See Figure 4-5.) Various nasal structures filter, warm, and moisten incoming air, preparing it for internal use. Nasal hairs just inside the nostrils trap large foreign particles.

Blood circulating in the lining of the nasal cavities helps warm the air. Specialized cells in the lining of the nasal passageways secrete a sticky mucus that performs a dual role. It filters the air by trapping small, foreign particles, and also moistens the air as it passes from the nasal cavities into the pharynx or throat area. In the pharynx, air is further warmed and moistened. This preparation of air for the lungs is possible through the combined action of cilia, mucus, and the many blood vessels surrounding the respiratory tract.

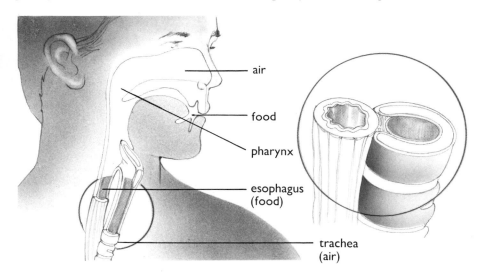

FIGURE 4-5 Nostril hairs filter large particles from incoming air, while the convoluted shape of the nasal passages provides a large, mucus-covered surface to moisten it and trap small particles.

Structure and Function of the Trachea and Bronchi

The **pharynx** is a common passageway for both food and air. Two major passageways branch from the end of the pharynx. (See Figure 4-6.) The

LEFT: FIGURE 4-6 The pharynx branches into two separate tubes—one for air (trachea) and one for food (esophagus).

BELOW: FIGURE 4-7 The trachea is lined with cilia that may beat up to 16 times per second.

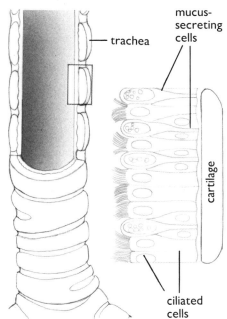

esophagus carries food, and the **trachea** carries air. The trachea is a hollow tube, kept permanently open by rings of a firm, yet flexible, material called cartilage. This structural support allows the neck to bend or twist without interrupting air flow. The tissue lining the trachea continues the process of filtering, warming, and moistening inhaled air.

Small particles are trapped and eventually expelled by the beating of microscopic, hair-like cilia that line this part of the respiratory tract. (See Figure 4-7.) A single cell may possess hundreds of these cell projections. The cilia beat simultaneously to move trapped particles upward, pushing foreign material into the pharynx to be swallowed or expelled. Breathing polluted air can clog up the cilia, strip them away, or impair their ability to beat.

Because the pharynx is a common passage for air, food, and saliva, it is important that swallowed solids and liquids be prevented from entering the trachea. A flap of tissue called the **epiglottis** functions as a barrier by covering the upper trachea during swallowing. During inhalation, however, the epiglottis remains open, allowing air to travel down either the trachea or the esophagus. Figure 4-8 shows the co-ordination of this swallowing action.

FIGURE 4-8 The epiglottis prevents food from entering the trachea when you swallow.

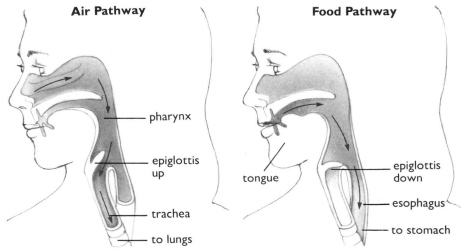

FIGURE 4-9 Your vocal cords produce sound when air is forced between the tightly stretched bands of tissue.

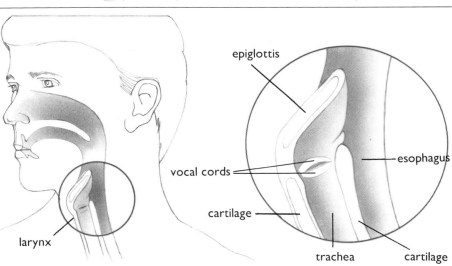

The vocal cords remain apart when you breathe and come close together when you talk.

At the top of the trachea, just below the epiglottis, is the voice box or **larynx.** The vocal cords of the larynx consist of two bands of tissue stretched across the top of the trachea. Sound is produced when air is forced between the vocal cords, causing them to vibrate. (See Figure 4-9.) The pitch of your

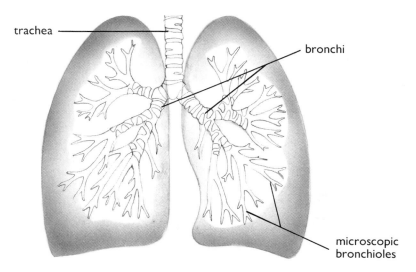

trachea

bronchi

microscopic
bronchioles

voice varies according to the amount of tension you exert on these vocal cords.

The trachea divides into two **bronchi,** which are tracheal extensions consisting of muscle and cartilage. The bronchi are lined with cilia and coated with mucus. Each bronchus conducts air to one of your lungs. Both bronchi branch into smaller and smaller ducts, and eventually lead to a very large number of microscopic tubes called **bronchioles.** (See Figure 4-10.) The bronchioles deliver the warm, moist, filtered air to the lungs.

Structure and Function of the Lungs

The typical mammalian gas-exchange system has a pair of large, soft, baglike organs called **lungs.** In humans, the right lung has three lobes, but the left lung has only two. (See Figure 4-11.) Lung tissue consists mainly of

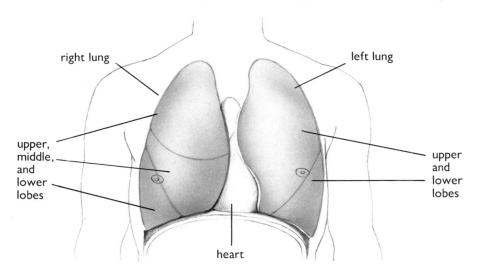

right lung

left lung

upper,
middle,
and
lower
lobes

upper
and
lower
lobes

heart

FIGURE 4-11 The right lung of a human has three lobes, but the left lung has only two.

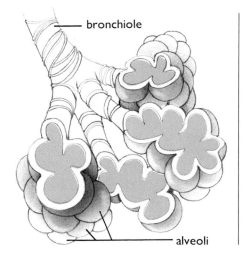

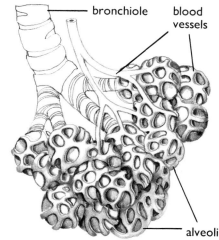

bronchiole

bronchiole   blood vessels

alveoli

alveoli

LEFT: FIGURE 4-12 Each bronchiole leads to three or four clusters of air-filled alveoli.

RIGHT: FIGURE 4-13 The thin-walled alveoli are surrounded by a network of numerous thin-walled blood vessels.

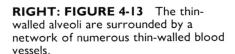

A double membrane system called the pleura covers the lungs and lines the chest cavity. The pleura membranes secrete a lubricating fluid that allows the lungs to move within the chest cavity. Pleurisy is an infection of the space between the two membranes.

hollow, thin-walled **alveoli.** Alveoli are microscopically small air sacs located at the ends of the bronchioles. (See Figure 4-12.)

This structural arrangement gives the lungs a spongy texture and maximizes the amount of lung surface that can be packed into the chest cavity. The average adult has about 300 million alveoli, with a total area of 70 m², which is about the same amount of surface area a classroom floor would cover. A gas-exchange surface this large would not be possible if the lungs were simply hollow bags.

The large alveolar surface is where gas molecules are exchanged. The thin walls of the alveoli are just one cell layer thick, and their inner surfaces are moist. Oxygen molecules from inhaled air dissolve in this moisture, which consists almost entirely of water. In this way, the alveoli form a thin, moist membrane. This membrane is surrounded by so many thin-walled blood vessels that the dissolved oxygen can pass readily into the blood. Similarly, dissolved carbon dioxide from the blood can pass into the hollow space of the alveolus. The membrane's large surface area and its thin walls allow for a maximum gas exchange between the air in the alveoli and the circulating blood. (See Figure 4-13.)

The Mechanics of Breathing

The lungs are contained within an enclosed body space called the chest cavity. The volume of the chest cavity, and that of the lungs, depends on the action of the movable walls that surround it. One wall is formed by the rib cage and the muscles connecting the rib bones. Contracting these muscles makes the rib cage move up and out, expanding the chest cavity. Relaxing them allows the ribs to slide down and in, collapsing the chest cavity.

The other wall of the chest cavity is formed by the diaphragm, a thin sheet of muscle that is shaped like an inverted bowl when it is relaxed. This upward

96   II ANIMALS

curve of the diaphragm reduces the volume of the chest cavity. When contracted, the diaphragm flattens to a shape that is more like a plate, resulting in an expanded chest cavity. Because lung tissue is elastic, the lungs expand and contract along with the chest cavity.

Breathing involves two main stages: **inspiration** (inhalation) and **expiration** (exhalation). (See Figure 4-14.) During inspiration, the rib muscles and the diaphragm contract simultaneously. This action increases the volume of the chest cavity. The lungs expand, and the air inside them spreads out, reducing the internal air pressure below that in the external environment. As a result, outside air rushes into the lungs. This occurs because air tends to flow away from regions of higher pressure toward regions of lower pressure, for example, out of a tire or into a vacuum-sealed coffee container.

During expiration, relaxation of the diaphragm and rib muscles reduces lung volume and increases internal air pressure. As a result, air rushes out of the trachea until the pressures inside and outside the lungs are equal.

The mechanics of breathing can be influenced by changes in atmospheric pressure. At high altitudes, for example, atmospheric pressure is very low. This means that the pressure difference between the internal and external environments is smaller than usual. As a result, air cannot rush in and out of the lungs as rapidly as it does under normal conditions. In addition, each lungful of low-pressure air contains fewer oxygen molecules than usual. The human body responds to low air pressure with an increased breathing rate that helps maintain stable internal conditions.

The regulation of a stable state within a living organism is called **homeostasis.** (You will learn more about homeostasis in Chapter 7.) In humans, breathing rate is an important homeostatic mechanism. For example, during intense physical activity such as running or jumping, muscle cells need an increased supply of oxygen to release extra energy. The breathing rate quickly speeds up in response to this internal requirement. Besides bringing in extra oxygen, rapid breathing removes the additional carbon dioxide produced during periods of heightened cellular respiration. Both of these processes help to maintain a stable internal state.

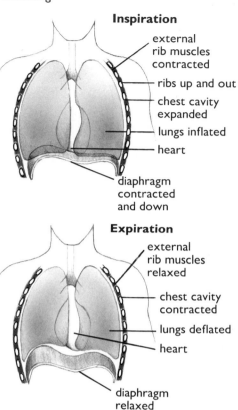

FIGURE 4-14 The mechanics of breathing

Inspiration

external rib muscles contracted

ribs up and out

chest cavity expanded

lungs inflated

heart

diaphragm contracted and down

Expiration

external rib muscles relaxed

chest cavity contracted

lungs deflated

heart

diaphragm relaxed and up

Lung Capacities

The efficiency of gas exchange is affected by how much air can be moved in and out of the lungs. This depends partly on the size of the lungs and the chest cavity, and partly on how the breathing muscles are used. Figure 4-15 illustrates how much variation is possible. Each numbered peak on the graph shows a single breath. The amount of air that moves into the lungs during each normal inspiration (Peaks 1 and 2) is called the **tidal volume.** The same volume moves out of the lungs during a normal expiration.

Peak 3 is made up of two parts, a normal inhalation followed immediately by a deeper breath to fill the lungs as full as possible. The *extra* volume of inhaled air is called the **inspiratory reserve volume.** The total amount of air

FIGURE 4-15 A comparison of lung capacities

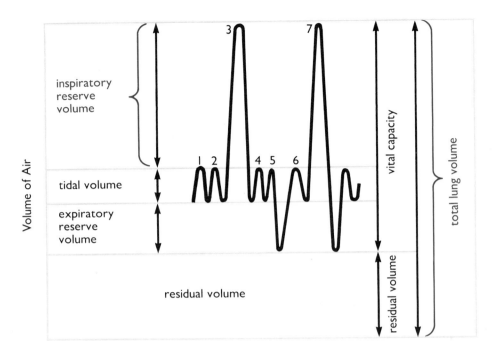

TABLE 4-1 Lung Capacities for Average Adults

	Male (cm³)	Female (cm³)
Inspiratory Reserve Volume	3100	2100
Tidal Volume	500	500
Expiratory Reserve Volume	1200	800
Vital Capacity	4800	3400
Residual Volume	1200	1000
Total Lung Capacity	6000	4400

that is moved into the lungs to produce Peak 3 includes both the tidal volume and the inspiratory reserve volume. Peak 4 shows a normal breath, but the depression between Peaks 5 and 6 is produced by pushing out as much air as possible after a normal expiration. The *extra* volume of expelled air is called the **expiratory reserve volume.** The total amount of air expelled between Peaks 5 and 6 includes both the tidal volume and the expiratory reserve volume.

Peak 7 is produced by taking a very deep breath and then pushing out as much air as possible. The total volume of air expelled after Peak 7 is called the **vital capacity.**

Even after a massive exhalation, the lungs remain partly expanded because they cannot be emptied completely by the breathing muscles. The volume of air remaining is called the **residual volume.** It can only be expelled after death by opening the chest cavity. (See Table 4-1 for a comparison of male and female lung capacities.)

LABORATORY EXERCISE 4-2
Determining Lung Capacities

The lung capacities shown in Table 4-1 are averages. Actual values vary according to age, sex, body type, and fitness level. Vital capacity is often used as an indicator of physical fitness, because it represents the largest amount of air that can be pulled into the lungs at one time during exercise. The maximum possible volume depends on the smooth functioning of the breathing tubes and passages, the elasticity of the lung tissue in the alveoli, and the strength of the rib muscles and the diaphragm. In this exercise, you will measure your own lung capacity and compare your measurements with those obtained by other students in your class.

First Aid for Breathing Disruptions

Each year, accidents such as choking, drowning, electrical shock, or suffocation by poisonous gases cause breathing disruptions. In some cases, a victim's breathing can be restored by using appropriate resuscitation techniques or equipment. Trained personnel are seldom immediately available, but the following first-aid rules can help you assist the victim of a breathing disruption until professionals arrive.

1. Stay calm, especially if you are the only person available to take charge.
2. Analyze the situation. If you are alone, decide whether to help the victim first or call for assistance.
3. Avoid moving the victim unless the immediate environment is life-threatening. Do not risk your own life.
4. Make sure that someone calls for help. Describe the victim's symptoms and give directions to the accident site.
5. While waiting, administer artificial respiration or other appropriate first aid. (Ideally, someone with up-to-date first-aid training should do this. If no one with this training is present, an immediate effort to restore breathing should be made since brain damage from lack of oxygen begins within a few minutes.)

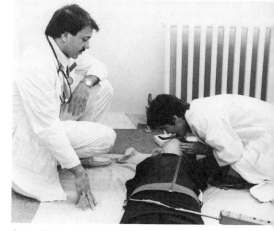

A medical student learns how to administer mouth-to-mouth resuscitation.

The Heimlich manoeuvre

Artificial respiration forces air into a victim's lungs until normal breathing resumes. The mouth-to-mouth method is most common. This procedure involves tilting the victim's head back to open the air passages, pinching the nostrils, and blowing air into the mouth. If air cannot be blown into the lungs by this method, the airway is probably blocked. In this case, a technique called the Heimlich manoeuvre may help.

To perform the Heimlich manoeuvre, the rescuer "hugs" the victim from behind and clasps both hands to form a double fist just below the victim's breastbone. A sharp upward movement with the clenched fist causes a sudden rise of internal air pressure, forcing air back out of the lungs. If the victim has choked on a piece of food, this simple action may be enough to expel the food from the trachea. First-aid measures for other breathing disruptions are usually more extensive.

Adapting to Life in a Low-Oxygen Environment

Millions of people around the world live easily at elevations where most Canadians would become exhausted by hypoxia (low oxygen levels). After a few weeks at high altitudes, most lowlanders do acclimatize to the thin air. Adjustments include altered hemoglobin with more oxygen-carrying capacity, more red blood cells, greater gas exchange in the lungs, and faster breathing. However, these adaptations fade within a month of returning to lower altitudes.

By contrast, people whose ancestors have lived in a hypoxic environment for thousands of years appear to have more permanent adaptations. To study these adaptations at low altitudes, a research team headed by Dr. Peter Hochachka of the University of British Columbia recently brought a group of Quechua Incas to Vancouver from their Peruvian home, which is 4200 m above sea level.

Most Incan adaptations to hypoxia were already known or suspected: large efficient lungs, high-capacity hemoglobin, more red blood cells, and extremely strong hearts. After six weeks at sea level the Incas' hemoglobin capacity and red cell count had dropped significantly, and their hearts had to pump harder to do the same job of delivering oxygen. Their lung adaptations, however, appeared to be permanent.

The study's most important finding was its answer to the "lactate paradox." Imagine exercising until your muscles can no longer get enough oxygen. Past this aerobic limit, energy must be supplied by anaerobic respiration, which produces a lactate-containing acid. Given the Incas' highly efficient oxygen-delivery system, one would expect them to reach their aerobic limit later than lowlanders, then to produce lactate in comparable amounts. The paradox is that both predictions are wrong. The Incas reach their aerobic limit

much *sooner* than lowlanders and beyond that limit produce much *less* lactate.

All previous attempts to understand the lactate paradox were based on the following explanation. Animal cells run on an energy-rich molecule known as ATP. When oxygen is plentiful, ATP is produced in large amounts by aerobic respiration. This enables muscle cells to store ATP during periods of low demand. To contract, the cells use the stored ATP while aerobic respiration replaces the reserves. If energy demand increases sharply, both stored ATP and oxygen quickly run out. Biochemical adjustments in the cell automatically trigger anaerobic respiration, which produces large amounts of lactate but only small amounts of ATP.

This explanation is correct for the muscle cells of lowlanders, but not for those of the Incas. Their muscle cells produce ATP aerobically, almost as soon as it is needed. Response is so rapid that anaerobic pathways are never relied on to the same extent as in lowlanders, even though they are triggered earlier. This finely tuned adaptation operates at any altitude and appears to be permanent.

By combining the Incan data with Hochachka's earlier studies of Weddell seals and Andean llamas, researchers hope to find treatments that selectively protect human tissues from hypoxia.

RESEARCH PROJECT
Rescue and Resuscitation Techniques

Your objective in this research project is to conduct an up-to-date survey of the rescue and resuscitation techniques used by medical or first-aid professionals. To maximize the benefits of this survey, you should work in groups. Each group should investigate a different topic, then summarize their findings as a class.

Choose a topic from the following list or one suggested by your teacher. Present the results of your research in a poster, a written report, a short talk, or as a "how-to" demonstration. Be sure your presentation explains the biological basis of the method or device you have chosen.

- How to rescue a drowning victim without risking your own life or exposing the victim to further injury.
- How to rescue a victim of electrical shock without risking your own life or exposing the victim to further injury.
- How to rescue a victim from suffocation by poisonous gases without risking your own life or exposing the victim to further injury.
- CPR: what it is, how it's done, and who should do it.
- Tracheotomy: what it is, how it's done, and who should do it.
- Mechanical resuscitation devices: how they work and who should use them.
- Electrical resuscitation devices: how they work and who should use them.
- Oxygen masks, tubes, and tanks.
- First-aid courses: types available and what they teach.

You might contact St. John Ambulance, the Canadian Red Cross, the local public health nurse, lifeguards at a local pool, and the public information officer of an electrical utility company for information.

Section Review Questions

1. a) Describe the two major functions of the human gas-exchange system.
   b) What other name is sometimes given to the gas-exchange system, and what does it reveal about the system's overall function?
2. a) List the structures that filter, warm, and moisten inhaled air.
   b) Describe the types of tissue that enable these structures to perform their function.
3. a) What is the primary function of the trachea and the bronchi?
   b) Both the trachea and the bronchi contain cartilaginous rings. How do their structures help them serve their primary function?
4. a) Identify two parts of the human gas-exchange system that are not directly involved with bringing oxygen into the body.
   b) Describe the structure and function of each part.

5. What parts of the human gas-exchange system are directly involved with bringing oxygen into the body? Briefly describe the structure and function of each.

6. a) What muscle movements occur during inspiration?
   b) How do these movements affect internal air pressure and lung volume?

7. Describe the first-aid steps that should be taken to help someone who is choking or drowning.

4.3 The Physiology of Human Gas-Exchange Systems

While anatomy is the study of body structures, **physiology** is the study of body processes. Physiologists investigate how body parts perform vital life functions. And gas exchange is an example of a vital life function. Physiologists use microscopes to examine preserved tissues, perform chemical tests on body tissues or body products, and employ special techniques that allow them to observe living cells or entire systems in action.

In Section 4.2, you learned about the anatomy of the structures involved in breathing and gas exchange. In this section, you will focus on how these structures function.

The function of body parts is always closely related to their structure. The size, shape, and characteristics of each part must be suited for the role it plays in the processes of the body. For example, the structures of the upper respiratory tract perform three functions: warming, filtering, and moistening incoming air. However, none of these structures would seem to affect either breathing or gas exchange because they do not move air or transfer gas molecules to the blood. But the structures of the upper respiratory tract play an important role in the overall functioning of the gas-exchange system.

If cold air was allowed to reach the lungs, the rate of gas exchange would be reduced. This would occur because cool molecules move more slowly and blood vessels constrict when chilled, reducing their ability to carry oxygen through the body. The distance air must travel through the air passages, however, warms it, thereby preventing the introduction of cold air into the lungs.

Unfiltered air in the lungs might introduce foreign particles that could damage the alveolar surface available for gas exchange. But nasal hairs and tracheal cilia trap most of these particles before they reach the lungs.

The introduction of unmoistened air into the lungs would dry the delicate alveolar tissue, preventing oxygen from dissolving. However, mucus-secreting glands in the upper passages ensure that air is thoroughly moistened before it enters the lungs.

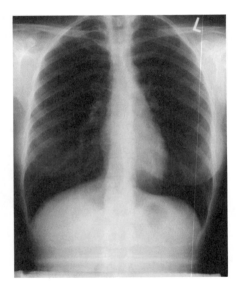
Movies taken with an X-ray camera reveal the role of the diaphragm, ribs, and lungs in breathing. The action of cilia lining the trachea can be observed with a microscope attached to a long, flexible light probe. The composition of air and exhaled breath can be determined through chemical tests. These are just three examples of the many tools and methods physiologists can use to understand the operation of a moving, living system.

Alveoli: The Site of Gas Exchange

The alveoli, or air sacs, are the actual site of gas exchange in humans. The lungs contain an estimated 300 million alveoli, which are arranged in clusters at the ends of the bronchioles. Dissolved gas molecules are transferred between the internal and the external environments by diffusing across the membranous lining of the alveoli.

This lining is made up of epithelial tissue similar to that lining the inner side of your cheeks. The flat epithelial cells form a very thin layer through which dissolved gases can diffuse easily. (See Figure 4-16.) This tissue is interlaced with fine elastic fibres that stretch during inhalation and rebound during exhalation. The limited elasticity of the fibres determines how far the air sacs can inflate and deflate. The fibres also form a kind of "skeleton" that helps to support the lungs by enabling the alveoli to remain open until the next inhalation.

Gas Exchange and Breathing

Since only half a litre of air is exchanged with each breath, you might think there is a pocket of air somewhere down at the bottom of your lungs that never gets exchanged. But gas molecules in the lungs move about constantly and are stirred up by the currents that accompany each breath. The molecules in the residual volume change constantly because diffusion mixes them with gas molecules in the rest of the lungs. This ensures the maximum possible degree of gas exchange.

About 4-6 L of blood are delivered to the lungs every minute. This blood is distributed around the internal environment side, or the "body side," of the lung tissue so evenly that the alveoli seem to be bathed in a thin film of blood. When the lungs are fully inflated with fresh air, the oxygen level in the moisture on the external environment side, or the "gas side," of the lungs is much greater than the oxygen level in the blood on the body side. As a result, the oxygen molecules diffuse across the lung tissue into the blood.

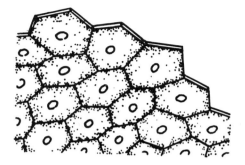

FIGURE 4-16 Epithelial tissue in the alveoli is a single layer of flat epithelial cells that are broad in area but very thin. Epithelial cells are fitted closely together, somewhat like the tiles on a bathroom wall.

DID YOU KNOW?

The oxygen needed for cellular respiration comprises just over 20% of the air volume you take in with each breath. The oxygen content of exhaled breath is only 15%, but this amount is sufficient for continued gas exchange in a drowning victim who is receiving mouth-to-mouth resuscitation.

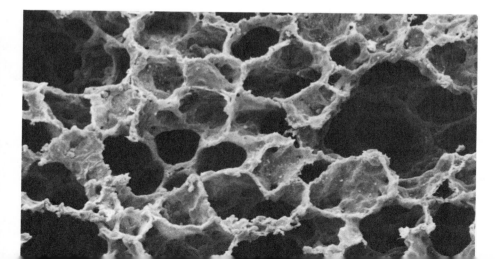

This cross section of a mouse lung shows the alveolar sacs surrounded by a lattice-like arrangement of alveoli. Each sac is almost completely surrounded by capillary blood.

103

Exchange of Gases in the Lungs

One hundred millilitres of blood can carry 20 mL of oxygen.

The transfer of gas molecules across the alveolar membrane is dependent on the process of diffusion. Each gas moves from a region of higher concentration to a region of lower concentration. Oxygen diffuses through the thin alveolar walls into the capillaries that surround each air sac. Carbon dioxide diffuses outward through the capillary walls and then through the alveolar walls into the alveolar spaces, where it is eliminated by the next exhaled breath. (See Figure 4-17.)

FIGURE 4-17 A magnified vein of the alveolar tissue and surrounding capillaries as seen from the body side. You can see that the direction of oxygen diffusion is from the alveolar tissue, which has a higher oxygen concentration, toward the blood, which has a lower concentration. Carbon dioxide moves in the opposite direction from a region of higher concentration to one of lower concentration.

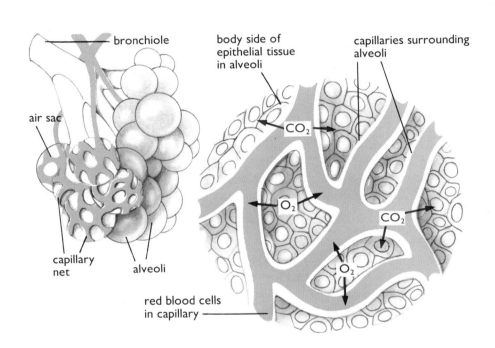

However, only dissolved molecules can diffuse. Oxygen molecules dissolve in the water on the surface of the alveolar walls. The molecular motion of the water molecules moves the dissolved oxygen through the thin alveolar membranes and then through the thin walls of the blood capillaries. The oxygenated blood is carried away to the body cells and replaced in the lung capillaries by deoxygenated, carbon dioxide enriched blood from the body cells.

Oxygen molecules enter the body cells by diffusion. As the cells carry out respiration, their internal oxygen level drops below that of the tissue fluid bathing the cells. First, more oxygen diffuses into the cells from the fluid. Then more oxygen diffuses into the fluid from nearby capillaries. Meanwhile, the carbon dioxide molecules produced by cellular respiration move in the opposite direction.

When blood containing carbon dioxide reaches the lung capillaries, the dissolved carbon dioxide diffuses into the alveolar space and eventually is exhaled.

All of these movements ultimately depend on the specialized gas-exchange tissues that allow gas molecules to enter or leave the internal environment. In the following activity, you will examine some of the specialized gas-exchange tissues responsible for the respiratory process.

INQUIRY ACTIVITY
Examining Gas-Exchange Tissues

Both of the photomicrographs on this page show cross sections of lung tissue, magnified 175×. Study the photomicrographs and answer the following questions.

Discussion Questions
A. Look at the photomicrograph that shows healthy lung tissue.

1. a) About how many distinctly separate air sacs can you see?
   b) Are most of these sacs inflated?
   c) Estimate the air-to-tissue ratio of this cross section.

2. a) Identify the alveolar membrane forming the surface of each air sac.
   b) Which areas represent the surface of alveoli that were not cut when the cross section was made?

3. The tissue between the air sacs is permeated with dark-coloured dots and streaks.
   a) What structures normally surround healthy alveoli in large numbers?
   b) Explain why these structures look like dots when viewed in cross section.
   c) What colour would they be in living tissue?

B. Look at the photomicrograph that shows diseased lung tissue.

1. a) Approximately how many distinctly separate air sacs can you see?
   b) Are most of these sacs inflated?
   c) Estimate the air-to-tissue ratio of this cross section.

2. a) Compare the air-to-tissue ratio in diseased and healthy tissue.
   b) How will this difference affect gas exchange?

3. a) Compare the total surface available for gas exchange in diseased tissue and healthy tissue.
   b) How will this difference affect gas exchange?

4. a) What evidence is there that blood circulation in the diseased tissue has been impaired?
   b) How will this affect gas exchange?

Healthy lung tissue

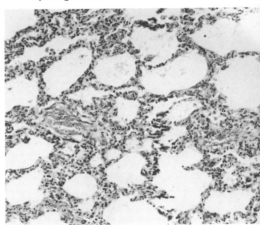

Diseased lung tissue

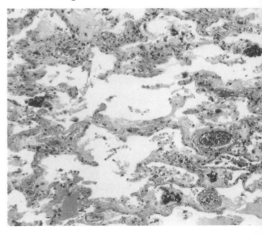

5. This diseased tissue came from a patient who died of asbestosis. The dark islands are asbestos particles surrounded by scar tissue.
   a) How would these regions affect the patient's ability to exchange gases?
   b) How would they probably affect breathing ability? Discuss.
6. a) What would you expect to observe in the trachea of workers exposed to asbestos over a long period? Discuss.
   b) What would you expect to observe in the lungs and tracheas of coal miners and smokers? Discuss.
7. a) What symptoms would you expect in patients with lungs damaged by asbestosis and similar ailments?
   b) How could these patients be treated to relieve their symptoms?
   c) Would this treatment repair the damaged tissue? Discuss.

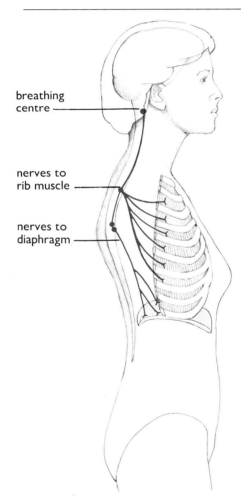

FIGURE 4-18 Nervous control of breathing

Breathing and Homeostasis

All organisms must maintain a constant internal state, or homeostasis, even though they may live in a constantly changing external environment. Your breathing rate is your body's major mechanism for regulating internal levels of oxygen and carbon dioxide. Your breathing rate is regulated by both nervous and chemical controls, which operate simultaneously but independently of one another.

Nervous Control of Breathing

A network of nerve fibres connects the breathing muscles to a breathing centre in the brain. (See Figure 4-18.) The rate at which these muscles contract, however, is affected by internal body conditions.

The **breathing centre** contains cells that act as chemical detectors. High levels of carbon dioxide in the blood stimulate these cells, which, in turn, trigger more frequent impulses to speed up the rate of contraction. The result is a more rapid breathing rate. Carbon dioxide is expelled more rapidly, and internal conditions soon return to normal, maintaining homeostasis.

You can consciously control your breathing rate, but only in a limited way. You can decide to breathe faster, slower, deeper, or more shallowly. You can even hold your breath, but not for long because the increasing level of carbon dioxide will soon stimulate the breathing centre. The breathing centre then sends a stream of impulses so strong that you cannot consciously overcome them. As a result, your body maintains homeostasis even without your co-operation.

The breathing centre is also affected by emotions and influenced by impulses from elsewhere. Laughter, sadness, excitement, and fear can affect your breathing rate. For example, when something frightens you, you usually experience a sharp intake of breath. An irritant such as dust, pollen, or soot in the

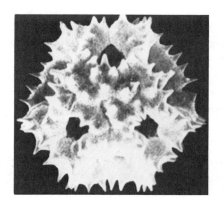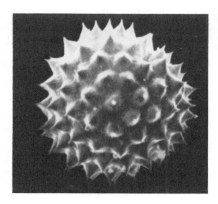

Electron micrographs of pollen, one of the major irritants to the human respiratory system. **Left:** Dandelion pollen. **Right:** Ragweed pollen.

upper respiratory tract may cause you to cough or sneeze. In both situations, you will inhale deeply and exhale rapidly. Expelled air in a cough or a sneeze may travel as fast as 160 km/h.

A yawn is another respiratory adjustment to a lack of oxygen or an excess of carbon dioxide in your body. The deep inhalation associated with a yawn brings more air into the lungs for gas exchange. A hiccup, or a spasm of the diaphragm, can result when the nerves to the diaphragm are irritated, for example, by indigestion or by food that is too hot.

Gas Exchange and the External Environment

Both plants and animals must carry out cellular respiration to release energy for their life functions. Cellular respiration requires two starting materials: glucose and oxygen. Plants can obtain both of these materials through photosynthesis, but animals must obtain glucose and oxygen from the external environment. However, only very simple animals can obtain oxygen by diffusion from the air or water that surrounds them. Most animals need specialized systems to obtain oxygen from their external environments. But gas exchange can proceed normally only if all parts of an animal's respiratory system are functioning smoothly, and if the external environment is free of poisonous substances and maintains its usual oxygen level.

A malfunction of any part of an animal's gas-exchange system can threaten the animal's health. So can the presence of pollution in the air. In Section 4.4, you will examine how these two factors affect the respiratory health of humans.

Section Review Questions

1. a) Define anatomy and physiology.
   b) Use an example from the human gas-exchange system to explain how the two terms are related.

Diving Whales

Professional shell divers can descend to depths of 45 m, about the height of a 15-storey building, and survive 2-3 min on one breath while working. However, these feats pale in comparison to the records set by whales. The sperm whale, for example, may go up to 75 min on one breath, dive up to 1 km below the surface, and within 5 min of surfacing be ready for another long dive.

Several adaptive mechanisms account for the whale's remarkable ability to spend long periods under water. Whales and other diving animals make adjustments to their cardiovascular systems during a dive that prevent the rapid depletion of oxygen in blood. Total blood flow is reduced through a dramatic reduction in heart rate. Arteries constrict to maintain blood pressure and shunt blood to organs such as the brain and heart, which cannot survive long without oxygen. Arteries to muscle, kidney, and intestine become greatly constricted.

The whale's respiratory system is also highly adapted to diving. Ironically, whale lungs are relatively small—50% smaller than a human's, proportionally. They are, however, very efficient. Gas exchange takes place very quickly with each breath. In fact, below a depth of 100 m, external water pressure collapses the lungs, pushing air into the whale's windpipe and nasal passages, preventing gas exchange. This seemingly impractical system is actually an ingenious solution to a problem that plagues human divers—the bends.

As external water pressure increases around a human diver, the lungs contract so that the pressure of air in the lungs is approximately equal to the water pressure. Under these conditions, nitrogen diffuses from the lungs into the bloodstream. If external water pressure decreases too rapidly during surfacing, the nitrogen diffuses out of solution and forms bubbles in the blood. Severe cases of the bends may be fatal. By cutting off access to their air supply below 100 m, whales avoid this problem.

The real secret to the whale's abilities, however, is in its muscles, which are extraordinarily rich in myoglobin. Like hemoglobin, this protein can bind and store oxygen within the body. Myoglobin is found in muscle, where it transports oxygen from blood capillaries to mitochondria. The dynamics of myoglobin-oxygen binding make possible the transport and release of oxygen when needed. At normal partial pressures of blood oxygen, myoglobin has a far greater affinity for oxygen than does hemoglobin, so oxygen is transferred from hemoglobin to myoglobin. At very low partial pressures, like those inside working muscle cells, oxygen is released.

While myoglobin is present in all mammalian muscles, whales carry far more than land animals do. A resting land animal will carry about 25% of its oxygen store in its muscles. A whale carries twice as much. Table 4-2 shows what percentage of oxygen is stored in whale tissues in comparison to that in human tissues. While diving, whales rely on this built-in oxygen tank, which allows blood oxygen to be diverted to less self-sufficient organs.

TABLE 4-2 Oxygen Levels in Human and Whale Tissues

	Human (%)	Whale (%)
Lungs	34	9
Blood	41	41
Muscle	13	41
Other Tissue	12	9

2. a) Define homeostasis.
   b) Explain how gas exchange contributes to homeostasis.

3. a) Describe how breathing rate is controlled in humans.
   b) List some external and internal factors that affect breathing rate.

4. a) Describe the tissues that make up the alveoli.
   b) What features maximize the surface area of the alveoli? Explain why a large surface area is important.
   c) What other features help the alveoli perform their function?

5. Describe the process by which oxygen moves
   a) across the alveolar walls
   b) away from the lungs
   c) into body cells

6. Describe the process by which carbon dioxide moves
   a) out of body cells
   b) back to the lungs
   c) across the alveolar walls

4.4 Factors Affecting Respiratory Health

To function effectively, gas-exchange surfaces must be moist, thin, and shaped to maximize surface area. In humans, these surfaces are also warm. Unfortunately, these are the very features that also make the human gas-exchange system vulnerable to airborne contaminants such as bacteria, mould spores, and other pollutants. The alveolar tissue lining your lungs has a surface area of about 70 m^2 and is only one cell layer thick. This means that every cell of the lining is exposed constantly to foreign particles in the air. One common contaminant is industrial smoke.

Industrial smoke consists of gases, liquid droplets, and solid particles. Toxic gases such as methane, ammonia, carbon monoxide, hydrogen sulphide, and nitrous oxide may be introduced into the body through the respiratory tract. These gases dissolve in the mucus, and most of them form irritating acids. In addition to directly causing inflammation of respiratory tissues, these gases also pass into the bloodstream, and may cause headaches, dizziness, weakness, and sickness.

Industrial smoke also contains microscopic, solid particles such as pollen, ash, carbon, and metallic dust. Most of these particles are too fine to be filtered by the nasal hairs. They are trapped by the mucus lining the upper respiratory tract, and then they are moved to the pharynx, where they can be expelled by coughing. However, constant exposure to such particles eventually will lead to a buildup of excess mucus on respiratory surfaces, and debris-clogged cilia will be unable to function normally.

DID YOU KNOW?
Carbon monoxide is a particularly dangerous air contaminant because red blood cells prefer it to oxygen. So, inhaling air that contains carbon monoxide quickly deprives body tissues of oxygen for cellular respiration, even though there is plenty of oxygen inside the lungs. Because carbon monoxide has no colour, taste, or odour, people can be unaware that they are inhaling it. Lethal concentrations cause unconsciousness and death. Treatment involves the use of a mechanical respirator and 100% oxygen. Even after recovery, heart, nerve, or brain damage may result.

LEFT: Claude Guay of Ottawa wears an army-surplus gas mask to relieve his asthma symptoms in areas that are heavy with car exhaust fumes. Urban air can be hazardous to the health of people with respiratory problems.

RIGHT: A pollution control plant at Powell River, British Columbia. The plant filters out cinders and ash from mill wastes so they will not enter the ocean. Similar filtering systems are now being used by other companies to catch pollutants before they enter the water or air.

Once the filtration system no longer functions normally, fine smoke particles can reach the fragile gas-exchange membrane. Alveolar tissue has no cilia, so airborne smoke particles become permanently trapped in the alveolar spaces. As the airborne particles accumulate in the air sacs, they cover up the respiratory surface and interfere with gas exchange. Repeated exposure to contaminants leads to further lung deterioration, and general weakening of the lungs or other tissues may result in disease.

RESEARCH PROJECT
Workplace Pollutants and Respiratory Health

Choose an occupation from the following list or one suggested by your teacher. Research the effects on human respiratory tissue of any airborne pollutants associated with the workplace for the occupation you select.

Your report should identify the job-related pollutant(s), the source(s) of the pollutants, and the respiratory diseases or disorders associated with the occupation you have chosen.

- miner (coal, asbestos, or other)
- grain-elevator operator
- traffic-control officer
- lumber-mill sawyer
- crop sprayer
- hospital laboratory technician

- sewage-treatment worker
- auto mechanic
- steel-mill worker
- hairdresser
- oil-refinery worker

- chemistry teacher
- night-club singer
- dry cleaner

Respiratory Diseases and Disorders

Airborne pollutants are not the only cause of respiratory diseases and disorders. Many result from infection by airborne micro-organisms such as bacteria or viruses that inflame the respiratory lining. Excessive flow of mucus, fever, and headache are common symptoms of respiratory problems.

The Common Cold and Influenza

The two most familiar respiratory infections are probably the common cold and influenza. (See Table 4-3.) Both are caused by viruses. Colds occur repeatedly because the immunity you acquire from one cold virus will not protect you from another cold virus. Pneumonia is a possible complication of a cold or flu.

The inflammation caused by common colds may be in the nasal area (rhinitis), the pharynx (pharyngitis), the larynx (laryngitis), or the bronchial tubes (bronchitis).

TABLE 4-3   The Common Cold and Influenza

	Common Cold	Influenza
Cause	• over 200 viruses	• 3 virus strains
Onset	• a period of days	• within hours
Duration	• 1–2 weeks	• 3–5 days
Transmission	• airborne droplets (see influenza) • direct contact with contagious people	• airborne droplets sprayed by sneezing or coughing of infected persons
Symptoms	• sore throat, sneezing, runny nose	• fever, headache, lung congestion, cough, malaise
Treatment	• rest, fluids • relief of symptoms with over-the-counter remedies	• rest, fluids • Type-A flu can be cured by the prescription drug Amantadine if taken immediately after symptoms occur
Prevention	• avoid people with colds	• vaccine is 60–70% effective; protects for one flu season

Pneumonia is an acute infection of the alveolar sacs. Symptoms include chest pain, fever, coughing, and accumulation of mucus in the lungs. In most cases, the cause is bacterial, but viruses, fungal spores, or severe allergic reactions may also cause pneumonia.

DID YOU KNOW?
Tuberculosis was once the major cause of death in North America and is still a killer in poor countries, where it is prevalent in children and young adult females.

A skin test can be administered to discover if a person has been exposed to the tuberculin bacteria. A positive test, with a swelling and redness near the injection site, indicates previous exposure, but does not necessarily mean the presence of an active infection. Further tests, usually chest X-rays, are needed to determine whether treatment for the disease is required.

Emphysema is a degenerative lung disease that frequently results from cigarette smoking or other air pollutants. The condition is characterized by overinflation of the lungs, loss of lung elasticity, and reduced gas exchange.

Three main strains of influenza virus have been identified. As a result, laboratories are able to prepare effective vaccines. However, viruses mutate regularly. Mutation means that the internal structure of a virus alters slightly. But this slight alteration is enough to make previous immunization ineffective, so new vaccines must be developed each year. As new mutations emerge, they are usually named after the geographical location where they are first identified. You may be familiar with Asian, Taiwan, or Hong Kong flu. Influenza viruses have acquired these names because they are usually seen in the Far East before they spread to North America.

Tuberculosis

Tuberculosis is usually caused by *Mycobacterium tuberculosis* and is transmitted to the lungs by the inhalation of live *Mycobacterium tuberculosis*. These bacteria are found in the droplets that are sprayed into the air when an infected person sneezes or coughs. Lung tissue reacts to the invading bacteria by producing protective cell clusters that engulf the bacterial organisms. These clusters are called tubercules. If the infection is untreated, the tubercules continue to grow, eventually dropping off into the lung cavities. Symptoms of tuberculosis include chest pain, fever, weight loss, and hemorrhaging of the lungs.

Tuberculosis can also spread through the circulatory and lymphatic systems to other organs. Treatment involves drug therapy for at least one year. Frequent checkups after treatment are vital because the infection may reoccur at any time.

Maintaining Respiratory Health

There are many things you can do to maintain your respiratory health. You can choose not to smoke. Smoking greatly increases your chances of contracting respiratory diseases such as emphysema and lung cancer. It can also be a factor in heart disease. If you have allergies or asthma, smoking may further aggravate these conditions.

You can decide to get more exercise such as walking, running, swimming, and cycling. Physical exercise on a regular basis can greatly improve your respiratory health by making more oxygen available to your body. Regular exercise can also lower your heart rate.

Generally, people do not die as a direct result of air pollution, unless there is some environmental catastrophe such as a poisonous gas leak into the environment. However, long-term exposure to air pollution contributes to the death rate from diseases such as emphysema, lung cancer, stomach cancer, and heart disease. Despite the presence of body structures to filter and eject pollutants, some damage to the gas-exchange system is inevitable. The kinds and amounts of air pollution in Canada vary according to the level of industrial activity and population density.

People often feel they have little influence over the quality of the air they breathe in the places where they live and work. However, the air-pollution laws of a city often reflect the importance its citizens place on respiratory health. Many cities have passed by-laws that prohibit smoking in public places, in office buildings, and on public transportation. Many restaurants also have no-smoking sections.

Public opinion has also had an impact on government awareness about air pollution. Although the emission of polluting substances has not been eliminated, some legislation has been created to reduce the amount industry can release into the air. Further co-operation between governments and industry, and the development of cost-efficient technologies, could improve air quality significantly.

In some urban areas, people have chosen to rely on public transportation instead of their cars. Automobile exhaust is one of the major contributors to air pollution. By joining a car pool, riding a bicycle, or travelling on a subway, these people are making a commitment to cleaner air and better respiratory health.

Running is an excellent aerobic activity that helps maintain respiratory health.

Section Review Questions

1. What features of the human gas-exchange system make it vulnerable to airborne contaminants and infectious organisms?

2. Briefly explain how air pollutants interfere with gas exchange in the lungs.

3. The human gas-exchange system has several features to screen out airborne contaminants. Briefly describe how industrial smoke affects each of these features.

4. Prepare a simple table to compare the cause, symptoms, and treatment of influenza, the common cold, and tuberculosis.

5. A common cold that starts in the nasal passages may spread to the bronchial tubes. How do you think this happens?

6. a) State an example of the impact public opinion has had on air quality.
   b) What steps can you take to maintain your own respiratory health?

Meet Gordon Sussman

Gordon is head of the Allergy Division of Immunology at Wellesley Hospital in Toronto. He is also on staff at two other hospitals and is an assistant professor at the University of Toronto in the Department of Medicine.

Q. Why did you decide to become an allergist?

A. At university, I became interested in immunology. The research in immunology is in the forefront of every aspect of medicine. Allergy is a branch of immunology.

Q. How many years did it take to become an allergist?

A. I studied biology at university, and obtained a medical degree, and then I did two years of internal medicine. After that, I trained in immunology. To specialize in medicine takes about ten years of education and training.

Q. What are the most common allergic problems that you see?

A. Respiratory allergies such as allergic rhinitis and asthma, skin allergies such as eczema and hives, adverse reactions to drugs and foods, and severe allergic reactions are the four primary categories of allergies.

Q. What do you do when a patient with a respiratory allergy comes to you?

A. I do a physical examination, take a medical history, and then run tests. We use blood tests to look for hypersensitivity in the

antibody called IgE. But skin tests are most common. We take a standardized extract of dust, pollen, animal dander, or whatever substance we want to test for, and inject a small amount into the patient's skin to see if the skin reacts.

Q. When you discover the cause of the allergy what is the next step?

A. I decide on the best form of treatment. Sometimes it's as simple as finding an environmental

control, such as getting rid of a pet if the patient is allergic to animals. Medication such as antihistamines can sometimes control the problem. There are also nose sprays and eyedrops to control inflammation. If none of these is successful, we can immunize the patient.

Q. What does immunizing the patient involve?

A. For example, if the patient is allergic to ragweed, we will inject the patient with small doses of ragweed, increasing the dosages over time, until the body builds up an immunity to ragweed. We're trying to turn immune responses on and off. Sometimes it's easier in mice than in people.

Q. Have there been many changes in the respiratory-allergy field since you entered it?

A. There have been no major breakthroughs and no cures. But, there has been an improvement in drugs and in the development of new drugs to control allergic conditions. In the last 15 years, immunology has advanced faster than any other branch of medicine. Many new treatments in all areas of medicine are due to immunology research.

Q. What do you like best about being an allergist?

A. It's interesting and the research is fun. You can help people and the treatments are improving all the time.

4.5 Gas-Exchange Systems in Other Vertebrates

Much can be learned about human body systems by comparing them with those of other vertebrates. Because there are many vertebrate species, biologists usually choose one representative from each major class for intensive study. (See Table 4-4.) For example, the anatomy and physiology of a cat can reveal a great deal about structure and function in lions and tigers. Mice, rats, and pigs are often used instead of human subjects. Although each representative animal has specialized adaptations for its own environment, it is similar enough to other members of its class to reveal general patterns in structure and function among these animals.

Patterns for Gas Exchange in Terrestrial Vertebrates

Terrestrial vertebrates have gas-exchange systems that enable them to obtain oxygen from the air. Most vertebrate systems include internal lungs, or air sacs, that are directly connected to the external environment. Inspiration fills the air sacs, which are surrounded by blood capillaries. These capillaries absorb oxygen from the inspired air and release carbon dioxide, which can be collected for exhalation.

Most mammalian gas-exchange structures are similar to those found in humans, but each species has adaptations that suit it to its environment. Camels, for example, are adapted to dry desert conditions. Compared to humans, camels have many more nasal hairs to trap dust particles. They also have much longer passageways to moisten air before it reaches their lungs. A camel's nostrils have muscles that cause them to close during sandstorms.

The Arctic fox is adapted to exchange gases in extremely cold temperatures (-40°C or lower). The flow of blood around its air passageways is much greater than that of other foxes. This feature warms the cold air enough to prevent damage to an Arctic fox's delicate lung tissue.

TABLE 4-4 Representative Vertebrates

Class	Usual Representatives
Mammalia	• human, pig, rat, cat
Aves	• pigeon
Reptilia	• garter snake, turtle
Amphibia	• frog
Osteichthyes	• perch

DID YOU KNOW?
Lemmings are adapted to Arctic conditions. Although lemmings live under the snow during winter, they still require a great deal of heat energy to survive. Lemmings survive because they have an increased breathing rate that supplies them with the oxygen they need to maintain their high metabolic rate. Lemming lungs are proportionally larger than human lungs, which allows for this extensive gas exchange.

Would the adaptations of an Arctic fox enable it to survive in a camel's environment?

Like mammals, birds have a pair of lungs, but they also have extra air sacs that play an important role in adapting them for flight. Birds must have high rates of gas exchange to provide enough oxygen for the energy they need to fly. Their lungs and air sacs are connected, giving them about twice as much gas-exchange surface as a mammal of similar size. (See Figure 4-19.) Birds breathe by contracting both their chest and their abdominal muscles to force exhaled air out. As the muscles relax, outside air rushes in.

Reptiles such as lizards and turtles also have a pair of lungs to receive inhaled air. However, these lungs are much smaller than those of birds or mammals of similar size. (See Figure 4-20.) Reptiles do not need larger lungs because they are cold-blooded, meaning that their body temperatures are the same as their surroundings. Since they do not need to maintain a warm body temperature, less oxygen is needed for cellular respiration, and less surface area is required for gas exchange.

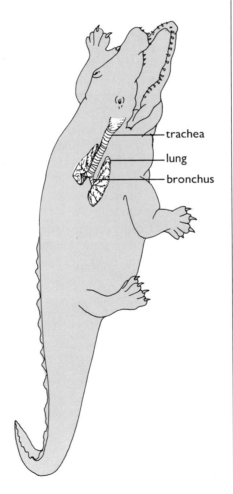

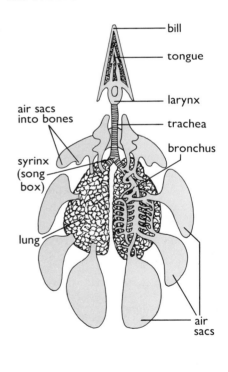

FIGURE 4-19   The gas-exchange system of a bird

bill
tongue
larynx
trachea
bronchus
air sacs into bones
syrinx (song box)
lung
air sacs

trachea
lung
bronchus

FIGURE 4-20   Lung tissue makes up only 0.9% of an alligator's body mass. By comparison, lung tissue makes up 1.1% of a human's body mass. Other reptiles, especially snakes, have even less gas-exchange tissue, which limits the ability of these cold-blooded vertebrates to release heat through cellular respiration.

Patterns for Gas Exchange in Aquatic Vertebrates

There are two basic patterns for gas exchange in aquatic vertebrates. Aquatic mammals such as whales and seals breathe air, as do the land-dwelling members of the mammalian class. Aquatic reptiles such as sea snakes and turtles must also surface for air. Although most of these air-breathers possess adaptations for breath-holding, their gas-exchange systems are quite similar to those of land-dwelling vertebrates. Like humans, these aquatic vertebrates have lungs to extract oxygen molecules from the air they inhale. However, aquatic vertebrates such as fish and tadpoles have gills instead of lungs. Gills enable these animals to extract the oxygen molecules that are dissolved in the surrounding water, so they do not need to surface for air.

Fish, for example, have two gill chambers that contain rows of tiny projections called gill filaments. Each gill filament is surrounded by part of a continuous thin membrane through which dissolved materials diffuse easily. Each filament contains large numbers of blood capillaries. Water entering a fish's mouth is forced out through the gill openings. As the water passes over and around the gill filaments, gas exchange occurs. Dissolved oxygen from the water diffuses into the capillaries. Carbon dioxide from the capillaries diffuses into the water, which is eventually pushed out of the gill openings. A constant flow of water over the gill filaments is required for gas exchange to occur continuously.

Amphibians such as frogs exhibit gas-exchange structures characteristic of both aquatic and terrestrial vertebrates. As tadpoles, frogs are entirely aquatic, extracting dissolved oxygen from the water with their gills. As adults, frogs rely mainly on their lungs to breathe air. Compared with similar bird or mammal structures, a frog's lungs are small both in volume and in surface area. However, this small size is adequate for the needs of the cold-blooded frog. (See Figure 4-21.) In addition, a frog can exchange gases through its mouth and skin surfaces. Its skin is thin and moist enough to transfer oxygen whether the frog is surrounded by water or by air. In late autumn, frogs burrow into pond mud. During the winter, frogs remain dormant, relying on their skin to provide the small amount of oxygen they require.

The gill filaments of this salmon fan out to maximize surface area for the diffusion of oxygen.

The frog's skin must remain moist at all times. Desert-dwelling amphibians such as the toad have specialized skin cells that secrete moisture.

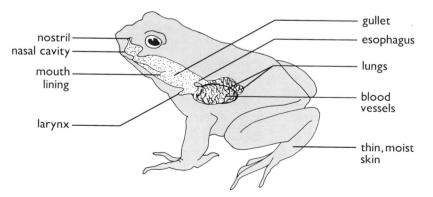

nostril
nasal cavity
mouth lining
larynx

gullet
esophagus
lungs
blood vessels
thin, moist skin

FIGURE 4-21 An adult frog's gas-exchange system. The lungs are simple sacs without any alveoli to increase surface area.

You will examine the physical structures of a vertebrate's respiratory system more closely in the following laboratory exercise.

LABORATORY EXERCISE 4-3
Exploring a Vertebrate's Gas-Exchange System

The fundamental purpose of this laboratory exercise is to examine the gas-exchange structures of a representative vertebrate. Following the dissection, you will prepare a chart comparing the gas-exchange system of your specimen with that of a human and one other vertebrate.

A dissection can be a valuable learning tool in biology. It is important to learn as much as possible from each dissection by practising careful, precise dissection techniques. If you follow correct procedures, observe carefully, keep complete records, and make detailed diagrams, you can help maximize the educational value of each dissection and minimize the number of specimens you will need.

Since the same vertebrate specimen will probably be used to study other internal systems, it is important that you work with only one system at a time. The use of one specimen for several dissection exercises reduces the overall number of specimens that are required for this biology course.

Your teacher may choose to use display models of vertebrate systems instead of laboratory dissections or in addition to them.

Section Review Questions

1. a) Describe the basic pattern of gas-exchange systems in terrestrial vertebrates.
   b) Describe how this basic pattern is adapted to suit the gas-exchange needs of a bird.

2. Compare the gas-exchange systems of a reptile with that of a mammal.

3. a) Describe the two basic patterns of gas-exchange systems in aquatic vertebrates.
   b) Which type of system is found in nonmammalian aquatic vertebrates?
   c) Which type of system is found in aquatic mammals. What is its advantage?

4. a) Gills and lungs perform a similar function. Describe this function.
   b) List two similarities and two differences in the structure and operation of gills and lungs.

5. a) Frogs have rather small lungs when compared with those of mammals or birds of similar size. Explain why this small size is not a disadvantage.
   b) How does the gas-exchange system of a tadpole differ from that of an adult frog?

Oceans in Danger?

Oceans cover nearly 70% of Earth's surface and provide humanity with food, transportation, and surprisingly, much of the oxygen we breathe. The source of this oxygen is phytoplankton. Phytoplankton are tiny marine organisms that are important because of their photosynthetic ability and overwhelming quantity. Oceanic phytoplankton produce more atmospheric oxygen than land plants do. They are also the base of marine food chains, ultimately supporting ocean ecosystems. Of the approximately one hundred billion tonnes of organic material produced by photosynthesis every year, two thirds is attributed to oceanic phytoplankton.

Some scientists are trying to determine the importance of phytoplankton in global ecosystems. One controversial theory suggests that phytoplankton are one of the most important factors in maintaining the stability of the atmosphere. While many other scientists feel that this claim is exaggerated, or simply wrong, it is generally accepted that more information needs to be gathered.

Under these circumstances, what would be the effects of increasing ocean pollution? Could ocean pollution decrease worldwide populations of phytoplankton, destroying marine food chains and lowering oxygen levels worldwide? At the moment, an answer of ''yes'' would be speculative since no evidence of global phytoplankton depletion has been reported. However, given the potential seriousness of such consequences, speculation and early action may be the only way to avert disaster.

Pollution does affect phytoplankton. In lakes, rivers, and coastal waters, pollutants produced by humans such as sewage, fertilizers, and biocides have destabilized and harmed phytoplankton populations, as well as the ecosystems that they support. Some people say that if pollution can adversely affect phytoplankton locally, it could have a disastrous effect globally. Others argue that the oceans are too large to be affected seriously by pollution. Coastal pollution, they say, seems very serious because we rely on the coastal area of the oceans (which accounts for only 2% of the total area of the earth's oceans) for 88% of our economic benefits.

The remaining 98% of oceans, it is argued, has yet to be affected by pollution. Yet, one hundred years ago, it was believed that the Great Lakes could also absorb any amount of waste without adverse effects. News reports on the effects of industrial wastes in Lake Erie, sewage in Lake Ontario, and pollution from motor boats and cottages on Lake Huron prove conclusively that this assumption was wrong. Is it reasonable to make comparisons between the Great Lakes and the oceans? Why or why not? Consider bodies of water such as Lake Erie, Hamilton Harbour, and northern acidified lakes. How long has it taken for them to become seriously damaged? Do these bodies of water ever recover? How long does it take? How do these examples compare to ocean pollution?

What questions need to be answered to judge the extent of the danger to our oceans from pollution? What studies might be done? If you determine that ocean pollution must be stopped, how could this be done, and at what cost? Given the work that still must be done by scientists, are we justified in incurring economic and social hardship to keep the oceans clean? Can we afford to protect the oceans? Can we afford not to?

4.6 Gas-Exchange Systems in Invertebrates

Invertebrates have the same need for energy and oxygen as vertebrates do, and must possess specialized structures for obtaining oxygen from air or water and disposing of carbon dioxide. However, invertebrates exhibit a much greater diversity in gas-exchange structures than vertebrates.

Grasshoppers and earthworms are both terrestrial, but they have very different structures for obtaining oxygen from the air. Like most insects, grasshoppers have a complex gas-exchange system of moist internal passages, and special structures to pump air in and out of their bodies. (See Figure 4-22.) In contrast, the earthworm has no special respiratory structures apart from a rich blood supply just beneath its skin. The earthworm, therefore, requires a moist environment so oxygen can diffuse through the surface of its skin. However, the earthworm cannot live in an aquatic environment.

The earthworm requires a moist environment at all times.

FIGURE 4-22 The grasshopper pumps air in and out through its spiracles by moving its wings and abdomen. Oxygen diffuses directly into the tissue surrounding the air sacs.

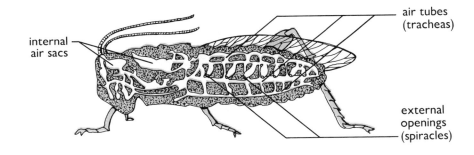

internal air sacs

air tubes (tracheas)

external openings (spiracles)

Except for insects and a few other arthropods and annelids, most invertebrates are aquatic. Despite similarities in the way aquatic invertebrates obtain oxygen from water, each kind displays particular adaptations that suit it to its environment.

Gas Exchange in the Phylum Porifera

The phylum Porifera includes some of the very simplest of animals. All of its members are sponges—either marine or freshwater. Each sponge consists of a hollow, vase-shaped body with a double-layered cell. The sponge shown in

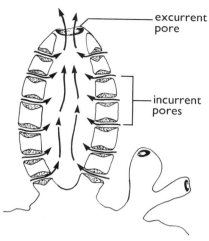

FIGURE 4-23 A sponge obtains fresh supplies of food and dissolved oxygen by circulating water through its hollow body. Beating flagella on specialized cells move water in through incurrent pores and out through excurrent pores.

Figure 4-23 draws water through the incurrent pores in its wall. The sponge collects its food and its oxygen from the water it takes in. Dissolved oxygen from the incoming water diffuses directly into the cells that make up the sponge. Waste carbon dioxide from cellular respiration diffuses outward and is disposed of by water flowing out through the excurrent pore.

Structurally, the bag-like sponge resembles a vertebrate's lung. The sponge's walls are permeated by numerous tiny tubes and hollow chambers formed by repeated folds in the body tissues. The large surface area that is created permits rapid gas exchange, especially since the tissues themselves are only two cell layers thick. The cells lining the chambers have beating flagella that keep water moving, and ensure the rapid inflow of oxygen and outflow of carbon dioxide.

Gas Exchange in Other Invertebrate Phyla

Although all the invertebrates in Table 4-5 are aquatic, they live in different types of aquatic environments, and each has different structures and systems for gas exchange.

RESEARCH PROJECT
Invertebrate Gas-Exchange Systems

Select representatives from two invertebrate phyla listed in Table 4-5. Check with your teacher and other class members to make sure that all phyla in the table are represented.

Consult reference books in your library to learn about the gas-exchange systems of each organism. Remember that you may have to look under "respiration" or "respiratory systems" in some books.

TABLE 4-5   Representative Aquatic Invertebrates

Phylum	Usual Representatives
Phylum Porifera	• sponge
Phylum Coelenterata	• hydra, jellyfish
Phylum Platyhelminthes	• flatworm, tapeworm
Phylum Mollusca	• clam, snail

Write a description of the structure and function of the gas-exchange system of each phylum. Be sure to include a suitable diagram. Devise a chart to compare the gas-exchange systems of the two invertebrates you have selected. Then compare the features of these systems to the human respiratory system and to the gas-exchange system of the sponge.

Gas Exchange and the Environment

All animal gas-exchange systems are adapted for a pollution-free environment. Just as air pollution endangers the health of humans and all other air-breathers, water pollution endangers aquatic animals. Acid rain, for example, can cause such severe pollution in a small lake that neither the fish nor the small invertebrates on which they feed can survive. Industrial effluents dumped into lakes or rivers also reduce the variety of animals that can inhabit the water.

Pollutants of this type directly result in the death of organisms because they interfere with vital life functions. Mercury, for example, may destroy the nervous system. Other forms of water pollution destroy animals and plants by removing oxygen. When garbage and raw sewage are dumped into streams, large colonies of bacteria flourish on the rich food supply. Like most other living things, bacteria need oxygen for cellular respiration, and can deplete even large lakes of oxygen in a surprisingly short time. In order to preserve water quality in the future, more attention will have to be paid to the disposal of human and industrial wastes.

Oxygen alone, however, is not enough for cellular respiration. The purpose of cellular respiration is the release of energy that is stored in the bonds of glucose molecules obtained from food. Few natural foods, however, contain pure glucose. All animals must process the food they ingest in order to obtain glucose from it. You will learn about the body systems that enable animals to perform this function in Chapter 5.

This lake in northern Ontario is being tested for its acidity level. Increased acidity levels caused by pollution are suspected to increase algal populations. When this happens, the algae use up the oxygen supply needed by the other animal and fish populations that depend on the lake.

Section Review Questions

1. Explain how the earthworm and the grasshopper demonstrate the diversity of invertebrate gas-exchange systems.

2. a) How does the earthworm's gas-exchange system limit it to a moist environment?
   b) How does the grasshopper's gas-exchange system enable it to move faster than the earthworm?

3. a) Describe the structure of the sponge's gas-exchange system.
   b) In what ways does it resemble the gas-exchange system of a terrestrial vertebrate? How does it differ?

4. What adaptations suit the gas-exchange systems of the earthworm, the sponge, and the grasshopper to their usual environments?

Chapter Review

Key Words

alveoli
anaerobic respiration
anatomy
aerobic
basal metabolic rate
breathing
breathing centre
bronchi
bronchioles
cellular respiration
epiglottis
expiration
expiratory reserve volume

gas exchange
homeostasis
inspiration
inspiratory capacity
inspiratory reserve volume
larynx
metabolism
pharnyx
physiology
residual volume
tidal volume
trachea
vital capacity

Recall Questions

Multiple Choice

1. The chemical reaction that combines glucose and oxygen to produce carbon dioxide, water, and usable energy is called
   a) metabolism
   b) homeostasis
   c) breathing
   d) cellular respiration

2. The transferring of oxygen into the blood is known as
   a) breathing
   b) cellular respiration
   c) gas exchange
   d) anaerobic respiration

3. Vital capacity is
   a) the volume of air remaining in the lungs at all times
   b) the total volume of air that can be expelled after a deep breath
   c) the air you are exchanging now
   d) the extra volume of air inhaled into the lungs

4. The actual site of gas exchange in humans is the
   a) trachea
   b) pharynx
   c) bronchi
   d) alveoli

5. When gas exchange occurs in fish
   a) dissolved oxygen from the water diffuses out of the capillaries
   b) water is carried into the gill openings
   c) water passes through the gill filaments
   d) carbon dioxide in the water passes into the capillaries

6. In anaerobic respiration, the substance produced is
   a) water
   b) oxygen
   c) lactic acid
   d) carbon dioxide

7. Food is prevented from entering the trachea by the
   a) pharynx
   b) epiglottis
   c) larynx
   d) cilia

8. In adult frogs, gas exchange occurs through the
   a) gills, skin
   b) lungs, mouth
   c) lungs, mouth, skin
   d) lungs, gills, skin

9. Oxygen molecules enter body cells by
   a) diffusion
   b) cellular respiration
   c) inspiration
   d) circulation

Fill in the Blanks

1. _____ is the volume of air that always remains in the lungs.

2. _____ are tiny microscopic hairs that help purify the air going through the respiratory tract.

3. The maintenance of a constant state in living things is called _____ .

4. _____ is administered when breathing has stopped.

5. _____ draw in dissolved oxygen in water by incurrent pores and dispose of carbon dioxide in water through excurrent pores.

6. During a state of emergency, energy is obtained by _____ .

7. Gas exchange occurs in the earthworm through its _____ .

Short Answers

1. How does a change in altitude affect breathing rate?

2. Respiration for the human body occurs at three levels. What are these three levels?

3. What is the role of the mucus in the respiratory tract?

4. How do fish gills perform gas exchange with their environment?

5. How does your gas-exchange system help your body fight bacteria?

6. Explain why you cannot hold your breath for very long.

7. Why is immunization against cold and flu viruses effective for only a short period of time?

Application Questions

1. Use your knowledge of the human gas-exchange system to explain why cigarette smoking is a health hazard.

2. A puncture to the chest cavity is treated with pressure to seal the opening. Why is this first-aid procedure so important?

3. A coroner examines a body found in a river and finds that there is dirty water in the mouth, nasal passages, and upper trachea. The lungs, however, still contain air. What is the probable source of this air? What does its presence tell the coroner about the probable cause of death?

4. Why might a smoker find it more difficult to adjust to a higher altitude?

5. Hyperventilation (rapid breathing) increases oxygen levels and decreases carbon dioxide levels in the bloodstream. What problem might hyperventilation cause?

6. A student, who often hyperventilates when excited or under stress, breathes in and out of a paper bag until his breathing returns to normal. How would breathing into a paper bag help the student in this situation?

7. Why do space vehicles carrying humans need a system to remove carbon dioxide from the air?

Problem Solving

1. The liver has a mass of 1.8 kg. The lungs have a much larger volume, but their combined mass is only about 1.1 kg. What structural characteristic of lung tissue explains this relatively small mass? What is the functional advantage of this structural arrangement?

2. Laboratory rats, who were given a saline solution to breathe instead of air, were nevertheless able to stay alive. Explain how this is possible.

3. a) Do talking, singing, and laughing occur during inhalation or exhalation?
   b) How are the vocal cords of the larynx controlled by air flow and muscles to produce sound?

4. Emergency personnel sometimes cut a hole in the trachea to allow air to enter directly. This procedure is called a tracheotomy. For what reason might it be performed? Support your answer.

Extensions

1. a) What is the "bends"? Find information on how the bends is related to breathing.
   b) Why is helium used as a substitute gas for nitrogen gas?

2. a) Sudden Infant Death Syndrome, or crib death, is a respiratory problem in infants. What are some possible causes of this respiratory syndrome?
   b) How are potential SIDS victims being identified and monitored?

3. Use your knowledge of gas-exchange systems in land-dwelling animals to explain why earthworms come to the surface of the soil during heavy rainfalls.

4. Breathing is influenced by the pH of the blood. Find out how breathing and blood pH are related and how they help regulate breathing rate.

CHAPTER

5

Digestion

In the last few decades, the eating habits of people in developing countries have changed. Where indigenous crops such as cassava, yams, millet, and sorghum once satisfied nutritional needs, now white bread made from imported wheat flour has become popular. Between 1961 and 1981, wheat consumption in tropical countries grew by an average of 3% every year, while consumption of local roots and tubers dropped. In these countries, eating traditional foods is now regarded with derision. Unfortunately, this shift in eating habits is accompanied by serious side effects that the Food and Agriculture Organization of the United Nations (FAO) is now trying to remedy.

Bread's advantages over traditional staples are clear. One traditional staple easily grown in tropical countries is cassava. This tuber, often served as tapioca, may be prepared in a number of ways, all of which require a great deal of time and effort. By comparison, bread is a convenience food, which requires little preparation and has a long shelf life.

Although bread is cheap and convenient, its main ingredient, wheat, is difficult to grow in the tropics because wheat grows best in temperate zones. As well, modern wheat production usually requires a European style of land use that is ill-suited to tropical geography and cultures. Recent Canadian efforts to establish wheat cultivation in northern Tanzania have so disrupted the livelihood of local herding tribes that they have appealed to the FAO to stop the project before they starve.

Developing countries normally import wheat to produce bread. But unfortunately, the increased use of bread decreases the popularity of local staples. The price of these staples falls and production soon declines. The country quickly loses the ability to feed its population, making the demand for imports even greater. A developing nation dependent on imported food is very vulnerable.

As one solution to these problems, the FAO has developed methods to make bread from nonwheat staples such as cassava. The FAO researchers set out to imitate the function of the protein gluten, which is found in wheat, but in few other cereals or tubers. Gluten's elastic properties give bread its texture. One successful gluten-imitating agent that has been discovered by the FAO is xanthan gum, a food additive previously used as a fast-food thickening agent. Dough made from cassava flour with xanthan gum added produces tasty breads with long shelf lives.

If we are to satisfy the nutritional needs of both developing and industrial nations, we need to use technology to create projects such as the development of large-scale processing of cassava flour.

Digestion and nutrition are not just physical concerns. Economics, technology, and politics play a great part in determining how, or whether, nutritional needs are met.

Chapter Objectives

When you complete this chapter, you should:

1. Appreciate the importance of good nutrition and a properly functioning digestive system to human health, and describe the role of a balanced diet in meeting these aims.

2. Be able to identify the major animal nutrients that must be supplied by a balanced diet, describe the role each nutrient plays in an animal's body, and identify a human food source for each nutrient.

3. Know how to perform chemical tests to identify which nutrients are present in different foods and to determine how enzymes such as amylase act on these nutrients.

4. Apply the principles of nutrition to analyze your own diet for balanced nutrition and energy intake.

5. Be able to describe the four basic steps that must be carried out by every animal digestive system and appreciate the intricacy of vertebrate systems as compared to invertebrate systems.

6. Based on laboratory investigations, be able to draw and identify the structures of a vertebrate digestive system and explain how the individual parts are suited to their function.

7. Be able to compare the digestive structures of a human to those of other mammals and nonmammalian vertebrates.

8. Be able to describe the physical and the chemical breakdown of foods by a vertebrate digestive system, identify the end products of digestion, and describe how they are absorbed by the internal environment.

9. Be able to describe how food is moved along the digestive tract, and how the sequential release of digestive chemicals is controlled.

10. Appreciate the advantages and the disadvantages to nutrition and digestion of preserving and processing foods.

11. Understand the biological basis for digestive disorders, and state the causes, symptoms, and cures for at least three different types of disorders.

5.1 Nutritional Requirements of Animal Cells

You probably think more about what you are eating than why you are eating it. But understanding the nutritional content of the foods you eat can help you develop a healthy body and maintain it throughout your life. All organisms need a variety of materials to carry out their life functions. Examples of the materials that organisms need include: substances for growth, maintenance, and renewal of body tissue; substances for regulating essential chemical reactions; and substances high in stored chemical energy for use in cellular respiration. Humans require thousands of different materials. But most of these materials can be manufactured by the body itself, provided it is supplied with a much smaller number of basic materials known as **nutrients.** Nutrients are elements and compounds an organism needs but cannot manufacture for itself.

What constitutes a nutrient varies from one organism to another. For example, the nutritional needs of plant cells are fairly simple. Given basic nutrients —carbon dioxide, water, a few dissolved minerals, and some soluble nitrogen compounds — plants can manufacture everything else they need. They can make carbohydrates and fats such as starches and sugars for energy storage, and proteins for building body tissues. Therefore, carbohydrates, fats, and proteins are plant products not plant nutrients.

Animals also require carbohydrates, fats, and proteins, but they cannot manufacture them from such simple raw materials. For animals, these three materials are major nutrients, substances that must be obtained from food manufactured by producers such as plants or from other animals that eat producers.

Plants growing in the wild obtain soluble nitrogen from compounds produced by soil bacteria. Cultivated plants often obtain this nutrient from nitrogen-containing fertilizers.

Fruits and vegetables are essential for a balanced diet.

128

LABORATORY EXERCISE 5-1
Testing Foods for Nutrient Content

All animal cells require carbohydrates, fats, and proteins. Good health requires the consumption of adequate amounts of these major nutrients on a regular basis and in the correct proportions. To make sure your cells are properly nourished, it is important to know which foods contain these nutrients and in what amounts. In this exercise, you will learn how to test common foods for the presence of carbohydrates, fats, and proteins.

Carbohydrates

Most of the energy in animal diets is derived from carbohydrate-containing foods such as grains, potatoes, and fruits. All **carbohydrates** contain the same three chemical elements: carbon, hydrogen, and oxygen, combined in different ways to form molecules ranging from small and simple to large and complex. The smallest and simplest carbohydrate molecules are **monosaccharides** (single sugars). The most common monosaccharides in human food are glucose, fructose, and galactose. Sources of these three single sugars are listed in Table 5-1. As Figure 5-1 shows, their ring-like molecules are very similar. All three monosaccharides can be used directly in cellular respiration with very little change to their molecular structure.

TABLE 5-1   Summary of Carbohydrates

Type of Carbohydrate	Name of Carbohydrate	Food Source	Monosaccharide Present
Monosaccharide	• glucose	• honey	• glucose
	• fructose	• fruit	• fructose
	• galactose	• none	• galactose
Disaccharide	• sucrose	• table sugar	• glucose/fructose
	• lactose	• milk	• glucose/galactose
	• maltose	• malted milk shakes	• glucose/glucose
Polysaccharide	• starch	• potatoes	• glucose
	• glycogen	• liver	• glucose
	• cellulose	• bran	• glucose

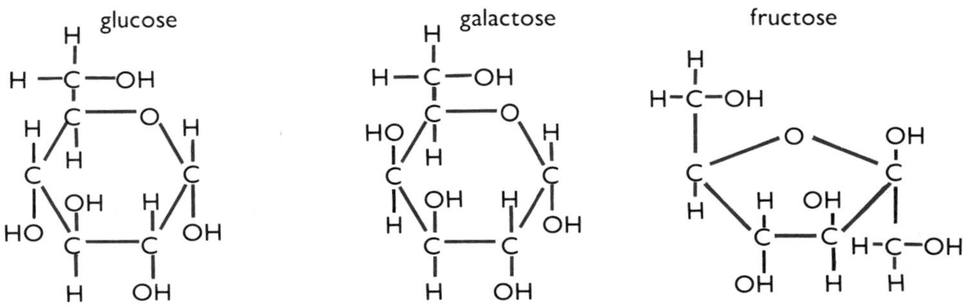

FIGURE 5-1 Each of these monosaccharides contains six carbon atoms, 12 hydrogen atoms, and six oxygen atoms. But each monosaccharide has a different arrangement.

Disaccharides, or double sugars, are larger carbohydrate molecules that contain two ring-like monosaccharide units bonded together. Before humans can use a disaccharide as a source of energy, it must be converted to single sugars. For example, when your body's digestive system breaks down maltose, the natural sugar used to sweeten malted milk shakes, two glucose molecules are formed. (See Figure 5-2.)

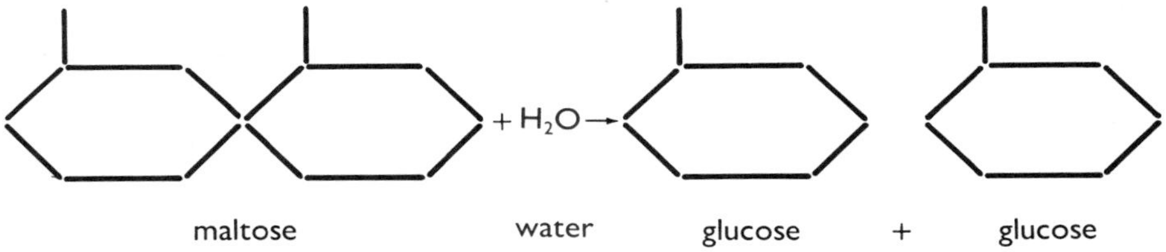

FIGURE 5-2 Water is needed to break down a disaccharide such as maltose into usable monosaccharides such as glucose.

Polysaccharides are large, complex carbohydrate molecules in which long chains of monosaccharide units are linked together by chemical bonds. Foods such as bread and potatoes contain **starch,** a polysaccharide containing 200 or more glucose-like monosaccharide units. Green plants store much of the glucose they produce in polysaccharides, which are well-suited for storage. First, their chain-like structure takes up less space than a collection of individual monosaccharides. Second, starch is insoluble. The formation of starch takes the glucose units out of circulation so that the plant cells are forced to produce more glucose for their own use.

Animals can store limited amounts of excess glucose in a polysaccharide called **glycogen.** In humans, glycogen is found in the liver and the muscles. Both starch and glycogen must be broken down into monosaccharides before animal cells can make use of the stored energy.

Green plants also produce polysaccharides called **cellulose.** (See Figure 5-3.) Cellulose forms the fibrous material that helps support the walls of plant

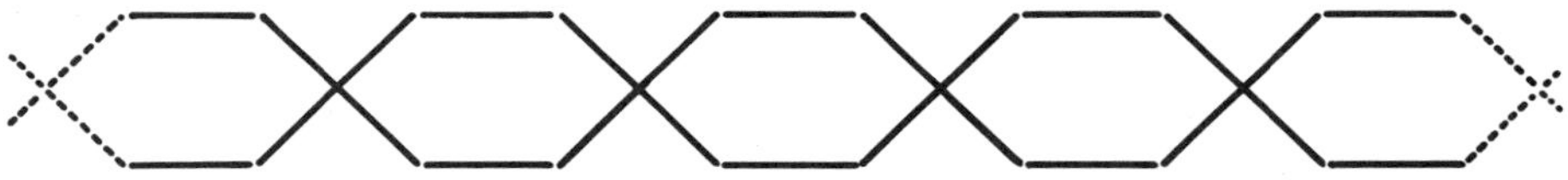

FIGURE 5-3 Each starch molecule is a long chain of glucose-like units. A cellulose molecule contains several chains, which are twisted and linked side by side.

cells, stems, and tree trunks. Each cellulose chain contains at least 1500 glucose units, and the chemical bonds between them are harder to break than those in starch. The digestive systems of some plant eaters such as cows and termites contain bacteria that can break down cellulose into glucose molecules. The bacteria found in the human digestive system cannot do this, so plant cellulose in human diets remains undigested. However, plant cellulose does provide roughage, which stimulates the movement of wastes and food through the intestine.

Even plants cannot use the glucose units in cellulose as food. Like humans, plants lack the enzymes needed to break the cellulose chains into individual glucose units again.

Fats

Like carbohydrates, **fats** provide an energy source for animal cells. Like starch and cellulose, fats are complex molecules made up of smaller building blocks containing carbon, hydrogen, and oxygen. However, one gram of fat contains twice as much energy as one gram of carbohydrate. This is because the arrangement of the three elements is very different: a fat molecule contains three fatty acid units attached to a glycerol "spine." (See Figure 5-4.)

Differences in the fatty acids determine the characteristic taste of each kind of fat. Butterfat, for example, contains many more short, fatty acid units than lamb fat. Differences in fatty acids also determine whether the fat is solid or liquid at room temperature.

Liquid fats are often referred to as oils. The molecules in plant fats such as corn or canola oil are said to be unsaturated because they contain much less hydrogen than most animal fat molecules of similar size. Fat molecules such as those found in lard have a high hydrogen content for their size and are said to be saturated. Pure saturated fats tend to be solid at room temperature, and pure unsaturated fats are usually liquid. (See Table 5-2.)

Fats are an important part of your diet. Besides being an energy source,

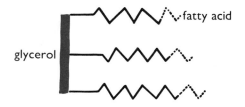

FIGURE 5-4 All fat molecules have the same glycerol spine (colour). The length and exact composition of the fatty acid side arms differ for each type of fat.

TABLE 5-2   Saturated and Unsaturated Fats

Food Source	Estimated Saturated Fatty Acids %	Estimated Un-saturated Fatty Acids %
Coconut Oil	90	10
Palm Oil	47	53
Lard	42	58
Cod Liver Oil	14	86

DID YOU KNOW?
A cultural preference for using solid fats in cooking has created a North American market for hydrogenated or solidified vegetable oils such as Crisco vegetable shortening.

FIGURE 5-5 Cholesterol is needed to manufacture sex hormones and other essential molecules. If no cholesterol is ingested, the body will make its own from digested fats.

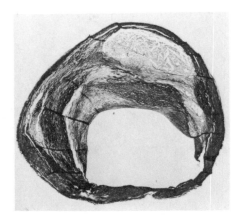

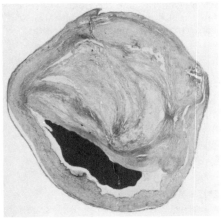

Artery degeneration is often caused by cholesterol deposits.

A few proteins contain additional elements such as sulphur and phosphorous.

fat is also used to manufacture structures such as the cell membrane. The fat stored under your skin functions as an insulator and a shock absorber. Fats aid the absorption of vitamins. But fat can cause problems.

The liver collects fatty acids to make various types of necessary lipids, including cholesterol. (See Figure 5-5.) Too much cholesterol production can result in plaque deposits on the walls of arteries, which interfere with blood circulation. The amount of fat consumed and the type of fat consumed have been linked to cholesterol deposition. Diets high in saturated fatty acids have been linked to increased cholesterol levels, but the significance of research findings is not yet conclusive. However, most nutritionists agree that many North Americans eat too much fat, and less than 40% of our daily energy intake should be derived from it.

Proteins

The molecules of **proteins** are even larger and more complex than those of carbohydrates and fats. (See Figure 5-6.) Each protein molecule is a very long chain of smaller units called **amino acids** that contain nitrogen as well as carbon, hydrogen, and oxygen. If an animal's diet includes too much protein, the excess will be converted to fat. If an animal's diet is deficient in other energy sources, proteins will be broken down and used as a source of energy. Usually, however, protein is not a primary source of energy. Instead, animals need to take in proteins because they perform several important functions that carbohydrates and fats do not.

First, proteins are the basic building blocks from which all cells, tissues, and organs are constructed. The human body assembles thousands of different proteins, each with a different function. For example, protein chains formed in red bone marrow combine with iron to form hemoglobin, which carries

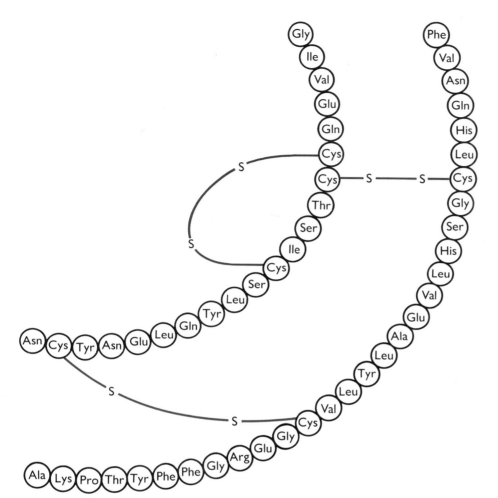

FIGURE 5-6 The insulin molecule shown in this figure is one of the simplest proteins. How many amino acid units does it contain (see circles)? How many different amino acids can you identify?

oxygen throughout the bloodstream. Protein chains formed in heart muscle cells function by contracting in unison to make the heart beat. However, not all proteins are used to build body parts. Some proteins perform important regulatory functions.

Enzymes are proteins that accelerate chemical reactions in the cell. Each different body reaction requires its own special enzyme, and complex reactions need a different enzyme for each step. Cellular respiration, for example, requires about 30 different enzymes. All enzymes are produced inside living cells, and usually remain in the same cell to do their work.

Most **hormones** are also proteins. Hormones are carried far from the cells that produce them to distant body parts, where they regulate, or control, some body function. Human growth hormone, for example, is produced at the base of the brain, but it controls the growth of the limbs. (See Figure 5-7.)

FIGURE 5-7 Hormone growth, which is produced by the pituitary gland, travels to all parts of the body through the bloodstream.

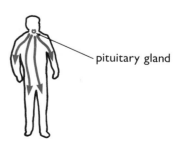

pituitary gland

These foods have a high protein content.

Babies also need a ninth essential amino acid called histidine.

Beverages high in additives such as sugar, caffeine, or alcohol should not be counted as part of your daily water intake. These solutes create more thirst than they satisfy, and they also interfere with the water balance in your body.

DID YOU KNOW?
Many desert animals such as the camel and the kangaroo rat have adaptations that help them reduce their need for scarce water supplies.

Usually, the protein molecules in food cannot be used immediately as building blocks, enzymes, or hormones by the animal that eats the food. This is because no two species, regardless of their kingdom, contain exactly the same proteins. For example, the proteins assembled by humans differ from those assembled by pigs for a similar purpose, even though both consume food containing the same amino acids. After ingestion, the protein molecules in food must be broken down into separate amino acids and then carried to the cells. There the amino acids are reassembled to make entirely new proteins such as insulin, which regulates blood glucose levels. Both pigs and humans make insulin, but the precise sequence of amino acids in pork insulin is slightly different from the sequence in human insulin.

Humans need 20 amino acids to assemble all body proteins. Twelve of these acids are called *nonessential* amino acids because the body can manufacture them from nonprotein foods. The other eight are *essential* amino acids, which must be present in the human diet.

Animal products such as meat, milk, and eggs are often called *complete protein* foods because they contain all eight essential amino acids. Plant products such as rice, beans, and wheat are *incomplete protein* foods because they lack one or more essential amino acids. But much of the world's human population obtains all or most of its protein from plant food by combining two incomplete proteins.

Water

Water may not seem very nourishing, but it does fit the definition of a nutrient because all organisms need water to carry out their life functions. In general, all life functions involve water either directly or indirectly. For example, water is a chemical reactant in most body reactions, including those of the digestive process. Water is also important as a solvent. Only materials dissolved in water are able to pass into or out of cells through cell membranes. Water also acts as a lubricant, bathing cells and protecting them from damage. Water is an integral part of the cytoplasmic liquid in which the various cell organelles are suspended. Its movement transports the products of these organelles. In humans, water helps regulate body temperature by evaporating from the skin and cooling the blood underneath.

Water in your diet is derived from drinking fluids such as milk, juice, *and* water or from the moisture content of the foods you eat. Most nutritionists recommend a minimum intake of 1.5 L of water daily.

Vitamins and Minerals

Carbohydrates, fats, proteins, and water are regarded as **macronutrients** because they must be consumed in large amounts every day to provide materials for body parts and energy for life functions. For example, growing teenagers need up to 100 g of protein each day. However, **micronutrients** are essential nutrients needed in minute amounts. Vitamins and minerals are examples of micronutrients. For example, your body requires only 0.01 g of Vitamin D daily. But **vitamins** play an important role in body metabolism by co-operating with enzymes to carry out chemical reactions. For this reason, vitamins are often referred to as co-enzymes. Vitamin C, for example, assists in the metabolism of iron, while Vitamin D is needed for proper absorption of calcium. Table 5-3 summarizes other important facts about the role of vitamins in your diet.

Both iron and calcium are examples of **minerals,** chemical elements used by the body as micronutrients. The mineral iron is required to make that part

Fat soluble vitamins like vitamins A, D, E, and K are measured in International Units. For example, 0.01 g of vitamin D is 400 I.U., but 0.24 g of carotene are needed to supply 400 I.U. of vitamin A.

DID YOU KNOW?

Most vitamins must be obtained from the external environment, but vitamin D can be manufactured in the human body. Vitamin D is formed by the action of ultraviolet rays from the sun on a cholesterol compound in the skin.

TABLE 5-3 Some Important Vitamins in the Human Diet

Vitamin	Dietary Sources	Function	Symptoms of Vitamin Deficiency
A	• milk • liver • eggs	• promotes good night vision and resistance to infections	• night blindness • low resistance to infection
B_1 (thiamin)	• meat • cheese • nuts	• releases energy from carbohydrates	• nerve disease and muscle weakness (beriberi)
B_2 (riboflavin)	• liver • milk • cereals • bread	• helps maintain healthy skin • releases energy from carbohydrates	• skin tissue damage • fatigue
B_3 (niacin)	• wholegrain cereals • poultry	• aids in energy release from carbohydrates	• headaches • insomnia • backache
B_{12}	• meat • fish • eggs	• helps nervous system function • red blood cell formation	• anemia • bowel disorders • poor appetite
C	• citrus fruits • leafy vegetables	• maintains healthy teeth and gums	• bleeding gums • low resistance to infection • scurvy
D	• milk • fish • liver	• helps absorb calcium and phosphorous for bones and teeth	• softening of bones • poor teeth (rickets)
E	• vegetable oils • whole grains	• helps in formation of red blood cells and muscles	• anemia • loss of energy
K	• green leafy vegetables	• promotes normal blood clotting	• poor blood clotting

of the hemoglobin molecule enabling red blood cells to carry oxygen. The mineral calcium is required for bone and teeth development, the normal clotting of blood, and also for the normal functioning of muscles and nerves. Table 5-4 summarizes other important facts about minerals in your diet.

TABLE 5-4   Some Important Minerals in the Human Diet

Mineral	Dietary Sources	Function	Symptoms of Mineral Deficiency
Calcium	• milk • cheese • cereals	• forms teeth and bones • aids blood clotting	• poor teeth and bones • osteoporosis
Iodine	• iodized salt • seafood	• controls hormone activity of thyroid gland	• goitre • swollen thyroid gland
Iron	• liver • nuts • meat	• needed to form hemoglobin in red blood cells	• iron deficiency anemia • lack of energy
Phosphorous	• meat • grains • fish	• forms teeth and bones	• poor teeth and bones
Sodium	• table salt	• regulation of water level in body tissue • used in nerve transmission	• dehydration • fainting spells

INQUIRY ACTIVITY
A Personal Food Survey

How much food energy do you take in during a typical week? Are you getting enough micronutrients and all essential amino acids? One way to find out is to keep a personal record of the types of food you eat and the quantities you consume. When your record is complete, your teacher will provide nutrition tables so you can analyze your diet to determine its nutritional value. Then you can compare your intake with the amounts recommended for your body size.

Choosing a Balanced Diet

Following the Canada Food Guide should ensure that your diet is balanced. (See Figure 5-8.) A balanced diet is one that supplies your cells with the glucose, amino acids, vitamins, minerals, and water they require to build body protein and release energy for life functions.

FIGURE 5-8 The Canada Food Guide. Choosing a variety of foods from each major food group will ensure that your diet contains appropriate amounts of different nutrients. Correct amounts vary according to your build, and whether you are still growing.

No human diet is truly balanced unless it also includes an important non-nutrient, dietary fibre. Dietary fibre consists of indigestible material such as the cellulose in the cell walls of the plant foods you eat. Humans lack the enzymes needed to break cellulose into small nutrient molecules. Therefore, fibre cannot be absorbed by your cells and is not a nutrient. However, fibre plays an important role in your digestive system. (You will learn more about the importance of fibre in Section 5.2.) Whole grains, fruits, and vegetables are the best source of dietary fibre. But how much fibre is enough? This is a

A well-balanced diet should not require daily vitamin supplements.

controversial question among nutritionists, and it is possible to consume too much. However, most experts believe that the average North American eats too many highly processed foods and consumes too little fibre.

Most nutritional experts also agree that the average North American is overnourished. If you consume more food than your body needs, your digestive system will still process it. Regardless of whether the extra food is fat, carbohydrate, or protein, your cells will convert the excess nutrient molecules into body fat. In addition to obesity, the health problems caused by an overly abundant diet include heart disease and overstressed joints.

Nutritional Deficiencies and Disorders

Nutritional deficiencies in the human diet may be due to a lack of macronutrients, micronutrients, or both, which may result in a deficiency disorder. For example, kwashiorkor is a nutritional disorder caused by a lack of protein in the diet. Kwashiorkor occurs most often in poor countries when a child is weaned from its mother's milk. Symptoms of the disorder include retarded growth, change in skin texture and hair pigmentation, diarrhea, and loss of appetite. Often the lack of protein at a critical time of development results in permanent underdevelopment of the brain. Victims of kwashiorkor often display a distended abdomen because of a buildup of tissue fluid. Treatment involves providing the child with a balanced diet and a skim milk formula.

Nutritional deficiency disorders seldom show up alone. For example, a child deprived of protein is probably also lacking sufficient amounts of B vitamins. This is because B vitamins are commonly found in high-protein foods such as meat. Consequently, the child will have kwashiorkor in addition to other problems. Some of the B-vitamin deficiency disorders that could occur with kwashiorkor are listed in Table 5-3.

The diet of a child afflicted with kwashiorkor is also likely to be deficient in fats, minerals, and vitamins, although it may provide enough carbohydrates. These deficiencies are usually associated with general starvation, a condition that is not only restricted to poor countries. School-age children anywhere who have inadequate diets will have great difficulty learning in school.

Section Review Questions

1. a) What is a nutrient? What are the three principal functions of nutrients in living systems?
   b) List four basic nutrients required by plants. Where possible, identify the elements found in each.
   c) List three major nutrients required by animals and identify the elements found in each.
2. a) Carbohydrate molecules are classified according to size. List the three size categories and state at least one example for each category.

Anorexia Nervosa

Anorexia nervosa is a frightening, sometimes fatal eating disorder that has become more common in Canada in the last 20 years. It is most prevalent among white females 15-25 years of age. Researchers in the United States estimate that 20% of college women suffer to some degree from anorexia or a related disorder, bulimia.

Bulimics gorge and purge; anorexics avoid food. Anorexia is a relentless pursuit of thinness. Its victims seem addicted to starving. Anorexics say they feel wonderful and refuse to eat normally, even though they may be on the verge of death from starvation.

It is commonly believed that a web of social, parental, and self-imposed pressures are factors in the development of anorexia nervosa. Our society, preoccupied with fitness and beauty, is obsessively self-conscious about body weight. Studies indicate that eating disorders are epidemic in the beach states of the United States, where appearance is a way of life.

Anorexia usually develops during the teenage years. Anorexics typically have low self-esteem, above average intelligence, and a perfectionist streak that pushes them to excel physically and mentally. Control is a major issue. Dieting is a demonstration of control. However, after a short period of starvation, the body's electrolyte levels (minerals, nutrients, and vitamins) become unbalanced, and soon the body controls the victim.

Some researchers in the United States have recently suggested a physiological factor in anorexia. Prolonged starvation may release endogenous (self-produced) drug-like substances known as opioids, which could cause the euphoria or "high" anorexics feel. The compulsive behaviour of anorexics is very like that of drug addicts or alcoholics; they focus their lives on dieting the way drug addicts focus on a fix or alcoholics on a drink.

Amy is 23. When interviewed, her mass was dangerously low at 36 kg, only two-thirds of what it should be for her height. She says, after a nine-year struggle with anorexia: "My life is a nightmare. I'm afraid of dying. I haven't had a period for two years. . . . I'm still afraid of gaining weight. I'm under the control of my little voice upstairs. I always do what it says: run, restrict, purge. Nobody can know what it's like."

At age 15 Amy weighed 66 kg. She began dieting at the beginning of Grade 10. "I was sick of being teased. To start with, I just cut back. By the end of Grade 10, I was down to 55 kg. The compulsive behaviour started that summer. I would skip breakfast, cut back at lunch, and go jogging right after supper."

The obsession continued and the condition worsened until one day a stranger stopped her in the street and asked why she was so thin. "I guess that opened a door for me. I thought what she said must be true." This admission was the first step; Amy checked herself into a treatment program with a determination to address her condition.

The most advanced treatment for eating disorders takes a multi-faceted approach. Each patient is treated by a team of health-care professionals. There is an emphasis on admitting and taking responsibility for your condition in a supportive environment similar to Alcoholics Anonymous. In many cases, as for Amy, several years may pass before the anorexic will admit he or she is starving to death. By that time, it may be too late to restore damaged organs and tissue.

b) Briefly describe the structure of each carbohydrate molecule named in part (a). Identify the molecular components from which each is made.

3. a) What nutritional function do fats share with carbohydrates?
   b) What other roles do fats play in living systems?
   c) Describe the structure of a fat molecule. Identify the molecular components from which it is made.

4. a) Briefly discuss the three nutritional functions of proteins. Explain how these functions differ from the roles played by fats and carbohydrates.
   b) Describe the structure of a fat molecule. Identify the molecular components from which it is made.

5. Compare the following pairs of terms. State what they have in common and how they differ.
   a) hormones and enzymes,
   b) essential and nonessential amino acids,
   c) complete and incomplete protein foods,
   d) starch and glycogen.

6. a) What is a balanced diet? What principles should be followed in choosing one?
   b) What does it mean to be overnourished, and what are some associated health risks?

7. a) What is a nutritional deficiency?
   b) Which disorder is associated with a deficiency of protein?

5.2 Structures for Digesting Food

All living things require nutrients, but animals have a functional need that green plants do not share. Like all heterotrophs, animals must be able to digest their food. **Digestion** involves the conversion of food from its original form in the external environment into nutrient molecules small enough to enter body cells and participate in cell functions. Most animals, especially large vertebrates such as humans, have a system of specialized organs to perform digestion.

LABORATORY EXERCISE 5-2
Exploring the Digestive System of a Representative Vertebrate

Much of modern understanding about the structure and function of the human digestive system has been derived from human autopsies, from the study of digestive disorders, and from the dissections of representative vertebrates. Such dissections make comparative studies possible, and the one in this exercise is the first part of an ongoing study of vertebrate body systems that will continue throughout Unit II. Pig embryos, rats, or frogs make suitable representatives for this purpose.

Human Digestive Structures

The human digestive system shown in Figure 5-9 is, as you would expect, similar in many ways to the vertebrate digestive system you observed in the above dissection. In humans and in all other vertebrates, the digestive system is really just one long tube, which is open at both ends. Food enters at one end, and indigestible wastes are expelled at the other, leaving many nutrients

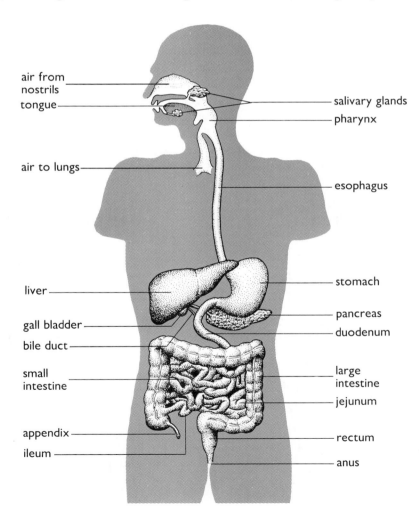

FIGURE 5-9 Main structures of the human digestive system

air from nostrils
tongue
air to lungs
liver
gall bladder
bile duct
small intestine
appendix
ileum

salivary glands
pharynx
esophagus
stomach
pancreas
duodenum
large intestine
jejunum
rectum
anus

behind for the body cells. Side pockets and tributaries located at various sites along the digestive tube contribute to the breakdown of large food particles into small nutrient molecules. In humans, the major sites of digestion are the mouth, the stomach, the small intestine, and the large intestine.

Mouth

In all vertebrates, food enters the digestive system by way of the **mouth.** This first step is called **ingestion.** In humans, the digestive process begins as soon as food enters the mouth, which is equipped with teeth that initiate the physical breakdown of food. The structure of the teeth determines their function. The incisors, or front teeth, cut food into smaller pieces. The adjacent pointed canine teeth and bicuspids pierce and tear food while the molars crush and grind it. (See Figure 5-10.)

The muscular action of chewing stimulates the salivary glands that surround the mouth. A gland is an organ or group of cells that manufactures chemicals such as enzymes and hormones. The **salivary glands** secrete saliva, a mixture of water, mucus, and amylase. Amylase is an enzyme that breaks the carbohydrate starch down into the simpler carbohydrate maltose.

The **tongue** is a muscular organ that moves the food around for thorough chewing and mixing with the saliva, until it forms a ball called a bolus, which the tongue pushes back to the pharynx. The pharynx is a dual-purpose passage that receives both food from the mouth and air from the nose. A flap-like structure called the epiglottis ensures that food will travel down the digestive tract instead of the trachea. Each time you swallow, the epiglottis covers the trachea so that the bolus of food passes into the esophagus. (See Figure 5-11.)

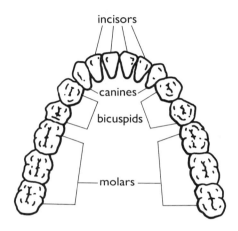

FIGURE 5-10 Human teeth. How does the position of each type of tooth suit it to its function?

incisors
canines
bicuspids
molars

DID YOU KNOW?

The tip of the tongue is sensitive to sweet and salty, the edges to sour and salty, and the back to bitter tastes.

The esophagus, a collapsible tube, is about 25 cm long.

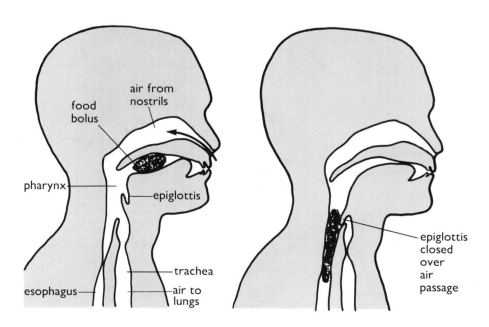

food bolus
air from nostrils
pharynx
epiglottis
esophagus
trachea
air to lungs
epiglottis closed over air passage

FIGURE 5-11 During swallowing, the epiglottis lowers, covering the air passage.

The **esophagus** is a muscular tube that carries partially digested food to the stomach through the action of two muscle layers. One layer has fibres arranged in a circular pattern; the other has longitudinal fibres. These layers contract and relax, creating a rhythmic, wave-like motion called **peristalsis,** which pushes the bolus toward the stomach. (See Figure 5-12.)

Stomach

At the bottom of the esophagus is a muscular valve called the **cardiac sphincter.** A sphincter is a ring-like muscle that surrounds an opening or a passage of the body. When sphincter muscles contract, the opening closes. In this case, the sphincter muscles control the entry of food into a J-shaped, bag-like organ called the **stomach.**

The stomach has three muscle layers arranged in circular, longitudinal, and oblique patterns. The rhythmic contraction and relaxation of these muscle layers churns the partially digested food and mixes it with gastric juice. (See Figure 5-13.) Gastric juice is a mixture of hydrochloric acid, mucus, and enzymes secreted by three types of gland-like cells in the stomach's innermost lining or mucosal layer.

The hydrochloric acid assists in the physical breakdown of fibrous tissue in the food and destroys foreign organisms such as bacteria. The acid also promotes chemical digestion because some digestive enzymes can function only in an acid environment.

The stomach enzyme pepsin initiates protein digestion by breaking down large protein molecules into long amino acid chains called polypeptides. The mucus-secreting cells produce a thick layer that protects the stomach itself from the hydrochloric acid and the pepsin. Without mucus, the juices would digest the stomach lining. Damage to this mucous barrier results in gastric ulcers.

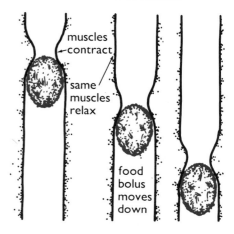

FIGURE 5-12 Peristaltic action by the muscles of the esophagus moves the food bolus toward the stomach.

muscles contract

same muscles relax

food bolus moves down

Your stomach produces about 0.5 L of gastric juice during and after an average meal.

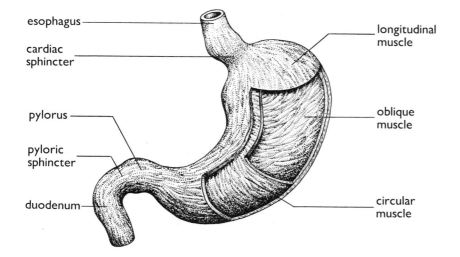

esophagus

cardiac sphincter

pylorus

pyloric sphincter

duodenum

longitudinal muscle

oblique muscle

circular muscle

FIGURE 5-13 The human stomach has three layers of muscle.

The release of hydrochloric acid, mucus, and protein-digesting enzyme molecules is co-ordinated by special sensory cells located near the cardiac sphincter. When food passes through the cardiac sphincter, the specialized cells produce a chemical messenger hormone called gastrin. Gastrin, which is carried by the bloodstream, stimulates the stomach cells to produce secretions for the food they will soon be receiving.

The lower region of the stomach is called the pylorus. The partly digested food in the pylorus has the same texture as porridge and is called chyme. **Chyme** consists of partially digested food, water, and gastric juice. From the stomach, the chyme is squirted through a gateway called the **pyloric sphincter** into the next digestive site — the small intestine.

Small Intestine

In humans, the **small intestine** is approximately 6.2 m in length and 2.5 cm in diameter. This convoluted tube is surrounded by two muscle layers arranged like those of the esophagus, which are able to perform peristalsis. For convenience, biologists subdivide the small intestine into three segments: the duodenum, jejunum, and the ileum. (See Figure 5-14.)

The jejunum and ileum are 2.5 m and 3.5 m in length, respectively.

FIGURE 5-14 The digestive organs shown here have been separated for greater clarity.

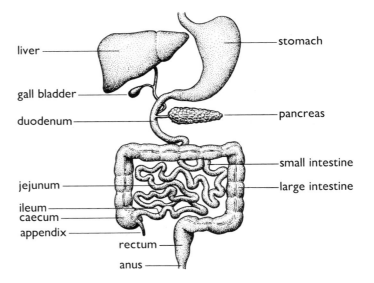

The **duodenum** is the segment closest to the stomach. Its first few centimetres are coated with a very thick layer of mucus that protects the lining from the acidic chyme. Although the duodenum is only 25 cm long, it is the site of a great deal of digestive action. Most of the chemical breakdown occurring in the duodenum results from the action of digestive juices that enter through the common duct. The common duct is a narrow tube that carries secretions from the liver and the pancreas. These two glandular organs play a major role in the digestive process.

Having an average mass of 1.5 kg, your **liver** is the largest gland in your body. Your liver produces a single digestive juice, a substance called **bile.** Bile is an emulsifying agent needed for the physical digestion of fats. It breaks large fat globules into small ones and prevents them from clumping together again. The smaller the size of the globules, the larger their total surface area becomes. As a result, emulsification exposes a larger number of fat molecules to the digestive enzymes farther down the intestine. Bile is secreted continuously by the liver and stored in the sac-like gall bladder until it is needed.

The **pancreas** produces several digestive secretions, including a neutralizer, a fat-digesting enzyme, a protein- digesting enzyme, and a carbohydrate-digesting enzyme. All are carried from the pancreas via the pancreatic duct to the common duct, which empties both bile and pancreatic juices into the duodenum. The pancreatic neutralizer is sodium bicarbonate, the compound found in common, household baking soda. Within the duodenum, the sodium bicarbonate neutralizes the acidic chyme, forming a basic mixture. This change allows the intestinal enzymes to continue the chemical breakdown of food.

The second segment of the small intestine is the **jejunum.** Structurally, the jejunum is much like the duodenum, except that it has more intestinal folds and glands. These intestinal glands secrete the enzymes that chemically break down any remaining protein and carbohydrate chains into amino acids and glucose molecules. These end products of digestion are small enough to be absorbed by the **villi.** (See Figure 5-15.) These finger-like projections on the intestinal folds transfer the end products to the bloodstream for circulation to cells throughout the body.

The third segment of the small intestine is the **ileum.** It is similar to the jejunum, except that it produces few enzymes, and its villi are smaller and fewer in number. The main function of the ileum is absorption. Its peristaltic action pushes any remaining undigested material into the large intestine.

Large Intestine

The **large intestine** is little more than 1.5 m long, but it is considered to be large because its diameter is about twice that of the small intestine. The small intestine joins the large intestine about 7 cm from the top end of the large intestine. This arrangement forms a pouch called the caecum which has a worm-shaped extension called the vermiform appendix. In humans, the appendix is not involved in the digestive process, but it does play a role in digestion in horses and some other vertebrates.

The main function of the large intestine is to reabsorb usable materials. Its second function relates to vitamin production and absorption. Vitamin K and some B vitamins are produced by harmless bacteria that live in the intestinal tract. These micronutrients are absorbed by the walls of the large intestine along with dissolved minerals and excess water.

As the water is removed, and the contents of the large intestine are absorbed

Your liver is a multi-purpose organ that is also involved in many functions such as carbohydrate storage and energy release, detoxification, and waste processing.

DID YOU KNOW?
Many people enjoy eating the pancreas from beef cattle. This delicacy is called sweetbread.

FIGURE 5-15 Numerous villi form the velvet-like inner surface of the small intestine. Each villus contains a network of blood vessels surrounded by a single layer of cells that allows nutrients to pass through.

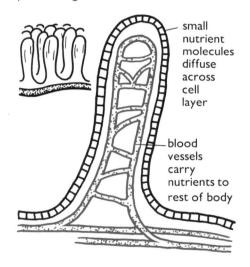

small nutrient molecules diffuse across cell layer

blood vessels carry nutrients to rest of body

DID YOU KNOW?
Appendicitis is the inflammation of the appendix, and an appendectomy is the removal of the appendix.

and pushed down the tube by peristalsis, the liquid mass slowly becomes firmer. The firm material, which consists primarily of living and dead bacteria, cellulose, and water, is called **feces.** Problems such as diarrhea and constipation can occur if there are irregularities involving the absorption of water. Diarrhea results if not enough water is reabsorbed from the feces, and constipation results if the feces remain in the large intestine too long.

As feces are formed in the large intestine, they are pushed down by peristalsis. A weak sphincter muscle at the entrance to the **rectum** prevents fecal matter from entering until it is ready for elimination. Eventually, the feces in the intestine are pushed into the rectum and toward the **anus.** Two sphincter muscles, an internal and an external one, control the final elimination of feces. When the rectum is full of feces, the internal sphincter relaxes. But the external sphincter remains contracted until it relaxes voluntarily for elimination.

Disorders of the Digestive Structures

Three types of digestive disorders result mainly from the impairment of the digestive structures themselves. These disorders are classified as structural, inflammatory, or malabsorptive disorders.

Structural disorders occur when an abnormality in the size or the shape of a digestive structure interferes with the normal functioning of the structure and interrupts the digestive process. Two common structural disorders are pyloric stenosis and hiatus hernia. Pyloric stenosis is caused by a buildup of muscle tissue around the pyloric sphincter. This buildup obstructs the flow of food into the small intestine. Pyloric stenosis occurs in one out of 200 newborns. Babies having this condition usually vomit a great deal. In adults, pyloric stenosis is often linked to scars from stomach ulcers. Treatment involves surgery, where some of the muscle fibres are cut and the pyloric opening is enlarged.

A hiatus hernia may occur if there is a gap, or a hiatus, between the esophagus and the esophagal opening in the diaphragm. Such gaps are found in about 40% of the population, but not all people with this condition are troubled by an active hiatus hernia. A hiatus hernia occurs only if a portion of the stomach pushes through the gap. The major symptoms are pain and heartburn, which is a burning sensation caused by the backward flow of the acidic contents from the stomach into the esophagus. Heartburn can be alleviated by the intake of antacids that reduce the acidity.

A hiatus hernia is both a structural and an inflammatory disorder. Surgical treatment is not usually required since the disorder can be controlled by diet. Bland foods help reduce stomach acidity, and dividing the daily food intake into several small meals reduces the stomach's tendency to push through the gap.

Blockage of the bile duct by gallstones is also regarded as a structural disorder, although the gall bladder's tendency to form these stones may indicate a chemical imbalance. In addition to holding back bile, which is needed

An average person eats 1.5 kg of food daily and produces about 0.4 kg of solid wastes in the form of feces.

II ANIMALS

for the physical digestion of fats, gallstones can cause severe pain. Surgical removal of the gall bladder may be necessary.

Inflammatory disorders are often associated with bacterial toxins or the ingestion of chemicals, drugs, or certain types of food. For example, excessive intake of aspirin, which is an acid, can cause inflammation and possible bleeding of the stomach lining.

Malabsorptive disorders occur when digested nutrients cannot be absorbed by the small intestine. Symptoms may include diarrhea, weight loss, muscular weakness, and bone pain. Malabsorptive disorders are caused by defects in the intestinal wall, in its mucosal lining, or in the tiny circulatory vessels just inside the lining. In celiac disease, for example, the proteins in wheat and rye grain products damage or destroy the villi so that they cannot absorb any nutrients. Celiac disease is an inherited disorder that first appears in children 6-18 months of age. Treatment involves a diet that excludes all grain products except rice and corn.

These foods have been prepared with a special wheat and starch mixture that is a substitute for the grain products celiac patients cannot digest.

Normal villi are about 1 mm in height.

Section Review Questions

1. a) Define digestion. What is a digestive system?
   b) Why do animals require digestive systems?

2. List, in order, the structures food must pass through in a typical vertebrate digestive system.

3. For each structure you identified in Question 2, list the cells or glands that act on food as it passes through the digestive system. Briefly describe how each structure functions.

4. Which structures or tissues in a vertebrate digestive system act to
   a) move food through the system
   b) control the rate at which food moves?

5. Identify the segments of the small intestine, and briefly describe how they differ in structure and function.

6. a) Compare the length and diameter of the small and large intestine.
   b) Briefly describe the digestive function of the large intestine. What other roles does it play?

7. a) How are disorders of human digestive structures classified?
   b) For each type of disorder, state one example with a brief description of its cause and treatment.

Food Additives

You made instant noodle soup for lunch. The ingredients of that soup included wheat flour, salt, palm oil, tetrasodium pyrophosphate, sodium carbonate, potassium carbonate, and guar gum. The four ingredients after the palm oil are known as food additives.

Under Canada's Food and Drug Regulations, the federal government currently approves about 380 additives for use in or on our food. They maintain or improve nutritional value, prevent spoilage, assist in processing or preparation, and make food more appealing.

Nutritional deficiency diseases such as goitre, rickets, or pellagra have vanished from North America over the last 50 years because food manufacturers fortify everyday foods with vitamins and minerals important to the human diet.

Mould, bacterial, fungal, or yeast contamination of food can cause severe or fatal digestive disorders such as ptomaine poisoning or botulism. Salt or sodium nitrates and nitrites are used to preserve meat, fish, and poultry. Sugar is used to preserve canned and frozen fruit. Ascorbic acid (vitamin C) and other anti-oxidants help prevent food from turning brown or losing its colour, flavour, or texture when exposed to air.

Additives like the ones in your soup help with processing or preparation. They give body and texture to foods, control pH, retain moisture, or help prevent caking and lumping.

Other additives make food look and taste better by colouring, flavouring, or sweetening. MSG (monosodium glutamate) is a widely used flavour enhancer. Scientists think that MSG works by increasing nerve impulses responsible for flavour perception. It can also cause adverse reactions such as tightness in the chest, headaches, and a burning sensation in the neck and forearms.

Food additives, for all their obvious benefits, remain at the centre of heated public debate about the safety of the food we eat. Additives like nitrites and the artificial sweetener Saccharin (which has been banned in Canada) have been linked to cancer in laboratory animals. As well as additives, our food may also contain traces of agricultural chemicals, chemicals from packaging materials, environmental contaminants, or natural toxins.

Regulation of food safety is the responsibility of Health and Welfare Canada. Development and approval of a new additive and the required package of supporting toxicology and reproductive studies can take ten years and cost the manufacturer ten to thirty million dollars. For the range of substances that can legally be added to or appear on our food, Health and Welfare sets Acceptable Daily Intake levels at $\frac{1}{100}$ of the amount where *no* effects are found on laboratory animals.

On the other hand, there are still some genuine unknowns. No one can know how, during the lifetime of an individual, different foods and additives will react synergistically (enhancing each other) or antagonistically (cancelling each other out). Our food today may be safer than ever, but it will never be risk free.

Contains 56% skim milk from concentrate.

Ingredients: Skim milk from concentrate (concentrated skim milk, water), sugar, water, hydrogenated vegetable oil, modified tapioca starch, dextrose, cocoa, corn starch, caramel, salt, sodium stearoyl-2-lactylate (for smooth texture), vanillin.

5.3 Chemical Digestion of Major Nutrients

The primary function of digestion is to convert food into nutrients for the body. So many different physical and chemical changes occur at each digestive site that it is sometimes difficult to keep track of the nutrients themselves. In this section, you will focus only on chemical digestion, examining one nutrient at a time.

The chemical digestion of carbohydrates, fats, and proteins is greatly dependent on the action of enzymes. Enzymes are catalysts, agents that accelerate reactions without the need for high temperatures. The enzyme molecules are not used up in the reactions they accelerate. Chemically, this means that each enzyme molecule can be used again and again, a feature that saves both materials and energy. Biologically, digestive reactions, which must take place at body temperature, can nevertheless proceed rapidly enough to sustain life.

The chemical compound on which an enzyme acts is called its **substrate.** Any material that results from the reaction is called a product. Enzymes are very specific in their action. (See Figure 5-16.) For example, human salivary glands secrete an enzyme called amylase. The only substrate amylase can act on is starch. The product of the resulting reaction is maltose. Amylase is specific to this one reaction—it acts only on starch. It cannot break down any other substrate, not even other carbohydrates. The further breakdown of maltose requires a completely different enzyme.

Two important factors that influence enzyme activity are temperature and acidity. Human digestive enzymes are most active at normal body temperature (37°C). The protein structure of a digestive enzyme alters when body temperature approaches 40°C, and enzyme action stops entirely at temperatures

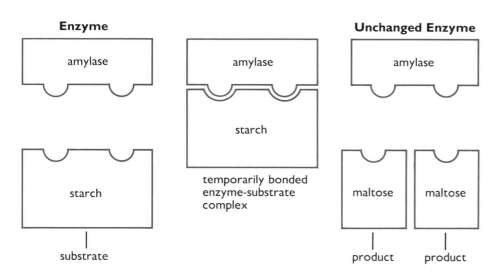

Enzyme

amylase

starch

substrate

amylase

starch

temporarily bonded enzyme-substrate complex

Unchanged Enzyme

amylase

maltose

maltose

product   product

FIGURE 5-16 A "lock-and-key" model of enzyme action. Like a key, the enzyme (amylase) enables the substrate (starch) to "open." Also like a key, the enzyme can be used again for the same purpose.

beyond 40°C. Enzymes are also sensitive to acidity. For example, salivary amylase works best in the almost neutral environment of the mouth. Once the amylase in the food reaches the stomach, it is inactivated by the strong acid in the stomach and can no longer function as a carbohydrate-digesting enzyme. Any further starch digestion requires a new enzyme that can operate in the new environment.

Because digestion involves so many different chemical and physical changes at so many different digestive sites, biologists often attempt to isolate a single reaction for examination. Often this requires performing similar chemical reactions outside of the human digestive system. These studies are called *in vitro* studies. (*In vitro* means ''in glass.'')

LABORATORY EXERCISE 5-3
Preparing *In Vitro* Models for Study

Digestion is a process where carbohydrates, fats, and proteins are chemically changed from complex food molecules to simpler nutrient molecules. In this exercise, you will prepare *in vitro* test-tube models to study the action of enzymes and other digestive chemicals.

Chemical Digestion of Carbohydrates

Salivary amylase is chemically identical to pancreatic amylase. Both are needed to ensure the complete digestion of starch because salivary amylase is destroyed once it reaches the acidic conditions of the stomach. Any undigested starch passes into the small intestine, where it is acted on by pancreatic amylase.

The chemical digestion of starch, a polysaccharide carbohydrate, begins in the mouth. Here the enzyme amylase assists in breaking down the starch substrate into separate molecules of maltose, which is a disaccharide. Ideal conditions for the chemical digestion of starch include a temperature near 37°C and an almost neutral environment, which is neither acidic nor alkaline. The mouth satisfies both of these conditions.

For the chemical digestion of starch, the time you take to chew your food is also important. The starch-containing food must be moistened and thoroughly mixed with the amylase. Any starch that leaves the mouth undigested will not be broken down until it reaches the small intestine. In the duodenum, pancreatic amylase completes the breakdown of starch into maltose.

Maltose is a disaccharide. But only monosaccharides are small enough to pass through the intestinal lining into the bloodstream. The chemical digestion of disaccharides is carried out by several enzymes produced in the glands of the jejunum. Each enzyme is specific for a different disaccharide substrate. For example, the disaccharides maltose, lactose, and sucrose are chemically digested by the enzymes maltase, lactase, and sucrase, respectively. The end products of this final stage of carbohydrate digestion are monosaccharides such as glucose, fructose, and galactose. These monosaccharides are readily absorbed by the villi and enter the bloodstream for transport to body cells.

Chemical Digestion of Fats

Fats, or lipids, consist of molecules that are much too large to pass through the intestinal wall. Since fats do not dissolve in water, they cannot be broken down chemically until they undergo several physical changes. (See Figure 5-17.) First, chewing, churning, and mixing in the mouth and stomach convert pieces of fat to large globules. In the duodenum, these globules are subdivided into much smaller fat globules by the action of bile from the liver. Bile is an emulsifying agent that spreads the smaller fat globules evenly through the chyme and prevents them from coming together again.

These physical changes increase the surface area of the fat, exposing the fat molecules to the action of lipase. This enzyme is produced by the pancreas, but is active only in the alkaline environment of the duodenum. Lipase acts to split the fat into glycerol and fatty acids. Both of these products pass readily through the wall of the small intestine.

The action of bile is similar to the action of an egg yolk in salad dressing. Ingredients in the yolk emulsify the oil, which means that small droplets of oil remain evenly distributed throughout the vinegar.

FIGURE 5-17 The digestion of fats

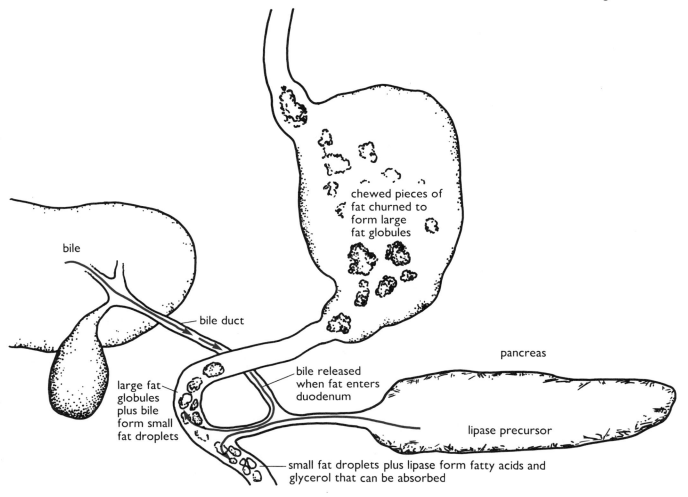

chewed pieces of fat churned to form large fat globules

bile

bile duct

large fat globules plus bile form small fat droplets

bile released when fat enters duodenum

pancreas

lipase precursor

small fat droplets plus lipase form fatty acids and glycerol that can be absorbed

Chemical Digestion of Proteins

Protein digestion in heterotrophs presents a puzzling biological question. What prevents a digestive system from digesting itself? After all, any chemical that is able to break down protein in food also has the ability to digest protein in living cells. In humans, this outcome is prevented by a multi-step sequence of interactions between digestive hormones and enzyme precursors.

Digestive hormones are produced by glands in one part of the digestive system. Then they travel by way of the bloodstream to stimulate other digestive structures. Enzyme precursors are inactive enzymes. If protein-digesting enzymes were manufactured in an active form, they would digest the enzyme-secreting cells themselves. Precursors do not become active until they reach the digestive tube, which has a continuous mucous lining for protection. Figure 5-18 shows the complex sequence that finally converts proteins to separate

FIGURE 5-18 The digestion of protein

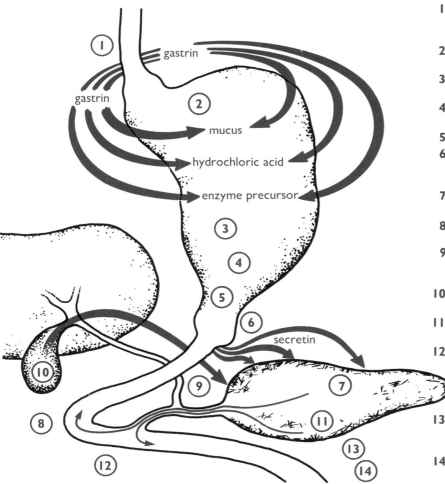

1. Protein-containing food stimulates cardiac sphincter cells to release hormone gastrin into blood.

2. Gastrin stimulates stomach lining cells to release secretions into stomach.

3. Acid converts precursor into active enzyme pepsin.

4. Pepsin breaks protein molecules into long amino acid chains.

5. Acidic chyme enters duodenum.

6. Acid in chyme stimulates duodenal gland cells to release hormone secretin into blood.

7. Secretin stimulates pancreas to send sodium bicarbonate into duodenum.

8. Sodium bicarbonate neutralizes contents of duodenum, turning them alkaline.

9. Protein in chyme stimulates duodenal gland cells to release hormone cholecystokinin.

10. Cholecystokinin stimulates gall bladder to contract and release bile into duodenum.

11. Cholecystokinin stimulates pancreas to release precursor enzymes.

12. Chemicals in duodenum convert pancreatic precursors into active enzymes trypsin and chymotrypsin, which break long amino acid chains into short ones.

13. Enterokinase, produced in the small intestine, stimulates the intestinal glands to produce peptidase.

14. Active peptidase splits the short-chain amino acids into single amino acids.

TABLE 5-5   Summary of Chemical Digestion in Humans

Digestive Structure	Digestive Site	Digestive Chemicals	Function of Chemicals
Salivary Glands	• mouth	• salivary amylase	• converts starch to disaccharides
Stomach Lining Cells	• stomach	• hydrochloric acid • pepsin and similar enzymes	• breaks down connective tissue and cell membranes in food • break food proteins into shorter chains
Liver	• small intestine	• bile	• causes physical breakdown of fats
Pancreas	• small intestine	• pancreatic amylase • lipase • trypsin and similar enzymes	• continues breakdown of starch into disaccharides (maltose) • neutralizes acidic chyme as it enters small intestine • convert fats to fatty acids and glycerol • continue breakdown of protein by converting short chains to amino acids
Small Intestine Lining Cells	• small intestine	• maltase and similar enzymes	• continue breakdown of carbohydrates by converting disaccharides such as maltose to glucose

amino acid molecules for absorption. Table 5-5 compares the structures, sites, secretions, enzymes, substrates, and end products of protein digestion with those for the digestion of carbohydrates and fats.

Regulation and Co-ordination of Digestion

Extracting nutrients from the complex food mixtures that most of us eat every day is a full-time job for the digestive system and for other body systems, too. For example, during and after a full-course meal, all of the following digestive events might be happening simultaneously.

• Chemical and physical digestion of baked potato in the mouth
• Chemical and physical digestion of lean meat in the stomach
• Conversion of fat globules of meat to small molecules by bile and pancreatic lipase in the duodenum
• Absorption of monosaccharide glucose from butter tart by villi in the jejunum
• Peristaltic movement of cellulose from corn kernels along the large intestine

Co-ordinating all of these events is the combined task of the nervous and endocrine systems. You will learn more about these systems in Chapter 8. Their role in digestion is carried out by numerous specialized endocrine glands that secrete digestive hormones and by numerous nerve fibres embedded in the digestive tract. If any part of this complex arrangement fails, digestion will not proceed normally.

Chemical Digestive Disorders

Most chemical digestive disorders are classified as metabolic because they interfere with the chemical reactions necessary for normal digestion. Usually, such disorders are caused by the body's failure to produce all of the acids, enzymes, and hormones it needs to convert food into usable nutrient molecules.

There are two very different types of health problems caused by metabolic disorders. The first type involves nutritional deficiencies that occur despite ingestion of a balanced diet. For example, a person whose diet includes adequate iron may develop iron-deficiency anemia if any of the enzymes involved in iron metabolism are absent or do not function normally. Most disorders of this type are easily treated by prescribed diets or medications.

The second type of metabolic digestive disorder results from poisoning through the accumulation of incompletely digested food components. The inherited metabolic disorder phenylketonuria (PKU) is an example. PKU causes a deficiency of the enzyme phenylalanine hydroxylase. This enzyme is needed to break down the amino acid phenylalanine. Without the enzyme, phenylalanine accumulates in the bloodstream and gradually damages brain tissue. Since phenylalanine is found in milk, affected infants gradually become developmentally handicapped. Although the retardation that occurs as a result of PKU is irreversible, preventive measures are now available to detect PKU before damage can occur. In Canada, all hospital-born babies are routinely screened for PKU through urine or blood tests to detect phenylalanine levels. Treatment to prevent retardation involves strictly limiting phenylalanine intake for the first 20 years of life. PKU is most common among people of Irish ancestry.

Tay-Sachs is a fatal metabolic disorder that strikes children after six months of age. Babies who seem healthy and normal until this age start to show signs of paralysis, mental retardation, and blindness. As yet, there is no cure for this tragic inherited disorder, which occurs most frequently among Jewish people of eastern European descent. Researchers believe that the cause of Tay-Sachs is an enzyme deficiency in the lysosomes of cells. This enzyme deficiency is thought to cause a deadly accumulation of fatty tissue around the nerve cells, which interferes with nerve transmissions in the body.

Untreated PKU patients have very fair hair, eczema, progressive mental retardation, and an unpleasant odour to their urine and perspiration.

II ANIMALS

Investigating Digestive Disorders

Scientists often find it useful to summarize written articles with a short statement called an abstract. Your task in this activity is to write an abstract for each of three digestive disorders selected from the following list or from those suggested by your teacher.

- gingivitis
- gastroenteritis
- Crohn disease
- ulcerative colitis
- diverticulosis
- acute appendicitis
- dysentery

Find an article in a medical encyclopedia or in a similar reference work for each of the disorders you have chosen. Follow a format similar to that used to discuss PKU on the previous page. Be sure to describe the cause, the symptoms, and the treatment of each disorder in its respective abstract.

Section Review Questions

1. a) What are enzymes?
   b) Which two important factors influence enzyme activity?
   c) Describe the relationship between an enzyme and its substrate.

2. a) Trace the chemical digestion of carbohydrates in the human digestive system from the mouth to the point of absorption.
   b) There is a radical change in acidity as food enters the stomach and again as it leaves. How does this change affect carbohydrate digestion?

3. a) What important physical change must fats undergo before chemical change can take place?
   b) Where and how does this physical change occur?

4. a) Where does the chemical digestion of fats begin?
   b) Which digestive chemical is involved?
   c) What are the end products? Where are they absorbed?

5. a) Why does the action of the digestive system have to be co-ordinated?
   b) Which chemicals co-ordinate this action?
   c) Which body systems interact to co-ordinate digestion?

6. a) Where does the chemical digestion of proteins begin? Where does it end?
   b) The digestion of proteins is much more complex than the digestion of fats or carbohydrates. Explain why.
   c) What role do enzyme precursors play in the chemical digestion of proteins?

7. How is it possible to eat a balanced diet yet suffer from a nutritional deficiency?

Frederick Banting

Dr. Frederick Banting was chosen the greatest living Canadian in three separate polls in the 1920s and 1930s. Banting was hailed as the discoverer of insulin, a hormone capable of controlling diabetes mellitus. Until the discovery, thousands of people died every year because they were unable to metabolize sugar.

In many ways, it was remarkable that Banting succeeded where some of medicine's greatest researchers had failed. Born in 1891 in Alliston, Ontario, he trained as a doctor and surgeon. In the early years of his medical practice, his goal was to learn about advances in surgery. He was not an experienced researcher, nor did he specialize in the treatment of diabetes.

In 1920, after reading a journal in preparation for a pancreas lecture, Banting had an idea. He knew that diabetic symptoms could be triggered by damaging or removing the islets of Langerhans in the pancreas. This had led many researchers to believe that a substance secreted by the islet cells prevented the disease. Banting also knew that blocking the main pancreatic duct would cause the pancreas to atrophy and stop secretion of digestive enzymes. But it would not affect the islets of Langerhans. Banting wondered whether the islet secretion could be collected from such an atrophied pancreas, free of digestive enzymes.

Dr. J.J.R. MacLeod of the University of Toronto agreed to supply space and a research assistant for Banting to test his idea. In May of 1921, Banting and Charles

Best, a graduate biochemistry student, began their work. Within a year, they had confirmed the effectiveness of the islet cell secretion in relieving diabetic symptoms in dogs, and had partially purified the active ingredient, which they called insulin. Only one year later, Banting and MacLeod were awarded the Nobel Prize in medicine.

The team of Banting, MacLeod, Best, and Dr. James B. Collip, a biochemist, had made one of the most spectacular breakthroughs in medical history. Banting is widely praised as the discoverer of insulin, but all the researchers were indispensable and deserve acclaim. Banting provided the idea that set the research in motion and, with Best, performed the tests that verified the islet secretion's ability to control blood sugar. MacLeod supplied the research facilities. As well, MacLeod knew the history of diabetes research and used his background to guide the team's research. Collip refined the crude pancreatic extract supplied by Banting and Best, so a pure insulin solution could be used on test patients without the serious reactions the impure extract caused.

Within months of the discovery, there was a worldwide demand for insulin. In the following years, Banting's team, in collaboration with others, concentrated on further purifying the hormone and mass producing it.

5.4 Digestion in Other Animals

Given the great diversity of gas-exchange systems in the animal kingdom, you might expect a similar variety in digestive structures. However, although animal digestive systems do vary somewhat, there are more similarities among them than there are differences.

- Digestion in all animals requires the same four basic steps: ingestion, chemical and physical breakdown of food absorption of small nutrient molecules, and egestion of indigestible matter. (See Figure 5-19.)
- All animals require the same major nutrients — carbohydrates, fats, and proteins — to supply the amino acids needed to assemble the protein molecules from which their body cells are constructed.
- As heterotrophs, all animals must obtain these nutrients from the same basic food sources: either producer organisms such as plants or products from consumer organisms such as other animals that eat plants.
- All animals must produce substances such as acids, antacids, enzymes, and hormones to break large food particles down into small nutrient molecules.

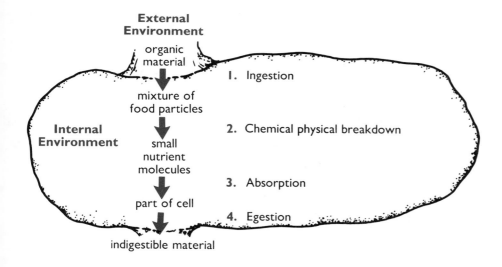

FIGURE 5-19 The four basic steps of digestion

Patterns for Vertebrate Digestive Systems

The digestive systems of other vertebrates are very much like your own. Their digestive structures and processes parallel those found in humans. Often, the contrasts that do exist are related more to variations in external body shape than to any fundamental difference in the digestive process. (See Figure 5-20.)

The most outstanding contrasts are between the digestive systems of carnivores and herbivores. In general, herbivores have much longer digestive

FIGURE 5-20 Can you identify the major differences between the digestive system of a snake and that of a human? Do you think these differences affect the digestive process?

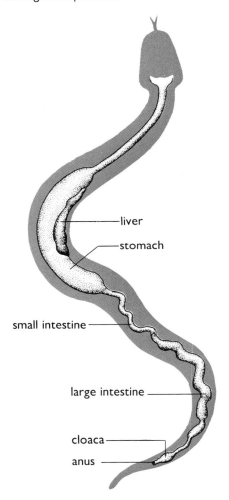

- liver
- stomach
- small intestine
- large intestine
- cloaca
- anus

DID YOU KNOW?

One reason the panda is dying out is that it is built like a carnivore but eats like a herbivore. Since a panda's mass is approximately one-third that of a cow's, the digestive tract of a panda should be at least one-third as long to meet its nutritional needs. In fact, the panda's digestive tract is only one-fifth as long, and its ability to digest plants is limited to certain types of bamboo and related species.

systems than carnivores of the same size. For example, the digestive tract of an antelope, a herbivore, is three to four times longer than that of the cheetah, which preys on antelopes. Since plant products are more difficult to digest than meat, the longer digestive tract of a herbivore allows enough time and surface area for a more complete breakdown of foods and absorption of nutrient molecules. Such contrasts can also be seen at different developmental stages of the same animal. (See Figure 5-21.)

Large predators such as this cheetah can go for days without eating, gaining the necessary nutrients in large, easily digested kills. The antelope's digestive system, however, requires more time to absorb the required nutrients. It must spend most of its waking hours eating and searching for food.

Tadpole's Digestive System   **Frog's Digestive System**

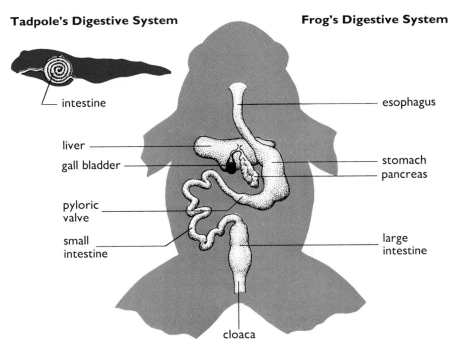

- intestine
- liver
- gall bladder
- pyloric valve
- small intestine
- esophagus
- stomach
- pancreas
- large intestine
- cloaca

FIGURE 5-21 Can you identify the changes that take place in the digestive structures when a tadpole develops into a frog?

INQUIRY ACTIVITY
Comparing Vertebrate Digestive Patterns

An understanding of vertebrate digestion is important for many reasons. The study and research of vertebrate digestion leads to a better understanding of human digestion. Greater understanding of the diets and the digestive systems of vertebrates also has significant agricultural and economic importance. Animal products such as milk and eggs are important food sources for many humans. Both of these products depend on the ability of other vertebrates to digest food types that humans cannot.

In this activity, you will read the following data section, which outlines digestion in five representative vertebrates. Using this data as a basis, you will prepare a chart comparing all aspects of digestion in at least two vertebrates with digestion in humans. You will then answer the discussion questions that follow, referring to other resource materials where necessary.

Data Section on Vertebrate Digestion

The Cow: A Representative Mammal

A ruminant ungulate such as the cow is an important food source for humans. The cow is called a ruminant because its digestive system has four stomach compartments. (See Figure 5-22.) The first two segments, the rumen and the reticulum, harbour bacteria, which produce enzymes that assist in the chemical breakdown of cellulose in plant materials such as leaves or grasses.

The cow cannot produce the enzymes needed to break the long cellulose polysaccharide into separate monosaccharides. Even the bacterial enzymes cannot break down all of the cellulose after the cow has chewed it only once. Further physical breakdown of the grass or leaves is necessary. Partially digested material from the rumen and reticulum is regurgitated back into the cow's mouth, where it can be chewed over again and reswallowed, thereby increasing the amount of plant surface exposed to bacterial enzymes.

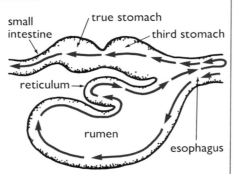

FIGURE 5-22 Which structures of the cow's digestive system are unlike those of the human system?

When most of the cellulose in the plant material is broken down, the partially digested food moves into the third stomach, where it is churned. The gastric juices of the true stomach prepare the food for the final stages of digestion in the small intestine.

Nonruminant ungulates such as the horse have a blind pouch called the caecum at the end of the small intestine. The caecum provides an environment for bacteria that break down the cellulose in the horse's high roughage diet.

The Chicken: A Representative Bird

Like all birds, domesticated chickens have beaks for collecting food. Very little physical digestion occurs in the mouth because a chicken does not have teeth, and the food it collects is swallowed quickly. (See Figure 5-23.) The esophagus carries the swallowed food to a storage pouch called the crop. As food leaves the crop, it passes into the first stomach segment, where digestive juices are added.

The resulting mixture then passes into a specialized stomach segment called the gizzard. The gizzard usually contains small stones or grit that help grind the food mixture as its thick, muscular walls contract. The ground-up food then passes through a pyloric valve into the intestine. From this point, digestion is similar to that of mammals — chemical breakdown by intestinal enzymes followed by absorption of nutrients and egestion of solid wastes.

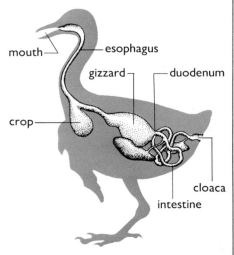

FIGURE 5-23 Compare the digestive structures of a bird with those of a human. What adaptations suit a bird's digestive system to its way of life?

The Garter Snake: A Representative Reptile

Like many other nonpoisonous snakes, the garter snake seizes live prey in its mouth, and then swallows it whole. A snake is capable of swallowing an animal four or five times larger in diameter than its own body. This phenomenal feat is possible because of a structural adaptation that enables a snake's jaw to "walk" the prey down its throat. The garter snake's lower jaw is subdivided into two parts that work independently. As one side pulls the prey down the snake's throat, the other side moves forward to apply a new hold on the prey. The garter snake's teeth assist by holding the prey firmly during the swallowing action.

The snake's stomach and intestine secrete strong digestive enzymes that gradually break down its huge, unchewed meal. Otherwise, digestion is similar to that in other vertebrates.

The snake's two-part lower jaw is an adaptation that enables it to grip its prey firmly, even without limbs or claws.

All snakes are carnivorous. Therefore, they have much shorter intestines than herbivores of similar size. A large holding cavity called the cloaca is located at the end of the large intestine. At different times, the cloaca may hold feces, urine, sperm, or eggs. Undigested skin and bones may either pass out as feces or be regurgitated.

Some nonpoisonous species squeeze their prey to death before swallowing them. Poisonous snakes inject a nerve poison that paralyzes their prey so they can be swallowed at a later time. The snake itself is not affected by the poison.

The Leopard Frog: A Representative Amphibian

An adult leopard frog's mouth is specially adapted to capture prey. Its long tongue is attached to the floor of its mouth. To catch prey, the leopard frog uses strong muscles to flick its tongue out faster than the eye can see. Prey is caught on the tongue's sticky surface and then drawn into the mouth. The leopard frog has two types of teeth on its upper jaw that assist in holding the prey as it is swallowed. Frogs have no teeth on their lower jaw and so they cannot chew their food. However, a frog can hold large amounts of food in its wide, elastic esophagus or gullet. The remainder of the leopard frog's digestive system is similar to other vertebrate systems. However, the leopard frog also has a cloaca similar to that of the snake.

The diet of a frog changes during its life cycle. As a tadpole, it is a herbivore. But as an adult frog, it is a carnivore, eating mostly insects. This dietary change occurs because structural and functional changes take place that convert the tadpole's herbivore digestive system into the adult's carnivore digestive system.

The frog's sticky tongue is an adaptation that enables it to capture high-protein foods without the need to run or swim after its prey.

The adult perch eats smaller fish by seizing them by their tails with its sharp teeth. Once the tail of its prey is damaged, the perch turns the smaller fish around and swallows it head first.

The Perch: A Representative Fish

Only a few fish species are herbivores. These species survive mainly on algae and water plants, but they may also eat animals. Most fish are carnivores. Like the perch, they have mouths with sharp teeth to grasp and to swallow their prey.

Most fish consume other fish and invertebrates such as insects and crayfish. The long, straight stomach of the perch allows it to swallow a fish almost the same size as itself. (See Figure 5-24.) At the junction of a fish's stomach and its intestine, short, finger-like tubes called the pyloric caeca carry out much of the digestion and absorption processes. Any remaining digested nutrients are absorbed by the intestinal wall. Undigested fecal matter is egested through the anus.

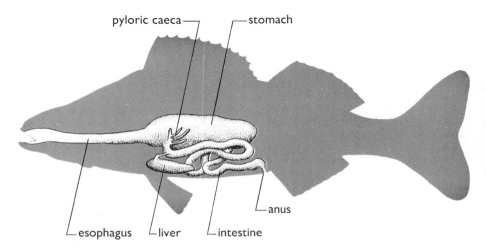

Smaller fish are an important food supply for larger carnivorous fish.

FIGURE 5-24 How does the digestive system of a perch reflect its dietary habits?

Discussion Questions

1. a) Which of the four representative vertebrates does not chew its food?
   b) Which structures or processes do these vertebrates have that serve the same purpose?
2. a) All four vertebrates ingest a considerable amount of roughage. Explain how each digestive system processes this roughage.
   b) Which vertebrate digestive system(s) seem most like the human digestive system in this respect?

3. Which of the representative vertebrates is a herbivore? A carnivore? An omnivore? A top carnivore?

4. Which of the four vertebrates has the most complex digestive system? State reasons for your answer.

5. a) Imagine a world in which cows, chickens, frogs, and humans all had the same mass. Which animal would have the largest stomach? Rank the remainder and state your reasons.

   b) Which animal would have the longest intestine? Rank the remainder and state your reasons.

   c) Which digestive system would be most like a human digestive system? Explain why.

6. Discuss the apparent relationship between food-gathering methods and the digestive structures of each representative vertebrate.

Patterns for Invertebrate Digestive Systems

Over 95% of all members of the animal kingdom are invertebrates or animals without backbones. Invertebrates such as clams, oysters, and lobsters are important food sources for humans. But grasshoppers, aphids, and beetles consume vast quantities of food intended for human consumption.

The simplest invertebrate digestive system is found in the phylum Porifera. Simple sponges have hollow bodies that act as living filters. Water containing various nutrients enters through incurrent pores. Any food in the water is ingested by specialized cells lining the cavity of the sponge. Nutrients are chemically broken down inside this cavity and absorbed by surrounding cells. Waste products and undigested materials are forced out of the sponge through a large excurrent pore by the rhythmic beating of hair-like cilia. (See Figure 5-25.)

All other invertebrate digestive systems can be classified as being one of two basic patterns: a bag-like system or a tube-like system. (See Figure 5-26.) Most simple invertebrates have a bag-like system with only two organs: a digestive sac and a single opening that functions as both mouth and anus. No physical breakdown of food occurs. Instead, food is ingested whole, stimulating gland cells in the lining of the sac to release digestive enzymes. When chemical breakdown is complete and most of the nutrients have been absorbed, the indigestible materials are egested.

Most complex invertebrates have a tube-like digestive system. As in vertebrate systems, food enters the tube at one end and indigestible wastes leave at the other. In most tube-like systems, digestive organs help carry out physical or chemical digestion. Table 5-6 compares digestion in representatives of five different invertebrate phyla.

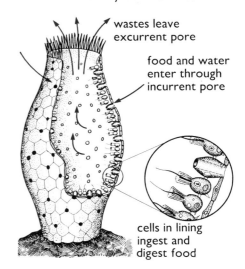

FIGURE 5-25 The simple, "flow-through" digestive system of a sponge is unlike that of any other animal.

wastes leave excurrent pore

food and water enter through incurrent pore

cells in lining ingest and digest food

DID YOU KNOW?
Earthworms do not have teeth to aid physical digestion. Instead, like birds, they have gizzards.

FIGURE 5-26 Compare the bag-like digestive system of the hydra with the tube-like system of the earthworm.

Hydra

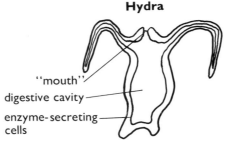

"mouth"

digestive cavity

enzyme-secreting cells

Earthworm

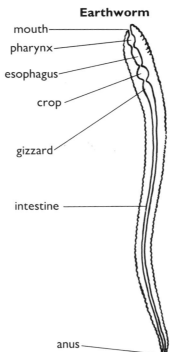

mouth

pharynx

esophagus

crop

gizzard

intestine

anus

TABLE 5-6 Comparison of Invertebrate Digestive Systems

Invertebrate	Type of Digestive System
Sponge	• bag-like
Hydra	• bag-like
Flatworm	• tube-like
Roundworm	• tube-like
Earthworm	• tube-like
Clam	• tube-like
Starfish	• tube-like

RESEARCH PROJECT
How Invertebrates Interact with the Human Digestive System

The health of the human digestive system is often adversely affected by invertebrates. Some of the world's most significant health problems are caused by human-invertebrate interactions. Choose an invertebrate from the following list and prepare a written report that explains how its digestive needs interact with those of humans.

- liver fluke
- hookworm
- tapeworm
- intestinal roundworm

Organize your report under these headings, writing no more than one or two paragraphs on each topic. Be sure to include a life-cycle diagram of the invertebrate you have chosen.

a) Classification of invertebrate
b) Method of introduction to human host
c) Life cycle of invertebrate
d) Adaptations of invertebrate to its environment
e) Effects on human health
f) Treatment methods

Section Review Questions

1. List and explain briefly the four basic functions that must be performed by all animal digestive systems.

2. Is there evidence of diversity among vertebrate digestive systems? Among invertebrate digestive systems? Discuss.

3. a) What is the basic pattern of digestion in vertebrates?
   b) What factors appear to have the greatest influence on digestive structures? On digestive processes?

4. a) Identify the two basic digestive patterns found among most invertebrates.
   b) State an example of each digestive pattern. Explain how the four basic digestive functions are performed by each system.

5. a) Which simple invertebrate has a completely different digestive system?
   b) Describe this system.

Turning the Tables

If you saw a wasp, a mountain chinch bug, an oak-boring beetle, a locust, or a red ant larva on your dinner plate, you would swat it. People in Mexico would eat it. Entomologists find that aboriginal peoples all over the world include insects in their diets. The Tukanoan Indians of Colombia, for example, eat over 20 species of insects, including weevil larvae, ants, and termites. The insects usually appear in their diet as alternatives to fish and game.

Your bias against eating insects is cultural rather than practical. David Madsen, an American archaeologist, did some research in the mid-1980s into the nutritional value and food efficiency of grasshoppers. Members of his team decided to eat grasshoppers in a spirit of scientific curiosity. Soon they were referring to them as "desert lobster."

Madsen and his associates became curious about insect eating when they found tens of thousands of grasshopper fragments in one of their digs near Great Salt Lake in Utah. In 1985, they found millions of naturally dried, salted grasshoppers along the shores of the lake and they realized that collecting them might be quite easy.

Nutritional analysis of one of the grasshoppers—*Melanoplus sanguinipes*, the migratory grasshopper—showed it contained 60% protein, 11% carbohydrate, and 2% fat. Although the grasshopper protein was not analyzed, the

cricket, a close relative, is known to contain all the amino acids required in the human diet. A kilogram of grasshoppers produced 5711 kJ, which compares to about 5188 kJ for a kilogram of cooked, medium-fat beef.

Madsen's group also studied kilojoules returned in relation to the amount of time invested in gathering the insects. They found that in 1 h a person could gather about 9 kg of sun-dried grasshoppers, equal in food energy value to 10 kg of meat or 43 Big Macs.

Although you don't live in a hunter-gatherer society, you may find in the next ten years that insects form a greater part of your diet. Eating insects may not be your preference, but it may become a necessity. In its *State of the World 1989* report, the World-

watch Institute notes that the continuing rapid growth of world population during the last few years combined with reduced harvests has led to a record fall in world per capita output of grain. It has also resulted in a corresponding fall in world supplies of protein. There are over 900 000 known species of insects in the world and, as you have seen, some of them are very rich in protein. To date they represent a generally untapped food resource.

Professional groups like the Entomological Society of America study and report on the future of insects as a food resource, among many other entomological topics. At a December 1989 symposium hosted by the Society, papers on insects as food were presented from Brazil, Colombia, India, Japan, Mexico, New Guinea, Thailand, and Zaire.

Insects could be reared and harvested on insect farms. For those of us who still wince at the idea of a bowl of salted grasshoppers instead of a bowl of peanuts, insects could be processed and packaged as a high-protein powder. This could be added to other foods to improve their nutritional value.

We go to great lengths to poison many edible insects with pesticides when they threaten to eat our food crops. Perhaps we are missing the obvious: could we serve ourselves better by turning the tables and eating the insects instead?

Chapter Review

Key Words

amino acids
bile
carbohydrates
digestion
disaccharides
duodenum
enzymes
fats
feces
ileum
jejunum

large intestine
monosaccharides
nutrients
peristalsis
polysaccharides
proteins
salivary glands
small intestine
substrate
villi

Recall Questions

Multiple Choice

1. Which of the following carbohydrates is a disaccharide?
   a) glucose
   b) maltose
   c) glycogen
   d) fructose

2. The jejunum, the ileum, and the duodenum are sections of the
   a) stomach
   b) large intestine
   c) small intestine
   d) esophagus

3. Salivary amylase and pancreatic amylase are enzymes responsible for the chemical breakdown of
   a) starch
   b) glucose
   c) maltose
   d) lactose

4. Which of the following micronutrients is produced by the human body from food through bacterial action?
   a) vitamin C
   b) vitamin K
   c) calcium
   d) iron

5. The emulsifying agent that physically breaks down fats into smaller fat globules is called
   a) lipase
   b) amylase
   c) bile
   d) chyme

6. Which of the following do animals use to build cells and repair body tissues?
   a) amino acids
   b) fatty acids
   c) hydrochloric acid
   d) sodium bicarbonate

7. Which of the following vertebrate digestive structures is *not* involved in physical digestion?
   a) incisor
   b) crop
   c) liver
   d) pancreas

Fill in the Blanks

1. Proteins, fats, and carbohydrates are classified as _____ because they must be consumed in large amounts every day.

2. _____ is the wave-like motion of muscles that pushes a bolus of food through the stomach.

3. A chemical compound on which enzymes act is called _____ .

4. Most physical digestion in humans occurs in the _____, and the _____ .

5. Simple invertebrates have a _____ -type digestive system.

6. _____ in your diet is needed to help the large intestine retain _____ .

7. The _____ are small, finger-like structures found in the lining of the _____ .

8. Two glands that play important roles in vertebrate digestive systems are the _____ and the _____ .

Short Answers

1. a) At what point is food fully digested on its way through a vertebrate's digestive system?
   b) What is the function of the remainder of the system?

2. Although absorption of nutrients has occurred in the small intestine, the large intestine still contributes to the digestive process. Explain its contribution.

3. At what point in the human digestive system does the chemical environment surrounding food change from nearly neutral to strongly acidic? From acidic to strongly alkaline?

4. The pancreas plays a very important role in the digestive process. Summarize this role.

5. How does a vertebrate digest the protein in food without also breaking down the tissues and cells of its own digestive system?

6. Both enzymes and hormones regulate chemical reactions. How does the action of enzymes differ from the action of hormones?

7. Which foods enable animals to manufacture all enzymes and most hormones?

8. What is a balanced diet, and why is a balanced intake of food nutritionally important?

9. What are the two major types of metabolic digestive disorders? State an example of each.

10. a) A potato is mostly starch. Describe the physical and the chemical breakdown of a potato by the human digestive system.
    b) Which molecules will finally be absorbed by the small intestine?

Application Questions

1. Normal milk is comprised of a carbohydrate (lactose), a protein (casein), and a fat (butterfat). Summarize the steps involved in the complete digestion of this food.

2. If you chew a cracker long enough without swallowing it, it will begin to taste sweet. Explain what has happened in your mouth.

3. a) Describe the role of the liver in the human digestive process.
   b) Do you think the liver plays a similar role in other vertebrates? Explain your answer.

4. a) Describe the role of the mouth in human digestion.
   b) Does the mouth play a similar role in the digestive systems of other vertebrates? Explain your answer using at least two nonhuman vertebrate examples.

5. Prepare a four-column chart with the following headings.

Facts	Proteins	Fats	Carbohydrates

In the Facts column, list the following points: Elements Present, Molecular Components Present, Nutritional Role. Complete the chart, adding any other points you may need to summarize the most important facts about the three major nutrients.

6. a) Explain the difference between essential and nonessential amino acids.
   b) What does this difference imply about the dietary choices you should make to ensure that you have a balanced diet?

7. a) What is the recommended daily intake of water, and why do nutritionists recommend such an amount?
   b) Which sources do you obtain water from?
   c) Do you think your friends and family are obtaining enough water? Explain.

8. a) How do plants and animals obtain the fats, carbohydrates, and proteins they need for their life functions?
   b) Explain how this difference affects the complexity of animal body structures.

9. A popular reducing diet recommends the consumption of meat or fish in increased amounts every day. Individuals who follow this diet do lose several kilograms in only a few weeks. Why would physicians warn that this diet is a dangerous ''fad'' diet? What is the safe way to reduce body mass?

Problem Solving

1. During a hockey game, why would it be better for a player to consume a glucose-containing beverage instead of one containing sucrose?

2. a) Some of the methods used to reduce obesity include stapling the stomach or removing a segment of the small intestine. What effects would gastric stapling have on food intake?
   b) Which part of the intestine would probably be removed?

3. A person sits down to a dinner of fish, rice, and carrots. A glass of wine is also consumed with the meal. Immediately after the meal, the alcohol is already in the bloodstream. Why is the alcohol able to be absorbed into the bloodstream much faster than the nutrients in the food?

4. a) Consider dogs, cats, mice, canaries, goldfish, and turtles. Which would you expect to have the longest digestive system relative to their size?

   b) Which pair of animals would you expect to have very similar digestive systems? Why?

5. The onset of sexual maturity in female humans depends in part on the body's ability to manufacture sex hormones. A century ago, the average age of onset in North American females was sixteen. Today, the average age is twelve. Why do you think biologists attribute this change to nutrition?

Extensions

1. Bulimia has both similarities to and differences from anorexia nervosa. Research the cause, symptoms, and treatment of this digestive disorder, and compare it to anorexia nervosa.

2. The digestive system is a tube that extends from the mouth to the anus and is sometimes called the alimentary canal. Calculate its length in humans.

3. The diets of astronauts during long space flights have to be carefully planned. A major consideration when preparing space-flight menus is the minimization of the amount of wastes egested. Which foods do you think would be best? Which ones do you think would not be appropriate? Explain reasons for your answers.

4. In North America, duodenal ulcers occur eight times more frequently than gastric ulcers. Why do you think such a high incidence of duodenal ulcers occurs?

5. Radioisotopes are used to trace certain nutrients through the digestive system. Research the names of some radioisotopes and explain how they are used to study the digestive process.

6. You may have heard the saying: "You are what you eat." In what ways do the digestive systems of various organisms and their diets reflect this statement?

7. One of the hazards of worldwide travel is the digestive upsets and diarrhea that often accompany drinking different water. Why does this occur?

CHAPTER

6

Transport

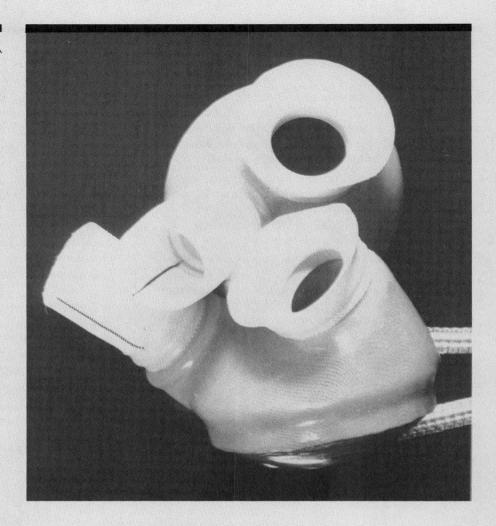

When sixty-one year old Barney Clark, who suffered from heart disease and chronic lung disease, was rejected as a heart transplant candidate, he became the first recipient of the world's first total artificial heart (TAH). Unfortunately, Clark died 112 days after his transplant.

Three other patients soon received Jarvik-7 hearts, but they all succumbed eventually to post-operative complications. Despite the limited success of these first permanent implants, researchers such as Dr. William DeVries, Barney Clark's surgeon, argue that funding of further human studies is necessary. DeVries's position in the face of opposition begs the question, "Are artificial replacement organs the way of the future?"

For now, the answer appears to be "no." First of all there are some moral objections. "Why is it that technological fixes or solutions seem more attractive than preventable activities?" asks Barton Bernstein, a historian at Stanford University. Bernstein suggests that because prevention is not dramatic it is less able to attract funding. Even with many fees waived, Clark's operation and treatment cost over $300 000, money which might have yielded a greater benefit had it been spent on preventive medicine, Bernstein says.

DeVries's critics have also accused him of performing implants in humans as an experiment rather than for his patients' benefit. They claim that serious problems experienced by calves using the Jarvik-7 were not solved before human trials began. But DeVries argues that nothing more could be learned from calf studies.

DeVries's claim that the quality of life for TAH recipients will improve with subsequent trials is hotly contested. Critics of the TAH believe the number, degree, and complexity of complications encountered by DeVries's patients cannot be solved with present technology. The most serious of these complications is infection. The air hoses that provide the power to run the Jarvik-7 lead from the external drive system through a hole in the patient's side. The hole and hoses allow microbes easy entrance to the body. Once inside the body, bacteria find an ideal surface area for colonization—the implant itself—from which more extensive infection may develop. With current technology and biomaterial, many believe that serious infection is almost inevitable during long-term implantation.

A less contentious and more beneficial role for TAH's may be in their original use, as a bridge to heart transplantation. This operation, in which the TAH replaces a failed heart until a suitable donor organ can be found, is more acceptable because the TAH is used only temporarily to lead to a procedure that has a high long-term success rate. Also, this operation decreases the risk of serious infection since the body is open for only a limited time.

While the temporary use of TAH's is relatively rare, heart transplants are not. Because of the high success rate of transplants, the demand for donors far outstrips the supply. As long as this discrepancy persists, researchers must seek other solutions to prevent or to treat heart disease.

The heart is only one of the many components of the circulatory system. How do these components interact in maintaining health and in leading to disease? How can an understanding of the circulatory system be used to prevent diseases or to treat them?

Chapter Objectives

When you complete this chapter, you should:

1. Appreciate the structure and the function of the vertebrate transport system.

2. Be committed to developing and maintaining cardiovascular fitness.

3. Be curious about the causes and the symptoms of circulatory disorders.

4. Know how to dissect vertebrates to identify and examine the major parts of their transport systems.

5. Be able to identify and compare heart structure and pulmonary circulation in mammals with other vertebrates.

6. Know how to examine and analyze photomicrographs of blood, blood cells, and circulatory system tissue.

7. Be able to describe in general terms the various roles of the circulatory system in vertebrates.

8. Be able to describe the flow of blood in a closed circulatory system in mammals.

9. Be able to describe and compare the structure and the function of arteries, veins, and capillaries.

10. Be able to describe the pulmonary, cardiac, and systemic circulatory system in humans.

11. Understand the structure of the mammalian heart and be able to compare it with that of a fish and an amphibian.

12. Trace the flow of blood through the human heart and be able to explain the mechanics of its flow.

13. Be able to describe how heartbeat is initiated and controlled in humans.

14. Be able to compare diastolic and systolic blood pressure in humans.

15. Be able to describe the origin, the structure, and the function of the lymphatic system.

16. Understand the causes, the effects, and the treatments of various circulatory diseases, and be able to describe methods of reducing susceptibility to these diseases.

6.1 The Problem of Transport

For unicellular protists such as the paramecium, the transport of materials required for life functions is simple. Molecules of oxygen, water, and nutrients diffuse directly into the cell of the paramecium. Cytoplasmic streaming then circulates the materials to all cell parts. (See Figure 6-1.) Any wastes produced in the cell also circulate and eventually diffuse into the external environment.

Multicellular animals have the same transport needs as unicellular protists, but many of their cells do not have direct contact with the external environment. Only very small, thin-bodied aquatic animals can obtain the materials they need without having a specialized system for transporting them. The planarian, for example, is only three cell layers thick. All of its inner cells are close enough to the surrounding water to exchange gas molecules directly. (See Figure 6-2.) The outer cells of the planarian are close enough to its corrugated gut to absorb nutrients directly.

RIGHT: FIGURE 6-1 In unicellular protists, materials diffuse through either the outer cell membrane or the membrane lining the vacuoles (coloured arrows). Cytoplasmic streaming is shown by black arrows.

BELOW: FIGURE 6-2 The planarian can absorb nutrients, and exchange gas and molecules with the surrounding water without a specialized system for transport.

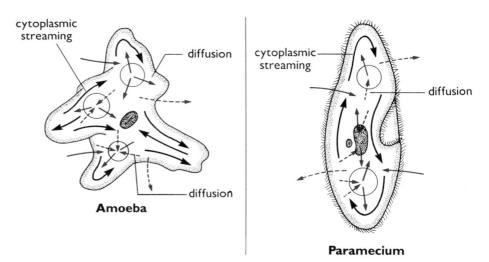

Amoeba

Paramecium

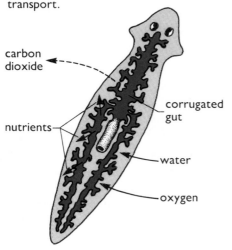

In larger animals, however, most cells do not have immediate access to the sites where supplies of oxygen, water, and nutrients enter their bodies. For these animals, solving the problem of transport requires an internal system to perform the following functions.
- A transport system must handle required materials and wastes in a form that can diffuse through cell membranes. This requirement can only be met by a fluid.
- A transport system must link every cell with the body sites that supply materials and discard wastes.

Many of this elephant's cells are located more than 1 m away from its lungs or intestinal walls. Even the smallest flea on the elephant's back also needs a system for transporting oxygen, nutrients, and wastes.

- A transport system must circulate the fluid, moving it around so that each cell receives a share of needed materials and also rids itself of wastes.

In vertebrates and many other animals, all of these functions are performed by an internal circulatory system with three principal components. These components are a fluid called blood, a network of tube-like blood vessels, and a circulatory pump or heart. These three parts are completely internal. Blood, for example, can only be seen if you damage your body covering in some way. Despite this, you can easily observe external evidence of your own internal transport system.

LABORATORY EXERCISE 6-1
External Evidence of an Internal Transport System

The walruses in the photograph in the colour section for Unit II undergo a dramatic change in external appearance when their environment changes. This phenomenon occurs when the walruses' internal transport system responds to the change in environment. Can you explain why the walruses' external appearance changes in this way? In this exercise, you will be looking for external evidence that your own internal transportation system responds to changes in the environment.

Structure and Function of Blood

If you cut yourself, the blood that oozes out of the wound looks like a uniform fluid. Microscopic examination, however, reveals that **blood** has a complex structure corresponding to the numerous functions it must perform. One

A centrifuge separates blood into its liquid and solid components. Notice the clear plasma on top.

Plasma does carry a little dissolved oxygen, but the amount it can hold is only 1% of the oxygen required by the body.

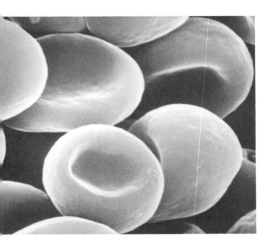

The number of red blood cells often indicates the general health of the individual.

obvious function of blood is the transport of nutrient molecules from the digestive tract to cells throughout the body. Another function is the transport of oxygen molecules from the lungs for use in cell respiration. But blood is also responsible for the transport of wastes from respiration and other body reactions to an organ that can eliminate these products. In addition, blood must be able to clot quickly to prevent excessive loss when you cut your skin. Blood can perform these functions because it contains many different components. However, only the four most important components of human blood will be discussed in this section: plasma, red blood cells, white blood cells, and platelets.

The Nature and Function of Plasma

Approximately 55% of blood volume is a pale yellow fluid called **plasma.** Plasma is about 92% water, and it carries dissolved nutrients throughout the body. These nutrients include minerals, amino acids, fats, and carbohydrates such as glucose and fructose. Dissolved wastes such as urea and carbon dioxide are carried by the plasma to such organs as the kidneys and the lungs for disposal.

Plasma also contains several kinds of protein molecules: albumin, fibrinogen, and globulins. Albumin, the most abundant plasma protein, helps regulate the amount of water in the plasma so the blood can flow smoothly through the blood vessels. Albumin also helps the plasma transport fatty acid molecules by binding to them. Fibrinogen plays an important role in the blood-clotting mechanism.

Globulins include several types of large protein molecules. One type acts as a carrier, transporting body chemicals such as hormones, nutrients such as copper, or waste substances such as iron from broken-down hemoglobin. A second type of globulin acts to disable potentially harmful enzymes such as those manufactured to break down scar tissue. A third major function of globulins is the defence against foreign invaders. The globulin proteins that perform this function are known as immunoglobulins or **antibodies.** Hematologists think that globulins also perform other functions, but these are not yet fully understood.

Structure and Function of Red Blood Cells

Red blood cells, or **erythrocytes,** make up approximately 44% of human blood volume. (See Figure 6-3.) Erythrocytes are produced in the red bone marrow, where they have all the usual structures found in a normal cell. However, as each cell matures and enters the bloodstream, its nucleus and most of its organelles disappear. At this point, the cell is composed primarily of the iron-containing protein hemoglobin.

Hemoglobin enables the red blood cells to carry oxygen from the lungs to other body cells. The "heme" in hemoglobin refers to its four iron-con-

FIGURE 6-3 The dimensions of an erythrocyte

|←—7.5 μm—→| 2 μm |←→|

FIGURE 6-4 A heme group. Each ten-thousand-atom hemoglobin molecule contains four of these groups. Each red blood cell contains approximately 280 million hemoglobin molecules.

taining groups. (See Figure 6-4.) Each heme is surrounded by a globulin "arm," a long protein chain of amino acids. One hemoglobin molecule can combine with four molecules of oxygen to form oxyhemoglobin. Bright red blood contains a great deal of oxyhemoglobin. As the oxygen is released to the body cells, a dark red colour appears, indicating that the red blood cells have picked up the waste gas carbon dioxide instead. The life span of a red blood cell is approximately 120 days. Dead cells are broken down in the liver, where the iron is recycled for future red blood cell production.

Structure and Function of White Blood Cells

White blood cells, or **leukocytes,** are also manufactured in the red bone marrow, but they make up less than 1% of blood volume. White blood cells play no part in the transport of nutrients, gases, or wastes. Their main functions are defending the body against invaders, and cleaning up dead cells and foreign matter at injury sites. The pus that collects around an infected wound contains many white blood cells.

All white blood cells are colourless and larger than red blood cells. Some white blood cells contain granules and some do not, but all possess distinct nuclei. Those cells that contain granules are manufactured in red bone marrow. They live only a few hours or a few days. Nongranular cells are produced in lymphatic tissues such as the tonsils. These cells may live up to four months.

As Figure 6-5 illustrates, there are five different types of white blood cells. Most are **phagocytes**; they are able to change shape much as amoebas do. Phagocytes act by surrounding and "swallowing" bacteria, dead cells, and other foreign materials. (See Figure 6-6.) To perform these functions, white

Red blood cells outnumber white blood cells 600 to 1 under normal conditions.

FIGURE 6-5 Percentages of the five types of human white blood cells

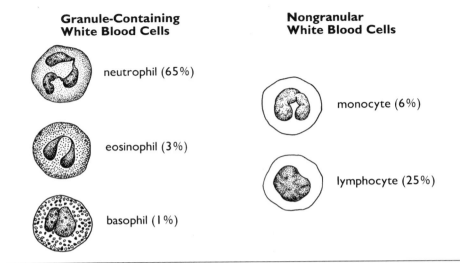

Granule-Containing White Blood Cells

neutrophil (65%)

eosinophil (3%)

basophil (1%)

Nongranular White Blood Cells

monocyte (6%)

lymphocyte (25%)

FIGURE 6-6 The phagocytic action of a neutrophil. These sketches were made 30 s apart.

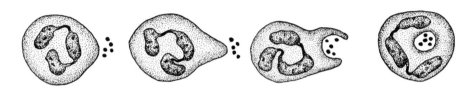

blood cells must leave the blood vessels to reach invasion or injury sites. They do this by squeezing through tiny pores in the walls of the blood vessels. (See Figure 6-7.) Eosinophils are only moderately phagocytic, but they play a major role in allergic reactions. Lymphocytes function differently. They are involved in the multistage process that produces custom-made antibodies to destroy foreign substances such as the protein coats of viruses. The function of basophils is not completely understood, but their numbers become elevated in some forms of leukemia.

Usually, white cells make up less than 1% of blood volume. During illness, the white blood cell count increases significantly. In pneumonia, the neutrophil

FIGURE 6-7 White blood cells can squeeze through the tiny pores in the walls of the narrowest blood vessels. You can see that the rigidly shaped red blood cells remain inside the circulatory system.

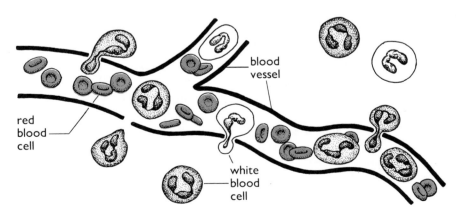

blood vessel

red blood cell

white blood cell

II ANIMALS

count increases by 25%. In tuberculosis, the monocyte count increases by 500%. Why do you think patterns such as these help physicians diagnose illnesses?

Structure and Function of Platelets

Blood **platelets** are small fragments of larger cells found in red bone marrow. Platelets have no nuclei but are surrounded by membranes. There are about 250 000 platelets in each cubic millimetre of blood, one for approximately every 20 red blood cells.

The primary function of platelets is to initiate blood clotting. The rupturing of platelet membranes during an injury releases a substance that reacts with plasma proteins such as fibrinogen to form a mesh of fibres. The mesh traps blood cells and forms a clot that prevents further blood flow. The fibres gradually contract and close the wound. Platelets that are not used in this way die after about ten days. Platelets can be separated from the whole blood of a donor and added to the blood of a patient whose own blood is not clotting properly.

A normal skin cut takes approximately 4 min to form a clot.

DID YOU KNOW?
The Canadian Red Cross uses donated blood for the following.
- *Whole blood*: to replace blood lost through bleeding
- *Red blood cells*: to treat anemia
- *Platelets*: to help form blood clots
- *Albumin*: to treat burns (present in plasma)
- *Factor VIII or IX*: to treat hemophilia (present in plasma)
- *Immunoglobulin*: to boost the immune system (present in plasma)

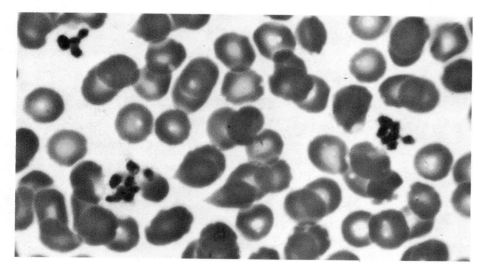

These platelets are greatly outnumbered by much larger red blood cells.

INQUIRY ACTIVITY
Cells, Tissues, and Vessels of the Circulatory System

Although blood is a fluid, biologists regard it as a tissue because it contains a collection of similar cells that are organized to carry out particular functions. The electron micrographs on the following page show blood cells in action. Study these micrographs, interpret them, and use your findings to answer the Discussion Questions.

Photomicrograph 1   Photomicrograph 2

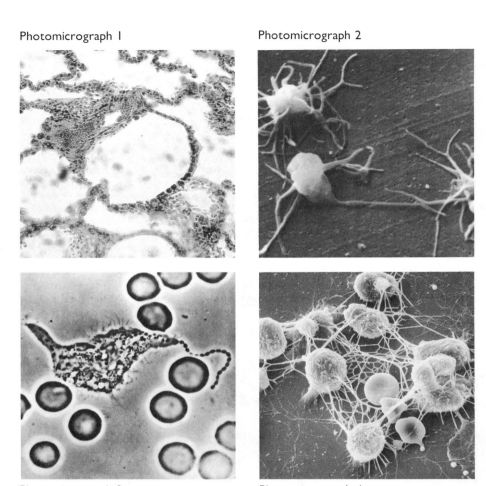

Photomicrograph 3   Photomicrograph 4

Discussion Questions

1. Which photomicrographs show the following?
   a) blood platelets shortly after they have been ruptured during an injury
   b) the formation of a blood clot
   c) the flow of blood cells through lung capillaries
   d) how blood cells defend the body from foreign invaders
2. a) Identify the three kinds of blood cells or cell fragments shown and rank them from largest to smallest.
   b) Describe any relationship between cell size and cell function.
3. a) Describe the shape of each kind of blood cell or cell fragment.
   b) Describe any relationship between cell shape and cell function.

4. a) In healthy individuals, the most abundant kind of blood cell outnumbers the least abundant by approximately 750:1. Which cells are being compared in this ratio?
   b) Which cells or cell fragments are being compared if the ratio is approximately 20:1?
5. a) Which of these three cells or cell fragments can move on its own without the help of the circulating fluid?
   b) How does this extra mobility enhance the cell's ability to perform its main function?
6. One kind of cell usually has to slow down and twist to pass through the narrowest of the capillaries. How does this tight fit affect gas exchange in lung tissue?

Blood Types

Transfusions of whole blood can be used to replace circulatory fluids lost from serious wounds or during major surgery. However, human blood is not universally interchangeable. Prior to a transfusion, blood from a donor and a recipient must be cross-matched to check for compatibility. Tests for this purpose identify four major blood groups or types: A, B, AB, and O.

If the two blood types are not compatible, antibodies in the recipient's blood will attack proteins on the donor's red blood cells. The antibody action causes the foreign red blood cells to clump. If this happened in the recipient's body, it would block the normal flow of blood and probably cause death.

Table 6-1 indicates which combinations of A, B, AB, and O blood are safe. However, transfusions must also be matched for the presence (positive) or absence (negative) of a red blood cell protein known as Rh. An Rh negative recipient who receives Rh positive blood will produce antibodies to fight the foreign protein. However, antibody production is a slow process. Usually, most of the donated cells have died by the time there are enough antibodies to cause a serious problem. Once the body "learns" how to make these

Many Canadians carry blood-donor cards that indicate their blood type for donations or transfusions.

TABLE 6-1   Safe Combinations of A, B, AB, and O Blood Types

Blood Types			Can Receive Blood From		Can Donate Blood To	
Blood Type	Protein	Antibody	Best Match	Emergency	Best Match	Emergency
A	A	anti-B	A	O	A	AB
B	B	anti-A	B	O	B	AB
AB	A, B	none	AB	A, B, O	AB	none
O	none	anti-A anti-B	O	none	O	A, B, AB

antibodies, large numbers can be manufactured in a short time. If the person receives Rh positive blood again, the antibodies will cause clumping almost immediately. This response is much different from those in Table 6-1. Anti-Rh antibodies do not appear until after the blood has been exposed to Rh protein. A, B, and AB blood, however, carry the corresponding antibodies whether they have been exposed to donated blood or not.

The Problem of Transporting Circulatory Fluids

When you are at rest, blood is distributed to your body in various ways. For example:
- 25% to the kidneys
- 15% to the digestive tract
- 10% to the liver
- 8% to the brain
- 4% to the heart muscle
- 13% to the lungs

The many different components of human blood enable it to defend the body against invaders, transport body chemicals, supply raw materials for growth, repair, and cellular respiration, and absorb waste products for eventual disposal. Moving blood around so it can meet the needs of the human body's 50 trillion or so cells requires a highly efficient transport system. This system must have tubes that lead to all parts of the body and a pump to distribute the circulatory fluid at high speed. The network of tubes making up the circulatory system will be discussed in Section 6.3. Other animals also need to transport fluids. You will learn about the circulatory systems of representative vertebrates and invertebrates in Section 6.4.

Section Review Questions

1. Explain why multicellular organisms require an internal transport system.
2. What are the three principal components required for an internal circulatory system?
3. List the four major components of blood and state at least one function for each.
4. Explain how and why red blood cells differ from other cells in the bloodstream.
5. a) List the five types of leukocytes.
   b) How do lymphocytes differ in structure and function from other leukocytes?
6. a) What are the three major protein components in blood plasma?
   b) State one function of each component.
7. a) What is hemoglobin?
   b) Explain why hemoglobin is so important to the transport system.
8. One person has Type O negative blood. Another person has Type A positive blood.
   a) Which antibodies does each person have?
   b) In an emergency, who could act as a donor and who could be a recipient? Explain the reasons for your answer.

Rh Incompatibility

Every child differs genetically from its parents. On rare occasions, these differences can be deadly. It is rarely a problem if a child's blood differs from its mother's in its ABO system of antigens. But, a difference in the Rh system between a child's blood and its mother's can have serious consequences. When an Rh negative mother carries an Rh positive fetus, a condition called erythroblastosis fetalis may develop. On rare occasions, the condition may be fatal to the fetus, whose erythrocytes are attacked and destroyed by its mother's immune system.

Rh negative erythrocytes lack the Rh antigen. When exposed to the antigen found on Rh positive erythrocytes, the Rh negative person produces antibodies to attack these foreign erythrocytes in a process called sensitization. If an Rh negative woman has been sensitized to the Rh antigen, her antibodies may cross the placenta when she becomes pregnant. If her fetus is Rh positive, the mother's antibodies will attack and destroy fetal erythrocytes. In extreme cases, the destruction of red blood cells is so extensive that the fetus becomes anemic and suffers heart failure. Less severely affected newborns may suffer from jaundice, a yellowing of the body caused by large amounts of bilirubin derived from the breakdown of hemoglobin. Severe cases of jaundice can cause brain damage.

Fortunately, erythroblastosis fetalis is rare. Also, the mother must have had previous exposure to Rh positive blood in order to be sensitized. Sensitization sometimes occurs during a blood transfusion. But sensitization more often develops during the delivery of an Rh positive child when the child's Rh positive blood may enter the mother's body. Because fetal blood does not readily cross the placenta earlier in pregnancy, the first Rh positive fetus of an Rh negative mother rarely contracts erythroblastosis fetalis.

Erythroblastosis fetalis was once a tragic cause of fetal and infant mortality, but it has been brought under control by highly effective prevention, detection, and treatment techniques. Today, it develops in only 1 in 20 Rh positive fetuses of Rh negative mothers. Rh negative mothers who are given anti-Rh antibodies after they have given birth to Rh positive babies can avoid sensitization. Fetal erythrocytes in maternal blood are destroyed before the mother's immune system can produce antibodies against them.

If sensitization does occur, monitoring maternal anti-Rh antibody levels during later pregnancies may anticipate the condition. If antibody levels rise, the extent of fetal anemia and erythrocyte destruction can be monitored through amniocentesis, a procedure in which placental fluid is withdrawn with a needle.

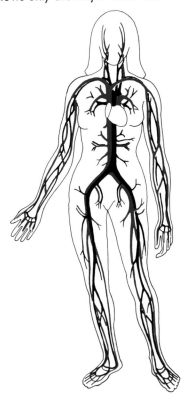

6.2 A System for Transporting Fluids

Figure 6-8 shows the extensive network of tubes involved in circulating blood through the human transport system. This figure is a representational diagram, one that represents the true shape, arrangement, and relative size of all components. The complexity of these diagrams can make it difficult to understand them. So, biologists often use schematic diagrams like Figure 6-9. Schematic diagrams do not attempt to show the true size or shape of the structures. Instead, they focus on the function of the structures and how they are connected to each other. This figure shows clearly the need for different kinds and sizes of blood vessels.

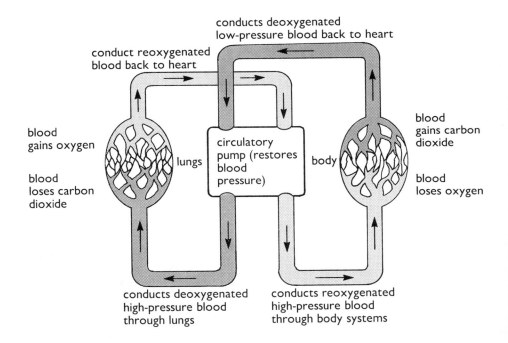

conducts deoxygenated low-pressure blood back to heart

conduct reoxygenated blood back to heart

blood gains oxygen

blood loses carbon dioxide

lungs

circulatory pump (restores blood pressure)

body

blood gains carbon dioxide

blood loses oxygen

conducts deoxygenated high-pressure blood through lungs

conducts reoxygenated high-pressure blood through body systems

FIGURE 6-9 A schematic diagram of blood circulating through the human transport system

Types of Blood Vessels

The main types of blood vessels are arteries, capillaries, and veins. **Arteries** are vessels that carry blood *away* from the heart. As you can see in Figure 6-10, arteries have thick walls made of elastic and muscle tissue that stretch when large volumes of blood under high pressure pass through them. Arteries carry blood to narrower vessels called **arterioles.** Together, arteries and arterioles carry blood from the heart to even smaller vessels called **capillaries.** (See Figure 6-11.) Capillaries are distributed throughout body tissues. Capillary walls are only one cell thick. Therefore, they are thin enough to allow

FIGURE 6-10 A cutaway view of an artery, showing the relative thickness of each layer

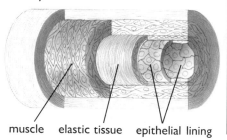

muscle   elastic tissue   epithelial lining

FIGURE 6-11 The structure of a capillary

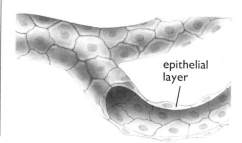

epithelial layer

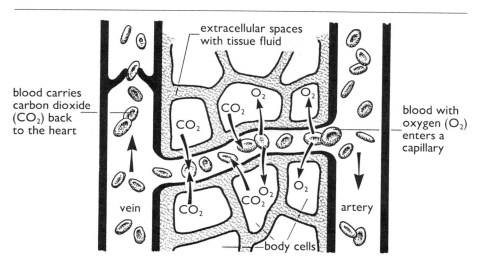

extracellular spaces with tissue fluid

blood carries carbon dioxide (CO_2) back to the heart

O_2 O_2

CO_2 CO_2 CO_2

blood with oxygen (O_2) enters a capillary

CO_2 O_2 O_2

CO_2

vein CO_2 body cells   artery

LEFT: FIGURE 6-12 Body cells are nourished by the diffusion of dissolved nutrients and oxygen from tissue fluid.

BELOW: FIGURE 6-13 A cutaway view of a vein, showing the relative thickness of each layer

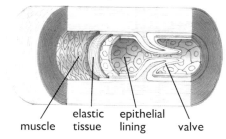

muscle   elastic tissue   epithelial lining   valve

blood plasma to pass through to the extracellular spaces. Cells are nourished by the inward diffusion of dissolved nutrients and oxygen from this tissue fluid. (See Figure 6-12.)

Cell wastes and carbon dioxide diffuse outward from individual cells into the tissue fluid. Waste products are carried away when the tissue fluid diffuses into nearby capillaries. The capillaries carry the waste-laden blood to larger vessels called **venules**. Blood from the venules is collected by still larger vessels called **veins**. (See Figure 6-13.) A vein is a vessel that carries blood *toward* the heart.

Venous blood is under much less pressure than arterial blood, so circulation in the veins is much slower. As illustrated in Figure 6-13, vein walls have fewer muscles and very little elastic tissue compared with arteries. Contraction of the surrounding skeletal muscles squeezes the veins and moves the blood toward the heart. Many veins have one-way valves that help prevent the low-pressure venous blood from draining backward. (See Figure 6-14.) Together, arteries, capillaries, and veins comprise a closed system for transporting materials and wastes in the body. (See Figure 6-15.)

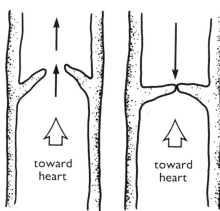

toward heart   toward heart

blood flows toward heart; valve is open

blood flows away from heart; valve is closed

FIGURE 6-14 A series of valves in the veins prevents blood from flowing away from the heart.

FIGURE 6-15 A schematic diagram, showing how different types of blood vessels are related

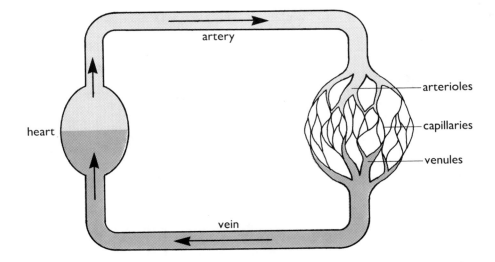

LABORATORY EXERCISE 6-2
The Circulatory System of a Representative Vertebrate

In this exercise, you will continue the ongoing dissection of a representative vertebrate, focussing on its circulatory system. Preserved laboratory specimens can be specially prepared for artery and vein examination. Liquid latex rubber is injected into the blood vessels of the dead animal. Arteries are usually injected with a red latex and veins with blue latex. If your specimen is double injected, you will be able to trace its entire circulatory system easily.

The Human Circulatory System

In humans, the circulation of blood is carried out by three interconnected subsystems: the pulmonary, the systemic, and the cardiac subsystems.

Pulmonary Subsystem
Before blood can perform its main function, it must carry waste carbon dioxide to the lungs and pick up fresh oxygen. The circuit of vessels that does this is called the **pulmonary subsystem.** (See Figure 6-16.) Deoxygenated blood enters the heart on the right side and is pumped to the lungs where oxygenation occurs. The carbon dioxide in the blood is also collected and exhaled out through the lungs. (See Figure 6-17.) The reoxygenated blood is now carried back to the heart, where it can be distributed by the systemic subsystem.

FIGURE 6-16 The pulmonary
subsystem

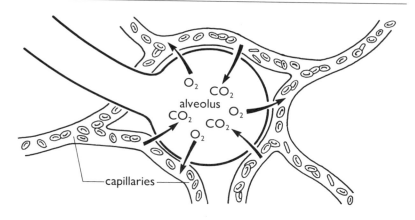

FIGURE 6-17 Gas exchange in the
lungs occurs between the capillaries and
the alveoli.

Systemic Subsystem

The **systemic subsystem** carries blood from the heart to all other body systems
and organs except the lungs. (See Figure 6-18.) The oxygenated blood is
pumped out of the left side of the heart to the body's largest artery, the **aorta.**
The aorta branches into major arteries to the head, the heart, the chest, and
the lower body. These arteries branch into arterioles and capillaries, the sites

FIGURE 6-18 The systemic subsystem. The aorta, which has a diameter of 2.5 cm, is the largest blood vessel in the body.

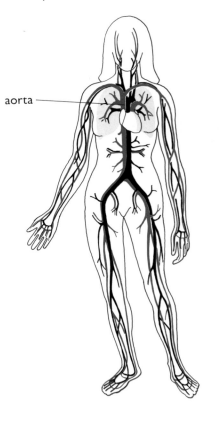

aorta

FIGURE 6-19 In this diagram, you can see how the systemic and pulmonary subsystems are connected.

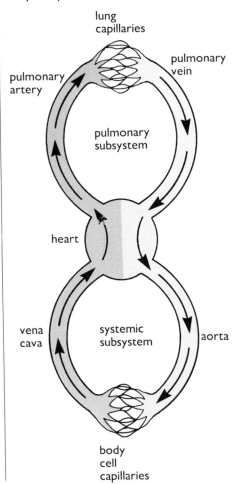

lung capillaries

pulmonary artery

pulmonary vein

pulmonary subsystem

heart

vena cava

systemic subsystem

aorta

body cell capillaries

of gas exchange. Venules and veins return the blood to the heart, where it enters pulmonary circulation again. (See Figure 6-19.)

Cardiac Subsystem

Pushing blood through all the vessels of the pulmonary and systemic subsystems is hard work. A great deal of energy is required by the heart muscle itself to contract rhythmically, 70-80 times each minute, for an entire lifetime. To meet this energy requirement, the heart muscle requires an abundant supply of nutrients and oxygen for cellular respiration. This need is met by the **cardiac subsystem,** a system of specialized coronary vessels that branch off the aorta

Your heart is so strong that it can continue to pump even when one half of its muscle mass is dead.

II ANIMALS

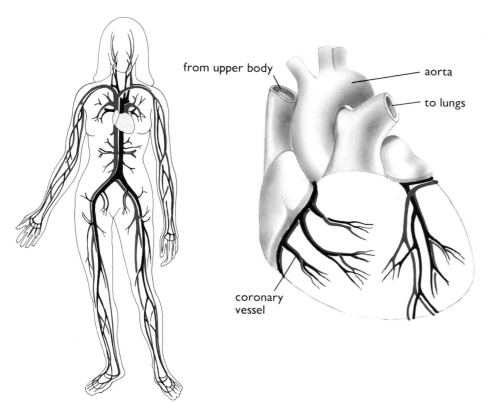

from upper body

aorta

to lungs

coronary
vessel

FIGURE 6-20   The cardiac subsystem
depends on the coronary vessels that
distribute blood to all parts of the heart
muscle.

and carry blood to the heart muscle. (See Figure 6-20.) Coronary arteries and
arterioles carry the blood to the capillaries where the exchange occurs. Coronary venules and veins collect the venous blood and return it to the right, or
pulmonary, side of the heart.

LABORATORY EXERCISE 6-3
Investigating Your Pulse Rate

Pulse sites are located throughout the human body. (See Figure 6-21.) Each
of these pulse sites has artery blood flow near the skin's surface. If you place
your fingers on top of a pulse site, you will feel the pulsation of arteries. The
movement of the artery corresponds to the ventrical contractions of the cardiac
cycle. So, pulse rate can be used as an indicator of heart rate for a given
period of time. In this exercise, you will investigate pulse rate at various sites
on your body.

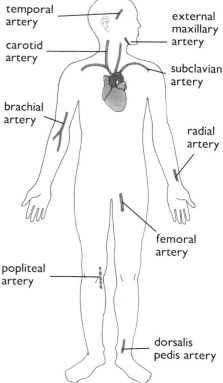

temporal
artery

external
maxillary
artery

carotid
artery

subclavian
artery

brachial
artery

radial
artery

popliteal
artery

femoral
artery

dorsalis
pedis artery

FIGURE 6-21   The location of pulse
sites throughout the body

The Circulatory Role of the Lymphatic System

After a wound stops bleeding, it may leak an almost colourless liquid. This liquid is evidence of another system for circulation — one that does not circulate blood. Such a system is needed to help the body maintain homeostasis because not all of the tissue fluid between body cells returns to the capillaries. Remember that tissue fluid is formed by plasma that leaves the capillaries. Without some way of restoring tissue fluid to the bloodstream, the plasma liquid content of the blood would soon drop to very low levels. The job of collecting the tissue fluid is performed by the **lymphatic system.** The lymphatic system is a network of very fine, thin-walled tubes leading to larger vessels and ducts. (See Figure 6-22.)

The fluid inside this network is known as **lymph.** It is almost identical to blood plasma but contains large numbers of lymphocytes (up to 20 000/mm^3). Highly permeable walls allow the vessels to collect large foreign particles such as bacteria. Many vertebrates have muscular "lymph hearts" that pump lymph through the lymph vessels. In humans, the movement of lymph through the tubes is very slow. However, contractions of nearby muscles help push the lymph along, and one-way valves help prevent it from backing up until it reaches the lymph nodes. (See Figure 6-23.)

Your tonsils and adenoids are lymph nodes in the throat area.

FIGURE 6-22 Lymph nodes in humans are concentrated in the armpits, groin, elbows, and knees.

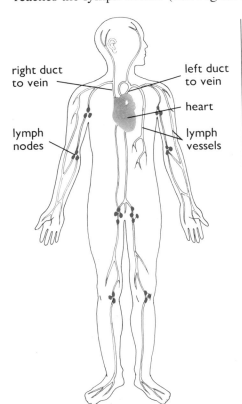

right duct to vein

left duct to vein

heart

lymph nodes

lymph vessels

FIGURE 6-23 Lymph nodes are responsible for filtering the lymph fluid.

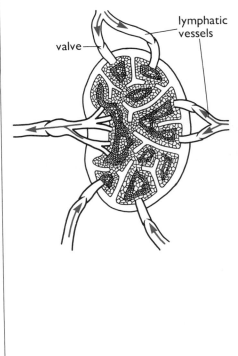

valve

lymphatic vessels

Lymph nodes are enlarged clusters of knotted tubes containing cells that destroy foreign organisms. The filtered liquid is then carried to a major duct that adds it to the venous blood at a point near the heart. Because of this connection, the lymphatic system can be regarded as a fourth subsystem, even though it does not usually carry any red blood cells.

Each of the four subsystems discussed in this section requires the movement of blood or fluid. All movement requires some form of driving force. The driving force behind the movement of all circulating fluids, blood and lymph alike, is the heart. You will learn more about the heart in Section 6.3.

Section Review Questions

1. Explain the differences between plasma, tissue fluid, and lymph.
2. Why are valves essential in veins and lymph vessels but not in arteries?
3. a) Explain how the systemic and pulmonary subsystem differ.
   b) Explain how these subsystems are interconnected.
4. Shown a vessel attached to the heart, how could you tell if it was an artery or a vein?
5. How does the lymphatic system assist the pulmonary, the systemic, and the cardiac subsystem?

6.3 Structure and Function of the Human Heart

Pushing blood through the interconnected vessels of the human circulatory system requires a multi-purpose pump, one that can continue pumping at all times. The human **heart** is this kind of driving force. Even the circulation of lymph ultimately depends on the heart's ability to pump blood throughout the body. Usually, the heart's pumping action is not heard, but in the following laboratory exercise, you will amplify its sounds with a simple instrument called a stethoscope.

LABORATORY EXERCISE 6-4
Investigating Heart Sounds

You can hear the familiar ''lub-dup'' sound of the heart clearly when you use a stethoscope. This sound results from the closure of the two sets of valves in the heart. A stethoscope is an amplifying device that transfers sound from its flat, thin diaphragm to your ear pieces. In this exercise, you will position a stethoscope at various listening sites around the heart and at other parts of the body to investigate the sounds produced at these locations.

How Blood Flows through the Heart

The schematic diagram in Figure 6-24 shows that the human heart is actually a double pump in one organ. One pump, or "right heart," is associated with pulmonary circulation. It receives blood from the body and pumps it to the lungs. The other pump, or "left heart," is associated with the systemic and the cardiac subsystem. It receives oxygenated blood from the lungs and pumps it back to the body.

FIGURE 6-24 The human heart acts like a double pump. Compare this schematic diagram with Figures 6-9 and 6-15.

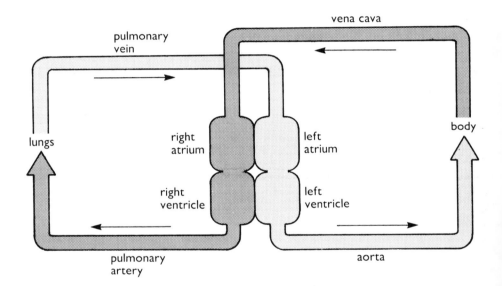

The representational cutaway view in Figure 6-25 shows that the human heart has four distinct muscular chambers, each somewhat different in size and shape. Two thin-walled upper chambers, or **atria,** receive blood from the major veins. Two thick-walled lower chambers, or **ventricles,** pump blood into the major arteries. A thick dividing wall called the **septum** separates the chambers of the "right heart" from those of the "left heart."

The two hearts beat with the same rhythm. Both atria contract while both ventricles relax. Then the ventricles contract while the atria relax. These contractions make little sound. The "lub-dup" of a beating heart is made mostly by two sets of valves that control the flow of blood through its chambers.

The openings to the atria have no valves and thereby receive a constant

FIGURE 6-25 The human heart is not symmetrical—its left side is larger. The right ventricle's less muscular walls are strong enough to push blood around the nearby lungs. Pushing blood through the much larger systemic-cardiac circuit, however, requires much more strength. This is provided by the much thicker muscle in the walls of the left ventricle.

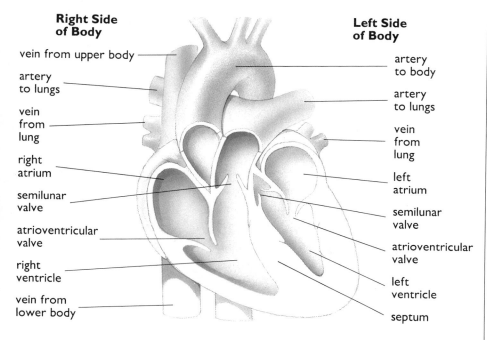

Right Side of Body

vein from upper body

artery to lungs

vein from lung

right atrium

semilunar valve

atrioventricular valve

right ventricle

vein from lower body

Left Side of Body

artery to body

artery to lungs

vein from lung

left atrium

semilunar valve

atrioventricular valve

left ventricle

septum

inflow of blood from the major veins. (See Figure 6-26a.) Once the atria are filled to their stretching point, they contract, forcing blood through the **atrioventricular valves** into the ventricles. (See Figure 6-26b.) These one-way valve gates remain open, and blood continues to flow through until the ventricles reach their stretching point. Then the ventricles contract sharply. (See Figure 6-26c.) The blood inside them pushes outward, forcing the atrioventricular valves to close. (See Figure 6-26d.) This action causes the "lub" sound.

For an instant, the ventricle chambers are completely closed. However, ventricular contraction continues, so that the blood inside exerts an even greater outward pressure on the muscular walls. This pressure shuts the one-way atrioventricular valves even more firmly, but forces the **semilunar valves** open. (See Figure 6-26e.) Because of its high pressure, the blood rushes through these one-way valves into the arteries. When the ventricle starts to relax, the greater pressure of the blood in the arteries forces the semilunar valves shut. This action causes the "dup" sound. The heart valves have now returned to their original state shown in Figure 6-26a.

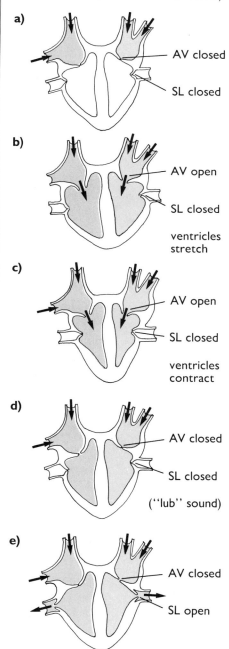

FIGURE 6-26 In this figure, the vessels leading to and from the heart have been "straightened out" so the sequence of valve action can be seen clearly. You can see that blood flows into the atria at all times. (AV = atrioventricular valve; SL = semilunar valve.)

a)
AV closed
SL closed

b)
AV open
SL closed
ventricles stretch

c)
AV open
SL closed
ventricles contract

d)
AV closed
SL closed
("lub" sound)

e)
AV closed
SL open

The alternating cycle of contraction and relaxation keeps the blood circulating around the body, through the heart, around the lungs, and back through the heart again. The blood's route through the body and the lungs is revealed by the pattern of vessels you saw in Figure 6-8. However, the heart's closely packed arrangement of chambers and vessels makes it difficult to follow the blood's route through the heart itself. The "route map" in Figure 6-27 should help you to understand the following description.

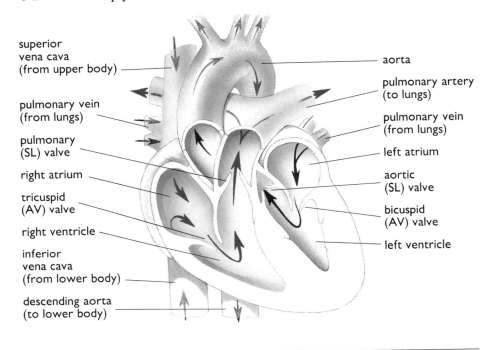

FIGURE 6-27 The flow of blood through the human heart

superior
vena cava
(from upper body)

pulmonary vein
(from lungs)

pulmonary
(SL) valve

right atrium

tricuspid
(AV) valve

right ventricle

inferior
vena cava
(from lower body)

descending aorta
(to lower body)

aorta

pulmonary artery
(to lungs)

pulmonary vein
(from lungs)

left atrium

aortic
(SL) valve

bicuspid
(AV) valve

left ventricle

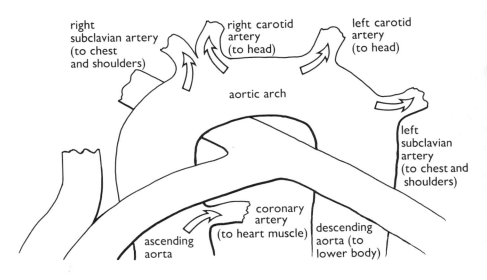

FIGURE 6-28 Several arteries branch upward from the aorta to carry freshly pumped blood toward upper body.

right
subclavian artery
(to chest
and shoulders)

right carotid
artery
(to head)

left carotid
artery
(to head)

aortic arch

left
subclavian
artery
(to chest and
shoulders)

coronary
artery
(to heart muscle)

ascending
aorta

descending
aorta (to
lower body)

Deoxygenated blood enters the right atrium through the **superior vena cava** (the major vein from the head and the upper part of the body), and the **inferior vena cava** (the major vein from the legs and the lower part of the body). As the right atrium contracts, blood passes through the **tricuspid valve** (right-hand atrioventricular valve) into the right ventricle. From the right ventricle, blood is pumped out through the **pulmonary semilunar valve** into the **pulmonary artery** and on to the lungs. There the waste carbon dioxide diffuses out as fresh supplies of oxygen diffuse in.

Oxygenated blood from the lungs returns through the **pulmonary vein** to the left atrium, which pumps the blood through the **bicuspid valve** into the left ventricle. From the left ventricle, blood is pumped out through the **aortic semilunar valve** into the aorta. The aorta's branching arteries carry the oxygenated blood throughout the body. (See Figure 6-28.)

You have probably heard of the jugular vein. It carries blood from the head to the superior vena cava.

LABORATORY EXERCISE 6-5
Anatomy of a Mammalian Heart

The hearts of all other mammals have the same basic structural features as the human heart, and they function in much the same way. In this exercise, you will examine a nonhuman mammalian heart (or a model), and draw a diagram to illustrate its structure and function. You will also compare its features with those of the representative vertebrate you examined in Laboratory Exercise 6-2. (If your representative vertebrate *was* a mammal, you will examine the heart of *another* class of vertebrate and make the same type of comparison.)

Blood Pressure

Continuous contraction by the heart's ventricles, at an average rate of 70 beats per minute, maintains a high pressure in the blood that enters the body's main arteries. The pressure is so great that a cut artery can spurt blood up to a metre away. But two factors operate to reduce the pressure as blood travels away from the heart. The first is frictional resistance from blood vessel walls. The second is the ever-increasing area blood encounters as it spreads into the smaller but more numerous vessels. By the time blood reaches the capillaries, it is spread across an area 700 times that of the aorta, and its pressure is very low. (See Figure 6-29.) This is why blood merely oozes from a pinprick or a small gash that does not cut an artery.

High pressure in the arteries ensures that blood is moved to all parts of the body. Low pressure in the capillaries ensures that tissue fluids have time to exchange materials with the cells. Low pressure in the veins ensures that venous blood will not be forced back into the capillaries. (The veins also have

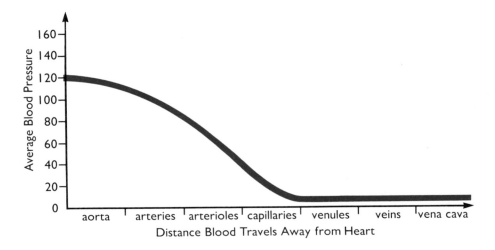

FIGURE 6-29 How blood pressure changes as blood travels away from the heart

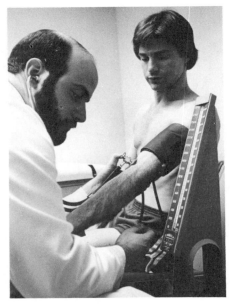

Measuring blood pressure with a sphygmomanometer. Notice the pressure gauge.

Until recently, sphygmomanometers were connected to mercury tubes that measured the blood pressure. These tubes were awkward to use and posed a toxic waste problem if they were broken. Today, mechanical or electrical gauges have replaced them, but blood pressure is still measured in mm Hg (millimetres of mercury).

one-way valves that prevent back flow.) Even when the rate at which blood is circulated increases sharply, the veins can maintain their low pressure by expanding to hold excess blood until the heart can handle it. Expansion is possible because the veins have little elastic tissue.

Since pressure in the capillaries and the veins is always low, doctors measure blood pressure in the arteries. Blood pressure readings always include two numbers. For example, normal resting blood pressure for an average healthy individual is 120 over 80 or 120/80. The higher number is always given first. It represents the **systolic pressure,** which is the pressure of arterial blood when the ventricles contract. The lower number represents the **diastolic pressure,** which is the pressure exerted by the arterial blood while the ventricles are relaxed.

The instrument used to measure blood pressure is called a sphygmomanometer. To use it, a doctor or a nurse tightens a band around a patient's arm, places a stethoscope above a nearby artery, and slowly releases the band. The pressure gauge is read twice: once when a pounding sound made by the contracting ventricles is first heard (systole), and again when the ventricles relax and the pounding sound stops (diastole).

Blood pressure readings are taken because their values have great significance for human health. Readings greatly above or below the normal range are a cause for concern. High blood pressure causes damage to the brain, the kidneys, the blood vessels, and the heart itself. The heart must work much harder to pump out blood against the high pressure of blood already present in the arteries. High pressure can also weaken blood vessel walls, so that they may bulge or even rupture. The bursting of blood vessels can damage the delicate tissues of body organs such as the kidneys. Ruptured vessels in the heart cause heart attacks. Ruptured vessels in the brain cause strokes. The exact cause of high blood pressure is not known, but it can usually be controlled by diet and medication.

II ANIMALS

Low blood pressure may result from large blood losses due to an injury or as a result of surgery. This condition is called shock. Prompt treatment is essential to prevent vital organs such as the brain from being permanently damaged due to a lack of oxygen. Any ailment such as a severe allergic reaction that lowers blood pressure severely can result in shock.

Heart Rate and Homeostasis

The normal rate at which your heart beats when it is resting is set by the **pacemaker,** or sinoatrial node, a cluster of specialized nerve cells in the right atrium. The pacemaker sends out a wave-like electrical impulse that stimulates both atria to contract. It also stimulates a second cell cluster called the **atrioventricular node (AV node).** The AV node sends out new impulses that stimulate both ventricles to contract. (See Figure 6-30.)

Normally, the average heart beats about 70 times per minute, but it can pump faster or slower according to the circulatory needs of the body. Two sets of nerves lead to the pacemaker from a control centre in the brain. One set speeds up the heart rate while the other set slows it down. Your heart rate also responds to adrenaline, a hormone or body chemical released by glands near the kidneys whenever the brain perceives an emergency situation that will require increased blood flow. (You will learn more about the nervous control and chemical regulation of heart rate in Chapter 8.)

An artificial pacemaker can be used if the body's own pacemaker fails. There are two types: the fixed pacemaker, which emits a set number of impulses per minute, and the demand pacemaker that varies with cardiovascular demands.

DID YOU KNOW?

Fibrillation is a term physicians use to describe irregular and chaotic contractions of the heart muscle. The atria, for example, may contract as many as 300 times per minute when fibrillating. Prolonged fibrillation must be treated quickly by applying controlled impulses from an external electrical source. Otherwise, death will result.

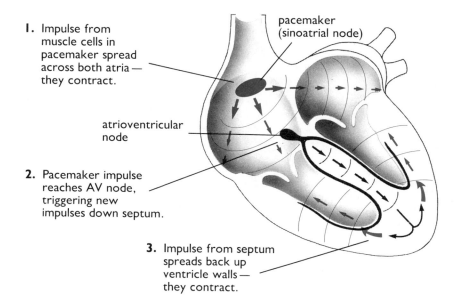

I. Impulse from muscle cells in pacemaker spread across both atria — they contract.

pacemaker (sinoatrial node)

atrioventricular node

2. Pacemaker impulse reaches AV node, triggering new impulses down septum.

3. Impulse from septum spreads back up ventricle walls — they contract.

FIGURE 6-30 How the pacemaker sets heart rate. Impulses travel down the septum and back up the ventricles by way of specialized muscle cells called Purkinje's fibres.

New Techniques in Heart Surgery

Although heart disease remains the most common cause of death in Canada, it is no longer on the rise. Since 1950, the number of people killed yearly by heart disease, hypertension, and stroke has dropped from 410 to 310 per 100 000. New surgical techniques have contributed to the decrease in heart-disease mortality. Percutaneous transluminal coronary angioplasty is one of the more effective of these techniques.

The major cause of heart disease, atherosclerosis, is caused by a buildup of cholesterol and other fatty material along the inner walls of heart-blood vessels. These deposits, called plaque, narrow the vessels, making it difficult for oxygen-carrying blood to flow. Heart-muscle cells that are deprived of oxygen eventually die, impairing heart function.

Three different conditions may result from the death of heart-muscle cells, depending on the location and extent of blood-flow restriction. In angina, small areas of damage cause heart pain. Arteriosclerotic heart disease is caused by widespread, low-level damage. The most serious consequence of atherosclerosis, the heart attack, is caused by a severe reduction in blood flow to the heart, which is usually the result of a blood clot in the plaque of the coronary artery.

In severe cases of heart disease, transplantation is the only way to save the patient. Angioplasty provides a less traumatic solution in less serious circumstances. A flexible tube called a catheter is inserted through a skin incision into an artery. The catheter is then manoeuvred through the circulatory system until it reaches the section of artery narrowed by plaque. Here, a balloon at the end of the catheter is inflated, which squeezes the plaque against the arterial wall,

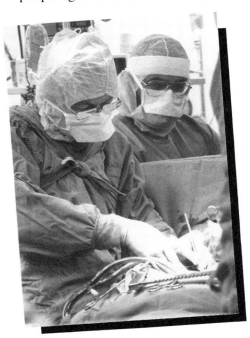

widening the passage available for blood flow.

The advantage of angioplasty is that blood flow in the coronary artery is increased without major surgery. It can be an effective preventive measure because narrowed arteries can be widened before the risk of heart attack becomes high. In fact, angioplasty is most often used to relieve angina, which results from only partial blockage of blood vessels. Researchers are now developing methods for equipping angioplasty catheters with lasers to open holes in total blockages. Once a hole is produced, conventional angioplasty can be performed to increase the size of the hole.

Between 1984 and 1986, use of angioplasty tripled. According to one researcher, by the end of 1986 the procedure was successfully increasing blood flow in 94.4% of all cases. Regardless of the increasing success of angioplasty and other surgical procedures, reparative techniques are not as effective as prevention, and our reliance on them should be decreased. Lifestyle plays an important part in the development of heart disease. If people exercise and avoid harmful habits such as smoking and eating foods high in saturated fats and salt, the incidence of heart disease will fall dramatically.

Section Review Questions

1. Identify the heart valve that separates
    a) the pulmonary artery and the right ventricle
    b) the left atrium and the left ventricle.
2. List the steps necessary for a heartbeat to occur.
3. a) Why is blood pressure higher in the arteries than in the capillaries and veins?
    b) Why is it important that the pressure in the capillaries be lower?
4. Define the terms systolic pressure and diastolic pressure.
5. a) Why are the artery walls always pulsating?
    b) What causes this pulsation?

6.4   Transport in Other Animals

The common function of all animal transport systems is to circulate blood throughout the body so that each cell obtains a share of the nutrients and oxygen consumed by the organism. In nonhuman vertebrates, blood circulates through a closed network of tube-like vessels much like the human circulatory system. The major difference in vertebrate systems is the complexity of the heart that pumps the blood.

INQUIRY ACTIVITY
A Comparative Study of Vertebrate Hearts

While vertebrate hearts all perform the same basic function in a transport system, they may differ in design and structure. In this activity, you will examine a variety of vertebrate hearts and comment on their different structures.

Discussion Questions

1. Which heart in Figure 6-31 (see next page) is most similar to a human heart?
2. a) Which hearts keep oxygenated blood separate from deoxygenated blood?
    b) What would the advantage be in having oxygenated blood pumped through the heart?
3. Which of the hearts would be most efficient? Most inefficient? State reasons for your answers.

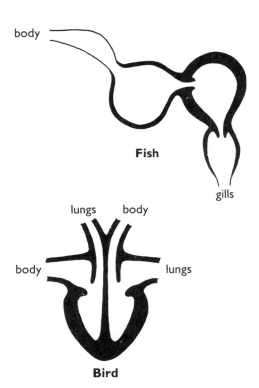

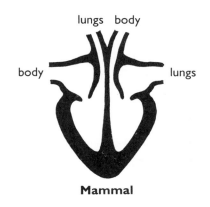

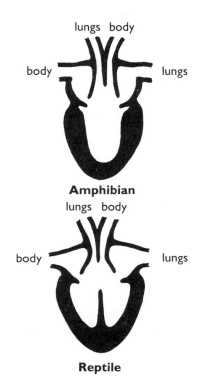

FIGURE 6-31 Comparative anatomy of vertebrate hearts

4. Some vertebrate hearts mix oxygenated and deoxygenated blood. How would this affect the efficiency of the circulatory system? Explain.

5. Explain how the efficiency of the heart is often paralleled with the size and complexity of the vertebrate organism.

Invertebrate Transport Systems

Some small invertebrates do not require a complex circulatory system with vessels, blood, and a heart. A simple sponge, for example, takes in water through its pores, and cilia circulate fresh water past its cells. Nutrients and oxygen diffuse inward while waste products diffuse outward. Circulation in the hydra, a cnidarian, is similar. (See Figure 6-32.) Neither a sponge nor a hydra needs blood to transport materials, but most more complex animals do.

The earthworm, for example, has several muscular heart chambers (aortic arches) that pump its blood through a ventral blood vessel to its body cells. (See Figure 6-33.) Blood returns to the heart by way of a dorsal blood vessel. This system is called a **closed circulatory system** because blood remains inside the vessels or the heart of the animal at all times. Plasma may leave the capillaries and enter the tissue spaces, but the red blood cells stay inside the vessels or heart chambers. Closed circulatory systems are considered to be

The earthworm's hearts are really muscular chambers connecting the two main vessels.

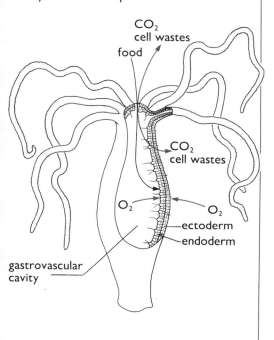

FIGURE 6-32 Like the planarian in Figure 6-2, the hydra is only three cell layers thick and needs no specialized system for transport.

CO₂
cell wastes
food

CO₂
cell wastes

O₂   O₂
                      ectoderm
                      endoderm
gastrovascular
cavity

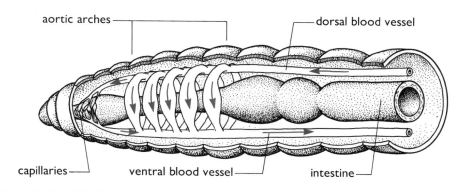

FIGURE 6-33 How does blood flow through the aortic arches of the earthworm?

aortic arches   dorsal blood vessel

capillaries   ventral blood vessel   intestine

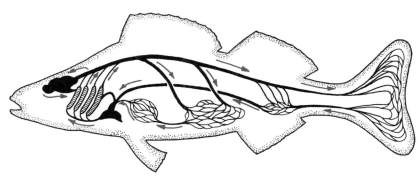

FIGURE 6-34 Fish and all other vertebrates have a closed circulatory system, which actively moves blood through vessels throughout all parts of the body. As a result, the cells are continuously exposed to fresh supplies of blood.

efficient because all of the blood circulates near body cells almost all of the time. (See Figure 6-34.) This means that nutrients, gases, and wastes can be exchanged frequently. But despite these advantages, only 10% of all animal species have closed circulatory systems. These species include all vertebrates and a very small number of invertebrates.

All other invertebrate species have **open circulatory systems.** Examples of these species include all members of the phylum Arthropoda: lobsters, spiders, crabs, scorpions, and insects. Figure 6-35 illustrates the open circulatory system of a grasshopper. The circuit of tubes and vessels is incomplete, and the circulating fluid pours out of the tubes into the body cavity. This forms slow-moving pools of blood that bathe the animal's tissues and exchange materials with the cells, but at a much slower rate than occurs in a closed circulatory system. Continued pumping by the animal's heart or hearts (there are often several), eventually brings the pooled blood back into the tubes and the cycle continues.

You might expect that the slow rate of an open circulatory system would be a great disadvantage for air-breathers, especially large ones. It is not a problem for insects, however, partly because they are small, and partly because an insect's blood functions primarily to deliver nutrients and to collect

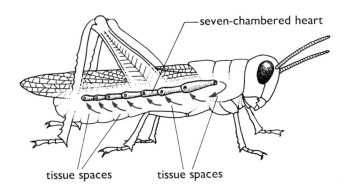

FIGURE 6-35 Grasshoppers, all other arthropods, and many other invertebrates have open circulatory systems. Pooled blood moves sluggishly through the spaces between the cells that lie above the long, seven-chambered heart.

seven-chambered heart

tissue spaces   tissue spaces

cell wastes. Insects transport oxygen molecules through a separate system of air tubes and not through the circulatory system.

Observing open circulatory systems by the same methods you would use to investigate closed circulatory systems is difficult. Because the circuit is incomplete, dissecting a preserved specimen reveals little of how the system actually works in a living animal.

LABORATORY EXERCISE 6-6
Investigating an Open Circulatory System

In this exercise, you will observe the structures of an open circulatory system in a crayfish. The crayfish is a ten-legged crustacean. It plays an important role in aquatic ecosystems.

Section Review Questions

1. Explain the difference between an open and a closed circulatory system.
2. Why is the closed circulatory system considered to be more efficient than the open circulatory system?
3. A sponge is like a living filter that circulates water internally. In what way is water circulation in the sponge similar to blood circulation in more complex animals?
4. In most organisms, oxygen is dissolved in the blood and transported by the circulatory system. How does the transport of oxygen in insects differ?
5. Large organisms could not exist with an open circulatory system. Explain why.

On February 16, 1986, animal-rights activists broke into a laboratory at the University of Toronto to free test animals being used by researchers. Although the activists were unsuccessful, they left spray-painted messages accusing Dr. Barry Sessle, the school's assistant dean, of torturing animals in his studies on tooth pain.

Acts of vandalism and violence have occurred wherever animals are being used in medical research. In 1987, nine British members of the Animal Liberation Front, an international animal-rights organization, were sentenced to prison for raiding research labs and fire-bombing a department store that sold furs. Although violence in support of animal rights is unusual, the debate over animal testing and research evokes strong emotions.

In Canada, approximately two million animals are used in medical research every year. Most researchers consider this necessary because some important medical studies can only be carried out on live subjects. Animals can be used to study systems, measure the effectiveness and side effects of drugs, and perfect surgical techniques, without risking human lives. Because mammalian physiology is similar to human physiology, knowledge gained from these tests can often be applied to humans.

Animals and Medical Research

Animal testing and research in the field of heart physiology has a long and successful history. Frog hearts were used to discover the link between the autonomic nervous system and the control of heart function. Horses were the subjects of early blood pressure studies. The link between diet and atherosclerosis was first established in rabbits. Pioneering work on the heart-lung machine was

done with dogs. Animal tissues can even be transplanted into humans. Pig-heart valves, for example, sometimes replace damaged human valves.

Animal-rights activists are concerned that animal testing is cruel and painful, despite government regulations designed to protect test animals. According to animal-rights activists, animals' social instincts and ability to feel pain are ignored by researchers, so animals are tortured in the lab. Confinement is a form of torture for some animals, because animals need open spaces to maintain their emotional health. Even though regulations prohibit inflicting pain on test animals, many experiments still produce degrees of discomfort and disorientation.

Because the use of animals in research is taken for granted, activists claim that animals are killed in trivial research. Researchers, they say, rarely explore alternatives to animal testing or approach their research with an eye to minimizing animal suffering.

Some believe animal lives should be treated with the same respect as human lives. However, most Canadians (84 % according to a 1987 Gallup poll) approve of animal testing if there is a reasonable chance of future benefit to humans. What is your opinion? Should animals be tested and even killed to save human lives?

6.5 Factors Affecting Cardiovascular Health

The heart and the blood vessels are called the **cardiovascular system** by most health and fitness experts. The cardiovascular system is a good indicator of overall body health because its performance is easy to measure. Like your breathing rate, your heart rate naturally increases during exercise in response to an increased need for oxygen by your muscle cells. Also, your heart rate, like your breathing rate, reflects your internal state.

Cardiovascular Health and Personal Choice

"Heart disease clearly begins in childhood," says Dr. Gerald Berenson, a New Orleans cardiologist. His research shows that those who are likely to have a heart attack later in life can be identified when they are as young as 6 months of age. Dr. Berenson recommends early testing of all children so those found to be at risk can be educated about good health habits in time to prevent damage. It is especially important for susceptible individuals to avoid smoking and dietary fats, and to exercise regularly.

Aerobic exercise is important for maintaining a healthy cardiovascular system.

Some people are predisposed to cardiovascular problems such as high blood pressure, blood clots, or heart attacks caused by the blockage of blood vessels, especially in the coronary artery. These people benefit from early detection, enabling them to modify their behaviour and increase their chance of living a normal lifespan. People with no family history of heart problems should also assess their cardiovascular health. Heart attacks and related cardiovascular disorders are the leading cause of death in North America. Many of these deaths could have been prevented because cardiovascular disease develops slowly over many years.

Exercise is a good way to help prevent heart disease. It has a positive effect on blood circulation, both through your heart and through the rest of your body. Many heart attack victims lead a sedentary life with little physical activity. Like all muscles, the heart becomes flabby if it doesn't do enough work. Exercise stimulates the heart and the control centres in the brain that regulate heartbeat. A carefully planned exercise program increases blood flow through the heart and the volume of blood pumped per beat. Ultimately, exercise can reduce your resting heart rate, so your heart doesn't have to work as hard. Exercise also increases the rate and depth of your breathing, making more oxygen available to all muscles, including your heart. A sensible exercise program helps to build a stronger, healthier heart.

Another factor affecting cardiovascular health is diet. For example, a diet low in fat and salt may inhibit the formation of cholesterol deposits that narrow major blood vessels. Diet can also help control high blood pressure. Statistics indicate that only half of the people with high blood pressure know that they have it. These individuals are unaware of the risk they run by consuming fatty and salty foods.

A sensible diet can also help reduce excess body mass. Overweight people put stress on their cardiovascular systems in several ways. Every extra kilogram of fat increases the total length of the blood vessels through which blood must be pushed every time the heart beats. In addition, the heart has to do more work for any activity simply because the skeletal muscles must exert more force to move the body around. Finally, the diets of overweight people are usually high in fats and salt, foods that clog arteries and block blood flow.

Alcohol consumption can also affect cardiovascular health because it causes an abnormal heartbeat. This abnormal heartbeat is accompanied by a decrease in the pumping force of the heart. The ethyl alcohol in an alcoholic beverage is absorbed into the bloodstream, primarily in the small intestines. Once the ethyl alcohol is in the bloodstream, it starts to affect all body cells. The liver takes in and chemically breaks down the ethyl alcohol into usable body energy. Excess levels of alcohol that cannot be metabolized by the liver circulate in the bloodstream. The circulation of alcohol in the bloodstream causes vasodilatation, which is the opening of blood capillaries and a slowing down of brain activity. Alcohol acts as a depressant, causing a reduction in thought processes, judgement, and self-control.

Cigarette smoking presents a double threat to cardiovascular health. The carbon monoxide in tobacco smoke binds to the hemoglobin in red blood cells more quickly and more effectively than oxygen. This reduces the amount of oxygen the blood can carry, and a smoker's heart rate speeds up to compensate.

The best conditioning for an already fit cardiovascular system is aerobic exercise. Swimming, bicycling, cross-country skiing, and running are four examples. Those who are "out of shape" should consult a physician before embarking on an exercise program.

DID YOU KNOW?
The heart of a long-distance runner can increase its pumping capacity to five or six times its output at rest.

People with high blood pressure should not eat french fries.

Within 2 min of consuming an alcoholic beverage, about 20% of the ethyl alcohol is quickly absorbed into the blood by way of the stomach lining.

25 FILTER CIGARETTES KING SIZE

Smoking reduces life expectancy

25 CIGARETTES KING SIZE

Smoking during pregnancy can harm the baby

25 CIGARETTES · KING SIZE

Smoking is the major cause of lung cancer

Many smokers do not take the health warnings on cigarette packages seriously.

The nicotine in tobacco smoke dissolves in the plasma, causing an immediate constriction of the blood vessels. The narrowing of blood vessels, or vasoconstriction, causes both increased blood pressure and increased heart rate. Smokers are much more likely than nonsmokers to develop high blood pressure and other cardiovascular problems. Many insurance companies now charge smokers a higher premium for life insurance because they may die early from smoking-related disorders. (See Figure 6-36.)

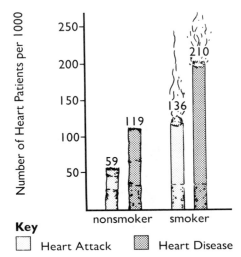

RESEARCH PROJECT
Diseases and Disorders of the Transport System

Choose a disease or disorder from the following list. Your teacher may also have suggestions. Gather information about the cause, symptoms, and possible treatment for the disease or disorder you have selected. Present your findings in a poster, a short essay, or a brief talk as suggested by your teacher.

- sickle cell anemia
- pernicious anemia
- iron deficiency anemia
- leukemia
- hemophilia
- mononucleosis
- Hodgkin's disease
- aneurysm
- dropsy
- hypertension
- phlebitis
- cerebral thrombosis
- elephantiasis
- septicemia

The Interaction of the Transport System with Other Systems

The cardiovascular system is linked to all other body systems and especially to the gas-exchange system. However, if one body system does not function properly, another must work harder. Because of the extra work, the second system may develop problems, too. For example, overly rapid heart rates often result from the overly rapid breathing rates associated with lung disorders. Such disorders reduce the ability of the lungs to dispose of carbon dioxide. Increased levels of this waste gas trigger the brain's breathing centre and also stimulate chemical receptors in the blood vessels. The increased heart rate helps to dispose of the waste gas and restores homeostasis.

However, blood must also carry wastes that cannot be disposed of at the lungs. These materials must be carried by the circulatory system to another system of organs that can remove waste molecules from the blood. In Chapter 7, you will examine the excretory system, which specializes in removing these wastes.

Section Review Questions

1. How does aerobic exercise improve cardiovascular health?
2. What are three risk factors associated with heart and vascular problems?
3. Explain what vasoconstriction is and how it affects blood pressure. What avoidable factors cause vasoconstriction?

Chapter Review

Key Words

aorta
antibodies
arteries
arterioles
atria
blood
capillaries
closed circulatory
  system
erythrocytes
heart
hemoglobin
inferior vena cava
leukocytes

lymph
lymphatic system
open circulatory
  system
pacemaker
phagocytes
plasma
platelets
pulmonary artery
pulmonary vein
superior vena cava
veins
ventricles
venules

Recall Questions

Multiple Choice

1. Albumin, fibrinogen, and globulins are found in the
   a) platelets
   b) red blood cells
   c) plasma
   d) white blood cells

2. Waste-laden blood coming from the capillaries flows into the
   a) arterioles
   b) venules
   c) arteries
   d) veins

3. The engulfing of bacteria, or phagocytosis, is performed by
   a) platelets
   b) plasma
   c) erythrocytes
   d) leukocytes

4. A person with AB negative blood requires a blood transfusion. Which of the following blood types would a donor have to be?
   a) AB positive
   b) A negative
   c) B positive
   d) O negative

5. The movement of blood from the left atrium to the left ventricle means the blood has to pass through the
   a) aortic semilunar valve
   b) tricuspid valve
   c) pulmonary semilunar valve
   d) bicuspid valve

6. The "dup" sound for the heartbeat is attributed to
   a) the opening of the semilunar valves
   b) the closing of the semilunar valves
   c) the opening of the atrioventricular valves
   d) the closing of the atrioventricular valves

7. Erythroblastosis fetalis results from
   a) low platelet count
   b) protein deficiency in the plasma
   c) Rh incompatibility
   d) abnormally high white blood cell count

8. An open circulation system is found in
   a) earthworms
   b) humans
   c) spiders
   d) birds

9. The iron protein found in the erythrocyte is called
   a) globulin
   b) thrombocytes
   c) hemoglobin
   d) lymph

Fill in the Blanks

1. The heart and the blood vessels are part of the _____ system.

2. The _____ divides the human heart into a left and a right side.

3. The filtering units of the lymphatic system are called _____.

4. _____ are one of the major blood components responsible for initiating blood clot formations.

5. _____ is the pressure of arterial blood when the heart ventricles contract.

6. The _____ is a specialized group of nerve cells in the wall of the right atrium that initiates each heartbeat.

7. Excess circulation of alcohol in the bloodstream causes _____, which is the opening of blood capillaries.

8. The _____ is the major vein that returns blood to the right atrium from the head and the upper body parts.

9. A _____ is an instrument used to hear heart sounds.

Short Answers

1. Briefly describe how blood flow, blood pressure, and heart contractions are synchronized in the human body.

2. Blood clots can be life saving, but how can they also be life threatening?

3. The human heart is very asymmetrical. Why are the chambers and walls so different in size and thickness?

4. What threat would arteries pose if they were too close to the skin's surface? Briefly explain your answer.

5. List the major components of blood and state one major function of each.

6. The three major blood vessels are arteries, capillaries, and veins. How does the structure of each vessel suit it for performing its specific function?

7. The human heart is really two hearts in one. Clearly explain this statement.

8. Larger, more complex organisms require a closed circulatory system rather than an open circulatory system. Explain why.

Application Questions

1. You should never exert yourself physically after consuming a large meal. Explain why doing so could threaten your circulatory system.

2. The adenoids and the tonsils are examples of lymph tissue that can be removed if necessary. What is the function of these structures, and why can you live without them?

3. Why is hypertension called the "silent killer"?

4. Why is an inflammation site often warm, red, swollen, and painful?

Problem Solving

1. On a cold winter day, a person is sitting in a hot tub, smoking a cigarette, and drinking a martini. Explain in detail what might be occurring in this person's circulatory system.

2. Red blood cells usually perform their function in the blood, while white blood cells perform their function in the blood or in body tissue. Explain why there is a difference.

3. "Blood doping" is a controversial method of enhancing performance by removing blood from an athlete a week or so before an athletic event. Prior to the event, the athlete receives a transfusion of his or her blood. Blood doping can provide an unfair advantage. Explain why.

4. The liver is an important glandular organ that performs as many as 500 different body functions daily. What are five functions of the liver that are related to the transport system?

5. Blood clots are often formed after surgery. Why would a blood clot form at this time? What could be done to help prevent the formation of blood clots?

Extensions

1. Contact the Red Cross and investigate the following questions. Write a summary of your findings.
   a) How is blood processed into its different components?
   b) How is each blood component used?
   c) How long can blood components be stored?
   d) How are prospective donors screened for antibodies?

2. A coronary by-pass has become a common surgical method to correct cardiovascular problems. Research this treatment and write a report covering the following questions.
   a) Which vessels are surgically removed?
   b) Which vessels can be used as replacements? How?
   c) How does this corrective surgery save lives?
   d) Are there any controversies surrounding this treatment?
   e) What advances are being made?

3. Cholesterol is often linked to high blood pressure and cardiovascular problems. Write a report about cholesterol after examining the following questions.
   a) What is cholesterol?
   b) What are the different types of cholesterol?
   c) What specifically is its function in the body?
   d) How can cholesterol levels in the blood be controlled?

CHAPTER

7

Excretion

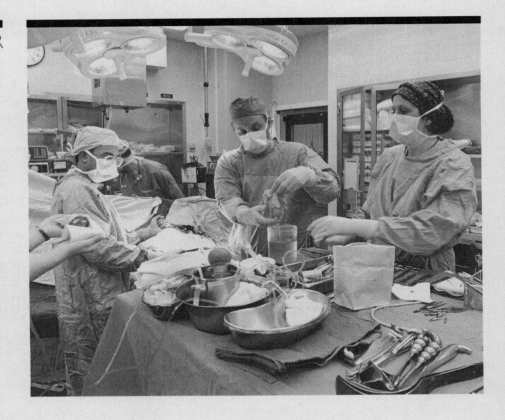

After the devastating 1988 earthquake in Armenia, a call went around the world to provide emergency supplies for the survivors. Dialysis machines were among the essential items needed to keep some survivors alive. Severe shocks to the body such as those experienced in an earthquake can cause temporary renal failure. Renal failure occurs when the kidneys no longer function.

Untreated renal failure, whether temporary or chronic, is inevitably fatal. As recently as fifty years ago, many people died because no treatment was available. When we realize how completely we depend on the proper functioning of an essential organ such as our kidneys, we realize how vulnerable our bodies are to dangers around us. At the same time, we are equally vulnerable to the dangers within us.

There are a multitude of toxins within our bodies at any one time. Urea, a waste product of protein decomposition, is toxic and must be excreted from the body as quickly and efficiently as possible. We also frequently ingest toxins. If all the caffeine in a cup of coffee were absorbed into our bloodstream, it would kill us. Fortunately, caffeine is not easily absorbed by the body and most of the caffeine is excreted. You may notice that after drinking large quantities of caffeinated drinks, you actually get more thirsty. This is because your body needs water to dilute and flush the caffeine into your kidneys.

Excreting harmful substances from our bodies is one critical function that our kidneys perform. An equally critical function is to maintain a precise balance between the multitude of substances in our body fluids. Regardless of how much milk you drink, the calcium levels in your blood are always about 1 pp 10 000; a drop of 0.5 pp 10 000 would kill you. In spite of food binges or diets, blood glucose levels are typically 7 pp 10 000. A steady level of 12 pp 10 000 makes you diabetic, causing numerous health problems. A drop to 3 pp 10 000 could threaten your life.

Most of us take for granted that the major organs of our bodies function properly. Yet in Canada today, there are over 9000 people with end-stage renal failure, which means that these people have less than 10% of normal kidney function. They are alive today because treatment in the form of constant dialysis treatment or kidney transplants is available. Almost 5000 patients require some form of weekly dialysis treatments. The remaining 48% have had kidney transplants.

However, roughly 11% of Canadians who receive dialysis treatment choose to die every year because they voluntarily discontinue dialysis treatment. This fact suggests that there is still much to be done to improve the life of these people.

The kidney transplant is the best treatment for most patients. Fortunately, kidney transplants are among the most successful of all organ transplants. There would be even more transplant recipients if more kidneys were available.

There are approximately 1200 Canadians on a waiting list for a kidney at any time. If there are no emergencies, a kidney will be given to the recipient whose body-tissue type most closely matches that of the available kidney. The closer the match, the less risk there is that the recipient's body will reject the kidney. Once the threat of rejection is overcome, a transplanted kidney will function as if it were the original.

Chapter Objectives

When you complete this chapter, you should:

1. Appreciate the need for homeostatic mechanisms in living organisms.
2. Be able to describe homeostasis and explain its importance in the body.
3. Be able to explain the processes of osmosis, diffusion, and active transport in living cells, and relate these processes to the formation of urine in the nephron.
4. Be able to explain the term excretion and how excretion occurs in the lung, skin, colon, and kidney.
5. Be able to describe the structure of the human kidney and nephron.
6. Be able to describe briefly how and why urea is formed in the liver.
7. Be able to describe how urine is eliminated from the body.
8. Be able to explain how concentrations of water, salts, and other chemicals are regulated, and how homeostasis is maintained by the excretory system in humans.
9. Understand the excretory process in humans and its role in maintaining homeostasis in the human body.
10. Recognize the relationship between the excretory process of different vertebrates and the environmental conditions under which they live.
11. Be able to compare the excretory systems of a freshwater fish, a marine fish, a reptile, and a desert mammal, and describe how the excretory process of each animal is adapted to its environment.
12. Be able to research and report on the causes, the effects, and the treatments for several diseases and disorders of the human excretory system.
13. Be able to describe the influence of chemicals such as alcohol on the process of water reabsorption by the nephron.
14. Know how to dissect, identify, draw, and describe the parts of vertebrate excretory systems.

Homeostasis and Regulation in Animal Cells

FIGURE 7-1 The pH of human blood in relation to the pH of some common foods and household products

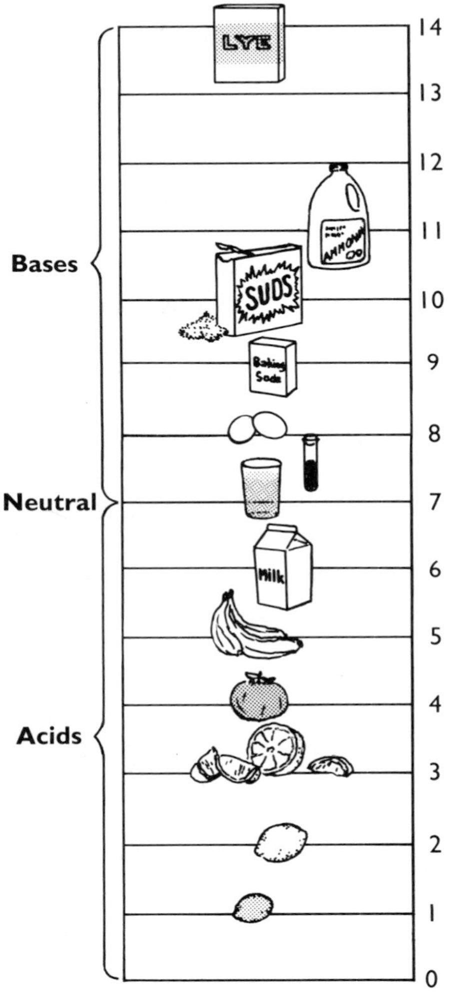

The pH scale indicates the strength of acids or bases on a scale ranging from 0 (extremely acidic) to 14 (extremely basic). Pure water has a pH of 7, which means it is chemically neutral. A pH of 7.4 means that normal blood is very slightly basic.

Homeostasis is the process by which living organisms maintain a stable internal environment. For example, birds and mammals must maintain a constant internal temperature, even though temperature conditions in their external environment may vary from day to day or hour to hour. The chemical composition of body fluids such as cell cytoplasm, extracellular fluid, and blood must also be maintained within narrow limits. For example, human blood has a pH of about 7.4. (See Figure 7-1.) Beyond a range of pH 7.0 to 7.8, proteins such as hemoglobin may become inactive, drastically reducing the oxygen-carrying capacity of red blood cells.

To maintain a constant internal environment, every animal, from the smallest invertebrate to the largest vertebrate, must regulate the inflow and outflow of material from its body. In humans, homeostasis involves several body systems. The respiratory, digestive, and circulatory systems work together to supply the raw materials for cell reactions such as respiration. As cell metabolism uses up these materials, more must be provided to keep the chemical composition of body fluids constant.

Cell metabolism also produces unwanted waste products that become dissolved in the cytoplasm. These wastes interfere with normal cell activity, and may even cause death if they are allowed to accumulate.

In most vertebrates, metabolic wastes are disposed of by excretion. **Excretion** involves two main steps: first, separating dissolved wastes from body fluids, and second, removing the wastes from the body.

Excretion is sometimes confused with elimination, but the two processes are quite different. In humans, elimination is the process that removes undigested materials from the large intestine. Because these solid wastes never leave the digestive tube, they can be eliminated simply by egesting them through the anus. Excretion, however, must remove dissolved metabolic wastes from cells throughout the internal environment. In humans, excreting such wastes involves dissolving them in urine and then draining them from the body. Before this can happen, however, the wastes must first leave the cell cytoplasm and enter the blood.

How Materials Enter and Leave Cells

The movement of materials into and out of cells is called **cell transport**. Biologists recognize two types of cell transport: passive transport and active transport.

Passive transport refers to the natural spreading out of mobile molecules from regions of high concentration to regions of low concentration. The diffusion of molecules such as glucose from the bloodstream into the extracellular fluid and then into body cells is an example of passive transport. The term passive is used because no energy from the cell is needed to move the materials. The molecules spread out because of their own random motions and collisions. (See Figure 7-2.)

In fact, the cell membrane has very little control over passive transport. Both the rate and direction of diffusion are determined by concentration. Biologists say that dissolved glucose follows a **concentration gradient** as it diffuses into body cells. (See Figure 7-3.) A concentration gradient for glucose develops because cell mitochondria constantly use up glucose dissolved in cell cytoplasm. When the glucose concentration drops below that of the surrounding extracellular fluid, more glucose diffuses into the cell. As glucose concentration drops below that in nearby capillaries, more glucose diffuses through the capillary walls. Other nutrients and oxygen also follow a concentration gradient into cells, while dissolved wastes follow a different concentration gradient out of cells.

Water moves in and out of cells along a concentration gradient by passive transport. However, because water is such an important substance to living organisms, the diffusion of water across a cell membrane is given its own name—**osmosis**.

Active transport refers to the movement of substances from regions of

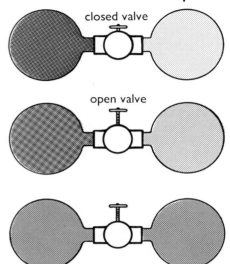

A Model for Passive Transport

closed valve

open valve

FIGURE 7-2 Once the valve is open, molecules diffuse spontaneously along the concentration gradient until concentrations are equal on both sides.

LEFT: FIGURE 7-3 A concentration gradient for glucose

BELOW: FIGURE 7-4 Energy is needed to pump molecules against the concentration gradient.

A Model for Active Transport

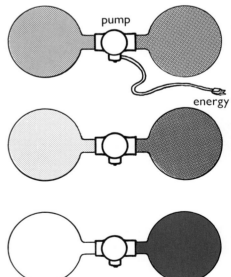

pump

energy

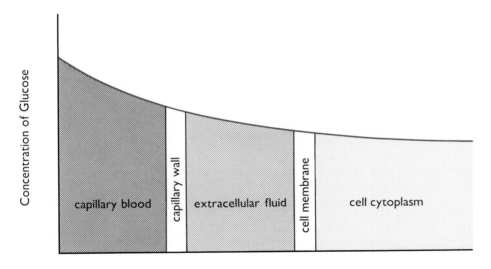

low concentration across a membrane to regions of high concentration. Forcing materials *against* a concentration gradient does not take place spontaneously, and the energy needed for active transport must be supplied by the cells themselves. The ability of cells to perform active transport is important for human excretion because the concentration of waste molecules in urine must be built up to a much higher level than that in surrounding body fluids such as blood. (See Figure 7-4.)

The Nature of Metabolic Wastes

Some metabolic wastes are small, simple molecules that cells dispose of with no specialized structures or systems. For example, the metabolism of glucose by cellular respiration produces water and carbon dioxide as by-products. Both of these substances can be passively transported from the cells to the lungs, where they can be excreted along with exhaled air.

Metabolizing most other nutrients, however, results in molecules that are much larger than water and carbon dioxide molecules. In addition, many processed foods contain additives that the human digestive system cannot break down. To maintain homeostasis, all of these waste molecules must be removed from the body, along with excess vitamins and salt. But most waste molecules are too heavy or too complex to be carried away in exhaled breath. Such wastes can only be excreted from the body after they have been dissolved in urine.

Sodium is the most common waste found in urine, but nitrogen is the most important. (See Table 7-1.) Animals such as humans consume nitrogen in the form of amino acids, but they have no way to store this vital nutrient. Any amino acids that exceed the needs of the human body are deaminated. **Deamination** breaks excess amino acids down into two products: reusable carbon-rich molecules and toxic nitrogenous wastes.

Different animals produce different types of nitrogenous wastes. Fish produce ammonia. Insects, reptiles, and birds produce uric acid. And mammals produce urea. (See Figure 7-5.) All three of these nitrogen-containing compounds are poisonous and must be removed from an animal's tissues as quickly as possible. In animals such as fish, ammonia simply diffuses outward from the gills along with carbon dioxide. Air-breathers, however, need specialized excretory structures and systems to maintain homeostasis. In humans, the most important excretory product is urine.

Of the three major nutrients, only amino acids cannot be stored. After the nitrogen-containing amine group has been removed, however, the carbon-rich molecule that remains can be used by the body for energy or converted to fat and stored.

TABLE 7-1   Composition of Normal Urine (1 L)

Substance	Quantity (g)
Sodium	13.0
Nitrogen	11.7
Chlorine	5.8
Phosphorus	2.0
Potassium	2.0
Sulphur	1.5
Calcium	0.2
Magnesium	0.2
Iron	0.003

LABORATORY EXERCISE 7-1
A Test-Tube Model for Urinalysis

In order to maintain homeostasis, the body deposits unwanted materials into urine. Urinalysis, which is the process of testing urine samples, can detect the presence, or absence, and relative concentrations of poisons, drugs, and pregnancy hormones, as well as abnormal levels of body wastes. In this exercise, you will test a sample of simulated urine for the presence of some of these substances.

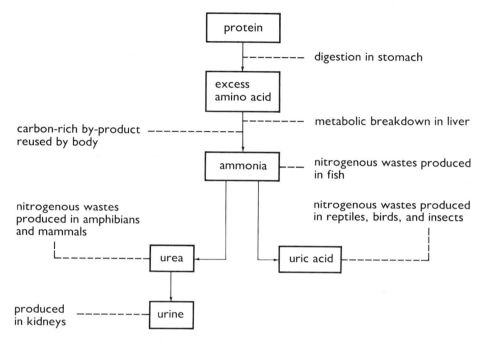

The Formation of Nitrogenous Wastes

protein

------ digestion in stomach

excess amino acid

------ metabolic breakdown in liver

carbon-rich by-product reused by body ------

ammonia

--- nitrogenous wastes produced in fish

nitrogenous wastes produced in amphibians and mammals

nitrogenous wastes produced in reptiles, birds, and insects

urea

uric acid

produced in kidneys ------ urine

FIGURE 7-5 Ammonia is the most toxic nitrogenous waste formed. Urea is less toxic, and uric acid is the least toxic.

Urine, Excretion, and Homeostasis

Urinalysis is an invaluable diagnostic tool for physicians because it reveals the materials the body had to excrete to maintain homeostasis. A laboratory technician would expect a healthy adult to produce about 1.5 L of urine daily, which would contain approximately 30 g of assorted mineral salts, 30 g of dissolved urea, and 2 g of unconverted amino acids. Anything else detected by the urinalysis might indicate an abnormality. (See Table 7-2.)

TABLE 7-2 Possible Significance of Urinalysis Results

Substance in Urine	Normal Amount	Actual Amount	Possible Significance
Glucose	• none	• traces	• diabetes mellitus • high sugar diet
Alcohol	• none	• traces	• liver damage
Human Chorionic Gonadotropin	• none	• traces	• pregnancy
Sodium	• 13 g/L	• above normal	• Addison disease

The chorion, the outer embryonic membrane that surrounds the fetus and becomes part of the placenta, produces a hormone that is indirectly responsible for maintaining the lining of the uterine wall during the early stages of pregnancy. The hormone is called human chorionic gonadotropin, and its level peaks about two months after implantation. Commercial pregnancy tests make use of this hormone to diagnose pregnancy because it can be detected in the urine by an immunological test.

A Role for Urinalysis

"You are what you eat" is a truism, and while what goes into your body is an indicator of its contents, so is what comes out. Changes in body chemistry are reflected in excretions such as exhaled air, sweat, and urine. Urine is the most versatile indicator of internal changes. New laboratory techniques have dramatically increased the capabilities of urinalysis. But, the benefits of urinalysis have also created controversy.

Urinalysis is an important diagnostic tool. As part of a physical examination, urine samples are compared to norms for colour, odour, clarity, volume, specific gravity, protein content, pH, sugar, bile, red blood cells, white blood cells, and bacteria. Deviations from norms, or the presence of unexpected elements, may indicate that a disease or abnormality exists. However, urinalysis rarely identifies the problem specifically. For example, increased volume may indicate nervousness, diabetes, or the use of diuretic drugs. Decreased volume could be caused by diarrhea, nephritis, or heart failure. Further tests are usually needed to pinpoint the cause of an unusual urinalysis.

Although diagnosis is its most important function, urinalysis is better known for its role as a biological detective. Many drugs alter urine in distinguishable ways. Some drugs and drug metabolites are detected directly.

Other drugs alter proportions of the body's chemicals in recognizable patterns, which urinalysis *may* reveal.

Most athletes and organizers of sporting events support testing for performance-enhancing drugs at competitions to ensure fairness. At the same time, the sensitivity of new testing techniques has revealed that banned drug use is far wider than was at first suspected. A positive urinalysis for banned steroids uncovered Ben Johnson's drug use and stripped him of his medal at the 1988 Seoul Olympics. New strategies will be needed to fight drug use in sports.

Outside the athletic world, drug testing is also controversial.

Hundreds of North American companies use urinalysis to test their employees for drug use. While everyone agrees that airline pilots, rail workers, and other workers responsible for hundreds of lives should not be allowed to work under the influence of alcohol or drugs, the ethics of mandatory urinalysis raise many questions.

Drug-testing supporters argue that employee performance and public safety are at risk if drug users work in certain positions. Opponents object to the criteria used to initiate tests. While some companies test only workers in safety-related jobs, or those whose performance has noticeably declined, others test all job applicants, or test employees randomly, without specific suspicions. Many consider this a humiliating invasion of privacy.

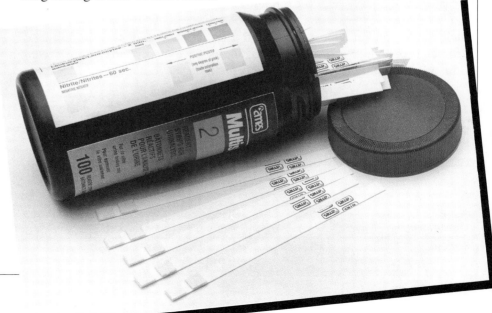

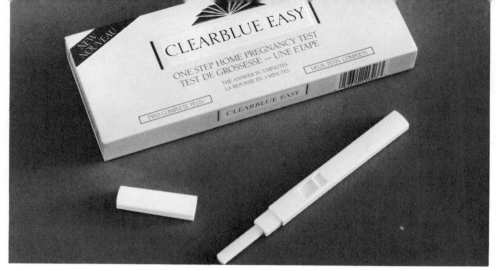

Pregnancy tests can now be performed at home with test kits available in drug stores. If a blue line forms on the test stick 3 min after the stick has been placed in the woman's urine, the test result is positive.

Section Review Questions

1. a) Define homeostasis.
   b) List several factors that must be kept constant in order for organisms to survive.
2. a) What is excretion?
   b) How do excretion and elimination differ?
3. Compare active and passive transport. State an example of each.
4. Excess amino acids cannot be stored. What happens to them in the human body?
5. Ammonia is the most poisonous form of nitrogenous waste. How do fish excrete ammonia?

7.2 Structures for Excretion

The human excretory system is made up of several structures and organs that co-ordinate to regulate the concentration of materials dissolved in the blood. These structures and organs collect and dispose of wastes. (See Figure 7-6.) Some excretory organs such as the **kidney** and the **bladder** are specialized for excretion. Other organs such as the lungs, the skin, the colon, and the liver are multi-purpose structures that perform a variety of functions in addition to excretion.

For example, a major function of your **lungs** is to bring in oxygen for cellular respiration. However, the lungs also function as excretory organs by releasing carbon dioxide into the external environment before it builds up to extremely toxic levels internally. A certain amount of excess water is also excreted from the lungs in the form of vapour.

DID YOU KNOW?
The right kidney rests slightly lower than the left kidney to accommodate the presence of the liver on the right side.

Another toxic compound that may be excreted with exhaled breath is alcohol. The concentration of alcohol in the blood may be measured indirectly from a sample of exhaled breath.

FIGURE 7-6 The kidney and the bladder are specialized organs for excretion. The liver, skin, lungs, and colon are multi-purpose organs designed for excretion and other functions.

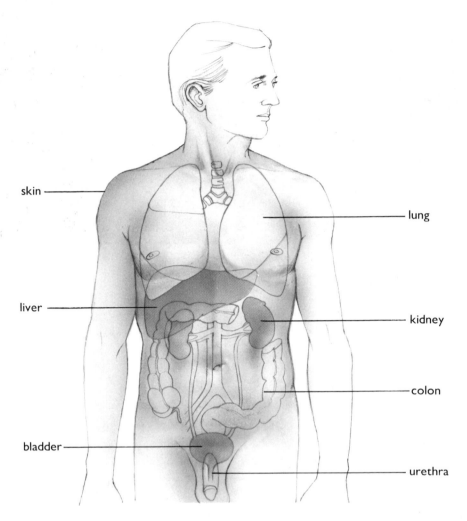

FIGURE 7-7 Sweat glands aid in the excretion of salts, water, and other wastes.

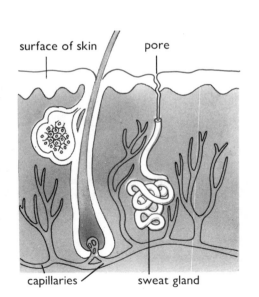

The largest organ of the human body is the **skin**. This multi-purpose organ contributes to homeostasis in several ways. As a tough but elastic covering, the skin protects fragile internal tissues from the external environment and prevents dehydration. In humans, the skin also helps regulate internal body temperature through the evaporation of sweat from the skin's surface, which produces a cooling effect.

The **sweat glands** allow your skin to act as an excretory structure as well. (See Figure 7-7.) The sweat glands collect fluid from nearby capillaries and excrete it to the skin's surface through pores. Sweat is mostly water. Only small amounts of other compounds, which are mainly mineral salts such as sodium chloride, are excreted through your skin. (This is why sweat tastes salty.)

The large intestine, or **colon**, is also involved in removing metabolic wastes from the body. These wastes come from another multi-purpose organ — the liver.

The Liver's Role in Excretion and Homeostasis

Besides its importance as a digestive organ, the **liver** also has three major excretory functions.

- The breakdown of red blood cells
- The detoxification of harmful and foreign substances
- The deamination of amino acids

The liver breaks down the hemoglobin in old red blood cells. This breakdown reaction forms two products: an iron compound that the body reuses to make new red blood cells, and pigment molecules that are metabolic wastes. These wastes dissolve in bile and are eventually passed on to the colon, which egests them from the body along with the feces.

As blood passes through the liver, many kinds of dissolved molecules diffuse from the capillaries into the liver tissue. Chemical reactions in the tissue detoxify harmful ingested substances such as poisons and drugs by breaking the large, actively toxic molecules into smaller, less active ones. These less active molecules then diffuse back into the blood, leaving the liver. Eventually, they will be dissolved in the urine and carried away from the body.

Urine derives its name from the waste product **urea**, which is produced in the liver from amino acids. Often, after a meal high in protein, the blood contains more amino acids than necessary for growth and repair. Deamination of excess amino acids takes place in the liver.

During the first step of deamination, the nitrogen-containing amine group (NH_2) of each amino acid is converted into ammonia, which is an extremely toxic substance. In the second step, a series of enzyme-controlled reactions quickly converts the ammonia into urea, which is a less toxic compound. In the third step, urea diffuses into the blood and leaves the liver. Then it is transported to the urinary system for excretion from the body.

DID YOU KNOW?
Because urine is almost free of bacteria, it has been used in emergencies as a disinfectant to clean wounds.

The Human Urinary System

Although the lungs, skin, colon, and liver play a significant role in excretion, most dissolved wastes leave the blood by way of more specialized excretory structures.

The urinary system includes only those excretory structures that are directly involved in the production and excretion of urine. (See Figure 7-8.)

A pair of **renal arteries** that branch off the aorta carry waste-laden blood from the rest of the body into the kidneys. Humans have two kidneys, each about the size of a clenched fist, which are located at the back of the abdominal cavity just below the rib cage. The kidneys form urine by filtering wastes and excess water from the blood without removing essential blood components or usable nutrients such as glucose. Urine trickles into the hollow, interior **renal pelvis** of the kidney. The purified blood is returned to the circulatory system by a pair of **renal veins**.

DID YOU KNOW?
Pregnant women urinate more often as the growing fetus increases pressure on the bladder.

FIGURE 7-8 The human urinary system

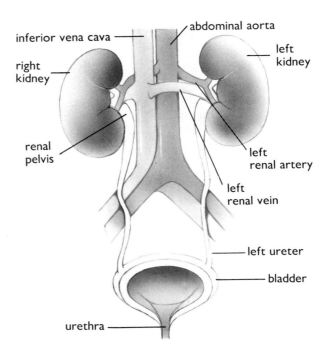

inferior vena cava

abdominal aorta

right kidney

left kidney

renal pelvis

left renal artery

left renal vein

left ureter

bladder

urethra

The human body has several sphincters. All are rings of muscle that guard or close an opening or tube. Some, such as the pyloric sphincter, are automatically controlled. Others such as the sphincter that guards the urethra are usually voluntarily controlled.

Urine formed in the kidneys is carried away from the pelvis by the peristaltic action of the ureters, two long, thin muscular tubes that lead to the bladder. The bladder is an elastic, thin-walled muscular sac near the bottom of the abdominal cavity. As the urine collects, it is held in the bladder by a tightly contracted ring of muscle known as the **sphincter**.

When the volume of urine stored in the bladder builds up to about 250 mL, rhythmic contractions of the bladder wall give warning of the need to void. This "urge" can be suppressed for a while, but eventually the sphincter relaxes while the bladder contracts and releases the urine into the **urethra**, a duct that carries urine to the external environment.

LABORATORY EXERCISE 7-2
Investigating the Urinary System of a Representative Vertebrate

In this exercise, you will continue to dissect a representative vertebrate to locate, describe, sketch, and label its major urinary structures in order to compare them with the human urinary system already described.

DID YOU KNOW?
Both sphincter and sphinx are derived from the Greek verb *sphingein*, which means "to hold tight."

The Most Important Excretory Organ

The lungs, liver, colon, and skin all play necessary roles in the excretory process. The kidney, however, is the primary organ of excretion. Other urinary structures function as feeding tubes and storage units, but only the kidney can perform the difficult task of filtering waste materials from the blood, concentrating them in the urine, while returning useful materials back to the body. How the kidney accomplishes this will be discussed in Section 7.3.

Section Review Questions

1. How do the lungs and skin aid in excretion?
2. What functions does the liver perform in the excretory process?
3. How is the colon involved in excretion of wastes?
4. Describe how urea is formed in the liver.
5. Trace the production of urea from amino acids.
6. a) What are the functions of the renal arteries and veins?
   b) Trace the path of urine from its production in the kidneys to its release into the external environment.

7.3 Structure and Function of the Human Kidney

The renal arteries deliver about 1200 mL of waste-laden blood from the body cells to each kidney every minute of the day. The kidneys remove wastes and any other solutes your body does not need, but they conserve the solutes your body can use. The structure of the human kidney is uniquely suited to this important function.

The interior view of the kidney in Figure 7-9 shows three distinct regions. An outer **renal cortex** and **renal medulla** are composed of approximately one million **nephrons**. Nephrons are the functional units that enable the kidney to filter blood and form urine. The cup-shaped, receiving ends, or **Bowman's capsules**, of the nephrons lie in the cortex. The tubular, urine-collecting ends lie in the medulla and drain into the renal pelvis, where urine is collected and passed on to the ureters. Understanding blood filtration and urine formation requires a closer look at a single nephron.

DID YOU KNOW?
The million or more nephrons of one kidney would reach over 100 km if they were stretched out and laid end to end.

Structure and Function of the Nephron

Blood vessels leaving the renal artery branch out repeatedly, channelling waste-laden blood into a million tiny arterioles. There is one arteriole for

FIGURE 7-9 An interior view of a human kidney, including details of the nephron and the Bowman's capsule

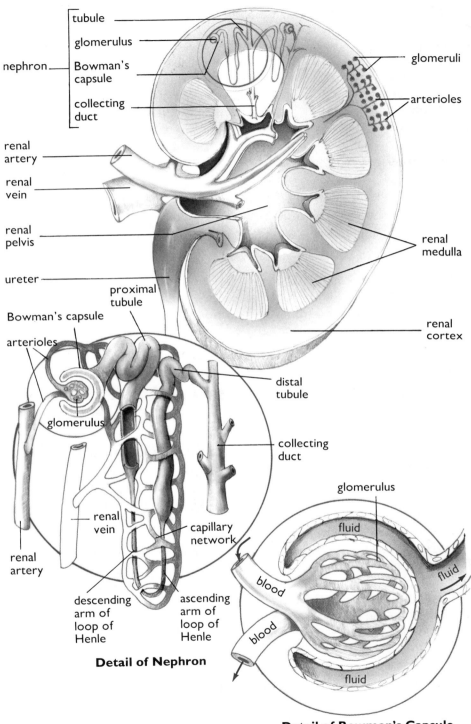

nephron
- tubule
- glomerulus
- Bowman's capsule
- collecting duct

glomeruli

arterioles

renal artery

renal vein

renal pelvis

ureter

renal medulla

renal cortex

proximal tubule

Bowman's capsule

arterioles

glomerulus

renal vein

renal artery

distal tubule

collecting duct

capillary network

descending arm of loop of Henle

ascending arm of loop of Henle

Detail of Nephron

glomerulus

fluid

blood

fluid

blood

fluid

Detail of Bowman's Capsule

every nephron in the human kidney. Each nephron is a long, winding tube surrounded by a capillary network. As the detail of the nephron in Figure 7-9 shows, the tube and capillaries are so intertwined, it is difficult to distinguish the various parts of the nephron. Figure 7-9 shows a simplified view of the nephron, with the tube and capillaries extended for clarity. Table 7-3 lists the function of each part, according to the direction in which fluid travels through the nephron tube.

Materials move between the capillaries and the nephron tube by three processes: filtration, reabsorption, and secretion. **Filtration** transfers part of the blood plasma from the capillaries into the tubule at the cup-shaped end of the nephron. This transfer is accomplished by passive transport aided by the pressure of the blood. The transferred fluid is called the **filtrate** because large

TABLE 7-3 Structure and Function of the Nephron

Name of Part	Structure	Function
(A) Glomerulus	• knot of capillaries • pressure of blood inside is very high because exit tube is narrower than entrance tube	• *Filtration.* Pressure of blood forces about $1/5$ of its plasma out through capillary walls, along with everything small enough: urea, glucose, amino acids, but no red blood cells or large proteins.
(B) Bowman's Capsule	• hollow, cup-shaped end of nephron with double walls one cell thick	• *Filtration.* Plasma with dissolved solutes diffuses into hollow space and is passed on to the tubule.
(C) Proximal Tubule	• hollow, winding, large diameter tube • cells in thin walls have numerous mitochondria	• *Reabsorption.* Active transport pumps glucose, sodium, and amino acids back into capillaries: most urea stays inside tubule
(D) Henle's Loop (descending arm)	• tubule narrows and straightens, and then takes a hairpin turn	• *Reabsorption.* Concentration of water in filtrate inside tubule now greater than in surrounding blood. • Water flows out by osmosis, urea stays inside.
(E) Henle's Loop (ascending arm)	• tubule straightens	• *Reabsorption.* Active transport pumps sodium out of tubule. • Walls here are impermeable to water so it remains inside.
(F) Distal Tubule	• hollow, winding, large diameter tube	• *Reabsorption.* Final adjustment of water and solutes. • Permeability of tubule walls controlled by hormones. • If body is dehydrated, permeability increases to let water return to capillaries by osmosis. If not, permeability decreases to let water dilute urine and leave body.
(G) Collecting Duct	• system of urine-collecting ducts that widen as they near the renal pelvis	• *Secretion.* Potassium and ammonia move from capillary network into duct by active transport. • *Reabsorption.* Water moves by osmosis from duct into surrounding blood.

particles such as red blood cells and protein molecules have been left behind in the capillaries. However, filtration does not sort wastes from useful substances. Besides urea and excess salts, the filtrate also contains useful substances such as water, glucose, and amino acids.

Reabsorption is the transfer of useful materials from the nephron back to the capillaries by passive or active transport at several locations along the tube. **Secretion** is the transfer of additional wastes from the capillaries to the nephron after the filtration step. Secretion involves active transport. By the time the filtrate reaches the collecting duct at the far end of the nephron, it has become urine, and consists mainly of water, salts, dissolved urea, and a few other molecules.

INQUIRY ACTIVITY
Examining the Structure of the Human Nephron

Nephrons are microscopic in size. In this activity, you will examine the photomicrograph on this page, or a prepared slide of kidney tissue, to practise identifying, drawing, and labelling the parts of nephrons.

Procedure

1. Study the photomicrograph on this page and compare it with Figure 7-9.
2. Try to identify the parts of individual nephrons within the tissue sample.
3. Sketch one nephron as completely and accurately as possible based on your observations. Do not draw what is not visible or recognizable to you.
4. Label your sketch.
5. Repeat Steps 1-4 with a prepared slide if available.

Discussion Questions

1. Which parts of the nephron were easy to identify?
2. Which structures were difficult to see or were not observable at all?
3. a) Which parts of the nephron are found in the renal cortex?
   b) Which parts are found in the renal medulla?
   c) Which parts are found in the renal pelvis?

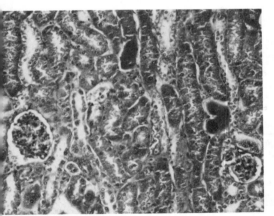

Kidney tissue from a rabbit (100×)

The Kidney and Homeostasis

The human kidney plays three major roles in homeostasis by controlling the volume, composition, and pressure of body fluids. First, the kidney prevents waste products from building up to toxic levels, so the blood that returns to the body from the kidney is cleaner than the blood that entered the kidney.

You should drink up to eight glasses of water each day to help your body excrete wastes.

However, dissolved wastes cannot be removed completely by a single pass through the nephrons. Since your kidneys receive 25% of your heart's blood output each minute, several sweeps can be made in a short time. With each pass, the blood becomes cleaner, and the urine becomes more concentrated. The nephron's ability to carry out active transport prevents most of the concentrated waste solutes in the urine from diffusing back into the blood.

Second, active transport by the nephron also returns materials such as glucose and amino acids to the rest of the circulatory system. This process maintains high nutrient levels in the blood, making it unnecessary for you to eat continually. Third, almost 99% of the water that enters the nephron is reabsorbed by the blood, which reduces the total amount of water that must be replaced to about 2 L each day. Urination accounts for about 1.5 L of this daily loss. Other excretory processes such as perspiration, exhalation, and defecation make up the rest.

The kidney cannot maintain homeostasis by itself. As Figure 7-10 shows, the excretory system must interact with the circulatory, nervous, and endocrine systems to achieve the required levels of water in the human body.

Receptors in the brain (nervous system) are sensitive to the concentration of water in the surrounding blood (circulatory system). If these receptors detect a drop in water concentration, they send signals to the pituitary gland (endocrine system). The pituitary gland releases an antidiuretic hormone, ADH, into the blood. The blood carries the hormone to all parts of the body,

DID YOU KNOW?
When you sleep, filtration in the kidney slows down.

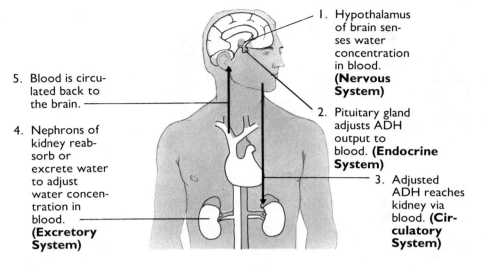

5. Blood is circulated back to the brain.

4. Nephrons of kidney reabsorb or excrete water to adjust water concentration in blood. **(Excretory System)**

1. Hypothalamus of brain senses water concentration in blood. **(Nervous System)**

2. Pituitary gland adjusts ADH output to blood. **(Endocrine System)**

3. Adjusted ADH reaches kidney via blood. **(Circulatory System)**

DID YOU KNOW?

Despite active transport, some urea does return to the blood. When the body is dehydrated, and large amounts of water are reabsorbed to maintain homeostasis, up to 80% of the filtered urea in the tubule may diffuse back into the capillaries. This is only one reason why health experts urge you to drink six to eight glasses of water each day.

including the kidneys (excretory system). In the kidneys, the antidiuretic hormone alters the permeability of the distal tubule to allow more water through to the capillaries for reabsorption by the blood.

Under these conditions, the nephrons will produce a concentrated, deep yellow urine, and the concentration of water in the blood will increase. When brain sensors detect that the water level has returned to normal, they signal the pituitary gland to stop producing and secreting the hormone. The concentration of salt in body fluids is controlled in a similar way—through the action of hormones produced by the adrenal glands, which rest on top of the kidneys.

Section Review Questions

1. What part of the nephron is in the renal cortex? What function does it perform?

2. What part of the nephron is in the renal medulla? What function does it perform?

3. List the structures, in order, through which urea passes from the renal artery to the renal pelvis.

4. a) What materials move into the Bowman's capsule from the glomerulus? By what process do they move?

   b) What materials move back into the blood from the proximal tubule? By what process do they move?

   c) What waste materials move into the collecting duct from the capillaries? By what process do they move?

5. If you drink excess water, your blood will contain more water than usual. What events will occur in the excretory system to compensate for this increased amount of water?

Overcoming Kidney Failure

The invention of the dialysis machine is a tribute to the ingenuity of Dr. Willem Kolff, a Dutch physician who was working at the time in Nazi-occupied Holland. Among the usual war injuries, Kolff treated many cases of kidney failure. Until 1946, anyone who suffered from kidney failure became comatose and died. Although diffusion, the principle behind the working of the dialysis machine, is quite simple, the technical problems in simulating the work of the kidney had defeated previous researchers.

By the end of World War II, Kolff had built eight working dialysis machines. Each was made with 20 m of cellophane tubing (similar to tubes used for sausage casings) wrapped around a vibrating wooden drum. Seals from the water pumps of Ford cars were used to prevent leakage where blood entered and left the drum. Since that time, dialysis machines have become more sophisticated, but essentially they operate on the same diffusion principles as the glomerulus inside a real kidney.

During the procedure, the patient's blood is circulated through a dialyzing fluid in a tube made of a semipermeable membrane. Blood cells, blood proteins, and glucose molecules are too large to diffuse across the membrane. However, smaller waste molecules such as urea, uric acid, and ammonia pass through the membrane from a higher concentration in the blood to a lower concentration in the dialyzing fluid.

Circulating blood outside the body creates serious problems. For example, formation of even the smallest lethal bubbles, the tendency for blood to clot outside the body, and possible hypothermia from even slightly cooled blood are among the countless complications to overcome in improving dialysis treatment.

One complication is that many dialysis patients suffer from anemia, which is partially caused by the absence of erythropoietin, a hormone secreted by healthy kidneys that stimulates blood-cell production. Blood transfusions every few months can alleviate, but not cure, the problem.

Perhaps the most serious problem is that the intermittent nature of dialysis treatment cannot maintain blood homeostasis—stable concentrations of blood chemicals—as well as real kidneys. Treatment incidence and duration vary with the severity of the failure. It is not unusual for patients to require two to three 5 h treatments per week. Between treatments, the levels of blood constituents are effectively out of control. Some results of this variable blood chemistry are infection and higher incidences of heart attack and strokes from high blood pressure. Researchers are trying to develop a portable dialysis machine, but for now the only permanent solution is a kidney transplant.

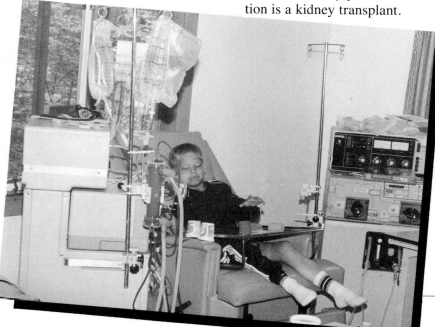

7.4 Excretion in Other Animals

The human excretory system provides a basis for understanding the nature of excretion in other animals. However, there is a surprising degree of diversity in the excretion process within the animal kingdom. Even among members of the same phylum, the excretory system may vary much more than the respiratory, digestive, or circulatory systems.

Excretion in Vertebrates

As Table 7-4 shows, vertebrates display a wide range of excretory adaptations that suit them for life in their particular environments. In aquatic vertebrates such as fish, the liver deaminates excess amino acid molecules in a single step, producing ammonia, just as it does in humans. However, fish need no specialized structures to excrete nitrogenous wastes because the ammonia never builds up to toxic levels. Instead, ammonia simply diffuses outward through the gills along with carbon dioxide. Fish do, however, need excretory structures to regulate the concentration of salt.

By contrast, reptiles and birds are air-breathers, and most are land dwellers. Their excretory systems are adapted to minimize dehydration. Both birds and reptiles excrete uric acid, a nitrogen compound that is almost insoluble in water. Therefore, these vertebrates do not produce anything like urine at all. Instead, they push out crystals of solid uric acid mixed with just enough water to make them movable. As a result, water losses from excretion are minimized.

Most mammals have an excretory system similar to that of humans. The liver breaks down excess amino acids in two steps. In the first step, a highly

Guano islands are produced from the nitrogenous wastes of birds such as these cormorants. This island is over 30 m thick.

TABLE 7-4   Excretory Adaptations of Some Vertebrates

Vertebrate	Excretory Adaptations
Freshwater Fish (trout)	• tissues have lower water concentration than surrounding medium • takes in water by osmosis through gills (passive transport) • loses salt from tissues by diffusion (passive transport) from high to low concentration • salt reabsorbed by gills and kidneys (active transport) from low to high concentration • much diluted urine is excreted to remove excess water
Marine Fish (cod)	• tissues have higher water concentration than surrounding salt water • tends to lose water by osmosis through gills (passive transport) • attempts to replace water by drinking sea water, which leads to high salt concentration in tissues • extra salt is excreted by gills (active transport) from low to high concentration • kidney reduces water loss by excreting small quantities of concentrated urine
Amphibian	• **in water** — tissues have low concentration of water, take in water by osmosis (passive transport) • kidneys excrete excess water in urine, reabsorb salt needed to survive (active transport) • **on land** — tissues have high concentration of water, tend to lose it by osmosis (passive transport) • kidneys reabsorb water from tissues and store in bladder as a reserve
Reptile	• tissues have high water concentration compared to surroundings • loses water by osmosis and evaporation (passive transport) • replaces water by drinking and eating • converts nitrogenous waste to insoluble uric acid, which can be excreted with little water loss (active transport)
Bird	• tissues have high water concentration compared to air • tends to lose water by osmosis and evaporation (passive transport) • converts ammonia to insoluble uric acid, which needs little water for excretion, so can be reabsorbed and conserved by kidneys

toxic ammonia is formed. In the second step, the ammonia is converted to urea, a less toxic nitrogen compound. Urea is then separated from the blood by the kidneys and dissolved in water along with other wastes. The resulting urine is stored until it can be excreted from the body. This system of excretion causes large water losses, and most mammals need to drink much more water than reptiles or birds of the same size.

Safe Laboratory Techniques

You may not think of the blood or urine sample you leave at the medical laboratory as hazardous material, but the people who test it do. They risk infection from whatever bacteria or viruses the sample contains. Your safety as a patient and their safety as workers are protected by a set of strict precautions.

Every sample is assumed to be hazardous because technologists do not know what it contains until it is tested. In the parts of a laboratory where testing is done, technologists wear plastic aprons and gloves, which they must remove when they leave the "contaminated" area. Sample containers are sealed in packages or covered and sealed with lids or corks. The clear test tubes used for blood samples are made of specially treated glass so they won't break if they are dropped. Any spills are wiped up with a 1% bleach solution, which is strong enough to kill bacteria or viruses.

Used testing materials must be specially disposed of. Swabs go into waste containers with one-way tops. Samples on slides and in petri dishes and other containers are put in special boxes marked "contaminated." These boxes are sealed and removed from the building for burning.

The testing process is governed by stringent protocols that ensure thoroughness and accuracy. From the moment your sample is collected to the moment when the results are given to your doctor, everything is done in a specific sequence. Samples are destroyed a few days after testing, but every decision and step taken is recorded for possible future reference.

Every laboratory test is performed as a control experiment. Let's say your doctor has sent in a throat swab to be tested for Group A Streptococcus. The technologist will use the swab to grow a culture, and then extract an antigen from the cultured bacteria. This antigen will then be tested with a preparation containing the specific antibody for Group A Streptococcus. As a positive control, a standard reagent known to contain Group A antigen will also be tested with the antibody preparation. As a negative control, a standard reagent containing a different streptococcal antigen will

be tested with the antibody. The patient's original sample is only considered positive for Group A if the test results are identical to the positive control and different from the negative control.

The patient's test can only be reported if the expected results are obtained. If something different happens, the technologist must question whether the test procedure was done correctly, whether the test materials worked correctly, or whether there was some other problem such as contaminated equipment.

Quality control is monitored constantly. A laboratory is accredited by the provincial government and must continue to meet high quality control and safety standards to maintain its accreditation. Supervisors in the laboratory run regular checks. For instance, they compile a daily record containing details of every test performed and the number of controls performed on it.

Everyone who tests samples is a registered technologist. Within the medical technology field a person can focus on special areas like virology, bacteriology, cytology, or hematology.

Integrity is important because the health of patients and laboratory personnel is at stake. Medical technologists must be conscientious and honest enough to admit a mistake promptly so it can be corrected. They have no doubt about the value of their work.

Up to 90% of the water needed by the kangaroo rat comes from metabolic processes such as cellular respiration. By contrast, it loses only about 25% of water through urination.

TABLE 7-5 Water Intake and Output in Human and Kangaroo Rat

Intake of Water	Human	Kangaroo Rat
Drinking	48%	0%
From Food	40%	10%
From Metabolic Process	12%	90%

Output of Water	Human	Kangaroo Rat
Urine	60%	25%
Perspiration and Breathing	34%	70%
Feces	6%	5%

The kangaroo rat, however, does not drink at all. Like most desert mammals, its excretory system is different in several ways from the human excretory system. (See Table 7-5.) The kangaroo rat subsists on a diet of seeds and vegetable matter that is high in fat and low in protein. Its only source of moisture is the small amount of water produced by the metabolism of fat and by cellular respiration. Because the kangaroo rat's diet is low in protein, it produces few nitrogenous wastes, needs very little water to dissolve them, and urinates infrequently. Kangaroo rats have no sweat glands from which water might evaporate. They are active only at night when the air is cooler and more humid.

RESEARCH PROJECT
Excretory Systems in Invertebrates

Invertebrates also have a variety of methods for regulating internal water levels. For this project, your class will work in groups to conduct a comparative study of excretion among the following invertebrates: hydras, planarians, earthworms, and grasshoppers.

A. Have your group select one of the invertebrates above or one suggested by your teacher. Based on library research conducted by your group, summarize the methods used by the invertebrate to regulate water content. Develop a 5-min presentation to convey the findings of your group to your class. Use visual aids where possible.

B. Draw a large chart similar to Table 7-3 (see page 221) on newsprint or on the chalkboard. Record the findings of each group. Compare the adaptations used for water regulation among the invertebrates researched. Compare the methods of water regulation used by one invertebrate and those used by humans. Repeat the comparison between two different invertebrates.

Excretion and Homeostasis

What sort of excretory adaptations would you expect to find in salmon? Salmon spend their first few months of life in fresh water followed by several years in salt water. Then they return to fresh water to mate and to lay their eggs.

Regardless of whether an animal is an invertebrate or a vertebrate, its excretory system must fulfill two important functions. First, it must remove potentially harmful waste materials from the animal's body before they reach toxic levels. Second, it must regulate the amount of water inside the animal's body so that dehydration does not occur. Therefore, both wastes and water concentration are maintained at fairly constant levels, and homeostasis is maintained.

Section Review Questions

1. Compare the methods of water regulation in a freshwater fish and a marine fish.
2. How do the gills of freshwater and marine fish maintain homeostasis with respect to salt?
3. List organsims that excrete nitrogenous wastes as a) ammonia, b) urea, or c) uric acid.
4. Why do most mammals need to drink more water than birds or reptiles of the same size?
5. Describe how a kangaroo rat maintains a constant internal water level despite the fact that it never drinks.

7.5 Human Excretory System Disorders

The organs of your excretory system are designed for a lifetime. With attention to proper diet, exercise, and lifestyle, there is no reason why they shouldn't remain healthy and efficient. Sometimes, however, diseases or disorders hamper the excretory process.

Urine often reveals the health of the excretory system. Normal urine is yellow—any other colour may indicate the presence of disease. Red to brown discolouration may indicate the presence of blood. Cloudiness may also indicate a problem. Most healthy adults pass between 700-1500 mL of urine daily, voiding four to six times a day. Much larger or smaller urine volumes, more frequent voiding, or painful urination are all signs of a possible illness of the excretory system.

Kidney Failure

Because of the kidney's importance to excretion and homeostasis, kidney failure is the most serious excretory disorder. Kidney failure, which is also called renal failure, is the inability of the kidneys to produce and excrete wastes from the body. This condition can be caused by the formation of cysts within kidney tissue, high blood pressure, diabetes mellitus, obstructions such as kidney stones (see Figure 7-11), or by infections.

Kidney stones often cause frequent urination and severe pain when voiding. Their composition varies according to diet and geographical location, but 90% contain calcium. The shape of kidney stones varies according to where they were formed. (See Figure 7-11.) Large stones may cause kidney failure by blocking the urinary system completely. Once treatable only by surgical methods, today many kidney stones can be fragmented by ultrasound into pieces small enough to pass with urine.

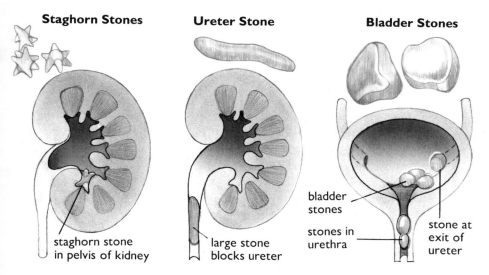

Staghorn Stones

staghorn stone in pelvis of kidney

Ureter Stone

large stone blocks ureter

Bladder Stones

bladder stones

stones in urethra

stone at exit of ureter

FIGURE 7-11 Two examples of kidney stones. Notice that bladder stones are usually much larger than kidney stones.

Kidney failure can result in uremia, a condition where urea and nitrogenous wastes build up in the blood. This buildup of wastes can be fatal if left untreated.

Depending on the cause, several treatments for kidney failure are possible. Obstructions may be surgically removed or chemically dissolved. Dialysis, the process of cleansing the blood of waste materials by using a machine, is another alternative. Dialysis requires that a patient remain hooked up to a machine for 4-6 h several times a week. A kidney transplant can be another solution for kidney failure. But unfortunately the recipient's immune system often reacts to the foreign tissue of the donor kidney and rejects it. In order to avoid organ rejection, the tissue of the donor kidney must be carefully matched to the recipient's immune system. Organ donation from a relative will also decrease the risk of rejection. Both the donor and the recipient can survive with one healthy kidney as long as it is not overworked by an overactive lifestyle.

Excretion and General Health

Because the excretory system is so important to homeostasis, it is often affected by disease in other parts of the body. Many diseases, other than those of the excretory system, cause the urine to have an abnormal colour. Blackwater fever, for example, gets its name from the very dark urine it produces. Blackwater fever is a complication of malaria. The dark colour is caused by extensive internal bleeding. Dark urine is also a symptom of alkaptonuria, which is a metabolic disorder. Alkaptonuria is caused by the lack of the enzyme needed to break down tyrosine, an amino acid.

Extremely large or very small volumes of urine may indicate disorders such as dysuria, which makes urination painful or difficult, thereby decreasing the volume excreted. Diabetes insipidus decreases the production of a pituitary hormone, ADH, which is responsible for controlling urine production, so the volume of urine passed is increased.

Even when urine seems normal in colour and volume, urinalysis may reveal the presence of abnormal solutes or abnormal amounts of normal solutes. People suffering from diabetes mellitus are unable to utilize glucose properly, which results in high quantities of glucose being passed in the urine.

The amounts of sodium and potassium in the body must be in balance with each other. They help keep body fluids neutral, attract nutrients into the blood, and maintain osmotic pressure within the body. An excess of either sodium or potassium in the diet causes the other to be lost in urine.

Influence of Diet and Lifestyle on Excretion

Discoloured urine on a baby's diaper may be a sign of illness or nothing more serious than that the baby ate strained beets the previous day. Berries and

DID YOU KNOW?
Stress can increase urine output, but smoking decreases it.

other richly coloured foods may also affect the colour of urine, but these effects are usually temporary and do not indicate a problem.

Consistently dark yellow urine may be a sign of inadequate water intake, a habit that can cause long-term problems. Your kidneys can continue to function when you do not have enough water, but eventually they can break down because they must overwork to prevent dehydration. Also, urea and excess salts are soluble in water and must be dissolved in order to be excreted. A lack of water can cause these substances to accumulate in blood and kidney tissues, eventually poisoning them. Most of the two or more litres of water you lose each day by urinating, sweating, and exhaling, you must replace partially by drinking 1.0-1.5 L of water daily.

You can meet some of your body's water requirement by drinking milk or by eating fruit with a high moisture content. However, many water-based beverages contain substances that interfere with normal kidney function. The caffeine found in cola, coffee, or tea, for example, increases urinary output and reduces internal water levels.

The consumption of alcoholic beverages also places a burden on the excretory system. Even though beer, wine, and mixed drinks all contain water, none of these beverages contains enough water to replace the extra water loss caused by the alcohol. Alcohol inhibits normal hormone production, making the nephron less able to reabsorb water. The result is an increased flow of urine and a need to drink more water to compensate for the extra loss. This cycle is especially noticeable in people who drink large quantities of beer.

Alcohol consumption over an extended period can lead to more serious consequences for the liver. Accumulated alcohol will cause liver tissue to break down, reducing its ability to convert drugs, alcohol, and other poisons into less harmful molecules.

Alcohol and liquids containing caffeine can have a harmful effect on kidney function.

Making sure that your body gets enough water and avoiding harmful substances are important for life-long health benefits. A properly functioning excretory system needs your care to maintain a stable internal environment for other body systems.

Section Review Questions

1. Suppose your urine has a reddish colour. List several possible causes for this discolouration.
2. a) What is kidney failure?
   b) List several causes of kidney failure.
3. Explain how dysuria and diabetes insipidus affect the volume of urine passed.
4. Describe two complications resulting from not drinking enough water over extended periods of time.
5. Explain why drinking beer does not quench thirst.
6. Describe the effects of alcohol consumption on the liver over long periods of time.

Meet
Greg Manger

Greg works in the burn and plastic surgery unit at Toronto's Hospital for Sick Children. As the clinical instructor on the ward, part of his job involves training new staff.

Q. What does your job involve?

A. I work as part of a team in the burn unit. When a child comes into the hospital with a burn injury, one of the nurses is put in charge of the treatment and care of the child and his family. Other people on the team include the surgeon, the physiotherapists and occupational therapists, the dietitian, the bacteriologist, the hospital school teacher, and the orthotist who makes special splints if they are necessary.

Q. How important is team work in nursing?

A. You must be good at working with others as a team. You need good communication skills and you have to be a bit assertive, too. The nurse acts as a co-ordinator, and is usually closest to the patient and most aware of that child's needs.

Q. How are burn injuries described?

A. First-degree burns are superficial injuries affecting only the outermost layer of skin. These burns heal in a few days and leave no scars. Second-degree burns affect deeper layers of skin. Skin grafting may be necessary, and the patient is usually in hospital for about six weeks. Third-degree burns involve the depth of the skin. These burns can take months to heal if they are not grafted, and they always leave scars.

Q. How do you care for these children?

A. They come in as emergency cases, and I would work on their initial treatment. The day-to-day care involves a lot of wound care. The patient goes into the burn tub two or three times a day. The wound is washed and ''debrided'' to remove loose skin and bacteria. Then the wound is dressed. This treatment can take all morning.

Q. What are other aspects of burn treatment?

A. In the first few days, we are concerned with maintaining fluid balance. Urine losses are measured and so is fluid intake. Children with large injuries have a feeding tube placed through the nose to the stomach to provide extra nutrition. This is very important for healing.

Q. How do you prepare the child for leaving the hospital?

A. We have a plan for getting the child back into the community. First, we might just walk around inside the hospital. Then, we'll go to the cafeteria. Then we'll go outside for a walk around the block. Finally, we start taking them to McDonalds or to the museum. It's hard for these children to get used to being scarred.

Q. Do you teach the children how to treat their wounds at home?

A. We counsel the children and their parents on how to reduce scarring by fingertip massage and by wearing pressure garments. These pressure garments force the skin fibres to lie flat and therefore reduce scarring. They must be worn 24 h a day, except when bathing, for two years. Some children also wear orthotic splints that keep the damaged skin areas from shrinking.

235

Chapter Review

Key Words

active transport	passive transport
bladder	reabsorption
Bowman's capsule	renal arteries
deamination	renal cortex
excretion	renal medulla
filtrate	renal pelvis
filtration	renal veins
homeostasis	secretion
kidney	urea
liver	urethra
nephrons	urine

Recall Questions

Multiple Choice

1. The most toxic form of nitrogenous waste is
   a) urea
   b) ammonia
   c) uric acid
   d) urine

2. Which of the following groups of vertebrates rely primarily on skin for the excretion of carbon dioxide?
   a) fish
   b) amphibians
   c) reptiles
   d) birds

3. Filtration of blood occurs at the
   a) Bowman's capsule
   b) proximal tubule
   c) loop of Henle
   d) distal tubule

4. Which of the following explains the reabsorption of water by the capillaries from the tubules?
   a) osmosis
   b) passive transport
   c) active transport
   d) all of the above

5. The element that is excreted in greatest quantity in normal urine is
   a) nitrogen
   b) sodium
   c) chlorine
   d) potassium

Fill in the Blanks

1. The _____ is an organ responsible for maintaining salt and water balance in a fish.

2. The _____ is the functional unit of the kidney.

3. Nitrogenous wastes are produced by the metabolism of _____ in the body.

4. The formation of _____ allows birds and reptiles to excrete nitrogenous wastes but helps them conserve water.

5. The _____ conducts urine from the kidney to the bladder.

6. The fluid in the nephron tubule after filtration is referred to as _____ .

7. The loop of Henle is located in the _____ of the kidney.

Short Answers

1. a) How does the excretion of uric acid conserve water?
   b) List several organisms that rely on this method of excretion.

2. Describe the deamination process that occurs in the liver.

3. a) What are the three main components of urine?
   b) Where in the kidney does each component become part of excreted urine?

4. Which part(s) of the nephron is/are found in the renal cortex? The renal medulla? The renal pelvis?

5. Describe the path urine takes from the renal pelvis to the external environment.

6. List the substances that filter from the glomerulus into the Bowman's capsule.

7. a) What effect does ADH have on the kidney?
   b) How is the production and release of ADH controlled?

8. List four ways excess water is removed from the human body.

9. What substances are normally reabsorbed from the nephron by the capillary network?

Application Questions

1. How does the production of uric acid benefit egg-laying vertebrates?

2. If the frog used only its skin as an excretory surface, how would this limit its lifestyle?

3. Explain how a high-protein diet would affect the liver.

4. What effect would damage to the pituitary gland have on kidney function?

5. Many birds are able to excrete uric acid while they are flying. How does this process maintain the lightest possible body weight?

Problem Solving

1. What would happen if the walls of the Bowman's capsules completely lost their permeability?

2. How does the excretory system respond in a person who is exposed on a hot day with nothing to drink?

3. Explain how a diet high in salt might affect water retention in a human.

4. Reptiles and birds develop in an egg that provides them no way to excrete nitrogenous wastes. How do they survive without poisoning themselves?

Extensions

1. Research and report on the excretory processes of one of the following invertebrates.
   a) paramecium
   b) clam
   c) sow bug

2. Research how to build a simplified working model of a dialysis machine and demonstrate it to your class.

3. Research the progress being made in the area of kidney transplants. Include in your report how donors and recipients are selected, the kind of preparation that is necessary, how the operation is performed, the post-operative care required, and how organ rejection is controlled.

4. Discuss or debate the ethical, moral, and legal issues surrounding kidney and other organ transplants.

CHAPTER

8

Nervous Control

It can take only seconds to completely change your life if your spinal cord is damaged. A missed tackle, a shallow dive, a motorcycle accident—all could leave you paralyzed to some degree.

Every spinal-cord injury is different in location and severity. Paralysis occurs below the injury site, so the higher up the cord is damaged, the greater the resulting disability. People whose arms and legs are paralyzed are called quadriplegics. People whose legs only are paralyzed, like these basketball players, are called paraplegics.

The severity of a spinal-cord injury depends on whether the cord has been compressed, stretched, crushed, or completely severed. In a damaged but not severed cord, some nerve fibres and signals remain. Neurosurgeons try to save as many of these fibres as possible from further damage. Physiotherapists then teach the patient how to use them.

Using biofeedback, psychologists try to trace the connections between the brain and the spinal cord in order to help the brain locate nerve pathways that are still alive in the cord. Electrodes placed on the patient measure the electrical energy being sent to the muscles. The patient views target and actual levels of muscle activity on a computer screen. The patient

works at getting the level of muscle activity to or over the target level. The body's neurons learn—and remember—what works.

Functional Electrical Stimulation (FES) is a technique that helps paralyzed people move around more freely. It also helps to ward off muscle atrophy. In a person who isn't paralyzed, muscles move in response to low-level electrical impulses carried to them by the nerves. FES duplicates that situation mechanically with electrodes, which, placed on the patient and wired to a computer, fire muscles in a specific order. The patient and computer can be wired for a wide variety of activities from stationary cycling to walking with the aid of a walker. Neuroscientists and electrical engineers are now experimenting with the implantation of electrodes and wires right into patients' limbs to make the controls less intrusive.

Biomedical engineers are also investigating the connections between thought and action. They are developing devices that can detect neural commands either in the brain or along the neural pathways and transform them into electronic commands. Such electronic thought commands could control external devices or assist in FES. However, detecting neural signals is difficult, and this work is still in its formative stages.

These efforts to minimize the degree of paralysis, to improve rehabilitation techniques, and to develop sophisticated aids such as lightweight wheelchairs make an active life more possible than ever for those with spinal-cord injuries.

But better still would be the ability to walk again, and researchers around the world have been working toward this goal for years. The most exciting breakthrough so far has been reported by scientists at the University of Zurich. They have discovered a way to regrow damaged spinal nerves in the laboratory.

The inability of human brain and spinal nerves to regenerate themselves has long puzzled neurologists. Fish and amphibian spinal nerves do regenerate when cut, and human peripheral nerves also regenerate when given enough time. The Swiss researchers have discovered that human spinal nerves do not regrow because cells surrounding the nerve fibres produce a growth inhibitor. When artificial antibodies are added to block the inhibitor, severed spinal nerves can grow rapidly.

The scientists warn that their research is still preliminary, and they foresee many problems that must be solved before their discovery can be used to help paralyzed people walk. But at long last, the hope of a cure has been given a realistic basis.

Chapter Objectives

When you complete this chapter, you should:

1. Appreciate that all animals need systems for control and regulation to maintain stable internal conditions.

2. Be able to describe the structure of a neuron and explain its function.

3. Be able to explain the nature of nervous and endocrine signals, and how they travel to target organs or body parts.

4. Based on experimental findings, be able to compare brain structure and function in humans and other vertebrates.

5. Know how to carry out experimental procedures to demonstrate typical human reflexes and map sensory receptors.

6. Appreciate the complexity of the human nervous system, and describe the structure and function of its subsystems.

7. Based on experiment, be able to identify nervous system components in a representative vertebrate and compare them with humans.

8. Collect experimental data relating to homeostatic mechanisms in humans and other animals.

9. Be able to describe briefly the human endocrine system and compare it to the nervous system.

10. Understand how co-ordination of the nervous system and the endocrine system contributes to the maintenance of homeostasis in humans.

11. Be able to describe some nervous and endocrine disorders in humans, and explain the importance of co-ordination to personal health.

12. Be able to describe briefly the potential benefits and risks of drugs that affect the nervous system.

8.1 Nervous Control in Animals

The robots used in assembly lines require a complex control system for co-ordination of movement. This system is based on the transmission of electrical impulses, which are waves of charged particles that travel along copper wires linking the "hands" of the robot with the central processing unit.

The control system that enables animals to detect stimuli and co-ordinate responses is called the **nervous system.** The nervous system is also based on the transmission of electrical impulses. In animals, however, the impulses travel through **nerves,** which are long, thin strands of living tissue. Nerves are connected to each other and to the organs and tissues of an animal's body.

The simplest type of nervous system is the crudely organized nerve net observed in cnidarians such as the hydra. Because all the nerves in the net are two-way conductors (see Figure 8-1), every stimulus from the external environment can be felt everywhere in the hydra's body. Therefore, the resulting response involves the entire organism.

A nerve net has two disadvantages. First, a single nerve impulse cannot reach all body parts at exactly the same time. This effect causes a noticeable delay in the reactions of large sea anemones, although it cannot be observed in the tiny hydra. Second, a nerve net produces an all-or-nothing response. Either all of a hydra's tentacles move at once to their fullest extent, or none of its tentacles move at all. A hydra cannot move just one tentacle at a time.

By contrast, the planarian displays a wide range of localized, specific responses. Its nervous system is much more organized, and has two major nerve cords and numerous minor nerve endings. (See Figure 8-2.) The planarian has an enlarged nerve cluster at one end that functions as a simple **brain** or central processing unit. Each nerve transmits impulses in only one direction — body to brain, or brain to body.

The planarian's nervous system also includes specialized **sensory receptors** that convert stimuli from the external environment into nerve impulses. The planarian's brain processes this information and signals other body parts to take appropriate action. For example, when light strikes its eyespot, a planarian's brain sends an "avoid" signal to its muscles. The planarian also has sensory receptors that can detect touch, heat, dissolved chemicals, and water currents.

As you can see in Figure 8-2, the arrangement of the planarian's nervous system provides it with a recognizable head end, and enables it to test its environment before moving forward. In the next laboratory exercise, you will investigate the nervous system of annelids.

A balance of electrical input and output signals keeps the robots on this car assembly line operating in co-ordination.

The slow conduction characteristic of nerve nets also causes delayed responses in large echinoderms such as starfish.

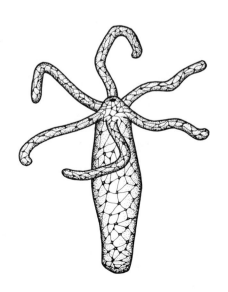

FIGURE 8-1 The hydra's nerve net has no central processing unit, or brain, so the hydra has no distinct head.

II ANIMALS

When one tentacle is stimulated by its prey, all parts of the hydra's body contract. Each tentacle simultaneously releases a "poison dart," all of which work together to push the prey into the hydra's mouth opening.

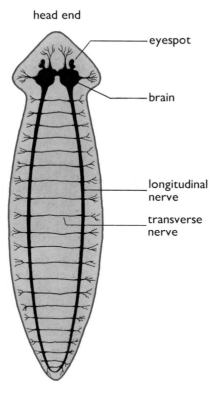

head end

- eyespot
- brain
- longitudinal nerve
- transverse nerve

FIGURE 8-2 Notice the ladder-like structure of the planarian's nervous system.

Flatworms such as the planarian belong to the phylum Platyhelminthes. All of the members of this phylum have a similar body plan.

LABORATORY EXERCISE 8-1
The Nervous System of Annelids

In this exercise, you will investigate the nervous system of the earthworm and compare it to the nervous system of a typical vertebrate. You will also compare the nervous system of the earthworm to those of other invertebrates.

Structure of the Neuron

In animals, electrical impulses move through nerves containing a series of separate, long, thin cells called **neurons.** The neuron is the basic functional unit of the nervous system.

Regardless of differences in appearance, all neurons have the same basic structure. (See Figure 8-3.) Each has a large **cell body** that houses the nucleus. Many short-armed **dendrites** carry nervous signals from outside the neuron toward the cell body. A single, long-armed **axon** carries these nervous signals away from the cell body and toward other cells. In most vertebrates, and in some invertebrates, many axons are covered by a nonliving, fatty white **myelin**

The axon is extremely long compared to the dendrites, and extremely thin compared to its own length. Most axons are only a few micrometres wide. In some large vertebrates, axons may be up to a metre long.

LEFT: FIGURE 8-3 All neurons have the same basic structure shown here. However, some do not have a myelin sheath.

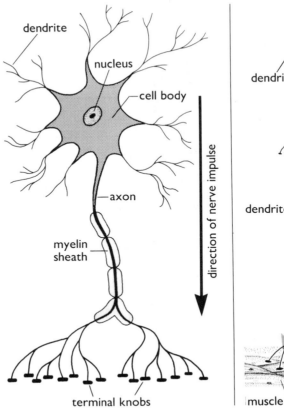

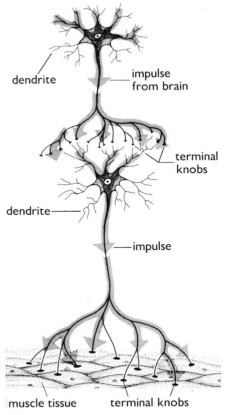

RIGHT: FIGURE 8-4 A nerve impulse from the brain is relayed from neuron to neuron until it reaches its destination. In this case, the impulse is relayed to a muscle.

The insulating myelin sheath enables the fastest human axons to transmit impulses at speeds up to 120 m/s. By comparison, cars at top highway speeds travel only 25 m/s.

sheath that functions as an electrical insulator and keeps the charged particles inside.

When an impulse reaches the **terminal knobs** at the end of the axon, it is relayed onward until it eventually reaches the brain or a body part such as a muscle. (See Figure 8-4.)

Nerve impulses that carry information to the brain originate in receptors. Some receptors are specialized for detecting internal stimuli such as the carbon dioxide content of the blood. Others detect various external stimuli such as light or odour.

LABORATORY EXERCISE 8-2
Mapping Sensory Receptors in Human Skin

Human skin contains several types of receptors, each specialized for sensing a different kind of external stimulus. In this exercise, you will design and demonstrate a procedure to map the density of pressure receptors in skin.

The Nature of Nervous Control and Co-ordination

All animals with a brain possess three main types of neurons. **Sensory neurons** carry nerve impulses from receptors toward the brain. The brain processes the information, identifies the stimulus, and initiates a second impulse in response. (See Figure 8-5.) **Motor neurons** carry the new impulses from the brain toward a muscle or a gland that then carries out the appropriate response. **Interneurons** in the brain or spinal cord link the sensory and motor neurons.

All electrically based systems for control and co-ordination depend on the smooth transmission of impulses. The copper wiring in robots and household appliances must be continuous. Any gap in a copper circuit would interrupt the flow of electricity. In animal nervous systems, however, tiny gaps called **synapses** prevent individual neurons from touching each other. Nevertheless, electrical impulses flow smoothly along a circuit of neurons as shown in Figure 8-5. This difference between living and nonliving control systems raises several important questions. Just what *is* a nerve impulse? How does it get started? How does it move along a neuron, and how does it jump the synapse from one neuron to the next?

Transmitting electrical impulses through neurons involves the movement of charged particles called **ions.** Ions are formed when ordinary neutral atoms acquire a positive or a negative charge. Both the cytoplasm inside a living neuron and the extracellular fluid around it contain positive ions of sodium and potassium.

Although these ions are dissolved, they cannot move freely across the cell membrane of a "resting" neuron — a neuron that is not conducting a nerve impulse. This is because a resting neuron is actually very active, constantly pumping sodium ions out of the cell while pumping potassium ions back in. As a result, sodium ions are more numerous outside the neuron, and potassium

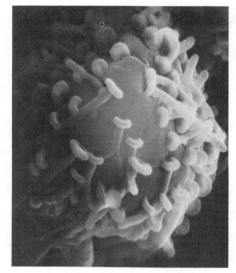

Terminal knobs meeting a nerve cell within the ganglion of a sea slug. The terminal knobs do not make direct contact with the next nerve cell.

Neutral atoms contain equal numbers of protons (+) and electrons (−). Negative ions are formed when extra electrons are gained. Positive ions are formed when electrons are lost.

DID YOU KNOW?
Electrical devices such as car batteries and dry cells also depend on the movement of dissolved ions to carry an electrical charge. In a car battery, sulphuric acid provides the dissolved ions.

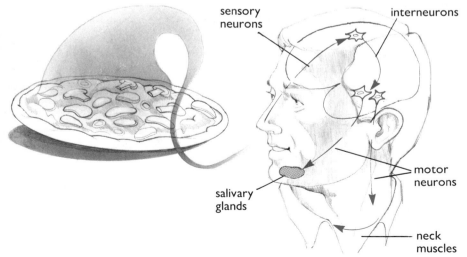

sensory neurons

interneurons

salivary glands

motor neurons

neck muscles

FIGURE 8-5 Sometimes the aroma of freshly baked pizza can cause you to salivate or turn your head to determine where the odour of pizza is coming from. These are responses to impulses received from the brain.

FIGURE 8-6 A nerve impulse is set in motion when a region of reversed polarity travels along the axon like a wave.

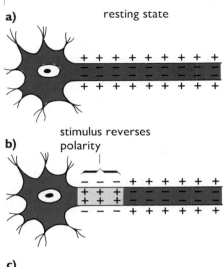

a) resting state

b) stimulus reverses polarity

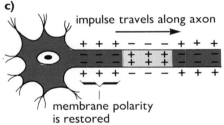

c) impulse travels along axon

membrane polarity is restored

ions are more numerous inside. In addition, the overall concentration of positive ions outside the neuron is greater than it is inside. (See Figure 8-6a.) This difference in concentration results in a slight positive charge outside the cell. For this reason, a resting neuron is said to be polarized.

A nerve impulse starts when the dendrite end of a neuron is stimulated, for example, by a sensory receptor. This disruption makes the nearest part of the membrane more permeable. Extra sodium ions sweep in and potassium ions rush out, temporarily reversing the polarity in a short segment of the cell membrane. (See Figure 8-6b.) This sudden exchange of ions produces the actual nerve impulse.

This sharp change of charge stimulates the adjacent cell membrane. More sodium and potassium ions change places, and the region of reversed polarity spreads like a wave. Meanwhile, the ions in the first section return to their original positions, restoring the polarized condition. (See Figure 8-6c.) Because the change in polarization is temporary, a new impulse can travel along the same neuron within a few milliseconds.

You should remember that the ions themselves do not travel the length of the neuron. They only cross and recross the cell membrane. What moves along the neuron is the nerve impulse, which is a region of reversed polarity caused by successive, alternating waves of ions. This wave action keeps the impulse moving until it reaches the terminal knobs at the end of the axon, where it stimulates the knobs to release chemicals called **neurotransmitters.** As the neurotransmitter molecules diffuse across the synapse, they stimulate the nearby dendrites and initiate a new nerve impulse in the next neuron. (See Figure 8-7.) In this way, the impulse is relayed from neuron to neuron until it reaches its destination—the brain, a target muscle, or a gland.

Biologists call the above pattern of nervous transmission electrochemical because it depends on both electrical and chemical energy. Both kinds of energy are supplied by a neuron's mitochondria, especially those in the terminal knobs. Each time a nerve impulse reaches the end of an axon, energy from the mitochondria boosts the strength of the impulse for transmission through the next neuron. Even a resting neuron uses energy to transport the excess sodium ions around it to the external environment.

The basic principles of nervous control discussed in this section are similar throughout the animal kingdom, but vertebrates share several features not found in invertebrates. You will learn more about the nervous systems of vertebrates in Section 8.2.

Section Review Questions

1. a) What is the simplest type of animal nervous system?
   b) What are the disadvantages of this system?

2. How is the nervous system of a planarian more advanced than the nervous system of a hydra?

II ANIMALS

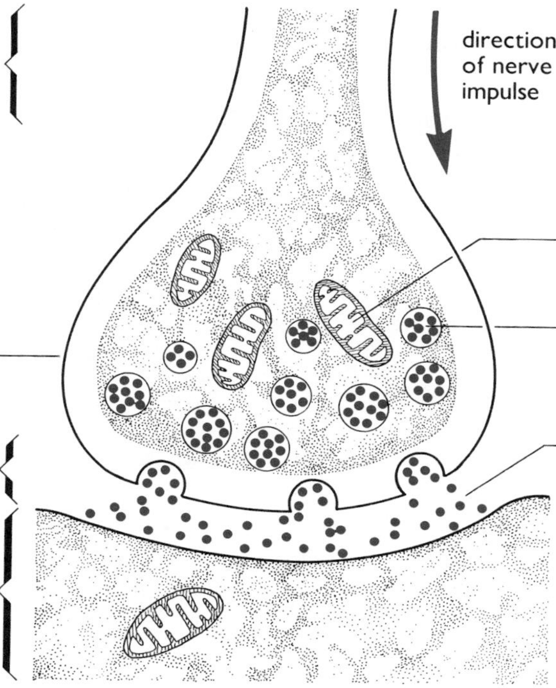

FIGURE 8-7 Neurotransmitter molecules crossing synapse

Labels in figure:
- axon of sending neuron
- direction of nerve impulse
- mitochondrion
- vacuole containing neurotransmitters
- neurotransmitters diffusing across synapse
- terminal knob
- synapse
- dendrite of receiving neuron

3. Draw a simple diagram of a neuron and label its parts.

4. Compare the functions of sensory neurons, motor neurons, and interneurons.

5. a) What are ions?
   b) Describe the role of ions in the transmission of nerve impulses.

6. a) What are neurotransmitters?
   b) Describe how neurotransmitters relay nerve impulses from neuron to neuron.

8.2 Structure of the Vertebrate Nervous System

In most animals, the main nerve cord or cords lie near the animals' ventral surfaces. Only chordates have a nerve cord that lies near the dorsal surface or back. (See Figure 8-8.) Most chordates are classified as vertebrates because their dorsal nerve cords are protected by a spine composed of hollow bones called vertebrae.

Although there are some differences, all vertebrates have a **central nervous system** made up of a brain and a long **spinal cord.** (See Figure 8-9.) Besides a protective bony skull and spine, both the brain and the spinal cord

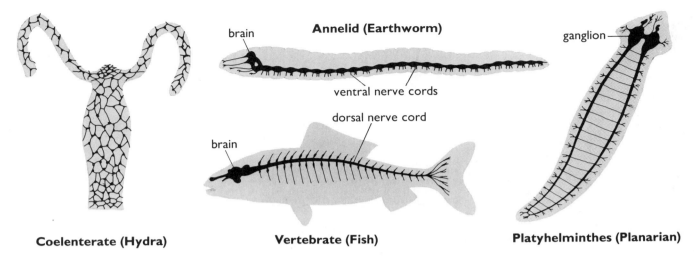

Coelenterate (Hydra)

Annelid (Earthworm)

brain

ventral nerve cords

dorsal nerve cord

brain

Vertebrate (Fish)

ganglion

Platyhelminthes (Planarian)

FIGURE 8-8 A dorsal nerve cord encased in a protective bony spine distinguishes vertebrates such as fish from invertebrates such as coelenterates, platyhelminthes, and annelids.

Cerebrospinal fluid is similar to blood plasma or lymph but contains almost no proteins. It also has much lower concentrations of all other solutes except sodium chloride and bicarbonate. These compounds provide the dissolved sodium ions needed for transmission of nerve impulses.

are surrounded by a tough outer membrane and two inner membranes that enclose a layer of **cerebrospinal fluid.** This clear liquid also fills hollow brain chambers called **ventricles** and the hollow central canal of the spinal cord. (See Figure 8-10.)

Cerebrospinal fluid has two functions. It cushions the brain and the spinal cord from blows, and also carries oxygen, nutrients, and wastes between the blood and the central nervous system. Cilia lining the ventricles keep the cerebrospinal fluid circulating within the brain and the spine.

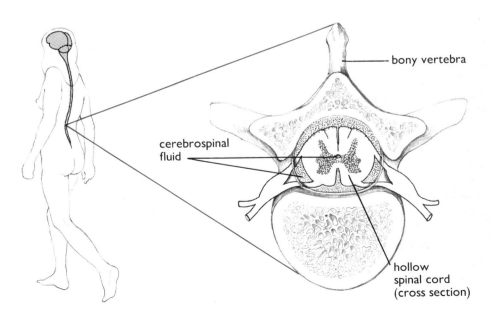

bony vertebra

cerebrospinal fluid

hollow spinal cord (cross section)

FIGURE 8-9 The central nervous system of a vertebrate includes a brain and a hollow dorsal nerve tube.

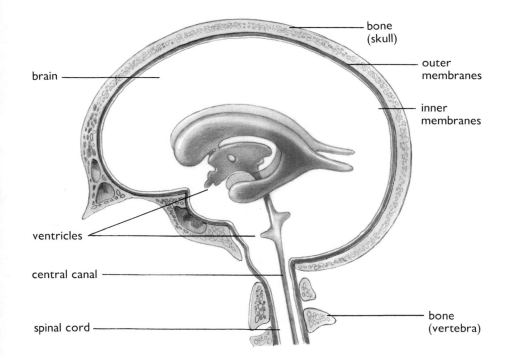

FIGURE 8-10   The human skull and brain

bone (skull)

outer membranes

inner membranes

brain

ventricles

central canal

spinal cord

bone (vertebra)

The Vertebrate Brain

In all very young vertebrate embryos, the central nervous system begins as a long dorsal tube. During development, the tube's front end swells to form a brain with three distinct sections: a **forebrain,** a **midbrain,** and a **hindbrain.** (See Figure 8-11.) As the embryo matures into an adult, these sections develop into specialized regions that enable the brain to act as a co-ordinating centre for the entire nervous system. Table 8-1 summarizes the functions of these brain structures. The relative sizes of vertebrate brain structures vary from one class to another, each being adapted to suit a particular way of life. (See Figure 8-12.)

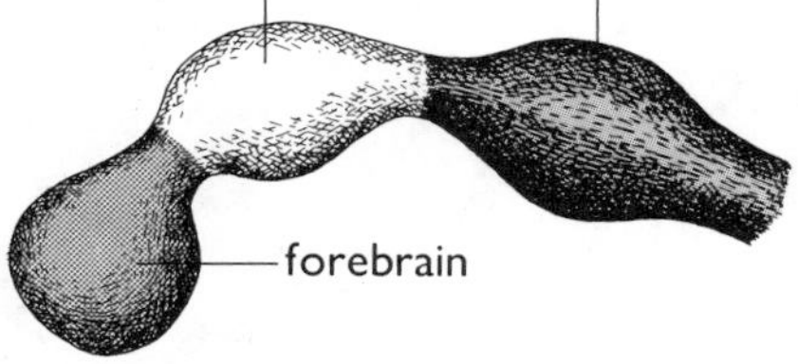

midbrain   hindbrain

forebrain

FIGURE 8-11   In the earliest embryonic stages, all vertebrate brains look similar.

LABORATORY EXERCISE 8-3
Exploring a Vertebrate Brain

Much of what is known about the human brain has been learned by studying the structures and tissues of other vertebrate brains. In this exercise, you will examine the external and internal features of a representative nonhuman vertebrate brain in order to produce a diagram identifying its component parts. You will also compare these parts to a diagram or to a model of the human brain.

TABLE 8-1 Functions of Vertebrate Brain Structures

Structure	Region	Generalized Functions
Forebrain	• cerebrum	• thought and memory; area of sensory input; origin of voluntary actions
	• thalamus	• sense integration; emotion
	• hypothalamus	• link between endocrine system and nervous system
Midbrain	• optic lobe	• involved with sensory nerve impulses from the eye in lower vertebrates
Hindbrain	• cerebellum	• muscular co-ordination and balance
	• pons	• receives stimuli from facial areas
	• medulla oblongata	• co-ordination of impulse from ear; taste and touch; contains centres for control of heart rate and breathing

FIGURE 8-12 All vertebrate brains have the same basic parts, but their relative sizes vary from class to class. Notice especially the variations in the olfactory lobe and the cerebrum, and the absence of midbrain structures in the adult mammal.

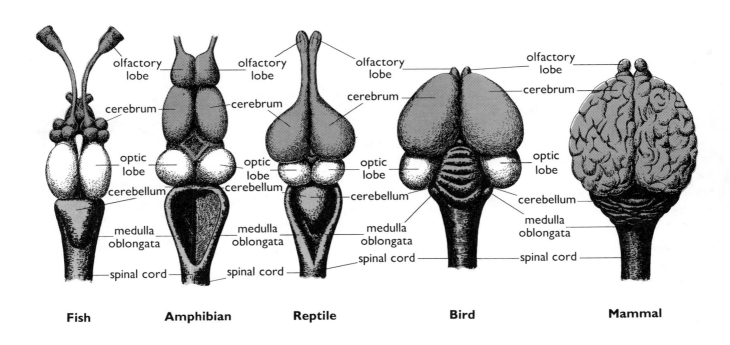

Fish   Amphibian   Reptile   Bird   Mammal

Walrus/
Odobenus rosmarus

Giant panda/*Ailuropoda melanoleuca*

Garter snake/
Thamnophis sirtalis

Red-eyed tree frog/
Hylidae

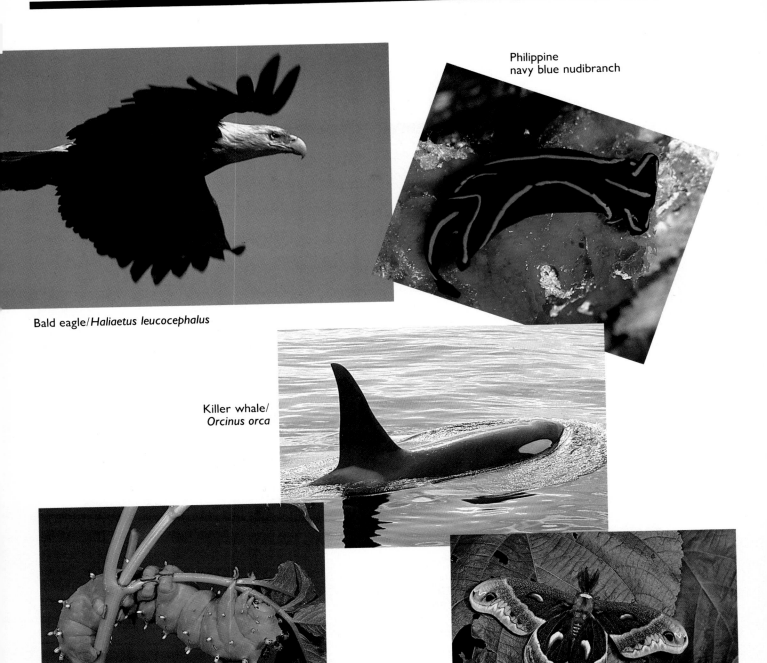

Philippine
navy blue nudibranch

Bald eagle/*Haliaetus leucocephalus*

Killer whale/
Orcinus orca

Cecropia moth caterpillar/
Hyalophora cecropia

Cecropia moth/
*Hyalophora
cecropia*

The Human Brain

The human brain is similar in structure and function to other vertebrate brains. But certain components such as the **olfactory lobe** are very small by comparison, while others are much more developed. One major difference between the human brain and other vertebrate brains is the comparative size and structure of the **cerebrum.**

The human cerebrum is almost completely divided into halves or hemispheres. (See Figure 8-13.) Its numerous folds and fissures provide enough surface area for the ten billion neurons needed to receive, process, and respond to sensory input from all over the body. The cell bodies, dendrites, and synapses of these neurons make up the outer layer of **grey matter.** The inner **white matter** of each hemisphere mainly consists of nerve fibres — axons bundled together by whitish myelin sheaths. These nerve fibres connect the neurons in the hemispheres with each other and with the rest of the brain and the body. Each cerebral hemisphere contains four lobes. The functions of these lobes are shown in the brain maps of Figure 8-14. The frontal lobe, which contains centres for personality, learning, thought, and speech, is much more highly developed in humans than in other mammals.

The human cerebrum has more neurons than any other animal brain of similar size.

DID YOU KNOW?
The expression "Use your grey matter" suggests that the surface layer of the cerebrum is the site of logical thinking. However, the white matter is equally important. Without its connections, there would be no nervous control or co-ordination.

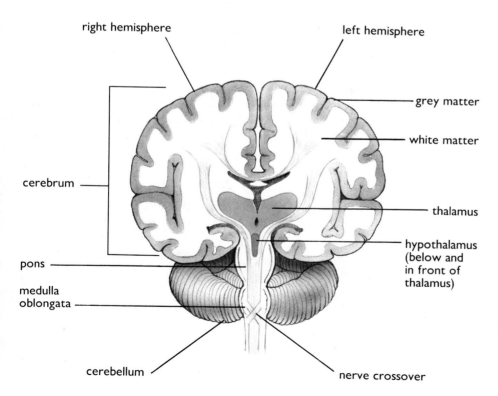

FIGURE 8-13 This vertical cross section shows the back half of the human brain.

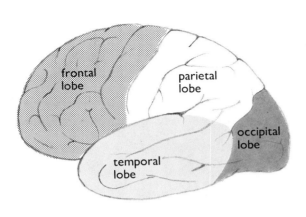

The Four Major Lobes

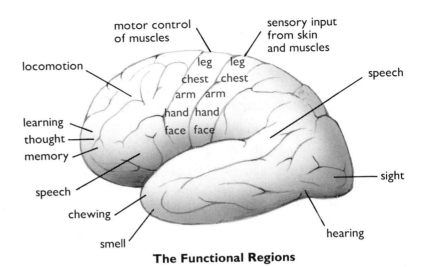

The Functional Regions

FIGURE 8-14 Each hemisphere of the cerebral cortex includes four major lobes and several functional regions.

Athletic helmets are designed and tested to reduce the risk of head injury.

The **thalamus** screens all nerve impulses before they can reach the cerebrum, allowing only essential messages through. This feature makes it possible for you to ignore unimportant sensations such as those caused by your clothing or the chair you are sitting on. The thalamus also controls sleeping and waking. It screens out the sound of a person delivering the morning paper every day, but lets the unaccustomed sound of a prowler through to waken a sleeping householder. The body's response to possible danger is then controlled by the **hypothalamus,** which monitors the release of chemicals, especially those relating to emotions such as fear and anger.

In humans, the hindbrain functions much as it does in other vertebrates. So, damage to the **cerebellum** interferes with muscular co-ordination, while damage to the **medulla oblongata** interferes with heartbeat and breathing. The medulla is also the site where many nerve connections between the brain and the body cross over. That is why damage to the motor region of the *right* cerebral hemisphere—by a stroke, for example—causes paralysis on the *left* side of the body. The pons relays messages from one part of the brain to another and is also the origin of several **cranial nerves.**

In humans, twelve pairs of cranial nerves connect the brain directly with structures in the head, neck, heart, lungs, and digestive tract. (See Table 8-2.) All other body parts are connected to the brain indirectly by 31 pairs of **spinal nerves** that lead from the spinal cord.

The Spinal Cord

The vertebrate spinal cord is continuous with the brain. Both are bathed in cerebrospinal fluid, and both contain grey and white matter. In the spinal cord, however, grey matter lines the inside of the cord, while white matter surrounds the outside. (See Figure 8-15.)

TABLE 8-2   The Twelve Cranial Nerves

Location	Number	Nerve	Functions Controlled
Midbrain	1	• olfactory (sensory)	• sense of smell
	2	• optic (sensory)	• sense of sight
	3	• oculomotor (motor)	• movement of eyes • size of iris opening
Pons	4	• trochlear (motor)	• movement of eyes
	5	• trigeminal (sensory and motor)	• sensation in face, eyes, nose, tongue • movement of jaw (chewing) • movement of eyes
	6	• abducens (motor)	
Medulla Oblongata	7	• facial (sensory and motor)	• sense of taste • movement of muscles in face, scalp, neck • stimulation of salivary flow
	8	• auditory (sensory)	• sense of hearing
	9	• glossopharyngeal (sensory and motor)	• sense of taste • sense of touch and temperature in mouth and throat • stimulation of salivary flow
	10	• vagus (sensory and motor)	• movement of muscles in larynx and pharynx • stimulation of heart, bronchi, stomach, pancreas, gall bladder, intestines • movement of muscles of neck and upper back and larynx
	11	• accessory (motor)	• movement of muscles of neck and upper back and larynx
	12	• hypoglossal (motor)	• movement of tongue muscles

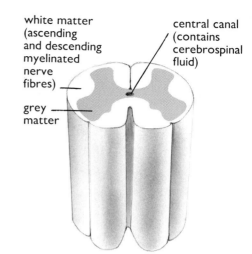

FIGURE 8-15 This illustration shows a segment of a human spinal cord. The spinal cord is actually about as thick as your index finger and 40-50 cm long.

white matter (ascending and descending myelinated nerve fibres)

central canal (contains cerebrospinal fluid)

grey matter

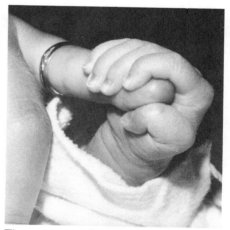

The grasping reflex in a three-day-old human infant. A baby monkey has a similar but much stronger reflex that enables it to cling to its mother's back as she moves.

The spinal cord has two main functions. One is to conduct sensory nerve impulses from all parts of the body to the brain for processing, and to carry motor signals from the brain to the body. The other function is to provide a nerve pathway for reflex actions. A **reflex action** is a rapid response that occurs when certain sensory neurons are stimulated. Reflex actions are predictable, automatic, and unlearned. For example, touching the palm of a newborn baby's hand initiates a grasping reflex by the baby in response. In the next exercise, you will investigate reflex actions that can be safely and easily demonstrated.

LABORATORY EXERCISE 8-4
Investigating Human Reflexes

In this exercise, you will investigate a variety of human reflexes — body responses that occur without conscious thought. You will also be asked to consider how these reflex actions aid in human survival.

The Reflex Arc

The **reflex arc** is the structural basis for all reflex actions. The most common reflex arc is composed of the five parts shown in Figure 8-16. One or more nerve receptors sensitive to a stimulus such as heat initiate a nerve impulse. Sensory neurons carry the nerve impulse and its message — HOT! — to the

FIGURE 8-16 A reflex arc

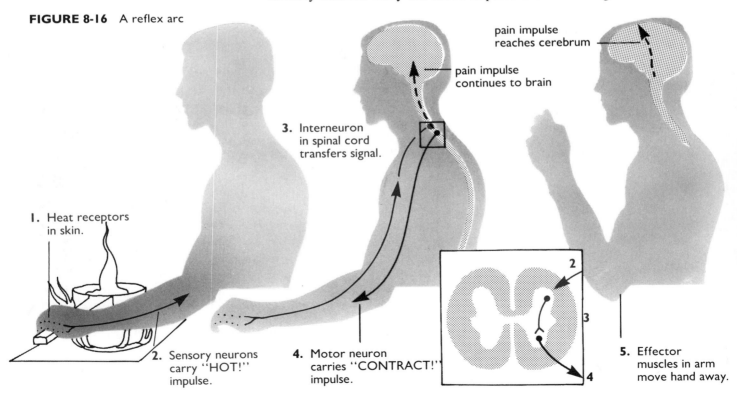

1. Heat receptors in skin.

2. Sensory neurons carry "HOT!" impulse.

3. Interneuron in spinal cord transfers signal.

pain impulse continues to brain

pain impulse reaches cerebrum

4. Motor neuron carries "CONTRACT!" impulse.

5. Effector muscles in arm move hand away.

spinal cord. Interneurons and synapses transfer the impulse directly to the appropriate motor neuron without any brain involvement. Motor neurons carry the responding impulse — CONTRACT! — from the spinal cord to the muscles. Effector muscles contract and complete the reflex action. An **effector** is any cell or body part that responds to an impulse from the central nervous system. For example, in some people the smell of pizza stimulates a response by two types of effector: neck muscles and the salivary glands. (Recall Figure 8-5 on page 243.)

Reflex arcs like the one shown in Figure 8-16 enable the body to respond rapidly to a dangerous stimulus. No time is lost waiting for the HOT! message to travel to the brain for processing and response. The brain does eventually receive a PAIN! message, but after the hand has already been withdrawn. At that point, the thinking ability of your cerebrum is useful in deciding what to do next. Should you call the fire department, an ambulance, or a doctor? Should you plunge your hand in cold water, grab a fire extinguisher, or rescue the family pet and run? The nervous interactions involved in making such decisions and carrying them out are much more complex than a simple reflex arc. In Section 8.3, you will consider the components that enable the human nervous system to function in such a co-ordinated manner.

Section Review Questions

1. Identify and briefly describe the components of the central nervous system.
2. a) Where is cerebrospinal fluid found?
   b) What is the function of cerebrospinal fluid?
3. a) Compare the size and structure of the human cerebrum with that in other vertebrate brains. Why is this difference important?
   b) What is the difference between the white and grey matter observed in the vertebrate brain? Why is the amount of grey matter significant?
4. a) What is the function of the thalamus?
   b) Why is this function important?
5. Why does damage on one side of the brain cause paralysis on the opposite side of the body?
6. a) What are reflex actions?
   b) How do reflex actions protect you?
7. List the five components of a common reflex arc and describe how they interact to perform the appropriate reflex action.

Migraines

For most people, headaches are an annoying, but hardly debilitating, fact of life. When most headaches strike, they can be treated with a mild painkiller and then forgotten. But for migraine sufferers, who make up 5–20% of the population, escape is not so easy. Migraines are generally more severe than other headaches, and although symptoms vary in both kind and intensity, they are often debilitating. Currently, researchers are exploring a new understanding of migraines to produce more effective drugs and treatments, which may ease the suffering of migraine victims.

Migraine pain can be intense. The first stage of some migraines may last up to 30 min and involves a variety of perceptual distortions. The sufferer may see flashing lights or lose vision altogether. Brief abnormalities in speech and body movement may also occur. The second more common stage features intense, throbbing pain over one temple, nausea, and increased sensitivity to light and sound. Mood disorders, as well as difficulty in thinking and sleeping, are also common. These symptoms may persist for a full day and may recur once every two to six weeks.

Recently, migraine has been recognized as a biological disease of the central nervous system. Previously, migraine sufferers

were told their pain was largely psychosomatic. The theory responsible for this view holds that stress induces constrictions and dilations of blood vessels. These blood-vessel alterations cause the pain of the migraine by altering blood supply to the brain. In people prone to migraines, attacks may be triggered by many different factors: stress, flashing lights, red wine, chocolate, cheese, and air-pressure changes.

There is now increasing agreement among researchers that a disturbance in the function of one of the brain's chemical messengers, serotonin, is the real cause of the migraine reaction, no mat-

JOURNEY THROUGH
MIGRAINE

ter how the migraine is caused. Serotonin is involved in controlling body functions such as sleep, mood, digestion, and constriction or dilation of blood vessels. These are the body functions disturbed during migraine attacks. In addition, all of the most effective medications for relief of migraine symptoms work by either enhancing or restricting the action of serotonin in different parts of the brain.

Researchers are using this new insight to focus their efforts in migraine treatment. In Britain, preliminary tests are now underway on a drug that stimulates at least one of serotonin's actions. Researchers hope that this new drug will be successful in treating migraine headaches without causing disturbing side effects. The drug, currently known only by its serial number GR43175, was developed by subtly changing an earlier drug that had alleviated migraine pain, but that had also raised blood pressure and caused other undesirable side effects.

While this and other drugs are developed for the relief of migraine pain, the next step for researchers will be to sort out the multitude of biochemical changes the brain experiences during the migraine attack, with the intent of discovering the cause of serotonin dysfunction.

8.3 Co-ordination of Nervous Control and Chemical Regulation in Humans

True nervous co-ordination is much more complex than a preprogrammed reflex response. To pick and eat an apple, for example, you must decide which apple is ripest and move several muscles in the correct sequence — first to detach the apple and then to chew it. But the need for co-ordination does not end here. Salivating, swallowing, peristalsis, secreting digestive juices, adjusting the heartbeat and breathing to permit the absorption of nutrients, and providing the oxygen needed for metabolizing these nutrients are only some of the processes that require action by the nervous system.

Components of the Human Nervous System

The human nervous system is made up of several component subsystems, all of which are co-ordinated by the central nervous system. (See Figure 8-17.) All nerves other than the brain and spinal cord belong to the **peripheral nervous system.** (See Figure 8-18.) Some peripheral nerves are attached to the brain by the cranial nerves, but most are attached indirectly by the spinal nerves. Biologists classify the peripheral nerves according to the type of nervous control each one exercises.

The **somatic nervous system** includes the motor nerves serving body parts that are under conscious control. This system also includes all sensory nerves. The sensory neurons that tell you your nose is itchy and the motor neurons that stimulate the muscles you move to scratch your nose both belong to the somatic nervous system.

The **autonomic nervous system** includes all motor nerves that function *without* conscious control. This system regulates automatic or involuntary responses such as heartbeat, glandular secretions, and body temperature. The motor neurons that stimulate peristalsis in the digestive tract when you eat, and the motor neurons that dilate your pupils in the dark all belong to the autonomic nervous system. (You should remember that the autonomic nervous system includes *only* motor neurons.) All sensory neurons are considered part of the somatic nervous system, even those that monitor internal conditions you usually are not aware of. Blood pressure is an example of an internal condition monitored by sensory neurons.

The autonomic nervous system includes two completely separate nerves for each body part: a **sympathetic nerve** and a **parasympathetic nerve.** (See Figure 8-19.) In general, parasympathetic nerves counteract the effects of sympathetic nerves. For example, the heart's sympathetic nerve speeds it up, while its parasympathetic nerve slows the heart down. However, the bladder's sympathetic nerve causes it to relax, while its parasympathetic nerve causes contractions.

Not all reflexes involve the spinal cord. The most direct reflex arc involves only a synapse linking a sensory neuron in the skin with a motor nerve connected to a skin muscle. This is the reflex that causes goose bumps when you feel cold.

RIGHT: **FIGURE 8-17** The central
nervous system and its subsystems

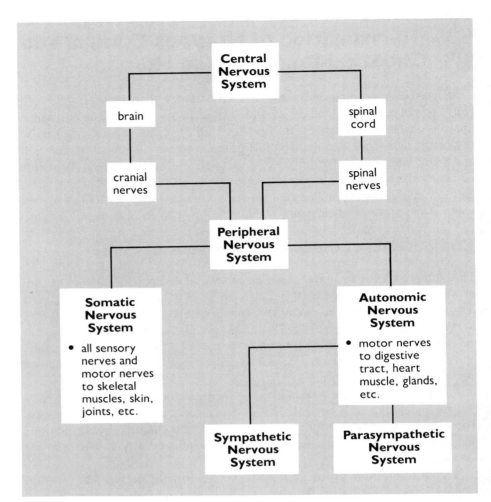

RIGHT: FIGURE 8-17 The central
nervous system and its subsystems

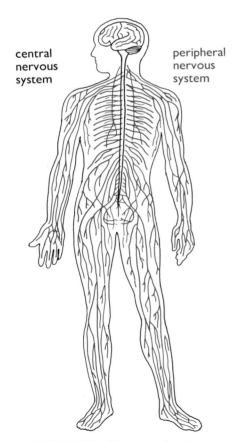

central
nervous
system

peripheral
nervous
system

FIGURE 8-18 The central and
peripheral nervous systems

The sympathetic nerves act directly to prepare body organs for a "fight
or flight" response to danger by accelerating the heartbeat, redistributing
blood through the dilation of vessels in the muscles and constriction of those
in the skin, and improving peripheral vision through the dilation of the pupils.
The sympathetic nerves also stimulate the adrenal glands to release adrenaline
and noradrenaline into the bloodstream. As these chemicals travel throughout
the body, they enhance and maintain the changes caused by the sympathetic
nerves themselves.

Adrenaline, for example, stimulates heart activity, improves muscle
power, prolongs muscle action, and increases breathing rate and the volume
of air taken in with each breath. Adrenaline also inhibits digestion and excretion. The adrenal glands are part of the endocrine system, which also produces
many other chemicals that regulate body activities.

The changes caused by adrenaline would be harmful to the body if they

II ANIMALS

Parasympathetic Nerves

Sympathetic Nerves

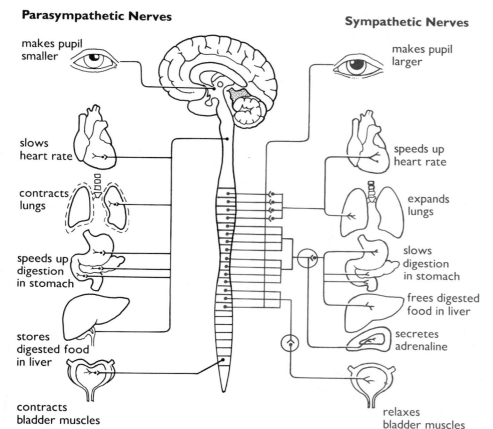

makes pupil smaller

slows heart rate

contracts lungs

speeds up digestion in stomach

stores digested food in liver

contracts bladder muscles

makes pupil larger

speeds up heart rate

expands lungs

slows digestion in stomach

frees digested food in liver

secretes adrenaline

relaxes bladder muscles

FIGURE 8-19 This illustration of the autonomic nervous system shows the antagonistic roles of the sympathetic nerves in colour and the parasympathetic nerves in black.

DID YOU KNOW?
Although the autonomic system is considered to be involuntary, amazing control over autonomic functions such as heartbeat has been demonstrated. During periods of meditation, some practitioners of Buddhism and Yoga have been able to reduce their heart and breathing rates below the levels that usually occur during sleep.

lasted for an extended period of time. The parasympathetic nervous system prevents this from occurring by returning the body to its normal, steady state when the danger or other stress has ended. Together with the endocrine system, the sympathetic and parasympathetic systems play a major role in maintaining homeostasis.

LABORATORY EXERCISE 8-5
Nervous Control and Chemical Regulation of Body Functions

In the first part of this exercise, you will observe how blood pressure changes when heart and breathing rates are altered. You will also determine how long it takes the body to return to its normal, steady state and identify factors that influence this time period.

In the second part, you will observe the effect of adrenaline on the heart rate of a daphnia, which is an invertebrate belonging to the phylum Arthropoda.

Nervous Control and Homeostasis

Nervous control plays a major role in homeostasis. For example, maintaining fairly constant levels of oxygen in the blood depends on an alternating pattern of inspiration and expiration. This pattern is controlled by nerve impulses from a breathing centre in the medulla oblongata. Figure 8-20 describes how each inspiration triggers the centre to send out impulses that eventually trigger the next expiration.

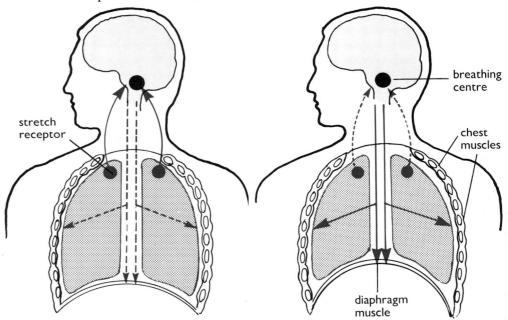

Expiration
Fully inflated lungs stimulate the stretch receptors. The result is an increase in impulses to the medulla (solid arrows). This increase signals the breathing centre to send fewer outgoing impulses (dotted arrows). The lack of stimulus from the medulla allows the muscles of the chest and diaphragm to relax. Relaxing the external chest muscles allows the lower ribs to fall back down and in. Relaxing the diaphragm allows it to resume its dome shape, move toward the lungs, and bulge into the chest cavity. Both movements compress the chest cavity, so lung volume is reduced and air is expelled.

Inspiration
Fully deflated lungs do not stimulate the stretch receptors. The result is a decrease in impulses to the medulla (dotted arrows). This decrease signals the breathing centre to send more outgoing impulses (solid arrows). The extra impulses from the medulla stimulate the muscles of the chest and diaphragm. The resulting contractions shorten the dome-shaped diaphragm, flatten it, and pull it away from the lungs. Contractions of the external chest muscles pull the lower ribs up and out. Both actions enlarge the chest cavity, allowing the lungs to expand so that air rushes in from outside.

FIGURE 8-20 Nervous control of breathing. You can see that the lungs are passive. They inflate or deflate according to the volume of the chest cavity. The work of breathing is performed entirely by the muscles of the chest and diaphragm.

Ordinarily, nervous control of breathing is involuntary. This is because your breathing rate is determined by the level of carbon dioxide in your blood. High carbon dioxide levels trigger the medulla to send out extra impulses that excite the breathing muscles. This feature limits the extent to which you can consciously control your breathing rate. The longer you hold your breath, for example, the more the medulla stimulates your breathing muscles, even though you may be fighting their action. The excess carbon dioxide will then be removed by gas exchange, and homeostasis will be restored.

As Figure 8-21 shows, nervous control of your heart rate is more complex. Heart muscle contracts only when stimulated by the **pacemaker,** a nerve cluster in the wall of the right atrium. The pacemaker is controlled by nerves that lead from an accelerating centre and an inhibitory centre, both located in the medulla oblongata.

The accelerating centre is under dual control. It responds to high blood levels of carbon dioxide in the neck arteries by sending more frequent signals to the pacemaker. Thus, vigorous activity speeds up the heart by increasing production of carbon dioxide from cellular respiration. The accelerating centre also responds to nerve impulses from the heart. The faster it beats, the more its walls stretch. Stretch receptors in the walls stimulate the accelerating centre to send more signals to the pacemaker. The result is a still faster heartbeat.

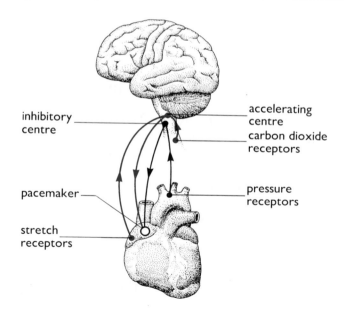

inhibitory centre

accelerating centre

carbon dioxide receptors

pacemaker

pressure receptors

stretch receptors

FIGURE 8-21 Nervous control of heart rate. The rate at which the heart muscle beats is set by impulses from the pacemaker. The coloured arrows show the nerve pathways involved in accelerating the pacemaker. The black arrows show those involved in decelerating it.

Control of heart rate by the accelerating centre is an example of **positive feedback**. A more familiar example will illustrate this term. Technicians who set up the sound system for a concert must ensure that no system output (sound from the speakers) can reach the microphones. Any system output that does re-enter becomes system input. The result is an unbearable screeching noise known as feedback because the original sound is fed back into the system several times. This feedback is positive because the sound is amplified further each time it re-enters.

In a biological system, positive feedback occurs whenever an increase in output causes a system to speed up and increase its own output still further. This definition describes the action of the accelerating centre. The faster your heart beats in response to the centre, the more the centre speeds up your heartbeat. This could cause your heart rate to become dangerously high.

The inhibitory centre, however, maintains homeostasis by responding to different nerve impulses. As your heart rate increases, so does your blood pressure, activating pressure receptors in the aorta to stimulate the inhibitory centre. The centre then signals the pacemaker to reduce the rate at which the heart muscle contracts. The faster your heart beats in response to the accelerating centre, the more the inhibitory centre reduces the action of the pacemaker. This type of control is an example of **negative feedback** because increased output in this case causes the system to slow down. Negative feedback through the inhibitory centre prevents your heart rate and blood pressure from increasing to dangerous levels. The nervous control of breathing is also an example of negative feedback.

Chemical Regulation and Homeostasis

Only animals have nervous systems to control movement. Rapid movement in plants such as the Venus flytrap results from changes in the water content of its cells. The slow response seen as a house plant gradually "leans" toward the stimulus of light results from growth. Plant growth is regulated by dissolved chemicals called **hormones.** A hormone is a substance produced in one part of an organism and transported throughout its body to act on another part. For example, hormones produced by the leaves of a plant affect growth in its stem.

Hormonal regulation in plants is limited to growth. In animals, however, hormones also affect most other life functions, thereby playing a major role in the maintenance of homeostasis. Animal hormones help to co-ordinate and regulate nearly all body systems, and may also cause profound changes in the structure of certain organs. For example, the dramatic transformation of a caterpillar into a butterfly is caused by hormones produced in the animal's brain.

In vertebrates, most hormones are produced by the endocrine glands and secreted into the bloodstream. (See Figure 8-22.) The human **endocrine system** includes several glands that manufacture a variety of hormones. (See

FIGURE 8-22 Hormone secretion by an endocrine gland. Hormones are produced in the glandular cells and then diffuse through the walls of the capillary network.

blood enters capillary network of gland

hormone-secreting gland cells

capillary network

hormone-laden blood leaves gland

Hormones in the growing tip of the plant cause it to bend toward light. A monarch butterfly's metamorphosis is controlled by levels of juvenile hormone in the insect's body.

Figure 8-23.) In most cases, each hormone has a specific target. (See Figure 8-24.) For example, the antidiuretic hormone, ADH, which is secreted by the posterior lobe of the pituitary gland, acts only on the kidney, even though it travels past numerous other organs and tissues along the way. Only the kidney has chemical receptor molecules with the correct shape to "trap" ADH molecules.

Chemical regulation is generally much slower than nervous control. Nerve impulses are electrical and travel rapidly along the neurons. Chemical signals are limited to the speed at which the bloodstream can carry the dissolved hormones.

A small number of hormones are produced by specialized nerve cells. Some of these hormones are secreted into the bloodstream; others directly into a target tissue or organ.

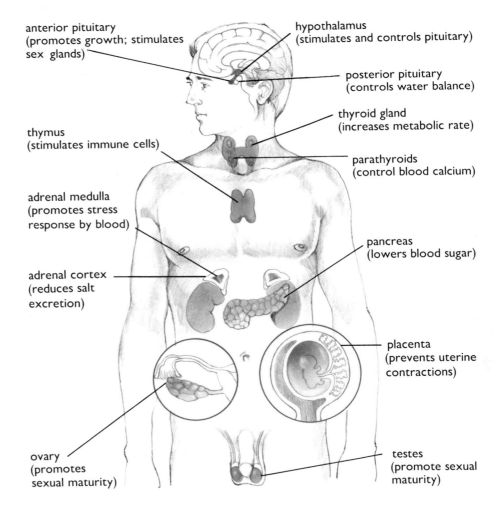

anterior pituitary
(promotes growth; stimulates
sex glands)

hypothalamus
(stimulates and controls pituitary)

posterior pituitary
(controls water balance)

thyroid gland
(increases metabolic rate)

parathyroids
(control blood calcium)

thymus
(stimulates immune cells)

adrenal medulla
(promotes stress
response by blood)

pancreas
(lowers blood sugar)

adrenal cortex
(reduces salt
excretion)

placenta
(prevents uterine
contractions)

ovary
(promotes
sexual maturity)

testes
(promote sexual
maturity)

FIGURE 8-23 The major glands of the human endocrine system and their most important functions

II ANIMALS

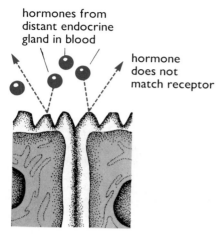

hormones from distant endocrine gland in blood

hormone does not match receptor

Nontarget Cells

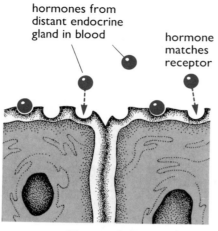

hormones from distant endocrine gland in blood

hormone matches receptor

Target Cells

FIGURE 8-24 Hormones do not affect nontarget cells because the receptors do not match in shape. However, target cells "recognize" hormones that have the correct shape to be trapped by the receptors.

Body responses to hormones are usually much slower and much less localized than responses to nerve impulses. Examples of long-term responses to hormones include growth and sexual development. Adrenaline is one of only a few hormones that act quickly. Perhaps the most versatile endocrine gland is the pancreas. It secretes digestive chemicals into the duodenum, and it also secretes the hormones insulin and glucagon into the bloodstream.

Insulin acts to decrease the amount of glucose in the blood, while glucagon acts to increase it. Together, they keep blood glucose at a fairly constant level by means of a feedback cycle. (See Figure 8-25.)

Although it is only the size of a pea, the **pituitary gland** secretes more kinds of hormones than any other endocrine gland. (See Table 8-3.) Two of these hormones are produced by the adjacent hypothalamus. (See Figure 8-26.)

The hypothalamus and the pituitary gland interact to exert a variety of effects on distant parts of the body. Human growth hormone, for example, regulates the growth of the skeleton and the muscles. It stimulates the production of bone materials that increase the length of the limbs, and also promotes the manufacture of proteins that increase the amount of muscle.

The levels of the hormones and many other chemicals are regulated by feedback control. This type of interaction helps the endocrine system to maintain a stable internal environment or homeostasis.

Co-ordination of Chemical Regulation and Nervous Control

The endocrine system and the nervous system act together in a co-ordinated way. For example, under the stress of an emergency that may require a rapid physical response such as running, the brain signals the sympathetic nervous

DID YOU KNOW?

If your diet is deficient in iodine, your thyroid gland cannot manufacture the hormone thyroxin. Under these conditions, the thyroid gland enlarges to form a visible neck swelling called a goitre. This deficiency disorder is now rare in Canada because all table salt sold here is "iodized." Iodized table salt contains a small quantity of sodium iodide.

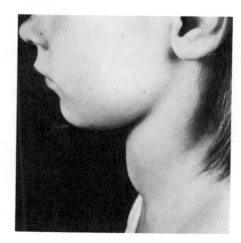

FIGURE 8-25 Feedback control of blood glucose is only one of many hormone-regulated cycles that help maintain homeostasis. Is the feedback illustrated here positive or negative?

The importance of insulin in controlling glucose levels was first demonstrated in 1922 by the Canadian scientists Frederick Banting and Charles Best. Banting later shared a Nobel Prize for his part in the discovery. In 1955, insulin became the first protein to be analyzed as to its amino acid sequence.

Plants also produce hormones that affect their growth. Among animals, hormonal regulation of body functions is much more common in vertebrates than in invertebrates.

1. High level of glucagon in blood stimulates conversion of glycogen to glucose, releasing it into blood.

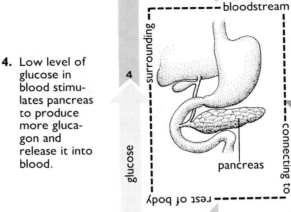

4. Low level of glucose in blood stimulates pancreas to produce more glucagon and release it into blood.

2. High concentration of glucose in blood stimulates pancreas to produce more insulin and release it into blood.

3. High level of insulin in blood promotes intake of glucose by cells that convert glucose to glycogen.

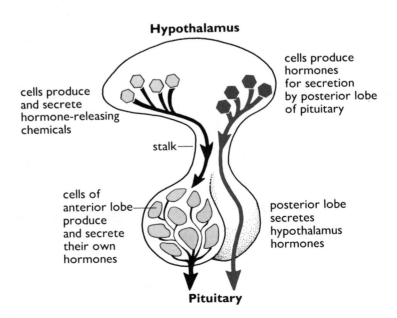

FIGURE 8-26 The hypothalamus controls hormone secretion by the pituitary. The two glands are connected by blood vessels (both lobes) and nerves (posterior only).

cells produce and secrete hormone-releasing chemicals

cells produce hormones for secretion by posterior lobe of pituitary

stalk

cells of anterior lobe produce and secrete their own hormones

posterior lobe secretes hypothalamus hormones

Hypothalamus

Pituitary

II ANIMALS

TABLE 8-3 Pituitary Hormones

Lobe of Gland	Hormone	Target Organ/Tissue	Effects
Anterior	• growth hormone (GH)	• liver	• stimulates growth of muscle, cartilage, and bone
	• thyroid stimulating hormone (TSH)	• thyroid gland	• stimulates thyroid to produce and secrete thyroxin
	• adrenocorticotropic hormone (ACTH)	• adrenal glands	• stimulates cortex to produce corticoid hormones
	• prolactin	• mammary glands	• stimulates the production of milk in mammary glands
	• melanocyte stimulating hormone (MSH)	• skin	• controls production of melanin in skin
	• follicle stimulating hormone (FSH)	• ovary • testes	• stimulates development of follicles in females • stimulates development of seminiferous tubules in males for sperm production
	• luteinizing hormone (LH)	• ovary • testes	• stimulates the maturation and expulsion of follicle from ovary • stimulates the secretion of sex hormones by ovaries and testes
	• interstitial cell stimulating hormone	• testes	• stimulates production of testosterone in males
Posterior	• antidiuretic hormone (ADH)	• kidney tubules	• stimulates the walls of the tubules to be more permeable to water, decreasing urine volume • stimulates constriction of smooth muscles of blood vessels, increasing blood pressure
	• oxytocin	• uterus • mammary glands	• causes uterus muscles to contract, signalling the onset of labour in childbirth • causes the release of milk by mammary glands into central milk duct

system, which, in turn, stimulates the adrenal glands to secrete adrenaline. While adrenaline expands blood vessels in the muscles, sympathetic nerves constrict blood vessels in the skin and shut down digestion. This combination makes more blood available for the heart, which both systems stimulate to beat faster, and for the muscles needed for running.

You learned earlier that these effects are called the ''fight or flight'' response. Your body responds in the same way to many other types of stress. That is why your heart may pound when your teacher hands out exam papers, and why you may feel angry when a bus door closes right in your face. The flight response helped early humans deal with marauding animals, but it is not always appropriate for the stresses of modern life. At such times, it can help to realize that homeostasis will soon be restored. When the emergency is over, the nervous system will signal the endocrine system to stop producing adrenaline, and the body will gradually return to normal.

The nervous system and the endocrine system interact in many other ways that help maintain homeostasis. Any disruption of either system can have far-reaching effects. You will learn about some of the diseases and disorders that can result from such disruptions in Section 8.4.

Section Review Questions

1. a) Use a simple diagram to show how the subsystems of the human nervous system are related.
   b) Identify each subsystem as either voluntary or involuntary.
   c) Briefly describe the function of each subsystem.

2. a) Explain one example of co-ordination by negative feedback.
   b) Explain one example of co-ordination by positive feedback.

3. Why can you only hold your breath for a limited time?

4. a) Where is the pacemaker located, and what is its function?
   b) How is the pacemaker controlled?

5. a) What are hormones?
   b) State an example of a hormone and its effect.
   c) Explain what is meant by specific targets in relation to hormone activity.

6. a) Where is the pituitary gland located?
   b) Identify the body system this gland belongs to.
   c) List the functions of the pituitary gland.

7. Explain how the ''fight or flight'' response provides an example of co-ordination.

8. List as many differences as you can between nervous control and chemical regulation.

Stephen Hawking is widely considered the greatest theoretical physicist since Albert Einstein. As the Lucasian Professor of Mathematics at Cambridge University, Hawking occupies the position Isaac Newton did three centuries ago. Hawking's accomplishments are especially impressive because for much of his adult life he has been unable to walk or speak.

Hawking has Amyotrophic Lateral Sclerosis (ALS), and his case is both unusual and typical of this degenerative nerve disease. The disease is usually fatal within four years, but Hawking has been fighting it since the late 1960s. Although he is now restricted to a wheelchair and able to communicate only through a computer-controlled voice synthesizer, Hawking continues to work, and he has written a best-selling book. According to Hawking, although the disease has made his achievements more difficult, it has allowed him to focus more intensely on his research, and he continues to explore the universe with his mind.

In ALS, the neurons controlling the body's muscles degenerate, causing a progressive loss of muscle control. Atrophy and muscle weakness develop as muscle use declines. Manual clumsiness, slurred speech, and difficulty in walking and eating are early symptoms of ALS. ALS is pro-

Amyotrophic Lateral Sclerosis

gressive and irreversible, affecting all the body's muscles. Eventually, the ALS sufferer becomes too weak to move. Death is usually caused by respiratory failure when the muscles that control breathing fail.

The variety of symptoms is so confusing that some researchers believe the syndrome may in fact be several related diseases. Most ALS patients are diagnosed in their forties, but some, like Hawking, contract ALS in their twenties. In nine of ten ALS victims, the disease is not genetically inherited, but the remaining 10% do show an inheritance pattern. And although some ALS victims

like Hawking survive for over 20 years, the vast majority die quickly. Among these was Lou Gehrig, the New York Yankee star of the 1920s and 30s, after whom ALS is popularly called "Lou Gehrig's Disease." In 1939, Gehrig was diagnosed as having ALS, retired from baseball, and died within two years.

The cause or causes of ALS are unknown. Theories with some supporting evidence propose everything from a transmitted viral infection, an enzyme abnormality, a nerve cell reaction, to an antibody attack as possible causes.

In the absence of a foreseeable cure, physicians focus on controlling ALS symptoms to improve the patient's quality of life. ALS patients may need psychological counselling to help them cope with the severe depression that accompanies the disease. Physical symptoms can usually be controlled or alleviated to make the patient more comfortable. But the progress of the disease cannot be stopped. Even respiratory failure can be controlled. Much of the work of breathing can be taken over by mechanical devices that preserve the patient's strength. However, eventually reliance on these devices for survival becomes complete. The patient must choose between death or life on permanent support systems.

267

8.4 Disorders of the Nervous and Endocrine Systems

Disorders affecting any part of the nervous or endocrine system can be caused by a variety of agents: inheritance, physical injury, pressure from a tumor, or infection by a micro-organism. Some disorders can be treated with drugs, while others are caused by drugs or chemicals. In all cases, however, the symptoms are determined by the organ or tissue that is affected.

Nervous System Disorders

Of the disorders described in Table 8-4, multiple sclerosis is the most common among young people. (See Figure 8-27.) It strikes its victims any time from their late teens to their late thirties, affecting more women than men. However, spinal-cord injury is a far more common cause of nervous dysfunction in this age group, especially among men.

TABLE 8-4   Disorders of the Nervous System

Disorder	Part of Nervous System Affected	Symptoms	Treatment
Poliomyelitis	• anterior horns of spinal cord in cervical and lumbar area	• fever, severe headache • paralysis, muscular atrophy	• vaccination • drug treatment
Multiple Sclerosis	• myelin sheaths of neurons in spinal cord and brain	• exaggerated reflexes; higher than normal muscle tone • loss of balance	• drug treatment with ACTH • physical therapy
Parkinson Disease	• degeneration of basal ganglia in the brain	• rigidity of muscles • unable to swing arms while walking • muscle tremors	• drug treatment
Amyotrophic Lateral Sclerosis (Lou Gehrig's disease)	• degeneration of motor nerves in spinal cord and brain	• hands first to suffer paralysis • spreading paralysis of organs	• no treatment
Meningitis	• inflammation of the meninges that cover the brain and spinal cord	• high fever • stiff neck • severe headache	• antibiotics
Encephalitis	• inflammation of the brain	• high fever • paralysis • coma	• antibiotics • antiviral agents

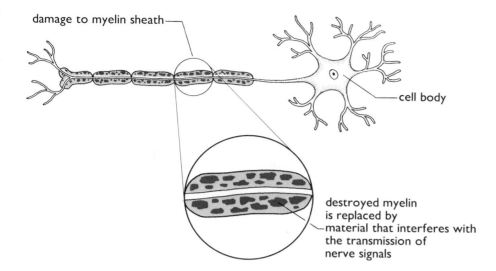

damage to myelin sheath

cell body

destroyed myelin is replaced by material that interferes with the transmission of nerve signals

FIGURE 8-27 Damage to myelin sheath occurring in multiple sclerosis

Most spinal-cord injuries are caused by motor vehicle and motorcycle crashes, or by accidental falls during sports such as diving. Suspected spinal-cord injury patients should be immobilized by specially trained emergency personnel before they are transported to a hospital for treatment. If the victim is not treated properly at the scene of the accident, further damage can occur.

Serious injuries to the spinal cord usually cause some form of permanent damage to the nervous system. In many cases, the spinal cord is either crushed or severed. Nerve function in the area below the injury is affected. (See Figure 8-28.) Injury to the lower end of the spine impairs nerve function in the legs, bladder, and bowel. Damage to the upper end of the spine impairs the arms as well. In some cases, surgery is necessary to stabilize the spine or to remove broken vertebrae. Rehabilitation requires many years of physical and occupational therapy to help retrain muscles that are only partially paralyzed.

Much research is now being devoted to spinal-cord damage. This research is aimed at discovering why the cells of the peripheral nervous system can regenerate, but the cells of the central nervous system cannot. Many of the procedures are experimental and controversial in nature. Some researchers are using electrical energy to stimulate nerve-cell growth. Others have designed experiments to transplant fetal tissue into damaged sites in the hopes of starting the regeneration process of nerve cells.

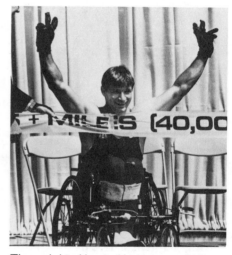

Through his *Man in Motion* tour, Rick Hansen demonstrated the potential of people who have had serious spinal-cord injuries.

Endocrine Disorders

Table 8-5 lists several disorders of the endocrine system. For young people, the most common disorders are those involving abnormalities in the production of human growth hormone. Under-secretion of growth hormone by the pituitary gland causes a condition called pituitary dwarfism. Pituitary dwarfs have normal intelligence levels, and their bodies have normal proportions.

FIGURE 8-28 The higher up the spinal cord an injury occurs, the greater the loss of nervous control.

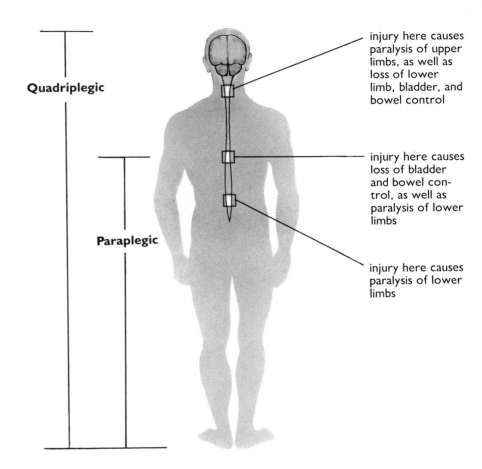

Quadriplegic

injury here causes paralysis of upper limbs, as well as loss of lower limb, bladder, and bowel control

injury here causes loss of bladder and bowel control, as well as paralysis of lower limbs

Paraplegic

injury here causes paralysis of lower limbs

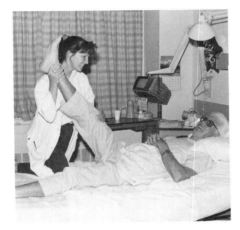

Patients with spinal-cord injuries must undergo extensive rehabilitation therapy.

TABLE 8-5 Disorders of the Endocrine System

Disorder	Endocrine Gland Affected	Symptoms	Treatment
Hyperthyroidism	• thyroid: overproduction of thyroxin	• tendency to thinness • nervous, irritable • thyroid gland enlarged • eyeballs protrude	• surgical reduction of thyroid
Hypothyroidism	• thyroid: underproduction of thyroxin	• before maturity victim fails to achieve normal physical or mental development • after maturity low metabolic rate, tendency to be overweight	• administration of thyroxin

TABLE 8-5——Continued

Disorder	Endocrine Gland Affected	Symptoms	Treatment
Goitre	• thyroid	• swelling of thyroid caused by lack of iodine in diet	• consumption of iodized salt • consumption of seafoods
Diabetes Mellitus	• pancreas: beta cells do not produce enough insulin	• sugar in urine • excessive urination • body cannot burn sugar, so must burn fat and protein, causing buildup of acids in blood, resulting in coma	• injections of insulin
Diabetes Insipidus	• pituitary anterior lobe: inability to produce ADH	• lack of ADH causes large amounts of urine to be produced, up to 20 times normal amount per day	• treatment with antidiuretics
Addison Disease	• adrenal cortex: underproduction of aldosterone, which regulates excretion, and cortisol, which regulates nutrient metabolism	• increased skin pigmentation • apathy, weakness, fatigue • increased potassium level in blood • decreased sodium level in blood • weight loss • low blood pressure	• treatment with aldosterone, cortisol (i.e., hormone replacement therapy)
Giantism	• pituitary: overproduction of human growth hormone (HGH) during childhood	• bones grow beyond normal length • body grows beyond normal size (2.5 m and 180 kg)	• reducing number of HGH-secreting cells through surgery, freezing, or radiation
Acromegaly	• pituitary: overproduction of HGH after skeletal development has been completed	• existing bone and cartilage thicken but do not lengthen • face, feet, hands widen considerably • erosion of joints	• reducing number of HGH-secreting cells through surgery, freezing, or radiation
Dwarfism	• pituitary: underproduction of HGH during childhood	• normal intelligence and body proportions • however, body much smaller than normal • premature senility • short life span (50 a)	• treatment with HGH produced through genetic engineering

The Cape Breton giant, Angus Mac-Askill, and the dwarf Tom Thumb. The pair toured with the Barnum and Bailey circus in the 1850s.

The very small stature of pituitary dwarfs makes it difficult for them to lead normal lives as adults. Fortunately, most pituitary dwarfs can attain near normal heights through hormone replacement therapy during childhood.

Originally, human growth hormone was scarce and expensive because it had to be obtained from the glands of deceased donors. Now, thanks to biotechnology, human growth hormone is produced inexpensively by genetically engineered bacteria. This makes plentiful supplies available for the medically guided treatment of pituitary dwarfism. Unfortunately, human growth hormone can be abused. An example is its nonmedical use by athletes who risk their health to grow bigger muscles for competition.

Chemically Induced Disorders

Some disorders of the nervous system are brought on by the inhalation or ingestion of substances that can damage nerve function. Some of these disorders are caused by chemicals in the environment. Some are caused by prescription drugs taken for other disorders. Others are self-inflicted, caused by legal drugs such as alcohol or illegal drugs such as cocaine.

Many of these so-called ''recreational'' drugs were actually developed to help treat nervous disorders. Some were formulated to block the sensation of pain. Such drugs fall into three general categories: depressants, stimulants, and hallucinogens.

Depressants slow down the functioning of the thalamus to promote sleep, muscle relaxation, or unconsciousness. Examples include anaesthetics such

A field of opium poppies

as chloroform and alcoholic beverages. Although some people drink alcoholic beverages to "get high," the ethyl alcohol these drinks contain is actually a depressant that impairs vision, speech, and hearing, and inhibits the sensory and motor actions of the cerebral cortex. Tranquilizers also depress the thalamus, reducing anxiety without inducing sleep. Tranquilizer treatment has enabled many formerly psychotic patients to lead satisfying lives without institutional care. Tranquilizers may also be prescribed for nonpsychotic patients suffering from severe, short-term anxiety. Inappropriate use, however, leads to dependence and unwanted side effects.

Opiate depressants such as morphine, codeine, methadone, and heroin block the sensation of pain by binding to receptor sites on the surface of sensory neurons. (See Figure 8-29.) While these sites are occupied, the neurons cannot transmit strong pain signals. The opiates fit the receptors because their molecules imitate the shape of the body's own pain-blocking chemicals. Opiates are very addictive because they produce two effects: tolerance and dependence. Tolerance creates the need for an ever-increasing dose to produce the same effect. Physical and psychological dependence make withdrawal from the opiate an unpleasant or sometimes fatal experience.

Stimulants such as the caffeine in cola drinks and the nicotine in cigarette smoke cause mild stimulating effects on the sympathetic nervous system. Stronger stimulants such as amphetamines and cocaine have legitimate medical uses, but they can damage the heart muscle and valves if they are abused because they increase the heart rate for long periods. Constant stimulation of the sympathetic nervous system causes a *deterioration* in an individual's psychological and physical well-being.

Even very small doses of hallucinogens such as extracts of peyote cactus or lysergic acid diethylamide (LSD) can cause powerfully distorting effects on a person's vision and hearing centres. Scientists think that hallucinogens work by imitating the molecular substances in the brain. This mimicry can be observed by comparing the molecular structure of brain transmitters with those of hallucinogens.

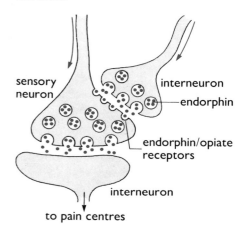

FIGURE 8-29 Endorphins released by the interneurons inhibit the transmission of signals from sensory neurons to interneurons, blocking pain signals to the brain.

Occasionally, alcoholics or other addicts attempt to "get high" by drinking solvents or fluids containing methyl alcohol. Methyl alcohol is a poison so toxic that just 100 mL (two or three mouthfuls) is fatal to adults. Smaller doses cause blindness by paralyzing the optic nerve.

Brain Chemistry and Nervous Function

In recent years, our understanding of brain function has been greatly increased by two very different groups of chemists: those who carry out scientific research, and those who manufacture illegal drugs. The first group are the neurophysiological researchers who identified a previously undiscovered class of brain chemicals now known as endorphins. Unlike the brain chemicals previously known, these "new" neurotransmitters occur in very low concentrations. Further study showed them to be similar to the opiate drugs morphine, opium, and codeine but much more powerful in their effect.

In the brain, the endorphins cause an increased tolerance to pain and promote a feeling of well-being. Scientists think that endorphins are responsible for the ability to withstand extreme pain during accidental limb amputations and other severe body injuries. Strenuous physical exercise has also been found to promote the release of endorphins, which helps explain the enjoyment some people find in sports such as running.

Endorphins may also explain why acupuncture or acupressure relieve pain at distant sites. Scientists have suggested that stimulating certain points on the body can cause the release of endorphins in the brain. People who have benefited from acupuncture hope that the Canadian medical establishment will find acupuncture more acceptable now that there is a physiological explanation of how and why it works.

Recent research has discovered that laughter stimulates the release of endorphins in the brain. Patients experiencing chronic pain are now taking a "laugh" treatment. The natural endorphins that are released into the brain by laughing can block pain for up to 2 h, so that a patient can have relief without having to use strong drugs such as morphine. Morphine and other opiates have to be introduced into the body orally or by injection. They also have to be taken in large doses to ensure that enough drug will reach the brain to block pain. Endorphins have the advantage because they are produced in the brain of the patient and can work effectively when only minute amounts are produced.

The second group of chemists who have increased our understanding of brain chemicals are the "underground" chemists who manufacture so-called "designer drugs." These chemists work in unlicensed laboratories with readily available chemicals. These synthetic drugs are produced to mimic the shape of opiate molecules. Designer drugs are popular with drug addicts because they can be 1000 to 2000 times as strong as heroin.

However, underground labs lack quality control, and slight imperfections in their products are often discovered. In 1982, a batch of a designer drug

Jogging stimulates the release of endorphins in the brain. Endorphins are natural opiates that promote a feeling of well-being.

called MPTP was sold to addicts in northern California. This batch had been improperly produced and was found to cause frightening side effects. Young users of MPTP began to display most of the symptoms of Parkinson's disease, a nervous disorder usually found in middle-aged and elderly people. These drug users had unwittingly become laboratory evidence for the causes of Parkinson's disease.

Acupuncture may release endorphins that relieve pain.

RESEARCH PROJECT
Nervous and Endocrine Disorders

Through library research, identify and report briefly on one neurological disorder, one endocrine disorder, and two chemically induced disorders. Research one chemically induced disorder caused by an environmental chemical, and one caused by a prescription or "recreational" drug.

Be sure to obtain your teacher's approval for your research topics. Appropriate nervous disorders include epilepsy, Alzheimer's disease, and Parkinson's disease. Suitable endocrine disorders include Cushing's disease and Addison's disease. Chemically induced disorders you might research include alcoholic cerebellar degeneration, fetal alcohol syndrome, and Minimata disease. Organize your findings under the following headings.

- Cause of the disorder
- Symptoms of the disorder and its effects on the nervous system
- Control or cure of the disorder
- Current state of research and medical knowledge

Section Review Questions

1. State the causes of two disorders that affect the nervous system and two that affect the endocrine system.
2. How can serious spinal cord injuries affect other parts of the body?
3. How do depressants affect the nervous system?
4. How do stimulants affect the nervous system?
5. How do hallucinogens cause powerful distorting visual and auditory effects?

Meet William Sauter

William works as a prosthetist at the Hugh Mac-Millan Medical Centre in the rehabilitation-engineering department. He is the Co-ordinator of Myoelectric Prosthetic Services.

Q. *What is a prosthetist?*

A. A prosthetist designs, manufactures, and fits artificial limbs. At this centre, we deal with external prosthetics such as artificial arms, hands, legs, and feet. There are also internal prosthetics such as artificial hip and knee joints.

Q. *Describe the kind of prosthetics you specialize in.*

A. I work with upper-extremity (meaning hands and arms) electrically powered limbs. About 83% of our patients have below-elbow amputations. Some patients are accident victims but some, particularly the children, were born this way.

Q. *What can you do to help these people?*

A. We fit them with a lifelike, electrically powered artificial arm that can move and grip objects.

Q. *How are they electrically powered?*

A. These limbs are myoelectric. *Myo* means muscle in Greek. The electricity comes from muscle tissues. All muscles produce a small electric current before contraction, and this electric current powers the artificial limb. Electrodes are used to pick up the electric signal.

Q. *Where are the electrodes placed?*

A. The electrodes are dime-sized, stainless-steel discs that are placed on the skin over a muscle. The patient learns to control the muscle where the electrode has been placed in order to activate the artificial limb. The power for the myoelectric control system comes from battery packs built into the prosthesis. The battery packs must be recharged every night.

Q. *What an improvement over the steel hook!*

A. Yes, and a major advantage of modern prosthetics is that the stigma surrounding artificial limbs has been removed. There have been dramatic changes since I came into the field. Canada is at

the leading edge of pediatric prosthetics. Although the majority of our patients are adults, we are currently treating about 150 children at this clinic. Our youngest patient is just 15 months old.

Q. *Describe the procedure for a patient.*

A. After registration, the patient sees me and a therapist. We present our findings to a doctor who generates a prescription for a prosthesis. Next, the patient is assessed for the most appropriate control site—that is, the muscle where an electrode will be placed to control the artificial limb. Then measurements and a plaster cast of the stump are taken.

Q. *Is the prosthesis made here?*

A. Usually. We buy the hands and the batteries, but other parts are made here. First, we make the socket, the part that connects to the body. This must be carefully fitted so that it is both comfortable and secure. It takes about four weeks to make the prosthesis. Then the patient must be trained to use it and to take care of it.

Q. *Are more people needed in the field?*

A. There are about 243 prosthetists in Canada and about 40 accredited facilities that hire prosthetists. With an aging population and more road and industrial accidents, there will be an increasing demand. It's an interesting field, and we always need more people.

Chapter Review

Key Words

autonomic nervous system
axon
central nervous system
cerebellum
cerebrum
dendrites
effector
endocrine system
hormones
hypothalamus
interneurons
medulla oblongata
motor neurons

neurons
neurotransmitters
parasympathetic nerve
peripheral nervous system
pituitary gland
reflex actions
sensory neurons
sensory receptors
somatic nervous system
spinal cord
sympathetic nerve
synapses
thalamus

Recall Questions

Multiple Choice

1. The gaps between neurons are called
   a) myelin
   b) dendrites
   c) synapses
   d) neurotransmitters

2. The typical vertebrate nervous system consists of
   a) brain, sensory nerves, motor nerves
   b) brain, spinal cord
   c) sensory nerves, motor nerves
   d) brain, spinal cord, sensory nerves, motor nerves

3. The function of cerebrospinal fluid is to
   a) protect the body from electric shock
   b) cushion the brain and spinal cord
   c) make the transmission of nervous signals faster
   d) aid the balance centre of the brain

4. A reflex arc is made up of the following sequence of events
   a) effector, sensory neuron, interneuron, motor neuron, sensory receptor
   b) interneuron, sensory receptor, motor neuron, effector
   c) sensory receptor, sensory neuron, interneuron, motor neuron, effector
   d) sensory receptor, sensory neuron, brain, motor neuron, effector

5. Nervous control of the heart is an example of negative feedback because
   a) increased cardiac output causes the system to slow down
   b) decreased cardiac output causes the system to slow down
   c) increased cardiac output causes the system to speed up
   d) decreased cardiac output causes the system to speed up

Fill in the Blanks

1. The basic functional unit of the nervous system is the _____.

2. Neurons can be divided by function into three groups: _____, _____, and _____.

3. A wave of depolarization in the neuron is called an _____.

4. The substance that transmits nerve impulses across the synapse is called _____.

5. Simple nerve responses that protect you from harmful stimuli are called _____.

6. The three major divisions of the vertebrate brain are the _____, _____, and the _____.

7. Most depressant drugs act by depressing the _____ in the brain.

8. Stimulants work by exciting or stimulating the _____

9. Hallucinogens act by _____ normal brain chemicals, causing mind-altering effects.

10. Nervous control is _____ in nature, while hormonal regulation is _____.

Short Answers

1. How can you differentiate between the dendrites and the axon?

2. Outline the functions and locations of a) the sensory neurons, b) the interneurons, and c) the motor neurons.

3. What is the difference between grey matter and white matter in the brain?

4. a) What is the purpose of the cerebrospinal fluid?
   b) How is this fluid circulated throughout the central nervous system?

5. a) What is a reflex action?

b) Describe a typical reflex action seen in humans.

6. Describe the nervous co-ordination involved in the inspiration-expiration cycle.

7. Compare the functions of the sympathetic and the parasympathetic nervous systems.

8. a) What are the symptoms of multiple sclerosis?
   b) What structure does this disease damage?
   c) How does the damage affect nerve function?

9. a) State the names of three different classes of depressant drugs.
   b) What part of the nervous system do these drugs affect?

10. How do opiates block pain?

Application Questions

1. a) List all of the possible stimuli that cause the eye to blink.
   b) List the sensory receptor, sensory nerve, and motor nerve in this reflex arc. How do they affect the effector muscle?

2. Why is the saying ''practice makes perfect'' true? Explain in terms of repeated muscle motions that are controlled by the brain.

3. What does the maintenance of the resting membrane potential in a neuron depend upon?

4. Explain the relationship of the thalamus to the cerebral cortex.

5. Why do chemicals that mimic neurotransmitters disrupt the body's normal systems when they are introduced into the body?

6. a) State examples of stimuli that have caused the ''fight or flight'' response in your body.
   b) Describe how your body responded to these stimuli.

7. State an example of the nonmedical abuse of human growth hormone. What are the risks of such abuse?

Problem Solving

1. a) Which part of your nervous system is being examined when your doctor performs the familiar ''knee-jerk'' test?
   b) What can this test reveal about the health of other parts of your body?

2. Why are the adrenal glands important to the functioning of the autonomic nervous system?

3. a) What would happen to your breathing rate if you were forced to re-breathe your own expired air?
   b) Suppose all the carbon dioxide could be removed from the expired air before you re-breathed it. Explain what would happen to your breathing rate in this case.

4. What would happen to the heartbeat under the following conditions?
   a) the nerve from the inhibitory centre to the pacemaker was surgically cut
   b) the nerve from the accelerating centre to the pacemaker was cut
   c) the nerve from the aorta to the medulla was cut
   d) the nerve from the stretch receptors to the medulla was cut
   e) the blood supply to the pacemaker was cut off during surgery or a heart attack

5. Use your knowledge of endorphins to give a possible explanation of the pain-blocking effects of acupuncture.

Extensions

1. What does it mean if a person is right- or left-brained? Research your answer in a library.

2. a) What effect does caffeine have on the nervous system? On other body systems?
   b) List at least five common beverages in order of their caffeine content.
   c) What foods contain caffeine?

3. Obtain information from an addiction research foundation or other reliable source about a ''recreational'' drug such as marijuana, cocaine, or crack. What are the health risks associated with the use of this drug?

4. Interview someone who has been fitted with an artificial pacemaker. Find out the medical problem it solves, how it works, and how it was installed.

CHAPTER 9

Protection, Support, and Movement

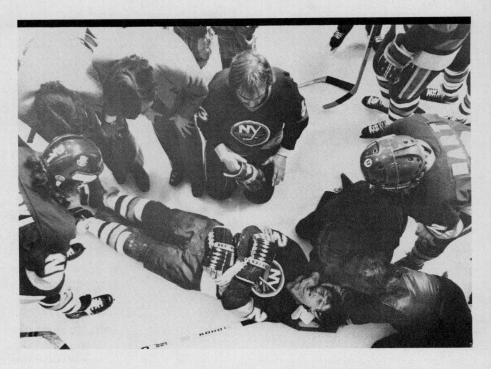

A professional tennis match is a study in extremes. On one hand, the spectators are almost completely inactive, while on the other hand, the athletes are working to their physical limits. In fact, both athletes and spectators should modify their activities.

The effects of underuse on a body can be described by contrasting them with the benefits of exercise. Through a wide range of cardiovascular and skeletal muscle changes, exercise improves the body's ability to do work and cope with stresses. An individual in good physical condition faces less risk of coronary heart disease and mortality from almost all causes. Exercise makes you healthier. Full-time spectators miss the benefits

exercise brings.

However, professional athletes face other risks. A typical professional football player may absorb over 15 000 hits per season. Professional hockey players average three injuries per year, ranging from stick- and puck-induced cuts to broken bones, and bruised muscles and internal organs.

The case of Craig Hartsburg, who played for ten years in the NHL, is grim but not unique. Among his everyday aches and pains, Hartsburg suffered a fractured hip, severe ankle bone bruises, two hernia injuries, and ligament damage in his left knee. He also had his shoulder joint reconstructed twice following injury.

Competitors in noncontact sports such as tennis and baseball are also plagued with injuries. Although the actions involved in noncontact sports are not in themselves harmful, they must be performed so often that they may lead to injuries as a result of overuse.

Between 20-30% of professional tennis players develop tennis elbow, tendonitis or painful inflammation of a tendon running past the elbow. The dominant factor in development of tennis elbow is frequency of play. One study has shown that 45% of people who play daily will eventually develop the condition. Among those who play two or three times per month, the incidence is only 7%. Tendonitis of the shoulder or rotator cuff is caused by excessive repetition of what is another unusual motion for the body: an overhand sweep of a serve in tennis, a throw in baseball or football, a spike in volleyball, and a freestyle stroke in swimming. In addition, many professionals are plagued by regular pain in their feet, ankles, and the most frequently injured of joints, the knees, caused by the constant running, jumping, and changing of directions involved in nearly all sports.

Perhaps the healthiest people are those who exercise and compete in moderation, and who understand how their bodies work. What are the components of the body that are used in movement and exercise? How do they work together? What happens to your body when you exercise? How can you get the maximum benefits from exercise and avoid injury?

Chapter Objectives

When you complete this chapter, you should:

1. Appreciate the various roles of vertebrate integumentary systems.

2. Understand the interrelationships of vertebrate integumentary systems and other organ systems.

3. Be concerned about the effects of solar radiation and the use of chemicals on the skin.

4. Be able to describe the functions of vertebrate skeletal and muscular systems.

5. Be able to describe the structure of bone, muscle, and connective tissues.

6. Be able to explain how body parts are moved and how that movement is controlled.

7. Be able to compare the structure and function of at least one homologous structure on three or more different vertebrates.

8. Understand the cause, effects, and treatment of three or more disorders, diseases, and injuries of the human skeletal and muscular systems.

9. Be able to explain the terms homeostasis, homoiothermic, and poikilothermic, and relate them to the integumentary system.

10. Know the functions of vertebrate integumentary systems and be able to describe the structure of the human integumentary system.

11. Be able to describe the structural and functional aspects of one or more epidermal characteristics unique to mammals, amphibians, reptiles, and birds.

12. Be able to explain the mechanisms of temperature regulation in humans and understand the role played by the integumentary system.

13. Know how the human integumentary system acts as a barrier to the harmful effects of external agents.

14. Understand how the integumentary system acts as a sense organ.

15. Be able to describe skin pigmentation, referring to moles, freckles, liver spots, and tanning.

16. Be able to describe the cause, effects, and treatment of three or more skin disorders, diseases, or injuries.

17. Know how to dissect a vertebrate for examination of muscle masses, and the movement of appendages and movable joints.

18. Know how to use prepared slides or electron micrographs to examine and describe the structure of bone, muscle, connective tissue, and integumentary system tissue.

9.1   **Structures for Support**

Your survival depends mainly on your ability to move around in your environment. Without a strong support system, all of your soft tissues and organs would collapse, making rapid locomotion impossible. The internal framework that supports the human body in an upright position is called the **skeletal system**.

Structure and Function of the Human Skeletal System

The human skeletal system contains over 200 bones that function together to support the human body and its appendages. The skeletal system also supports many internal organs in the lower abdomen. Figure 9-1 shows other important functions performed by the skeleton.

Protection
The brain is protected by the skull. The heart and lungs are protected by the rib cage, and the spinal cord is protected by the bones of the vertebral column. Even a baby developing in the uterus of a female is partially protected by the bones of its mother's pelvis.

The people forming a human pyramid in this beach scene of the 1930s show evidence of strong, healthy bones and muscles.

Mineral Storage

Minerals such as calcium and phosphorus are stored in the bones, giving them strength and rigidity. If your diet is deficient in calcium, your body will use the minerals stored in your bones and will weaken them. For this reason, you should maintain a calcium-rich diet throughout your life.

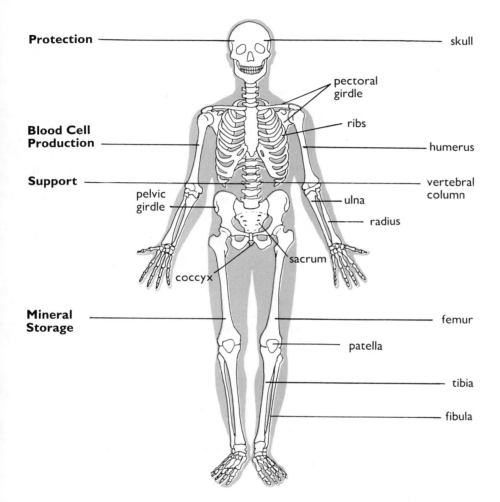

Protection — skull

pectoral girdle

ribs

Blood Cell Production — humerus

Support — vertebral column

pelvic girdle

ulna

radius

sacrum

coccyx

Mineral Storage — femur

patella

tibia

fibula

FIGURE 9-1 The human skeleton performs a number of important functions.

Connections between muscles and bones form joints (here marked by x) that allow this gymnast to perform a variety of movements.

Blood Cell Production

Red blood cells are produced in the bone marrow of many large, flat bones such as the ribs and the sternum, and in the ends of the long bones in your arms and legs.

Muscle Attachment

Locomotion and movement depend on the ability of muscles to move the bones of the skeleton. Joints in the skeleton flex or extend as the muscles attached to them contract and relax. The way muscles and bones are arranged allows you to execute a variety of movements.

Structures for Strength and Flexibility: Bones and Cartilage

The bridge shown in the photograph is made of many individual structural parts. Some parts such as the girders and cables are made of steel. Others are made of concrete. Each part is shaped in a particular way to perform a specific function. During construction, the parts are arranged and attached together in a pattern that allows the bridge to support the forces exerted on it by daily traffic.

The human skeleton resembles a bridge in many ways. Each bone is shaped to perform a particular function in the skeletal system. For example, the short, cylindrical **vertebrae** are stacked in a column. This arrangement gives the spine maximum flexibility, while allowing it to support the load exerted by the upper body. The hollow centres of the vertebrae provide a protective casing for the spinal cord. The bones of the foot are shaped and arranged to form an arch, a structure that is often used in bridges because it supports large loads efficiently. The thin, flat, fused bones of the **skull** form a protective covering for the brain while minimizing the extra load on the rest of the skeleton.

Like a bridge, the human skeleton is made of more than one material. (See Figure 9-2.) Bones are covered by a tough membrane called the **periosteum**. Beneath this membrane lies a layer of **compact bone** that consists of living bone cells embedded in a concrete-like mixture, or matrix of minerals, such as calcium phosphate and protein fibres called **collagen**. But not all bone tissue is alike. Toward the ends of many long bones, or femurs, is tissue called **spongy bone**, which is lighter and more porous than compact bone. Much of the bone marrow is found in the spongy bone.

Some parts of the skeleton such as the ears and the tip of the nose are **cartilage** and not bone. Cartilage is a supporting tissue made of cells embedded in a strong but flexible mixture of collagen fibres and polysaccharides. The skeleton of a developing human embryo begins as a framework of cartilage. As the baby grows, the cartilage is replaced by permanent bone in a gradual process called **ossification**. Cartilage cells are replaced by bone cells that

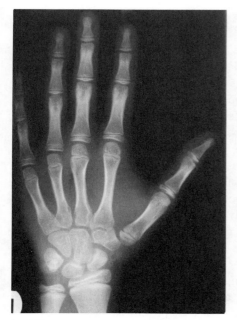 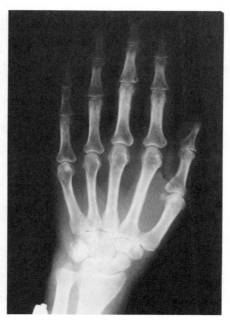

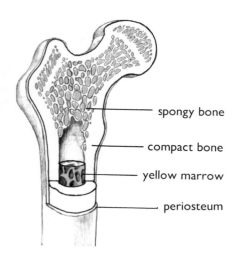

FIGURE 9-2 A cross section of a human femur showing bone composition

- spongy bone
- compact bone
- yellow marrow
- periosteum

LEFT: The progress of ossification in a child's hand. (Only bones are shown — the empty space between the bones is cartilage.) Ossification in the child's bones begins at the diaphysis (bone centre) and continues at the epiphysis (bone ends), which have not yet joined. **RIGHT:** In the adult, the wrist is solid and the ossification centres have fused to form single bones.

secrete minerals and calcium compounds to solidify the bone. Ossification continues well into the late teens and early twenties. Proper formation of bone during this period depends largely on an adequate intake of minerals and proteins.

In a bridge, the joints between structural parts are welded or bolted together to minimize movement. In the human skeleton, some joints such as those between the bones of the skull must also be immovable. In joints such as those in the hand, however, the bones must be free to move.

LABORATORY EXERCISE 9-1
Examination of Bones and Joints

The function of locomotion is possible because bones are arranged to form joints that are moved by muscles attached to them. Unlike the parts of a bridge, bones are living tissue that must be connected with other structures such as blood vessels and nerves in order to function.

In this exercise, you will examine vertebrate bones, joints, and associated structures such as those found in a chicken leg or wing. If you have time, try to test the strength of some of these bones.

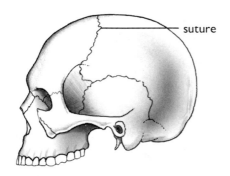

FIGURE 9-3 The sutures of an adult human skull are examples of immovable joints.

Connective Structures: Joints and Ligaments

Any place in the skeleton where two or more bones meet is called a **joint**. A joint includes all associated tissues, as well as the ends of the bones. The range and direction of joint motion depend on the shape of the bone ends.

Immovable joints are formed by bones fused so closely together that little or no movement is possible. Such bones are usually held together by short fibres of connective tissue. The fused bones of the adult human skull form immovable joints, or sutures, but these bones are not fused in a fetus. (See Figure 9-3.) As a result, the loose bones can shift, changing the shape of the baby's head during the birth process. Young babies typically have "soft spots" in their skulls until the bones fuse together permanently. Other immovable joints are found in the coccyx, and between the sacrum and the pelvis.

Most joints, however, permit some type of movement. The names of the **movable joints** in Figure 9-4 indicate the type of motion they allow. The bones of movable joints are held together by **ligaments**. Ligaments are strong, stretchable bands of connective tissue made of the proteins elastin and collagen. Ligaments act like the cables on a crane, allowing the parts to move

FIGURE 9-4 Four examples of movable joints. What other kind of joint might you consider the elbow to be?

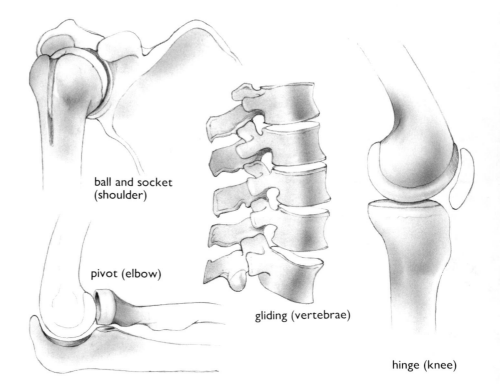

ball and socket (shoulder)

pivot (elbow)

gliding (vertebrae)

hinge (knee)

without separating. Pads of cartilage on the ends of the bones function as shock absorbers to cushion the force of movement and prevent the bones from wearing down. A **synovial sac** between the bones secretes a fluid that acts as a lubricant. (See Figure 9-5.) Although the function of most joints is to permit movement, bones cannot move by themselves. In vertebrates such as humans, bones are moved by the contracting and relaxing action of muscles.

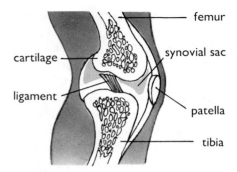

FIGURE 9-5 The synovial sac is a membrane that surrounds the synovial fluid of this knee joint.

LABORATORY EXERCISE 9-2
Investigating the Movement of Appendages and Joints

In this exercise, which is part of an ongoing vertebrate dissection, you will expose, examine, and identify the large muscles of your specimen's limbs. You will also try to determine which limb actions will result when particular muscles contract or relax.

Interaction of the Skeleton with Other Body Systems

The combination of strength and flexibility enables your skeletal system to support other body structures and permits a wide range of movements. However, your bones cannot move unless the right muscles contract and relax in the correct sequence. Co-ordinating muscle action is the job of the nervous system. Providing muscle cells with the nutrients and oxygen they need for energy is the job of the circulatory system. Since neither your bones nor your muscles can operate independently of each other, biologists often refer to them as the **musculoskeletal system**. The muscular component of this system will be discussed in Section 9.2.

Section Review Questions

1. List four functions of the human skeletal system.
2. Describe the structure and characteristics of the following tissues: a) compact bone, b) spongy bone, c) cartilage, and d) ligaments.
3. a) What is ossification?
   b) How long does ossification take in a human?
4. a) State an example of an immovable joint and describe its function.
   b) List four types of movable joints and state an example of each.
   c) Describe the movement of each example above.
5. Describe the function of the labelled parts in Figure 9-5.

Arthroscopic Surgery

If you perform strenuous exercise, chances are you will sooner or later suffer from pain in your knees. Like many, you may hobble to your doctor to ask for arthroscopic surgery. But this may or may not be the best treatment for your problem. Some people now feel that expectations of arthroscopy, fueled by tales of miracles with athletes' knees, are greatly exaggerated.

Arthroscopy is the insertion of a rigid tube 2 mm in diameter into a body to view internal features. Additional instruments inserted near the scope can be used in surgery. Arthroscopes have come a long way since 1964, when arthroscopy was first performed in North America by Dr. Robert Jackson of Toronto. Then arthroscopes consisted of small tungsten bulbs and complicated lens systems. Now, they use fibre optics to project a brightly illuminated image on television screens.

Arthroscopy is a new way to perform old procedures. Because much smaller incisions are made, arthroscopy has many advantages over conventional open surgery, or arthrotomy. In addition, an arthroscope can explore cavities that normally cannot be reached with conventional techniques.

With small incisions there is less disruption to the body — quicker surgery, less anesthetic, fewer complications, reduced stiffness, and less immobilization and muscle atrophy. All these factors result in shorter down-time for the body, so rehabilitation can begin sooner. Arthroscopy patients often walk out of the hospital, while arthrotomy patients may spend weeks in a cast.

With all of these dramatic advantages, how can anyone speak out against arthroscopy? But there are limitations. Not all surgery can be done by arthroscopy. Above all, it is a useful diagnostic technique. Some surgery to repair damage can be done at the same time, but the kinds of repairs are limited. Most repairs consist of cleaning and removing damaged tissue. A problem of arthroscopy

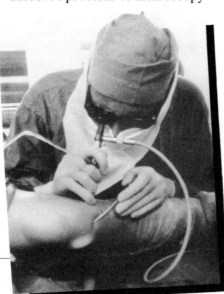

is the lack of peripheral vision the technique allows the surgeon. As well as restricting the surgeon's work, this flaw sometimes leads to damage and scuffing of normal tissue from cutting instruments.

Also, arthroscopy is not without complications. Arthroscopic surgery is still surgery, so common surgical risks exist — infection, blood vessel and nerve damage, and painful swelling. As well, patients are often unaware that when some surgical procedures such as tissue suturing are performed, recovery times from arthroscopy and arthrotomy are comparable. Phenomenal recovery times reported by some athletes after arthroscopy can be attributed to the trained athlete's motivation to work at therapy, and to the possibility that only minor procedures were performed.

Because of complications, doctors feel that even for diagnostic purposes arthroscopy should not be substituted for noninvasive but more time-consuming techniques. Clinical examination will usually reveal the nature of a joint problem; some knee problems will heal without surgery. But as long as people are in a hurry, doctors will probably be pressured by patients to use arthroscopy.

9.2 Structures for Movement

All body movement results from muscle action. The human body has three kinds of muscle. **Cardiac muscle** is found only in the heart and is controlled automatically by the nerves of the autonomic nervous system. The pumping action of the heart is the most important muscular action in the body. Many factors affect the rate at which the heart beats, but the beating itself is not under voluntary control.

Smooth muscle is found in the walls lining internal organs such as the bladder and the esophagus. Smooth muscle is also controlled automatically. The movement of food along the digestive tract is caused by the rhythmic involuntary action of the smooth muscles.

The muscles that enable a tennis player to serve and volley are referred to as **skeletal muscle** because they are attached to the bones of the skeleton. Only skeletal muscle is under the voluntary control of the peripheral nervous system. (See Figure 9-6.)

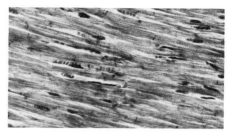
Cardiac muscle

Smooth muscle

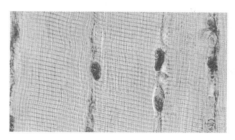
Skeletal muscle

Structure and Function of the Skeletal Muscular System

Your body has over 600 muscles, and most of them are skeletal. Many of the large skeletal muscles are used for gross body movements such as running, walking, climbing, and throwing. They are arranged so the action of a muscle or a group that moves a body part one way can be corrected by the action of another muscle group that returns the body part to its original position. Other skeletal muscles are very small, and enable you to perform fine manipulations with your hands or to raise your eyebrows. All of these actions are voluntary and are consciously controlled by the brain.

Skeletal muscle must be attached to bone in order to cause movement. Muscles are attached to bones by **tendons**. Tendons consist of connective tissue made mostly of collagen fibres with little or no elastin. Tendons are extremely tough, and they stretch very little, if at all. Individual muscles are usually attached to two bones. One bone moves and the other remains stationary. The place where the muscle is attached to the stationary bone is called the **origin**. The place where the muscle is attached to the moving bone is called the **insertion**. The tendon at the insertion is usually longer than the tendon at the origin.

Muscles shorten as they contract and lengthen as they relax. Only contraction is active; relaxation is totally passive and exerts no force on the bone. A body part moves only when it is pulled by a contracting muscle. But that same muscle cannot push on the bone to return the body part to its initial position. This shortcoming does not limit movement, however, since many skeletal muscles are arranged in antagonistic pairs that have the opposite effect

The muscles that control eye blinking can be controlled voluntarily or involuntarily. The eye-blink reflex helps protect the eye from foreign particles and lubricates its surface. Blinking your eyes is an involuntary action. You can stop blinking and hold your eyes open, but only for brief periods of time.

FIGURE 9-6 Biceps and triceps are muscles that are attached to bone by tendons. Why are they examples of antagonistic muscles?

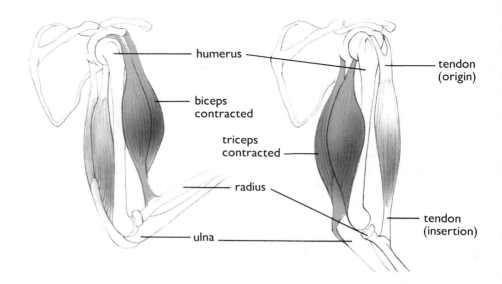

on a body part. One muscle flexes the joint by bringing the bones closer together. The other muscle extends the joint by returning the bones to their original position. These pairs of muscles are referred to as **antagonistic muscles** because they work against each other to make the bones of a joint move.

INQUIRY ACTIVITY
Investigating Antagonistic Muscles

In this activity, you will investigate the action of several pairs of antagonistic muscles in your own body. Refer to Figure 9-7 for the location of the muscles used in this activity.

Procedure

1. While standing, let your right arm rest straight at your side. Measure and record the origin to insertion length of the biceps muscle.

2. Place the index finger of your left hand at the insertion of the biceps muscle. (Remember that the insertion is on the bone that will move.)

3. Without moving your index finger, slowly bend your right arm until it is completely flexed. Watch the action of the biceps muscle.

4. a) Measure and record the approximate distance between the origin and the insertion when your arm is flexed.
   b) Calculate the difference between extended and contracted muscle length.

5. Repeat Steps 1-4 for the triceps muscle at the back of your arm. You may need the help of a partner.

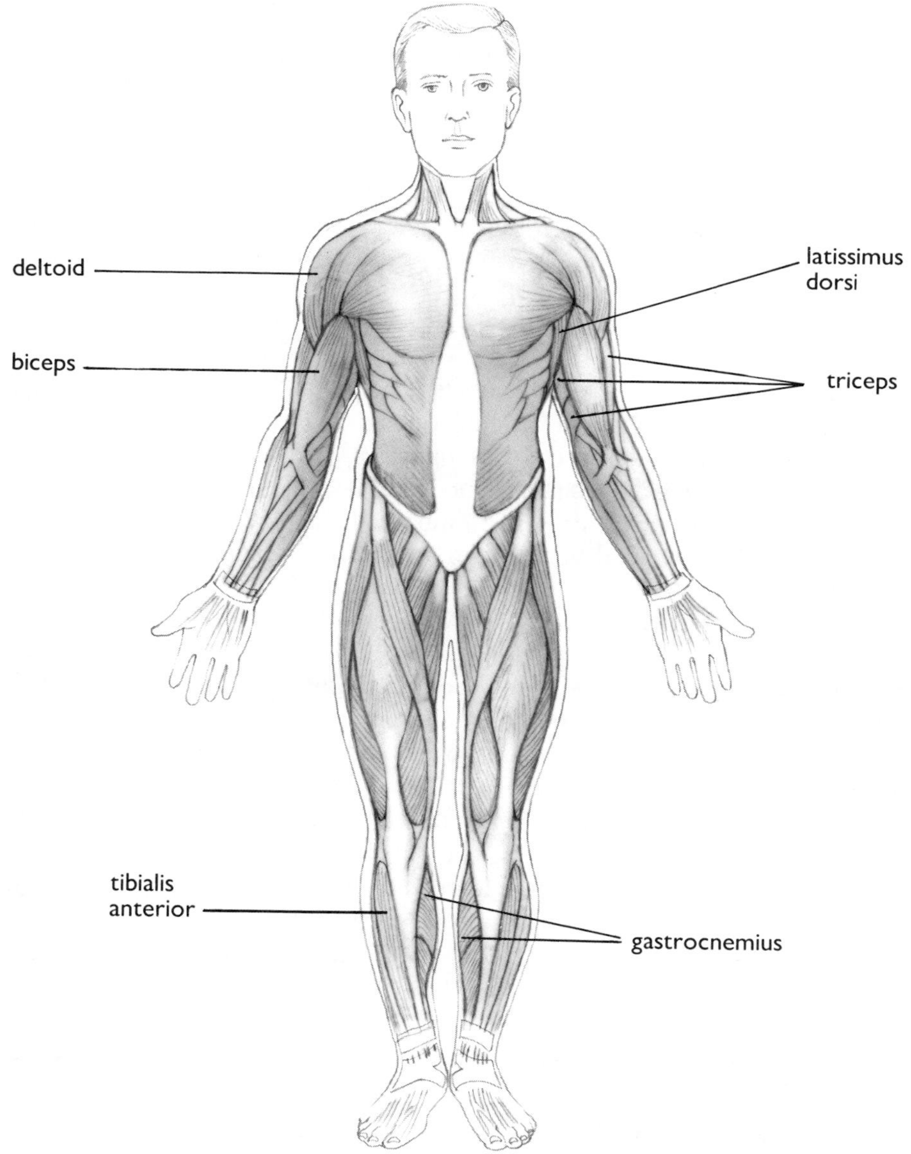

FIGURE 9-7 Muscles of the human body

deltoid

biceps

latissimus dorsi

triceps

tibialis anterior

gastrocnemius

6. Using Figure 9-7 as a guide, select another set of antagonistic muscles in your body and repeat Steps 1-5. Record your observations.

Discussion Questions

1. Describe what must happen to one member of an antagonistic pair of muscles as the other contracts. Explain why this is necessary.

2. The muscle that must contract to bend a joint is called a flexor. The muscle that must contract to straighten the joint is called the extensor. List three flexors and three extensors in the human body. Test the action of these muscles if you have not done so already.

3. Muscles are never completely relaxed. They are always in a state of partial contraction known as muscle tone. Can you think of two reasons why good muscle tone in your body is essential?

Biophysics

Most of your voluntary body movements result from forces produced by the interaction of the muscular and skeletal systems. The study of these and other interactions is called **biophysics**. In biophysics, body movements are compared to the movement of mechanical models. Many movements can be understood by comparing the action of the limbs to the action of simple machines called levers. Muscles and bones form a system of levers in the body that allow you to do work.

In a first-class lever, the fulcrum, or pivot point, is located between the load and the effort force. To lift the load, the effort force must be applied in the same direction as the load force. Look at Figure 9-8a. Which body part acts as the fulcrum? As the load? As the effort force?

In a second-class lever, the load is located between the fulcrum at one end and the effort force at the opposite end. To lift the load, the effort force must be applied in the opposite direction to the load force. Look at Figure 9-8b. Which body parts correspond to the parts of a second-class lever?

In a third-class lever, the effort force is applied between the fulcrum and the load, which are located at opposite ends. The effort force must act in the opposite direction to the load force. Look at Figure 9-8c and determine where the fulcrum, load, and effort force are located in the body parts illustrated.

INQUIRY ACTIVITY
Models of Muscle and Bone Interaction

A. Construct a model of a knee joint. Use wood for the bones, sponge for cartilage, a small, water-filled balloon for the synovial sac, elastic bands for the ligaments, string for the tendons, and balloons for the muscles. Use this model to explain how a typical joint functions.

B. Using suitable materials, construct models of first-class, second-class, and third-class levers to represent parts of the human body. Compare the actions of these models to those observed in the human body.

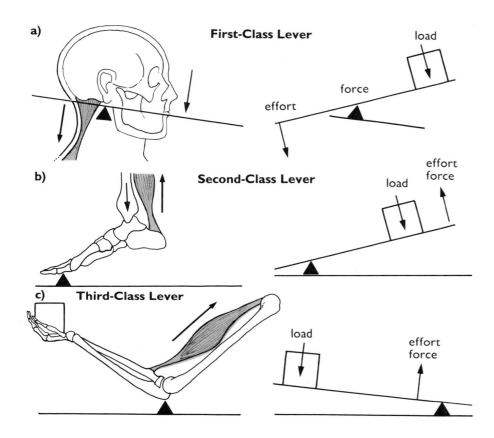

a) **First-Class Lever**

load

force

effort

b) **Second-Class Lever**

effort force

load

c) **Third-Class Lever**

load

effort force

FIGURE 9-8 The bones and muscles of the body act as levers that allow you to do work.

Muscles, Movement, and Work

The ability of the musculoskeletal system to exert forces while moving enables you to do work. Athletes often enhance the levers of their own bodies with tools that extend their reach. This tennis player is using her right forearm as a first-class lever and her racket as a third-class lever. Hockey players use their sticks in much the same way to shoot rapidly. People who do curls in weight training use their forearms as third-class levers.

How many levers do you think are involved in this shot?

Section Review Questions

1. List the three types of muscle in the human body and state the location of each.
2. a) What is the difference between the origin of a muscle and the insertion of a muscle?
   b) How are muscles attached to bones?

Muscles in Space

The drugs that have been a centre of controversy on Earth may someday help humans survive lengthy journeys in space. In spite of the reputation anabolic steroids have acquired through their illegal use in athletics, steroids do have legitimate medical uses. Muscle growth and tissue regeneration in post-operative and geriatric patients can be stimulated with anabolic steroids. If astronauts are to survive low-gravity space flights, the use of anabolic steroids may be required for the same purposes.

Astronauts returning from missions in orbit regularly experience difficulty readjusting to Earth's gravity, despite vigorous on-board exercise regimens. In 1973, American Skylab astronauts reported a 10-15% loss in muscular strength after three months in space. In 1979, two Soviet cosmonauts returning to Earth after a record-breaking 175 days in space required four days of massage, heat treatments, and breathing exercises before they were even capable of standing unassisted.

Originally, this loss of muscle strength was blamed on lack of use. Since there is little gravity in space, even working muscles experience only a small fraction of the load they must carry constantly on Earth. When muscles are inactive, they atrophy and shrink.

However, evidence is mounting that factors other than atrophy may be involved. In a 1987 joint Soviet-American-Australian study, muscles taken from rats after 12.5 days in space showed 40% shrinkage due to atrophy. In addition, researchers found a number of symptoms similar to human nerve-muscle disorders. For example, swollen muscle fibres had been invaded by white blood cells, broken blood vessels had caused internal bleeding, and nerve endings were damaged. Cosmic radiation, stress, reduced blood circulation, and muscle disuse were cited as possible causes. Another possible explanation suggests the rats' natural repair mechanisms, which are accustomed to operating in full gravity, may have shut down in the absence of gravity.

While exercise can help prevent loss of muscular strength due to atrophy, the kind of damage witnessed in the rat muscle requires a different approach. Exercise will not stimulate muscle that has become disconnected from nerves, nor can it help muscles that are unused in space. Anabolic steroids, which are synthetic chemicals similar to the male hormone, testosterone, promote muscle repair as well as muscle growth. Together with exercise, these drugs have been proposed as one method of preventing extreme muscle deterioration in astronauts.

The shrinkage of heart muscle, loss of balance and co-ordination, and bone deterioration experienced by astronauts on long low-gravity missions must be overcome before more ambitious space projects can be undertaken.

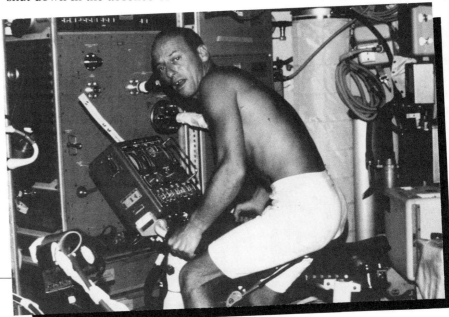

3. a) Why are antagonistic pairs of muscles needed in the human body?
   b) List and describe the action of one pair of antagonistic muscles in the human body.
4. a) What is biophysics?
   b) How might a knowledge of biophysics help a tennis player or a hockey player?

How do hockey players' sticks enhance the levels of their bodies?

9.3 Structures for Protection

All of the systems you have studied so far must interact with each other to maintain a stable internal environment. But animals live in an external environment that is constantly changing and can be very dangerous. Without some means of protection, exposure to invading micro-organisms, harmful pollutants, chemicals, radiation, and climate changes can upset the stability of their internal systems. All animals, however, get some degree of protection from an **integumentary system**.

Structure and Function of the Human Integumentary System

In humans, the integumentary system includes the skin and all of its **accessory structures**. Some accessory structures grow out of the skin. These structures include hair and fingernails. Other accessory structures such as glands and

The snake's integumentary system is made up of a covering of hard scales, which protects it from its environment.

sensory receptors are embedded in the skin. (See Figure 9-9.) Your skin consists of two layers. The upper **epidermis** is a thin layer from which all accessory structures develop. Structures such as sweat glands, oil glands, hair follicles, and receptor nerves extend downward into the lower dermis layer. The **dermis** is several times thicker than the epidermis and also contains numerous receptor nerve endings and capillaries. A layer of fat cells lies between the dermis and the underlying muscle attached to it.

FIGURE 9-9 A cross section of human skin

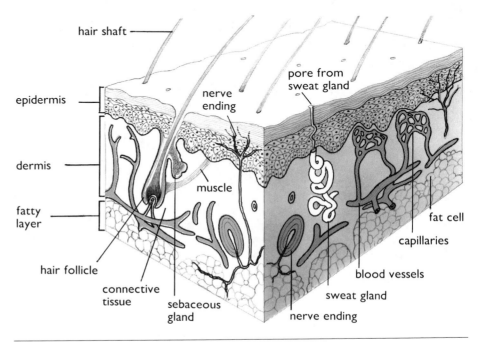

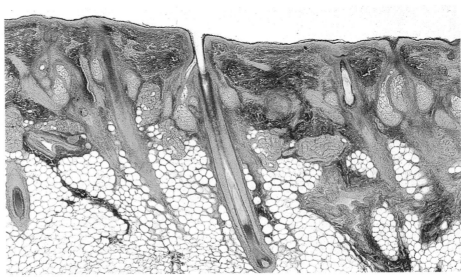

A cross section through the skin showing hair follicles. Can you identify any other structures?

The epidermis is thin enough to allow the receptors below to detect changes in external temperature, pressure, and touch. The outer layer of the epidermis forms a protein called keratin, which toughens and waterproofs the skin, but leaves it flexible enough to permit joints to move. The epidermis also prevents micro-organisms and harmful chemicals from entering the body and attacking healthy tissue. The lower epidermis is responsible for producing the pigment **melanin**, which helps protect you from the sun's harmful ultraviolet radiation.

LABORATORY EXERCISE 9-3
Examination of Skin and Accessory Structures

The skin does not have the same characteristics in all locations of the body. Factors affecting the appearance of the skin include the amount of time exposed to the environment and the primary function of the body in that particular area.

In this exercise, you will compare the surface structure and characteristics of your skin at different locations on your body using a hand lens or magnifying glass. You will also use a microscope to examine slides of your own hair and compare your observations with those of other students.

Skin Colour

Skin colour is a result of two factors: the amount of melanin present, and the amount of blood brought to the skin's surface by the capillaries. Emotions such as fear and anger can change the colour of the skin by moving blood toward or away from the skin's surface. Medical conditions such as anemia, which reduces the hemoglobin or the number of red blood cells, can also affect skin colour. Exposure to ultraviolet radiation causes a temporary increase in the amount of melanin in the skin. This produces the darker skin tone associated with suntans. Although suntans are often thought of as a sign of health, they really indicate that the skin has been damaged.

All patterns of skin pigmentation are caused by the distribution of melanin. Differences in overall skin colour are related to the amount of melanin usually present. Moles occur where the skin has a higher density of melanin-producing cells. Freckles are tiny areas of increased pigment production. Liver spots occur in old age when melanin production becomes uneven.

The Role of Skin in Homeostasis

The skin contributes to the maintenance of a stable internal environment in a number of ways.

DID YOU KNOW?
The low energy ultraviolet light used in suntanning machines was once thought to be relatively harmless. Studies of cell cultures have shown that exposure to this light can damage DNA molecules in a way that could change the structure or the function of a cell.

DID YOU KNOW?
Birthmarks are patches of lighter or darker skin, which are sometimes raised and bumpy in appearance. The discolouration may be due to patterns of capillaries under the skin, as well as differences in pigmentation. Birthmarks are inherited, and most people have one somewhere on their bodies.

FIGURE 9-10   The lubricating glands of the skin

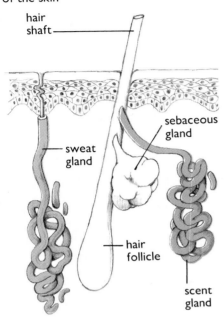

hair
shaft

sebaceous
gland

sweat
gland

hair
follicle

scent
gland

Scent glands also branch off many hair follicles. They produce a secretion that becomes odourous when it is exposed to air. In many vertebrate species, odours help attract mates, and may play a role in attracting humans to each other as well.

Protection

Besides screening out harmful radiation, the skin forms a continuous barrier surrounding all internal structures, thereby preventing the entrance of disease-causing microbes or harmful chemicals and pollutants. The skin is also thick and tough enough to protect muscles and other internal structures from minor physical contact.

Lubrication

Your skin contains sebaceous glands and scent glands that branch off the hair follicle and share the same skin opening. (See Figure 9-10.) Scent glands do not aid in homeostasis, but sebaceous glands secrete an oil that lubricates the skin, keeping it healthy and flexible.

Fluid Regulation

The waterproof nature of your skin helps prevent the dehydration of moist, delicate, internal tissues. Your skin does, however, permit controlled evaporation of fluids excreted by the sweat glands. If water is limited, the sweat glands will close to preserve it. Sweating helps to release excess water and a certain amount of waste material such as salt.

Temperature Regulation

Humans and all other mammals are **homoiothermic**. Homoiothermic mammals are ''warm-blooded'' animals that maintain a nearly constant body temperature regardless of the temperature in their external environments. Many mammals, including humans, regulate their body temperatures during hot weather by the evaporation of sweat from the skin. Evaporation is an energy-absorbing process, which helps cool both the skin and the internal environment. As heat energy is absorbed from capillaries near the skin's surface, the cooled blood returns to the body's interior, helping maintain a stable internal temperature.

Insulation

There is not enough hair on your body to have much insulating value, but fat deposits beneath your skin help prevent the loss of body heat in cold weather. Humans whose ancestors have lived in cold climates for thousands of years tend to develop thicker layers of fat beneath the dermis as a form of insulation.

Accessory Structures

In some vertebrates, the accessory structures form thick layers that completely cover the skin. Arctic mammals typically have heavy layers of long, shaggy hair. The spaces between the hairs trap air close to the surface of an animal's body. Heat from the body warms the air, which insulates the animal and keeps it warm. Oil from the skin helps keep the hairs from matting together. In most

After a workout, boxer Lennox Lewis must sweat to help reduce his internal body temperature. What other purpose does sweating serve?

These distinctive features of the Inuit are a result of fat stored around the cheekbones. The fat insulates sensitive facial tissues from the cold winter temperatures of the Arctic.

The Arctic fox's fluffed-up fur helps insulate the animal by trapping a layer of air against the skin.

cases, the hair can be fluffed up to increase the amount of trapped air. This type of protection is especially vital for small mammals that have a much greater amount of surface area for each kilogram of body mass than do larger animals.

In humans, tiny muscles attached to each hair cause the hair to stand on end when they contract. Usually, this is a response to fright or to air that cools the body such as wind. However, there is not enough hair on the human body to have much insulating value. Hair is nonliving and is made of a shaft of dead cells containing keratin. Hair colour results from pigments in the cells. Each hair develops and grows from its own living follicle. Men and women have about the same distribution of hair follicles in their skin. The hair of women tends to be thinner and more transparent than that of men, making men appear to have more hair. In fact, chimpanzees have about the same number of hair follicles as humans. They look hairier because their hair shafts tend to be thicker and more heavily pigmented.

Eyelashes are made of hair arranged in a pattern that helps protect the eyes from dust and other airborne particles.

Nails are hard structures that protect the upper surface of the sensitive fingertips. Nails are made of keratinized cells that are continually replaced from layers of living cells in the epidermis at the base of the fingernail. Toenails are formed in the same way.

Section Review Questions

1. Which structures are associated with the epidermis and the dermis of the skin?

2. a) Which two factors are responsible for skin colour?
   b) Describe several factors that may temporarily alter the colour of your skin.

Skin Replacement Technology

Skin replacement technology is a combination of old and new techniques that are used to treat severe burn victims. Traditional techniques include the autograft, the allograft, and the heterograft.

The autograft involves taking skin from an unburned part of the patient's body and using it to cover the burned area. This method can be successful as long as there is enough undamaged skin to graft. There is no danger of tissue rejection because the skin is the patient's own. The allograft uses the skin of a donor, which is usually taken from a cadaver. These grafts are often difficult to obtain, and tissue rejection is a possibility. The heterograft uses skin from animals—typically pigs —or artificial skin that combines plastics with fibres from organic sources such as cowhide. Allografts and heterografts are temporary and eventually must be replaced with natural skin.

New techniques are being perfected to provide skin for grafting when other sources are unavailable. Two doctors at the Harvard Medical School have developed a process for growing skin from small samples taken from the unburned areas of a victim. The samples are ground and mixed with enzymes in a flask to separate the cells. Growth stimulators are then added to the mixture. The patches of skin that grow from the culture are used for grafting when they are large enough. Within a week, new skin is growing over the burned area. This manufactured skin is smooth and shiny, and it lacks hair follicles and sweat glands. Although there is no danger of tissue rejection, the three-week period needed to grow the skin can create complications.

A second technique has been pioneered by doctors in Massachusetts. It is called "the hundred-minute procedure" because it takes 100 min from the time a patient enters the hospital until a skin graft is in place. A small patch of unburned skin from the victim is centrifuged to separate young skin cells. These skin cells land on a membrane that is applied to the burned area, and new skin begins to grow. The membrane acts as a template to guide the skin's growth. This procedure eliminates the waiting period for skin grafts to grow.

In a third process, healthy donors provide skin samples that are used to grow larger skin grafts. These skin grafts are stored in skin banks until they are needed. Enzymes have been used in this process to remove particular skin cells that may trigger an immune response in a burn victim, causing tissue rejection.

The ideal skin replacement of the future must meet certain criteria. It must be flexible enough to fit anywhere on the body. It must prevent the creation of air pockets that can lead to infection. And it must be durable enough to stand up to operating procedures. Skin replacements of the future must be biodegradable, and they must allow enough water to escape from tissues without causing a patient to suffer dehydration.

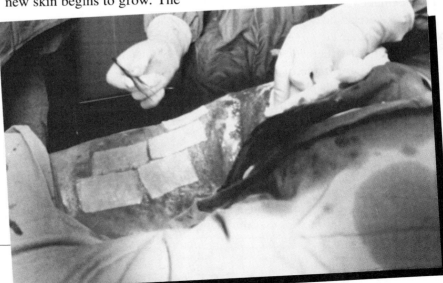

3. Describe five ways the skin helps maintain homeostasis.

4. Explain how the hair of Arctic mammals helps maintain their internal body temperatures.

5. a) What substance is common to the structure of hair and nails?
   b) What function does this substance serve?

9.4 Tissues

The musculoskeletal and integumentary systems contain several different kinds of tissues. Each tissue is made of groups of specialized cells that give the tissues their characteristics and allow them to perform their functions.

Structure and Function of Epithelial Tissue

The general function of **epithelial tissue** is to cover and protect other tissues. In humans, skin is made of layer upon layer of epithelial tissue. Its flat cells fit together tightly like the pieces of a jigsaw puzzle. The number of layers of epithelial tissue in the skin varies from location to location. For example, the palm of your hand has more layers of epithelial tissue than the back of your hand.

The upper layers of the epidermis are made of keratinized cells that are continually rubbed off when you wash, dress, or rub your skin against other materials. Underlying layers of the epidermis consist of sheets of living epithelial cells that reproduce rapidly, pushing new cells toward the skin's surface. These new cells replace those that have been rubbed off.

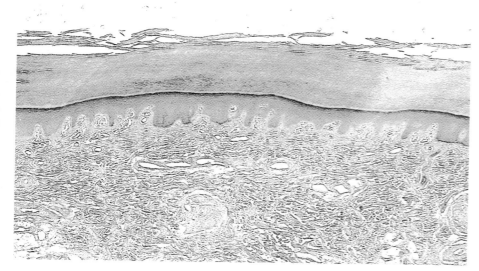

The arrangement of cell layers in the epidermis of a human foot. Notice how the dead outer layers peel away.

Structure and Function of Skeletal Muscle Tissue

Skeletal muscle tissue is made up of many parallel bundles of muscle fibres. Both the bundles and the fibres are parallel to each other and to the muscle itself. Each fibre is actually a long, thin muscle cell containing several nuclei and numerous mitochondria, which supply the large amounts of energy needed for muscle contraction.

Each muscle cell, or fibre, contains smaller functional units called **myofibrils**. Myofibrils enable a muscle to contract. Within each myofibril, thick protein filaments called **myosin** alternate with thin protein filaments called **actin**. The parallel arrangement of actin and myosin gives skeletal muscle its striped appearance. (See Figure 9-11.)

Relaxed Muscle

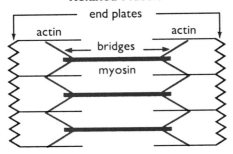

Contracted Muscle

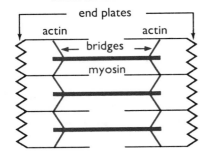

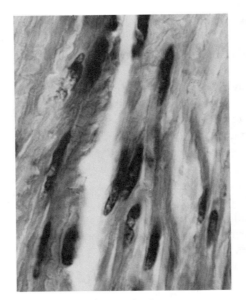

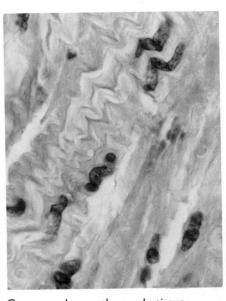

Relaxed smooth muscle tissue   Contracted smooth muscle tissue

FIGURE 9-11 The contraction of skeletal muscle. Note that protein filaments do not shorten. Instead, bridges slide actin past myosin, pulling the end plates closer together.

Bridge-like structures connect the myosin to the actin, which, in turn, are attached to end plates. When a muscle cell receives a signal from the nervous system, the electrical stimulus causes the myosin bridges to pull on the actin filaments. This action draws the end plates closer together, shortening the myofibril. When all the myofibrils shorten simultaneously, the muscle fibre contracts.

Individual muscle fibres display what biologists call an "all or nothing" response. Either all of the myofibrils contract fully, or none do. However, muscles themselves do not show this response. The intensity of a muscle contraction depends on how many muscle fibres contract at one time. For this reason, you are able to perform tasks requiring fine motor co-ordination.

Structure and Function of Connective Tissue

There are many types of connective tissue, several of which play important roles in the musculoskeletal and the integumentary systems. In general, **connective tissue** consists of a few cells and protein fibres embedded in a matrix. A matrix is a nonliving mixture of materials in which living cells are embedded. The arrangement of the fibres and the matrix give the different tissues their unique properties. Bones, cartilage, ligaments, tendons, and adipose tissue are all connective tissues.

The cells of bone tissue are arranged in concentric rings and are embedded in a matrix of protein fibres and minerals. (See Figure 9-12.) The protein fibres are collagen, and the minerals are mainly calcium phosphate. Both give the bone its characteristic hardness.

Tendons and ligaments are examples of fibrous connective tissue. (See Figure 9-13.) The protein fibres of these connective tissues are arranged in a parallel pattern. Tendons and ligaments both contain tightly packed collagen fibres. Ligaments contain an additional protein, elastin, which makes them more stretchable than tendons. This stretchability is important because ligaments hold the bones of joints together and must be able to stretch somewhat if the joint is stressed.

Cartilage is similar to bone in its structure except that it lacks the hardening minerals. (See Figure 9-14.) Its collagen and polysaccharide matrix is flexible, yet firm enough to support structures such as the nose and the outer ear. Cartilage also has good shock-absorbing qualities, which make it useful between bones in the spine and large joints like the knee.

Adipose tissue contains large, rounded, fat-storage cells in a sparse, low-fibre matrix. (See Figure 9-15.) Adipose tissue is found beneath the dermis, between the skin and the underlying muscle. Adipose tissue is a good insulating tissue, and its fat reserves can be used as a source of energy.

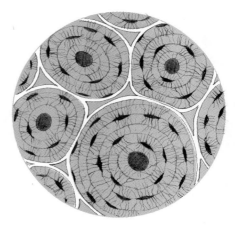

FIGURE 9-12   Bone tissue

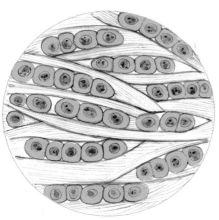

FIGURE 9-13   Fibrous connective tissue in tendons and ligaments

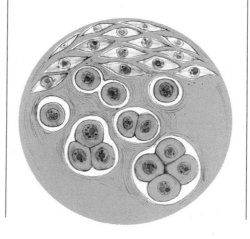

FIGURE 9-14   Cartilage

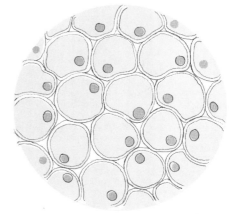

FIGURE 9-15   Adipose tissue

Microscopic Examination of Musculoskeletal and Integumentary Tissues

In this exercise, you will examine prepared slides of different types of epithelial, muscular, and connective tissues to determine how they differ in structure. You will also relate these differences to tissue function.

Tissue Injuries

Small cuts to healthy skin tissue usually heal quickly. If the cut is small, the layer of the epidermis that forms new cells will create new tissue to seal the wound. If the cut is deep enough to cause bleeding, the blood will first clot to seal the opening from infectious bacteria. The resulting scab should not be removed because the moist underlying tissues will be exposed. As new tissue forms, the scab will eventually fall off.

If a cut is very large, and the two sides of the wound are far apart, stitches may be needed to close the wound. Stitching a wound helps control blood loss and reduces both the amount of new tissue that must be formed and the time needed for repair. Since nerve tissue usually cannot be regenerated once it is damaged, the skin that forms over scar tissue tends to have no "feeling" because it lacks sense receptors and nerve endings.

Small burns are often much more painful than a cut of the same size. This is because extreme heat stimulates many more pain receptors in the skin than a narrow cut. A first-degree burn damages only the epidermis, but a second-degree burn damages the dermis as well. In these cases, the damaged skin can usually regenerate.

Third-degree burns cause extensive damage to tissues so they cannot regenerate. Since the skin is the largest organ of the body, it cannot control fluid loss if too much of it is damaged by severe burns. As a result, homeostasis is disturbed, and the loss of fluid through leakage and increased evaporation from exposed tissues can lead to dehydration, shock, and kidney malfunction. Also, exposed tissues may develop infections caused by bacteria and other microbes.

Section Review Questions

1. Describe the tissue that makes up the epidermis.
2. a) Describe the structure of skeletal muscle tissue.
   b) What roles do actin and myosin play in muscle contraction?
3. Compare the structure of cartilage and bone tissue.

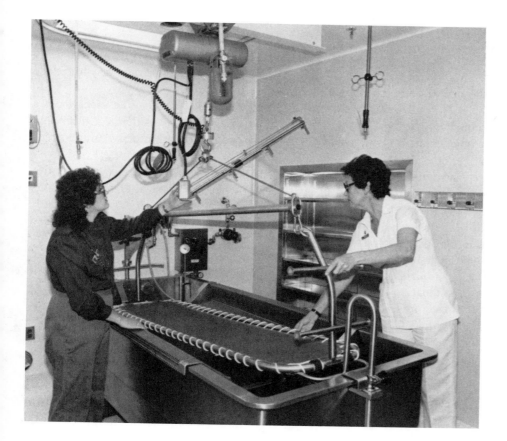

This special tank at the Wellesley Hospital in Toronto is used to shower burn patients.

4. How do the matrix structures of the four connective tissues discussed in this section differ?

5. a) How do third-degree burns differ from first-degree and second-degree burns?

   b) What effect can some third-degree burns have on homeostasis?

9.5 Fitness, Health, and Disorders of Muscle, Skin, and Bone

Muscle, skin, and bone, like all living tissue, require constant nourishment from a complete and balanced diet. Your bones need a continuous supply of calcium both as you grow and throughout your adult life. Muscle and skin tissues need a constant supply of protein for daily maintenance and repair even after you reach your adult height.

Musculoskeletal Fitness

Many people besides athletes are concerned about fitness. Exercise is not only for muscles but for bones as well. Astronauts must exercise regularly to reduce the rate of bone loss they undergo while in space.

People who do not get enough exercise need to make fitness activities a regular part of their day. Twenty minutes a day is considered a minimum requirement. It is important that a fitness program is appropriate to the needs of an individual.

Musculoskeletal injuries caused by heavy work or exercise can be prevented. Be sure to warm up and cool down before and after any strenuous activity or sport. Torn muscles and muscle cramps during extended periods of heavy exercise can result if your muscles are not warmed up. You can also injure your muscles by improperly lifting heavy objects. Stretched tendons, torn ligaments, joint sprains, and strains are common sports injuries. More serious injuries such as joint dislocations and bone fractures can be the result of participation in contact sports. Figure 9-16 shows some common types of bone fractures. Knee, ankle, and elbow injuries are common in football, hockey, and baseball. A good diet, training, and protective equipment can help you reduce the possibility and severity of any injuries you might sustain during a fitness activity.

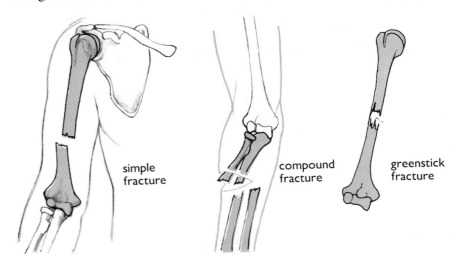

FIGURE 9-16 Three types of common bone fracture

simple fracture

compound fracture

greenstick fracture

Caring for Your Skin

Oily secretions from sebaceous glands, as well as secretions from sweat and scent glands, tend to remain on your hair and on the surface of your skin. Dirt, dust, and bacteria also accumulate on your skin. Daily cleansing removes these secretions and stimulates your skin.

II ANIMALS

Overexposure to the sun can seriously damage your skin. Skin cancer and premature aging of the skin can result. If you must stay out in the sun, a sunscreen lotion containing para-aminobenzoic acid, or PABA, can be used to protect your skin. Such lotions have a "protection factor" rating on the label. This rating indicates how much longer you can stay in the sun. For example, a rating of 8 means if you normally burn in fifteen minutes, you may remain in the sun eight times longer, or up to two hours.

PABA, or para-aminobenzoic acid, is a member of the B-complex family of vitamins. Good natural sources of PABA include liver, brewer's yeast, and whole grains. Internally, PABA helps the body utilize proteins. Externally, the sun-screening properties of PABA are utilized in many suntan lotions. PABA also helps reduce the pain of burns, delays wrinkling, and keeps skin smooth and healthy.

RESEARCH PROJECT
Personal Care of Your Muscles, Skin, and Bones

Students who do Part A of this project will investigate and report on several topics related to the musculoskeletal system. Students who do Part B will gather information and report on personal-care products.

A. Collect information and report on one of the following topics, or research another topic suggested by your teacher. Investigate the most recent information available for your subject and prepare a summary of your findings. Present the summary to your class in a 5-10 min seminar, or submit it as a written report to your teacher.

- The harmful effects of jogging on bones and muscles versus its beneficial aspects
- The development of prosthetic devices, for example, artifical arms or legs
- The causes of lower back injuries, their treatment, and prevention

B. Choose a topic related to the use, manufacture, or sale of personal-care products. These products include hair-care products, skin-care products, perfumes, and colouring agents such as makeup and hair tints. Select only one product and investigate the physical and psychological effects of using the product. You might also research the process of developing new products, or the nature of the industry and its dependence on advertising. Present your findings to your class in the form of a poster, a display, or a short talk. As an alternative, submit a written report to your teacher.

Musculoskeletal Disorders

Table 9-1 on pages 308–309 lists the disorders and diseases of the human musculoskeletal system that can occur regardless of the quality of an individual's lifestyle. There are several types that may affect muscles, bones, or joints. These disorders and diseases may be inherited, or they may develop from an infection.

TABLE 9-1 Disorders and Diseases of the Human Musculoskeletal System

Muscles	Characteristics and Symptoms	Cause	Treatment
Muscular Dystrophy (Duchenne)	• healthy muscle fibre is destroyed and replaced by scar tissue and fat; affects mainly legs • affects male children only	• inherited (sex-linked recessive)	• no cure • symptoms relieved by surgery, physiotherapy
Myasthenia Gravis	• progressive muscular weakness and eventual paralysis • affects eye and facial muscles, respiration, chest, limbs	• unknown • breakdown between nervous system transmission and muscles	• drugs may restore transmission • surgical removal of thymus gland may cure
Poliomyelitis (Infantile paralysis)	• affects children and young adults • headache, fever, sore throat, back and limb pain, muscle tenderness • muscles atrophy; leads to paralysis and sometimes death	• viral infection of nervous system	• vaccination can prevent • bed rest, nursing care, and isolation • passive muscle treatment and exercises

Bones	Characteristics and Symptoms	Cause	Treatment
Osteoporosis	• bone loss; bones become less dense • risk of fractures (especially hip fractures) increases • affects mostly post-menopausal females • can also affect adolescent females who over-exercise	• reduced estrogen levels caused by inadequate calcium intake and lack of exercise	• estrogen replacement therapy • proper dietary intake of calcium • increased exercise (for older females); decreased exercise (for younger females)
Scoliosis	• abnormal curve of spine to one side of body • decreases lung capacity, causes back pain, degenerative arthritis of spine, intervertebral disk disease, and sciatica	• can be functional: poor posture or leg length discrepancy • can be structural: deformity of vertebral bodies or congenital malformations	• can be corrected in adolescence through exercise, bracing, surgery

Joints	Characteristics and Symptoms	Cause	Treatment
Arthritis (Rheumatoid)	• very painful • joints swell, become stiff and deformed • can be accompanied by fever, anemia, fatigue, and inflamed arteries • inflammation of bursa (fluid-filled sac between bones)	• cause unknown	• no known cure • physiotherapy • anti-inflammatory drugs • steroids

TABLE 9-1—Continued

Joints	Characteristics and Symptoms	Cause	Treatment
Bursitis	• inflammation of bursa • affects any age or sex • affects shoulders, elbows, wrists, knees • joint is tender, painful • movement limited	• prolonged over-use of muscles through repetitive activity (e.g. sports), injury, or infection • anti-inflammatory drugs • physiotherapy	• anti-inflammatory drugs • physiotherapy
Gout	• in primary stage, sudden, severe joint pain with pain-free periods • affects toes, fingers, knees • if chronic, malformations may result • affects mostly males	• excess uric acid forms crystals in joints • primary stage caused by minor trauma, surgery, excessive alcohol consumption • often runs in families	• anti-inflammatory drugs • physiotherapy • controlling uric acid levels • mass reduction, joint rest, reduced alcohol consumption

Skin Disorders

Skin disorders are usually noticeable and may cause embarrassment to the sufferer. Because the skin contains so many sense receptors, even a minor disorder can cause discomfort in the form of pain and itching. Table 9-2 lists some common skin disorders.

TABLE 9-2 Common Skin Disorders

Disorder	Symptoms	Cause	Treatment
Athlete's Foot	• itching; skin can break and bleed • contagious	• fungus growing between toes	• foot powders, foot sprays with anti-fungal agents • preventable by keeping feet clean and dry
Warts	• raised bump on face, fingers, elbows, feet • plantar warts (feet) may be painful due to bearing body weight	• virus invading skin	• most disappear spontaneously • paste to dissolve outer layer and cauterize rest, then scraped off
Psoriasis	• reddish patches of scaly skin • very itchy • affects scalp, arms, legs • scratching causes bleeding • tends to appear at adolescence	• unknown • stress and nervousness bring on in those predisposed	• no cure • itching relieved with creams and ointments
Impetigo	• inflammation and swelling due to pus below skin • pus sacs rupture leaving yellow crust on skin • contagious	• bacterial infection of epidermis	• antibiotic creams
Boil	• pus-filled abscess in skin • swelling	• bacterial infection through cut or hair follicle	• antibiotics may reduce swelling • boil must sometimes be lanced to open

Acne is a disorder of the hair follicles and sebaceous glands. Its onset is stimulated by the increased production of androgens, or sex hormones, which coincides with the beginning of puberty. These hormones cause the walls of the hair follicle to thicken, blocking the sebaceous gland and trapping an increasing amount of oil that is produced during adolescence. Bacteria decompose the trapped oils by converting them to fatty acids. The fatty acids irritate the glands and hair follicles, resulting in pimples and blackheads. The skin around these areas may also be reddened and infected.

Most teenagers experience acne to some extent during their adolescence. Mild cases can be annoying and embarrassing. Most commercial treatments are not very effective, and efforts to cover acne with cosmetics may only aggravate the condition. Frequent washing is still the best way to prevent the spread of the bacteria, but it will not cure existing pimples. More serious cases of acne should be attended to by a physician as improper treatment may lead to disfiguring scars.

Multisystemic Disorders

Multisystemic disorders affect more than one body system at a time. An example of a multisystemic disorder is dermatomyositis, which is a connective tissue disorder that causes inflammation and deterioration of both the skin and the skeletal muscles. The most disabling symptom of dermatomyositis is extreme muscle weakness. Some patients seem paralyzed, unable to raise their heads. Other symptoms include fever, muscle pain, tender skin, and eventually, extremely painful skin eruptions. Skin ulcers and gastrointestinal ulcers are often seen in children. Microscopic examination of the affected tissue shows a thinning of the epidermis and a degeneration, or even death, of muscle fibres.

Dermatomyositis affects twice as many females as males. The onset of the disorder usually occurs between five and fifteen years of age and again between thirty and sixty. Usually, severe flare-ups alternate with periods of remission. Death in adults results from either malignant tumours (20% of cases), or respiratory complications worsened by the patient's inability to swallow or clear the throat. Death in children usually results from bowel damage.

Dermatomyositis is not as rare as doctors once thought. But the disorder is difficult to diagnose because few family doctors see more than six cases in their careers. Until skin lesions appear, patients are sometimes considered neurotic. The cause of dermatomyositis is unknown, but many specialists feel it is probably an auto-immune disorder in which the patient's own immune system attacks other parts of the body. At present, there is no cure; however, some symptoms can be relieved with anti-inflammatory drugs such as cortisone. Drugs that suppress the immune system are also helpful in some cases.

Meet Lynda Dunal

Lynda is an occupational therapist who works for COTA (Community Occupational Therapy Associates). She enjoys working in the community and helping people in their own homes.

Q. *What does an occupational therapist do?*

A. Occupational therapists help people with physical and mental health problems maximize their physical, psychological, social, and emotional abilities.

Q. *How is this different from what a physiotherapist does?*

A. Physiotherapists treat disease by using massage, exercise, or heat. Physiotherapists deal with physical problems and more directly with bone, muscle, or joint problems.

Q. *What studies are required?*

A. Most occupational therapists have a B.Sc. in Occupational Therapy. This is a four-year course with three of those years spent at the School of Rehabilitation.

Q. *Did you get a job right after graduation?*

A. Yes. There are plenty of jobs in this field. I first worked at the Workers' Compensation Board treating injured workers.

Q. *What sort of work was that?*

A. I helped people recover from injuries. For example, for a patient with an injured shoulder, I would find a purposeful and enjoyable activity such as weaving on a wall loom to help strengthen the patient's shoulder.

Q. *What kind of patients do you see?*

A. Some occupational therapists specialize, but I prefer being a generalist. One of my patients is a man who has had a head injury. I'm trying to encourage him to write poetry, which he enjoys and can still do despite his injury. Another patient who has multiple sclerosis has poor co-ordination and little strength, so I'm helping her find ways to manage in the kitchen. I had a patient with AIDS who had gone blind. He needed some short-term remedies for dealing with blindness.

Q. *Does this job require much scientific and medical knowledge?*

A. Much of the course to become an occupational therapist is based on biology, anatomy, and the study of disease. We often have to educate patients about their conditions, so we need to have medical knowledge.

Q. *Is there special equipment you need to know about?*

A. Yes, because we use equipment to compensate for lost physical ability. We have long-handled hair brushes and shoe horns, and reachers with pincers for people who can't bend over to pick things up. There is also the larger mobility equipment such as scooters, wheelchairs, and walkers. People need this equipment to be independent.

Q. *What do you like best about your career?*

A. I like helping people help themselves to achieve their own goals and be able to do what's important to them. This is very different from patient care in a hospital, where often a medical team decides what's good for the patient.

Q. *What opportunities exist for occupational therapists?*

A. The need is great everywhere. There are many jobs to choose from. You can work in a hospital, in a rehabilitation centre, in private practice, or in a school for children who have learning disabilities. Some occupational therapists work in government setting policy and procedures.

Section Review Questions

1. What can you do to ensure that your musculoskeletal system remains healthy?
2. What positive effects do daily washings have on your skin?
3. Describe the cause, symptoms, and treatment for one skeletal disorder, one muscular disorder, and one joint disorder.
4. a) Explain why acne affects teenagers more than other age groups.
   b) What is the best way to prevent the spread of acne? Why does it work?
5. a) What is a multisystemic disorder?
   b) State an example of a multisystemic disorder and explain its effects.

9.6 Protection, Support, and Movement in Other Animals

The most easily observed part of any animal is its integument. Differences in accessory structures are integumentary adaptations that help animals survive in their environments.

Vertebrate Integumentary Systems

The integumentary systems of aquatic vertebrates are adapted for survival in water. For example, the combination of overlapping bony scales and mucus-secreting skin glands helps fish swim by reducing water resistance. The mucus also makes a fish difficult to hold if caught by a predator, and it presents a barrier to water and micro-organisms such as water moulds and bacteria.

The scales of cartilaginous fish such as sharks are tooth-like. These scales are made of dentine, have a pulp-filled cavity, and are covered with enamel. Lungfish and coelacanths, both regarded as "living fossils" because they are almost identical to fish that lived millions of years ago, have similar scales that contain an inner layer of bone. The scales of most common fish such as trout, smelt, perch, and salmon are bony plates.

The overlapping scales of this fish are an adaptation that help it to swim.

By contrast, the smooth, thin, moist skin of amphibians is permeable to water, and it has no accessory structures except glands that secrete a mucous layer. The mucus slows down water loss and makes the animal difficult to catch. Most amphibians live near water or dig deep into the soil to avoid dehydration.

Most reptiles are land dwellers. Their thick, dry, scale-covered skin is impermeable to water. This skin enables reptiles such as snakes and lizards to live in very dry climates with no danger of dehydration, while allowing alligators and crocodiles to stay submerged in swamps without risk of infection from water-borne micro-organisms.

Reptiles, fish, and amphibians are **poikilothermic**. Poikilotherms do not maintain a constant internal temperature. Poikilotherms are often called "cold-blooded," but their blood is not always cold. Instead, their internal body temperatures are dependent on conditions in the external environment. In cold weather, poikilotherms cool off, and all of their body reactions slow down. This reaction to cold weather leads to sluggish behaviour because the cells cannot metabolize glucose quickly enough to release the energy needed to remain active. In warm weather, cell metabolism speeds up, internal temperatures rise, and reptiles are once again able to hunt prey and escape from predators.

As you have learned, birds and mammals are homoiothermic. Their internal body temperatures are kept at relatively high and constant levels regardless of the external temperature. As a result, cell metabolism proceeds at a fairly rapid rate even in cold weather. The heat released by these metabolic processes helps maintain high body temperatures. In addition, the integumentary systems of most birds and mammals contribute to homeostasis with accessory structures that help regulate internal temperature.

This Mexican beaded lizard is a poikilotherm.

Huskies are homoiotherms.

To help camouflage themselves, weasels can change the colour of their fur, depending on the season.

FIGURE 9-17 Four examples of homologous structures in a bird, a whale, a lion, and a human

Bird skin is covered with feathers made of keratin. Air trapped in spaces throughout the feathers helps insulate a bird's body and aids in preventing heat loss. A gland at the base of the tail secretes oil that a bird spreads over its feathers with its beak when it preens. This oil waterproofs and protects the feathers from damage. In very cold weather, birds fluff up their feathers, trapping even more air and providing greater insulation.

Mammals display a range of integumentary adaptations for regulating their body temperatures. During hot weather, mammals with sweat glands cool both their skin and the blood just beneath their skin through evaporation. The cooled blood keeps the internal environment from overheating. Mammals without sweat glands usually look for shade during hot weather.

Most mammals have hair or fur that insulates them against cold weather. Many northern mammals grow an extra layer of fur as winter approaches, then shed it when warmer weather returns. Integumentary features can also help animals hunt, escape from predators, or win mates. Both hares and weasels undergo a complete colour change each winter, while deer and mountain sheep grow accessory structures that help them compete for mates.

Vertebrate Musculoskeletal Systems

Vertebrate musculoskeletal systems are also adapted to different environments. But some vertebrates move the same way humans do—by contracting muscles anchored to an internal skeleton. Comparing vertebrate skeletons reveals likenesses that are otherwise masked by differences in shape, function, and integumentary covering.

For example, the forelimbs of a whale look very different from those of a lion or a bird, and they are used for entirely different purposes. Figure 9-17, however, shows that the underlying skeletal structure is remarkably similar to that of the human forearm. In the embryonic stages, resemblance is even

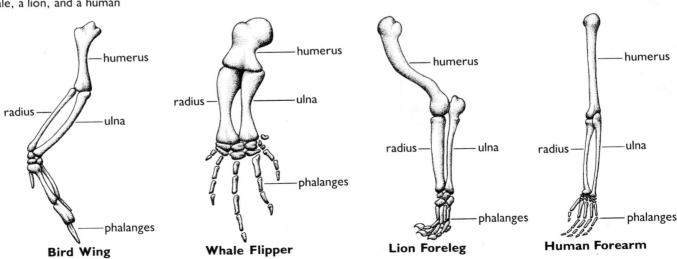

Bird Wing   **Whale Flipper**   **Lion Foreleg**   **Human Forearm**

closer, but function becomes specialized as the animals mature. The wing is adapted for flight, the flipper for swimming, the foreleg for running, and the forearm for grasping. Body parts that compare in arrangement and embryonic development, but differ in shape and function are called **homologous structures**. The bird's wing, the whale's flipper, the lion's foreleg, and the human forearm are all homologous structures, so much alike that some of the individual bones are given the same names.

LABORATORY EXERCISE 9-5
Investigation and Comparison of Homologous Structures in Vertebrates

Homologous structures are structures that develop in the same way in different organisms, but may have different functions depending on the environment in which the organism must survive.

In this exercise, you will investigate homologous skeletal structures such as a forelimb in different vertebrate groups, using models, diagrams, or mounted skeletons. You will also examine the microscopic differences in the accessory structures of vertebrate integumentary systems.

Protection, Support, and Movement in Invertebrates

Invertebrates may look very different from vertebrates, but they have the same need for protective coverings, support structures, and some means of moving around in their environments.

In most invertebrates, both protection and support are provided by a rigid **exoskeleton** made of a complex carbohydrate called chitin. The exoskeleton covers and protects the invertebrate from its external environment and also functions as an attachment point for muscles. For example, the exoskeletons of arthropods are hinged at various points with muscles attached to either side of the joint. (See Figure 9-18.) As in vertebrates, contraction of one set of muscles flexes the joint, while contraction of another set straightens it out.

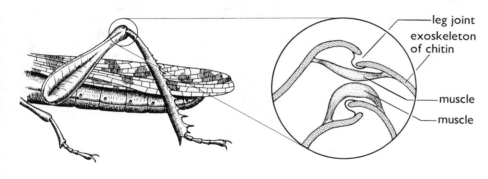

leg joint
exoskeleton of chitin
muscle
muscle

FIGURE 9-18 The grasshopper is a typical arthropod with an exoskeleton made of chitin. Notice the muscle attachment in the leg joint.

The exoskeletons, or shells, of clams, oysters, and snails are highly protective and even help in locomotion. (See Figure 9-19.) Many aquatic invertebrates, however, do not have an exoskeleton. The squid, for example, has only a stiff internal structure of cartilage that gives it its shape and provides a point for muscle attachment. But this internal cartilage offers no protection. Sea slugs and garden slugs also lack shells. Their soft bodies make them vulnerable to predators.

All of this diversity occurs in the phylum Mollusca. But there are twelve invertebrate phyla, and each shows a wide variety of adaptations for survival. Although the integumentary and musculoskeletal structures may differ, these structures enable animals to protect themselves, support their bodies, and move around.

FIGURE 9-19 The muscular foot of the clam is anchored to its shell at only one end. Blood flowing into the foot forms a swelling that anchors the other end in the sand. Muscle contractions then pull the clam down.

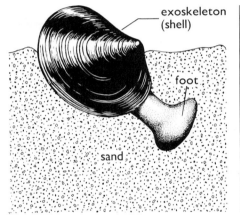

exoskeleton (shell)

foot

sand

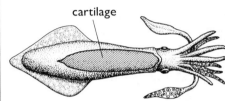

cartilage

FIGURE 9-20 Squid move by expelling a jet of water from their mouths. The cartilaginous core gives the squid its body shape and provides a support for muscle attachment.

A sticky substance secreted by the snail's skin protects it from injury as it glides over a razor blade.

Section Review Questions

1. Briefly describe how the integuments of fish, amphibians, and reptiles are adapted to their particular environments.

2. a) What is the difference between a poikilothermic animal and a homoiothermic animal?
   b) State an example of one animal of each type.

3. How is a bird's integumentary system specially adapted to help it maintain a constant internal temperature?

4. Explain how mammals with and without sweat glands keep cool during hot weather.

5. a) What are homologous structures?
   b) State an example that supports your definition of homologous structures.

6. Describe how arthropods protect, support, and move themselves.

Chapter Review

Key Words

accessory structures
antagonistic muscles
biophysics
cardiac muscle
cartilage
compact bone
connective tissue
epithelial tissue
homoiothermic
homologous structures
immovable joints
insertion

integumentary system
joint
ligaments
movable joints
origin
poikilothermic
skeletal muscle
skeletal system
smooth muscle
spongy bone
tendons

Recall Questions

Multiple Choice

1. Muscles are attached to bones by a connective tissue known as
   a) cartilage
   b) ligaments
   c) tendons
   d) adipose tissue

2. Bone performs all of the following functions except
   a) protecting soft internal organs
   b) allowing the rib cage to expand
   c) producing red blood cells
   d) storing minerals like calcium.

3. Which of the following animals is homoiothermic?
   a) salmon
   b) frog
   c) bird
   d) snake

4. The muscle type that is responsible for moving bones is called
   a) smooth muscle
   b) striated muscle
   c) skeletal muscle
   d) voluntary muscle

5. Production of new cells in the skin occurs in the
   a) epidermis
   b) integument
   c) sebaceous gland
   d) dermis

Fill in the Blanks

1. The skeletons of developing human embryos begin as _____.

2. _____ connects bones to other bones in movable joints.

3. A muscle that straightens out a joint is called a _____.

4. The hip joint is an example of a _____ joint.

5. _____ secrete oily substances that lubricate and protect the skin and the hair.

Short Answers

1. Describe the difference in the accessory structures in the integument of fish, amphibians, reptiles, birds, and mammals.

2. a) What is the difference between a homoiothermic and a poikilothermic animal?
   b) Describe how each responds when the external temperature drops.

3. Compare the structure and function of epithelial, skeletal muscle tissue, and connective tissue.

4. Use an example to describe how an antagonistic pair of muscles moves the bones of a joint.

5. How do the functions of melanin and keratin differ in the skin?

Application Questions

1. Explain why cartilage is found only in certain key locations in an adult human skeleton. Support your explanation with examples.

2. If the contraction of muscle fibres is an ''all-or-nothing'' phenomenon, why are you able to flex your arm half way and stop?

3. Why are antagonistic pairs of muscles associated with each joint?

4. Explain why cardiac muscle never becomes fatigued to the point where it stops contracting or pain is felt.

5. Compare the range of movement allowed by the ball-and-socket, pivot, and hinge joints.

6. Describe how the skin helps maintain homeostasis in a human.

Problem Solving

1. Suppose that the motor nerve stimulating the triceps muscle was severed in an accident. How would this affect arm mobility?

2. Ligaments and tendons do not have the same characteristics, but both are considered to be connective tissues. How are their structures related to their different functions in the skeletal system?

3. Glycogen is converted to glucose and then into lactic acid in the absence of oxygen in an overworked muscle. The buildup of lactic acid creates pain in the muscle, which is not the same as pain from a muscle tear. Why does it take a day or two for the pain to go away?

4. Everyone has experienced an arm or a leg that has ''fallen asleep.'' What causes this sensation? Why do you temporarily lose voluntary control of the limb's movement?

5. What would probably happen to you if the hot and cold temperature receptors of your skin ceased to function?

6. Why should milk be such an important part of your regular diet and not only while you are growing?

Extensions

1. Learn the common names and the scientific names for the main bones of the human skeleton.

2. Construct and demonstrate working models of joints that represent the three classes of levers.

3. Investigate how to show experimentally what happens to bone when calcium phosphate is removed. Perform the experiment and present your results to your class.

4. Obtain a cross section and a longitudinal section of a long bone of an animal such as a cow from a butcher. Include a knee joint if possible. Study the structure and write a report on your findings.

5. Sports injuries involving bones, muscles, and joints occur frequently in our fitness-conscious society. Research the causes, treatments, and prevention of some of these injuries. Make a presentation to your class about your findings.

6. Research fingerprint patterns and investigate how they are used in criminology.

CHAPTER 10

Reproduction and Development

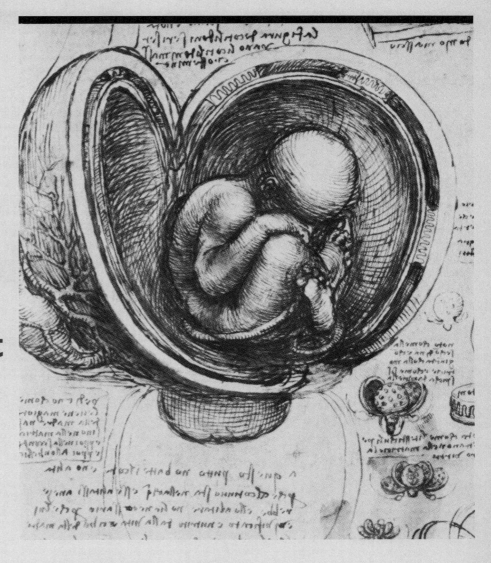

How and when does life begin? In the centuries before anything was known about cells, theories about human development were purely speculative. The philosopher Aristotle suggested that the substance for the development of a child is provided by the mother, but the creative principle (form, sex, characteristics) is supplied by the father. This implied the necessity of fertilization.

It was not until the fifteenth century, during the Renaissance in Europe, that scientists began to address questions about the origins of life, which had previously preoccupied philosophers and theologians. Leonardo da Vinci, like other Renaissance artists, made dissections to increase his knowledge about the human body. These dissections were performed on corpses. This illustration is an example of what he observed and drew around 1490. Leonardo's observations, unprecedented in their mathematical and quantitative detail, make him the founder of embryology as an exact science.

Leonardo looked at fetal functions and the relative sizes of body parts. He was the first investigator to make quantitative observations about embryonic growth. He noted that the rate of growth decreases as the size of the embryo increases.

However, scientists still did not know where the embryo came from. It was thought to result from the combination of semen with menstrual blood. In the sixteenth century, the philosopher Paracelsus outlined a recipe for making a homunculus—a miniature human—by mixing semen and blood and allowing them to putrefy. In other words, he thought that human embryos developed from rotting material.

The theory of preformation, common in the seventeenth and eighteenth centuries, held that if an embryo develops in the mother's uterus, it must have been there all the time, but so tiny at first as to be invisible. When Leeuwenhoek first observed sperm in 1677, some scientists said they could see a homunculus in the head of the sperm. This led to a heated and protracted debate over whether the homunculus was in the sperm or in the womb.

Scientists continued to investigate and experiment. The human egg was first observed in 1827. By 1855, the cell theory had helped to explain how cells divide and multiply. Discovering the role of chromosomes in reproduction around 1900 and the role of DNA in heredity during the 1950s led to an even better understanding of how fertilized eggs develop into embryos and eventually form fully differentiated organisms.

Today, in embryology you hear about techniques such as *in vitro* fertilization and the pre-screening of test-tube embryos before implantation in the mother's womb. Embryologists have answered the question about how life begins; but they, and all of us, are still debating when it begins. This question has preoccupied people throughout history. What you will learn in this chapter represents our current understanding about the mystery of life's beginnings.

Chapter Objectives

When you complete this chapter, you should:

1. Be able to explain the differences between sexual and asexual reproduction, and the advantages and disadvantages of each.

2. Understand the similarities and differences between the ovulation cycle, fertilization process, and gestation period of humans and other vertebrates.

3. Be able to describe the structure and function of a male and a female mammalian reproductive system.

4. Be able to describe the process of fertilization in mammals and the stages of embryonic development to the fetal stage.

5. Understand and compare the structure and function of the reproductive systems of male and female humans, a marsupial pair, and another mammalian pair.

6. Be able to describe the hormonal, uterine, and ovarian changes of the human menstrual cycle.

7. Understand how hormones control puberty and be able to describe the physiological changes that take place during puberty.

8. Appreciate the importance of good health habits during pregnancy.

9. Be able to list and describe several natural and artificial methods of preventing or facilitating fertilization in humans.

10. Be able to describe briefly the physiology of at least three malfunctions of the human reproductive system and three sexually transmitted diseases.

11. Know how to use laboratory techniques to examine prepared slides and electron micrographs of vertebrate gonadal tissue, sperm, eggs, and embryos.

12. Know how to perform a dissection to observe the reproductive system of a representative vertebrate.

13. Appreciate the contributions and limitations of science concerning moral and ethical issues associated with the human reproductive process.

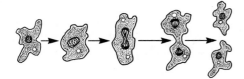

FIGURE 10-1 Asexual reproduction in an amoeba by binary fission. Each new cell is identical to the original parent cell.

Principles of Reproduction in Animals

Digestion, excretion, gas exchange, and all other life functions you have studied so far in this unit are necessary for the survival of individual organisms. Reproduction is not necessary for individual survival; however, all individuals eventually die. Unless most members of a species reproduce during their lifetime, the species will become extinct.

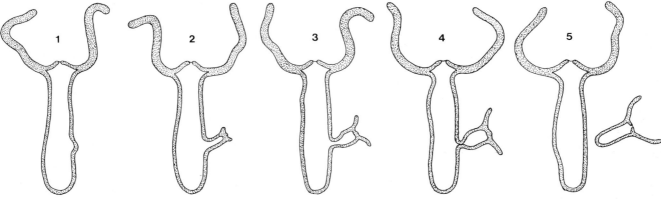

1. Parent Hydra.

2. Bud enlarging, shares parent cavity.

3. Bud getting larger. Common cavity beginning to seal off.

4. Common cavity completely sealed off.

5. Bud breaks off to exist as an independent organism.

FIGURE 10-2 Asexual reproduction in a hydra occurs by budding.

Asexual and Sexual Reproduction

In **asexual reproduction,** a new individual is formed directly from the body or some body part of a single parent organism. In some kingdoms, asexual reproduction is common. For example, in unicellular protists such as the amoeba, one parent cell splits, forming two offspring identical to each other and to the parent. This process is called **binary fission.** (See Figure 10-1.)

In the animal kingdom, asexual reproduction is much less common, but it does occur in some species. Figure 10-2 shows **budding** in the hydra. Each bud eventually forms a miniature hydra, which detaches from the parent and lives independently. Figure 10-3 illustrates **regeneration** in a planarian. Each half of the original planarian grows the missing body parts it needs to become a complete individual. In more complex animals, regeneration is usually restricted to the replacement of missing limbs or the healing of wounds. **Fragmentation** is a specialized type of regeneration that occurs in some simple animals such as the sea anemone. In this process, pieces of a parent organism break off and regenerate into complete, new individuals.

FIGURE 10-3 Planarians can split spontaneously in two. Each half grows the missing body parts it needs by regeneration.

A single starfish arm, accidentally removed from the parent organism, is regenerating its missing arms to form a complete, new starfish.

These greyhound puppies display obvious variations from their mother.

Complex behaviours that occur between a queen bee and the workers ensure the fertilization of her eggs.

For most of the animal kingdom, however, reproduction is usually sexual, even for animals that can reproduce by asexual means. In **sexual reproduction,** a new individual is formed by the union of two nonidentical cells from two nonidentical parents. Although the offspring is of the same species as its parents, it is not identical to either. Instead, an offspring has a combination of characteristics from both parents.

Sexual Reproduction in Animals

Producing offspring by sexual reproduction is a complex process involving specialized body systems, cell processes, and behavioural patterns. Although the particulars may differ, all animal phyla, including our own phylum Chordata, share many reproductive features.

Two Sexes
Most animal species come in two body types or sexes: male and female. Each sex is specialized for a particular role in reproduction. In some species such as mollusks, the two sexes appear the same and can be distinguished only by an internal examination. In other species, the two sexes are noticeably different in appearance, a characteristic that is called **sexual dimorphism.** (See Figure 10-4.)

Gamete Production
A **gamete** is a specialized reproductive cell that must be combined with another gamete before a new individual can be formed. Most animal species produce two types of gametes: eggs and sperm. **Eggs** are the female gametes. They are generally round, contain a nucleus with hereditary material, and a large amount of stored food called the yolk. **Sperm,** the male gametes, are much smaller by comparison. They contain only a nucleus with hereditary material, a mid-section with numerous mitochondria, and a tail called a **flagellum.** The

FIGURE 10-4 Sexual dimorphism is apparent in roundworms, where the female is larger than the male.

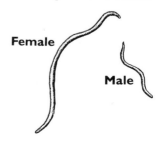

Female

Male

A sea urchin egg and sperm at the moment of fertilization

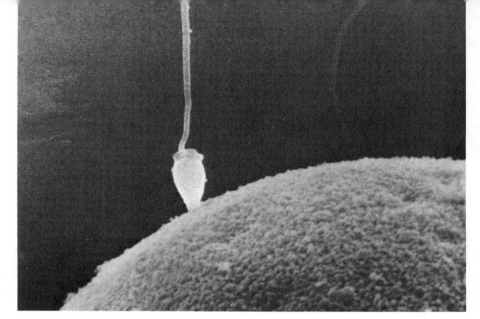

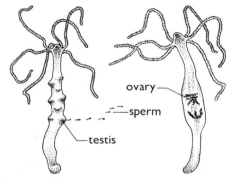

ovary

sperm

testis

FIGURE 10-5 Gonads in the male and female hydra. The released sperm swim through water to the ovary to fertilize the eggs internally.

FIGURE 10-6 Earthworms are hermaphrodites (each contains both male and female gonads). However, the sperm and eggs of a single worm cannot unite. So, zygote formation depends on the exchange of sperm-carrying semen (see arrows) between two worms.

flagellum allows the sperm to swim toward the egg, which has no structures for locomotion of its own. Both types of gametes are fragile and die quickly if exposed to air.

Gametes are produced in sex organs called **gonads.** Female animals have gonads called **ovaries** that produce the eggs. Males have gonads called **testes** that produce sperm. (See Figure 10-5.) In some organisms, **seminal fluid** is released along with the sperm. Seminal fluid contains fructose, a glucose-like sugar that provides energy for the mitochondria, and chemicals that help the sperm survive in a female's reproductive system. The mixture of sperm and seminal fluid is called **semen.** (See Figure 10-6.)

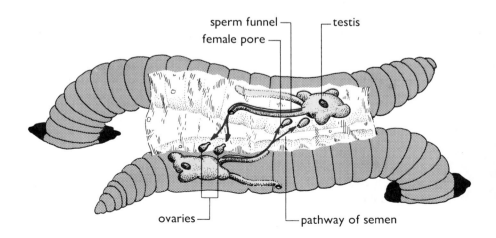

sperm funnel

female pore

testis

ovaries

pathway of semen

Zygote Formation

Producing a new offspring requires uniting an egg with a sperm from the same species. During fertilization, the two gametes fuse, forming a single cell called a **zygote** that will eventually grow into a new individual.

If gametes contained the same number of chromosomes as other body cells, the zygote would contain twice the number of chromosomes normal for the species. The abnormal amount of DNA and the resulting imbalance of chemicals produced in the zygote would cause it to malfunction or die before it could develop normally.

This doubling of chromosomes does not happen because each gamete contains only half the usual number of chromosomes for the species. Therefore, the combination of two gametes results in a complete set of chromosomes that contain all the information a zygote needs to develop into a new individual. (See Figure 10-7.)

Embryonic Development

Soon after fertilization, the zygote begins to divide repeatedly by **mitosis**. From this point until it hatches or is born, the developing animal is called an **embryo.** Since mitosis produces exact copies of the original nucleus, each

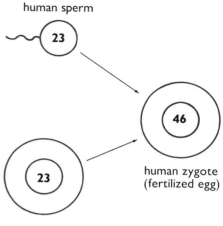

FIGURE 10-7 In humans, all ordinary body cells contain 46 chromosomes. Each egg and sperm, however, contains only 23 chromosomes. When two gametes fuse, the newly formed zygote will contain a complete set of chromosomes or 46.

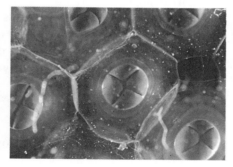

The development of a frog embryo. The embryo divides into two cells, then four, then eight, and finally into multiple cells.

FIGURE 10-8 Repeated mitosis forms all body systems and cells of the developing embryo.

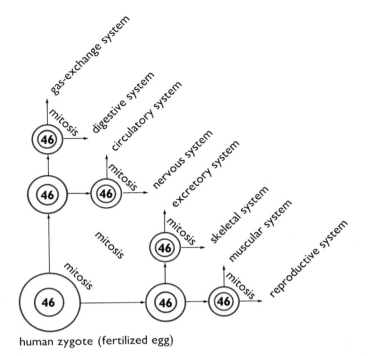

human zygote (fertilized egg)

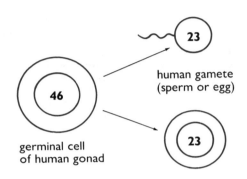

germinal cell of human gonad

human gamete (sperm or egg)

FIGURE 10-9 Gametes have only half the usual number of chromosomes.

new embryo cell receives a complete set of chromosomes identical to those in the original zygote.

At first, the embryo is simply a ball of identical cells, but eventually these cells differentiate to form different body systems. (See Figure 10-8.) An unborn human is usually called a **fetus** once it develops recognizable features. When a fetus or an embryo emerges from the egg or the mother's reproductive system, it is called an **offspring.** The offspring becomes sexually mature when its gonads begin to produce gametes with only half the usual number of chromosomes. (See Figure 10-9.)

The Need for Meiosis

Mitotic division accounts for embryonic development, growth, and repair in all ordinary body cells and structures. However, mitosis always results in a full set of chromosomes for each new cell. Producing gametes with only half a set of chromosomes requires a specialized cell process called **meiosis**.

In males, meiosis occurs only in the germinal cells of the testes. (See Figure 10-10.) Before sperm production begins, each germinal cell contains the same number of chromosomes as any other body cell. Half of these chromosomes, the maternal chromosomes, can be traced back to the organism's female parent. The other half, the paternal chromosomes, come from the male parent. During sperm formation, meiosis reduces the number of chromosomes in each sperm to half, and regroups the maternal and paternal chromosomes. (See Figure 10-11.) The end result is four sperm cells, each with a different half-set of chromosomes.

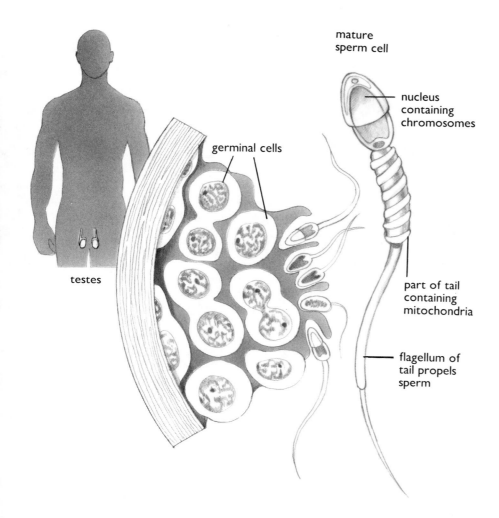

mature
sperm cell

nucleus
containing
chromosomes

germinal cells

part of tail
containing
mitochondria

flagellum of
tail propels
sperm

testes

FIGURE 10-10 Before meiosis, each germinal cell in a male testis has the normal chromosome number for the species. After meiosis, each mature sperm cell has only half the usual number of chromosomes.

Meiosis in the female ovary is similar, except that only one cell survives to become an egg. (See Figure 10-11.) Each egg cell that is produced has a different half-set of chromosomes, even though all of the germinal cells in one ovary are identical. Therefore, when eggs and sperm from the same pair of parents unite, each zygote gets a slightly different combination of chromosomes. This new combination differentiates offspring from each other and also from either parent. (Remember the greyhounds in the photograph on page 323.)

Fertilization

Fertilization is the process that transfers sperm to the vicinity of the eggs so that the two gametes can unite to form a zygote. Egg and sperm cells are delicate, so timing is critical. A few species can store eggs or sperm, but for

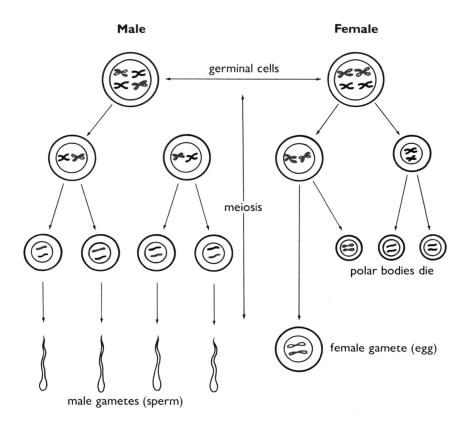

FIGURE 10-11 Meiosis in the germinal cells of males and females produces gametes with different half-sets of chromosomes. Random union in fertilization produces offspring with different chromosome combinations than either parent.

Salmon can reproduce only after they return to the river where they were born.

Earthworms are hermaphrodites and contain both types of sex organs. However, they do not fertilize their own eggs. During mating, two earthworms line up beside each other and double copulation takes place. The sperm of one worm is transferred to the receptacles near the ovaries of the other. Chromosomes are exchanged and new genetic combinations occur by this method. Very few hermaphrodites fertilize their eggs with their own sperm.

most, gametes must unite within hours of release. Animals have developed a variety of methods for ensuring that sperm and egg cells arrive in the same place, at the same time. Many species have a mating season, a short time period when large numbers of males and females gather in the same place to fertilize eggs.

Except for mammals, fertilization in aquatic animals is usually external, occurring outside the body of either parent. In most mollusks such as clams and oysters, the sexes are separate. Males and females come close together and release hundreds of eggs and sperm at the same time. The large number of parents releasing huge numbers of gametes at the same time in the same location ensures that reproduction will occur. However, many gametes will be washed away by currents, consumed by other animals, or die before fertilization takes place.

Land animals maximize zygote formation through internal fertilization. Internal fertilization prevents the delicate gametes from drying out. Fertilization of the eggs takes place within the female's body after the male deposits sperm inside her reproductive tract. This process is called **copulation.** (See Figure 10-12.)

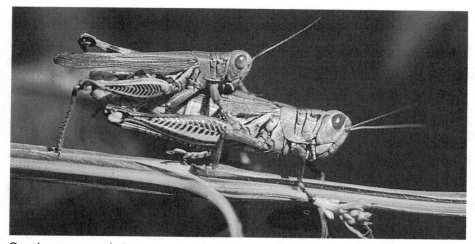

Grasshoppers copulating

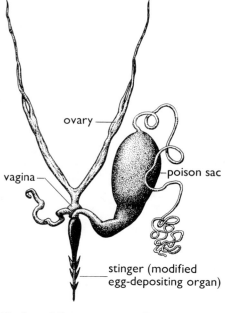

ovary

vagina

poison sac

stinger (modified
egg-depositing organ)

**Reduced Reproductive Organs
of Female Worker
(modified for defence)**

internal penis
extends only
during copulation

ovaries
contain
many egg
tubules

sperm develop
inside abdomen

developing egg
cells descend as
they mature

FIGURE 10-12 Fertilization in bees. Several mating flights over a two-day period provide the queen with enough stored sperm for her whole lifetime, but not all eggs are fertilized. Unfertilized eggs (N) produce male drones. Fertilized eggs (2N) develop into workers or queens, depending on how larvae are fed.

mature egg cells complete
meiosis in oviduct

semen ejaculated
into bulb of penis

storage vessel holds
live sperm

**Abdomen and Partly Extended
Penis of Male**

bulb of penis
remains in vagina

stored sperm fertilizes
mature egg in vagina

vagina contracts, forcing
sperm into storage vessel

male body parts ejected
through opening of vagina

fertilized eggs leave through
external body opening

**Fully Developed Reproductive
Organs of Female Queen**

Life Cycle

All animals that reproduce sexually pass through a life cycle with at least five stages: (1) fertilization of an egg by a sperm, (2) zygote formation, (3) embryonic development, (4) immature juvenile form, and (5) mature adult form capable of producing gametes for fertilization. This basic pattern is repeated throughout the animal kingdom. (See Figures 10-13 and 10-14.)

FIGURE 10-13 The five main stages of development in the life cycle of a jellyfish

DID YOU KNOW?

Not all species reproduce only when they are sexually mature. The axolotl, the larval form of the tiger salamander of Mexico, can produce gametes while still in the juvenile stage. The axolotl is aquatic. A lack of iodine in the ponds it inhabits prevents the axolotl from fully developing into a land-dwelling adult.

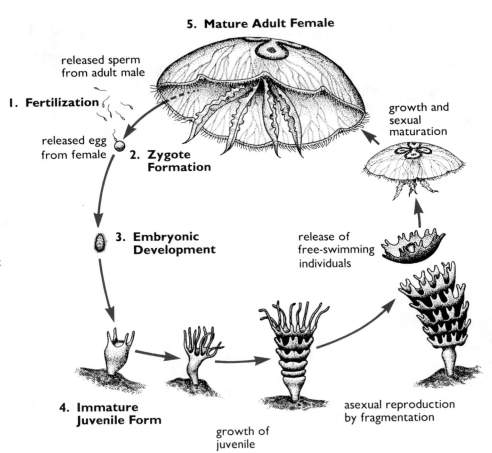

5. **Mature Adult Female**

released sperm from adult male

I. **Fertilization**

released egg from female

2. **Zygote Formation**

growth and sexual maturation

3. **Embryonic Development**

release of free-swimming individuals

4. **Immature Juvenile Form**

growth of juvenile

asexual reproduction by fragmentation

Microscopic Examination of Reproductive Cells, Tissues, and Embryos

Recognition of cell types and tissues in actual specimens of reproductive tissue

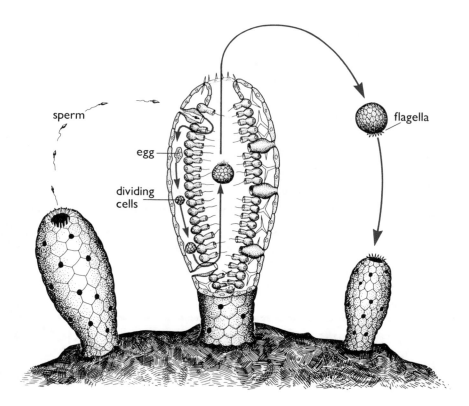

sperm

egg

dividing
cells

flagella

is quite different from recognizing photographs in a text since some detail may be lost or obscured during the preparation of a tissue slide.

In this exercise, you will practise examining and drawing samples of reproductive tissues and cells. These samples will include germinal tissue from ovaries and testes, sperm cells, egg cells, and embryos in different stages of development.

The Significance of Sexual Reproduction

Sexual reproduction occurs in all known kingdoms: animals, plants, fungi, protists, and monerans. Since sexual reproduction occurs in every kingdom, it must have great advantages. Scientists believe that the primary advantage of sexual reproduction is new chromosome combinations that become possible in offspring. These new combinations ensure variations among individuals of the same species, increasing the likelihood that at least some individuals will survive and reproduce if the environment changes.

Section Review Questions

1. Describe four methods of asexual reproduction and state an example for each from the animal kingdom.

2. a) What is sexual dimorphism?
   b) State one example of sexual dimorphism.

3. Define the following terms: a) gamete, b) gonad, c) egg, d) sperm, e) flagellum, f) ovaries, g) testes, and h) semen.

4. a) Why is meiosis necessary in animals that reproduce sexually?
   b) How does meiosis in males and females differ?

5. List the five stages of development in the life cycle of a typical animal.

6. a) In which kingdoms does sexual reproduction occur?
   b) What do scientists think is the main advantage of sexual reproduction?

10.2 Patterns of Vertebrate Reproduction and Development

All 40 000 vertebrate species reproduce sexually. In most of these species, the sexes are separate and have two reproductive features in common: a pair of gonads and a pair of tubes that enable gametes or fertilized eggs to leave the body. In addition, each vertebrate species has characteristic body structures and behavioural patterns that ensure enough eggs become fertilized and enough offspring survive to perpetuate the species.

Seasonal mating is perhaps the most widespread reproductive pattern among vertebrates. Early each spring, huge schools of grunion gather near the California coast. The continued survival of the grunion depends on their ability to produce and fertilize more eggs than their predators can eat. This

Grunion mate and lay their fertilized eggs in the beach sand when they are washed ashore at high tide. Adults are exposed to predators when the tide retreats, so a great number of eggs are required for the species to survive.

ability to reproduce in large numbers is especially important because fish do not provide parental care for their young.

Most vertebrates, sea mammals, birds, and larger fish that follow the herring to feed on their eggs or their offspring also breed on a seasonal basis. Only humans do not breed seasonally. They produce offspring throughout the year regardless of climate or availability of food.

Patterns for Reproduction in Water

Except for mammals, virtually all aquatic vertebrates lay many eggs and display behaviour patterns that maximize zygote formation. (See Figure 10-15.) Water plays a vital role in the reproductive patterns of aquatic vertebrates. First, sperm must be able to swim to the eggs once they are released in order to fertilize them. Second, since fertilization is external, water prevents the zygotes and developing embryos from drying out. Third, water provides an environment in which offspring can move about and find food readily. Even tree frogs, which spend much of their adult lives on land, need water for reproduction.

If not enough water is available, tree frogs create a foam nest, a moist environment that allows their eggs to be fertilized.

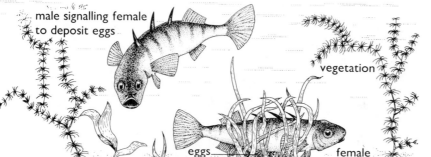

male signalling female to deposit eggs

vegetation

eggs

female

pond bottom

FIGURE 10-15 The female stickleback deposits eggs inside a nest built by the male. When she leaves, the male enters the nest and releases sperm. The fertilized eggs are partially protected by the nest. An elaborate sequence of events during the mating of stickleback fish maximizes the number of eggs that are fertilized.

External fertilization means that eggs are vulnerable to predation and environmental conditions. However, since thousands of eggs are laid simultaneously, and courtship behaviour brings males and females close together at the same time, most of the eggs that are released are fertilized.

LABORATORY EXERCISE 10-2
Vertebrate Reproductive Structures

The reproductive systems of most vertebrates have common structural features. In this exercise, you will dissect and study the reproductive system of a mammalian vertebrate. You will also compare the structure of the mammalian system to that of other vertebrates illustrated in this chapter.

Patterns for Reproduction on Land

Reptiles and birds are terrestrial vertebrates. Although many terrestrial vertebrates such as sea turtles and ducks spend much of their adulthood in water, they must return to land to reproduce. Internal fertilization enables the sperm to swim to the eggs and protects the gametes and the zygotes from drying out. Mating behaviour in both groups includes copulation, which occurs in much the same way for both reptiles and birds. The male mounts the female from the rear and bends his posterior underneath the female's so that their cloacal openings touch. The male releases semen into the moist surroundings of the female's cloaca, enabling the sperm to swim up the oviduct. (See Figure 10-

Copulation in turtles facilitates internal fertilization.

Some turtles lay their eggs in sandy hollows on beaches near water. Since the mother will not be present when the eggs hatch, she must cover them for added protection.

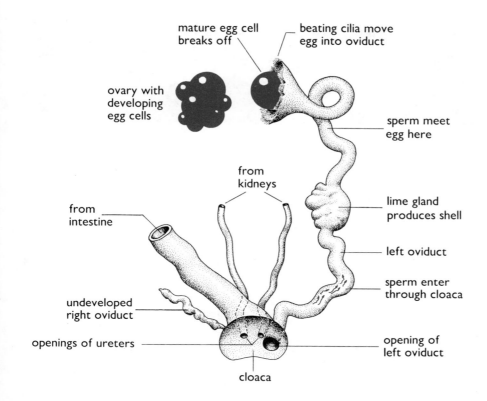

mature egg cell breaks off

beating cilia move egg into oviduct

ovary with developing egg cells

sperm meet egg here

from kidneys

from intestine

lime gland produces shell

left oviduct

sperm enter through cloaca

undeveloped right oviduct

openings of ureters

opening of left oviduct

cloaca

FIGURE 10-16 Internal fertilization in birds takes place in the upper part of the left oviduct. The undeveloped right oviduct is a weight-saving adaptation. Fertilization in reptiles is similar, but structural details may differ. For example, the snake's reproductive structures are adapted to suit its elongated body.

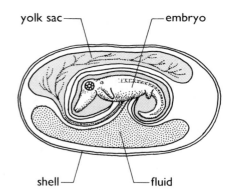

yolk sac

embryo

shell

fluid

FIGURE 10-17 Reptile eggs have waterproof shells, large yolks, and several membranes to protect the developing embryo.

16.) After fertilization, the egg is surrounded by a shell and passed out through the cloaca.

Although reptiles do not usually care for their eggs, they do ensure that most will hatch by laying the eggs in a hole that they fill in. The eggs also have thick, leathery, waterproof shells that protect the developing embryos from water loss. Large yolks and several membranes improve the embryos' chances of survival. (See Figure 10-17.) Once born, however, the young reptiles must feed themselves. Bird eggs are similar to reptile eggs except that they are enclosed in a hard shell and contain a second stored food source — the **albumen** or egg white. Unlike reptiles, birds incubate their eggs and feed their young until they can care for themselves.

Table 10-1 indicates that the number of eggs laid by vertebrates that provide some form of parental care is smaller than the number of eggs laid by vertebrates that do not. The number of eggs laid during one mating cycle is much lower for reptiles and birds than for fish and amphibians. Internal fertilization increases the percentage of eggs fertilized and also protects the embryos. Structural adaptations such as thick egg shells and behavioural adaptations such as parental care also ensure that more offspring will survive to reproductive age.

DID YOU KNOW?
Domesticated birds such as chickens may lay more than 300 eggs each year.

Because birds take care of their young, fewer offspring per mating pair are necessary to perpetuate the species.

TABLE 10-1   Number of Eggs Laid by Vertebrates

Vertebrate	Number of Eggs Laid (a)	Parental Care	Survival Pattern
Fish	• thousands	• none	• most eggs are eaten or die before hatching
Frog	• hundreds	• none in most cases	• most eggs are eaten or die before hatching
Reptile	• over 12	• eggs laid in nest and covered	• most eggs hatch, but many offspring are eaten before adulthood
Bird	• 1–20	• eggs tended by parents, hatchlings fed until able to fly	• most hatchlings survive to adulthood

The display of plumage in peacocks to attract mates is a sign of sexual maturity.

Vertebrate Reproductive Cycles

Vertebrates must release their sperm and their eggs at the same time and in the same place to maximize the possibility of fertilization. Although behavioural adaptations may differ among species, all vertebrates display courtship rituals and mating patterns that help them accomplish fertilization. All vertebrates except humans mate on a seasonal basis. These seasonal patterns usually begin at a time of year when environmental conditions are favourable for the survival of offspring, and an abundant supply of food is available.

A typical vertebrate reproductive cycle begins with the courtship and mating behaviour of the adults. The next cycle does not begin until the offspring are sexually mature and are able to produce offspring of their own.

The reproductive system of a juvenile animal is usually the last system to mature. Some simple vertebrates may become sexually mature within the first year. Others may take several years to mature. Sexual maturity is usually controlled by sex hormones. In birds, for example, hormones stimulate the development of adult plumage, indicating that the reproductive system has matured. Other hormones responsible for egg production and courtship behaviour are not released until the mating season begins.

A New Twist on Breeding Technology

During World War II, military transports from the Philippines introduced to the Pacific island of Guam a new predator—a brown tree snake. The snake liked Guam and was so successful it pushed a native species of bird, the Guam rail, to the edge of extinction. In 1960, there were 40 000 rails on Guam; by 1984, there were only 18. In 1984, biologists who hoped to save the species captured 16 of the survivors to be bred in captivity. Soon, the population had increased to 120, but the biologists were still worried.

Without knowing how closely two individuals are related, mating success is unpredictable. Individuals such as siblings, who are very similar genetically, often produce weakened offspring because of inbreeding and depression. At the other extreme, individuals who are extremely dissimilar genetically produce offspring that may be weakened by what is called off-breeding depression. The Guam researchers were worried because many of the captured Guam rails had been siblings or close relatives. Researchers plan to return 100 rail offspring to the wild on Rota, an island similar to Guam that has no brown tree snakes. But would such a highly inbred group of birds survive when released to the wild?

In an attempt to ensure the survival of the Guam rail, they turned to an emerging technology, DNA fingerprinting. With this technique, the DNA of two individuals is compared. The degree of similarity of the DNA is a measure of how close the two individuals are related genetically. These comparisons may be used to determine the likelihood of mating two birds to produce strong, diverse offspring. The researchers hope that DNA fingerprinting will reveal which birds in the population of 120 rails should be bred to maximize the diversity and health of the next generation.

The primary use of DNA fingerprinting is the positive identification of individuals by examining their DNA. Samples of DNA are mixed with enzymes and molecular tags, which cut and label DNA segments that have specific sequences. These DNA fragments are then sorted by size on a gelatin strip. Eventually, the strip of DNA fragments resembles the bar codes on grocery packages. Any two samples of an individual's DNA fingerprint will produce identical ''bar codes,'' and can be used as ''fingerprints'' in criminal investigations.

Currently, DNA-fingerprinting technology is being used to help other threatened species such as the African elephant. According to John Patton, a conservation biologist, although some African countries have few elephants, they allow ivory exports despite the endangered status of elephants. Patton hopes to use the breeding and migration patterns of elephants to develop a system that will identify the geographical origin of an ivory piece by its DNA.

Section Review Questions

1. Describe the reproductive features common to sexually reproducing vertebrates.
2. What three advantages does an aquatic environment provide vertebrates that reproduce using external fertilization?
3. a) What advantage is internal fertilization to vertebrates that reproduce on land?
   b) Which structural and behavioural adaptations ensure that some reptile eggs will hatch?
4. a) Which factors help vertebrates release their sperm and their eggs at the same time for fertilization?
   b) What role do hormones play in the reproductive cycle?

Mammals such as beluga whales feed their offspring milk from the female's mammary glands.

10.3 Mammalian Reproductive Patterns

All mammals have the ability to feed their young with milk from the female's **mammary glands.** These glands are modified sweat glands that release a liquid containing all of the nutrients required for a young mammal's growth. In addition to mammary glands, mammals have many other reproductive features in common.

Mammalian Reproductive Structures

The reproductive systems of all vertebrates include two gonads and a pair of tubes leading to the outside of the body. In mammals, these reproductive structures are adapted to suit a different reproductive pattern.

The oviducts of the female mammal are called **Fallopian tubes** and do not lead directly out of the body. (See Figure 10-18.) Instead, they join to form the **uterus,** a chamber-like organ where the zygote will develop until birth. The **vagina,** a tube leading from the uterus to the outside, receives the sperm from the male. The major adaptation of the male mammal is the **penis,** a structure that facilitates internal fertilization by depositing the sperm as close as possible to the opening of the uterus, which is called the **cervix.**

Almost every mammal species has a reproductive system very similar to that described above. Although the precise shape of the reproductive parts may vary from species to species, their basic structure and function are similar.

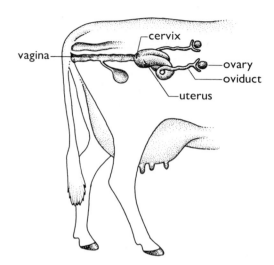

Sexual readiness in female baboons is signalled by changes to the external genital area that correspond to peak hormone levels during the ovulation cycle.

Patterns of Fertilization

All mammals reproduce by internal fertilization. Even aquatic mammals such as seals must copulate. Unlike fish, they do not depend on water to allow the sperm to swim to the female for fertilization.

Female mammals usually produce fewer than 12 eggs at a time. A typical mammalian egg is microscopically small and contains a very small yolk. The release of an egg from an ovary is called **ovulation,** which occurs during **estrus,** the hormonal peak of the reproductive cycle. In some species, estrus and ovulation occur only once during a mating season. If estrus occurs more than once a season, an ovulation cycle results, with eggs released at the peak of each cycle. In some species, copulation is needed to stimulate ovulation.

Hormones controlling the ovulation cycle are also responsible for bodily changes that signal the female's state of readiness and stimulate the male's desire to mate. These signals range from scent molecules such as those released by cats and cows to changes in physical appearance such as those seen in some apes.

Internal Embryonic Development

In most mammals, the embryo develops and grows inside the uterus instead of inside an egg. But the extent of embryonic development prior to birth varies widely. Newborn horses and deer are ready to run within a few hours of birth. Bear cubs are born naked, blind, and completely helpless in mid-winter, and they may rely on their mother for a year or more.

The period of time between fertilization and birth is called **gestation.** Gestation periods also vary greatly. (See Table 10-2.) In the following activity, you will investigate the significance of these differences in four representative mammals, including humans.

TABLE 10-2 Gestation Periods in Mammals

Mammal	Average Gestation Period (d)
Opossum	13
Mouse	21–28
Grey Kangaroo	40
Cat	60–63
Tiger	90
Pig	112–115
Cow	270
Human	270
Elephant	600–660

Mammalian Reproductive Patterns

Almost all mammals have the same basic pattern of reproduction. The details and timing of the process, however, may differ. In this activity, you will study the reproductive patterns of four different mammals, make some preliminary observations, and draw some conclusions about the extent to which the patterns are the same or different.

Procedure

1. In your notebook, set up an observation chart that has the following five headings.

Reproductive Feature	Monotreme (Platypus)	Marsupial (Opossum)	Placental (Cat: multiple)	Placental (Human: single)

In the first column, list the following points for comparison. Be sure to leave enough space for your observations.
- Structure(s) for producing sperm
- Structure(s) for ejecting sperm
- Structure(s) for receiving sperm
- Structure(s) for producing eggs
- Structure(s) for transferring eggs
- Site of fertilization
- Site of embryo development
- Mode of embryo nutrition
- Structure(s) for birth of offspring
- Structure(s) for feeding newborn

2. Study the illustrations in Figure 10-19 on pages 342–343, and fill in your observation chart.

3. Using the observations in your chart and other information provided with the diagrams, answer the Discussion Questions.

Discussion Questions

Ovulation Cycle

1. a) In some mammals, the ovulation cycle limits mating to a particular season. In others, the ovulation cycle permits mating throughout the year. Which ovulation pattern is more common among mammals, and what are its advantages?
   b) How does the human pattern differ? What are its advantages?

Fertilization Process

2. In vertebrates such as fish and frogs, fertilization is generally external. What is the general pattern of fertilization in mammals, and what are its advantages?

3. a) What common function does the uterus have in all four representative mammals?
   b) Describe any structural differences.
   c) What is the most important functional difference?

4. Which differs more from one mammal to another, the male reproductive system or the female reproductive system?

Development of Embryo or Fetus

5. a) In some mammals, the embryo or fetus shares its mother's body systems throughout gestation. What structure makes this arrangement possible?
   b) To what order do such mammals belong?

6. State the two mammalian orders in which the embryo does not share its mother's body systems. How do the young of these mammals survive the embryonic development period?

7. a) Which of the developmental patterns described in Questions 5 and 6 is more common in mammals?
   b) What is its advantage?

Period of Dependency

8. a) How are young mammals nourished immediately after birth?
   b) What is the main advantage of this pattern of nourishment to the infant and to the parent(s)?

9. Newborn fish, frogs, and snakes generally receive no parental care after hatching. Newborn birds receive intensive parental care until they can fly. Describe the general pattern of parental care among mammals (apart from nourishment).

10. a) Platypus, opossum, cat, and human infants are all helpless when they are born. Is there any relationship between litter size and the length of the dependency period?
    b) How does litter size in mammals compare to the number of offspring produced by other vertebrates?

FIGURE 10-19   Reproduction in four types of mammals

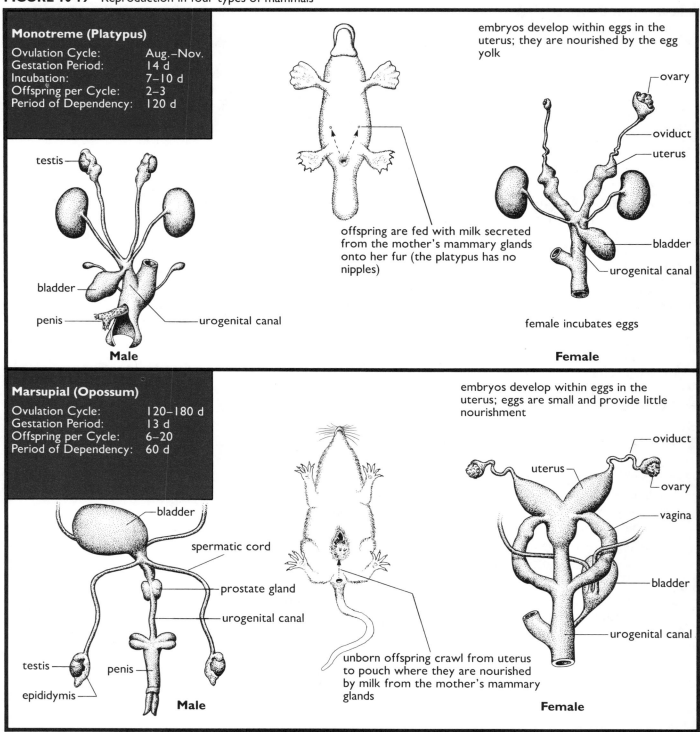

Monotreme (Platypus)

Ovulation Cycle:	Aug.–Nov.
Gestation Period:	14 d
Incubation:	7–10 d
Offspring per Cycle:	2–3
Period of Dependency:	120 d

testis

bladder

penis

urogenital canal

Male

embryos develop within eggs in the uterus; they are nourished by the egg yolk

ovary

oviduct

uterus

bladder

urogenital canal

offspring are fed with milk secreted from the mother's mammary glands onto her fur (the platypus has no nipples)

female incubates eggs

Female

Marsupial (Opossum)

Ovulation Cycle:	120–180 d
Gestation Period:	13 d
Offspring per Cycle:	6–20
Period of Dependency:	60 d

bladder

spermatic cord

prostate gland

urogenital canal

testis

penis

epididymis

Male

embryos develop within eggs in the uterus; eggs are small and provide little nourishment

oviduct

uterus

ovary

vagina

bladder

urogenital canal

unborn offspring crawl from uterus to pouch where they are nourished by milk from the mother's mammary glands

Female

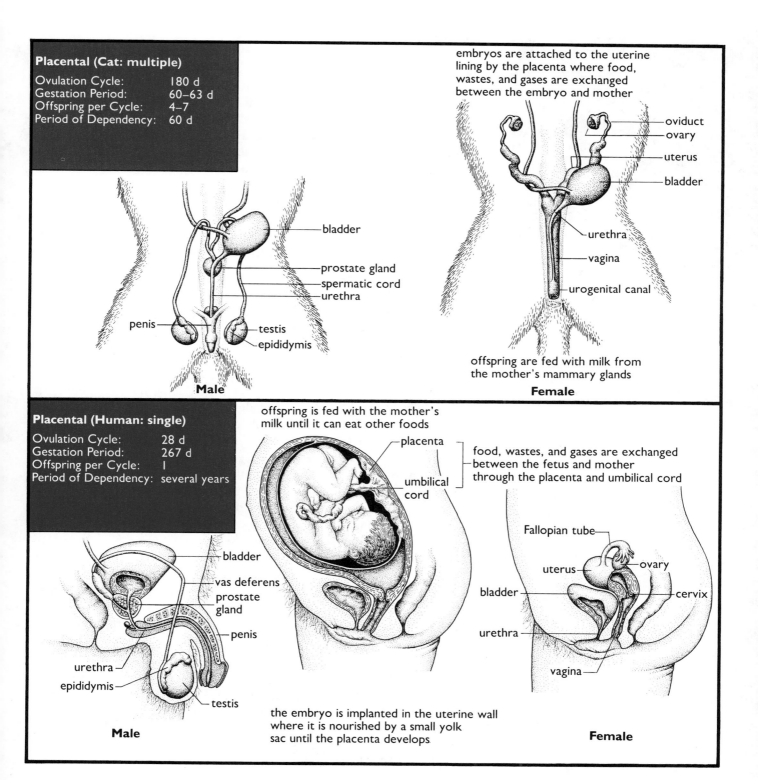

Placental (Cat: multiple)

Ovulation Cycle: 180 d
Gestation Period: 60–63 d
Offspring per Cycle: 4–7
Period of Dependency: 60 d

embryos are attached to the uterine lining by the placenta where food, wastes, and gases are exchanged between the embryo and mother

oviduct
ovary
uterus
bladder
urethra
vagina
urogenital canal

offspring are fed with milk from the mother's mammary glands

Female

bladder
prostate gland
spermatic cord
urethra
penis
testis
epididymis

Male

Placental (Human: single)

Ovulation Cycle: 28 d
Gestation Period: 267 d
Offspring per Cycle: 1
Period of Dependency: several years

offspring is fed with the mother's milk until it can eat other foods

placenta
umbilical cord

food, wastes, and gases are exchanged between the fetus and mother through the placenta and umbilical cord

bladder
vas deferens
prostate gland
penis
urethra
epididymis
testis

Male

Fallopian tube
uterus
ovary
bladder
cervix
urethra
vagina

Female

the embryo is implanted in the uterine wall where it is nourished by a small yolk sac until the placenta develops.

An adult beaver protecting her kittens

Parental Care

Mammals feed and care for their young until they can fend for themselves. In the very early stages after birth, the female provides all the necessary nutrients for her offspring from her own body. In mammals such as cats and cattle, males do not participate in rearing the young. However, no parental care is given after these animals stop feeding on their mothers' milk. In a few species such as wolves, both male and female parents participate in rearing the young and in training them to hunt for food.

The length of time until the offspring of mammals set out on their own or are forced out by their parents varies. Young mice are ready to leave their nests within several days. Beavers have a family group that includes parents, newborns, and year-olds. Two-year-old beavers are usually driven from the family den or leave on their own. Of all mammals, human infants have the longest childhood.

Applications of Reproductive Patterns

The reproductive system of a cow is adapted to provide a calf with milk for up to a year after its birth. As the young calf becomes better able to feed itself on grasses, it demands less milk, resulting in a drop off of milk production by the mother. Since the calf requires less milk, some milk remains in the udder, which is a signal for the female to stop production. Humans take advantage of this adaptation by milking a cow twice a day during the time it would normally be feeding its offspring. Provided the udder is emptied each time, the female will continue to produce large quantities of milk. About ten months after the birth, however, the milk dries up. Another pregnancy will have to be planned to stimulate renewed milk production.

Raising cattle for meat and dairy products is a major industry in Canada. Attempts are continually being made by scientists and agronomists to increase production. One way to do this is through selective breeding. Selective breeding allows only the heaviest beef cattle or the best milk producers to reproduce.

Until recently, three factors limited the extent to which farmers could improve their herds by selective breeding. One factor was cost. Mating the best cows in a herd with prize-winning bulls involved either buying a very expensive animal, or paying high stud fees and the cost of transporting the animals. This limitation has been largely overcome in recent years with the widespread use of **artificial insemination.** In this technique, semen is collected from male animals with desirable characteristics and frozen in liquid nitrogen. Frozen semen is inexpensive, and shipping costs are low, so most breeders can afford to improve their herds in this way. A single bull might sire thousands of offspring across the country in its lifetime. Artificial insemination is now used for breeding many kinds of domestic animals, even bees, although their semen cannot be frozen.

This calf is the outcome of artificial insemination, crossing a cow with a buffalo. It is a new hybrid called a beefalo that will yield more meat than a cow.

The second factor inhibiting herd improvement was the slow rate of reproduction. The long gestation period for cattle limits the number of offspring a single female can produce in her lifetime. No way has yet been found to shorten the gestation period, but this limitation has been overcome with embryo-implantation technology. First, a cow with desirable features is injected with hormones to stimulate the production of several eggs at once. (Cattle normally produce only one egg per cycle.) These eggs are collected and fertilized in a laboratory. Several embryos result, which are provided with nutrients and allowed to develop until they reach a suitable stage for freezing. Later, each frozen embryo is implanted in a different cow. This cow becomes a surrogate mother, nourishing the developing embryo and feeding the calf after birth. However, a surrogate does not pass on any of its own characteristics. Implantation allows one superior cow to parent many offspring each year instead of just one.

The third limiting factor farmers faced was the timing of their animals' natural reproductive cycle. In nature, most animals ovulate at a time that ensures springtime births, so the young can become fairly independent by the following winter. The success of both artificial insemination and implantation technology depends on the use of hormones to control reproductive cycles.

RESEARCH PROJECT
Controlling Animal Reproductive Cycles

Breeders who raise domestic animals sometimes want to control the ovulation cycles of their herds for a variety of reasons. They may want to ensure continuous delivery of an animal product that is consumed year-round such as milk. Or they may want to ensure delivery of a large number of animals for a particular date such as turkeys for Christmas.

Sheep farmers, for example, prefer synchronized ovulation cycles. If all females ovulate at the same time, a veterinarian can inseminate the entire herd

One of the most common causes of mental retardation in humans is entirely preventable. Impaired intellectual development is the most common symptom of Fetal Alcohol Syndrome or FAS. A syndrome is a group of symptoms found to occur simultaneously and to characterize a particular abnormality. The cause of a syndrome may be unknown. However, the cause of FAS has been identified as alcohol consumption by the pregnant mother.

The link between maternal drinking and the health of unborn children was dismissed for centuries. As recently as 1955, a report by the Rutgers Center of Alcohol Studies said ''the old notions about children of drunken parents being born defective can be cast aside.'' Indeed, when reports began to appear in the early 1970s that such links could be proven, they were greeted with skepticism.

FAS is diagnosed by the presence of three characteristics found in the child of a mother who was an alcoholic during her pregnancy. These characteristics are mental retardation, small birth length and

Fetal Alcohol Syndrome

weight, and facial deformities such as shortened eyelid openings. Less common congenital abnormalities include small head circumference, defective joints in hands and feet, heart defects, and cleft palates. Children who suffer from FAS cannot overcome these disabilities through treatment or education.

No safe level of alcohol consumption during pregnancy has been demonstrated. Indeed, some controversy still revolves around this issue. Although links between heavy drinking and the syndrome are firm, the risk involved in occasional drinking is not clear. Total abstinence is recommended by many doctors to minimize the risk.

How alcohol causes the abnormalities is also unclear. It has not yet been established with certainty whether it is alcohol or its metabolites that are responsible for fetal damage. However, the timing of heavy alcohol consumption has

been related to the type and extent of damage. Heavy drinking in the first trimester of pregnancy causes the congenital deformities described above, because this is when the body's organs are being formed. Brain damage in the fetus may be caused by consumption throughout the pregnancy.

Physicians face many difficulties in preventing Fetal Alcohol Syndrome. Unlike syndromes caused by chromosomal abnormalities, the likelihood of a baby being affected by FAS is difficult to predict. Although alcoholism in the mother is the major warning sign, alcoholic pregnant women often do not report or sometimes do not even recognize their alcoholism because of the social stigma attached to it. FAS is estimated to affect approximately 1 in every 500 babies. Fetal Alcohol Effects, an incomplete set of FAS symptoms, is about three times as prevalent. Education and counselling are the only ways likely to reduce the incidence of FAS. The tragedy of lifelong impairment in 1% of all children born every year demands action.

with frozen semen during one visit. As a result, a breeder can arrange a birth date that suits the local climate and minimizes the loss of lambs to late winter storms. With dairy cattle, however, staggered ovulation cycles are needed because breeding must take place every month of the year.

Your objective in this research project is to learn how the reproductive cycles of three domestic mammals are controlled. For each animal, gather information about the timing, sequence, and pattern of the natural reproductive cycle, and the reasons and methods for altering the natural cycle. Present your findings in a detailed chart, an illustrated poster, a short written report, or a brief talk as instructed by your teacher.

In addition to library books on animal breeding and animal husbandry, other information sources include federal and provincial ministries of agriculture, manufacturers of veterinary medicines, agricultural colleges, veterinarians, animal breeders, farmers, and the 4-H Club.

Section Review Questions

1. How do the structures of male and female mammalian reproductive systems differ from those of other vertebrate groups?
2. a) Define the terms ovulation and estrus.
   b) Describe ovulation in animals that experience estrus more than once during a mating season.
3. What role do hormones play in the ovulation cycle?
4. a) Compare the parental care mammals give their young with that of other vertebrates.
   b) Compare the parental care wolves give their young with that of cats.
5. Explain why farmers can continue to milk a cow after the calf has stopped feeding on the cow's milk.
6. Describe three technologies that have helped farmers improve the quality of their herds.

10.4 Human Reproductive Patterns

Although humans have all the structures needed for reproduction at birth, these structures remain nonfunctional until **puberty.** At puberty, sex hormones are released that cause the gonads to become functional. The same hormones stimulate the appearance of secondary sexual characteristics.

Male Reproductive Structures and Their Functions

In males, the sex hormone, **testosterone,** causes the appearance of secondary sexual characteristics. These include increased facial and body hair, deepening

Of all mammals, humans take the longest to reach sexual maturity. Females reach puberty several years before males. Females reach puberty, on average, between 10 and 14 years of age. In males, puberty usually occurs between 13 and 16 years of age.

FIGURE 10-20 The male reproductive system

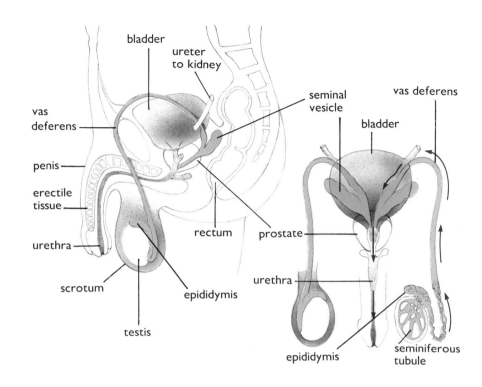

Sperm are most efficiently produced at a temperature slightly below internal body temperature. The scrotum ensures that the testes are held away from the body, resulting in a lower temperature.

Seminal fluid is added as the sperm pass through the vas deferens. The secretion from the seminal vesicle provides nutrients and protects the sperm from acidic conditions in the vagina. The prostate gland and Cowper's glands add fluids that also protect the sperm from acids encountered in a female's system and in a male's urethra.

Semen travels out of the penis through the same duct that carries urine from the bladder. However, contraction of the bladder sphincter prevents urine from leaking into the semen.

of the voice, and muscular development. Testosterone also stimulates sperm production in the testes, which are outside the body contained in a sac called the **scrotum.** (See Figure 10-20.)

Mature sperm are produced in the **seminiferous tubules** and stored in the **epididymis.** If fertilization is to take place, the sperm must be deposited in the female reproductive tract. Sexual excitation causes blood to flow into the spongy erectile tissues of the penis, causing it to become erect and fairly rigid. This enables the penis to enter the vagina with its opening as close as possible to the uterus. As sexual stimulation continues, a series of rhythmic contractions of the muscles surrounding the male's urethra causes the sperm to be ejected, along with the glandular secretions that make up the seminal fluid. The urethra carries the semen through the body of the penis to deposit it inside the vagina of the female. This method of transferring sperm is called **sexual intercourse.**

Female Reproductive Structures and Their Functions

The reproductive structures of female humans are similar to those of other mammals. (See Figure 10-21.) All structures are present from birth, but the reproductive system remains dormant until puberty when the ovaries start to

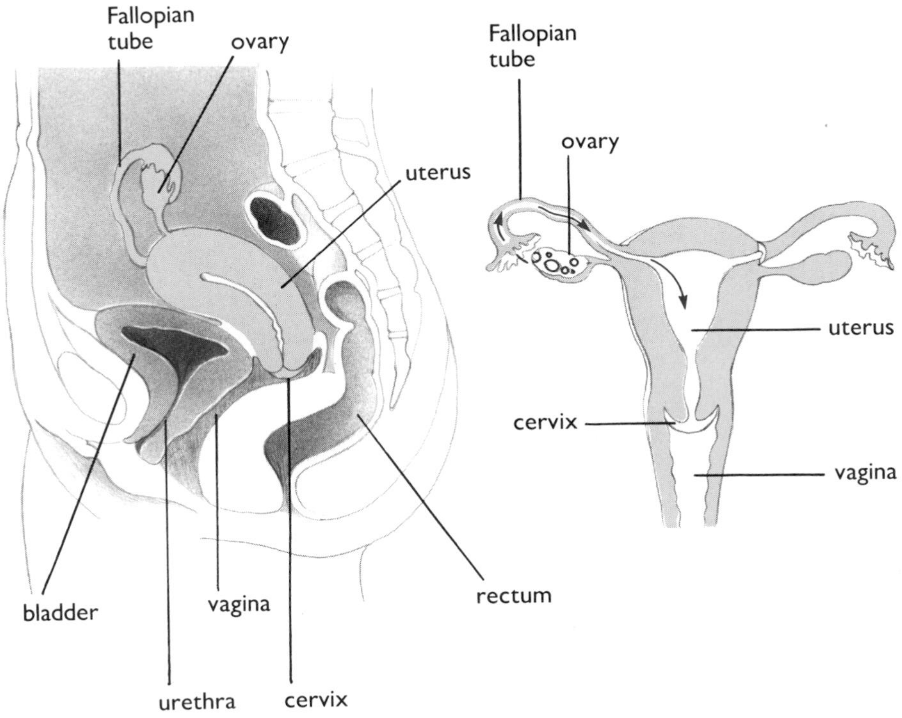

FIGURE 10-21 The female reproductive system

release **estrogen,** a female sex hormone. As it travels throughout the body, estrogen stimulates the development of secondary sexual characteristics. These characteristics include enlarged breasts, pubic and underarm hair, extra fat deposits under the skin, and wider hips that allow for childbirth. Other hormones produced at the same time interact with estrogen to stimulate important internal changes, including egg production. (See Figure 10-22.)

At birth, the ovaries already contain thousands of partially developed egg cells. Each egg is surrounded by a cell layer called a **follicle.** About once a month, the pituitary gland releases the **follicle-stimulating hormone (FSH),** which triggers further maturation of a single egg. This egg is released from the ovary when the follicle ruptures. Cilia lining the nearby mouth of the Fallopian tube create a current that carries the egg into and along the tube. Meanwhile, the **lutenizing hormone (LH)** produced by the pituitary gland acts on the remaining follicle cells. A yellowish body called the **corpus luteum** forms and starts to release the hormone **progesterone.**

Progesterone causes dramatic structural changes in the **endometrium,** which is the lining of the uterus. The endometrium thickens as new blood vessels form, small arteries coil up, epithelial cells multiply rapidly, and secretory glands enlarge and become more active. All of these changes prepare the uterus for a possible pregnancy. However, if the egg is not fertilized within

By the time a baby girl is born, the germinal cells in her ovary have already proceeded part way through meiosis. Mature eggs, however, will not begin to form until the ovary is stimulated by hormones at puberty.

FIGURE 10-22 Hormones produced by the pituitary gland, ovaries, and uterus interact during the menstrual cycle.

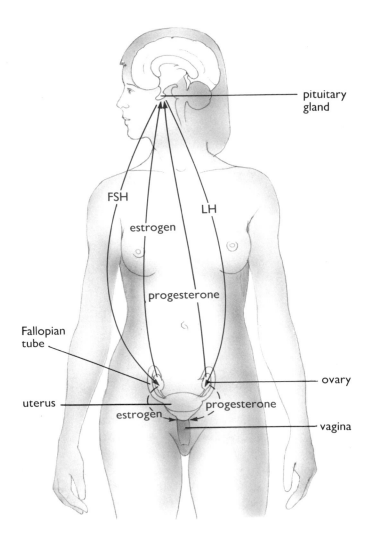

pituitary gland

FSH

LH

estrogen

progesterone

Fallopian tube

ovary

uterus

progesterone

estrogen

vagina

48 h of its release, it disintegrates. A few days later, the corpus luteum also disintegrates. The endometrium then breaks down and is shed through the vagina. The resulting flow of blood and tissue, called **menstruation,** is just one stage of an ovulation cycle that repeats itself about once a month.

The main functions of a mammal's ovulation cycle are egg maturation and the preparation of the uterus should a zygote be formed. Ovulation cycles in human females are controlled by hormones as they are in other mammals. However, the human ovulation cycle is not limited to a particular breeding season. It occurs more or less regularly throughout the year. The human ovulation cycle is often referred to as the **menstrual cycle** because the repetitive menstrual flow provides external evidence of internal changes.

INQUIRY ACTIVITY
Investigating the Menstrual Cycle

In this activity, you will use diagrams and graphs to investigate and describe the hormonal, uterine, and follicular changes that occur during the menstrual cycle of the human female. Study Figures 10-22 and 10-23 carefully, and observe how hormone levels affect the follicle, the endometrium, and each other. Answer the Discussion Questions based on your findings.

Discussion Questions

1. The average length of one menstrual cycle is 28 days. This period may be divided into three stages. Given the following description of each stage, determine its length in days. (Notice that Figure 10-23 shows one complete cycle and the first four days of the next.)

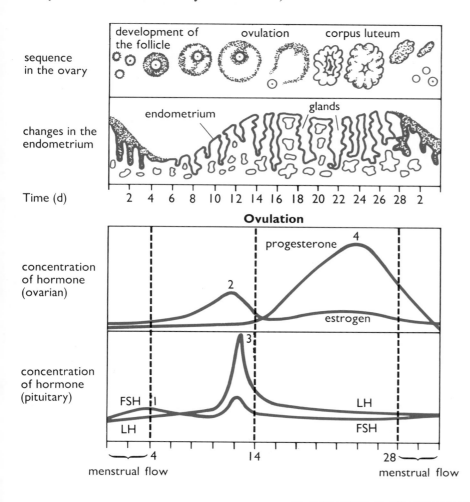

FIGURE 10-23 Changes in the ovaries, uterine lining, and hormone levels during the menstrual cycle

- *Follicle stage*: from the end of menstrual flow to ovulation. The egg matures, the follicle ruptures, and the egg is released.

- *Corpus luteum stage*: from ovulation to the beginning of menstrual flow. The remnants of the ruptured follicle secrete the hormone progesterone and the endometrium thickens.

- *Menstrual stage*: from the beginning of menstrual flow to its end. The endometrium disintegrates and leaves the body.

2. a) Identify the hormones produced by the pituitary gland and those produced by the ovary itself.
   b) Which ovarian and pituitary hormones tend to peak at about the same time?
   c) What major event in the cycle corresponds to this peak?

3. a) How many days after the first day of menstrual flow does ovulation occur?
   b) What hormonal change(s) occurs immediately after ovulation?

4. a) On what day of the cycle does progesterone production reach a peak?
   b) Where is progesterone produced?

5. What effect do high levels of progesterone seem to have on the endometrium and the pituitary hormones?

6. a) On what day of the cycle does estrogen production reach a peak?
   b) Where is estrogen produced?

7. a) What effect do high levels of estrogen seem to have on the pituitary hormones?
   b) What effect do falling levels of estrogen seem to have on the pituitary hormones?

8. Most contraceptive pills contain a mixture of estrogen and progesterone. These pills are taken for 21 consecutive days in fairly high concentrations. What effect would these pills have on a) pituitary hormone levels, b) follicle development, and c) the endometrium?

9. After 21 days, contraceptive pills are discontinued for seven days. What effect does discontinuing the pills have on a) pituitary hormone levels, b) follicle development, and c) the endometrium?

Fertilization and Implantation

Fertilization in humans takes place within the Fallopian tube. During sexual excitation, the vagina secretes fluids that facilitate the entry of the erect penis and enable the sperm to swim freely. Sperm deposited in the vagina swim through the cervical opening into the uterus and on to the Fallopian tubes. If there is an egg in one of the tubes, fertilization may result.

Although millions of sperm are released at one time, acidic conditions in the female reproductive system will kill most of them before they reach the egg. Fertilization will not occur unless numerous sperm do reach the egg, allowing the enzymes they secrete to soften the egg's membrane enough for one sperm to penetrate it. If this happens, the nuclei of the egg and the sperm will unite to form a zygote. Almost instantly, a membrane will form around the new zygote, preventing any other sperm cells from entering.

The newly formed zygote has enough yolk to allow it to survive until it reaches the uterus. Over the next few days, while remaining in the Fallopian tube, the zygote undergoes a series of mitotic divisions called **cleavage.** (See Figure 10-24.) The first result of these mitotic divisions is a **morula,** a solid ball of cells no bigger than the zygote itself.

The morula enters the uterus, where it grows and divides until it becomes a hollow, fluid-filled ball of cells called a **blastocyst.** A small mass of cells inside the blastocyst will form the embryo. The outer layer of the blastocyst secretes enzymes that eat into the lining of the uterus, allowing the embryo to become embedded in the lining. This process is called **implantation,** which marks the beginning of pregnancy.

Pregnancy and Embryonic Development

The blastocyst continues to grow and change until it becomes a **gastrula.** The embryonic cell mass inside the gastrula forms three cell layers: **endoderm, mesoderm,** and **ectoderm.** Each layer of cells will eventually result in the formation of the tissues and organs of the fetus. (See Figure 10-25 and Table 10-3.)

At the time of implantation, the stored egg yolk has almost been exhausted by the embryo. The embryo must now rely on the body systems of the mother

FIGURE 10-24 Through cleavage, the human zygote develops into a blastocyst ready for implantation.

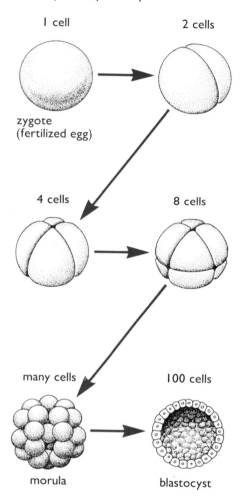

TABLE 10-3 Organ and Tissue Development

Endoderm	• pancreas • liver • lining of digestive system • lungs
Mesoderm	• skeleton • muscles • gonads • excretory system • inner layer of skin
Ectoderm	• brain • spinal cord • nerves • outer layer of skin • some parts of eye • nose • ears

FIGURE 10-25 The development of specialized tissues and organs from the three germinal layers of the embryo

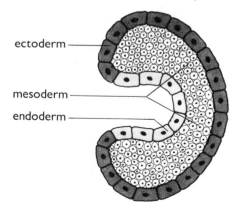

FIGURE 10-26 The placenta forms between the uterine wall and the embryo. Gas and nutrient exchanges take place at the placenta.

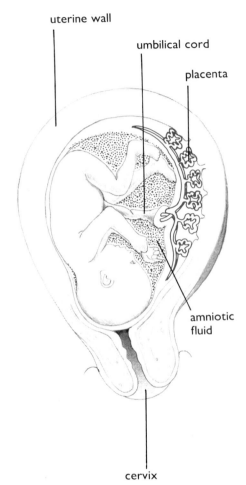

uterine wall

umbilical cord

placenta

amniotic fluid

cervix

DID YOU KNOW?
A Swedish study has found that babies born to mothers who smoke more than ten cigarettes a day while pregnant are twice as likely to become victims of Sudden Infant Death Syndrome (SIDS).

An embryo becomes a fetus when it develops features that are recognizably similar to those of an adult. In humans, this occurs at about eight weeks.

for nutrition, gas exchange, and waste excretion. A specialized organ called the **placenta** develops between the uterine lining and the finger-like extensions of the membrane surrounding the embryo. Blood vessels from the embryo reach the placenta through the **umbilical cord.** The circulatory systems of the mother and the embryo are brought close together at the placenta, although the blood of each system does not mix. Gases, nutrients, and wastes cross the placenta by diffusion. (See Figure 10-26.) The placenta also secretes hormones that are necessary to prevent menstruation during pregnancy.

Although the placenta is able to protect the embryo from some harmful substances in the mother's blood, alcohol, nicotine, and drugs can pass through the placenta and harm the embryo. The carbon monoxide in cigarette smoke that the mother may inhale actually becomes more concentrated in the embryo's tissues than in the tissues of the mother.

Human babies are born with their future reproductive roles already determined, although males and females are structurally identical in the very early stages of embryonic development. At around seven or eight weeks of development, the chromosomes of the male embryo guide the production of male hormones, causing the reproductive structures to develop into testes. Embryos without these hormones develop female reproductive structures such as ovaries. Many other adult features also become recognizable at about the same time. From this point on, the embryo is called a fetus, and continues to grow and develop as a male or as a female.

After birth the structures of the reproductive system develop more slowly than those of other body systems. For example, a baby's circulatory and excretory systems are fully functional at birth, but the maturation of its nervous system continues throughout childhood. However, the reproductive systems of males and females remain dormant until the hormones produced at puberty prepare them for reproduction.

Section Review Questions

1. a) What effects does the sex hormone testosterone have on males?
   b) What effects does the sex hormone estrogen have on females?

2. a) Describe the path sperm take from where they are produced to where they are released.
   b) Describe the path a released egg takes from where it is produced to the uterus if no fertilization occurs.

3. Where and how do fertilization and implantation occur?

4. Briefly describe a) the morula, b) the blastocyst, and c) the gastrula.

5. a) How does the placenta develop?
   b) What is its function?

6. a) Why do you think good health habits are important during pregnancy?
   b) State one example of a poor health habit and its effect on an embryo.

II ANIMALS

Meet
Susan Weiss

Susan works at The House, a health clinic for young adults that is sponsored by Planned Parenthood of Toronto. Over 4000 young people come to The House every year for counselling in birth control, nutrition, and other concerns.

Q. Is this clinic unique?

A. Yes, because here we deal with adolescent health needs — both physical and emotional. Our clients range in age from 13 to 25 years old.

Q. Do you counsel them about birth control?

A. I deal with psychological and emotional problems, and I talk with my clients about values and communication. We have trained volunteer counsellors who give information on contraception.

Q. What led you into this field?

A. I always knew that I enjoyed working with people in some sort of helping capacity. Social work is an open field — you can do many different things with a degree in social work.

Q. What is a typical day like?

A. Most of my day is spent one on one with a client. I try not to schedule more than four clients a day because the sessions can be quite intense. I don't see my clients as people who drop into my office once a week. I try to be aware of what their lives are like in other places, so I do liaison work with other agencies and with school staff. Our work in The House is a team effort. We consult each other about clients. There are also reports to be written.

Q. What is a typical client like?

A. Most are young women 18 or 19 years old. Men are less practised at talking about emotional and sexual issues. However, that's not always the case. One of my clients is a 16-year-old boy who is involved with a young girl in a serious sexual relationship. I am encouraging them to come together for a session with a birth-control counsellor.

Q. But they haven't done this yet?

A. No. It's hard for adolescents to look at long-range consequences. Even though they may have all the accurate birth control information, getting them to use a

contraceptive method is the challenge. There's still an ingrained belief that women are responsible for birth control.

Q. Do you see any changes in sexual responsibility?

A. Maybe because of AIDS, issues related to sexuality and sexual responsibility are more openly discussed. But most kids still don't think AIDS will affect them.

Q. What's the most challenging part of your job?

A. Nearly everyone who comes to me is in the midst of what they consider a crisis. I try to give kids the sense that they are able to influence what happens to them. This can be hard, because often they're too young to live on their own, drive, or vote. I also help them to see themselves as part of a larger whole — the family and the community.

Q. What qualities are required for a job like yours?

A. Any job where you deal with other people demands tolerance. You have to be comfortable with yourself, so that your own biases don't get in the way of professional goals.

Q. Is there a need for more clinics like this one?

A. There should be many more that deal with family planning within the context of the whole person. In the United States, school health-care clinics have been successful. Maybe school clinics should be adopted in Canada, as well.

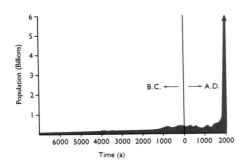

FIGURE 10-27 The dramatic increase in world population in the last century is partly due to the high fertility of humans. Sexually active females have an 80% chance of becoming pregnant if no method of contraception is used.

DID YOU KNOW?
Fertility awareness methods are also valuable to those who wish to conceive a child. Having intercourse during the woman's most fertile period greatly increases the chance that a pregnancy will result.

The contraceptive sponge is now available in Canada. Whether inserted 24 h in advance, or only minutes before intercourse, it works three ways to prevent conception: by blocking the cervix, by absorbing sperm, and by killing them with a self-contained spermicide that also protects against some sexually transmitted diseases. The sponge can be obtained without a prescription, but users should seek professional advice on correct insertion. For effective contraception, the sponge must be left in place for 6 h after intercourse.

10.5 Reproductive Medicine and Technology

Despite the convoluted path sperm must follow to fertilize an egg, and the complex sequence of events that must precede the birth of a healthy baby, humans are amazingly fertile. (See Figure 10-27.) In the past, the earth's human population was controlled by a high death rate, especially among children. Today, improved nutrition, sanitation, and medical treatment for infectious diseases ensure that most babies born in rich countries such as Canada survive childhood. Even in poor countries, a much larger percentage of children now survive to adulthood. In some regions, these changes have contributed to a serious overpopulation problem.

Controlling Fertility

Controlling fertility is an important issue in many poor countries, which fear becoming unable to feed a growing population. It is also important in many richer countries, especially among individuals who want to limit the size of their families. Often, however, controlling fertility presents emotional or ethical problems. In some cultures, children are seen as a form of wealth, ensuring that elderly parents will be cared for.

In other cases, moral or religious objections preclude the use of most artificial methods for preventing pregnancy. However, many people who have such objections do find it acceptable to control fertility by abstaining from intercourse during the most fertile days of each menstrual cycle. This method involves recognizing the day when ovulation occurs. Fertility awareness is possible because the hormonal changes of the menstrual cycle result in two observable clues that signal the onset of the fertile period.

First, the woman's body temperature peaks sharply at ovulation and remains higher than average for the rest of the cycle. Second, the mucus that is always present inside the vagina changes in quantity, colour, and texture as ovulation approaches. Keeping track of these natural body signals for several cycles enables many women to predict ovulation accurately. However, intercourse must be avoided for several days because the sperm can survive in the mucus for up to 3–5 days.

Successful use of this *body awareness* method of fertility management requires instruction from a specialized counsellor or physician. It also requires commitment from both partners using the method. Among consistent, reliable users, the risk of pregnancy can be reduced to 8% or less. Among poorly trained or uncommitted users, the risk of pregnancy can increase to 40%.

TABLE 10-4 Comparing Contraceptive Methods

Contraceptive Method	Used by Male or Female	How Conception is Prevented	Possible Side Effects	Number of Pregnancies per 100 Women per a	Reasons for Failure
None	• both	• chance		• 80 or more	
Douching	• female	• sperm are washed out of vagina after intercourse	• irritation	• 50 or more	• sperm already past cervix • may force sperm into uterus or fail to reach sperm • sperm present in folds of vagina hard to wash out
Rhythm	• both	• refraining from intercourse during part of cycle when egg is travelling to uterus	• none	• 30–35	• dates are never exact • variation in cycle • variation in length of time sperm and ovum stay alive
Withdrawal	• male	• ejaculation occurs outside vagina	• none	• 25–30	• leakage of small amounts of semen at early stages of intercourse • withdrawing penis too late
Spermicides, Jellies, Creams, and Foams	• female	• kills sperm and/or blocks entry to uterus for about 1 h	• irritation	• 20–25	• may not completely block the cervix • loses effectiveness if left too long • some require waiting period • douching before 8 h have passed
Diaphragm with Contraceptive Cream	• female	• blocks entry to uterus for several hours • kills sperm that do get by	• irritation	• 15–20	• not correctly placed • spermicide not used • not left in place for 8 h after intercourse
Condom (alone)	• male	• prevents sperm from entering vagina	• none	• 15–17	• not put on penis before contact with the vagina • insufficient care in removal
Condom (with spermicide)	• male	• kills sperm that do enter	• none	• 3–5	• as above

TABLE 10-4—*Continued*

Contraceptive Method	Used by Male or Female	How Conception is Prevented	Possible Side Effects	Number of Pregnancies per 100 Women per a	Reasons for Failure
I.U.D (coil, loop)	• female	• prevents implantation	• cramps • irregular bleeding	• 2–8	• some women do not retain the device
Birth-Control pill	• female	• inhibits ovulation	• nausea • weight gain • irregular bleeding	• up to 5	• forgetting to take pill • not following instructions • hormone content not high enough to suppress ovulation

Contraceptive Methods

Contraception is the prevention of fertilization or implantation so pregnancy will not occur. Table 10-4 on pages 357–358 summarizes a variety of contraceptive methods that interrupt the sequence of events leading to pregnancy in one or more of the following ways.

1. Blocking the path of the gametes to prevent them from meeting.
2. Preventing implantation of the zygote in the uterine wall.
3. Blocking the production of gametes by the gonads.
4. Upsetting the timing of egg and sperm release.

Some individuals may choose sterilization as a permanent method of contraception. In both males and females, sterilization can be accomplished by cutting and tying specific tubes in the reproductive system. (See Figure 10-28.) In males, the operation is called a **vasectomy,** and in females it is referred to as a **tubal ligation.** Gametes can no longer travel uninterrupted through the male or female reproductive system after a vasectomy or a tubal ligation. As a result, gametes cannot unite, and fertilization does not occur. However, sexual function remains unimpaired in both sexes. Most physicians suggest counselling prior to deciding on sterilization because the operations usually cannot be reversed.

Several other contraceptive methods exist for people who want to remain fertile but avoid pregnancy. All of these methods have advantages and disadvantages. Choosing the best contraceptive method is sometimes a matter of balancing the risk of pregnancy against other risks to an individual's health.

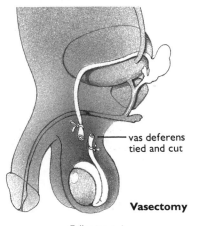

vas deferens tied and cut

Vasectomy

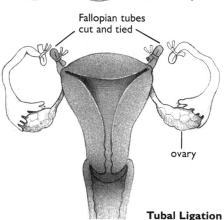

Fallopian tubes cut and tied

ovary

Tubal Ligation

FIGURE 10-28 Vasectomies in males and tubal ligations in females are permanent methods of contraception.

Probably the most widely used contraceptive methods are the birth-control pill and the condom. Birth-control pills contain a combination of hormones, which, taken over a 21-day period, prevent ovulation from taking place. Menstruation occurs sometime during the next seven days of the sequence. The use of birth-control pills requires a doctor's prescription, and not all women are able to take them.

The condom is a sheath placed over the penis prior to intercourse. It functions as a barrier to sperm, preventing them from entering the vagina and reaching the egg. A condom must be placed correctly on the penis so the semen collects in the reservoir at the condom's tip. Neither the birth-control pill nor the condom is completely effective, and it is best to seek medical advice before using any contraceptive method.

Disorders of the Human Reproductive System

All of the human reproductive disorders summarized in Table 10-5 on page 360 are serious. Many of these disorders affect young people, but they go undetected because the symptoms are nonexistent or difficult to recognize. Serious consequences may result if affected persons do not consult a physician.

The testes of males usually descend into the scrotum at some point during fetal development. Undescended testicles may result in sterility because the high internal temperature of the abdominal cavity reduces the production of active sperm. There is also a danger of malignant tumors developing in the testes, and they may have to be removed surgically.

Some males may experience difficulty or pain when passing urine. In some cases, the problem is caused by the presence of a venereal disease such as gonorrhea. A medical examination can determine the cause of the problem and the treatment that should be followed.

In females, abnormal menstrual cycles or irregular periods may indicate hormone imbalances caused by malfunctioning ovaries, problems with the pituitary gland, bacterial infections, or psychological problems. Complications may become more serious if medical help is not sought.

Cervical cancer in females affects the cervix, which is the opening to the uterus. Some scientists think that cervical cancer is caused by a virus, although other factors may also be responsible in some cases. The presence of abnormal cells can be detected by a Pap test, which is a microscopic examination of cells scraped from the surface of the cervix. If Pap tests are performed on a regular basis, cervical cancer can usually be detected early enough for effective treatment.

Pelvic inflammatory disease is caused by a bacterial infection that swells and clogs the Fallopian tubes. It is most common among sexually active women in their late teens and early twenties. Acute flare-ups may cause severe abdominal pain. Often, the symptoms are mild and may even subside for long periods, but the infection continues to spread. If left untreated, permanent infertility due to blocked Fallopian tubes may result.

TABLE 10-5 Summary of Human Reproductive System Disorders

Disorder	Symptoms	Causes	Effects	Treatment
Prostate Disorders (male)	• difficult urination • abdominal tenderness	• bacterial infection • aging • complications of gonorrhea	• cancerous tumors • obstructed urethra • thickening of bladder walls	• antibiotics • partial or whole removal of gland
Infertility (male)	• inability to fertilize egg	• low sperm count • abnormal sperm • exposure to radiation, heat, malnutrition, mumps, STD	• sterility	
Infertility (female)	• inability to produce egg	• failure to ovulate • uterine abnormalities • Fallopian tubes too narrow • hormonal defect • tubal disorder (STD) • hostile cervical environment	• sterility	• hormonal therapy in some cases
Impotence (male)	• inability to produce and maintain erection	• diseases such as alcoholism or diabetes • spinal injury • psychological/ emotional causes	• inability to copulate	• dialogue with family physician • psychotherapy
Abnormal Menstruation (female)	• absence of menstruation • painful menstruation	• infections of reproductive system • malfunctioning ovaries or pituitary gland • emotional or psychological problems	• difficulty in becoming pregnant • infections may spread	• hormone therapy • allieviate emotional/ psychological pressures
Tumors (female)	• none in early stages • may be detected by Pap test	• develop spontaneously • individuals may be genetically predisposed	• cancer may spread • malfunctioning reproductive system	• surgery, drugs, or radiation to remove tumor
Undescended Testicles	• testicles not contained in scrotum • poor sperm production	• unknown	• sterility • malignant tumors	• surgery to remove testicle
Ectopic Pregnancy	• abdominal pain • bleeding from uterus • blackouts	• implantation of embryo in Fallopian tube usually resulting from previous tubal infection	• shock • severe abdominal pain • death unless embryo removed	• diagnostic operation (laparotomy) necessary • surgery to remove tube containing embryo

Infertility differs from impotence. Impotence is an inability to perform sexual intercourse and affects only males. Infertility is an inability to reproduce and can affect either males or females. Fertility depends on the proper functioning of both the male and female reproductive systems. Today, many young people are becoming infertile before they begin to think about parenthood due to the effects of sexually transmitted diseases.

Sexually Transmitted Diseases

Sexually transmitted diseases, or STD's, are passed on by sexual contact with infected persons. Some STD's cause serious long-term consequences such as infertility or eventual death if left untreated. Often, however, the symptoms are nonexistent or difficult to detect, so treatment is not sought. Meanwhile, the infected person may be passing the disease on to others. It is even possible for an infected person to have more than one disease at a time. Each sexually transmitted disease is caused by a different organism, which is usually a bacteria or a virus.

Herpes genitalis is a viral disease transmitted by sexual contact. The virus is similar to the one that causes cold sores. An infected person develops a group of small, intensely painful blisters on the genitals. The female cervix can also be affected by the disease. The sores will eventually disappear, but they may reoccur from time to time. There is no cure for herpes, and no completely effective treatment has yet been found.

Gonorrhea is a bacterial disease that affects the inner mucous membranes of the reproductive tract. It often causes painful urination and a yellowish discharge, but some people experience no symptoms at all. These carriers may spread the disease for a long time before they are diagnosed. Untreated cases may develop more serious symptoms such as arthritis and infertility. Gonorrhea can be cured with antibiotics such as penicillin, but only a physician can decide when a patient is cured.

Until recently, syphilis was regarded as the most serious of the sexually transmitted diseases because of the long symptom-free periods experienced by infected individuals. Syphilis is caused by a bacterial infection, and once contracted, it progresses through three stages. Within the first few weeks, hard sores develop on the genitals, fingers, or lips at the point where the bacteria entered the body. These sores clear up without treatment, but several weeks or months later, the second stage of the disease begins. During the second stage, infected persons experience sore throats, headaches, ulcers, and rashes among other symptoms. Again, these symptoms will disappear without treatment. The third stage of the disease can occur several months or years later. During this stage, more serious symptoms affecting the heart, brain, liver, skin, and blood vessels appear. Neurological damage, blindness, and paralysis can also result. If treated with antibiotics in the earliest stage, syphilis can be cured.

Sexually transmitted diseases can be passed on even without sexual intercourse. Any contact of a sexual nature may transfer the organism that can cause a sexually transmitted disease to another host.

The condom offers some protection against sexually transmitted diseases, but no more than it does against pregnancy.

Syphilis and gonorrhea are also called venereal disease or VD.

A baby can contract gonorrhea while passing through the birth canal of an infected mother. Gonorrhea can cause blindness in the infant if it is not treated. Syphilis and AIDS can also be passed on by an infected mother to her unborn offspring.

TABLE 10-6   Summary of Other Sexually Transmitted Diseases

Disease	Symptoms	Effects	Treatment
Chlamydia	• possible urethral discharge in males • possible vaginal discharge in females; abdominal pain in advanced cases • 20% of infected persons are symptom-free, but suffer the same internal effects and can infect others	• inflammation of reproductive tubes leading to scarring, blockage, and sterility • may spread to eyes, bladder, or other body parts	• antibiotics (doxcycline, tetracycline) • sexual partners must also be treated • condoms prevent spread of infection • permanent damage can be prevented through early detection by regular checkups
Chancroid	• small, red sores on genitals in two days to two weeks • skin breaks down and drains pus, leads to slow healing, painful ulcers • lymph glands in groin may swell • abscesses leave ulcers and scars on genitals and groin • usually affects males	• can be confused with primary stages of syphilis • must be diagnosed early for proper treatment • urethral stricture and tissue destruction	• drugs (sulfonamides) effective if begun early
Nonspecific Urethritis	• similar to gonorrhea but milder • painful urination • discharge from penis or vagina • males usually have more symptoms than females	• may be confused with gonorrhea but requires different treatment • infection may spread to uterus in females before pain is felt	• antibiotics are used, but they differ from those used to treat gonorrhea • tetracycline can be used if uncomplicated by other diseases
Vaginitis (*Trichomonas vaginalis*)	• discharge from vagina • burning and itching of external genitals • usually affects women, though men can be carriers of organism responsible	• infection can be passed back and forth between partners if not treated • infection sometimes occurs with gonorrhea	• metronidazole is most effective • both sexual partners should be treated

Table 10-6 summarizes several other sexually transmitted diseases. Anyone who suspects they have contracted a sexually transmitted disease should obtain medical treatment as soon as possible. Since many diseases have stages that are asymptomatic, it is also important to have regular follow-up appointments. Remember that only a doctor can determine whether or not an infected person has been cured.

AIDS

AIDS stands for Acquired Immune Deficiency Syndrome. AIDS is caused by the human immunodeficiency virus (HIV), which attacks the immune system and prevents the body from mounting its normal defence against all other disease-causing organisms, as well as the AIDS virus itself. Infected persons

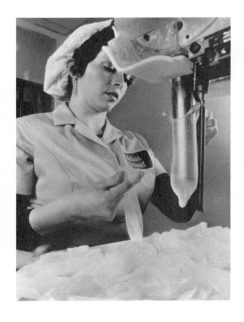

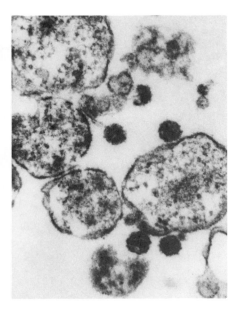

For sexually active individuals, latex condoms such as the one being tested here offer the best defence against the AIDS virus. Abstinence from both sexual activity and intravenous drug use offers the only completely effective defence against the virus.

The AIDS virus

may have symptoms ranging from fever, chills, weight loss, and colds. They may also be susceptible to a variety of rare cancers.

AIDS is mainly a sexually transmitted disease, although it can also be passed on by blood transfusions if the blood had been originally obtained from an infected person. (In Canada, however, all blood for transfusions is screened for the presence of the AIDS virus.) The sharing of needles among infected drug users is another way AIDS can be transmitted. Most experts believe that AIDS will become an increasingly serious public health problem in the next two decades. (See Chapter 18 for a more in-depth study of AIDS.)

Treating Infertility

Infertility is a problem for about 10% of couples who want to have children. In males, infertility may be caused by a shortage of sperm in the semen, the production of defective sperm, or an obstruction along the ducts. These problems may be caused by mumps, malnutrition, or sexually transmitted diseases. Female infertility may be caused by blocked Fallopian tubes, a disease of the uterus, or by a malfunctioning ovulation cycle.

Some infertile males can be helped by surgical expansion of the tubes associated with sperm release. But similar surgery does not help females with blocked Fallopian tubes. *In vitro* fertilization may allow some women to become pregnant. (See Figure 10-29.) If failure to ovulate is the problem, hormone therapy may stimulate the production and the release of eggs. If a low sperm count in the male is the problem, artificial insemination, the introduction of sperm from a donor into the uterus by a doctor, may enable the female partner to become pregnant.

FIGURE 10-29 *In vitro* fertilization in humans

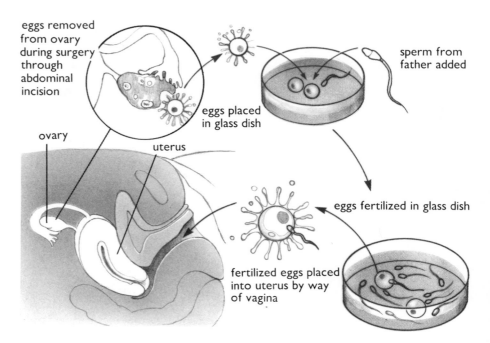

eggs removed from ovary during surgery through abdominal incision

ovary

uterus

eggs placed in glass dish

sperm from father added

eggs fertilized in glass dish

fertilized eggs placed into uterus by way of vagina

This party was held in 1988 to celebrate the tenth anniversary of *in vitro* fertilization, first introduced in 1978. The guests of honour included 168 "test-tube" babies and their parents.

Advancing medical technology has created many other techniques to promote or control fertility. However, some reproductive technologies have proven to be very controversial. The use of surrogate mothers, the existence of sperm banks, and the production of frozen embryos for implantation are three examples of controversial reproductive technologies.

Cervical Cancer

Canadian women stand a 1% chance of contracting cervical cancer in their lifetime, possibly from a common, sexually transmitted virus. That's the bad news. The good news is that the death rate from cervical cancer has declined 80% since 1955.

Canada has one of the world's best programs for screening and treating cancers. The Cytology Screening Laboratory at the Cancer Control Agency in Vancouver, British Columbia, is now the largest laboratory of its kind in Canada. It was developed in the 1950s by pathologist Dr. Herb Fidler and gynecologist Dr. David Boyes. Dr. Boyes recently received the Order of Canada for his contribution to cancer screening and surgery.

Cancer of the cervix — the neck of the uterus which opens into the vagina — is one of the most curable of cancers, if it is caught early. In their pre-cancerous stage, cells on the surface of the cervix become dysplastic, exhibiting larger nuclei and less cytoplasm than normal cells. This stage can be observed in a simple procedure called a Pap test.

A Pap test is quick and painless. A sample of cells is scraped from the surface of the cervix and smeared on a microscope slide. Patient information is forwarded with the slide to the screening laboratory. Medical technologists search the 50 000 — 300 000 cells on the slide for abnormalities.

Any suspect slides are sent to a pathologist, who classifies the slide into one of five types from normal to cancerous. Abnormal cells may develop into a localized cancer. About two-thirds of these pre-invasive cancers are treated with cryotherapy or laser therapy.

Doctors recommend that all women who are or have been sexually active should have a Pap test and a pelvic exam once a year. Studies show that women who become sexually active when they are teenagers or who have multiple sex partners are at higher risk for cervical cancer. In the last 25 years, the number of pre-cancerous cervical abnormalities in Canadian women aged 16 to 20 has increased dramatically.

Three factors in addition to sexual activity have been identified as contributing to cervical cancer: the hormone diethylsilbestrol (women whose mothers took

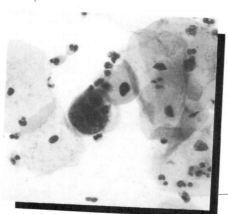

DES, a morning-sickness drug, during pregnancy are at higher risk); active or passive smoking; and the sexually transmitted human papilloma virus, HPV.

Researchers estimate that HPV infection in the general population is far more common than infection with the viruses that cause genital herpes or AIDS. More than 50 different types of the HPV virus have been identified to date. Fifteen are commonly found in genital infections, and seven of these have been linked to cervical cancer.

HPV is known as the "wart virus" because it can cause tiny growths anywhere on the body. The warts may or may not be visible in men or in women, but they do show up in an abnormal Pap test. With two types of the virus, abnormal cells and cancers can develop from the warts. Removing the warts is difficult and does not necessarily eliminate the virus.

The best treatment for cervical cancer is prevention. Women should avoid smoking. If they are sexually active, they should use a condom or a diaphragm. (Other contraceptive devices will not provide protection against HPV.) Women should also know their partners and limit the number they have.

An annual Pap test for women is important. If a woman is tested every year, any problems she develops will be caught early and treated quickly.

The Implications of Reproductive Technology

Newspapers often report legal, moral, and ethical debates about the repro-ductive technologies mentioned above. For example, who are the "real" parents of a baby conceived by *in vitro* fertilization using donor sperm and a donor egg, implanted in the uterus of a surrogate mother, and finally adopted by a different couple?

Research one contemporary issue related to reproductive technology. Explore the societal implications of the technology you have chosen. (Make sure the material you use is current.) What are the values and opinions expressed by the people who are involved in the issue? Consider your own values and opinions concerning the technology. Write a report presenting your own feelings and the viewpoints of other groups or individuals.

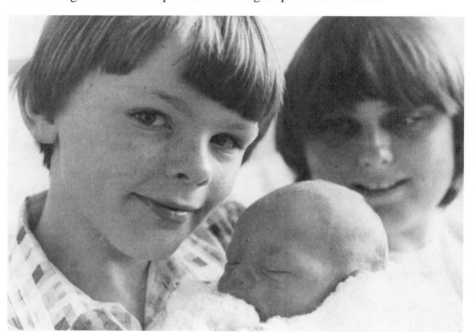

Ten-year-old Adrian Short holds his newborn brother, Martin, who was conceived by *in vitro* fertilization.

Section Review Questions

1. a) List three factors that have contributed to overpopulation problems in some countries.
   b) State two reasons why some people might want to control fertility.

2. All contraceptive methods are intended to prevent fertilization or implantation. List four ways contraceptive methods work and provide one example of each.

3. Identify and describe a permanent contraceptive method for both males and females.

4. What is the difference between impotence and infertility?

5. a) What are sexually transmitted diseases?
   b) State two reasons why these diseases are so dangerous.
   c) Describe the three stages in the progression of syphilis.

Chapter Review

Key Words

asexual reproduction	implantation
contraception	menstrual cycle
copulation	menstruation
embryo	ovulation
estrogen	puberty
estrus	sexual reproduction
fertilization	sexually transmitted
fetus	diseases
gamete	testosterone
gestation	zygote
gonads	

Recall Questions

Multiple Choice

1. Which of the following terms is not related to sexual reproduction?
   a) fertilization   c) copulation
   b) fragmentation   d) zygote formation

2. The eggs of which animal groups contain albumen as a food source?
   a) fish   c) birds
   b) amphibians   d) reptiles

3. In which structure of the female mammalian reproductive system does the zygote usually develop?
   a) uterus   c) cervix
   b) vagina   d) Fallopian tube

4. Which hormone is responsible for producing secondary sexual characteristics in female humans?
   a) progesterone   c) LH
   b) FSH   d) estrogen

5. Which of the following sexually transmitted diseases are caused by a viral infection?
   a) gonorrhea   c) syphilis
   b) herpes genitalis   d) all of the above

Fill in the Blanks

1. _____ refers to the two sexes of a species being noticeably different in appearance.

2. The process by which a male deposits sperm inside the female reproductive tract is called _____ .

3. The hormonal peak of the reproductive cycle of animals is called _____.

4. Blood vessels from an embryo reach the placenta through the _____.

5. The inability of humans to reproduce is called _____ , which affects both males and females.

Short Answers

1. What is the main advantage of sexual reproduction over asexual reproduction?

2. How does the seasonal mating of animals maximize fertilization and the survival of offspring?

3. Briefly describe the structures of typical male and female reproductive systems in mammals.

4. Compare the changes brought on by the onset of puberty in male and female humans.

5. What is the relationship between hormone levels and estrus?

6. Describe each of the following according to its structure and its role in human reproduction: a) morula, b) blastocyst, and c) gastrula.

7. a) Compare impotence and infertility.
   b) How can infertility be treated in males and in females?

Application Questions

1. How would studying the reproductive processes in mammals other than humans help you understand human reproduction?

2. In most animals, the reproductive system is the last system to mature after birth. What is the advantage, if any, of this developmental pattern?

3. a) The young of mammals such as horses are able to walk and run within hours after birth, although they are still dependent on their mothers' milk for a period of time. Based on what you have learned in this textbook and what you already know, identify three other mammals whose young are able to do this.

b) Explain how you would expect their gestation period to compare with that of an opossum.

4. How does sexual reproduction help a species survive environmental change?

5. Do male or do female organisms produce more gametes? Explain.

Problem Solving

1. a) Why would separation of the cell mass into two or more parts in the blastocyst stage be less damaging than in the gastrula stage?
   b) What would be the most likely outcome in each case?

Extensions

1. Obtain some frog eggs from a local pond and place them in an aquarium filled with pond water and plants. Observe the stages in the development of the fertilized eggs. Report your observations to your class using a series of drawings or photographs. (Use a series of prepared slides if live specimens are not available.)

2. Research one of the following topics and submit a report to your teacher or make a presentation to the class.
   a) The first 16 weeks of development following the fertilization of a human egg.
   b) The effect of chemicals such as alcohol or nicotine on the development of the fetus.

3. Research a sexually transmitted disease in more detail to determine the present status of the disease in Canada.

4. Research the advances being made in one of the following methods of reproductive technology.
   a) *in vitro* fertilization
   b) artificial insemination by partner or donor
   c) surrogate motherhood
   d) sperm banks
   e) use of fertility drugs

Plants and Fungi

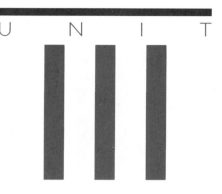

CHAPTER

11

Diversity in Two Kingdoms

The kingdom Plantae includes the largest organisms that have ever lived. Trees such as the sequoia far surpass animals such as the blue whale in mass and volume. In addition, the number of plants on Earth is so large that they are the first living things to be seen as Earth is approached from space. Plants supply half of Earth's oxygen, and almost all of the food used by humans and other land animals.

But many plant populations are now seriously threatened by human activities. Whole forests are being levelled to provide fuel, farmland, construction materials, or living space. The resulting environmental damage endangers all life on this planet.

The negative impact of deforestation in Africa, Asia, and the Americas has been greatly publicized in recent years. As a result, many people now recognize the value of maintaining large tracts of trees. But the fungi living on the forest floor are seldom considered as important. As a result, few people realize that Canada's rain forest is being threatened by the overharvesting of wild fungi as much as it is by the overharvesting of trees.

No forest can remain healthy for long without fungi. They play a vital vole in the forest ecosystem by decomposing fallen leaves and other litter, thereby recycling nutrients needed by trees. The poisonous *Amanita*, whose fruiting body is shown here, is seldom disturbed. But each autumn, hundreds of tonnes of wild mushrooms are gathered and sold to foreign markets. The pine mushroom is an especially popular gourmet food. This species is most numerous in the old-growth rain forests of coastal British Columbia.

Once the autumn rains begin, the edible fruiting bodies of the pine mushroom emerge by the thousands from a complex underground system of mycelium threads. The underground mycelium lives year-round, its threads intertwined with the roots of trees. Tree roots provide the fungi with sugars, and the mycelium threads pass water and minerals to the trees. The mycelium under a populous patch of pine mushrooms may be hundreds of years old. When mushroom pickers use rakes to search for mushrooms, they damage the mycelium, upsetting the entire forest ecosystem.

The market for wild mushrooms has grown so quickly that some scientists are calling for a ban on exports in order to have time to assess the environmental impact of harvesting. The only short-term solution appears to be a program of public education. A society that understands the vital role the kingdom Fungi plays in maintaining plant life may be less willing to tolerate activities that can cause permanent harm to both fungi and plants.

Chapter Objectives

When you complete this chapter, you should:

1. Be able to explain the historical context for using the term division instead of phylum when classifying fungi and plants.

2. Be able to explain how taxonomists justify grouping fungi and plants into two separate kingdoms.

3. Be able to list the characteristics that define the kingdom Fungi, state the basis on which this kingdom is sorted into divisions, and name the divisions.

4. Be able to list the characteristics that define the kingdom Plantae, and identify the five divisions into which plants can be classified.

5. Be able to name the three divisions of multicellular algae and describe the distinguishing characteristics of each.

6. Be able to list the characteristics that define the division Bryophyta, understand why bryophytes are said to be nonvascular, and describe the reproductive cycle of a typical bryophyte such as moss.

7. Be able to list the characteristics that define the division Tracheophyta, understand why tracheophytes are said to be vascular, name the four tracheophyte subdivisions, and describe the identifying characteristics of each.

8. Be able to identify the subdivision Pteropsida as the most successful and important group of plants, name its three classes, and describe the characteristics of each.

9. Know how to use a dichotomous key to identify tree-sized vascular plants.

FIGURE 11-1 The sequence of classification levels for plants and fungi

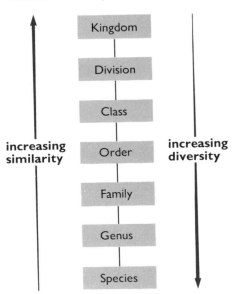

increasing similarity → Kingdom → Division → Class → Order → Family → Genus → Species ← increasing diversity

In this textbook, plants and fungi have been classified into divisions, but be aware that you may encounter some reference books that classify all kingdoms into phyla. You should realize that the names of individual species are unaffected by such variations in classification systems.

11.1 Classifying Fungi and Plants

Originally, the study of plants and fungi was considered to be quite separate from the study of animals. And traditionally, most zoologists have used the term *phylum* to describe the major groups of the animal kingdom. Botanists, however, use the term *division* for major groups of plants and fungi. A **division** is a group of similar classes and therefore represents the same degree of similarity as a phylum. (See Figure 11-1.)

Seaweed is a general term that describes many different species of multicellular algae.

This crop of mushrooms is being grown in the dark on a bed of sterilized manure. How does this kind of farming differ from the way green crops are grown?

Problems of Plant Classification

Biologists hold a variety of opinions about plant classification. There are three main areas of contention: how to classify algae, how to classify fungi, and the appropriate number of plant divisions. The term *algae* is left over from an era when cell chemistry was not well understood. Aquatic species such as seaweeds are still called algae, but modern taxonomists no longer regard them as a distinct, kingdom-like group. The algae divisions have therefore been reassigned—one to Monera, three to Protista, and three to Plantae.

Early biologists classified fungi as plants because they are nonmotile and have cell walls, and because many species grow out of the ground. Today, however, most taxonomists feel that fungi differ too greatly from plants to be assigned to the same kingdom. Biologists also disagree about how many distinctly different plant divisions are appropriate. Some classification systems list twelve or more, and others list only two.

By now, you have probably realized that there is no one "correct" way to classify living things. This should not be surprising given that all classification systems are a compromise between convenience and an accurate representation of similarities, differences, and relationships. The system used in this textbook attempts to strike a practical balance by sorting the kingdom Plantae into five divisions (including three divisions of multicellular algae), and placing fungi in a separate kingdom.

Both bracket fungus and corn smut belong to the same fungal division — Basidiomycetes.

Unity and Diversity in the Kingdom Fungi

Fungi are unicellular or multicellular heterotrophs. The smallest members of the kingdom **Fungi** consist of single cells, but most are multicellular and can be seen with the unaided eye. Some multicellular species consist of sprawling, thread-like structures such as the mycelium of the forest fungi described at the beginning of this chapter. In other species, however, closely packed cells form firm-textured structures called fruiting bodies. These fruiting bodies may grow to 0.5 m in width. Fungal shapes range from shelf-like brackets that grow on tree trunks to formless powdery smuts that infect corn and other food crops. Colours include white, grey, brown, red, and yellow, but not green.

Despite these differences, fungi share many characteristics that set them apart from members of other kingdoms.
- Unlike plants, fungi are heterotrophs. They cannot make their own food.
- The cell walls of fungi are made of chitin, a nitrogen-containing polysaccharide that differs in composition from plant cellulose.
- Unlike animals, fungi are sessile. They cannot hunt for food.
- Fungi cannot ingest food; they must either live in it or on it, and absorb nutrients through their walls.
- Unlike the cells of any other kingdom, some fungal cells contain multiple nuclei embedded in an unusually large mass of cytoplasm.

Fungi also differ from other kingdoms in their reproductive methods. In fact, reproductive structures provide the primary basis for classifying fungi into the divisions shown in Figure 11-2. For example, the sexual spores of the division **Ascomycetes** form inside a finger-like sac known as an ascus. Ascomycetes includes many single-celled species called yeasts. In the division **Basidiomycetes,** sexual spores are produced on club-shaped reproductive cells called basidia. Some club fungi form conspicuous fruiting bodies. Examples include mushrooms and bracket fungi. But Basidiomycetes also includes rusts and smuts, which do not produce noticeable fruiting bodies.

Most fungi excrete digestive chemicals that break their food into molecules they can absorb. Plants also absorb materials through their cell walls but only small, simple molecules such as water. Fungi absorb much larger molecules such as amino acids.

Very few protist species have two nuclei per cell. Plants and animals seldom have more than one.

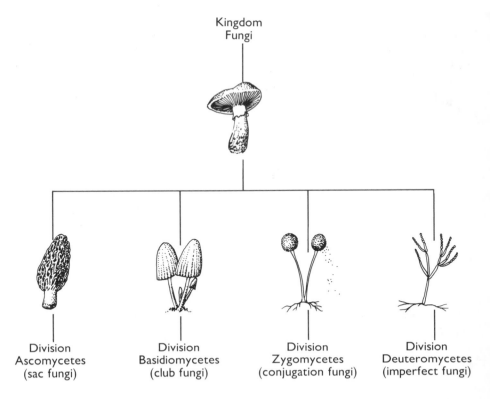

FIGURE 11-2 Classification of the kingdom Fungi

Kingdom Fungi

Division Ascomycetes (sac fungi)

Division Basidiomycetes (club fungi)

Division Zygomycetes (conjugation fungi)

Division Deuteromycetes (imperfect fungi)

The truffle is an edible member of Ascomycetes. Its large fruiting bodies grow underground and are harvested by specially trained pigs or dogs.

Not all plants are able to photosynthesize. The dodder in the colour section for Unit III is a parasite. It takes its nourishment from other plants, killing them in the process. The bright orange threads choking the mesquite bush resemble carelessly discarded plastic packing, but they are actually the body parts of a living dodder plant.

The division **Zygomycetes** is named for the thickly coated, zygote-containing spores produced by sexual reproduction. These zygospores form when branches of two different fungi meet and fuse. This process is called conjugation. Bread mould is the best-known example of the conjugation fungi. The division **Deuteromycetes** is made up of fungi that do not reproduce sexually. Parasites such as the fungal species that causes athlete's foot belong to this division.

Together with bacteria, fungi are the biosphere's primary decomposers. Their ability to break down materials such as dead trees is vital to the continued survival of plants and animals alike. You will learn more about the four fungal divisions and their environmental roles in Chapter 14.

Unity and Diversity in the Kingdom Plantae

Members of the kingdom **Plantae** are defined as multicellular autotrophic organisms, which have membrane-bound nuclei and walls made of cellulose. All but a few plants contain chlorophyll. Chlorophyll enables plants to manufacture their own food by photosynthesis, a process that stores solar energy in nutrient molecules such as sugars and starches. About 250 000 plant species fit this definition. They range from large to small, terrestrial to aquatic, and

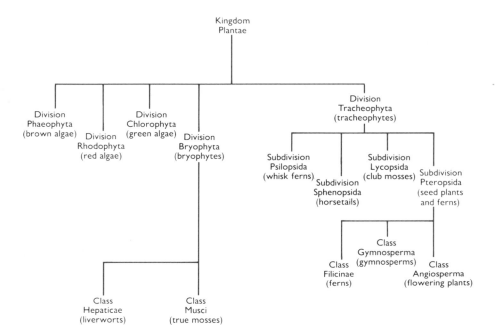

FIGURE 11-3 Classification of the kingdom Plantae

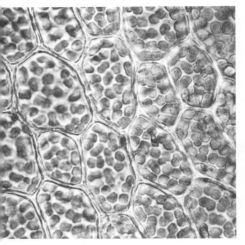

Chlorophyll-containing chloroplasts dominate these plant cells and give the plant its overall green colour.

The giant saguaro cactus could never reach heights of 3 m or more without specialized vascular tissues to conduct its scant water supply to the top of its "arms."

common to rare, but all of these species can be grouped into only five divisions: Tracheophyta, Bryophyta, Chlorophyta, Rhodophyta, and Phaeophyta. (See Figure 11-3.)

Tracheophytes are called **vascular plants** because they have specialized vascular tissues that conduct water and nutrients throughout their bodies. All

Many bryophytes have parts that resemble leaves, stems, and roots, but biologists use these terms only for structures that contain vascular tissue.

Bryophytes are important ecologically because they can grow where there is no soil, thereby contributing to soil formation. Their ability to hold water is also a major influence on the environment in which they grow.

The free-floating brown algae of the genus *Sargassum* have accumulated in tangled, island-like mats that cover millions of square kilometres of the Atlantic Ocean. This region is called the Sargasso Sea.

A single strand of kelp may be many metres long. Like most brown algae, kelp becomes attached to objects near the shoreline.

large land plants belong to this group. Bryophytes are called **nonvascular plants** because they lack comparable conducting tissues. The low, moss-like plants of this group can grow only in damp surroundings. Rhodophytes, phaeophytes, and chlorophytes are mainly multicellular algae, which also lack vascular tissue. Since all algae are aquatic, they do not require structures to transport liquids. You will learn more about these five plant divisions in the following text. You might also find that referring to Figure 11-3 will help you as you read.

Characteristics of Multicellular Algae

Multicellular algae are grouped into three divisions according to the composition of their stored food, and to the presence of pigments other than chlorophyll.

The division **Phaeophyta** includes approximately 1000 aquatic species commonly known as **brown algae.** Phaeophytes are the biggest and the most complex algae, and include some of the very largest seaweeds. All brown algae have chlorophyll, but they also contain so many brown pigment molecules that their overall colour is brown instead of green. This effect is often called masking. The cell walls of brown algae contain a sticky, water-retaining material that prevents them from drying out between tides. They store the food they make as fat or as a nonstarchy polysaccharide called laminarin.

The division **Rhodophyta** has close to 2500 species that are commonly called **red algae.** Some rhodophytes are microscopic and unicellular, but most are macroscopic seaweeds that live in deep water. The colours of red algae actually range from red to purple or black because the chlorophyll is masked by red and blue pigments. These pigments absorb the dim light that penetrates

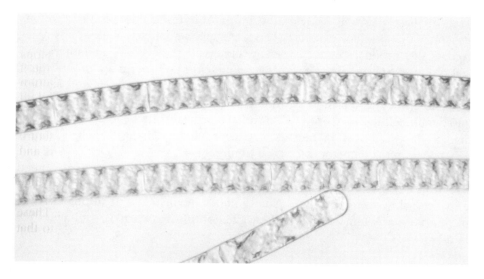

DID YOU KNOW?

Here is another list of root words derived from Greek and Latin. Refer to this mini dictionary to help you understand the classification terms used in this chapter.

Root	Meaning
bryon	moss
chloro	green
lycos	wolf (as in the claw shape of the roots)
musci	moss
opsis	appearance
phaios	brown
phyton	plant
psilos	bare (as in bare branches)
pteron	feather (as in the feathery shape of some leaves)
rhodon	rose
sphen	wedge (as in the shape of emerging leaf bundles)
tracheia	windpipe

deep water. Then they pass the collected energy to the chlorophyll molecules for photosynthesis. Rhodophytes store food in the form of a unique polysaccharide called floridean starch.

The division **Chlorophyta** has about 6000 species, most of which inhabit fresh water, although some species live in salt water, and a few are found in damp locations on land. Chlorophytes are called **green algae** because they usually have no other pigments to mask the colour of their chlorophyll. Green algae store their food as starch just as most land plants do. Some green algae are unicellular. Multicellular species vary from flat, sheet-like seaweeds to long threads and hollow balls of cells.

Characteristics of Nonvascular Plants

The nonvascular terrestrial plants of the division **Bryophyta** are small and low growing. Although adapted to suit life on land, they thrive only in moist environments. This is because bryophytes lack vascular tissue, so their cells can only obtain water by simple diffusion.

The class **Musci** includes about 15 000 species, which are generally called the true mosses to distinguish them from other low-growing plants that are quite different in structure. Mosses are often found on forest floors because they can produce food in very dim light. The root-like rhizoids that anchor moss plants and help them to absorb water are not regarded as true roots. This is because they have no vascular tissue and cannot transport water to other plant parts. Above-ground cells and tissues obtain moisture by diffusion from the water droplets trapped between the close-growing, individual plants.

Mosses reproduce by **spores.** A spore is a single reproductive cell that can germinate and grow into a new organism. Moss spores sprout into masses of green threads, which then develop into the familiar spongy bed of moss plants.

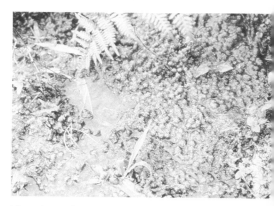

Most bryophyte species are mosses. The numerous, tiny individual plants in this bed of moss trap water droplets to keep their environment damp.

Each of these plants is known as a **gametophyte** because its tip develops structures that produce gametes. The female gametophyte develops an archegonium that produces eggs. The male gametophyte develops an antheridium that produces sperm. (In some species, both eggs and sperm are produced on the same gametophyte.) Fertilization occurs only if there is enough surface water to allow the sperm to swim to the egg. The resulting zygote develops into a multicellular **sporophyte,** so called because its tip develops a structure that produces spores. In mosses, the sporophyte remains attached to and dependent on the gametophyte. (See Figure 11-4.)

The class **Hepaticae** has about 8500 species, which are commonly called liverworts. Most liverworts are inconspicuous flat masses of green tissue that grow very low to the ground, usually under other plants or in bogs. These plant bodies are gametophytes. Reproduction in liverworts is similar to that in mosses.

FIGURE 11-4 The life cycle of a moss

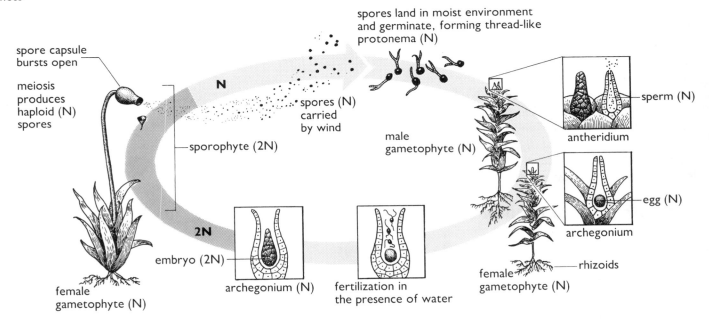

Characteristics of Vascular Plants

The division **Tracheophyta,** or vascular plants, includes the largest and most complex plants. Tracheophyta has such a wide range of species that many taxonomists sort it into four subdivisions: Psilopsida, Sphenopsida, Lycopsida, and Pteropsida. The roots and stems of all four subdivisions are regarded as true because they contain vascular tissue. Most vascular plants also possess true leaves. By transporting water, the vascular tissues enable tracheophytes to grow much taller than nonvascular plants.

The subdivision **Psilopsida** has only three living species, which are commonly known as whisk ferns. Psilopsids as big as trees have been found in fossil form, but modern species range in size from 1–30 cm and are found only in warm climates. Whisk ferns are the simplest vascular plants living today. They have no leaves; the bare stems carry out photosynthesis. The spores develop in small cases studding the branches.

Subdivision **Sphenopsida** has 32 species, which are commonly known as horsetails. Fossil evidence found in coal seams shows that tree-like sphenopsids existed when the earth's climate was wetter, but most modern species are less than 1 m in height. Both the roots and the ''horsetails'' grow from horizontal underground runners. The hard, hollow, upright stems are ringed with tiny scale-like leaves, from which the bright green ''horsehairs'' emerge. Spores are produced only at the tips of specialized shoots.

The subdivision **Lycopsida** includes approximately 1100 species, many of which are called club mosses, although they are quite different from true mosses. The ''club'' refers to the spore-bearing cones at the tips of the upright branches. Club mosses have true roots on their horizontal stems and true, needle-like leaves on their upright branches. There is fossil evidence showing that tree-size lycopsids existed in the past, but all living species are small and inconspicuous.

Whisk ferns, horsetails, and club mosses have certain reproductive features in common. Like mosses, all produce eggs and sperm on plant bodies called gametophytes, which depend on the presence of water for fertilization. But the gametophytes of vascular plants are so small and inconspicuous that they are seldom noticed. Some even form underground. The plant bodies you know as whisk ferns, horsetails, and club mosses are all sporophytes.

The middle stalk of this horsetail shows its specialized spore-producing structures. The other stalks bear the familiar green ''horsetails.''

Some lycopsid species known as ground pines are becoming rare because of over-harvesting for use as holiday decorations.

Only the feathery sporophytes are large enough to be noticeable in most ferns. The tiny gametophytes are usually hidden in the litter on the forest floor.

Traditionally, the class Gymnosperma has included the cycads (which resemble cone-bearing palm trees), gingkoes (which resemble deciduous shade trees), and gnetophytes. One desert-adapted gnetophyte is shaped like a low, round coffee table. It has cones at its rim and sprawling split leaves about 2 m in length. Some taxonomists think these plants should be placed in completely separate classes, and a few think they should be placed in separate subdivisions.

TABLE 11-1 Full Classification of the Red Maple

Taxonomic Group	Identifying Characteristics
Kingdom	Plantae
Division	Tracheophyta
Subdivision	Pteropsida
Class	Angiosperm
Order	Sapindales
Family	Aceraceae
Genus	Acer
Species	Acer rubrum

A Very Successful Subdivision: Ferns and Seed Plants

With over 210 000 species, the subdivision **Pteropsida** is by far the most widespread, successful, and diverse group of plants living today. The most outstanding feature common to pteropsids is their leaves, which are both larger and more complex than the leaves of other tracheophytes. Pteropsida is composed of three classes: Filicineae, Gymnosperma, and Angiosperma.

The class **Filicinae** consists of the true ferns and includes 10 000 species. The bodies of fern plants are sporophytes. Their feathery leaves spring directly from underground stems that live through the winter. Cold-climate ferns are seldom more than 1 m in height, but some warm-climate species have strong, thick, vertical stems and grow to tree size. Fern spores develop on the underside of the leaves and sprout on the forest floor into inconspicuous gametophytes. Like whisk ferns, horsetails, and club mosses, true ferns require water for sexual reproduction.

The class **Gymnosperma** has 700 species, which are mostly coniferous trees. The class **Angiosperma** is composed of nearly 200 000 flowering-plant species, including all grasses, grain plants, vegetables, and deciduous trees. Gymnosperms and angiosperms share two outstanding features that have enabled them to dominate the plant kingdom on land—pollen grains and seeds.

Pollen Grains

The sperm produced by seed plants are encased in tough, waterproof structures called **pollen grains.** Pollen grains prevent the sperm from drying out, even when they must travel long distances in dry conditions to reach the eggs. This means that seed plants do not require water for sexual reproduction.

Seeds

Seeds are multicellular structures that contain an embryonic plant and a small food supply which are encased together in a protective coat. The seeds of angiosperms are also surrounded by a fruit. Gymnosperm seeds do not have the added protection of a fruit. However, they do develop within a protective cone, which does not release them until they are mature.

Table 11-1 is a complete classification of the red maple, an angiosperm found throughout much of eastern Canada. The table reveals much about the maple's relationship to other plants. However, this formal approach to classification is not very helpful if you need to identify a particular specimen. For this purpose, scientists often prepare a **dichotomous key.** This key guides the user to a correct identification through a series of carefully sequenced steps. Dichotomous keys are so named because they offer the inexperienced user only two choices at each step. Dichotomous keys are available for identifying birds, snakes, seaweeds, wildflowers, fungi, minerals, rocks, and trees.

Identifying Tree-Sized Vascular Plants Using a Dichotomous Key

In this activity, you will identify some of the native trees in your environment, using the dichotomous keys provided by your teacher. Since most tree-sized gymnosperms in Canada retain their leaves through the winter, the same set of keys can be used throughout the year. But most tree-sized angiosperms are deciduous. Consequently, the Canadian Forest Service has developed two sets of keys for deciduous trees. The summer keys are based on differences in leaf shape and structure. The winter keys are based on differences in the way buds and leaf scars are arranged on the bare twigs. The simple dichotomous key below will help you choose the appropriate keys for your own identification exercise.

1. Does the tree have needle-like leaves?
   a) If yes, go to the *Keys for the Conifers*.
   b) If no, go to Question 2.
2. Does the tree have broad leaves?
   a) If yes, go to the *Summer Keys for Deciduous Trees*.
   b) If no, go to the *Winter Keys for Deciduous Trees*.

The Importance of Vascular Plants and Fungi

The goal of biological classification is to simplify the study of functioning organisms. This very short survey of the kingdom Plantae is a necessary first step for a more detailed exploration of Tracheophyta. The study of this division is of considerable practical importance since tracheophytes are the major producers of food for humans and all other land animals. But a more detailed study of the kingdom Fungi is also important, since some fungi are major food decomposers, while others play a vital role in returning nutrients to the soil for reuse by the kingdom Plantae. In Chapter 12, you will consider structure and function in vascular plants, particularly in ferns and seed plants. In Chapter 13, you will investigate how ferns and seed plants grow, develop, and reproduce. In Chapter 14, you will learn more about structure, function, and reproduction in fungi.

Canada's landscape is dominated by seed plants.

Chapter Review

Key Words

Angiosperma
Ascomycetes
Basidiomycetes
brown algae
Bryophyta
Chlorophyta
Deuteromycetes
dichotomous key
division
Filicinae
Fungi
gametophyte
green algae
Gymnosperma
Hepaticae
Lycopsida

Musci
nonvascular plants
Phaeophyta
Plantae
pollen grains
Psilopsida
Pteropsida
red algae
Rhodophyta
seeds
Sphenopsida
spores
sporophyte
Tracheophyta
vascular plants
Zygomycetes

Recall Questions

Multiple Choice

1. The term algae refers to
   a) a distinct kingdom of aquatic organisms
   b) a distinct division of plants
   c) a division of nonvascular plants
   d) none of the above

2. A seed contains which of the following structures?
   a) spore   c) zygote
   b) gamete   d) embryo

3. True mosses lack
   a) cell walls
   b) chloroplasts
   c) vascular tissue
   d) the ability to reproduce sexually

4. Which of the following vascular plants lack true leaves?
   a) whisk ferns   c) club mosses
   b) horsetails   d) all of the above

5. Which of the following vascular plants do not produce seeds?
   a) whisk ferns   c) club mosses
   b) horsetails   d) all of the above

Fill in the Blanks

1. The multicellular algae of the division _____ may reach several metres in length. These algae are _____ in colour and store their food as _____.

2. The algae of the division _____ are adapted for very deep water. These algae are _____ in colour and store their food as _____.

3. The algae of the division _____ contain only one kind of pigment, which gives them their _____ colour. These algae store their food as _____.

4. The low-growing land plants of the division _____ thrive only in _____ environments because they lack _____ tissue.

5. All large land plants belong to the division _____. Its members possess _____ roots and stems that help transport _____ to the uppermost parts of the tallest species.

Short Answers

1. List the characteristics that distinguish the kingdom Plantae from the kingdom Fungi.

2. Which characteristic of fungi is used to classify the kingdom into separate divisions?

3. Briefly describe the characteristics used to classify green, red, and brown algae into separate divisions.

4. Briefly describe the characteristics used to classify tracheophytes and bryophytes into separate divisions.

5. Explain why ''moss'' is an imprecise name.

6. a) Briefly describe the appearance of true mosses.
   b) Which factors limit their size?

7. For each of the following pairs of terms, explain what the two terms have in common and how they differ.
   a) phylum, division
   b) sporophyte, gametophyte
   c) spore, seed
   d) angiosperm, gymnosperm

8. Match the group name in Column A with the descriptions in Column B.

Column A	Column B
i) Angiosperma	a) class of cone-bearing plants
ii) Bryophyta	b) class of feathery-leafed plants
iii) Basidiomycetes	c) class of flowering plants
iv) Gymnosperma	d) division of aquatic plants
v) Filicinae	e) division of fungi
vi) Lycopsida	f) division of nonvascular plants
vii) Phaeophyta	g) subdivision of leafless plants
viii) Psilopsida	h) subdivision of leafy plants
ix) Pteropsida	i) subdivision of scaly leafed plants
x) Sphenopsida	j) subdivision of cone-bearing plants

Application Questions

1. The complete classification for a particular kind of rose is listed as Plantae, Tracheophyta, Angiosperma, Rosales, Rosaceae, *Rosa, canina.*
   a) Identify the classification level for each group name.
   b) The chokecherry, *Prunus virginiana*, belongs to the same family as the rose. Write a complete classification list for the chokecherry.

2. A sick family member receives as a gift a plant with numerous large, green, feathery leaves that seem to spring directly from the soil.
   a) Which plant division, subdivision, and class does this plant belong to?
   b) Is it a sporophyte or a gametophyte? Explain how you know.

3. a) If you were asked to classify a "mystery organism" that is multicellular, in which three kingdoms might you place it?
   b) If the mystery organism is also heterotrophic, in which two kingdoms might you place it?
   c) What additional information would you need to make a final kingdom assignment? Explain.

4. a) What problems must land plants overcome that are not faced by aquatic plants?
   b) Discuss the adaptations that have allowed land plants to thrive despite these problems.

Problem Solving

1. Study the moss life cycle in Figure 11-4.
   a) In which structure does meiosis occur? What clue would help you answer this question even if the term meiosis did not appear on the diagram?
   b) How does the final outcome of meiosis in mosses differ from the final outcome of meiosis in animals such as humans?
   c) In which structures do you think mitosis is occurring? Explain.

2. The life cycles of multicellular algae were not discussed in this chapter. How do you think their gametes reach each other for fertilization?

3. Much of the world's food supply comes from angiosperms such as rice, wheat, corn, and millet. Farmers harvest the seeds of these plants instead of their roots or stems. Explain why seeds might be a more important food source.

4. "Alternation of generations" is often used to describe a life cycle such as that of true mosses. Study Figure 11-4 and comment on the factors that might have led to the use of this term. How does its significance apply to what you have learned about the meaning of generation in humans and other animals?

Extensions

1. Obtain a copy of a modern college biology textbook and a biology or botany textbook that is at least 25 years old. Compare the classification systems in these two books with each other and with the system used here.

2. Sometimes freshwater algae in a lake or pond "bloom," turning the entire body of water green. An algae bloom is the result of a population explosion. Find out what causes algae to bloom, what problems an algae bloom causes for the lake and its other inhabitants, and what steps can be taken to prevent algae blooms.

CHAPTER

12

Plant Structure and Function

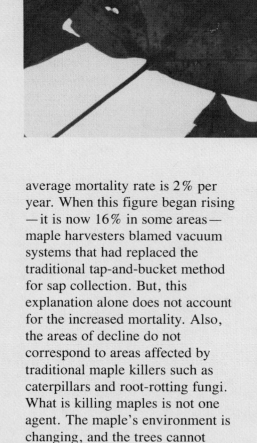

Eastern Canada's maple forests are dying. The killer works so gradually that a tree's reduced growth rate, smaller leaves, and decreased sap production may not be evident at first. This pattern of decline was first noticed in eastern Canada early in the 1980s, and has become more common since. In 1984, 28% of Quebec maple stands showed signs of decline. The next year, over 50% did. The decline of maples will have drastic consequences for organisms dependent on these large trees for food and shelter, as well as for the maple-sugar and forestry industries.

In a healthy maple bush, the average mortality rate is 2% per year. When this figure began rising — it is now 16% in some areas — maple harvesters blamed vacuum systems that had replaced the traditional tap-and-bucket method for sap collection. But, this explanation alone does not account for the increased mortality. Also, the areas of decline do not correspond to areas affected by traditional maple killers such as caterpillars and root-rotting fungi. What is killing maples is not one agent. The maple's environment is changing, and the trees cannot cope.

The environment is being changed by pollutants made by humans, especially acid precipitation and ozone. Ozone, combined with acidic precipitation and other airborne chemical irritants, can dissolve the cuticle, or protective coating, of maple leaves. Once the cuticle is weakened, acids may enter the leaf cells and leach out stored sugars and proteins, as well as trace minerals necessary for photosynthesis. The destruction of leaves reduces the maple's ability to create and store energy.

Below the ground, high soil acidity decreases the tree's absorption of nutrients and water. High acidity and metals deposited by air pollution are suspected causes of moss and lichen death.

These organisms break down dead leaves and organic litter, and release nutrients into the soil. As moss and lichen populations decrease, so do soil-nutrient levels. When the soil becomes acidic, essential minerals are washed deep into the soil out of reach of the maple's root system. Acidic soil also allows the release of toxic aluminum from natural rock and soil compounds in a form easily absorbed by the roots. Beneficial microbes and fungi that live along tree roots are also harmed by increasing acidity.

Pollution reduces the tree's ability to photosynthesize, decreases soil nutrient levels, and hampers absorption of these nutrients and water. The weakened tree may also be attacked by a traditional enemy, a cold winter, or high winds, and die. Since maples grow slowly and need the shade and protection of older trees to compete with more light-loving, fast-growing plants, each maple death makes it more difficult for other maples to grow.

As you read about plant structures and functions, think about these issues. Can the environmental changes and stresses be eliminated or minimized?

Chapter Objectives

When you complete this chapter, you should:

1. Be curious about plant growth and the structure and function of plant parts and tissues.

2. Appreciate the sophistication of plant structure, function, and growth.

3. Appreciate the adaptations of plants that help them survive in a variety of environments.

4. Be interested in the uses of vascular plants in industry.

5. Be able to prepare plant material for experimentation.

6. Be able to identify, measure, compare, and draw plant parts, tissues, and cells.

7. Know how to perform experiments to examine plant growth and germination.

8. Be able to infer the adaptive value of the various plant structures.

9. Be able to compare the structures of a monocot and a dicot stem and the structures of a herbaceous and a woody stem.

10. Be able to describe and compare the structure and function of xylem and phloem tissue.

11. Be able to describe how the structure of root hairs complements their function.

12. Be able to account for the movement of liquids through xylem cells.

13. Be able to state one theory explaining the movement of liquids through phloem cells.

14. Be able to describe the location and development of meristematic regions in a herbaceous and a woody plant.

15. Be able to compare the structural features of plants from different environments and infer their adaptive value.

16. Know how to identify several plant species common to two Ontario biomes and infer the relationship between the species and the abiotic conditions.

12.1 Organs and Tissues in Vascular Plants

Like animals, plants have specialized organs to carry out their life functions. **Vascular plants** have three major sets of organs: leaves, stems, and roots. Although these organs have specialized tissue for their own particular function, they all contain vascular tissue that forms an interconnected network. This network transports substances such as water and food throughout plants much as the circulatory system transports materials in animals.

Some plant organs are permanent and others are temporary. For example, tree roots and stems may live for 100 years or longer. Maple leaves, however, live for only a few months. The maple tree sheds these temporary organs in autumn and replaces them with a new set of organs in spring.

In some vascular plants, both the stems and the leaves are temporary organs that must be replaced each spring. Such plants are called perennials. Examples include chrysanthemums, shasta daisies, and violas. Many other vascular plants die completely at the end of the growing season and rely on seeds to grow a complete new set of organs. These plants are called annuals because they last only one growing season and must be replanted each spring. Examples of annuals include marigolds, geraniums, garden peas, beans, and grains such as oats, wheat, and corn.

Plants of all types must be able to grow rapidly to replace these parts when the growing season starts. They meet this need with a feature that is not found in animals. In plants, all specialized tissues grow from a single, unspecialized tissue type called the **meristem**. Meristematic tissue is composed of small, actively dividing cells that eventually produce all of the different tissues seen in the roots, stems, and leaves of a plant. Meristematic tissues near the tips of roots and shoots are referred to as **apical meristems**.

LABORATORY EXERCISE 12-1
Locating Meristematic Regions in Roots

In this exercise, you will examine bean seedlings to determine the location of meristematic tissue in roots. You will attempt to determine where new cells are formed and where they increase in length.

Differentiation

Meristematic tissue is found wherever new tissue may be needed for the growth of roots, stems, and leaves. All cells in the meristem are identical at first but, as they divide repeatedly, they become specialized for functions such as protection, support, storage, photosynthesis, and transportation. This division of cells in the meristem is called **differentiation**. Through differentiation, cells begin to look and act differently as they become specialized for their particular functions. How this process occurs is not completely understood, and differentiation is the subject of intensive research.

Specialized Plant Tissues

All plant tissues develop from the meristems that are found in various regions in a plant. (See Figure 12-1.) The specialized structures of these tissues allows the organs to carry out their special functions.

Parenchyma tissue is soft because it is composed of large, thin-walled, loosely packed cells. In roots, stems, and fruits, the cells and the spaces between the cells provide storage for sugars and starches. The edible part of an apple or a potato is mainly parenchyma. In leaves and young stems, the parenchyma cells contain chloroplasts. (See Figure 12-2.) The spaces between the cells allow the rapid exchange of gases involved in photosynthesis. Parenchyma tissue in leaves and young stems is called green parenchyma or chlorenchyma.

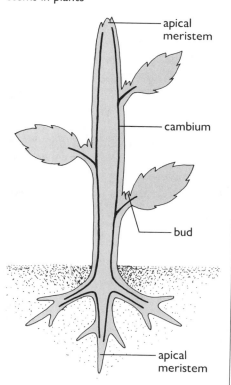

FIGURE 12-1 The location of meristems in plants

- apical meristem
- cambium
- bud
- apical meristem

FIGURE 12-2 Green parenchyma cells

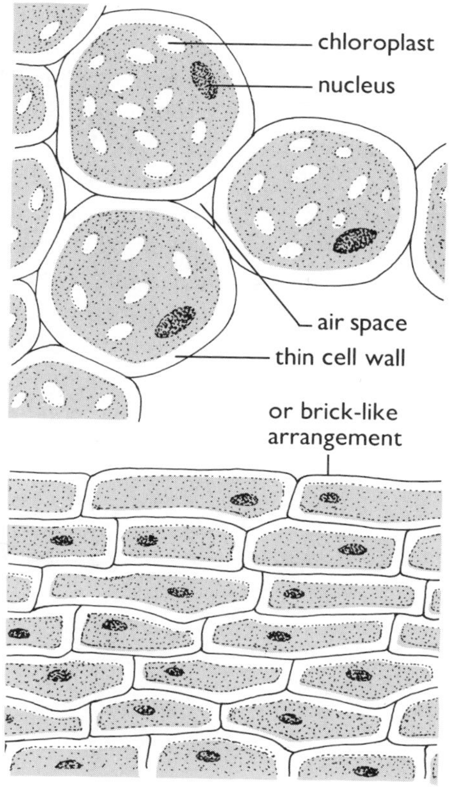

- chloroplast
- nucleus
- air space
- thin cell wall
- or brick-like arrangement

FIGURE 12-3 Sclerenchyma cells

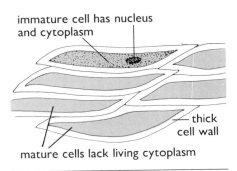

immature cell has nucleus
and cytoplasm

thick
cell wall

mature cells lack living cytoplasm

Sclerenchyma tissue is a strengthening tissue found wherever support is needed in roots, stems, and in the veins of leaves. The cells of mature sclerenchyma usually contain no cytoplasm, and their walls are so thick that there is almost no internal space inside each cell. (See Figure 12-3.) The thick, strong walls of the sclerenchyma cells are composed of cellulose and permeated with a glue-like substance called lignin that increases the strength of sclerenchyma.

Epidermal tissue covers the outer surface of roots, stems, and leaves. Epidermal tissue protects a plant's organs. In roots, specialized epidermal cells form the root hairs that absorb water from the soil. In leaves, the epidermal cells secrete a waxy substance called cutin that forms a layer called the **cuticle**. The cuticle helps to reduce water loss and protect leaves from injury. However, it can be damaged by acid rain and air pollution. Airborne pollutants and acid rain allow bacteria and fungi to infect the tissues of leaves. This type of damage may be partly responsible for the decline in Canada's maple tree population.

Vascular Tissue

Vascular tissue forms a network of tube-like structures that carry materials to and from a plant's organs. There are two types of vascular tissue: xylem and phloem.

Xylem tissue transports water, minerals, and other water-soluble materials. In gymnosperms such as pines, xylem tissue consists primarily of long, tapered tracheid cells. The walls of the tracheids are quite thick and perforated with many holes called pits. (See Figure 12-4.) At maturity, the living parts of the cells die, leaving only the hollow cell walls. Because the cells overlap, water can move from one tracheid to another through the pits in the walls. Any dissolved materials move along with the water.

In angiosperms such as maples, xylem tissue consists mainly of long vessel cells arranged in an end-to-end pattern. (See Figure 12-5.) When mature, the contents of the cells die and the end walls dissolve, leaving behind one continuous tube-like vessel up to a metre in length. Vessels are also much larger in diameter than tracheids and conduct water more efficiently.

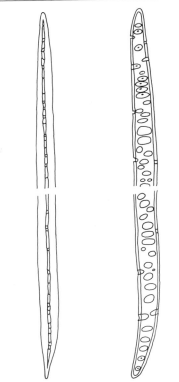

FIGURE 12-4 Left: Outside view of a pine tracheid. Notice the long, thin shape. **Right:** Internal view of a pine tracheid. Notice the hollow interior and thick, pitted walls.

FIGURE 12-5 In the vessel cells of angiosperms, the end walls dissolve, leaving a tubular structure that can conduct water.

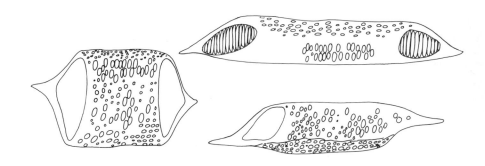

Transportation of water is only one of the functions performed by the dead cells that make up the xylem tissue. Both types of xylem also serve to strengthen the stems of vascular plants. The walls of the tracheid cells contain extra lignin and cellulose that strengthen the wood of trees. The strength of the lumber used in building construction depends mainly on the structure of xylem tissue.

Phloem tissue forms a network of tubes in vascular plants that transports dissolved nutrients such as sugar. Phloem is composed of two types of living cells. Sieve tube cells are long and tubular. They have perforated seive plates and a smaller companion cell attached to their side walls. (See Figure 12-6.) At maturity, the sieve tubes lose their nuclei but do not die. Scientists think that the companion cell nuclei probably regulate the activities of the sieve tube cells since strands of living cytoplasm connect the two cell types.

Xylem and phloem tissues are grouped together in vascular bundles. These bundles form a continuous transportation network extending from the roots of a vascular plant through its stem to its leaves. Some vascular bundles such as the veins of a leaf, or the "ribs" of a celery stem, are easy to see. In most stems and roots, however, the vascular bundles can be seen only by cutting a cross section. Figure 12-7 shows that the way the vascular bundles are arranged differs from organ to organ. The vascular tissue itself, however, is similar throughout.

All vascular plants depend on efficient functioning of their vascular tissues for survival. Another reason why maple trees are dying is that the xylem in their roots does not absorb water as well as it should. If the xylem cannot transport water and other needed substances upward to the leaves of a tree, the tree may become dehydrated. Dehydration reduces both the number of leaves and the amount of food a tree can produce. Continued dehydration inevitably leads to death.

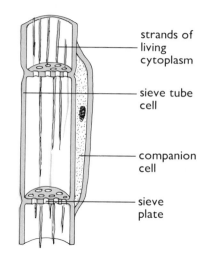

FIGURE 12-6 Phloem tissue consists of living sieve-tube cells.

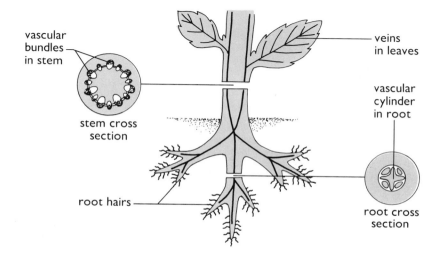

FIGURE 12-7 In the root of this dicot plant, there is only one bundle of vascular tissue, which is in the vascular cylinder. In the stem, the vascular tissue is separated into several distinct bundles.

The vascular bundles of this celery stalk are smaller, but similar in function, to the vascular bundles of the tree.

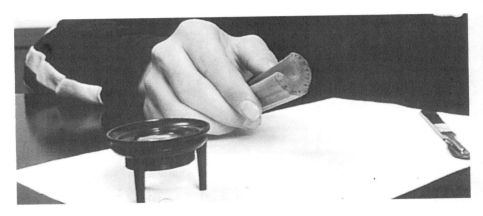

Section Review Questions

1. a) What are the three major sets of organs found in plants?
   b) Describe the function of each set of organs.
   c) Which of these organs are permanent, and which are temporary in annuals and perennials?

2. Where is meristematic tissue found in plants, and what is its function?

3. Compare parenchyma, sclerenchyma, and epidermal tissues using the headings: Description of Cell, Location of Tissue, and Function of Tissue.

4. How does xylem tissue in angiosperms differ from xylem tissue in gymnosperms?

5. Compare the fluids transported through xylem tissue with the fluids transported through phloem tissue.

6. Mature phloem cells lack a nucleus. How do scientists think they are directed to function?

12.2 Roots

In most vascular plants, **roots** lie below the surface of the soil. These roots serve three main functions. They anchor plants in the ground, absorb water and water-soluble substances from the soil, and transport these materials upward to other plant organs. An additional function of many roots is the storage of food materials made in the leaves and stems. Some plants such as cacti maintain themselves with a very small root mass. Other plants such as trees have a root mass equal to the mass of the tree parts above ground. For example, the roots of the maple tree spread far beyond the leaf canopy and grow down to a depth of approximately 2 m.

Designing
Plant Fibres

If biologist Joe Goodin of Texas Tech University has his way, cotton harvesters may soon be out of work. Goodin does not think cotton will be replaced. On the contrary, he thinks the versatile plant fibre, which has been used for thousands of years, will continue to be popular. However, Goodin thinks cotton fibre production may change. In the future, cotton fibre may come from a laboratory, instead of from the mature boll of a cotton plant.

Cotton is the most widely used plant fibre. Although it is finer than wool, cotton fibre is very strong. Also, cotton fabrics "breathe." Air and moisture pass between the cotton fibres in a garment, keeping the wearer cool and dry. Another advantage is cost. Cotton can be grown, spun, and woven inexpensively. Goodin believes the cost may be lowered even more by eliminating the cost of growing the cotton plant. He has accomplished this by exploiting a peculiar property of cotton fibre.

Under a microscope, cotton fibres appear as flattened, rough, corkscrew tubes. Each fibre is really a single cell. By contrast, linen, rayon, and other plant fibres are not. Linen is produced by drying, crushing, and beating flax stalks. Each linen fibre is composed of numerous long cells from the stalks. Rayon is produced from cellulose extracted from softwood or other plant materials.

While trying to regenerate whole cotton plants from single cells, Goodin noticed that some cells elongated into cotton fibres. Eventually, by manipulating growth conditions such as temperature, pH, oxygen, sugar, salt, and hormone concentrations, Goodin found he could force nearly all cotton cells to become cotton fibres. Since all cotton cells carry the same genetic information, each has the potential to become any part of the plant if the cells are given the proper stimulus. Goodin discovered it is possible to identify the conditions during which cotton cells grow into fibres.

Goodin has identified a potential use for his test-tube cotton: the production of designer fibres. Cotton fibres of specific lengths, widths, and shapes may be produced when growth conditions are varied.

Goodin admits his method is not yet economical. But test-tube cotton will have some advantages over the natural variety. First, fibre can be produced in about half the time required by field-grown cotton. Second, test-tube cotton will be produced indoors with no special lighting or pesticides, and will require little space. Bad weather and natural disasters, which can ruin a traditional cotton producer's harvest, will not affect a test-tube cotton farmer. Goodin's method gives the producer complete control of the entire process.

Root Types

Figure 12-8 shows two types of roots: the taproot and the fibrous root. Each type of root is adapted to different environmental conditions and soil types.

FIGURE 12-8 Fibrous root and taproot systems

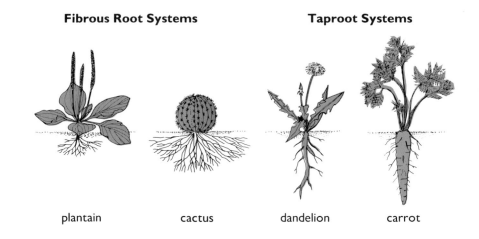

Fibrous Root Systems

plantain   cactus

Taproot Systems

dandelion   carrot

Taproots and Fibrous Roots

When a seed germinates, it first sends out a primary root. If this primary root enlarges to become the major root, the plant has a taproot system. The **taproot** can reach deep into the soil for water and anchors the plant quite efficiently. The dandelion, for example, has a taproot system that is hard to pull out of the soil. The taproot system of the oak tree helps it survive drought conditions. Other plants such as grasses and maple trees send out secondary roots that very quickly outgrow the primary root. These roots are called **fibrous roots**. The fibrous root system is characterized by a shallow mass of tangled roots that spread throughout a large area of soil.

How Roots Grow

Roots grow by increasing their length. Figure 12-9 shows the growing tip of a root has a protective root cap and three distinct growth regions: the meristematic region, the elongation region, and the maturation region. Two factors contribute to the increase in root length. First, in the meristematic region, continual cellular reproduction adds new cells that help push the root cap through the abrasive soil. As the root cap cells are worn away, they are replaced by the dividing meristematic cells. Second, cells of the elongation region increase in length, forcing the root cap and meristem farther into the soil.

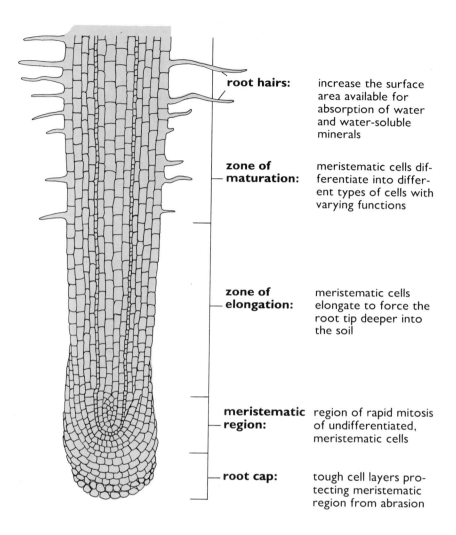

FIGURE 12-9 The growing tip of a root

root hairs: increase the surface area available for absorption of water and water-soluble minerals

zone of maturation: meristematic cells differentiate into different types of cells with varying functions

zone of elongation: meristematic cells elongate to force the root tip deeper into the soil

meristematic region: region of rapid mitosis of undifferentiated, meristematic cells

root cap: tough cell layers protecting meristematic region from abrasion

In the maturation region, the elongated cells that came originally from the meristem finally begin to differentiate. Vascular tissues form inside the root, while epidermal tissue forms on the outside. Specialized epidermal cells form extensions called root hairs, which greatly increase the amount of root surface available for absorption. As the root grows, the hairs farthest from the tip die and fall off, while new root hairs form closer to the root tip.

Water moves passively into root hairs by osmosis whenever the water concentration of the surrounding soil is greater than the water concentration inside the root hairs. Studies have shown that minerals can enter root hairs even when no water is being absorbed by the plant, and even when the mineral concentration inside the root is greater than it is outside the root. This indicates that the plant itself must be supplying energy to transport these minerals.

LABORATORY EXERCISE 12-2
Investigating Root Systems and Root Structure

In this exercise, you will investigate the two types of root systems by examining samples of taproots and fibrous roots. Microscopic examination of a root tip will allow you to observe the different zones found within a root tip and to observe root hairs.

Structure and Function in Roots

The cells in the maturation region of a young root develop into three concentric layers of tissue: the epidermis, the cortex, and the vascular cylinder. In cross section, these layers appear as rings. (See Figure 12-10.)

The **epidermis** is a single layer of cells that surrounds a root and protects it from bacteria and fungi. Epidermal cells are permeable by water and dissolved minerals.

Most of the **cortex** of a root is composed of parenchyma tissue. (See Figure 12-10.) The intercellular spaces permit water to move freely between the cells. In some plants, the parenchyma cells store plant food as insoluble starch for future use by the plant. The innermost boundary of the cortex is composed of a single layer of endodermis tissue. A waxy material between these cells limits the flow of water into the vascular cylinder of the root.

The **vascular cylinder** is the innermost region of a young primary root. As Figure 12-10 shows, it contains four distinct types of tissue. A ring of parenchyma cells forms the outer boundary of the cylinder. At the centre of

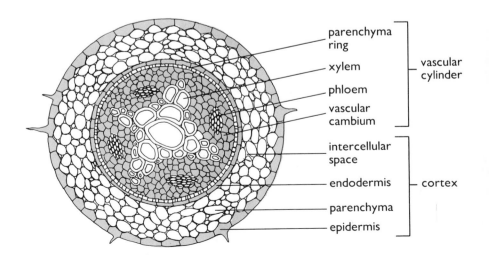

FIGURE 12-10 A cross section of a buttercup root showing the major tissue types

parenchyma ring

xylem

phloem

vascular cambium

vascular cylinder

intercellular space

endodermis

parenchyma

epidermis

cortex

the vascular cylinder, a single large bundle of xylem tissue transports water and minerals upward to other plant organs. Several smaller bundles of phloem tissue transport food made in the leaves back down for use by the root cells. Between these bundles lies a thin layer of **vascular cambium**, a type of meristematic tissue that is responsible for increasing the diameter of a root as it matures. During the growing season, the vascular cambium produces new xylem cells on its inner side and new phloem cells on its outer side.

Older roots develop a second meristematic layer beneath the epidermis. This layer, the **cork cambium**, forms a tough, waterproof outer surface. Once the cork cambium is in place, roots can no longer absorb water, although they can still conduct water and store food. These mature roots still maintain young growing tips that continue to grow and absorb water.

Root Adaptations

Factors such as soil type and the location of a plant can affect the type of root a plant develops and the adaptations of its root system.

Many tropical plants live on trees and are not rooted in the soil. For example, orchids grow **aerial roots** that absorb water from dew and moist tropical air. Dust and particles of bark that collect on the surfaces of these roots are sources of minerals. The common spider plant, which is a popular house plant, grows aerial roots at the ends of its hanging runners.

Adventitious roots grow directly from the stems of many plants. English ivy often develops adventitious roots that help it cling to walls and climb upward. **Prop roots** are adventitious roots that grow downward from plant stems. Large tropical banyan trees send out many prop roots to support their large upper canopy of leaves. Most adventitious roots provide only support for plants.

Spider plants have aerial roots.

Section Review Questions

1. What are the three main functions of roots?
2. Describe the taproot and explain the special environmental conditions it is adapted to.
3. Describe the fibrous root and explain the important ecological role it plays.
4. Where is the meristematic region found in a growing root tip?
5. a) How do root hairs form?
   b) Where are root hairs located on a root, and what is their purpose?
6. What type of cells make up the cortex of a root, and what substance is stored there?
7. List three types of root adaptations and identify a plant that is an example of each adaptation.

Banyan trees have prop roots for support.

Saving
the Maples

Science and technology are being used in an attempt to rescue eastern Canadian maples. Syrup producers whose livelihoods are threatened by the effects of acid precipitation and air pollution may now be able to protect their trees temporarily.

Two proposed solutions to the problem seem logical. The first proposes liming the forests to raise the pH levels. Lime, which is composed of calcium oxide, can improve soil quality. Liming has been used to decrease the acidity of lakes affected by acid precipitation. Now some success has been achieved in reviving maple stands by liming forest floors. The second strategy bypasses the issue of soil acidity and attempts to replace lost nutrients. Canagro Agricultural Products has developed an antacid fertilizer that replaces micronutrients leached from soil by high acidity. This fertilizer also contains a calcium component that binds up toxic aluminum in the soil, preventing its absorption by trees.

Unfortunately, neither of these solutions is universally practical. Since soil conditions vary from place to place, responses vary with each situation. Problems may result from indiscriminate liming or fertilization of maple stands, since careless use of any chemical can upset the delicate nutrient balance of soil and damage plant life.

Use of folial, or leaf, analysis to determine optimum responses is a better solution. In Quebec, scientists at private and public laboratories are analyzing the nutritional needs of maple trees in each maple stand. In the autumn, maple owners gather leaves from trees on their property and submit them for folial analysis. The next spring, a recommendation for custom-made fertilizer can be made. When a specific nutrient is needed, it can be concentrated in the fertilizer. If a broad range of nutrients is lacking, liming may be recommended along with fertilization. Liming decreases soil acidity, and so aids the growth of mosses and lichens and the subsequent release of nutrients into the soil.

Unfortunately, folial analysis is slow. In the six months it takes to decipher a tree's nutritional needs, the tree may die. In serious cases, time can be saved by injecting fertilizer directly into the tree. However, at $15 per tree large-scale direct injection programs are not economical. Although an injection may save the tree for another year, it does nothing to cure the causes of the maple's decline.

Indeed, even wide-scale folial analysis, if proven accurate and effective over time, will still be just a stopgap measure. The only sure way to save the maples and other trees of eastern Canada is to remove from the air and soil the poisonous agents responsible for their decline.

12.3 Stems

In most plants, the **stems** are upright organs that function to support the leaves and expose them to sunlight. Stems have two additional functions that are common with roots: they transport materials such as water, and they may be used as storage sites for plant food. In some plants, stems also take on a fourth function, that of photosynthesis.

The tissues present in roots extend upward through the stems with modifications that permit the stems to grow above the surface of the soil. The vascular tissue of roots and stems is continuous, providing a direct path for water travelling upward through the xylem to the leaves, and for food molecules travelling downward through the phloem to the root.

How Stems Grow

The pattern of growth in stems is similar to that of roots. Meristematic tissue located at the tip of a stem forms new cells. As the new cells elongate, the stem grows upward. Later, the cells differentiate to form the various types of stem tissue. Stem tissues are similar to those in roots except that the xylem and the phloem are arranged in **vascular bundles.** (See Figures 12-11 and 12-12.)

Above: What functions are performed by the massive stem of the Douglas fir? **Below:** What functions are performed by the thick, green stems of the broccoli?

LABORATORY EXERCISE 12-3
The Transportation of Water through Stems

In this exercise, you will observe the transportation of water through a herbaceous stem. The pathway of water will be made evident by a red dye called eosin. You will take cross sections of the stem at measured intervals to observe how quickly the eosin dye moves upward in the plant.

Types of Stems

Early biologists recognized only two different types of plant stems: woody and herbaceous. These names are still used to describe the stems of angiosperms, along with newer terms based on internal structure. However, woody and herbaceous stems are found only in angiosperms.

Soft, fleshy **herbaceous stems** are found in angiosperms such as flowers, weeds, grasses, and food plants. The green colour of herbaceous stems indicates that they contain chlorophyll and can undergo photosynthesis. Like leaves, these stems normally die back to the ground in winter. Herbaceous stems can be further classified as monocots or dicots according to the internal arrangement of their vascular bundles.

Monocot and dicot are terms derived from seed structure. The seeds of dicotyledons have two embryonic leaves inside. Monocotyledon seeds have only one embryonic leaf.

FIGURE 12-11 A cross section of a
herbaceous monocot stem

Corn is a herbaceous monocot.

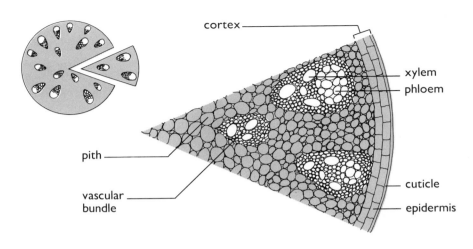

FIGURE 12-12 A cross section of a
herbaceous dicot stem

Sunflowers are herbaceous dicots.

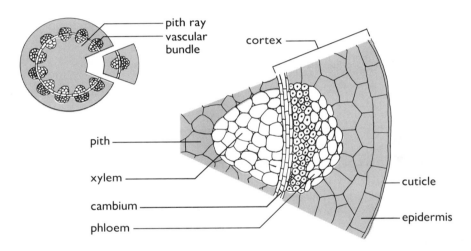

The vascular bundles of herbaceous monocot stems are scattered through-out a spongy parenchyma tissue called pith. (See Figure 12-11.) Monocot stems are surrounded by epidermal cells that produce a waxy, waterproof cuticle. Examples of herbaceous monocots include tulips, onions, and grasses. Much of the food consumed by humans and domestic animals is produced from herbaceous monocots such as wheat, corn, and rice.

The vascular bundles of herbaceous dicot stems are arranged in the form of a ring. (See Figure 12-12.) The xylem and the phloem in the vascular bundles are separated by a continuous ring of meristematic tissue called cambium. The pith rays are thought to be areas where food and water can be exchanged between vascular bundles. The entire stem is surrounded by chlorophyll-containing epidermal cells and a waxy cuticle. The cambium layer increases the width of a dicot stem by forming extra xylem on the inside of the ring and extra phloem on the outside. However, the stems of herbaceous

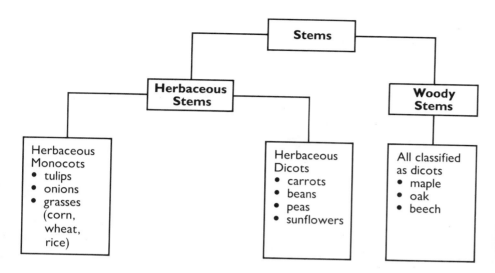

```
                    ┌─────────────┐
                    │   Stems     │
                    └─────────────┘
            ┌──────────────┴──────────────┐
    ┌───────────────┐              ┌──────────────┐
    │  Herbaceous   │              │    Woody     │
    │    Stems      │              │    Stems     │
    └───────────────┘              └──────────────┘
   ┌────────┴────────┐                    │
┌─────────────┐ ┌─────────────┐   ┌─────────────┐
│ Herbaceous  │ │ Herbaceous  │   │ All classified│
│ Monocots    │ │ Dicots      │   │ as dicots   │
│ • tulips    │ │ • carrots   │   │ • maple     │
│ • onions    │ │ • beans     │   │ • oak       │
│ • grasses   │ │ • peas      │   │ • beech     │
│   (corn,    │ │ • sunflowers│   │             │
│   wheat,    │ │             │   │             │
│   rice)     │ │             │   │             │
└─────────────┘ └─────────────┘   └─────────────┘
```

FIGURE 12-13 Stem classification in angiosperms

This chestnut tree is hundreds of years old, but few woody dicots live that long. Some sequoias and sitka spruces on the west coast of North America are at least 1000 years old, but these forest giants are gymnosperms, not angiosperms.

dicots never grow very large because they die back when the weather turns cold. Nevertheless, herbaceous dicots are an important food source. Examples include vegetables such as carrots, peas, and beans; soft fruits such as strawberries and cantaloupes; and oil-producing plants such as sunflowers.

Tough, rigid **woody stems** are found in shrubs and trees. (See Figure 12-13.) The stems of these plants do not die back in cold weather. In fact, the stems of some trees may live up to a century or even longer. All angiosperms with woody stems are classified as dicots because they all have a cambium ring between the xylem and the phloem.

The meristematic tissue in the cambium produces new layers of xylem and phloem each year. The new phloem crushes the old phloem against the outer bark. However, much more xylem is produced than phloem, so the central part of the stem develops a thicker core, which helps to support the ever-increasing mass of the tree. This thick xylem layer is commonly called wood.

The xylem vessels produced in the spring, when water is more plentiful, are much larger than those formed in the drier summer months. The spring xylem appears as a light band and the summer xylem appears as a dark band. Together, they form an annual ring. The width of the two xylem bands in each ring indicates what the weather conditions for that growing season were like. Tree-ring records also reveal climate changes, droughts, insect infestations, and forest fires.

Only the most recently formed xylem bands actually transport materials upward. This xylem is called sapwood because it is saturated with tree sap. The inner, older xylem that functions only as support is called heartwood. Heartwood is darker in colour than sapwood and is of greater economic value to the lumber industry.

The outer bark on the stem is formed by a second layer of meristematic tissue that develops around the outside of the stem. This new meristem, the

In trees, more xylem is produced to supply the massive amount of water that is lost in transpiration. Only 2% of the water that is transported through the xylem is actually used in photosynthesis, and 98% is lost in transpiration.

The strength of wood made it one of the earliest and most widely used building materials.

cork cambium, forms two types of tissue: cork on the outside of the stem and parenchyma on the inside next to the phloem. As the stem grows, the outer layers of cork cells die and become impregnated with a waxy material that protects the stem from diseases and insects, and also reduces water loss.

Palm trees are monocots that have successfully adapted to a warm growing climate.

LABORATORY EXERCISE 12-4
Investigating Stem Structure

In this exercise, you will use slides and a microscope to compare the tissues of herbaceous monocot and dicot stems. You will also examine cross sections and prepared slides of woody dicot stems to observe the growth of spring and summer xylem.

Stem Adaptations

Some stems have structural adaptations that enable them to survive and reproduce successfully in their usual environments. A **stolon**, for example, is a slender modified stem that grows into the air and then curves downward. (See Figure 13-15 on page 441.) Wherever a stolon touches the soil, it sends out roots and produces a complete new plant at that point. This feature enables strawberry plants, for example, to spread rapidly.

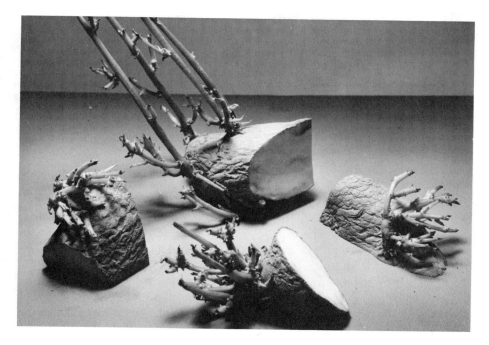

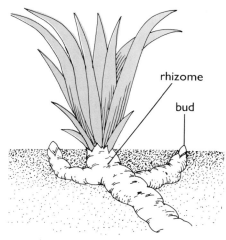

FIGURE 12-14 The rhizome of an iris plant

Underground stems called **rhizomes** grow horizontally through the soil but never appear above ground. (See Figure 12-14.) The thick, fleshy rhizome of the flowering iris produces leaves that grow upward and roots at nodes along its length. The starch stored inside this modified stem provides food for rapid, early spring growth.

A more familiar plant with underground stems is the common potato. The edible part of the potato is a swollen, starch-filled tuber. Tubers differ from rhizomes because they appear only at intervals. The rest of the potato plant's underground stem is quite slender. If a tuber is left in the ground or replanted, new shoots and roots will grow from the nodes or "eyes."

Many spring flowers grow from **corms** or **bulbs**. Both are specialized underground stems, but their structures are somewhat different. (See Figures 12-15 and 12-16.) Corms are short, thick, fleshy underground stems that later develop leaves and roots. Bulbs consist mainly of numerous thick, fleshy leaves that surround a very small, flattened stem. Like other underground stems, corms and bulbs provide the food needed for rapid, early spring growth. Crocuses and gladiolas develop corms; onions and daffodils develop bulbs.

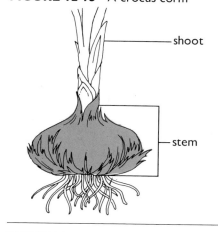

FIGURE 12-15 A crocus corm

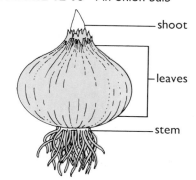

FIGURE 12-16 An onion bulb

Section Review Questions

1. What are three important functions of stems?
2. Where is the meristematic tissue located in growing stems?
3. a) Why are herbaceous stems green?
   b) What function can they perform given the above?

Papermaking

A plant's strength is found in its cellulose fibres. These fibres, which raise a plant's flower to the sun or hold a tree steady in the wind, have been used for centuries to make a substance that is both strong and flexible, even when pressed to a great thinness. In paper, cellulose fibres have been detached and then meshed to form an interlocking, smooth, flat mat.

Papermaking technology has advanced, but the basic principles have not changed since its invention by the Chinese nearly 2000 years ago. Now as then, the plant's cellulose fibres must first be separated and diffused throughout a liquid pulp. The Chinese inventors of papermaking accomplished this by boiling rags and plant fibres until a homogenous, hot liquid was formed.

Today, pulp is commonly made in one of two ways. Mechanical pulping involves crushing and grinding coniferous woods between rotating grindstones until loose cellulose fibres can be washed away with water. The chemical method of pulping is more efficient. As well as separating cellulose fibres, chemicals dissolve the lignin glue that holds cellulose fibres together in a living plant. As a result of this process, a lower yield of higher quality pulp is produced.

Papermaking from pulp is also essentially unchanged. In the ancient Chinese method, a horizontal sieve was dipped into the pulp, and the resultant thin layer was left to drain before pressing. Today, the horizontal sieve is sometimes made of wire or plastic, and the screen is vibrated

rapidly to mesh the pulp fibres together. This vibration strengthens the paper and removes water. A vacuum underneath the screen dries the paper efficiently. Then the thin pulp sheet is passed between massive pressure rollers and over cylinder driers.

The pulp and paper industry in Canada is important and profitable, but it consumes approximately 90 000 000 m^3 of wood annually. Concern over depletion of forest resources has raised interest in recycling, but recycling alone will not reduce the use of forests for paper products. Demand for paper should continue to increase as populations rise. Also, certain papers cannot be made from recycled material because of impurities in the recycled material. Even if effective recycling programs were in place, it is uncertain how much paper would be recycled. As yet, recycling programs have not been successful in Canada.

4. How do the vascular bundles of monocot and dicot stems compare?

5. How are woody stems different from herbaceous stems?

6. a) How do the xylem vessels produced in a tree change with the seasons?
   b) What do these bands of xylem tell you about the environment the tree exists in?

7. List four stem adaptations and state an example of a plant that demonstrates each adaptation.

12.4 Leaves and Photosynthesis

Leaves are the final destination for the water and the dissolved minerals that enter a plant through its root hairs and travel upward through its stem. The principal function of leaves is the manufacture of food for all other plant organs and parts through a process called **photosynthesis**.

carbon dioxide + water + light energy $\xrightarrow{\text{chlorophyll}}$ glucose + oxygen

To carry out this chemical reaction, a leaf must be able to gather the raw materials it needs, collect the required light energy, transport the manufactured food to other plant parts, and dispose of any waste products.

Structures for Collecting Energy

Leaves come in a variety of shapes and sizes. Leaf variety, combined with the way leaves are arranged on a plant, maximizes the total leaf area exposed to sunlight. Exposure to sunlight is critical since photosynthesis cannot take place without adequate light.

Left: A tree in autumn after it has lost its leaves. **Right:** The same tree in summer with new leaves.

How do the adaptations of tropical jungle plants help them obtain sunlight?

How do the adaptations of desert plants help them survive in their environment?

The epidermis of a leaf is transparent, which allows a maximum amount of light to pass through it to the chlorenchyma cells that make up most of a leaf's spongy internal tissues. The chlorenchyma cells also contain **chlorophyll**, a chemical compound that absorbs and traps light energy for use in photosynthesis.

In addition to these features, many leaves have special adaptations that suit them for collecting sunlight in their usual environments. Tropical jungle plants, for example, generally have large, flat leaves suited for collecting the diffuse sunlight that filters through the thick forest canopy. By contrast, the leaves of desert plants are usually small. Cactus leaves are mere thorns, and photosynthesis takes place in the chlorenchyma cells of the thick, fleshy stem.

Structures for Transporting Liquids

Most leaves have highly visible veins, which are firm, tube-like structures that are continuous with the vascular tissue of a plant's roots and stem. The veins provide some support for soft leaf tissue, but their main function is to transport the liquids involved in photosynthesis. Xylem tissue in the veins conducts water and dissolved minerals into the leaf. Phloem tissue conducts a water solution of glucose away from the leaf into other plant organs. This efficient two-way transportation enables leaves to manufacture glucose or other plant sugars continuously during daylight hours.

Water is vitally important to photosynthesis, and all leaves have a waterproof outer coating called the cuticle. The cuticle is a waxy layer that is secreted by the outer epidermis. It helps prevent dehydration of a leaf's delicate internal tissues. The cuticle also blocks the entry of disease-causing fungi and bacteria. Acid rain and other airborne pollutants can break down the

The veins in this maple leaf make up its complex transportation system.

The fine, fuzzy hairs on the leaf of the African violet help it conserve water.

cuticle layer. Scientists think this breakdown may be an important contributing factor in the early death of maples and other tree species in areas where acid rain is a problem.

Many plants have other leaf adaptations that help them conserve the water they need for photosynthesis. The leaves of desert plants, for example, are fleshy rather than thin, with surface areas that seem quite small. The leaves of most desert plants also have an extra-thick cuticle. The African violet conserves water with a fuzzy layer of fine hairs that grow from its outer epidermis. The hairs help retain any moisture near the epidermis, and protect the plant from air currents that might dry it out. Some cacti have numerous fine thorns that function in a similar way.

LABORATORY EXERCISE 12-5
Investigating Leaf Structure

In this exercise, you will examine and compare prepared slides of leaf tissue from various aquatic and terrestrial environments.

Structures for Exchanging Gases

When examined with a microscope, the epidermis of a leaf shows the presence of pores called **stomata**. These openings allow gases to enter and to leave the internal tissues. The carbon dioxide gas needed for photosynthesis comes from

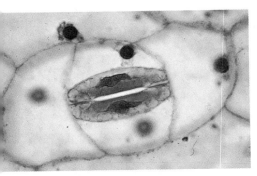

A stomata is a plant structure for exchanging gases.

the air surrounding the leaves. The oxygen gas produced by photosynthesis passes out through the stomata into the air. Guard cells around the stomata adjust the size of the openings to suit the plant's needs. Most plants keep their stomata open only during the day.

The amount of oxygen produced during photosynthesis far exceeds that needed by the plant for cellular respiration. To the plant, the excess oxygen is a waste product, but heterotrophs such as humans use oxygen for cellular respiration, then exhale carbon dioxide gas, which may be used by plants. Therefore, the atmospheric levels of these two vital gases remain nearly constant.

Adaptations for the Canadian Environment

The photographs below are of the same species, *Pinus banksiana*, or common jack pine. The jack pines that grow in the Northwest Territories never reach a great size, and are not suitable as shade trees or for forest products. Yet, on favourable sites northwest of Lake Superior, the same species grows so large that the trees are harvested for manufacturing pulp and paper. The jack pine is an example of a relatively unspecialized vascular plant, which can thrive in a variety of environments, but reaches its full potential only where growing conditions are most favourable.

There is a sharp contrast between the jack pine and the cactus, a vascular plant so specialized that it can live in only one biome. A **biome** is a large geographical area with a distinctive climate and a dominant type of natural vegetation. Tropical rain forests and deserts are examples of biomes. The cactus is well adapted for life in the desert biome, but it is poorly adapted to survive in Canadian biomes.

Left: A stunted jack pine growing in unfavourable conditions. **Right:** Favourable growing conditions encourage greater growth for jack pines.

INQUIRY ACTIVITY
Adaptations for Canadian Biomes

In this activity, you will examine photographs of several native Canadian plants and match each species with the biome to which it seems best adapted. Write your answers on a copy of the following chart. Beside each choice, list the structural adaptations that suit the plant to that particular environment.

Tundra

Prairie

Boreal forest

Temperate forest

Table 12-1   Adaptations for Canadian Biomes

Biome	Environmental Conditions	Plant Species	Structural Adaptation
Tundra (lichens, mosses, herbs; small, woody plants)	• precipitation:less than 250 mm/a • avg. wintertemp.: −27°C • avg. summertemp.: 5°C • soil: shallow, and poorly drained		
Prairie (tall grasses; few trees)	• precipitation:250-750 mm/a • avg. wintertemp.: −18°C • avg. summertemp.: 19°C • soil: deep, nutrient-rich, and well-drained		
Boreal Coniferous Forest (black spruce, white spruce, trembling aspen, willow)	• precipitation:380-1000 mm/a • avg. wintertemp.: −20°C • avg. summertemp.: 20°C • soil: deep, nutrient-poor, and poorly drained		
Temperate Deciduous Forest (beech, maple, walnut, hickory, oak)	• precipitation:750-1250 mm/a • avg. wintertemp.: 2°C • avg. summertemp.: 24°C • soil: deep, nutrient-rich, and well-drained		

Discussion Questions

1. a) Which of the biomes in the chart exist in your province?
   b) Which biomes exist in Canada?
2. Which biomes do you live in? How do you know?
3. Conduct library research to identify a vascular plant that is adapted to live only within your biome.

Section Review Questions

1. What is the principal function of leaves?
2. a) What is chlorophyll?
   b) Where is it found in leaves?
   c) What does chlorophyll have the ability to do?
3. a) What are the veins of a leaf composed of?
   b) What are two important functions of veins?
4. Where is the cuticle located in a leaf, and what is its function?
5. a) What are the stomata?
   b) What leaf structure adjusts their size?

Why does water condense on the inside of this plastic bag?

12.5 Transpiration, Transportation, and Translocation

Despite the presence of structures and adaptations to minimize water loss from leaf tissues, plants release surprisingly large amounts of water vapour into the air. If a small, potted house plant is sealed in a plastic bag and left in the light, you would observe numerous droplets of condensed water on the inside of the bag in a very short time. Water loss by plants is called **transpiration**. Careful measurements have shown that an average hectare of corn will transpire 900 000 L of water in one growing season. Imagine how much water is transpired by the rain forests of British Columbia.

LABORATORY EXERCISE 12-6
Factors Affecting Transpiration Rate

In this exercise, you will manipulate a variety of factors and observe how they affect the rate of transpiration in a vascular plant.

The Problem of Transpiration

For many years after it was first observed, transpiration presented biologists with a puzzling problem. In order to manufacture food, all plant leaves must receive adequate amounts of water. But transpiration measurements showed clearly that vascular plants deliver far more water than their leaves need for photosynthesis.

Why would a Douglas fir that is 70 m in height transport thousands of litres of water to its upper branches, only to release it through the stomata on its needle-like leaves? What are the physical forces that lift water to such a height?

Figure 12-17 demonstrates how remarkable these forces are. It summarizes the results of experiments comparing the height water can be raised to by a mechanical pump to that achieved by living plants. The plant is able to "out-lift" the best vacuum pump. But how is this possible?

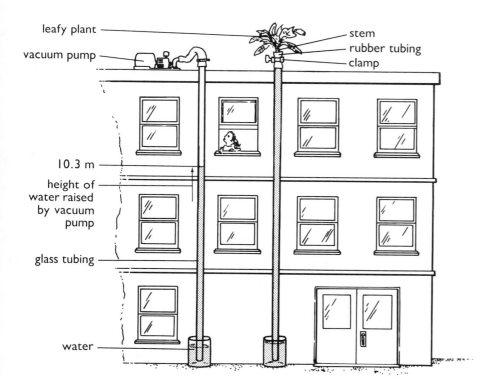

leafy plant
vacuum pump
stem
rubber tubing
clamp

10.3 m
height of water raised by vacuum pump
glass tubing
water

FIGURE 12-17 The height of water raised by a vacuum pump is less than that raised by a leafy plant.

Explaining Transpiration

Understanding the forces behind transpiration is important to scientists because the same forces deliver the water vascular plants need for photosynthesis. Transpiration also has a profound effect on the earth's water cycle and

FIGURE 12-18 A demonstration of root pressure in a tomato plant

FIGURE 12-19 A demonstration of capillarity

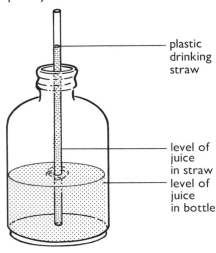

plastic drinking straw

level of juice in straw

level of juice in bottle

consequently on its weather. As a result, scientists have put forward several hypotheses to explain transpiration.

One hypothesis suggests that water is pushed upward by **root pressure**. Root pressure develops because the concentration of water in the soil around a root is much greater than the concentration of water inside the root. Therefore, water diffuses from the soil into the root. Experimental measurements show that tomato plants develop large root pressures that are enough to make the main stem squirt water when it is cut. (See Figure 12-18.)

However, root pressure cannot explain the transportation of water in most other plants. First, few plants other than the tomato develop large root pressures. Second, even the largest measured root pressures are not enough to lift water to the top of a Douglas fir. Third, root-pressure values are always lowest in summer, even when transpiration is at its peak.

Root pressure as a major factor in transpiration was finally discredited in 1960 when a team of plant physiologists conducted an experiment with rattan vines in the Australian jungle. They severed a vine close to the ground and placed the cut end in a pail of water. With no connections to its roots, the vine continued to deliver water to its upper foliage—50 m above the jungle floor.

Capillarity has also been suggested as an explanation for transpiration. Capillarity can be observed whenever a narrow tube is placed in a liquid. You have probably noticed the level of juice in a plastic drinking straw rising above the level of juice in the bottle. (See Figure 12-19.) The force behind capillarity is caused by two physical properties of water molecules: adhesion and cohesion.

Adhesion is the force of attraction between two unlike molecules. Adhesion between water molecules and the molecules in plastic is relatively high. As a result, water tends to cling to plastic. **Cohesion** is the force of attraction between like molecules. Cohesion between water molecules is relatively high.

Together, adhesion and cohesion cause capillarity. Adhesive forces attract water molecules at the top of the liquid column inside the straw toward the plastic. Cohesive forces make the water molecules farther down the column stick to the ones at the top and follow them upward, like links in a chain. The narrower the tube, the higher the water will rise, but there is an upper limit. Juice in a straw rises only so far and then stops. To make it move higher, you must exert a force at the top of the straw.

Since xylem forms narrow tube-like structures, capillarity must contribute to the upward movement of water in vascular plants. However, capillarity alone is not enough. Even the narrowest xylem tube cannot conduct water upward indefinitely without a force at its top.

Today, the most widely accepted explanation for transpiration is the **Transpiration-tension theory**. This theory states that water is pulled upward from the roots of a plant by the energy of the sun. (See Figure 12-20.) During photosynthesis, any water molecules near the open stomata of the leaves are likely to evaporate in the sun's heat. As each water molecule evaporates, it exerts a cohesive pull, or tension, on the molecule behind it, which, in turn,

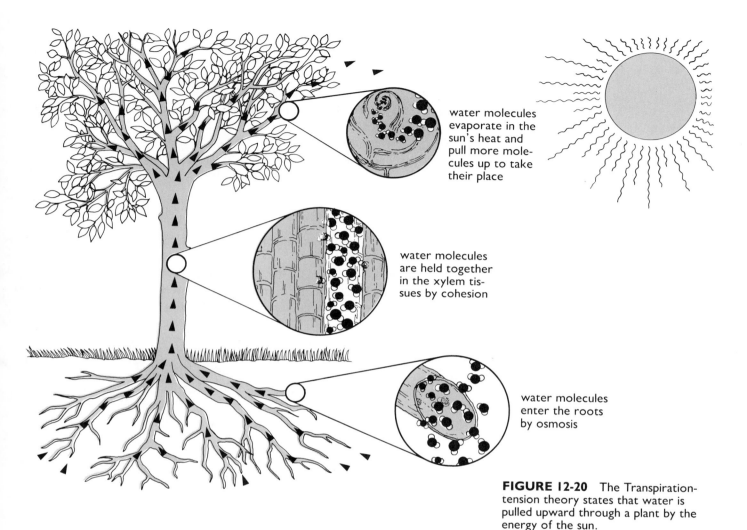

water molecules evaporate in the sun's heat and pull more molecules up to take their place

water molecules are held together in the xylem tissues by cohesion

water molecules enter the roots by osmosis

FIGURE 12-20 The Transpiration-tension theory states that water is pulled upward through a plant by the energy of the sun.

pulls on the molecule behind it and so on, all the way down the stem to the roots. This upward movement lowers the concentration of water molecules inside the root, so more water diffuses inward from the surrounding soil.

Translocation of Food

Translocation refers to the transportation of materials such as water, minerals, and food within a plant. In vascular plants, the translocation of water and dissolved minerals takes place within the xylem tubes. The translocation of dissolved food, or sap, takes place within the elongated sieve tubes of the phloem.

Food manufactured in the leaves is needed by every living cell in a plant to provide materials for growth and energy for all of its life functions. Any food that remains after these needs are met will be stored. In some plants, excess food is stored in the roots or the stem, so translocation is mainly a downward moving process. In other plants, food must be translocated upward for storage in fruits or seeds.

Upward translocation also occurs when spring sap rises in deciduous trees, providing food for growth of the next season's leaves. This upward movement cannot be explained by the Transpiration-tension theory, since sap rises at a time when the trees do not have any leaves. As yet, there is no explanation that satisfies all scientists, but biologists do have several clues to the puzzle.

- They know that phloem tissue is made of living cells (unlike xylem, which is made of dead cell walls).
- Phloem moves sap 1000 times more rapidly than it could move by simple diffusion.
- Damage to the phloem such as a browsing deer "girdling" a tree stops all movement.
- Simple diffusion should make sugar molecules spread out, but translocation moves sap into plant parts that already have high sugar levels.
- Experiments have shown that phloem cells use oxygen while translocating food.

Researchers have concluded that the phloem cells themselves somehow provide the energy for the translocation of food. This idea is sometimes referred to as bulk transport or mass transport, but the exact mechanism is not yet understood. If researchers can find an explanation for translocation soon, they may be able to explain why Canada's sugar maples are dying and understand how to apply the scientific knowledge needed to save them.

Section Review Questions

1. a) What is transpiration?
   b) How can the forces involved in transpiration be demonstrated?
2. How can the process of transpiration affect water cycle and weather patterns?
3. What are the two forces that cause capillarity in plants?
4. How does the Transpiration-tension theory explain the upward movement of fluids in plants?
5. a) Through which tissue does the translocation of plant food take place?
   b) In which direction(s) does this transportation occur?
6. What do researchers know about the transportation of foods through the phloem cells of plants?

Sugar Making

Certain plants store sugar in a more concentrated form than others do. This discovery, made in different places around the world at different times, has led to the extraction of sugar from a number of plants for use as a sweetener and food preservative.

At one time, all of Canada's sugar came from the sugar maple. Native people in North America were tapping maple trees long before Europeans arrived. Although technology has improved, the process of maple-sugar production remains essentially the same today. In early spring, maple sap, containing up to 2% sugar, begins to flow upward from the maple's roots through its phloem. Native people made axe cuts in the trees to drain sap. Successive freezings and boilings of the sap concentrated the sugar and removed water until maple butter, syrup, taffy, or sugar remained.

European settlers continued the maple-tapping tradition so that Canada's maples fulfilled the colonies' sugar needs until the mid-1800s. At this time, however, cane sugar from the West Indies became cheaper to import than domestic maple sugar was to produce, and maple-sugar producers switched to producing more expensive specialty products for export.

Sugar cane was first used to produce sugar in India in approximately 3000 B.C. From there, the practice spread east and west with the spread of the plant, until Europeans brought sugar cane to the Caribbean. Cane sugar is now the major source of sugar for Canada. Cane sugar and sugar beets account for most of the world's sugar production.

Sugar cane is a tall, bamboo-like grass that grows in tropical areas. Once mature, the sugar-cane stems are cut and stripped of leaves, then sent to a mill where they are cleaned and crushed between large rollers. The sap from inside the hollow canes is strained before lime is added to remove impurities. This sugary liquid is boiled in a vacuum until

crystals appear. More water is removed in a centrifuge, which spins the raw sugar crystals until they are dry. At a refinery, the crystals are sorted by size and colour into different grades such as granulated, golden, and brown.

In western societies, we are obsessed with sweetness. In his book, *The Scotch*, Canadian-born economist John Kenneth Galbraith writes that as a boy he loved the taste of maple syrup so much that the dead leaves, brown moths, and drowned field mice in the sap buckets did not bother him. The syrup tasted better with the additions, he said. Although we know the amount of sugar we consume —about 47 kg per person per year —is excessive, instead of changing our lifestyles and cutting down on sugar, we search for artificial sweeteners that more closely resemble sugar.

Chapter Review

Key Words

apical meristems
biome
fibrous roots
herbaceous stems
leaves
meristem
phloem
photosynthesis
rhizomes
roots
stems
stolon
stomata

taproot
translocation
transpiration
Transpiration-tension
  theory
vascular bundles
vascular cambium
vascular cylinder
vascular plants
vascular tissue
woody stems
xylem

Recall Questions

Multiple Choice

1. The plant tissue in the stem that specializes in continued reproduction and differentiation is called
   a) pith   d) cambium
   b) xylem   e) sieve tubes
   c) phloem

2. The major difference between stems and roots
   a) is the absence of xylem in stems
   b) is the arrangement of the tissues
   c) is the absence of phloem in roots
   d) is both a and b
   e) is none of the above

3. The absorption of materials by root hairs takes place by
   a) osmosis   d) a and b only
   b) diffusion   e) a, b, and c
   c) active transport

4. Food produced in the leaves is transported to the roots by the
   a) cambium   d) pith
   b) phloem   e) cortex
   c) xylem

5. Which statement concerning xylem and phloem is not correct?
   a) Phloem cells consist of dead conducting cells.
   b) Phloem cells transport sugars in the plant.
   c) Xylem cells are responsible for the transportation of water.
   d) Xylem cells make up the wood in a typical tree.
   e) Xylem cells are composed of vessel cells and tracheids.

6. Which of the following statements comparing fibrous and taproot systems is incorrect?
   a) Fibrous root systems are characteristic of grasses.
   b) Fibrous root systems absorb water less efficiently than taproots.
   c) Plants that have taproots are more effective at preventing erosion than plants that have fibrous roots.
   d) Taproots are able to reach deep into the soil for water.

Fill in the Blanks

1. All plant tissues originate from one type of tissue called _____.

2. The primary purpose of any root system is _____.

3. The root hair is actually a specialized _____ cell.

4. Cork cells on the stem are impregnated with a waxy substance that protects the cells from _____.

5. The inactive central xylem found in certain plants is called _____. This material is found in plants such as _____ but not in _____.

6. The loss of water in a plant through evaporation is also known as _____.

Short Answers

1. What is differentiation and why is it important to plants?

2. Distinguish between parenchyma and sclerenchyma.

3. How is the function of a sieve tube cell and a companion cell linked?

4. Compare the arrangement of the vascular tissues in herbaceous monocot and dicot stems.

5. a) What is the function of the cork cambium?
   b) How does cork form?
6. a) What is the bark of a woody dicot composed of?
   b) How does this bark form?
7. How do the leaves of tropical plants and jungle plants differ? Why?
8. a) What is transpiration?
   b) Explain how transpiration can affect the water cycle and the weather.
9. a) How does the Transpiration-tension theory differ from the root-pressure theory?
   b) On what physical properties of water is the Transpiration-tension theory based?

Application Questions

1. Predict the effect an increase in rainfall would have on woody dicots in a tundra biome.
2. Explain the effect of hot dry weather on coniferous forests in northern Ontario.
3. Describe a type of stomata that would better suit a desert plant to its natural habitat.
4. Describe the effect on a leaf of a mysterious disease that weakens the cells in the leaf's spongy layer.

Problem Solving

1. Some algae found in lakes grow to a length of 50 m. These plants lack a vascular system and supportive tissue. Explain how this occurs.

2. The leaf can be described as the functional organ of the plant. Look up the definition of the word organ and explain why such a statement can be made.
3. a) What is the eventual outcome of too much transpiration in a plant?
   b) What have some plants developed to prevent this from occurring?
4. How might the guard cells of plants in a desert biome differ from the guard cells of plants in a deciduous forest?
5. A plant that has been left in direct sunlight too long has wilted. Describe how you would revive the plant, and explain how you might modify the factors affecting its environment to speed the plant's recovery.

Extensions

1. Research the logging industry in relation to the production of pulp and paper. Comment on the use of new hybrid poplar trees for pulp use.
2. Visit an arboretum and use a classification key to help you identify the various species of conifer and deciduous trees.
3. Make a collection of the leaves from your neighbourhood. Construct a leaf press and preserve the specimens, identifying each with its proper scientific name.
4. Write letters to major logging and lumber companies in Canada asking for data about the number of trees being cut compared to the number of trees being planted. What conclusions can you draw from this data?

CHAPTER

13

Plant Growth and Reproduction

Agriculture is one of Canada's most successful and stable industries. Canada's well-being depends on the success of modern farming. This success, in turn, depends on agriculturalists' thorough understanding of plant growth and reproduction.

Continued efforts to increase crop yields will ensure an abundance of food for the future.

An understanding of plant reproduction is used in a number of ways. An apple-orchard owner can arrange for a local beekeeper to pollinate the orchard so that as many apple blossoms develop into

mature fruits as possible. This co-operative effort will improve crop yield. Such arrangements are possible only through careful observation of the process and timing of sexual reproduction in flowering plants.

As well, insight into plant reproduction has been used to

protect and strengthen certain crop species. For example, researchers have developed strains of wheat and oats resistant to their natural enemies. In Canada, research has also produced crops capable of high yields in a short growing season. Techniques to improve crops are constantly multiplying and becoming more sophisticated, and include an increasing number of genetic engineering techniques.

Understanding plant-growth conditions allows agriculturalists to manipulate these conditions in search of higher yields. Although climatic conditions cannot be controlled, agriculturalists have learned to control some factors. Soil conditions are rarely perfect, but with a knowledge of a crop's optimum soil conditions, improvements can be made. Canadian farmers regularly apply fertilizers to help match the soil's nutrient content to the needs of the target crop. The soil's moisture content can also be altered through the use of drainage and irrigation systems.

Agriculture has moved indoors where researchers have more control over plant-growth factors. Greenhouses can be used to control temperature to exact specifications. As well, crops can be protected from natural enemies. More advanced controlled environments, in which the amount of light reaching the plant can be controlled, are now being developed. An environment designed to grow lettuce has been tested successfully. A greenhouse may yield ten times the produce of a farmer's field, but a completely controlled environment may yield ten times more than a greenhouse. For some crops, food factories where crops are grown from seed to maturity under artificial light and completely controlled conditions may be the future.

As you read this chapter, consider other plant characteristics that might be used by agriculturalists to improve crops. Can you think of techniques that might be developed to take advantage of these characteristics?

Chapter Objectives

When you complete this chapter, you should:

1. Appreciate the environmental factors that affect plant growth.

2. Appreciate and understand the importance of flower structure and function in the sexual reproduction of plants.

3. Be able to explain the role of pollination, fertilization, seed dispersal, and seed germination in the sexual reproduction of plants.

4. Know how to compare the structure of a dicotyledon and a monocotyledon seed through laboratory examination.

5. Be able to describe the role in the germination process of the seed coat, micropyle, endosperm, cotyledons, radicle, apical meristems, and hypocotyl.

6. Be able to describe the conditions necessary for seed germination.

7. Be able to describe the effects of two plant-growth regulators other than auxins. (For example, gibberellins or cytokinins.)

8. Be able to describe two or three examples of tropisms in plants and explain the role of auxins in these responses.

9. Be able to describe several methods of asexual reproductive methods used to reproduce plants.

10. Be able to perform experiments to study germination and early plant growth.

11. Be able to use the scientific method to study plant responses to external stimuli.

The largest group of gymnosperms are the conifers, which include cedars, spruces, and pines. Although conifers make up only a small percentage of the plant kingdom, their populations are large and widespread, especially in northern Canada. Conifers have great economic importance as sources for lumber and pulp and paper.

13.1 Reproduction in Vascular Plants

Several hundred million years ago, when the earth was a much wetter place than it is today, huge forests of tree-sized ferns dominated the plant world. Today, the landscape is dominated by **angiosperms**, or flowering vascular plants, which account for approximately 85% of all plant species and almost 95% of all vascular plant species. (See Figure 13-1.) The great success of flowering plants can be attributed to their reproductive methods. A brief discussion of reproductive methods in other vascular plants will help you understand what gave the flowering plants their competitive advantage.

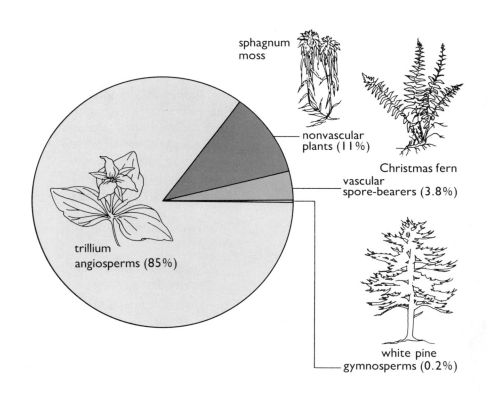

FIGURE 13-1 Approximate percentages of different plant groups making up the plant kingdom

Reproduction in Spore-Bearing Vascular Plants

Today, ferns and other spore-bearing vascular plants such as whisk ferns, horsetails, and club mosses make up only about 4-5% of all vascular plant species. Figure 13-2 shows the life cycle of a typical fern. Sexual reproduction in ferns follows a life cycle similar to that in mosses. **Spores** from the fern do not develop directly into young **sporophytes** (spore-producing plants).

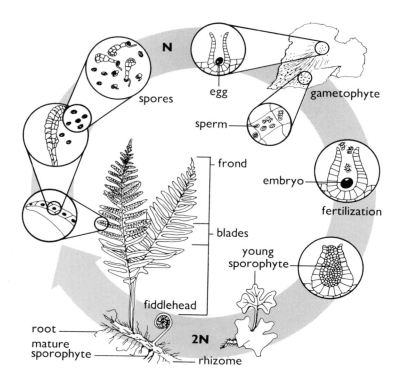

FIGURE 13-2 The life cycle of a typical fern

Instead, the spores germinate into **gametophytes**. These specialized, independent plant bodies produce **gametes**, which are sex cells with half the usual number of chromosomes for the species (N for each gamete).

Fern gametophytes contain both types of sex organs. Male sex organs produce sperm that fertilize eggs from the female sex organ. The resulting zygote contains a full chromosome count (2N) and eventually develops into another sporophyte. This is the mature plant you know as a fern. The gametophyte bodies are quite small and usually grow unnoticed in the litter on the forest floor.

Ferns and other spore-bearing vascular plants no longer dominate the plant world because they require water for fertilization. Since the sperm must be able to swim to the egg, these plants can only grow well in a wet climate. Today's world, much drier than it was millions of years ago, favours plants that can carry out fertilization without water.

Reproduction in Seed-Bearing Vascular Plants

Gymnosperms make up less than 5% of all vascular plant species, but they have great economic and ecological importance because they grow so large and in such huge numbers. Such growth is possible because the male gametes

Most gymnosperms are tree-sized and tend to grow in huge forests with only one or two species. Tree-sized angiosperms such as maple, beech, oak, and hickory tend to grow in mixed stands with small populations of each.

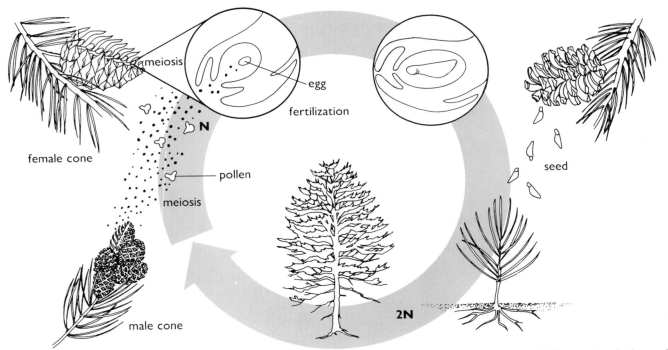

female cone

N

pollen

meiosis

male cone

meiosis

egg

fertilization

seed

2N

FIGURE 13-3 The life cycle of a typical gymnosperm

of gymnosperms are embedded in grains of pollen, which are tiny, independent structures that can be spread by the wind.

The life cycle of a conifer such as the pine is typical of gymnosperms. (See Figure 13-3.) The tree itself is the sporophyte stage. It produces two kinds of cones: small, soft male cones and larger, hard female cones. The male cones produce millions of pollen grains that contain sperm cells with half the usual number of chromosomes (N). Similarly, the female cones produce egg cells with half the chromosome count (N). When released, the pollen enters the open scales of the female cone, and the sperm fertilize the eggs to form zygotes with a full chromosome count (2N).

Inside the female cone, the zygote develops into an embryo plant enclosed in a seed coat with a wing-like structure. When released, the winged seeds can be carried great distances by the wind. Each seed has the potential to develop into a new sporophyte plant if it lands on a site that offers suitable growing conditions.

Reproduction in Flowering Vascular Plants

Flowers are specialized reproductive structures that form the seeds from which all angiosperms develop. Flowers give angiosperms several reproductive advantages over gymnosperms. First, relying on wind to transfer pollen means that much of the pollen produced by gymnosperms never fertilizes an egg. But the brightly coloured and scented flowers of angiosperms attract insects and other animals that carry pollen directly from flower to flower. This means of transferring pollen greatly increases the likelihood that gametes will unite. Second, most flowers contain both male and female reproductive parts, which makes self-fertilization possible. Third, angiosperm seeds develop in and are protected by a fruit. In fact, the term angiosperm means ''covered seed.'' The term gymnosperm means ''naked seed.'' These ''naked'' seeds, although not totally exposed, are not as well protected as the seeds of angiosperms. The fruit of an angiosperm helps to increase a plant's chances of survival because it provides food for the embryo and has structures that help spread the seeds.

Flower Structure and Function

Figure 13-4 shows the structure of a typical flower. A flower consists of male and female reproductive parts, which are surrounded by specialized leaf-like structures held on the widened tip of a stem. The male structure, the **stamen**, is made up of two parts. The stalk-like **filaments** support the **anthers**, where pollen grains containing male sex cells are formed.

The female structure, the **pistil**, is made up of three parts. Its enlarged **ovary** is connected by a tube-like **style** to the wide, sticky **stigma** at the top. **Ovules** containing female sex cells develop within the ovary.

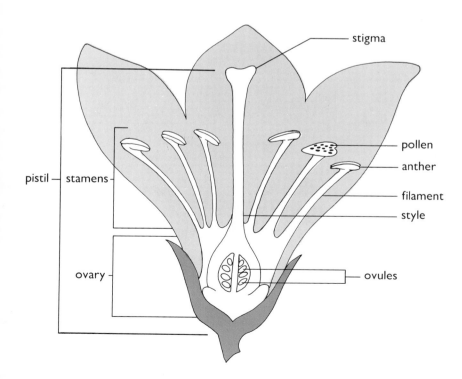

FIGURE 13-4 The structure of a typical flower

Flowers with both male and female reproductive parts are called **perfect flowers**. Flowers with only male or female parts, but not both, are called **imperfect flowers**.

The function of these reproductive structures is to produce gametes with half the number of chromosomes usual for the species. The pollen grains themselves are not actually gametes. Rather, they are very small gametophytes. These pollen grains do eventually form sperm cells, but not until they reach a stigma. Figure 13-5 shows the development of mature pollen grains, each of which contains only two cells. The **generative cell** will develop into sperm, and the **tube cell** will help the sperm reach the egg.

The female gametophyte develops inside the ovule, where the nucleus of a specialized cell divides repeatedly. (See Figure 13-6.) The resulting gametophyte consists of three haploid cells. One is an egg cell ready to be fertilized. The other two eventually produce food for the seed.

FIGURE 13-5 The formation of pollen grains in the anther

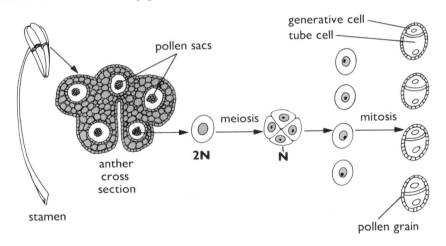

FIGURE 13-6 Ovule formation within the ovary of the pistil

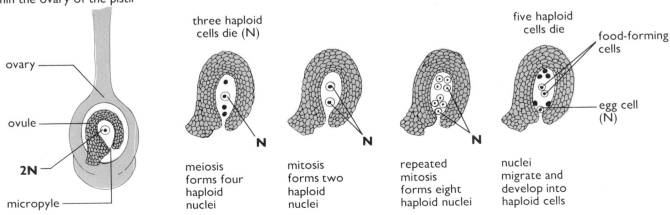

UNIT III

Plants and Fungi

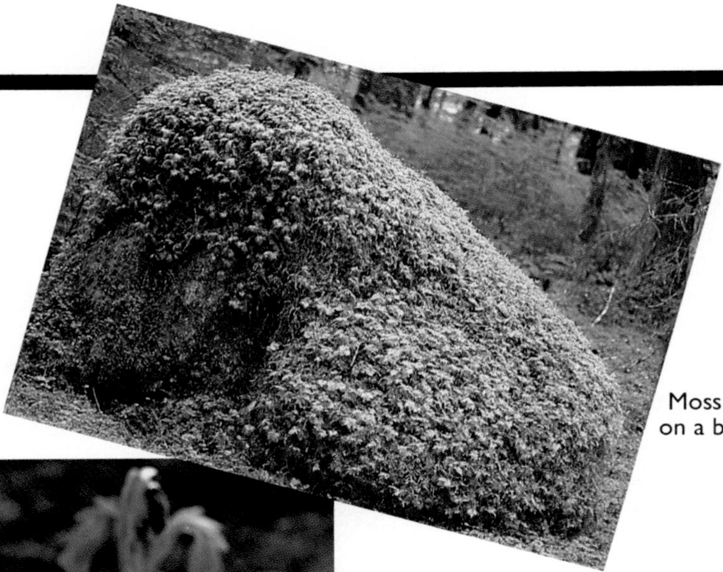

Moss mat on a boulder

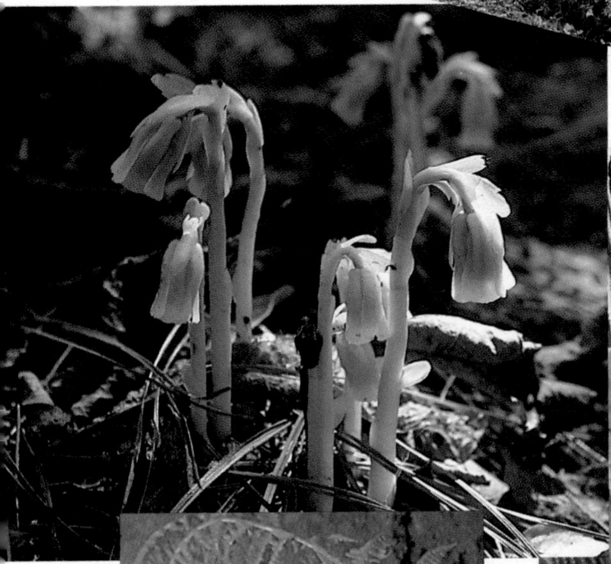

Indian pipes/ *Monotropa uniflora*

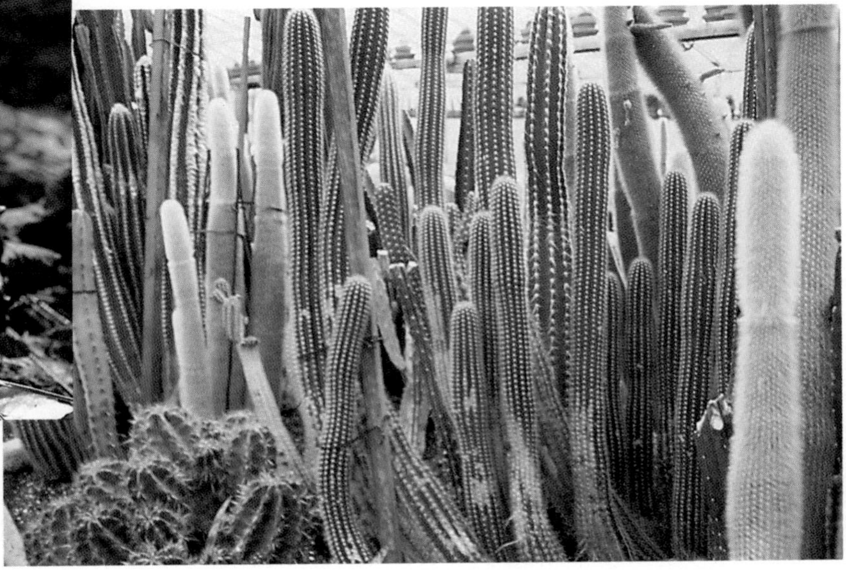

Cacti

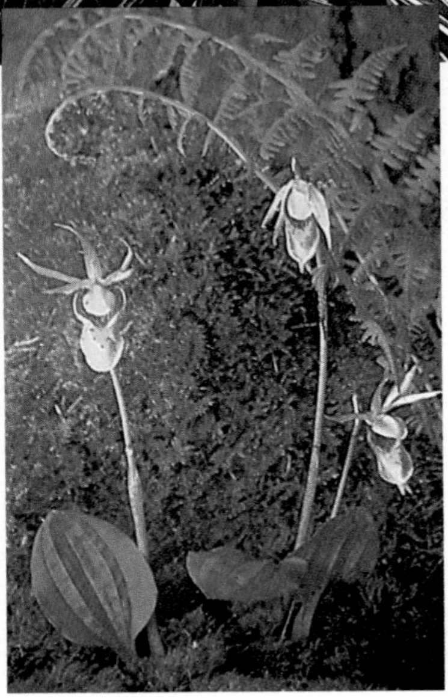

Orchids on a tree trunk

Chanterelle/*Cantharellus cibarius*

Red cup fungus/ *Sarcoscypha coccina*

Vermillion chanterelle/ *Cantharellus cinnabarinus*

Penicillium mould on tangerines

Dodder/*Cuscuta*

Slime mould/ *Physarum polycephalum*

Pollination

Pollination is the process by which mature pollen is transferred from anther to stigma. External agents often assist in this process. Insects such as bees may be attracted to brightly coloured, scented flowers. As these insects search for nectar, pollen sticks to their legs and abdomens. The pollen is then transferred from the anther to the stigma of the same flower or to that of a different flower. Birds such as the hummingbird transfer pollen with their long beaks and tongues as they look for nectar in the flower.

In a few angiosperms such as grasses and grains, pollen is carried by the wind from one flower to another. Such flowers are usually dull and may even lack petals. This is an adaptation that exposes the anthers ensuring that their pollen grains are easily caught by the wind.

DID YOU KNOW?
Hummingbirds seem to be particularly attracted to red. Flowering plants such as the red-hot poker in the garden will increase your opportunities for watching these interesting birds.

When pollen is transferred within the same flower, **self-pollination** has occurred. This method limits the amount of variation possible in the offspring since all characteristics are inherited from the same parent plant. **Cross-pollination** occurs when pollen from one flower is transferred to the stigma of another flower. This method increases the likelihood of variation since the offspring can inherit characteristics from two different parent plants. Many floral adaptations increase the chances of cross-pollination occurring, therefore maximizing the chances of variation from one generation to the next. For example, flowers such as the sage flower cannot self-pollinate because their anthers and ovaries mature at different times. Other flowers such as those of willow and poplar trees are imperfect and, having only male or female reproductive structures, are unable to pollinate themselves.

Researchers can often control pollination for their own purposes. When experimenting to create new hybrid species, researchers can use small paintbrushes to transfer the pollen of one species to the pistils of a second species. Small bags are placed over the flowers to prevent unwanted pollen from other species contaminating the combination being tested. In this way, reseachers can be sure that the new hybrid species is a result of a combination of characteristics from the two selected parent species.

Flower shape, colour, and arrangement facilitate pollination. **Left:** The everlasting pea's asymmetrical, self-enclosing petals help in self-pollination. **Centre:** The rose's brightly coloured, symmetrical petals attract insects. **Right:** Manitoba maples have only flowers with stamens or flowers with pistils.

The development of a cherry from flower to fruit

Fertilization and Seed Formation

When you bite into an apple, a cherry, or a tomato, you are eating a **fruit**. A fruit is the ripened seed container, or ovary, of what was once a flower. But what has occurred since the pollen landed on the stigma? First, special chemicals in the stigma cause the tube cell in each pollen grain to form a **pollen tube**. (See Figure 13-7.) The pollen tube works its way down the style toward the ovary. Inside the tube, the generative cell divides to produce two identical **sperm nuclei**.

When the pollen tube reaches the ovule, its contents enter through the **micropyle**. One sperm nucleus fertilizes the egg cell to produce a zygote. The zygote will become the embryo of a new plant. The second sperm nucleus joins other nuclei in the ovule to form a mass of tissue called the **endosperm**. The embryo will feed on the endosperm until the seed is planted and begins to germinate. The embryo, endosperm, and surrounding membranes, or seed coat, will eventually form the mature seed. As the surrounding ovary matures, it forms a fruit that helps protect the seed, or seeds, and aids in dispersal.

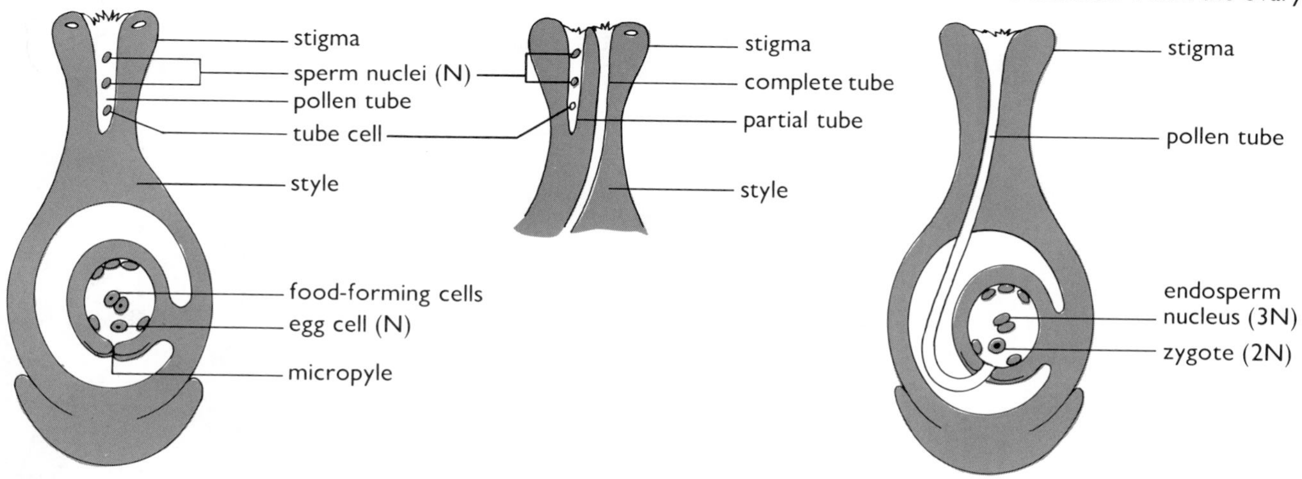

FIGURE 13-7 Pollen tube formation and fertilization within the ovary

LABORATORY EXERCISE 13-1
Investigating Seed Structure

Angiosperms are classified into two groups on the basis of seed structure. Plants with seeds that separate easily into two sections are called dicots. Those with seeds that do not separate naturally are called monocots. In this exercise, you will dissect, identify, and compare the parts of representative dicot and monocot seeds.

Seed Structure and Function

A bean seed splits naturally into halves. Each half, called a **cotyledon**, digests and stores food from the endosperm. In the bean seed, all of the endosperm has been converted into stored food for the embryo. Because bean seeds have two cotyledons, a bean plant is referred to as a **dicotyledon** or **dicot**. A corn seed contains only one cotyledon, an embryo, and some endosperm that has not yet been converted by the cotyledon into stored food. Corn is a **monocotyledon** or **monocot**. As Figure 13-8 shows, dicots and monocots also have other structural differences.

The tiny embryonic plant that develops within the seed is made up of three sections. The **epicotyl** holds the first set of leaves and will become the first growing shoot of the new plant. The centre section, the **hypocotyl**, will

FIGURE 13-8 Structural comparison of a typical dicot and a typical monocot

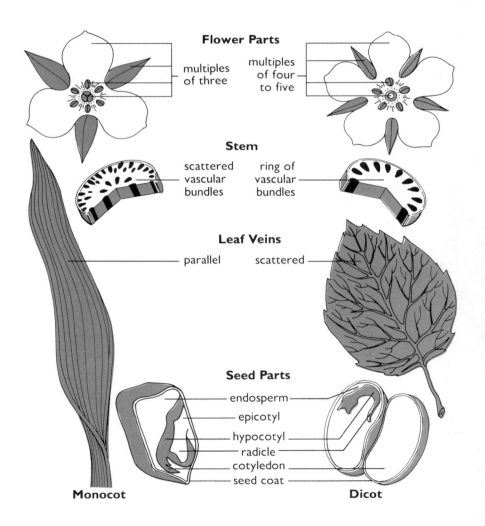

Flower Parts

multiples of three

multiples of four to five

Stem

scattered vascular bundles

ring of vascular bundles

Leaf Veins

parallel   scattered

Seed Parts

endosperm
epicotyl
hypocotyl
radicle
cotyledon
seed coat

Monocot   Dicot

develop into the lower stem in some plants and the upper root in others. The **radicle** is the lower part of the embryo and eventually forms the roots of the plant. The **seed coat** protects all other parts from dehydration.

All angiosperm seeds are contained within a protective fruit. **Simple fruits** develop from a single ovary of a single flower. **Aggregate fruits** form from many ovaries of one flower. **Multiple fruits** develop from single ovaries of a cluster of flowers. Figure 13-9 shows examples of all three fruits.

Seed plants provide a source of raw materials for paper, textiles, and building materials. Angiosperms are especially important as the primary source of nutrition for the world's human population. The rest of this chapter will focus on how seeds germinate and how seed plants grow and develop. An understanding of germination and growth has helped humans to increase crop yields and to produce better and hardier strains of many plant species.

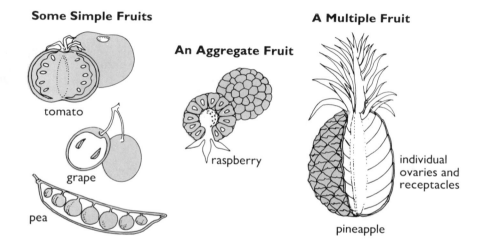

Some Simple Fruits

tomato

grape

pea

An Aggregate Fruit

raspberry

A Multiple Fruit

individual ovaries and receptacles

pineapple

FIGURE 13-9 Examples of different types of fruits

Section Review Questions

1. Why do ferns only survive in a moist location?
2. What adaptation of the male gametes of conifers allows them to be dispersed without the presence of water?
3. What are the functions of the anther and the ovary of a flower?
4. a) Compare self-pollination and cross-pollination.
   b) List three agents that help pollination occur.
5. What functions do a) the seed coat, b) the endosperm, and c) the embryo serve?
6. State two functions of the fruit.

Asian Bee Mites

In Canada, beekeepers annually produce fifty million dollars worth of honey. In Ontario alone, there are 6000 registered commercial beekeepers. The bee's role in agriculture is just as important economically as its role in producing honey. By renting beehives, farmers can efficiently pollinate millions of dollars worth of crops such as apples, cucumbers, tomatoes, beans, and almonds each year. In the United States, many millions of dollars of crops are pollinated this way annually. When bee populations decrease, crop yield does as well.

But Canadian bees that are used commercially are now threatened. In 1987, the Asian bee mite, *Varroa jacobsoni*, was detected in Florida—the first known occurrence in North America. The tiny mite—less than 1 mm long—is all but invisible. It drinks the blood of bees for nourishment, and may attack either the larvae, pupae, or adult bees. Depending on the time of infection, an infected bee will either die or develop deformities that will eventually bring about death.

Canadian beekeepers are worried because the bee mite infestation has spread from Florida to most of the United States, and has proven difficult to contain. Because victims exhibit no symptoms during the first two years of infection, the spread of the infestation is invisible. By the time malfunctions are visible in a bee colony, the colony is already lost. Spread of the mite has been aided by both bees and beekeepers. As beekeepers move their colonies from area to area pollinating crops, bees from an infected colony may encounter those from one that has not yet been infected. The mite also spreads easily when an infected bee becomes lost and joins a new uninfected colony.

Because of the speed with which the threat has developed, preventive measures have not yet been perfected. Canadian beekeepers have relied on common sense to keep the mite out of the country. Until recently, few large-scale beekeepers wintered their bees, preferring to import new stocks each spring from the United States. To prevent the Asian bee mite from entering with imported bees, Canada has closed its borders to American imports.

Infection prevention is now being studied. Recent experiments have been undertaken with a miticide that seems to be almost 100% effective. The miticide is placed on a strip, which is hung inside the hive and kills mites before they cause an infection. Unfortunately, the miticide's environmental effects have yet to be determined. Should environmental concerns prevent miticide use, Canada's bees will eventually have to contend with the Asian bee mite. Our border with the United States is long, and free-flying bees cannot be kept out by customs officials.

13.2 Germination and Growth of Seed Plants

If all seeds fell on the ground directly beneath the parent plant, it would not be long before numerous small plants would be competing for water, light, and nutrients. When this happens, not many offspring survive. Many plants have seed dispersal adaptations that help spread the seeds over a wide area, increasing each new plant's chance of survival.

Adaptations for Seed Dispersal

Some plants disperse seeds directly. For example, bean and pea plants have seed pods that burst open when they become mature. The force of the bursting pod releases seeds over a broader area than would be possible if the seeds simply fell. But these seeds seldom fall more than a couple of metres away. Much greater distances are achieved by plants that disperse their seeds with the help of outside agents.

Animals frequently act as dispersal agents for seeds that are contained within fruits. Squirrels and other seed eaters may carry seeds such as acorns far from the parent plant. These animals often bury the seeds, and the forgotten seeds may develop into new plants.

Many birds and animals eat fleshy fruits like berries for nourishment. The seeds pass unharmed from the animal's digestive tract along with solid wastes wherever the animal happens to defecate. Sometimes seeds are transported kilometres away from the parent plant in this way.

Less tasty seeds often have some other adaptation that makes dispersal by an outside agent possible. For example, the seed coats of plants such as wild carrot and sandbur have tiny hooks or barbs. The hooks or barbs may attach themselves to the fur of a passing animal, and the seeds may fall off later in some distant location.

The fruit of plants that depend on wind to disperse their seeds also have special adaptations. You have probably seen the winged fruit of the maple tree twirling like a helicopter propeller as the wind carries it to a new location. The tiny "sails" attached to the seeds of a dandelion plant perform the same function.

Water can also be an effective agent of dispersal, even if a fruit does not have a special adaptation. Coconuts, for example, can be carried long distances once they have fallen into a body of water. Later, they may be washed up onto a beach or a shoreline where they can germinate. A driving rainstorm can also scatter seeds as the raindrops splash on a ripe fruit that is ready to release its seeds.

Explain the methods of seed dispersal you see here.

Some seeds have developed thick seed coats or layers of special chemicals that must decay or be worn away naturally before a seed will germinate. The seeds of lotus and locust plants have thick, hard coats that must be worn away. Many annuals have seeds covered with chemicals that must be broken down during the winter in order to germinate in the spring.

Conditions for Germination

If seeds do not encounter suitable growing conditions where they fall, they may go through a period of **dormancy** when processes such as cellular respiration slow down. Some seeds such as corn will not germinate at all without a dormant period. Seeds may remain dormant through one winter season, or several years, depending on the species. However, the ability of seeds to germinate after a period of dormancy may be inhibited.

LABORATORY EXERCISE 13-2
Investigating Germination and Growth

Seeds must encounter a suitable combination of water, temperature, and light in order to germinate and to grow into healthy plants. If any of these three factors is not present, a seed may not be able to germinate. In this exercise, you will investigate the effect of each of these factors on the process of germination and initial plant growth.

Germination and Growth

The **germination** of seeds begins once they absorb water. Water absorption causes the tissues to swell and the seed coat to split. In dicot seeds such as beans, the radicle emerges first and grows down to anchor the plant and to form roots. (See Figure 13-10.) As the fine root hairs absorb water from the soil, the hypocotyl grows in an upward curve, causing it to break through the surface of the soil, pulling the two cotyledons with it. Finally, the epicotyl

FIGURE 13-10 Germination and early growth of a bean plant

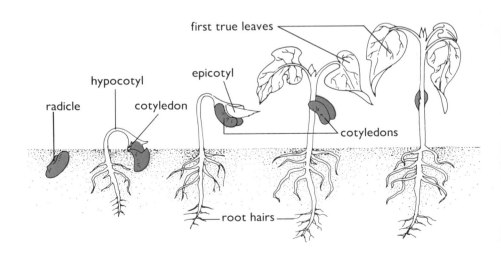

first true leaves

hypocotyl

epicotyl

radicle

cotyledon

cotyledons

root hairs

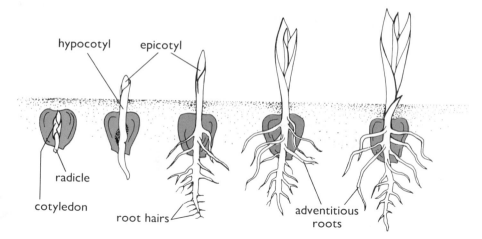

hypocotyl   epicotyl

radicle

cotyledon

root hairs

adventitious
roots

FIGURE 13-11 Germination and
early growth of a corn plant

emerges and develops the first set of leaves. The stored food in the cotyledons
nourishes the plant until its leaves begin to photosynthesize. Eventually, the
cotyledons shrivel and drop off.

Monocot seeds develop somewhat differently. (See Figure 13-11.) For
example, the cotyledon of the corn seed remains underground after the seed
coat splits and never breaks through the surface. The hypocotyl, which also
remains underground, produces a second set of roots after the first set from
the radicle develops.

The new plant increases in size through rapid cell division in the meristems.
Apical meristems at the tips of the roots and stems allow those structures to
grow longer by increasing the length and number of the cells. (See Figure 13-
12.) The new roots and stems grow thicker through rapid division of meristematic tissue in the cambium layer near their outer surfaces. All of these
meristems will eventually differentiate into the specialized tissues discussed
in Chapter 12. Each performs a particular function for the new plant's roots,
stems, and leaves.

Farmers can attempt to enhance the germination rate of their next year's
crop by storing seeds in a cool, dry place. The ability of a seed to germinate,
or its viability, often depends on a suitable dormancy period. By controlling
the oxygen, heat, and moisture at planting time, which can be done in greenhouses, seed germination rates and initial plant growth can be enhanced.

Section Review Questions

1. Describe three different ways that animals can help to disperse seeds.
2. What is the time period between seed dispersal and seed germination called?
3. In what two ways are the germination of dicot and monocot seeds different?
4. What is the function of the apical meristems and the cambium in plants?

DID YOU KNOW?
When the bean seed's two cotyledons
first emerge, they contain chlorophyll.
The green pigment makes them
resemble leaves, but their shape is quite
different from that of the bean's first
true leaves.

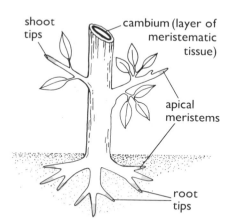

shoot
tips

cambium (layer of
meristematic
tissue)

apical
meristems

root
tips

FIGURE 13-12 Locations of meristematic tissue in a typical plant

Meet
Robert Coffin

Robert works for Agriculture Canada at the University of Guelph. He is an adjunct professor in Horticultural Science and Food Science. For the past seven years he has been looking after the potato-breeding program at the university. He develops new potato breeds for processing and for the table-stock market.

Q. *What's involved in breeding potatoes?*

A. First, we decide what kinds of qualities we want to produce in a potato. For instance, we might want to crossbreed a potato with good chipping quality, that is, a potato that produces good potato chips, with a potato that has a high yield. Then, we remove the anthers from the flower of a male plant, shake off the pollen, and put the pollen on the stigma of a female plant. If the pollen unites with the eggs from the female plant, then fertilization has occurred. However, only a small number of plants that are pollinated by this method are successfully fertilized.

Q. *What happens if fertilization occurs?*

A. We open the seed balls and plant the potato seeds first in flats, and later we transfer them to pots. We grow approximately 10 000 plants a year. From the pots, we harvest tubers, which are then planted outside in the spring.

Q. *Does it take long to produce a new potato breed?*

A. It takes from 12 to 15 years from the time of cross-pollination until a new potato variety is licensed. Years of field and quality trials have to take place. Only one in 10 000 new varieties of potato is good enough to achieve registration. To register a new breed, you must show development-performance data from field trials, lab information on dry-matter content, and you must also prove that the new breed is free from disease. The data must include results from many years and from many growing locations to show consistency. The new potato must also be as good as, or better in some way, than existing standard

varieties. Last year, five or six new varieties were registered.

Q. *Have you produced any registered varieties?*

A. I have four new varieties registered. In a lifetime, a potato breeder might produce six to ten varieties. I'm especially enthusiastic about a new potato called *Saginaw Gold* that was developed in part by the University of Guelph.

Q. *What is special about the Saginaw Gold potato?*

A. It has a low sugar level, which means it stays light even when it is stored and then fried for potato chips. Most of our potatoes will eventually be processed. Forty percent of Ontario's potato crop ends up in a potato-chip bag. The average consumer in North America eats approximately 55 kg of potatoes a year, and most of this amount is in the form of processed potatoes.

Q. *How do you organize your time throughout the year?*

A. The seasons play a role in the work I do. In May, we plant potato trials in the field. In July, we harvest the early potatoes, but the main harvest is in September. In October and November, we grade the potatoes. We look for marketable yields and defects. From then until April, I work in the lab, boiling and baking different varieties, making potato chips and french fries. I eat a lot of potatoes!

13.3 Growth Regulation and Environmental Response

A plant can only grow to its full potential under ideal conditions of light, temperature, and moisture. Too much or too little of any of these factors can severely retard plant growth.

Light is necessary to stimulate the formation of chlorophyll, the green pigment that makes photosynthesis possible. Plants grown in a poorly lit environment show a growth pattern called etiolation. These plants are taller and thinner than normal, as if stretching to find a source of light. Their leaves are underdeveloped and yellow. Such plants are unable to manufacture their own food and soon die.

Temperature is also a critical factor in plant growth. Most plants grow best within an optimum temperature range. If the temperature gets too high, the rate of photosynthesis and transpiration may increase so much that a plant will lose water more quickly than the vascular system can replace it. Long periods of high temperature can eventually lead to plant death. Conversely, if the temperature drops too low, photosynthesis may slow down so much that plant growth stops completely.

Water is one of the raw materials plants use to produce the glucose they need. Plants use glucose as an energy source for all life functions, including growth. A water shortage will slow down glucose production, leading to a lack of energy and retarded growth. A shortage of carbon dioxide or insufficient chlorophyll in a plant's leaves will produce the same effects.

The effect of light deprivation on a plant. The plant on the left is etiolated, while the plant on the right was grown in ideal conditions.

Hormones and Plant Growth

Plant growth is also affected by internal growth regulators such as **hormones**. Hormones are the natural chemical compounds that influence the division and elongation of cells. Three general types of hormones are auxins, gibberellins, and cytokinins.

Auxins are produced in the growing tips of stems and roots, and are transported to all parts of the plant through the vascular tissue. Auxins affect the growth of all plant tissues. They stimulate cell differentiation in roots and shoots. Auxins produced in the meristem of a shoot cause it to increase in length. But auxins also inhibit the growth of lateral branches. One way to make a plant more full is to cut off the shoot tip. This will allow the lateral buds to form and create new branches. The development of flowers, fruits, and roots can also be promoted by auxins. However, very high concentrations of auxins can actually inhibit the growth of roots.

Gibberellins were first discovered in Japan when rice plants infected by a fungus grew extraordinarily tall. After the hormone responsible for this growth was extracted from the fungus and identified, scientists realized that plants manufacture the same hormone. Gibberellins produced in the leaves of plants are transported to the stems. Here they promote stem growth through the lengthening of cells. Dwarf plants can be stimulated to grow taller by applying extra gibberellins to the meristems of the shoots. Gibberellins have also been found to promote the development of seeds and fruit.

Bean seedlings treated with gibberellic acid (an extract of the plant hormone). **Left:** Untreated plants. **Centre:** Plants treated with 500 ppm. **Right:** Plants treated with 5000 ppm.

Cytokinins are growth regulators that stimulate cell division but only in the presence of auxins. Cytokinins increase the rate of cell division and influence the size of leaves, roots, and fruits.

Some synthetic hormones are used to enhance plant growth. The synthetic auxin, 2, 4-D, which is in weed killers, stimulates broad-leaved plants like dandelions to grow so quickly that their vascular tissues cannot deliver enough raw materials, which results in their death. Development of fruit without pollination and fertilization can be stimulated in plants like tomatoes and cucumbers by spraying their flowers with auxins. The fruits, of course, are seedless. Fruit trees can be sprayed with auxins to prevent the fruit from falling off early, which increases the yield of mature fruit.

One of the most important plant auxins is IAA (indoleacetic acid). This auxin was first isolated from human urine.

LABORATORY EXERCISE 13-3
Hormones and Plant Growth

In plants, as in animals, the production and circulation of hormones plays an important role in regulating normal growth. In this exercise, you will perform experiments to investigate the effects of plant-growth hormones on plant growth.

Tropisms

Even though they lack muscle-like tissue, plants must sometimes respond with movement to environmental stimuli in order to survive. For example, plants kept on a sunny windowsill will gradually bend as they grow toward the light. In plants, any movement toward a helpful stimulus, or away from a harmful one, is called a **tropism**. Tropisms are both slow and nonreversible because they involve cell growth.

The movement of a plant toward a stimulus is called a **positive tropism**. The movement of a plant in response to light is called a **phototropism**. Therefore, plants on a sunny windowsill exhibit a positive phototropism when they grow toward the light. All positive tropisms result from the action of auxins regardless of the nature of the stimulus. Plants bend toward the light because auxins collect on the dark side of the stem, stimulating those cells to elongate faster than the cells on the bright side of the stem. (See Figure 13-13.)

The movement of a plant away from a stimulus is called a **negative tropism**. Roots can display a negative phototropism if they are exposed to light. Auxins collect on the side of the root that is not exposed to light, but the effect is opposite to that seen in stems. The high concentration of auxins inhibits cell growth on the dark side of the root. But the low concentration of auxins on the exposed side of the root stimulates those cells to grow longer. As a result, the root grows away from the light.

An example of plant tropism

FIGURE 13-13 Auxins cause this stem tip to bend toward the light.

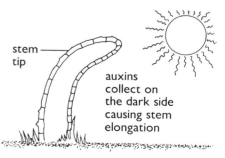

stem tip

auxins collect on the dark side causing stem elongation

FIGURE 13-14 The effect of auxins on roots is opposite to their effect on shoots.

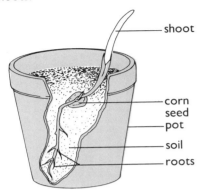

- shoot
- corn seed
- pot
- soil
- roots

Thigmotropism in a bean plant

Positive and negative tropisms are adaptations that ensure roots will grow down, regardless of how a seed is planted, and stems will grow up.

The response of a plant to the force of gravity is called **geotropism**. As the root and shoot emerge from a seed planted sideways, gravity causes auxins to gather on the undersides of both structures. This causes the cells of the underside of the shoot to elongate faster than the cells of the upper side, making the shoot grow upward. Conversely, the auxins in the lower side of the root slow cell growth in that location, causing the root to grow downward. (See Figure 13-14.)

Some plant parts show a response to touch called **thigmotropism**. The tendrils of climbing plants such as the bean will wind around any object they touch. In this case, auxins collect on the side of the tendril away from the point of touch. Since tendrils are made of stem tissue, the cells on the outside elongate more rapidly, forcing the tendril to curl around the object as it grows.

LABORATORY EXERCISE 13-4
Investigating Irritability in Plants

The ability of living things to respond to stimuli in their environment is called irritability. Many factors such as light, gravity, touch, and chemicals can cause a response in a plant or a plant part. In this exercise, you will design and perform experiments to study the response of plants or plant parts to one or more external stimuli.

Nastic Movements

All tropisms are dependent on the direction of the environmental stimulus. They are also slow and nonreversible because cell growth, which is a permanent change, is involved. **Nastic movements** are faster, reversible, and independent of stimulus direction.

Changes in temperature trigger nastic movements in plants such as the morning glory. Its flowers open as the temperature of the air increases during the day and close toward evening as temperatures drop.

Changes in light intensity or touch may trigger nastic movements in some other species. A species of cactus blooms in response to nighttime darkness and closes during the day. Rapid response to touch can be seen in the *Mimosa pudica*, which is commonly called the "sensitive plant." Touching any part of the leaves causes them to fold up and droop immediately. In a short time, the leaves return to their normal, open position. This example illustrates the reversibility and speed of nastic movements.

A *Mimosa* plant before being touched **(left)** and after **(right)**

All nastic movements result from absorption or elimination of water by the cells of the plant. As cells absorb water, they become more rigid, a condition known as cell turgor. As cells eliminate water, they become less turgid or flaccid. Changes in cell turgor cause some plant parts to open, some to close, and others to droop or straighten. Water can enter and leave a cell quite easily by osmosis. This explains why such movements are both rapid and reversible.

Section Review Questions

1. State the three factors required for plant growth and explain why each is important.
2. What may happen to a plant if the temperature gets too high?
3. How do auxins affect plant growth?
4. Identify the stimulus responsible for the following tropisms: a) phototropism, b) thigmotropism, and c) geotropism.
5 Describe an example of each tropism you have identified in Question 4.
6. Compare tropisms with nastic movements by stating examples.

13.4 Asexual Reproduction in Seed Plants

Many seed plants have the ability to reproduce asexually. In asexual reproduction, there is only one parent organism. No union of sex cells, or gametes, is needed to produce more plants. Instead, a small part of the plant's body grows all the organs needed to form a complete new individual. For example, a spider plant grows roots when it is placed in water near sunlight. Many other house plants can be propagated, or multiplied, in this manner by similar methods. Asexual reproduction also occurs in the natural environment.

The propagation of a plant by a cutting is an example of asexual reproduction.

Photoperiodism

In planning a garden, landscape architects consider the garden's appearance throughout the year. To extend the garden's appeal, they take advantage of the fact that some plants flower like clockwork at different times of the year. Why are these plants so reliable? How does a plant know when it is time to flower?

The effect of day length on plant flowering was first noticed in the 1920s by Garner and Allerd, two researchers who discovered that soybeans planted at different times flowered virtually simultaneously. After varying temperature, nutrition, and soil without effect, the researchers varied the length of time in which the plants were exposed to sunlight. Eventually, they were able to describe photoperiodism—the series of plant responses to changing lengths of daylight and darkness that occurs as the seasons change. In addition to flowering, photoperiodic effects can influence internode length and the growth and fall of leaves in woody plants. It can also affect tuber and runner formation in other plants.

Photoperiodic plants are classified according to the length of daylight needed to induce flowering. Short-day plants such as poinsettias and goldenrod bloom during the spring and autumn. Long-day plants such as irises and radishes flower in the summer. Day-neutral plants such as roses and tomatoes are unaffected by night and day length and show no photoperiodism. Among plants that do show photoperiodism, there is a wide variation in sensitivity to the effect. Some plants will never flower unless the proper photoperiod is established for a number of days. Others are much more tolerant to variation. One species, *Xanthium strumarium* (cocklebur), requires only one presentation of the proper photoperiod to set off 12 months of flowering.

It is actually the proper length of uninterrupted darkness that sets off flowering in photoperiodic plants. If a light is flashed briefly during the dark period of a short-day plant, in effect interrupting the night, the plant will not flower. Short-day plants might better be called long-night plants. Likewise, long-day plants are really short-night plants.

Photoperiodism is a complex phenomenon, and although researchers have made progress in understanding it, its exact mechanisms remain unclear. It is now believed that a pigment in leaves is sensitive to the relative amounts of light and dark that the plant experiences in a 24 h cycle. Through a complex set of chemical reactions, and the release of a plant hormone as yet unidentified, this sensitive pigment can affect the natural rhythms of the plant and bring about flowering at the proper time.

Adaptations for Asexual Reproduction

By skipping the steps involved in seed formation and germination, asexual, or vegetative, reproduction speeds up the rate at which new plants can be produced. Plant species with the ability to reproduce rapidly can form large populations more quickly than competing species. Any adaptation that promotes asexual reproduction can give plants an advantage in competing for limited ecosystem resources. Therefore, many plant species have roots, stems, or leaves that are adapted for the purpose of asexual reproduction.

Stem Adaptations

Strawberry plants develop horizontal stem extensions called stolons, or runners, that grow above and close to the surface of the ground. When the tip of the stolon touches fertile soil, new roots develop at the point of contact. (See Figure 13-15.) Many independent offspring can be formed in this manner. Other berries such as blackberries and raspberries, as well as grass and spider plants, also reproduce asexually in this way.

Root Adaptations

Elderberry roots send out horizontal growths that radiate from the parent plant beneath the surface of the ground. At points along the root extensions, vertical shoots may develop that lead to the formation of a new plant. Lilac, milkweed, and sumac roots are also able to reproduce asexually using their roots in this way.

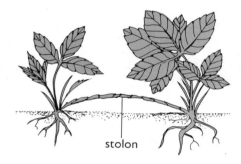

FIGURE 13-15   The strawberry plant uses stolons to reproduce asexually.

Leaf Adaptations

The house plant, *Bryophyllum*, forms tiny, new plants along the edges of its leaves. If these small plants encounter good growing conditions when they drop off, they grow into new, independent adult plants. African violets and begonias also use their leaves to reproduce asexually. When a parent leaf from an African violet or a begonia contacts the soil, a new plant may develop from the edge or the surface of the leaf.

All of the plants in the above examples also form flowers and seeds to reproduce sexually. However, asexual reproduction is an important factor in their survival in the natural environment.

A *Bryophyllum* plant growing new plants along the edge of its leaves

Applications of Asexual Reproduction

Close observation of asexual reproduction in nature enabled early farmers to increase crop yields by using similar methods. For example, white potatoes are the enlarged parts of underground stems, which contain stored food and "eyes." Each eye is a node, or bud, of meristematic tissue that can form a shoot and roots. A farmer can cut a potato into pieces, ensuring that each piece has at least one eye. Then the farmer plants each piece. Each eye will develop into a new potato plant. Today, this technique is just one of many ways asexual reproduction is applied to the problem of growing large amounts of food for human consumption. Since potatoes grown from seed take much longer to reach the harvesting stage, some methods simply speed up reproduction. Other methods allow growers to propagate unusual or desirable plants such as seedless oranges that cannot reproduce by natural methods.

Cutting can be used to propagate new plants from a parent plant. (See Figure 13-16.) In this method, a piece of stem with several leaves is cut from the parent plant. The cut end of the stem is then placed in water. When the roots develop, the cutting is ready for an independent life and can be planted. Sometimes the tips of the roots are dipped in hormones to stimulate root growth. Commercial crops such as bananas and grapes can be reproduced by this method. Ornamental plants such as roses and ivy are other examples.

FIGURE 13-16 Reproducing plants asexually by cutting

The cutting should retain the top three or four leaves.

The cutting should be watered regularly until rooting is completed.

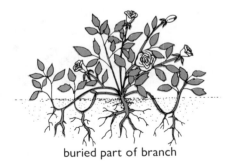

buried part of branch

FIGURE 13-17 Layering in a rosebush

Layering is commonly used to reproduce climbing rose bushes. While it is still attached to the parent plant, part of the stem is buried, leaving only its growing tip exposed. Eventually, the buried part of the stem will develop roots of its own and the tip will grow new shoots. (See Figure 13-17.) The new plant can then be separated from the parent plant and planted. Raspberries, blackberries, and honeysuckle can be propagated by the layering method.

Grafting involves attaching a small branch or bud — a **scion** — from a desirable plant, to the branch of a rooted host plant — the **stock**. (See Figure 13-18.) Successful grafting occurs when the vascular tissues of the stock and the scion are carefully aligned and touching. This ensures that materials can pass back and forth between the two parts. Usually, the graft is taped or sealed with wax to prevent water loss and to protect the exposed branch ends from diseased organisms. Many seedless fruits such as oranges and grapes, and many seed-containing fruits, such as pears, peaches, and apples are propagated by this method.

Technically, all new plants produced asexually from a parent plant are **clones** because their cells have chromosomes identical to those of the parent. In advanced cloning techniques, strains of identical plants are stimulated to form from individual cells or tissue samples of a parent plant. New plants produced in this way are identical to the parent plant. Cloning could be used to reduce the chances of inherited variability through sexual reproduction in plants already considered "perfect." Cloning may also help researchers to create new plant strains by combining traits from two species that might not come together by natural or selective breeding methods. New types of wheat and carrots have been produced in this way.

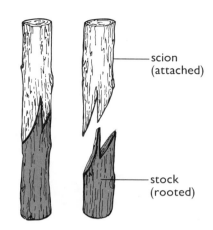

FIGURE 13-18 Grafting a scion to a stock

RESEARCH PROJECT
Applications of Asexual Reproduction

Modern scientific understanding of plant tissues and the factors that regulate growth has led to some amazing applications of asexual reproduction. Choose one of the following projects to increase your personal understanding of these applications.

A. Use what you have learned in this chapter about plant hormones to design an experiment to compare the effects of plant hormones on various methods of asexual plant propagation techniques. Decide which hormones and methods you will investigate. Prepare a detailed experimental procedure. Obtain approval from your teacher before performing your experiment.

B. Visit a greenhouse or a nursery to observe the relative importance of asexual and sexual reproduction in modern agriculture. For example, how are new strains of apples or grapes developed? How are these plants usually propagated? Prepare a short written report, a poster, or give a brief classroom presentation about your findings.

C. Invite a guest speaker such as a horticulturist to speak to your class about the latest methods of reproducing plants. Prepare a list of questions for the guest speaker to stimulate discussion after his or her speech.

DID YOU KNOW?
In recent years, it has been possible to cause the protoplasm of two unrelated plant cells to fuse once the cell walls have been removed by enzymes. The new hybrid cells have a mixture of traits from both unrelated parents. Less frequently, the hybrid cells can generate a new plant. This technique is called "protoplast fusion."

Asexual versus Sexual Reproduction

All angiosperm species can reproduce sexually. But often the time required for seed formation or germination is lengthy. Asexual reproduction allows these plants to multiply more quickly. Since each new individual is formed from a single parent plant, it possesses exactly the same hereditary information as the parent plant. Offspring are identical to the parent. There can be no variation in characteristics except for those caused by mutation.

Asexual reproduction has both advantages and disadvantages. A major advantage of asexual reproduction is that a species will continue to thrive in its natural environment through many generations. Eventually, the entire population might be genetically identical. However, if the environment changed, there would be no variants in the plant population that might be more suited to the new conditions. This could lead to the extinction of the species in that area.

Section Review Questions

1. What is the main difference between asexual and sexual reproduction in plants?
2. Describe one example of a root, a stem, and a leaf adaptation for asexual reproduction.
3. Describe three applications of asexual reproduction to the growth of food for humans.
4. What are the advantages and disadvantages of asexual reproduction?

Restoring Kew Gardens

A natural disaster is giving British botanists an opportunity to study artificial plant propagation. The Royal Botanical Gardens, more commonly known as Kew Gardens, is situated just west of London, England. Founded over 225 years ago, it is probably the oldest and most famous of the world's botanical gardens. Kew Gardens covers over 120 ha and contains one of the most outstanding plant collections in the world.

On October 16, 1987, Kew Gardens was devastated by one of the worst storms in Britain's history. Hurricane-force winds uprooted, destroyed, or damaged over 1000 trees, some of which are impossible to replace. Among them were an Iranian elm planted when the gardens opened in 1761, and an elm from the Himalayas that had survived Dutch elm disease only to perish in the storm. Attempts are being made to save between 50-60 of the damaged trees by a variety of means.

Conditions for propagation by conventional means were not favourable since the storm took place in October, and destroyed mostly mature trees. Mature trees grow more slowly than young trees do, and their growth rate is lowest in autumn. Since young, fast-growing shoots are best-suited for artificial propagation, the timing of the storm could not have been worse. Kew's staff had to persuade some trees to ignore the signals of age and seasonal change. Those specimens refusing to propagate without winter were given winter conditions. Packages of twigs and branch tips were wrapped in moist newspapers, placed in plastic bags, and stored in refrigerators until spring, in the hope of producing successful cuttings.

Timing and age also worked against the propagation of trees by other means. Cloning technology is in its infancy, and has had limited success, but since conventional techniques have never been very successful on trees with hard or pithy wood, botanists at Kew Gardens decided to try raising some whole plants from cell cultures. Again, young, quickly dividing cells are needed for this propagation technique. Since most culture cells were in a low-growth phase of development, division was forced for some stock tissues by immersion in a high-sugar solution. This strategy was meant to stimulate growth and division, and succeeded in breaking the dormancy of some cells.

Other research efforts inspired by the storm are ongoing at Kew Gardens. Root material of destroyed trees is being used to study the complex workings of tissue. As well, tree-ring research is under way, using the garden's recently enlarged wood collection. Ironically, in providing scientists with material for studying the practice and problems of propagation of a variety of species, as well as other processes, the storm at Kew Gardens may yet be seen as a beneficial event.

Chapter Review

Key Words

cotyledon
cross pollination
dicot
dicotyledon
endosperm
flowers
fruit
germination
monocot

monocotyledon
nastic movements
pistil
pollination
radicle
seed coat
self-pollination
stamen
tropism

Recall Questions

Multiple Choice

1. Which of the following is a natural method of asexual reproduction in plants?
   a) layering
   b) stolon formation
   c) grafting
   d) cutting
   e) budding

2. All of the following are involved with sexual reproduction by flowers except
   a) anther
   b) style
   c) stamen
   d) cambium
   e) stigma

3. Which embryonic plant part first emerges from the seed during germination?
   a) radicle
   b) hypocotyl
   c) plumule
   d) epicotyl
   e) endosperm

4. The ability of a seed to germinate is called
   a) dormancy
   b) germination
   c) viability
   d) etiolation
   e) tropism

5. When touched, the leaves of the *Mimosa pudica* fold and droop. This is an example of
   a) phototropism
   b) meristematic response
   c) thigmotropism
   d) geotropism
   e) nastic movement

Fill in the Blanks

1. Grafting is a method of _____ asexual reproduction.

2. The female structure of the flower is the _____.

3. A _____ is the ripened ovary of a flower.

4. The tissue the embryonic plant feeds on until it can photosynthesize is called _____.

5. Dicot plants are protected by the _____ until they break through the surface of the soil.

6. _____ plants blossom in response to long nights.

Short Answers

1. a) List two natural and two artifical methods of asexual reproduction.
   b) Describe how each method is performed.

2. Describe the structures of the stamen and the pistil.

3. Distinguish between the following pairs of terms
   a) layering and cutting
   b) monocotyledon and dicotyledon
   c) epicotyl and hypocotyl

4. Describe three seed dispersal agents.

5. State three factors that can affect the germination of a seed.

6. Where are the meristems located in a developing plant?

7. Explain how auxins play a major role in plant tropisms.

8. What is the stimulus responsible for the following tropisms: a) thigmotropism, b) geotropism, and c) phototropism.

9. Describe one example of a nastic movement in a plant.

Application Questions

1. How would knowing about asexual reproduction methods in plants save the average homeowner money?

2. What would happen to a species of flowering plant if its natural insect pollinator were destroyed by a pest-control program?

3. Why would soaking seeds in water too long before planting be detrimental to their germination?

4. Discuss the effect on bean seedlings if the cotyledons are removed as soon as the young plants break through the soil.

5. Why do rose bushes produce flowers during the entire growing season?

6. What would happen to roots if auxins had the same effect on them as they do on shoots?

7. How could you tell whether a movement observed in a plant is a nastic movement or a topism?

Problem Solving

1. How could an economically poor country increase the availability of food from plants if it could not buy any more seeds?

2. Why would the seeds of plants from a tropical area tend not to germinate in Canada?

3. How would you ensure that plants placed in front of a well-lit window would grow straight and not bend?

4. Describe several steps a farmer could take to maximize his or her harvest from a kilogram of seeds.

Extensions

1. Visit a greenhouse to find out what techniques are used to multiply plants and to keep them healthy.

2. Design and perform one of the following experiments.
   a) Test whether a flower responds to light or to temperature when it opens in the morning.

b) Test and compare the responses of several different plants to the same stimulus.

c) Test the effects of the length of time seeds are pre-soaked before planting on their germination.

3. Perform one of the following investigations related to plant growth.
   a) Investigate the factors that initiate flowering.
   b) Report on the experiments of Darwin, Boysen-Jensen, and Went. How did they contribute to knowledge about the chemical regulation of plant growth?

4. Research and report on the use of plant hormones in agriculture.

5. Investigate the advantages and disadvantages of using herbicides such as 2, 4-D; 2, 4-5-T; and agent orange to control weed growth.

6. Research the method of plant growth known as hydroponics. Report on its advantages and disadvantages.

7. Research and compare plant adaptations found in the following North American biomes: tundra, desert, grassland, coniferous forest, and deciduous forest.

CHAPTER

14

Fungi

In 1844, new varieties of potatoes were introduced to Europe from the Americas. In the following year, something mysterious happened to potatoes in Europe. The leaves of potatoes in the ground became covered in strange, dark lesions; potatoes in storage turned black with rot in a few days. The spread throughout Europe of Late Blight, as the disease came to be called, was phenomenally rapid.

Ireland, unlike continental Europe, had no alternative sources of food. When the blight arrived, potato crops failed for years on end. The Irish did not know how to protect their potato crops from Late Blight, and by 1851, thousands had died of starvation or malnutrition.

We can explain the tragedy today, and to a great degree we can prevent further tragedies. Ireland had been invaded by a member of the kingdom Fungi, *Phytophthora infestans*. Little was known at the time about fungi, but the potato famine in Ireland provided the impetus for research. However, despite the progress made by research, fungal infections still cause extensive crop damage every year.

Canada is no stranger to the problem. One of the country's most vital crops is wheat. Canada is the world's second largest wheat exporter, so it is essential to guarantee a stable and abundant wheat crop from year to year.

The wheat in this photograph has been infested by a parasitic fungus known as wheat rust. This coppery-coloured growth attacks the stems and leaves of wheat plants. It lives off the plant it infects, diverting its host's resources to ensure its own survival and reproduction. The infection causes fewer and smaller grains to be produced, so a farmer may see a huge reduction in yield—up to 50%.

In the 1940s, biologists were somewhat successful in limiting the spread of wheat rust by developing resistant strains of wheat. But in the mid-1950s, a new variety of wheat rust appeared that had adapted to the new wheat strains and spread rapidly through susceptible hosts. Eight million tonnes of wheat were destroyed in a year. Today, carefully timed applications of fungicide are used to interrupt the wheat rust's life cycle. This strategy, along with the use of resistant wheat strains, has been successful in controlling wheat rust destruction. Still, no solution can guarantee success.

It is hardly surprising then, that the term ''fungus'' has negative connotations, but it would be unfair to condemn the entire kingdom. In fact, many fungi are incredibly useful. The most obvious examples are yeast and edible mushrooms. Another member of the kingdom Fungi is used by pharmaceutical companies to produce penicillin, a powerful antibiotic.

What, then, does a mushroom have in common with *Phytophthora infestans*, the fungus that,

indirectly, sent thousands of people to their graves in Ireland? How can such small, simple organisms, which seem so insignificant, cause so much damage and so much good? How can biologists protect us from one kind and utilize another? This chapter will help you answer questions like these.

Chapter Objectives

When you complete this chapter, you should:

1. Appreciate the variety of roles played by fungi on earth, and understand how fungi are used by and affect humans.

2. Understand the structure, reproduction, growth, and importance of fungal decomposers.

3. Understand the problems caused by fungal decomposers such as those causing food spoilage.

4. Be able to describe the differences in structure and function between flowering plants and fungi.

5. Be able to explain the terms saprophyte, parasite, and symbiont using examples from the kingdom Fungi.

6. Be able to describe how fungi obtain nutrients.

7. Know the three divisions of true fungi. Be able to describe the structural and reproductive characteristics used to classify them and give examples of each.

8. Know and describe the features characteristic of imperfect fungi, slime moulds, and lichens.

9. Be able to explain the importance of fungi in lichen growth.

10. Be able to describe the effects, methods of control, and economic impact of several plant diseases caused by fungi. Also, understand the impact of food spoilage and mildew formation caused by fungi.

11. Be able to describe the causes and the effects of these fungi on humans.

12. Be able to describe how fungi are used by humans.

13. Know how to design and perform experiments to investigate the factors that affect the growth of fungi.

14. Have developed laboratory skills such as culturing, dissecting, and preparing fungal tissue for examination with a compound microscope.

14.1 Characteristics of Fungi

DID YOU KNOW?
Mushrooms rank second to potatoes as the most valuable vegetable crop for Canadian farmers. Mushroom production results in annual domestic sales of over $136 million.

Fungi vary in form and size from microscopic, one-celled organisms such as yeast, to giant, multicellular puffballs that can reach up to 1 m across. Fungi can range in colour from white- or brown-capped toadstools to coppery wheat rust, bright red chanterelles, or purple *Cortinarius glaucopus*. Nevertheless, all fungi have features in common with commercial mushrooms you can buy in grocery stores.

LABORATORY EXERCISE 14-1
The Anatomy of a Commercial Mushroom

DID YOU KNOW?
The most common variety of mushroom grown by Canadian farmers is the *Agaricus bisporus*. Domestic production of more exotic types such as the Shiitake mushroom from Asia and the oyster mushroom is increasing.

In this exercise, you will examine the structure of selected parts of the fruiting body of a fungus. (The fruiting body is the part of the fungus that produces reproductive spores.) You will also make a spore print from a mushroom cap.

It is always dangerous for anyone except an expert to pick mushrooms in the wild. The two mushrooms in the photographs on this page, for example, look very much alike. One of these mushrooms is safe to eat, but the other is highly toxic. Many mushrooms that look harmless can be fatal if you eat them. Just touching some species can cause severe skin irritation. Therefore, the mushrooms used in this exercise will be the commercial variety.

DID YOU KNOW?
Domestic mushrooms must be grown indoors under shelter. The buildings for Canada's first mushroom farm were erected in Waterloo, Québec, by Fred and Charles Slack in the 1920s. By the mid-1950s, the Slack brothers were producing almost 1000 t of mushrooms annually. Today, over 50 000 t of mushrooms are produced each year by Canadian farmers.

Only an expert can tell the difference between the poisonous *Amanita virosa* (**left**) and the edible *Lepiota naucina* (**right**). You should eat only store-bought mushrooms.

How Fungi Differ from Vascular Plants

By examining a mushroom, you can see that there are several major differences between fungi and flowering vascular plants. (See Table 14-1.) Perhaps the most important difference between them is that fungi lack chlorophyll, and are unable to manufacture their own food by photosynthesis. Fungi are **heterotrophs** and must rely directly or indirectly on food produced by **autotrophs** such as green plants as their source of nutrients.

Most fungi are made of thin, thread-like filaments called **hyphae**. As a hypha grows in length and branches out, cross walls may or may not develop between nuclei, depending on the species. As a result, some hyphae appear to be chains of cells, while others look like long, uninterrupted strands of cytoplasm with many nuclei. (See Figure 14-1.) Many species of fungi such as mushrooms and toadstools have cell walls made of a substance called **chitin**. Chitin is a carbohydrate similar in many ways to cellulose.

The hyphae of a fungus may take on the appearance of a tangled mass of threads called a **mycelium**. Some varieties of fungi have a very loose mycelium that gives them a "fluffy" appearance. This is typical of species such as bread mould. In other species such as mushrooms and bracket fungus, the mycelium is more compact and forms fairly solid bodies. Often, the greater portion of the mycelium cannot be seen because it lies under the surface of the material the fungus grows on. The parts of a fungus you see are usually the structures responsible for producing and releasing reproductive spores.

The fluffy, thread-like appearance of the bread mould *Rhizopus* is the result of a loose arrangement of hyphae.

The firm, fleshy body of a mushroom is formed by a dense, compacted mycelium. The black spore fluid of *Coprinus comatus* was once used as a substitute for Indian ink.

TABLE 14-1   Comparison of Fungi and Flowering Vascular Plants

Characteristic	Fungi	Flowering vascular plants
Tissue Types	• unspecialized (hyphae)	• specialized (vascular, epidermal parenchyma, chlorenchyma sclerenchyma)
Colour	• varies, but never green	• mostly green
Body Structures	• loose mycelium • compact mycelium	• roots, stems, leaves
Flower	• absent	• present
Reproduction	• sexually by means of zygospores • asexually by means of spores or fragmentation	• sexually by means of seeds • asexually by means of runners, etc.
Nutrition	• heterotrophic: rely on food produced by plants and other autotrophs	• autotrophic: produce their own food using solar energy collected by chorophyll

FIGURE 14-1 The hyphae of two types of fungi

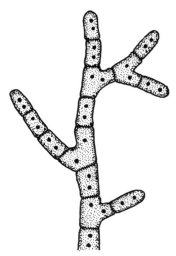

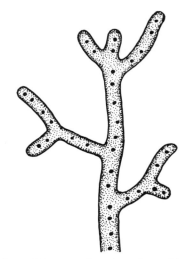

This puffball has a mass of 7 kg. When mature, its fruiting bodies will release millions of tiny spores into the air.

Most fungi can also reproduce asexually by fragmentation. Floods, storms, or animal activity may break away part of the mycelium of the parent organism. The fragment can develop into a complete new individual.

The hyphae of fungi such as morel mushrooms are chains of subdivided cells with distinct cross walls.

The hyphae of fungi such as bread mould do not have cross walls and resemble long, thin branched tubes.

How Fungi Reproduce

Fungi normally reproduce by means of **spores**. These spores can be either sexual or asexual. Some kinds of fungi produce both types. Sexual spores are produced by the union of gametes, much as the seeds of flowering plants are formed. Asexual spores, however, form directly from the body of an individual parent fungus. Flowering plants have no structure comparable to asexual spores.

In most fungi, spores form in a specialized **fruiting body** and are released in large numbers to be carried away on air currents. Only the water moulds produce spores with their own means of locomotion. All spores are capable of developing into new fungi under suitable growing conditions.

How Fungi Grow

Fungi grow so rapidly that they often seem to appear overnight. Perhaps you have noticed mushrooms on a lawn after a rainstorm where there were none the day before. If spores from a parent plant are carried to a moist, nutrient-rich location such as a well-kept lawn, they will begin to germinate, and the new mycelium will spread out in all directions as the older, central part dies. (See Figure 14–2.) When the toadstools or mushrooms emerge through the lawn, they form a circle around the original location of the spores.

DID YOU KNOW?
Since your body is moist and full of nutrients, it is an ideal growth medium for some fungi. If not for your skin and other body defences, you would be a perfect medium for the growth of moulds.

spore begins to germinate

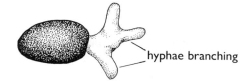

hyphae branching

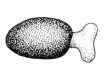

growth of hyphae

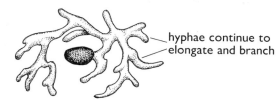

hyphae continue to elongate and branch

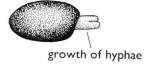

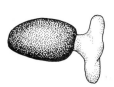

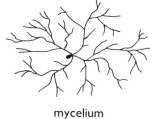
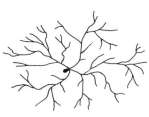

mycelium

FIGURE 14-2 The formation of mycelium from a germinating spore

The mushrooms in this "fairy ring" all came from the same parent mycelium.

LABORATORY EXERCISE 14-2
Investigating Bread Mould

Another fast-growing fungus that is all too familiar in most homes is the bread mould *Rhizopus*. There are many bread-mould spores in the air and they land on everything, including exposed food. *Rhizopus* is an ideal species for studying how fungi grow because of its ability to grow rapidly from spores. And air is a convenient source of spores for culturing a bread-mould mycelium.

In this exercise, you will gather spores, grow a mould, and observe its mature spore-producing structures with a hand lens and a compound microscope.

How Fungi Feed

Like humans, fungi are heterotrophs that must locate, digest, and process food in order to survive. Fungi are referred to as **saprophytes** if their source of nutrition is dead vegetable or animal matter. Saprophytes act as agents of decay, breaking down dead organic matter. This process recycles the nutrients back into the earth, where they can be used by green plants. Toadstools and mushrooms are saprophytic fungi that thrive in the leaf litter on the forest floor.

Organisms that obtain their nutrients from living hosts are called **parasites**. Bracket fungi and rusts are examples of parasitic fungi. For example, the parasitic bracket fungus feeds on the living tissues of conifers such as pines. Parasitic fungi are the cause of many plant diseases such as wheat rust, as well as a few human diseases such as athlete's foot.

Regardless of their food source, most fungi use extracellular digestion to obtain their nutrients. The hyphae making up the mycelium penetrate the organic matter of the food source by secreting digestive enzymes. These enzymes break down the large food particles into smaller, soluble nutrient molecules. The nutrients then diffuse across the membrane into the cytoplasm of the hyphae to be used for energy and growth. The action of these enzymes causes the organic matter to soften and rot. That is why a fruit becomes slimy when it is attacked by a mould.

Right: Bracket fungi growing out of cracks in the bark of a host tree derive nourishment from the tree's vascular tissue. **Below:** White morels growing on leaf litter

Antibiotics

Medicines against bacterial infections are a recent development. Until the 1800s, it was not even known that illness could be caused by infections of bacteria. By the 1920s, bacterial diseases had been identified, but little could be done to stop these diseases once they had started.

A breakthrough came in 1928. Alexander Fleming, a British-born microbiologist, was working with bacteria when he discovered that a blue mould, *Penicillium notatum*, had infected one of his cultures. Cultures had been ruined by mould before, but Fleming noticed something others had missed. Around each mould growth was a circular area with no bacterial colonies. Fleming concluded a chemical agent secreted by the mould was inhibiting the growth of the bacteria in his culture. He named this agent penicillin. It took researchers Howard Florey and Ernst Chain 20 years of work to isolate penicillin, prove it effective and safe for use in humans against a wide range of bacterial agents, and produce it in quantity. In 1948, Fleming, Florey, and Chain were awarded the Nobel Prize in medicine and physiology for their work.

Penicillin revolutionized the practice of medicine, but the struggle against harmful bacteria did not end in the 1940s. New antibiotics were immediately in demand since some harmful bacteria were unaffected by penicillin.

Streptomycin was developed in 1943 for use against tuberculosis. New antibiotics are still constantly required to combat resistant strains of bacteria. Resistant strains are formed when bacteria adapt to an antibiotic through natural changes, or mutations, of their DNA. These resistant strains are no longer affected by that antibiotic. Scientists have tried to combat this by finding new antibiotics and developing semi-synthetic variations of old ones for treating specific problems. The monocylic beta-lactam antibiotic in the photograph is a new antibiotic developed to fight infections in hospital patients.

Prescribing antibiotic medication is never easy. Because bacteria can develop resistance to antibiotics, each infection must be treated with the correct dose of the appropriate antibiotic. Trivial use of antibiotics is dangerous because the more often an antibiotic is used, the more likely a resistant strain will develop. The relative effect on the patient of each antibiotic must also be considered. Penicillin is nontoxic, but it does cause allergic reactions. Streptomycin must be used with greater care since its overuse may cause vertigo or deafness. Other antibiotics are safe for use against surface infections, but are highly toxic when taken internally. To determine which antibiotic will be most effective, doctors run a standard test called a bioassay.

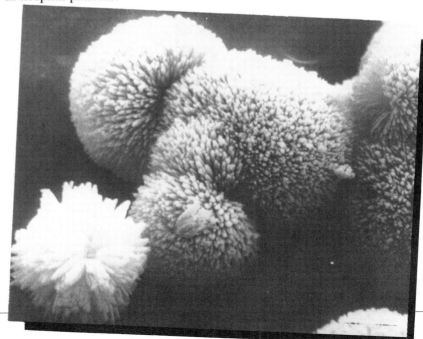

Section Review Questions

1. State three important ways fungi differ from vascular plants.
2. State the functions of the following fungal structures: a) hyphae, b) mycelium, c) fruiting body, and d) spores.
3. Compare the mycelium of a bread mould with that of a mushroom.
4. a) Explain how fungi obtain their nutrients.
   b) Which other kingdom is similar to fungi in the way nutrients are obtained? Explain your answer.
5. a) Explain how fungi reproduce.
   b) Compare reproduction in fungi to reproduction in flowering vascular plants.
6. Why is *Rhizopus* a good species to use to study how fungi grow?

14.2 Life Cycles of the True Fungi

Most fungi are classified in a group known collectively as true fungi. All true fungi display a sexually reproducing stage at some point in their life cycle. (See Figure 14-3.)

Life cycles play an important part in **mycology**, which is the study of fungi. Knowing about the life cycles of fungi enables humans to control the reproduction and growth of many fungal species. We may want to prevent the growth of a harmful fungus such as wheat rust, or promote the growth of a useful fungus such as the commercial mushroom or *Penicillium* mould. We can control these fungi if we know the conditions under which they grow best.

LABORATORY EXERCISE 14-3
Factors Affecting the Growth of Fungal Moulds

Fungal moulds can grow on any type of organic matter such as dead plants and animals, food, or your skin. Moulds can also grow on a prepared culture medium such as agar.

In this exercise, you will design controlled experiments to identify some of the factors that affect the growth of fungal moulds. In this way, you will be able to determine optimum conditions for their growth.

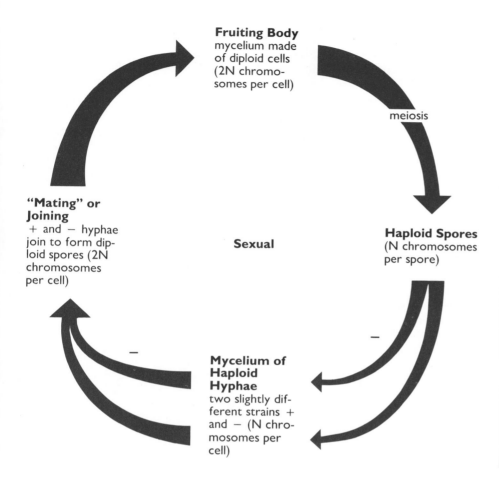

Fruiting Body
mycelium made
of diploid cells
(2N chromo-
somes per cell)

meiosis

Haploid Spores
(N chromosomes
per spore)

−

**Mycelium of
Haploid
Hyphae**
two slightly dif-
ferent strains +
and − (N chro-
mosomes per
cell)

Sexual

**"Mating" or
Joining**
+ and − hyphae
join to form dip-
loid spores (2N
chromosomes
per cell)

−

FIGURE 14-3 All fungi that reproduce sexually follow this life cycle. Of
course, the fruiting bodies and spore-
producing structures differ among
divisions.

When the mature spore cases of the
bread mould, *Rhizopus*, turn black, the
spores are ready to be released.

Division Zygomycetes: Conjugation Fungi

True fungi share other characteristics besides the ability to reproduce sexually. All true fungi are made of hyphae that form either a loose or a compact mycelium. True fungi have cell walls made of chitin, and their hyphae secrete digestive enzymes. True fungi are classified into three divisions according to the type of reproductive structure they have that produces the sexual spores.

Fungi that produce spores from a zygote-based structure belong to the division **Zygomycetes**. The bread mould *Rhizopus* is a typical zygomycete. A mature bread-mould mycelium contains three types of hyphae. Root-like hyphae called **rhizoids** penetrate the surface of the organic material the bread mould grows on. (See "start here" on Figure 14-4.) These rhizoids break down the organic material, which is not always bread, by secreting digestive enzymes. Then the rhizoids absorb the resulting small nutrient molecules. **Stolons** are hyphae that grow horizontally above the surface of the growth medium. They allow the mould to spread. At points where the stolons touch

Biologists often use the same term for similar structures in two very different organisms. Rhizoid and stolon also describe underground and above ground stems in many flowering vascular plants.

the surface, vertical **erect hyphae** sprout up. Spore cases develop on the tips of the erect hyphae.

The spores produced in these cases are asexual because they form from a single parent by mitosis. As a result, these spores have the same number of chromosomes as the cells of the parent mycelium. Mycologists call this chromosome count the **haploid number**, and they use the symbol N to represent it. When the spores are mature, the spore cases turn black and erupt, releasing the spores to the air. Upon germination, the spores develop into new mycelium with N chromosomes per haploid cell. (See Figure 14-4.)

FIGURE 14-4 Sexual and asexual reproduction in the bread mould *Rhizopus*

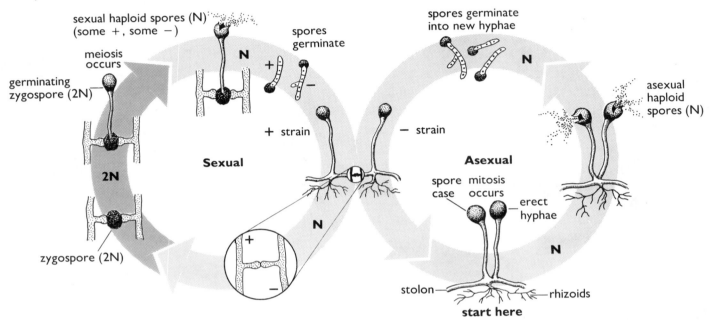

Asexual spore formation accounts for most cases of reproduction of *Rhizopus*. Sexual reproduction of bread mould usually occurs only when conditions for growth are unfavourable. Sexual reproduction is possible because there are actually two mating strains of hyphae in bread mould, even though neighbouring patches of mycelium appear to be identical. The two strains are designated by "+" and "−". When plus and minus hyphae of opposite mating strains grow close together, they join and form a thick-walled zygote with 2N chromosomes (the **diploid number**). Because the joining of two mating strains is called **conjugation**, the zygomycetes are sometimes called **conjugation fungi**.

The diploid zygospore remains inactive until suitable growing conditions return. Then an erect hypha with a spore case emerges and forms ordinary haploid spores by meiosis. When these haploid spores germinate, they grow into ordinary *Rhizopus* mycelium with N chromosomes per cell.

Important Conjugation Fungi

If food is left exposed to the air for too long, bread-mould spores will begin to germinate. The spread of bread mould can be controlled by keeping food in airtight, waterproof containers. Refrigerating food also helps control *Rhizopus* as low temperatures retard its growth.

Besides bread, *Rhizopus* attacks fruit such as strawberries and grapes. The mycelium grows over the moist organic material in a fluffy mass. As it digests the organic material and absorbs the nutrients, rapid decay occurs.

Another famous conjugation fungus is the late blight fungus, *Phytophthora infestans*. This fungus caused the Irish potato famine from 1845-1847. The potato was an important staple in the diet of the Irish, and many people died as the fungus destroyed both the mature potatoes and other plant parts such as the leaves. Extremely wet growing seasons during those years contributed to the rapid spread of the disease. Late blight fungus also attacks other crops such as tomatoes.

The potato blight fungus begins its life cycle when its spores land on the wet leaves of the potato plant. Knowing this, farmers can control the spread of the disease by spraying the leaves with a fungicide. Biologists may also develop new strains of the potato plant with leaves that are more resistant to attacks by the late blight fungus.

Several species of water mould such as *Saprolegnia* are also included in the division Zygomycetes. These moulds usually appear as a light-coloured fluff, which is caused by the growth of the mycelium on the bodies of fish and other water animals. The spores of water fungi are well adapted to their aquatic environment. The spore-producing bodies of water moulds form motile spores that can swim with the use of flagella. (See Figure 14–5.) *Saprolegnia* often attack aquarium fish. The mycelium grows into the body tissues of the fish and absorbs its nutrients. The fungal infection enables bacteria to enter the fish more easily. When the fish dies, the mould continues to feed off the dead matter. Water moulds can also destroy fish in ponds and lakes, upsetting natural food chains.

In a home aquarium, fungal infections of fish can be controlled by using commercially available drops containing a fungicide to treat the water, and by swabbing the infected area with a 10% iodine solution. A more permanent solution is to use fish food laced with medication. Fungal infections of fish are often caused by overly acidic water, which results in weakened resistance to infection. Most freshwater fish thrive in nearly neutral water, so controlling the acidity of aquarium water helps reduce infections. Of course, controlling the acidity of freshwater lakes and ponds is much harder to do. Reducing acid rain could keep conditions in natural bodies of water within tolerable levels.

Mycelium of the water mould, *Saprolegnia*

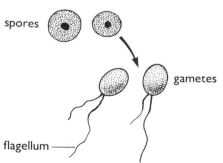

FIGURE 14-5 The spores of water moulds develop flagella that allow them to swim and spread over a wide area.

Division Ascomycetes: Sac Fungi

Fungi in the division **Ascomycetes** produce sexual spores in long, thin sac-like structures called **asci**. The divsion name is derived from this structure, but members are more commonly called **sac fungi**. The asci are often contained inside cup-shaped fruiting bodies like those in the cup fungus, *Peziza*, or in the foldings on the surface of the edible morel.

Sac fungi can also reproduce asexually by fragmentation or by the production of asexual haploid spores. These spores form on the ends of hyphae growing up from the surface of the organic matter containing the main mycelium. In yeast, which is also a sac fungus, asexual reproduction takes place by budding. (See "start here" in Figure 14-6.)

Sexual reproduction in yeast normally occurs only when environmental conditions are not suitable for growth. When conditions are unfavourable, two yeast cells of opposite mating strains (+ and −) fuse to form a cell with two nuclei, one from each parent strain. The two nuclei then join and form a diploid nucleus. The resulting zygote-like cell can survive until better growing conditions return, at which time meiosis will form ordinary haploid **ascospores**.

In other multicellular ascomycetes, hyphae of opposite mating strains may unite to form new hyphae with two nuclei per cell. (See "start here" in Figure 14-7.) The nuclei in the ends of some hyphae may join to form a diploid nucleus, which, in turn, will undergo meiosis to produce haploid ascospores.

FIGURE 14-6 Sexual and asexual reproduction in the unicellular ascomycete yeast

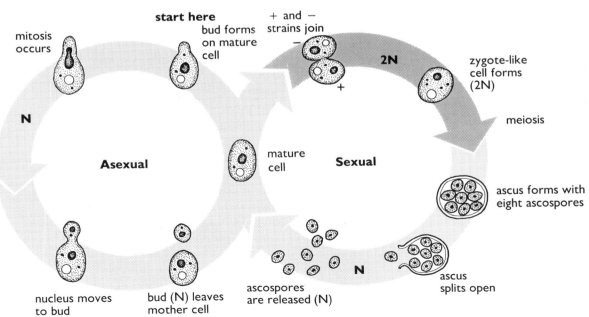

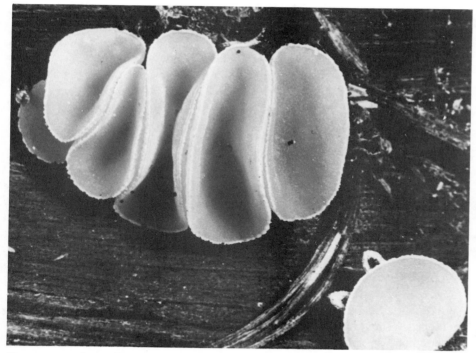

Common sac fungi. Spore-producing sacs are found in the cups or folds of these mushrooms. **Left:** Scarlet cup fungi. **Right:** Morel.

FIGURE 14-7 Sexual and asexual reproduction in a typical ascomycete

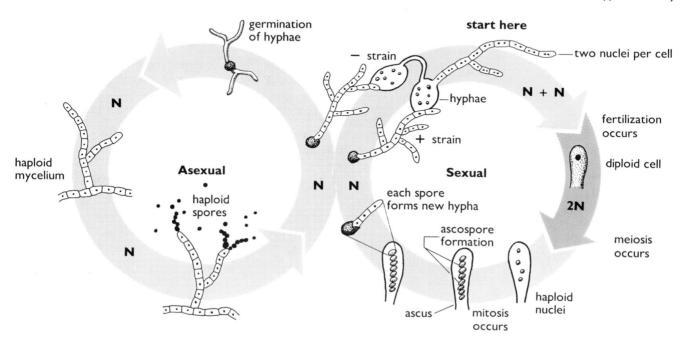

germination of hyphae

start here

− strain

two nuclei per cell

hyphae

N + N

+ strain

fertilization occurs

diploid cell

N

haploid mycelium

Asexual

haploid spores

N

N

Sexual

each spore forms new hypha

ascospore formation

2N

meiosis occurs

haploid nuclei

ascus

mitosis occurs

Spores released by the mildew on these lilac leaves cause the powdery appearance. The inset shows new mycelium spreading over the surface of a lilac leaf.

Important Sac Fungi

Yeasts are the only ascomycetes that exist as single cells. They do not form mycelia. Yeasts obtain their energy from the breakdown of glucose in a process called **fermentation**. Fermentation occurs in the absence of oxygen and produces carbon dioxide and alcohol as waste products. So, yeasts are very useful in bread-baking and alcohol-based industries. It is the carbon dioxide bubbles trapped in bread dough that make bread rise when it is baked. Some kinds of rubbing alcohol and beverages such as wine and liquor make use of the alcohol produced during the fermentation of plant materials.

Not all sac fungi are useful. Some can cause considerable damage to whole populations of trees such as the parasitic ascomycete responsible for Dutch elm disease. Dutch elm disease is carried by the Japanese bark beetle and enters the tree trunk through openings in the bark. The damage caused by the disease has resulted in the virtual disappearance of Dutch elms from many parts of North America.

Powdery mildews are other examples of parasitic fungi that can attack grapes, apples, and roses. When the spores of one of these fungi land on a wet leaf of a host plant, they germinate and form a mycelium on the surface of the leaf. The fungus covers the leaf and obtains nourishment from the leaf's tissues. The spores produced by the hyphae give the surface of the leaf a powdery appearance. Leaves damaged in this way can no longer photosynthesize, and the growth of the host is affected.

Division Basidiomycetes: Club Fungi

All members of the division **Basidiomycetes** produce spores in club-shaped structures called **basidia**. The best known club fungus is the common mushroom. The mushroom has a typical life cycle. (See Figure 14-8.)

The part of the mushroom that you eat is only the fruiting body, not the whole organism. The rest of the mushroom's mycelium grows unseen in the organic material the fungus feeds on. During sexual reproduction, haploid hyphae of two opposite mating strains fuse to form diploid cells. After a rainstorm, the diploid hyphae compact into small, round **buttons** that push their way through the soil. As the buttons grow in size, a stem-like stalk forms, which is topped by an umbrella-shaped cap. The expanding cap will eventually tear away from the stalk leaving a ring behind. Under the cap is a series of vertical plates called **gills** on which the basidia form.

Meiosis occurs in the tip of each basidium to produce haploid spores. These haploid spores are released and dispersed by the wind when they are mature.

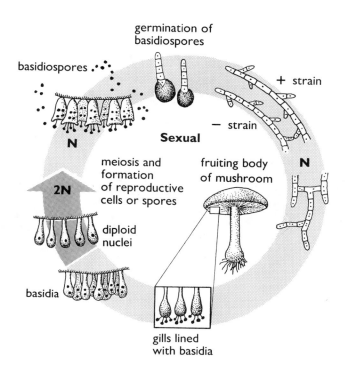

germination of
basidiospores

basidiospores

+ strain

− strain

Sexual

N

N

meiosis and
formation
of reproductive
cells or spores

fruiting body
of mushroom

2N

diploid
nuclei

basidia

gills lined
with basidia

FIGURE 14-8 Sexual reproduction in a basidiomycete such as the mushroom. Asexual reproduction usually occurs by fragmentation of the underground mycelium.

Important Club Fungi

Club fungi include some of the largest fungi such as mushrooms, toadstools, bracket fungi, and puffballs.

Rusts and **smuts** are an interesting but harmful group of club fungi. These parasitic fungi can grow on and destroy crops such as wheat, corn, barley, and oats. Rusts and smuts can also harm several species of decorative plants.

Wheat rust has a very peculiar life cycle that involves two host plants at different times of the year. During the early growing season, wheat rust mycelium can destroy much of a healthy wheat crop. Toward the end of the growing season, the wheat rust releases spores that can drift onto neighbouring wild barberry bushes. The spores that land on these bushes remain inactive over the winter. But in the spring, these spores produce new mycelia on the barberry plant. These mycelia release spores that, in turn, infect the next season's wheat crop.

Farmers have attempted to stop the spread of wheat rust by destroying the barberry bushes before the fungi become active. But destroying these bushes is not always possible since they may be growing in fields not owned by the farmer. Effective control involves co-operation among farmers since all secondary hosts in the region must be eradicated at the same time.

Programs funded by the government to help destroy barberry bushes have helped control the spread of wheat rust. The Department of Agriculture has

CAUTION!

Although there are many edible types of club fungi such as the mushroom *Agaricus*, there are just as many species that are deadly and should never be eaten. These include such varieties as the destroying angel and the fly agaric. Accidentally ingesting these mushrooms can cause death.

Corn that has been infected by corn-smut fungi

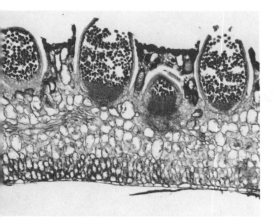

Wheat rust spores are seen here being released from the cup-like structures invading a barberry leaf.

also supported efforts to help scientists develop strains of wheat that are hardier and more resistant to infection by wheat rust.

Corn smut infects the stems and leaves of the corn plant, affecting its health and growth. The ears of the corn plant can also be destroyed by the corn-smut fungus. Since the corn plant is the only host, farmers try to control the spread of the disease by burning the infected plants or by plowing them under. Developing strains of corn that are more smut-resistant has helped reduce the problem in North America.

Corn and wheat make up a large percentage of the world's food supply. Club fungi, therefore, can have a devastating effect on the economy of countries, like Canada, which rely on these crops for food and export.

Section Review Questions

1. Which common characteristics do true fungi share?
2. a) Describe how each of the three divisions of true fungi acquired its name.
   b) Describe the life cycle of a representative member of each division.
3. State two reasons why it is important to study the life cycles of fungi.
4. a) List one useful species for each of the three true fungi divisions. Choose one species and describe how it is used.
   b) List one harmful species for each true fungi division. Choose one species and describe how it causes damage.
5. a) How does the life cycle of wheat rust differ from that of other members of the same division?
   b) How does an understanding of the life cycle of wheat rust enable farmers to combat infestations?

Fungus Kills Dandelion!

Environmentally concerned homeowners should take heart. The war against dandelions may soon be waged in a new way. A biologist at the University of Guelph is aiming a different kind of weapon at dandelions — a fungus.

In 1989, a colleague of Dr. Lee Burpee, a biologist at the University of Guelph, discovered an afflicted patch of dandelions. Investigation of the plants soon revealed the roots of the plants were infected by a damaging fungus. The dandelion on the right in the photograph shows the effects of this fungus, in contrast to the healthy dandelion on the left. When the virulence of the fungus was discovered, Dr. Burpee was eager to develop it as a naturally occurring biological control for the weed. Although chemical herbicides must be certified by Agriculture Canada as safe to use, naturally occurring biological controls are considered by many to be even safer because they add nothing new and potentially damaging to the environment. Another advantage of biological controls, Dr. Burpee says, is that a perennial population of the control organism may become established in an area, making annual application unnecessary. Chemical herbicides do not develop this kind of residual control of a weed.

However, the most virulent fungal weed controls have been only 80% effective in comparison to chemical herbicides. Researchers are altering growth and spreading conditions of the cultured fungus in an attempt to increase its virulence.

A further goal of these alterations will be to improve the effectiveness of the fungus against the dandelion taproot. Currently, the taproot of established dandelions is resistant to fungal attacks. After the rest of the dandelion has died, this taproot often remains as a base for regrowth. Younger seedlings, which have poorly developed taproots, can be successfully killed. This suggests the fungus may best be used as a preventive agent.

Fungal agents pose problems that chemical herbicides do not.

Chemical herbicides directly affect only areas of application. Although seepage of herbicides into groundwater causes problems, their initial action is specifically located. By contrast, biological controls are living organisms that can either move or grow into areas where they are not wanted.

In the case of Dr. Burpee's fungus, this danger is compounded because its lethal effect is not specific to dandelions. Broadleaf crops such as tomatoes and beans are killed as well. Sporulating fungi could not be used commercially since crops might be threatened by the fungus spreading by way of spores. Dr. Burpee has solved this problem by finding a strain of the fungus that cannot sporulate. Since the fungus can grow only through its mycelium, and it grows only a few millimetres without a food source, the effect of the fungus is confined to the root on which it grows.

Mycologists still debate the classification of several species of fungus that do not display all the structural and reproductive characteristics of true fungi. *Penicillium*, for example, is sometimes classified as an ascomycete and sometimes as an imperfect fungus.

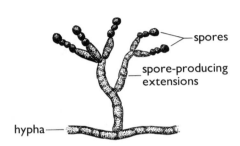

FIGURE 14-9 The structure of the blue-green mould *Penicillium*

14.3 Imperfect Fungi, Lichens, and Slime Moulds

Imperfect fungi, lichens, and slime moulds have often caused problems for taxonomists, and controversy about their classification still exists. The life cycles of imperfect fungi are apparently different from those of true fungi. Lichens are *made up* of two separate organisms. Slime moulds *behave* like two different organisms. Perhaps as the tools and methods of science improve, biologists will understand these three groups better, and be able to classify them more accurately.

Imperfect Fungi

Several species of fungi exist for which biologists have observed no sexual stage of reproduction. For this reason, these species are referred to as **imperfect fungi**. However, the placement of species in this group may reflect only an inability to observe accurately. In fact, many species have been reclassified as improved instruments have allowed scientists to observe sexual reproduction in fungi formerly thought to be imperfect.

However, each species of imperfect fungi is ideally suited to reproduce and survive in its environment. Most imperfect fungi are plant parasites that thrive on farm crops such as apples, beans, and cabbages. But some imperfect fungi can be helpful as well as harmful. The blue-green mould, *Penicillium*, for example, is a widespread imperfect fungus that attacks food, paper, and other organic material. (See Figure 14–9.) However, some types of *Penicillium* are used to colour and flavour blue cheese. And *Penicillium* is also used to produce the powerful antibiotic penicillin.

Asexual reproduction of imperfect fungi occurs when spore-producing extensions of the hyphae develop. The spores are released when they are mature and travel through the air. The spores of imperfect fungi such as *Penicillium* are numerous, widespread, and germinate easily. Therefore, they can grow and feed on any moist organic material including clothes, leather, and human food.

Some skin disorders in humans are caused by parasitic imperfect fungi. Ringworm and athlete's foot, for example, are both caused by the same fungus. They differ only in the location of the infection.

Lichens: Primitive Pioneers

Lichens are sometimes referred to as **pioneers** because they are the first living things to invade uninhabited areas and prepare the way for future plants. In carrying out their life processes, lichens convert rock into soil over long periods of time. The soil that farmers use to grow their crops was probably created by the action of lichens ages ago. But how does this change occur? To answer this question, you will collect samples of lichen for laboratory examination.

LABORATORY EXERCISE 14-4
Collecting and Examining Lichens

In this exercise, you will study the structure of lichens to determine how they survive, and how they help form soil from rock. Lichens are usually found on bare rock or on the bark of trees in areas far removed from the city environment. A field trip may be necessary to collect lichens in their natural environment. If a field trip is not possible, your teacher may be able to provide you with lichen samples and prepared slides.

Lichens: Primitive Partners

Scientists once thought each type of lichen was a single plant species. By using the microscope, scientists eventually understood the true nature of lichen. Instead of existing as a single species, each lichen is really a close association of two distinct species—one a fungus and the other a green alga. (See Figure 14–10.) A close association between two species is known as **symbiosis**. In the lichen, both **symbionts** — the organisms in the symbiotic partnership — benefit from their relation to each other. This type of symbiosis is called **mutualism**. The green algae, through photosynthesis, provide a source of food for both fungi and algae. The ability of the fungal mycelium to retain water prevents dehydration of either species. For this reason, lichens can live on rocks where neither fungi nor algae could survive on their own.

Lichens secrete acidic enzymes to obtain mineral nutrients from the rocks they grow on. The enzymes cause the rock to break down and crumble. The action of the enzymes gradually forms a thin layer of soil, which eventually allows slightly larger organisms such as shallow-rooted plants to invade the area.

The Life Cycle of Slime Moulds

Perhaps the strangest fungi of all are the **slime moulds**. They present a different classification problem than lichen because they exhibit both an active and an inactive stage during their life cycle. Active slime moulds look so little like inactive slime moulds because of the structural and behavioural characteristics displayed by each at these two stages of their life cycle. As a result, biologists used to think the two forms were two different organisms.

Lichens such as the orange lichen covering this rock can break down rock, thereby beginning the process of soil formation.

There is still no final agreement about the classification of slime moulds. Some biologists classify them as protists. Others classify slime moulds as fungi.

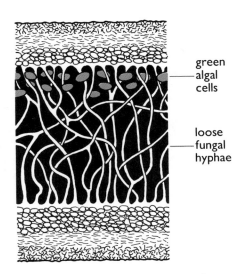

green
algal
cells

loose
fungal
hyphae

FIGURE 14-10 Cross section of a lichen that shows the symbiotic association between algal cells and fungal hyphae

FIGURE 14-11 Sexual reproduction in a slime mould

During the active phase of its life cycle, a slime mould moves about the moist, warm forest floor like an overgrown amoeba, feeding on dead and rotting trees and leaves. The **plasmodium**, or main body of the slime mould, is not much more than a mass of protoplasm, containing many nuclei surrounded by a flexible membrane. As the plasmodium moves over the rotting vegetation, it takes in small bits of organic matter, digesting this material in its food vacuoles. Asexual reproduction may occur by fragmentation during this phase of its life cycle.

When growing conditions are unsuitable such as during droughts or cool weather, the plasmodium becomes inactive and stops moving. The plasmodium then forms many vertical fruiting bodies in much the same way as other fungi do. These fruiting bodies produce haploid spores that are released when better growing conditions return. (See Figure 14–11.) The spores develop into flagellated cells that join together to form a zygote. The zygote then grows to form a new plasmodium.

The problem of classifying a slime mould exists because it behaves like a protist during the active stage of its life cycle and a fungus during the inactive stage. Further study of this organism may help clarify its position in the living world.

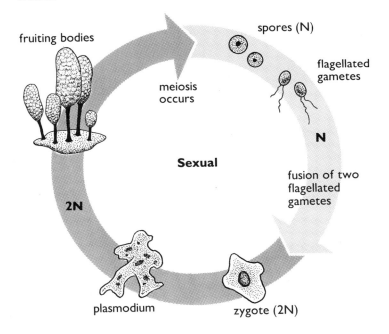

fruiting bodies

spores (N)

flagellated gametes

meiosis occurs

N

Sexual

fusion of two flagellated gametes

2N

plasmodium

zygote (2N)

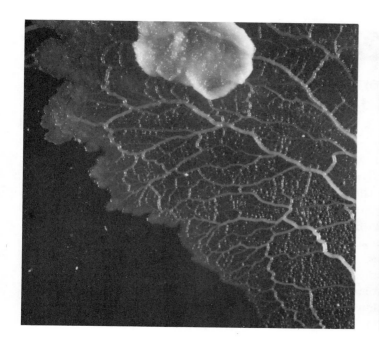

LEFT: The plasmodium of a slime mould engulfs an oat flake (top). The slime mould will soon absorb and digest the flake.

RIGHT: Fruiting bodies of a slime mould

Section Review Questions

1. a) How did imperfect fungi get their name?
   b) Explain why the name is not entirely suitable.

2. State how *Penicillium* can act as both a useful and a harmful fungus.

3. a) List the two symbionts that make up a lichen.
   b) What is the nature of the relationship between the two symbionts?
   c) Which characteristics probably led early scientists to suppose lichens were plants?

4. Describe the role lichens play in the formation of soil from rock.

5. Explain how a slime mould may be classified as a protist at one stage and a fungus at another stage of its life cycle.

Lichens as Pollution Indicators

On April 26, 1986, an accident at the Chernobyl nuclear power station in the USSR shocked and frightened the world. Although much of the radioactive fallout from the accident was deposited over central Europe and Scandinavia, other northern countries are also expected to receive fallout due to long-range transport of radioactive isotopes in the atmosphere. A recent Canadian study found increases in levels of the radioactive isotope cesium-137 of between 0-19% in various locations as a result of fallout from the Chernobyl accident. Surprisingly, radiation counters were not used in the field. Instead, researchers took samples of slow-growing mosses and lichens that were then dried and counted for cesium-137 decay in the lab.

Although all life forms are affected by pollution, only lichens are routinely used by researchers as reliable indicators of environmental pollutants. Lichens' peculiar method of taking in nutrients is a key reason for this. Plant surfaces are protected from the atmosphere by either bark or cuticle. But lichens, which lack similar physical barriers, readily absorb airborne substances. Soil can also act as a buffer between the environment and a plant's internal environment by filtering many undesirable substances from rain and ground water. Lichens have no roots, so they have no such buffer. Instead, lichens absorb rainwater and dissolved substances directly, and for the most part, indiscriminately. As a result of their lack of filtering systems, lichens often have levels of pollutants similar to that of the surrounding area.

Pollution studies make use of lichens' peculiar abilities. Although variations in the effect of air pollution on individual lichen growths depend on the species and the material on which the lichen grows, the relationship between the intensity of air pollution and the destruction of lichens is clear. Today, observation of lichen growth is used to map the locations of airborne pollutants such as sulphur dioxide, heavy metals, and nitrous oxides. Three levels of increasing pollution can be determined by visually examining the condition of lichens. The first level of pollution results in diminished luxuriance of growth; the second, in stunted growth; the third, in sterility. Extremely polluted areas are lichen deserts, which support no growth at all.

Concern over radioactive material in northern food chains was the impetus for the cesium-137 study. An increase in lichen radioactivity might lead to an increase in caribou radioactivity since caribou eat the affected lichens. The exposure of humans who hunt caribou, in turn, would be expected to increase. The Chernobyl accident caused increases between 12.7 and 37% in cesium-137 concentration in caribou at different locations across northern Canada.

14.4 Fungi in the Biosphere

Because fungi are heterotrophs and must rely on material produced by other organisms for nutrition, they have a profound effect on the biosphere. Fungi function as **decomposers**, perhaps their most important ecological role. Dead plants and the bodies of dead animals would quickly accumulate and choke the natural environment if it were not for the action of fungi.

Saprophytic fungi such as mushrooms, toadstools, and slime moulds break down dead plant and animal matter with the enzymes they secrete to digest their food. Some nutrients are absorbed directly by these fungi and used as a source of energy. Other materials produced through the decomposition process are returned to the soil to be used by green plants. This recycling of organic matter by fungi is important because it helps free the earth of wastes. Decomposition also helps keep the soil fertile.

Although *Penicillium* is essential for producing the antibiotic penicillin, it can also destroy foods such as this orange once it begins to grow.

However, not all decomposition by fungi is beneficial. Bread mould and some blue-green moulds can survive in your refrigerator and spoil leftover food. Other types of fungi attack rare books, leather, and clothing if these items are stored in a damp, warm place. Large libraries often keep rare books in a climate-controlled room designed to prevent the growth of fungi.

Parasitic fungi act as agents of plant and animal diseases. Many parasitic rusts, smuts, and blights destroy a variety of plant crops such as wheat and corn annually. Apple scab is a parasitic fungi that attacks apple crops in Canada. Apple scab infects plant structures at the early growth stage, and appears later as circular scabs on the fruit or the leaves. Damaged leaves inhibit photosynthesis, affecting the quality of the apples. Infected apples are difficult to sell because of their appearance. Apple scab can be controlled by burning the leaves, by plowing infected parts under, or by spraying trees with a fungicide.

In order to decide how to control one of these diseases, it is useful to know where and how the fungus attacks specific plant parts.

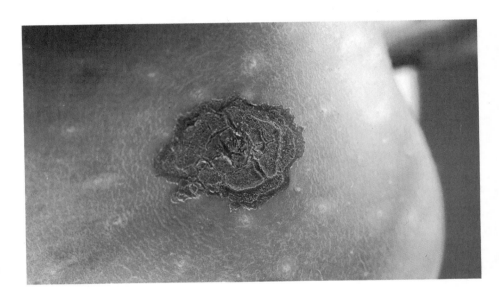

The brown spots on this apple show the effects of apple scab.

LABORATORY EXERCISE 14-5
Fungal Infections of Plant Tissues

Certain fungi are responsible for causing many diseases of plant tissue. In this exercise, you will examine prepared slides of diseased plant tissues to determine what type of damage is caused by the fungal mycelium infection. You may be able to use this information to determine how best to control the particular infection.

Fungal Infections of Humans

Several human diseases are caused by fungi. Most of these diseases are merely annoying, but some of them can be deadly.

Ringworm is a skin infection caused by *Microsporum*, a species of imperfect fungus that usually affects the skin of the groin, the scalp, and the beard. *Microsporum* can cause severe itching, and the fungus is contagious. If left untreated, *Microsporum* can spread rapidly by spores and may be passed to others by direct or indirect contact. Sprays and powders containing fungicides can be used to help control its spread.

Athlete's foot is caused by the same species of imperfect fungus as ringworm and usually affects the skin between the toes. The athlete's foot fungus exists on dirty shower floors and in running shoes, and the disease may be contracted from these sources. Keeping your feet clean and dry, and using foot powders and sprays when necessary, can help prevent the disease from occurring or spreading.

Eating mushrooms picked in the wild can be a dangerous undertaking since many of these mushrooms are poisonous. The most harmful and potentially fatal mushrooms belong to the genus *Amanita*. (See page 372 for photograph.) Accidentally ingesting only one or two destroying angels can, for example, lead to abdominal pain and cramps, vomiting, and eventually death. These effects are caused by toxins in the mushroom that can enter the bloodstream within hours of ingestion.

Another type of *Amanita* produces poisons that can affect the nervous system and cause hallucinations and behaviour similar to drunkenness. These neurotoxins may cause coma and eventual death. The first step in effective treatment involves emptying the stomach and intestines before the poisons enter the bloodstream. Further treatment for mushroom poisoning depends on knowing which *Amanita* species was ingested. If *Amanita muscaris* was eaten, atropine is injected to counteract overstimulation of the nervous system. If *Amanita phalloides* was ingested, however, an intravenous solution of sugar and salt is necessary to combat possible liver damage. If the species is not known, it is difficult for doctors to determine which treatment is needed. Remember that you should eat only store-bought mushrooms.

Practical Uses of Fungi

Although there are many harmful species of fungi that exist, there are just as many species that are useful. Some fungi are edible and add variety to your diet. Several species of fungi such as *Penicillium* are used to produce a variety of antibiotics that combat certain diseases and infections.

Many antibiotics are produced by the fermentation process carried on by some species of fungi. The fungi used to produce antibiotics are placed in

DID YOU KNOW?
Ringworm fungus is so named because of the raised, circular or concentric sores in the skin that resemble coiled worms.

DID YOU KNOW?
Dermatophytes are fungi that cause skin diseases in humans and animals. Four genera (*Epidermophyton*, *Trichophyton*, *Microsporum*, and *Keratinomyces*) of dermatophytes are responsible for these skin diseases or dermatomycoses.

DID YOU KNOW?
Mushrooms are an excellent source of vitamins (thiamine, riboflavin, niacin) and minerals (calcium, iron, potassium, phosphorus). They are also low in fat, sugar, and sodium.

The word equation for fermentation, the energy releasing process occurring in yeast cells, is as follows.

$$\text{glucose} \xrightarrow{\text{enzymes}} (\text{energy}) + \begin{array}{l}\text{ethyl}\\\text{alcohol}\end{array} + \begin{array}{l}\text{carbon}\\\text{dioxide}\end{array}$$

This process occurs in the absence of oxygen, which explains why fruit drinks that are first exposed to air and then sealed tightly can still ferment.

The wonderful aroma of freshly baked bread is mostly alcohol vapour.

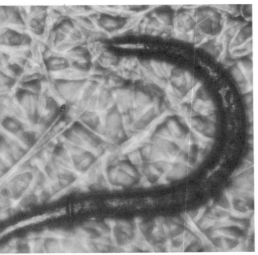

A predatory fungus trapping a nematode worm with a noose made from its hyphae

tanks containing a culture medium where fermentation can take place. The antibiotics are then isolated and removed from the culture medium.

Yeast is a fungus that is very useful in the bread-baking process. Using yeasts to make bread is possible because of the way they feed. As yeast cells break down glucose molecules to release energy for their life functions, they also produce two by-products—carbon dioxide and alcohol. You have already learned that this process is called fermentation. The carbon dioxide formed by baker's yeast gets trapped in the dough and expands when it is heated, causing the dough to rise. Several types of yeast are used to form the alcohol content of commercial beverages such as wine, beer, and liquor.

Predatory fungi have recently been discovered that attack insects and other pests. Spores land on an insect's body, germinate, and form a mycelium that penetrates the living tissues of the insect in search of nutrition. The insect is destroyed in the process. Spore-producing structures emerge from the corpse, releasing spores as the cycle begins again. Agriculturists might be able to use spores from predatory fungi to control crop pests. The spores would be contained in insecticides and sprayed on crops.

Section Review Questions

1. How do saprophytic fungi help recycle organic matter?
2. What methods can farmers in Canada use to help control the spread of apple scab?
3. Describe the cause, effects, and treatment of ringworm in humans.
4. a) List several harmful effects resulting from the ingestion of poisonous mushrooms such as those belonging to the genus *Amanita*.
   b) How can such harmful effects be avoided?
5. How does the process of fermentation performed by yeast benefit humans?
6. a) What are predatory fungi?
   b) How might predatory fungi be used by agriculturalists?

Meet Lori Marshall

Lori is a pharmacist who works in the Pharmacy Department of Women's College Hospital. She provides drug information to doctors, nurses, and other health-care workers.

Q. *What does your work as a pharmacist involve?*

A. My priority is to answer drug-information questions. The drugs are labelled by name only, so it's my job to know, or be able to find out, all the information about that drug.

Q. *What kind of information do doctors usually need?*

A. Doctors need to know about the side effects of drugs. For example, certain fungal infections are hard to kill and require multiple drug regimens. Because some of these drugs have nasty side effects, we can suggest appropriate doses.

Q. *How do you find information?*

A. We use what's called a "systematic approach to drug information." This is a three-level research approach. First, we consult textbooks for information on older drugs. But because things change so quickly in this field, even books published in the 1980s can be out of date.

Q. *What's the second step?*

A. We consult indexing and abstracting services such as the *Index Medica*, which is a monthly publication that lists drugs and drug information. The third step is to check primary literature such as journal and magazine articles about drugs.

Q. *What are some of the other aspects of your job?*

A. I sit on a Pharmacy and Therapeutics committee that devises policies and procedures for drugs to be used in the hospital. Because a hospital is run under budget restraints, it does not have an entire range of drugs of a certain type, unlike a drugstore. So, the committee decides which drugs will be used for certain conditions. It's my job to prepare unbiased drug reviews for this committee.

Q. *What do you mean by "unbiased"?*

A. I look into all the research and information about the drug, and not just the information provided by the pharmaceutical company that produces that drug. The manufacturer's information could be biased.

Q. *Do you have to keep learning new things all the time?*

A. Yes. There is also a lot of interdepartmental education. For example, we have a journal club that meets to share and discuss new information. Each club member must read and keep up to date with a journal. We also write and publish a bimonthly newsletter for the physicians and nurses.

Q. *What types of work, other than hospital, can pharmacists choose?*

A. A pharmacist can work for a drug company, in a drug-store pharmacy department, or set up a pharmacy.

Q. *Why did you choose hospital work?*

A. I felt I would be able to use my education to more advantage, because more interesting kinds of drugs are used in hospitals. For example, intravenous drugs are often used in hospitals.

Q. *Is there a demand for pharmacists?*

A. There's a shortage of pharmacists in Canada. There are only eight schools in Canada and not nearly enough graduates.

Chapter Review

Key Words

asci	hyphae
ascomycetes	heterotroph
autotroph	mycelium
basidia	mutualism
basidiomycetes	parasite
buttons	pioneers
chitin	plasmodium
conjugation	rhizoids
decomposer	saprophyte
fermentation	symbiont
fragmentation	symbiosis
fruiting body	zygomycetes

Recall Questions

Multiple Choice

1. Which of the following is not a structural characteristic of fungi?
   a) hyphae
   b) spores
   c) roots
   d) mycelium

2. The bread mould *Rhizopus* belongs to the division
   a) Ascomycetes
   b) Basidiomycetes
   c) Imperfect Fungi
   d) Zygomycetes

3. Joining of + and − strains of hyphae is characteristic of which reproductive process?
   a) conjugation
   b) budding
   c) fragmentation
   d) spore formation

4. Symbiosis in fungi is best seen in
   a) slime moulds
   b) bracket fungi
   c) lichens
   d) *Saprolegnia*

5. A mass of moving protoplasm, as seen in slime moulds, is referred to as a
   a) fruiting body
   b) plasmodium
   c) mycelium
   d) smut

Fill in the Blanks

1. A carbohydrate that is similar to cellulose and is found in the walls of some fungal cells is called _____.

2. The _____ that forms in bread mould by the fusion of opposite mating strains is diploid (has 2N chromosomes per cell).

3. Ascospores are _____ produced by sac fungi during asexual reproduction.

4. The symbiotic association between two species in lichens is an example of _____.

5. Fungi are considered _____ if their source of nutrients is dead organic matter.

Short Answers

1. Summarize the differences between fungi and flowering vascular plants.

2. Describe how *Saprolegnia* acts as both a saprophyte and a parasite.

3. What is the main structural difference among the three divisions of true fungi?

4. Describe how fungi can be both directly and indirectly harmful to humans.

5. Explain the characteristics of yeast cells that make them useful in the baking and alcohol-related industries.

Application Questions

1. a) Why do you think many fungi were originally classified in the plant kingdom?
   b) Why did scientists eventually decide to classify fungi as a separate kingdom?

2. How do saprophytic and parasitic fungi differ in the ways they obtain nutrients? State two examples of each.

3. Which fungi help keep the earth free of wastes? How?

4. How can you prevent moulds from growing on leftover food?

5. List several methods that could be used to control the spread of fungal plant diseases.

Problem Solving

1. Describe how fungi enhance the survival of green plants in the natural environment.

2. How might farmers make use of fungi in their fields?

3. What steps could people who are allergic to fungal spores take to ensure that their living environment is relatively spore free?

Extensions

1. Research one of the following topics and make a report to your class.
   a) the Irish potato blight of 1845-1847
   b) the use of fungi in the production of antibiotics
   c) the physiological effects of poisonous fungi on the human body

2. Investigate how to safely produce a pure mould culture (a culture containing only one species). Consult higher level biology texts and library sources to learn how to perform the technique. Try the procedure with your teacher's approval and assistance.

3. Visit a mushroom farm and obtain samples of several varieties of edible mushrooms. Make spore prints for each type and compare them. Compare spore prints according to colour of spores, arrangement of gills, shape of print, and so on. Report how suitable growing conditions are maintained on the farm. If possible, set up your own mushroom-growing location.

Microscopic Life

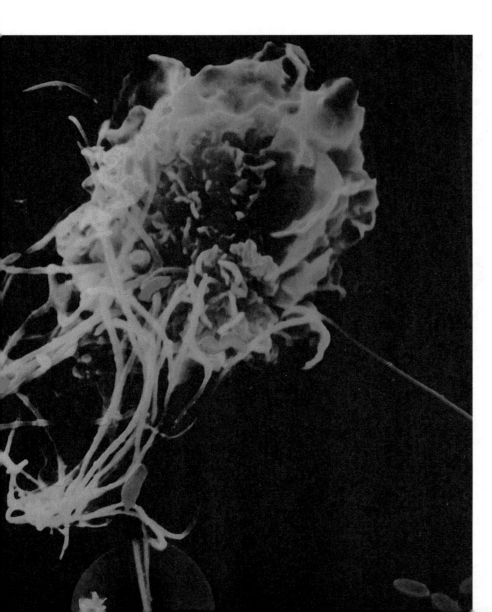

CHAPTER

15

Diversity in the Microscopic World

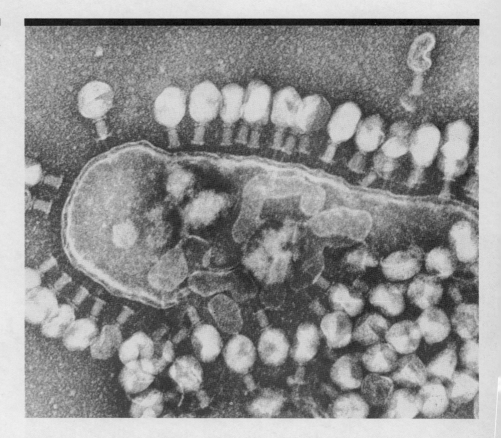

For most people, the term micro-organism means "disease-causing germ." Biologists now know that many micro-organisms are ecologically beneficial, but much of this understanding was reached through research into the origins of disease.

As early as the 1400s, a few physicians speculated that certain diseases might be caused by tiny, invisible "living seeds" in the blood. By the 1500s, some thought that these living seeds could spread disease. In the 1600s, Leeuwenhoek published numerous drawings of micro-organisms, but nobody associated Leeuwenhoek's

"beasties" with the idea of living seeds, and widespread belief in supernatural origins of disease persisted. In fact, the relationship between micro-organisms and disease was not made clear until late in the nineteenth century.

By 1864, the French microbiologist Louis Pasteur had already shown that the air is filled with micro-organisms that could cause decay unless removed or destroyed. When asked to investigate a wine spoilage problem that threatened the French wine industry, Pasteur detected micro-organisms in the "sick" wine. He then found that spoilage could be

prevented by using heat to kill the organisms before they multiplied, a process still called pasteurization. This experience led him to hypothesize that micro-organisms might also cause plants, humans, and other animals to become sick.

Although Pasteur's hypothesis was untested, the English surgeon Joseph Lister immediately began sterilizing instruments and spraying disinfectant into the air of his operating rooms. Improved survival in Lister's surgical patients provided indirect support for Pasteur's idea.

More direct evidence came from experiments by the German

physician Robert Koch. Koch isolated and cultured the bacterial species responsible for causing anthrax in sheep, and later the species responsible for tuberculosis in humans. Koch's research eventually supported Pasteur's hypothesis so well that it became known as the Germ Theory of Disease. Microbiologists still use Koch's methods to establish whether a biological agent is causing a disease.

We now know that not all diseases are caused by bacteria. For example, protists cause dysentery and malaria, both of which are major public health problems in some parts of the world. But influenza and other viral diseases are generally the most difficult to treat or control. Viruses are not considered to be alive, but their activities have an enormous impact on living things. Electron micrographs like this one show why.

This bacterium was originally invaded by a single virus, which converted the bacterial cell into a kind of factory for manufacturing new viruses. These viruses destroyed the cell as they burst through its wall, ready to invade neighbouring bacteria. An invasion like this is fatal to unicellular organisms, and can make multicellular organisms extremely sick as the viruses burst out of infected cells to infect many others.

Electron microscopes are far too costly for use in high schools, but you can culture protists and bacteria, and use a compound microscope to see them in much the same way as Koch and Pasteur did. In this chapter, you will become more familiar with the wide range of microscopic entities that are associated with disease. You will also learn that microscopic organisms play many other roles in the biosphere.

Chapter Objectives

When you complete this chapter, you should:

1. Be able to describe the characteristics that define and distinguish prokaryotes and eukaryotes.

2. Appreciate the simple yet effective unicellular structure that enables protists to carry out all life functions.

3. Be able to describe the general structure of a bacterium and explain how it differs from that of a protist.

4. Know how to establish and maintain a culture of mixed protists.

5. Know how to use a microscope to monitor a protist culture, use a key to identify species, and keep records of all observations.

6. Know how to use sterile techniques to prepare growth media and culture nonpathogenic bacteria.

7. Be able to describe the number, variety, and appearance of bacterial colonies that appear on the growth medium.

8. Be able to describe the general structure of viruses, and identify their usual shapes.

9. Be able to explain how viruses can play an important role in the biosphere even though most biologists do not regard viruses as living things.

10. Appreciate the characteristics that distinguish reproduction in protists and bacteria from replication in viruses.

Each streak on the surface of the culture medium contains numerous bacterial colonies. The medium provides food and moisture, but the clear spot surrounding one of the test disks shows that it contains a substance that inhibits the growth of this species.

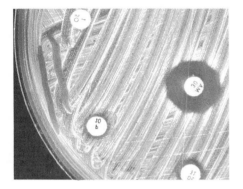

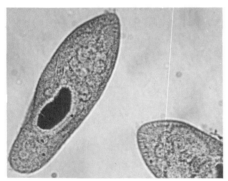

This unicellular eukaryote is a complete organism. It has all the structures and abilities it needs to carry out its life functions.

DID YOU KNOW?
The Greek root *eu* means true; *pro* means before; and *karyon* means kernel or nucleus.

Multicellular eukaryotes, which have not already been classified as plants, animals, or fungi, are also assigned to Protista.

Volvox is a colonial protist that contains several thousand identical cells. The smaller spheres are new colonies that will eventually break free of the larger one surrounding them.

15.1   Classification of Micro-Organisms

The kingdoms Animalia, Plantae, and Fungi consist mainly of multicellular, macroscopic organisms. Some kinds of worms and other multicellular organisms are microscopic in size, but most micro-organisms are unicellular. They are visible to the unaided eye only if present in very large numbers. Therefore, the classification of unicellular micro-organisms is based on similarities and differences in the cells themselves.

Microbiologists identify two fundamentally different cell types: prokaryotic cells and eukaryotic cells. **Prokaryotic cells** do not possess a true nucleus. Instead, a single, loop-like DNA molecule lies in twists and folds in the cytoplasmic fluid, unprotected by a nuclear membrane. Prokaryotic cells also lack membrane-bound organelles such as mitochondria and chloroplasts. Organisms made up of prokaryotic cells are called **prokaryotes.** For example, the bacteria that cause tooth decay are prokaryotes. All prokaryotes are grouped together in the kingdom **Monera.**

Eukaryotic cells have a true nucleus, one in which a nuclear membrane separates the DNA from the cytoplasm. Organisms made up of eukaryotic cells are called **eukaryotes.** For example, plants and animals are eukaryotes. But some eukaryotes are unicellular. Examples include organisms such as the amoeba and the paramecium. All unicellular eukaryotes are grouped together in the kingdom **Protista.**

Classification of the Kingdom Protista

The organisms assigned to the kingdom Protista share the following characteristics.
- *Unicellular or colonial*: Most protists are independent single-celled organisms. Colonial species are simply groups of identical cells. They do not have any specialized tissues.

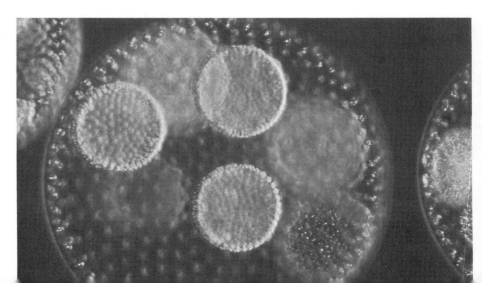

- *Eukaryotic*: All protist cells have a membrane-bound nucleus, and most contain membrane-bound organelles such as vacuoles and mitochondria. Many also contain chloroplasts.
- *Aquatic*: All protists live in moist surroundings such as fresh water, salt water, animal fluids, or very damp terrestrial environments.
- *Reproduction by mitotic cell division*: Most protists reproduce asexually by mitotic cell division. Some also exchange DNA in a form of sexual reproduction, but the process differs considerably from that observed in plants and animals.

FIGURE 15-1 Most of these protists are heterotrophs. They must ingest or absorb food produced by autotrophic organisms.

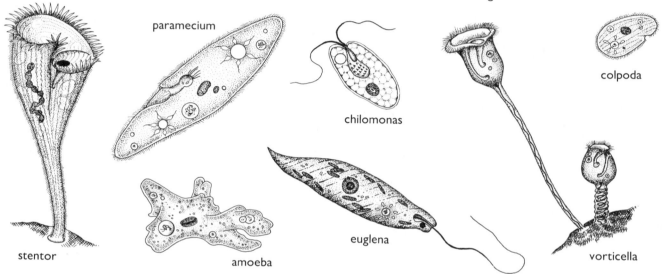

paramecium

chilomonas

colpoda

stentor

amoeba

euglena

vorticella

Since almost 50 000 species fit the above description, Figure 15-1 only suggests how great the diversity of cell shapes and structures observed among protists is. Some biologists compare Protista to a "junk drawer," because it includes all the species that don't seem to fit anywhere else. The result is an unusually low degree of similarity at the kingdom level. Taxonomists continue to use the kingdom Protista because it is convenient, not because it shows functional or structural relationships particularly well.

Because the cells of protists are relatively large, their structures and activities can be observed with an ordinary compound microscope. Such observations provide a basis for dividing Protista into two subkingdoms. Species that use light energy to manufacture their own food are assigned to the subkingdom **Algae.** Those that hunt or gather food, and ingest it, are grouped in the subkingdom **Protozoa.** Algae and Protozoa are further divided into phyla, based on observed differences in cell structure. The classification chart in Figure 15-2 shows only the best-known phyla of the protist kingdom. You will learn more about these phyla in Chapter 16.

Some authorities group slime moulds in Protista because of their resemblance to protozoans such as amoebas.

Some protists simply absorb nutrient molecules from their surroundings in the same way most fungi do. Many biologists think that fungi may have developed from some of these protists.

DID YOU KNOW?
The Greek root *protos* means first and *zoion* means animal.

FIGURE 15-2 Protist classification

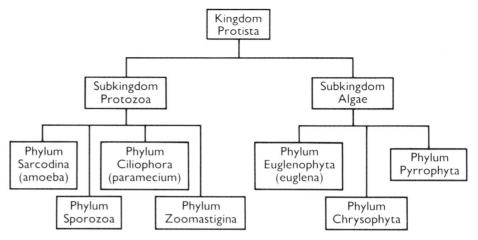

Both protozoans and algal protists are plentiful in ponds.

Understanding protists is important because they interact with the rest of the biosphere in many ways. Some protozoans cause serious diseases in humans and in other animals. Algal protists are major producers of food for aquatic ecosystems, and they also produce oxygen for the entire biosphere. In order to have living protists available for your studies in Chapter 16, you should begin culture preparations a few days in advance.

LABORATORY EXERCISE 15-1
Culturing and Classifying Protists

In the first part of this exercise, you will establish a protist culture. In the second part, you will observe the protist culture at regular intervals and keep records of your observations, using a classification key to identify the species you see. Specimens to start your culture can be collected from a nearby pond and maintained by setting up a hay infusion. If winter weather or your school's location make a pond visit impractical, starter specimens can be obtained commercially.

Classification of the Kingdom Monera

The organisms assigned to the kingdom Monera share the following characteristics.
- *Unicellular or colonial*: All monerans are unicellular, but many species stick together in clusters, strings, or colonies. Such colonies consist of identical cells. They do not have any specialized tissues.
- *Prokaryotic*: Monerans lack membrane-bound internal structures. They have no organized nucleus, and no vacuoles, mitochondria, or chloroplasts.

- *Aquatic*: Monerans thrive only in moist surroundings. If the environment dries up, the cells become inactive.
- *Reproduction by simple cell division*: Monerans reproduce asexually by simple cell division, a process that differs from mitotic cell division in eukaryotes. Some monerans occasionally exchange DNA, but the process differs from that seen in protists, and bears no resemblance to sexual reproduction in plants and animals.

Despite the apparent simplicity of their prokaryotic cells, monerans are a remarkably diverse kingdom. Classifying monerans into smaller, similar groups has always been a problem for taxonomists. This is partly because prokaryotic cells are generally much smaller than eukaryotic cells. Since few internal details of moneran structure could be seen with a light microscope, early microbiologists had to depend on other clues to identify them.

Clues found in the past have included the characteristic patterns formed by those species that clustered into colonies, the shapes of individual cells, the colour of cell contents or walls, and the capacity of cell walls to absorb certain dyes. For example, a technique called **Gram staining** involves treating bacteria with a series of stains and other chemicals. Those bacteria that appear blue-purple after treatment are described as Gram-positive; those that appear pink are Gram-negative. This method of classifying bacteria is useful to medical scientists because Gram-positive bacteria are generally more susceptible to antibiotics. However, a system that divides bacteria into two very large groups does little to help biologists understand how monerans carry out their life functions.

One fundamental barrier to biological understanding of monerans has been the great difficulty of distinguishing different species. You have already learned that a species is defined as a group of organisms so similar that they can mate and produce fertile offspring. This definition, however, cannot be applied to monerans, because they do not mate and produce offspring as multicellular plants and animals do. Until recently, it was difficult even to clarify relationships among different genera.

In the past decade, increasingly sophisticated techniques in taxonomy have revolutionized the classification of monerans. Microbiologists now focus on the chemical characteristics of a moneran—the composition of its cell wall, the molecules in its cytoplasm, and the chemical reactions with which it uses nutrients, produces body materials, and releases energy. By comparing proteins, enzymes, and chemical processes, researchers can now discriminate between similar genera with reasonable certainty. The number of moneran species is much less certain, but most microbiologists now think that it is not likely to exceed 1600.

Two groups of monerans that have been reclassified because of new biochemical data are cyanobacteria and methanogens. **Cyanobacteria** are named for the cyan, or blue-green, colour of those species that contain blue pigments as well as chlorophyll. But not all cyanobacteria are blue-green. Some species

Moneran reproduction does *not* involve either mitosis or meiosis. Both terms refer to events that take place in the nucleus. Since prokaryotic cells do not have true nuclei, monerans cannot divide by mitosis or meiosis.

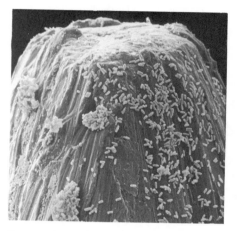

Even with an electron microscope, it may not be possible to see more than the external shape of a prokaryotic cell. These prokaryotes are bacteria, which are shown on the head of a pin to indicate size.

DID YOU KNOW?
Gram staining was developed in 1884 by Hans C.J. Gram, a Danish physician. Although the technique has been modified slightly, it is still used by medical scientists to classify bacteria.

DID YOU KNOW?
Alexander Fleming's interest in antibiotics did not stop with the discovery of penicillin. He also discovered the presence of a bacteria-killing enzyme called lysozyme in human fluids such as nasal secretions and tears when he noticed that bacteria died after he sneezed on them. Gram-positive bacteria are more susceptible to lysozyme than Gram-negative bacteria are.

Increasingly, microbiologists use chemical techniques as well as microscopes in their investigations.

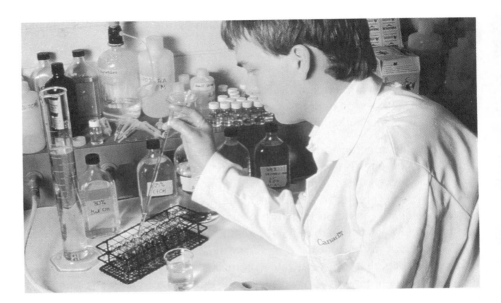

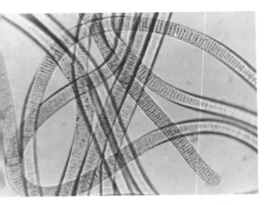

Many cyanobacteria are motile, able to glide, bend, or rotate. The Oscillatoria shown here is a typical example. Its thin strands wave gently back and forth, even when there is no water current. The strands consist of identical coin-shaped cells.

The bubbles that often appear on the surface of a pond are usually produced by methanogens.

contain red pigments instead of blue, and others have coloured cell walls. All cyanobacteria, however, contain green chlorophyll.

Previously, cyanobacteria were thought to be fundamentally different from "true" bacteria. Today, modern techniques have provided convincing evidence that they are simply true bacteria that happen to contain chlorophyll. Like plants, cyanobacteria carry out photosynthesis using light, water, and carbon dioxide to produce sugar and oxygen.

Cyanobacteria have great ecological importance for two reasons. They produce oxygen, and they form "blooms" that disrupt the ecological balance of many bodies of water. The Red Sea was named for the colour of the red cyanobacteria that cause frequent blooms on its surface. Despite modern techniques, cyanobacteria are still not well understood and are presently under intensive investigation. So far, researchers cannot say exactly how many species exist, but they predict the number will probably be less than 200.

Methanogens are so named because they produce methane gas. These prokaryotes are found only in anaerobic, or oxygen-free, environments such as the mud on pond bottoms. Researchers have known about methanogens for a long time, but they have been difficult to study. Since contact with oxygen kills them, methanogens cannot be cultured using ordinary techniques. Recent studies reveal that the chemical characteristics of methanogens differ greatly from those of other prokaryotes. Some researchers think methanogens should be placed in a separate, sixth kingdom.

At present, the criteria for the classification of monerans continue to change. The harder microbiologists look at prokaryotic cells, the more they question earlier ideas about relationships among the various groups. For this reason, a classification chart like the ones you have studied for other kingdoms is not appropriate. Instead, Table 15-1 lists the best-known groups of monerans

TABLE 15-1 Major Groups of Monerans

Group	Form	Locomotion	Nutrition	Ecological Role	Other Features
Actinomycetes (*Mycobacterium tuberculosis*)	• branching filaments	• nonmotile	• heterotrophic	• decomposers (fats) • some pathogens (e.g., tuberculosis)	• resemble fungi; mould-like appearance • some produce antibiotics
Cyanobacteria (*Oscillatoria*)	• unicellular	• nonmotile and motile (unknown mechanism)	• autotrophic by photosynthesis	• manufacture food • produce oxygen	• plant-like photosynthesis
Methanogens	• unicellular	• nonmotile	• heterotrophic	• make methane from carbon dioxide	• live in anaerobic environment
Mycoplasmas (*M. pneumoniae*)	• unicellular • lack cell walls	• nonmotile	• heterotrophic	• pathogens	• smallest known cells • live as parasites in other cells • do not swell and burst from osmosis even without cell walls
Myxobacteria (*Chrondromyces crocatus*)	• rod-like filaments	• motile by unknown gliding mechanism	• heterotrophic	• decomposers	• some form fruiting bodies like slime moulds
Nonphotosynthetic Eubacteria (*Streptococcus*)	• unicellular • simple, branched cells with rigid walls	• nonmotile and motile by contracting flagella	• heterotrophic • autotrophic by photosynthesis	• decomposers • many pathogens (e.g., scarlet fever)	• can be further classified by shape (i.e., rods, spheres, spirals)
Photosynthetic Eubacteria (purple and green sulphur bacteria; purple nonsulphur bacteria)	• unicellular • unbranched cells with rigid walls, containing brightly coloured pigments	• nonmotile	• autotrophic by photosynthesis	• decomposers of sulphur compounds, alcohols, fatty acids	• nonplant-like photosynthesis using nonvisible infrared light • do not produce oxygen • sulphur types produce solid sulphur
Rickettsia (*R. prowazekii*)	• very small cells	• nonmotile	• heterotrophic	• pathogens (e.g., typhus)	• live as parasites in other cells • so small that several can live in a single animal cell
Spirochetes (*Treponema pallidium*)	• very long, flexible helical cells	• motile (twisting caused by contracting axial filament)	• heterotrophic	• decomposers • pathogens (e.g., syphilis)	• many are anaerobic • some live in warm-blooded animals

and summarizes their characteristics as they are understood today. In the next decade, researchers expect that new technology will help them clarify much that is now uncertain.

Table 15-1 also shows that most monerans are bacteria. Understanding bacteria is important because they interact with the rest of the biosphere in many ways. Together with fungi, bacteria are the biosphere's primary decomposers. Their ability to break down dead organisms is vital to the continued survival of plants and animals. In addition, some bacteria produce nitrogen compounds that are essential for plant growth. Some produce food for heterotrophs. And some bacteria cause serious diseases in plants and animals, including humans. You will learn more about bacteria in Chapter 17. In order to have living bacteria available for your studies, you should begin culture preparations a few days in advance.

LABORATORY EXERCISE 15-2
Culturing and Classifying Bacteria

In the first part of this exercise, you will prepare a suitable growing medium for a bacterial culture. In the second part, you will observe and classify the bacteria that appear in your culture. The most easily obtained source of bacteria is the surface film of a hay infusion. Bacteria are also plentiful in decaying materials of all kinds.

However, it is unwise to culture specimens that may be pathogenic, and there is no way of knowing which bacterial species are present in natural sources. Therefore, it is safest to use pure, nonpathogenic cultures obtained from commercial suppliers. Classroom cultures should be started about three days before they will be needed for bacterial studies. It is vital that you use sterile techniques throughout this investigation.

A Taxonomic Puzzle: The Submicroscopic World of Viruses

The first indication of the existence of viruses occurred in 1892 when the Russian biologist Dmitri Ivanowsky found that healthy plants could be infected with mosaic disease by rubbing them with the juice of diseased plants. Ivanowski assumed that the infection was being passed on by bacteria. But even after the juice had been passed through a filter with pores small enough to trap the smallest known bacteria, it was still able to infect healthy plants. Ivanowski concluded that the filtered juice must contain an infective particle of unusually small size.

Similar findings by other investigators supported Ivanowski's conclusion. In 1896, the particles were called **viruses** by Martinus Beijerinck, a Dutch

Although the germ theory was well established by 1892, it was still very new and exciting to biologists. It was natural for Ivanowski to think of bacteria as a cause for the plant disease.

botanist, but their nature remained a mystery. Unlike bacteria, viruses couldn't be seen, cultured, or deactivated by disinfectants such as alcohol. In 1935, the American biochemist Wendell M. Stanley showed that the tobacco mosaic virus could be purified and stored in a powder form, then reactivated by adding water. This confirmed that viruses were solid particles, but the first direct look at viruses had to await improvements in the newly invented electron microscope.

Electron micrographs show that viruses are very small, simple particles. Their sizes range from 17-300 nm, only slightly bigger than the very smallest monerans. Structurally, each virus consists of a protein coat surrounding a core of nucleic acid such as DNA. The shape of a virus varies according to how the protein molecules in its coat fit together. For example, the tobacco mosaic virus resembles long, thin rods because its protein molecules are wound in a helix. Many viruses are polyhedral instead of helical, and others combine the two shapes.

The main function of the protein coat is to protect the nucleic acid inside. The nucleic acid contains all the instructions needed to manufacture new viruses. But the virus itself does not have the structures that could carry out these instructions. New viruses can only be manufactured inside a living cell. For this reason, biologists prefer to use the term **replication** to describe the formation of new viruses.

Viruses cannot be assigned to a kingdom because they lack most of the features associated with living things. They are said to be submicroscopic because they cannot be seen with a light microscope. Nevertheless, viruses are enormously important to biologists because they invade and take over living things. They cause a wide variety of diseases in living things and even attack bacteria.

Several systems exist for classifying viruses, each based on the needs of those using the system. One system classifies viruses according to whether they attack plants, animals, or bacteria. Viruses that invade bacteria are called **bacteriophages.** Most viruses are host-specific. This means they can invade only one kind of organism and often only one kind of cell. The animal virus that causes polio in humans is specific to one kind of nerve cell in the brain and the spinal cord. Other systems classify viruses according to the nature of the diseases they cause, the severity of the diseases, or the kind of nucleic acid in their cores.

Until recently, most of what was known about viruses came from studying bacteriophages like those in the photograph at the beginning of this chapter. More recently, virologists have been making intensive efforts to understand the viruses that cause human diseases, especially AIDS. In Chapter 18, you will investigate the structure and functioning of viruses in greater detail.

A bean plant infected by the mosaic virus. Notice the leaves mottled with light and dark patches. Because insects can carry viruses to healthy plants, all diseased plants must be destroyed by burning.

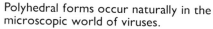

Polyhedral forms occur naturally in the microscopic world of viruses.

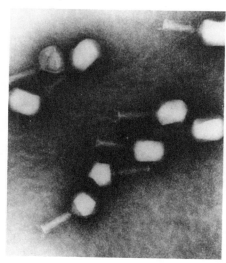

Chapter Review

Key Words

Algae
bacteriophages
cyanobacteria
eukaryotes
eukaryotic cells
Gram staining
methanogens

Monera
prokaryotes
prokaryotic cells
Protista
Protozoa
replication
viruses

Recall Questions

Multiple Choice

1. Which of the following statements is true for protists but not for monerans?
   a) They are microscopic.
   b) They are unicellular.
   c) Some are photosynthetic.
   d) They are eukaryotic.

2. A protozoan is
   a) an autotrophic protist
   b) a heterotrophic protist
   c) a prokaryotic protist
   d) a unicellular prokaryote

3. A bacterial colony is
   a) a multicellular eukaryote
   b) a multicellular prokaryote
   c) many unicellular eukaryotes clustered together
   d) many unicellular prokaryotes clustered together

4. The core of a virus consists of a strand of
   a) protein   c) enzyme
   b) nucleic acid   d) chlorophyll

5. A bacteriophage is
   a) a virus that attacks bacteria
   b) a disease-causing bacterium
   c) a bacterium that attacks viruses
   d) a disease-causing prokaryote

Fill in the Blanks

1. Any organism that is single-celled and prokaryotic belongs to the kingdom _____.

2. Any organism that is single-celled and eukaryotic belongs to the kingdom _____.

3. Protists reproduce by _____ cell division, and monerans reproduce by _____ cell division.

4. _____ bacteria are more susceptible to antibiotics than are _____ bacteria.

5. In the past, monerans were classified by characteristics such as _____, _____, and _____, but microbiologists now prefer to focus on _____ characteristics.

Short Answers

1. What is the difference between the following?
   a) a prokaryotic organism and a eukaryotic organism
   b) a colonial eukaryote and a multicellular eukaryote

2. Briefly describe the structure of a protist, a moneran, and a virus.

3. a) On what basis are protists classified into subkingdoms?
   b) List the subkingdoms of Protista.

4. Which kingdom is more diverse — Monera or Protista? Support your answer.

5. Monerans and protists live in similar habitats. Describe the type of habitat they require and explain why.

6. Which structure contains the instructions needed to manufacture new protists? New monerans? New viruses?

7. What term do biologists use to describe the formation of new protists? New monerans? New viruses?

8. a) What do cyanobacteria and methanogens have in common?
   b) How do they differ?

9. a) Identify one protist and one moneran that make an important contribution to the world's oxygen supply.
   b) What is the chemical reaction each one uses to produce the oxygen?

10. On what basis are viruses classified?

11. Match the terms in Column A with the descriptions in Column B.

Column A

  i) Algae
 ii) cyanobacteria
iii) methanogens
 iv) Monera
  v) Protista

Column B

a) photosynthetic eukaryotes
b) photosynthetic prokaryotes
c) lack membrane-bound organelles
d) possess true nuclei
e) anaerobic prokaryotes

Application Questions

1. a) Prepare a simple chart that compares protists and monerans under the following headings: Number of Cells per Organism, Form of Hereditary Material, Usual Habitat, and Type of Reproduction.
   b) Based on this chart, identify the most significant difference between the two kingdoms. Explain your answer.

2. a) Which kingdom is better understood by microbiologists at present—Protista or Monera? Explain why there is such a difference in understanding.
   b) What implications does this difference have for taxonomists?

3. The kingdom Protista has been described as a collection of ''misfits.'' Write a short paragraph commenting on the meaning and accuracy of this statement.

Problem Solving

1. a) Study Table 15-1. Identify the moneran groups that are described as photosynthetic. Which group carries out photosynthesis in much the same way as plants do?
   b) How does the outcome of photosynthesis in other monerans differ?

2. Viruses contain both proteins and nucleic acids such as DNA. These chemicals are found in all living things. Why are viruses considered to be nonliving particles?

3. A sample of greenish scum is examined with a compound microscope. The scum consists of threads made up of identical cells. A single cell is isolated and examined under high power. However, it is difficult to see whether or not the cell has a true nucleus because it contains so many oval-shaped, bright green organelles.
   a) To which kingdom would you assign this organism? Explain why.
   b) Can the organism be classified further without conducting additional tests? Explain.

Extensions

1. Under favourable conditions, an individual bacterium can divide once every 20 min. Suppose a single bacterium is placed on a culture medium at 12:00 on Monday. Assume that no bacteria die, and all reproduce every 20 min. How many bacteria would there be by 12:00 on Tuesday? How likely is it that the total population would reach this number? Explain.

2. Monerans called mycoplasmas are thought to be the smallest cells possible. Biologists think nothing smaller could contain all the molecules needed by a living cell. Investigate and report on the characteristics of *Mycoplasma pneumoniae* and the illness it causes.

3. Infective particles even smaller than viruses have now been detected. These viroids consist of short segments of nucleic acid without a protein coat. Viroids are known to cause several plant diseases and are suspected of causing diseases in animals, including humans. Investigate and report on the latest findings concerning viroids.

CHAPTER

16

The Protist Kingdom

D o plankton control global climate? A group of British scientists led by Dr. James Lovelock proposed that members of the kingdom Protista, the planktonic algae found in all oceans, are essential in controlling global temperature. This hypothesis is part of Lovelock's theory that chemistry and physics alone cannot explain the earth's environment. In his book, *The Gaia Hypothesis*, Lovelock claims that all organisms have modified conditions on Earth to sustain life.

Lovelock has suggested that algae control temperature by a mechanism known as a feedback loop, a cycle in which changes in one part of the cycle cause changes in another part of the cycle. This in turn leads to changes in yet another part, and so on back to the starting point. In this particular loop, the components are plankton, a substance they emit called DMS (dimethyl disulfide), water vapour, clouds, and air temperature.

According to the theory, an increase in DMS emission leads to higher atmospheric DMS concentration. In the atmosphere, DMS is oxidized to form tiny particles of sulphate, which can act as condensation centres for water vapour to form clouds. Unlike air over land masses, the air over oceans has little dust and few solid particles, so cloud formation over oceans would be limited by the availability of sulphate. With increased atmospheric sulphate, water would condense in more, but smaller droplets. Such clouds would have a high albedo or reflectivity. These clouds appear whiter than clouds with few condensation centres. Clouds with higher albedo reflect more of the sun's radiation away from the earth, thus cooling the planet.

For a feedback mechanism to be complete, the loop must be closed. In this case, changing atmospheric temperature and the amount of sunlight striking the oceans should, in turn, affect plankton DMS emissions. The researchers were unable to suggest how the loop is closed and left several questions unanswered. If the theory is an explanation of a climate control mechanism, cooling of the earth would lead plankton to emit less DMS, and therefore produce a warming effect. However, these scientists could not say whether this is the case.

Since the theory was proposed, another researcher, Stephen Schwartz, questioned the theory's assumption that atmospheric sulphate concentrations influence cloud albedo. Schwartz reasoned that sulphate resulting from fossil-fuel combustion is twice that of marine plankton, so it too should have an effect on cloud albedo. Also, since the majority of these sulphate sources are in the northern hemisphere and atmospheric sulphate concentrations are greater here, clouds in the northern hemisphere should be brighter than those in the south. However,

Schwartz found no discernible cloud-albedo difference between the two hemispheres. Schwartz concluded that it is unlikely cloud albedo and temperature are controlled by gaseous sulphur compounds.

But Schwartz's findings have also been called inconclusive since a number of variables he had not taken into account might have influenced his readings.

Do plankton control the global climate? We will have to wait to see. Should Lovelock's theory be rejected, however, it can never be considered a complete failure. The very process of the theory's rejection will demand research into the system, and will promote a greater understanding of plankton, the nature of ecosystems, and issues in related fields.

Chapter Objectives

When you complete this chapter, you should:

1. Be able to name the representative protists, explain how they were chosen, and explain how they are used in the study of the protist kingdom.

2. Be able to describe cell structure in representative protists, and compare them as they relate to nutrition, reproduction, and homeostasis.

3. Maintain a protist culture and observe fluctuations in populations.

4. Based on observations with a microscope, be able to draw and label diagrams of protist cells and cell parts.

5. Based on observations with a microscope, be able to compare locomotion by cilia, flagella, and pseudopods.

6. Know how to design and conduct experiments to study stimulus and response in protists.

7. Be able to explain the role of protists in the biosphere and appreciate their importance to all living things.

8. Be able to describe the composition of plankton and appreciate its importance to aquatic food webs and the rest of the biosphere.

9. Be able to explain the role of nonplanktonic protists in the biosphere and appreciate their importance.

10. Be able to identify several human diseases that are caused by protists, describe their transmission, symptoms, and treatment, and explain how they can be controlled.

16.1 Structure and Sensitivity in the Protist Kingdom

When biologists want to study a diverse group of living things, they usually choose representative organisms for their investigations. Later, they apply what they have learned to other members of the same group, looking for similarities and differences among them.

In this chapter, you will begin the study of the kingdom **Protista** by investigating three representative **protists**: two from the subkingdom Protozoa and one from the subkingdom Algae. (See Figure 16-1.) The phylum **Sarcodina** is represented by *Amoeba proteus* (see Figure 16-2), the phylum **Ciliophora** by *Paramecium caudatum* (see Figure 16-3), and the phylum **Euglenophyta** by *Euglena spirogyra* (see Figure 16-4). These three species have been chosen as representatives because they are easy to obtain, grow, and feed. Other less common members of the same phyla have similar structures and features.

In this chapter, *Amoeba proteus*, *Paramecium caudatum*, and *Euglena spirogyra* will be referred to by their common names: amoeba, paramecium, and euglena.

FIGURE 16-1 The kingdom Protista includes seven main phyla.

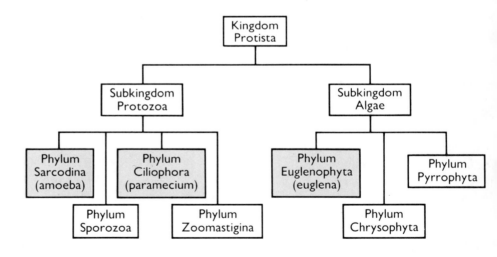

Structure of Three Representative Protists

As a single-celled organism, each protist has all the organelles it needs to maintain life, but these organelles are not identical. You can see in Figures 16-2, 16-3, and 16-4 that all three representative protists have a nucleus,

The amoeba's shape is constantly changing.

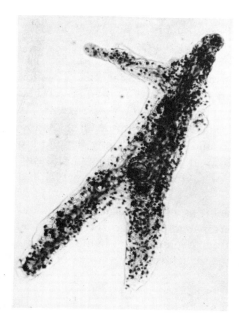

The paramecium's beating cilia propel it rapidly through the water.

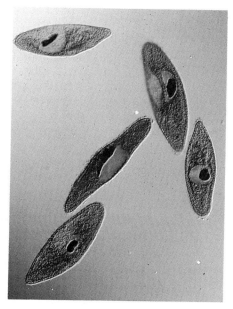

Euglenas are active swimmers and collect in large numbers where light is available.

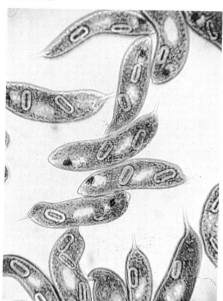

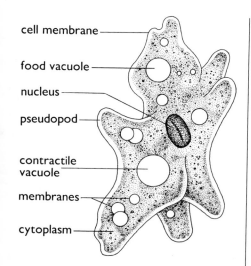

cell membrane

food vacuole

nucleus

pseudopod

contractile vacuole

membranes

cytoplasm

FIGURE 16-2 The structural features of *Amoeba proteus*

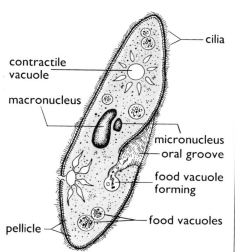

cilia

contractile vacuole

macronucleus

micronucleus

oral groove

food vacuole forming

food vacuoles

pellicle

FIGURE 16-3 The structural features of *Paramecium caudatum*

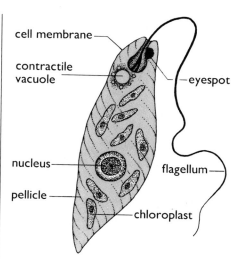

cell membrane

contractile vacuole

eyespot

nucleus

pellicle

flagellum

chloroplast

FIGURE 16-4 The structural features of *Euglena spirogyra*

contractile vacuoles, and cytoplasm, which are surrounded by a semipermeable membrane. But each protist also has its own unique structure. Both the paramecium and the euglena have a firm but elastic protein **pellicle** around the cell membrane. This structure gives these organisms their characteristic shape, but is flexible enough to allow slight changes in these shapes.

The amoeba lacks a pellicle, so its shape is constantly changing. The amoeba has cytoplasmic extensions called **pseudopods**, or "false feet," which the cytoplasm flows into as the organism moves. (See Figure 16-2.) The paramecium and the euglena have smaller, specialized cytoplasmic extensions called **cilia** and **flagella**, respectively. These extensions protrude through minute pores in their pellicles. Cilia are short and numerous while flagella are long and few in number. But both cilia and flagella are able to beat vigorously. Paramecia have specialized openings for taking in food. Amoebas and euglenas do not.

Large collections of protists may be visible as a group because they colour or cloud the water they live in. (See the marginal note on page 511.) Individual protists, however, can only be viewed through a microscope. In the following laboratory exercise, you will examine the structure of a variety of living protists.

Paramecia is the plural form of paramecium. Amoeba and euglena retain the same spellings when they are pluralized — amoebas and euglenas.

LABORATORY EXERCISE 16-1
Structure of Living Protists

The close relationship between structure and function is one that recurs frequently in biology. In this exercise, you will examine and compare the structure of amoebas, paramecia, and euglenas. You will also use your knowledge of structure and function in the plant and animal kingdoms to infer the functions of the features you observe in these protist cells.

Response to Stimuli

All types of living things are able to respond to stimuli, a characteristic of life known as irritability. Large multicellular animals detect changes in their environments and respond to them by means of a nervous system. Although unicellular protists do not have nervous systems, they also display irritability. Even organisms as simple as the amoeba and the paramecium can respond to stimuli such as touch or exposure to dissolved chemicals by moving toward or away from them. (See Figure 16-5.) Euglenas and many other protists have **eyespots,** which are specialized cell clusters capable of detecting light. Amoebas and paramecia do not have eyespots, yet they are also capable of responding to light. How would you expect their response to compare to that of the euglena? In the following activity, you will investigate irritability in protists.

DID YOU KNOW?
There is evidence that the trumpet-shaped protozoan stentor can "learn." If poked once, a stentor will bend away from the stimulus and stop feeding. If poked repeatedly, it ignores the stimulus and returns to normal feeding.

IV MICROSCOPIC LIFE

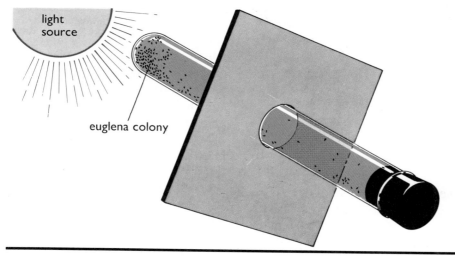

INQUIRY ACTIVITY
Designing an Experiment to Study the Responses of Protists to Stimuli

Although their speed and method of locomotion differ, amoebas, paramecia, and euglenas are constantly in motion. For simple organisms, these protists exhibit surprisingly complex behaviours. In this activity, you will design and perform your own experiments to identify some of the stimuli that various protists respond to. In your experiments, you will also investigate how protists respond to these stimuli. If a protist moves toward a stimulus, its response is said to be positive. If a protist moves away from the stimulus, the response is negative.

Some examples of the stimuli you might test are solids such as a solid barrier or chemicals such as a weak acidic solution. Ask your teacher about references for other stimuli that you could test safely in the laboratory.

Since all of your observations will be made with a microscope, you will need to devise ways to introduce the stimuli to the organisms on the microscope slide.

In your experimental design, be sure to state the purpose of your experiment and your hypotheses. Develop a data table suitable for recording your observations and include sketches as part of your observations. Remember to obtain your teacher's permission before performing your experiments.

A Question for Further Research

Both paramecia and amoebas respond to stimuli such as food or light almost instantly. Yet, neither protist possesses any observable structures for detecting a stimulus or for co-ordinating a response. How such simple organisms can

Stimulus and Response in Protists

Amoebas detect and approach food without being able to smell it. Paramecia respond to light without eyespots. Protists respond to many external cues and conditions, apparently without organelles that might make these responses possible.

How do protists respond quickly and appropriately to external stimuli? Biologists have no real answers yet, although they have isolated molecules from protist cytoplasm that may be responsible for protist response and control. Remarkably, the same molecules carry information in humans as well.

Adrenaline, dopamine, serotonin, and acetylcholine are produced by many kinds of living things, but their functions differ in different organisms. In vertebrates, they are called neurotransmitters and are responsible for carrying information throughout the nervous system. For example, acetylcholine is used in humans to transmit sensory information to the brain and to stimulate muscle action. Insects use the same molecule but only in sensory functions. The plant known as the stinging nettle uses acetylcholine for defence. In the kingdom Monera, blue-green algae are thought to use acetylcholine in photosynthesis.

Some evidence suggests that in protists acetylcholine and similar molecules control cilia and flag-

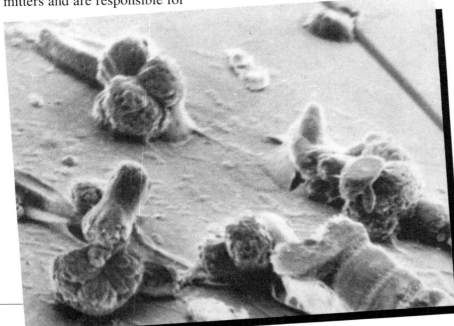

ella in the same way they control muscle action in humans. When exposed to these molecules, protists react dramatically. Small amounts of adrenaline repel one kind of dinoflagellate. Acetylcholine decreases sensitivity to light in another kind of dinoflagellate, and also causes some amoebas to collect together.

Pathways by which these molecules might act in protists have yet to be uncovered. In humans, messages that initiate muscle action must travel through millions of nerve cells from sensory organs to the brain. Transmission of impulses across the gap between nerve cells requires three elements: a neurotransmitter molecule, a transmitter to produce and release it, and a receptor to receive it and pass along the signal. However, in protists only the molecules that act like neurotransmitters have been detected so far. No structures similar to the transmitter and receptor structures in human nerve cells have been identified in protists.

Many serious human diseases are caused by nervous-system malfunctions that are not yet understood. Although the role of neurotransmitters in humans has been identified, neurotransmitter molecules may have other functions that have not yet been discovered. Researchers hope that by discovering how neurotransmitters function in protists, more will be revealed about their operation in humans.

perform these functions without a nervous system is a question that has puzzled biologists for many years. Hopefully, further research will increase our understanding of this important life function, not only in protists but also in animals such as humans. In Section 16.2, you will investigate how protists carry out their other life functions.

Section Review Questions

1. a) What is meant by the term representative organism?
   b) State the complete names of the three species chosen to represent the protist kingdom in this chapter.
   c) Identify the phylum each species belongs to.
2. a) State the common names of the three representative protists.
   b) Prepare a simple chart that summarizes the structural similarities and differences among these protists.
3. Which of the three representative protists has structures for locomotion that suit it for
   a) life as an active hunter? Explain.
   b) life as a consumer of dead organisms? Explain.
4. Define irritability and state an example of irritability in protists.

16.2 Life Functions in the Representative Protists

Although single-celled protists do not have separate organs or organ systems, their organelles and cytoplasmic chemicals enable them to perform the same basic life functions as larger, multicellular organisms. Digestion, excretion, gas exchange, and reproduction all occur in protists but in a much simpler manner.

Gas Exchange

Oxygen for cellular respiration is an essential requirement of most organisms. Humans and other terrestrial animals have complex gas-exchange systems, but protists have only a thin cell membrane. Oxygen first diffuses across the cell membrane into the cell from the external environment. Oxygen diffuses in this direction because its concentration outside the cell is higher than it is inside. The higher concentration of oxygen in pond water is maintained by diffusion of oxygen from the air, and also by the production of oxygen by green pond plants through photosynthesis. The concentration of oxygen in a protist cell is kept low by its metabolic activity.

FIGURE 16-6 The stentor's thin, cone-shaped body increases its surface area-to-volume ratio so that it receives an adequate supply of oxygen.

Once inside the cell, the oxygen molecules spread by diffusion and cytoplasmic streaming (currents in the cytoplasm), until they reach the mitochondria, which carry out cellular respiration. As the reaction proceeds, the concentration of carbon dioxide inside the protist cell becomes higher than that in the water outside the cell. As a result, the waste carbon dioxide diffuses out of the cell into the pond water. Some of this carbon dioxide is used by aquatic plants for photosynthesis, and some of it diffuses out of the water into the air, so the concentration of carbon dioxide in pond water remains lower than that inside the cell.

The need for gas exchange limits the maximum possible size of unicellular protists. This is because gas exchange can only take place at the surface of a cell. Therefore, the amount of oxygen that can enter a protist cell depends on the surface area. But the surface area-to-volume ratio gets smaller as cell size increases. (See Figure 16-6.) The larger a single cell grows, the greater the length of time needed for oxygen to diffuse into its centre. Only if a protist cell remains very small can sufficient oxygen diffuse inward quickly enough to supply its needs. Because of this limitation, all unicellular protists are microscopic in size. Even the largest amoeba can barely be seen without a microscope, and most protists are visible to the unaided eye only when present in very large numbers.

Nutrition and Digestion

Food for use in cellular respiration and growth is another important requirement of organisms. Each of the three representative protists has its own means of obtaining food. The amoeba engulfs food particles by extending its pseudopods. (See Figure 16-7.) (This process, which is called phagocytosis, is similar to that used by white blood cells to engulf bacteria.) Once inside the amoeba, the food particles are surrounded by a pinched-off part of the cell membrane. The membranous bubble and its contents are called a **food vacuole.** Digestive enzymes produced in the amoeba's cytoplasm then diffuse into the food vacuole through the membrane, and the food inside gradually breaks down into small nutrient molecules. Once the nutrients have diffused into the cytoplasm, only undigested wastes remain. The vacuole then migrates to the surface of the amoeba, and the wastes are expelled to the external environment.

Food particles enter the paramecium and other ciliates through an **oral groove,** swept in by the beating cilia that line it. (See Figure 16-8.) At the base of the oral groove is a funnel-like **gullet** where the food becomes enclosed in a membrane-bound vacuole as it enters the cytoplasm. This food vacuole breaks away from the gullet and circulates throughout the cytoplasm. Once a food vacuole forms, a paramecium digests the food and absorbs nutrients in the same way as an amoeba does, but it disposes of wastes differently. After digestion, any remaining waste particles pass out through the anal pore, a tiny opening in the pellicle.

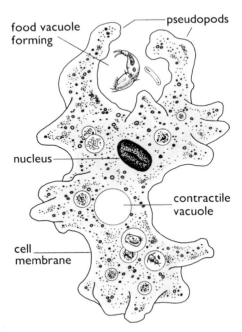

food vacuole forming

pseudopods

nucleus

contractile vacuole

cell membrane

FIGURE 16-7 Phagocytosis in an amoeba. Compare this process with phagocytosis in human white blood cells.

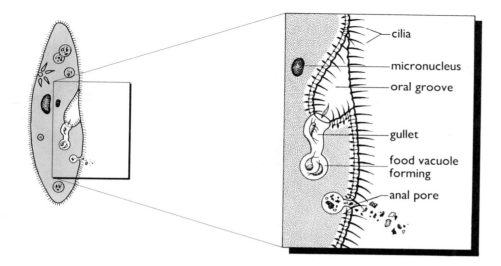

FIGURE 16-8 The oral groove and gullet of a paramecium

cilia

micronucleus

oral groove

gullet

food vacuole forming

anal pore

Euglenas are easily recognized by their large central nuclei and the green colour of their numerous, small chlorophyll-containing chloroplasts. When light is available, euglenas produce their own food by photosynthesis. In the absence of light, euglenas live as heterotrophs. However, euglenas have never been observed taking in food particles through their gullet-like structures. Instead they absorb dissolved nutrients directly from the water they live in.

Maintaining Homeostasis

For most protists, the external environment consists of fresh water containing dissolved oxygen. Like oxygen molecules, water molecules diffuse inward across the cell membrane. This is because the concentration of water molecules in the surrounding environment is much higher than it is in the cell cytoplasm, which contains numerous other molecules in addition to water. The resulting continual inward diffusion of water makes maintaining a stable internal environment difficult. Some water is needed for cell reactions such as digestion, and some is required to maintain correct water levels in the cytoplasm. However, far more water moves into the cell than it can use up. Without a way to remove the excess water, the protist cell would soon swell and burst.

The organelle that excretes excess water is the **contractile vacuole.** Excess water entering a euglena collects in its contractile vacuole. The vacuole fills and expands until the cell membrane fuses with that of the vacuole. The vacuole then contracts, releasing excess water through the gullet. The empty vacuole then begins to fill again as water continues to diffuse into the cell. The entire cycle shown in Figure 16-9 usually takes about 1 min. This homeostatic mechanism enables amoebas, euglenas, paramecia, and many other protists to maintain stable internal conditions.

FIGURE 16-9 The contractile vacuole

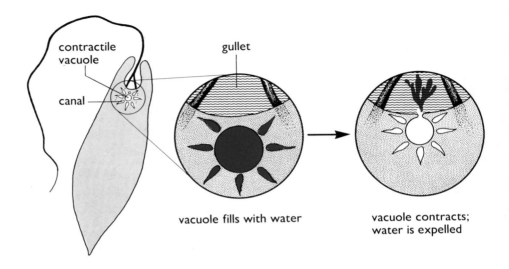

contractile vacuole

gullet

canal

vacuole fills with water

vacuole contracts; water is expelled

Locomotion

The members of the protist kingdom vary considerably in their ability to move. Almost all members of the subphylum Protozoa have some special means of locomotion, but most protists of the subkingdom Algae do not; they simply drift with the ocean current. However, algae such as those in the phylum Euglenophyta are able to move about in search of food and to move away from unsuitable conditions in their environment.

At first glance, the amoeba does not seem to have any specialized structures for locomotion. However, the cytoplasm of an active amoeba is constantly streaming and forming pseudopods. Figure 16-10 shows how the cytoplasm flows into the pseudopods, enlarging them until the entire organism moves. This type of locomotion is called **amoeboid movement.** After careful observation, however, the cytoplasm of an amoeba can be seen to consist of two different types. These two types of cytoplasm differ in the way they flow because one type is less fluid than the other. However, the amoeba can quickly

FIGURE 16-10 The amoeba's pseudopods, which form when cytoplasm streams and becomes stiff, allow it to move.

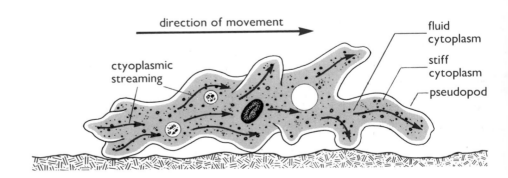

direction of movement

ctyoplasmic streaming

fluid cytoplasm

stiff cytoplasm

pseudopod

IV MICROSCOPIC LIFE

convert the less fluid cytoplasm into the more fluid type. This ability to vary cytoplasmic flow rate enables the amoeba to form its pseudopods. The amoeba's shape constantly changes as new pseudopods form and others disappear. Many other protozoans also exhibit amoeboid movement, as do certain vertebrate white blood cells such as those you studied in Chapter 6.

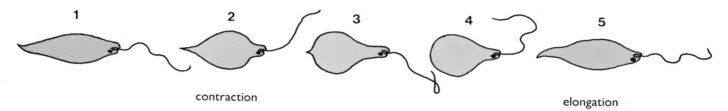

1   2   3   4   5

contraction   elongation

FIGURE 16-11   Euglenoid movement

Euglenas are capable of a type of locomotion called **euglenoid movement.** (See Figure 16-11.) Euglenoid movement resembles amoeboid movement, but it has a different structural basis. Beneath its pellicle, the euglena has a layer of delicate fibres that can contract. These fibres enable the organism to change its shape. The euglena alternately contracts and elongates to crawl along a surface such as an underwater leaf.

Euglenas also have flagella, which are specialized structures for locomotion that enable them to move freely through the water. Each euglena has two flagella, but only the larger one is active in locomotion. Its whip-like motion causes the euglena to move forward and to rotate slightly. The result is a spiralling motion through the water.

The paramecium also swims freely with a spiralling motion, but it moves much more rapidly, propelled by the rhythmic beating of numerous cilia arranged in rows. On the action stroke, the cilia are rigid enough to push the water backward and propel the organism forward. (See Figure 16-12.) On the

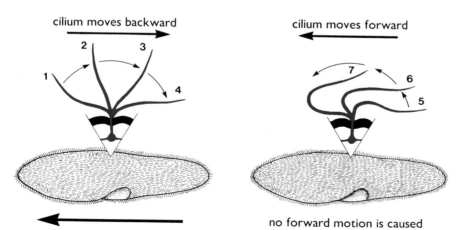

cilium moves backward

2   3
1   4

action helps to move
paramecium forward

cilium moves forward

7   6
5

no forward motion is caused

FIGURE 16-12   The beating of a single cilium. The cilium is rigid during the action stroke (left). Then the relaxed cilium returns to its original position to prepare for the next action stroke (right).

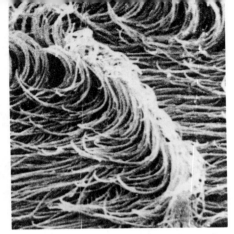

Cilia beat rhythmically and continuously in a co-ordinated movement.

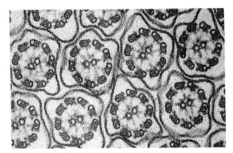

All cilia and flagella found in protists have the same structure (60 000 ×).

FIGURE 16-13 Movement in paramecia

return stroke, the cilia are relaxed, exerting very little force on the water. The strokes of the cilia occur in co-ordinated waves as action strokes alternate with return strokes. It is not known exactly how the beats are co-ordinated, but biologists believe that a network of fibres under the cell membrane is involved.

The cilia beat at an angle, and the organism rotates on its longitudinal axis. Also, because the oral groove of a paramecium has more cilia than other parts of its pellicle, and they move more quickly, the front end of the organism moves in a large circle. Figure 16-13 shows how these two motions combine to produce the distinctive spiralling pattern seen as the paramecium swims forward.

Despite differences in size and number, cilia and flagella have the same basic internal structure. They both have nine pairs of microtubules in a ring with two microtubules in the centre. Microtubules are long, thin tubes of protein. Like muscle fibres, microtubules can contract. These contractions cause the beating movement of the cilia or the flagella.

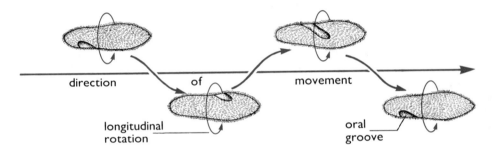

direction   of   movement

longitudinal rotation

oral groove

LABORATORY EXERCISE 16-2
Observing Structures for Locomotion and Reproduction in Protists

Functions such as locomotion are best studied by observing living specimens. However, living protists move so quickly that it is difficult to observe structural details at the same time. In this exercise, you will observe the structure and location of cilia and flagella in the representative protists by examining prepared slides. You will also examine slides or photographs showing reproduction because reproduction in amoebas, paramecia, and euglenas is difficult to observe over a short time period.

Reproduction in the Representative Protists

All three of the representative protists are able to reproduce asexually by a process called binary fission. First, the nucleus replicates itself, then the cytoplasm divides so that each of the two offspring has an equal share of cytoplasm and a nucleus identical to that of the original cell.

The paramecium has two kinds of nuclei: a large macronucleus that directs most cell activities, and a smaller micronucleus that directs cell division. Both nuclei are located near the centre of the cell. When a paramecium reproduces by binary fission, both nuclei divide, providing one macronucleus and one micronucleus for each new cell. (See Figure 16-14.) A second oral groove and two more contractile vacuoles become visible. A constriction forms across the centre of the cell, splitting the original paramecium into two complete, identical offspring cells.

FIGURE 16-14 Binary fission in a paramecium

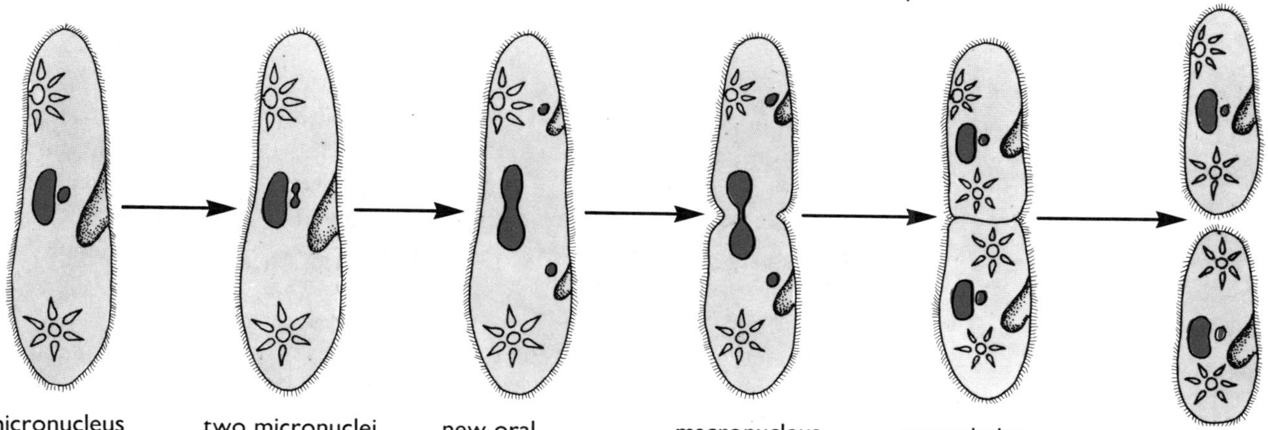

| micronucleus directs process of separation | two micronuclei form | new oral groove forms; micronuclei move to opposite ends of cell | macronucleus divides | constriction forms near middle of cell | paramecium divides into two new paramecia |

Binary fission is similar in both the euglena and the amoeba. However, these unicellular protists have only one kind of nucleus to replicate and distribute to each of the offspring cells.

At present, biologists believe that reproduction in the euglena is entirely asexual. And, until recently, they also thought that amoebas only reproduced asexually. New findings, however, suggest that some amoebic species probably do exchange hereditary material under certain circumstances. Research into sexual reproduction by the amoeba is continuing. (You can read about this research on page 508.) By contrast, sexual reproduction in the paramecium is common, and the process is well understood by biologists.

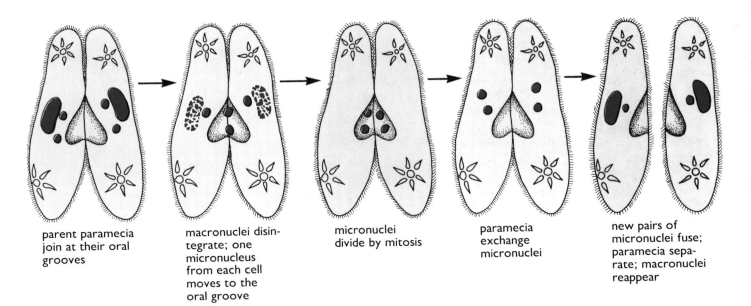

parent paramecia join at their oral grooves

macronuclei disintegrate; one micronucleus from each cell moves to the oral groove

micronuclei divide by mitosis

paramecia exchange micronuclei

new pairs of micronuclei fuse; paramecia separate; macronuclei reappear

FIGURE 16-15 Conjugation in a paramecium

Paramecia reproduce sexually by **conjugation.** (See Figure 16-15.) During this process, two paramecia of the same species (but slightly different strains) press together at their oral grooves. Within each cell, the macronucleus disintegrates. Only the micronuclei are involved in sexual reproduction. The micronuclei undergo a series of divisions followed by an exchange of hereditary material. Each paramecium donates a micronucleus containing half of its chromosomes (N) to its partner and receives half of the partner's chromosomes in exchange. When the two cells separate, each has a full set of chromosomes (2N). However, the new chromosome combination differs from that in the original parent cells.

The exchange of hereditary material allows for variations within a species. Since each individual inherits a slightly different combination of chromosomes, each has slightly different characteristics. These variations increase the likelihood that some individuals will have the characteristics they will need to survive a major environmental change. Although many individuals may die as a result of environmental change, the species itself will survive. The ability of some protist species to reproduce sexually is only one factor contributing to the widespread success of the protist kingdom.

Protists are found throughout the biosphere, wherever there is enough water. They live in oceans, lakes, streams, and ponds. But many ponds and small streams dry up in the summer and freeze in the winter. However, when a pond fills with water or its ice melts, it is soon repopulated with protists. This happens because some kinds of amoebas and other protists are able to form **cysts** when living conditions become unfavourable. The cytoplasm of the amoeba takes on a spherical shape, then a thick protective covering forms around the cell. When favourable conditions return, the cyst breaks open and the amoeba resumes its active motile form. The ability to form cysts is a great advantage for the survival of some species of protists.

If food is plentiful, and other conditions are favourable, protists reproduce rapidly. The ability of protists to reproduce quickly is also important to their survival. Under ideal conditions, paramecia can undergo fission every 6-12 h, while euglena and amoebas can divide once a day. A controlled environment such as the hay infusion described in Chapter 15 provides the food and temperature conditions needed for maximum rates of growth and reproduction. But even in the laboratory, protist populations fluctuate in size just as they do in nature. Populations of some protists can increase rapidly, while the populations of others drop dramatically. This fluctuation in population size occurs because any sharp increase in the numbers of one protist species will soon provide food for the predators that feed on it. Therefore, individual protists do not survive long. But the chromosomes of the protists that do escape predators long enough to reproduce live on in their offspring, ensuring the survival of the species.

Section Review Questions

1. a) Briefly describe gas exchange in protists.
   b) What causes oxygen to move into protist cells and carbon dioxide to move out?
2. a) Identify each representative protist as autotrophic or heterotrophic.
   b) Which representative protist does not ingest or digest food? Explain how this protist obtains nutrients.
   c) Describe food ingestion, food digestion, nutrient absorption, and waste disposal in the amoeba. Compare these processes with those of the paramecium.
3. Describe one way protists maintain homeostasis.
4. a) Identify the specialized structures for locomotion possessed by each of the representative protists. Explain how each structure performs its function.
   b) Describe amoeboid movement and compare it to euglenoid movement.
   c) Describe how cilia help protists move and compare this movement to that of flagella.
5. a) Define binary fission.
   b) Describe the process of conjugation in paramecia.
6. a) Define a cyst.
   b) Why is the ability to form cysts an advantage to certain protists?

Contrary to the widely accepted belief that amoebas reproduce asexually, some amoebas may, in fact, reproduce sexually. Amoebas have long been considered incapable of exchanging genetic material. Amoeba reproduction was believed to be asexual only. But P.G. Sargeaunt of the London School of Hygiene and Tropical Medicine has discovered evidence that some *Entamoeba hystolytica* differ from their parents, a fact inconsistent with asexual reproduction.

E. hystolytica is studied because it causes amebiasis, an infectious disease causing over 100 000 deaths every year in developing nations. Poor sanitary conditions aid transmission of *E. hystolytica* through cysts in drinking water and by hand-to-mouth contact. Once ingested, the amoeba can cause ulcers, diarrhea, acute amoebic dysentery, and other potentially fatal complications. To characterize each amoeba, Sargeaunt first cultured individual amoebas into populations large enough for analysis. The distinctive gel electrophoresis banding pattern of the enzymes of each cloned culture was then used to characterize each individual amoeba. (You will recall gel electrophoresis was discussed in Chapter 2.) In this way, Sargeaunt distinguished 18 varieties of amoeba (labelled I–XVIII) of *E. hystolytica* in the world. Only

Do Amoebas Mate?

seven varieties of these amoeba were pathogenic.

In 1981, Sargeaunt was surprised to discover small numbers of a previously unknown variety, XIX, with a completely new banding pattern. At first, Sargeaunt speculated that the new variety was a spontaneous mutation, a natural change caused by small DNA copy errors during cell division. However, in nine previous years of cloning *E. hystolytica*, no change in banding pattern had ever been attributed to mutation. Later, Sargeaunt found XIX in amoeba samples from both India and Africa. This discovery was further evidence against Sargeaunt's first hypothesis of spontaneous mutation since identical mutations on two continents would be highly improbable.

Sexual reproduction seemed the most likely origin of XIX. But since this had never before been seen in amoebas, Sargeaunt's team needed to test the hypothesis. Two varieties, II and XIV, were chosen as the most likely parents for XIX because of their electrophoresis patterns and geographical distribution. Fifty mixtures containing the two varieties were

incubated for 48 h. Then 152 amoeba were selected for cloning. Three resulting varieties would confirm the theory of sexual reproduction. And three varieties were found, but they were not the ones expected. Instead of II, XIV, and XIX, the two parent amoeba were found along with another new variety, XX.

Again, sexual reproduction was seen as the only reasonable explanation of the results. Spontaneous mutation was discounted when the experiment was repeated successfully. Subsequent tests by Sargeaunt's group using rats as biological hosts support the sexual reproduction hypothesis. These tests also revealed that one of the previously identified varieties could be produced sexually from other varieties.

In addition to its interesting theoretical implications, the possibility of sexual reproduction in amoebas has grave social consequences. Any species capable of reproducing sexually is not nearly as predictable as one reproducing asexually. When different amoeba varieties that would not normally meet are brought together as a result of modern travel, they might produce new pathogenic varieties, making control and treatment of amebiasis even more difficult.

16.3 Protists in the Biosphere

Protists are found almost everywhere in the biosphere, and they play a variety of ecological roles. One of their most important roles is the provision of food for other organisms. Although protists are very small, they occur in extremely large numbers. Therefore, they are an important part of aquatic food chains, food webs, and food pyramids. Protists can provide a food source for large heterotrophs such as baleen whales. And they can even become food for other protists. Small protists such as the didinium, for example, can catch and consume a much larger paramecium.

A protist population can grow rapidly if there are no predators, but only as long as its food supply lasts. Over time, the protist population in a pond ecosystem, for instance, will fluctuate. One species may flourish for a time and then fade out, as another becomes prominent.

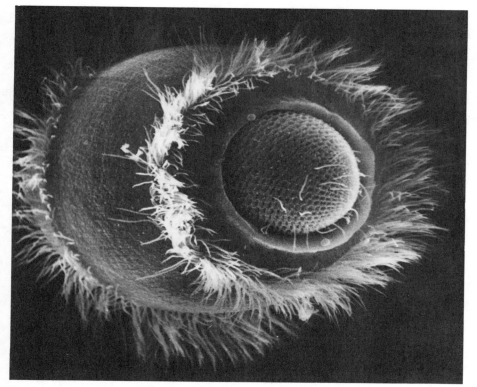

A unicellular didinium feeds on a paramecium almost as large as itself. Once inside the didinium, the paramecium is completely surrounded by a membrane that forms a food vacuole. A didinium can consume as many as 12 paramecia each day.

LABORATORY EXERCISE 16-3
Observing Protist Population Fluctuations

Many factors affect the growth and size of protist populations. Temperature, available oxygen, and competition for space and food are only a few examples. In this exercise, you will maintain and observe a mixed culture of protists over an extended period of time. You will determine and record the relative number of each type of organism in the culture. When you have obtained sufficient data, you will graph the population growth curve and interpret it.

Protists as Food Producers

Amoebas, paramecia, and euglenas are mostly heterotrophic. That is, they act as consumers of food rather than as producers. The "fire algae" of the phylum **Pyrrophyta,** however, are mainly autotrophic. (See Figure 16-16.) Like plants, most pyrrophytes have chlorophyll-containing chloroplasts and can produce food by photosynthesis. Unlike plants, some pyrrophytes are able to perform locomotion.

The most common pyrrophytes are the marine algae known as dinoflagellates. Most dinoflagellates are active swimmers, and most have chloroplasts containing green chlorophyll. However, they also contain so many brown and red pigment molecules that their overall colour is reddish instead of green. Those without chloroplasts are heterotrophs that feed mainly on smaller protists and monerans. Dinoflagellates reproduce asexually by binary fission. Each of the two offspring cells receives only one flagellum from the parent cell. A second flagellum develops as the offspring matures. A few species of dinoflagellates also reproduce sexually.

The flagella of a typical dinoflagellate

DID YOU KNOW?
Some species of dinoflagellates can produce light. This ability is called bioluminescence. Many sightings of ghost ships can be attributed to this phenomenon. Disturbances in the water such as large fish, boats, or waves often trigger bioluminescence, causing the water to glow at night with an eerie blue or green light.

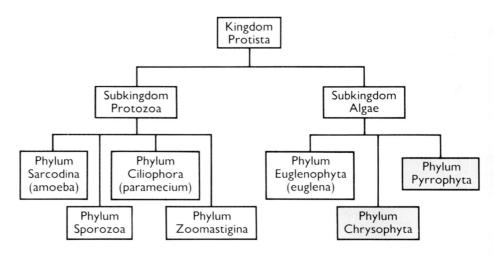

FIGURE 16-16 Members of the phyla Pyrrophyta and Chrysophyta are autotrophs.

The phylum **Chrysophyta** includes a wide variety of algal species, most of which are diatoms. Diatoms are found in both fresh and salt water, but are especially abundant in oceans. Their cell walls are made of silica, which forms a shell-like covering. Silica is a glassy material that contains an abundance of the element silicon. Each cell contains a nucleus and one or more chloroplasts, but they lack flagella. Diatoms usually reproduce asexually, although sexual reproduction does occur.

Diatoms exist in a variety of beautiful and interesting shapes.

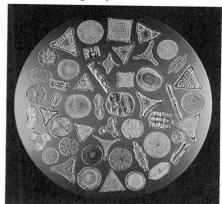

The phylum Chrysophyta also includes several species of golden-brown and yellow-green algae. These species are photosynthetic and contain green chlorophyll. Their characteristic golden colours result from the presence of other pigments such as carotenoids. All of these species have either one or two flagella that function in locomotion, and most are found in fresh water.

Large populations of protists that drift in the ocean are often called **plankton.** Heterotrophic types are called **zooplankton,** while photosynthetic types are known as **phytoplankton.** The planktonic organisms of the phylum Pyrrophyta and the phylum Chrysophyta are mainly photosynthetic. These organisms are the major producers in many aquatic ecosystems. Their extremely large numbers form the base for many aquatic food chains, food webs, and food pyramids. (See Figure 16-17.) If the population of these planktonic algae were seriously affected by pollution or other environmental changes, huge filter-feeding baleen whales would be directly affected since their diet consists primarily of plankton. Aquatic carnivores such as tuna would also be affected because they depend on plankton as the major producers in their food chains. (See Figure 16-18.)

A close look at this beached grey whale reveals the baleen plates, which act as the whale's filtering system.

FIGURE 16-17 A food web in an aquatic ecosystem

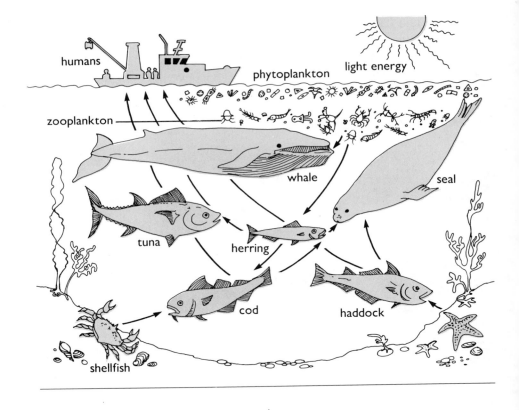

humans

phytoplankton

light energy

zooplankton

whale

seal

tuna

herring

cod

haddock

shellfish

DID YOU KNOW?

The word plankton comes from the Greek word *phagktos*, which means wandering.

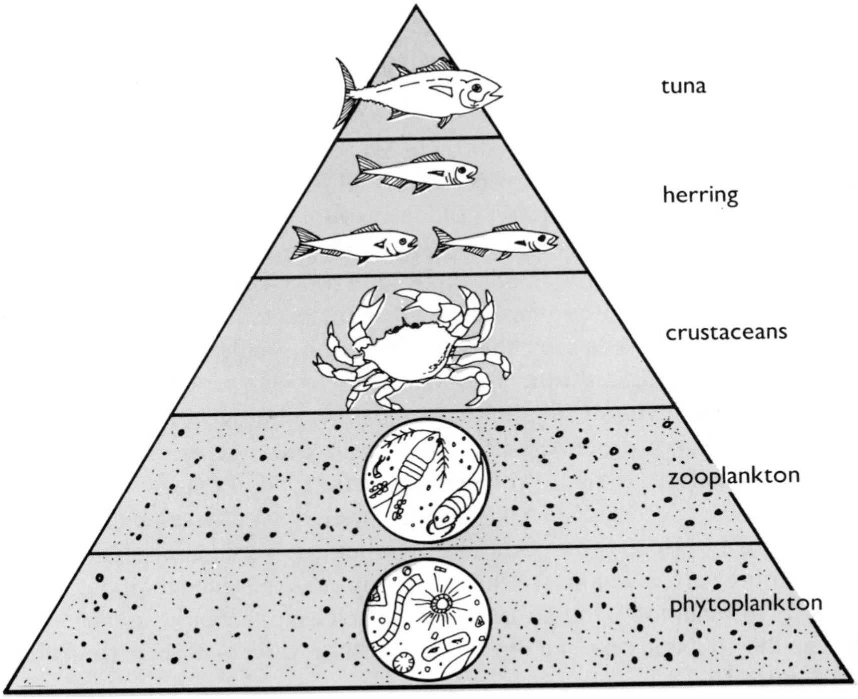

tuna

herring

crustaceans

zooplankton

phytoplankton

FIGURE 16-18 Plankton are an essential part of the energy pyramid for many aquatic communities.

IV MICROSCOPIC LIFE

Protists, Oxygen, and the Environment

Although they are very small and inconspicuous, protists are widespread, and have a major effect on both the biotic and the abiotic environments. Whether autotrophic or heterotrophic, all protists are involved in a variety of ecological relationships with other organisms, including humans. (See Table 16-1.)

As the major photosynthetic organisms in oceans, pyrrophytes and chrysophytes are also important contributors to the world's oxygen supply. Land plants also produce significant amounts of oxygen, but there are not enough terrestrial plants to maintain present-day oxygen levels in the atmosphere.

The distinction between a commensal organism and a parasite is not always easy to make. Most parasites live in a commensal relationship to their hosts the majority of the time. For example, *Entamoeba histolytica* is considered to be a parasite. Yet, dysentery carriers are quite unaffected by the spores that reside in their body. Therefore, the spores of *E. histolytica* can be regarded as commensals.

TABLE 16-1 Ecological Relationships Involving Protists

Type	Description
Predator-Prey	• Plankton forms the basis of many aquatic food chains. Blue whales feed mainly on plankton. • Didinium feeds on paramecium.
Parasitism	• *Entamoeba histolytica* causes amoebic dysentry in humans. • *Plasmodium vivax* causes malaria in humans and other organisms. • *Trypanosoma gambiense* causes African sleeping sickness.
Mutualism	• *Trichonympha* lives in the digestive tract of termites. It digests the wood that termites eat. Termites cannot digest cellulose.
Commensalism	• *Endolimax nana* lives in the digestive tract of humans. It feeds on intestinal contents that humans do not use. It has never been known to be harmful.

Most atmospheric oxygen diffuses into the air from the oceans. As major producers of oxygen and food for other aquatic organisms, protists are important to both the oxygen cycle and the carbon cycle. Any major disturbance, such as extensive water pollution, which would seriously affect the phytoplankton populations in oceans, would also have serious consequences for humans and most other organisms.

In addition to producing oxygen, protists also contribute to the abiotic environment in some unexpected ways. For example, some members of the phylum Sarcodina, the foraminifers, surround themselves with shells made of calcium carbonate. In some areas, accumulations of these tiny shells over millions of years have formed geologically important limestone deposits. Samples of limestone found in different areas have different characteristics. Some harder limestone is quarried, cut into stones, and used for buildings. Other softer types of limestone are crushed and used in various industrial processes such as winemaking and pharmaceutical manufacturing. Limestone, when heated, is converted into quicklime, which is used in the steel industry. Quick-

Water pollution in the Kaministikwia river near Thunder Bay, Ontario, has killed aquatic plants and oxygen-producing diatoms. The resulting lack of oxygen has had catastrophic effects on the fish.

This limestone deposit near Jasper, Alberta, shows the sedimentary layers that were formed as the tiny shells of foraminifers and other creatures piled up over thousands of years.

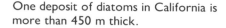

One deposit of diatoms in California is more than 450 m thick.

Limestone is often used as building stone, but it can be damaged by the sulphur dioxide in acid rain.

Oil rigs produce petroleum that is used for fuel and many other products.

lime is mixed with water to form slaked lime, which is used to make building materials such as cement, mortar, and plaster.

The cell walls of most diatoms contain silica. When diatoms die, their shells sink to the bottom of the ocean floor. In other locations, the skeletons of long-dead diatoms have accumulated in deposits many metres thick. Over millions of years, the glassy silica of the skeletal cell walls turns into rock. These rock-like deposits are known as diatomaceous earth. Although originally formed underwater, many of these deposits are now on land. Diatomaceous earth is mined and used to produce the fine abrasives in metal polishes and toothpaste. It is also used to manufacture insulation and filtration materials.

Scientists also believe that planktonic protists are a large part of the original living material that formed petroleum. The formation of petroleum is thought to have started over 500 million years ago in the warm, shallow seas that covered much of the earth's surface. Fossils found in the rocks around present-day oil deposits suggest that these seas contained large populations of protozoans. As these organisms died and sank to the sea bottom, they were buried by sediments. A combination of decay, pressure, heat, and time converted their cytoplasm into energy-rich hydrocarbon molecules. Today, substances such as petroleum are recovered from the earth and burned as a fuel, or used to produce plastics and other synthetic materials.

Pamela Stokes

Dr. Pamela Stokes believes that a new, interdisciplinary approach to science is the key to understanding and solving environmental problems. "The boundaries between many of the disciplines are boundaries of convenience, which have developed over time," says Stokes.

Stokes, until recently the director of the University of Toronto's Institute for Environmental Studies (IES) and a professor of botany, is involved in a research project that demonstrates the need for an interdisciplinary approach.

As some northern Ontario lakes become acidic, Stokes says, they become susceptible to blooms. These large algal slimes, which coat docks, boats, and cover fish spawning grounds, are a sure sign that the lake system is out of balance. Stokes believes blooms may be caused indirectly by acid rain, which may reduce populations of animals that normally control algal populations.

To understand and correct the problem, expertise in more than one discipline will be needed, Stokes says. A botanist might be expected to focus on the algae's relationships with predators, and their reactions to increased water acidity. However, as Stokes points out, this approach leaves important questions unanswered. How are predator populations affected by acidity and why? Why does the acidity develop? What is the source of the pollution and how might the pollution travel? How might the lake pH be normalized?

None of these questions falls within the traditional sphere of the botanist. To understand the complex relationships between the pollution, its sources, the lake water, and its various inhabitants, Stokes says, a synthesis of research in disciplines as diverse as chemistry, physics, meteorology, ecology, toxicology, and physiology may be required.

Although no one can be expected to have expertise in all of these disciplines, researchers can learn to benefit from the abilities of other scientists. As director of the IES, Stokes was responsible for supplying support services and leadership to research groups

working in many other university departments. She promoted an interdisciplinary approach as "the key to intelligent environmental management."

Pamela Stokes was born in England, and received a Ph.D. in fungal physiology from the University of Bristol. She taught in England and did research at the University of Illinois before coming to the University of Toronto in 1969. Here she studied metal tolerance, a field that remains important to her research today.

"I have always had a fascination for the capacity of living things to survive when pushed to their limits," Stokes said. In 1973, she studied resilient algae that had survived years of intense pollution in lakes in northern Ontario. Stokes's major concerns have been the responses of freshwater phytoplankton to both trace metals and lake acidification, the processes by which trace metals are cycled in lakes, and the long-range airborne transport of pollution. Through her research, and the influence of her colleagues at the IES, Stokes found herself developing into a mission-oriented environmental scientist.

Stokes is gratified by the public's raised environmental awareness. There is a noticeable difference in attitude, today, she says, and real changes are being made. "There is a sense developing," Stokes says, "that we're all in this together."

Section Review Questions

1. a) Briefly describe three ecological roles performed by protists.
   b) State one example of each ecological role you have described.
2. a) Which substance is found in the protists of the phylum Pyrrophyta that enables them to photosynthesize? What colour is this substance?
   b) What is the common name of the pyrrophytes, and what is their usual colour?
   c) Explain why the colour identified in part (a) is not the same as the colour identified in part (b).
3. Repeat Question 2 for the protists of the phylum Chrysophyta.
4. a) Why are pyrrophytes and chrysophytes important to aquatic animals, including carnivores?
   b) Why are these protists important to terrestrial animals, including humans?
5. List three materials in use today that were produced by protists that lived millions of years ago.

16.4 Pathogenic Protozoans

Pathogens are micro-organisms that cause disease in other organisms. For example, some very serious human diseases are caused by pathogenic protozoans that live in the human intestine. These kinds of pathogenic protozoans are a major concern in underdeveloped countries where drinking water is often contaminated by human waste.

Amoebic dysentery, for example, is caused by *Entamoeba histolytica*, a member of the phylum Sarcodina. This amoeba lives in the large intestine of humans and feeds on the intestine walls, causing fever, chills, bleeding ulcers, diarrhea, and abdominal cramps. The disease is spread when some amoebas form cysts that pass out of an infected person in digestive wastes. Another person becomes infected by eating food or drinking water contaminated by these cysts. The cysts can survive for long periods of time, making eradication of the parasite very difficult. The parasite is also difficult to eliminate because of a high incidence of **carriers.** Carriers are infected persons who do not become ill, but who do pass on cysts. In some countries where amoebic dysentery is prevalent, up to 50% of the population are carriers.

The sanitary disposal of human waste is the best way to prevent widespread transmission of dysentery. To avoid dysentery in areas where human wastes are not properly handled, any water used for drinking, cooking, or washing food must be boiled. In many poorer parts of the world, however, neither clean water nor fuel is easily obtained, and many people do become infected.

Amoebic dysentery can be treated with drugs, but several follow-up tests are required to ensure that the intestine is cyst-free.

Sarcodina is not the only protozoan phylum associated with human diseases. Both Sporozoa and Zoomastigina also include pathogenic members. (See Figure 16-19.)

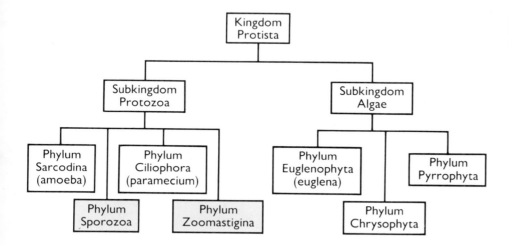

FIGURE 16-19 Members of the phyla Sporozoa and Zoomastigina cause diseases in humans.

Phylum Sporozoa and Malaria

The members of the phylum **Sporozoa** are characterized by the absence of cilia or flagella, and by their complex life cycles. The best known sporozoans are members of the genus *Plasmodium*, which cause malaria in humans. Like other protists, sporozoans are independent, single-celled organisms, but they differ in their method of reproduction. A distinguishing feature of sporozoans is the ability of their cells to multiply asexually in human tissues by forming spores.

The malaria parasite, *Plasmodium vivax*, has a complex life cycle that involves two hosts: humans and mosquitoes of the genus *Anopheles*. (See Figure 16-20.) Malaria is transmitted to humans when a female mosquito infected with the plasmodium pierces the skin to feed on blood. The plasmodium cells that are injected into the bloodstream travel to the liver, where they reproduce asexually by spore formation. The newly formed plasmodium cells return to the blood, where they eventually invade red blood cells and reproduce asexually again. Within 48–72 h, the infected red blood cells burst, releasing even more new plasmodium cells to infect more red blood cells. Usually, infected red blood cells burst simultaneously, causing the patient's temperature to soar for a few hours, then to drop suddenly. The fever and chills of malaria coincide with the reproductive cycle of the parasite.

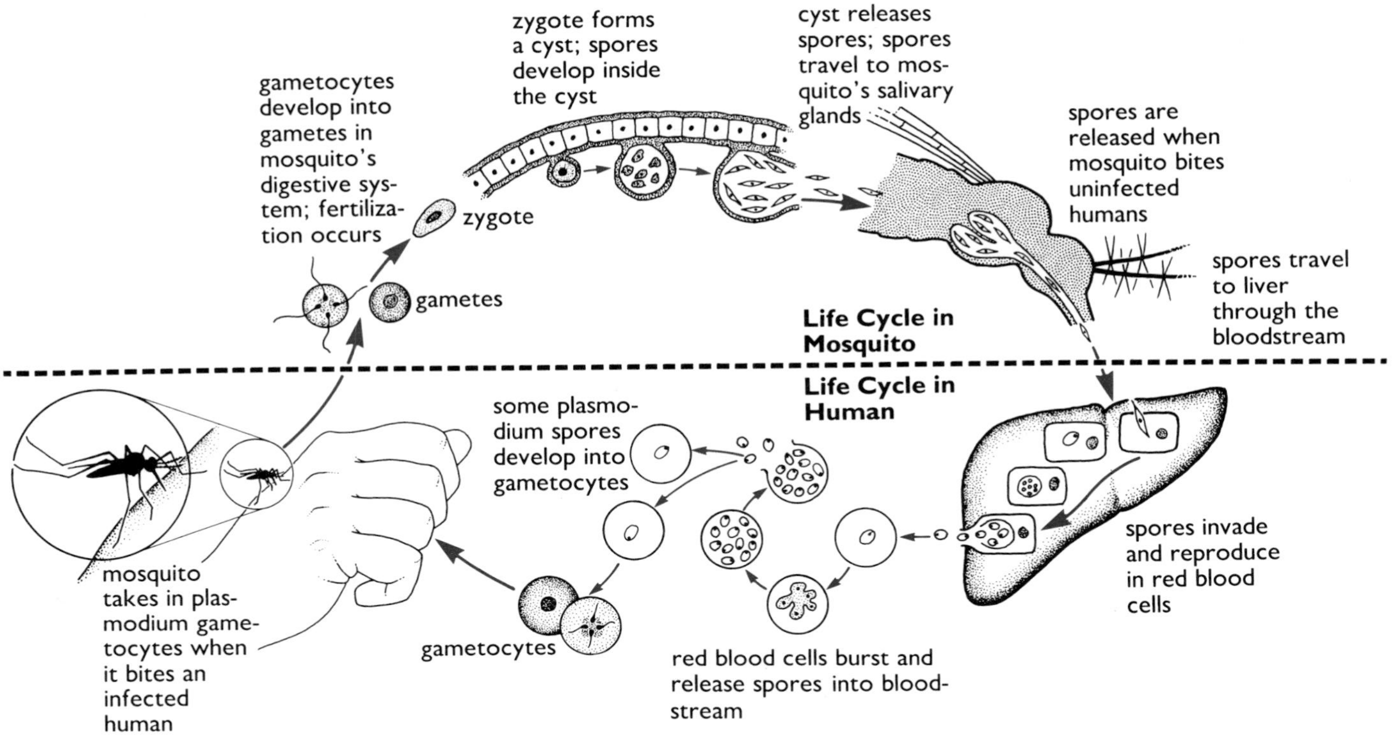
gametocytes develop into gametes in mosquito's digestive system; fertilization occurs
zygote forms a cyst; spores develop inside the cyst
cyst releases spores; spores travel to mosquito's salivary glands
spores are released when mosquito bites uninfected humans
zygote
gametes
spores travel to liver through the bloodstream
Life Cycle in Mosquito
Life Cycle in Human
some plasmodium spores develop into gametocytes
spores invade and reproduce in red blood cells
mosquito takes in plasmodium gametocytes when it bites an infected human
gametocytes
red blood cells burst and release spores into bloodstream

FIGURE 16-20 The life cycle of the malaria parasite, *Plasmodium vivax*

DID YOU KNOW?

The drug quinine, which occurs naturally in the bark of the cinchona tree, has been successfully used since the early seventeenth century for the treatment of malaria. Tonic water contains quinine hydrochloride.

After several cycles of asexual reproduction in the red blood cells, some of the plasmodium spores develop into gametes. When a mosquito ingests the blood of an infected human, it takes plasmodium gametes into its intestine. Fertilization occurs and a zygote is formed. The zygote then reproduces asexually to form thousands of spores. These spores develop into cells that travel to the mosquito's salivary glands. The next human to receive a mosquito bite will also receive some plasmodium cells, and the life cycle will begin again. The *Anopheles* mosquito is an example of a **vector,** an animal that transmits parasites from one animal to another.

Malaria can be treated with drugs, but so far the most effective way to deal with the disease is to eliminate the vector. In many tropical countries where malaria is common, pesticides were widely used to eliminate the *Anopheles* mosquitoes during the 1950s and 1960s. However, because of variability, some mosquitoes were naturally resistant to the pesticide. These few mosquitoes survived and passed their resistance to the pesticide on to their offspring, which have now multiplied to numbers approaching the original population. Today, researchers are attempting to develop a vaccine to control malaria. Meanwhile, the disease continues to be a serious human health problem in many tropical areas.

Phylum Zoomastigina and African Sleeping Sickness

The members of the phylum **Zoomastigina** are often called zooflagellates. Unlike the autotrophic dinoflagellates, zooflagellates lack chlorophyll, and thus are heterotrophic. Zooflagellates move by beating their long, whip-like flagella, but only a few species feed by ingesting dead organic matter, live bacteria, or other organisms smaller than themselves. These species are said to be free-living because they can move about independently. Most zooflagellates, however, are parasites that live in the bodies of animals and plants.

African sleeping sickness is caused by the pathogenic protozoan *Trypanosoma gambiense*. This zooflagellate multiplies in the blood of humans, releasing toxins that affect the nervous and the lymphatic systems. (See Figure 16-21.) Symptoms include irregular fever, chills, headache, skin eruptions, swollen lymph nodes, weakness, and sleepiness. If diagnosed at an early stage, African sleeping sickness can be treated with drugs. Without medical treatment, a diseased person eventually dies because of damage to the central nervous system. *Trypanosoma* inhabits the blood of wild and domestic mammals throughout much of Africa, but it does not affect them. The vector that transmits *Trypanosoma* from other animals to humans is the tsetse fly, which bites both to feed on their blood.

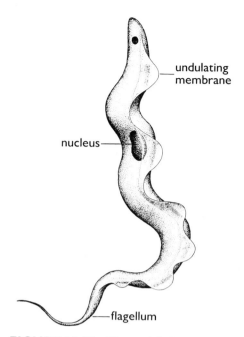

FIGURE 16-21 The undulating membrane of *Trypanosoma gambiense*, which allows it to move like an eel, is one of the many modifications that differentiate the protozoan from other unicellular protists.

RESEARCH PROJECT
The Social Impact of Pathogenic Protists

Suppose you are an employee of a charitable organization that has been asked to help underdeveloped countries. Your organization is considering the funding of projects to help reduce disease caused by pathogenic protists. Your director is too busy to read lengthy reports, and asks your research team to prepare a *brief* on the social impact of each pathogenic protist listed below.

- *Entamoeba histolytica*
- *Leishmania donovani*
- *Leishmania tropica*
- *Leishmania braziliensis*
- *Leishmania mexicana*
- *Plasmodium falciparum*
- *Plasmodium malariae*
- *Plasmodium ovale*
- *Toxoplasma gondii*
- *Trypanosoma brucei gambiense*
- *Trypanosoma brucei rhondesiense*
- *Trypanosoma cruzi*

A brief summarizes what is known about a particular subject, but focusses only on aspects related to a specific problem. It must be clear and concise, yet convey enough information to help solve the problem. In this case, the director's problem is deciding whether or not to release funds for the projects the organization has been asked to develop.

Your class will be the research team. The director could be your teacher or a guest from a foreign relief agency. Your class should do the research in small groups with each group responsible for the preparation of one brief based on three or four protists. (Your teacher may be able to provide suggestions about how to format your brief.)

When the briefs are ready, conduct a meeting of the entire research team to discuss the following questions.

1. Which three protists have the greatest social impact?
2. If only one project can be funded this year, which protist should be the target of that project?

Based on this discussion, prepare a team recommendation and present it to your director.

Importance of the Protist Kingdom

All six protist phyla consist of one-celled organisms, but otherwise they have little in common. The members of these phyla differ greatly in shape, structural complexity, feeding habits, locomotion, and reproduction. Protists also display great ecological diversity, occupying almost every known niche and habitat.

The impact of protists on the biosphere is enormous. They provide aquatic consumers with food; they provide both aquatic and terrestrial heterotrophs with oxygen; and they cause some of the world's most serious diseases. Therefore, despite their small size and deceptively simple structure, the members of the protist kingdom are extremely important to the members of all other kingdoms. In fact, the only rival to the kingdom Protista in population size and ecological importance is the kingdom Monera, whose members are so small that they often provide food for heterotrophic protists. You will learn more about the most familiar and important monerans — the bacteria — in Chapter 17.

Section Review Questions

1. a) Define pathogens.
   b) State three examples of pathogenic protists that affect humans.

2. a) Which species causes amoebic dysentery? To which kingdom, subkingdom, and phylum does it belong?
   b) Which feature of this species makes control of dysentery difficult?
   c) Which environmental conditions contribute to the spread of dysentery?

3. a) What is the disease caused by *Plasmodium vivax*?
   b) Define vector.
   c) Which organism is a vector of *Plasmodium vivax*?
   d) Which organisms are hosts of *Plasmodium vivax*?

4. List the cause, vector, and symptoms of African sleeping sickness.

Chapter Review

Key Words

amoeboid movement
carriers
Chrysophyta
cilia
Ciliophora
conjugation
contractile vacuole
cysts
euglenoid movement
Euglenophyta
eyespots
flagella
food vacuole
gullet

oral groove
pathogens
pellicle
phytoplankton
plankton
Protista
protists
pseudopods
Pyrrophyta
Sarcodina
Sporozoa
vector
Zoomastigina
zooplankton

Recall Questions

Multiple Choice

1. Which of the following is not a means of locomotion in the protist kingdom?
   a) pseudopods
   b) flagella
   c) cilia
   d) pellicles

2. Paramecia move by means of
   a) flagella
   b) pseudopods
   c) cilia
   d) pellicles

3. Euglena obtain food through the
   a) gullet
   b) cell membrane
   c) oral groove
   d) pseudopods

4. The representative protists maintain homeostasis with the help of the
   a) contractile vacuole
   b) contractile fibres
   c) food vacuole
   d) microtubules

5. Which of the representative protists is heterotrophic?
   a) amoeba
   b) euglena
   c) (a) but not (b)
   d) both (a) and (b)

Fill in the Blanks

1. Ciliates have a protective covering called _____.
2. Amoeba move by means of _____.

3. The two methods by which euglena move are _____ and _____.
4. Oxygen enters paramecia, amoebas, and euglenas by the process _____.
5. Amoeba reproduce only by means of _____.
6. Sexual reproduction in paramecia occurs by _____.
7. The protective stage that an amoeba can form during unfavourable conditions is called a _____.
8. The ability to respond to a stimulus is called _____.
9. The structure that allows euglena to detect light is the _____.
10. The substance that gives the cell walls of diatoms a glassy appearance is _____.
11. The rapid reproduction of dinoflagellates can cause _____.
12. African sleeping sickness is caused by the pathogenic protist _____.
13. Malaria is caused by the zooflagellate _____. The vector of malaria is _____.

Short Answers

1. a) List all the phyla in the protist kingdom and state one member of each.
   b) Prepare a simple chart that compares the main structural features of the protists you identified in part (a).
2. Describe how each protist in your chart maintains homeostasis.
3. a) What are the structural similarities between cilia and flagella?
   b) How do cilia and flagella differ?
4. Compare amoeboid movement with euglenoid movement.
5. How does an amoeba feed?
6. List three types of sarcodines.
7. Briefly describe the life cycle of *Plasmodium vivax*.
8. State three examples of ecological diversity in the protist kingdom.
9. Compare amoeboid movement with euglenoid movement.
10. How does an amoeba feed?

11. List three types of sarcodines.

12. Briefly describe the life cycle of *Plasmodium vivax*.

13. List three ways in which diatomaceous earth is useful to humans.

14. State two functions of the cilia in paramecia.

Application Questions

1. a) In what way(s) do euglenas resemble plant cells?
   b) In what way(s) do they resemble animal cells?
   c) How do euglenas differ from either plant or animal cells?
   d) How do they differ from most other algal protists?

2. Discuss the following statement. "All producer protists are green because food production requires the presence of the photosynthetic pigment chlorophyll." State whether you agree and explain why.

3. a) What are the human diseases caused by *Plasmodium vivax*, *Trypanosoma gambiense*, and *Entamoeba histolytica*?
   b) Explain how each disease identified in part (a) is transmitted, describing the role of vectors and carriers where appropriate.
   c) At what stage in the life cycle of each protist listed in part (a) do you think treatment methods would be most effective?

4. a) What conditions encourage rapid growth and reproduction in amoebas?
   b) What is the main factor that limits the maximum size of an amoeba, and what happens when maximum size is reached?
   c) How does an amoeba respond when conditions become unfavourable for growth and reproduction?
   d) Do your answers to parts (a), (b), and (c) apply to protists other than amoebas?

5. a) Briefly explain how planktonic and nonplanktonic protists differ in structure.
   b) Identify the two types of planktonic protists, and explain how their ecological roles differ.
   c) Discuss the ecological role(s) of at least three nonplanktonic protists.

6. Suppose water pollution in the oceans was allowed to become so serious that it affected the plankton populations. List ways in which this would affect humans.

7. Dysentery occurs mainly in countries where unsanitary living conditions prevail. However, isolated cases do appear occasionally in countries such as Canada where sanitary standards are high. What is the most likely explanation for this pattern?

8. If a protist possesses a contractile vacuole, what is its probable habitat?

Problem Solving

1. a) Paramecia are sometimes thought of as animal-like protists. Explain why.
   b) Compare conjugation in paramecia with sexual reproduction in animals. What do the two processes have in common, and how do they differ?

2. While using a microscope to examine pond water, a biology student observed three distinctly different protist species. Although the protists moved too fast for certain identification, the student did observe that protist A had chloroplasts, while protist B had flagella, and protist C had a variable shape.
   a) Name every phyla to which each protist could possibly belong.
   b) What can you conclude about the possible ecological role(s) of each protist?

3. Some biologists have compared the protist kingdom to a "junk drawer," a useful category in which to classify organisms that do not clearly belong to any other kingdom. Now that you have completed Chapter 16, state whether you agree with this comparison. Explain why.

4. Compare the response to light of the euglena, the paramecium, and the amoeba. What does the response of each protist reveal about the organism? What is the advantage of each type of response?

5. a) State two types of protist fossils that are currently used for practical purposes.
   b) Which protists alive today are most likely to leave fossil evidence for future biologists to study? Explain wh

6. Some classification systems include slime moulds in the protist kingdom. The system used in this book, however, classifies slime moulds in the fungi kingdom. Write two short paragraphs, one supporting the first position and one supporting the second.

Extensions

1. Obtain samples of pond water containing protists. Use a microscope and reference materials to identify the organisms present in your samples.

2. Research one of the following topics and submit a report to your teacher or make a presentation to your class.
   a) the concept that protists may be an evolutionary link between prokaryotic and eukaryotic organisms
   b) the importance of protists in the digestive tract of termites and herbivorous mammals

3. Research the techniques for preparing fixed and stained slides of protists. With your teacher's permission, prepare slides of various protists.

17

The
Bacteria

For most of history, the major part of humanity's struggle for health was against an enemy it suspected but did not know existed. An ancient Greek writer speculated that "tiny animals," invisible to the eye, might cause disease. Before the existence of bacteria was discovered, doctors protected themselves from infectious diseases by wearing the clothing shown in this illustration. This doctor is clothed entirely in leather. His mask holds sweet-smelling spices for filtering polluted air. His wand was used for feeling the patient's pulse.

Louis Pasteur's proposal, in 1878, of the germ theory, clarified the problem and revolutionized medicine. Pasteur showed that disease, infection, putrefaction, and fermentation were all caused by micro-organisms.

Research in the light of the germ theory soon revealed the hidden mechanisms of transmittal, infection, and action of pathogenic bacteria. This knowledge, in turn, has led to measures that control bacterial populations in three ways —decreasing exposure, increasing resistance, and fighting bacteria in the body. Public health measures, including efficient sewage control and water treatment, control bacterial populations in the environment and limit our exposure to harmful bacteria. Defences against certain diseases can be strengthened by individual immunization. As a final defence, antibiotics kill or weaken bacteria within the body.

The effectiveness of these measures is dramatic. In 1900, six of the ten leading causes of death in the United States were bacterial agents. Today, only one of the top ten causes of death—pneumonia— is bacterial. In addition, widespread immunization is credited with the virtual disappearance of once dreaded diseases such as smallpox.

The second area of medicine revolutionized by the germ theory was surgery. Before 1846, surgery was rarely performed. The greatest danger to patients was infection during the operation. Surgeons performed with bare hands, wearing street clothes, and in front of curious audiences. The most common surgeries were amputations of damaged limbs. The mortality rate following amputation was approximately 40%. Since operations were performed without anesthesia, surgeons operated

quickly to minimize the patient's discomfort.

The discovery of bacteria's role in infection and disease, and the development of anesthesia completely changed surgery. Within twenty years, surgery was transformed from a near death sentence (and a painful one, at that) to a life-saving option. As anesthetic and antibacterial techniques developed, surgical safety improved further, and surgeons became more ambitious and more skilled. By 1890, abdominal surgery, which had rarely been attempted before 1866, was being performed on an elective basis. Today, surgeons operate on almost all of the body's structures without undue risk.

To appreciate how great an impact the germ theory has had, think about our views of disease. How many of our actions and decisions are based on our understanding of bacteria and infection?

Chapter Objectives

When you complete this chapter, you should:

1. Appreciate the importance of bacteria in the biosphere, and describe the roles played by autotrophic, heterotrophic, nitrogen-fixing, and pathogenic species.

2. Appreciate the importance of public health regulations and personal hygiene to minimize

harm from normal exposure to bacteria, and understand why aseptic techniques are some-times needed.

3. Use aseptic techniques to pre-pare bacterial cultures, observe and identify the colonies that develop, and investigate factors affecting their growth.

4. Based on microscopic investi-gations and data, label diagrams showing the characteristics of bacterial colonies and individ-ual bacterial cells.

5. Appreciate that bacteria display great diversity despite their apparently simple structure.

6. Be able to explain why bacteria are classified as prokaryotes, and compare their structural characteristics and reproductive methods with those of eukar-yotic cells.

7. Be able to describe the role of conjugation, transformation, and transduction in bacterial reproduction, and appreciate how these processes can be applied to biotechnology.

8. Be able to describe the method of transmission, symptoms, social importance, and treat-ment of some representative bacterial diseases.

9. Be able to describe how the human body defends itself against bacteria, and explain the role of vaccines, antibiotics, and antiseptics in the prevention or cure of bacterial disease.

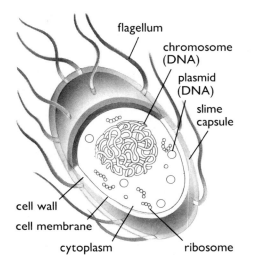

flagellum

chromosome (DNA)

plasmid (DNA)

slime capsule

cell wall

cell membrane

cytoplasm

ribosome

FIGURE 17-1 A generalized diagram of a bacterial cell. Part of the slime capsule and the cell wall have been cut away to reveal the multiple folds of the single chromosome loop.

17.1 Characteristics of Bacteria

Bacteria are among the smallest living organisms in the world. Even the largest bacterium is much smaller than any cell of a protist, plant, or animal. Yet, bacteria are able to perform the same basic life functions as complex living things composed of thousands or millions of cells.

Like an amoeba or a paramecium, each bacterium contains all it needs to carry on normal life functions in a single cell. But bacteria differ from unicellular protists in many ways both structurally and functionally. (See Table 17-1.)

Figure 17-1 is a *generalized* diagram of a bacterial cell. In other words, the diagram combines the features usually observed in the most common kinds of bacteria. You should remember that not all bacterial cells will look exactly like this. Many bacteria have whip-like flagella that extend from their cell walls. Each bacterial flagellum contains a single twisted fibre of the protein flagellin. A protist flagellum differs from a bacterial flagellum because it contains 11 fibres in the form of microtubules.

Most bacterial cells are surrounded by an outer **slime capsule,** which is a thick gelatinous layer that helps bacteria cling to surfaces. The slime capsule also protects the cell from drying out and from attack by phagocytes such as

TABLE 17-1   Comparison of Bacteria and Protists

	Bacteria	Protists
Locomotion	• flagellum if motile	• all are motile and use cilia, flagellum, or amoeboid movement
Reproduction	• fission, conjugation, spore formation	• fission, conjugation, cyst formation
Digestion	• heterotrophic types excrete digestive juices onto organic material in external environment and absorb nutrients	• heterotrophic types secrete digestive juices into food vacuole and absorb nutrients
Gas Exchange	• some need oxygen; some do not	• all need oxygen for cellular respiration
Excretion	• by diffusion across membrane	• by diffusion into contractile vacuole or across membrane
Sensitivity	• some species sensitive to light and oxygen levels	• some species sensitive to contact, heat, light, chemicals

white blood cells. The thicker the slime capsule, the more virulent the bacterial species.

All bacterial cells have a cell wall that is composed of amino acids and sugar molecules joined together. The amino acids and sugar molecules form a rigid material that gives bacteria their characteristic shape. A cell membrane just inside the cell wall keeps the cell contents inside but allows nutrients, wastes, and other substances to move in and and out of the cell.

Viewed through a microscope, the cytoplasm of bacterial cells appears granular, but it lacks the specialized, membrane-bound organelles found in **eukaryotes** such as humans and paramecia. Like them, bacteria do contain ribosomes, which are tiny, grainy cell structures that manufacture protein. However, the ribosomes of eukaryotes are firmly attached to a membranous organelle (the endoplasmic reticulum). By contrast, bacterial ribosomes float freely in the cytoplasmic fluid. The cytoplasm also contains water, wastes, vacuoles, granules of stored food, and DNA.

The DNA of eukaryotes is arranged in rod-like chromosomes, which normally have no contact with the cell cytoplasm because they are enclosed by a membrane-bound nucleus. Bacteria, however, are **prokaryotes**. Their DNA is arranged in loops and is always in direct contact with the cell cytoplasm. Research has shown that most of a bacterium's DNA is actually a continuous loop that forms a single circular chromosome. Twisting and folding may make this chromosome appear as a clump in the cytoplasm. Small rings of additional DNA called **plasmids** float freely in the cytoplasm. The exposed nature of the plasmids makes it easy for scientists to manipulate their DNA, rearranging and recombining it by means of techniques collectively called genetic engineering.

In the following activity, you will use your knowledge of the structure of bacteria to study electron micrographs and distinguish between bacterial cells and other types of micro-organisms.

The walls of plant and fungal cells contain cellulose, and therefore differ in their chemical nature and surface texture from the walls of bacterial cells. These differences form the basis for the selective action of many drugs that destroy bacteria but not plant or fungal cells.

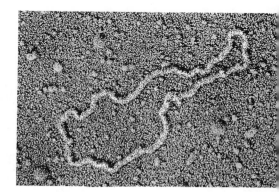

Additional DNA in bacterial cells is found in a closed loop called a plasmid.

INQUIRY ACTIVITY
Analyzing Electron Micrographs

Bacteria have certain cellular features that make their identification quite unmistakable. Structural features such as the lack of cellular organelles or a membrane-bound nucleus are clues that will help you to differentiate between bacteria and other micro-organisms.

Procedure

1. Examine the electron micrographs on page 528. Pay particular attention to the magnification of the organisms represented and consider their actual size. (Your teacher may choose to provide you with additional examples.)

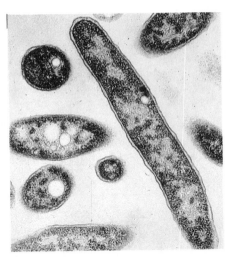

(261 000 ×)

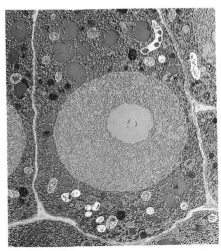

(3842 ×)

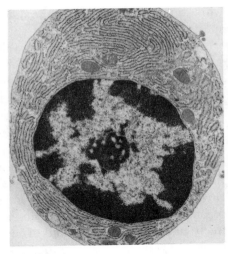

(13 638 ×)

2. From your examination of the cellular features you can identify, which micrographs show bacterial species and which ones do not?

3. For each micrograph, note your observations and make a concluding statement about each.

Discussion Questions

1. Which of the micrographs are of bacterial species? How do you know?

2. Which features of the organisms in the other micrographs distinguish them as nonbacterial organisms?

3. How did considering the size of the organisms help you to identify them?

Asexual Reproduction in Bacteria

In most cases, bacteria reproduce asexually by binary fission. As in protists, one unicellular organism divides and produces two complete new organisms. However, protists divide by mitosis. Bacterial cells divide by a much different process. (See Figure 17-2.)

In the first step of bacterial binary fission, the loop of DNA in the bacterium's single chromosome attaches itself to the cell membrane. Then the DNA makes an identical copy of itself. Next the cell grows longer so that the two chromosomes move apart. Then the membrane pinches inward, dividing the plasmids and cytoplasm into two approximately equal portions. Finally, new cell walls form to complete the division process. Unlike paramecia, the two

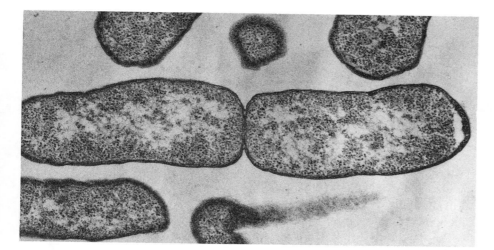

Binary fission in *E. coli* bacteria

FIGURE 17-2 Binary fission in bacteria

DNA molecule attaches itself to cell membrane

cell membrane

DNA molecule

DNA replicates

cell membrane grows

cell membrane indents

cell divides to form two new cells

new bacteria are fully grown, each about the same size as the parent. Each offspring of a paramecium is only half as large as the parent.

Under ideal conditions, binary fission of bacteria can take as little time as 20 min. Such rapid reproduction requires sufficient moisture, a temperature that is neither too warm nor too cool, and a plentiful food supply. Food used to grow bacteria in the laboratory is called a growth medium. In the following exercise, you will prepare a growth medium, and use it to culture bacteria.

LABORATORY EXERCISE 17-1
Culturing Bacteria

To culture bacteria, you will deposit a small bacterial sample on a growth medium in a sterilized plate and control its environment. Bacteria for culturing may be obtained either from a bean infusion such as that described in Chapter 15, or from commercial suppliers in sealed containers. Over a period of several days, you will observe your culture daily, noting the number, size, and characteristics of the colonies that develop. The entire laboratory exercise must be performed using strictly sterile techniques to prevent exposure to hazardous strains of bacteria.

Sexual Reproduction in Bacteria

Bacteria are capable of three types of sexual reproduction: conjugation, transformation, and transduction. All of these types of sexual reproduction involve some degree of DNA recombination. None of these processes involve meiosis or the fusion of gametes.

FIGURE 17-3 Conjugation in bacterial cells

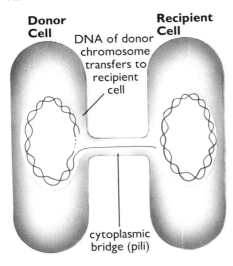

Donor Cell

Recipient Cell

DNA of donor chromosome transfers to recipient cell

cytoplasmic bridge (pili)

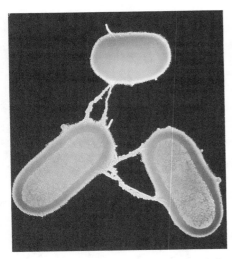

The *E. coli* bacterium in the bottom left is conjugating with two other *E. coli* bacteria. The transfer of DNA takes place through the long, hollow surface hairs called pili.

FIGURE 17-4 In transduction, a virus transfers DNA from one bacterium to another.

In **conjugation,** a segment of DNA is transferred from a donor bacterial cell to a recipient bacterial cell. (See Figure 17-3.) This transfer is accomplished by specialized protein filaments called **pili,** which are anchored in the cell membrane and project through the cell wall. The photograph on this page shows the long pili of the bacterial species *Escherichia coli*. Bacterial DNA can be observed as a granular material passing through this microtubule from donor to recipient.

Transformation occurs when a segment of DNA from a dead bacterial cell is picked up and incorporated into the single chromosome of a living bacterial cell. This process is called transformation because the DNA from the dead bacterial cell is added to the DNA of the living bacterium and transforms its function. The transformed bacterium can now perform some of the functions previously performed only by the dead species.

Transduction differs from the other two methods of DNA recombination because it requires the activity of a type of virus known as a bacteriophage. The bacteriophage attacks and destroys a host bacterium, picking up some of its DNA. (See Figure 17-4.) When the bacteriophage attacks a second bacterium, the extra DNA may be added to one of the new bacterium's plasmids or to its chromosome. If the new host is immune to the bacteriophage, the new DNA will be replicated and passed on to its offspring through ordinary asexual binary fission.

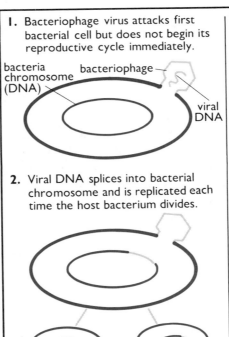

1. Bacteriophage virus attacks first bacterial cell but does not begin its reproductive cycle immediately.

bacteria chromosome (DNA)   bacteriophage

viral DNA

2. Viral DNA splices into bacterial chromosome and is replicated each time the host bacterium divides.

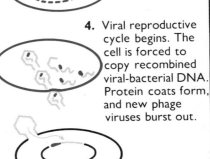

3. Some external factor reactivates the viral DNA. It breaks loose, taking along a small segment of bacterial DNA. The rest of the bacterial chromosome disintegrates.

4. Viral reproductive cycle begins. The cell is forced to copy recombined viral-bacterial DNA. Protein coats form, and new phage viruses burst out.

5. New phage virus attacks a second bacterial cell. Recombined DNA from first bacterium replaces comparable segment in second bacterium.

Aseptic Techniques

In the 1840s, a Hungarian physician, Ignaz Semmelweis, discovered a novel way to decrease mortality rates in his maternity wards; he asked his doctors to wash their hands. At the time, one in six women giving birth in hospitals died of puerperal fever, a highly contagious infection that attacks the uterus after the victim has given birth.

Puerperal fever was only a minor concern until doctors began taking over from midwives in assisting at births. Doctors, their instruments, and hospitals were infested with bacteria. In fact, patients were more likely to contract an infectious disease in hospitals than to be cured of one. When Semmelweis's doctors kept their hands clean, mortality in his maternity ward dropped to less than one in fifty.

The uncleanliness of hospitals and their staff made surgery as risky as giving birth. Any open wound was susceptible to infection carried by dirty fingers, instruments, or bacteria in the air. Although surgeons and doctors had tried a number of measures to prevent infection, they lacked a sound knowledge of the real cause of infection, so their attempts to control infection were inevitably unsuccessful. Louis Pasteur's germ theory showed the world the root of the problem. However, a British surgeon, Joseph Lister, was largely responsible for showing how to overcome bacterial infection.

In his earlier work, Lister had tried various means of washing infectious agents away from wounds. But his lack of success and Pasteur's findings led him to believe that antisepsis, the killing of infectious agents present in a wound, could not by itself prevent infection. In 1865, Lister began dressing fracture wounds with lint soaked in carbolic acid, a chemical he believed to be effective in inhibiting bacterial growth. Constructing a barrier to shield the wound from infectious bacteria had never been tried before. In

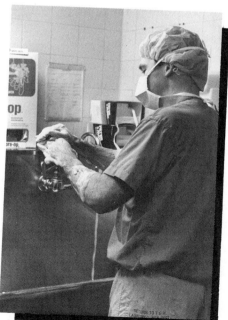

trial after trial, fracture wounds treated with Lister's principle of antisepsis (wound-cleansing) plus asepsis (wound-shielding) healed successfully without infection.

Later, Lister expanded the scale of his asepsis by spraying carbolic acid over the operating instruments, the entire operating team, and into the air of the operating room, thereby killing air- and surface-borne infectious agents.

Today, Lister's principles have been developed into a set of rules governing surgical procedure called the sterile-field technique. The open operating theatres of the past, with their crowds of curious, bacteria-infested spectators, have long been abandoned. Today, all operating room equipment, from the instruments, sutures, bandages, and sheets, to the clothing worn by the patient, doctors, and nurses, is sterilized by intense heat in vessels, called autoclaves, which produce steam under pressure. Doctors and nurses wear masks to prevent bacteria on their own breath from infecting the patient, and rubber gloves to allow them to touch the patient. Even operating room air is filtered to remove dust and particles as small as bacteria. When followed conscientiously, the sterile-field technique almost completely eliminates the risk of infection in most operations.

Survival of Bacteria

Given ideal growing conditions, one bacterium could produce two million kilograms of bacterial cells in only 24 h. But such rapid reproduction never occurs in nature. The reproductive rate of bacteria is limited by factors such as the availability of food, and the accumulation of waste materials that poison the environment of bacteria.

When growing conditions become unfavourable, bacteria cease to reproduce and enter an inactive state by forming **endospores.** (See Figure 17-5.) Endospore formation does not increase the number of bacteria, but it does enhance their chances of surviving unfavourable environmental conditions.

An endospore contains the bacterium's single chromosome, and some ribosomes and enzymes, all of which are wrapped in a double layer of plasma membrane. Most of the water leaves, virtually stopping metabolic activity such as cellular respiration. A cell wall several layers thick surrounds the capsule, providing additional protection from the environment.

The endospores of some bacterial species can survive extreme environmental stresses such as temperatures that range from 100°C to −250°C. Once the external environment becomes suitable for growth again, the endospore absorbs water, which splits the cell wall. A single bacterium emerges from the endospore case ready to resume its normal life functions.

Understanding how bacteria survive adverse conditions has helped bacteriologists develop **aseptic techniques.** Aseptic techniques are used in the study of bacteria and are useful for the treatment of patients in hospitals. Hospitals follow strict procedures to ensure that operating rooms, surgical instruments, linen, and bandages are free from bacteria or bacterial endospores.

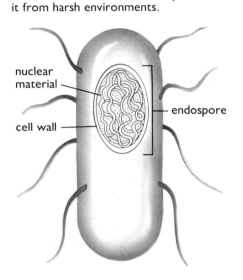

FIGURE 17-5 The endospore encloses the bacterial cell and protects it from harsh environments.

nuclear material

cell wall

endospore

Section Review Questions

1. a) What is a generalized diagram?
   b) List the cell features usually found in a generalized diagram of a bacterium.
2. a) What is the function of the slime capsule that surrounds most bacteria?
   b) What is the significance of this capsule?
3. a) Where is DNA found in bacterial cells?
   b) How does the arrangement of DNA in bacterial cells differ from that in eukaryotic cells?
   c) How does this arrangement facilitate genetic engineering?
4. a) State the process by which bacteria usually reproduce.
   b) State the process by which protists usually reproduce.
   c) What do the above processes have in common? How do they differ?

5. a) State the three processes by which bacteria may reproduce sexually.
   b) How does sexual reproduction in bacteria differ from that in eukaryotes?
6. a) What conditions favour rapid reproduction in bacteria?
   b) How do bacteria survive when growth conditions are not favourable?

17.2 Bacteria in the Biosphere

Bacteria are widespread in the living world and are also found from ocean depths to the upper atmosphere. Frozen endospores discovered in glaciers in the Antarctic show that an abundance of bacteria existed there at one time. Even the digestive tracts of animals such as cows, horses, and humans are inhabited by bacteria.

Fossil evidence indicates that bacteria have been a part of the biosphere for at least three billion years. Early bacteria were well suited for living conditions on Earth billions of years ago. Present-day bacteria have adapted to a wide variety of habitats, enabling them to populate every ecological niche in the biosphere. Perhaps the most important factor contributing to their success is the ability of bacteria to obtain the nutrition they need for growth and energy.

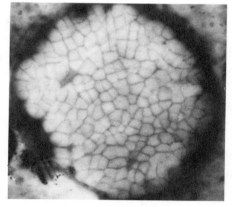

A fossilized colony of cyanobacteria. This fossil was found in China and is over 570 million years old.

How Bacteria Meet Their Nutritional Needs

Of the approximately 1500 species of bacteria present on Earth, only a very few are autotrophic. Most autotrophic bacteria carry out photosynthesis by trapping solar energy and using it to manufacture their own food. Purple and green sulphur bacteria, for example, manufacture glucose using energy from the sun. However, bacterial photosynthesis differs from plant photosynthesis in two important ways.

First, the photosynthetic pigments of bacteria are scattered throughout their cytoplasm instead of being contained within the chloroplasts. The chemical makeup of these pigment molecules resembles the chlorophyll found in plants and algae. However, bacterial pigments are able to capture solar energy at wavelengths so long they can neither be seen by humans nor absorbed by plants and algae. This ability to trap ''invisible'' light enables sulphur bacteria to produce food in locations that are too dark to support other autotrophs. The pigments also give these bacteria their unusual colours.

Second, both purple and green sulphur bacteria live in swamps where hydrogen sulphide is abundant. The bacteria use hydrogen sulphide as a raw material instead of water. Like plant photosynthesis, bacterial photosynthesis also produces the glucose needed for cellular respiration, but otherwise yields very different end products.

Compare the reactants and the products of bacterial photosynthesis with those for plant photosynthesis.

$$\text{carbon dioxide} + \text{water} \xrightarrow[\text{chlorophyll}]{\text{visible solar energy}} \text{glucose} + \text{oxygen}$$

$$\text{hydrogen sulphide} + \text{carbon dioxide} \xrightarrow[\text{photosynthetic pigments}]{\text{``invisible'' solar energy}} \text{glucose} + \text{sulphur} + \text{water}$$

The sulphur crystals formed by this reaction accumulate within the cells of purple and green sulphur bacteria, while excess water diffuses outward into the swamp.

Perhaps the most important difference between plant photosynthesis and bacterial photosynthesis is that bacterial photosynthesis produces no oxygen, and therefore does not contribute to the world's oxygen supply.

Other types of autotrophic bacteria manufacture food by **chemosynthesis.** That is, they use energy from chemical reactions to convert carbon dioxide and water into food. For example, iron bacteria obtain the chemical energy they need to manufacture food by oxidizing iron in their environment. These bacteria are responsible for the brownish scale you can sometimes see inside the water tanks of toilets. The rusty brown by-product of this reaction is iron oxide.

All other bacterial species are heterotrophs. They consume food produced by other organisms. Some of these bacteria are saprophytes. Saprophytic bacteria are decomposers that feed on dead organic material and act as agents of decay. Like fungi, these bacteria release digestive enzymes into the dead organic material around them. The enzymes break down the material into nutrient molecules that the bacterial cell can absorb. This process causes the material to decay. Decay is a vital link in all nutrient cycles. Without it, the dead matter from once living organisms would accumulate and choke the biosphere.

But decay can also be an undesirable process. Food products are composed mainly of plant or animal substances that can decay through the action of bacteria. The current level of world food production would be sufficient to feed all the planet's inhabitants if food spoilage could somehow be prevented. The methods now used for this purpose can be grouped into two major categories: those that slow down bacterial growth and those that kill bacteria.

Refrigerating, freezing, and dehydrating food are examples of the first category. These methods slow down normal growth and activity by exposing food bacteria to an unfavourable environment. Heating food to extremely high temperatures, adding chemical preservatives, and irradiating it with high-energy light waves are examples of the second category. Both of these methods kill the bacteria completely, although treated foods may spoil later if contaminated by new saprophytic bacteria.

Lush communities of ocean organisms live at depths of 2500 m, where hot water and minerals issue forth from the earth's interior and mix with the frigid ocean water. Special chemosynthetic bacteria use chemical substances in the water as a source of stored energy to make food for themselves. These bacteria take the place of green plants and form the basis of the food chain in these deep-sea communities.

Scientists can only propose solutions to scientific problems, but world hunger is a social problem affected by many factors other than spoilage. Even if spoilage could be completely eliminated, distribution would continue to be a problem. Political and economic conditions would still prevent available food from reaching many of those who need it.

To slow the growth of bacteria on its way from the farm to the dairy, milk is transported in refrigerated trucks. At the dairy, pasteurization kills the bacteria in unprocessed milk.

Ecological Interactions of Bacteria

Many heterotrophic bacteria obtain their nutrition through symbiotic relationships with other living things in the ecosystem they inhabit. These symbiotic relationships are of three different types: mutualism, commensalism, and parasitism.

Mutualism is a mutually beneficial relationship between two organisms of different species. The close association of nitrogen-fixing bacteria such as *Rhizobium* with legume plants is an example of a mutualistic relationship. *Rhizobium* bacteria invade the roots of legumes and live in swellings called root nodules. These bacteria are chemosynthetic — they obtain the chemical energy they need to manufacture food from gas. The chemical reaction that releases energy for the bacteria also produces nitrogen compounds that can be used by the plant to manufacture food. The plant benefits by obtaining needed nutrients, and the bacteria benefit from having a habitat in which to live. In this case, the benefits from the mutualistic relationship extend far beyond the legume partner, since the entire ecosystem of the soil also obtains nutrients.

In **commensalism**, two organisms of different species live together in a close association, but only one partner benefits. The other is neither helped nor harmed. For example, the enormous population of *Escherichia coli* that normally lives in the human intestine causes no ill effects. These bacteria feed on leftover cellulose and other food products that humans cannot digest. In their metabolic processes, they produce gases and other wastes that leave the body with the fecal mass. Thus, *E. coli* live in a commensal relationship with humans.

In **parasitism**, two organisms of different species live in a close association that benefits one partner (the parasite) but harms the other (the host). Usually,

The round nodules on this bean-root system house colonies of nitrogen-fixing bacteria. These bacteria can turn atmospheric nitrogen into a nitrogen compound that the plant can use.

Proper home-canning techniques can prevent botulism. If you are unsure about the safety of any canned food, you can destroy the toxins by cooking the food at 80°C for at least 30 min.

The production of biogas is a new energy source on many farms. This large cylindrical bag is used to store methane gas produced through the action of anaerobic bacteria on animal manure.

a parasite consumes only enough food or living tissue to survive without destroying the host and reducing its chance of survival. Human diseases caused by parasitic bacteria are discussed in Section 17.3

How Bacteria Obtain Energy from Their Food

Many heterotrophic bacteria require oxygen for cellular respiration to release energy for their life functions. The need for oxygen means these bacteria must live in airy environments, or in water with an abundance of dissolved oxygen. Such bacteria are called **obligate aerobes.** For example, tuberculosis is caused by *Mycobacterium tuberculosis*, an obligate aerobe that lives in the lungs of an infected person. A high oxygen concentration makes the lung tissues a good place for obligate aerobes to live. If untreated, tuberculosis is usually fatal, but it may take years for the patient to die, ensuring a continuous oxygen supply and a long life for the parasite.

To many bacteria, however, oxygen acts as a poison. Such bacteria are called **obligate anaerobes** because they must live in an oxygen-free, or anaerobic, environment. This means they cannot carry out ordinary cellular respiration because it requires oxygen. Instead, obligate anaerobes obtain their energy from a different chemical reaction called **anaerobic respiration.** Anaerobic respiration does not require oxygen. Many obligate anaerobes are saprophytic decomposers. They live in compost heaps or in the low-oxygen sediments of bogs or marshes, where they produce gaseous by-products. These include hydrogen sulphide ("rotten egg" gas), or methane, a compound also found in natural gas.

Many industrial applications harness the activity of anaerobic bacteria. For example, anaerobic bacteria are used to digest sewage in modern treatment facilities. These obligate anaerobes produce vast amounts of methane, a gas that can be used to supply energy.

Some obligate anaerobes, however, are harmful. *Clostridium botulinum*, for example, produces a paralyzing neurotoxin that can cause botulism, a type of food poisoning. Endospores of *C. botulinum* are widespread. If food is not heated properly when it is canned, a few spores may survive. Then sealing the jar or the can creates a low-oxygen environment where surviving bacteria can thrive. As they reproduce, these obligate anaerobes release large amounts of the neurotoxin, which is very difficult to destroy once it is present. Eating the contaminated food, even in small amounts, can cause symptoms such as tingling limbs and blurred vision. Larger amounts cause paralysis and death. Heating the canned food after the toxin has been formed does not help because heating destroys only the bacteria not the toxin they produce.

Facultative bacteria thrive whether oxygen is present or not. They are not restricted to one type of environment, and thus are found in many more habitats than either obligate aerobes or obligate anaerobes. *E. coli* is an example of facultative bacteria. This species thrives equally well in the anaerobic environment of the human intestine or in the aerobic environment of lake water.

Section Review Questions

1. a) How do autotrophic bacteria differ from heterotrophs? Which are more common?
   b) What do chemosynthetic bacteria have in common with photosynthetic bacteria? How do they differ?
2. a) What is the role of saprophytic bacteria in the environment?
   b) Are they helpful or harmful to humans? Explain.
3. The methods used to prevent food spoilage form two distinct categories. State an example of each and explain how it works.
4. a) What is mutualism? State an example of mutualism involving a bacterial species.
   b) What is commensalism? State an example as above.
   c) What is parasitism? State an example as above.
5. a) Differentiate between obligate aerobes and obligate anaerobes. State an example of each.
   b) Which bacteria is helpful to humans? Explain.

17.3 Pathogenic Bacteria

Pathogenic bacteria are parasitic species that cause disease in the host organism. Inside the host, the pathogen's life functions cause symptoms that result from the body's response to the bacterial invasion. Human diseases caused by pathogenic bacteria include rheumatic fever, typhoid, dysentery, cholera, diphtheria, tuberculosis, some types of pneumonia, several sexually transmitted diseases, leprosy, gastroenteritis, and food poisoning.

How Bacteria Make People Sick

All pathogenic bacteria act in much the same way. Once they gain entrance to the body, they begin to produce chemicals called **toxins.** These toxins are harmful to the human hosts and are able to travel throughout the body via the circulatory system, causing fever, chills, and other related symptoms.

Sometimes these effects may be observed in tissues distant from the site where the bacteria first entered. If you step on a rusty nail contaminated with endospores of *Clostridium tetani*, an anaerobic species, the endospores that enter deep into the tissue of your foot may find favourable conditions for resuming an active bacterial form. As the bacteria multiply, they produce a neurotoxin that causes spasms and locking, or tetanus, of the muscles, especially those in the jaw. For this reason tetanus is often called "lockjaw." The spasms spread to the breathing muscles, causing convulsions or even asphyxiation and death.

The species that causes diphtheria, *Corynebacterium diphtheriae*, produces a very different toxin, one that prevents cell organelles from manufacturing proteins. The host's cells are disabled because most cell reactions except respiration involve the production of proteins. So, the effects of diphtheria are felt far beyond the initial site of infection in the throat.

Fighting Bacterial Diseases

The human body has many defences against bacterial invasion. But the most visible defence is the skin. Unless broken, human skin forms an almost impenetrable barrier against bacteria, although some species do enter hair follicles or sweat glands through skin pores. Sweat, however, contains salts and amino acids that are poisonous to most bacteria found on the skin.

Many bacteria enter the body through the nasal passages or the pharynx, both of which are equipped with defensive features. Specialized cells in the

FIGURE 17-6 External features of the body fight bacteria before they can enter the internal environment.

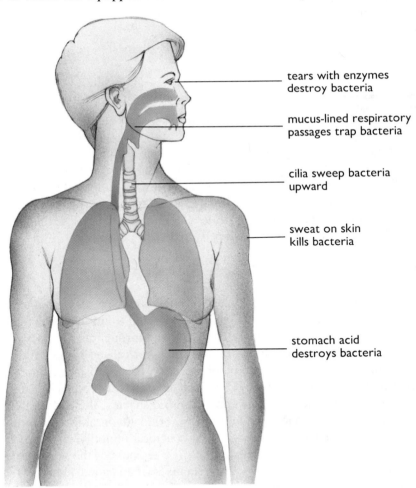

tears with enzymes destroy bacteria

mucus-lined respiratory passages trap bacteria

cilia sweep bacteria upward

sweat on skin kills bacteria

stomach acid destroys bacteria

lining of these passages secrete mucus, a sticky substance that traps the inhaled bacteria. Mucus also contains digestive enzymes that destroy the cell walls of many bacteria. The lining of the nasal passages and the pharynx also contains specialized cells equipped with cilia. Debris from the trapped bacteria are swept upward by the rhythmic beating of the cilia to the throat, where they are either swallowed or expelled by coughing.

Bacteria also enter the body through the mouth in food and water, but acids in the stomach kill most of them. (See Figure 17-6.) Bacteria that enter the eyes are attacked by the enzymes contained in tears, which continually bathe eye surfaces, cleaning them of bacteria and dust. Usually, tears drain into the upper nasal passages, where any bacteria they have not destroyed are attacked by the enzymes in mucus.

Despite these external defences, even the healthiest body can be invaded by bacteria. When this occurs, internal body defences are activated, beginning with white blood cells called **macrophages.** These white blood cells are motile and able to travel across body membranes seeking infection sites. Macrophages engulf foreign bodies such as bacteria and destroy them with digestive enzymes. The white blood cells themselves may be killed by these enzymes. The mass of dead white blood cells and dead bacteria produced at the site of an infection is called pus. But some bacteria may escape being digested.

The second line of internal defence is **antibody** formation. (See Figure 17-7.) Antibodies bind to the surface of invaders and render them ineffective.

FIGURE 17-7 The production and action of antibodies

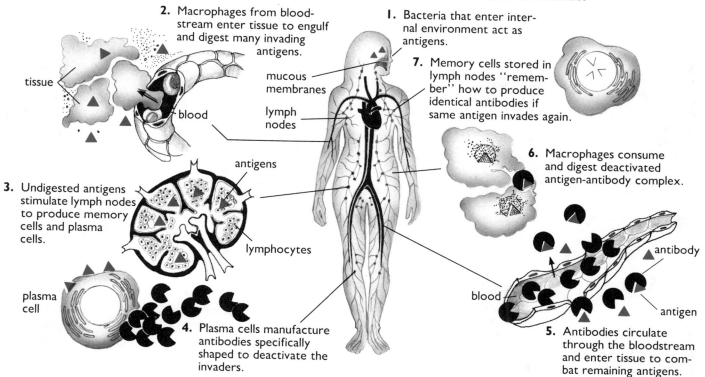

2. Macrophages from bloodstream enter tissue to engulf and digest many invading antigens.

tissue

blood

mucous membranes

lymph nodes

1. Bacteria that enter internal environment act as antigens.

7. Memory cells stored in lymph nodes "remember" how to produce identical antibodies if same antigen invades again.

6. Macrophages consume and digest deactivated antigen-antibody complex.

3. Undigested antigens stimulate lymph nodes to produce memory cells and plasma cells.

antigens

lymphocytes

plasma cell

4. Plasma cells manufacture antibodies specifically shaped to deactivate the invaders.

blood

antibody

antigen

5. Antibodies circulate through the bloodstream and enter tissue to combat remaining antigens.

Vaccinations are an important part of our public health system. Students must be vaccinated several times during their school career.

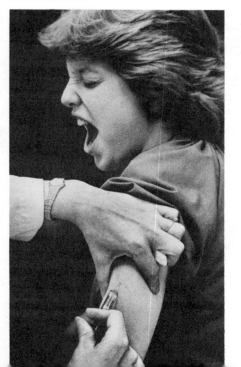

Then the macrophages move in to engulf the masses of immobilized bacteria. In general, any foreign material that causes the formation of antibodies is called an **antigen.** Each antigen requires its own specific antibody. It has been estimated that an average human body may contain over ten million different antibody types, each ready to repel future antigen invasions.

Active and Passive Immunity to Bacterial Diseases

The production of antibodies to counteract foreign bodies is called an immune response. In **active immunity,** the body itself manufactures antibodies to combat a specific disease. This active immunity can be acquired naturally when an individual suffers from a bacterial disease and recovers because his or her body has produced antibodies. Usually, the person will have a lifelong immunity because any future infection with the same pathogen will trigger an immune response.

Active immunity can also be acquired artificially by the injection of **vaccines** made of dead or weakened bacterial cells. These bacterial cells stimulate the production of antibodies without causing the disease itself. For example, tetanus vaccine is administered to people who have suffered a severe cut or puncture wound. It stimulates the production of antibodies specific to the tetanus bacterium. Tetanus shots usually provide immunity for less than ten years, but many other vaccines provide lifetime immunity against bacterial diseases such as diphtheria.

In **passive immunity,** the antibodies themselves are introduced directly into the bloodstream of an individual. Passive immunity can be acquired naturally when antibodies pass from a woman to her unborn child during the last month of pregnancy. The newborn baby also receives maternal antibodies for about two days in the thick, yellow fluid secreted by its mother's breasts prior to the onset of milk production. The child will then be immune to the same bacteria as its mother for a short period of time. The protection lasts only a few weeks or months, so babies usually begin receiving immunization shots when they are still quite young.

Passive immunity can also be acquired artificially by the injection of a serum containing antibodies to a specific antigen. Women who want to become pregnant and who have never had German measles (rubella) should receive the rubella vaccine. Contracting rubella while pregnant can cause severe malformations in the fetus. The rubella vaccine, however, provides only short-term immunity.

Antibacterial Agents

Antibacterial agents are substances that can either be injected into the bloodstream or applied to body surfaces to inhibit or kill bacteria. **Antibiotics** are substances that can be taken internally either by mouth or by injection. Antibiotics are produced mainly by fungi or other bacteria, and act to inhibit or destroy disease-causing bacteria. Penicillin is an antibiotic that works by preventing bacteria from constructing a normal cell wall. Another antibiotic, streptomycin, works by preventing bacteria from manufacturing proteins such as the enzymes needed to digest food.

Antiseptics are chemicals that can be used on the surface of the human body to kill bacteria or slow down their growth. Most wound-cleansing agents contain an antiseptic to prevent the infection of wounds, scrapes, or burns. Many mouthwashes contain an antiseptic to inhibit the action of bacteria in the mouth that cause bad breath or tooth decay. Examples of antiseptics include soap and alcohols such as propanol.

Disinfectants are strong chemical solutions that are used to sterilize surfaces that need to be bacteria free. Hospital operating rooms and dairy or pig farms use disinfectants to prevent bacterial growth. Examples of substances used as disinfectants range from sodium hydroxide (lye), to phenol (carbolic acid), and formaldehyde.

The frozen corpses of Arctic explorers who died of lead poisoning in 1848 have forced microbiologists to re-examine theories about drug-resistant bacteria. It has been supposed that resistance develops only after exposure to specific drugs. But bacteria from the corpses were already resistant to antibiotics developed a century later. These findings suggest two lines of research for microbiologists to follow. One is the growth of modern bacteria in lead-contaminated food to determine if they develop resistance. The other is the examination of tissue from the corpses for natural substances similar to modern antibiotics.

LEFT: Characteristic growth pattern of a colony of *Penicillium* mould. This mould is the parent of many varieties used to make the antibiotic penicillin.

RIGHT: Disinfectants are used to sterilize the walls, floors, instruments, and machinery used in an operating room.

LABORATORY EXERCISE 17-2
Antibiotic and Antiseptic Action on Bacteria

In this exercise, you will observe how antibacterial agents affect the growth of the bacteria you cultured in Laboratory Exercise 17-1. You will compare common antiseptics and disinfectants to determine which are most effective in preventing bacterial growth. You will also use commercially prepared antibiotic disks to compare their effects on the growth of various bacterial species.

Workers in food industries must wear gloves and hairnets to prevent the contamination of food products.

The Importance of Sanitation

Most North Americans are relatively safe from illnesses caused by pathogenic bacteria in drinking water. Strict public health regulations in most municipalities have virtually eliminated the risk of infection. In underdeveloped countries, where enforcement of such regulations is difficult, outbreaks of bacterial disease such as typhoid or cholera sometimes occur when pathogens from raw sewage contaminate drinking water.

To prevent bacterial diseases, sanitary procedures must also be followed in food preparation, especially when large amounts of food are being prepared. For example, canneries, school cafeterias, hospitals, and institutions must adhere to public health regulations. These regulations ensure that bacteria are not spread to food and to the people who consume it.

Personal hygiene is extremely important in preventing the spread of diseases among your own family and friends. Some hygiene practices are simply common sense. Regular hand washing, especially before meals, prevents the transfer of bacteria to food during preparation or to your mouth during meals.

Section Review Questions

1. a) What name is given to bacteria that cause diseases in humans?
   b) How do these bacteria make people sick?
   c) Explain why their harmful effects may occur far from the site of infection.
2. a) Describe how each of the following defends the body against bacterial invasion: the skin (two ways), the upper respiratory passages (two ways), the stomach, and the eyes.
   b) Explain why the body defences listed above are considered to be external.
3. a) Describe the body's first line of internal defence against bacterial invasion.
   b) Describe the body's second line of internal defence. Explain how it differs from the first.
4. What do the following types of immunity have in common, and how do they differ?
   a) active immunity and passive immunity
   b) natural active immunity and artificial active immunity
   c) natural passive immunity and artificial passive immunity
5. a) Identify the three different types of antibacterial agents and state an example of each.
   b) Which of the three antibacterial agents is safe for internal use by humans? What effect does it have on bacteria?
   c) Where and how are the other two agents used? What effect do they have on bacteria?

Coliform Counts

An unquestioned pleasure of summer in Canada is swimming in our many lakes and rivers. Unfortunately, water near many towns and cities has become too dangerous for swimming. According to Estelle Mo-Wong, an official with Toronto's Department of Health, high bacterial concentrations in polluted water can cause serious skin, eye, ear, mouth, nose, and intestinal infections.

The bacteria responsible for these infections come from feces. Sewage and liquid waste are normally cleaned of harmful substances before being released from municipal water systems into the environment, but in some municipalities such as Toronto, rainfall can overburden the water system. Throughout much of Toronto's sewer network, conduits carrying sewage and surface run-off from rain flow together. Ideally, sewage and surface run-off should be separate. Rainwater should flow immediately into Lake Ontario, and sewage should be directed to treatment facilities.

But when it rains in Toronto, treatment facilities are often not able to cope with the combined volume of run-off and sewage, so fecal material flows into the lake without treatment. So far, there are still no methods of storing excess sewage until treatment facilities can recover. According to Mo-Wong, if even 2 mm of rain falls, some Toronto beaches are automatically considered polluted for 48 h afterward.

Over 1000 beaches across Ontario are inspected daily for safety. Health officials do not test for the harmful bacteria themselves since bacteria responsible for most infections, even in dangerous waters, are found in low concentrations. Testing for harmful bacteria is not only expensive,

but so time-consuming the test results are outdated before they arrive.

By contrast, bacteria found in human and animal feces, called coliform bacteria, persist in greater numbers outside the body and are easier to test for. These bacteria, particularly *Escherichia coli*, which is the most common human coliform bacteria, are used as an indicator of fecal contamination. The presence of *E. coli* may also indirectly reveal the possible presence of other fecal bacteria that are pathogenic. Toronto-area swimming water, Mo-Wong says, is considered safe if it contains less than 100 coliform bacteria per 100 mL of water.

A more vital concern for health officials is the purity of drinking water. In 1885, 80 000 Chicagoans died of typhoid when summer rains washed human waste from the Chicago River, where the city's sewage was dumped, into Lake Michigan, where its drinking water was gathered. Bacteria in drinking water can also cause dysentery, Asiatic cholera, and diarrhea.

Incidents like the Chicago typhoid epidemic, which proved that dilution of waste in huge water bodies like the Great Lakes could not assure the safety of drinking water, led to the building of treatment facilities for drinking water in cities and towns around the world.

17.4 Applications of Bacteriology

Humans have been using helpful bacteria to solve practical problems for thousands of years without even knowing that bacterial action was involved. For example, meat that has been allowed to "hang" for a few days becomes tastier and easier to chew because bacterial enzymes act to break down the fibres. Bacterial fermentation of food products has been used for centuries to improve their taste or storage life. Milk that has been fermented by certain types of bacteria is commonly known as yogurt. Bacteria that produce lactic acid impart a characteristic flavour to cheese, which is another fermented milk product. Cheese remains fresher longer than milk because the lactic acid inhibits micro-organisms that cause spoilage. Approximately 20 different species of bacteria are used to produce the vast array of cheese types now available.

All of these processes were well known long before scientists understood about the action of bacteria or enzymes. In the time since Pasteur's germ theory first gained wide acceptance, the study of bacteria has developed into a distinct branch of biology called **bacteriology.** Bacteriology has helped make surgery safer. It has also enabled scientists to realize the potential of bacteria as agents of chemical change. Many ingenious uses for bacteria have been developed since Pasteur's day.

Bacteria and Biotechnology

Biotechnology is the use of living things, their cell parts, or their chemical components to manufacture materials or perform services. Using blue-green moulds to produce penicillin is an example of biotechnology. The methods for making yogurt and cheese are also examples of biotechnology using bacteria even though they were developed a long time ago. Using bacteria to produce silage is a more recent example of bacteriology based on a scientific understanding of how bacteria function.

The silage process was first developed in Europe and brought to North America around 1870. Green plants such as corn, grasses, and alfalfa are harvested, chopped into small pieces, and blown into a silo. If this material is packed firmly, anaerobic conditions are created in the silo. Anaerobic bacteria can then digest the sugars in the green plant material, converting them to lactic acid. This silage takes on a characteristic smell and taste, and the acid prevents spoilage by other micro-organisms. Silage makes up a large part of the diet of dairy cattle in many parts of the world.

A much more recent application of bacteriology is the use of certain bacterial species to perform services for the mining industry. Some worked-out mines can be made operational again through flooding and the addition of sulphuric acid-producing bacteria to dissolve any useful minerals still left in

Bacterial fermentation in milk produces cheese. The type of cheese produced depends on the species of bacteria used, and on the storage and production procedures.

Dairy cattle are fed green plant material (mostly chopped corn plants) that is packed into a silo, where special anaerobic bacteria convert the plant sugars and starches into lactic acid. Cattle feed produced in a silo is called silage.

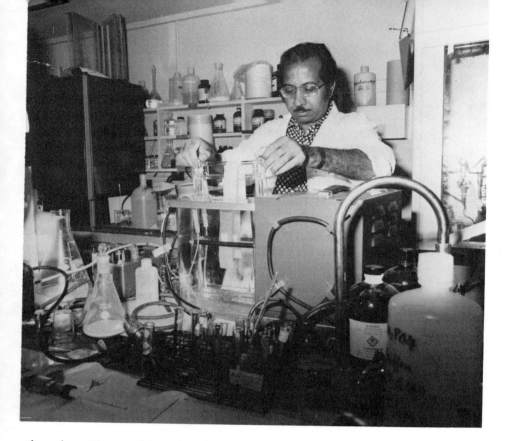

Dr. Sarang Narang, a scientist at the National Research Council in Ottawa, has created a new linker molecule that allows researchers to plug new genetic information into bacterial cells.

the mine. The resulting material is pumped out of the mine and the desired minerals are chemically separated from the mixture. Copper, uranium, iron, nickel, and gold have been extracted using this technology. Other bacterial species have been discovered that can use petroleum for food. These bacteria can be used to help clean up oil spills.

By far the most exciting modern developments in biotechnology are based on understanding bacterial reproduction, and on understanding the structure and function of bacterial DNA. Using this knowledge, microbiologists have perfected methods for inserting DNA from other organisms into bacteria. This procedure is called **recombinant DNA technology.** A bacterium with recombinant DNA will still produce all the proteins it needs for its own life functions. In addition, it will produce the foreign protein specified by the inserted DNA. This enables the bacteria to produce proteins usually found only in organisms of other kingdoms.

One important example of recombinant DNA technology is the manufacture of human insulin for use by diabetics. Formerly, insulin for diabetics has been obtained from pork or beef pancreatic tissue. The purification process is long and costly, and both pork and beef insulin differ slightly from human insulin. Because the molecules of pork and beef insulin are foreign to humans, they can trigger an immune response in some diabetics and cause undesirable side effects.

DID YOU KNOW?

Microbiologists have developed a weakened strain of salmonella bacteria to use in preparing an anti-salmonella vaccine. This vaccine could prevent dangerous and costly bacterial infestations affecting both the meat and the eggs of domestic chickens. It is also hoped that a wider range of human vaccines can be manufactured using the nonvirulent salmonella as a vector to carry other pathogens.

FIGURE 17-8 Producing human insulin through recombinant DNA technology

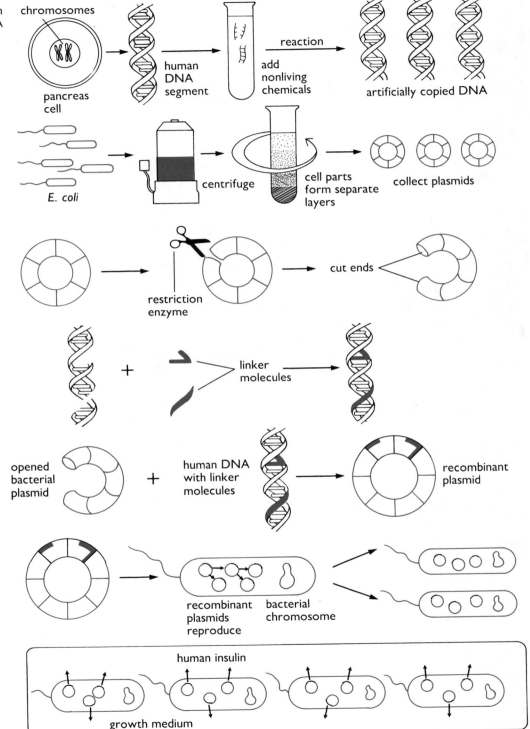

1. Isolate DNA segment coding for insulin from human pancreas cell. Use biochemical reactions to manufacture multiple copies of coding segment.

2. Isolate plasmids from *E. coli* by crushing bacteria in a blender and spinning cell parts in a centrifuge.

3. Use specialized enzymes called restriction enzymes to cut plasmids open in a place where foreign DNA can be inserted.

4. Add linker molecules to human DNA so coding segments will match cut ends of plasmids.

5. Mix human DNA and opened plasmids so linker molecules can bond to cut ends.

6. Insert resulting recombinant plasmid into living *E. coli* bacterium. Plasmid will now reproduce itself, and copies will be passed on when bacterium divides.

7. Spliced-in human DNA directs production of human insulin.

To manufacture human insulin using recombinant DNA technology, the section of DNA that controls the production of insulin must be isolated from the chromosomes of a normal human pancreatic cell. (See Figure 17-8.) This DNA is then "spliced" into the single chromosome of an *Escherichia coli* bacterium. When the *E. coli* bacteria are cultured under suitable growing conditions, they can produce human insulin in substantial amounts. The insulin must then be separated from the bacterial cells and purified. Human insulin produced by this method is already being used by diabetics across North America. There is evidence that using human insulin will decrease some of the problems associated with using animal insulin.

RESEARCH PROJECT
Advances in Biotechnology

There is tremendous potential for applications of biotechnology in medicine and agriculture. Biotechnology may help feed the world through the production of food proteins for humans and animals, and by improvements in soil fertilizers and animal health products. Malaria, a protist-caused disease that has so far resisted control, may eventually be prevented through the use of monoclonal antibodies, which are protein molecules able to recognize and combat foreign substances.

But biotechnology advances so rapidly that today's "big news" quickly becomes outdated. You may find that the best way to learn about the latest biotechnological developments and their significance is through a research project. Start by choosing a topic that interests you. Consider the following list, or scan newspapers and magazines for research topics.

- human medicine
- veterinary medicine
- agricultural science
- soil fertilizer technology
- food production
- chemical products
- mining and mining extraction
- waste management
- pollution control
- energy conversion

Begin your research in your school or public library. Government agencies or the public relations office of local industries may also provide you with information.

Investigate the latest biotechnological advances concerning your topic. Are there problems with the technology? What new related research is planned? Has this advance saved money, resources, or the environment? Has it improved human health or the quality of human life? Present your findings in a talk, a short essay, or a bulletin-board display. Your teacher may also have other suggestions for presentations.

Biotechnology, Bacteria, and Viruses

One of the most efficient ways to kill bacteria is to infect them with viruses. Viruses that destroy bacteria are called **bacteriophages.** The Greek word *phag* means eat, but bacteriophages are much too tiny to eat a bacterium. Instead, they lock onto the bacterium's cell wall and deposit their DNA inside its cytoplasm. The viral DNA then controls the functioning of the bacterium's cell parts. This ability of viruses provides microbiologists with an important way to probe and alter bacteria. Much biotechnology of today and of the future is based on this ability of viruses.

Viruses also invade the cells of large organisms such as humans, and some of the most serious diseases are caused by viruses rather than bacteria. In Chapter 18, you will learn more about viruses and viral diseases, especially the human immunodeficiency virus that causes AIDS. AIDS is a disease that is expected to rival the worst bacterial plagues before it is brought under control.

Section Review Questions

1. List three ways humans have used helpful bacteria to solve practical problems.
2. List three ways developed by scientists of solving practical problems with helpful bacteria.
3. a) What is recombinant DNA technology?
   b) What role do bacteria play in this technology?
4. a) Until recently, how has insulin for diabetics been obtained?
   b) Outline the steps required to remodel a bacterium so it can manufacture human insulin.
   c) What practical problem is solved by the method described above?
5. a) What are bacteriophages, and how do they affect bacteria?
   b) What special ability of bacteriophages makes them important to present and future biotechnology?

Meet Bob Pickett

Bob is the Assistant Director for water-pollution control in Toronto. He is in charge of four sewage treatment plants.

Q. *Describe the process of sewage treatment.*

A. Sewers bring sewage, which is 99% water, from houses and buildings to the treatment plant. The method used to treat the sewage is called the activated sludge process, which begins with a screening to remove sticks and nonorganic material from the sewage flow. Then the sludge in the raw sewage settles to the bottom of the primary sedimentation tanks, and from there it is pumped into aeration tanks.

Q. *What happens in the aeration tanks?*

A. Air blowers provide an aerobic environment for biological growth. The biomass in the tank will feed on the organic material in the sewage. To measure organic material, we conduct a test called a biochemical oxygen demand test (the BOD test), which tells us the amount of organic material in the sewage. We want to remove solids and organic material from the sewage before the sewage enters the lake, because these solids will exert an oxygen demand on the lake. If this happened, there would be no oxygen for aquatic life.

Q. *What happens after the aeration tank?*

A. The sewage enters the final sedimentation tanks, where the effluent is treated with chlorine, which destroys most of the microorganisms and all pathological life, and makes it suitable for disposal into Lake Ontario. It's a continuous operation of recycling activated sludge into aeration tanks.

Q. *Where does this sludge go?*

A. Into digestion tanks, where it's allowed to digest for 30 days at a regulated temperature. During digestion, methane gas is generated and used as fuel in the plant. Digested sludge is conditioned and incinerated.

Q. *Is it unpleasant to work in a treatment plant?*

A. If you work in a perfume factory you smell perfume. People who tour the treatment plants are surprised to find that they are just like any other industrial plant.

Q. *What are the capacities of the four plants?*

A. The main treatment plant is the largest secondary-treatment plant in Canada. It has the capacity to handle 817 000 m of sewage a day.

Q. *Why does this field interest you?*

A. I saw a technical challenge in operating a treatment plant that also provides a benefit to society. The challenge is to repair and replace equipment. I'm always reviewing new processes and equipment. I also find satisfaction in serving the public.

Q. *Has there been increasing focus on pollution lately?*

A. Yes. The public is more aware of pollution now. We're responsible to the provincial Ministry of the Environment, which has to answer to the public.

Q. *What do you like best about your job?*

A. It's an exciting field with tremendous variety. There are opportunities to use many different talents in sewage treatment. We work with chemists, biologists, mechanical experts, electricians, and lab technicians.

Q. *Would you advise young people to go into this field?*

A. Absolutely. Every town and city has a sewage treatment facility, so there's lots of work. It's a field that will always be with us. We have a saying here, "If you're bored in sewage treatment, you must be dead!"

Chapter Review

Key Words

active immunity	facultative bacteria
anaerobic respiration	macrophage
antibiotics	obligate aerobes
antibody	obligate anaerobes
antigen	passive immunity
antiseptics	pathogenic bacteria
aseptic techniques	plasmids
bacteria	recombinant DNA
bacteriology	technology
bacteriophages	slime capsule
biotechnology	toxins
chemosynthesis	transduction
conjugation	transformation
disinfectants	vaccines
endospores	

Recall Questions

Multiple Choice

1. Which statement concerning bacteria is incorrect?
   a) Bacteria are prokaryotic organisms.
   b) Bacteria have lived on Earth for at least three billion years.
   c) Bacteria are eukaryotic organisms.
   d) All bacteria are motile.
   e) Bacteria lack a true nucleus.

2. By which means do bacteria reproduce?
   a) sexual means only
   b) asexual means only
   c) endospore formation
   d) asexual and sexual means
   e) asexual means and endospore formation

3. To which of the following groups does *Escherichia coli* belong?
   a) saprophytic bacteria
   b) parasitic bacteria
   c) autotrophic bacteria
   d) commensal bacteria
   e) chemosynthetic bacteria

4. Which of the following statements concerning antibodies is correct?
   a) Antibodies are specific for one antigen.
   b) Antibodies are produced by red blood cells.
   c) Antibodies act by consuming the antigen.
   d) Antibodies remain active only until the antigen has been eliminated.
   e) Antibody formation stops in adulthood.

5. To acquire active immunity naturally you must
   a) receive antibodies from your mother prior to birth
   b) suffer from a disease and recover through an immune response
   c) receive antibody inoculations from your doctor
   d) receive a vaccination from your doctor
   e) receive an antibiotic from your doctor

Fill in the Blanks

1. When bacteria, protists, and viruses are ranked according to size, _____ are the largest, _____ are next largest, and _____ are the smallest.

2. Bacterial DNA is exposed to the cell _____ and is arranged in _____ or _____.

3. The cytoplasm of bacteria contains no _____, but it does contain _____ for the production of protein.

4. Most bacteria reproduce _____; however, some bacteria do reproduce _____.

5. To escape harsh environmental conditions, some bacteria can enter the _____ stage.

6. In _____ DNA technology, a _____ from one organism is transferred into another.

7. Bacteria that can produce their own food from inorganic molecules are called _____.

8. An important chemosynthetic bacterium that lives in the soil helps convert _____ into _____.

9. Bacteria that cannot live in the presence of oxygen are called _____, and bacteria that cannot live in the absence of oxygen are called _____.

10. Pathogenic bacteria are _____ species that produce _____ harmful to humans.

Short Answers

1. Draw and label a generalized diagram of a bacterium.

2. What does the slime capsule indicate about the virulence of a bacterium?

3. Describe the process of binary fission in bacteria.

4. a) How rapidly can binary fission take place in bacteria?
   b) Why doesn't binary fission take place rapidly all the time?

5. What is the function of the pili in a bacterial cell?

6. What conditions must be met for bacterial transduction to take place?

7. a) Describe the range of environmental conditions that endospores can withstand.
   b) What structural features make their survival possible?

8. How do bacteria make people sick?

9. How does the human body prevent bacteria from entering its internal environment?

10. How does the body attack bacteria that do enter the internal environment?

11. What is the second line of defence used by the body to combat bacteria?

12. Describe three important ecological roles played by bacteria in the biosphere.

13. List at least three examples of harmful bacteria and three examples of beneficial bacteria.

14. Define bacteriology and biotechnology and explain how the two are related.

Application Questions

1 Bacterial endospores contain very little cytoplasm. How does this help the endospores withstand harsh environmental conditions?

2. Make an organized list of all body defences that exist to fight bacteria.

3. Prepare a chart to compare bacteria with protozoans. Organize your information under the following headings:

Generalized Cell Structure, Components of Cytoplasm, Nutrition, Locomotion, Asexual Reproduction, Sexual Reproduction, Habitat, and Ecological Niche.

4. Compare the outcome of binary fission in bacteria and protists.

Problem Solving

1. a) How does the structure of a typical bacterium compare with that of a typical plant cell?
   b) Which parts do they have in common and which parts are different?

2. Why are saprophytic bacteria important in all ecosystems?

3. In a mutual relationship, both organisms must benefit in some way. Explain how this is true in the mutual relationship between a legume and a rhizobium.

4. Explain why bacterial cells such as *E. coli* are useful for biotechnological applications.

Extensions

1. With your teacher's permission, contact the supervisor of a bacterial laboratory in a hospital to plan a visit with one of your classmates. When you return, make an oral presentation about the kind of work performed in a bacterial laboratory.

2. a) Conduct library research to find out who administered the first rabies vaccination.
   b) How was this vaccination prepared and to whom was it given?
   c) What are the origins of the word vaccination?

3. In a group of four, make up two posters: one based on helpful bacteria and the other on harmful bacteria. Use pictures from magazines and short paragraphs to illustrate the posters.

4. Visit a sewage treatment plant and observe the testing procedures used to detect coliform bacteria.

5. Ask a student who lives on a farm to bring in a sample of silage to test the odour of the bacterial product. If the student is from your class, ask him or her to explain the workings of a silo.

CHAPTER

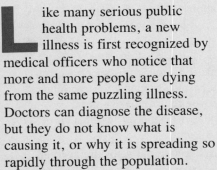

18
The
Viruses

Like many serious public health problems, a new illness is first recognized by medical officers who notice that more and more people are dying from the same puzzling illness. Doctors can diagnose the disease, but they do not know what is causing it, or why it is spreading so rapidly through the population.

Soon everyone knows that a pandemic (a country-wide or worldwide epidemic) is underway. The disease becomes prevalent everywhere, and public unrest and uncertainty grow because the causative agent is unknown. There is no effective treatment, and the outcome is likely to be agonizing death, lifelong scarring, or permanent disability.

Rumours and panic spread even faster than the disease. Infected individuals try to hide their symptoms as long as they can. And those who are still well shun the sick.

Overcrowded hospitals struggle to treat the disease, but millions die. Meanwhile, researchers scramble to find a cause, a cure, or some way to stop the disease from spreading. Eventually, an untested vaccine is ready for trial. At first, no one understands how the vaccine works, and there is some public resistance to it. Gradually, however, the vaccine's success rate changes public opinion. Soon no new cases occur in richer countries, where most of the population is vaccinated in childhood, but outbreaks continue in poorer parts of the world.

Eventually, after intensive research, a virus is identified as the cause of the disease. The World Health Organization (WHO) launches a publicly funded vaccination campaign and sends medical teams anywhere in the world where outbreaks occur until no more cases are reported.

This story describes our successful 200-year fight against smallpox, a viral disease that became a serious health problem in Europe around 1600. The first child was vaccinated with a serum prepared from cowpox sores in 1796, and smallpox was finally eradicated in 1977. The only smallpox viruses remaining in the world are securely stored in laboratories in Great Britain, the USSR, and the United States. The only cases reported since 1977 have been the result of laboratory accidents.

Occasionally, rumours circulate that suggest smallpox has returned. These are passed on to WHO in Switzerland. To date, each of these reports has been thoroughly investigated and found to be false. Almost all are a case of honest but incorrect diagnosis. In one atypical case, a persistent rumour was traced to the parents of a dead child who believed a reward was involved.

The story of polio has not yet passed through all these stages. For centuries, polio was a much feared but relatively uncommon childhood disease called ''infantile paralysis'' because of its crippling effects. Then, in the 1940s, large numbers of North Americans, most of them children, became infected in a polio epidemic. Some died, and many were paralyzed so severely that they required artificial respirators to keep them alive. Since nobody knew what caused polio, and rumours spread like wildfire, parents kept children away from movies, swimming pools, and each other.

Intensive research identified the polio virus and an effective vaccine was developed by 1954. As polio vaccinations became a routine part of childhood, the disease largely disappeared in North America. However, there are still infective pockets in poorer parts of the world, and a few cases here among those who refuse to be vaccinated. WHO is currently conducting a vaccination program aimed at eradicating polio completely.

The story of AIDS is near its beginning. We are confronted with a pandemic and are spending millions of dollars to find a prevention and a cure for this disease.

Chapter Objectives

When you complete this chapter, you should:

1. Recognize the harmful effects of viruses on most types of organisms, and appreciate the importance of their role in the biosphere, particularly the extent of their impact on humans.

2. Be able to describe how viruses infect host cells, understand how this process makes humans sick, and explain how the immune response promotes recovery.

3. Be able to describe the role of vaccines in minimizing the impact of viral diseases on the health of individuals and on the public.

4. Be able to compare structure and reproduction in DNA and RNA viruses, identify which viruses are also called retroviruses, and explain why the diseases they cause are so virulent.

5. Identify the virus that causes AIDS, classify it as a retrovirus, and identify the specific features of this retrovirus that make AIDS so difficult to treat and control.

6. List several human diseases caused by RNA viruses, several caused by DNA viruses, and compare one from each group with AIDS according to transmission, symptoms, and treatment.

7. Be able to compare past methods used to control or eradicate other serious viral diseases with current efforts now being made to bring AIDS under control.

8. Based on current research findings, be able to explain the probable link between viral agents and some forms of human cancer.

Ryan White, a young AIDS victim who acquired the disease through a blood transfusion, was banned from his school in Kokomo, Indiana. A telephone link to his classrooms was the only way he could keep in touch with his school.

18.1 AIDS

AIDS (*A*cquired *I*mmune *D*eficiency *S*yndrome) was first recognized in 1981 by a sudden increase in the incidence of previously rare forms of cancer. As its serious nature rapidly became obvious, AIDS research around the world proceeded so intensively that the causative virus had been isolated and identified by 1983. Research is now proceeding along two main fronts: the development of a vaccine to prevent infection of healthy people, and the development of effective medical treatment, both for those who are already ill, and for the millions likely to become infected before AIDS is eradicated.

Because AIDS *is* a frightening disease, the thought that the world is on the verge of another **pandemic,** or worldwide epidemic, makes it seem even more so. You have probably heard some of these "facts": only homosexuals get AIDS (not true); AIDS can be contracted by donating blood (not true); the AIDS virus kills everyone it infects (not proven). The list goes on and on, and the misinformation does a great deal of harm because it encourages people to make unwise decisions.

Learning about AIDS

Accurate, up-to-date information is vital since AIDS will probably be a major health problem around the world for most of your adult life. For most young people, however, becoming informed is difficult because there is too much raw data to interpret. AIDS seems to be in the news every day. How can you decide what is important about the disease and be able to tell fact from fiction? To evaluate new information properly, you need a basic understanding of what is currently known by biologists about viruses and their role in causing diseases such as AIDS. To help you acquire this basic understanding, this chapter has been set up as a series of questions about viruses, focussing on the AIDS virus in particular. These questions, and the discussions they stimulate, will provide the data you will need to conduct the AIDS research project at the end of the chapter.

WHAT IS AIDS?

Early signs of AIDS include any or all of the following symptoms.

- Fatigue and loss of appetite
- Diarrhea
- Unexplained rapid loss of body mass (10% or more)
- Thick white coating on the mouth and tongue
- Open sores in the mouth or on the genitals
- Fever and/or night sweats
- Dry cough and shortness of breath
- Swollen lymph nodes in neck, groin, or armpits

- Purplish red lumps that seem to increase in size
- Loss of memory or co-ordination

You should remember that some of these symptoms are similar to flu symptoms. In AIDS, however, the symptoms persist longer than a month and are eventually followed by more serious disorders, which eventually lead to death. The progress of the disease is variable. Some patients remain relatively well for years while others decline rapidly. The reasons for this variability are not yet clear, but researchers are investigating two factors that may be responsible: either some inherited characteristic activates the virus more quickly, or another existing infection is present.

Unlike smallpox or polio, AIDS is a completely new disease. From 1978 onward, African doctors began to see increasing numbers of patients who wasted away from a disease they called "slim." Some died from bacterial infections, but the deaths of others were more puzzling. Doctors were unable to treat the disease or to identify its cause.

In North America, the presence of a new disease was first recognized in 1981 when small but significant numbers of previously healthy homosexual men began to die of unusual lung infections and rare cancers. As ever-increasing numbers of these cases were reported, health officials at the Center for Disease Control in Atlanta, Georgia, recognized the characteristics of a completely new disease. (See Figure 18-1.) Because this new disease attacked the

FIGURE 18-1 These figures show the global statistics on AIDS as of June 5, 1989. Some countries, however, do not report all AIDS cases. How could you find out how much these numbers have changed? (*Source*: WHO)

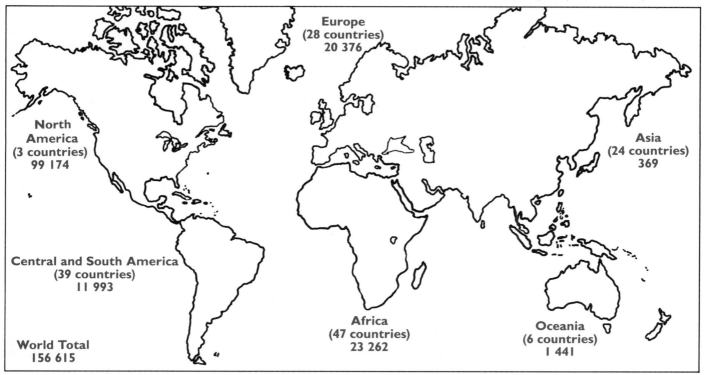

Europe
(28 countries)
20 376

North America
(3 countries)
99 174

Asia
(24 countries)
369

Central and South America
(39 countries)
11 993

Africa
(47 countries)
23 262

Oceania
(6 countries)
1 441

World Total
156 615

FIGURE 18-2 These figures show the distribution of AIDS cases in Canada as of June 5, 1989. How do they compare with current data on AIDS? (*Source*: Ontario Ministry of Health)

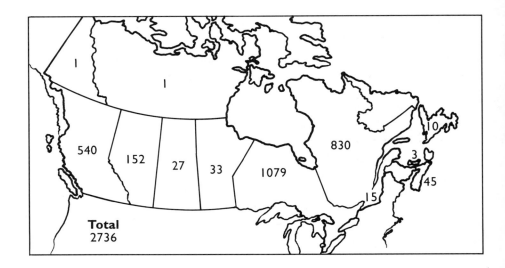

immune system and made the body vulnerable to potentially fatal infections, it was called AIDS.

At first, doctors thought that AIDS affected only homosexuals. By 1983, however, other groups of infected individuals began to emerge: drug addicts who shared or re-used needles, and hemophiliacs who required frequent blood transfusions to survive. A similar disease was also being noticed among homosexual men in Europe. Medical researchers there began to test the blood of African patients. They discovered that AIDS and "slim" were identical except for one feature: over 75% of African patients were heterosexuals. This finding dispelled the idea that AIDS was restricted to homosexuals.

Since then AIDS has become a pandemic, spreading to every country in the world, including Canada. (See Figure 18-2.) Researchers estimate that the number of North Americans already infected but not yet showing symptoms may be fifty times as great. The numbers are far greater in the "AIDS belt" of central Africa, where between five and ten million people may be infected. (See Figure 18-3.)

Scientists may never know how AIDS began. One hypothesis suggests that the disease may have originated in the African green monkey. About 60% of these animals are infected with a virus remarkably similar to the one that causes AIDS in humans. This virus does not make the monkeys ill, and it does not give humans AIDS, but it might have been transformed into the AIDS virus if the following had occurred.

- Its DNA underwent a spontaneous rearrangement. This type of change is called a **mutation** and frequently occurs in flu viruses, for example.
- The mutation altered the virus so it could live and multiply in human cells.
- The mutant viruses were then transmitted to humans, perhaps through a bite or the consumption of monkey flesh.

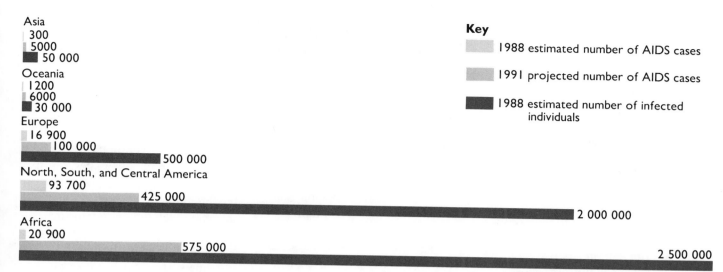

Asia
| 300
| 5000
■ 50 000

Oceania
| 1200
| 6000
■ 30 000

Europe
| 16 900
| 100 000
| 500 000

North, South, and Central America
| 93 700
| 425 000
| 2 000 000

Africa
| 20 900
| 575 000
| 2 500 000

Key
1988 estimated number of AIDS cases

1991 projected number of AIDS cases

1988 estimated number of infected individuals

FIGURE 18-3 This graph compares the projected worldwide 1991 figures on the spread of AIDS to the number of cases reported at the end of 1988. However, the projected figures do not include the estimated number of individuals who may be infected with the AIDS virus but, as yet, show no symptoms. (*Source*: WHO)

Discussion Questions

1. a) What does AIDS stand for?
   b) In what way(s) does AIDS resemble other illnesses?
   c) In what way(s) does it differ?

2. a) When did doctors first recognize the existence of AIDS?
   b) How did doctors know that AIDS was a completely new disease?
   c) Explain why the spread of AIDS is being called a pandemic.

3. a) Where did AIDS probably originate?
   b) State one hypothesis that may explain how the AIDS virus originated.

4. a) What is the link between AIDS and cancer?
   b) What is the link between AIDS and blood transfusions?

5. a) Why is there such widespread fear of AIDS?
   b) Who is at risk from AIDS?
   c) Record and save your answers to parts (a) and (b). Reconsider them after you complete this chapter. Do you still agree with your original responses?

Even before the cause of AIDS could be identified, researchers suspected a virus was responsible for causing the disease. The spread of AIDS among people receiving transfused blood or blood products confirmed early on that whatever caused AIDS was carried in the blood. The spread of AIDS through sexual contact made it clear that the causative agent could also be found in other body fluids such as semen or vaginal secretions. But no sign of previously unknown protists or bacteria could be found in the body fluids of AIDS

HOW DO WE KNOW THAT AIDS IS CAUSED BY A VIRUS?

Fighting the Common Cold

At this moment, chances are at least one of your classmates is fighting a cold. The inability of science to cure the common cold is legendary.

A number of factors make the common cold difficult to defeat. Viral infections, unlike bacterial infections, are not usually treated with drugs because anti-viral drugs are too harmful to the body except for use in emergencies. Instead, prevention is stressed. However, vaccination, the most effective way of preventing viral infections, is useless against colds because they can be caused by over 200 different viruses. An effective vaccine would have to stimulate immunity to all 200 viruses simultaneously. Since this is not possible, we must rely on our own immune-system responses to repel colds.

Although colds are self-limiting, and symptoms usually subside within two weeks of the original infection, this in itself shows a surprising persistence. An American molecular biologist, Dr. Michael Rossmann, has explained this persistence by constructing a three-dimensional model of a rhinovirus, one member of a family of 100 cold-causing viruses.

A virus's survival depends on its ability to do two things. First, it must evade attack from its host's immune system. The immune system usually works by recognizing viral surface features and producing antibodies to attack these structures. Second, the virus must multiply. To multiply, the virus must have recognizable surface features that act as binding sites to interact with the target cell's surface features. If the virus needs recognizable binding sites, what prevents the immune system from recognizing these sites and attacking them?

The persistence of rhinovirus infections, Rossmann found, could be traced to surface changes the virus makes with each generation. Using computers, a high-powered X-ray device, and the virus's ability to crystallize, Rossmann found the rhinovirus looks like a mountain-covered planet. While the "valleys" remain consistent, the shape of the "mountains" changes in each generation.

Rossmann believes this is a way of evading immune system recognition. Mountain formations in the parent virus are absent in the next generation, so antibodies produced for the first generation will have no effect on the second. The unchanging valley sites are of no use to the antibodies because they are huge Y-shaped molecules that can reach the mountain sites, but are simply too large to fit into the valleys. Eventually, the immune system catches up and overwhelms the virus, but only after several generations.

Rossmann's work is important because it suggests that immune-system responses cannot be used to defeat colds caused by rhinovirus infections. Instead, preventive treatment must be developed to interfere with the attachment of viruses to target cells, or to interfere with virus function within the target cells.

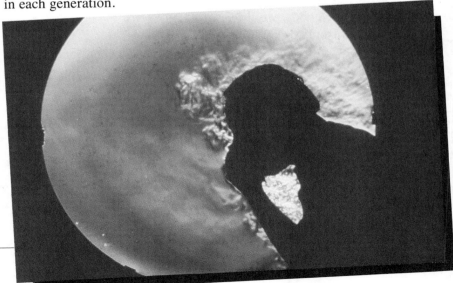

patients. These findings suggested that AIDS must be caused by an agent too small to be seen with a microscope. So, researchers were looking for a virus from the outset.

In 1983, French researchers at the Pasteur Institute in Paris isolated a previously unknown virus from the swollen lymph nodes of known AIDS patients. They called it LAV for Lymphadenopathy-Associated Virus. Months later, an American team at the National Cancer Institute in Bethesda, Maryland, isolated the same virus, which they called HTLV-III. The World Health Organization, recognizing the importance of clear communication, decided to call the virus **HIV** for **Human Immunodeficiency Virus.**

The photograph on this page shows what AIDS researchers saw in their electron microscopes: a protein-coated particle only 100 nm in diameter poised on the surface of a cell many times larger. The size and shape of the particle together with a dark shadow revealing its internal package of nucleic acids confirmed its classification. For most scientists, these findings confirmed the assumption that AIDS is caused by a virus.

The discovery of HIV quickly helped to solve a serious problem — blood intended for transfusion could be tested for the AIDS virus. All blood stored in Canadian blood banks had been screened and declared free from the virus by November 1985.

Scientists focussed on developing a vaccine against HIV and on devising treatments for those already infected. In order to advance in these areas, scientists reviewed what they already knew about viruses to see what prior knowledge could be applied to HIV.

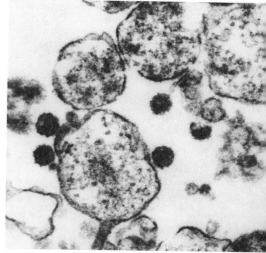

The AIDS virus

Discussion Questions

1. a) When did researchers first suspect that AIDS was caused by a virus? Why?
   b) What is the link between AIDS and body fluids?
2. a) Can you get AIDS by donating blood? Explain.
   b) Can you get AIDS from a blood transfusion? Explain.
3. a) State the full name of the virus that causes AIDS and its abbreviation.
   b) Usually, a new virus is named by the researcher who discovers it. Who named the virus that causes AIDS? Why?

Practical and ethical considerations limit the ways scientists can study the viruses that cause human diseases. Until recently, much of what was known and taught about viruses was based on what researchers had discovered about bacteriophages. From these studies, biologists know that the amount of hereditary information stored in a virus is incredibly small. A typical human cell

WHAT DO WE ALREADY KNOW ABOUT OTHER VIRUSES?

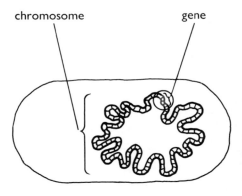

chromosome   gene

bacterium

Infection of *E. coli* bacterium by a phage virus. Some of the viral DNA has already invaded the bacterium, while some viral DNA remains attached to the bacterium's cell wall.

has around 40 000 **genes** in its 46 chromosomes. Each gene is a short segment of DNA that contains instructions for one specific function such as the manufacture of a particular enzyme, hormone, or other protein molecule. (See Figure 18-4.) Relative to the smaller size of a bacterium, the single chromosome of *Escherichia coli* contains only 2000 genes. The DNA of a typical phage virus, however, contains only 75 genes.

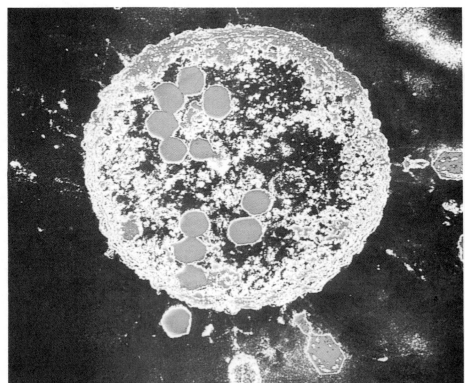

The term bacteriophage means "bacteria eater," although the electron microscope shows that phage viruses do not kill bacteria by eating them. When a bacteriophage attacks a bacterial cell, its protein coat stays outside the cell. Only the DNA of the phage enters the cell's cytoplasm. Even though the number of genes of a phage virus is small, the DNA they contain is enough to prevent the host bacterial cell from performing its normal life functions.

Viral genes redirect the host cell from producing the materials it needs to performing only three functions: manufacturing hundreds of copies of viral DNA, producing proteins for new viral protein coats, and producing a powerful enzyme that dissolves the bacterium's cell wall. When the DNA and the protein coats have been assembled, the newly formed phage viruses burst, infecting nearby cells and repeating the cycle. (See Figure 18-5.)

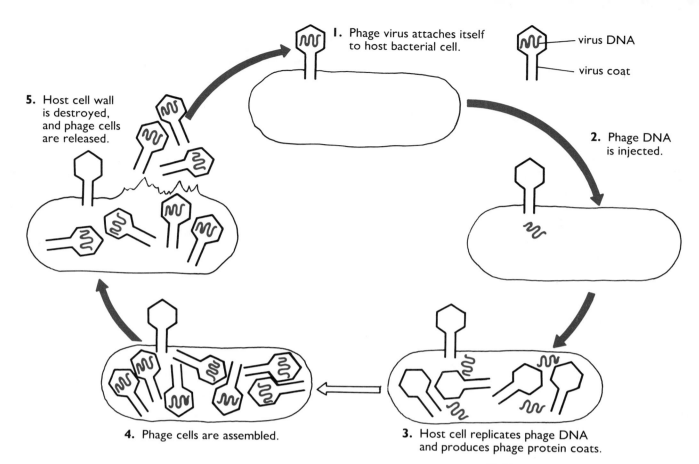

1. Phage virus attaches itself to host bacterial cell.

virus DNA

virus coat

5. Host cell wall is destroyed, and phage cells are released.

2. Phage DNA is injected.

4. Phage cells are assembled.

3. Host cell replicates phage DNA and produces phage protein coats.

FIGURE 18-5 The life cycle of a bacteriophage may be completed in only 30 min.

FIGURE 18-6 A cross section of a typical DNA virus

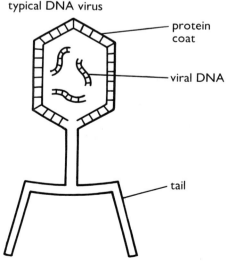

protein coat

viral DNA

tail

All **viruses** have the same basic structure and composition as bacteriophages. They have a protein coat surrounding a core of nucleic acid that stores the hereditary information needed for the virus to reproduce inside a living cell. In bacteriophages and most other viruses, the nucleic acid is DNA, the molecule found in human and bacterial chromosomes. (See Figure 18-6.)

Some viruses contain RNA instead of DNA. **RNA** stands for **ribonucleic acid**, a chemical very similar to DNA. The only other structural difference between an RNA virus and a DNA virus is that the RNA virus contains a few molecules of a specialized enzyme. (See Figure 18-7.) Although the differences between the two viruses are small, they must be significant. As Table 18-1 shows, human diseases caused by RNA viruses are generally much more serious than those caused by DNA viruses. Understanding why depends on understanding the role of RNA in normal, uninfected cells.

All living cells produce their own **messenger RNA (mRNA)** to carry instructions from the chromosomes to the ribosomes. Figure 18-8 shows the usual cell DNA ⟶ cell mRNA ⟶ cell ribosome ⟶ cell protein sequence

FIGURE 18-7 A cross section of a typical RNA virus

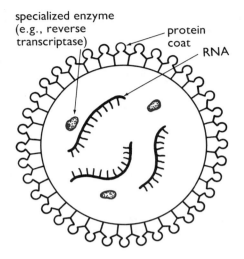

specialized enzyme (e.g., reverse transcriptase)

protein coat

RNA

TABLE 18-1   Diseases Caused by DNA Viruses and RNA Viruses

DNA Virus	Disease	RNA Virus	Disease
Epstein-Barr Virus	• mononucleosis	HIV	• AIDS
Herpes Simplex	• cold sores	Rubella Virus	• rubella (German measles)
Herpes Varicella-zoster	• chicken pox	Rubeola Virus	• measles (red measles)
Herpes Varicella-zoster	• shingles	Poliovirus	• polio
Papillomavirus	• warts	Rhinovirus	• common cold
Adenovirus	• respiratory infection	Rabies Virus	• rabies

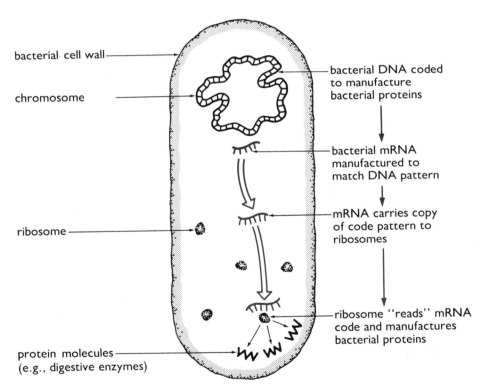

bacterial cell wall

chromosome

ribosome

bacterial DNA coded to manufacture bacterial proteins

bacterial mRNA manufactured to match DNA pattern

mRNA carries copy of code pattern to ribosomes

ribosome "reads" mRNA code and manufactures bacterial proteins

protein molecules (e.g., digestive enzymes)

FIGURE 18-8 Messenger RNA (mRNA) carries this bacterium's genetic code from its chromosome to its ribosomes.

in a bacterial cell. Viral DNA interrupts this sequence by deactivating the host cell's mRNA and forcing the host ribosomes to produce viral proteins instead of those needed by the cell itself. (See Figure 18-9.) Viral RNA, however, cannot interrupt the sequence so directly.

FIGURE 18-9 How a DNA virus interrupts the production of host protein in a host cell

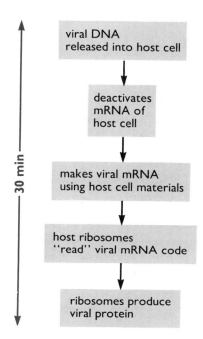

viral DNA released into host cell

↓

deactivates mRNA of host cell

↓

makes viral mRNA using host cell materials

↓

host ribosomes "read" viral mRNA code

↓

ribosomes produce viral protein

30 min

FIGURE 18-10 How an RNA retrovirus interrupts the production of host protein in a host cell

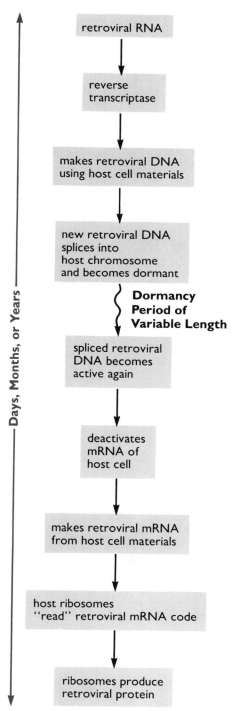

retroviral RNA

↓

reverse transcriptase

↓

makes retroviral DNA using host cell materials

↓

new retroviral DNA splices into host chromosome and becomes dormant

Dormancy Period of Variable Length

↓

spliced retroviral DNA becomes active again

↓

deactivates mRNA of host cell

↓

makes retroviral mRNA from host cell materials

↓

host ribosomes "read" retroviral mRNA code

↓

ribosomes produce retroviral protein

Days, Months, or Years

Before an RNA virus can take over a host cell's machinery, its viral RNA must be converted into a form that the cell's ribosomes can recognize. This process is carried out by the specialized enzyme that all RNA viruses contain. The enzyme found in RNA viruses like HIV is called **reverse transcriptase** because it reverses the usual DNA-to-RNA sequence. RNA viruses with this unusual ability are often called **retroviruses.**

In fact, it is this ability that makes RNA retroviruses especially lethal since the retroviral DNA produced by the enzyme often splices itself into the host's DNA. (See Figure 18-10.) In other words, the host's chromosomes now contain DNA copies of the retroviral genes. Once this happens, the retroviral DNA may remain dormant, or latent, for months or even years before becoming active. This effect is possible because the spliced genes can hide in the host cell without stimulating the host organism's immune system. Since the hidden genes have no protein coat, the immune system cannot recognize that they are foreign and does not produce antibodies against them. During the **latency period**, an infected individual looks and feels healthy. However, nothing can remove the spliced genes. Every time the host cell divides by mitosis for tissue growth or repair, the retroviral DNA divides, too.

This process increases the number of infected cells, allowing the retroviral genes to reproduce even though they stay hidden. When the dormant genes become active again, the infected cells will produce and release retroviruses with protein coats. Now the immune system can begin to produce antibodies. By that time, however, the number of infected cells and the number of retroviruses they release may be very large. The sudden surge of viruses may tax the immune system to its limit. As a result, the host organism may become very sick or even die before enough antibodies can be made to counteract the retroviruses.

Few DNA viruses can remain hidden in the same way as RNA retroviruses. Most DNA viruses stimulate the immune system to produce antibodies soon after invasion while the number of viruses is still small enough to be destroyed easily. Therefore, the diseases caused by DNA viruses are usually much less serious than those caused by RNA retroviruses.

Discussion Questions

1. a) Which viruses did biologists study most intensively in the past?
   b) Why were human viruses not studied more often?
   c) Why are human viruses being studied so intensively now?

2. a) What is a gene? List the number of genes in a typical human cell, a bacterial cell, and a bacteriophage virus.
   b) What do these numbers suggest about the relative complexity of viruses?

3. a) What is a retrovirus? How does it differ structurally from other viruses?
   b) What makes the diseases caused by retroviruses especially serious? State three examples.

4. Prepare a simple chart to describe and compare the following.
   a) how a phage virus attacks a bacterial cell
   b) how a DNA virus attacks a human cell
   c) how an RNA retrovirus attacks a human cell

5. a) What is reverse transcriptase, and where is it found?
   b) What is a latency period?
   c) How are reverse transcriptase and latency linked?

WHAT DO WE ALREADY KNOW ABOUT OTHER VIRAL DISEASES?

To understand AIDS more quickly, researchers compared it with what they already knew about other viral diseases. All viruses act by forcing the host cell's machinery to manufacture hundreds or thousands of copies of the infecting virus. While this is going on, the host cell can no longer manufacture the materials it needs to carry out its normal functions. When the new viral particles are released, the host cell is destroyed. If the host cell is one of many in a multicellular organism, the host organism may become sick as a result.

In humans, the respiratory tissues of the lungs and the throat are the first hosts for many viruses. For example, a flu virus may attack the ciliated cells lining the upper respiratory passages. (See Figure 18-11.) If these cells are destroyed, the lining can no longer sweep mucus and foreign particles out of

FIGURE 18-11   How a flu virus affects the body

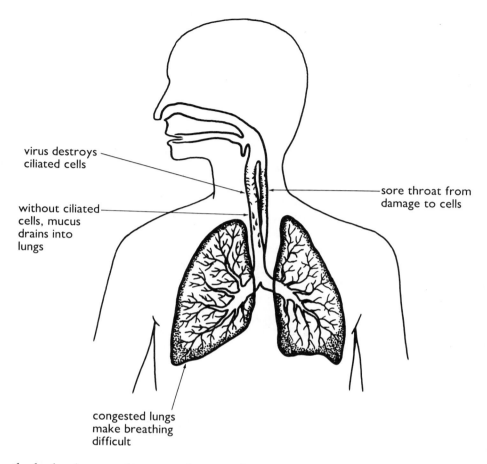

virus destroys ciliated cells

without ciliated cells, mucus drains into lungs

sore throat from damage to cells

congested lungs make breathing difficult

Small lesions on the trunk and face of this child are symptoms of the common childhood disease, chicken pox.

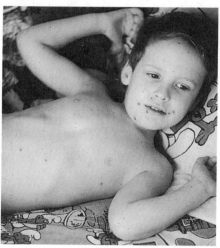

the body. As a result, a sore throat and congested lungs are the first signs of many viral infections. Meanwhile, the same virus may spread through the body to other host cells in the muscles, nerves, or blood.

Herpes varicella-zoster is a DNA virus that enters the body by way of the respiratory passages. It causes both chicken pox and shingles. Chicken pox is more common and is usually seen only in children. Early symptoms of headache, nausea, and fever begin about 36 h before the pox erupt. These itchy, blister-like lesions on the torso, neck, and upper limbs develop a crusty covering, and may leave scars if knocked off prematurely. Successive crops of pox form over two to five days. Healing time varies from one to three weeks depending on the severity of the attack.

Although it causes skin eruptions, the virus spreads mainly by airborne particles that escape from the nose and throat of an infected person. Chicken pox can also be transmitted through contact with pus from the lesions, but this is less common. The first symptoms of chicken pox do not appear until 14-21 days after infection. This elapsed time is called an **incubation period** because the virus is actively multiplying and spreading to new host cells

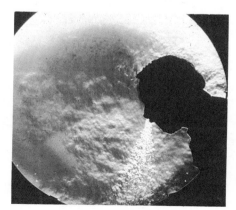

An unmuffled sneeze can spread viral particles great distances from the infected person.

throughout the body. However, it takes many days before there are enough viruses to cause noticeable symptoms.

Shingles is normally seen only in adults. The disease is characterized by a thick crop of small but intensely painful blister-like skin lesions usually occurring on the trunk.

Chicken pox and shingles are usually considered to be mild diseases, although complications can arise if the virus invades the central nervous system. No vaccine is available, but after a person recovers, they usually have a lifetime immunity against the virus. However, re-infection can occur in cancer patients presumably because their immune systems are already over-stressed.

Rabies is caused by an RNA virus that affects humans and a wide range of other animals, both wild and domesticated. The virus spreads by means of three body fluids: saliva, milk, and urine. Humans usually become infected through a bite from a rabid animal. At first, the rabies virus infects only skin cells around the site of entry, but its preferred target host is nervous tissue.

In humans, the first symptoms of rabies are headache and fever, followed by uncontrollable excitement, excessive salivation, and painful spasms of the throat muscles. The victim is thirsty, but cannot swallow water, a characteristic that gives the disease its common name of hydrophobia. Recovery is very rare, and death from asphyxiation or paralysis can occur within a week. The development of these symptoms usually can be prevented by the injection of a vaccine soon after exposure to the virus.

Rabies has been brought under control in the island nations of Britain, Australia, and New Zealand through the use of strict quarantine regulations and mandatory vaccination programs. In North America, the control of rabies is difficult because there is such a large population of wild animals to serve as hosts for the virus. However, domesticated animals can be protected by annual vaccinations.

Veterinarians and animal health technicians are also vaccinated on an annual basis because they frequently handle animals with unknown health histories. No one else requires routine protection, but anyone bitten by an animal that may be rabid should seek immediate medical attention.

The time span between the viral infection and the first noticeable symptoms is much longer for rabies than it is for chicken pox. In rabies, this time span is known as a latency period instead of an incubation period. This is because rabies is caused by an RNA virus, which passes through a latent, or dormant, period. During the first stages of infection, the virus multiplies actively and quickly spreads to the host organism's nerve cells. In the nerve cells, the viral RNA remains dormant for 30-50 days on average, although latency periods of up to a year have been observed in humans. The latency period for rabies is shorter in people who have been bitten several times, and presumably have been infected with a greater number of viral particles. A variable latency period is typical of diseases caused by RNA viruses. This is especially true for retroviral diseases such as AIDS.

Annual booster shots are vital for protecting pets against rabies and other viral diseases such as distemper.

Discussion Questions

1. a) Which tissues are often the first site of attack by human flu viruses?
   b) What does your answer to part (a) suggest about how the flu virus spreads from one person to another?

2. a) What are the usual early symptoms of the flu? What causes these symptoms?
   b) How does the flu virus spread to other body tissues?

3. a) What two human diseases are caused by Herpes varicella-zoster? Compare their symptoms.
   b) Which tissues are the main target of the virus in both cases?
   c) How does Herpes varicella-zoster spread from one person to another? Explain why this is surprising given your answer to part (b).

4. a) Although people can contract rabies, it is not primarily a human disease. How does rabies spread to humans from infected individuals?
   b) Which tissues are the main target of the rabies virus in humans?
   c) How does the rabies virus spread from the entry site to the target tissues?

5. a) Two different terms are used to describe the period between a viral infection and the first noticeable symptoms. Identify both periods.
   b) Which period identified in part (a) is typical of a DNA virus? An RNA virus?
   c) What is the virus doing in each period identified in part (a)? How would this difference affect the ability of health officials to control outbreaks?

HOW DOES THE BODY DEFEND ITSELF AGAINST OTHER VIRAL DISEASES?

Usually, the skin and the mucous membranes form an effective barrier to microscopic invaders. However, viruses can enter the body's internal environment if their protein coats happen to match one of the many **receptors,** or surface protein molecules, on the host cells. (See Figure 18-12.) When this happens, it becomes the job of the immune system to prevent these viruses from using host cells to reproduce.

To do so, the immune system must be able to tell the difference between host cells and foreign invaders. Your immune system is able to make this distinction because all of your body cells share the same distinctive pattern of surface proteins. No other organism has exactly the same protein arrangement unless you have an identical twin. To your immune system, surface proteins act like a chemical flag that recognizes which cells are yours and identifies which cells or other particles are invaders.

Figure 18-13 illustrates the human immune system. Two parts are of special importance in understanding the link between AIDS and immunity: the bone marrow and the thymus. Both are involved in producing specialized immune cells that detect or destroy foreign proteins.

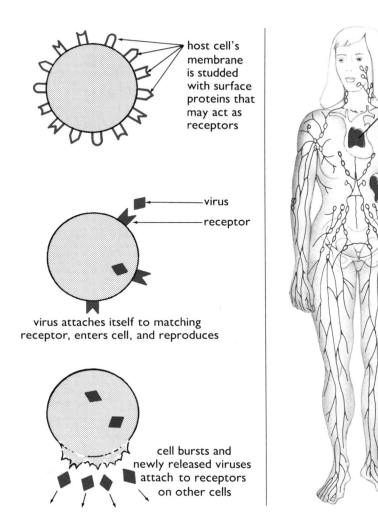

host cell's membrane is studded with surface proteins that may act as receptors

virus

receptor

virus attaches itself to matching receptor, enters cell, and reproduces

cell bursts and newly released viruses attach to receptors on other cells

FIGURE 18-12 Viruses enter the internal environment and spread by attaching themselves to cell receptors.

Thymus
T-helpers
T-killers
T-suppressors

lymph nodes

spleen

Bone Marrow
monocytes
T cells
B cells

FIGURE 18-13 The human immune system

Bone marrow produces three main types of immune cells: **monocytes, T cells,** and **B cells.** All of these cells are highly mobile, able to move around the body by way of the circulatory system, or squeeze out through the capillary walls to fight infections in body tissue. Immune cells that leave the blood vessels eventually enter the lymph vessels. Some return to the blood while others stay in the lymph nodes of the neck, armpits, and groin. The nodes are small clumps of lymphatic tissue that filter foreign material from the lymph fluid and often swell when they are fighting an infection.

When first released from the bone marrow, monocytes, T cells, and B cells are immature. All must undergo changes before they can function to defend the body. Once released by the bone marrow, monocytes circulate in

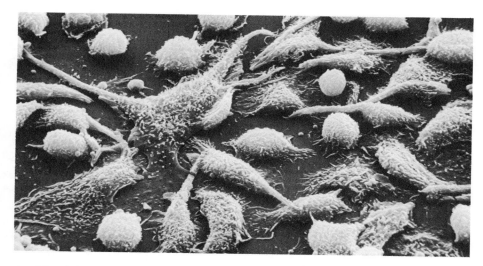

Human macrophages engulfing foreign invaders that have entered the body

the blood for several days before they are transformed into active macrophages. Macrophages are especially active near the skin, spleen, and lymph nodes. These large, amoeba-like cells are the first to meet foreign invaders, which they engulf and consume. Macrophages also stimulate the first in a series of important events involving the T cells.

T cells remain nonfunctional until they migrate to the thymus gland for maturation. There the cells are altered so that each can recognize only one type of invader. T cells mature into three different forms: **T-helpers, T-killers,** and **T-suppressors.** T-helpers are often described as the cornerstone of the immune system because they interact with all other immune cells, beginning with the macrophages. (See Figure 18-14.)

Hormonal signals from the macrophages stimulate the T-helpers to multiply and send their own hormonal message to the T-killers. (See Figure 18-15.) The T-killer cells then multiply and destroy infected host cells, a step that prevents the invading virus from reproducing.

FIGURE 18-14 T-helpers are stimulated by hormones from the macrophages.

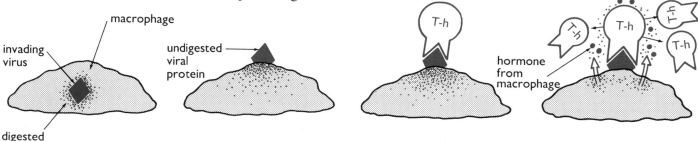

macrophage surrounds and digests viruses found in bloodstream

small amount of undigested viral protein is ejected onto surface of macrophage

mature T-helper cell recognizes viral protein and binds to surface of macrophage, stimulating hormone production

macrophage releases a hormone that signals T-helper cell to multiply

FIGURE 18-15 Hormones from
T-helpers stimulate reproduction by
T-killers, which, in turn, destroy
infected cells.

T-helper cells also send different hormonal messages to the B cells. B cells are specialized for the production of antibodies, which are protein molecules that deactivate the invaders by binding to their surface proteins. B cells mature into two specialized forms: **plasma-B cells** and **memory-B cells.**

Plasma-B cells manufacture new types of antibodies to fight new types of invaders. (See Figure 18-16.) Each invader has its own distinctive pattern of surface proteins, and therefore requires a different antibody. The first time your immune system encounters a new virus or bacteria, the plasma-B cells may need up to 25 days to manufacture the specific type of antibody needed to render the invader harmless. Once that happens, however, identical antibodies can be produced within hours if the same invader enters again. This is possible because memory-B cells store the protein patterns created by the plasma-B cells.

Once the infection is over, the T-suppressor cells act to return the immune system to a stable state. They send out chemical signals to slow down and stop the production of T-helper, T-killer, and plasma-B cells. (See Figure 18-17.) Only the memory-B cells remain to provide lasting immunity against reinfection by the same viral or bacterial invader.

For some viral diseases, the lasting protection of a successful immune response can be acquired artificially by the injection of a vaccine. The first vaccination was given in 1796 by Edward Jenner, an English physician. Jenner

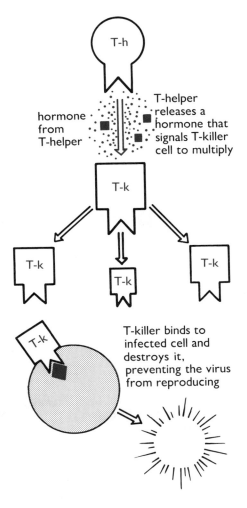

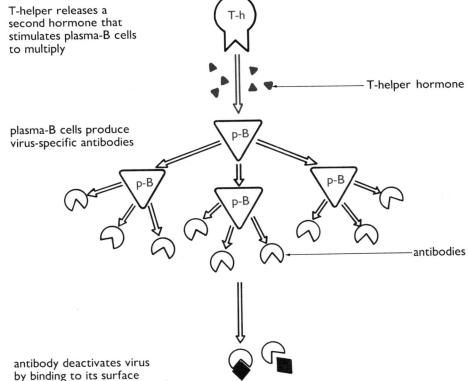

FIGURE 18-16 Other T-helper hormones stimulate plasma-B cells to reproduce and manufacture antibodies.

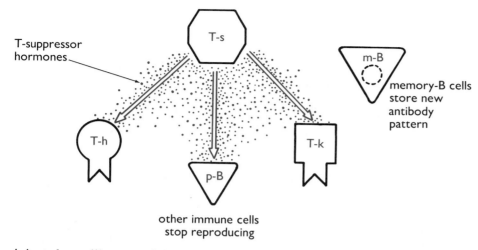

FIGURE 18-17 Once the virus has been destroyed, T-suppressor cells signal other T cells and plasma-B cells to stop reproducing.

memory-B cells store new antibody pattern

other immune cells stop reproducing

injected pus-like material from the sores of a girl who had cowpox into a healthy human subject. The subject did not develop cowpox symptoms. Later, this subject was injected with material from smallpox sores but remained healthy. Similar experiments yielded similar results. Apparently, the subjects had acquired protection against a viral disease without ever becoming ill.

Today, scientists realize that the injected pus probably contained dead or weakened viral particles that triggered an immune response. The healthy subject's plasma-B cells manufactured antibodies, and the memory-B cells stored the instructions for manufacturing the same antibodies if the same virus struck again. Jenner's experiment was successful even though the cowpox and smallpox viruses are not identical. In this case, the surface proteins are so much alike that antibodies to cowpox can also bind to smallpox viruses. Most vaccines must be prepared from the target viruses themselves to be successful. Figure 18-18 summarizes modern methods of manufacturing antiviral vaccines. All such vaccines provide long-term immunity by stimulating an immune response. (See Figure 18-19.)

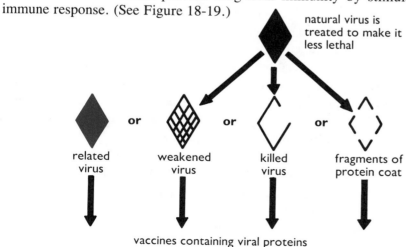

natural virus is treated to make it less lethal

related virus   or   weakened virus   or   killed virus   or   fragments of protein coat

vaccines containing viral proteins

FIGURE 18-18 Modern vaccines contain proteins or fragments from dead, weakened, or related viruses.

FIGURE 18-19 How long-term artificial immunity is acquired

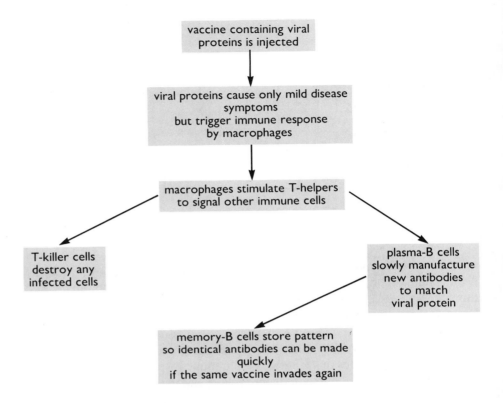

Discussion Questions

1. a) How does your immune system recognize a viral invader in your body?
   b) Which immune cell is first to attack the invader? How does it alert other parts of your immune system to the invasion?

2. a) Outline the three types of immune cells manufactured in the bone marrow and discuss their functions.
   b) Which cell can be called the cornerstone of the immune system?

3. a) What product of the immune system finally ends a viral infection?
   b) How do T-suppressor cells and memory-B cells provide lasting immunity against re-infection?

4. a) What are surface proteins? What are receptors?
   b) How does a virus use surface proteins to infect your cells?
   c) How does your body use viral surface proteins to combat viruses?

5. a) What is the name given to a preparation containing weakened or dead viruses?
   b) What is the purpose of this preparation, and how does it perform this function?

Figure 18-20 shows the structure of the HIV retrovirus as it is currently understood. Like other retroviruses, its RNA and the enzyme that converts the RNA to DNA are surrounded by a protein-studded capsule. Compared to a bacterium or a multicellular animal, the HIV retrovirus seems quite simple. For a retrovirus, however, HIV is amazingly complex, primarily because it contains so much hereditary information. Most animal retroviruses have only three genes. This means that their RNA contains codes for only three functions: producing more viral RNA, producing more protein coats, and producing more viral enzymes.

HOW DOES HIV COMPARE TO OTHER VIRUSES?

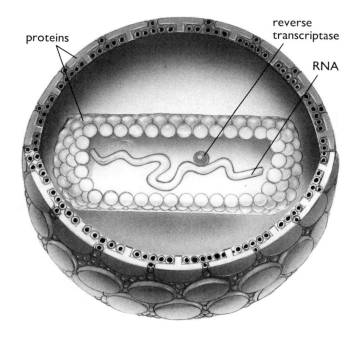

FIGURE 18-20   The structure of the HIV retrovirus

By contrast, HIV has at least eight genes, and some experts think there may be even more. Despite intensive research, the function of the extra genes is not yet completely understood, but one is known to accelerate reproduction. Without an accelerator gene, the retrovirus cannot be reproduced at all. Therefore, some researchers are trying to design a drug to deactivate this gene. Others are focussing on the fact that RNA retroviruses must carry out an extra enzyme step to reproduce. A drug to deactivate reverse transcriptase could interrupt the reproduction cycle of a retrovirus by preventing the formation of viral DNA.

Complexity is only one important difference between HIV and other viruses. Another is that HIV attacks the immune cells, thereby preventing the production of antibodies against HIV or anything else. Once this happens, many other microscopic invaders can enter the body and multiply unchecked.

As a result, AIDS patients die from a wide range of infections, most of which are not fatal in people who do not have AIDS. For example, one common AIDS-related infection is a pneumonia caused by a parasitic protozoan. The parasite is widely found in nature, but it is harmless to healthy individuals. Only when the immune system is depressed can the parasite cause a fatal lung infection.

Discussion Questions

1. a) How many genes are found in a typical bacteriophage? How many are in a typical retrovirus?
   b) How does this difference limit the usefulness of bacteriophages as a model for understanding retroviral diseases?

2. a) How many function codes do the genes in a typical retrovirus contain? Describe these codes.
   b) How many additional function codes do HIV genes contain? Describe one of these extra functions.

3. What features of HIV are some researchers hoping will help them develop a drug against AIDS?

4. Why do AIDS patients die from infections that are usually not fatal to others?

HOW DOES THE BODY'S RESPONSE TO HIV DIFFER FROM ITS RESPONSE TO OTHER VIRUSES?

Usually, the body can defend itself against a viral invasion by the immune response. The body's response to HIV is entirely different because HIV attacks the immune cells themselves, especially the pivotal T-helper cells. Whether a virus can invade a particular cell depends on how the outer coat of the virus compares to the surface proteins of the cell. T-helper cells happen to have receptor sites that are a perfect match for HIV's protein coat.

These receptor sites normally function as mouth-like inlets that bring hormones into the cell. If HIV becomes attached to its "mouth," the inlet swallows the entire retrovirus instead. Inside the cell, the protein coat is cast off, and the retroviral RNA enters the cell's cytoplasm. There the RNA is transcribed into DNA by the enzyme action of reverse transcriptase. (See Figure 18-21.)

The newly formed DNA genes then enter the cell nucleus, where they splice themselves into the host's DNA and remain dormant for a latency period that may last weeks, months, or years. Once the retroviral DNA is reactivated, however, reproduction of new viruses is a thousand times faster than that of any other known virus.

As the new viruses leave a T-helper cell, their protein coats pick up pieces of T-helper surface proteins. This step makes HIV unrecognizable to the immune system and enables the retroviruses to infect other T cells easily. Each infected cell dies, leaving the T-helper population depleted and the

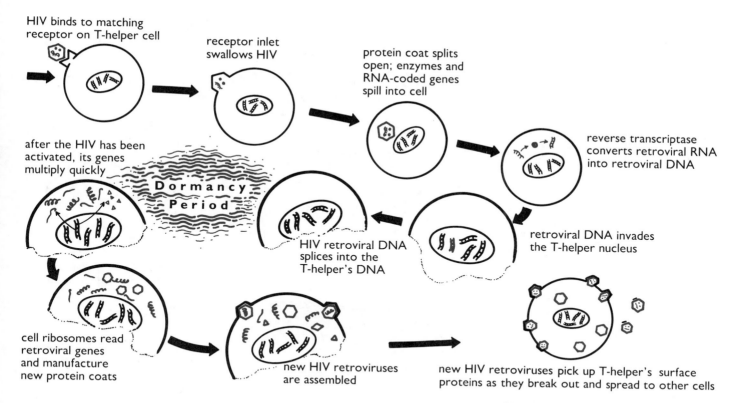

HIV binds to matching receptor on T-helper cell

receptor inlet swallows HIV

protein coat splits open; enzymes and RNA-coded genes spill into cell

reverse transcriptase converts retroviral RNA into retroviral DNA

after the HIV has been activated, its genes multiply quickly

Dormancy Period

HIV retroviral DNA splices into the T-helper's DNA

retroviral DNA invades the T-helper nucleus

cell ribosomes read retroviral genes and manufacture new protein coats

new HIV retroviruses are assembled

new HIV retroviruses pick up T-helper's surface proteins as they break out and spread to other cells

FIGURE 18-21 How the HIV retrovirus invades a T-helper cell, reproduces, and picks up T-helper surface protein

immune system devastated because it lacks the co-ordinating action of the T-helpers.

All early AIDS research focussed on T-helper cells because most viruses found by detection methods then available were located in AIDS patients' T-helpers. AIDS researchers, therefore, assumed that T-helper cells were the principal target of the retrovirus. However, these researchers were puzzled by finding HIV in some people whose T cells showed no signs of infection, and who had no antibodies.

Now there is increasing evidence that T-helpers may not be the only target of HIV or even the primary one. New findings show that HIV can hide inside macrophages without being consumed and without giving any external evidence of their presence. With no HIV particles on their surface, infected macrophages cannot signal the T-helpers to trigger the normal immune response, and no HIV antibodies are produced. Meanwhile, the HIV retrovirus inside the macrophage multiplies without killing its host. Once an infected macrophage leaves the bloodstream, HIV can emerge and infect other cells directly. (See Figure 18-22.) No antibodies are produced because the retrovirus is no longer in the bloodstream. Researchers differ on the other kinds of host cells HIV can attack, but likely targets include certain cells in the brain and in organ linings.

Another major difference in the body's response to HIV as compared to

FIGURE 18-22 Direct and indirect infection by HIV

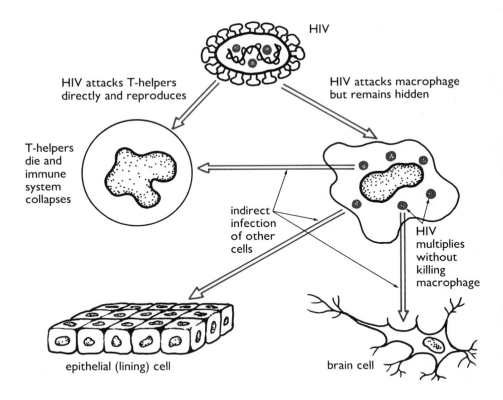

HIV

HIV attacks T-helpers directly and reproduces

HIV attacks macrophage but remains hidden

T-helpers die and immune system collapses

indirect infection of other cells

HIV multiplies without killing macrophage

epithelial (lining) cell

brain cell

other viruses is the length and variability of the latency period. The virus that causes rabies never remains dormant for more than a year, and the disease follows the same pattern in all infected people once the symptoms begin. With AIDS, however, some people carry HIV genes for years with no obvious ill effects. But others become sick and die very quickly. Researchers are still trying to solve a fundamental puzzle — What activates HIV?

This research could eventually provide an answer to a very practical question: Does HIV always kill? Some doctors think that everyone infected with HIV will eventually die of AIDS. Others feel that it is much too early in the pandemic to make such a definitive statement.

Discussion Questions

1. a) Why did researchers first assume that T-helper cells were the primary target of HIV?
   b) How does the destruction of T-helper cells cripple the immune system?
2. HIV disguises itself from detection by the immune system in three different ways. Briefly describe each method and explain how it prevents the formation of antibodies.

3. a) The body's response to HIV differs from its response to other retroviruses. Briefly describe two of these differences.
   b) How would you expect each of these differences to affect the treatment and control of AIDS?
4. List two important questions about HIV that researchers are still trying to answer. Explain why the answers are important.

Several characteristics of AIDS make it exceptionally difficult to treat or to control. First, AIDS is both very new and very deadly. Doctors have little past experience to guide them when they treat patients with AIDS. Many patients die before new treatments and drugs can be developed.

Second, AIDS is an extremely complex disease. A syndrome rather than a disease, AIDS is a diverse combination of symptoms and secondary infections that eventually leads to more serious medical problems.

- Infection with HIV
- Persistently swollen lymph glands
- Diverse array of infections and symptoms
- Dementia and motor co-ordination disorders
- Full-blown AIDS
- Death from cancer, pneumonia, or other major infection

Third, AIDS is spread mainly by sexual contact. It is extremely difficult to alter sexual behaviour and often impossible to get frank answers from patients about their sexual history. This aspect of AIDS hinders the efforts of public health officers to advise those who may have been exposed to the retrovirus and are unaware of it. In addition, many people have strongly held sexual attitudes that interfere with AIDS education programs intended to

WHAT PROBLEMS MAKE AIDS MORE DIFFICULT TO TREAT OR TO CONTROL THAN OTHER VIRAL DISEASES?

Members of the AIDS Committee of Toronto meet at their headquarters to plan an educational campaign. Armed with pamphlets and up-to-date facts on AIDS, the staff and volunteers counsel people about protection through safe sex practices.

A campaign launched in Toronto featured Bleachman, who showed intravenous drug users how to clean used needles with bleach. AIDS can be spread by drug users who share unsterilized needles.

inform the general public. For example, many North Americans still think that only homosexuals get AIDS. This is *not* true. AIDS can be spread by any kind of sexual activity that enables HIV to enter the bloodstream.

HIV can also be spread among intravenous drug users who share needles. These individuals are especially resistant to health education. Since many work as prostitutes to earn money for drugs, they are major transmitters of HIV into the general population.

AIDS can also be transmitted from mother to child during birth, and until North American blood banks were screened for HIV, some cases of AIDS were caused by the transfusion of infected blood. There is still a risk of infection by blood transfusion in countries that cannot afford screening.

A fourth problem in dealing with AIDS is detection. The first AIDS tests depended on the detection of antibodies. But HIV can hide in macrophages without alerting the immune system to begin producing antibodies. HIV genes can linger in the T-helper cells for months or years, again without producing antibodies in detectable quantities.

Detection is made even more difficult because the most accurate tests have been so expensive that few public health bodies can afford to use them. (See Figure 18-23.) In addition, certain medical conditions or medications can cause test results, or "false positives," that seem to indicate AIDS but are later proven to be inaccurate. The detection problem could be solved with a test to detect HIV itself, even when the virus is hidden inside immune cells. Recent reports announce the development of a reliable but expensive new test

FIGURE 18-23 In this antibody-sensitive AIDS test, blood samples are mixed with purified HIV proteins. If there are any HIV antibodies in the sample, they will stick to the retroviral proteins. Further treatment changes the colour of any samples in which binding has occurred. The test is only 75% accurate, partly because testing materials can vary from batch to batch, and partly because the chemicals can migrate from one well to another, making negative specimens look positive.

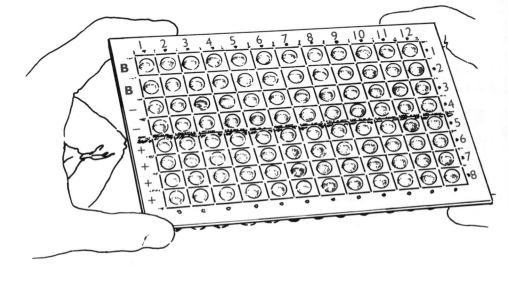

to spot HIV in blood. If costs can be reduced, this test could lead to the early detection of HIV, and help to slow down the rate at which AIDS spreads.

Other recent reports, however, indicate that the testing problem will not be solved so easily. Canadian virologists have already identified a few patients infected with a *new* AIDS-causing retrovirus that appears to have originated in Africa. This development is not surprising. Mutations occur frequently and naturally among the viruses that cause influenza. For purposes of classification and testing, the original AIDS-causing virus is called HIV-1. The new virus is called HIV-2. The symptoms caused by the two retroviruses are similar, but tests for HIV-1 do not always detect HIV-2.

At present, most virologists doubt that HIV-2 will make much difference to the overall AIDS problem. They say they are more concerned with HTLV-1, a retrovirus that appears to be responsible for certain types of cancer in Japan and the Caribbean.

Discussion Questions

1. a) How does HIV enter the body?
   b) List several ways HIV can spread from one person to another.
   c) Who is at risk for contracting AIDS? Who is at most risk?

2. Which characteristics of AIDS make it
   a) difficult to detect?
   b) difficult to treat?
   c) difficult to control?

3. a) What word does the S in AIDS stand for?
   b) What is the medical meaning of this term, and what does it imply about AIDS?
   c) How does this aspect of AIDS make it difficult to treat?

4. a) What do you think the goals of an AIDS education program should be?
   b) Which groups are in the greatest need of effective AIDS education?
   c) What sort of program do you think might be effective for the groups you identified in part (b)?

Cancer is the abnormally rapid and uncontrolled reproduction of cells that divide without specializing to form normal body tissue. The resulting clump of cells is called a **tumor.** Tumors are classified as one of two types. **Carcinomas** grow in the tissues that form skin and organ linings. **Sarcomas** are found in connective tissue such as bone. Blood is also considered to be a connective tissue, but the cancerous growth of white blood cells is called **leukemia.**

Scientists have been trying to pinpoint a cause for cancer since 1911. An experiment conducted at that time linked viruses with cancer in chickens.

ARE AIDS AND CANCER CONNECTED?

TABLE 18-2 Virus-Caused Plant and Animal Diseases

Virus Type	Disease
Animals	
Vaccina	• cowpox
Cytomegalovirus (feline, canine, bovine)	• stomatitis, encephalitis
Adenovirus (canine)	• hepatitis (dogs)
Papillomavirus	• malignant parotid tumors in mice
Rabies Virus	• rabies (mammals)
Picornaviruses	• foot and mouth disease
Avian Leukovirus	• leukemia in fowl
Plants	
Tobacco Ringspot Virus	• many plant hosts and diseases (e.g., soybean bud blight)
Tobacco Mosaic Virus	• many plant hosts and diseases (e.g., wrinkled, mottled tobacco leaves)
Apple Stem Grooving Virus	• disease of apple stems
Potato Mep-top Virus	• potato irregularities
Wheat Mosaic Virus	• mosaic disease in wheat

Healthy birds were injected with a filtered extract from the tumors of cancerous chickens. Sarcomas soon developed in the previously healthy birds, suggesting that a cancer-causing virus must have been present in the tumors. Since then virologists have compiled a long list of virus-caused plant and animal cancers. (See Table 18-2.)

Are any human cancers caused by viruses? Scientists know that cancer is linked to the presence of cancer-causing genes in the cells of tumors. They are still trying to determine whether cancer genes are introduced by a viral agent or are already present in the host cell's DNA. If cancer genes are already present, what activates them? Some researchers think that studying HIV may help to answer these questions since there is a definite link between AIDS and a formerly unusual cancer called Kaposi sarcoma.

Kaposi sarcoma is characterized by multiple reddish, purple, or black tumors in the connective tissue beneath the skin and the lining of the digestive tract. The tumors swell, often resulting in great deformity before death, which is usually caused by bleeding from internal tumors. Prior to the late 1970s,

Kaposi sarcoma was found only in elderly men of southeastern European descent and in patients receiving medical treatments that suppressed the immune system.

Researchers believe that HIV is not the only virus linked to human cancers. No one has yet observed a virus actually causing cancer in humans, and most related research is limited to viruses that cause cancer in other organisms. But scientists think that much of this research can be applied to humans. Furthermore, there is such a strong statistical link between cervical cancer and the human papilloma virus (HPV) that researchers no longer doubt the connection. Medical experts now classify cervical cancer as a sexually transmitted disease that is caused by a virus. There is also strong evidence to suggest a connection between the Epstein-Barr virus and lymphoma. This cancer of the lymphatic system occurs only in people whose immune systems are already depressed. In patients with healthy immune systems, the Epstein-Barr virus causes mononucleosis, an acute but seldom fatal disease.

Many scientists think there may be a relationship between HIV and the retroviruses that cause cancer in other animals. The most obvious connection is that both AIDS and cancer involve genetic changes at the cellular level. Therefore, AIDS research may also uncover facts that will be useful in understanding cancer. Similarly, cancer research may help scientists to understand AIDS better. Understanding these interrelationships more fully will require further advances in cellular biology, molecular biology, and genetics.

Discussion Questions

1. a) Describe the earliest research linking animal cancers to viruses.
   b) Why is it difficult for researchers to establish definite links between human cancers and viruses?

2. a) What is the link between genes and cancer?
   b) What major questions are cancer researchers asking about these links?
   c) Which of these questions is similar to one being asked about AIDS?

3. a) List all of the viruses that have been linked to human cancers. Beside each, write the name of the associated cancer.
   b) Briefly describe the cancer that develops in some AIDS patients. Suggest reasons why not all patients develop this cancer.

4. Why do scientists think AIDS research may further their understanding of cancer?

IS THERE ANYTHING BENEFICIAL ABOUT AIDS?

There cannot be anything good about a disease as devastating and widespread as AIDS. However, some benefit may be derived from the intensive human, economic, and scientific effort now being made to find a treatment, a cure, or a way to prevent the disease.

Viral diseases have been a health problem throughout human history. Before 1981, most viral research was focussed on viruses that attack plants, other animals, and bacteria. Despite great medical advances in many fields, including immunization against viral diseases such as polio, very little was known about how viruses worked in human cells. Insufficient funding and ethical considerations are two factors that have contributed to this lack of knowledge. Funding for basic research has always been limited, and the kind of research that can be carried out on human subjects is also limited.

Now that fundamental research into the nature of viruses has an immediate application, scientists can expect to learn much more about them before AIDS is finally eradicated. In the process, considerably more about cells will be learned. Understanding viral diseases, and any possible link they may have with cancer, depends on understanding how normal cells reproduce, obtain materials, produce energy, and pass on their genetic code. These very important functions of normal cells will be the main focus of Unit V.

RESEARCH PROJECT
Inquiring about AIDS and Other Viruses

This chapter has provided some basic answers to several important questions, but AIDS research is ongoing and new discoveries are frequently reported. Your task in this project is to examine reports of recent research related to AIDS, HIV, other viruses, or cancer. Based on what you have learned in this chapter, evaluate reports in newspapers, magazines, and scientific journals. Use the following questions to help you in your evaluation.

- What is the focus of the research being reported? Cells, genes, or molecular biology? The virus or the disease? Treatment or prevention?
- What questions does the research attempt to answer?
- Is the research being carried out on animal subjects? If so, can the results be applied to humans?
- Are the researchers biased? Are they starting out with a fixed idea and trying to prove it, or do they seem to be approaching the problem with open minds?
- How reliable are the newspapers, magazines, or scientific journals you are reading? Are the publishers trying to inform and educate the public, or are they trying to increase sales with sensational stories?
- Are the articles and reports biased? Do they try to prove a particular point? Do they suppress any relevant information?

Meet
Rose Sheinin

Rose teaches microbiology and is Vice-Dean of the School of Graduate Studies at the University of Toronto. Most of her time, however, is spent in a laboratory studying cancer-causing viruses.

Q. Why did you become interested in a science career?

A. When I was only three years old, a favourite uncle died of lung and liver cancer. Since then I've wanted to be in cancer research.

Q. What did you study at university?

A. I did a Ph.D. in biochemistry and then did a two-year fellowship. By that time, it was possible to study cancer-related viruses so I became a virologist.

Q. Is the theory that viruses cause cancer now generally accepted?

A. We now know that viruses cause the largest number of cancers in the world. But it took a long time before doctors (who are trained to treat and cure, not to do preventive medicine) would accept this. Our health-care system is not concerned enough with prevention — there's not enough money for research.

Q. What have been the most startling discoveries in your field?

A. The discovery of the Hepatitis B Virus, which is the primary cause of liver cancer in the world. Another important discovery is the human papilloma virus (HPV), which causes cervical cancer in women and which we should be able to treat with a vaccine.

Q. What about the AIDS virus?

A. The HIV virus was the first discovered retrovirus in humans (it's widespread in animals) and is the most virulent of cancer-causing viruses. The HIV virus has made the medical world aware that we need to know more about viruses.

Q. Do you believe that viruses are the major cause of cancer?

A. Yes, although there are exceptions such as lung cancer, which is caused by smoking. I believe that a vaccine may be possible for a majority of cancers. But, this is all relatively new information. The discoveries of

human viruses have only occurred in the last 50 years. Although there's more concern now, there still isn't much understanding.

Q. Will there be more money for research in the future?

A. I think the government will increase funding because the cost of treating cancer is so high. One in four or five people will eventually have cancer.

Q. What are you studying in your laboratory?

A. I'm studying the basic mechanism by which these viruses work — that is, how they become part of the genetic machinery of the cell. I'm interested in how viruses change the inheritable properties of the cells and animals they infect. This work is also important in the development of molecular probes for the diagnosis of cancer and for the discovery of oncogenes, cancer-causing genes.

Q. What is the most gratifying part of your work?

A. Making a discovery. But also being part of a science that is essential to our culture. I believe that with virus vaccines and an educated population, most cancers will disappear.

Q. What other qualities, other than educational, are required?

A. You have to be curious and interested in life. You have to be disciplined because the work is hard. You need a good knowledge of math, physics, and chemistry.

- What further research seems to be needed in the area you are investigating? What more would you like to know that the articles and the reports don't tell you?

Write a report about your investigation. Include the information you consider to be accurate, and state reasons why you have formed this evaluation. List the sources you obtained your information from in a bibliography. Make your report available to other members of your class.

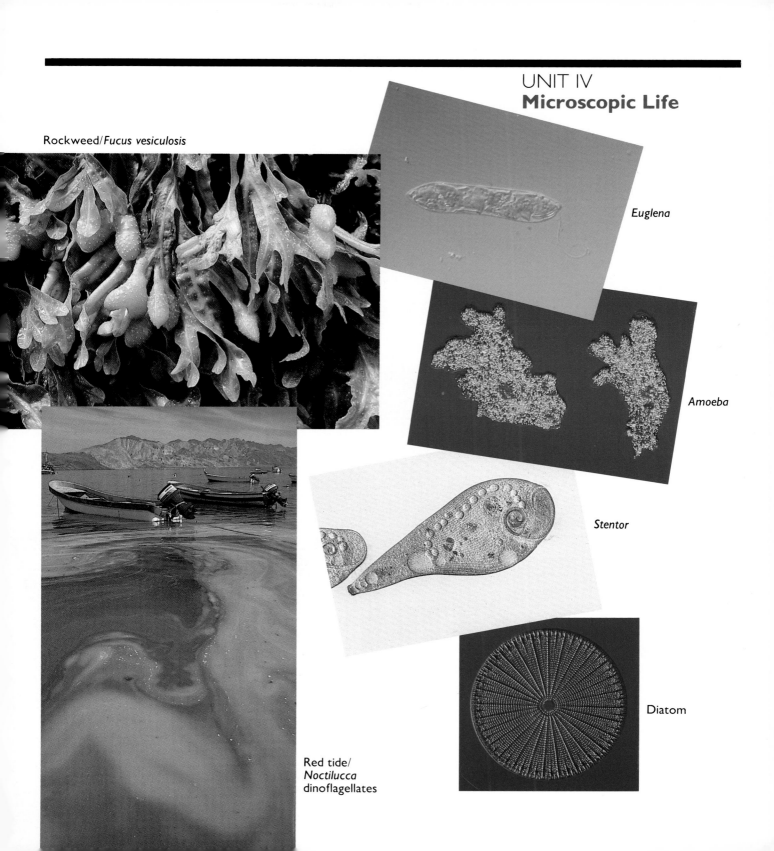

Rockweed/*Fucus vesiculosis*

Euglena

Amoeba

Stentor

Red tide/
Noctilucca
dinoflagellates

Diatom

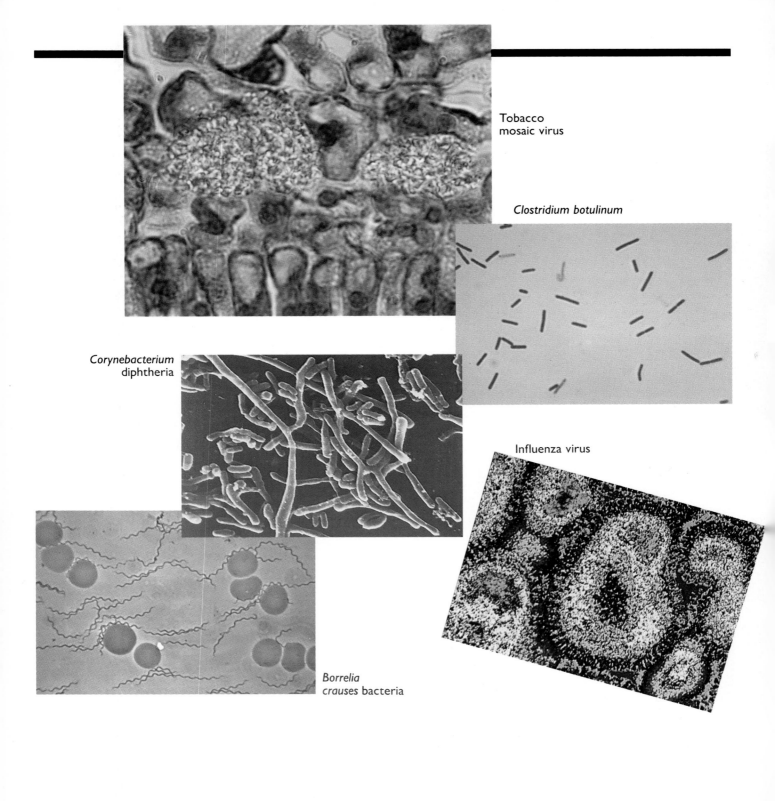

Tobacco
mosaic virus

Clostridium botulinum

Corynebacterium
diphtheria

Influenza virus

*Borrelia
crauses* bacteria

Review Questions

Key Words

Acquired Immune Deficiency Syndrome (AIDS)
B cells
cancer
carcinomas
genes
Human Immunodeficiency Virus (HIV)
incubation period
latency period
leukemia
monocytes
pandemic

plasma-B cells
memory-B cells
messenger RNA (mRNA)
RNA (ribonucleic acid)
receptors
retroviruses
reverse transcriptase
sarcomas
T cells
T-helpers
T-killers
T-suppressors
tumor
viruses

Recall Questions

Multiple Choice

1. A retrovirus contains all of the following features *except*
   a) deoxyribonucleic acid
   b) ribonucleic acid
   c) a protein coat
   d) a specialized enzyme

2. The three types of immune cells produced by bone marrow are
   a) monocytes, T cells, and memory-B cells
   b) monoctyes, macrophages, and T cells
   c) T cells, monocytes, and B cells
   d) B cells, bacteriophages, and plasma-B cells

3. The DNA of a typical phage virus contains
   a) 75 genes   c) 40 000 genes
   b) 2000 genes   d) no genes

4. The function of mRNA is to
   a) make host ribosomes produce viral protein
   b) carry instructions from the chromosomes to the ribosomes
   c) manufacture copies of viral DNA
   d) allow retroviral genes to reproduce

5. The function of T-suppressor cells is to
   a) "eat" bacteria
   b) manufacture new types of antibodies
   c) produce protein coats
   d) stabilize the immune system after infection

6. The function of plasma-B cells is to
   a) manufacture antibodies to fight infection
   b) store antibody protein patterns
   c) consume foreign invaders
   d) send hormonal messages to T-killer cells

7. Carcinomas are found in
   a) bone tissue   c) blood
   b) skin and organ tissue   d) lymph nodes

Fill in the Blanks

1. The outer layer of a virus is composed of _____, while its core contains either _____ or _____.

2. AIDS is caused by _____ , which contains the nucleic acid _____ and the enzyme _____.

3. The symptoms of chicken pox develop after a short _____, while the symptoms of AIDS develop after a _____ of variable length.

4. The virus that causes AIDS has more _____ than any other retrovirus and can _____ a thousand times faster.

5. _____ are the first immune cells to fight a viral infection, but _____ cells co-ordinate the rest of the immune response.

6. The retrovirus that causes AIDS is usually called _____, which stands for _____.

Short Answers

1. a) What is messenger RNA?
   b) What is mRNA used for in normal living cells?

2. a) List two important structural differences between DNA and RNA viruses.
   b) State two examples of diseases caused by each viral type.

3. a) How do DNA viruses interrupt the normal sequence of protein production in living cells?
   b) How do RNA retroviruses interrupt this sequence?

4. a) Why are some retroviruses able to lie dormant for a variable period of time?
   b) What is the variable period of time called?

5. a) Describe the structure of HIV.
   b) Why is HIV classified as a retrovirus, and what diseases does it cause?

6. a) List three ways HIV can hide in the body.
   b) Why does this ability make AIDS difficult to detect?

7. a) Which T cell is the most important?
   b) What is its function?

8. a) Who gave the first recorded vaccination?
   b) What was the vaccination for, and what were the results?

9. a) What do most vaccines contain?
   b) How do they provide lasting immunity to viral diseases?

10. a) What host cell is destroyed by the AIDS retrovirus?
    b) Why is this so devastating to the immune system?

11. a) Which virus has been linked to cancer?
    b) What type of cancer does this virus seem to produce?

12. Why do scientists think AIDS research may help doctors understand cancer better?

Application Questions

1. a) List all the different types of immune cells your body produces to fight viral infections.
   b) Arrange them according to the cells that become involved first, second, and so on.
   c) Which immune cells remain after a viral infection has been conquered? What is the significance of these cells?

2. a) Identify two viral diseases that develop after a variable latency period.
   b) Which type of virus causes these diseases?
   c) Explain how a latency period makes these diseases especially serious.

3. a) Which features of HIV make early detection of AIDS difficult?

   b) What are the potential advantages of early detection?
   c) What are the potential disadvantages?

4. a) How do your cells differ from those of all other organisms, including humans?
   b) How does this difference enable your immune system to fight off invasions by micro-organisms?

5. a) How does HIV gain entry to the human body?
   b) How does HIV gain entry to individual cells?
   c) How can HIV spread from one cell to another without triggering the production of antibodies by the immune system?

6. All active immune cells develop from monocytes, B cells, and T cells.
   a) Where are monocytes first produced?
   b) Where do monocytes undergo further development?
   c) Which active immune cells do monocytes produce as they develop?
   d) What role do the cells that develop from monocytes play in the immune response?
   e) Repeat parts (a) to (d) for B cells and for T cells.

7. Arrange the following terms in a diagram to show that you understand how they are linked: AIDS, cancer, carcinoma, Epstein-Barr virus, HIV, HPV, Kaposi sarcoma, leukemia, lymphoma, sarcoma, and tumor.

8. a) Which groups were vulnerable to Kaposi sarcoma before HIV became well established?
   b) Which answer to part (a) suggests an obvious reason why many AIDS patients develop Kaposi sarcoma? Explain.
   c) The other answer to part (a) may suggest why only some AIDS patients develop Kaposi sarcoma. Explain.

Problem Solving

1. a) Potato plants, pigs, and bacteria are all affected by viruses. Are these effects harmful or beneficial?
   b) What are the roles of potato plants, pigs, and bacteria in the biosphere? Use ecological terms to describe the role, or niche, of each organism.
   c) Use ecological terms to describe the role of viruses in the biosphere. Is there any potential benefit that can result from viral action?

2. a) Describe the impact of viruses on human health.
   b) Describe the role of vaccines in minimizing this impact. State specific examples of viral diseases.
   c) Why is it important to weaken or kill the viruses used to manufacture a vaccine?

3. a) At what point in its reproductive cycle is a retrovirus most vulnerable?
   b) What does this suggest about a focus for anti-AIDS research that may produce positive results?

4. Suppose it became possible to test the safety of vaccines without using human subjects. What problems would still confront researchers trying to develop an effective vaccine against AIDS?

5. a) What ability do retroviruses have that might make them useful in genetic engineering?
   b) Which characteristic might make them unreliable?

6. a) Dr. Jonas Salk, who developed the first successful vaccine against polio, is actively investigating a vaccine against AIDS. What factors do you think make an AIDS vaccine more difficult to develop than a polio vaccine?
   b) Salk's own AIDS research has focussed on vaccines for those who are already infected with HIV. How does this focus overcome some of the difficulties described in part (a)?
   c) Salk thinks multiple strategies will be needed to defeat AIDS. What strategies do you think might produce positive results? What facts about AIDS form the basis of your opinions?

7. a) Organ transplants often trigger an immune response in the recipient. Explain why.
   b) Drugs that suppress the immune system are given to transplant patients to prevent rejection of the donor organ. What are some potential risks to patients who take these drugs?

Extensions

1. Investigate the causes and the symptoms of a disease called Kuru. Prepare a brief report that discusses the following questions.
   a) Is Kuru a widespread public health problem?
   b) How might a Kuru research program contribute to knowledge about AIDS and cancer?
   c) What other human disorders might Kuru research help scientists to understand?

2. Who administered the first vaccination against the rabies virus? When? Visit a local animal hospital and inquire about rabies vaccinations. Contact the local office for the Ministry of Natural Resources and ask about the rabies control program in your area.

3. Research the virus that causes warts in humans. In what way do these warts resemble tumors? How do they differ?

4. Contact the local office for the Ministry of Health to find out why there are periodic outbreaks of rubella, even though an effective vaccine has been developed. What are the usual symptoms of rubella? Are they serious? Who is at greatest risk of being harmed by the rubella virus?

The Unity of Life

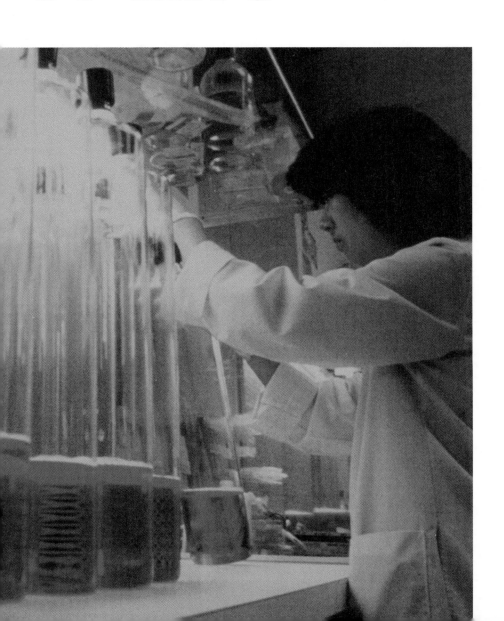

CHAPTER

19

Understanding Diversity

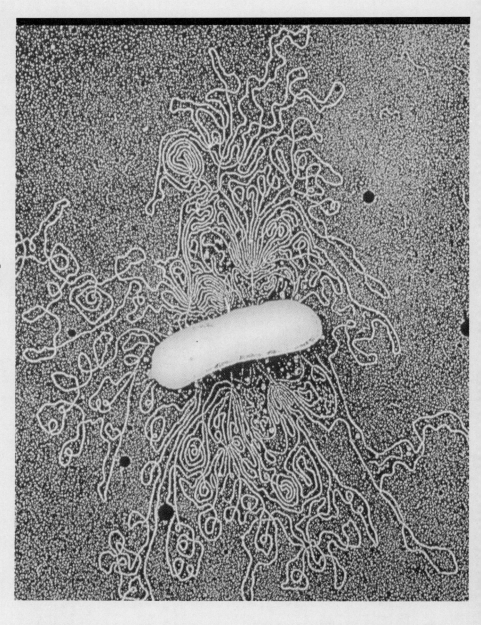

The bacterial species *Escherichia coli* is a common subject for many biological experiments. The thread-like material streaming out of this *E. coli* bacterium is its DNA. Bacterial DNA usually lies in a fairly compact cluster within a cell's cytoplasm. In preparation for the electron micrograph above, the bacterium was placed in distilled water. Eventually, so much water moved into the cell that its membrane burst, despite the compensating pressure of the surrounding cell wall. The cell's DNA was ejected, and it spread out on the surface of the water.

The length of *E. coli*'s single DNA molecule is astounding when compared to the length of the

590   V   THE UNITY OF LIFE

bacterium itself. But larger, more complex species have even longer strands of DNA. For example, the DNA from a single human cell would stretch out to a length of nearly 2 m. It would, however, still be invisible to the unaided eye because it is extremely thin.

DNA was discovered in 1869, when the German biochemist Friedrick Miescher found an acidic substance in the cell nucleus. Miescher called the acid "nuclein." Once its composition had been determined, nuclein was renamed deoxyribonucleic acid or DNA.

Almost a century passed before scientists realized that DNA is the unifying structure that makes the diversity of the biosphere possible. That understanding arose from numerous biochemical investigations conducted in the century following the discovery of DNA. The most important of these studies unravelled the structure of DNA. In this chapter, you will explore the structure of DNA, how it was discovered, and its significance to living cells and organisms.

Chapter Objectives

When you complete this chapter, you should:

1. Appreciate that the cell is the basic unit of structure and function in both unicellular and multicellular organisms.

2. Understand that species differ in structure and function because of differences in the way their cells organize amino acids to form proteins.

3. Recognize that DNA's role in directing protein production makes it the source of both biological continuity and biological diversity.

4. Be able to describe the structure of DNA in simple terms and explain how this structure enables DNA to serve as a master set of instructions for assembling and operating a complete organism.

5. Be able to describe the structure of RNA in simple terms and explain RNA's role in protein production.

6. Using the discovery of DNA's structure and function, be able to explain how major scientific breakthroughs usually involve many scientists of differing backgrounds and nationalities.

19.1   The Search for Biological Unity

So far, your kingdom-by-kingdom exploration of the biosphere has focussed on diversity. Emphasizing how living things differ can make you lose sight of their commonalities. But Figure 19-1 emphasizes the features that are common to all five kingdoms. Emphasizing similarities helps remind you that all living things must carry out the same basic life functions, regardless of how much their structures or abilities may differ. This similarity in life functions is evidence of a fundamental unity among living things. By taking a closer look at cell parts and the chemical components that make up living things, you will acquire a greater understanding of this unity.

The Cellular Basis of Life

"What does the earth resemble most? . . . A living cell." — *Lewis Thomas*

All organisms are made up of one or more cells, and most living cells contain similar cell parts. These common characteristics provide more evidence of the unity among living things. But what is behind this unity? When scientists want to look for underlying patterns or regularities, they often organize their observations in a different way. When observations are presented as in Table 19-1, you can see more clearly that the only feature all five kingdoms have

FIGURE 19-1 A summary of the characteristics of the five kingdoms

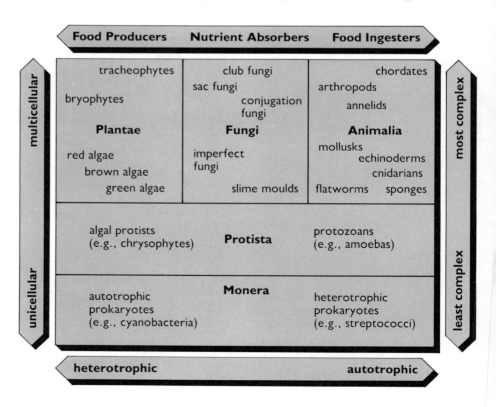

V   THE UNITY OF LIFE

TABLE 19-1   A Comparison of Cells from Five Kingdoms

Feature	Monera	Protista	Fungi	Plantae	Animalia
Cell Type	• prokaryotic	• eukaryotic	• eukaryotic	• eukaryotic	• eukaryotic
Nuclear Membrane	• absent	• present	• present	• present	• present
Chromosome Content	• DNA only	• DNA plus protein	• DNA plus protein	• DNA plus protein	• DNA plus protein
Cell Wall Content	• polysaccharide	• variable where present; absent in most species	• chitin	• cellulose	• absent
Nutrition	• heterotrophic and autotrophic	• heterotrophic and autotrophic	• heterotrophic only	• autotrophic only	• heterotrophic only
Motility	• by gliding or by flagella where present; absent in many species	• by cilia/flagella • by amoeboid motion • absent in many species	• by cilia or flagella where present • cells nonmotile	• by cilia or flagella where present, as in swimming sperm cells • most cells nonmotile	• by cilia/flagella • by amoeboid motion • many cells such as skin cells nonmotile
Dependence on Other Cells	• independent, unicellular	• most independent, unicellular	• interdependent, multicellular structure in most species	• interdependent, multicellular structure in most species	• interdependent, multicellular structure in all species

in common is chromosomal DNA. Paradoxically, it is this common chemical that makes their diversity possible.

The Chemical Basis of Life

All structural and functional characteristics observed in living things are the end products of numerous chemical reactions. Many of the most fundamental reactions are remarkably similar from one kingdom to another. For example, the series of reactions known as cell respiration proceeds in much the same way in almost all living cells.

At first, you might think that the molecules making up living things seem very different from each other. Humans, for example, have thousands of body chemicals, each with its own formula. Closer inspection shows that these thousands of formulas fall into just a few categories. The molecules in each category are assembled according to a similar pattern—a few basic chemical sub-units are used repeatedly in different arrangements. (See Table 19-2.) The greatest variations occur in protein molecules. These chain-like molecules differ in length and also in the sequence of the amino acids they contain. Since there are 20 different amino acids, the number of different proteins that can be assembled is almost unimaginably large.

The 20 amino acids listed below are needed to assemble human proteins. Those shown in black are considered to be nonessential because they can be made from other molecules commonly found in the human diet. The eight shown in colour are essential. They must be obtained from the food you eat.

Nonessential Amino Acids
- alanine
- asparagine
- cysteine
- glutamine
- serine
- histidine
- aspartate
- glutamate
- glycine
- proline
- tyrosine
- arginine

Essential Amino Acids
- isoleucine
- lysine
- phenylalanine
- tryptophan
- leucine
- methionine
- threonine
- valine

TABLE 19-2 Characteristics of Some Important Biological Molecules

Category	Type of Sub-unit	Arrangement of Sub-units	Function	Example
Carbohydrates	• simple sugars (e.g., glucose)	• linked in chains of variable length but consistent composition	• energy source • structural components	• glucose, sucrose • cellulose in plant cell walls
Lipids (complex)	• glycerol plus fatty acids with long hydrocarbon chains	• one glycerol unit linked to three fatty acids with hydrocarbon chains of variable length but consistent composition	• energy storage • waterproofing	• body fat under the skin • waxy cuticle on leaves
Lipids (simple)	• based on hydrocarbon made of four fused rings	• various small molecular groups linked to four-ring hydrocarbon	• regulation • digestion	• sex hormones (testosterone) and adrenal hormones (adrenaline) • bile acids
Proteins	• amino acids (22 kinds)	• linked in chains of variable length and sequence	• structural components • digestion • regulation	• fingernails • digestive enzymes (salivary amylase) • nonlipid hormones (insulin) and most nondigestive enzymes

Arginine and histidine are sometimes listed as essential amino acids because they are required by very young children who cannot synthesize these molecules in large enough amounts to sustain rapid growth.

Not all hormones are protein molecules. For example, the molecules sex hormones are made of are closely related to fats.

DID YOU KNOW?

Dogs and most other animals require different essential amino acids from humans. This is why veterinarians discourage the practice of feeding dogs a human diet because it may not contain the balance of amino acids dogs need.

You will recall from Chapter 5 that humans ingest protein-containing foods because they are a source of amino acids. Until the protein in a plant or animal food source has been broken down into separate amino acids, it cannot be used. After digestion, your blood carries the amino acids to your cells, where specialized organelles rearrange them to make human proteins. These proteins include enzymes, hormones, and structural proteins. The enzymes facilitate the reactions that produce all other body chemicals, and the hormones help regulate and co-ordinate these reactions.

The way human cells assemble amino acids distinguishes humans from other animals such as pigs. Pigs and humans eat similar food, and their digestive systems break proteins down in much the same way. But after digestion, a pig's cells rearrange the amino acids to form pig proteins. Organisms such as pigs and humans differ from each other because the cells of each species contain a unique set of instructions. Your cells contain instructions for making and operating a human. A pig's cells contain instructions for making and operating a pig. Initially, the master set of instructions for making pig proteins is contained in the nucleus of the zygote. As the zygote divides and develops into a pig embryo, the instructions are duplicated so that each cell receives its own set.

V THE UNITY OF LIFE

Although pig proteins contain the same amino acids as human proteins, pig cells assemble the amino acids in different sequences, according to the master set of instructions contained in the nucleus.

The Source of Diversity

Biologists now know that the master set of instructions for every living thing is directed by a single type of molecule—**DNA.** Most biologists rejected this idea when it was suggested in the early 1940s. They thought the composition of DNA was too simple to carry instructions for assembling 20 amino acids in an almost endless array of proteins. Since the nuclei of all eukaryotic cells contain protein as well as DNA (see Table 19-1), many biologists thought the instructions must be encoded on a master set of protein molecules contained within the nucleus.

In 1951, the American biologists Alfred Hershey and Martha Chase conducted a two-part study using two sets of tagged bacteriophages to infect *E. coli*. (See Figure 19-2.) In one part, they tagged the protein coats of the phages

Alfred Hershey and Martha Chase. Hershey later shared the 1969 Nobel prize in physiology and medicine for his work with bacteriophages. Chase was a research assistant—her first job after obtaining a degree in biology and chemistry.

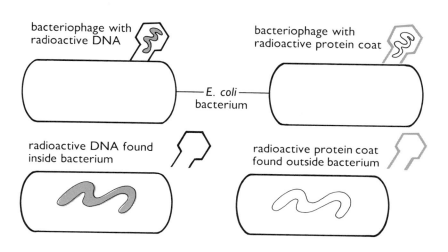

bacteriophage with radioactive DNA

bacteriophage with radioactive protein coat

E. coli bacterium

radioactive DNA found inside bacterium

radioactive protein coat found outside bacterium

FIGURE 19-2 The Hershey-Chase experiment

James Watson **(left)** and Francis Crick **(right)** with their now famous double helix model of DNA.

Rosalind Franklin. Her work contributed greatly to the unravelling of DNA's structure. She died the same year that Watson, Crick, and Wilkins won the Nobel prize for their work.

with radioactive atoms. In the second part, they tagged the DNA cores. At the end of the experiment, tagged DNA was found inside the bacteria. The tagged protein coats were left outside. Hershey and Chase concluded that the instructions forcing the bacterium to manufacture new viruses were carried on the viral DNA, not on its protein coats.

The evidence was so compelling that biologists everywhere had to accept it, even though they could not explain the scientific basis for the observations. Clearly, DNA was the molecule responsible for directing the manufacture of all cell proteins, including enzymes and hormones. In turn, the enzymes and hormones directed the assembly of all other cell chemicals and controlled all cell functions. By the time the Hershey-Chase experiment had been duplicated and verified by other scientists, the same question was on almost every biologist's mind. *What structure enables the DNA molecule to carry a complete set of instructions for making a living thing?* The answer to this question came much sooner than anyone expected.

The Quest for the Double Helix

In 1951, the same year that Hershey and Chase conducted their landmark experiment, many scientists embarked on a quest to determine the structure of the DNA molecule. Competition was keen because those who succeeded could win a Nobel prize. The young American biologist James Watson joined forces with the British physicist Francis Crick. And the British chemist Rosalind Franklin began working in the laboratory of British biophysicist Maurice Wilkins. Franklin's research focussed on probing the DNA molecule with X-rays to search for clues to its structure.

Unlike the other scientists who were trying to determine the structure of the DNA molecule, Crick and Watson did no experiments. Instead, they gathered, analyzed, and reorganized data from DNA experiments conducted by other scientists. Their eventual success illustrates the scientific value of good research skills *outside* of the laboratory. Crick and Watson had to gather data from a variety of sources before they could solve the problem. Some of the information they needed had been reported in scientific journals, but much was still being gathered in various laboratories and had to be obtained directly from the investigators. These methods enabled Crick and Watson to gather the following facts.

- DNA is composed of phosphate, sugar (deoxyribose), and four weak nitrogenous bases: **adenine, thymine, cytosine,** and **guanine.**
- These components are grouped together to form four different DNA subunits called **nucleotides.** Each nucleotide contains one phosphate, one deoxyribose, and one base. The four nucleotides are labelled A, T, C, or G according to the base they contain. (See Figure 19-3.)
- The DNA molecule has a very large mass when compared to other molecules and even to proteins.

V THE UNITY OF LIFE

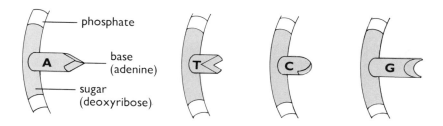

phosphate

base (adenine)

sugar (deoxyribose)

A T C G

FIGURE 19-3 Four different nucleotides are found in DNA. The composition of DNA was identified in the 1880s by Albrecht Kossell, a German biochemist. The composition of DNA's nucleotides was determined in the 1920s by Phoebus Levere, a student of Kossell's.

- The nucleotide proportions of DNA are variable; they differ from species to species. However, the number of A and T nucleotides always equal each other. Similarly, the number of C and G nucleotides always equal each other. That is, A = T and C = G. (See Table 19-3.)
- New measurements made by Maurice Wilkins showed that the DNA molecule was very long and extremely thin. The dimensions and shape of each component in the various nucleotides had also been measured.

Watson and Crick used this information to do something nobody else seems to have thought of. They built large-scale models of all four nucleotides, and used them to build trial models of DNA. However, they were unable to build a model that agreed with all the known facts, until 1952, when they saw Franklin's latest X-ray photograph. This picture, which showed a pattern produced by passing X-rays through a specially prepared sample of DNA, gave Crick and Watson the final clues they needed. To those who knew how to read it, the photograph showed clearly that DNA was a **double helix,** with the phosphate ends of its nucleotides on the outside, and the base ends on the inside.

Crick and Watson assembled their model nucleotides according to this new data and produced the now familiar double-helix DNA model that is still used by biologists today. Three-dimensional models are still favoured by biochemists to help them understand all biological molecules. You will also understand the structure of DNA much better once you have built a mechanical model.

TABLE 19-3 Base Content of DNA in Several Organisms

Organism	A %	C %	G %	T %
Bacterium (*E. coli*)	25	25	25	25
Yeast	32	18	18	32
Carrot	27	23	23	27
Sea Urchin	33	17	17	33
Human	30	20	20	30

Note: Percentage figures have been rounded off to reflect limits of experimental error.

LABORATORY EXERCISE 19-1
A Model of the Structure of DNA

The DNA molecule is so big that a model showing all of its atoms would be too complex to be easily understood. For most students, models using simple shapes to represent the four nucleotides are more meaningful. In this exercise, you will have the opportunity to make a flat model of DNA. If your school owns a commercial DNA modelling kit, you may be able to see for yourself how the helical turns of DNA affect the orientation of the various components.

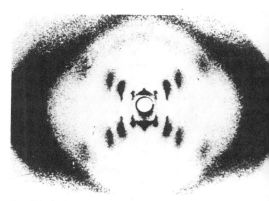

Franklin's X-ray diffraction photograph of DNA. The crossed bars in the middle indicate that DNA is helical. The dark regions at top and bottom indicate that the bases are arranged in "stacks."

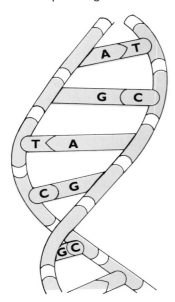

FIGURE 19-4 The Watson-Crick model of the DNA molecule resembles a twisted ladder with sugar-phosphate rails and base-pair rungs.

Diversity and DNA

Figure 19-4 shows a simplified version of the Watson-Crick model. Its main features are summarized below.

- DNA's double helix structure resembles a twisted ladder.
- The outside "rails" of the ladder are formed by bonding the sugar-phosphate ends of the nucleotides in a long chain. These bonds are very strong.
- The inner "rungs" of the ladder are formed by bonding the base ends of the nucleotides together. Each rung formed in this way is referred to as a **base pair.** The bonds that hold base pairs together are fairly weak.
- Only two nucleotide combinations are possible within the structural framework of DNA: A with T or C with G. (If A paired with G, the rung would be too long to fit between the rails. The rung formed if T paired with C would be too short.)

Although there are only two possible nucleotide combinations, the result is four different base pairs: AT, TA, CG, and GC. (See Figure 19-5.) These four base pairs are the only variables in the DNA molecule. Therefore, the instructions DNA carries are "written" in a code composed of four base-pair "symbols."

Four symbols do not seem like very many, especially when compared with the 26 symbols used for the English alphabet. However, the diversity of a code does not depend on the number of different symbols. For example, the entire English language could be written in Morse code instead of the usual alphabet. Morse code has only two symbols, a dot and a dash, but these can be used in various combinations to send any message that can be written using the English alphabet.

The secret to the diversity and the complexity possible with the DNA code is size. The great length of the molecule allows numerous combinations involving the same four base pairs. When thousands of base pairs are arranged along the molecule's length, an almost limitless variety of sequences becomes possible. And DNA is very long. Even a simple *E. coli* has four million base pairs.

Cracking the DNA Code

Biologists spoke of a "code of life" long before Crick and Watson showed that it was made up of only four base pairs. After that, another decade passed before researchers discovered that the code of life was written in triplets — groups containing three base pairs each. Four base pairs arranged in groups of three can form up to 64 different triplets. Most triplets specify a particular amino acid, but some are "punctuation marks." These signal the end of a set of instructions for assembling one chain of amino acids. Some protein molecules consist of a single chain. Others, such as insulin, are made of two or more chains linked together.

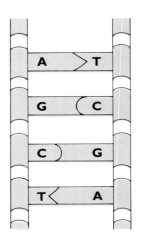

FIGURE 19-5 Read from top to bottom, this DNA segment has four different base pairs. (The model has been untwisted for easier viewing.)

Reading the DNA Code

In eukaryotic cells, the "master copy" of the DNA code is encased by a nuclear membrane most of the time. But proteins are assembled by **ribosomes**, which are tiny granular organelles located in a cell's cytoplasm. The instructions encoded on the DNA are transported to the cytoplasm by a related nucleic acid commonly called RNA. **RNA** is an abbreviation for **ribonucleic acid.** It differs from DNA in the following ways. (See Figure 19-6.)

- RNA is single stranded.
- RNA's sugar-phosphate "rail" contains ribose instead of deoxyribose.
- RNA contains no thymine. Instead, it has a nucleotide that contains the nitrogenous base **uracil** (U). Its other three nucleotides are identical to those found in DNA.
- RNA strands are usually much shorter than an entire DNA molecule.

Most RNA is made in the nucleus. It carries "disposable" copies of the DNA code through the pores in the nuclear membrane to the cytoplasm. The structure of DNA is well suited for the production of RNA copies. Its weak base-pair bonds allow it to "unzip" and provide a master pattern from which the RNA copies can be assembled. As with DNA, the RNA copy of the DNA code is written in triplets along the length of the RNA molecule. Each RNA strand produced in this way is just long enough to carry the code for one amino acid chain. By the early 1960s, biologists had identified which RNA triplets corresponded to which amino acids.

For nearly two decades, scientists believed that the RNA code was universal, that is, all living things used exactly the same RNA triplets to manufacture their proteins. Now scientists have determined that the mycoplasmas and at least one paramecium species use slightly different triplet codes for some amino acids. In other words, the code is not entirely universal. Over the next decade, some researchers will focus intensively on identifying other organisms with unusual triplet codes. No doubt what they find will raise more questions about the code of life.

As you progress through this final unit of your biology course, you should remember that living things can sometimes surprise biologists. Even the very best theories can only explain the facts biologists know at the time the theories are formed. As the use of new technologies reveals new facts, biologists may have to revise old theories. Regardless of what we learn about the code of life, there will always be new questions to answer.

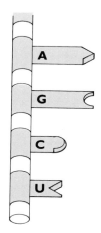

FIGURE 19-6 How does this strand of RNA resemble DNA? How does it differ? **(Hint:** Compare this figure with Figure 19-5.)

Some sample RNA triplet codes are shown in the left column and the corresponding assembly instructions are in the right column.

UUU	• phenylalanine
CCC	• proline
GAG	• glutamate
AAU	• arginine
UAA	• end of chain

Chapter Review

Key Words

adenine
base pair
cytosine
DNA (deoxyribonucleic acid)
double helix
guanine

nucleotides
ribosomes
RNA (ribonucleic acid)
thymine
uracil

Recall Questions

Multiple Choice

1. Protein molecules consist of
   a) long chains of nucleotides
   b) long chains of amino acids
   c) long chains of DNA
   d) long chains of RNA

2. Pigs and humans are made of
   a) the same amino acids
   b) the same proteins
   c) the same DNA
   d) the same RNA

3. The master set of instructions for making a living thing is contained
   a) on the protein in its nucleus
   b) on the DNA in its nucleus
   c) on the RNA in its nucleus
   d) on the RNA in its ribosomes

4. Enzymes are protein molecules that
   a) store energy
   b) build cell structures
   c) regulate cell functions
   d) contain the code of life

5. DNA is composed of
   a) adenine, cytosine, guanine, and thymine
   b) adenine, cytosine, guanine, and uracil
   c) phosphate, ribose, and nitrogenous bases
   d) phosphate, deoxyribose, and nitrogenous bases

Fill in the Blanks

1. DNA was first discovered in _____, but the role it plays in living things was not convincingly demonstrated until 19____ by _____ and _____.

2. That same year, _____ and _____ began series of experiments using X-rays to probe the structure of DNA. However, the first DNA model to explain what was then known about DNA was eventually worked out by _____ and _____.

3. This team did _____ experiments. Instead, they built trial _____, using data from _____.

4. The structure of DNA was shown to resemble a _____.

Short Answers

1. What do the cells of all five kingdoms have in common?

2. What is an amino acid? How many different amino acids are known?

3. What is a protein? How many different proteins are known?

4. What is the relationship between amino acids and proteins?

5. Proteins can be classified into three main groups. List the groups and describe the role each plays in living things.

6. Why is the structure of DNA referred to as a double helix?

7. a) Identify the components found in the "ladder rails" of a DNA molecule.
   b) Identify the components found in the "ladder rungs."

8. a) Which components of DNA are strongly bonded together?
   b) Which are weakly bonded?

9. a) What is a nucleotide?
   b) Describe the parts of a DNA nucleotide.

10. a) How many different DNA nucleotides are there?
    b) Explain what they have in common and how they differ from each other.

11. a) How many different RNA nucleotides are there?
    b) Explain what they have in common and how they differ from each other.

12. How does RNA differ from DNA?

13. a) In which cell structure is the DNA code stored?
    b) In which cell structure is the DNA code used to manufacture proteins?
    c) How is the code carried from the cell structure in part (a) to that in part (b)?

Application Questions

1. a) Which chemical substance is responsible for the diversity of living things?
   b) Which chemical substance is responsible for the unity of living things?
   c) Explain how your answers to parts (a) and (b) are related.

2. Study Figure 19-5 again. If this DNA segment were replicated in a cell, how would the resulting DNA compare with that in the diagram?

3. A segment of the left-hand strand of a DNA molecule has the following base sequence: A, T, G, C, C, T, T, A. List the base sequence you would expect to find on the right-hand strand.

4. Prepare a concept map showing how the following scientific researchers, specimens, tools, techniques, and events are related: Martha Chase, Francis Crick, Rosalind Franklin, Alfred Hershey, James Watson, Maurice Wilkins, bacteriophages, *E. coli*, laboratory research, library research, measurement, mechanical models, radio-active atoms, X-rays, discovery of DNA's role in living things, discovery of DNA's structure, discovery of the code of life.

Problem Solving

1. Study Figure 19-6 again. Sketch the single DNA strand from which this RNA strand must have been copied. (The DNA has to split into two strands before RNA copies can be made.) Sketch the entire double-stranded DNA as it must have appeared before it split.

2. For many years, biologists thought that the four nitrogenous bases (A, C, G and T) of DNA were present in equal proportions. Suggest how they might have reached this incorrect conclusion. What do you think might have made biologists realize that DNA *could* act as a code-carrying chemical?

Extensions

1. Read *The Double Helix* by James D. Watson. Write a brief commentary that explains how the discovery of DNA differs from the usual list of steps given to describe the scientific method.

2. During the early 1940s, a group of American researchers headed by O.T. Avery produced evidence from bacterio-phage experiments that DNA is the molecule that carries the ''code of life.'' Consult an encyclopedia, college biology text, or other reference work to find out why few biologists found Avery's work convincing.

CHAPTER
20

Cell Structure and Function

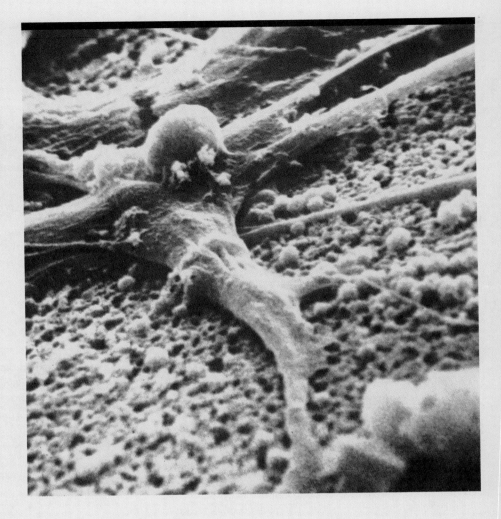

In ancient Mesopotamia, medicine was practised by priest-physicians who performed chants and incantations as well as surgery. The Mesopotamians believed that disease was caused by evil spirits entering the patient's body.

Many cultures have shared the Mesopotamians' beliefs. Ancient peoples could not draw conclusions about the causes and nature of disease because they could not observe the body at the microscopic level. The Mesopotamians, as well as other ancient peoples, knew little about anatomy and nothing about cellular structure.

Although the ancient Greeks saw no more than the Mesopotamians, they employed a more rational analysis. They made careful observations and correlated disease symptoms with their observations of time, place, season, and the physical workings of the body. The Greeks established a theory of illness that dominated western medicine for centuries.

The Greeks had observed that the expulsion of body fluids often preceded a patient's improvement. This led them to conclude that a balance of bodily fluids was required for health. The Greeks believed the four elements of which everything was composed — earth, air, fire, and water — corresponded to the four bodily "humours" of blood, phlegm, black bile, and yellow bile. Health was maintained by the proper balance among these bodily fluids or humours.

Understanding of the body's internal physiology was slow in coming. For centuries, anatomical study was prohibited by Christianity, Judaism, and Islam. Even when organs were described anatomically, their functions were misinterpreted in the light of humouralism. Organs with cavities such as the heart, bladder, and kidneys were believed to attract and trap humours. Spongy organs such as the lungs absorbed humours from surrounding tissues.

The development of the light microscope along with detailed anatomical study eventually discredited the theory of humouralism. Only when microscopists were able to study life at a scale thousands of times smaller than had previously been possible were cells recognized as the units of life. This was followed by studies of the function of organs, of the chemistry of body function, and of bacteria's role in causing disease. The discovery that bacteria are associated with certain illnesses completed the rejection of the theory of humours.

Modern understanding of illness starts at the chemical and cellular levels. Whether they are caused by internal or external factors, diseases are the products of alterations in cell structure and function that affect organs, tissues, and complex systems within the body.

Despite these technological advances, medical science still does not completely understand the causes and cures of disease. Further advances in electron microscopy and biochemistry should reveal structure in even finer detail and lead researchers to a greater understanding of cellular structures and processes.

Chapter Objectives

When you complete this chapter, you should:

1. Appreciate the role of cells as the smallest units of life, and be able to explain how features common to all cells underlie the great structural and functional diversity of living things.

2. Be able to identify and to describe several tools and techniques used by cytologists in the study of cellular structure and function.

3. Appreciate both the limits and the tentative nature of current cytological knowledge.

4. Know how to prepare and to stain a variety of tissues for viewing with a compound microscope, and be able to draw labelled diagrams of the cellular structures you observed.

5. Be able to name all cell organelles presently known, identify them in prepared slides, photomicrographs, or electron micrographs, and describe their structure and function.

6. Be able to relate the presence and number of certain organelles to overall cell function.

7. Be able to identify the generalized cell as a useful scientific model, list its characteristics, and explain how it differs from real cells.

8. Based on an understanding of their structural and functional differences, be able to distinguish between plant and animal cells in prepared slides, photomicrographs, or electron micrographs.

9. Be able to identify several vital cell processes, understand why all life depends on them, and explain how they depend on the relationship between cell structure and function.

The study of the cell is called **cytology.** From 1590 until early in this century, cytologists depended on the compound microscope to reveal the details of cell structure. Although more powerful microscopes are now available, the compound microscope is still a much valued tool in modern testing laboratories, which use it to examine many types of tissue and to observe the cells within these tissues.

However, using the compound microscope to study individual cells and organelles presents a considerable challenge. Since large organisms are made up of millions and millions of cells layered one on top of another, it is often difficult to isolate and view single cells. Individual cells are small, and their organelles and subcellular structures are smaller still. To further complicate the problem, cell parts are essentially transparent and are not easy to distinguish from one another. To overcome these challenges, cytologists have developed techniques to slice large cell masses into very thin sections or to break them down into smaller fragments.

You have probably used a compound-light microscope in many of the laboratory exercises in this textbook. Unlike electron microscopes that use electron beams to form images, compound microscopes use light. Compound microscopes are called "compound" because they have a system of lenses rather than the single lens of the simple microscope.

LABORATORY EXERCISE 20-1
Observing Cell Organelles with a Compound Microscope

In earlier studies, you learned that cells contain many different organelles. However, no one cell actually shows all of these types. In this exercise, you will examine several types of cells to observe the organelles prominent in each. To do this, you will need to use a variety of staining and preparation techniques. For this reason, your teacher may decide to have you carry out these procedures over several class periods.

Tools for Extending the Senses

As a tool for extending human vision, the compound microscope is limited by its restricted resolving, contrasting, and magnifying ability. **Resolving power,** or resolution, is the ability of an instrument to produce separate images of two objects that are very close together. Even the best compound microscope cannot distinguish between objects closer than 0.2 μm, which is about 20 times the thickness of a cell membrane.

The limited resolving power of the compound microscope results because it depends on visible light to form images. The image-forming behaviour of visible light can be compared to the behaviour of water waves with a long wavelength (waves with their crests far apart). In Figure 20-1, the wave pattern

The micrometre (μm) and the nanometre (nm) are units of measurement biologists use to measure objects they observe under a microscope. A micrometre is $\frac{1}{1000}$ of a millimetre and a nanometre is $\frac{1}{1000}$ of a micrometre.

- 1 μm = 10^{-6}m
- 1 nm = 10^{-9}m

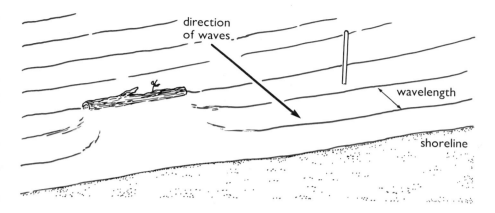

FIGURE 20-1 The wave pattern reaching the shore forms an indistinct "image" that reveals the presence of the log. However, the wavelength is too great for the water waves to form an image of the narrow post.

reaching the shore clearly shows the presence of the large obstacle, but gives no indication that a small obstacle is also present. Similarly, light waves are noticeably disrupted by large objects such as whole cells or nuclei, but not by cell membranes or by any other feature smaller than 0.2 μm across.

In addition, the ability of a compound microscope to show any contrast between cell organelles and the fluid surrounding them is limited because both are transparent. Another limitation of the compound microscope is that the maximum magnification it is capable of is only 1500×, which is not enough to see most cell organelles.

Throughout the history of science, however, there has been a strong link between the search for fundamental knowledge and the invention of related technology. As a result, tools have either been based on the acquisition of new knowledge or developed to probe it more deeply. Between 1930 and 1939, the quest for greater knowledge about the internal structure of cells led to the development of more powerful microscopes. The superior resolution, contrast, and magnification of these microscopes have resulted in an explosion of new information for cytologists.

Under ideal conditions with a geometric test specimen such as a printed grid or field of regular dots, a perfectly shaped human eye can resolve objects only 0.1 mm apart. But with biological specimens under average viewing conditions, the resolving power of an average human eye is about 0.2 mm or 200 000 nm. Therefore, the eye can only appreciate the resolving power of a microscope when the object under view is magnified until its resolution reaches 200 000 nm.

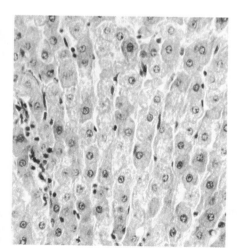 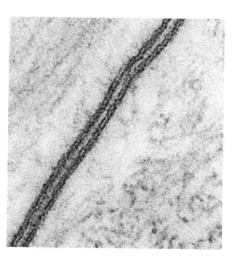

LEFT: Low magnification and low resolving power limit the amount of detail that can be seen of a cell membrane with a compound microscope.

RIGHT: High magnification and high resolving power enable the electron microscope to reveal much more of the cell membrane's structural details.

The phase contrast microscope uses the wave properties of light to make many small details more visible. **Left:** Liver cells without phase contrast. **Right:** The same cells with a phase contrast microscope.

Phase Contrast Microscope

Cytologists often fix and stain tissues to make their transparent organelles visible under a compound microscope. However, this process kills the cell. The **phase contrast microscope** provides contrast and definition to the organelles of still-living cells without the need for staining. Its operation depends on two important characteristics of light. First, light behaves like waves that travel in alternating peaks and valleys of energy intensity. Second, light travels at different speeds through different transparent materials. (For example, the speed of light through diamond is only 40% of its speed through air.)

A phase contrast microscope rearranges the incoming light by breaking it into pairs of beams whose peaks and valleys are perfectly aligned. The matching beams are then sent through the cell sample from different angles and recombined afterward by a powerful condensing lens. Only beams that remain aligned can be viewed through the lens. If one beam slows down as it passes through a cell organelle, its peaks and valleys may no longer match the other beam. Where they cancel each other out, a dark patch will be observed. This method makes some organelles and other cell structures shine out like stars against a dark background.

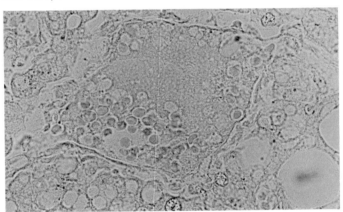
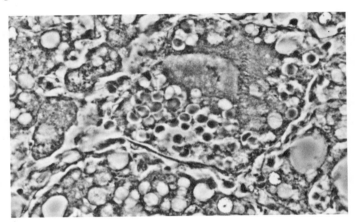

Transmission Electron Microscope

More detail of cell structure can be observed with a **transmission electron microscope.** (See Figure 20-2.) The magnification and resolution of a transmission electron microscope is much greater than that of a compound microscope. The transmission electron microscope uses a beam of electrons instead of light to form the image of a specimen. Electron beams have much shorter wavelengths than visible light. (See Figure 20-3.) So, they can pass between and bounce off objects that are very close together. As a result, the electron microscope provides much better resolution.

Since electrons do not travel well through air, a vacuum must be maintained in the body of the microscope. To maintain the vacuum, the electron microscope must be airtight and strongly built. (As a result, electron microscopes are extremely expensive.) Electron beams are focussed by electromagnets

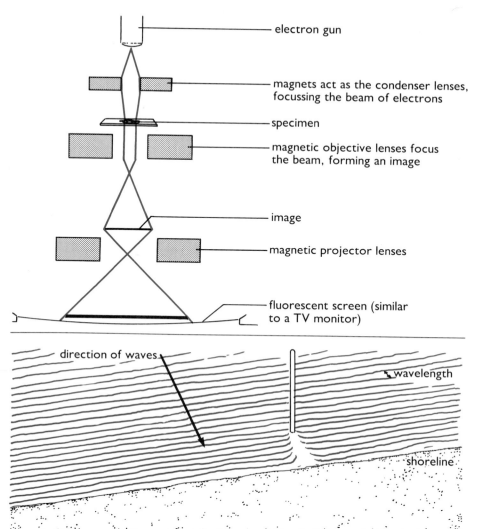

electron gun

magnets act as the condenser lenses, focussing the beam of electrons

specimen

magnetic objective lenses focus the beam, forming an image

image

magnetic projector lenses

fluorescent screen (similar to a TV monitor)

FIGURE 20-2 A schematic diagram of a transmission electron microscope. As the electrons pass through the specimen, their original wave pattern is altered. The rearranged pattern is displayed when the electrons strike the coated inside of a fluorescent screen.

direction of waves

wavelength

shoreline

FIGURE 20-3 Passing water waves are deflected by the post when their wavelength is shortened to half the post's width. Similarly, a short wavelength beam of electrons is deflected by the smallest cell features.

A transmission electron microscope

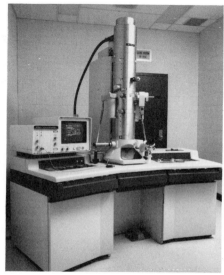

instead of by the glass lenses used to focus beams of light in compound microscopes. The image formed by the transmission, deflection, and absorption of electrons is displayed on a fluorescent screen similar to a television screen. Modern transmission electron microscopes can magnify objects well in excess of $200\ 000\times$. They can also distinguish objects as close together as 1 nm, about $\frac{1}{100\ 000}$ the thickness of a pinpoint.

The main disadvantage of the transmission electron microscope is that specimens must be dead, dehydrated, and very thinly sliced. These preparation techniques minimize the random scattering of electrons, which are easily deflected or absorbed. However, these preparation techniques may also alter the specimen, resulting in an image that is not an accurate representation of the living material.

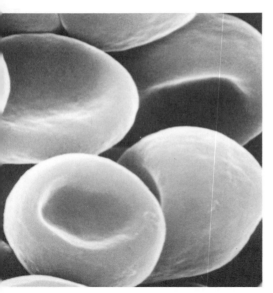

Blood cells seen through a scanning electron microscope

Scanning Electron Microscope

The **scanning electron microscope** has two main advantages over the transmission electron microscope. First, it allows direct observation of surface features and, second, the images have a three-dimensional appearance. However, the resolution of a scanning electron microscope is not as high as that of a transmission electron microscope, but it is ten times greater than that of a compound microscope.

In a scanning electron microscope, electrons are bounced off the surface of a specimen. (See Figure 20-4.) So, the specimen does not have to be cut into thin sections. Instead, it is coated with a very thin layer of metal such as gold. Then the specimen is scanned, back and forth, by a thin beam of high-energy electrons. The rebounding electrons are captured by an amplifier and used to form an image on a monitor. Because they appear to be three-dimensional, scanning electron micrographs are easier to interpret than the two-dimensional transmission electron micrographs. Recently, a type of scanning electron microscopy that allows for the examination of living specimens has been developed.

FIGURE 20-4 A schematic diagram of a scanning electron microscope. As the electron beam moves back and forth, it excites the surface atoms of the specimen, which emit secondary electrons. Their pattern varies according to the surface features of the specimen. An electron detector relays this pattern to a fluorescent screen.

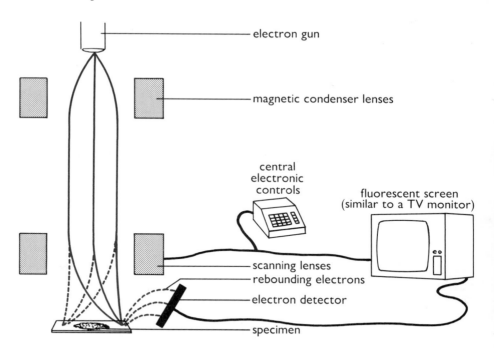

Techniques for Preparing Biological Specimens

Preparing individual cells and cell parts for observation with an electron microscope is much more challenging than preparing specimens for viewing under a compound microscope. The procedures most commonly used are fixation, embedding, thin sectioning, and differential centrifugation.

Fixation involves the use of various chemicals to preserve and dehydrate a specimen. The process must be done quickly so the specimen does not change from the time it is killed until it is viewed. Fixatives coagulate the cell proteins, harden the gels, and deactivate most enzymes. Fixatives can also affect tissue, causing it to react better to certain stains. Electron microscopists have experimented with a wide variety of chemical solutions to find those that will stop cell activity quickly and still provide clear, accurate images of the cells.

Embedding is a technique used to suspend a soft specimen in a block of material so it can be cut into thin slices. Usually, embedding consists of pouring a liquid such as melted wax, agar medium, or epoxy resin around the specimen, and allowing it to solidify. The resulting block holds the specimen in a stationary position ready for thin sectioning.

In **thin sectioning,** the block containing the specimen is mounted on the holder of a **microtome,** which has a very sharp glass or diamond blade. As the specimen block moves back and forth across the blade, very thin slices, or sections, are cut from it. The gear mechanism of the microtome can be adjusted to cut sections to the desired thickness, which is usually between 0.025 and 0.1 μm.

Differential centrifugation separates and isolates cell organelles, making it possible to study their individual structures and functions. The cells are broken up in preparation for this process by placing them in a cold sugar solution and grinding them in a blender. The resulting mixture is then spun in a centrifuge at various speeds. (See Figure 20-5.) Cell organelles and fragments of broken cells settle to the bottom of the centrifuge tubes at rates relative to their size and density. Larger and denser organelles such as nuclei settle faster than fragments of cell membrane or smaller, less dense organelles such as mitochondria. The isolated organelles can then be viewed with an electron microscope or used in biochemical tests.

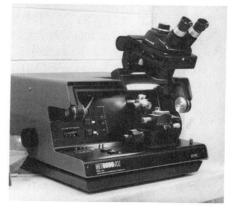

A microtome

An average cell yields about 200 sections when it is sliced as thinly as possible for viewing under an electron microscope.

FIGURE 20-5 Cell organelles can be isolated using differential centrifugation.

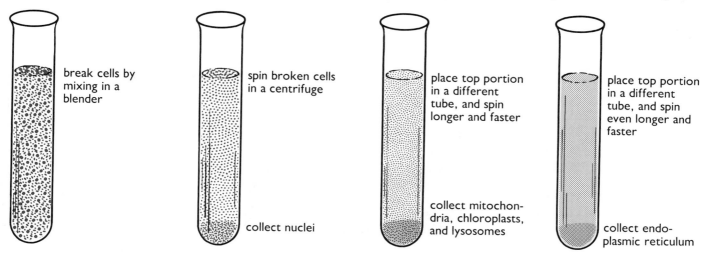

break cells by mixing in a blender

spin broken cells in a centrifuge

collect nuclei

place top portion in a different tube, and spin longer and faster

collect mitochondria, chloroplasts, and lysosomes

place top portion in a different tube, and spin even longer and faster

collect endoplasmic reticulum

Meet
Marika Winnett

Marika works as an electron microscopist in the Pathology Department of Women's College Hospital in Toronto. With the electron microscope, she examines tissue to help doctors diagnose diseases.

Q. *What is an electron microscope?*

A. An electron microscope produces high magnification by using a beam of electrons instead of light. There are two types—one that creates an image on a fluorescent screen, and one that uses a scanning beam that is measured electrically and feeds a signal to a television monitor.

Q. *What are you looking for?*

A. We examine cell structure for abnormalities. When a diagnosis of a piece of tissue can't be done with a light microscope, we do it with the electron microscope. With a light microscope you can magnify up to 3000×, but with the electron microscope we can magnify up to 300 000×. People find it hard to grasp that it's possible to see a cell in such detail.

Q. *What kind of tissue do you examine?*

A. For example, a tissue sample from an enlarged lymph node will first be examined by the histology lab (where organic tissues are studied), using the light microscope. But if the histology lab can't make a diagnosis with the light microscope, we will then examine it with the electron microscope.

Q. *How do you prepare the tissue for examination?*

A. We put small pieces of tissue (about 1 mm in size) in a universal fixative for a few hours. Then the samples are rinsed and post-fixed in a solution of osmium tetroxide and distilled water. The tissue pieces are then put through a series of processes so that they end up in the form of a block. A section is sliced from the block and examined, using the light microscope. If necessary, a doctor will look at the tissue in the light microscope to determine if it should be examined in the electron microscope.

Q. *Does the electron microscope require even smaller sample sizes?*

A. Yes—10 000× thinner. These are then mounted on tiny copper grids just a bit bigger than a pinhead. We then examine, or do what's called a "scoping" of the section. The final step is developing and printing the film of the sample.

Q. *What is a typical day like in this laboratory?*

A. Depending on what stage of the processing we've reached, we will either be preparing the tissue specimen and cutting it into thin slices or scoping.

Q. *Are there any hazards?*

A. We use hazardous chemicals and deal with diseased tissue, so there are dangers. We have safety procedures to follow. Because of AIDS, we now take even more precautions. Also, working on the electron microscope can be hard on the eyes, so we don't use the microscope for more than 4 h.

Q. *What qualities are important for this work?*

A. You have to be patient and neat. Cleanliness is essential, because if anything gets dirty it has to be thrown out. You have to be well co-ordinated and have good small-motor control, especially when slicing thin tissue sections. The tissue samples are so tiny it can be frustrating, but I don't know any other branch of technology that is as fascinating.

Cell Biology and the Nature of Science

Current scientific knowledge about cells is the result of centuries of study. Continuing development of more sophisticated tools and techniques has dramatically altered our view of the cell during the past 50 years. You can probably expect a similar broadening of knowledge about cells in your lifetime, and some of what you learn now may not be current in the future.

Much of scientific knowledge is simply the best explanation for what scientists understand today. A future discovery might alter slightly, or change completely, scientific views in a particular field. If existing theories cannot explain new scientific evidence, then the theories must be modified to reflect the new evidence.

Section Review Questions

1. a) Which branch of biology concerns the study of cells?
   b) What instrument first made this study practical? When?

2. a) How does the resolving power of a microscope affect its usefulness?
   b) How does the contrast of a microscope affect its usefulness?
   c) How does the magnification of a microscope affect its usefulness?

3. a) What advantage(s) does a phase contrast microscope have over a compound microscope?
   b) What advantage(s) does an electron microscope have over a compound microscope?

4. Briefly explain the procedures for preparing a specimen for observation under an electron microscope.

5. Compare the transmission electron microscope and the scanning electron microscope.

20.2 A Survey of Cell Parts

The cell is often described as the basic structural and functional unit in all living things. But tremendous diversity in structure and in function can be observed at the cellular level. For example, muscle cells exert contractile forces; stomach cells secrete digestive juices; and nerve cells conduct electricity. Whatever function an organism may require, a cell seems to exist that can perform that function.

The tools and techniques of modern cytology have revealed in great detail the nature of the components that enable cells to assume so many forms and play so many roles. In this section, you will examine what cytologists currently know about the structure and function of each cell part or organelle. As you

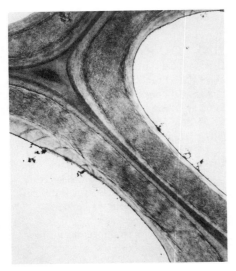
Thick and sturdy plant cell walls help cells retain their shape.

Some membrane carbohydrates are combined chemically with proteins. These molecules remain embedded in the phospholipid layers. Other carbohydrates form short chains that extend beyond the phospholipids. These carbohydrate chains help to hold adjacent cells together. They also act as receptors for hormones, antibodies, and any viruses with a similar shape.

read, look for evidence of a relationship between the structure of each organelle and its specific function. You should also realize that the information presented here reflects what scientists know today. As investigative tools and methods improve, some aspects of scientific thinking about cell structure may also change.

Cell Walls

Cell walls are found around the cells of plants, fungi, many protists, and all bacteria. The rigid cell wall gives the cell its shape, and provides protection and support for all other cell parts. Cell walls must therefore be strong, yet porous enough to let materials pass between the cell and its external environment. Chemical studies show that most plant cell walls are composed primarily of cellulose (a polysaccharide). Fungal cell walls are mainly chitin, a nitrogen-containing polysaccharide. Bacterial cell walls contain amino acids as well as polysaccharides. Animal cells do not have walls.

Cell Membrane

Cells must be able to absorb and retain the materials necessary for life but also rid themselves of toxic wastes. To do this, a cell possesses a selectively permeable barrier between itself and the surrounding environment called a **cell membrane.** The structure of the cell membrane enables it to control substances entering and leaving the cell.

The cell membrane is only about 7.5 nm thick and cannot be seen clearly with a compound microscope. Through an electron microscope, it appears as two parallel lines or layers. Chemical tests on isolated fragments of cell membranes show that these layers contain a few proteins and carbohydrates but consist mainly of complex, double-ended molecules called **phospholipids.** (See Figure 20-6.)

FIGURE 20-6 Each phospholipid molecule has two ends with distinctly different characteristics. The phosphate head is attracted to water, while the lipid tail is repelled by water. When surrounded by watery fluids (such as those inside and outside a cell), these molecules line up as shown with the lipid ends inside.

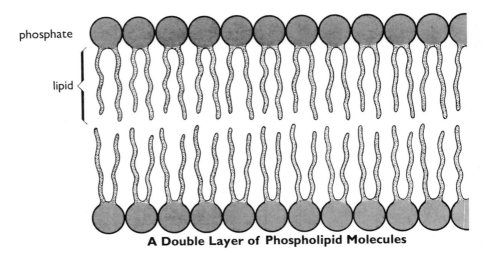

A Double Layer of Phospholipid Molecules

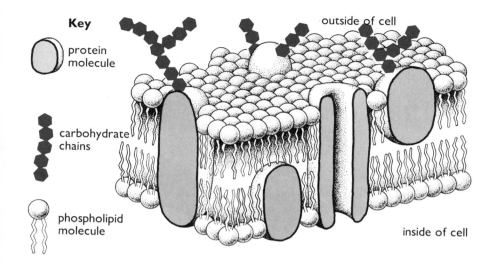

Key

⬭ protein molecule

⬡ carbohydrate chains

🦠 phospholipid molecule

outside of cell

inside of cell

FIGURE 20-7 The fluid mosaic model of the cell membrane. A double phospholipid layer is studded with large proteins formed by twisted chains of amino acids. Carbohydrates (chains of sugar molecules) extend from the outside proteins.

DID YOU KNOW?

The fluid mosaic model in Figure 20-7 followed years of debate about the structure of the cell membrane. It was first proposed by S.J. Singer and J.L. Nicholson in 1972 after years of research. All other models biologists use today are very similar.

Figure 20-7 shows the most widely accepted explanation of the structure of the cell membrane put forward so far. The **fluid mosaic model** suggests that the phospholipid molecules lie side by side in two layers. The "lipid" ends of the molecules face each other, while the "phospho" ends face away, thereby forming the inner and the outer surfaces of the membrane. Cytologists believe that the proteins and carbohydrates are embedded in the phospholipid layers similar to the way tiles are embedded in a mosaic—hence the model's name. The "fluid" part of the model's name is derived from the fact that the components of the membrane are always moving. Phospholipid molecules are able to migrate sideways along the membrane's surface, and certain proteins remain embedded in the membrane only temporarily. When they leave, other protein molecules move in to take their place. The fluid nature of the membrane allows it to seal itself when it is broken.

The structure of the cell membrane allows it considerable control over the materials that enter and leave the cell. It does not, however, control the movement of water. Whether water moves in or out of the cell depends on how the concentration of water molecules inside the cell compares to the concentration of those outside the cell.

The membrane surrounding a cell accounts for only one-tenth of the membranous material it contains. In fact, the cell interior is divided into distinct regions by systems of internal membranes. The most visible such region, the nucleus, is separated from the rest of the cell by a membranous nuclear envelope. (Organelles such as mitochondria and chloroplasts are also enclosed by membranes very similar in structure to the cell membrane.)

The cell membrane is also known as the plasma membrane.

DID YOU KNOW?

The cell membranes of animals and some other organisms also contain molecules of cholesterol, but most bacterial membranes do not.

A cross section showing cell membranes in a cat's intestine

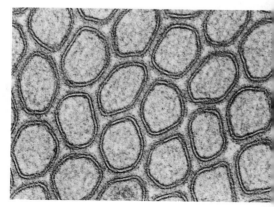

Cytoplasm

Cytoplasm is the complex mixture that lies between the cell membrane and the nuclear envelope. Several types of cellular components called cytoplasmic

Cytoplasmic organelles include only those structures within the cytoplasmic space. Therefore, although the nucleus is also an organelle, it is not a cytoplasmic organelle.

The cytoplasm and nucleus together are sometimes referred to as protoplasm.

FIGURE 20-8 The nuclear envelope consists of a double membrane with many pores, or openings, which allow passage of large molecules.

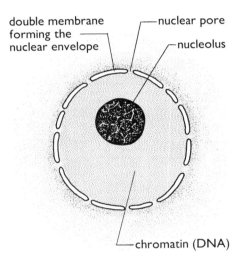

double membrane forming the nuclear envelope — nuclear pore

— nucleolus

— chromatin (DNA)

organelles are suspended in a fluid consisting of water, dissolved substances such as minerals, carbohydrates, and proteins, and numerous, large molecules that are nonsoluble. These substances circulate in the cytoplasmic space and are used by the organelles in various metabolic reactions. The exact composition of the cytoplasm changes somewhat as materials move into or out of the cell, and as new cell products or wastes are produced.

Nucleus

As the cell's largest organelle, the **nucleus** is easily seen through a compound microscope. The electron microscope has revealed that the nucleus is surrounded by a **nuclear envelope** consisting of two membranes separated by a narrow space as illustrated in Figure 20-8. The numerous small pores of the nuclear envelope allow certain materials to pass between the nucleoplasm inside the nucleus and the cytoplasm outside it. The nucleoplasm contains the cell's DNA and one or more spherical masses called **nucleoli.** (The singular form is nucleolus.)

Even under an electron microscope, DNA cannot be seen clearly. DNA usually appears as a scattered collection of tangled strands called **chromatin.** Chromatin is so named because these strands absorb coloured stains easily. Only when the cell is dividing do the strands of chromatin coil up to form **chromosomes** that can be seen under a compound microscope. The chemical code embedded in the DNA provides all the instructions the cytoplasmic organelles need to manufacture cell products. The nucleoli, which are not membrane-bound, are present only when cells are not undergoing cell division. They consist of protein and nucleic acids, and play an important role in the production of ribosomes.

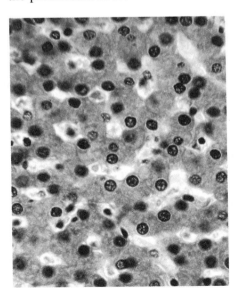
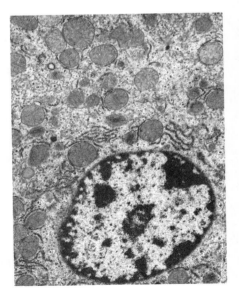

LEFT: The nuclei of mammalian liver cells seen through a compound microscope
RIGHT: The nucleus of a mammalian liver cell seen through an electron microscope

V THE UNITY OF LIFE

Ribosomes

Ribosomes are roughly spherical cytoplasmic organelles that are either free-floating or attached to internal membranes. (See Figure 20-9.) At less than 30 nm in diameter, they are too small for even electron microscopes to reveal much detail. Chemical studies of samples purified by centrifugation show that ribosomes are composed of proteins and nucleic acids, and that their function is protein synthesis. In other words, ribosomes produce all cell proteins. Some proteins will become structural components of the cell, and others will be used as enzymes or hormones. Free-floating ribosomes manufacture proteins for use within the cell. Attached ribosomes manufacture proteins for use outside the cell.

Protein production is an extremely vital cell function. Even bacteria, which lack all other cytoplasmic organelles, do have ribosomes. Viruses, which have no means of producing their own proteins, must invade living cells to gain control of the cells' ribosomes.

Endoplasmic Reticulum

The **endoplasmic reticulum** is a membranous system of long tubules and canals that connects the nuclear envelope to the cell membrane. As you can see in Figure 20-9, there are two types. Rough endoplasmic reticulum has

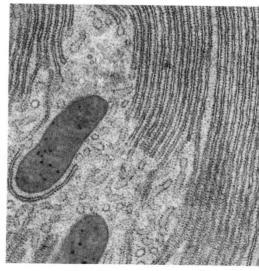

Rough endoplasmic reticulum (the straight lines) is dotted with numerous ribosomes (the black dots). If there are no ribosomes, it is called smooth endoplasmic reticulum.

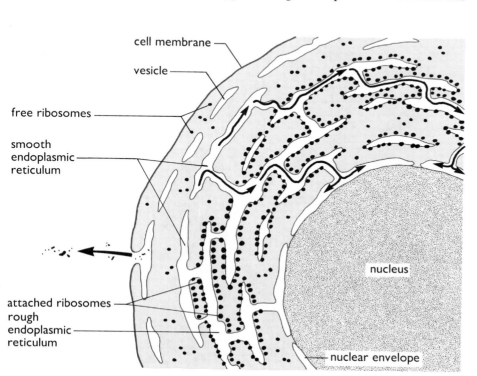

FIGURE 20-9 Proteins and lipids are transported both within the endoplasmic reticulum and within vesicles.

FIGURE 20-10 A cut-away model of a Golgi apparatus

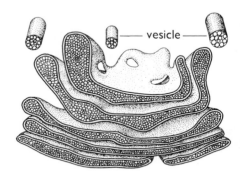

A cross section of the Golgi apparatus

ribosomes attached to the membrane. Smooth endoplasmic reticulum lacks ribosomes. Both types function in the transport of proteins and lipids. Proteins manufactured by the ribosomes on rough endoplasmic reticulum travel through the membrane network until they reach the smooth endoplasmic reticulum. At this point, a small portion of the smooth membrane pinches off, forming a membrane-bound sac called a **vesicle.** The vesicle then carries the protein directly to the membrane for secretion outside the cell or to the Golgi apparatus for further processing.

Golgi Apparatus

The **Golgi apparatus,** or Golgi body, usually takes the form of a system of membrane-bound vesicles arranged like a stack of saucers. (See Figure 20-10.) It often appears to be connected with the endoplasmic reticulum. Cytologists think that the Golgi apparatus adds fat and sugar molecules to the proteins produced by the ribosomes on the rough endoplasmic reticulum. The finished products collect in membranous vesicles, which pinch off and are then expelled through the cell membrane. The Golgi apparatus is especially prominent in cells such as the pancreatic cells that secrete hormones or enzymes.

Mitochondria

Mitochondria are the site of cellular respiration in all organisms except bacteria. Under a compound microscope, mitochondria are barely visible. Under an electron microscope, most mitochondria appear as rod-shaped structures approximately 3 μm long and 1 μm wide, although their sizes and shapes may vary considerably. Like the nucleus, each mitochondrion has two separate membranes with a space between each. (See Figure 20-11.)

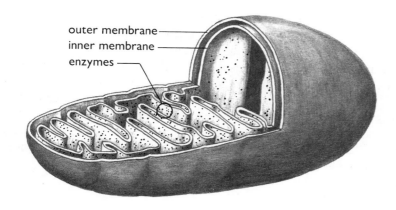

outer membrane
inner membrane
enzymes

FIGURE 20-11 A mitochondrion has two membranes. Convoluted extensions of the inner membrane are studded with the enzymes needed for cellular respiration.

Mitochondria at work in the heart muscle

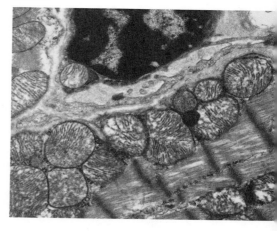

The inner membrane is enfolded many times to form finger-like projections called cristae. Cristae are covered with the enzymes required for cellular respiration. The extensive folding provides a very large surface area on which the chemical reactions of respiration can take place. The degree of folding of the inner membrane varies with the energy requirements of the cell. Cells that are very active such as those in the heart muscle or in the growing tips of plant roots have mitochondria with extensively folded inner membranes. In less active cells such as fat-storage cells the inner membranes are folded to a lesser degree. The number of mitochondria present in cells also varies according to need. For example, the average heart-muscle cell contains far more mitochondria than the average skin cell.

Mitochondria have their own DNA to direct their functions. In humans, mitochondria are inherited quite separately from the chromosomes that determine all other inherited characteristics. They also reproduce independently from the chromosomal reproduction that occurs in the nucleus. In fact, all of your mitochondria are direct descendents of your mother's mitochondria, which, in turn, were direct descendents of her mother's mitochondria and so on. This happens because all the cytoplasm of a newly formed zygote comes from the egg.

Plastids

Plants and some unicellular autotrophs contain membrane-bound organelles called **plastids.** There are two types: leukoplasts and chromoplasts. Cytologists think that plastids can change from one type to another. Leukoplasts are colourless plastids that store the energy-rich products of photosynthesis in the form of starch. Chromoplasts contain pigments such as the red, orange, or yellow molecules that give colour to many different flowers and fruits. Chloroplasts belong to this group. But they contain chlorophyll, which is the pigment responsible for the green colour of most plants, many algae, and some protists.

Chloroplasts

Chloroplasts are the organelles responsible for photosynthesis, the process that manufactures glucose from water, carbon dioxide, and solar energy. Easily seen with a compound microscope, chloroplasts vary in size and shape. Often they are oval, usually 5-8 μm in length. (See Figure 20-12.) Some algae have only one chloroplast per cell, whereas some plants have hundreds. The electron microscope reveals that a chloroplast has a double membrane and contains an elaborate system of internal membranes surrounded by an enzyme-rich fluid. These membranes form stacks of plate-like structures with hollow interiors that contain dissolved ions (electrically charged particles). The chlorophyll molecules needed for photosynthesis are embedded in the membranes themselves. Membranous connections can be seen between adjacent stacks. The membranes, fluid, and chlorophyll each play a different role in photosynthesis. You will learn more about photosynthesis in Chapter 21.

Chloroplasts also contain their own DNA, and reproduce independently of the nucleus much as mitochondria do.

FIGURE 20-12 A chloroplast also has two membranes. Extensions of the inner membrane contain the chlorophyll needed for photosynthesis.

A tomato plant showing the chloroplast's large membranous surface area

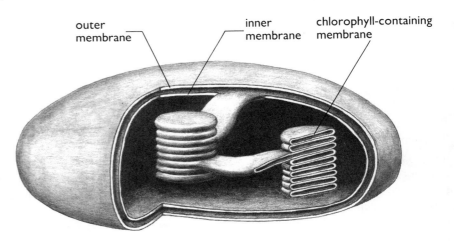

outer membrane   inner membrane   chlorophyll-containing membrane

Vacuoles

Vacuoles are not usually regarded as part of the cytoplasm. They are fluid-filled spaces surrounded by a membrane identical to that surrounding the cell. Like cell membranes, vacuole membranes are able to control the materials that pass through them. Vacuoles occur in many cell types, but they are most prominent in the cells of plants and plant-like organisms. (See Figure 20-13.)

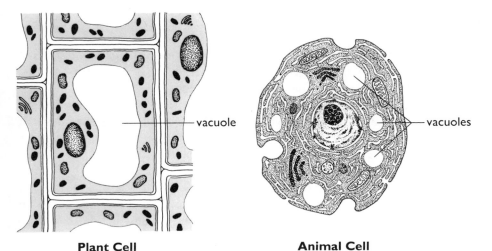

Plant Cell   **Animal Cell**

In plants, pressure from the fluid inside the vacuoles helps keep the cell's outer membrane pressed firmly against the cell wall. Plant vacuoles also help regulate the amount of water to the cytoplasm.

In heterotrophic protists, food vacuoles are prominent. (See Figure 20-14.) Food vacuoles contain water-laden food particles that become membrane-bound as they pass in through the cell membrane. Food vacuoles circulate in the cytoplasm until the food is digested. Undigested materials are held back until they are eventually expelled from the cell.

In many protists, excess water and dissolved wastes accumulate in contractile vacuoles, which periodically contract to expel their contents. Contractile vacuoles serve a homeostatic function by maintaining stable conditions in the cell cytoplasm, and some biologists do regard them as organelles.

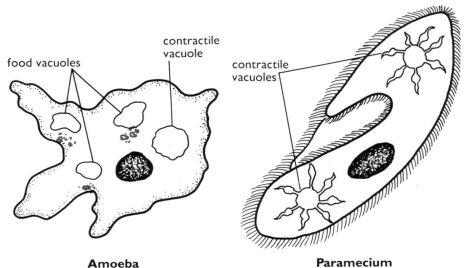

FIGURE 20-14 This amoeba has several food vacuoles as well as a contractile vacuole. The paramecium has two contractile vacuoles surrounded by collecting tubules.

Amoeba   **Paramecium**

Lysosomes

Lysosomes are roughly spherical membrane-bound organelles cytologists think are formed by the Golgi apparatus. (See Figure 20-15.) Lysosomes do not have a significant internal structure, but they do contain a variety of enzymes. Lysosomes have three main functions. First, in unicellular organisms, they combine with food vacuoles and release digestive enzymes that break down food particles. Second, in some animals, lysosomes assist the immune system. For example, lysosomes are abundant in human white blood cells. When white blood cells engulf disease-causing bacteria, lysosomes release enzymes that digest the foreign organisms. Third, in many organisms, lysosomes appear to cause old, malfunctioning cells and cell organelles to destroy themselves. The products of this cellular self-destruction move into the extracellular fluid and are then used by other living cells.

Lysosomes also appear to perform an important role in the development of some animals. For example, a tadpole loses its tail and grows legs as it develops into a frog. During this process, lysosomes digest certain existing cells such as those in the tail. The products that result from this breakdown are then absorbed by the tadpole's bloodstream, and used as nutrients to help produce the new cells needed to form the legs of the frog.

Cells must manufacture all of their own organelles. Enzymes in lysosomes are manufactured on ribosomes. They then travel to the Golgi apparatus via the endoplasmic reticulum.

FIGURE 20-15 Lysosomes contain powerful digestive enzymes able to destroy entire cells. They are much more common in animal cells than in plant cells.

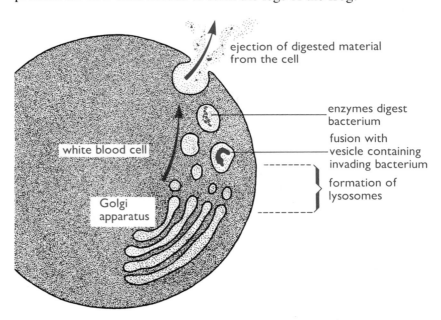

ejection of digested material from the cell

enzymes digest bacterium

fusion with vesicle containing invading bacterium

formation of lysosomes

white blood cell

Golgi apparatus

Microfilaments and Microtubules

Microfilaments are long, thin protein fibres that are able to contract. (See Figure 20-16.) Microfilaments are similar in composition to actin, a protein

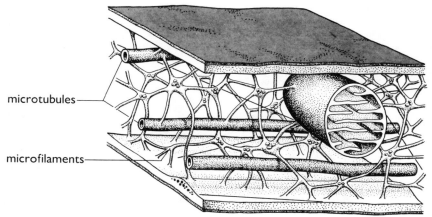

microtubules

microfilaments

FIGURE 20-16 Microfilaments and microtubules form a network throughout the cell. They appear to be attached to both the membrane and to various organelles, and function both in maintaining the shape of the cell and in cell movement.

FIGURE 20-17 A microtubule is a thin cylinder composed of spherical protein molecules.

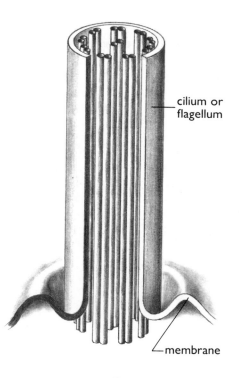

cilium or flagellum

membrane

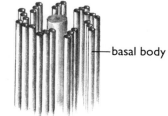

basal body

FIGURE 20-18 Although cilia and flagella grow from basal bodies, the microtubules from which they are formed differ in number and arrangement. The "core" of the basal body is not a microtubule.

that is involved in the contraction of muscle cells. Biologists think that cytoplasmic streaming in amoebas or paramecia results from the contraction of microfilaments in the cytoplasm.

Microtubules are long, hollow, fairly rigid cylinders composed of protein molecules. (See Figure 20-17.) Their cylindrical structure enables them to perform a variety of functions. First, they form the **cytoskeleton,** which helps give the cell its shape. Second, microtubules help support long, thin cell parts such as those found in nerve cells. Third, microtubules are used in the construction of basal bodies, cilia, flagella, and centrioles. (See Figure 20-18.)

Centrioles and Basal Bodies

Centrioles occur in most animal cells and in the cells of some simple plants. They are formed by a bundle of nine microtubule triplets. Centrioles occur as short pairs of cylinders arranged at right angles to one another. A pair of

LEFT: The microtubules of centrioles are arranged like the spokes of a wheel.

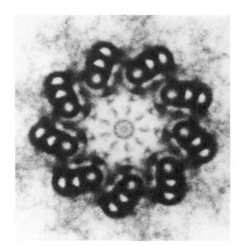

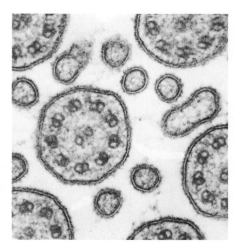

RIGHT: A cross section of basal bodies

centrioles is often called a centrosome and is located close to the nucleus of the cell. Centrioles are most active during cell division when they help redistribute chromosomes. You will learn more about cell division in Chapter 22.

Basal bodies have the same structure as centrioles and are produced by them. Flagella and cilia grow out of basal bodies. When the cilia and flagella are complete and ready to move, the basal body provides an anchor or a support base.

INQUIRY ACTIVITY
Interpreting Electron Micrographs

The electron microscope, because of its much greater magnification and better resolving power, has provided scientists considerably more information about cells and tissues than they were able to obtain using the compound microscope. It is important for biologists and biology students to be able to read and interpret pictures taken using the electron microscope.

This activity will help you improve your interpretation skills. Study the electron micrographs on pages 623–624 and answer the following Discussion Questions.

Discussion Questions

A. Look at electron micrograph 1, which shows all but a small portion of a single cell.

1. a) Identify cell part A.
   b) What enabled you to identify it?
   c) What is the principal function of cell part A?
   d) How does A's structure and composition suit it to perform this function?

V THE UNITY OF LIFE

2. Repeat Question 1 for cell parts B to H.

3. a) Which kingdom is this cell sample probably taken from?
   b) Which structural features suggest that the cell sample is from this kingdom? Explain how you were able to eliminate the others.
   c) Identify the largest single structure in the cell and describe its function. What part of this structure enables it to perform this function?
   d) Identify the dominant cytoplasmic organelle (the one that occurs most often). What does its dominance suggest about the overall function of the cell?

Electron Micrograph 1

B. Look at electron micrograph 2, which shows three cells but only a small portion of each one.

1. a) Which structural feature makes it possible to count the cells?
   b) What is this structure made of, and what is its main function? What other functions does it also perform?
2. a) Identify the largest organelle shown. What is its function?
   b) Which characteristics confirm this identification?
3. a) Which kingdom is this cell sample probably taken from?
   b) How do the structures referred to in Questions 1 and 2 suggest that the cell sample is from this kingdom rather than from another kingdom?
   c) Which other visible organelle confirms the kingdom you have identified? Describe the structure and function of this third organelle.

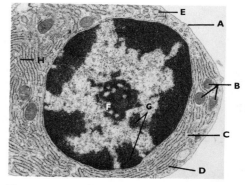

Electron Micrograph 2

C. Look at electron micrograph 3, which shows several bumpy structures (J) attached to a relatively smooth surface (K).

1. a) Identify the bumpy structures.
   b) What are they made of, and what is their function?
2. a) The smooth surface is also a cell part. What is it called?
   b) What is it made of, and what is its function?
3. a) In some cells, unattached structures like J are found scattered through the cell cytoplasm. Compare their function with the function of J.
4. a) Some cells also contain a smooth-surfaced part that resembles K but lacks the attached bumpy structures. What is the name of this smooth-surfaced part?
   b) What is it made of, and what is its function?
   c) Compare its function with the function of K.

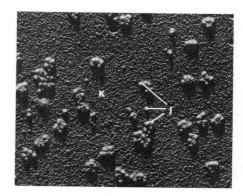

Electron Micrograph 3

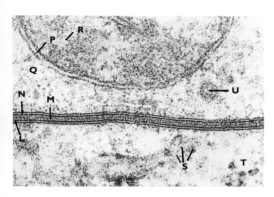

Electron Micrograph 4

D. Look at electron micrograph 4, which shows a close-up view of a tissue sample.

1. How many cells does this micrograph show in whole or in part? Explain how you know.

2. a) Look closely at the stripe running down the middle of the image. What does it represent?
   b) The stripe includes three distinct regions: L, M, and N. Which cell part makes up regions L and N? Briefly describe the model biologists use to explain the appearance of this cell part.
   c) Explain how you know that region M is *not* a cell part. Identify region M and describe its probable composition.

3. a) Identify structure P. Identify the structure surrounded by P.
   b) Why is region R so much darker in colour than region Q?
   c) Compare the structure and function of P to the structure and function of N.

4. a) Identify the scattered dark structures marked S. Why are there so many of these structures?
   b) What is the probable identity of structure T? Of structure U? Explain why you may find it difficult to be sure.
   c) Which would be more helpful in confirming the identity of T and U— greater magnification or greater resolution? Explain why.
   d) Identify the type of electron microscope used to take this micrograph and explain how you know. Repeat this question part for electron micrographs 1, 2, and 3.

Section Review Questions

1. a) What is cytoplasm?
   b) List the components of cytoplasm briefly and describe their general function.

2. Prepare a simple chart that shows how structure and function are related for the following organelles: a) cell membrane, b) Golgi apparatus, c) mitochondrion, and d) chloroplast.

3. a) Which organelles are found in plant cells but not in animal cells?
   b) Relate the function of these organelles to their presence in plants.

4. a) Identify the two types of endoplasmic reticulum and explain how they differ.
   b) What is the overall function of the two types?

5. How does the nucleus differ from other cell organelles in structure and in function?

V THE UNITY OF LIFE

The Microtrabecular Lattice

The electron microscope is the principal tool of the cell biologist. Although electron microscopes give scientists the ability to study cellular structures in minute detail, they do so at the expense of depth. To produce high resolutions, standard electron microscopes require material to be sliced to a thickness of less than 0.2 μm. The result reveals little of the cell's three-dimensional structure.

Recently developed high-voltage electron microscopes permit researchers to view cell specimens several micrometres thick. The effect produced is like an X-ray.

This change in perspective has produced a controversy. Cytoplasm appears almost entirely empty of structures when it is viewed in thin sections. But when it is viewed in thick sections, it appears to be crowded with microtubules, microfilaments, and other proteins.

Some researchers have used these thick sections as evidence for the existence of a three-dimensional network of protein filaments called the microtrabecular lattice. This lattice, which is believed to span the cytoplasm, includes those filaments normally associated with the cytoskeleton microtubules, microfilaments, and intermediate filaments. Established theory says these filaments function with relative independence to produce cell shape, loco-motion, elasticity, division, internal organization, and movement. However, according to the lattice theory, short, thin proteins called trabeculae link these filaments with each other as well as with virtually all other cytoplasmic components. The result is a shifting, but highly organized protein lattice in which cellular organelles are embedded.

Proponents of the microtrabecular lattice theory think the lattice not only stabilizes cytoplasmic organelles, but may also facilitate cellular processes. Scientists suspect many enzymes, which are important for easing protein synthesis and other cellular processes, may be associated with the lattice just as organelles are. This possibility is attractive. By arranging the opposition of organelles and enzyme systems, the microtrabecular lattice would ensure a high rate of efficiency for cellular processes.

However, the evidence of thick sections from high-voltage electron micrographs has been questioned. Some researchers believe the numerous filaments seen in thick sections are an illusion created by the techniques used in sample preparation. Also, the trabeculae proteins, which appear to be between 2–4 nm in diameter, have yet to be isolated. Critics of the lattice theory believe that if these proteins were essential to the lattice, then it would be possible to isolate them from the cytoplasm.

More research will be required to determine whether the microtrabecular lattice is an important part of cytoplasm or an optical illusion.

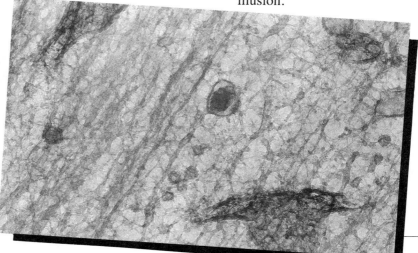

20.3 Cell Models and Living Cells

In biology, as in other sciences, models are used to visualize objects that are difficult to observe or ideas that are difficult to understand. Cytologists find a model of a "generalized" cell useful. The generalized cell is a composite picture of all known cell organelles. Although no real cell contains all of these features, the generalized cell is a useful model for understanding the structure and function of real living cells.

The Generalized Cell

Each specific type of cell has features that make it different from other types of cells. However, biologists find it useful to generalize that all animal cells

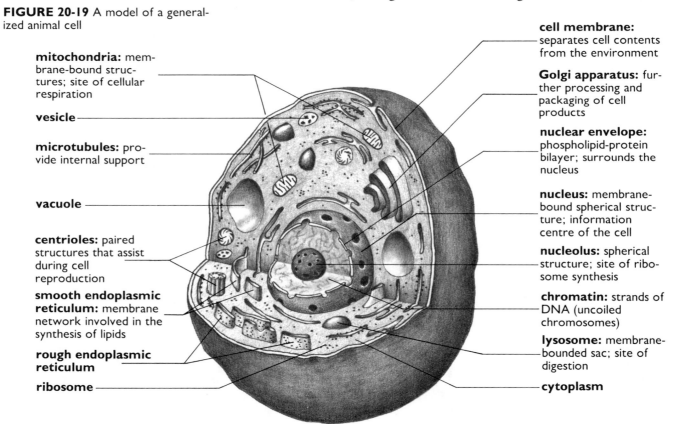

FIGURE 20-19 A model of a generalized animal cell

mitochondria: membrane-bound structures; site of cellular respiration

vesicle

microtubules: provide internal support

vacuole

centrioles: paired structures that assist during cell reproduction

smooth endoplasmic reticulum: membrane network involved in the synthesis of lipids

rough endoplasmic reticulum

ribosome

cell membrane: separates cell contents from the environment

Golgi apparatus: further processing and packaging of cell products

nuclear envelope: phospholipid-protein bilayer; surrounds the nucleus

nucleus: membrane-bound spherical structure; information centre of the cell

nucleolus: spherical structure; site of ribosome synthesis

chromatin: strands of DNA (uncoiled chromosomes)

lysosome: membrane-bounded sac; site of digestion

cytoplasm

have certain features in common, and all plant cells also share certain characteristics. The models in Figures 20-19 and 20-20 provide a generalized view of animal and plant cells. But while biologists speak of "typical" plant cells and "typical" animal cells, there are no real cells like the ones in the models. Except for examples like the unspecialized meristematic cells found in plants, most cells are specialized, and the organelles they contain reflect their specialization.

Heart muscle cells illustrate clearly how much a real animal cell may differ from the model. While the typical animal cell has some mitochondria to provide energy for the cell's functions, heart muscle cells must have many more. Heart muscle cells work constantly for an animal's lifetime. Therefore, they require far greater amounts of energy than many other kinds of cells. Also, heart muscle cells contain far more protein fibres, elements that enable muscles to contract.

FIGURE 20-20 A model of a generalized plant cell. Which features of the generalized animal cell do not appear here? Which features appear in this model but not in the other? What do these differences imply about cell functions?

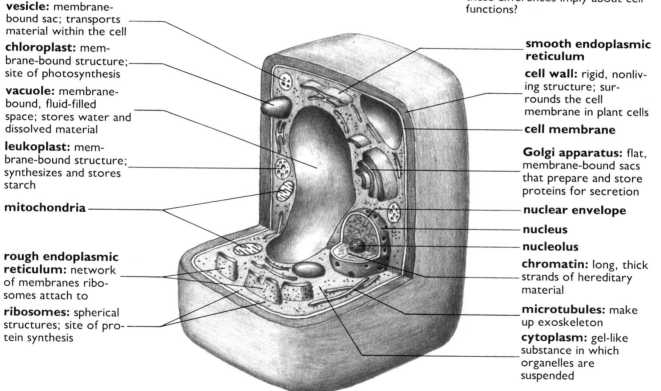

vesicle: membrane-bound sac; transports material within the cell

chloroplast: membrane-bound structure; site of photosynthesis

vacuole: membrane-bound, fluid-filled space; stores water and dissolved material

leukoplast: membrane-bound structure; synthesizes and stores starch

mitochondria

rough endoplasmic reticulum: network of membranes ribosomes attach to

ribosomes: spherical structures; site of protein synthesis

smooth endoplasmic reticulum

cell wall: rigid, nonliving structure; surrounds the cell membrane in plant cells

cell membrane

Golgi apparatus: flat, membrane-bound sacs that prepare and store proteins for secretion

nuclear envelope

nucleus

nucleolus

chromatin: long, thick strands of hereditary material

microtubules: make up exoskeleton

cytoplasm: gel-like substance in which organelles are suspended

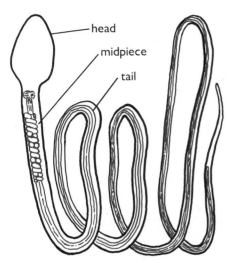

FIGURE 20-21 An animal sperm cell is highly specialized.

Sperm cells are even more specialized. (See Figure 20-21.) Unlike typical animal cells, sperm cells are divided into three regions: the head, the midpiece, and the tail. The head of the cell has a cap containing enzymes that enable sperm to penetrate an egg cell. The head also contains the nucleus. The midpiece is packed with mitochondria that produce the energy required for the sperm's constant, rapid motion. Behind the midpiece is a single flagellum, consisting of bundles of microtubules enclosed in a sheath. This tail section is used for locomotion, and very few other animal cells are capable of such independent locomotion. Overall, a sperm cell bears little resemblance to a typical animal cell.

Highly specialized plant cells also seem to differ from the model of a typical plant cell. For example, the green chlorenchyma cells that form the inner layers of a leaf are specialized for food production. These cells contain large numbers of chloroplasts to carry out photosynthesis. However, their cell walls are thin, and chlorenchyma tissue is spongy and delicate as a result.

By contrast, the transparent epidermal cells that form the top and bottom layers of a leaf are specialized for protection. Their extra-thick cell walls prevent the delicate inner tissues from being crushed. In addition, many epidermal cells exude a waxy coating that prevents dehydration, and their lack of colour lets light through to the chlorenchyma layers.

However, regardless of their exact structure and function, all plant cells and all animal cells have many features in common. The models enable biologists to visualize all that is known about each type of cell. However, as improved observational tools and techniques yield new data, these models may change.

RESEARCH PROJECT
The Cell Model So Far

Although the compound microscope and the electron microscope have provided biologists with enormous amounts of information about cells over the years, much remains to be discovered. For example, cytologists know that skin cells, nerve cells, and muscle cells in an organism have identical sets of DNA. But cytologists do not know exactly why skin cells develop into *skin* cells and not into nerve or muscle cells.

Many areas of cell biology like the previous example are the subjects of current research in the laboratories of universities, hospitals, and research institutes all over the world. The findings of researchers are shared around the world through scientific journals. Keeping informed of new developments through such journals is an important part of every researcher's work.

Review a variety of scientific publications in your school's resource centre or in your local library. Identify an area of cell biology in which new discoveries are being made. After some preliminary reading, select a specific topic for more intensive research. Present a report on your research topic to your class. Be sure to follow your teacher's suggestions about the length and format of your report.

The Living Cell

Just as organs enable your body to carry out your daily activities, organelles enable a cell to carry out its life functions. In the following laboratory exercise, you will observe living cells as they take in molecules from their surroundings, alter them chemically, and return new substances to the external environment.

LABORATORY EXERCISE 20-2
Observing Cell Activity

Yeast cells are microscopic, unicellular fungi that live on the surfaces of fruits and seeds. As single-celled organisms, they are capable of the same cellular processes as other types of cells. Yeast cells take in nutrients from their environment, perform respiration, grow, and reproduce. In this exercise, you will observe yeast cells carrying out these important life functions.

Cell Processes

The living yeast cells you observed in the previous exercise carry on at a cellular level most of the functions associated with life. These functions are often called cell processes because they must be carried out by all living cells. There are four main cell processes you can observe in yeast or in any other type of cell: production of substances, storage and release of energy, transport of materials, and cellular reproduction. Each process is associated with particular organelles. Biologists often compare these organelles to factories, powerhouses, and transport systems.

Cellular Factories

The primary function of certain organelles is the production of chemical substances. Some organelles such as lysosomes break down large molecules into smaller, simpler ones. Others such as ribosomes take simple building-block molecules and use them to *assimilate*, or build up larger, more complex chemical substances. Ribosomes take simple amino acids from the cytoplasm and use them to manufacture protein molecules. Some of these molecules are structural proteins that are used for cell growth or the production of new cells. Other proteins are enzymes or hormones that may be used directly by the cell to regulate chemical changes, or they may be stored and secreted from the cell for use elsewhere in the organism.

The chloroplasts found in the cells of plants and algae also function as cellular factories. These organelles are able to convert the simple raw materials—carbon dioxide and water—into glucose. The glucose can then be used directly as a source of energy by the plant or algal cell, or it may be stored and used later by the same organism or by another organism if it is eaten.

Cellular Powerhouses

All cells obtain the energy they need for their life functions from chemical reactions. Plant cells store the sun's energy by means of photosynthesis, a chemical reaction that takes place in the chloroplasts. The sugars and starches produced by photosynthesis are used by other organisms as food—a source of stored energy. In most organisms, mitochondria are the organelles that release this stored energy. Through the process of cellular respiration, mitochondria convert the food energy stored in glucose into a form of energy that can be used directly by other cell parts. Both the manufacture of chemical substances and the release of usable energy involve numerous chemical reactions. These processes are referred to collectively as cellular metabolism.

Cellular Transport

If the major function of a cell is to produce a complex chemical substance, it must be able to transport raw materials into itself. Similarly, all cells produce metabolic wastes and must be able to rid themselves of these harmful products. The organelles that play important roles in cell transport include the cell membrane, the endoplasmic reticulum, and the Golgi apparatus. You will learn more about the important roles played by these organelles in Chapter 21.

Cellular Reproduction

All living things including cells need to reproduce. Whenever growth occurs or damaged tissues are repaired, new cells are produced. For most organisms, the cell parts involved in reproduction include the nucleus and the microtubules of the centrioles.

In Chapters 21 and 22, you will learn more about these four vital cell processes.

Conclusion

Throughout this chapter, you have observed the close relationship between structure and function in various cell organelles. In Chapters 21 and 22, you will learn how the processes that take place in living cells depend on this relationship.

Section Review Questions

1. a) What is a model and how can it be used in science?
   b) Briefly describe the generalized cell model and explain why it is useful to biologists.

2. a) Which organelles do a typical plant cell and a typical animal cell have in common?
   b) List the organelles that are unique to plant cells and those that are unique to animal cells.

3. How do living animal cells differ from the generalized cell? Explain why, using specific examples to support your answer.

4. a) What is a cell process?
   b) Which four cell processes must be performed by all living cells?
   c) List the organelle(s) most closely associated with each process in part (b).

The Giant Axon
of the Squid

Of all the incredibly varied types of cells found in our bodies, perhaps none has greater impact on our lives than the nerve cell. Nerve cells gather information from the environment; they carry and pass along electrical messages; and, ultimately, in their many millions, form the brain itself.

Yet the average nerve cell is a small, delicate bit of membrane, organelles, and extensions. Studying individual nerves was considered impossible until 1936 when an anatomist dissected an odd string of whitish tissue from the mantle of a squid. This tissue appeared at first to be part of the blood system. It turned out to be a bundle of giant nerve fibres or axons.

The squid has one defence against its many predators. When alarmed, the animal ejects water and ink from a siphon in a form of jet propulsion, pushing itself away from danger with blinding speed and leaving a confusing cloud behind. Its muscles must react extremely rapidly and powerfully for this method to be effective. Since larger nerves transmit impulses more quickly, evolution in the squid has led to the development of truly immense axons, allowing its ''flight'' instructions to travel the entire length of its body within a millisecond.

Almost everything discovered to date about nerve action—and probably much of what is left to find out—has been learned using the living model provided by the giant axons of the squid. Microscopic tools, including voltmeters, can be placed inside the membrane to measure the chemical and electrical changes taking place during a nerve impulse. In a technique called patch clamping, a tiny glass tube containing a fine electrode is placed directly on the surface of the squid's nerve membrane. The glass seals tightly, isolating a patch. This process is fine enough to record the movement of ions through only one membrane channel.

One of the most recent discoveries was made by just looking at a living axon. Recorded by a video camera, tiny sacs called vesicles could be seen moving about in the axoplasm, the jelly-like fluid that lies just inside the axon's outer membrane. These vesicles were found to carry important proteins, including neural transmitters, from the body of the nerve to its extensions. They move along a network of microtubules drawn by the action of a protein called kinesin.

The squid is a creature long valued for its tasty flesh. Now the opening of each year's squid fishing season has a whole new meaning as scientists investigate the operations of a most unusual and important cell.

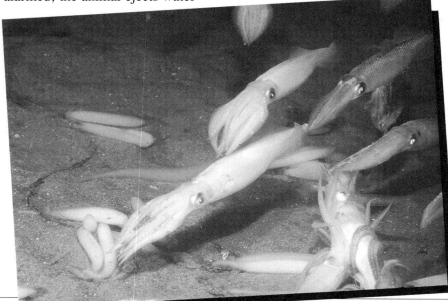

Experiments on the giant axon of the squid revealed much about nerve cells.

Chapter Review

Key Words

basal bodies	microtubules
cell membrane	mitochondria
cell walls	nuclear envelope
centrioles	nucleoli
chloroplasts	nucleus
chromatin	plastids
chromosomes	resolving power
cytology	ribosomes
cytoplasm	scanning electron
cytoskeleton	microscope
endoplasmic reticulum	transmission electron
fluid mosaic model	microscope
Golgi apparatus	vacuoles
lysosomes	vesicle
microfilaments	

Recall Questions

Multiple Choice

1. The organelle that is not present in animal cells is the
   a) nucleus
   b) cell wall
   c) mitochondrion
   d) ribosome

2. The "powerhouse of the cell" is the
   a) ribosome
   b) mitochondrion
   c) endoplasmic reticulum
   d) Golgi apparatus

3. Which of the following is used to prepare a specimen for viewing with the scanning electron microscope?
   a) thin sectioning
   b) metallic coating
   c) fixation
   d) embedding

4. During centrifugation, cell organelles and fragments are separated on the basis of
   a) function
   b) structure
   c) size and density
   d) mass

5. Which of the following is not a membrane-bound organelle?
   a) nucleus
   b) chloroplast
   c) Golgi apparatus
   d) centriole

6. Which of the following synthesizes proteins for use within the same cell?
   a) free-floating ribosomes
   b) attached ribosomes
   c) endoplasmic reticulum
   d) Golgi apparatus

Fill in the Blanks

1. _____ function as the site of photosynthesis in plant cells.

2. An electron microscope has greater _____ power and greater _____ than a compound microscope.

3. The electron microscope uses a beam of _____ rather than light to illuminate the object.

4. The _____ prepares proteins for secretion.

5. The _____ supports and protects the softer parts of the cell.

6. The _____ are the site of protein synthesis.

7. The internal membranous cell structure dotted with ribosomes is called _____.

8. The finger-like projections inside the mitochondria are called _____.

9. _____ contain powerful digestive enzymes capable of breaking down an entire cell.

10. Cilia, flagella, and centrioles all contain _____as part of their internal structure.

Short Answers

1. a) Define resolving power and explain how it differs from magnification.
   b) Which is more important to cytologists? Why?

2. List several similarities and several differences between the compound microscope and the electron microscope.

3. Compare the structure and function of the cell membrane with the structure and function of the cell wall.

4. Compare the structure and function of plant-cell vacuoles with protist-cell vacuoles.

5. Describe the relationship between ribosomes and the endoplasmic reticulum.

6. a) Briefly describe the fluid mosaic model of the cell membrane.
   b) How was the evidence that supports this model obtained?

7. Why is it important that cell membranes are selectively permeable?

8. Identify three types of plastids. Briefly describe the structure and function of each type.

9. Which organelle packages protein products such as hormones for secretion from the cell? Briefly describe how these products are secreted.

10. Identify five cell organelles that are membrane-bound. Identify one that is not.

11. Summarize the function of the following cell structures in a table: a) cell membrane, b) microfilaments, c) ribosomes, d) centrioles, and e) chloroplasts.

12. Identify the cell structures that perform the following functions: a) locomotion, b) internal transportation, c) waste disposal, and d) energy production.

Application Questions

1. a) Compare the advantages and the disadvantages of the compound microscope with those of the electron microscope.
   b) Which microscope has had the greatest impact on cytology? State reasons for your answer.

2. a) Compare image formation by a phase contract microscope with image formation by a transmission electron microscope.
   b) Which microscope would be most useful to a cytologist? Explain why.

3. a) Compare specimen preparation for viewing with a scanning electron microscope with specimen preparation for a transmission electron microscope.
   b) Which microscope would be most useful to a cytologist? Explain why.

4. Heart cells and sperm cells are not typical animal cells. List several other kinds of plant or animal cells that are atypical. In each case, state reasons for your selection.

5. Would you expect the degree of specialization to be greater in the cell of a unicellular organism or in a single cell from a multicellular organism? State specific examples to support your answer.

Problem Solving

1. You are a forensic scientist. A small piece of tissue has been found at the scene of a crime. How would you determine the nature of the specimen? In particular, what would you look for to determine whether the specimen is plant or animal tissue?

2. a) Suppose the main function of a certain group of plant cells is to perform photosynthesis. What evidence would exist for this function if a microscopic examination were made of the cells?
   b) What type of microscope would be needed to observe this evidence? Describe how the specimen would be prepared for viewing.

3. a) Hormones are chemical secretions produced by specialized cells in glands. The hormones can then enter the bloodstream to perform specific functions in the body. Which cell organelles would be evident in the cells that produce hormones?
   b) What preparation technique might help to reveal the presence of these organelles, and what type of microscope would be best for viewing them?

4. Invent a new type of cell that is able to perform photosynthesis, perform locomotion in a water environment, produce protein secretions, and feed itself when sunlight is not available. Ensure that the new cell has all of the necessary organelles and cellular specializations. Draw a diagram of the new cell.

5. a) List the organelles that are found in bacterial cells. List those that are not found.
   b) Do bacterial cells perform any of the functions associated with the "missing" organelles? If so, explain how those functions are performed. If not, explain why bacteria do not need to perform those functions.

6. There are no blood vessels near mature sperm cells when the sperm are released. Where do the mitochondria of the sperm obtain the raw materials they need for cellular respiration?

Extensions

1. Use the library resource centre in your school and other available resources to research the structure of some highly specialized animal cells. Choose one type of specialized cell and do the following.
   a) Draw a diagram of the cell.
   b) Write a brief description of the cell.
   c) Compare the cell with a typical animal cell.
2. Write a report about the involvement of Canadian scientists in the development of the electron microscope.

CHAPTER

21

Cell Physiology: Transport and Energy

Globally, less food is consumed by humans than is lost to insects, plant diseases, and spoilage during distribution. Researchers are helping solve this problem by developing technology such as Modified Atmosphere Packaging (MAP). With this new technology, meat, fish, poultry, pasta, baked goods, and fresh produce can be safely stored much longer under various modified atmospheres.

To deliver food to market in consumable condition, two processes must be controlled. First, stored food of any kind must be protected from pathogenic organisms—bacteria and fungi that use the product as their own food. Additional control is necessary to store fruits and vegetables. These foods continue cellular respiration after harvest, and eventually, they can become overripe.

Modified Atmosphere Packaging uses a modified gaseous environment as a preserving agent. Gases such as carbon dioxide, nitrogen, oxygen, argon, and helium are used in proportions tailored to the product being preserved.

MAP is effective because respiratory enzymes do not function efficiently at high concentrations of carbon dioxide or low concentration of oxygen. Ripening slows, and growth of bacteria and fungi is inhibited. While either reduced oxygen or elevated carbon dioxide can slow respiration and ripening, the two effects are additive. Fresh colour does not deteriorate because modified atmospheres slow the loss of green chlorophyll, as well as the production of other plant pigments. Bumps and other physical injuries to fruit under modified atmospheric conditions do not develop unsightly bruising. As well, watertight packaging slows the spread of pathogens.

There are some harmful effects that may result from storage atmospheres that vary from the optimum. Although low oxygen may slow aerobic respiration in apples, if the oxygen concentration falls below a certain level, anaerobic processes that produce off-flavours and tissue breakdown begin. There is a strict range of requirements that define optimum storage conditions for each kind of food. If conditions deviate from these parameters, MAP effectiveness becomes unreliable.

Safety is one concern that remains about MAP. In general, the same conditions that slow cellular respiration in food slow respiration in bacteria and fungi. However, optimum conditions for each of these two desired effects may differ. Some health officials fear certain conditions might inhibit the growth of the micro-organisms that warn consumers of spoilage— organisms that produce conspicuous effects and off-odours—but may not inhibit pathogenic organisms whose presence may be undetectable to the senses. Research into the relationship between spoilage and pathogens continues.

MAP technology is the direct result of an understanding of cellular processes. What other aspects of our lives are the result of such knowledge?

Chapter Objectives

When you complete this chapter you should:

1. Be able to define cell physiology, list three related cell processes, and explain their role in living cells.

2. Be able to use the basic principles of cell transport to explain how a living cell interacts with its external environment to maintain homeostasis.

3. Be able to identify both types of passive transport, construct simple models to demonstrate them, and determine how they are affected by changes in temperature and concentration.

4. Correctly use the terms isotonic, hypotonic, and hypertonic to describe and explain how concentration differences affect the net movement of substances across cell membranes.

5. Use your understanding of passive transport to predict the net movement of water through cell membranes under various conditions.

6. Be able to define active transport, list several types of active transport processes, and describe the models scientists use to explain them.

7. Be able to distinguish between passive and active transport, and describe some practical applications of the basic principles behind them.

8. Be able to list the main stages of photosynthesis, use word equations to describe it, identify the types of cells that perform photosynthesis, and explain its role in providing cellular energy.

9. Be able to list the main stages of cellular respiration, use word equations to describe both the individual stages and the overall process, identify the types of cells that perform respiration, and explain its role in providing cellular energy.

10. Use word equations to describe how some types of cells can obtain usable energy from food when no oxygen is available, and be able to explain how these energy-releasing processes differ from each other and from cellular respiration.

11. Be able to describe how the interactions between photosynthesis and cellular respiration help to maintain a constant environment for the entire planet.

21.1   The Role of Transport in Cell Physiology

Biologists classify the study of living things such as plants and animals into two related but distinct categories. Anatomy is the study of body structures. Physiology is the study of how the structures perform life functions. These terms are also used by cytologists. **Cell anatomy** is the study of structure in individual cells. In Chapter 20, you learned that each cell part is associated with one particular function. The study of these functions is called **cell physiology.**

Each living cell has the same basic biological needs, whether it is an independent unicellular organism or simply a single unit in a multicellular organism. These needs are met by the following cell processes.

Cell Division

All organisms depend on the division of individual cells for growth and reproduction. You will learn more about this important topic in Chapter 22.

Cell Metabolism

In order to grow, a cell must be able to carry out hundreds of different chemical reactions at the same time. The sum total of these reactions is called **metabolism.** You will examine those metabolic reactions that provide energy for cell activities in Section 21.3. (The reactions that manufacture cell parts and products are a topic for more advanced studies.)

Cell Transport

Each cell must maintain a suitable internal environment for its metabolic reactions. To do this, a cell must obtain the materials it needs for metabolism from its external environment. It must also dispose of waste products. Without efficient transport methods, the cell cannot obtain materials for reactions or growth, or energy for activities and cell division. In this section, you will consider how the simplest and smallest molecules enter and leave living cells, and you will investigate the transport of larger particles in Section 21.2.

Homeostasis and the Cell Environment

All living things are affected by their environment and must interact with it in order to survive. Similarly, the individual cells of a multicellular organism are also affected in the same way. The immediate environment of a cell is the extracellular fluid that surrounds it. (See Figure 21-1.) Individual cells must obtain the nutrients they need from this fluid and release the wastes they produce into it. Extracellular fluid is a solution. The solvent is water. The dissolved solutes include sugars such as glucose, gas molecules such as oxygen and carbon dioxide, and ions from salts such as sodium chloride.

Ions are charged particles. Examples of small ions include the sodium and potassium ions that play such an important role in the transmission of nervous impulses. A sodium ion consists of a single sodium atom from which one electron has been removed, resulting in a positive charge for the ion. Sodium ions can pass readily across cell membranes.

     V THE UNITY OF LIFE

The amount of solute in a solution is usually expressed in terms of concentration. Concentration compares the amount of solute in equal volumes of solution. For each solute dissolved in extracellular fluid, the concentration varies from place to place in the body. For example, oxygen is more concentrated near the aorta than near the feet. Concentration also varies from time to time. The concentration of oxygen in an athlete's extracellular fluid is greater just before a race than just after.

Despite these variations, each living cell must maintain a stable internal environment. Even though its external environment may be changing, solute concentrations inside the cell must remain nearly constant. Maintaining relatively stable conditions, whether in an entire organism or in a single cell, is called homeostasis.

The Problem of Homeostasis

Maintaining a constant internal environment is a major problem for large organisms, especially warm-blooded birds and mammals. Most human body functions, for example, operate efficiently only at a temperature close to 37°C. This temperature must therefore be maintained despite daily and hourly variations in outside temperatures since much variation will speed up or slow down or stop vital body functions. Internal water levels must also remain nearly constant, even though water is continually lost through perspiration and used up by processes such as digestion.

Like the organisms of which they are a part, individual cells must also maintain homeostasis. For cells, regulating the chemical composition of internal cell fluids despite concentration changes in the surrounding extracellular fluid and in the cell itself is a continuing problem. Without some method of transporting materials in and out of the cell, the concentration of essential solutes would change rapidly. For example, the mitochondria are constantly using the cell's own dissolved glucose and oxygen. More must be quickly obtained from the fluid outside the cell so the release of energy can continue. Meanwhile, the cell must dispose of the carbon dioxide being produced before it builds up to toxic levels. Similar in-and-out activity is needed to maintain correct levels of all other solutes.

In a way, the term homeostasis is misleading, since it suggests a static, stable, unchanging set of conditions. Therefore, it is important to realize that maintaining homeostasis is an active process. For a living cell, regulating a steady internal state involves never-ending activity, most of it centred on the cell membrane.

Diffusion across a Membrane

Diffusion plays a major role in transporting solutes across the cell membrane. **Diffusion** is the spontaneous movement of particles throughout a solution from

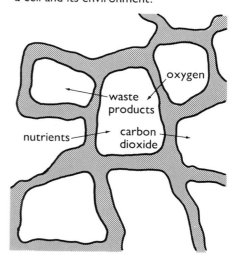

FIGURE 21-1 The extracellular fluid between cells contains solutes that must be exchanged between the contents of a cell and its environment.

This cocker spaniel is panting in an attempt to keep its body temperature constant on a hot summer day.

Eventually, the solute molecules diffuse throughout the water.

a region where the molecules are more concentrated to a region where the molecules are less concentrated. For example, if you add a spoonful of instant tea to a glass of water, the two materials will eventually produce a uniform solution even without stirring. This happens because the kinetic energy of the water molecules carries the flavour and colour molecules all through the water. Unless there is a barrier to their movement, the particles in a solution will diffuse randomly in all directions until the concentration is uniform everywhere.

The only barrier separating a cell's interior from its surroundings is the cell membrane, which defines the cell's limits and keeps its contents inside. The raw materials needed for cell activities must move across the cell membrane on their way into the cell. Useful cell products, as well as cell wastes, must move across the cell membrane on their way out of the cell. The cell membrane is able to control the movement of materials across it because it is semipermeable.

Homeostasis and Membrane Permeability

Many important solutes move across the cell membrane by means of diffusion. Substances differ in their ability to diffuse across cell membranes. Cell membranes are said to be selectively permeable because they allow some particles to pass through freely but restrict the passage of others.

A cell membrane can be compared to the paper sieve around a tea bag. The "holes" are big enough to allow only the small flavour and colour particles to pass through. The much larger tea leaves are held back. Similarly, a cell membrane will only let small molecules such as water or carbon dioxide diffuse across it. Larger molecules such as proteins and amino acids cannot diffuse across cell membranes. (See Figure 21-2.)

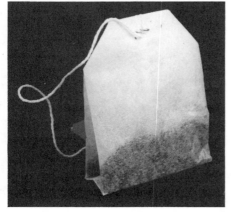

The gauze of this tea bag functions like a selectively permeable membrane.

V THE UNITY OF LIFE

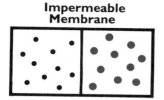
Impermeable Membrane

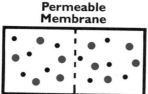
Permeable Membrane

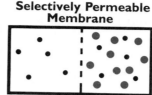
Selectively Permeable Membrane

FIGURE 21-2 Which of these membrane models is most like a cell membrane?

Permeability is determined by the properties of the cell membrane and the size and characteristics of the molecules involved. Small molecules can move more freely across cell membranes than large ones. Also, since the cell membrane is composed of phospholipid molecules, substances that are soluble in lipids move across cell membranes more easily than substances which are not. (See Figure 21-3.) There is also evidence that the selectivity of the cell membrane can change depending on the homeostatic needs of the cell.

In the tea-bag model of the cell, water and solute particles move through the pores of the sieve-like bag. The **selectively permeable membrane** of a living cell performs a similar function. Its pores permit molecules such as water to diffuse freely while blocking larger particles such as protein molecules and bacteria. In a tea bag, membrane selectivity depends entirely on the size of the pores. In a living cell, pore size is only one factor affecting diffusion across a cell membrane.

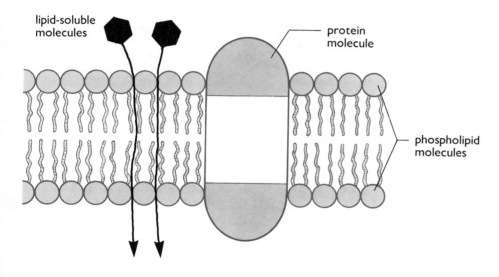

lipid-soluble molecules

protein molecule

phospholipid molecules

FIGURE 21-3 Substances that are lipid soluble move easily across cell membranes.

LABORATORY EXERCISE
21-1 Factors Affecting Diffusion

The rate at which flavour and colour molecules of tea move through a tea bag is greatly affected by temperature. Hot water "makes" tea much faster than cold water does. But a tea bag is a crude model of a cell. In this exercise, you will construct a more sophisticated model to investigate a variety of factors affecting diffusion across a selectively permeable membrane.

Passive Transport in Living Cells

In a simple cell model such as a tea bag, your laboratory model, or the one shown in Figure 21-4, all movement is caused by diffusion. Water molecules diffuse readily because they are already moving. Their own kinetic energy is enough to move them through the pores of the membrane into the bag. The coloured solute molecules diffuse outward, helped along by kinetic energy of the water molecules. Both the water and the solute move from regions of higher concentration to regions of lower concentration until concentrations inside and outside the membrane are identical. This process is called **passive transport** because it takes place without the need for energy from the cell.

FIGURE 21-4 The diffusion of water and food colouring through the cellulose membrane is an example of passive transport.

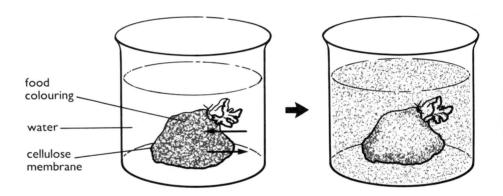

food colouring

water

cellulose membrane

Passive transport in living cells moves solutes such as gas molecules, minerals, and small ions across the membranes. Because the kinetic energy required for this movement is supplied by the molecules themselves, the cell does not have to supply any energy from its own mitochondria. As a result, many biologically important substances such as water, carbon dioxide, and oxygen can diffuse quickly across most cell membranes.

Consider the effect of passive transport on the animal cell in Figure 21-5. As the mitochondria carry out cellular respiration, they use up oxygen from the cytoplasm and release carbon dioxide at the same time. This means that the oxygen concentration inside the cell is always less than the oxygen concentration outside the cell. As a result, oxygen molecules diffuse inward— from the region of higher concentration (the extracellular fluid) toward the region of lower concentration (the cell cytoplasm). The carbon dioxide molecules also diffuse according to concentration. This means that the carbon dioxide molecules diffuse outward— from the region of higher concentration (the cell cytoplasm) toward the region of lower concentration (the extracellular

In plant cells that contain chloroplasts, the direction in which gas molecules diffuse is opposite to that observed in cells that do not photosynthesize. As the chloroplasts lower the cytoplasmic concentration of carbon dioxide, it diffuses inward from the extracellular fluid, providing the fresh supplies needed for photosynthesis.

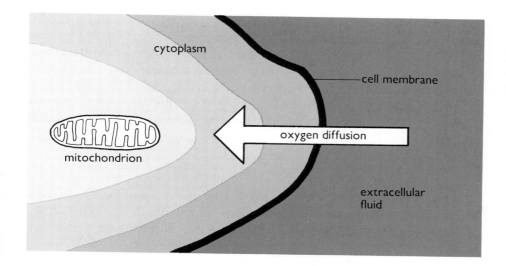

FIGURE 21-5 In this figure, colour intensity shows the concentration gradient that causes oxygen to diffuse into the cell. Carbon dioxide diffuses outward because its concentration gradient goes the other way.

fluid). All of this movement occurs spontaneously. Both the gas molecules and the water molecules in which they are dissolved possess kinetic energy.

Passive transport also moves the water itself in and out of the cell. Water makes up more than 70% of the mass of most organisms and 99.1% of the fluid in most cells. These levels reflect its great biological importance. First, water serves as a solvent that keeps many vital materials dissolved and ready to take part in cell reactions. Second, water plays a vital role in the metabolism of all cell types in all living things. In fact, the diffusion of water molecules across cell membranes is so common and so important that it has been given the special name of **osmosis.** Osmosis is the movement of water molecules across a selectively permeable membrane from a region of higher concentration of water molecules to a region of lower concentration of water molecules. You should remember that this concentration is the concentration of the water, not the concentration of any solutes that may be dissolved in the water.

Figure 21-6 shows a model for osmosis in a cell surrounded by pure water.

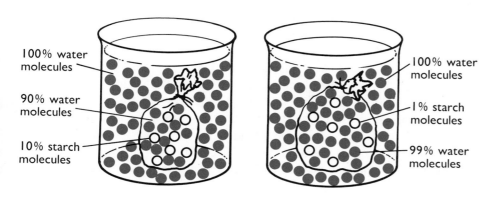

100% water molecules

90% water molecules

10% starch molecules

100% water molecules

1% starch molecules

99% water molecules

FIGURE 21-6 The pressure that develops as osmosis continues could eventually burst this model cell.

The solution inside the model cell is only 90% water. As you might expect, water molecules diffuse from the 100% pure water outside the bag into the region of lesser concentration inside the bag. This model cell differs from Figure 21-4 because it contains starch molecules, which are too large to move through the pores of the bag. As a result, the concentration of water outside the bag remains higher than the concentration of water inside the bag. Osmosis continues to move water into the bag, but conditions inside and outside will never be exactly the same.

Osmosis in Living Cells

If you have ever tried to keep house plants alive, you have probably seen how leaves shrivel and droop when a plant does not receive enough water. If the plant is watered in time, the leaves will resume their normal shape. If the plant is left without water too long, the leaves will die. These changes result directly from the movement of water by osmosis into the plant.

The same is true of many other types of cells. Human red blood cells, for example, change shape noticeably if they gain or lose some of their water content. But osmosis occurs only when the water concentration inside the cell differs from that outside the cell. If red blood cells are placed in a solution that has exactly the same concentration of water molecules as red blood cell cytoplasm, they neither lose nor gain water by osmosis. The surrounding solution is said to be isotonic to the cytoplasm of the cells.

Isotonic, hypotonic, and hypertonic are terms that biologists use to compare solutions. These terms are usually used to describe how the solution surrounding a cell compares to the cytoplasmic solution inside the cell. An **isotonic solution** has the same concentration of solutes and water molecules as the solution to which it is being compared. (See Figure 21-7.) Because the red blood cells in the above example are surrounded by an isotonic solution, osmosis does not occur.

When red blood cells are placed in distilled water, however, water molecules begin to diffuse into the cells. Osmosis occurs in this case because there is a greater concentration of water molecules outside the blood cells than there is inside the cells. Distilled water is said to be hypotonic to the cytoplasm of the cells. A **hypotonic solution** has a lesser concentration of solutes *and* a greater concentration of water molecules than the solution to which it is being compared. (See Figure 21-8.)

Because of osmosis, water accumulates inside the cells, exerting an outward pressure on their membranes. Pressure produced in this way is usually called **osmotic pressure.** Since red blood cells are very fragile, the buildup of osmotic pressure causes them to burst. This process is called hemolysis.

If red blood cells are placed in a highly concentrated salt solution such as sea water, water passes out by osmosis. The cells shrink by a process called crenation. This happens because sea water contains fewer water molecules than does an equal volume of cell cytoplasm. So, sea water is hypertonic

FIGURE 21-7 Osmosis does not occur when a red blood cell is placed in an isotonic environment. The cell maintains its normal size and shape.

Cytoplasm
99.1% water
0.9% other solutes

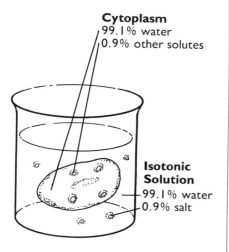

Isotonic Solution
99.1% water
0.9% salt

Blood cells in an isotonic solution

FIGURE 21-8 Osmosis moves water into a red blood cell placed into a hypotonic environment. The cell swells, becomes spherical in shape, and eventually bursts.

Cytoplasm
99.1% water
0.9% other solutes

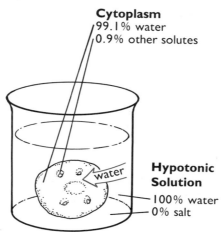

Hypotonic Solution
100% water
0% salt

Blood cells in a hypotonic solution

FIGURE 21-9 Osmosis moves water out of a red blood cell that has been placed in a hypertonic environment. The cell shrinks and dies.

Cytoplasm
99.1% water
0.9% other solutes

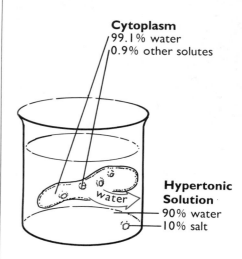

Hypertonic Solution
90% water
10% salt

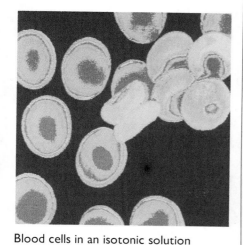

Blood cells in a hypertonic solution

compared to the cytoplasm of red blood cells. A **hypertonic solution** has a greater concentration of solutes *and* a lesser concentration of water molecules than the solution to which it is being compared. (See Figure 21-9.)

Most organisms live in nonisotonic environments. Animals, protists, and plants living in fresh water are surrounded by a hypotonic medium and tend to gain water by osmosis. This could easily cause cells to burst in organisms that lack cell walls. Organisms that live in sea water, however, are surrounded by a hypertonic medium. They tend to lose water by osmosis and could easily

When plant cells are placed in a hypertonic solution such as sea water, water from the cytoplasm diffuses outward along with water from the central vacuole. As the vacuole shrinks, the cell membrane pulls away from the cell wall, causing it to collapse. This process is called plasmolysis.

The starfish has specialized systems and structures to prevent its cells from shrinking in its hypertonic sea water environment.

become dehydrated even though they are surrounded by water. Many freshwater and marine organisms need special adaptations to suit them for survival in their usual environment.

Osmosis in Plant Cells

In addition to acting as a solvent and regulating the concentration of other substances in the cytoplasm, water plays another role in plant cells. As long as the solution surrounding a plant cell is hypotonic, water will enter the cell by osmosis, collecting in the central vacuole, which, in turn, presses the cell membrane against the cell wall. This effect is called **turgor pressure.** (See Figure 21-10.) Turgor pressure enables plant stems to remain upright despite the downward force of gravity. When the surrounding medium is hypertonic, however, plant cells lose their turgor pressure by plasmolysis. For example, cut celery stalks left standing in water stay rigid and crisp. When they are removed from water, they become limp and rubbery.

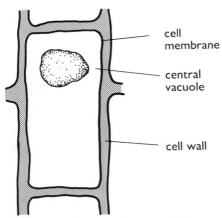

FIGURE 21-10 The plump, full shape of a healthy plant cell depends on a balance between turgor pressure, which pushes the cell membrane outward, and the inward pressure of the cell wall.

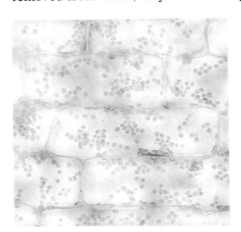

Elodea cells are turgid in fresh water.

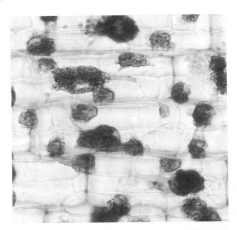

Plasmolysis occurs when *Elodea* cells are placed in salt water.

Applications of the Osmotic Effect

If you were to spill some chemical fertilizer on your lawn, the grass would turn brown and die. You have probably heard people say that the grass is "burnt," but the burnt effect is actually caused by osmosis. The solution that forms when fertilizer dissolves in dew has a very high concentration of solutes and a low concentration of water molecules as compared to cell cytoplasm. This solution is hypertonic to the cells in the blades of grass. Water moves out by osmosis, causing the blades of grass to dry up and die.

The effects of osmosis can be used for practical purposes. For example,

V THE UNITY OF LIFE

rinsing your mouth with an alcohol-based mouthwash kills bacteria in your mouth by osmosis. The concentration of water in the mouthwash is so much less than the concentration of water in the bacterial cytoplasm that crenation occurs and the bacteria become dehydrated and die. Bacteria can also be killed by surrounding them with highly concentrated sugar solutions (as in jams and preserves) or with salty brine solutions (as in pickles and corned beef). In either case, the bacteria are killed by dehydration.

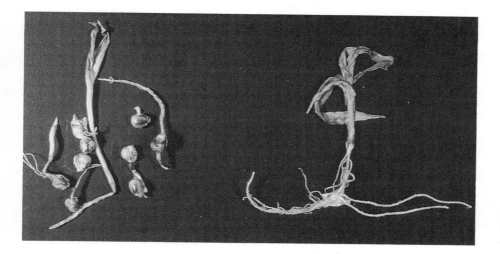

The roots of this corn plant have fertilizer burn. A concentrated solution of fertilizer around the roots caused dehydration of the root cells by osmosis.

Section Review Questions

1. How do selectively permeable membranes enable cells to maintain homeostasis?
2. a) What is the extracellular fluid?
   b) Why are conditions in the extracellular fluid so important to the cell?
3. a) Define the terms diffusion, osmosis, and passive transport.
   b) Explain how these terms are related.
4. Use sketches to explain the meanings of isotonic, hypotonic, and hypertonic.
5. a) Define turgor pressure and plasmolysis.
   b) Explain why they are important to plants.

Osmotically Speaking

Have you ever worried about osmosis? Probably not, since you know your body is protected from dangerous water loss or gain by your skin as well as by your body's excretory functions and behaviours. But think again. Osmosis, when understood, is a powerful tool. The dialysis machine is one of the most outstanding medical applications of osmosis.

Osmotic principles are important also to hospital patients who must be treated with a saline solution that drips directly into the patient's bloodstream through an intravenous (IV) tube. Saline solution, a mainstay of medicine, is nothing more than sodium chloride in water. The salt is necessary to make the liquid isotonic with blood and living cells. If the liquid's water concentration does not match the body's water concentration, potentially damaging water loss or gain will occur in cells and tissues.

Osmosis is also used to preserve food from the action of micro-organisms such as bacteria. To understand how, first consider a human red blood cell. When placed in a hypotonic solution (one that contains relatively more water than its cytoplasm), a red blood cell receives an influx of water molecules by osmosis until its membrane shatters. However, most bacteria, including those responsible for food spoilage, can survive in a hypotonic environ-

ment. This is because of the rigid wall surrounding each bacterial cell. As water enters the cell, the wall counters with its own pressure. The cells become turgid but rarely explode.

Hypertonic solutions pose a much more serious threat to bacteria. As water diffuses out of bacterial cells into a hypertonic solution, their cell membranes pull away from the enclosing wall. This is called plasmolysis. Plasmolyzed bacteria cannot function normally, and cell activity may stop altogether.

In fact, humans understood the relationship between osmosis and

food spoilage long before the presence of bacteria was even suspected. Food preservation techniques dating back to the earliest civilizations all depended on adding salt or sugar to foods. It is not surprising that in ancient times salt was worth more than gold, especially in warm climates where unpreserved food spoiled rapidly. In some regions of the world, 10-15% salt solutions are still used for killing the micro-organisms that cause food spoilage.

However, there are always exceptions to any rule—especially in biology. One such exception is the halophilic, or salt loving, bacteria. These hardy micro-organisms thrive under conditions of 30% or higher salt concentrations. They are found where little else survives—in the Dead Sea.

21.2 Active Transport

Passive transport by diffusion or osmosis can be compared to the natural movement of loose rocks down a slope or a gradient. In passive transport, the cell does not expend any of its own energy to move the molecules. Because diffusion and osmosis are passive methods, they can only move molecules *down* a **concentration gradient,** that is, from a region of greater concentration to a region of lesser concentration. (See Figure 21-11.)

In **active transport,** the cell must expend its own energy to move the molecules. Active transport methods are needed to move materials that would not diffuse naturally. (See Figure 21-12.) Root cells, for example, need active transport to maintain a mineral concentration greater than that in the dilute

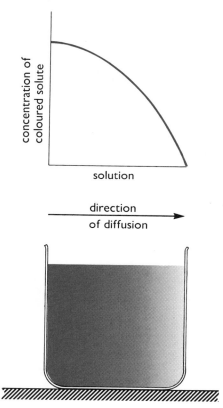

FIGURE 21-11 The graph shows the concentration gradient of a coloured solute. As the solute molecules diffuse from left to right, they will spread out evenly. Soon there will be no concentration gradient.

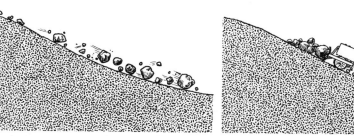

Passive transport requires no additional energy.

Active transport requires additional energy input.

FIGURE 21-12 Active transport requires additional energy to move materials against the concentration gradient.

solution surrounding the root. (See Figure 21-13.) Ordinary diffusion would transport these minerals out of the cell. Through active transport, the root cell continues to move mineral ions from the external environment against the concentration gradient. Energy to move rocks up a gradient can be supplied by a bulldozer's engine. Energy to move molecules or ions against a concentration gradient must be supplied by the cell's mitochondria. The actual process of moving the particles in or out, however, is performed by cell membranes.

Active transport is necessary whenever a cell must maintain internal concentrations that differ greatly from those surrounding the cell. For example, human red blood cells have a potassium ion concentration about 30 times greater than that in the surrounding blood plasma. Potassium ions are relatively small and pass readily across most cell membranes. Potassium ions normally

In some cases, active transport is needed to move materials *down* a concentration gradient. For example, the concentration of amino acid molecules is greater in blood cells than in body cells. However, the molecules are too large to diffuse across a membrane by passive diffusion. The cells themselves must supply the energy to pull the needed molecules inside.

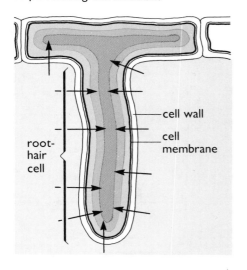

FIGURE 21-13 Active transport of minerals into a root hair (the deeper the colour, the greater the mineral concentration). Active transport is needed to move minerals against the concentration gradient. Which cell structure must be performing this function?

cell wall

cell membrane

root-hair cell

diffuse according to the concentration gradient. So, you would expect the potassium ions in a red blood cell to diffuse outward into the plasma. To maintain a higher potassium concentration, a red blood cell must actively transport potassium ions inward against the concentration gradient. But the concentration of sodium ions in a red blood cell is only one tenth that of the surrounding plasma. Pumping sodium ions out against the concentration gradient also requires active transport and the constant expenditure of energy by the cell. (See Figure 21-14.)

A further example of the vital role played by active transport is provided by the human kidney. Its function is to produce urine with much higher waste concentrations than the surrounding blood. This requires the constant expenditure of energy by the kidney cells. Not surprisingly, these cells contain many more mitochondria than average cells. If kidney cells are treated with a chemical that deactivates the mitochondria, the accumulated ions soon diffuse out until their concentration is the same on both sides of the cell membrane. Active transport can only take place when large amounts of energy are constantly available.

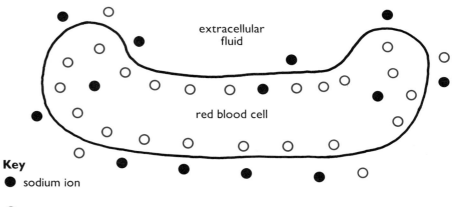

extracellular fluid

red blood cell

Key

● sodium ion

○ potassium ion

FIGURE 21-14 Red blood cells must transport both potassium ions inward and sodium ions outward against the concentration gradient.

A Model for Active Transport

The most recent model for active transport suggests that certain transport proteins embedded in the cell membrane help to move the ions or molecules from one side to the other. Cytologists think that the transport protein must first bind to the ion or molecule being transported. After that, there are two possible ways to move the ion or molecule across the cell membrane. Both methods involve changing the shape of the transport protein, which either pulls the molecule across or forms a channel for its passage. (See Figure 21-15.) Cytologists believe that this shape-changing stage is the step that requires

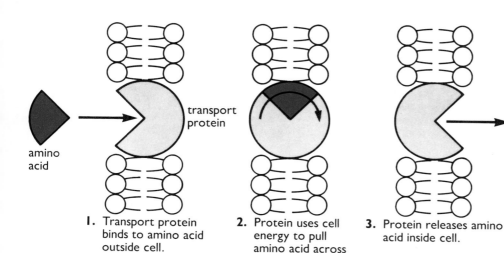

1. Transport protein binds to amino acid outside cell.

2. Protein uses cell energy to pull amino acid across membrane.

3. Protein releases amino acid inside cell.

4. Transport protein uses energy to return to original state.

transport protein

amino acid

FIGURE 21-15 A model for active transport

FIGURE 21-16 Endocytosis is a form of active transport.

the energy. Finally, the transport protein releases the ion or molecule on the other side of the membrane.

Endocytosis

Endocytosis is a form of cell transport in which the cell engulfs particles by folding a portion of its membrane around them. There are two types of endocytosis: phagocytosis and pinocytosis. (See Figure 21-16.)

Phagocytosis, or ''cell eating,'' is also shown in the photograph on this page. Part of the cell membrane wraps around the particle and pinches off to

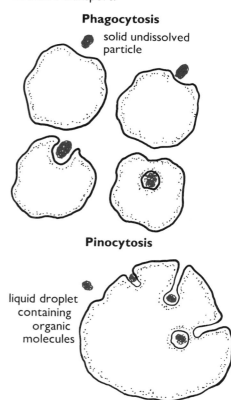

Phagocytosis

solid undissolved particle

Pinocytosis

liquid droplet containing organic molecules

This white blood cell is engulfing a bacterium by phagocytosis.

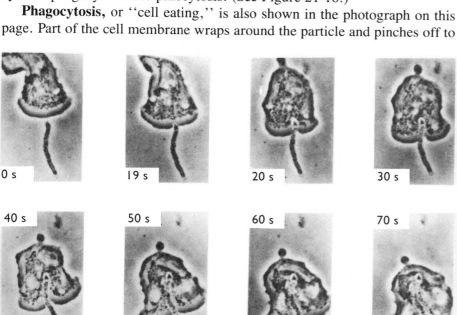

0 s   19 s   20 s   30 s

40 s   50 s   60 s   70 s

form a vesicle or vacuole that remains inside the cytoplasm. Relatively large particles can be engulfed by this process.

Pinocytosis, or "cell drinking," involves the ingestion of dissolved organic molecules that are too large to pass across a membrane by other methods. When the molecules contact the cell membrane, it bulges inward to form a narrow channel and a bulbous sac. Both the desired molecules and some extracellular fluid enter the cell by way of these channels. The cell membrane then pinches off, and the detached sac drifts through the cytoplasm until the molecules are broken down and the nutrients are absorbed.

Pinocytosis occurs in many kinds of animal cells including human intestine, kidney, liver, and blood cells. The main difference between the two types of endocytosis is that phagocytosis transports undissolved materials, but pinocytosis transports dissolved, extra-large molecules.

Exocytosis

Exocytosis is the disposal of waste material accumulated in a cell vacuole. When the vacuole contacts the cell membrane, the two join together and the waste material is dumped into the extracellular fluid. (See Figure 21-17.) Phagocytosis, pinocytosis, and exocytosis are active transport processes because energy is required to change the shape of the membrane. Cytologists do not completely understand the precise nature of the mechanism that causes active transport to occur, so research continues in this area.

Section Review Questions

1. Describe the difference between passive transport and active transport.
2. What is the energy source for passive transport? For active transport?
3. Materials that can diffuse across the cell membrane are sometimes moved by active transport instead of passive transport. Explain why.
4. State an example of an organ in which active transport plays an important role. Explain why active transport is needed.
5. a) Describe the differences between endocytosis and exocytosis.
   b) Explain how these processes differ from passive transport and from active transport.

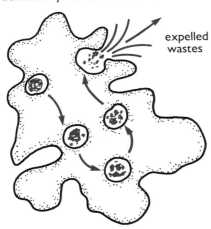

FIGURE 21-17 The amoeba expels wastes by exocytosis. Exocytosis occurs when the vacuole membrane touches and joins the cell membrane.

expelled wastes

Facilitated Diffusion

Simple diffusion fails to explain the movement of many substances across cell membranes, particularly those that cannot dissolve in, and so move through, the lipid layer. The transport of such substances is thought to involve the use of carrier molecules.

One way of imagining what happens is to think of these carrier molecules as individual ferry boats afloat within the cell membrane. Now, imagine a large river being travelled in both directions by ferries loaded with cargo. Travel downstream, with the current, would be an easy task. The same trip upstream, against the current, would of course require powerful engines.

In cell transport, the current to be contended with is the concentration gradient across the cell membrane (and its related electrochemical gradient). Where the carrier system must fight against this current, energy is expended. You will remember that this is called active transport.

Where the carrier system can go with the current, transporting molecules in the direction favoured by diffusion, energy is not needed. This is called facilitated diffusion. Molecules that could otherwise not pass through the membrane are, in effect, given a lift. For example, glucose enters most cells by facilitated diffusion. Experiments have shown that the carrier molecule for glucose in a human red blood cell is a protein located on about 300 000 sites on the cell membrane.

Much of the recent work on membrane transport has concentrated on small, nonprotein carrier molecules. Several of these are ion-carrying antibiotics called ionophores. For example, the antibiotic valinomycin helps the passage of potassium ion, normally present in high concentrations within cells.

Valinomycin is a ring-like compound with a hydrophobic (water-hating) exterior and a hydrophilic (water-loving) interior. This outer layer dissolves readily in the lipid layer, allowing the molecule to pass through the cell membrane. The inner layer forms a chamber within which the lipid-insoluble potassium ion is carried. The potassium binds with the valinomycin when the ion is in high concentration, and it is released when the ion is in low concentration.

Valinomycin is produced by certain fungi as a weapon against competing species. When valinomycin binds to a cell membrane, it essentially punches a hole through which the vital potassium ions bleed out of the cytoplasm. The cell must expend energy to replace this potassium. The loss of potassium coupled with the energy drain then inhibits or kills the cell.

Although ionophores are useful in stopping the growth of microorganisms, most cannot be taken internally as medication. This is because of their powerful, and indiscriminate, effect on cell membrane transport.

21.3 Energy for Cell Activities

All living things require energy to perform life functions such as growth and development, and the repair of damaged cells and tissues. Cell processes such as reproduction and active transport, as well as many chemical reactions, also require energy. In addition, motile organisms require energy to perform work. Walking and running both depend on the release of energy by the muscle cells that are performing the work.

The energy needed for all of these activities must be obtained at the cellular level from food. But where did the energy come from? And how did it get into the food? How do the cells of an organism use this energy? This section will help you find answers for these important questions.

Photosynthesis and Food Energy

Directly or indirectly almost all living things rely on energy originating from the sun. Most terrestrial food chains are based on plants. Most aquatic food chains begin with algae. (See Figure 21-18.) Both plants and algae are called producers because they can manufacture their own food by **photosynthesis.**

FIGURE 21-18 Through photosynthesis, the plants and the algae in this ecosystem produce food for all heterotrophs by storing solar energy in the bonds of glucose molecules.

The following word equation that describes this process is:

$$\text{solar energy} + \text{carbon dioxide} + \text{water} \xrightarrow[\text{enzymes}]{\text{chlorophyll}} \text{glucose} + \text{oxygen}$$

This equation makes photosynthesis look like a single chemical reaction. But photosynthesis is actually a complex series of chemical reactions. These reactions can be divided into two groups: **light reactions** and **dark reactions.** (See Figure 21-19.) Light reactions are so named because they can only take place in the presence of light. Dark reactions, however, do not require light.

During light reactions, solar energy is absorbed by the chlorophyll in cell chloroplasts. Some of the trapped energy is converted into chemical potential energy, and some is used to split water molecules. Two products result: oxygen gas and energized hydrogen atoms. The oxygen gas escapes into the atmosphere. The energized hydrogen atoms take part in the dark reactions. This

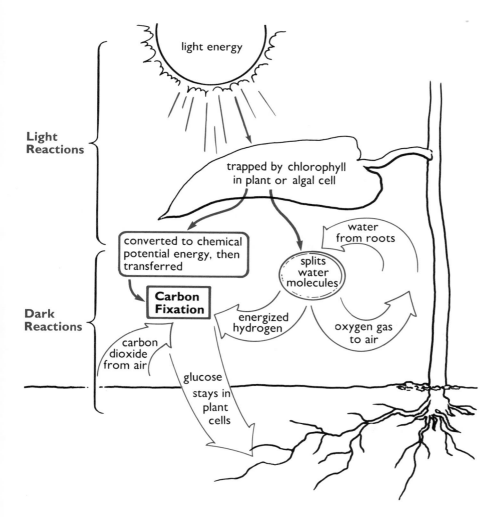

FIGURE 21-19 A simplified model of photosynthesis

Most of the potato's volume is occupied by starch storage cells such as this one.

stage is also called **carbon fixation** because the hydrogen and the carbon dioxide combine to form glucose molecules. The chemical energy from the light reactions and the energy of the hydrogen atoms is stored in the bonds of the glucose molecules.

Plants use up some of the glucose they produce for their other life processes such as growing and reproducing. However, most plants convert glucose to starch, which is much more compact and occupies less space. Animals make use of this stored food by eating the plants. Foods such as corn and potatoes are excellent sources of starch. The starch these plants contain was originally glucose produced in their green leaves by photosynthesis. The oxygen released by photosynthesis is also useful to animals, which need it to carry out cellular respiration.

Releasing Energy by Cellular Respiration

Only producers can store energy in the bonds of food molecules such as glucose and starch. But producers and consumers alike share the problem of releasing the stored energy in a form that can be used by their cells. The process by which most organisms break down glucose molecules and release the chemical potential energy stored in them is called **cellular respiration.** Like photosynthesis, cellular respiration involves a complex series of chemical reactions. Again, it is helpful to divide the reactions into two groups: the anaerobic stage and the aerobic stage.

Anaerobic Stage

The first stage of cellular respiration takes place in the fluid part of the cell cytoplasm. (See Figure 21-20.) It is called **anaerobic respiration**—*without air*—because it requires no oxygen. Anaerobic respiration involves splitting glucose into two identical molecules of a substance called pyruvic acid. Enzymes play an important role in this process.

$$\text{glucose} \xrightarrow[\text{enzymes}]{} \text{pyruvic acid} + \text{usable energy}$$

The energy released during the anaerobic stage is in a form that the cell can use directly. However, because this step breaks very few bonds, it releases only about 5% of all the energy stored in the bonds of the original glucose molecule.

Aerobic Stage

The second stage of cellular respiration is called **aerobic respiration**—*with air*—because it requires oxygen. During the aerobic stage, the pyruvic acid molecules split and move into the mitochondria. (See Figure 21-21.) Then

FIGURE 21-20 The anaerobic stage of cellular respiration takes place in the fluid part of the cell cytoplasm.

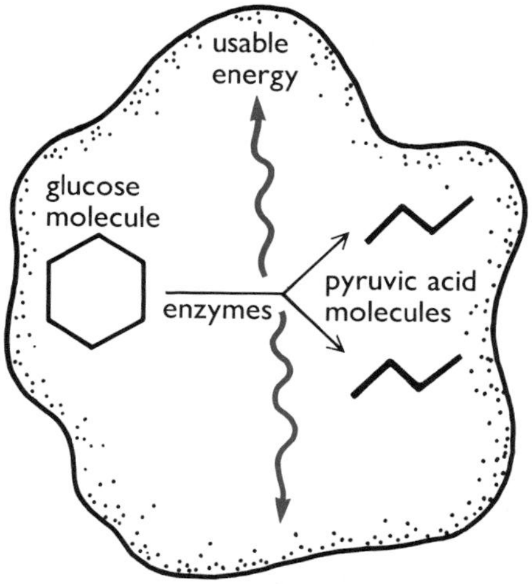

FIGURE 21-21 The aerobic stage of cellular respiration takes place in the mitochrondria, releasing over ten times as much energy.

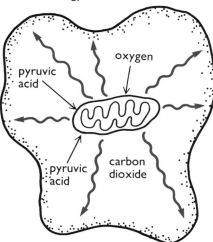

another complex series of enzyme-assisted reactions breaks more chemical bonds.

$$\text{pyruvic acid} \ + \ \text{oxygen} \ \xrightarrow[\text{enzymes}]{} \ \text{carbon dioxide} \ + \ \text{water} \ + \ \text{usable energy}$$

Carbon dioxide is produced when unbonded carbon and oxygen from the original glucose molecule join together. Water molecules are produced when unbonded hydrogen from the glucose combines with oxygen taken in by the organism from its surroundings. Formation of the new molecules completes the breakdown of the glucose and releases the other 95% of the energy stored in its bonds.

Over half of the energy released by the two stages of cellular respiration is needed to keep the reactions going. The fraction of energy that is actually available for cell activities is called usable energy. The following word equation sums up the two stages of cellular respiration.

$$\text{glucose} \ + \ \text{oxygen} \ \xrightarrow[\text{enzymes}]{} \ \text{carbon dioxide} \ + \ \text{water} \ + \ \text{usable energy}$$

Alcoholic Fermentation

The production of alcohol for beverages and fuels is a multibillion dollar industry that depends on a cellular process. People have known for thousands of years that wine and beer can be made by allowing yeast to feed on plant foods such as grapes and grains. Today, we understand why the process works and how to control it.

The reactions of the aerobic stage occur in two distinct sequences: the citric acid cycle (CAC) and the electron transport chain (ETC). Only the ETC uses oxygen directly. The CAC does not require oxygen molecules at all, but it does require a constant supply of molecules produced by the ETC. If the cell runs out of oxygen, *both* sets of reactions stop immediately. Therefore, the CAC is grouped with the aerobic stage, rather than with the anaerobic stage.

Yeast cells and anaerobic bacteria obtain energy from glucose in the food through a process called **alcoholic fermentation.** This process is entirely anaerobic, and its first stage is like that of cellular respiration.

glucose $\longrightarrow$ pyruvic acid + usable energy

This is the stage that releases energy for the yeast or bacteria. No further energy can be released without oxygen. Since these organisms cannot carry out aerobic respiration, they have already obtained all the energy they possibly can. However, if pyruvic acid builds up, the first-stage reaction would slow down and stop. So, a second stage is needed to remove pyruvic acid.

pyruvic acid $\longrightarrow$ ethyl alcohol + carbon dioxide

From the word equation, you can see that no energy is released by the second stage, and neither yeast nor bacteria can make use of the alcohol. The second stage is needed only to keep the first stage going, but it cannot last indefinitely. As the alcohol accumulates, water moves out of the cells by osmosis. The end result is cell crenation and death.

The two stages of alcoholic fermentation can be summarized in a single word equation.

glucose $\longrightarrow$ ethyl alcohol + carbon dioxide + energy

As an energy-releasing process, alcoholic fermentation is highly inefficient. About 93% of the energy in the original glucose molecule is still present in the bonds of the ethyl alcohol. This stored energy can be released by burning the alcohol in the presence of oxygen. Ethyl alcohol is widely used in industry, wherever a clean-burning, high-energy fuel is needed. Because ethyl alcohol is also a useful solvent, its production for industrial purposes is a major industry.

The production of alcohol for beverages is also a major industry. Regardless of what advertising campaigns for beer and wine may suggest, the ethyl alcohol these products contain is consumed for its intoxicating effects. Although the molecule is a neurotoxin, it can be broken down in the liver because its structure resembles that of a carbohydrate. Again, oxygen is needed to break the molecule down completely and energy is released. In a way, ethyl alcohol can be regarded as an "energy food," but one with serious side effects.

Lactic Acid Fermentation

Animal cells sometimes have to function without oxygen. For example, when you take part in a strenuous activity, your muscle cells need a great deal of energy. If the activity is sustained for a long time, your body systems may not

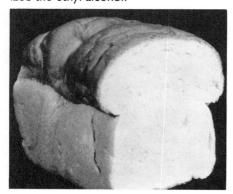

The bubbles of carbon dioxide that made this bread rise were produced by alcoholic fermentation. The heat of baking killed the yeast cells and vaporized the ethyl alcohol.

be able to provide enough oxygen for the aerobic stage of cellular respiration. When this happens, your cells can continue to release energy by another process called **lactic acid fermentation.** Lactic acid fermentation is also entirely anaerobic and occurs in two stages. Again, the first stage is like that for ordinary cellular respiration.

$$glucose \longrightarrow pyruvic\ acid\ +\ energy$$

If pyruvic acid builds up, the first-stage reaction would slow down and stop. This outcome is prevented by a second stage which breaks down pyruvic acid.

$$pyruvic\ acid \longrightarrow lactic\ acid$$

The second stage releases no energy. Its only function is to remove pyruvic acid so that the first stage can continue to release energy. This enables your muscles to keep working for a longer period, even though the cells are deprived of oxygen. As the activity continues, however, lactic acid accumulates in the cells. This buildup is a major cause of muscle soreness after prolonged exercise.

Both stages of lactic acid fermentation can be summarized in a single word equation.

$$glucose \longrightarrow lactic\ acid\ +\ energy$$

When the emergency is over, the lactic acid must be broken down to restore homeostasis in the muscle cells. This breakdown process requires oxygen. Athletes who have accumulated large amounts of lactic acid during a race are said to have an oxygen debt. For several minutes after the race, very deep breathing is needed to supply the extra oxygen needed to eliminate the remaining lactic acid.

DID YOU KNOW?

Factors other than lactic acid affect the degree of muscle soreness experienced after exercise. Torn muscle fibres also cause pain. Athletes, however, experience much less muscle soreness than people who exercise only occasionally. There are three reasons for this. First, athletes have much more efficient cardiovascular systems and can deliver much more oxygen to their muscle cells. This minimizes the amount of lactic acid produced and the amount of time needed to decompose it. Second, athletes' muscles are trained to stretch without tearing. Third, any tears that do occur heal much more rapidly because athletes maintain high concentrations of interleukin-I. This chemical of the immune system triggers the repair process by breaking down and disposing of the protein in the damaged muscle fibres.

As these sprinters become more fit, their ability to circulate oxygen will increase, and their oxygen debt will decrease.

Comparing Energy Processes

Cellular respiration is the most important of the energy-releasing processes you have just examined. Fermentation plays only a minor role in the release of energy for cell activities. Few organisms depend entirely on alcoholic fermentation, and lactic acid fermentation in animal cells is limited to periods of oxygen shortage.

Photosynthesis is the major energy-storing process. Some bacteria can obtain energy from sources other than sunlight, but their role in the biosphere is very limited. These bacteria could never support an animal population as large as the one now living on Earth. Most of Earth's inhabitants must obtain their energy from glucose produced by photosynthesis.

The comparison of cellular respiration and photosynthesis reveals many similarities and close relationships between the two cell processes. (See Figure 21-22.) Both take place inside living cells, and both involve the transport of materials. In terms of materials, photosynthesis and cell respiration are complementary. The elements and compounds involved are constantly recycled—the products produced by one become reactants for the other. If photosynthesis were interrupted on a global scale, cell respiration would soon cease. The reverse is also true. In a very real way, you depend on photosynthesis, not only for your glucose, but also for the oxygen you need to carry out cellular respiration.

Some chemosynthetic bacteria can obtain their energy from nitrogen gas molecules in the air or hydrogen sulphide molecules escaping from volcanic vents in the ocean floor and in the earth's surface.

FIGURE 21-22 Cellular respiration and photosynthesis. Which essential components are not recycled?

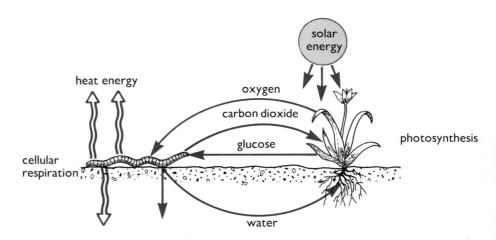

However, the energy relationship between the two processes is not complementary. This is because the energy produced by cellular respiration is eventually converted to heat, released into the atmosphere, and finally escapes from Earth. It cannot be recycled for use in photosynthesis, which requires energy in the form of light. Except for a few bacteria previously mentioned, all other processes in all other cells are dependent on the constant inflow of solar energy.

David Suzuki

During the last twenty years, David Suzuki has become one of our most prominent scientists and our best-known scientific conscience. The combination is not an accidental one. It was Suzuki's work in the field of genetics that first led him to ponder the role of science in our lives and the future of this planet.

As a scientist, Suzuki was acclaimed for his pioneering work with the *Drosophila* fruit fly at the University of British Columbia. Suzuki was looking for an alternative to chemical pest control. His studies of fruit-fly genetics led him to produce a strain that was sensitive to heat. These flies died at 29°C. This seemed to promise an environmentally safe method of pest control. Laboratory-bred flies carrying the heat-sensitive gene would be released to breed with their wild counterparts. Offspring inheriting the characteristic would die in the first period of hot weather instead of consuming human crops.

However, Suzuki was troubled by the broader, long-range implications of genetic tinkering with existing species. The ability to customize genes was becoming possible before our understanding of their function and operation in living organisms was complete. Just as the harmful effects of toxic substances such as DDT on natural food webs were not even imagined until falcon eggs failed to hatch, Suzuki warned, hazards beyond our current understanding could also occur as a result of genetic experimentation. Suzuki was concerned that information about genetic engineering proposals was not available to the public, so informed decisions could not be made. At the same time, scientists were too involved with individual approaches and topics of study to be able to make proper assessments of long-term effects.

In the 1970s, Suzuki began a second career as a science broadcaster. By presenting scientific information in an accessible and understandable way to the nonscientist, Suzuki hoped to encourage people to ask the right questions about new technologies and developments.

Suzuki's most recent effort has been his book *Genethics*, written in collaboration with Peter Knudtson. In *Genethics*, Suzuki addresses the nonscientist who must assess and make decisions about scientific issues. *Genethics* also represents Suzuki's efforts to

provide us with ethical guidelines for science.

Consider this statement from *Genethics*: "The information contained in genetic molecules is vulnerable to loss through mutations caused by sunlight, radioactivity, chemicals, and other external mutagenic forces. Each of us has a responsibility to develop an awareness of potential mutagens in our immediate surroundings and to seek to minimize environmentally induced damage to our DNA." Everyone must know and care about threats to the genetic makeup of ourselves and other life.

What of our planet? How can decisions concerning genetics have an effect on our survival? Suzuki states: "Genetic diversity, in both human and nonhuman species, is a precious planetary resource, and it is in our best interests to maintain and preserve that diversity." Imagine the irreplaceable genetic treasures being lost by the destruction of rain forests and other natural habitats.

Time may show that Suzuki's greatest contribution to science will turn out not to have come from his diligent work in the laboratory at all but rather from something else. He has given us a clearer sense of what we are and how human biology is part of the global ecosystem. He has also put the responsibility for the wise use of science, with all its wonder and power, into the hands of us all.

Section Review Questions

1. a) Write the simplified word equation for photosynthesis.
   b) Briefly describe the role of each term in the equation. (Explain where it comes from, what it does, or where it goes.)

2. The chemical reactions of photosynthesis can be divided into two groups or stages.
   a) Identify the two groups and explain the basis for their names.
   b) Briefly describe the changes that occur during each stage.

3. a) Write the simplified word equation for cellular respiration.
   b) Briefly describe the role of each term in the equation.

4. Cellular respiration also takes place in two distinct stages.
   a) Identify the two stages and explain the basis for their names.
   b) Write the complete word equation for the first stage and explain the significance of each term.
   c) Write the complete word equation for the second stage and explain the significance of each term.

5. a) List the three processes by which living cells may release energy.
   b) Prepare a simple chart to compare these three processes. Show differences as well as similarities.

6. Write the simplified word equation for photosynthesis. Skip one line and write the word equation for cellular respiration. Link each pair of identical terms with a single straight line. Circle each term that remains. What does this diagram demonstrate about the relationship between the two processes?

Chapter Review

Key Words

active transport
aerobic respiration
alcoholic fermentation
anaerobic respiration
concentration gradient
diffusion
endocytosis
exocytosis
hypertonic solution
hypotonic solution
isotonic solution

lactic acid
  fermentation
metabolism
osmosis
osmotic pressure
passive transport
permeability
phagocytosis
pinocytosis
selectively permeable
  membrane
turgor pressure

Recall Questions

Multiple Choice

1. The muscle soreness experienced after physical exertion is caused by
   a) lactic acid
   b) pyruvic acid
   c) acetic acid
   d) ethyl alcohol

2. A hypotonic solution, relative to the solution to which it is being compared, has
   a) a lesser concentration of water
   b) a lower concentration of solutes
   c) a greater concentration of water
   d) both a) and b)
   e) both b) and c)

3. During osmosis, water moves
   a) from an area of high concentration of solutes to an area of low concentration of solutes
   b) from an area of low concentration of water to an area of high concentration of water
   c) from an area of high concentration of water to an area of low concentration of water
   d) both a) and b)
   e) both a) and c)

4. Which of the following processes requires oxygen as a starting material?
   a) alcoholic fermentation
   b) cellular respiration
   c) lactic acid fermentation
   d) photosynthesis

5. Which of the following cannot be transported across a cell membrane by simple diffusion?
   a) carbon dioxide
   b) amino acids
   c) oxygen
   d) water

6. Which of the following processes does not take place in a cell organelle?
   a) light reactions
   b) dark reactions
   c) anaerobic stage
   d) aerobic stage

7. The small, protein-filled vesicles that break away from the Golgi apparatus fuse with the cell membrane and empty their contents into the extracellular space. This is an example of
   a) active transport
   b) endocytosis
   c) exocytosis
   d) osmosis

8. During photosynthesis, oxygen is separated from water molecules and is used to make
   a) oxygen gas molecules
   b) glucose molecules
   c) chlorophyll molecules
   d) both a) and b)
   e) both b) and c)

Fill in the Blanks

1. For continued survival, all cells and organisms must maintain a steady state called _____.

2. The outward pressure on the membrane of a cell is called _____.

3. _____ can occur when too much water inside a cell moves out by osmosis.

4. Hard breathing continues after vigorous exercise stops because extra _____ is needed to break down the _____ that accumulates in _____.

5. Cellular respiration is the process by which organisms obtain _____ from _____.

6. The first stage of cellular respiration differs from the second stage in that it is _____.

7. The anaerobic stages of cellular respiration occur in the _____.

8. The process of fermentation releases _____ in muscle cells, and _____ and _____ in yeast.

9. Fermentation is said to be _____ because it does not require _____.

Short Answers

1. a) Define passive transport and identify all methods of cell transport that can be considered passive.
   b) What do the methods you identified above have in common, and how do they differ?

2. Identify two substances that can move across a cell membrane by passive transport and two that cannot.

3. a) Define osmosis.
   b) Describe the role of osmosis in cell transport.

4. a) How are active and passive transport similar?
   b) How are active and passive transport different?

5. a) How are pinocytosis and phagocytosis similar?
   b) How are pinocytosis and phagocytosis different?

6. a) Briefly describe a simple model to explain passive transport.
   b) Describe the model biologists use to explain active transport.

7. How do conditions in the extracellular fluid affect conditions inside the cell?

8. a) What is osmotic pressure?
   b) What is turgor pressure? Explain its function in plants.

9. a) A healthy human body maintains almost constant levels of glucose in the blood. Which process is this an example of?
   b) Which type of cell transport makes this process possible? Explain your answer.

10. a) What is the process used by yeast cells to release energy?
    b) Which molecules are produced, and how are they put to practical use?

11. What is another name for the dark reactions of photosynthesis? Explain the basis for both names.

12. a) Write a word equation for lactic acid fermentation.
    b) Which organisms use this process to release energy and under what circumstances?

13. What role does chlorophyll play in photosynthesis?

Application Questions

1. Explain why a salt solution is a good antiseptic.

2. The solution that surrounds red blood cells is called blood plasma. Is blood plasma hypertonic, hypotonic, or isotonic compared to the cytoplasm of red blood cells? Explain briefly.

3. How would the response of an amoeba to distilled water differ from its response to salty sea water? Explain. (Remember that amoebas are single-celled organisms that live in freshwater ponds.)

4. How does the response of a plant cell to a hypotonic solution differ from the response of an animal cell to a hypotonic solution?

5. How would an ocean-dwelling algal cell respond if placed in fresh water?

6. What can be done to "freshen" celery sticks that have wilted? Explain the scientific basis for this household hint.

7. Compare the anaerobic stage of cellular respiration with the aerobic stage in regard to starting materials, end products, and the release of energy.

8. Cellular respiration involves a complex series of chemical reactions. Where do cells obtain the energy needed to rearrange the molecules during these reactions?

9. a) How do the light reactions of photosynthesis set the stage for the dark reactions?
   b) How does the anaerobic stage of photosynthesis set the stage for the aerobic stage?

Problem Solving

1. Trained athletes do not experience sore muscles after every strenuous game or athletic event they participate in. Explain why.

2. A concept map is a diagram that summarizes relationships among facts and ideas. Figure 21-23 illustrates an incomplete concept map for cell energy. Complete the map using additional boxes and lines to show how the following terms are linked to cell energy and to each other: solar energy, chemical energy, light reactions, dark reactions, aerobic, anaerobic, photosynthesis, fermentation, oxygen, carbon dioxide, and glucose.

FIGURE 21-23

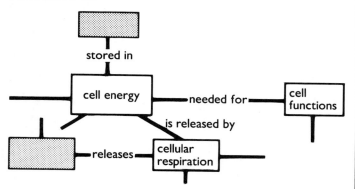

3. Construct a concept map for cell transport. Include the following terms: active transport, concentration gradient, diffusion, endocytosis, exocytosis, hypertonic, hypotonic, isotonic, osmosis, osmotic pressure, and passive transport.

4. Complete the chart using the appropriate letter from the following list.
   A. cellular respiration
   B. photosynthesis
   C. both cellular respiration and photosynthesis

	Plant Cells	**Animal Cells**
Day		
Night		

5. Most cookbooks, including those for microwave cooking, suggest adding salt to meat *after* cooking. What do you think would probably happen if salt were added to fresh meat?

6. Approximately 1% of the solar energy that strikes a leaf is converted by photosynthesis to chemical energy stored in food. What do you think happens to the other 99%?

Extensions

1. Identify and investigate two organisms that are able to live in both fresh water and in sea water. Explain what must occur to the cells of these organisms when they are in each environment.

2. Research one of the following topics. Write a report or make a presentation to your class.
   a) Specific methods of food preservation, the types of food that are preserved by each method, and how each method works.
   b) The importance of food preservation techniques in preventing food spoilage. State specific examples.

CHAPTER

22

Cell Division: Mitosis and Meiosis

J oey Moss has Down syndrome. But despite this, he works for the Edmonton Oilers. Although his speech is unintelligible, his work for the Edmonton Oilers is efficient. He is also popular with the players. Even though he has Down syndrome, Moss is leading a productive life.

Down syndrome produces varying degrees of mental retardation. People with the syndrome are educable according to their degree of retardation, and have a right to the richest life possible, but only recently have they been given a chance. Fifty years ago, Down syndrome

children were assumed to be so severely retarded they received little or no education. Only recently has the potential in Down syndrome children been explored.

People with Down syndrome do have serious medical problems. Some of the most serious symptoms include thyroid dysfunction, a high incidence of congenital heart malformations, and a relatively weak immune system. Mortality among people with Down syndrome is high, though decreasing with time. Today, fully 71% of Down syndrome births can be expected to live to age 30. Although this is much lower than the general population at 97%, it is a 20% improvement over a generation ago.

Two developments may improve the outlook for Down syndrome babies in the future. The first is early infant stimulation. It is believed that infants are born with surplus brain cells that will eventually die off if they remain unused. By intense early stimulation—talking, playing, and exercising—these excess cells can be called into use to maintain or increase an infant's physical and intellectual capacity. While applicable to any child, this technique is considered especially essential for a Down syndrome child.

The second development is the use of computers to help children with Down syndrome improve their language skills. For Down syndrome children, language problems do not stem from a simple lack of intelligence. Also involved are hearing loss brought on by a susceptibility to ear infections, and a perceptual problem that makes it difficult for people with Down syndrome to understand certain parts of speech. Educators believe that learning to write while learning to speak may help.

Our bodies are composed of many millions of cells. The faulty division of one of these cells may lead to Down syndrome. In other circumstances, it may lead to cancer and even death. The division process is extremely accurate and rarely errs. How would you construct such a nearly perfect replicating system? As you read this chapter, keep your ideas in mind.

Chapter Objectives

When you complete this chapter, you should:

1. Appreciate the significance of accurate cell division processes for growth and reproduction of plants and animals.

2. Be able to identify replication, mitosis, and cytokinesis as major events in mitotic cell division, and recognize the role played by each.

3. Be able to draw labelled diagrams of the stages of mitosis, explain the purpose of each stage, and state the final outcome.

4. Demonstrate skill in preparing, staining, and examining slides of plant tissue to observe various stages of mitosis.

5. Based on observations of commercially prepared slides, be able to draw labelled diagrams to compare mitosis in plant and animal cells.

6. Appreciate that cell division in plants is essentially similar to cell division in animals.

7. Be able to identify the major events of meiotic cell division and recognize the role played by each.

8. Be able to draw labelled diagrams of the stages of meiosis, explain the purpose of each stage, and state the final outcome.

9. Based on observations of commercially prepared slides, be able to draw labelled diagrams of the stages of mitosis and meiosis.

10. Be able to compare the stages of meiosis with the stages of mitosis.

11. Be able to identify, observe, and describe examples of sexual and asexual reproduction, relate them to mitosis or meiosis, and describe the advantages and disadvantages of each.

12. Appreciate the role of meiosis in sexual reproduction and explain how it ensures inherited variation in offspring.

22.1 Functions of Cell Division

The four basic functions of cell division are growth, maintenance, repair, and reproduction. Growth is a fundamental characteristic of all living things. Two cell-related factors contribute to the growth of an organism. One is an increase in cell size and the other is an increase in cell number. Some cells increase in size as they store the products they manufacture. Other cells store materials such as fat that are produced elsewhere in the organism.

However, no cell can continue to grow indefinitely because growth alters the surface area-to-volume ratio. (See Table 22-1.) The surface area of the cell membrane eventually becomes unable to transport materials in and out of the cell quickly enough to meet the needs of the cell contents. When this happens, the cell divides. At first, the two offspring cells are smaller than the parent cells. But they soon grow too large and divide again. This combination of cell growth and cell division causes the organism to grow.

TABLE 22-1 How Cell Growth Alters Surface Area-to-Volume Ratio

Dimensions of Cubic Cell	Surface Area (cm^2)	Cell Volume (cm^3)	Surface Area-to-Volume Ratio
1 cm cube (1 cm)	6	1	6:1
2 cm cube	24	8	3:1
3 cm cube	54	27	2:1

A second function of cell division is the production of new cells for maintenance. In humans, for example, millions and millions of new skin cells are produced every day to replace old cells that are lost from the skin's surface. (See Figure 22-1.) Cell division also produces new cells for repairing damaged tissue such as cuts in the skin, torn muscles, or broken bones.

Finally, as you will investigate further in this chapter, cell division is essential for reproduction. In the following laboratory exercise, you will observe cell division during the reproduction of yeast.

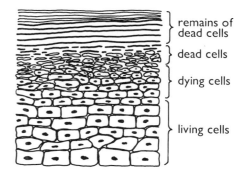

FIGURE 22-1 A cross section of skin that shows how dead cells at the surface are replaced by new cells.

remains of dead cells
dead cells
dying cells
living cells

LABORATORY EXERCISE 22-1
Observing Cell Division in Yeast

Unicellular organisms reproduce by mitotic cell division. Yeast cells reproduce asexually by budding. When a yeast cell reaches a certain size, an enlargement called a bud forms on the perimeter of the yeast cell. Mitosis occurs and one nucleus moves into the bud while the other remains in the parent cell. The bud slowly increases in size and eventually breaks away from the original cell.

Under certain conditions, when cell division is occurring rapidly, new buds begin to form on buds before they have broken away from the parent cell. Such rapid cell division may result in chains of yeast cells that are connected together. In this exercise, you will establish and grow a yeast culture, and observe cell division during the reproduction of yeast.

Cell Division and Biological Continuity

Whether the function of cell division is growth, maintenance, or repair, new cells must contain exactly the same DNA code as old cells. Maintaining the same DNA code is especially important during cell division for reproduction since only exact cell copies can ensure biological continuity. Biological continuity refers to the continued reproduction of offspring that resemble their parents. This concept is clearly illustrated by reproduction in unicellular organisms. In a suitable medium, a single yeast cell will soon produce thousands of offspring. All of these offspring will be identical in structure and function to the original yeast cell.

Biological continuity depends on accurate cell division. When yeast reproduces, each new yeast cell requires a complete copy of the parent cell's DNA code in order to grow, develop, look, and behave like yeast. The code is stored in DNA molecules carried on long, thin strands of **chromatin** contained in the nucleus.

Usually, the thread-like strands of chromatin are so scattered and tangled that they cannot be seen clearly even through an electron microscope. Only

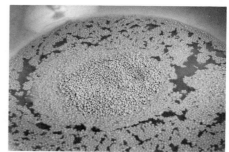

Sugar and warm water provide an ideal environment for the reproduction of yeast cells. You can see how much the yeast has expanded after only 1 h in the water and sugar solution.

during cell division does the chromatin coil up and thicken to form the distinctly visible nuclear bodies known as chromosomes. (See Figure 22-2.) If the new yeast cells are to be identical to their parents, each cell must receive its own complete set of chromosomes during cell division.

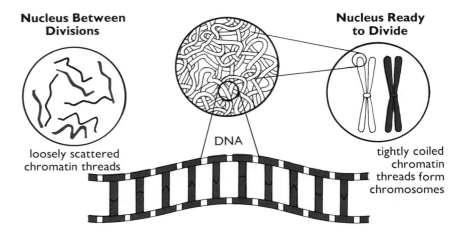

FIGURE 22-2 Chromosomes form from chromatin threads during cell division.

Chromatin Replication

Each parent cell has at least two copies of all cell organelles except the nucleus. When the cell divides, these organelles and the cytoplasm are shared between the two new cells. However, there is only one nucleus and only one set of chromosomes. Before the parent cell can begin to divide, the chromatin it contains must be duplicated so that each new nucleus receives its own set of chromosomes. This process is called **replication,** because the DNA on the new chromatin is a replica, identical to the original DNA.

Before the chromatin can replicate itself, all of the nucleotides needed for assembling the new DNA must already be present in the nucleus. These are called free nucleotides because they circulate freely throughout the nucleoplasm. In addition, the nucleus must also contain the enzymes that enable the process to take place rapidly.

The three-step replication sequence hinges on the ladder-like structure of the DNA molecule. (See Figure 22-3.) First, the DNA molecule separates into two strands much as a zipper does when you unzip it. This step breaks up the base pairs and exposes their unbonded ends to the free nucleotides. (See Figure 22-4.) Second, the base ends of nearby free nucleotides pair up with any exposed "rungs" that have matching base ends. Third, the sugar-phosphate ends of the new nucleotides bond to each other, completing the formation of two new DNA molecules.

The end result of chromatin replication is the formation of two complete sets of chromatin, which are identical to each other and to the original. The

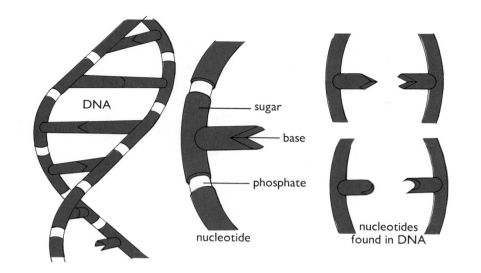

DNA

nucleotide

sugar

base

phosphate

nucleotides
found in DNA

FIGURE 22-3 The DNA molecule resembles a ladder twisted at both ends. It is made up of four types of T-shaped nucleotides that differ only at their base ends.

FIGURE 22-4 The three-step replication sequence of the DNA molecule. (The DNA ladder is shown here untwisted.)

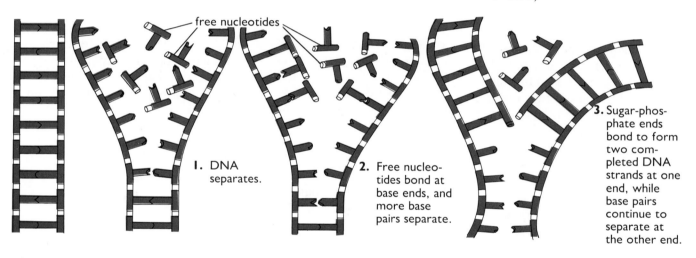

free nucleotides

I. DNA separates.

2. Free nucleotides bond at base ends, and more base pairs separate.

3. Sugar-phosphate ends bond to form two completed DNA strands at one end, while base pairs continue to separate at the other end.

nucleus now contains enough chromatin to form two complete sets of chromosomes. Cell division can now begin.

Section Review Questions

1. List the four functions of cell division and state an example of each.
2. Identify the two methods by which organisms grow.
3. a) What is the meaning of biological continuity?
   b) What role does cell division play in biological continuity?
4. a) Describe the structure and function of chromatin.
   b) How are chromatin and chromosomes related?
5. Define chromatin replication and describe its role in cell division.

Getting to the Root of Cancer

Every summer, people flock to beaches in search of the perfect tan, despite continual warnings that tanning not only wrinkles and toughens skin but may also increase the risk of developing skin cancer.

In its various forms, cancer strikes one in four Canadians and kills 1500 North Americans daily. While some types of cancers are being treated with success, others are still difficult to treat effectively. For instance, only 3% of people with pancreatic cancer live more than five years after diagnosis.

Although cancerous tumors or growths are found in all kinds of tissues, they are grouped together because all cancers result from abnormal cell growth. Normally, the growth, division, and position of cells is tightly controlled by factors within the cell and in its environment. These determine the nature of the organ or tissue of which the cell is a part. However, cancer cells grow and divide uncontrolled by limitations, and they can migrate to other tissues to create new tumors.

Until recently, the way in which cancer starts was a mystery. For example, what links the chemicals in tobacco smoke and the ultraviolet radiation in sunlight? They are both known to cause cancer, but what do they have in common? Although many cancer-causing agents have been identified, cancer deaths have not decreased in the last several decades. Simply identifying the agents that cause cancer evidently is not enough.

There is now progress in understanding how cancer starts. Researchers believe radiation and chemical carcinogens cause cancers by triggering genetic mutations. The ultraviolet radiation in sunlight, for example, creates kinks in DNA strands. Most mutations are benign and have little effect on the organism as a whole, since only one cell among many millions is affected. Mutations within two specific groups of genes, however, promote cancer. Not surprisingly, both groups produce proteins that regulate cell growth and division. The first group, called proto-oncogenes,

produces proteins that promote cell growth and replication. Some mutations of proto-oncogenes create cancer-causing genes or oncogenes. The second group, suppressor genes, normally produces proteins that inhibit cell growth and replication.

If a mutation produces an oncogene, the cell tends to grow and divide. If a simultaneous mutation damages suppressor genes, the cell has no ability to stop runaway growth. In reality, several mutations are probably necessary to create a cancerous cell. The systems regulating growth and division are poorly understood, but they likely involve complex interactions between proto-oncogene and suppressor-gene proteins.

Researchers hope effective cancer treatments will be developed when oncogenes and suppressor genes are better understood. Some benefits are already evident. Of patients who have had breast cancer tumors removed, 25% suffer relapse. The patients who experience relapse all carry a specific oncogene. A clinical trial is underway that identifies the women who carry that oncogene so they may be given further treatment. Future treatments may attempt to counteract the effects of cancer-causing mutations by blocking oncogene action with drugs and replacing the protein products of disabled suppressor genes.

22.2 **Mitotic Cell Division**

Growth and maintenance in multicellular organisms and reproduction in unicellular organisms all depend on **mitotic cell division.** The end result of this process is two new cells with nuclei identical to the original nucleus. Mitotic cell division involves three major events that occur in a sequence.

1. **Replication:** The production of an exact copy of all the chromatin in the original nucleus.
2. **Mitosis:** The separation of the chromatin copies and their even distribution to form two new nuclei, identical to each other and to the original nucleus.
3. **Cytokinesis:** The division of the cytoplasm such as fluid and organelles between the two new cells.

This three-part sequence is called mitotic cell division because it depends on mitosis to distribute the replicated chromatin. Each new cell receives an exact copy of the chromatin present in the original nucleus, and each cell is identical to the original except in size.

Interphase and Replication

As long as an organism remains alive, mitotic cell divisions continue to produce new cells to replace worn-out tissue such as skin, increase overall body size such as that of newborns, or increase the population of single-celled organisms such as yeast. Nevertheless, cells spend only a small amount of time participating in mitotic divisions. (See Figure 22-5.) Each cell spends most of its life in **interphase,** the period after a cell has been formed by mitotic division and before it divides again. (See Figure 22-6.)

When viewed under a compound microscope, a cell in interphase has a nucleus with a uniform appearance. Chromosomes are not visible because the chromatin is a mass of long, thin strands that are spread evenly throughout the nucleoplasm.

If you examine cells from a region of growth such as an onion-root tip, only about 10% of these cells will be dividing by mitosis. Even the fastest-dividing cells spend about 90% of the time in interphase.

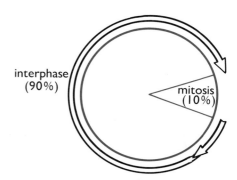

FIGURE 22-5 The cell cycle

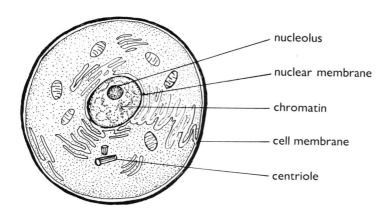

- nucleolus
- nuclear membrane
- chromatin
- cell membrane
- centriole

FIGURE 22-6 An animal cell in interphase

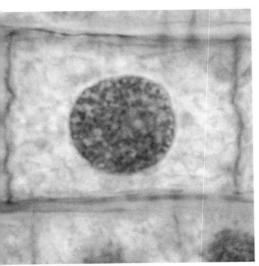

A cell in interphase. No chromosomes are visible.

A cell in prophase

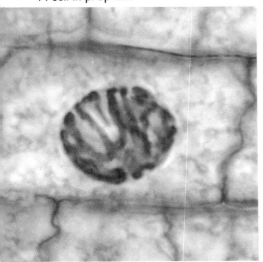

During interphase, the cell nucleus appears to be inactive because no movement or activity can be observed. However, the nucleus is performing its regular metabolic activity—sending codes for protein production to the ribosomes in the cytoplasm. Toward the end of interphase, chromatin replication occurs. If you were to examine the nucleus under a compound microscope during this step, you would be unable to detect changes taking place within the nucleus. It would continue to have a uniform appearance. However, the nucleus is now ready to undergo mitosis.

Stages of Mitosis

Actually, interphase is not a part of mitosis. Mitosis refers only to the process that divides the nucleus. For convenience, biologists describe mitosis as a series of four distinct stages: prophase, metaphase, anaphase, and telophase.

Although the end result of mitosis is the same in both plant and animal cells, the details of some stages differ slightly. The following subsections describe mitosis in plant cells. As you read them, refer frequently to the flow diagram in Figure 22-7.

Prophase
When prophase begins, the nucleus already has two complete, but intertwined, sets of chromatin. **Prophase** is the series of events that prepares the nucleus to distribute the replicated chromatin into two separate sets. Under a compound microscope, early prophase can first be observed when the nucleolus begins to disintegrate. The thin strands of chromatin begin to shorten and thicken, but do not yet appear as distinct chromosomes. (See Figure 22-8.)

By middle prophase, the chromosomes are becoming visible, and the nucleolus has completely disintegrated. The nuclear membrane also begins to break down. (See Figure 22-9.) Microtubules called **spindle fibres** then form

FIGURE 22-8 Early prophase

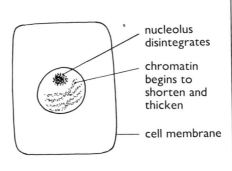

nucleolus disintegrates

chromatin begins to shorten and thicken

cell membrane

FIGURE 22-9 Middle prophase

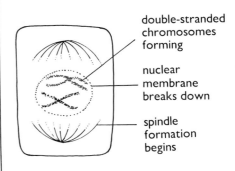

double-stranded chromosomes forming

nuclear membrane breaks down

spindle formation begins

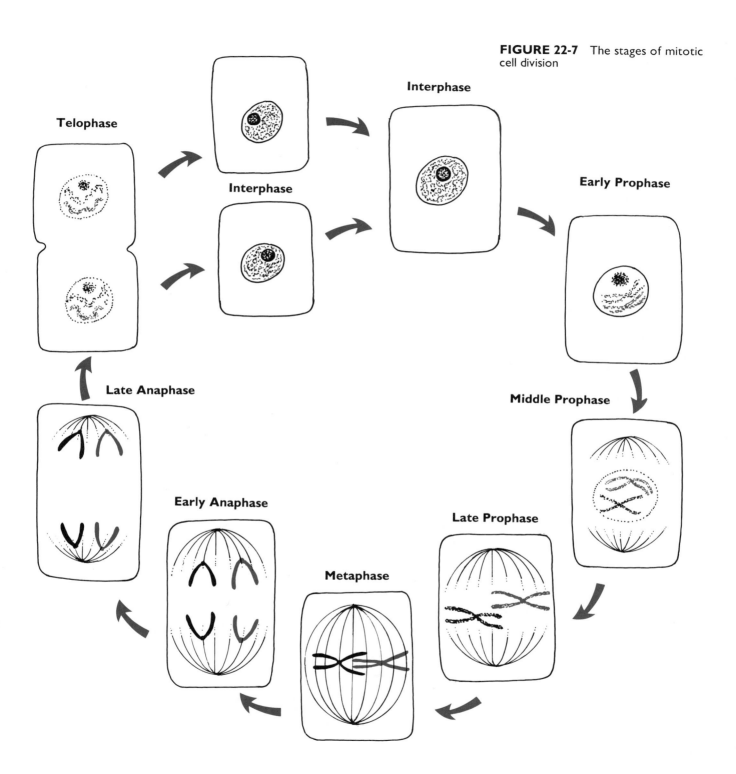

FIGURE 22-7 The stages of mitotic cell division

Telophase

Interphase

Interphase

Early Prophase

Middle Prophase

Late Prophase

Metaphase

Early Anaphase

Late Anaphase

between the two ends, or poles, of the cell. The resulting array of fibres is called the **spindle.** (See Figure 22-10.)

By late prophase, the nuclear membrane has disintegrated completely, and the chromatin has thickened to form distinctly visible **double-stranded chromosomes.** (See Figure 22-11.) Each chromosome has a pair of identical strands known as **chromatids,** which are linked close to the middle by a bead-like **centromere.** Near the end of prophase, the double-stranded chromosomes begin to move toward the centre of the cell.

LEFT: FIGURE 22-10 Late prophase

RIGHT: FIGURE 22-11 Each chromatid of a double-stranded chromosome contains copies of its DNA code.

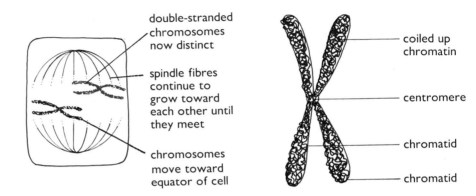

double-stranded chromosomes now distinct

spindle fibres continue to grow toward each other until they meet

chromosomes move toward equator of cell

coiled up chromatin

centromere

chromatid

chromatid

Metaphase

As the photomicrograph on the next page shows, metaphase is easy to identify. During **metaphase,** the double-stranded chromosomes line up along the equator of the cell. (See Figure 22-12.) Each pair of chromatids is attached by its centromere to a spindle.

In late metaphase, the centromeres split, and the double-stranded chromosomes begin to pull apart. As the paired chromatids separate, they move in opposite directions. Once this happens, the chromatids are called **single-stranded chromosomes.** (See Figure 22-13.) Each of these chromosomes has a half centromere somewhere along its length.

LEFT: FIGURE 22-12 Metaphase

RIGHT: FIGURE 22-13 Each single-stranded chromosome contains one copy of its DNA code. The nucleus now contains pairs of identical single-stranded chromosomes.

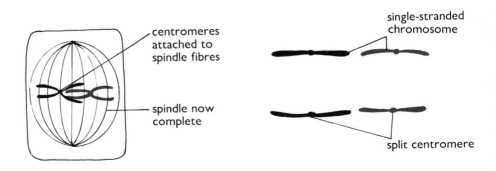

centromeres attached to spindle fibres

spindle now complete

single-stranded chromosome

split centromere

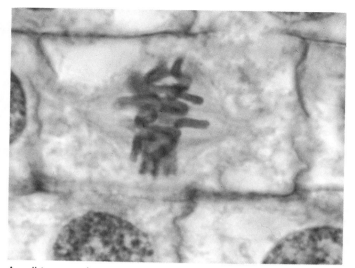
A cell in metaphase

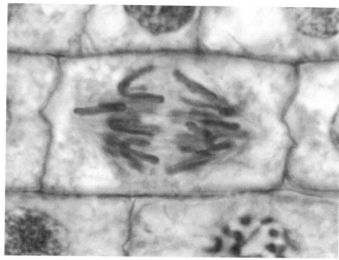
A cell in anaphase

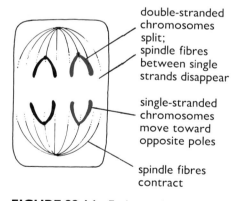

double-stranded
chromosomes
split;
spindle fibres
between single
strands disappear

single-stranded
chromosomes
move toward
opposite poles

spindle fibres
contract

FIGURE 22-14 Early anaphase

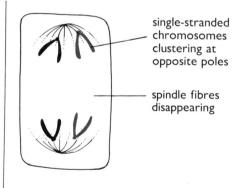

single-stranded
chromosomes
clustering at
opposite poles

spindle fibres
disappearing

FIGURE 22-15 Late anaphase

Anaphase

Anaphase is easily recognized in a photomicrograph because the single-stranded chromosomes form V-shapes that point toward the poles of the cell. The chromosomes look as if they are being pulled along by the spindle fibres, which remain attached to the half centromeres. (See Figure 22-14.) The exact cause of this movement is not fully understood, but biologists think it results from the contraction of protein molecules in the spindle fibres. At the end of anaphase, a complete set of single-stranded chromosomes is at each pole of the cell. (See Figure 22-15.)

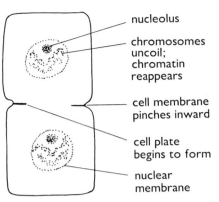

- nucleolus
- chromosomes uncoil; chromatin reappears
- cell membrane pinches inward
- cell plate begins to form
- nuclear membrane

FIGURE 22-16 Telophase

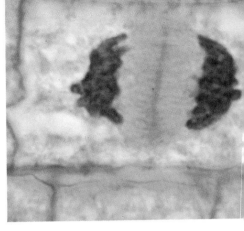

A cell in telophase

Telophase

Telophase is the final stage of mitosis. The first sign of telophase is the formation of a nuclear membrane around each set of chromosomes. Then a nucleolus reappears in each nucleus. Finally, the chromosomes begin to unravel. They lose their distinct shape and again begin to appear as a scattered mass of chromatin. (See Figure 22-16.) At the end of telophase, two complete, new nuclei are formed which are identical to each other and to the original nucleus.

Although telophase marks the end of mitosis, cell division is not yet complete. Complete cell division requires three processes: replication, mitosis, and cytokinesis.

Cytokinesis

Cytokinesis is the division of the cytoplasm in the original cell between the two new cells. During cytokinesis in plant cells, a structure known as the **cell plate** forms from tiny vesicles produced by the Golgi apparatus. These vesicles fuse to become the cell plate. The cell plate first appears as a very faint, thin line along the equator of the original cell. It gradually grows thicker as each new cell constructs its own cell wall from molecules of cellulose.

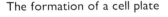

The formation of a cell plate

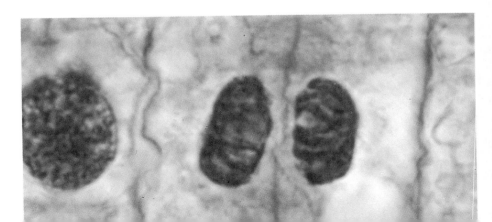

LABORATORY EXERCISE 22-2
Mitosis in Onion-Root Tips

The nucleus of a cell contains the hereditary material that directs the development of the organism. During cell reproduction, the nucleus and its contents undergo orderly changes and processes. The end result of these activities is the exact replication of the hereditary material and the formation of two new nuclei.

Mitotic cell division in plants and animals is most noticeable in regions of rapid tissue growth. In plants, new shoots and root tips are the main regions of mitotic cell division. In this exercise, you will prepare slides of the cells of onion-root tips to observe the various stages of mitosis.

Mitosis occurs at the tips of new roots.

Mitotic Cell Division in Animals

In animals, mitotic cell division begins in the same way as it does in plants with the replication of the chromatin in the cell nucleus. However, mitosis in animal cells differs in some respects from mitosis in plant cells. Most animal cells have a pair of **centrioles,** which are organelles most plant cells lack. Centrioles are cylindrical structures that play an important role in animal cell division.

During early prophase, the centrioles migrate to opposite poles of the animal cell. Microtubule fibres called **astral rays** form a prominent starlike arrangement around each centriole. (See Figure 22-17.) During late prophase, more microtubules develop to form spindle fibres extending between the centrioles. The resulting spindle is similar to the array formed in dividing plant cells, but plant cells do not have centrioles or astral rays.

Through metaphase and anaphase, mitosis in animal cells is the same as it is in plant cells. During late telophase, however, the centrioles in animal cells

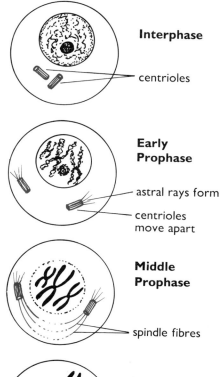

Interphase
— centrioles

Early
Prophase
— astral rays form
— centrioles move apart

Middle
Prophase
— spindle fibres

Late
Prophase

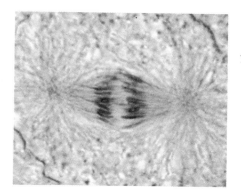

Mitosis in an animal cell. How does this differ from mitosis in a plant cell?

FIGURE 22-17 Centrioles play a role in spindle formation during mitosis in animal cells. (Plant cells do not have centrioles and do not form astral rays.)

The cleavage furrow in a frog embryo

replicate so that each new cell receives two. This step does not occur in plant cells because, as you have learned, they do not have centrioles.

Cytokinesis in animal cells is also very different from cytokinesis in plant cells. During telophase, just as the chromosomes reach the opposite poles and the nuclear membranes begin to re-form, the membrane of the animal cell begins to pinch together at the equator. This indentation, or groove formed around the middle of the cell, is called the cleavage furrow. The cleavage furrow becomes deeper and deeper until, eventually, the cytoplasm splits into two masses. Biologists think that contracting microtubule fibres exert the forces responsible for cytokinesis.

The Outcome of Mitotic Cell Division

In mitotic cell division, an original parent cell produces two identical offspring cells. (See Figure 22-18.) Regardless of whether the cell undergoing mitotic division is from a plant, a protist, or an animal, the outcome is the same. As a result of mitosis, each new nucleus contains an exact copy of the DNA present in the original cell nucleus. That is, each new offspring cell has exactly the same number and kind of chromosomes.

In the following laboratory exercise, you will observe and compare mitosis in a variety of plant and animal cells.

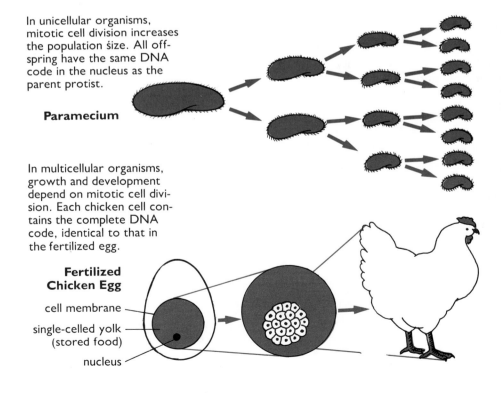

In unicellular organisms, mitotic cell division increases the population size. All off-spring have the same DNA code in the nucleus as the parent protist.

Paramecium

In multicellular organisms, growth and development depend on mitotic cell division. Each chicken cell contains the complete DNA code, identical to that in the fertilized egg.

Fertilized Chicken Egg

cell membrane
single-celled yolk (stored food)
nucleus

FIGURE 22-18 The outcome of mitotic cell division in unicellular (protist) cells and in multicellular (animal) cells.

LABORATORY EXERCISE 22-3
Mitosis in Plant and Animal Cells

As you have already learned, mitotic cell division is the way many unicellular organisms reproduce. It is also the process by which the body cells of multicellular organisms divide.

In multicellular organisms, mitotic cell division is best seen in regions where rapid growth occurs. In Laboratory Exercise 22-2, you made slides of onion-root tips in order to observe mitosis. In this exercise, you will examine slides of onion-root tips prepared in a different way. You will also observe a variety of other tissues to investigate further examples of mitotic cell division.

Rapid growth occurs in root tips when cells divide by mitosis, causing the root to lengthen.

The Need for Mitotic Cell Division

In humans, mitotic cell division begins when the sperm and the egg fuse at conception, and is repeated many millions of times until death. Because of mitotic divisions, a single-celled zygote can grow to become an adult with approximately *1 000 000 000 000* cells. Mitotic divisions also allow for the replacement of worn-out cells and the formation of scar tissue because any cut, break, or scrape stimulates adjacent cells to divide more rapidly.

The life span of a cell is the length of time between mitotic cell divisions. This period varies greatly, depending on the type of cell, the type of organism, and its age. In the rapidly growing embryos of many species, the number of cells can double every 15 min. In a newborn human, the number of new cells produced each day is enormous. Under ideal conditions, bacteria can divide every 20 min, and certain species of yeast can divide every 2 h. The rapidly growing cells at the root tips of certain plants divide every 14 h.

There may be a connection between a cell's ability to divide and the aging process. The exact nature of this relationship remains unclear, but some medical researchers think that human aging results from a limited ability of cells to continue making exact copies as they divide by mitosis. There is ample evidence that cells unavoidably accumulate poisonous wastes as the body ages. This accumulation slowly begins to interfere with the cell's ability to function normally and, as a result, the cell ages. The large amounts of pigment that can be found in the cells of aged people, especially in nondividing cells such as those in muscle and nerve tissue, support this hypothesis. In constantly dividing cells, such as liver cells, there is much less accumulation of pigment.

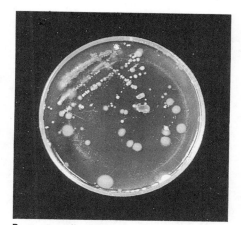

Bacteria cells divide rapidly to form the colonies seen here.

Currently, biologists do not know the exact chemical composition of the pigment that accumulates in cells. But they believe it is the remains of worn-out cell structures such as mitochondria that have been consumed by lysosomes. Interestingly, the organs that lose their ability to function, and therefore age most quickly, are those in which cells are not actively dividing. The brain, heart, kidneys, and muscles are examples. However, organs in which cells

Maureen is an internist who specializes in oncology, which is the study of cancer. She works at Women's College Hospital in Toronto. She spends most of her time in patient care and teaching students, but she also does clinical cancer research.

Q. *Since you began studying cancer, has there been much progress toward a cure?*

A. Cancer is abnormal mitosis. Cells replicate and continue to replicate uncontrolled. During the last 30 years, great advances have been made in cancer research. Now cancers that couldn't be cured before can be cured with chemotherapy. For breast cancer, there are now treatments that can actually prolong the patient's life.

Q. *What research are you doing?*

A. I work on clinical research. I test different drugs to be used for cancer treatment. We test three different treatments—hormone treatment, chemotherapy, and the newest treatment on the market, biologic-response modifiers.

Q. *What are they?*

A. Biologic-response modifiers are substances such as interferon. They make the body respond to cancer by using the body's own immune system to fight the disease.

Q. *Do you use information from your patients in these tests?*

A. For ten years, we have collected data and tissue from patients with breast cancer who

Meet Maureen Trudeau

have volunteered to take part in a research project on a new oncogene (a cancer-causing gene) called "her-z/neu," or "neu" for short. We're analyzing the tissue to find out if women with high oncogene levels are more likely to die of breast cancer than women with low levels.

Q. *What part of your job do you like best?*

A. I like the interaction with the patients, students, and residents. I like doing research. Medicine changes rapidly, so it's good to work in a teaching centre, where

there is access to everything new in the field.

Q. *Is it depressing working with patients who have cancer?*

A. Unfortunately, nice people get cancer. It is hard when your patients die. The problems you encounter with cancer patients take in the whole scope of medicine, including psychiatry. Patients need support, and you have to be content knowing that you made their lives more pleasant for a while.

Q. *Do you have to tell patients they're going to die?*

A. Yes, and it's always hard— there's no good way to do it.

Q. *What percentage of the doctors at this hospital are women?*

A. Half of the doctors and the students are women. Women in medicine are accepted and respected now. Men and women work well together in this field.

Q. *What do you recommend to a student interested in becoming a doctor?*

A. Medicine is a tough and competitive field. It requires hard work and responsibility. It's a good idea to do something else before going into medicine, to get some exposure to something other than science. I also recommend doing volunteer work in hospitals. Doing volunteer work will help you find out if you like the hospital atmosphere. Medicine is a dynamic and constantly interesting career.

continue to divide actively age more slowly and show far less loss of function. But there seems to be a limit to the number of times a cell can divide by mitosis. Consequently, the inability of cells to divide indefinitely limits the maximum possible human lifespan to little more than 100 years.

Section Review Questions

1. Describe the differences between
   a) chromatin and chromatid
   b) chromatin and chromosome
   c) single-stranded chromosome and double-stranded chromosome
2. List the three major events of mitotic cell division and briefly describe the main outcome of each.
3. Describe the differences between
   a) mitosis and mitotic cell division
   b) mitosis and interphase
4. List the four stages of mitosis and briefly describe the events that occur during each stage.
5. Compare cytokinesis in animal cells and in plant cells.
6. Explain the importance of mitotic cell division in humans.

22.3 Meiotic Cell Division

Mitotic cell division depends on mitosis to pass on exact and complete copies of the original DNA of a parent cell to new offspring cells. In addition to its importance to growth, maintenance, and repair of multicellular organisms, mitosis also ensures biological continuity in unicellular organisms. Because of mitosis, each offspring of an amoeba receives a nucleus like that of the parent cell. The budding of yeast and the asexual reproduction of plants from runners or cuttings also depend on mitosis. Mitosis occurs in every part of the human body and in all cell types but one. Cell divisions involving mitosis are the most common type. However, a second type, called **meiotic cell division** also occurs in organisms that reproduce sexually. In this section, you will investigate the importance and the process of meiotic cell division.

The Need for Meiotic Cell Division

Each species has a characteristic number of chromosomes per body cell. (See Table 22-2.) For example, fruit flies have *8* chromosomes in each body cell. This suggests that the fertilized egg the fruit fly developed from also had *8*

TABLE 22-2   Chromosome Number in Representative Plants and Animals

Organism	Body Cells: Diploid Number (2N)	Sex Cells: Haploid Number (N)
Human	46	23
Chicken	78	39
Fruit Fly	8	4
Crayfish	200	100
Garden Pea	14	7
Onion	16	8
Cat	38	19
Dog	78	39
Mouse	40	20
Rat	42	21
Corn	20	10
Lily	24	12
Sugar Maple	26	13
Scotch Pine	24	12

chromosomes. But only half of those chromosomes came from the unfertilized egg. The other half came from the sperm cell that fertilized it. Similarly, a fertilized human egg has *46* chromosomes: *23* **maternal chromosomes** from the mother's egg and *23* **paternal chromosomes** from the father's sperm.

Apparently, sex cells such as eggs and sperm contain only half the usual number of chromosomes. You have learned that all cells come from pre-existing cells. If every human grows from a fertilized egg with 46 chromosomes, how does the body produce cells with only 23 chromosomes? Mitotic cell division cannot produce such cells. No matter how many times a fertilized human egg divides by mitosis, all the resulting cells will still have 46 chromosomes. (See Figure 22-19.)

Therefore, if mitotic cell division produced eggs and sperm, each of these sex cells would contain a complete set of chromosomes. The result of conception would be a fertilized egg with two sets of chromosomes, and the chromosome number would double with each generation. But even one extra chromosome can cause serious developmental problems. Each body cell of a person with Down syndrome, for example, contains 47 chromosomes. For biological continuity, both the number and the kind of chromosomes must remain constant from one generation to the next. A fertilized egg with 92 chromosomes would not be able to develop at all.

Doubling of the chromosome number does not occur because egg and sperm cells are produced by meiotic cell division. During meiotic cell division, the chromosome number is reduced to half by a specialized process called **meiosis.** (See Figure 22-20.) In male humans, meiosis occurs only in the germinal cells of the testes. In females, meiosis takes place only in the ovaries. But although meiosis is limited to reproductive organs, it is vitally important for the biological continuity of all organisms that reproduce sexually, including plants and fungi, as well as animals such as fruit flies and humans.

Meiosis and Chromosome Number

Meiosis occurs in many different kinds of organisms, but chromosome number varies from one organism to another. To make one description of meiosis apply to different species, biologists use a code to describe chromosome number. (See Figure 22-21.) By understanding this code, you will find it easier to learn about meiosis.

FIGURE 22-19 Human egg and sperm join to form a 46-chromosome zygote. It divides by mitosis to form numerous 46-chromosome body cells. But mitotic division cannot produce 23-chromosome sex cells.

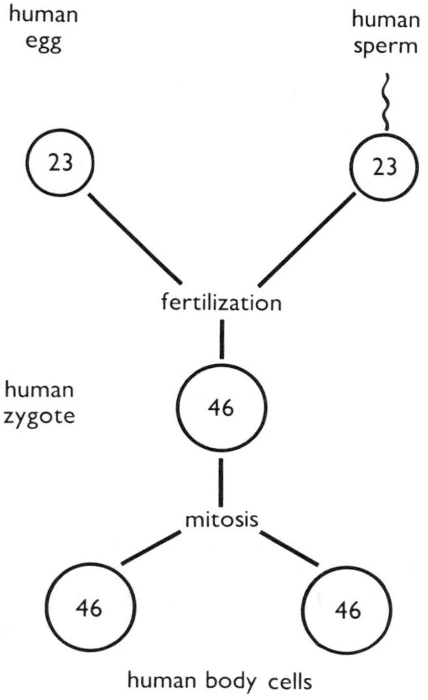

FIGURE 22-20 Meiotic division is needed to form human gametes with only 23 chromosomes each. Fertilization then brings together the 46 chromosomes characteristic of human body cells.

FIGURE 22-21 The chromosome code shown here uses 2N for body cells and N for sex cells. As a result, this description of sexual reproduction can be applied to many different species. (Figures 22-19 and 22-20 apply only to humans.)

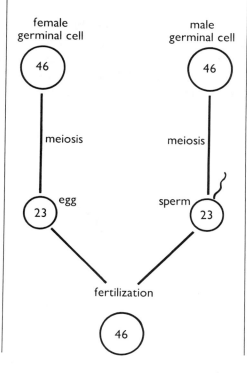

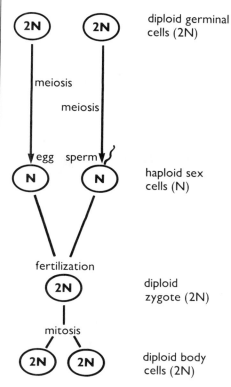

In this code, the number of chromosomes in a sperm cell or an egg cell is written as "N," and is called the **haploid number** because N represents a single set of chromosomes. (The prefix "hap-" is derived from the Greek word, *haplous*, meaning single.) When sperm and egg join, the number of chromosomes becomes "2N." This code is called the **diploid number** because it results from the combination of two sets of chromosomes. (The prefix "di-" is derived from the Greek word, *diploos*, meaning double.)

In fruit flies, N = 4 (the haploid number) and 2N = 8 (the diploid number). In humans, the haploid number (N) is 23, and the diploid number (2N) is 46. So, while all ordinary body cells contain 23 pairs of chromosomes, sperm and egg cells contain only 23 single chromosomes. These gametes are produced from specialized germinal cells in the gonads. Each germinal cell as 2N chromosomes but is divided by meiosis to produce sex cells with only N chromosomes.

Meiosis and Homologous Chromosomes

In Figure 22-22, you can see that for each paternal chromosome in the sperm cell, there is a corresponding maternal chromosome in the egg cell. For example, the maternal chromosome that carries DNA-coded instructions for eye colour is matched by a paternal chromosome that also carries instructions for eye colour. (See Figure 22-23.) These two corresponding chromosomes are **homologous chromosomes** or homologues of each other. The nucleus of a fruit-fly cell contains *4* pairs of homologous chromosomes. A human cell has *23* pairs of homologous chromosomes.

This means that all body cells, including the germinal cells, contain two complete DNA codes for every inherited characteristic. However, when a germinal cell divides by meiosis, the new sex cells receive only one chromosome from each pair of homologous chromosomes. In addition, meiosis

FIGURE 22-22 The diploid fruit-fly zygote contains 4 maternal chromosomes and 4 matching paternal homologues.

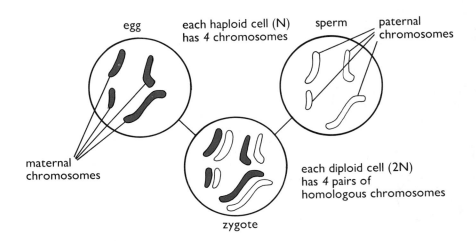

egg   each haploid cell (N) has 4 chromosomes   sperm   paternal chromosomes

maternal chromosomes

each diploid cell (2N) has 4 pairs of homologous chromosomes

zygote

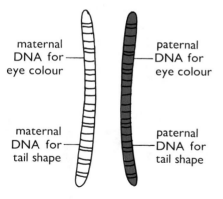

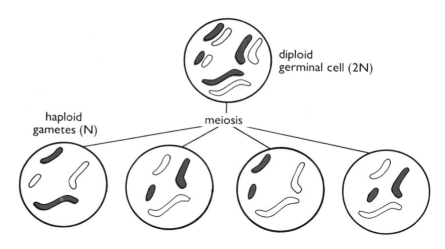

FIGURE 22-23 Each fruit-fly zygote receives two sets of instructions for each characteristic. Each homologue carries DNA codes for thousands of inherited features.

FIGURE 22-24 Haploid cells produced by meiosis contain only one homologue from each pair of homologous chromosomes. Random assortment results in many different homologue groupings.

rearranges the germinal cell's chromosomes so that its maternal and its paternal homologues are distributed randomly to the new sex cells. (See Figure 22-24.) For example, a human egg cell could receive the maternal chromosome for eye colour but the paternal chromosome for hair colour.

The end result of meiotic cell division is four new sex cells, each with only a single set of N chromosomes, the haploid number. This set contains one homologue from each pair of homologous chromosomes in the germinal cell, some of which are paternal, and others are maternal. This outcome is accomplished by three major events that occur in a sequence.

1. *Replication*: The production of an exact copy of all the chromatin in the original nucleus to provide enough chromatin copies for 4N chromosomes (double the diploid number).
2. *Meiosis*: The chromatin copies are divided twice and distributed randomly to form four completely different haploid nuclei.
3. *Cytokinesis*: The division of the cell cytoplasm into four parts. The new sex cells can then develop into mature eggs or sperm.

Stages of Meiosis

Meiosis occurs only in the nuclei of germinal cells, and only after the chromatin has already been replicated. During meiosis, the replicated DNA is divided twice. The first division is usually called Meiosis I, and the second division is Meiosis II. The individual stages of Meiosis I and Meiosis II have

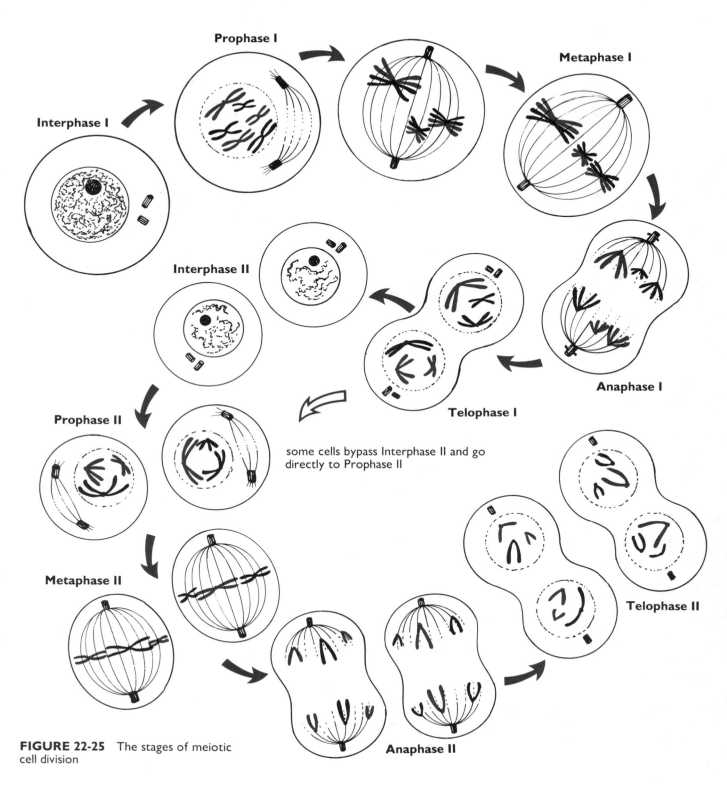

Interphase I

Prophase I

Metaphase I

Anaphase I

Telophase I

Interphase II

some cells bypass Interphase II and go
directly to Prophase II

Prophase II

Metaphase II

Anaphase II

Telophase II

FIGURE 22-25 The stages of meiotic
cell division

names like the stages of mitosis. However, the details of the stages of meiosis differ in several ways from the stages of mitosis. As you read the following subsections, refer frequently to the flow diagram in Figure 22-25.

Meiosis I: The First Meiotic Division

Before the first meiotic division can begin, the DNA in the cell nucleus must be replicated. As in mitosis, this first stage is called interphase.

Interphase I

Under a compound microscope, germinal cells in Interphase I can be identified by their uniform-looking nuclei. No chromosomes are visible because the chromatin remains scattered as it replicates. The germinal cell begins meiosis with a 4N set of chromatin, which is exactly enough to produce four haploid cells. (See Figure 22-26.)

Prophase I

At the beginning of Prophase I, the scattered chromatin slowly shortens and thickens to become distinctly visible chromosomes. Because the chromatin replicated during interphase, each double-stranded chromosome consists of two identical chromatids attached by a centromere. The germinal cell now has 4N chromatids but only 2N chromosomes. (See Figure 22-27.)

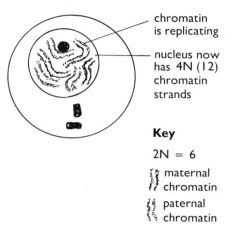

chromatin is replicating

nucleus now has 4N (12) chromatin strands

Key

2N = 6

maternal chromatin

paternal chromatin

FIGURE 22-26 The germinal cell of an animal prior to meiosis

FIGURE 22-27 Prophase I of meiosis in animal cells

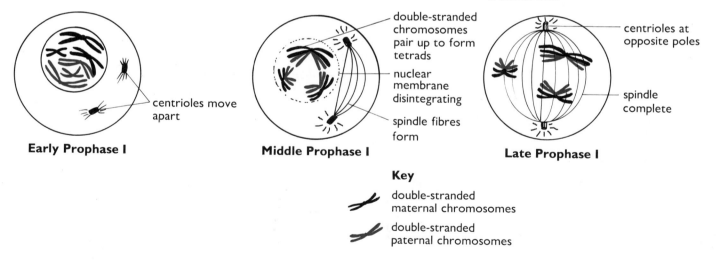

centrioles move apart

Early Prophase I

double-stranded chromosomes pair up to form tetrads

nuclear membrane disintegrating

spindle fibres form

Middle Prophase I

centrioles at opposite poles

spindle complete

Late Prophase I

Key

double-stranded maternal chromosomes

double-stranded paternal chromosomes

As Prophase I continues, each double-stranded chromosome pairs up lengthwise with its homologue. (See Figure 22-28.) The resulting structure is called a **tetrad** because it contains four strands. (The prefix "tetra-" is derived from the Greek word, *tetra*, meaning four.) The two homologous, double-stranded chromosomes in each tetrad line up so that corresponding points

FIGURE 22-28 The homologues in a tetrad line up so that corresponding DNA segments are paired exactly.

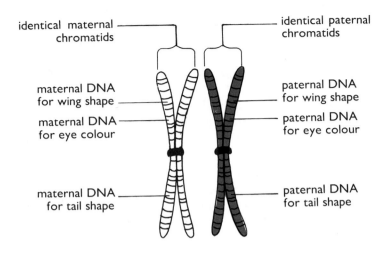

identical maternal chromatids

identical paternal chromatids

maternal DNA for wing shape

paternal DNA for wing shape

maternal DNA for eye colour

paternal DNA for eye colour

maternal DNA for tail shape

paternal DNA for tail shape

along their lengths are precisely matched up. (For example, DNA with the maternal code for eye colour lies beside the paternal DNA code for eye colour.)

The maternal and the paternal chromatids may then become connected at one or more points. At each of these points, the chromatids break and rejoin, exchanging entire segments. (See Figure 22-29.) This process is called **crossing over.** It allows the exchange of hereditary information between paternal and maternal chromosomes. (For example, DNA coding for blue eye colour may be replaced by DNA coding for brown eye colour.)

While these chromosomal changes are occurring, the nuclear membrane begins to disintegrate, and microtubules begin to form spindle fibres. As Prophase I ends, the tetrads can be seen moving toward the equator of the cell.

FIGURE 22-29 Crossing over changes chromatid structure.
Before (left): Wherever paternal and maternal chromatids touch each other, they break and form new links.
After (right): Three segments of maternal DNA have now exchanged places with three segments of paternal DNA.

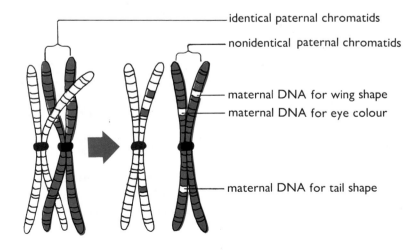

identical paternal chromatids

nonidentical paternal chromatids

maternal DNA for wing shape

maternal DNA for eye colour

maternal DNA for tail shape

Metaphase I

In Metaphase I, the tetrads line up lengthwise along the equator. (See Figure 22-30.) The nuclear membrane has completely disintegrated, and microtubules have formed a spindle. Each double-stranded chromosome is attached to a spindle fibre by its own centromere.

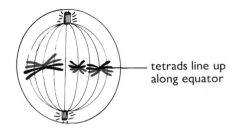

FIGURE 22-30 Metaphase I of meiosis in animal cells

Anaphase I

During Anaphase I, the tetrads break up into separate double-stranded chromosomes. (See Figure 22-31.) There are still 2N chromosomes, each with two chromatids joined by a centromere. Each centromere is still attached to a spindle fibre. Characteristic V-shapes are seen as each tetrad breaks up, and its two double-stranded chromosomes move along the spindle fibres to opposite poles. Each pole receives only N double-stranded chromosomes.

The direction in which maternal and paternal chromosomes migrate is determined purely by chance. Therefore, each pole receives a different and unpredictable grouping of the original chromosomes. This process of distributing chromosomes at random between the two new cells is called **random assortment.** Because of random assortment, many new homologue combinations are possible. This aspect of meiosis is important to the outcome of sexual reproduction.

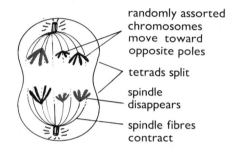

FIGURE 22-31 Anaphase I of meiosis in animal cells

Telophase I

During Anaphase I, each pole receives a total of N double-stranded chromosomes, one from each pair of homologous chromosomes. During Telophase I, these homologues are assembled into two new haploid nuclei. (See Figure 22-32.)

Telophase I marks the end of Meiosis I. This first meiotic division has caused three major changes.

1. *Crossing over*: Originally, the two linked chromatids on each chromosome were identical copies replicated from the same strand of chromatin. After crossing over, the copies are no longer identical.
2. *Random assortment*: The paternal and maternal homologues from the original nucleus have been distributed randomly to the new nuclei.
3. *Reduction division*: The number of chromosomes per nucleus is now N, half of what it was when meiosis began in the germinal cell.

Because Meiosis I produces two new offspring cells with haploid nuclei, it is often called **reduction division.** However, the N chromosomes have two chromatids each. So, there is still too much DNA in each nucleus for one sex cell. A second meiotic division is needed to complete the task of producing haploid sex cells.

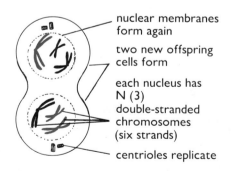

FIGURE 22-32 Telophase I of meiosis in animal cells

Meiosis II: The Second Meiotic Division

The starting point of Meiosis II is not as definite as it is in Meiosis I. Figure 22-25 on page 688 shows nuclear membranes forming at the end of Telophase I, which is then followed by a second interphase. However, not all organisms follow this sequence.

Interphase II

In organisms that do have a distinct Telophase I, cytokinesis forms two separate offspring cells. Inside the two nuclei, the chromatids uncoil, but the scattered chromatin does not replicate. In many organisms, however, the new nuclei skip these stages and go directly from Anaphase I to Prophase II.

Prophase II

As usual in prophase, the chromatin shortens and thickens, and double-stranded chromosomes become visible. Each offspring cell forms a spindle, and chromosomes migrate toward the middle of the cells. If a nuclear membrane has formed during Interphase II, it begins to disintegrate again. (See Figure 22-33.)

Metaphase II

Metaphase II is easily recognizable under a compound microscope because the chromosomes line up along the equators of the offspring cells. Each offspring cell has a total of N double-stranded chromosomes. The formation of the spindle is completed, and the paired chromatids are attached to the spindle fibres by their centromeres. (See Figure 22-34.)

Anaphase II

During Anaphase II, the centromeres split. The unpaired chromatids, now called single-stranded chromosomes, migrate in opposite directions. (See Figure 22-35.) Again, the chromosomes are distributed by random assortment. Under a compound microscope, this stage appears as four groups of V-shaped chromosomes moving toward the poles of the two cells. Each group contains N single-stranded chromosomes.

Telophase II

In Telophase II, the single-stranded chromosomes reach the opposite poles of the offspring cells. Under a compound microscope, they appear as four dense clusters, one at each pole. Then, as usual in telophase, the spindle disappears and nuclear membranes appear. There are now four complete haploid nuclei, each containing N single-stranded chromosomes. (See Figure 22-36.) Inside the nuclei, the chromosomes uncoil to form scattered chromatin once again.

Telophase II marks the end of Meiosis II, but meiotic cell division is not yet complete.

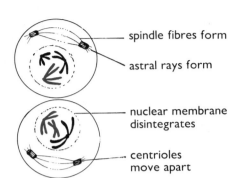

FIGURE 22-33 Prophase II of meiosis in animal cells

spindle fibres form

astral rays form

nuclear membrane disintegrates

centrioles move apart

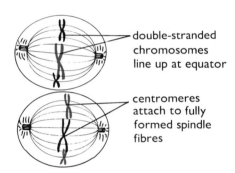

FIGURE 22-34 Metaphase II of meiosis in animal cells

double-stranded chromosomes line up at equator

centromeres attach to fully formed spindle fibres

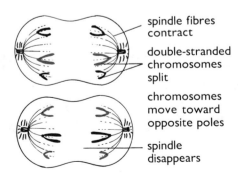

FIGURE 22-35 Anaphase II of meiosis in animal cells

spindle fibres contract

double-stranded chromosomes split

chromosomes move toward opposite poles

spindle disappears

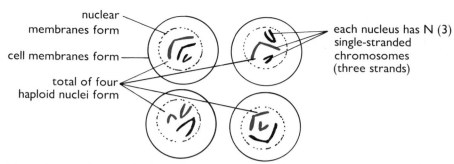

nuclear membranes form

cell membranes form

total of four haploid nuclei form

each nucleus has N (3) single-stranded chromosomes (three strands)

FIGURE 22-36 Telophase II of meiosis in animal cells

Cytokinesis and the Outcome of Meiotic Cell Division

Meiotic cell division involves three major events: replication, meiosis, and cytokinesis. Replication begins in a single germinal cell with a diploid nucleus. The two meiotic divisions produce four haploid nuclei. Cytokinesis actually occurs twice — once after Meiosis I and again after Meiosis II. Cytokinesis divides the cytoplasm of the germinal cell into four sections and surrounds each with a cell membrane.

In male humans, meiotic cell division results in four new cells of equal size. These cells eventually develop into four mature sperm cells, each containing N chromosomes. In females, both the process and the outcome are different. (See Figure 22-37.) Meiosis begins in a baby girl's germinal cells before she is born, but it stops before the cells actually divide. After puberty, at 28-day intervals, one germinal cell at a time completes the first meiotic division. This occurs one day before ovulation. The second meiotic division, however, proceeds to completion only if fertilization occurs. In that case, four cells with N chromosomes each are produced, but one cell receives almost all of the cytoplasm. The other three cells, which are called polar bodies, soon disintegrate. The single survivor eventually develops into an egg with a large quantity of stored nutrients and other molecules needed for development. (If fertilization does not occur, division stops at the two-cell stage.)

LABORATORY EXERCISE 22.4
Meiosis in Plant and Animal Cells

Chromosomes carry the hereditary material, DNA. When cells reproduce mitotically, the new cells receive an exact copy of the chromosomes in the parent cell. In organisms that reproduce sexually, sex cells, or gametes, are produced by meiotic cell division. Meiosis distributes one chromosome of each pair in the diploid nucleus to each new gamete. Meiosis is also called reduction division because it reduces the chromosome number to one half of the species number. In this exercise, you will be able to observe various stages of meiotic cell division in a variety of organisms by examining commercially prepared slides of plant and animal cells.

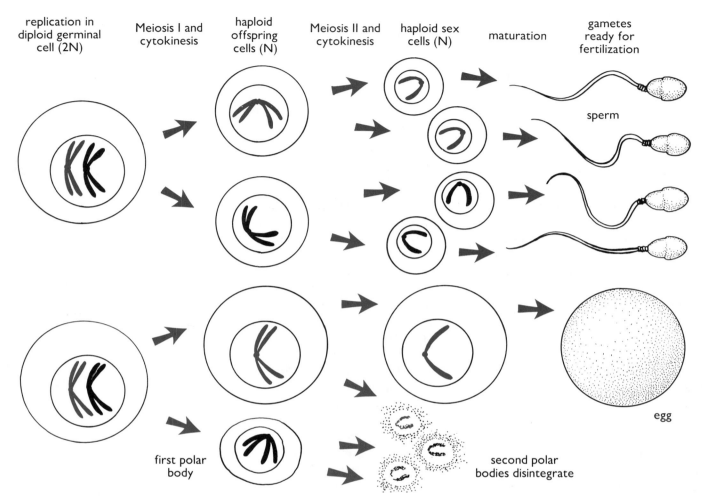

replication in diploid germinal cell (2N) · Meiosis I and cytokinesis · haploid offspring cells (N) · Meiosis II and cytokinesis · haploid sex cells (N) · maturation · gametes ready for fertilization

sperm

first polar body

second polar bodies disintegrate

egg

FIGURE 22-37 How sperm and eggs are formed

Section Review Questions

1. a) What is the primary function of meiosis?
   b) Why are two divisions necessary to complete meiosis?

2. a) At which stage in meiosis do homologous, double-stranded chromosomes line up next to each other?
   b) What is the function of this stage?

3. a) At which stage in meiosis does crossing over occur?
   b) What is the final result of crossing over?

4. Meiotic division of a germinal cell has a different outcome in male humans than in female humans. Explain this statement.

Down Syndrome

One in every 200 newborns suffers from some sort of chromosomal abnormality. The abnormality that causes Down syndrome, the most common chromosomal syndrome among newborns, belongs to a class of conditions called trisomies. Trisomies are created by errors in chromosome number: a trisomic person has one chromosome more than normal. People with Down syndrome, which is also known as Trisomy 21, have three rather than two copies of chromosome 21.

Trisomies are produced when one chromosome pair does not separate during meiosis. This phenomenon is called nondisjunction. Nondisjunction creates gametes that are haploid for all but one diploid chromosome. Zygotes to which one of these diploid gametes contribute are trisomic. Researchers believe nondisjunction can occur spontaneously, but they suspect carcinogens may increase its frequency.

Maternal age is the only factor known to affect the incidence of Down syndrome and some other trisomies. Males and females under 32 produce gametes that are diploid for chromosome 21 in equal frequencies. However, as a woman's age increases, her risk of having a Down syndrome child increases. The incidence of Down syndrome in the general population is approximately 1 in every 700 births. But for mothers over 45, it is 1 in every 16.

Trisomies cause pathological syndromes because the extra chromosomal material they carry upsets the delicate balance of gene expression required for normal human development. It is not surprising that the amount of genetic material added affects the severity of the trisomy. Down syndrome is less severe than other trisomies because chromosome 21 is one of the smaller chromosomes. Chromosomes 13 and 18 are slightly larger, a fact reflected in the syndromes associated with their trisomies. Both feature mental deficiencies, heart malformations, and physical deformities far more severe than those associated with Down syndrome. Also, life expectancies for both trisomies are short.

Trisomies of the largest chromosomes, 1 through 12, are found only in spontaneously aborted embryos. According to some sources, as many as half of all pregnancies are spontaneously aborted because chromosomal abnormalities interrupt fetal development.

Nondisjunction can also affect sex chromosomes, creating a variety of abnormalities of sex chromosome number. These generally have less severe effects than trisomies caused by other types of chromosomes. This is because cells having more than one X chromosome, like those in all women, use only one chromosome at any time. This helps to limit the damage caused by a trisomy of the X chromosome. Nevertheless, sex-chromosome abnormalities may cause abnormal sexual, intellectual, and behavioural development.

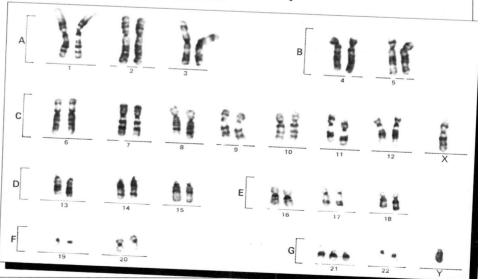

5. A germinal cell with *8* chromosomes undergoes a meiotic division. How many chromosomes will be in each cell at the end of Prophase I? Interphase II? Telophase II?

6. a) What clues would help you identify a cell at the end of Meiosis I under a compound microscope?

    b) How would the cell you identified above differ from a cell at the end of mitosis?

22.4 Mitosis, Meiosis, and Reproduction

Although mitosis and meiosis are similar in some ways, the details and final outcome of each process differ greatly. (See Table 22-3.) Both processes, however, play critical roles in reproduction and biological continuity.

Mitosis and Asexual Reproduction

Asexual reproduction allows individual organisms to reproduce without a mate. During asexual reproduction, one parent body divides into two or more parts, producing offspring that are identical to the parent except in size. Mitotic cell division ensures biological continuity in the three common types of asexual reproduction: binary fission, budding, and fragmentation.

Binary fission is usually seen in unicellular organisms such as the paramecium. Once a single cell grows so large that its cell membrane can no longer transport food efficiently, mitotic cell division begins. The end result

TABLE 22-3 Comparison of Mitotic and Meiotic Cell Division

Nuclear Division Process	Mitosis	Meiosis
Where Process Occurs	• in all zygotes after fertilization and all body cells thereafter	• in certain cells of reproductive organs
Number of Offspring Cells from One Parent Cell	• two	• four (three may die)
Chromosome Number of Parent Cell	• diploid (2N)	• diploid (2N)
Chromosome Number of Offspring Cells	• same as parent cell	• haploid (N)
Kind of Cells Produced	• various body cells	• gametes or certain spores
Function of Process	• biological continuity within same organism • ensures all new body cells have original DNA code	• biological continuity between generations • promotes variation among offspring

is two smaller but complete organisms, each with an exact copy of the original nucleus and half of the original cytoplasm.

Yeast cells reproduce by budding. (See Figure 22-38.) Each offspring first appears as a tiny bud on the parent cell. First, however, mitosis must produce two identical copies of the parent nucleus. So, although the cells differ greatly in size, the offspring's chromatin is identical to the parent's chromatin. Budding is also seen in multicellular animals such as the hydra.

Fragmentation is common in plants and animals such as flatworms and starfish. In fragmentation, each piece that breaks away from a parent body develops into a complete, new individual. Because all of the new cells result from mitotic divisions, all of the offspring are exact but smaller copies of the parent.

If the parent is a thriving organism and well suited to its environment, asexual reproduction can be a great advantage. The offspring will inherit all of the parent's successful traits and will also thrive. However, the offspring will also inherit any potential weaknesses. If the environment changes, these weaknesses could threaten the survival of the organism.

FIGURE 22-38 Yeast cells reproduce asexually by budding. They sometimes stay together long enough to form long chains of cells.

Yeast cells that feed on only one type of plant would die if an insect infestation destroyed the plant population. What characteristics would these yeast cells have to inherit to ensure their survival?

Lobsters, lizards, and salamanders can regenerate missing limbs, but they cannot produce new individuals by fragmentation.

Meiosis and Sexual Reproduction

Unless you have an identical twin, you do not look exactly like your brothers or sisters. Nor do you look exactly like either of your parents. Some of your characteristics are inherited from your mother and others from your father, but they are combined in a way that is unique. This effect is called **inherited variability,** and it occurs in all organisms that reproduce sexually.

In sexual reproduction, two parents contribute one reproductive cell each. During fertilization, the two sex cells unite, producing one offspring that differs from the parents and from other offspring. Meiosis plays two significant roles in achieving this result.

The hydra reproduces asexually by budding.

Even if a starfish is cut into fragments, each piece will regenerate by mitotic cell division.

Members of families, although they share obvious similarities, also exhibit inherited variability.

Once meiotic cell division has produced the haploid gametes needed for sexual reproduction, meiosis plays no further part in the formation of a new organism. After fertilization fuses the gametes, the diploid zygote develops and grows into a new individual through repeated mitotic divisions.

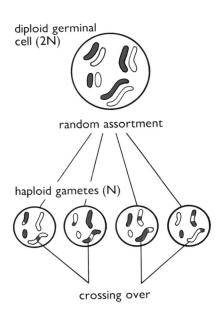

diploid germinal
cell (2N)

random assortment

haploid gametes (N)

crossing over

FIGURE 22-39 Each sex cell has a unique nucleus.

First, meiosis ensures that the number and the kind of chromosomes stays the same from one generation to the next. If sex cells were diploid, the chromosome number would double with each generation, and biological continuity would be impossible. Meiotic cell division, however, produces haploid sex cells. These cells develop into gametes such as eggs or sperm with N chromosomes each. When two haploid gametes unite, each zygote receives 2N chromosomes, the diploid number for the species. Since only half of the zygote's chromosomes come from each parent, it inherits a mixture of their characteristics. This process ensures that an offspring differs from either of its parents.

Second, meiosis shuffles the parents' chromosomes, producing four different nuclei from each germinal cell. As a result of crossing over and random assortment, no two gametes from the same individual are alike. (See Figure 22-39.) Therefore, the mother passes on a completely different set of homologues to each offspring as does the father. This process ensures that offspring of the same parents will differ greatly from each other.

Variability among offspring is the main advantage of sexual reproduction since even small variations provide organisms with the potential to adapt to environmental change. Consider a bird that inherits a slightly longer beak than its siblings. If the bird can use this beak to catch more bark beetles during a drought, it may have a better chance than its siblings of surviving long enough to reproduce. After a few generations, the longer beak may become more widespread in the population. Then this beak is described as an adaptation because it improves the likelihood of survival of the species.

For animals, the only significant disadvantage of sexual reproduction is the need for two members of the opposite sex to meet and to mate. Most species do this through adaptations such as mating seasons and hormonal cycles. Plants bring their gametes together through adaptations such as brightly coloured flowers that encourage bees to carry pollen from one plant to another.

Meiosis and sexual reproduction enable a species to become better adapted to the environment by making favourable features more common and by eliminating unsuccessful ones. Organisms limited to asexual reproduction lack this advantage because mitosis passes on exact copies of an original nucleus to each generation. Consequently, there is no opportunity for change or variety in the offspring. Many organisms that usually reproduce by asexual methods avoid this limitation by reproducing sexually when conditions in their environment become unfavourable. Several species of fungi, protists, and algae take advantage of sexual reproduction this way. The resulting variability in offspring means a chance to create new chromosome combinations, new characteristics, and perhaps a better, stronger organism.

Sexual reproduction provides the opportunity for offspring to inherit a new combination of chromosomes. You will learn about the ways in which organisms inherit the traits possessed by their parents in Chapter 23.

Pollination can result from the activity of bees. You can see the pollen grains on this bee's back.

Section Review Questions

1. a) What role does mitotic cell division play in the reproduction of unicellular organisms?
   b) What role does mitotic cell division play in the reproduction of multicellular organisms?

2. a) What role does meiotic cell division play in the reproduction of unicellular organisms?
   b) What role does meiotic cell division play in the reproduction of multicellular organisms?

3. a) Which two cell division processes occur in humans?
   b) What is the advantage of having both instead of only one?

4. Use the terms diploid and haploid to describe the major differences between mitosis and meiosis.

5. How are your body cells related to your mother's cells, your father's cells, and your grandparents' cells, respectively?

Chapter Review

Key Words

anaphase
astral rays
cell plate
centrioles
centromere
chromatids
chromatin
crossing over
cytokinesis
diploid number
double-stranded
   chromosomes
haploid number
homologous chromosomes
inherited variability
interphase

meiosis
meiotic cell division
metaphase
mitotic cell division
mitosis
prophase
random assortment
reduction division
replication
single-stranded
   chromosomes
spindle
spindle fibres
telophase
tetrad

Recall Questions

Multiple Choice

1. Mitotic cell division results in two cells that have
   a) N chromosomes and are genetically identical
   b) N chromosomes and are genetically different
   c) 2N chromosomes and are genetically identical
   d) 2N chromosomes and are genetically different

2. Which of the following observations identifies the metaphase stage of mitosis?
   a) chromosomes lined up on the equator
   b) nuclear membrane disappearing
   c) chromosomes shortening and thickening
   d) spindle fibres disappearing

3. Mitosis in plant cells differs from mitosis in animal cells in that plant cells
   a) have fewer chromosomes
   b) lack nuclear membranes
   c) lack nucleoli
   d) do not form spindle fibres

4. In Prophase I of meiosis, the pairing of homologous chromosomes is called
   a) cytokinesis
   b) synapsis
   c) random assortment
   d) replication

5. In tobacco, the diploid number of chromosomes is 48. For tobacco cells, N = ____?
   a) 96
   b) 24
   c) 48
   d) 12

6. The four products of meiotic cell division have
   a) 2N chromosomes and differ genetically from each other
   b) 2N chromosomes and are genetically identical to each other
   c) N chromosomes and are genetically identical to each other
   d) N chromosomes and differ genetically from each other

Fill in the Blanks

1. During _____, the event that precedes mitosis, the chromatin of a cell replicates. No _____ are visible at this point because the chromatin is scattered. At prophase, the chromatin strands shorten and thicken, the _____ begin to appear, and the _____ disappears. During _____, the chromosomes line up on the equator of the cell. They attach to the spindle fibres by their _____. During anaphase, the chromatids, now called _____, begin to move toward opposite _____ of the cell. When the chromosomes have reached their destination, the _____ disintegrates and the _____ begins to reappear. The products of mitosis are two _____ which are genetically _____. Following mitosis, _____ divides the cytoplasm into two portions, and mitotic cell division is complete.

Short Answers

1. List the three major events that occur during mitotic cell division and briefly describe each one.

2. List the three major events that occur during meiotic cell division and briefly describe each one.

3. a) What is the difference between mitotic cell division and mitosis?
   b) What is the difference between mitosis and cytokinesis?

4. How does mitosis in animal cells differ from mitosis in plant cells?

5. a) What is the diploid number of chromosomes in humans?

b) How many chromosomes does a human sperm cell have? A human muscle cell? Explain.

6. What is the most important difference between asexual and sexual reproduction?

7. Match the description of the phases of meiosis in Column A with the names of the phases in Column B.

Column A	Column B
i) single-stranded chromosomes reach opposite poles of the offspring cells	a) Prophase I
ii) tetrads line up on the equator	b) Metaphase I
iii) crossing over occurs	c) Anaphase I
iv) double-stranded chromosomes line up on the equator	d) Telophase II
v) each pole receives N double-stranded chromosomes	e) Metaphase II

Application Questions

1. Is mitosis occurring in your body right now? State two examples.

2. How is mitotic cell division involved in cancer?

3. a) What is biological continuity?
   b) How does mitosis contribute to biological continuity?
   c) How does meiosis contribute to biological continuity?

4. In a certain organism, the chromosome number in the muscle cells is 16.
   a) What is the value of N for this organism?
   b) How many chromosomes are in the sex cells of this organism? In the skin cells? Explain.

5. Explain the importance to future generations of
   a) crossing over
   b) random assortment

6. What evidence exists that indicates microtubules and microfilaments must play a role in cell division?

Problem Solving

1. a) Why are the offspring of sexual reproduction not identical to each other or to either of their parents?
   b) What is the advantage of inherited variability?

2. Compare the rate of recovery from a broken arm in a young boy with the same injury in his grandfather. Explain.

3. a) One bacterium enters your throat. How many organisms would be present after 24 h?
   b) Is this outcome likely? Explain.

4. a) Humans inherit all of their mitochondria from their mothers. What aspect of cell division makes this possible?
   b) Why isn't it possible for fathers to contribute mitochondria to the zygote?

Extensions

1. Draw and label a series of diagrams to illustrate mitosis in a cell where 2N = 8.

2. Prepare your own mitosis slides of mitosis from onion-root tips that you have grown. Draw and colour a series of diagrams to illustrate the stages of mitosis in the root tips or take photographs of the root tip cells with a camera and an adaptor.

3. Examine asexual reproduction in a variety of organisms. Use reference materials to find out about asexual reproduction in various protists, fungi, plants, and animals.

Principles of Heredity

Why do members of *Canis familiaris* vary so widely in size, shape, and temperament? Humans wanted a variety of dogs for a variety of needs, and went about shaping the species to their needs. Every breed of domestic dog has been bred with a purpose in mind.

Although the purpose of breeding dogs has varied from culture to culture, methods have been fairly consistent. The breeder usually has in mind certain features he or she would like to appear in offspring. Dogs today are bred for features such as a perfect curl of tail, a certain colour, intelligence, or an even disposition. The breeder then chooses two dogs likely to produce those features. Purebred dogs whose ancestors have been bred for a certain feature for several generations are best for this purpose, because offspring of two dogs purebred for a certain feature are almost certain to inherit that feature.

A second strategy, crossbreeding, uses dissimilar dogs in an attempt to combine positive features of both. The results of crossbreeding, however, are unpredictable. Offspring may have all or none of the desired features.

The dog is not the only animal whose breeding is controlled by humans. For 6000 years, important animals and plants have been bred to maximize their usefulness. Horses, once bred for riding, loading, and pulling, are now also bred for racing and other sports. Pigs are now specialized as either pork or bacon producers. Chickens are bred for either meat or egg production.

Controlling breeding is really controlling heredity, the transmission of structural and functional characteristics from parent to offspring. However, the benefits of controlled breeding are mixed. Until recently, human control of heredity has been limited to maximizing the incidence of features already existing within a population. For example, dairy cows have been bred to maximize milk production by breeding offspring of consistently high-yielding cows. This practice is well established and uncontroversial. But if breeding cattle to increase milk production is acceptable, is genetically altering the cow so it produces a different kind of milk also acceptable?

Through biotechnology, scientists today are capable of selecting and combining features not only within species, but between species as well. Already, mice have been created whose blood carries clot-dissolving protein for human blood. Bacteria are being altered to produce human insulin. Canadian researchers are trying to increase wheat's resistance to cold by transferring to it the "antifreeze" gene carried by the flounder. Are these and other developments of new life to be welcomed?

Although the economic benefits of biotechnology may be staggering, some critics abhor these experiments because they are cruel to their subjects, dangerous to the environment, and ethically questionable. If life is another tool for human advancement, where must we stop in bending it to our wills? As you uncover the principles of heredity, keep in mind how these principles might and ought to be applied.

Chapter Objectives

When you complete this chapter, you should:

1. Be curious about human knowledge of heredity and the scientific studies on which it is based.

2. Be able to describe the experiments of Gregor Mendel.

3. Be able to use a Punnett square to solve problems involving monohybrid and dihybrid crosses.

4. Using the pea-plant characteristics described by Mendel, be able to demonstrate a variety of monohybrid and dihybrid crosses, including the F_1 and F_2 generations.

5. Be able to explain the terms gene, allele, dominant and recessive alleles, incomplete dominance, homozygous, heterozygous, phenotype, genotype.

6. Be able to describe the relationships among a gene, a chromosome, and DNA in the transmission of traits from one generation to another.

7. Be able to describe how knowledge of heredity is used in breeding programs of domesticated plants and animals.

23.1 Discovering the Principles of Heredity

The study of **heredity** first assumed a scientific basis through the research of Gregor Mendel (1822-1884), an Austrian monk. Mendel investigated inheritance in pea plants through a series of breeding experiments he conducted between 1853 and 1861 in the garden of his monastery. Modern biologists highly regard Mendel's research methods because they illustrate a number of important aspects about the scientific process. These include sound experimental design, simple but powerful experiments, hundreds of repetitions, meticulous record keeping, quantitative as well as qualitative observations, and mathematical manipulation of numerical data to reveal underlying patterns.

As you read about these experiments, remember that Mendel knew nothing about meiosis, chromosomes, or DNA. His hypotheses were based entirely on what he could infer by observing external characteristics. Despite this, his conclusions have formed the foundation for much of what we understand about heredity today.

Mendel's Experimental Methods

A significant factor in the success of Mendel's experimental design was his selection of suitable experimental subjects. Pea plants are ideal because they are easy to grow, and they mature so quickly. As a result, several generations can be studied in only a few years. Pea plants also have several observable characteristics that express themselves as pairs of sharply contrasting traits. (See Table 23-1.) For example, tallness and shortness are contrasting *traits*. Both are expressions of the *characteristic* called height.

TABLE 23-1   Contrasting Traits in Mendel's Seven Pea-Plant Characteristics

Characteristic	Contrasting Traits	
Height	tall	short
Flower Position	side of stem (axial)	end of stem (terminal)
Seed Shape	round	wrinkled

TABLE 23-1——*Continued*

Characteristic	Contrasting Traits	
Seed Colour	yellow	green
Seed Coat	coloured	white
Pod Shape	inflated	constricted
Pod Colour	green	yellow

A further advantage of pea plants for hereditary research is that the structure of the pea flower and its natural method of pollination make it easy to use in controlled experiments. Pea flowers usually self-pollinate because the stigma and the anthers are enclosed by the petals as shown in Figure 23-1. For crossbreeding experiments, however, Mendel removed the anthers from a plant chosen as the ''female parent'' to prevent self-pollination. He then dusted the female parent's stigma with pollen from the anthers of a second plant chosen as the ''male parent.'' If Mendel wanted certain plants to self-pollinate normally, he simply left them alone.

FIGURE 23-1   Controlling pollination in pea plants

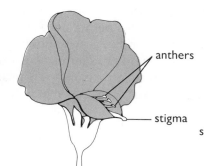

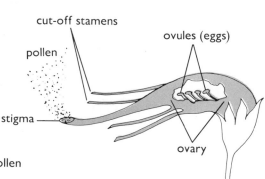

The pea flower's fused petals prevent external pollination by insects.

Removing the anthers before the pollen is mature prevents self-pollination. Lowering the fused petal cover protects the stigma from unplanned pollination.

Pollen from a second plant can then be added by hand when the stigma is ready.

Mendel's First Experiment

Earlier scientists who had performed experiments similar to Mendel's had reported an imbalance in the expression of contrasting traits. For example, tall pea plants were far more common than short pea plants. Mendel wondered if there was a pattern in the way contrasting traits were inherited. The purpose of his first experiment was to answer this question.

Mendel's Experimental Procedure

In designing his first experiment, Mendel realized that he would need plants that were purebred for contrasting traits such as tallness and shortness. To obtain purebred tall plants for his experiments, Mendel selected the tallest plants from his garden and allowed them to self-pollinate. He then repeated this procedure with the offspring for several generations. Eventually, all of the offspring were tall, indicating that tallness was being transmitted consistently from generation to generation. Mendel then considered these plants to be purebred for tallness. He used a similar technique to produce purebred short plants.

In his first experiment, Mendel crossed purebred pea plants with contrasting traits for the same characteristic. For example, he selected a pure tall plant as the female parent and dusted it with pollen from a pure short plant chosen as the male parent. Mendel referred to these two plants as the parental generation, which he designated by the letter "P."

Mendel also carried out the reciprocal cross. For example, he pollinated the stigma of a short pea plant with the pollen from the stamens of a pure tall plant. The outcome was unchanged.

After several weeks, Mendel picked the mature pods from the female parent and planted the seeds. Mendel considered these seeds to be **hybrid,** or crossbred, because the parents had unlike traits for the same characteristic. He referred to the hybrid plants that grew from the seeds as the **first filial (F$_1$) generation.**

Mendel's Observations

Mendel was a careful investigator, and he kept complete records of his procedures and observations for every experiment. When Mendel crossed a pure tall pea plant with a pure short one, he expected to see plants of intermediate height in the hybrid F$_1$ generation. Instead, the offspring were 100% tall. (See Figure 23-2.) Further experiments showed that the same was true for all other pairs of contrasting traits in pea plants. One trait was expressed in 100% of the F$_1$ generation while the other was not expressed at all.

Analyzing the Data

To Mendel, these observations suggested an obvious pattern, which can be described with the terms dominant and recessive. The trait expressed in the F$_1$ generation is called the **dominant trait.** (For example, tallness in pea plants is a dominant trait.) The contrasting trait which was *not* expressed in the F$_1$ generation is called the **recessive trait.** (For example, shortness in pea plants is a recessive trait.)

V   THE UNITY OF LIFE

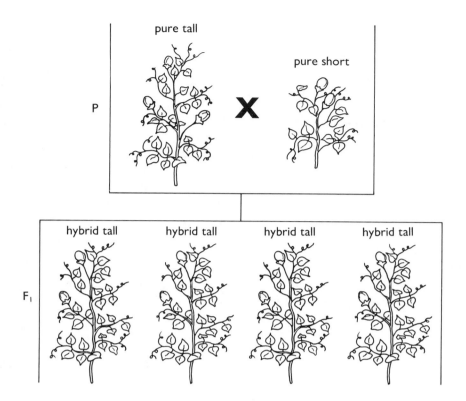

P

pure tall

pure short

X

F₁

hybrid tall   hybrid tall   hybrid tall   hybrid tall

FIGURE 23-2 Mendel crossbred pure tall and pure short parents (P). All hybrid offspring in the first filial (F₁) generation were tall.

Mendel's Conclusion

Mendel did not jump to a conclusion. He performed hundreds of similar experiments, eventually testing seven inherited characteristics. In every case, one contrasting trait proved to be dominant over the other. (See Table 23-2.)

TABLE 23-2   Dominant and Recessive Traits in the Seven Pea-plant Characteristics

Characteristic	Dominant Trait	Recessive Trait
Height	• tall	• short • dwarf
Flower Position	• side of stem	• end of stem
Seed Shape	• round	• wrinkled
Seed Colour	• yellow	• green
Seed Coat	• coloured	• white
Pod Shape	• inflated	• constricted
Pod Colour	• green	• yellow

Hundreds of repetitions of the same pattern led Mendel to the **Principle of Dominance.**

When an organism is hybrid (crossbred) for a pair of contrasting traits, it shows only the dominant trait.

Mendel's Second Experiment

As is often the case in scientific research, the results of Mendel's first experiment suggested questions for further investigation. Mendel wondered whether recessive traits were lost forever as a result of crossbreeding, or whether they were still present but not expressed. Consequently, he designed a second experiment to answer this new question.

Mendel's Experimental Procedure

You could think of the F$_2$ generation plants as the "children" of the F$_1$ plants and as the "grandchildren" of the P generation plants.

Mendel allowed the hybrid tall F$_1$ plants from the first experiment to mature and self-pollinate. He then collected and planted their seeds, and observed the traits expressed by the **second filial (F$_2$) generation.** (See Figure 23-3.)

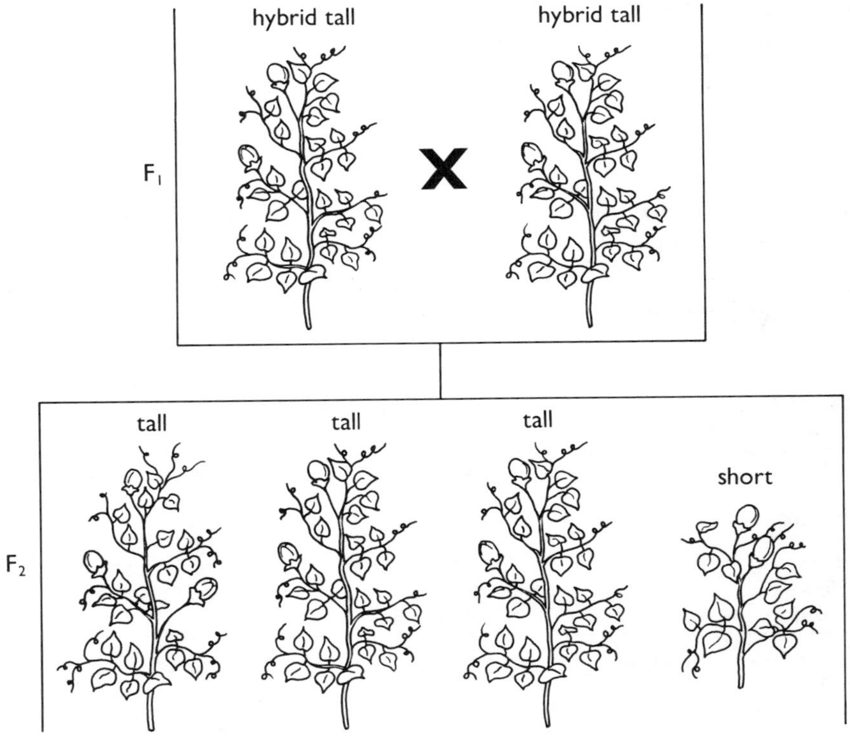

FIGURE 23-3 When Mendel crossed hybrid tall F$_1$ plants, the recessive trait reappeared. Only $\frac{3}{4}$ of the F$_2$ offspring were tall, while the other $\frac{1}{4}$ were short.

Mendel's Observations

While at university, Mendel had studied both biology and mathematics. So, it was natural for him to record his observations numerically. The numerical

TABLE 23-3   Results of Mendel's Second Experiment: Inheritance of Height

P generation	50% tall	50% short
F$_1$ generation	100% tall	0% short
F$_2$ generation	$\frac{787}{1064}$ = 74% tall	$\frac{277}{1064}$ = 26% short

data in Table 23-3 show clearly how often the "lost" shortness trait reappeared in the F$_2$ generation.

Analyzing the Data

Apparently, even though the F$_1$ plants showed no signs of shortness themselves, they were able to transmit the shortness trait from the P generation to the F$_2$ generation. In his search for a pattern that might explain this outcome, Mendel converted the numerical data into ratios. This helped him see that almost exactly $\frac{3}{4}$ (75%) of the F$_2$ plants were tall. The other $\frac{1}{4}$ (25%) were short. In other words, for every *3* offspring expressing the dominant trait, *1* offspring expressed the recessive trait. This 3:1 ratio reminded Mendel of his studies in mathematics. He began to suspect that the mathematical laws of probability could be applied to the study of heredity.

Mendel rounded off the numerical data to obtain these ratios

$$\frac{787}{1064} = 0.7397$$
$$= 73.97\%$$
$$75\% = \frac{3}{4}$$

$$\frac{277}{1064} = 0.2603$$
$$= 26.03\%$$
$$25\% = \frac{1}{4}$$

Rounding off is a common practice among statisticians (mathematicians who deal with probability), because it enables them to see patterns.

INQUIRY ACTIVITY
Investigating Probability

You will find it easier to understand the significance of Mendel's experimental results if you first understand the basic mathematics of probability. In fact, you already know more about the laws of probability than you realize. For example, if you flip a coin, you know the chance of it "turning up heads" is *1* out of *2*. A mathematician would say that the probability of this event is $\frac{1}{2}$ (50%). This means that if you were to toss the coin 1000 times, you would probably see about 500 heads and 500 tails. But what if you flipped the coin only ten times?

In this activity, you will investigate the relationship between predicted probability, actual results, and number of trials. Your teacher will provide you with a work sheet for this activity.

The outcome of a lottery or a card game depends on the laws of probability.

Mendel's Hypothesis: The Principle of Segregation

Mendel's first experiment showed that crossbreeding pure tall and pure short pea plants always produced offspring with the dominant trait of tallness. His second experiment showed that these tall offspring could pass on the recessive shortness trait even though they showed no external signs of it themselves. When Mendel tested inheritance in other characteristics, he found that the numerical results were always the same. (See Table 23-4.) If pure parents (P) with contrasting traits are crossed, 100% of the offspring will express the dominant trait. However, only 75% of the F_2 offspring express the dominant trait, while 25% express the recessive trait, a ratio of 3:1.

This 3:1 ratio convinced Mendel that inheritance could be compared to the outcome of coin tossing, an idea that he developed into a hypothesis. The main assumptions of Mendel's hypothesis are shown here as they would apply to the inheritance of height in pea plants.

1. Contrasting traits such as tallness and shortness are caused by internal "factors" that pass from parent to offspring by way of the seed.
2. Each offspring inherits two factors for a characteristic such as height, one from the male gamete (pollen) and one from the female gamete (ovule).
3. Purebred pea plants (P) inherit identical factors—either two tallness factors or two shortness factors.
4. Hybrid offspring (F_1) inherit contrasting factors—a shortness factor from the pure short parent and a tallness factor from the pure tall parent.
5. When both contrasting factors are present, the recessive factor is suppressed, and only the dominant factor (tallness) is expressed.

One test of a good hypothesis is its ability to explain all experimental observations. Mendel's assumptions passed this test because they explained why recessive traits such as shortness reappeared in the second experiment after disappearing in the first experiment.

TABLE 23-4   Results of Mendel's Second Experiment: Inheritance of Seven Characteristics

P₁ Cross	F₁ Plants	F₂ Plants	Ratio
Tall Stem × Short Stem	• 100% long	• 787 long: 277 short	2.84:1
Axial Flowers × Terminal Flowers	• 100% axial	• 651 axial: 207 terminal	3.14:1
Round × Wrinkled Seeds	• 100% round	• 5474 round: 1850 wrinkled	2.96:1
Yellow × Green Seeds	• 100% yellow	• 6022 yellow: 2001 green	3.01:1
Coloured Coat × White Coat	• 100% coloured	• 705 coloured: 224 white	3.15:1
Inflated Pods × Constricted Pods	• 100% inflated	• 882 inflated: 299 constricted	2.95:1
Green Pods × Yellow Pods	• 100% green	• 428 green: 152 yellow	2.82:1

According to Mendel's hypothesis, each purebred parent (P) in the first experiment had identical factors for height. Inheritance of these factors should not be affected by probability since gametes from the tall parent could not possibly contain anything but a tallness factor. Similarly, all gametes from a short parent must contain a shortness factor. Fertilizing short-factor gametes (ovules) with tall-factor gametes (pollen) would always form hybrid seeds. Because of the Principle of Dominance, the F_1 hybrid offspring would have to be 100% tall.

Another test of a good hypothesis is its ability to predict. Mendel's assumptions passed this test, too, by correctly predicting that inheritance in the second experiment *would* be affected by probability because the hybrid F_1 plants must have contrasting factors for height. According to the laws of probability, gamete formation in a hybrid parent is like a one-coin bet because a pollen grain, for example, has a 1:2 chance of receiving a tallness factor and a 1:2 chance of receiving a shortness factor. The same is true for the ovule of a hybrid parent.

Fertilization when hybrids self-pollinate is like a two-coin bet because a pea seed inherits two height factors, one from the pollen grain and one from the ovule. The combined probability of inheriting two recessive shortness factors is the product of the individual probabilities: $\frac{1}{2} \times \frac{1}{2} = \frac{1}{4}$. This prediction agrees with the outcome of the second experiment in which 25% of the F_2 offspring actually were short. This close agreement suggests that Mendel's assumptions were correct.

Eventually, Mendel stated his hypothesis as the **Principle of Segregation.**

Hereditary characteristics are determined by distinct units or factors that occur in pairs. When reproductive cells are produced, the two factors of each pair segregate (separate), and are distributed as distinct units or factors, one to each gamete.

Mendel published this hypothesis in 1866, but at that time it could not be verified since little was known about chromosomes, meiosis, or mitosis. Therefore, the importance of Mendel's research was overlooked. By 1900, however, cytologists had observed and named the paired chromosomes they observed in the nuclei of dividing cells. They had also described and recorded how chromosomes move during mitosis and meiosis. They could see that gamete formation separates paired chromosomes. Therefore, offspring must inherit one chromosome of each pair from the female parent and the other chromosome of each pair from the male parent. Mendel's experiments were rediscovered, and biologists soon found that his principles could be used to predict the outcome of many other experiments in heredity. Since that time, the term gene was adopted to replace factor. You will learn more about the concept of the gene and its role in heredity in Section 23.2.

Similar reasoning suggests identical probabilities for each of the other possible inherited combinations.

From the Ovule	From the Pollen	Combined Probability
tallness	shortness	$\frac{1}{2} \times \frac{1}{2} = \frac{1}{4}$
shortness	tallness	$\frac{1}{2} \times \frac{1}{2} = \frac{1}{4}$
tallness	tallness	$\frac{1}{2} \times \frac{1}{2} = \frac{1}{4}$

The total probability of inheriting at least one tallness factor is therefore $\frac{3}{4}$

Gregor Mendel

Gregor Mendel, the founder of modern genetics, was born to a peasant family in 1822 in Henzendorf, Austria. Mendel was a gifted student, but because the only educational opportunities available to the poor were provided by religious orders, Mendel joined an Augustinian monastery at Brno, in what is now Czechoslovakia. Eventually, he became a monk, but because he could not withstand the pressures of his position he tried to become a teacher. However, he was unable to pass his teaching examinations. Mendel was a substitute teacher for his entire teaching career at Brno.

Some believe that Mendel began his experiments in hopes of resolving a controversy he had witnessed in Vienna. There a professor had come under attack for teaching that the characteristics of species were unstable, a concept related to the theory of evolution. Official dogma claimed that species never changed. Mendel may have believed the dispute could be resolved by statistically analyzing the appearance of traits in hybrids from generation to generation. If the appearance of traits was consistent over time, then the species would be considered stable.

Whatever his reasons, Mendel achieved a breakthrough because he was the first researcher to look for statistical rules governing the distribution of traits in hybrids.

Other researchers had studied hybrids, but they used their results to try to determine how heredity worked for the organism as a whole. It had never occurred to anyone that Mendel's statistical analysis would reveal anything useful.

Unfortunately, Mendel did not live to see his work recognized. When his results were published in a journal in 1866, the paper was barely acknowledged. Several explanations for this have been proposed. Perhaps researchers' preoccupation with Darwin's theory of evolution was to blame.

Perhaps it was the obscurity of the journal in which the paper was published. Perhaps it was the fact that Mendel had no professional status; he may have been considered an amateur researcher by a tightly knit academic hierarchy. Some have suggested the very simplicity of Mendel's study doomed it to obscurity for decades. Mendel had established simple rules for the distribution of traits in hybrids; he made no grandiose claims.

However, 16 years after Mendel's death in 1884, three European botanists simultaneously and independently formulated their own versions of Mendel's laws. Only while they were preparing their own papers did they discover that Mendel had beaten them to the discovery.

Before Mendel, researchers had focussed on the inheritance of complex traits, and were therefore able to deduce little more than the fact that each parent contributed to the progeny. By simplifying the focus of heredity studies and submitting his results to statistical analysis, Mendel was able to lay the foundation upon which the modern study of heredity and genetics was built.

Section Review Questions

1. Define heredity.

2. Explain the difference between a trait and a characteristic.

3. Why was the pea plant a suitable organism for Mendel's heredity experiments?

4. a) State the Principle of Dominance.
   b) Briefly explain the experimental results that led Mendel to this principle.

5. State the Principle of Segregation.

6. What important numerical ratio always appeared in the F_2 generation of Mendel's hybridization experiments?

7. Briefly explain the terms a) hybrid, b) first filial (F_1) generation, c) dominant trait, and d) recessive trait.

23.2 Heredity, Genes, and Genetics

The scientific study of inheritance is now called **genetics,** after the gene, which functions as the basic unit of heredity. Formally defined, a **gene** is that part of a chromosome responsible for the inheritance of a single characteristic. Each gene consists of an uninterrupted segment of DNA. (See Figure 23-4.) The gene for any given characteristic is always found in the same location and in the same order along a particular chromosome.

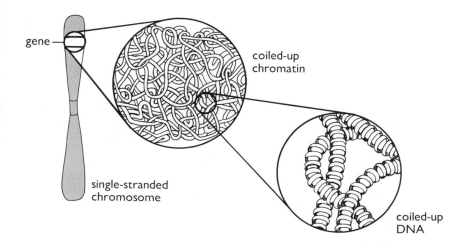

FIGURE 23-4 The coiled-up chromatin at any particular gene location contains all the DNA responsible for passing on a single characteristic. The DNA is wound around a protein core.

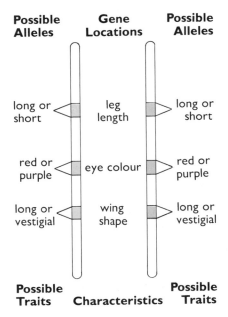

Possible Alleles	Gene Locations	Possible Alleles
long or short	leg length	long or short
red or purple	eye colour	red or purple
long or vestigial	wing shape	long or vestigial
Possible Traits	Characteristics	Possible Traits

FIGURE 23-5 A fruit fly inherits one gene for leg length from its mother and one from its father. The gene locations match, but they may be occupied either by an allele for long legs or an allele for short legs.

The letters used to represent alleles usually correspond to the dominant trait. R stands for round seed and r for wrinkled seed. Y stands for yellow seed and y for green seed.

The term genotype has also been used to refer to an organism's entire genetic makeup. Currently, geneticists prefer using the term genome to describe all of the genes in a complete set of chromosomes.

Alleles

Among sexually reproducing organisms, the offspring inherit two genes for each characteristic, one from each parent. In fruit flies, for example, the two genes for leg length are located at matching positions on homologous chromosomes. (See Figure 23-5.) However, although both genes are coded for the same characteristic, they are not necessarily identical. This is because most genes exist in an array of possible forms, which differ slightly in the arrangement of their DNA code. The particular DNA form that appears at a particular gene location is called an **allele.**

On the chromosome of a pea plant, for example, the gene location for height may be occupied either by an allele coded for the tallness trait or by an allele coded for shortness. For convenience, different alleles are usually symbolized by single letters. In pea plants, T stands for the tallness allele, and t stands for the shortness allele. You should remember that the same letter is used to represent both alleles. The capital letter is used for the dominant allele, and the lower-case letter is used for the recessive allele. An allele coded for a dominant trait such as tallness is called a **dominant allele.** An allele coded for a recessive trait such as shortness is called a **recessive allele.**

Genotypes

The separation, or segregation, of alleles during meiosis and their random recombination by fertilization determines which genes will be inherited by the offspring. The resulting combination is called the offspring's **genotype.** This term refers only to the pair of alleles present at the matching gene locations for a particular characteristic.

For example, the genotype of a pea plant that inherits two alleles for tallness is symbolized by TT. TT is referred to as a **homozygous** genotype because the zygote received two identical alleles. If both alleles are coded for shortness, the pea plant's homozygous genotype is tt. A hybrid pea plant that inherits different alleles for height has a Tt genotype. Tt is called a **heterozygous** genotype because the alleles are unlike.

Phenotypes

The outward physical appearance of an organism is called its **phenotype.** Phenotype is determined by the combination of alleles in an organism's genotype. For example, a pea plant with a homozygous dominant allele combination, TT, will have a tall phenotype. A homozygous recessive allele combination, tt, will result in a short pea plant. A heterozygous allele combination, Tt, results in a tall pea plant. (See Figure 23-6.) You can see that pea plants with the two genotypes TT and Tt have the same phenotype—both are tall. TT is referred to as pure tall, and Tt is called hybrid tall. Pea plants with the genotype tt are pure short.

The phenotype of an organism does not necessarily reveal its genotype. For example, there is no way to tell simply by looking at a tall pea plant whether its genotype is TT or Tt. A hybrid tall pea plant is just as big as a pure tall pea plant. However, *all* short pea plants have the same genotype, tt. This is because a recessive trait can only be expressed in the phenotype if the organism has two recessive alleles.

Punnett Squares

A **Punnett square** is a chart that makes it easier to predict the outcome of a crossbreeding experiment, using Mendel's principles of dominance and segregation. Consider, for example, the cross of a pure tall pea plant (TT) with a pure short plant (tt). The tall plant, as shown in Figure 23-7, can only produce gametes containing the dominant allele, T. The pure short pea plant can only produce gametes containing the recessive allele, t. The Punnett square for this cross is shown in Figure 23-8. The four boxes inside the Punnett square show all the possible genotypes that may occur in the offspring by recombining alleles from the two parent plants during fertilization. In this case, Tt is the only possible genotype. As a result, all the phenotypes will also be identical, and 100% of the offspring will mature into tall plants. (Remember, there will be no external evidence of their hybrid genotype.)

Compare this outcome with the results of crossbreeding two hybrid tall pea plants whose genotype is Tt. As the production of gametes takes place in their reproductive organs, meiosis will segregate the tallness allele from the shortness allele. Each of the gametes produced will receive only one of the two alleles. As a result, half of the gametes will contain the dominant allele,

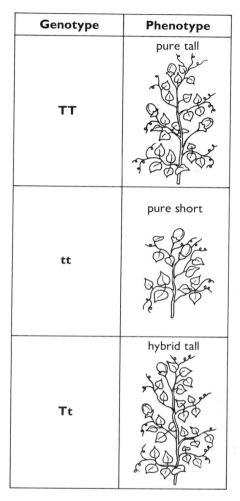

Genotype	Phenotype
TT	pure tall
tt	pure short
Tt	hybrid tall

BELOW: FIGURE 23-7 Gamete production in garden peas

RIGHT: FIGURE 23-6 Genotypes and phenotypes in pea plants

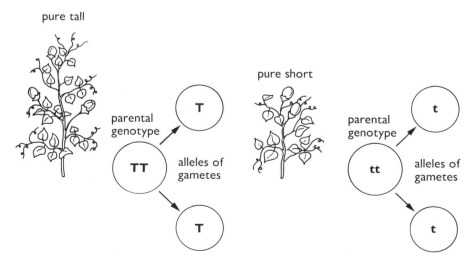

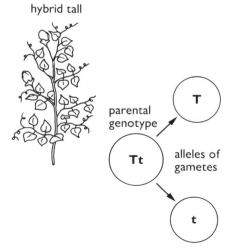

Pure Tall Parent (TT)
(alleles of gametes)

	T	T
t	Tt	Tt
t	Tt	Tt

Pure Short Parent (tt) (alleles of gametes) (left axis label)

FIGURE 23-8 A Punnett square. The shaded squares show all possible genotypes in the offspring.

LEFT: FIGURE 23-9 This Punnett square for a hybrid cross shows both the genotypes of the offspring and the genotypic ratio — I pure tall : 2 hybrid tall : I pure short.

RIGHT: FIGURE 23-10 The phenotypic ratio for this hybrid cross is 3 tall : I short. Two out of every three tall offspring will have a hybrid genotype, but their phenotype will be identical to the phenotype of the pure tall offspring.

T. The other half will contain the recessive allele, t. The Punnett square for this cross shows four possible genotypes for the zygotes (although Tt and tT are actually identical). (See Figure 23-9.)

According to the laws of probability, each of the four genotypes should occur with the same frequency if the number of crosses is large. Therefore, the Punnett square predicts that $\frac{1}{4}$ of the offspring's genotypes will be TT, $\frac{2}{4}$ will be Tt, and $\frac{1}{4}$ will be tt. This prediction can also be stated as a **genotypic ratio** of *1* pure tall to *2* hybrid tall to *1* pure short or 1:2:1.

Any zygote that receives Tt, for example, will then divide repeatedly by mitosis to form a multicellular adult. Each of the adult's cells will contain the genotype Tt. Since T is dominant, the resulting plant will be tall. Consequently, with respect to outward physical appearance, the Punnett square predicts that $\frac{3}{4}$ of the offspring will have a tall phenotype, and $\frac{1}{4}$ will be short. (See Figure 23-10.) This prediction can be stated as a **phenotypic ratio** of 3:1.

Hybrid Tall Parent (Tt)
(alleles of gametes)

	T	t
T	TT	tT
t	Tt	tt

Hybrid Tall Parent (Tt) (alleles of gametes) (left axis label)

Hybrid Tall Parent (Tt)
(alleles of gametes)

	T	t
T	TT (tall)	tT (tall)
t	Tt (tall)	tt (short)

Hybrid Tall Parent (Tt) (alleles of gametes) (left axis label)

The results of Mendel's second experiment confirm this predicted phenotypic ratio. When a large number of hybrid tall plants were allowed to crossbreed, Mendel observed that the ratio of tall phenotypes to short phenotypes in the offspring was about 3:1.

INQUIRY ACTIVITY
Solving Problems in Genetics

The Punnett square is a convenient way to visualize the results of a genetic cross. It is the simplest way to reveal the probability of a certain phenotype occurring in the offspring, or the ratio in which certain phenotypes are likely to occur. In some cases, you will be given the phenotypic results in the offspring, and you will be asked to deduce the genotype of one or both parents.

Generally, you will need to use a Punnett square to solve most genetics problems.

Sample Problem

When two heterozygous tall pea plants are crossed, what will the phenotypic ratio in the offspring be?

To answer the question:

1. Deduce the genotypes of the parents.
2. The genotype of a parent indicates the alleles it can contribute to an offspring. (See Figure 23-11a.) Determine the alleles that each parent can contribute to the offspring.
3. Construct the Punnett square. (See Figure 23-11b.)
4. Enter the symbols for the alleles that each parent can contribute to its offspring into the Punnett square. (See Figure 23-11c.)

FIGURE 23-11 Using Punnett squares to solve problems in genetics

a)

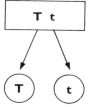

A heterozygous tall pea plant can contribute gametes with either a dominant allele, T, or a recessive allele, t.

b)

For monohybrid crosses, the Punnett square is a box containing nine smaller boxes.

c)

Both parents are heterozygous tall. Each one can contribute T or t to the offspring.

d)

Find the genotypes of the offspring by following the arrows.

5. Enter the genotypes of the offspring into the boxes of the Punnett square. (See Figure 23-11d.)

6. Determine the phenotypes of the offspring from their genotypes. Express this as a ratio.

Activity Problems

1. a) If a homozygous tall pea plant is crossed with a short pea plant, what will the appearance of the F_1 generation be?

   b) Use a Punnett square to determine the genotypes and the phenotypes in the F_2 generation.

2. What will the gametes produced by the parents be, and what will the height of the offspring be in each of the following crosses? Use Punnett squares in each case.

   a) TT × Tt   b) Tt × tt   c) Tt × Tt

3. A tall pea plant crossed with a short pea plant produces offspring of which about half are tall and half are short. What are the genotypes of the parents?

4. In guinea pigs, a rough coat (R) is dominant over a smooth coat (r). A particular rough-coated male guinea pig crossed with a smooth-coated female produces all rough-coated offspring. Another rough-coated male crossed with a smooth-coated female produces offspring of which about half are rough-coated and half are smooth-coated. Explain these results.

5. Assume that the allele for brown eyes (B) in humans is dominant over the allele for blue eyes (b). A brown-eyed man marries a blue-eyed woman and they have eight children. All eight children are brown-eyed. What are the genotypes of all individuals in the family?

6. A blue-eyed woman and a brown-eyed man have a blue-eyed child. What are their genotypes?

7. a) What is the probability that the first child of a marriage of two heterozygous brown-eyed parents will be blue-eyed?

   b) If the first child is blue-eyed, what is the probability that the second child will also be blue-eyed?

Monohybrid Crosses

A crossbreeding experiment that focusses on only one inherited characteristic is called a **monohybrid cross.** For example, when Mendel traced the inheritance of height in pea plants, he ignored other characteristics such as seed shape or colour. The Punnett square in Figure 23-10 describes a monohybrid cross as do all of the problems in the previous activity. A quick review of Mendel's first and second experiments shows that the principles of dominance and segregation are based on the outcome of many monohybrid crosses. In Section 23.3, you will consider Mendel's third experiment, which is more complex.

Cytoplasmic Inheritance

The flowers of the four o'clock plant inherit their colour from both parents, according to Mendelian principles. However, only the female parent determines colour inheritance in the green parts of four o'clock plants. Seeds from green branches produce green plants, seeds from pale green branches produce pale green plants, and seeds from dappled branches produce green, pale green, and dappled plants in unpredictable ratios. This pattern of colour inheritance depends on the female parent, on whose stems the egg-containing flowers grew. The green colouration of the plant that contributed the pollen has no effect on the green colouration of the offspring. Researchers have only recently discovered why such characteristics do not follow Mendelian patterns.

Mendel's laws apply only to characteristics controlled by DNA on the nuclear chromosome and distributed to the eggs and sperm by meiosis. However, not all DNA is located in the nucleus. Small rings of DNA called cytoplasmic DNA are also found outside the nucleus. Unlike chromosomal DNA, cytoplasmic DNA does not replicate during meiosis. If a characteristic shows an inheritance pattern that is distributed in patterns that do not conform to Mendel's laws, then cytoplasmic inheritance may be occurring.

Characteristics determined by cytoplasmic inheritance are transmitted from the parent contributing the most cytoplasm to the offspring. In plants, this is the female, since the egg cell contains a large amount of cytoplasm, while the sperm contains very little. Therefore, most cytoplasmic inheritance in plants is maternal. As in four o'clock plants, green-colour characteristics of the projeny mimic the mother's traits instead of the father's.

Cytoplasmic DNA occurs in two forms. The most common form is organelle DNA, which has been positively identified in chloroplasts and mitochondria. Researchers believe organelle DNA interacts with nuclear DNA to produce proteins needed by the organelle. These proteins cause additional effects. For example, the four o'clock plant's colour is

produced by its chloroplast colour, and this is determined by chloroplast DNA.

Foreign DNA from bacteria and viruses that sometimes live within the cytoplasm can also cause cytoplasmic inheritance. The paramecium, for example, can carry *kappa* particles, which cause their host to secrete a toxin lethal to other paramecia. *Kappa* particles, which resemble both bacteria and viruses, are passed on through asexual reproduction. During conjugation, paramecia exchange nuclear material, but they do not exchange much cytoplasm, so *kappa* particles are rarely transferred through conjugation.

Corn breeders rely on cytoplasmic inheritance in their work. Corn plants normally carry both male and female flowers and can either cross- or self-pollinate. However, some strains carry cytoplasmically inherited DNA that prevents male flowers from developing. These male-sterile strains can be cross-fertilized by male-fertile strains, but they cannot self-pollinate. As a result, breeders know that the cross will be pure. When necessary, breeders can restore male fertility by introducing a dominant chromosomal gene that overrides the cytoplasmic sterility DNA. With the capacity to eliminate self-pollination at will, breeders have more precise control over breeding.

Section Review Questions

1. Define the terms a) genetics, b) gene, c) allele, and d) monohybrid cross.
2. Explain the difference between a genotype and a phenotype and state examples of each.
3. State the genotypes for the following pea plants.
    a) homozygous tall
    b) heterozygous tall
    c) homozygous short
4. Construct and complete a Punnett square for each of the following crosses. State the genotypic and phenotypic ratio of the offspring in each cross.
    a) homozygous tall × homozygous short
    b) heterozygous tall × heterozygous tall
    c) heterozygous inflated pods × homozygous constricted pods
    d) homozygous green pod × yellow pod.

23.3 Mendel's Third Experiment

So far you have seen only inheritance in monohybrid crosses. However, Mendel also conducted **dihybrid crosses,** crossbreeding experiments that traced two inherited characteristics.

Investigating Dihybrid Crosses

Mendel's purpose in performing dihybrid crosses was to determine whether different characteristics were inherited independently of one another. For example, he wondered whether the inheritance of seed colour was linked in any way to the inheritance of seed shape. He designed his third experiment to answer this question.

Mendel's first step in his experimental procedure was to establish pure breeding lines of pea plants with contrasting traits for two characteristics. Through repeated selective breeding of round-seeded plants (genotype RR) with yellow-seeded plants (genotype YY), he developed a line of pea plants that always bore round, yellow seeds (genotype RRYY). By similar means, he developed a second line of pea plants that always bore wrinkled, green seeds (genotype rryy).

These purebred plants became the parental, or P, generation. Mendel crossbred them and planted their seeds to produce the F_1 generation. He allowed the F_1 generation to self-pollinate and then collected their seeds to grow the F_2 generation. When the F_2 plants matured, Mendel sorted them according to seed colour and shape, counted each kind, and recorded his observations. Before looking at Mendel's numerical data, stop and think about how the dominant and the recessive alleles are likely to recombine in a dihybrid cross.

INQUIRY ACTIVITY
Predicting the Outcome of a Dihybrid Cross

Mendel had to crossbreed his plants, wait for the results, and then search for patterns. But you can take advantage of the Punnett square to predict the probable outcome of Mendel's dihybrid crosses. Copy and complete Figure 23-12 in your notebook, then answer the Discussion Questions.

Gametes of Parent Pure for Round, Yellow Seeds (RRYY)

	RY			
ry	RrYy			

Gametes of Parent Pure for Wrinkled, Green Seeds (rryy)

FIGURE 23-12 A Punnett square for a dihybrid cross. This square has been started for you. Fill in the blanks for parental gametes and offspring genotypes. Then draw another square for the F_2 generation.

Discussion Questions

1. a) State the genotypes of the P generation.
   b) List all the predicted genotypes in the F_1 generation and state which phenotype will result in each case. Discuss reasons for your answers.
2. a) What percentage of the F_1 generation offspring will have round seeds? Wrinkled seeds? State this predicted outcome as a phenotypic ratio.
   b) What percentage of the F_1 generation offspring will have yellow seeds? Green seeds? State this outcome as a phenotypic ratio.

TABLE 23-5 Table of Observed F$_2$ Phenotypes in Dihybrid Crosses

315 with round, yellow seeds
108 with round, green seeds
101 with wrinkled, yellow seeds
32 with wrinkled, green seeds
556 F$_2$ plants observed

3. a) List all the possible genotypes in the F$_2$ generation.
   b) State a genotypic ratio for the F$_2$ generation.
4. a) Which phenotype will result from each F$_2$ genotype? Discuss reasons for your answer.
   b) State a phenotypic ratio for the F$_2$ generation.
5. Compare your predicted phenotypic ratio with Mendel's actual results as shown in Table 23-5. Discuss.

Interpreting Mendel's Third Experiment

Mendel's third experiment began with a dihybrid cross between parent plants that were pure for round, yellow seeds and plants that were pure for wrinkled, green seeds. Based on the Principle of Dominance, Mendel would have expected that 100% of the F$_1$ generation would express both dominant traits, and this is exactly what he observed. All plants in the F$_1$ generation had round, yellow seeds with no sign of wrinkled or green phenotypes.

To Mendel, the Principle of Segregation suggested that these recessive traits would reappear in some of the F$_2$ generation. To test this hypothesis, he carried out a dihybrid cross of the F$_1$ plants. The results confirmed his expectations. As Table 23-4 indicates, the F$_2$ phenotypes expressed every possible combination of seed shape and colour. When Mendel converted these numerical data to rounded-off phenotypic ratios, he found that $\frac{9}{16}$ of the F$_2$ seeds were round and yellow (dominant-dominant); $\frac{3}{16}$ of the F$_2$ seeds were round and green (dominant-recessive); and $\frac{3}{16}$ of the F$_2$ seeds were wrinkled and yellow (recessive-dominant); and $\frac{1}{16}$ of the F$_2$ seeds were wrinkled and green (recessive-recessive).

To Mendel, these results confirmed the hereditary role of probability. Here's how his thinking may have gone. Suppose only one characteristic is considered at a time, starting with seed shape. A monohybrid cross between a pure round-seeded parent (RR) and a pure wrinkle-seeded parent (rr) will result in 100% round-seeded but hybrid F$_1$ offspring (Rr). A second monohybrid cross between these hybrids will produce F$_2$ offspring with a $\frac{3}{4}$ (75%) chance of bearing round seeds (either RR or Rr). Similarly, a monohybrid cross between pure yellow-seeded parents and pure green-seeded parents will eventually yield F$_2$ offspring with a $\frac{3}{4}$ chance of bearing yellow seeds. Therefore, the combined probability of bearing seeds that are both round and yellow is $\frac{3}{4} \times \frac{3}{4}$, or $\frac{9}{16}$, exactly what Mendel observed.

The close agreement between predicted and observed results in the dihybrid cross suggested to Mendel that inheritance of seed colour is not linked to inheritance of seed shape. For example, a round seed may be either yellow or green. Mendel thought these results could be applied to all inherited characteristics. He stated his conclusion as a "law of independent assortment." This "law" claimed that inherited factors for different traits were always segregated and distributed to gametes independently of one another. However, more recent observations by other researchers show that this view of independent assortment is oversimplified.

Independent Assortment: A Modern View

For the seven pea-plant characteristics that he studied, Mendel's statement about independent assortment can be verified experimentally. It can also be verified for many other inherited characteristics in many other organisms. But modern studies of inheritance show that certain traits often occur together. In fruit flies, for example, long wings and a black body are usually found together, but stubby vestigial wings are usually found with a grey body.

Geneticists say the occurrence of the above traits together happens because the gene locations for wing shape and body colour are carried on the same chromosome. Genes on the same chromosome are said to be linked. **Linkage** refers to traits that are usually inherited together. In fruit flies, wing shape and body colour are linked. In pea plants, seed-coat colour and flower colour are linked. Linkage shows that Mendel's "law" does not apply to individual genes if they are on the same chromosome. Only genes on different chromosomes can assort independently during meiosis. Restated in modern terms, Mendel's "law" becomes the **Principle of Independent Assortment.**

The inheritance of alleles for one trait does not affect the inheritance of alleles for another trait unless both gene locations are on the same chromosome.

Linked genes do not always stay together on the same chromosome. During meiosis, crossing over causes homologous chromosomes to exchange equivalent segments. So, the segment coding for long wings could switch places with the allele for vestigial wings, while the alleles for a grey and black body remained in their usual location.

LEFT: Most black-bodied fruit flies have long wings.

RIGHT: Most grey-bodied fruit flies have stubby vestigial wings.

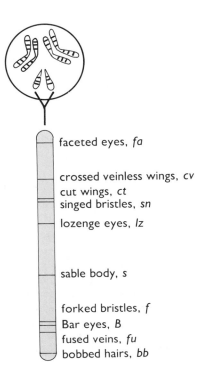

FIGURE 23-13 Careful analysis of gene linkages in hybrid fruit-fly offspring has been used to pinpoint the order and the location of genes in fruit-fly chromosomes. All four chromosomes have been partially mapped, but only one map is shown here.

In the chromosome (labels):
faceted eyes, *fa*
crossed veinless wings, *cv*
cut wings, *ct*
singed bristles, *sn*
lozenge eyes, *lz*
sable body, *s*
forked bristles, *f*
Bar eyes, *B*
fused veins, *fu*
bobbed hairs, *bb*

In some organisms, a single chromosome may carry genes for hundreds of characteristics. Geneticists have even determined the sequence of genes on some chromosomes in organisms such as fruit flies. The process of determining gene sequence is called **chromosome mapping.** (See Figure 23-13.)

Modernizing Mendel's Principles

The patterns of heredity uncovered by Mendel's research continue to be useful for predicting the results of crosses involving dominant and recessive alleles. However, there are many exceptions to the dominant-recessive pattern revealed by Mendel's research.

Incomplete dominance occurs when two different alleles control a characteristic, but neither is dominant. The resulting phenotype displays a blending of the two traits coded for by the alleles. For example, when red-flowered snapdragon parents are crossed with white-flowered snapdragon parents, the offspring always have pink flowers. Since neither colour is dominant, both the redness allele (R) and the whiteness allele (W) are shown as capital letters. The red-flowered parents have a homozygous genotype (RR) and so do the white-flowered parents (WW). Their pink-flowered F₁ offspring are heterozygous (RW). When two pink snapdragons are crossed, the F₂ generation shows a phenotypic ratio of 1 red:2 pink:1 white. (See Figures 23-14 and 23-15.)

Incomplete dominance also occurs in shorthorn cattle. A cross between a homozygous red shorthorn (RR) and a homozygous white shorthorn (WW) results in heterozygous offspring (RW) with a roan coat in which both red hairs and white hairs are present. This indicates that neither allele is completely dominant over the other. (See Figure 23-16.)

Pure White Parent (WW)
(alleles of gametes)

Pure Red Parent (RR) (alleles of gametes)	W	W
R	RW	RW
R	RW	RW

FIGURE 23-14 A cross of red and white snapdragons. Offspring are 100% hybrid pink.

Hybrid Pink Parent (RW)
(alleles of gametes)

Hybrid Pink Parent (RW) (alleles of gametes)	R	W
R	RR	RW
W	RW	WW

FIGURE 23-15 A cross of two pink snapdragons. Phenotypic ratio of offspring is 1 red : 2 pink : 1 white (1:2:1).

Red-Coated Parent (RR)
(alleles of gametes)

White-Coated Parent (WW) (alleles of gametes)	R	R
W	RW	RW
W	RW	RW

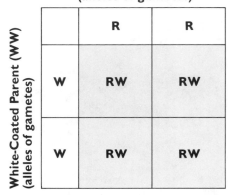

FIGURE 23-16 Incomplete dominance in shorthorn cattle

Multiple alleles also play an important role in heredity. Mendel's experiments suggested that each characteristic was determined by one pair of factors, and that only two contrasting traits were possible. In modern terms, this would mean that only one gene location was involved with only two different kinds of alleles to occupy it. Today, geneticists know that many inherited characteristics are controlled by multiple alleles, multiple gene locations, or both. In Chapter 24, you will learn about the role of multiple alleles in determining human blood types, and the role of multiple gene locations in determining human characteristics such as height, eye colour, and skin colour.

In Section 23.4, you will consider how the principles of heredity apply to breeding domestic plants and animals. This should enhance your understanding of Chapter 24 since much of what is now known about human heredity was first learned by observing inheritance in other organisms.

Section Review Questions

1. Define the terms dihybrid cross and linkage.
2. State three examples of dihybrid crosses of pea plants Mendel may have performed.
3. In a dihybrid cross of two pea plants, one homozygous for two dominant traits, the other homozygous for the corresponding recessive traits, what will the phenotypic ratio be in the F_1 generation? In the F_2 generation?
4. a) State the Principle of Independent Assortment.
   b) Explain briefly what is meant by independent assortment.
5. State two examples to explain incomplete dominance.
6. In four o'clock plants, red flowers are incompletely dominant over white flowers, the heterozygous plants being pink-flowered. If a red-flowered four o'clock plant is crossed with a white-flowered one, what will be the flower colour of
   a) the F_1 generation?
   b) the F_1 generation crossed with its red parent?
   c) the F_1 generation crossed with its white parent?

23.4 Applying the Principles of Heredity

Many successful breeding experiments took place long before genetics became an established science. For example, the sleek lines and great speed of thoroughbred racehorses are the outcome of a breeding program that began in England in 1700. However, early breeding programs also had numerous failures. Mating the fastest mares and stallions did not always produce winning

This foal of Secretariat, the famous racehorse, is chestnut-coloured with white stockings, just like his sire.

Generations of inbreeding produced the many dog breeds shown in Figure 23-17. Toy varieties are even more inbred. The toy poodle, for example, was developed by inbreeding the smallest offspring of larger poodles over successive generations.

offspring. Today, knowledge of genetic principles helps horse breeders to develop scientific breeding programs with a much higher success rate.

Modern agriculture also depends heavily on scientific breeding programs to preserve the desirable qualities of existing plant and animal varieties or to develop breeds with improved qualities. Strawberries with a longer shelf life and pork with a lower fat content are just two agricultural products improved by applying the principles of heredity.

Principles of Controlled Breeding

Mating plants or animals selected for their desirable traits is called selective or **controlled breeding.** There are three main types of controlled breeding: inbreeding, outbreeding, and crossbreeding.

Inbreeding is the mating of two closely related individuals such as brother and sister. Its objective is to preserve desired combinations of traits in future generations by bringing identical favourable alleles together. Thoroughbred racehorses were developed by inbreeding as were the dog breeds shown in Figure 23-17. Because inbreeding reduces the probability of unwanted variations, it is also used to maintain desired qualities in purebred fowl, sheep, cattle, and pigs.

V THE UNITY OF LIFE

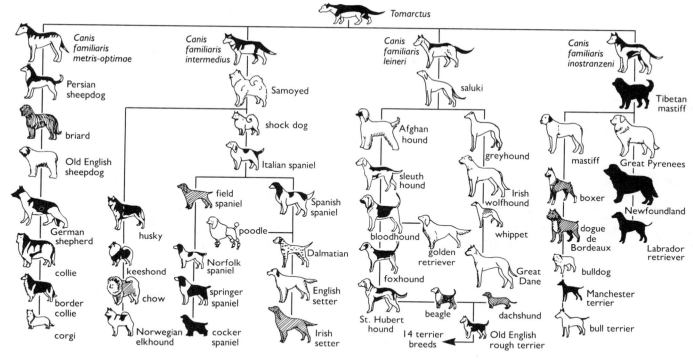

FIGURE 23-17   The development of dog breeds

Unfortunately, inbreeding also increases the probability that harmful recessive alleles will be brought together and expressed, a condition called **inbreeding depression.** Examples include deafness in Dalmations, hip dysplasia in German shepherds, deformed feet in Jersey cattle, and dwarfism in Hereford cattle. Inbreeding depression can sometimes be relieved by **outbreeding.** In outbreeding, an inbred organism is crossed with another inbred organism usually of the same breed but less closely related. The objective of outbreeding is to introduce favourable dominant alleles without altering the breed's distinguishing features.

By contrast, **crossbreeding** involves mating parents of distinctly different genotypes and phenotypes in order to produce hybrid offspring with entirely new combinations of features.

Hybridization and Hybrid Vigour

Crossbreeding unlike varieties to combine their best qualities is often called **hybridization.** For example, a variety of wheat that produces large and numerous grains may not grow fast enough to survive in a location with a short growing season. Crossbreeding it with a fast-growing variety may produce F_1 hybrids that are both fast growing and high yielding.

DID YOU KNOW?

Dog breeders often import dogs from another country to introduce alleles from a completely different breeding line. For example, a dachshund from a Canadian kennel might be bred with one from a British kennel. Sires with good health records can command large stud fees.

Canola was developed by plant-breeding techniques in Canada in the 1940s. It bred out several traits that had been linked with certain diseases, and bred in superior nutritional qualities.

Hybrid F_1 offspring can sometimes be inbred to establish a pure breeding line. More often, however, inbreeding causes unwanted recessive alleles to segregate independently and recombine in the F_2 generation (for example, slow-growing, low-yielding wheat plants). When this happens, the only reliable way to obtain the desired qualities is through repeated crossing of two purebred lines. This time-consuming process makes certified F_1 seed expensive.

An additional benefit of hybridization is that F_1 hybrids are often much healthier than either purebred parent, a quality called **hybrid vigour.** Hybrid vigour occurs because crossbreeding increases the chance that the hybrid offspring will inherit at least one favourable dominant allele for each trait. Many valuable plant and animal hybrids have been developed this way. (See Table 23-6.)

Hybridization between different species is unusual and occurs only if they are closely related. The best-known interspecies hybrid is the mule, which is produced by crossbreeding a female horse with a male donkey. The mule is a valued work animal because it combines the size of a horse with the endurance and disease resistance of a donkey. However, mules are usually sterile.

Most mongrels display hybrid vigour. A Dalmatian-German shepherd cross, for example, will probably produce pups with normal hearing and hips.

TABLE 23-6 Desirable Traits in Hybrid Plants and Animals

Hybrid	Desired Traits
Sweet Corn	• large cobs, numerous large kernels • sweet taste
Wheat	• ability to grow in colder climate • greater yield • resistance to disease
Tomato	• large fruits • increased fruit production
Rose	• increased flower production • larger flowers • variety in flower colour
Silver Fox	• attractive fur
Holstein	• increased milk production
White Leghorn	• increased egg production

TABLE 23-7 Rare and Unusual Breeds of Plants and Animals

Organism	Characteristics
Mule	• offspring of female horse and male donkey • superior physical endurance, strength, and resistance to disease
Beefalo	• offspring of male buffalo and beef cow • good quality beef • thick coat • ability to withstand cold weather
Liger	• offspring of female tiger and male lion • light ochre stripe • male has a mane
Geep	• offspring of goat and sheep • produced by genetic engineering

V THE UNITY OF LIFE

A leopon is the offspring of a leopard and a lion. Leopons have the mane of a lion and the spots of a leopard.

Interspecies hybrids are usually sterile because the chromosomes from the two parent species do not match and therefore cannot form homologous pairs at meiosis. As a result, the hybrid cannot produce normal gametes.

To obtain more mules, breeders must repeat the mating of a horse and a donkey. Table 23-7 lists some rare hybrids produced by crossing other closely related species.

Solving Breeding Problems: The Test Cross

Figure 23-18 illustrates a common problem breeders used to have trying to establish pure breeding lines. Is the long-haired dog really purebred for the dominant trait (homozygous genotype), or is it hybrid (heterozygous genotype)? There is no way to tell from its phenotype, but problems like this can sometimes be solved with a **test cross.**

The type of test cross needed to solve the above problem would cross the long-haired dog with a short-haired dog, and compare the results to the Punnett squares in Figure 23-19. If even one pup has short hair, the unknown long-haired parent's genotype can be inferred—it must be Hh. If all of the pups have long hair, the unknown genotype is probably HH, but this cannot be

hh

HH or Hh?

FIGURE 23-18 Left: Short hair is a recessive trait, so this smooth dog must have two copies of the recessive allele (hh). **Right:** Long hair is a dominant trait, so this fluffy dog's phenotype does not reveal whether it is purebred (genotype HH) or hybrid (genotype Hh).

FIGURE 23-19 These Punnett squares predict the outcome of crossing a short-haired dog (hh) with a long-haired dog of unknown genotype. **Left:** If the long-haired parent is purebred (HH), all of the offspring will have long hair. **Right:** If the long-haired parent is hybrid (Hh), the predicted phenotypic ratio is 1:1. On average, 50% will be short-haired.

Purebred Long-Haired Parent (HH)
(alleles of gametes)

Short-Haired Parent (hh) (alleles of gametes)

	H	H
h	Hh	Hh
h	Hh	Hh

Hybrid Long-Haired Parent (Hh)
(alleles of gametes)

Short-Haired Parent (hh) (alleles of gametes)

	H	h
h	Hh	hh
h	Hh	hh

Genetic defects that appear unexpectedly in a breeding line are usually caused by spontaneous mutations. One copy of a mutant allele is seldom harmful because the normal allele dominates it. The defect is only expressed if two mutant alleles come together, an outcome that is more likely when purebred lines are repeatedly inbred.

Spontaneous mutations are caused by seemingly simple mistakes during DNA replication. Just one mismatched, missing, or extra base pair can completely alter the code of an allele so that it cannot perform its normal function. (Imagine how a computer would respond to good, goo, or flood if the correct code is really food.)

known for certain because the genotype could be Hh. This uncertainty about genotype results because Punnett squares are based on the laws of probability, which are valid only for a large number of events. Just as a tossed coin may land tails up four times in a row, it is quite possible for an entire litter of long-haired pups to have the genotype Hh. If this occurred, the presence of the h allele in the pups would be undetectable.

Uncertainty is only one disadvantage of the test cross. A second is that results are slow in animals with small litters and long gestation periods. Fortunately, modern breeding records are so complete that the test cross is seldom needed. Today, its only common use by animal breeders is to detect carriers of genetic defects. Animal geneticists hope that chromosome mapping will eventually enable them to identify missing or defective genes in sample cells, and eliminate the need for test crosses entirely.

By contrast, test crosses on plants are fairly reliable since plants produce large numbers of offspring, and many generations can be observed in a short time. Test crosses to distinguish purebred plants from hybrids are made unnecessary by well-kept breeding records. However, plant researchers do use a different type of test cross to determine whether a particular characteristic is passed on by single-gene inheritance, two-gene inheritance, or multiple-gene inheritance.

This type of test cross involves three steps: crossbreeding parent plants (P) with contrasting traits, inbreeding the F_1 offspring, and observing the phenotypic ratios of the F_2 offspring. If there are only two distinct F_2 phenotypes in a telltale ratio of 3:1, the researcher knows that the characteristic under study is passed on by one pair of alleles at a single gene location on each chromosome. (Remember Mendel's second experiment.) If there are four distinct F_2 phenotypes in a ratio of 9:3:3:1, then two pairs of alleles at two gene locations are involved. (Remember Mendel's third experiment.) But if the characteristic is determined by alleles at multiple gene locations, the F_2

offspring will display a blending of traits. There will be no distinct phenotypes and no recognizable ratio. (See Figure 23-20.)

This type of test cross helps plant researchers decide whether their experimental design will have to allow for environmental effects. Single-gene inheritance is unaffected by environment. For example, seed colour in most plants is determined by alleles at a single gene location. As a result, all pea seeds are distinctly green or yellow regardless of soil conditions or the type of fertilizer used. Disease resistance is also passed on by single-gene inheritance. Experiments to test disease resistance can therefore be conducted indoors and on a small scale. There is no need to repeat the experiment many times under different conditions in many different environments.

If a test cross shows that the characteristic is passed on by multiple-gene inheritance, environment will be a much more important factor in experimental design. For multiple-gene characteristics such as yield, environmental effects may be almost as important as heredity. For example, so-called "high-yield" wheat seed will produce a poor crop if soil or rainfall is unsuitable. Large-scale experiments in many different environments are required to study multiple-gene characteristics such as yield.

Much of what plant and animal geneticists have learned from breeding experiments is also true for humans. In Chapter 24, you will learn how Mendel's principles and the ideas of modern genetics combine to help us understand human heredity.

FIGURE 23-20 All of these F$_2$ hybrid ears of corn had the same parents. How many different types of phenotypes do you see? How many pairs of alleles were involved in producing them?

This cob of corn represents an entire F$_2$ generation since each kernel grew from a different flower. Count the coloured and colourless kernels to determine the phenotypic ratio. Is kernel colour a single-gene, two-gene, or multiple-gene characteristic?

This F$_2$ hybrid shows four distinct phenotypes in a recognizable ratio of 9 coloured smooth: 3 coloured wrinkled: 3 colourless smooth: 1 colourless wrinkled. How many pairs of alleles were involved in producing these phenotypes? Which alleles are dominant and which are recessive?

Scientists are constantly trying to improve the characteristics of plants through crossbreeding experiments.

Genetic Research with *Brassica rapa*

Usually, it is difficult for high school classes to carry out genetic research because so much time is needed to trace inheritance in successive generations, even in plants. (Mendel's research lasted eight years.) However, if your class can obtain seeds from a small, yellow-flowered plant called *Brassica rapa*, you can observe Mendel's patterns of inheritance in only two months. *B. rapa* is closely related to cauliflower, turnip, cabbage, and broccoli, but its life cycle is much shorter. The seeds of rapid-cycling *B. rapa* germinate in 12 h. The plants emerge in two days, begin to flower in 13 and produce mature seeds in 36. Designing and conducting a monohybrid cross with contrasting forms of *B. rapa* will help you see what Mendel saw, but much faster and with much less trouble, since *B. rapa* does not self-pollinate. *B. rapa* seeds are usually sold in kit form complete with suggestions for experimental design.

Section Review Questions

1. Define the terms a) controlled breeding, b) inbreeding, c) outbreeding, and d) crossbreeding.
2. What harmful effect can occur in offspring after continuous inbreeding? State examples.
3. How does outbreeding reduce the harmful effects of repeated inbreeding?
4. What is hybrid vigour? Explain.
5. a) What is the purpose of a test cross?
   b) Explain briefly how a test cross is performed.

Saran Narang

Dr. Saran Narang, a researcher at the National Research Council (NRC) in Ottawa believes we have made progress toward unravelling the mysteries of DNA. "We can write the language of life," he says. Indeed, Narang has been involved in two of the most important developments in deciphering this language. The goal of molecular genetics today, he says, "is to understand the meaning in it."

Narang was born and educated in India, but he decided to emigrate to North America. Narang joined Dr. Har Gobind Khorana at the University of Wisconsin in 1963 to do work on cracking the genetic code. "Those were exciting days," says Narang, "especially as we were in a tight race with other laboratories. Eventually, we confirmed what biologists had inferred from purely mathematical considerations—that each amino acid is coded for by a triplet of three bases of DNA."

Once this work was finished, Narang felt the next step was to assemble a synthetic human gene. He brought this challenging idea to the NRC in 1966. Numerous difficulties stood in the way of synthesizing a human gene. Perhaps the most daunting were the slow, inefficient techniques available for synthesizing DNA. Producing a large gene would require huge amounts of material and time. Narang overcame this obstacle by developing a faster and more efficient approach to DNA synthesis—the modified triester approach.

The gene Narang had chosen to synthesize was proinsulin, the protein precursor to insulin. Narang believed the *E. coli* bacterium could be induced to incorporate the proinsulin gene into its own DNA. The bacteria would then be genetically coded to reproduce the protein. Therefore, an inexpensive, virtually infinite source of human insulin could be created.

Narang synthesized short segments of the gene that were joined with enzymes. The 258-base gene was then cloned and inserted into the *E. coli* genome. The experiment was so successful that some bacteria actually died by overproducing the proinsulin protein.

These bacteria were the culmination of over ten years of research for Narang. Today, his dream of inexpensive human insulin is a reality. His methods have been refined and are used around the world in the production of insulin and hundreds of other drugs.

Narang has moved on to another problem—the search for a universal vaccine. "I am trying to understand how nature evolved molecules used in immunity," he says. If he can decipher how nature arrived at the design of immunological molecules, he says, it may be possible to improve the immune system by producing antibodies capable of fighting more than one infection simultaneously.

Regarding the future, Narang says he would like to write a book entitled *What is Life?* that would explain the phenomena from a biochemical perspective. Narang will continue his work in science, he says, for the same reason that he started it—because it allows him, through his work, to enjoy "the poetry of life."

Chapter Review

Key Words

allele
chromosome mapping
controlled breeding
crossbreeding
dihybrid cross
dominant allele
dominant trait
first filial (F₁)
    generation
gene
genetics
genotype
heredity
heterozygous
homozygous
hybrid
hybrid vigour

hybridization
inbreeding
incomplete dominance
linkage
monohybrid cross
multiple alleles
outbreeding
phenotype
Principle of Dominance
Principle of Independent
    Assortment
Principle of Segregation
Punnett square
recessive allele
recessive trait
second filial (F₂)
    generation
test cross

Recall Questions

Multiple Choice

1. A gene is
   a) composed of chromatin
   b) a segment of a chromosome
   c) responsible for the inheritance of a single trait
   d) all of the above

2. In the F_2 generation of a monohybrid cross, the genotypic ratio would be
   a) 3:1
   b) 1:2:1
   c) 2:1:1
   d) 1:1:2

3. If a test cross is performed on a pea plant heterozygous for a particular trait, the resulting phenotypic ratio would be
   a) 1:0
   b) 1:1
   c) 3:1
   d) 0:1

4. Genes located on the same chromosome are said to be
   a) linked
   b) alleles
   c) homozygous
   d) heterozygous

5. Which of the following human characteristics is controlled by multiple alleles?
   a) blood type
   b) height
   c) skin colour
   d) all of the above

Fill in the Blanks

1. A _____ is a part of a chromosome responsible for the inheritance of one trait.

2. Organisms that are the offspring of parents possessing unlike traits for the same characteristic are called _____.

3. An organism that carries two identical alleles is _____ for that particular trait.

4. The set of alleles an organism has for a trait, or its complete set of alleles is its _____.

5. The ratio of one trait to the contrasting trait for the same characteristic in the offspring is called the _____ ratio.

6. The first group of offspring of a particular cross are called the _____, or the _____, for short.

7. The procedure used to determine whether an organism exhibiting a dominant trait is homozygous or heterozygous is called a _____.

8. A line of championship, purebred Alaskan malamute dogs has developed abnormally short, bowed legs. This could be an example of _____.

9. Heterozygous four o'clock flowers are _____ in colour.

Short Answers

1. Each parent has two alleles for a particular characteristic. How many does each parent give to each of its offspring?

2. What is the genotype of a pea plant with green pods? Explain.

3. a) What result did Mendel observe in the F_1 generation when he crossed pea plants that were homozygous for contrasting traits?
   b) What did he observe when two F_1 plants were crossed?
   c) What is meant by the term dominant allele?

4. a) Briefly explain the Principle of Independent Assortment.
   b) What is meant by the term linkage?
5. Identify a human trait that is controlled by multiple alleles.
6. Coat colour in shorthorn cattle is an example of incomplete dominance. The two homozygous genotypes produce red and white coats while the heterozygous genotypes produce a roan coat (a mixture of red and white). Use Punnett squares to show the results in the F_1 and F_2 generations when a white and a red shorthorn are crossed. State the phenotypic ratios.
7. a) What is the purpose of inbreeding?
   b) What problem sometimes results from continued inbreeding?
   c) How can the above problem be overcome?
8. a) What is hybrid vigour?
   b) How does hybrid vigour occur?

Application Questions

1. A black coat in guinea pigs is dominant over a white coat. How would you determine whether a black guinea pig is homozygous or heterozygous?
2. Suppose you are a dog breeder with a line of championship purebred Irish setters. Some of the dogs have developed a recessive trait known as hip dysplasia. How would you attempt to ensure that future generations of your dogs do not develop this condition?
3. How would you produce four o'clock seeds which would all yield pink-flowered plants when sown?

Problem Solving

1. Do all pea plants with the same phenotype have the same genotype? Explain briefly.
2. How would you determine whether a smooth-seeded pea plant is homozygous or heterozygous? Explain briefly.
3. A tall pea plant crossed with a short pea plant produces offspring of which one half are tall and one half are short. What are the genotypes of the parents?

4. If the tall parent in Question 3 self-pollinates, state the probable phenotypic ratio of the F_1 generation.
5. In four o'clock flowers, red flower colour (R) is completely dominant over white (r), the heterozygous plants having pink flowers.
   a) What flower colour will result in the offspring when a pink four o'clock plant is crossed with a red one?
   b) What flower colour will result in the offspring when a pink four o'clock plant is crossed with a white one?

Extensions

1. A trihybrid cross involves the alleles for three different traits. Select any three pairs of traits in pea plants considered by Mendel. Begin with two plants, one homozygous for all three dominant traits; the other homozygous for the recessive traits. Write the genotype for all F_1 plants. Use a Punnett square to show the cross of two of the F_1 plants.
2. Visit the genetics department of a university in your vicinity. Find out about the kinds of research being done there. Write a brief report.
3. Research the life and work of Luther Burbank. Produce a list of the many varieties of plants that he developed.
4. Research the history of several breeds of dogs or horses. Try to determine which traits of each particular breed were selected for the inbreeding and write a brief statement similar to the following example.

The curly haired, curly whiskered Rex cat was first recognized as a distinct breed in 1959. It was developed by inbreeding the offspring of a single curly haired individual first observed in 1943.

CHAPTER

24

Human Genetics

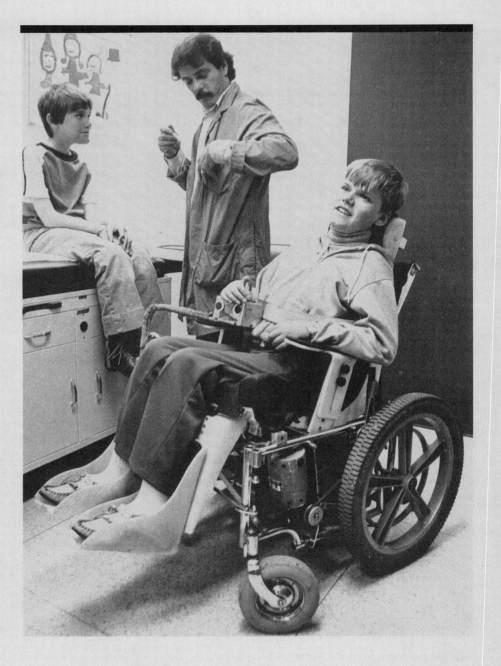

U ntil recently, medical researchers focussed on environmental causes of disease such as diet, infection, and pollution. Today, technological advances allow researchers to analyze genetic material. As a result, the genetic causes of diseases now receive equal attention. Genetic testing, one of the consequences of the attention, may spark a revolution in medicine.

When a genetic disease factor is recognized, one branch of research focusses on locating it on the human genome. So far, markers have been found to locate genes for more than 400 diseases. These markers make genetic testing possible. Although such testing is currently practical for only a few diseases, tests will eventually be developed for many more. Soon a small tissue sample may reveal a person's future health, identifying both the risk of disease, and any disease-causing genes he or she carries. Genetic testing may become a routine medical procedure.

Genetic testing allows physicians to diagnose some diseases long before symptoms appear, making their prevention possible. Screening for diseases caused by a combination of genetic and environmental factors helps patients minimize the risk they face. Some progress has already been made toward genetic screening for heart disease. Hyperlipidemia is one genetic disease that makes people susceptible to heart problems.

A further benefit of genetic screening is the control it gives people over their own lives. In the past, carriers and victims of genetic conditions such as hemophilia often avoided having children for fear of passing along the disease-causing gene. Through genetic screening of fetal tissue, parents will know whether their fetus is affected. They may choose to continue or terminate the pregnancy based on the diagnosis.

Genetic screening will bring both advances in health care and ethical dilemmas. The case of sickle-cell anemia illustrates both aspects. For this disease, one of the first widespread genetic screening programs was started in the United States in the early 1970s. The aim was to improve health care, but soon suspicions arose that screening results were being used to discriminate against disease carriers, most of whom were black. Despite the fact that most sickle-cell carriers are free of symptoms, some carriers found they were denied certain jobs and had their insurance premiums raised as a result of the diagnosis.

Some people fear this scenario might be repeated unless access to genetic information is strictly controlled. As you read this chapter, consider each new development in genetic knowledge. What consequences may each advance have beyond its immediate applications? How might increasing knowledge about human genetics affect society?

Chapter Objectives

When you complete this chapter, you should:

1. Appreciate the practical and ethical difficulties that have limited research into human genetics in the past, and be able to describe how modern techniques have alleviated some of these difficulties.

2. Be able to describe single-gene inheritance in humans, and identify several characteristics that are determined by this simple inheritance pattern.

3. Be able to describe inheritance patterns involving multiple genes or alleles, and identify several human characteristics that are determined by these more complex patterns.

4. Know how to use Punnett squares and pedigrees to predict genotypes and phenotypes of human offspring, and to infer parental genotypes and phenotypes.

5. Understand how sex is determined in humans, explain how irregularities in the usual chromosome pattern occur, and be able to describe their effect on phenotype.

6. Be able to explain the term sex-linked inheritance, list at least two sex-linked traits, and use Punnett squares or pedigrees to show how sex-linked traits are passed on.

7. Be able to describe at least three genetic disorders of humans and appreciate their impact on society.

8. Be able to describe some modern procedures for detecting, screening, and preventing genetic disorders.

9. Appreciate both the possible benefits and the potential risks of genetic research.

24.1 Investigating Human Genetics

In the past, geneticists have found it difficult to conduct studies of human inheritance using human subjects. From an ethical standpoint, using human subjects in controlled breeding experiments is unacceptable. From a scientific standpoint, the long time span between human generations is a significant drawback. Studies like Mendel's pea-plant experiments would take hundreds of years.

Consequently, the study of human genetics has been forced to rely on plant and animal investigations. By comparing the outcome of such studies to the patterns observed in humans, geneticists have realized that human heredity is governed by the same genetic principles that govern heredity in other organisms.

To identify patterns of inheritance in humans, geneticists have borrowed methods used by plant and animal breeders who rely on pedigrees to keep track of inherited characteristics. When applied to human heredity, a **pedigree** is a diagram that shows the inheritance of a single characteristic within a family. (See Figure 24-1.) Although human pedigrees do not provide as much information as large-scale, controlled breeding studies, they do play an important role in understanding human heredity.

FIGURE 24-1 A pedigree showing the inheritance of hairline shape over three generations

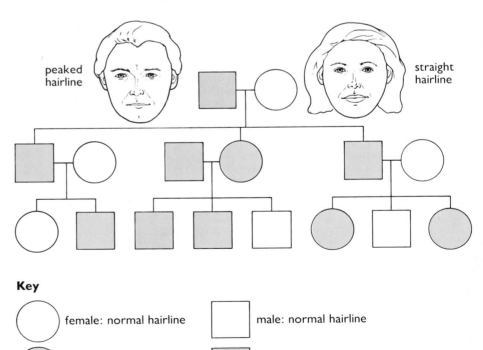

Key

◯ female: normal hairline   ☐ male: normal hairline

⬤ female: peaked hairline   ▣ male: peaked hairline

Single-Gene Inheritance in Humans

Like seed shape in pea plants, many human characteristics are determined by the inheritance of a single pair of alleles at a single gene location. The pedigree in Figure 24-1 provides two clues indicating that hairline shape is passed on by **single-gene inheritance.** The first clue is that only two distinct phenotypes exist for hairline shape: smooth or peaked. The second clue is the apparent dominance of one trait over the other in the children of contrasting parents.

The above pattern is reminiscent of that found in Mendel's first experiment. Mendel was able to test apparent dominance further by inbreeding F_1 offspring to obtain an F_2 generation. But in the case of hairline shape, humans are involved, not pea plants. Most societies have established customs that prohibit brother-and-sister marriages, and the children in this pedigree chose their mates without knowing their genotypes. As a result, the grandchildren do not show the characteristic 3:1 phenotypic ratio that could confirm single-gene inheritance of hairline shape. However, there are more grandchildren with a peaked hairline than there are without, which suggests that this trait may be dominant. Large-scale pedigree studies of several families have confirmed that a peaked hairline is, in fact, dominant while a smooth hairline is recessive.

The Principle of Dominance explains why recessive traits often skip generations. For those with smooth hairlines, only the homozygous recessive genotype (pp) is possible. But individuals with peaked hairlines may be either homozygous dominant (PP) or heterozygous dominant (Pp). Since there is no way of recognizing the heterozygous carriers, the recessive trait may show up unexpectedly in their offspring.

For example, Figure 24-2 predicts a smooth hairline for 25% of the offspring of two heterozygous carriers. But this prediction is based on probability.

You should not confuse dominance with high frequency. For example, most of the students in your school probably were born with exactly ten fingers and ten toes. Yet this trait is recessive. But polydactylism (having more than ten fingers or ten toes) is dominant. However, the allele for polydactylism is not very common in the general population. Consequently, the trait is not very common. It occurs frequently only among groups in which intermarriage has increased the frequency of the polydactyl allele.

Male Parent (Carrier)
Peaked Hairline Phenotype
Heterozygous Genotype

		P	p
Female Parent (Carrier) Peaked Hairline Phenotype Heterozygous Genotype	**P**	**PP** peaked hairline phenotype	**Pp** peaked hairline phenotype
	P	**Pp** peaked hairline phenotype	**pp** smooth hairline phenotype

FIGURE 24-2 Probability predicts a phenotypic ratio of *3* offspring with peaked hairlines to *1* offspring with a smooth hairline (3:1).

A real couple may have only one child who may also happen to be heterozygous. Given the small size of human families, it might be two or three generations before the smooth hairline shows up again. By that time, no one may be alive who remembers what great-great grandmother's hairline looked like.

Table 24-1 shows several other human characteristics that are transmitted by single-gene inheritance. Like hairline shape, all are easy to observe and are therefore well suited to the investigative procedures of the next activity.

TABLE 24-1 Contrasting Human Traits

Characteristic	Contrasting Traits	
	Dominant	**Recessive**
Hairline Shape	peaked	smooth
Mid-Digit Hairs	present	absent
Tongue Rolling Ability	can roll	cannot roll
Wrist Cords	two cords	three cords
Ear Lobe Shape	free	attached
Clasping Pattern	left thumb on top	right thumb on top

INQUIRY ACTIVITY
Investigating Single-Gene Inheritance

In this activity, you will investigate patterns of inheritance among the people around you. Part 1 explores the six pairs of contrasting traits identified in Table 24-1. Part 2 identifies a seventh inherited characteristic for further investigation in Parts 3 and 4. Only those students having large numbers of family members nearby should attempt the family survey described in Part 3. All others will help to conduct the large-scale public survey outlined in Part 4. Your teacher will supply a worksheet if you choose to do this activity.

CAUTION: Many people are reluctant to answer questions about personal family matters. When conducting a survey, be sure to explain what you are investigating. Ask permission before asking questions and accept that some individuals will prefer not to respond.

Understanding Human Diversity

Think of all the people you know, meet on the street, or see on television. Except for identical twins, no two people are exactly alike. This diversity results mainly from the great number of traits humans can inherit and the even greater number of ways traits can be combined. As a simplified example, consider only the characteristics in Table 24-1. With two contrasting traits for each of the six characteristics, the number of different combinations possible is $2 \times 2 \times 2 \times 2 \times 2 \times 2$, a total of 2^6 or 64. Since humans actually have 23 pairs of chromosomes and thousands of gene locations on all but the Y chromosome, the number of possible genetic combinations is almost unimaginable.

The shape of your hairline, ear lobe, and thumb play no significant role in your wellbeing. But many inherited characteristics do influence your health,

Even identical twins have different fingerprints, and they often differ in other small ways that enable family and close friends to tell them apart.

The expression of characteristics in the phenotype depends on both genotype and environment. For example, a child who inherits a tall genotype will not necessarily grow tall if he or she does not receive adequate nutrition to promote growth.

If you look carefully at the profiles of these students, you will see they have some similarities and some differences.

and the combination you inherit does affect your ability to function. However, most of these more important characteristics are difficult to isolate and observe. The simple patterns of single-gene inheritance provide a model for understanding the more complex patterns that make each of us a unique individual. You will consider some of these more complex inheritance patterns in the following sections of this chapter.

Section Review Questions

1. List two problems related to studying inheritance in humans.
2. What is a pedigree?
3. List three human traits that are passed on by single-gene inheritance.
4. From a genetic viewpoint, explain why brother-and-sister marriages and cousin-and-cousin marriages should not occur.
5. A peaked hairline is a dominant trait. If a man with a peaked hairline marries a woman with a smooth hairline, will their children have peaked hairlines? Explain briefly.
6. If each characteristic has two contrasting traits, how many different combinations are there in the inheritance of the following
   a) *2* characteristics
   b) *8* characteristics
   c) *n* characteristics

24.2 Sex-Related Inheritance

Around 1890, early investigators discovered that the chromosomes found in the cells of male humans were similar to those in females except for one pair. Because these unlike pairs were soon discovered to be responsible for determining sex, they are now called **sex chromosomes.** The identical pairs, called **autosomes,** determine nonsexual characteristics such as hair and eye colour. Sex-related traits such as heavier facial hair in men and slighter stature in women are determined by alleles on the sex chromosomes.

How Sex is Determined

Each human body cell contains 23 pairs of chromosomes: *22* pairs of autosomes and *1* pair of sex chromosomes. In females, the two sex chromosomes are identical to each other in size and shape. The symbol X is used to represent this type of sex chromosome. So, the normal body cells of female humans contain two X chromosomes (genotype XX). During meiosis, homologous pairs are split up, and each egg cell receives one X chromosome. (See Figure 24-3.)

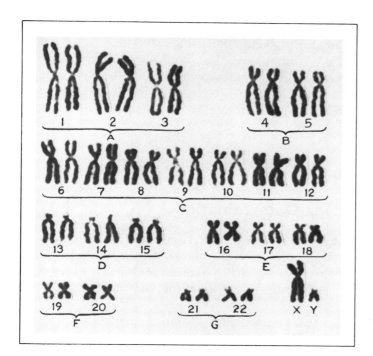

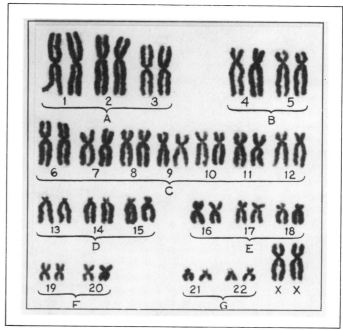

Left: The chromosomes of a normal male human. **Right:** The chromosomes of a normal female human. Only the sex chromosomes differ in size and shape.

father's sex chromosomes — **XY**

sperm cells — **X** **Y**

FIGURE 24-3 All human female gametes contain X chromosomes but only half of the male gametes do.

mother's sex chromosomes — **XX** → **X** **X**

egg cells

XX daughter	**XY** son
XX daughter	**XY** son

The Punnett square shows that 50% of human offspring should be male and 50% female. The actual ratio is not quite 1:1. Apparently, the uterine environment favours the Y-containing sperm. Consequently, more than half of all fertilized eggs are coded to become male.

    In males, the two sex chromosomes do not match. Only one chromosome is the same size and shape as the X chromosome found in females. The other, which is much smaller, is known as a Y chromosome. Each normal body cell of a male human contains one X chromosome and one Y chromosome (genotype XY). As sperm cells are produced, only half receive an X chromosome. The other half receive a Y chromosome. Therefore, there are two different types of sperm cells in male humans—those with X chromosomes and those with Y chromosomes.

When fertilization occurs, two offspring genotypes are possible, depending on which type of sperm cell fertilizes the egg. A zygote with the XX genotype develops into a female. A zygote with the XY genotype develops into a male. In humans, therefore, it is the sperm cell that determines the sex of the offspring.

Irregularities in Sex Determination

Irregularities may occur in meiosis that could result in egg cells with two X chromosomes or no X chromosomes at all. Similarly, sperm cells may form that have two sex chromosomes—X and Y—or no sex chromosomes at all. When such gametes participate in fertilization, the offspring develop abnormally.

Klinefelter syndrome is the combination of traits expressed when an XX egg cell unites with a normal Y sperm cell. The result is a male offspring with genotype XXY. In boys with this genotype, the penis and the testes are smaller than normal. At puberty they do not develop the usual secondary sex characteristics such as a deeper voice and male body hair. They may develop enlarged breasts. Men who have Klinefelter syndrome are sterile and may have below average intelligence.

Turner syndrome occurs if a sperm cell with no sex chromosome combines with a normal egg cell. The resulting female offspring will have just 45 chromosomes, including only one X chromosome (genotype XO). Girls who have Turner syndrome are usually shorter and stockier than most girls their age. They often exhibit webbing at the sides of the neck due to swelling under the skin. Their sex organs and breasts do not develop to the adult stage and as a result, they are sterile.

Triple-X syndrome occurs when an XX egg cell unites with an X sperm cell (genotype XXX). Most XXX females are normal in appearance. The most common problems associated with the syndrome are irregular menstruation, sterility, early onset of menopause, personality disturbances, and possible retardation. Most XXX females are normal in appearance, and some have produced offspring with normal chromosomes and phenotypes.

Sex-Linked Inheritance

Many entirely nonsexual traits appear to be inherited along with sex. Inheritance of these traits is referred to as **sex-linked inheritance.** For example, disorders such as colour blindness and hemophilia are much more common in one sex than in the other. The earliest clues to the nature of such disorders arose from studies of the inheritance of hemophilia in a royal family. Few other human families have kept such detailed records. In the following activity, you will use a royal pedigree to trace the sex-linked inheritance of hemophilia.

INQUIRY ACTIVITY
Tracing Sex-Linked Inheritance

Hemophilia is a hereditary condition in which the blood is slow to clot or does not clot at all. If cut or bruised, hemophiliacs bleed profusely externally or internally. Hemophilia is quite a rare disease, and the most famous cases of it occurred in the British royal family. Queen Victoria (1819-1901) had ten direct descendants with hemophilia, but neither she nor her husband, Prince Albert, had the disease.

Copy the pedigree in Figure 24-4 and use it to answer the Discussion Questions.

Discussion Questions

1. a) How many direct descendants are shown? How many have hemophilia?
   b) In which generations does hemophilia appear (P, F_1, F_2)?

FIGURE 24-4 The inheritance of hemophilia in the descendants of Queen Victoria and Prince Albert. Only branches with hemophilia are shown. The present British family is descended from Edward VII and has no hemophiliac members. (The black squares represent affected individuals.)

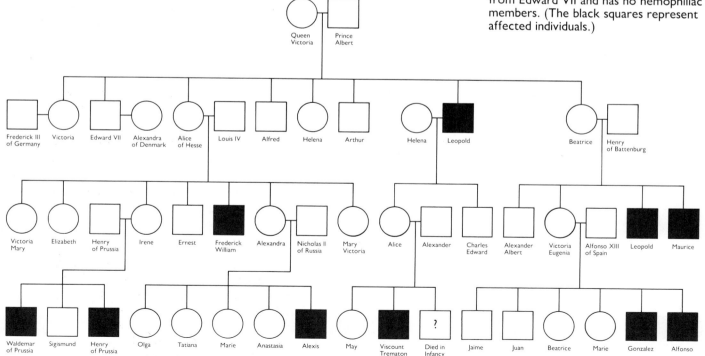

2. a) What do the hemophiliacs have in common in addition to their disorder?
   b) What do you notice about the descendants of the hemophiliacs?

3. a) For each hemophiliac, decide which parent transmitted the defect. Label these individuals as carriers. State reasons for your decision.
   b) Did the carriers have hemophilia? If not, how did you identify them as carriers?

4. a) What do all the carriers have in common?
   b) Could any other individuals shown in this pedigree be carriers? Can you be sure? Explain.

5. a) Whose gametes appear to be the source of hemophilia in this family?
   b) Did that person have hemophilia?

6. a) Based only on this pedigree, what evidence indicates that hemophilia is a sex-linked trait?
   b) Based only on this pedigree, what evidence indicates that hemophilia is passed on by single-gene inheritance?
   c) More recent evidence confirms that hemophilia is caused by a single defective allele. On which chromosome must that allele be located? Support your answer.

Explaining Sex-Linked Inheritance

An example of sex-linked inheritance is male-pattern baldness, which really has nothing to do with being male but is far more common in men than in women. The explanation for sex-linked inheritance lies in the structure of the sex chromosomes. The Y chromosome is very small, and most of its gene locations determine sexual characteristics. The much larger X chromosome has nearly 100 genes that control nonsexual characteristics such as hair pattern. Such characteristics are called **sex-linked characteristics** because they are carried on a sex chromosome. (See Figure 24-5.)

Since females receive two X chromosomes, they have two corresponding alleles for each of the 100 or so sex-linked characteristics. Such alleles are designated by adding a superscript to the letter X. For example, the allele for normal hair pattern is written as X^B to show that it occupies a gene location on an X chromosome. The B is capitalized because normal hair pattern is a

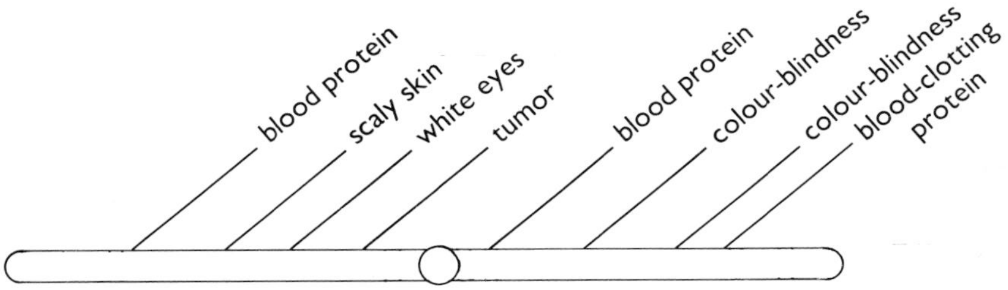

FIGURE 24-5 This map shows some of the gene locations that have already been determined for the human X chromosome.

blood protein   scaly skin   white eyes   tumor   blood protein   colour-blindness   colour-blindness   blood-clotting protein

dominant trait. The allele for baldness is written as X^b with a lower-case b to show that baldness is a recessive trait. A female who has a baldness allele (X^b) on one chromosome will probably have a dominant normal allele (X^B) on the other. Such females are carriers (genotype X^BX^b). They have a normal phenotype, but half of their eggs carry a baldness allele. (See Figure 24-6.)

Males inherit baldness from their mothers because the Y chromosome inherited from a male's father has no gene location for hair pattern. If the X chromosome from the male's mother happens to carry a baldness allele, the Y chromosome will have no corresponding normal hair pattern allele to compensate. The single baldness allele will be expressed. As Figure 24-7 shows, the male offspring of a normal father and a carrier mother have a 50% chance of becoming bald. Half of the female offspring will also inherit one X^b allele but will not express it.

A female carrier has only one baldness allele, which she may pass to either her daughters or her sons. Every bald male also has an X^b allele, but can only pass it on to his daughters not to his sons. A female offspring can only express baldness if she inherits the X^b allele from both parents. (See Figure 24-8.)

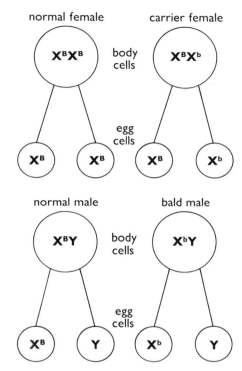

FIGURE 24-6 Baldness is a recessive inherited trait carried on the X chromosome.

Females who inherit male pattern baldness often go unnoticed. This is because the baldness usually does not occur until menopause when the level of female hormones is diminished.

FIGURE 24-7 The offspring of a female carrier of baldness and a normal male

FIGURE 24-8 The offspring of a female carrier and a bald male will be 25% bald females, 25% carrier females, 25% bald males, and 25% normal males.

	Normal Male (gametes)	
Female Carrier (gametes)	**X**	**Y**
X^B	X^BX	X^BY
X^b	X^bX	X^bY

	Bald Male (gametes)	
Female Carrier (gametes)	X^b	**Y**
X^B	X^BX^b	X^BY
X^b	X^bX^b	X^bY

Sex-linked inheritance such as that exhibited by baldness is observed in about 60 sex-linked disorders. These disorders are actually sex-linked traits that cause varying degrees of disability or disease in affected individuals. The most common example is colour-blindness, which is the inability to perceive or to distinguish certain colours, usually red and green. This condition is far more common in males than it is in females, but females may be carriers for the condition (genotype X^CX^c). Carriers are not colour-blind because the recessive defective allele (X^c) is counteracted by a dominant normal allele (X^C) on the other X chromosome. Such females have a normal phenotype, but they pass the colour-blindness trait on to their offspring.

As you already know, every male receives an X chromosome from his mother and a Y chromosome from his father. If the mother is a carrier of the red-green colour-blindness allele, there is a 50% chance that her son will receive it. (See Figure 24-9.) Since the Y chromosome has no corresponding gene location for colour vision, a son who inherits the defective allele on his X chromosome will be colour-blind. In this example, half of the daughters would also inherit a defective allele but would not be colour-blind.

A colour-blind father cannot transmit colour-blindness to his sons. He will, however, pass an X chromosome with a defective allele to each of his daughters. If the mother happens to be a carrier, each daughter has a 50% chance of being colour-blind and a 50% chance of being a carrier. (See Figure 24-10.) In this example, half of the sons will also be colour-blind, but they will have inherited this trait solely from their mother. If both parents are colour-blind, all their offspring will be colour-blind because neither parent is carrying a normal allele for colour vision.

Hemophilia is inherited in the same way as colour blindness is inherited. In most people, the X chromosome has an allele (X^H) coded for the production of an enzyme essential for blood clotting. Hemophiliacs have a defective allele (X^h). Queen Victoria's genotype was X^HX^h. She did not have hemophilia but she was a carrier. The male hemophiliacs in her family had the genotype X^hY. There were no female hemophiliacs. In order to have hemophilia, a female would have to have the genotype X^hX^h. This would only be possible if both her mother and her father carried a defective allele. Such matings are still rare, although many male hemophiliacs now survive to reproductive age.

DID YOU KNOW?

Queen Victoria was a mutant. There was no previous history of hemophilia in her parents' families or in their ancestors. Nor was there any evidence of the disease in Albert's family. Once present, however, a mutant allele can be as easily inherited as any other allele. If the mutant allele does not favour survival, it may eventually die out. Most mutant alleles have no effect because they are paired with a normal allele which dominates.

FIGURE 24-9 A cross between a normal male and a female who carries one defective allele for red-green colour vision.

Female Carrier (gametes) \ Normal Male (gametes)	X^C	Y
X^C	X^CX^C	X^CY
X^c	X^CX^c	X^cY

FIGURE 24-10 A cross between a red-green colour-blind male and a female carrier can produce colour-blind daughters.

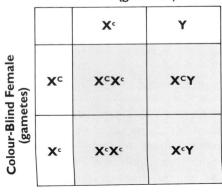

Colour-Blind Female (gametes) \ Colour-Blind Male (gametes)	X^c	Y
X^C	X^CX^c	X^CY
X^c	X^cX^c	X^cY

Hemophilia

Hemophilia is a rare blood disorder, but its hereditary transmission in an important and numerous family has made it seem far more prominent. Queen Victoria's son, three of her grandchildren, and six of her great-grandchildren, who were all male members of the royal families of England, Germany, Russia, and Spain, died of hemophilia. In the 1900s, little could be done to save hemophiliacs from an early death. Today, with improved treatments and methods of identifying hemophiliacs and the disorder's carriers, the prognoses of its victims have improved considerably.

Hemophiliacs are unable to produce a protein called factor VIII. Normally, injuries that cause bleeding are first plugged with platelets. Later, the plug is fortified with fibrin. In hemophiliacs, fibrin formation is incomplete, and the platelet plug eventually dissolves.

As a result, hemophiliacs may hemorrhage uncontrollably after even the most trivial injuries. Children may lose dangerous quantities of blood when they bite their tongues. Bleeding into joints, which is very common in severe cases, can cause crippling deformities. The most common cause of death for hemophiliacs is bleeding into the central nervous system. Such bleeding may be caused by a blow on the head so slight that, when symptoms arise after hours or days, the patient cannot even remember receiving it.

Hemophilia is a recessive trait transmitted by a gene on the X chromosome. As a result, almost all hemophiliacs are male. The disorder usually skips generations. It is passed from an affected male to an unaffected or mildly affected daughter before reappearing in a grandson. This pattern develops because the sons of a hemophilic man receive a Y chromosome from their father rather than an X chromosome carrying the abnormal factor VIII gene. All daughters of a hemophiliac receive the chromosome and become carriers. Carriers have equal chances of giving birth to normal or hemophilic sons and normal or carrier daughters.

Most carriers can be identified by comparing their relative levels of factor VIII and other blood-clotting agents. The plasma factor VIII levels in a carrier are usually about half those of normal women because only one of a carrier's chromosomes produces factor VIII. In fact, some carriers have plasma factor VIII levels nearly as low as those found in male hemophiliacs.

If these tests are inconclusive, genetic probes can be used to determine if a woman carries a hemophilia-causing mutation or not. Unfortunately, not all mutations capable of causing hemophilia have yet been catalogued. Within families long affected by hemophilia, physicians can identify carriers by comparing their factor VIII genes with the factor VIII genes of a hemophiliac in the family.

One reason for the greatly increased survival rate of hemophiliacs is that present understanding of both blood and genetics is much more advanced than it was in Queen Victoria's day. Blood is an extremely complex material. In addition to inheriting its clotting ability through an unpaired allele on one sex chromosome, blood also inherits many other characteristics through the pairing of alleles carried on homologous autosomes.

In Section 24.3, you will consider the genetics involved in the determination of blood types and other human traits that are more complex than those you have looked at in this section.

Section Review Questions

1. Describe the differences between autosomes and sex chromosomes.
2. a) Which human parent determines the sex of the offspring? Explain briefly.
   b) Use a Punnett square to show that the chances of a couple having a male offspring are equal to the chances of having a female.
3. a) Define sex-linked inheritance.
   b) Identify two well-known sex-linked traits.
4. a) On which chromosome is the gene for colour vision located?
   b) Would you expect to find colour-blindness and hemophilia more frequently in men or in women? Explain.
5. A hemophiliac man marries a female carrier. What is the probability of the following? Explain your answers.
   a) Their sons will be hemophiliacs.
   b) Their daughters will be hemophiliacs.
   c) Their daughters will be carriers.
6. A girl of normal vision whose father is colour-blind marries a man of normal vision whose father is also colour-blind. What type of vision can be expected in their offspring? Why?

24.3 Multiple Alleles and Genes

A diploid human cell contains 46 chromosomes. Even if each chromosome had only one gene location, and there were only two alleles available to occupy that location, the number of different genotype combinations would be 3^{23} or 9 414 317 910. However, most chromosomes actually carry thousands of genes, and inheritance is not always based on one gene location for each characteristic and two kinds of available alleles. Some characteristics are determined by multiple alleles, multiple gene locations, or both.

Multiple Alleles and Human Blood Type

Humans have only two sexes, two kinds of ear lobes, and two kinds of hairlines. But we do have four basic blood types: A, B, O, and AB. These blood types provide the best known examples of **multiple-allele inheritance** in humans. Table 24-2 shows that the four phenotypes result from different combinations of the three alleles—I^A and I^B, which are dominant, and i, which is recessive.

Only one gene location is available for these alleles. Consequently, each individual inherits two alleles for blood type, one on each homologous chromosome. As a result, there are six possible genotypes. However, only four phenotypes result. The heterozygous genotype I^Ai results in Type A blood. Type A blood contains red cells that have A protein on their surfaces because only the I^A allele is expressed. Genotype I^Bi results in Type B blood. The red cells of Type B blood have B protein on their surfaces. The homozygous genotype ii results in Type O blood. Its red cells have neither A nor B protein on their surfaces. Incompatibility of these surface proteins is what causes red cells to clump when unmatched blood is mixed. (See Table 24-3.)

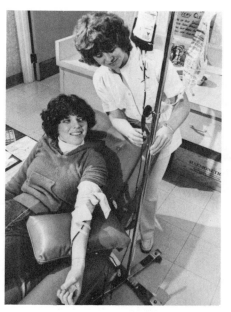

Until doctors understood blood types, many transfusions proved fatal because the recipient's red blood cells clumped, blocking blood flow through small blood vessels. Today, stringent testing ensures that the donor's blood type matches the recipient's.

TABLE 24-2 Inherited Genotype and Blood Type

Genotype (Inherited Combination of Alleles)	Phenotype (Resulting Blood Type)
I^AI^A I^Ai	Type A
I^BI^B I^Bi	Type B
I^AI^B	Type AB
ii	Type O

TABLE 24-3 Blood Type Compatibility

Type	Can Give Blood To	Can Receive Blood From
A	• A, AB	• A, O
B	• B, AB	• B, O
O	• A, B, O, AB	• O
AB	• AB	• A, B, AB, O

The Principle of Dominance explains the phenotypes that result from genotypes I^Ai, I^Bi, and ii. Dominance also explains why the homozygous genotype I^AI^A codes for Type A blood, and I^BI^B codes for Type B. But when I^A and I^B are paired in the same genotype, both alleles are fully expressed in the phenotype. The result is Type AB blood, which has both A and B proteins on the surface of its red blood cells. AB blood is not a blend. The red cells in Type AB blood have a full measure of A protein and a full measure of B protein. Geneticists use the term **co-dominance** to describe this effect, because both alleles are fully expressed.

Multiple alleles make the inheritance of blood type more complex than the inheritance of a characteristic such as hairline shape for which there are only

If Type A blood is donated to a Type O recipient, the "foreign" A protein stimulates anti-A antibodies in the Type O recipient's blood plasma to attack the donated cells, causing them to clump together. However, Type O blood can often be safely donated to a Type A recipient because Type O cells have no surface proteins that correspond to the antibodies in the Type A recipient's blood plasma.

FIGURE 24-11 This Punnett square predicts that two Type A parents with heterozygous genotypes will produce, on average, one offspring with Type O blood for every three offspring with Type A blood.

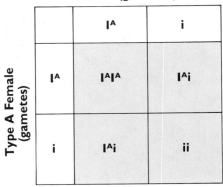

Type A Male (gametes)

	I^A	i
I^A	$I^A I^A$	$I^A i$
i	$I^A i$	ii

Type A Female (gametes)

two available alleles. However, Punnett squares are still useful for predicting the genotypes of offspring. Figure 24-11 shows that two Type A parents could produce Type O offspring. However, two Type O parents cannot produce Type A offspring. In the following activity, you will find out why.

INQUIRY ACTIVITY
Predicting the Blood Type of Your Offspring

In this activity, you will determine the possible blood types of your future offspring. You may be able to learn your own blood type from your parents, doctor, or local health unit. Another alternative is to test your blood with a blood-typing kit. But be sure you do so under your teacher's supervision. If none of these options is available, "adopt" a blood type for the following activity. (Be sure to use the same type for each step.)

Procedure

1. Determine your own genotype regarding blood type. (Some students will have more than one possible genotype.)

2. Determine the probable genotypes and phenotypes of your future offspring if the other parent has Type O blood. (Be sure to consider how many Punnett squares you will need and why.)

3. Repeat Step 1 for each of the other three blood types. Be sure to explore every possibility.

4. Compare your findings with those of other class members to answer the Discussion Questions.

Discussion Questions

1. Collect and classify the predictions for blood type made by your entire class. From this data, predict which blood type will predominate among the future offspring of your class members. Explain your prediction.

2. Suppose that a Type O child has a Type A mother.
   a) Could a Type B male be this child's father? Explain.
   b) Could a Type AB male be the father? Explain.

3. Suppose that emergency surgery must be performed on a Type B patient during a blood shortage. The patient's Type O mother cannot reach the hospital in time.
   a) Will blood from the father be suitable for transfusion? Discuss.
   b) Would blood from the mother have been suitable? Discuss.

4. a) Based on this activity, compare multiple-allele inheritance of blood type to inheritance of hairline shape and sex-linked inheritance of baldness.
   b) What do the three have in common, and how do they differ?

Multiple-Gene Inheritance

The pattern of heredity for human blood types is an example of single-gene inheritance. This means that each gamete has only one gene location on one chromosome that can carry a blood type allele. The zygote receives two homologous chromosomes, one from each parent. Consequently, although there are three different alleles for blood type, only two can be inherited by an individual. For this reason, single-gene inheritance limits the number of possible phenotypes. However, when more than one gene location is involved in determining a characteristic, a wide range of phenotypes becomes possible. This pattern of heredity is called **multiple-gene inheritance.**

For example, human eye colour is determined by multiple-gene inheritance. Eye colour depends on the amount of melanin in the pupils. More melanin means darker eye colour. Several different alleles are involved in melanin production. Some code for large amounts, and others code for small amounts. In varying combinations, these alleles occupy several gene locations. As a result, human eye colour ranges from light blue to very dark brown.

Two clues indicate that a characteristic results from multiple-gene inheritance. The first is the presence of a wide range of phenotypes. The second is the absence of any recognizable phenotype ratio. For example, Table 24-4 shows a survey of heights among 16-year-old students in a typical high school. Measurements range from 150 cm to 200 cm, yet there are no distinct short, medium, or tall groups. When these data are graphed, they produce what biologists call a normal distribution curve. (See Figure 24-12.) A graph of this shape is a telltale sign of multiple gene inheritance and an indication that Punnett squares cannot be used to predict offspring genotypes.

Knowing which inheritance pattern determines a characteristic is important for two practical reasons. First, the outcome of multiple-gene inheritance often

Some older genetics textbooks suggest that eye colour is determined by single-gene inheritance, where blue is recessive and brown is dominant. This theory has now been revised. Multiple-gene inheritance makes it possible for a blue-eyed couple to have a brown-eyed child, although the probability of such an event is low.

Human skin colour is also determined by multiple-gene inheritance. The greater the number of gene locations occupied by alleles coded for large amounts of melanin, the darker the skin colour. Like most multiple-gene characteristics, skin colour is also greatly affected by environment. Melanin production also varies according to exposure to sunlight.

TABLE 24-4   Height Range in 16-Year-Old Students at Heath High School

Height (cm)	Number of Students
150-154	3
155-159	5
160-164	8
165-169	9
170-174	12
175-179	11
180-184	10
185-189	8
190-194	4
195-199	2
200-205	1

Distribution Curve for Height

Number of Individuals / Height Measurement (cm)

FIGURE 24-12 The distribution of height among 16-year-old students. A similar graph would result from plotting the birth masses of all babies born on Christmas day or the yields from all corn plants in a field.

Meet Cheryl Shuman

Cheryl is a genetic counsellor at the Hospital for Sick Children in Toronto. In the prenatal genetic clinic, pregnant patients with possible genetic disorders come to Cheryl for counselling.

Q. How long have you worked at this hospital?

A. Since 1982. The department has grown since then. We now have a large research division. More people are becoming aware of the importance of genetics, and several medical centres now have genetic departments.

Q. What do you do when a patient comes to you?

A. My patients are usually pregnant women, who are referred to me by their doctors because their unborn children may have genetic defects. First, I take a family history of both the mother and father to find out if there's a hereditary factor. I review the medical information and discuss the prenatal tests. If prenatal tests have to be done, I book an appointment with an obstetrician who will do the tests.

Q. Is it part of your job to know which tests are suitable?

A. Yes, but I often consult a Ph.D. here or an M.D. at the clinic. For example, if a pregnant patient has a relative with spina bifida (a neural-tube defect), I might order a blood test to measure a protein called alpha-fetoprotein and an ultrasound for that patient. This combination of tests provides a high detection rate of open neural-tube defects.

Q. What other prenatal tests are there?

A. The most common test is amniocentesis, which involves inserting a needle through the patient's abdomen into the amniotic fluid surrounding the fetus. By removing some of the amniotic-fluid cells and growing them in the laboratory, their chromosomes can be analyzed. Down syndrome and other chromosomal disorders can be diagnosed in this way.

Q. Are there any other routine tests?

A. Chorionic Villus Sampling (CVS) is a newer test. Chorionic villi form a tissue surrounding the embryo. This tissue eventually becomes the placenta. The CVS test is an alternative to amniocentesis. It can be performed earlier in the pregnancy than amniocentesis. A narrow plastic tube, called a catheter, is inserted through the vagina into the uterus, and a small sample of chorionic villus is removed by suction and then analyzed.

Q. Has the field changed since you came into it?

A. It's changing all the time. We're using DNA technology to make more exact diagnoses. When I started, there was no prenatal test for cystic fibrosis or Duchenne muscular dystrophy. Now, we can test for both. This is great for couples with a family history of these diseases.

Q. Do you often have to give your patients bad news?

A. No. Many people think we're in the business of limiting families and aborting babies. But, in fact, some prenatal tests allow women to proceed with a pregnancy they might not have been able to without the knowledge from these tests. Most often, we give people good news.

Q. What qualities are required to be a genetic counsellor?

A. You must be interested in science and medicine. You must also be compassionate because you must deal with psycho-social problems. You must be nonjudgmental because in genetic counselling you must never tell patients what to do.

depends as much on environment as on genotype. For example, a child who inherits a tall genotype will require adequate nutrients and good general health to achieve his or her full height potential. Second, single-gene characteristics are usually expressed regardless of environment. A child who inherits hemophilia will become ill no matter how well nourished he or she is and regardless of living conditions. Understanding these differences is extremely important in the prediction, diagnosis, and treatment of genetic disorders, which you will investigate further in Section 24.4.

Section Review Questions

1. a) How many alleles are available for determining blood type in humans?
   b) How many alleles determine blood type in a single individual?
2. a) In describing inheritance of human blood type, how many different genotypes are possible?
   b) How many different phenotypes are possible? Explain why this number is not the same as the number of genotypes.
3. Define the term co-dominance.
4. a) Why does a wide range of eye colour occur in humans?
   b) Which inheritance pattern is human eye colour an example of?
5. Explain why the son of two tall parents who develops a bone disease in his legs as a child may not be a tall adult.

24.4 Medical Applications of Genetics

About 2600 human disorders are caused by defective alleles. Only 60 of these disorders are sex-linked. Because defective alleles are usually recessive, they seldom cause symptoms in carriers who have a normal allele present on the homologous chromosome. However, if the offspring of two carriers happens to receive two defective alleles, the disorder will develop. Because such disorders are surprisingly common, doctors and other medical workers need an understanding of genetics to diagnose, treat, and counsel their patients. (See Table 24-5 on page 756.)

Disorders of Genetic Origin

There are too many genetic disorders to investigate in this section. However, the following three have been selected to illustrate both the wide range of symptoms that defective alleles can cause and the restricted range of treatment options presently available. These three disorders result because the miscoded allele cannot guide the production of an essential protein such as a hormone, an enzyme, or some other functional molecule. Instead, the defective allele

TABLE 24-5 Some Genetic Disorders and Their Symptoms

Disorder	Symptoms	Dominant/Recessive
Cystic Fibrosis	• mucus clogs lungs, liver, and pancreas	• recessive
Sickle-Cell Anemia	• poor blood circulation	• recessive
Duchenne Muscular Dystrophy	• wasting away of muscles	• sex-linked recessive
Phenylketonuria (PKU)	• failure of brain to develop in infants	• recessive
Tay-Sachs Disease	• deterioration of central nervous system in young people	• recessive
Hemophilia	• failure of blood to clot	• sex-linked recessive
Huntington Disease	• deterioration of brain tissue in middle age	• dominant
Hypercholesterolemia	• high cholesterol levels in the blood leading to heart disease	• dominant

may code for the manufacture of a harmful protein, a harmless but unusable protein, or no protein at all. As a result, normal body function is seriously disrupted because the required protein is not available.

In phenylketonuria (PKU), an enzyme necessary for the normal breakdown of phenylalanine is missing. Phenylalanine is an amino acid present in milk. When it cannot be digested normally, it breaks down by a different metabolic process, forming products that damage the brain and cause mental retardation. In the past, early diagnosis of PKU was not possible. Now, however, PKU can be diagnosed at birth with a simple test of the infant's urine. If the test is positive, brain damage can be avoided by restricting the child to a diet low in phenylalanine. Infants with PKU must be fed a specially made formula since breast milk contains phenylalanine.

After brain development is complete, the child may eat a normal diet. However, a pregnant PKU adult female must eat a strictly controlled diet to help prevent the symptoms of PKU appearing in her offspring. The combination of early diagnosis and effective treatment has now eliminated the misery once caused by this genetic disorder.

By contrast, there is still no treatment available for Tay-Sachs disease, although it can also be detected at birth. Tay-Sachs is a hereditary disorder that results from the lack of an enzyme needed to break down lipids, or fats, in the brain. Without the enzyme, lipids accumulate in brain cells and destroy them. Affected children appear normal at birth and usually do not develop

The defective allele that causes PKU is rare in people of African descent and also in Jewish people from middle and eastern Europe. In most other populations, PKU occurs in one out of every 16 000 live births.

The defective allele that causes Tay-Sachs disease is rare in most populations but is carried by one in 30 Jewish people of middle and eastern European descent.

V THE UNITY OF LIFE

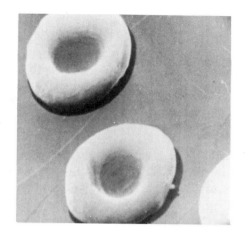
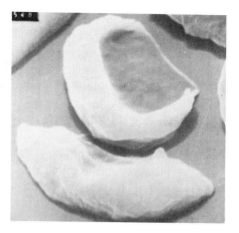

Left: Normal blood cells are smooth, rounded, streamlined and gel-like in consistency. **Right:** Sickle cells are too distorted and rigid to flow swiftly and smoothly.

symptoms until they are about eight months old. Within a year after birth, most children with Tay-Sachs disease are blind, and few live beyond five years of age.

Sickle-cell anemia is a genetic disorder characterized by the production of abnormal hemoglobin. Hemoglobin is the oxygen-transporting protein that makes up normal red blood cells. Abnormal hemoglobin molecules cause several harmful effects. First, they cannot transport as much oxygen as normal hemoglobin does. Second, they form defective, sickle-shaped blood cells that are so rigid and misshapen that they clump together to block small blood vessels. Third, the distorted shape of sickle cells causes large frictional forces that weaken them. As a result, sickle cells break down much more rapidly than they can be replaced. The loss of red cells further reduces the blood's ability to carry oxygen.

Sickle-cell anemia is caused by a defective recessive allele (s). Only homozygous recessive individuals (ss) have all the symptoms of the disease. These include stunted growth and low energy due to the lack of oxygen, and severe joint pain resulting from the clumping of sickle cells. There is no cure for this disorder, and treatment for symptoms is generally unsatisfactory. Few homozygous individuals live beyond the age of 40.

Heterozygous carriers (Ss) do not usually have symptoms, but they sometimes experience both sickling and anemia. These effects occur because the recessive allele (s) is able to produce small amounts of the abnormal hemoglobin, even though the dominant normal allele (S) is present. Larger amounts of abnormal hemoglobin are produced when the heterozygous carrier is under stress from a respiratory ailment or from lower oxygen levels during air travel. Many carriers avoid air travel for this reason. Figure 24-13 predicts genotype probability for the offspring of two carriers. On average, 25% will inherit two normal alleles, 25% will inherit two defective alleles, and 50% will be carriers like their parents.

Given the large number of genetic disorders, and the high frequencies of

Among North Americans of African origin, three in 1000 have sickle-cell anemia, and one in ten are carriers. The most likely explanation is that carriers are less susceptible to malaria than normal individuals. Under the stress of infection, even a single defective allele can cause sickling, but *Plasmodium* cannot reproduce in the rigid, sickled cells. This gives heterozygous individuals a survival advantage in malarial regions.

Key to Allele Symbols
S = normal hemoglobin (dominant)
s = abnormal hemoglobin (recessive)

FIGURE 24-13 A cross between two sickle-cell carriers. Such crosses are fairly common in the affected population.

		Male Sickle-Cell Carrier (gametes)	
		S	**s**
Female Sickle-Cell Carrier (gametes)	**S**	SS	Ss
	s	Ss	ss

Any disorder that results in below normal levels of red blood cells or hemoglobin is called an anemia. Sickle-cell anemia is only one of 16 common types. Causes of these various anemias range from dietary or digestive deficiencies to infections and cancer. Symptoms such as weakness are caused by the lack of oxygen in body tissues.

some, the chances that a newborn infant will inherit a disorder seem great. Many children who are born with a genetic disorder lead short and difficult lives, and the emotional upset caused for their parents is tremendous. Today, however, couples can learn through genetic testing before birth or even before pregnancy occurs about the likelihood of their children being healthy.

Detecting Genetic Disorders

There are four approaches to detecting genetic disorders: diagnosing those with symptoms of an inherited illness, screening those who are still well but may become sick later, screening fetuses for the presence of two defective alleles, and screening adults who may be carriers of one defective allele.

Diagnosing Genetic Disease
Once symptoms develop, diagnosis is usually straightforward. A physician who suspects that a patient has a genetic disease will usually take a family history, and may prepare Punnett squares or pedigrees based on the medical records of relatives. The absence of normal protein products or the presence of abnormal ones can be detected with laboratory tests.

Detecting Hidden Disorders
The symptoms of some genetic disorders do not become evident until later in life. Huntington's disease does not cause symptoms until age 30 or more, although two defective alleles have been present from conception. A newborn with Down or Turner syndrome looks much like other babies.

One method used to detect disorders before symptoms develop is through the preparation of a **karyotype.** (A karyotype is a picture showing the number and structure of all the chromosomes in a body cell arranged from largest to smallest.) The result is then compared with a normal human karyotype. This method can detect disorders caused by excess chromosomes, missing chromosomes, or deformed chromosomes. However, other methods must be used to detect disorders that do not affect the appearance of chromosomes.

Screening Unborn Patients
Several screening techniques are used to detect genetic, chemical, or structural abnormalities well before birth.

In **amniocentesis,** a sample of the amniotic fluid surrounding the fetus is withdrawn through a long, thin needle. (See Figure 24-14.) The fluid itself can be tested for the presence or the absence of certain enzymes. Genetic diseases such as Tay-Sachs can be detected in this way. The fluid sample will also contain some cells that have been sloughed from the fetus. These cells can be karyotyped to detect disorders caused by an abnormal chromosome number.

Amniocentesis can also determine the sex of the fetus. This information may be useful to a pregnant woman who is a carrier of a sex-linked disorder

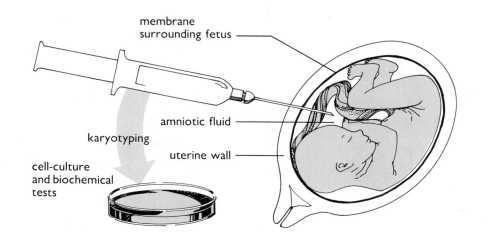

membrane
surrounding fetus

karyotyping

cell-culture
and biochemical
tests

amniotic fluid

uterine wall

FIGURE 24-14 Amniocentesis

Amniocentesis usually cannot be performed until the fourth or fifth month of pregnancy. Chorionic villus sampling can be done after nine weeks, although it does carry a slightly higher risk of causing a miscarriage.

such as hemophilia or Duchenne muscular dystrophy. On average, half of her male offspring would have the disorder and half of her female offspring would be carriers.

Chorionic villus sampling (CVS) can provide the same kind of information as amniocentesis, but it can be obtained earlier in the pregnancy. In the CVS procedure, a small fragment of one of the membranes surrounding the fetus is removed. This tissue can be karyotyped and tested within one day. Since these cells are genetically identical to those of the fetus, they can provide valuable information about the state of the fetus.

Because amniocentesis and CVS are invasive techniques, there is a risk of inducing a miscarriage. They are usually not advised unless a couple faces the possibility of having children with genetic defects. Couples at risk include those who have previously had a child with a genetic defect, those whose parents are known or suspected carriers of a genetic disorder, and couples where the woman is a carrier of a sex-linked disorder. Women over 35 years of age have a significantly higher risk of bearing a child with Down syndrome than younger women do, and are usually advised to undergo amniocentesis.

Ultrasound imagery is a technique that provides a picture of the fetus. High frequency sound waves are directed through the mother's abdomen. Those sound waves that reflect off the fetus are captured by a microphone, which converts sound impulses into electrical impulses. These impulses are eventually displayed as an image on a TV monitor. This procedure can determine the fetus's size and stage of development, which is critical for a safe delivery in difficult cases. Ultrasound images also detect certain kinds of structural abnormalities. This allows specialists to plan for corrective surgery immediately after birth. Ultrasound imagery poses little or no risk to the developing fetus.

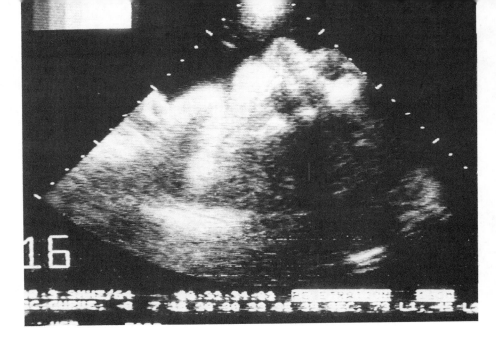

Ultrasound imagery allows doctors to view the progress of a developing fetus. In this image, the eyes and nose of a fetus at 32 weeks are clearly visible.

Fetoscopy provides a more direct view of the fetus but at greater risk. In fetoscopy, a long, slender tube with a light at its tip is inserted directly into the uterus. Samples for chemical or genetic analysis can also be taken at the same time.

Identifying Carriers

When a genetic disorder exists in a family, other family members may wish to know whether they are carriers of a defective allele before they have any children.

Carriers of Tay-Sachs can be detected by having their blood tested for levels of the enzyme needed to break down lipids in the brain. The single allele possessed by a carrier causes enough of the enzyme to be produced so that the disorder does not develop. However, carriers have lower levels of the required enzyme in their blood than normal individuals do.

For some genetic disorders, the DNA sequences of both the normal allele and the defective allele are known. A comparison of the DNA of a suspected carrier with the DNA of a normal individual can determine whether a person is a carrier. The comparison is performed using a **DNA probe.** (See Figure 24-15.) A DNA probe is a laboratory-manufactured segment of a nucleic acid that has been labelled with a radioactive element. Its single strand is designed to match the defective allele, much as a glove is designed to match a hand. The DNA probe is then mixed with a DNA sample from a suspected carrier. Because a DNA probe cannot combine with the normal allele, it can only combine with the DNA of a carrier. Therefore, if the human DNA becomes radioactive during this test, the person is then known to be a carrier for the disorder. Carriers of cystic fibrosis and sickle-cell anemia can be detected by using a DNA probe.

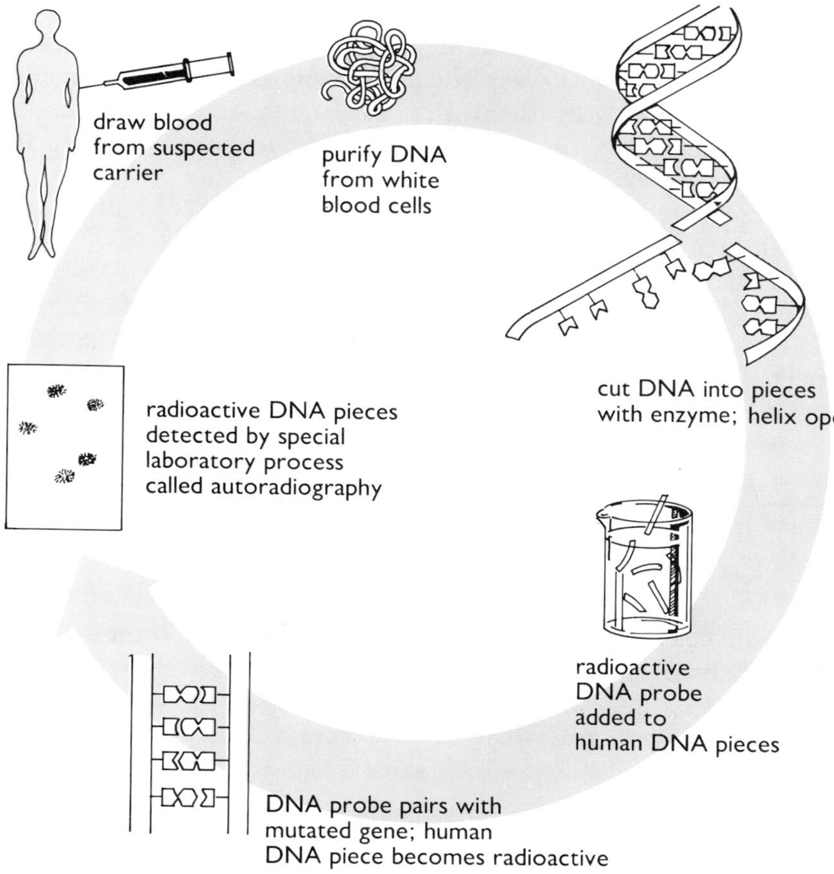

FIGURE 24-15 Defective genes can be detected by DNA probes.

draw blood from suspected carrier

purify DNA from white blood cells

cut DNA into pieces with enzyme; helix opens

radioactive DNA probe added to human DNA pieces

DNA probe pairs with mutated gene; human DNA piece becomes radioactive

radioactive DNA pieces detected by special laboratory process called autoradiography

Treating and Preventing Genetic Disorders

Most of the genetic disorders you have considered in this section are serious conditions. Some genetic disorders are so severe that affected fetuses die before birth or shortly after. Others are not immediately fatal, but they cause considerable misery for both the affected children and their families. Some disorders can be treated *in utero* by fetal blood transfusions, and certain chemical imbalances can be corrected if the mother takes prescribed drugs or eats a restricted diet. The disabling effects of PKU, which begin after birth, can be prevented by restricting the infant's diet. Most genetic disorders, however, cannot be prevented or treated.

Consequently, couples who suspect they might pass a genetic disorder on to their children often seek genetic counselling. The role of the genetic counsellor is to inform prospective parents about the probability that they might carry defective alleles. Genetic counsellors also inform couples how likely they are to have a child with a genetic disorder and the probable consequences

DID YOU KNOW?

Unsound medical knowledge about genetic disorders led Russia's last Czar and Czarina (Victoria's daughter) to seek help for their hemophiliac son from Grigori Rasputin, who was a faith healer. Rasputin's harmful influence on the royal family helped hasten the 1917 revolution.

Queen Victoria with one of her daughters. Historians think the disorder she passed on contributed to political instability in countries such as Russia, where the heir to the throne seemed likely to die of the "royal disease" before reaching adulthood. How might a genetic counseller advise a woman in her position today?

for the child and the family if they do. Genetic counsellors work in co-operation with family doctors and medical specialists. Their investigative methods include taking family histories, preparing pedigrees, and recommending appropriate laboratory tests. Counsellors interpret the results of enzyme tests or DNA probes, provide couples with the most up-to-date information available, and answer their questions.

Genetic counsellors, however, do not tell couples what to do. Based on the information they receive, couples must decide for themselves.

One couple might choose not to have children. Another couple might decide to risk a pregnancy, but screen and possibly abort a fetus exhibiting the genetic defect. If there is a 50-75% probability of having a healthy child, some couples will decide to go ahead and assume the risk.

INQUIRY ACTIVITY
You Be the Counsellor

Most genetic counsellors have to piece a picture together from incomplete family histories. But today's counsellors do have the advantage of modern medical knowledge. As you read the following stories, try to put yourself in the counsellor's place. Use what you have learned about human genetics to answer the questions that follow each story.

1. Gary and Joan are hesitant to start a family because they do not know Joan's background. She was adopted as an infant, and the health records she has been able to obtain are skimpy. Gary and Joan think there might be a problem because Joan became ill after a recent flight. That incident triggered a childhood memory. Joan remembered that a doctor once told her she shouldn't fly because of something related to her blood.
   a) Which genetic disorder might this history indicate? Why?
   b) What questions would you ask this couple?
   c) What tests would you recommend?
   d) Will the tests provide a definite answer? Why or why not?

2. Paul and Ricki are Jewish. Both of them are concerned that they might be Tay-Sachs carriers, although neither has had a brother or a sister with this disorder. They want to know whether they are at risk before they try to have a child.
   a) What questions would you ask this couple?
   b) What tests would you recommend?
   c) Will the tests provide a definite answer? Why or why not?
   d) If both Paul and Ricki are carriers, how likely are their children to have the disorder? To be carriers?
   e) What will you tell them if one proves to be a carrier but the other is not?

3. Kindi and Kal have sought genetic counselling because Kindi's brother and maternal uncle (her mother's brother) both have hemophilia. Kindi's family does not live in Canada. Kal has never met them and does not know anyone with hemophilia, so he is unfamiliar with the disorder.
   a) Draw a pedigree to show that Kindi's mother must be a carrier.
   b) Draw a Punnett square to show the probability that Kindi is also a carrier.
   c) Kindi asks if there is a test that will determine whether she is a carrier. What will you tell her?
   d) Kal asks about the probability of having a healthy child if Kindi does happen to be a carrier. What will you tell him?
   e) Kindi asks whether amniocentesis can detect hemophilia in the fetus. As a counsellor, you realize that this question really requires two answers: one to explain why amniocentesis cannot detect hemophilia, and one to explain what amniocentesis *can* tell this couple. What will you say?
   f) Part of the counsellor's job is to make sure a couple are fully informed even when they do not ask enough questions. What other information do Kindi and Kal need?
   g) A counsellor must not tell couples what to do. However, you get the sense that Kal is in favour of taking the chance while Kindi is reluctant. What recommendation could you make that might help them reach an agreement without compromising your position as a counsellor?

Section Review Questions

1. a) What is missing in individuals with phenylketonuria (PKU)?
   b) If it is diagnosed early enough, how is phenylketonuria treated?
   c) What result can occur if PKU is not detected early?

2. a) What is missing in infants with Tay-Sachs disease?
   b) What happens to affected individuals?

3. Sickle-cell anemia is caused by a defective recessive allele. What are the symptoms of the disease?

4. What are three things a doctor might do if a genetic disorder is suspected in a newborn infant?

5. Briefly describe each of the following medical procedures: a) amniocentesis, b) chorionic villus sampling, and c) fetoscopy.

6. How can carriers be detected? Briefly describe this procedure.

7. List three ways that some genetic disorders can be treated before an affected individual is born.

Mapping the Human Genome

Genome mapping and sequencing projects are beginning around the world. The most ambitious is the Human Genome Project (HGP), which is supported by the United States government. The director of the project is Dr. James Watson, co-discoverer of the structure of the DNA molecule. During the next 15 years, researchers hope to sequence all of the base pairs of the human genome.

The HGP is expected to revolutionize genetics and medicine. Advances will be made in the prediction and treatment of hereditary disorders. The HGP will provide a road map for scientists who are trying to locate a gene. The identification of thousands of disease genes will become much simpler as a result. And as more genetic causes of disease are recognized, the use of genetic screens to identify those at risk will increase also. Drug and gene therapies will be developed to deal with these conditions as our understanding improves.

As well, the HGP will enlarge our understanding of the basic processes of life. Researchers should learn how the expression of genes is controlled. Planners also expect new insight into the mechanisms of inheritance, gene mutation, and evolution, since other genomes will be sequenced for comparison as part of the project.

By the time the project is complete, the HGP researchers expect that current methods of gene mapping and sequencing will have been transformed.

Although critics acknowledge the value of the project's goals, they worry that the HGP may delay the resolution of many basic problems in biology. Many critics argue the goals of the project will be accomplished eventually by researchers working in the traditional manner of studying specific problems.

The focus of much of the opposition to the HGP is the second phase of the project. Most agree the first phase, mapping genes on the genome, will yield valuable information. However, the second phase, in which the entire genome is to be sequenced, has been attacked as wasteful. Researchers agree that only 5% of the genome has any role in producing proteins or in regulating the processes involved. Should millions of dollars be spent on sequencing the other 95%, which researchers commonly refer to as "junk DNA," critics ask? Sequencing speed and efficiency is increasing regardless of the HGP, they point out. Wouldn't it be cheaper to wait to sequence the entire genome?

The successful sequencing of the human genome will be a great feat of engineering, innovation and determination, but it may lead, some say, to a false sense of confidence in our ability to understand and control genetic material, as well as to an over-reliance on genetic solutions to medical problems. The data produced by the HGP, of course, will be a detailed map and an incredibly long list. It is essential that researchers remember these are but a first step toward understanding the intricate life processes the human genome controls.

Dr. James Watson, director of the Human Genome Project

24.5 The Future of Human Genetics

Research in human genetics is presently focussed on achieving two major goals: the identification of genes and alleles, and the treatment of hereditary disorders.

The continuing quest for improved methods of detecting harmful alleles is being pursued along several fronts. Karyotyping, for example, would be more informative if geneticists were able to identify DNA defects even when chromosome shape and number appear to be normal. This would allow them to detect homozygotes directly before symptoms caused by abnormal proteins develop. Improved karyotyping would also allow the direct detection of carriers. At present, carriers can be detected directly for only a few disorders, such as Tay-Sachs.

But simply recognizing a defective DNA sequence is not enough. Researchers also need to know the function that would be performed if a normal allele occupied the same gene location. Consequently, better chromosome mapping is needed because only a few hundred of the 100 000 gene locations on our 46 chromosomes are known by their functions.

All of the techniques now being researched will be much more effective if researchers can find an improved method to monitor fetal blood. Current methods for obtaining blood samples and giving transfusions are restricted to use in late pregnancy. Earlier, safer techniques would allow frequent testing of the blood of a fetus thought to be at risk. However, early detection must be accompanied by effective treatment. The development of improved methods for treating genetic diseases through biotechnology is the second major goal for researchers.

Genetic engineering, or gene splicing, involves transferring a piece of DNA from one organism into the chromosomes of another. The recipient's altered genetic material is referred to as **recombinant DNA** because it combines DNA from two sources.

Engineered bacteria are already being used to produce human insulin. First, the human allele that codes for insulin production is isolated. Then it is spliced into the chromosome of the familiar bacterial species, *Escherichia coli*. After splicing, the bacteria produce human insulin as well as their own protein products. When engineered bacteria reproduce, the human DNA is replicated along with the bacterial DNA, and the offspring bacteria continue to manufacture human insulin.

Many other human proteins are being manufactured using recombinant methods. Certain bacteria are selectively raised for the sole purpose of expressing human alleles.

Administering insulin to diabetics is an example of hormone replacement therapy. Some genetic disorders are caused by an inability to produce needed protein. Many geneticists think that these disorders can be treated with hormones or enzymes produced by engineered bacteria. But replacement therapy

Of the few gene locations geneticists do know, most are on the X and Y chromosomes. Can you suggest reasons why this is so?

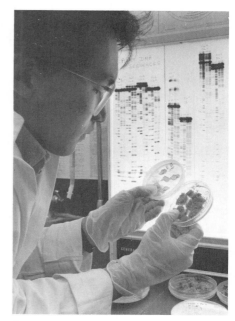

By inserting genes from one plant into the genetic structure of another, this geneticist can develop plants with the desired characteristics.

has negative aspects. For example, diabetics suffer serious side effects if they do not estimate their insulin needs exactly. But geneticists hope to overcome this type of problem by applying recombinant techniques directly to human cells.

Gene Therapy

Correcting genetic defects by transferring normal alleles to cells that lack them is called **gene therapy.** Geneticists have already demonstrated that donor DNA can be introduced into the chromosomes of animals as complex as mammals. In theory, some human hereditary diseases could be treated in this way. However, present-day gene-transplant techniques are limited. Usually, alleles are sorted out by meiosis and brought together at fertilization to form a complete set of chromosomes. The zygote then grows new sets by repeated mitosis. If all the needed alleles are not present at fertilization, inserting them into every cell after fertilization presents a major obstacle.

Nevertheless, most geneticists think that gene therapy will eventually become a reality. Several strategies have been proposed. Gene insertion would involve producing multiple copies of a normal allele and splicing them into the chromosomes of the target cells. The inserted allele would allow the cell to manufacture the protein it needs, and the miscoded allele could be left in place, providing it did not produce a harmful product. However, a defective allele that coded for a lethal protein would not be left in the cell. In that case, gene surgery would be used to remove the harmful allele from its chromosome and replace it with a normal allele. Gene modification, on the other hand, would leave the harmful allele in position, but alter its chemical composition to match the normal DNA code.

Of these three techniques, only gene insertion seems feasible in the immediate future. However, it may be practical only when replacement alleles can be inserted into cells of a single target organ rather than into cells all through the body.

Successful gene therapy would involve a complex series of steps.
1. Isolating the needed, normal allele from a human cell.
2. Determining the precise DNA sequence of the normal allele.
3. Using the DNA sequence as a blueprint to manufacture large numbers of artificial alleles.
4. Delivering correctly sequenced artificial alleles to the cell and splicing them into the chromosome. (In gene modification, the DNA sequence would be used to alter the chemical composition of the normal allele in each cell.)

Methods for implementing the first three steps of gene therapy are available now although not all have been perfected. Step 4 is also close to becoming a reality. Preliminary studies of gene therapy on other organisms indicate that alleles probably can be delivered to human cells by genetically engineered and tamed viruses.

Mapping the Human Genome

Today, the major stumbling block to gene therapy is that geneticists have an incomplete chromosome map of human gene locations. Isolating a needed allele from a living cell will only be possible if its gene location is known. Doing so for every genetic disorder means geneticists must know the DNA sequence of every chromosome. Geneticists are working to obtain this information, and some think that all DNA sequences will be known by the year 2000. But sequencing is only the first stage. Geneticists must identify every gene location and determine the function of every allele that can occupy each location.

Geneticists use the term **human genome** to describe the entire collection of human chromosomes, genes, and alleles. They think that a complete map of the human genome will enable us to understand much about human biology that is presently unclear, ranging from the genetic basis for normal structure and function to the genetic origin of disorders not now recognized as hereditary. Some people worry that this kind of knowledge could be abused. But the human genome will probably be fully mapped within your lifetime. Do you think society is ready for the implications of such knowledge?

RESEARCH PROJECT
The Great Debate: Risk versus Benefit

Recombinant techniques seem to promise many benefits: gene therapy, prenatal diagnostic tests, new drugs, new vaccines, and proteins for replacement therapy. Like all powerful technologies, however, genetic engineering and gene therapy could be used unethically. Only a well-informed citizenry can ensure that biotechnological decisions made by military, political, and scientific leaders maximize benefits to society and minimize risks.

In this research project, your task is to identify a recently announced biotechnological technique, process, or invention that has potential for both risk and benefit to society. Try to maintain an open mind as you research your topic. This may not be easy since controversial issues tend to attract vocal supporters and opponents, and you cannot count on either side to issue completely unbiased information. Prepare statements based on various viewpoints as outlined below and organize a class discussion.

- State three arguments that supporters of the technology might use.
- State three arguments that opponents of the technology might use.
- Ask three questions that an ordinary citizen might want answered about the risks and benefits of the technology.
- Try to provide unbiased answers to the three questions.
- State your personal opinion. How do you think this technology should be used? Do its potential benefits outweigh its risks?

The Future of Human Genetics

On August 24, 1989, the Hospital for Sick Children in Toronto announced what its geneticist-in-chief called "one of the most significant discoveries in the history of genetics." A research team led by Dr. Lap-Chee Tsui had identified the defective gene that causes cystic fibrosis, and had pinpointed a mutation responsible for 70% of cystic fibrosis cases.

Researchers had pursued this gene for years. Cystic fibrosis is the most common genetic disorder among whites, striking one in every 2000 people. However, the abnormal recessive gene responsible is carried by one in every 20 persons. Cystic fibrosis victims have cells that secrete an abnormally thick mucus. This can adversely affect the pancreas, liver, and gastro-intestinal and reproductive tracts, but it is most problematic in the lungs. Here, repeated infections eventually destroy the tissue. Lung infections claim many cystic fibrosis victims before the age of 30.

The task of finding the gene was huge. It was hidden somewhere within the many millions of base pairs in the human genome. In 1985, Tsui narrowed the search to only 150 million base pairs when he mapped the gene to chromosome 7. Still, much work had to be done.

To pinpoint the gene, Tsui's group first found marker sequences on chromosome 7 that they knew were inherited with the gene. Since the cystic fibrosis gene and the markers are rarely separated during recombination, Tsui knew the two were located close together. Tsui then used procedures called chromosome jumping and chromosome walking to sequence the DNA near the markers.

The researchers were looking for DNA sequences that matched those found in other organisms. These sequences usually indicate a gene coding for an essential protein. After jumping and walking over 280 kilobases of DNA, the researchers found the cystic fibrosis gene.

The gene is spread over nearly 250 kilobases. Sequence analysis revealed that the protein for which it codes is 2480 amino acids long. According to Tsui, 70% of cystic fibrosis cases are caused by the deletion of a single trinucleotide codon from the huge gene. The loss of one amino acid is enough to disrupt the protein's normal functioning.

Before the discovery of the gene, the cystic fibrosis protein was a mystery. Researchers now believe it is meant to regulate the movement of water and other chemicals across cell membranes. Once they fully understand its function, researchers hope to develop drugs that will compensate for its defect.

Dr. Lap-Chee Tsui with his research colleagues, Dr. Jack Riordan (left) and Dr. Francis Collins (centre)

Section Review Questions

1. What are the two major goals of research in human genetics?
2. a) What is recombinant DNA?
   b) How can a bacterium be engineered to perform a particular function?
   c) What kind of genetic defect can benefit from engineered bacteria?
3. Briefly describe how gene insertion, gene surgery, and gene modification could be used in the future.
4. What is meant by human genome?

Chapter Review

Key Words

amniocentesis
autosomes
DNA probe
gene therapy
genetic engineering
human genome
karyotype
multiple-allele
 inheritance
multiple-gene
 inheritance

pedigree
recombinant DNA
sex chromosomes
sex-linked
 characteristics
sex-linked
 inheritance
single-gene
 inheritance

Recall Questions

Multiple Choice

1. A colour-blind man marries a woman with normal vision. Their son is colour-blind. One of their daughters is colour-blind, but the other has normal vision. If the colour-blind allele is X^c and the normal allele is X, the genotype of the mother is
   a) X^cY^c
   b) XX^c
   c) X^cX^c
   d) XX

2. Determine the genotype of the parents if a blood Type A father and a Type B mother produce children in each of the four blood groups. The parents' genotypes are
   a) father I^Ai; mother I^BI^B
   b) father I^AI^A; mother I^BI^B
   c) father I^AI^B; mother I^Bi
   d) father I^Ai; mother I^Bi

3. A Type B female has a Type A child. Which of the following lists all possible blood-type genotypes of the father?
   a) I^AI^B, I^AI^A, I^Ai
   b) I^AI^B, I^BI^B, I^AI^A
   c) I^AI^B, I^Bi, I^Ai
   d) I^Ai, I^Bi^B, I^AI^A

4. Hemophilia is a sex-linked recessive trait in humans. If a father and a son are both hemophiliacs, but the mother is normal, her genotype must be
   a) X^hX^h
   b) X^HX^h
   c) X^HX^H
   d) X^hY

5. The type of genetic testing that involves taking cells from the fluid surrounding the fetus is called
   a) ultrasound imagery
   b) fetoscopy
   c) amniocentesis
   d) chorionic villus sampling

Fill in the Blanks

1. Humans possess 22 pairs of _____ and one pair of _____ chromosomes.
2. The sex genotype of male humans is _____, and for females it is _____.
3. Genes located on the sex chromosomes are called _____ genes.
4. A male human inherits sex-linked traits from his _____.
5. A female human who is heterozygous for a sex-linked recessive trait is called a _____.
6. The genotype of a colour-blind male is _____.
7. People who lack the enzyme that converts phenylalanine to another substance have the genetic disease _____.
8. A photograph of a complete set of chromosomes from a cell is a _____.
9. Stunted growth, shortness of breath, and lack of energy are all symptoms of _____.
10. DNA from one organism that is combined with DNA from another organism is called _____.

Short Answers

1. a) A couple has two daughters. What is the probability that their next child will also be a daughter? Use a Punnett square to illustrate your answer.
   b) Briefly explain what determines the sex of human offspring.
2. How is skin colour inherited in humans?
3. On which chromosome is the gene for colour vision located?
4. How many chromosomes does a person with Down syndrome have?
5. State the two genotypes that produce Type B blood.
6. List three genetic diseases in humans and describe the symptoms of each.

7. Describe how information about a fetus based on its chromosomes can be obtained.

8. State three examples of ways fetuses can be treated for genetic disorders.

9. What is the purpose of genetic counselling?

10. Describe how the processes of amniocentesis and karyotyping are used to diagnose genetic diseases.

Application Questions

1. Is it possible for Type B parents to have children who are not Type B? Explain.

2. Explain the difference between the way human eye colour is inherited and the way blood types are inherited.

3. Construct a pedigree of your family using one of the following traits.
   a) smooth hairline or peaked hairline
   b) tongue rolling
   c) free or attached ear lobes

4. Why might each of the following people want to consult a genetic counsellor? What type of test might the counsellor recommend for each patient?
   a) a woman whose father was a hemophiliac
   b) a pregnant woman of European Jewish descent
   c) a 40-year-old pregnant woman

Problem Solving

1. A boy's father is colour-blind. Will the boy necessarily be colour-blind? Explain.

2. A normal man marries a normal woman whose father is colour-blind.
   a) What is the probability that their sons will be colour-blind?
   b) What is the probability that their daughters will be colour-blind?

3. Explain why colour-blindness and hemophilia occur more frequently in men than in women.

4. A man with Type A blood (genotype unknown) marries a woman with Type B blood (genotype unknown). Which blood types could their children have? Explain briefly.

Extensions

1. Interview an obstetrician to investigate the positive and the negative aspects of amniocentesis.

2. Research a genetic disease and write a report. Aspects of the disease you should consider are the frequency of the disease, how it is inherited, the characteristics or symptoms of the disease, who is in the greatest risk, how the disease can be detected, and how it can be treated.

GLOSSARY

A

accessory structures: structures that grow out of the skin such as hair, and embedded structures such as glands

acquired immune deficiency syndrome: *see*: AIDS

actin: thin protein filaments in myofibrils

active immunity: lasting protection against a particular disease through the manufacture of antibodies in the body; may be acquired through infection or injection of a vaccine

active transport: the movement of molecules from regions of low concentration across a membrane to regions of high concentration; requires energy input from the cell

adaptations: specialized structures or abilities that suit an organism to its environment

adenine: one of four weak nitrogenous bases found in DNA

adhesion: the force of attraction between two unlike molecules

adventitious roots: roots that grow from the stems of plants

aerial roots: roots that are not anchored in the soil, which absorb water from dew and air; mainly occur in tropical plants

aerobic: requiring oxygen

aerobic respiration: the second stage of cellular respiration, which requires oxygen for its chemical reactions

aggregate fruits: fruits that develop from many ovaries of a single flower

AIDS (Acquired Immune Deficiency Syndrome): a disease caused by the HIV virus that attacks the immune system, making the body vulnerable to potentially fatal infections

albumen: water-soluble proteins found in blood, milk, and egg whites

alcoholic fermentation: a form of respiration used by yeast cells and anaerobic bacteria to obtain energy from glucose

Algae: a subkingdom of Protista; members use light energy to manufacture food

allele: the particular DNA form that appears at the gene location for an inherited characteristic; for example, tallness or shortness alleles at the gene location for height

alveoli: microscopic, hollow, thin-walled air sacs that make up lung tissue and are located at the ends of the bronchioles

amino acids: the building blocks of proteins, which contain nitrogen, carbon, hydrogen, and oxygen

amniocentesis: a procedure in which a sample of amniotic fluid is withdrawn through a long, thin needle for karyotyping or other testing

amoeboid movement: cell locomotion by pseudopods; occurs in white blood cells and protists such as amoebas

Amphibia: a vertebrate class containing amphibians

anaerobic respiration: a series of chemical reactions that release cellular energy from glucose in the absence of oxygen

anaphase: a late stage of mitosis or meiosis, during which chromosome strands separate and move toward opposite poles of the cell

anatomy: the study of the body structures of living things

Angiosperma: a class of plant species containing flowering plants

angiosperms: flowering vascular plants that produce covered seeds

Animalia: a kingdom containing multicellular heterotrophs, most of which move and reproduce sexually

animal kingdom: multicellular organisms that move about and hunt or gather food

Annelida: an animal phylum containing segmented worms

antagonistic muscles: pairs of muscles that produce opposite bone movements; when one contracts, the other relaxes

anthers: in flowers, structures at the ends of the filaments where pollen grains are formed

antibiotics: substances that inhibit or destroy disease-causing bacteria, which are taken by mouth or injected

antibody: a protein that destroys a foreign substance in the body by binding to its surface; also known as immunoglobulin

antigen: any substance that causes the formation of antibodies

antiseptics: chemicals that destroy or impede the growth of disease-causing organisms without harming body cells

anus: the opening at the end of the rectum through which feces are expelled

aorta: the body's largest artery; its branches carry blood to the head, heart, chest, and lower body

aortic semilunar valve: the valve that prevents blood pumped into the aorta from flowing back into the left ventricle

apical meristems: meristematic tissues at the tips of roots and shoots

Arachnida: a class of eight-legged arthropods such as spiders

arteries: vessels that carry blood away from the heart

arterioles: vessels that receive blood from the arteries and carry it to the capillaries

Arthropoda: an animal phylum containing organisms such as spiders and lobsters with a solid ventral nerve cord, jointed legs, an exoskeleton, and usually a segmented body

artificial insemination: the artificial introduction of semen from a male animal into the reproductive system of a female animal resulting in fertilization

asci: sac-like structures in which the spores of ascomycetes form

Ascomycetes: a division of fungi such as yeast that produce sexual spores in structures called asci

ascospores: haploid cells that develop in sac fungi as a result of meiosis

aseptic techniques: sterilization methods used in medicine to destroy bacteria and bacterial endospores

asexual reproduction: the formation of a new, identical individual from a single parent without the joining of two gametes

astral rays: short microtubule fibres radiating from each centriole during animal cell division

atria: the two upper chambers of the heart that receive blood from the major arteries

atrioventricular node (AV node): a cluster of specialized muscle cells in the right atrium that relay electrical impulses from the pacemaker, stimulating both ventricles to contract

atrioventricular valves: one-way valves through which blood is forced from the atria into the ventricles

autonomic nervous system: that part of a vertebrate's peripheral nervous system controlling muscles and glands, which functions without conscious thought

autosomes: all chromosomes other than sex chromosomes that determine nonsexual characteristics such as eye colour

autotrophs: organisms such as green plants that are able to manufacture their own food

auxins: plant-growth hormones produced in the growing tips of stems and roots, which affect growth in all plant tissues

Aves: a vertebrate class containing birds

axon: a single, long-armed branch of the neuron that carries nervous impulses away from the cell body

B

bacteria: extremely small unicellular prokaryotes

bacteriophages: viruses that invade and destroy bacteria

basal bodies: cell structures similar to centrioles from which cilia or flagella extend

basal metabolic rate: the rate at which energy is released by cellular respiration when the body is at rest

base pair: the inner ''rung'' of DNA's double helix structure formed when the base ends of the nucleotides bond together

basidia: club-shaped structures in which the spores of basidiomycetes are produced

Basidiomycetes: a division of fungi such as the common mushroom, which produces spores in club-shaped structures called basidia

B cells: immune cells that are produced in bone marrow and mature to form plasma-B or memory-B cells

bicuspid valve: the valve that prevents blood pumped into the left ventricle from flowing back into the left atrium

bile: a digestive juice produced in the liver necessary for the physical digestion of fats

binary fission: the splitting of one parent cell to form two offspring identical to the parent and to each other

binomial nomenclature: the system that gives each plant and animal a two-part name, consisting of the organism's genus and species

biologists: scientists who study the structure and function of living things

biology: the scientific study of living things

biome: a large geographical area such as a desert that has a distinctive climate and a dominant type of vegetation

biophysics: the study of the interaction of the muscular and skeletal systems

biosphere: a layer of Earth where living things exist and interact

biotechnology: the use of living things or their parts — chemical and cellular — to produce products such as penicillin or perform functions such as oil-spill cleanup

bladder: (1) a hollow, muscular organ specialized for the storage of urine in vertebrates; (2) other sac-like organs that store gas or liquid (for example, swim bladder)

blastocyst: in mammals, a fluid-filled ball of cells that results from the growth and division of the morula in the uterus

blood: a complex fluid that performs many functions, including the transport of oxygen, nutrients, and wastes

Bowman's capsules: the cup-shaped ends of kidney nephrons

brain: the central processing centre of the nervous system

breathing: the act of alternately inhaling and exhaling air

breathing centre: an impulse centre in the brain that controls breathing rate to meet the body's need for oxygen

breathing rate: the number of inhalations per unit of time

bronchi: two tracheal extensions that conduct air into each lung

bronchioles: microscopic tubes branching from the bronchi that deliver filtered air to the lungs

brown algae: large, multicellular aquatic plants included in the division Phaeophyta

Bryophyta: a plant division containing nonvascular terrestrial plants

budding: a type of asexual reproduction in which a group of cells forms a separate individual and detaches from the parent

bulbs: underground plant organs made up of many thick, fleshy leaf bases surrounding a small, flattened stem

buttons: small, round structures containing diploid hyphae, which push up through the soil and form the fruiting bodies of club fungi

C

cancer: the uncontrolled reproduction of abnormal cells resulting in destruction of healthy tissue

capillaries: small vessels that conduct fresh blood from the arterioles to the tissue

carbohydrates: molecules containing carbon, hydrogen, and oxygen; a major source of cell energy; foods such as sugar and flour

carbon fixation: in photosynthesis, the combination of hydrogen and carbon dioxide to form glucose molecules

carcinomas: cancerous tumors that grow in the tissues that form skin and organ linings

cardiac muscle: muscle located in the heart; its spontaneous contractions are stimulated by its own pacemaker, but the rate is controlled by the autonomic nervous system

cardiac sphincter: a muscular valve that controls the entry of food into the stomach

cardiac subsystem: a circuit of vessels that carries blood from the heart chambers to the heart muscle by way of the aorta

cardiovascular system: the circulatory system, including the heart and the blood vessels

carriers: infected individuals who carry disease but who do not become sick themselves

cartilage: a rubbery, connective tissue found in human ears and nose; also in regions where bones rub together

cell anatomy: the study of structure in individual cells

cell body: the part of the neuron that contains the nucleus

cell membrane: a selectively permeable membrane surrounding a cell that controls materials entering and leaving the cell

cell plate: a flat structure that forms along the equatorial plane during cytokinesis in plant cells

cell physiology: the study of cell function

cell theory: all living organisms are made up of cells; the cell is the basic structural unit of living organisms; the cell is the basic functional unit of living organisms; all cells come from pre-existing cells

cell transport: the movement of materials into and out of cells

cellular respiration: the chemical process by which living cells obtain usable energy from foods such as glucose

cellulose: a polysaccharide produced by green plants that cannot be easily broken down during digestion

cell walls: rigid structures surrounding the cell membrane; support and protect the cells of plants, fungi, bacteria, and some protists but not animals

central nervous system: in vertebrates, the brain and spinal cord; controls and co-ordinates all nerve functions

centrioles: pairs of cylindrical organelles prominent in most animal cells during cell division

centromere: a bead-like structure that links chromosome strands to each other and attaches them to the spindle fibres

cerebellum: the region of the vertebrate brain that controls balance and muscular co-ordination

cerebrospinal fluid: fluid in the hollow areas of the brain and spinal cord that protects them from shock

cerebrum: the largest part of the vertebrate brain, which controls reasoning, memory, and voluntary actions

cervix: the opening of the uterus that leads to the vagina

chemosynthesis: a chemical process by which certain autotrophic bacteria use energy from inorganic molecules to manufacture food

chitin: a carbohydrate similar to cellulose that is contained in the cell walls of many fungi species

chlorophyll: a chemical compound that collects light for photosynthesis in plants

Chlorophyta: a multicellular plant division containing green algae

chloroplasts: organelles that contain chlorophyll and are responsible for photosynthesis

Chordata: an animal phylum containing organisms such as mammals and reptiles with a dorsal nerve cord, a notochord, and gill slits

chorionic villus sampling (CVS): a procedure in which a fragment of one of the membranes surrounding the fetus is removed and karyotyped

chromatids: thickened rod-like strands of condensed chromatin; two identical chromatids form each double-stranded chromosome in early mitosis and meiosis

chromatin: long, thin DNA-containing strands scattered throughout the nucleus between cell divisions

chromatography: a technique used to separate substances according to their solubility

chromosome mapping: the process of determining gene sequence

chromosomes: structures containing one or two rod-like strands of condensed chromatin found in the nucleus during cell division

Chrysophyta: a phylum of the subkingdom Algae, which includes autotrophic protists such as diatoms

chyme: a mixture of partially digested food, water, and gastric juice

cilia: short, thin hairlike structures capable of contraction; (1) cilia extending from unicellular organisms such as paramecia allow them to move; (2) cilia extending from epithelial cells etc., that create currents in nearby fluids

Ciliophora: a phylum of the subkingdom Protozoa containing ciliated heterotrophic protists such as paramecia

class: a group of similar orders

classification: the sorting of large collections of data into smaller, more manageable groups

cleavage: a series of mitotic divisions undergone by a zygote in the Fallopian tube

clones: new organisms that are reproduced asexually; clones are genetically identical to their parents

closed circulatory system: one that retains a fluid such as blood within a complete circuit of tubes and vessels at all times

club fungi: members of the division Basidiomycetes

Cnidaria: an animal phylum containing organisms with stinging cells and a bag-like body pattern such as jellyfish and corals

co-dominance: occurs when two different alleles for the same characteristic are fully expressed in the phenotype; Type AB blood is an example

cohesion: the force of attraction between like molecules

collagen: protein fibres found in connective tissue

colon: the segment of the large intestine that absorbs water and minerals from undigested food

commensalism: symbiosis in which only one species benefits

compact bone: a layer of hard, strong tissue made of bone cells embedded in a mixture of protein fibres and minerals; lies beneath the periosteum

compound microscope: a microscope that uses visible light and a system of lenses to form an image

concentration gradient: refers to an increase or decrease in the concentration of solute or solvent molecules, especially across a cell membrane

conjugation: (1) the joining of two mating strains of zygomycetes; (2) the means of sexual reproduction for paramecia and bacteria

conjugation fungi: members of the division Zygomycetes

connective tissue: tissue that is composed of a few cells and protein fibres embedded in a noncellular matrix

continuity: the continued existence of living things through reproduction

contraception: the prevention of fertilization or implantation so pregnancy will not occur

contractile vacuole: an organelle found in the cytoplasm of some protists that excretes excess water to the external environment

control: in a controlled experiment, the set-up in which the variable being tested is absent (this variable is present in the experimental set-up)

controlled breeding: the crossbreeding of plants or animals selected for their desirable traits

controlled experiment: an experiment using two set-ups, where all factors are kept the same except one

copulation: the process of depositing sperm inside the female reproductive system

cork cambium: a layer of meristem surrounding a woody stem; produces bark-forming cork on its outer side and parenchyma on its inner side

corms: underground stems that are short, thick, and fleshy, which later develop leaves and roots

corpus luteum: a yellowish body that is formed inside a ruptured follicle; it releases progesterone

cortex: in plant roots and stems, tissue composed mostly of parenchyma cells; in animal organs, the outer region

cotyledon: a part of the embryo inside a seed; stores food and may form temporary leaves

cranial nerves: nerves that connect the brain with parts of the head, neck, heart, lungs, and digestive tract

crossbreeding: the mating of parents with distinctly different genotypes and phenotypes

crossing over: the exchange of hereditary information between homologous paternal and maternal chromosomes during meiosis

cross-pollination: the transfer of pollen from one flower to the stigma of another

Crustacea: a class of arthropods containing crustaceans such as lobsters

cuticle: a waxy substance secreted by the epidermal cells of leaves that protects them from disease and reduces water loss

cutting: propagating plants by detaching a small piece from a parent plant and rooting it in water or soil

cyanobacteria: autotrophic bacteria that contain either blue or red pigments as well as chlorophyll

cysts: protective structures formed by some protists in response to unfavourable conditions

cytokinesis: the division of a cell's cytoplasm following mitosis or meiosis

cytokinins: plant-growth regulators that affect leaves, roots, and fruits, which function only in the presence of auxins

cytology: the study of cells

cytoplasm: a complex mixture that lies between the cell membrane and the nuclear envelope

cytosine: one of four weak nitrogenous bases found in DNA

cytoskeleton: an internal structure of microtubules that provides support for a cell

D

dark reactions: in photosynthesis, the series of chemical reactions that take place in the absence of light

deamination: the breakdown of amino acids into carbon-rich molecules that can be used again, and toxic nitrogenous wastes that are transported to the urinary system for excretion

decomposers: organisms such as fungi that break down dead organic material, benefiting the biosphere

dendrites: the short-armed branches of a neuron that carry nerve impulses to the cell body

deoxyribonucleic acid: *see:* DNA

dermis: the thick skin layer found directly under the epidermis

Deuteromycetes: a division of fungi that do not reproduce sexually

development: in living things, the formation of adult body structures

diastolic pressure: the pressure of arterial blood when the ventricles are relaxed; the lower number in blood pressure readings

dichotomous key: a guide used in classification for specimen identification; it offers two choices at each step

dicot or dicotyledon: an angiosperm such as the pea plant that has two cotyledons per seed

differential centrifugation: spinning cell organelles in a centrifuge to separate them for viewing under an electron microscope

differentiation: the process of cell specialization through repeated division of cells in the meristems of plants or the embryos of animals

diffusion: the movement of gas or liquid molecules from a region of higher concentration to a region of lower concentration

digestion: the conversion of food into molecules small enough to enter body cells and take part in cell functions

dihybrid cross: a crossbreeding experiment that traces inherited characteristics

diploid number: the number of chromosomes (2N) found in each body cell of a given species; includes one pair of homologous chromosomes for each chromosome type

disaccharides: carbohydrate molecules containing two monosaccharides bonded together; double sugars such as sucrose

disinfectants: strong chemicals used to destroy or impede the growth of disease-causing organisms

diversity: the ways in which living things differ

division: a group of similar classes of plants or fungi

DNA (deoxyribonucleic acid): hereditary material found in the cell nucleus; DNA is a double-stranded nucleic acid that carries coded instructions for the operation of the entire organism

DNA probe: a procedure used to determine carriers of defective alleles

dominant allele: an allele coded for a dominant trait such as tallness

dominant trait: one that prevents the expression or the appearance of a recessive trait

dormancy: in many organisms, a period of inactivity during which normal life functions slow down or cease temporarily

double helix: a spiral consisting of two intertwined strands; describes the molecular structure of DNA

double-stranded chromosome: a nuclear structure containing two identical chromatids joined by a centromere; seen only during mitosis or meiosis

duodenum: the segment of the small intestine closest to the stomach

E

Echinodermata: an animal phylum containing saltwater organisms such as starfish, which have a five-way radial symmetry

ecologists: scientists who study how living things interact with their environments

ectoderm: the outermost cell layer of the gastrula, which eventually develops into the adult's skin and nervous system

effector: any cell or body part such as muscles or glands that responds to an impulse from the brain or the spinal cord

eggs: structures that contain female gametes

embedding: suspending biological specimens in a block of material, which is then cut into thin slices for viewing under an electron microscope

embryo: a developing animal from the time of fertilization to the time of hatching or birth

endocrine system: a chemical regulatory system, which includes glands that produce numerous types of hormones

endocytosis: a form of active transport in which a cell folds a portion of its membrane around particles and engulfs them; includes phagocytosis and pinocytosis

endoderm: the innermost cell layer of the gastrula, which eventually develops into the adult's digestive system

endometrium: the lining of the uterus

endoplasmic reticulum: a system of membranes connecting the nuclear envelope to the rest of the cell

endosperm: a mass of nutritive tissue around the embryo in the seed of a flowering plant

endospores: protective structures formed by bacteria during unfavourable environmental conditions

enzymes: proteins that accelerate chemical reactions in cells

epicotyl: the upper part of the embryonic plant within a seed that will become the growing shoot of the new plant

epidermal tissue: in plants, a thin protective tissue that covers the outer surface of roots, stems, and leaves

epidermis: in vertebrates, the thin upper layer of the integumentary system from which all accessory structures develop

epididymis: a tubule in the testes in which mature sperm are stored

epiglottis: a flap of tissue that covers the upper trachea when food and liquids are swallowed

epithelial tissue: in vertebrates, a sheet-like tissue that covers both the outer and inner surfaces of the body

erect hyphae: vertical structures that sprout up where the stolons of fungi touch their food; spore cases develop on the tips

erythrocytes: red blood cells

esophagus: a muscular tube that carries partially digested food to the stomach through the action of peristalsis

estrogen: a female sex hormone produced mainly by the ovaries

estrus: the hormonal peak of the female mammal's reproductive cycle

euglenoid movement: cell locomotion by the contraction of fibres beneath the pellicle occurs in protists such as euglenas

Euglenophyta: a phylum of the subkingdom Algae containing protists such as euglenas

eukaryotes: organisms such as humans, which are made up of eukaryotic cells

eukaryotic cells: cells that have a membrane-bound nucleus

excretion: the disposal of dissolved metabolic wastes by separating them from body fluids

exocytosis: a form of active transport in which a cell discharges the waste material accumulated in a vacuole

exoskeleton: a rigid outer covering that provides protection and support for invertebrates such as insects

expiration: the second main stage of breathing; exhalation

expiratory reserve volume: the extra volume of air that can be pushed out of the lungs after a normal expiration

external environment: everything surrounding the body of an organism

eyespots: specialized cell clusters found in simple organisms such as protists that allow them to detect light

F

facultative bacteria: bacteria able to survive in either aerobic or anaerobic environments

Fallopian tubes: slender tubes that carry eggs from the ovaries of female mammals to the uterus

family: a group of similar genera

fats: molecules containing long hydrocarbon chains; both plants and animals store surplus energy in fat; foods such as bacon and corn contain fat

feces: the firm product egested from the large intestine containing bacteria, cellulose, and water

fermentation: the breakdown of glucose in the absence of oxygen; releases energy and produces carbon dioxide and alcohol

fertilization: the union of one male gamete and one female gamete to form a zygote

fetoscopy: a procedure in which a tube with a light at its tip is inserted into the uterus in order to view the fetus

fetus: an unborn human embryo after about eight weeks of development when features become recognizable

fibrous roots: a system of roots that are all approximately the same size

filaments: the stalks of stamens that support the anthers in flowering plants

Filicinae: a class of vascular plants containing true ferns

filtrate: in excretion, the fluid filtered through the glomerulus into the Bowman's capsule

filtration: the passive transport of part of the blood plasma from the capillaries into the cup-shaped ends of the nephrons

first filial (F_1) generation: the first generation offspring of a crossbreeding experiment

fixation: the chemical preservation of biological specimens for viewing under a microscope

flagella: long, thin whip-like structures extending from cells such as euglenas, sperm, and certain bacteria that allow them to move

flowers: reproductive structures that form seeds from which angiosperms develop

fluid mosaic model: the most widely accepted explanation of cell membrane structure

follicle: in animals, a cell layer that protects and nourishes a structure inside it; examples include hair follicles and the follicle around a developing egg

follicle-stimulating hormone (FSH): in mammals, a hormone released by the pituitary gland that triggers the maturation of eggs in females, production of sperm in males

food vacuole: a sac-like membranous structure containing food particles; common in protists such as amoebas and paramecia

forebrain: the region of a vertebrate's brain that develops into the adult's cerebrum, hypothalamus, and thalamus

fragmentation: a type of regeneration in which new individuals are formed from fragments of a parent organism

fruit: the ripened ovary of a flower; it contains the seed(s)

fruiting body: a specialized part of a fungus that produces reproductive spores

function: refers to the abilities of an organism's body structures or materials

Fungi: a kingdom containing multicellular heterotrophic organisms that lack chlorophyll and do not carry out photosynthesis

G

gamete: a reproductive cell that contains half the usual number of chromosomes for the species

gametophytes: specialized plant bodies that produce gametes

gas exchange: the exchange of carbon dioxide and oxygen molecules between the internal and the external environments

gastrula: the cup-shaped cell cluster that results from the growth and the development of the blastocyst

gel electrophoresis: a technique used to separate substances according to their electrical charge

gene: a short segment of DNA containing instructions for a specific function such as the production of a hormone; the part of a chromosome responsible for the inheritance of a single characteristic

generative cell: one of two cells in a mature pollen grain; it forms sperm when it reaches the stigma

gene therapy: the correction of genetic defects by transferring normal alleles to cells that lack them

genetic engineering: the process of inserting genetic information from one organism into another; gene splicing

genetics: the scientific study of inheritance

genotype: the combination of alleles an offspring inherits for a particular characteristic

genotypic ratio: a mathematical statement predicting the genotypes expected from a crossbreeding experiment

genus: a group of similar species; *plural*: genera

geotropism: the growth of plants in response to gravity

germination: the sprouting of a plant seed after it has absorbed enough water to cause its seed coat to split; germination can only take place if a seed is viable and growing conditions are favourable

gestation: the time period between fertilization and birth

gibberellins: plant-growth hormones produced in the leaves and transported to the stems where they influence stem growth

gills: (1) a series of vertical plates under the cap of a club fungus on which basidia form; (2) an organ used by aquatic animals for gas exchange

glycogen: a polysaccharide found in the liver and the muscles of humans that stores excess amounts of glucose

Golgi apparatus: a system of membrane-bound vesicles in the cytoplasm that stores and transports cell products

gonads: sex organs in which gametes are produced

grafting: propagating plants by attaching a branch or a bud from the parent plant to a host plant

Gram staining: a technique used to classify bacteria as either positive or negative; Gram-positive bacteria are more susceptible to antibiotics

green algae: a species of mostly freshwater aquatic plants included in the division Chlorophyta

grey matter: the outer layer of the cerebrum; also lines the inside of the spinal cord

growth: an increase in body size in living things

guanine: one of four nitrogenous bases found in DNA

gullet: a funnel-like structure in protists such as paramecia in which food particles become enclosed as they enter the cytoplasm

Gymnosperma: a class of plant species containing mostly coniferous trees

gymnosperms: vascular plants such as conifers that produce seeds on the scales of cones; naked seeds

H

haploid number: the number of unpaired chromosomes (N) found in each egg or sperm cell of a given species; includes only one homologous chromosome for each chromosome type

heart: a muscular organ that pumps blood throughout the circulatory system

hemoglobin: the iron-containing protein in red blood cells that transports oxygen

Hepaticae: a class of nonvascular plant species containing liverworts

herbaceous stems: the green fleshy stems of angiosperms

heredity: the transmission of characteristics from one generation to the next

heterotrophs: organisms unable to manufacture their own food, which must rely on autotrophs for food

heterozygous: refers to an offspring that receives two unlike alleles for a given gene location

hindbrain: the brain region of a vertebrate embryo that develops into a cerebellum, pons, and medulla oblongata

HIV (Human Immunodeficiency Virus): the virus that causes AIDS

homeostasis: the tendency of living organisms to maintain a stable internal environment even though conditions in the external environment may vary

homoiothermic: refers to warm-blooded animals that maintain a constant internal temperature regardless of external conditions

homologous chromosomes: pairs of chromosomes that carry corresponding DNA codes; one member of each pair comes from the father and one from the mother

homologous structures: structures such as human arms and whale flippers that share a common embryonic development but differ in final shape and function

homozygous: refers to an offspring that receives two identical alleles for a given gene location

hormones: substances produced in one part

of an organism that are transported to regulate growth or function in another part of the organism

human genome: the sum of all human chromosomes, genes, and alleles

human immunodeficiency virus: *see*: HIV

hybrid: refers to offspring produced by crossbreeding purebred parents with unlike traits for the same characteristic

hybridization: crossbreeding unlike varieties to produce offspring that combine their best qualities

hybrid vigour: a quality possessed by hybrids, which are often healthier than either purebred parent

hypertonic solution: a solution that has a greater concentration of solutes and a lesser concentration of water molecules than the solution to which it is being compared; usually refers to the fluid surrounding a cell

hyphae: thin, thread-like filaments from which the bodies of most fungi are made

hypocotyl: the centre section of the embryonic plant within a seed; develops into the lower stem or upper root

hypothalamus: a region of the brain that regulates the release of hormones by the pituitary gland and thereby controls all other glands; helps to co-ordinate homeostasis

hypothesis: a possible solution to a problem; usually stated in the form of a prediction that can be tested

hypotonic solution: one that has a lesser concentration of solutes and a greater concentration of water molecules than the solution to which it is being compared; usually refers to the fluid surrounding a cell

I

ileum: the third section of the small intestine that pushes undigested material into the large intestine

immovable joints: joints where the bones are fused so tightly together that very little movement is possible

imperfect flowers: flowers that have only male or only female reproductive structures

imperfect fungi: species of fungi for which no stage of sexual reproduction has been observed

implantation: a process in which the mammalian embryo becomes embedded in the lining of the uterus

inbreeding: the mating of parents with similar genotypes and phenotypes

inbreeding depression: the expression of harmful recessive alleles as a result of inbreeding

incomplete dominance: occurs when two different alleles control a characteristic, but neither is dominant and both are partly expressed in the phenotype; pink colour in four o'clock flowers is an example

incubation period: the period of time between infection by a virus and the appearance of the first symptoms of a viral disease

inferior vena cava: the major vein conducting blood from the legs and the lower body back to the heart

ingestion: the first step of the digestive process when food enters the mouth

inherited variability: differences (for example, in colour or size) among offspring of the same parents in species that reproduce sexually; caused by the shuffling of parental chromosomes during meiosis

Insecta: a class of six-legged arthropods such as beetles and flies

insertion: the place where muscle is attached to a bone that does not move

inspiration: the first main stage of breathing; inhalation

inspiratory reserve volume: the extra volume of air that can be inhaled after a normal inspiration

integumentary system: a protective system that includes the skin and its accessory structures such as hair and fingernails

internal environment: everything inside the body of an organism

interneurons: neurons that link sensory and motor neurons

interphase: a period in a cell's life between nuclear divisions; chromatin replicate toward the end of interphase

invertebrates: animals without backbones

ions: charged particles (negative or positive) that help transmit electrical impulses through neurons

isotonic solution: a solution that has the same concentration of solutes and water molecules as the solution to which it is being compared; usually refers to the fluid surrounding a cell

J

jejunum: the second segment of the small intestine where remaining protein and carbohydrate chains are broken down

joint: a place in the skeleton where two or more bones meet

K

karyotype: a picture that shows the number and structure of every chromosome in a body cell arranged from largest to smallest

kidney: the main excretory organ in vertebrates

kingdom: the largest taxonomic grouping used in biological classification

L

lactic acid fermentation: an anaerobic process in animal cells that can release small amounts of energy from glucose when oxygen is not available; produces lactic acid

large intestine: a digestive organ situated between the small intestine and the rectum that reabsorbs water and minerals

larynx: in four-legged vertebrates, a structure containing vocal cords that is located at the top of the trachea

latency period: a period of time in which retroviral DNA remains dormant

layering: propagating plants by burying a stem in soil while it is still attached to the parent plant

leaves: the vascular plant organ in which food is manufactured through the process of photosynthesis

leukemia: cancer of the blood-forming tissues, leading to abnormal levels of red and white blood cells

leukocytes: white blood cells

lichens: plant-like organisms formed by the close association of two separate species (fungi and green algae)

life functions: the activities an organism must carry out to maintain homeostasis

ligaments: stretchable bands of connective tissue that hold the bones of movable joints together

light reactions: in photosynthesis, chemical reactions that take place only in the presence of light

linkage: refers to traits that are usually inherited together

liver: in vertebrates, a large lobed organ that detoxifies blood, deaminates proteins, stores excess glucose and iron, breaks down dead red blood cells, and produces bile, a digestive juice

lungs: sac-like organs that deliver oxygen for cellular respiration, and excrete carbon dioxide and excess water into the external environment

luteinizing hormone (LH): in mammals, a hormone that stimulates ovulation in females and sex hormone production in males

Lycopsida: a plant subdivision containing club mosses

lymph: fluid that circulates in the lymphatic system, similar to blood plasma

lymphatic system: a network of very fine, thin-walled tubes that collects tissue fluid and returns it to the bloodstream

lysosomes: membrane-bound organelles containing powerful enzymes that break down dead cells and also digest food in the vacuoles of living cells

M

macronutrients: nutrients consumed in large quantities to provide materials for the maintenance of body parts and energy for life functions

macrophages: white blood cells that develop from monotypes; they engulf and destroy foreign bodies such as bacteria; they also stimulate T-helpers to multiply

macroscopic: objects that can be seen by the unaided eye

magnification: the ability of a microscope to enlarge an image

Mammalia: a vertebrate class containing mammals

mammary glands: modified sweat glands in female mammals that produce a nutrient-containing fluid called milk

maternal chromosomes: the chromosomes in egg cells (female gametes); half of the chromosomes in ordinary body cells are maternal

medulla oblongata: the vertebrate brain stem that controls involuntary body processes such as breathing and heart rate

meiosis: a specialized division process that produces gametes with only a half-set of chromosomes per nucleus

meiotic cell division: a three-part cell division sequence: replication of chromatin, division of nucleus by meiosis, and division of cytoplasm by cytokinesis; produces four nonidentical haploid sex cells

melanin: a pigment produced by the lower epidermis, which protects against ultraviolet radiation

memory-B cells: B cells that store the new protein (antibody) patterns created by plasma-B cells

menstrual cycle: in females, repeated sequence of hormonal changes that cause ovulation and prepare the uterus to receive a fertilized egg

menstruation: the cyclical breakdown of the endometrium in human females causing a flow of blood and tissue

meristem: unspecialized plant tissue made up of rapidly dividing cells from which all plant tissues eventually develop

mesoderm: the middle cell layers of the gastrula, which eventually develop into the adult's muscles, circulatory tissues, and sex organs

messenger RNA (mRNA): a type of RNA that carries the DNA code from the chromosomes to the ribosomes

metabolism: the sum of all the processes a cell may use to store or obtain energy, and manufacture or utilize structural or functional materials

metaphase: an early stage of mitosis or meiosis, during which chromosomes line up along the equator at right angles to the spindle

methanogens: anaerobic prokaryotes that produce methane gas

microfilaments: long, thin protein fibres found in the cytoplasm that have the ability to contract

micrometres (μm): a unit of measurement equal to $\frac{1}{1000}$ mm or 10^{-6} m

micronutrients: essential nutrients needed only in very small amounts; vitamins and minerals are examples

micro-organisms: organisms that can only be seen through a microscope; mostly single-celled

micropyle: an opening in the ovule of a flowering plant that admits the pollen tube

microscopes: instruments used to examine objects that cannot be seen by the unaided eye

microscopic: refers to objects that are too small to be seen with the unaided eye

microscopy: the use of microscopes to examine objects

microtome: a very sharp blade of glass or diamond used to cut biological specimens into thin sections

microtubules: long, cylindrical protein structures that are hollow and fairly rigid; found in cilia, flagella, centrioles, and the cytoskeleton

midbrain: one of three brain regions in a vertebrate embryo; does not develop further in mammals, but may form optic lobes in nonmammals

minerals: chemical elements needed by living things for maintenance, development, and normal functioning

mitochondria: cell organelles that are the site of aerobic respiration

mitosis: a division process that ensures each offspring cell has a complete set of chromosomes in its nucleus

mitotic cell division: a three-part cell division sequence: replication of chromatin, division of nucleus by mitosis, and division of cytoplasm by cytokinesis; produces two offspring cells identical to each other and to the parent cell

Monera: a kingdom containing prokaryotes such as bacteria

monocot or monocotyledon: an angiosperm such as the corn plant that has only one cotyledon per seed

monocytes: immune cells that produce macrophages

monohybrid cross: a crossbreeding experiment that traces only one inherited characteristic such as height

monosaccharides: the smallest and simplest carbohydrate molecules; single sugars such as glucose

morula: a ball of cells that results from the first of a series of mitotic divisions in the zygote

motile: refers to organisms or cells that can move about freely

motor neurons: neurons that carry impulses from the brain to appropriate muscles or glands

mouth: a structure that ingests food and may initiate physical breakdown of food

movable joints: joints where at least one bone can move relative to the other(s)

multiple-allele inheritance: the inheritance of characteristics determined by multiple alleles, only two of which can occupy a single gene location

multiple alleles: refers to the existence of three or more different alleles for the same characteristic

multiple fruits: fruits that develop from the single ovaries of a flower cluster

multiple-gene inheritance: inheritance of a single characteristic such as height; determined by several pairs of alleles at different gene locations

Musci: a class of plant species containing true mosses

musculoskeletal system: a system of interacting bones and muscles that permit movement

mutation: the spontaneous rearrangement of genetic material

mutualism: a type of symbiosis in which both species benefit from their association

mycelium: a network of hyphae threads in fungi

mycology: the study of fungi

myelin sheath: the fatty white covering of an axon that prevents the charged electrical particles inside from escaping

myofibrils: functional units contained by muscle cells that enable a muscle to contract

myosin: thick protein filaments in myofibrils

N

nastic movements: plant responses to stimuli that are fast and reversible because they do not require cell growth

naturalists: individuals who study the natural world

negative feedback: a type of self-regulation by a biological system; an increase in system output acts as a signal that slows the system down; for example, an increase in body temperature triggers a decrease in heat production

negative tropism: the movement of a plant away from a stimulus

Nematoda: an animal phylum containing roundworms, which have unsegmented bodies

nephrons: microscopic sub-units that enable the kidney to filter blood and form urine

nerves: long, thin strands of tissue along which electrical impulses travel

nervous system: a control system based on the transmission of electrical impulses, which helps animals detect stimuli and co-ordinate responses

neurons: long, thin cells that are the basic functional units of the nervous system

neurotransmitters: chemicals released by the terminal knobs that initiate a new nerve impulse in the next neuron

nomenclature: in biology, the system of naming living things

nonvascular plants: plants that do not have specialized vascular tissues to conduct water and nutrients

nuclear envelope: a double membrane surrounding the nucleus

nucleoli: dense spherical masses found inside the nucleus

nucleoplasm: the complex fluid inside a cell's nucleus

nucleotides: the sub-units making up a nucleic acid; each contains a sugar, a phosphate, and a nitrogenous base

nucleus: the largest organelle of a cell; controls all cell activities

nutrients: elements and compounds an organism cannot manufacture itself, but which it needs to carry out its life functions

O

obligate aerobes: bacteria that require oxygen to perform their life functions

obligate anaerobes: bacteria that must live in oxygen-free environments to survive

offspring: a young animal after it has hatched from an egg or emerged from a female's reproductive system

olfactory lobe: the region of the brain that processes odour-related impulses

open circulatory system: one that allows a fluid such as blood to leave an incomplete circuit of tubes and vessels to bathe body tissues directly

oral groove: an entryway in protists such as paramecia through which food is swept by means of cilia

order: a group of similar families

organelles: internal cell structures found in the cytoplasm

origin: the place where muscle is attached to a stationary bone

osmosis: the natural diffusion of water molecules across a cell membrane from a region of higher concentration to a region of lower concentration

osmotic pressure: pressure resulting from the movement of water molecules by osmosis

ossification: the replacement of cartilage by permanent bone

Osteichthyes: a vertebrate class containing bony fish

outbreeding: the crossbreeding of one inbred organism with another, which is usually of the same breed but not as closely related

ovaries: the gonads of female animals that produce eggs; in flowers, female reproductive parts containing ovules

ovulation: the release of egg(s) from an ovary

ovules: structures containing sex cells that develop in the ovary of a flowering plant

P

pacemaker: a cluster of specialized muscle cells in the right atrium that sends out electrical signals, stimulating both atria to contract; also called the sinoatrial node

pancreas: a digestive organ that produces several important digestive enzymes and the hormone insulin, which controls glucose levels in the blood

pandemic: a worldwide or country-wide epidemic

parasites: organisms that obtain nutrients by living on or in other living organisms

parasitism: symbiosis in which one species benefits while the other is harmed

parasympathetic nerve: part of the autonomic nervous system; parasympathetic nerves usually counteract the effects of sympathetic nerves

parenchyma tissue: soft plant tissue made of loosely packed cells; the edible part of an apple is parenchyma

passive immunity: temporary protection against a particular disease by the introduction of antibodies; may be acquired through transfer from mother to fetus or by injection

passive transport: the natural movement of molecules across a cell membrane from regions of high concentration to regions of low concentration; no energy from cells is required

paternal chromosomes: the chromosomes found in sperm cells (male gametes); half of the chromosomes in ordinary body cells are paternal

pathogenic bacteria: parasitic species that cause disease in host organisms

pathogens: disease-producing micro-organisms

pellicle: a firm, elastic protein covering that surrounds the cell membranes of unicellular organisms such as euglenas

penis: a reproductive structure of male mammals that facilitates internal fertilization by releasing sperm into the reproductive system of a female

perfect flowers: flowers that have both male and female reproductive structures

periosteum: a tough membrane that surrounds all bones in the human skeleton

peripheral nervous system: all parts of the vertebrate nervous system except the brain and the spinal cord

peristalsis: a wave-like motion caused by the action of two muscle layers that pushes food along the digestive tract

permeability: the degree to which molecules can move freely across a membrane

Phaeophyta: a plant division containing brown algae

phagocytes: white blood cells that destroy bacteria

phagocytosis: a form of active transport in which the cell membrane engulfs undissolved particles and forms a vacuole that remains inside the cytoplasm

pharynx: in vertebrates, a common passageway for food and air

phase contrast microscope: a compound microscope that relies on co-ordinating wave-like energy pulses of light to produce an enhanced image

phenotype: the outward physical appearance of an organism that results from its genetic makeup

phenotypic ratio: a mathematical statement predicting the phenotypes expected from a crossbreeding experiment

philosophers: scholars who depend on thought and reason to acquire knowledge about the nature of the universe

phloem: a vascular plant tissue that transports dissolved food

phospholipids: complex molecules making up both layers of cell membranes

photosynthesis: a chemical process by which autotrophs such as plants use solar energy to manufacture food

phototropism: the movement of plants in response to light

phylum: a group of similar classes of animals or protists; *plural*: phyla

physiology: the study of how body structures perform vital life functions

phytoplankton: photosynthetic types of plankton

pili: specialized protein filaments that aid in the transfer of DNA between bacterial cells during conjugation

pioneers: living things such as lichens that are first to grow in areas where other plants have yet to establish themselves

pinocytosis: active transport of liquid droplets containing dissolved molecules too large to pass across the cell membrane; similar to phagocytosis

pistil: the female reproductive structure of a flower that holds the stigma

pituitary gland: the most important gland in the endocrine system, which interacts with the hypothalamus and produces more hormones than any other endocrine gland

placenta: a specialized organ in the uterus through which the embryo obtains nutrients, exchanges gases, and excretes wastes

plankton: large populations of free-floating organisms, which exist in oceans such as algal protists

Plantae: a kingdom including autotrophic organisms that contain chlorophyll and carry out photosynthesis

plant kingdom: multicellular organisms that grow from the ground and produce their own food

plasma: an important blood component that carries dissolved nutrients and contains several kinds of protein molecules

plasma-B cells: B cells that produce new antibodies to fight new types of invaders

plasmids: in a bacterium, small rings of extra DNA that exist and act independently of the much longer chromosome of bacteria

plasmodium: the main body of the slime mould

plastids: large membrane-bound organelles found in plants and some unicellular autotrophs; for example, chloroplasts

platelets: cell fragments found in blood, which initiate clotting; formed from larger cells in red bone marrow

Platyhelminthes: an animal phylum containing both free-living and parasitic flatworms

poikilothermic: refers to cold-blooded animals that do not maintain a constant internal temperature

pollen grains: waterproof structures that encase the male gametes of seed plants

pollen tube: a tube formed by the tube cell in a pollen grain that extends down the style to the ovary of a flowering plant

pollination: the transfer of pollen from anther to stigma

polysaccharides: complex carbohydrate molecules composed of long chains of monosaccharide units such as glucose

Porifera: an animal phylum containing sponges

positive feedback: a type of self-regulation in a biological system; an increase in system output acts as a signal that speeds the system up; control of heart rate by the accelerating centre in the brain is an example

positive tropism: the movement of a plant toward a stimulus

Principle of Dominance: when an organism is hybrid (crossbred) for a pair of contrasting traits, it shows only the dominant trait

Principle of Independent Assortment: the inheritance of alleles for one trait does not affect the inheritance of alleles for another trait unless both gene locations are on the same chromosome

Principle of Segregation: hereditary characteristics are determined by distinct units or factors that occur in pairs; when reproductive cells are produced, the two factors of each pair segregate (separate), and are distributed as distinct units or factors, one to each gamete

progesterone: a female hormone produced mainly by the corpus luteum that causes the lining of the uterus to thicken

prokaryotes: organisms such as bacteria, which are made up of prokaryotic cells

prokaryotic cells: cells that do not contain membrane-bound nuclei or membrane-bound organelles such as mitochondria and chloroplasts

prophase: the first stage of mitosis or meiosis, during which chromatin condenses to form chromosomes; spindle fibres form; chromosomes move toward the equator of the cell

prop roots: roots that grow downward from plant stems to provide support

proteins: large, complex molecules composed of long chains of amino acids; the building blocks of cells, tissues, and organs

Protista: a kingdom of autotrophic and heterotrophic eukaryotes that includes protists such as amoebas, paramecia, and euglenas

protists: mostly unicellular organisms belonging to the kingdom Protista

protoplasm: a complex fluid inside the cell membrane that contains everything a cell needs to live

Protozoa: a subkingdom of Protista in which the species hunt or gather food and ingest it

pseudopods: the cytoplasmic extensions of protists such as amoebas that enable them to move

Psilopsida: a plant subdivision containing whisk ferns

Pteropsida: a plant subdivision containing ferns and seed plants

puberty: the developmental stage at which male and female gonads become functional and secondary sexual characteristics develop

pulmonary artery: the artery that transports blood from the right ventricle to the lungs for oxygenation

pulmonary semilunar valve: a valve that prevents blood pumped into the pulmonary artery from flowing back into the right ventricle

pulmonary subsystem: a circuit of blood vessels that carries deoxygenated blood to the lungs for re-oxygenation

pulmonary vein: the vein that carries oxygenated blood from the lungs to the left atrium

Punnett square: a chart used to predict the outcome of a crossbreeding experiment

pyloric sphincter: a ring of muscle through which chyme is squirted into the small intestine

Pyrrophyta: a phylum of the subkingdom Algae containing autotrophic protists such as marine dinoflagellates

R

radicle: the lower part of the embryonic plant inside a seed that develops into the roots of the new plant

random assortment: occurs during the first meiotic division; replicated paternal and maternal chromosomes from the germinal cell are distributed randomly to the new nuclei

reabsorption: the passive or active transport of useful materials from the tubules of the nephrons to the capillaries for recirculation in the body

receptor: (1) a cell or group of cells specialized for detecting stimuli; (2) a protein molecule on a cell's surface that interacts with specific chemicals

recessive allele: an allele coded for a recessive trait such as shortness

recessive trait: one that is hidden or repressed by a dominant trait

recombinant DNA: the result of transferring a segment of DNA from one organism into the chromosomes of another

recombinant DNA technology: methods of inserting DNA from one organism into another

rectum: the end of the large intestine that holds fecal matter until it is ready for elimination through the anus

red algae: species of mostly macroscopic seaweed included in the division Rhodophyta

reduction division: occurs during the first meiotic division; the number of chromosomes per nucleus is reduced from 2N to N

reflex action: a rapid, unlearned response that occurs when particular sensory neurons are stimulated

reflex arc: a nerve circuit that forms the structural basis for reflex actions

regeneration: a type of asexual reproduction in which cells are regenerated to form the missing body parts of a separate individual

renal arteries: a pair of arteries branching off the aorta that carry waste-laden blood into the kidneys

renal cortex: the outermost layer of the kidney that is made up of numerous nephrons

renal medulla: the middle layer of the kidney that is made up of capillaries and tubes

renal pelvis: the hollow interior of the kidney; urine collects here

renal veins: veins that carry purified blood from the kidneys to the circulatory system

replication: the production of a complete, additional set of DNA-containing chromatin in a cell's nucleus prior to mitosis or meiosis

reproduction: the ability of living things to produce more organisms like themselves

Reptilia: a vertebrate class containing reptiles

residual volume: the volume of air that always remains in the lungs

resolving power: the ability of the human eye or an optical instrument to distinguish between objects that are extremely close together; also called resolution

retroviruses: RNA viruses in which the usual DNA-to-RNA sequence is reversed

reverse transcriptase: a specialized enzyme in RNA viruses that converts viral RNA to viral DNA

rhizoids: root-like hyphae in fungi

rhizomes: underground stems that grow horizontally through the soil

Rhodophyta: a plant division containing red algae

ribonucleic acid: *see*: RNA

ribosomes: cytoplasmic organelles that produce all cell proteins

RNA (ribonucleic acid): a single-strand nucleic acid related to DNA that plays a vital role in protein production

root pressure: a high pressure inside the root resulting from the inward diffusion of water from the soil

roots: specialized plant organs that anchor plants in the soil and absorb water and nutrients

rusts: harmful, parasitic club fungi

S

sac fungi: members of the division Ascomycetes

salivary glands: glands that surround the mouth, which secrete saliva

saprophytes: organisms that obtain nutrients from dead organic matter

Sarcodina: a protist phylum that includes amoebas

sarcomas: cancerous tumors that grow in connective tissue such as bone

scanning electron microscope: a microscope that produces a three-dimensional image using electrons emitted from the specimen's surface

science: the discovery of how the world works through observation, measurement, experiment, reason, and thought

scientific method: an orderly, logical system for solving problems

scion: a small branch or bud grafted to a host plant

sclerenchyma tissue: strengthening plant tissue found in roots, stems, and leaves

scrotum: in mammals, a sac outside the male body that contains the testes

second filial (F$_2$) generation: the offspring resulting from crossbreeding individuals of an F$_1$ generation

secretion: in a cell, the manufacture and discharge of substances such as hormones; in the kidney, the active transport of extra wastes from the capillaries to the nephrons after filtration

seed coat: the protective outer covering of a seed

seeds: multicellular structures containing an embryonic plant and a small food supply encased in a protective coat

selectively permeable membrane: the ability of a cell membrane to allow small molecules such as water to diffuse freely while blocking large particles such as proteins and bacteria

self-pollination: the transfer of pollen within the same flower

semen: a mixture of sperm and seminal fluid

semilunar valves: one-way valves through which blood is forced from the ventricles into the arteries

seminal fluid: a fluid released along with sperm that provides nutrients and chemicals that help the sperm survive in the female reproductive system

seminiferous tubules: tubules in the testes in which sperm are produced

sensory neurons: neurons that carry nerve impulses from sensory receptors to the brain

sensory receptors: specialized cells that convert external stimuli into nerve impulses

septum: any dividing wall in a plant or animal; for example, in humans a septum separates the chambers of the right heart from those of the left

sessile: refers to animals that are stationary

sex chromosomes: chromosomes that direct the development of sex organs

sex-linked characteristics: nonsexual characteristics that are carried on a sex chromosome

sex-linked inheritance: the inheritance of nonsexual traits along with sex; such traits appear more frequently in one sex; male pattern baldness is an example

sexual dimorphism: the existence of distinctly different male and female forms within the same species

sexual intercourse: the process of transferring sperm from the penis into the vagina

sexual reproduction: the formation of a new individual by the union of two nonidentical gametes from two different parents

sexually transmitted diseases (STD): diseases that are passed on by infected individuals through sexual contact

simple fruits: fruits that develop from the single ovary of a single flower

simple microscope: a microscope that uses only one lens to form a magnified image

single-gene inheritance: inheritance of a characteristic determined by a single pair of alleles at a single gene location

single-stranded chromosome: one of two structures formed when the chromatids of a double-stranded chromosome pull apart

skeletal muscle: muscle attached to skeletal bones and controlled by the peripheral nervous system

skeletal muscle tissue: tissue made up of many parallel bundles of muscle fibres

skin: the largest organ of the human body, which protects and regulates the internal environment

slime capsule: a protective gelatinous layer that surrounds many bacterial cells

slime moulds: fungi that have both an active and an inactive stage in their life cycle; slime moulds appear and behave differently in each stage

small intestine: a digestive organ situated between the stomach and the large intestine; most chemical digestion occurs here

smooth muscle: muscle located in the walls lining internal organs and controlled by the autonomic nervous system

smuts: harmful, parasitic members of club fungi

somatic nervous system: that part of a vertebrate's peripheral nervous system that controls the skeletal muscles

species: a group of similar organisms that can mate and produce fertile offspring

sperm: male gametes

sperm nuclei: the result of cell division in the generative cell in a flowering plant

Sphenopsida: a plant subdivision containing horsetails

sphincter: a ring of muscle that surrounds a body opening and can contract tightly to close it

spinal cord: a long, thick cord of nerve tissue extending from the brain

spinal nerves: nerves that lead from the spinal cord to those body parts that are not connected to the brain by the cranial nerves

spindle: a cage-like array of fibres on which chromosomes are carried to opposite poles of a cell during mitosis or meiosis

spindle fibres: microtubules extending from pole to pole in mitosis or meiosis

spongy bone: a light, porous bone tissue that

lies beneath the compact bone; found at the ends of femurs

spores: reproductive cells produced by plants, fungi, bacteria, and some protists but not by animals

sporophytes: specialized plant bodies that produce spores

Sporozoa: a protist phylum whose members do not have cilia or flagella; sporozoans

stamen: one of the male reproductive structures of a flower, which consists of an anther and a filament

starch: a polysaccharide found in most plants; used by animals as a major source of food energy

stems: upright plant organs that support leaves, transport materials, and store food

stigma: the top of the pistil where pollen collects

stock: the branch of a host plant to which a scion is grafted

stolon: in plants, a curving, modified stem that sends out roots wherever it touches the soil; in fungi, hyphae that grow horizontally above the ground

stomach: a bag-like organ that churns partially digested food through the rhythmic contraction and relaxation of its three muscle layers

stomata: pores in the epidermis of a leaf that allow gases to enter and leave its internal tissue

structure: the shape of an organism's body parts or the pattern in which they are arranged

style: the long tube part of a pistil that supports the stigma

substrate: the chemical compound on which an enzyme acts

superior vena cava: the major vein conducting blood from the head and the upper body back to the heart

sweat glands: glands that help the skin perform as an excretory organ by excreting water (sweat) through pores to the skin's surface

symbionts: the organisms in a symbiotic partnership

symbiosis: the close association of two species; lichens are an example

sympathetic nerve: part of the autonomic nervous system; the sympathetic nerves prepare the body for a fight or flight response

synapses: the tiny gaps between neurons; neurotransmitter molecules carry nerve impulses across the synapse

synovial sac: a sac between the bones of a joint, which secretes a lubricating fluid

systemic subsystem: a circuit of blood vessels that carries blood from the heart chambers to all body systems and organs except the lungs and the heart muscle

systolic pressure: the pressure of arterial blood when the ventricles contract; the higher number in blood pressure readings

T

taproot: a single, large primary root from which much smaller secondary roots develop

taxonomy: the science of classification

T cells: immune cells that are produced in bone marrow but mature in the thymus gland to form T-helpers, T-killers, and T-suppressors

technology: the knowledge, tools, and techniques societies employ to make use of natural resources

telophase: the final stage of mitosis or meiosis, during which chromosomes cluster to form new nuclei and are surrounded by new nuclear membranes

tendons: connective tissue that attaches muscles to bones

terminal knobs: clusters of cells at the end of the axon that relay nerve impulses

test cross: a breeding test to determine whether an individual is homozygous or heterozygous

testes: the gonads of male animals that produce sperm

testosterone: the male hormone that causes the appearance of secondary sexual characteristics and stimulates sperm production

tetrad: (1) a group of four chromatids formed in early meiosis when a double-stranded maternal chromosome pairs up with a matching double-stranded paternal chromosome; (2) a group of four haploid cells formed by meiotic cell division

thalamus: a part of the brain that screens nerve impulses before they reach the cerebrum, allowing only essential messages through

T-helpers: T cells that interact with all other immune cells, thereby co-ordinating the immune system

theory: a widely accepted explanation for a problem, which continues to explain new observations when tested

thigmotropism: the movement of a plant in response to touch

thin sectioning: a slicing technique used to prepare very thin biological specimens for viewing under an electron microscope

thymine: one of four weak nitrogenous bases found in DNA

tidal volume: the volume of air inhaled during each normal inspiration

T-killers: T cells that multiply and destroy host cells infected by a virus

tongue: a muscular organ that moves food around in the mouth, mixing it with saliva

toxins: poisonous chemicals produced by living organisms; bacterial toxins trigger an immune response in human hosts

trachea: the windpipe in air-breathing vertebrates; carries air from pharynx to bronchi

Tracheophyta: a plant division containing vascular plants

transduction: the recombination of bacterial DNA through the action of bacteriophages

transformation: the incorporation of DNA from a dead bacterial cell into a living bacterial cell; the living cell now performs some of the functions of the dead cell

translocation: the transportation of dissolved materials such as minerals or glucose in a plant

transmission electron microscope: a microscope that produces an image by passing a beam of electrons through thinly sliced specimens

transpiration: water loss through the leaves of plants

Transpiration-tension theory: a theory that explains the upward movement of water from the roots to the leaves of a vascular plant in terms of the sun's energy and the cohesive forces (tension) between water molecules

tricuspid valve: the valve that prevents blood in right ventricle from flowing back into the right atrium

tropism: the movement of a plant away from

or toward a stimulus; all tropisms involve cell growth

T-suppressors: T cells that return the immune system to a stable state after an infection

tubal ligation: an operation that causes sterility in females

tube cell: one of two cells in a mature pollen grain; it forms a pollen tube when it reaches the stigma

tumor: a dense clump of abnormal cells, which are either malignant or benign

turgor pressure: in plants, pressure resulting from the accumulation of water in the central vacuole, which causes the cell membrane to press against the cell wall

U

ultrasound imagery: a procedure that uses sound waves to provide an image of the fetus

umbilical cord: a long cord through which the blood vessels of the embryo reach the placenta

unity: refers to the features that all living things have in common

uracil: a nitrogenous base found only in RNA; corresponds to thymine in DNA

urea: a waste product produced in the liver from amino acids

urethra: a duct that carries urine from the bladder to the external environment

urine: the most important waste fluid produced by the excretory system, the main component of which is urea

uterus: a chamber in a female mammal where a zygote develops until birth

V

vaccines: solutions of dead or weakened bacterial cells that are injected to stimulate antibody production

vacuoles: fluid-filled spaces that circulate in the cytoplasm, which are surrounded by a membrane identical to a cell membrane

vagina: a tube or canal that leads from the uterus to the external environment

variable: in a controlled experiment, the only factor that is allowed to differ between the two set-ups

vascular bundles: groupings of xylem and phloem tissue to form long, continuous conducting vessels in seed plants and ferns

vascular cambium: meristematic tissue that increases the diameter of roots and stems as they grow

vascular cylinder: the innermost region of a young primary root, containing xylem and phloem; extends upward through stems

vascular plants: plants that have specialized conducting tissues for the transport of food and water

vascular tissue: a network of tube-like structures that transports materials through a plant

vasectomy: an operation that causes sterility in males

vector: an organism that transmits disease from one plant or animal host to another

veins: large vessels that collect blood from the venules; veins carry blood toward the heart

ventricles: (1) hollow, fluid-filled chambers in the brain and spinal cord; also; (2) the two lower chambers of the heart that pump blood into the major arteries

venules: vessels that receive waste-laden blood from capillaries

vertebrae: hollow, cylindrical bones that are stacked in a column, protecting the spinal cord

Vertebrata: an animal subphylum containing organisms with a flexible backbone consisting of a series of vertebrae

vertebrates: animals with backbones

vesicle: a membrane-bound cytoplasmic sac pinched off from the smooth endoplasmic reticulum

villi: finger-like projections on the intestinal lining that transfer digested food molecules to the bloodstream

viruses: particles that have a core of nucleic acid (RNA or DNA) surrounded by a protein coat; viruses require a living cell for replication

vital capacity: the total volume of air produced by expelling as much as possible from the lungs after a deep breath

vitamins: often referred to as co-enzymes because they co-operate with enzymes to control chemical reactions

W

white matter: (1) the inner portion of the cerebrum; (2) surrounds the outside of the spinal cord

woody stems: the tough, rigid stems of shrubs and trees

X

xylem: a vascular plant tissue that transports water and dissolved minerals

Z

Zoomastigina: a phylum of the subkingdom Protozoa containing heterotrophic protists

zooplankton: heterotrophic types of plankton

Zygomycetes: a division of fungi such as bread mould that reproduce sexually by forming a zygote-containing spore

zygote: the single cell formed when two gametes join

INDEX

animals, 91, 130, 172; and cell theory, 54; and heart research, 201; breeding of, 724, 725–6, 728, 729; cellular respiration in, 86, 107; digestion in, 140–65; diseases of, 472, 473, 556, 566, 579–80; domestic, 344, 345, 346, 566; gas exchange in, 86–122; nervous control in, 240–4, 245, 260; nutritional needs in, 128–34; reproduction in, 322–32, 698; role of in seed dispersal, 431
Annelida, (phylum), 74
annelids, 120; nervous system in, 241, 246
annual plants, 388
Anopheles mosquito, 517, 518
anorexia nervosa, 139
antacids, 157
antheridium, 380
anthers, 423, 425; of pea plants, 705
antibacterial agents, 540–1
antibiotics, 361, 362, 455, 466, 473–4, 485, 540–1
antibodies, 174, 176, 179–80, 539–40, 563, 564; prevention of production by HIV, 573, 575, 578; produced after vaccination, 571; produced by B cells, 570
antidiuretic hormone, (ADH), 223–4, 232, 233
antigens, 540
anti-inflammatory drugs, 308, 309, 310
antiseptics, 541
antiviral agents, 268
anus, 146, 163, 210
aorta, 185, 186, 193, 217, 260, 639
aortic arches, 198
aortic semilunar valve, 193
apical meristem, 388, 433
appendages, human, 282; *see also* arms; forelimbs; legs
appendix, 145
Arachnida, 76
archegonium, 380
Aristotle, 5, 6, 12, 22, 24
arms, bones of, 284
arteries, 108, 182–3, 191, 194, 217, 219; constriction of, 108; coronary, 187, 202; in endometrium, 349; inflamed, 308; major, 185, 190, 193; of neck, 259; plaque in, 132
arterioles, 182, 185, 187, 219, 221
arthritis, 308; degenerative, 308; of the spine, 308
Arthropoda, 76, 199
arthropods, 76, 120, 315
arthroscopic surgery, 288
artificial insemination, in cattle, 344, 345; in humans, 363

asci, 375, 460
Ascomycetes, 375, 460–1
ascospores, 460
aseptic techniques, 531, 532
asexual reproduction, 59, 322, 683, 696–7; advantages of, 444, 697; disadvantages of, 444, 697, 699; in bacteria, 528–9, 530; in fungi, 452, 457–8, 460, 466; in protists, 483, 505, 510, 511, 517–18; in seed plants, 439–43
Asian bee mites, 430
asthma, 112
astral rays, 679
athlete's foot, 309, 454, 466, 473
atrioventricular (AV) node, 195
atrioventricular valves, 191, 193
atrium, 190, 191, 193, 195; right, 259
atrophy, of muscles, 268, 308
auditory nerve, 251
auto-immune disorders, 310
autonomic nervous system, 255, 257, 289
autosomes, 742, 750
autotrophs, 18, 68, 451; algae as, 510; bacteria as, 533; plants as, 376; protists as, 510, 513
auxins, 436, 437; and tropisms, 437
Aves, 72, 80
axons, in brain, 249; of neurons, 241, 242, 244

backbone, 77; *see also* spine
bacteria, 109, 122, 143, 147, 176, 188, 306, 310, 312; anaerobic, 91, 536, 537, 544, 658, 681; as food, 519, 520; as prokaryotes, 482; cellular respiration in, 86; characteristics of, 526–7; classification of, 485; compared with protists, 526; destroyed by dehydration, 647; disease-causing, 112, 361, 537–41, 542; genetic engineering of, 272, 527, 545, 765; in human digestive system, 131, 145, 533; parasitic, 535–6; protection of plant parts from, 390, 396, 402, 406; reproduction of, 526, 528–9, 530
bacteria cell, 559, 560, 681; as host, 560; chromosome in, 560, 561; diseases of, 599–61, 582; genes in, 560; wall of, 612
bacterial infections, 304, 309, 310, 359–61, 537–41, 542; of fish, 459; of leaf tissue, 390, 406
bacteriology, 544–7
bacteriophages, 489, 530, 548, 559–61, 595; genes of, 560, protein coats of, 596
Banting, Sir Frederick, 156, 346
bark, 401
basal bodies, 621; function of, 622; structure of, 621–2

basal metabolic rate, 88
base pairs, of DNA molecule, 598, 670
basidia, 375, 462
Basidiomycetes, 375, 462–4
basophils, 176
beans, as dicot plants, 428, 432; dispersal of, 431; seeds of, 428
bees, 344; infection by Asian bee mites, 430; role in pollination, 425, 430
beetles, 462
behaviour, and reproduction, 323, 332, 333, 334, 336
behavioural adaptations, 336
Beijerinck, Martinus, 488
Best, Dr. Charles, 264
biceps, 290
bicuspid, 142
bicuspid valve, 193
bilateral symmetry, 74
bile, 145, 151, 153; wastes dissolved in, 217
bile duct, 146
binary fission, 322; in bacteria, 526, 528–9, 530; in protists, 505, 507, 510, 696–7
binomial nomenclature, 13–14, 71
biological classification, 18, 23–6; importance of, 27–8
biological continuity, 669, 683, 684, 685, 696, 698
biological research, 46–52
biological terminology, 41
biology, 13; basic assumptions of, 34–40, 43; branches of, 43–4; definition of, 34; tools and techniques of, 46–52, 60–3
bioluminescence, 511
biomes, 408–9; Canadian, 408, 409
biophysics, 292–3
biosphere, 4, 16, 17, 19, 513; bacteria in, 533; unity in, 592
biotechnology, 544–5, 765
birds, 639; brain of, 248; excretion in, 212, 226, 227; feathers of, 314, 338; gas exchange system in, 117; reproduction in, 333, 334–5, 336; role of in pollination, 425; role of in seed dispersal, 431; skin of, 313, 314
birth canal, 361
birth control, 356–9
birth control pill, 358, 359
bladder, urinary, 215, 218, 255, 269, 360, 362; lining of, 289; sphincter muscle of, 348
blastocyst, 353
bleeding, 3–4; from uterus, 360; internal, 232, 580; *see also* menstruation
blindness, 273, 361; *see also* colour blindness

blood, 93, 134, 198, 199, 210–11, 260, 297, 314, 350, 354; and erectile tissue, 348; as carrier of immune cells, 568; as connective tissue, 579; carbon dioxide in, 212, 259; circulation of, 132, 145, 173, 182–3, 184–7, 189, 198–200; clotting of, 135, 136, 174, 177, 304, 748; filtration of, 219–20, 221–2; function of, 173–7, 184; glucose in, 263–4; infected by *Plasmodium* cells, 517; infected by *Trypanosoma gambiense*, 519; in gas exchange, 96, 103–5; nutrients in, 223, 232; of annelids, 74; oxygen in, 88, 92, 102, 103–5, 108, 258; purified by kidneys, 217, 223–3, 227; structure of, 173–7; waste products in, 215, 217, 219, 242, 259; water in, 223, 224; *see also* plasma; platelets; red blood cells; white blood cells

blood cells, 652; defective, 757; production of, 284; *see also* red blood cells; white blood cells

blood donations, 554; screened for AIDS, 559, 578

blood flow, 192–3, 195

blood pressure, 108, 182, 183, 191, 193–5, 203–4, 221, 255; *see also* high blood pressure; low blood pressure

bloodstream, 133, 144, 145, 188, 203, 256, 260, 262

blood tests, 154, 760

blood transfusions, 179, 363, 556, 559, 578, 760; to fetus, 765

blood types, 179; as multiple-allele inheritance, 751

blood vessels, 173, 174, 176, 184, 193, 219, 264, 349; blockage of, 202, 203; constriction of, 108, 203, 204; damage to, 194; dilation of, 256, 265; disease of, 361; of earthworm, 198; of embryo, 361; types of, 182–3

blue-green moulds, 466, 472, 544

body temperature, 134, 210, 226, 348; control of, 255; regulation of, 298, 313, 639

bolus, 142, 143

bone marrow, 285; as producer of immune cells, 567, 568; red, 132

bones, 77, 135, 245, 246; as connective tissue, 303; diseases and disorders of, 307, 308, 579; effects of exercise on, 305; fractures of, 306; function of, 282–5; fusion of, 286; health of, 263, 265, 271, 284–5, 305; sarcoma of, 579; structure of, 284–5, 303

bony fish, 80

boreal forest, 409

botanists, 374

botulism, 536

bowel, *see* large intestine

Bowman's capsules, 219, 220, 221

bracket fungus, 375, 451, 454, 463

brain, 108, 133, 195, 202, 205, 223; breathing control centre in, 202, 203, 205, 248, 250, 255, 258, 259–60; chemicals in, 273–4; control of movement by, 289; damage to, 99, 154, 194, 195, 361, 756; disorders of, 268–9; function of, 250–1, 273; human, 247–51, 255, 273–4; interneurons in, 243, 253, 273; of animals, 242, 243, 244, 246; of annelids, 74; of planarians, 240, 241; of vertebrates, 245, 246, 247–8, 263; protection of, 282, 284; underdevelopment of, 138; ventricles of, 246

brain cells, affected by Tay-Sachs disease, 154, 756–7, 760; as targets of HIV, 575

bread mould, 451, 452, 457–8, 459, 472

breathing, 86–8, 94–8; disruption of, 537, 996; mechanics of, 96–7; nervous control of, 106–7; *see also* expiration; inspiration

breathing rate, 86, 87, 88, 97, 106, 115, 202, 203, 205; control centre for, 106, 202, 203, 205, 248, 250, 255, 258; nervous control of, 259–60

breeding, controlled, 726–7, 738, *see also* selective breeding; experiments in, 706–11, 716, 718, 725–6, 730; of animals, 337, 344–5, 724, 725–6, 727, 728, 729, 738; of cattle, 337, 334–5, 724, 727; of horses, 725–6; of plants, 443, 726, 727, 728, 730–1, 738

bronchi, 93, 95, 111; nervous control of, 251

bronchioles, 96, 103

Brown, Robert, 54

brown algae, 378

Bryophyta, 377, 379

bryophytes, 378

budding, 322, 460, 697

bulbs, 403

burns, 304

bursa, inflamed, 308, 309

bursitis, 309

buttons, of mushrooms, 462

cacti, adaptations of, 406, 407, 408

caecum, 145

caffeine, 233

calcium, 135; compounds, 285; deficiency of, 308; for healthy bones, 283, 305, 308; in diet, 136, 273, 283, 305; stored in bones, 283, 284

cambium layer, 433; of stems, 400, 401; *see also* cork cambium

cancer, 63, 360, 672; as stressor of immune system, 566; carcinoma, 579; Kaposi's sarcoma, 580–1; leukemia, 579, 580; of bone, 579; of connective tissue, 579; of cervix, 359, 365, 581; of lung, 112; of skin, 307; of stomach, 112; related to AIDS, 363, 554, 577, 581; related to viruses, 579–81, 582; research into, 579, 580, 581; sarcoma, 579, 580

cane-sugar making, 415

Canidae, (family), 71

canine teeth, 142

canopy, of forest, 406

capillaries, 108, 115, 182–3, 188, 193–4, 211, 216; gas exchange in, 104, 105, 185, 187, 217; in gill filaments, 117; in nephrons, 221, 222, 224; in skin, 296, 297; network of, 260; walls of, 568

capillarity, 412

carbohydrates, 61, 128–31, 138, 157, 174, 594; as energy source, 129–30, 135; complex, 315; digestion of, 142, 145, 149, 150, 153; in cell membrane, 613; in cytoplasm, 614

carbon, 89, 212; fixation of, 656; in nutrient molecules, 129, 130, 131, 132

carbon cycle, protists and, 513

carbon dioxide, 89, 226, 240; as by-product of metabolism, 212; as waste product of cellular respiration, 58, 500, 657; as waste product of fermentation, 462, 474, 658; carried by blood, 183, 184, 193, 242, 259; combined with hydrogen to produce glucose, 656; dissolved in water of extracellular fluid, 639; excreted by lungs, 215; for chemosynthesis, 534; for photosynthesis, 405, 407, 408, 534, 618, 630, 655; in breathing, 86, 87, 88, 91, 97; output of, 88, 91, 97, 106–7, 115, 117, 120, 121, 639; role of in plant growth, 435; transfer of in gas exchange, 96, 97, 104–5, 117; transport of, 174

carbon monoxide, 109, 193

carcinoma, 579

cardiac sphincter, 143, 144

cardiac subsystem, 186–7, 190

cardiovascular health, 202–4

cardiovascular system, 202–4, 205; of whales, 108

Carnivora, 71–2; features of, 71–2

carnivores, 19, 71–2; aquatic, 511; digestive system of, 157, 158

carotenoids, 511

carriers, identification of, 760, 765; of disease, 361, 516; of gene, 739, 747; of

374; of micro-organisms, 482; of plants, 374; of red maple, 382
cleavage, 353
cleavage furrow, 680
climate, of biome, 408, 409
cloaca, 334, 335
clones, 443
cloning, in plant breeding, 443
Clostridium botulinum, 536
Clostridium tetani, 537
club fungi, 375, 462–4
club mosses, 381, 420
clumping, of blood cells, 179–80, 751
Cnidaria, (phylum), 75
cnidarians, 75, 77, 198; nerve net of, 240
cocaine, 272–3
coccyx, fused bones in, 286
codeine, 273
co-dominance, 751
coelacanths, 312
coelenterates, 246
co-enzymes, 135
cohesion, of water molecules, 412
cold-blooded vertebrates, 116, 117, 313
cold sores, 361, 562
Cole, Harriet, 45
coliform counts, 543
collagen, fibrous nature of, 303; in bones, 303; in cartilage, 284, 303; in ligaments, 286; in tendons, 289
collecting duct, of nephron, 221, 222
colon, *see* large intestine
colonial organisms, 482, 484
colonies, 485
colour blindness, 744, 747–8
coma, 268, 271
commensalism, 513, 535
common cold, 558, 562
common duct, 144, 145
compact bone, 284
companion cells, of sieve tube cells, 391
complete protein, 134
compound microscope, 8–11, 46, 53, 60, 604, 673, 692
concentration, 640, 642; of solution, 58, 499, 501, 613, 639, 644–5, 646, 647
concentration gradient, 211, 649, 650
conception, 681, 684
conclusions, from experiments, 707
condom, 357, 359, 361, 362
conductors, two-way, 240
cones, in sexual reproduction, 422; of gymnosperms, 382
coniferous forests, 409
conifers, 382, 420; as hosts for bracket fungi, 454; life cycle of, 422
conjugation, in bacteria, 526, 529, 530; in fungi, 376, 458; in paramecia, 506

conjugation fungi, 458, 459
connective tissue, disorders and diseases of, 310, 579; function of, 303; in ligaments, 286; in tendons, 289; structure of, 303
consumers, *see* heterotrophs
contraception, 356–9; methods of, 357–8, 359
contractile vacuole, 496, 501, 505, 526, 619; homeostatic function of, 619
contrasting traits, 708, 725, 730; in pea plants, 704–5, 706, 707, 710
control, in an experiment, 51
convex lenses, 6, 8
co-ordination, fine motor, 302; muscular, 248, 250, 302; of nervous control and chemical regulation, 255–66
copulation, 328, 334, 339
corals, 75
cork, 402
cork cambium, of root, 397; of stem, 402
corms, 402
corn, as crop, 463, 464; as monocot plant, 428; seeds, 428, 432, 433
corn smut, 464, 472
coronary arteries, 187, 202
coronary veins, 187
corpus luteum, 349, 350
cortex, adrenal, 265; cerebral, 250, 273; of maturation region of root, 396
corticoid hormones, 265
cortisone, 310
Corynebacterium diphtheriae, 538
cotyledon, 428, 432
coughing, 107, 109, 111, 112
courtship behaviour, 334, 336, 339
Cowper's glands, 348
cowpox, 571, 580
cranial nerve, 250, 251, 255
crenation, 644, 647, 658
Crick, Francis, 596
cristae, 617
crossbreeding, 706, 708, 710, 714, 715, 727–9; and hybrid vigour, 728; in animals, 724, 725–6, 728, 729; in plants, 706, 708, 710, 715, 724, 727–8, 730; interspecies, 728–9
crossing over, 690, 691, 698
cross-pollination, 425; induced in pea plants by Mendel, 705, 706
Crustacea, 76
cuticle, function of, 390; of plants, 390, 400, 406–7
cutin, 390
cuttings, as application of asexual reproduction, 442; of plants, 439, 683
cyanobacteria, 485–6, 487; ecological importance of, 486

cystic fibrosis, 760
cysts, in kidney, 231; of amoeba, 506–7, 516, 526
cytokinesis, 59, 673, 678, 680, 687; after Meiosis II, 693; after mitosis, 678–80; in Interphase II, 692
cytokinins, 437
cytology, 604, 611
cytoplasm, 56, 390, 599, 629, 644, 652; and cell division, 505, 670, 673, 674, 678, 680, 687, 693; and cellular respiration, 656; function of, 57, 59, 614; in bacteria cells, 527, 528, 533, 548, 560; in eukaryotic cells, 482; in fungal cells, 375, 451, 454; in phloem tissue, 391; in protist cells, 496, 500, 501, 502, 506; ions in, 243; microfilaments in, 621; oxygen in, 642; structure of, 613–14; waste products in, 210
cytoplasmic inheritance, 719
cytoplasmic organelles, 613–14, 615
cytoplasmic streaming, 172, 500, 621
cytosine, 596
cytosine nucleotide, in DNA, 596–7, 598; in RNA, 599
cytoskeleton, 621

dairy cattle, 544
dandelions, 465
dark reactions, 655
data, analysis of in Mendel's experiments, 706, 708–9, 722; numerical, 709, 722
deamination, 212, 217, 226
death rate, 356
decay, bacteria as agents of, 534; fungi as agents of, 454, 459
deciduous trees, 408, 414
decomposers, 19, 74, 376; beneficial, 471, 536; fungi as, 19, 376, 454, 459, 471; harmful, 472, 536; obligate anaerobes as, 536
defecation, 223; *see also* elimination
deforestation, 372
dehydration, 170, 221; as means of destroying bacteria, 647; caused by burns, 304; of trees, 391; prevention of, 216, 226, 230, 233, 298, 313, 406, 628
dendrites, of neuron, 241, 242, 244, 249
dentine, 312
deoxygenated blood, 184, 193
deoxyribonucleic acid, *see* DNA
deoxyribose sugar, 596, 597, 598
dependence, on drugs, 273
depressants, 203, 272–3
dermatomyositis, 310
dermis, 296, 298, 303

hereditary information, 559, 561; exchange of, 505, 506, 690; in HIV retrovirus, 573; *see also* DNA; DNA code; genes

heredity, 704–5, 709, 725; experiments concerning, 706–11, 716, 718, 720, 722–3, 730; human, 738, 753; *see also* multiple-gene inheritance; sex-linked inheritance; sex-related inheritance; single-gene inheritance; two-gene inheritance

hermaphrodites, 324, 328

heroin, 273, 274

herpes genitalis, 361

Hershey, Alfred, 596

heterosexuals, and AIDS, 556

heterotrophs, 18, 20, 68, 70, 81, 152, 157, 408, 520; aquatic, 513, 520; bacteria as, 526, 534; classification of, 19; euglenas as, 501; fungi as, 375, 451, 454, 471; protists as, 509, 510, 526, 619; zooflagellates as, 519

heterozygous carriers, 757

heterozygous dominant phenotype, 739

heterozygous genotype, 714, 724, 729, 751

HGH, *see* human growth hormone

hiatus hernia, 146

high blood pressure, 194, 203, 204, 231

hindbrain, 247; function of, 248; in humans, 250; structure of, 248

histidine, 134

HIV, (human immunodeficiency virus), 262, 559, 562, 563, 573–6, 577; genes of, 573, 576; linked to cancer, 580; protein coat of, 574; spread of by sexual contact, 577–8; structure of, 573; testing for, 578–9

homeostasis, 38, 97, 106, 188, 195, 205, 501; and burns, 304–5; and kidneys, 222–4; and life functions, 36, 57; and nervous control, 258–60; explained, 36; in cell, 638–9, 659; maintained through excretion, 210, 212, 213, 230, 232; role of skin in maintaining, 297–8, 313–14

homoiothermic animals, 72, 73, 298, 313, 639

homologous chromosomes, 686–7, 689, 691, 698, 714, 742, 750–1, 753, 755

homologous structures, 314–15

homosexuals, not the only people with AIDS, 555, 556

homozygous dominant phenotype, 739

homozygous genotype, 714, 724, 729, 751

homozygous recessive phenotype, 739, 757

Hooke, Robert, 9, 34, 53, 54

hormonal cycles, 699; *see* also menstrual cycle; ovulation cycle

hormones, 574, 616, 765; and contraception, 357, 358; and excretion, 223–4, 232, 233; and reproductive system, 347, 350, 354, 363; as growth regulators in plants, 436–7, 443; as proteins, 133–4, 560, 594, 596, 629, 755; as signals from macrophages, 569; control of ovulation cycle by, 20; digestive, 142, 152, 154, 157, 174, 195; in animals, 260, 262, 263, 264; in plants, 260, 264, 436–7, 442

hormone therapy, 271, 272, 308, 360, 363, 765

horsetails, 381, 420; fossils of, 381

host, of a parasite, 454, 462, 463, 464, 535, 537

host cell, to virus, 560–4, 565–6, 569, 580

human chorionic gonadotropin, 213

human genome, 764, 767

human growth hormone, 133, 263, 265, 269, 271, 272

human immunodeficiency virus, *see* HIV

human papilloma virus, (HPV), 562, 580, 581

hummingbirds, role of in pollination, 425

hunter-gatherers, 4, 22

hunting, 71–2, 314

Huntington disease, 758

hybridization, *see* crossbreeding

hybrids, 426, 706, 708, 710–11, 714, 727, 728, 730

hybrid vigour, 728

hydra, 75, 154, 198; nerve net of, 240; reproduction in, 322, 324, 697

hydrocarbons, 514

hydrochloric acid, 143–4, 153

hydrogen, atoms, 89, 655; in air, 408; in nutrient molecules, 129, 131; produced by photosynthesis, 655, 656

hydrogen sulphide, 109, 536; as raw material for bacterial photosynthesis, 533, 534

hyperthyroidism, 270

hypertonic solution, 644–5, 646

hyphae, 451, 452, 457–8; and food source, 454, 457–8; of bread mould, 457–8; of imperfect fungi, 466; of sac fungi, 460, 462

hypocotyl, 428, 432, 433

hypoglossal nerve, 251

hypothalamus, 248, 250, 263, 264

hypothesis, in scientific method, 47–9, 50, 51

hypothyroidism, 270

hypotonic solutions, 644, 646

ileum, 144, 145

immune cells, 568, 569, 578; attacked by HIV, 573

immune response, 574; disabled by HIV, 574, 575; triggered by vaccine, 571

immune system, 177, 310, 564, 567, 568–71; and organ rejection, 231; assisted by lysosomes, 620; attacked by AIDS, 555–6, 567; deficiency of, 362; failure to recognize HIV as an invader, 574, 578; in latency period, 574, 575–6; not stimulated by retroviral DNA, 563; suppressed, 581

immunity, 540, 566

immunization, 541, 582

immunoglobulins, 174, 177

imperfect flowers, 424, 425

imperfect fungi, 466, 473

impetigo, 309

implantation, of zygote, 345, 353, 358, 360, 364; prevention of, 356–8

impotence, 360, 361

impulses, nervous, 240, 242, 244, 246, 251, 258

inbreeding, 726–7, 728, 730, 739

inbreeding depression, 727

incisors, 142

incomplete dominance, 724

incomplete protein, 134

incubation, 335

incubation period, 565–6

independent assortment, 723

infections, 175, 268, 356, 361–2; bacterial, 304, 359, 360, 362, 537–41, 542; fought by immune cells, 568–71; in AIDS patients, 574; microbial, 304; of kidney, 231; of muscles, 308; viral, 308, 313, 561, 562, 564, 565–6, 580, 582, *see also* HIV; water borne, 313

inferior vena cava, 193

infertility, (human reproductive), 359, 360, 361; treatment of, 363–4

inflammation, 308, 309; of brain, 268; of muscles, 310; of skin, 310

influenza virus, 111–12, 564–5; mutation of, 112, 556

ingestion, in pinocytosis, 652; of chemicals, 272–3; of food, 142, 157, 163

inhalation, *see* inspiration

inheritance, *see* heredity; multiple-gene inheritance; sex-linked inheritance; sex-related inheritance; single-gene inheritance; two-gene inheritance

inheritance patterns, 738, 739–41 742, 743–5, 746–8, 750, 751–2

inherited variability, 39–40, 697–8; example of, 39; in plants, 443; in protists, 506

mitotic cell division, 59, 483, 683, 696; in animals, 679–80, 697; in host cell of retrovirus, 563; in plants, 673–9, 697; need for, 681, 683; outcome of, 680

models, of cell membrane, 613; of DNA, 597, 598; use of, 626

molars, 142

moles, as skin blemishes, 297

Mollusca, 121, 316

mollusks, 323, 328

Monera, 374, 482, 484

monerans, as food for dinoflagellates, 510; characteristics of, 484–5; classification of, 485; groups, 487; interaction of with biosphere, 513; reproduction in, 331

monocots, 399, 400, 402, 428; development of from seeds, 433

monocytes, 177, 568–9; transformed into macrophages, 569

monohybrid cross, 718, 720, 722

mononucleosis, 562, 581

monosaccharides, 129, 130, 150, 153

monotreme reproduction, 342

morphine, 273, 274

morula, 353

mosquito, as host of malaria parasite, 517, 518

mosses, 379–80, 409

motility, 70, 75, 77, 374

motor co-ordination disorders, related to AIDS, 577

motor nerves, 243, 251, 253, 255, 268

moulds, 312, 451–2, 456–9, 466, 467, 468; spores of, 109, 457–8, 459, 468

mouth, in digestion, 142–3, 150, 151, 153, 163, 251

movement, 282, 284; and biophysics, 292–3; involuntary, 289; of joints, 286–7; voluntary, 289, 292; *see also* locomotion

mRNA, 561, 562

MSH, *see* melanocyte stimulating hormone

mucus, as defence, 539, 564; function of, 93, 95, 102, 109, 312, 313, 539; in digestion, 142, 143–4, 152

multicellular organisms, 70, 172, 374, 378, 379, 482, 673, 683, 697; and viruses, 564; fungi as, 450

multiple-allele inheritance, 751

multiple fruit, 429

multiple-gene inheritance, 730, 731, 753, 755

multiple sclerosis, 268, 269

multisystemic disorders, 310

Musci, 379–80

muscle fatigue, 89

muscles, 95, 115, 116, 203, 289–90, 292, 296; acidity of, 89, 90; and diet, 135, 136; and exercise, 305; attachment of,

284, 289, 315, 316; antagonistic pairs of, 289–90; blood supply of, 108; cardiac, 289, 302; cells in, 88, 287, 302, 620–1, 658–9; contractions, 265, 284, 287, 289, 302, 313, 314, 316, 348, 620–1, 627; co-ordination of, 248, 250; development of, 348; diseases, disorders, and dysfunctions of, 267, 268, 269, 307, 308, 310; effector, 253; effects of space travel on, 294; function of, 293; growth of, 263, 265; health of, 305; heart, 186, 187, 191, 202, 203, 259, 260, 273, 617, 627; in arterial walls, 182; in planarian, 240; insertion of, 289; involuntary, 289; in whales, 108; movement of, 284; nervous control of, 243, 244; of chest, 96, 98, 99, 258; of face, 251; of intestine, 144; of stomach, 143; origin of, 289; overuse of, 306, 308, 309; relaxation of, 273, 284, 287, 289; skeletal, 183, 203, 289, 302, 310; smooth, 265, 289; sphincter, 143, 144, 146, 218; storage of glycogen in, 130; tissue of, 302

muscular dystrophy, Duchenne, 308, 758

musculoskeletal system, connective tissue in, 303; disorders of, 307–10; human, 287, 291, 292; injury to, 306; invertebrate, 314–15; vertebrate, 315–316

mushrooms, 372–3, 375, 450–2, 454, 456 463, 471; life cycle of, 462; poisonous, 473

mutation, 443; of HIV-1 to HIV-2, 579; of viruses, 112, 556, 579

mutualism, 467, 513; of bacteria, 535

myasthenia gravis, 308

mycelium, 373–2, 375, 451, 452, 454, 457, 474; of bread mould, 457, 458, 459; of club fungi, 462; of sac fungi, 460, 462; of water mould, 459; of wheat rust, 563

Mycobacterium tuberculosis, 536

mycology, 456

mycoplasmas, 487, 599

myelin sheath, 241–2, 249, 268, 269

myofibrils, 302

myoglobin, 108

myosin, 302

myxobacteria, 487

Narang, Saran, 733

nasal hairs, 93, 109; function of, 102, 115

nasal passages, 538, 539; lining of, 539

nastic movements, of plants, 438–9

neck, arteries of, 259; human, 250, 251; lymph nodes in, 568; muscles in, 253; nervous control of, 250, 251

nectar, 425

negative feedback, 260

negative ions, 243–4

negative tropism, 437

Nematoda, 74

neon gas, 408

nephrons, 219, 223, 233; function of, 221–2; structure of, 220–1

nerve cells, *see* neurons

nerve cluster, of planarian, 240

nerve cord, of animals, 245; of annelids, 74; of arthropods, 76; of planarians, 240; of vertebrates, 77, 245–6

nerve endings, in skin, 296, 297; lacking in scar tissue, 304; of planarians, 240

nerve fibres, 106, 249

nerve impulses, 240, 243–4, 246, 250, 262

nerve net, of cnidarian, 240

nerves, 240, 255; longitudinal, 241; transverse, 241

nervous control, and chemical regulation, 255–66; and homeostasis, 258–60; in animals, 240–4; in humans, 249–53

nervous system, 154, 223, 246; affected by African sleeping sickness, 519; affected by poisonous mushrooms, 473; and diet, 135, 136; disorders of, 240, 268–9; human, 255–7, 258–60; interaction with musculoskeletal system, 287, 302; of cnidarians, 240; of planarians, 240–1; of vertebrates, 245–8

neurons, 154, 262, 269, 566, 621; function of, 243–4, 276; ions in, 243–4; in brain, 249, 268; in heart, 195; polarization of, 244; structure of, 243

neurotoxins, 536, 537, 658

neurotransmitters, 244, 273–4

neutrophils, 177

niacin, 135

nicotine, 204, 273; effects of on embryo, 354

nitrogen, 375; as nutrient, 128, 132, 212; as waste, 212, 226, 227, 231; compounds in air, 408, 535; in amino acids, 217, 226; in blood, 108; in urine, 212

nitrogen-fixing bacteria, 535

nitrous oxide, 109

nonvascular plants, 378, 379

noradrenaline, 256

nose, 93, 142, 251; cartilage in, 284, 303; function of, 93; structure of, 39

nostrils, 115

notochord, 73, 77

nuclear envelope, *see* nuclear membrane

nuclear membrane, 376, 482–3, 599, 614, 674, 676, 678, 680, 690–2; pores of, 599, 614

sporozoans, 517; in terrestrial vertebrates, 334-6; in unicellular organisms, 669, 696-7; in vascular plants, 379-82, 420-9; in vertebrates, 332-8; *see also* asexual reproduction; sexual reproduction
reproductive cell, 379; *see also* egg; gametes; germinal cells; sex cells; sperm
reproductive patterns, application of, 344-5, 347
reproductive system, human, 244; disorders of, 359-63, 365; female, 338, 348, 349, 353, 358; male, 347-8, 358; structures, 338, 347-50
reproductive technology, 364
reproductive tract, 328, 348, 361
reptiles, aquatic, 117; brain of, 248; excretion in, 212, 226, 227; gas-exchange systems in, 116; integumentary system in, 313; reproduction in, 334-5, 336
Reptilia, 72, 80
research, in genetics, 765-7; into AIDS, 554, 555, 556-9, 573, 575, 576, 581, 582; into viral diseases, 582
residual volume, 98, 103
resolving power, of microscope, 604
respiration, 100, 308, *see also* cellular respiration; external *see* breathing; internal *see* gas exchange
respiratory system, 90, 91-107, 108; disorders of, 111-13; functions of, 102-7; human, 210; infections of, 562, 564; inflammations of, 109; passages of, 93, 565
responses, "all or nothing," 302; "fight or flight," 256, 265-6; reflex, 251-2, 255, 268, 289; in plants to stimuli, 437-9; in protists to stimuli, 496; to impulses, 240, 243, 252-3
resuscitation, 99, 103
retroviruses, 563, 564, 573, 574, 581
reverse transcriptase, 563, 573, 574
rheumatoid arthritis, 308
Rh incompatibility, 179-80, 181
Rhinovirus, 558, 562
Rhizobium, 535
rhizomes, 403
Rhizopus, (bread mould), 457-8, 459
Rhodophyta, (division), 377
rhodophytes, 377, 378-9
rhythm method, of contraception, 357
rib cage, 96, 217; function of, 282
riboflavin, 135
ribonucleic acid, *see* RNA
ribose sugar, 599
ribosomes, 561-2, 563, 599, 616, 674; function of, 615, 629; of bacteria, 527, 532; structure of, 615

ribs, 96, 258, 284
rickettsia, 487
right cerebral hemisphere, 250
right heart, 184, 187, 190
ring records, of trees, 401
ringworm, 466, 473
RNA, 561; characteristics of, 599; formation of copies of DNA code by, 599; of virus, 561, 562, 563, 573, 574
RNA retroviruses, 563, 564, 566, 573, 574
RNA triplets, 599
RNA viruses, 561, 562, 563, 564
rock, breakdown of by lichens, 466-7; formed from deposits of dead protists, 496
root cap, 394
root hairs, 390, 395, 405, 432; function of, 390
root pressure, 412
roots, 387, 391, 392, 393-7; adaptations of, 397, 441; and anchorage of plants, 392, 394; and negative tropism, 437-8; effect of hormones on, 437; epidermal tissue in, 390; formation of, 429, 432; from stolon, 402; function of, 392, 396-7; growth of, 394-5; of vascular plants, 380, 381; nodules in legume plants, 535; parenchyma tissue in, 389; schlerenchyma tissue in, 390; storage in, 389, 392, 397, 399; structure of, 396-7; types of, 394; vascular tissue in, 395, 406
root tips, 387, 433, 436, 617
roughage, in diet, 131
roundworm, 74, 164, 323
rubella, 540
rubella virus, 562; vaccine for, 540
rubeola virus, 562
rusts, (fungi), 375, 450, 454, 463-4, 472

sac fungi, 460-1
sacrum, 286
safety, in laboratory techniques, 228
saliva, 94, 142, 566
salivary glands, 142, 149, 150, 153; of mosquito, 518
salivation, 251, 255; excessive, 566
salts, 222; dissolved in water of extracellular fluid, 639; excretion of, 212; in sweat, 216, 298; in urine, 213, 222, 224, 233; *see also* sodium
sanitation, 356, 542
sap, 401; rising in tree, 414
Saprolegnia, 459
saprophytes, 454, 471, 534, 536
sapwood, 401
Sarcodina, (phylum), 484, 494, 513, 516, 517

sarcoma, 579, 580
scanning electron microscope, 608
scar tissue, 174, 304, 308, 681
scent glands, 298, 306
scientific process, 704
sclerenchyma tissue, 390; function of, 390
scrotum, 348, 359, 360
sea anemones, 75; nervous response in, 240; regeneration in, 322
seasonal mating, 332, 333, 336
sebaceous glands, 298, 306, 310
secondary roots, 394
secondary sexual characteristics, female, 349; male, 347-8, 744
second filial generation, (F_2), 708, 709, 710, 721, 722, 724, 728, 730, 739
secretions, 153, 255, 264, 348, 352, 577; in kidney, 221, 222; of digestive juices, 102, 144-5, 149-50, 152, 163, 454, 457, 467, 526; *see also* glands
seed coat, 422, 427, 429, 431, 432, 433
seeds, 388, 436, 441; characteristics of, in pea plants, 704-5, 731; dispersal of, 422, 423, 427, 431; food storage in, 408; function of, 429; hybrid, 711; in Mendel's experiments, 706, 708, 710, 720; of conifers, 422; of flowering plants, 382, 423, 427; of trees, 382; structure of, 428-9
segregation, 715, 722; of alleles, 714, 715, 728
selective breeding, 337, 344-5, 347, 720, 726-7
selective permeability, 612, 640-1
self-fertilization, 423
self-pollination, 423; in hybrids, 711, 720; of pea plants, 705, 708
semen, 324, 334, 344, 347, 357, 359, 557
semilunar valves, 191
seminal fluid, 324, 348
seminiferous tubules, 265, 348
senses, 71-2, 248, 251
sensitivity, of bacteria, 526; of protists, 526
sensory nerves, 243, 251-2, 255, 273
sensory receptors, 244; in skin, 296, 297, 309; lacking in scar tissue, 304; of planarian, 240
septum, of heart, 190
sessility, 70, 75, 77, 374, 375
sewage, 119, 122; as contaminant of drinking water, 542
sex cells, 323, 684, 685, 686, 687, 697; chromosome count in, 684-5, 691; haploid, 691, 698; *see also* gametes; egg; sperm
sex chromosomes, 742, 743, 746, 750
sex hormones, 265, 310, 345, 347-8, 349, 354

sex-linked inheritance, 744–8, 749, 755, 758–60
sex-related inheritance, 742–50
sexual behaviour, and AIDS, 577
sexual dimorphism, 323
sexual intercourse, 348, 357, 361
sexual maturity, 336, 338
sexual reproduction, 323–30, 331–2, 382, 683, 685, 691, 697–8, 699; advantage of, 698–9; disadvantage of, 699; in amoebas, 505; in animals, 323–30, 331; in bacteria, 529–30, in dinoflagellates, 510; in fungi, 375, 376, 451, 452, 456, 457–8, 460, 462; in nonvascular plants, 379–80; in paramecia, 505, 506; in protists, 483, 511; in slime moulds, 468; in true fungi, 456, 457, 460, 462; in vascular plants, 380–2, 420–9, 451
sexually transmitted diseases, (STD), 361–2, 363, 581, 537
shells, 316, 511, 514; of eggs, 335; of foraminifers, 513
shivering, function of, 302
shock, 195, 360; as result of burns, 304
shoots, of plants, 388, 428, 436
shorthorn cattle, incomplete dominance in, 724
sickle-cell anemia, 757; carriers of, 760
sieve plates, 391
sieve tubes, 391, 413; companion cells of, 391
sight, sense of, 251
silage, 544
silica, 511, 514
silicon, (element), 511
similarity, of species, 70, 71
simple cell division, 485
simple fruit, 429
single-gene inheritance, 730, 731; in humans, 738–42, 753
sinoatrial node, 195
skeletal system, human, 282–7, 292; function of, 282–5; interaction of with other systems, 287; see also musculoskeletal system
skeleton, growth of, 263, 271; human, 283, 284, 289; of coral, 75; of diatom, 514; of embryo, 284; of vertebrate, 77, 314
skin, 134, 135, 295, 295, 300, 301, 303; accessory structures of, 295, 296, 298–9, 312, 313–14; as barrier to bacteria and viruses, 538, 567, 569; as tissue, 301; blood vessels in, 265; cancer of, 307; care of, 306–7; colour of, 297; damage to, 297, 304; diseases and disorders of, 307, 309–10, 361, 466; function of, 216, 295, 297, 298; health of, 305; human,

295–99; melanin in, 265, 297; of amphibians, 313; of fish, 312; of reptiles, 313; receptors in, 242, 255, 256, 296, 297, 304; role of in homeostasis, 297, 313–14
skin replacement technology, 300
skull, function of, 282, 284; human, 247, 285, 286; of baby, 276; of vertebrate, 245
sleep, 272
sleeping sickness, 513, 519
slime capsule, 526
slime moulds, 467, 471
small intestine, 144–5, 146, 147, 150, 151, 153, 203; see also intestine
smallpox, 571
smell, sense of, 71–2, 251
smoke, industrial, 109
smoking, 112, 113, 203–4, 273, 354
smuts, fungi, 375, 463, 464, 472
snapdragon plants, incomplete dominance in, 724
sodium, 136, 221; dissolved in sweat, 216; dissolved in urine, 212, 232, in blood, 271; see also salts
sodium bicarbonate, 145, 246
sodium chloride, 216, 246, 639
sodium hydroxide, 541
sodium iodide, 263
sodium ions, 243–4, 246, 650
soil, converted from rock by lichens, 468–9; erosion of, 394; fertility of, 471; water in, 390, 432
solutes, in cerebrospinal fluid, 246; in kidney, 219, 221, 223; in urine, 232; in water of extracellular fluid, 639; transport across cell membrane, 640, 642
solutions, 644–5; concentration of, 639, 642
somatic nervous system, 255
space travel, effects on bone, 306; effects on muscles, 294
species, 323, 324, 325, 327; motile, 70, 75, 77; sessile, 70, 75, 77; survival of, 322, 332, 506, 698–9
specimens, techniques for preparation, 608–9
sperm, 323, 336, 356, 357, 359; chromosomes of, 684, 686, 693, 698, 744; defective, 363; from gametophyte, 380, 381, 421; fusion with egg, 325, 327, 353, 681; in pollen grains, 382, 422; locomotion of, 324, 333, 334, 352; nucleus of, 427; production of, 265, 326, 348, 359, 360, 363; structure of, 628
sperm banks, 364
sperm duct, 363
spermicides, 357

Sphenopsida, (subdivision), 380, 381
sphincter, 143, 144, 146; of bladder, 218, 348
sphygmomanometer, 194
spinal cord, function of, 251–2, 253; human, 250, 251, 252, 255; injury to, 268–9, 270; interneurons in, 243; of vertebrates, 245–6; protection of, 282, 284; structure of, 250–1
spinal nerves, 250, 255
spindle, in meiosis, 691, 692; in mitosis, 674, 679
spindle fibres, in meiosis, 690, 691, 692; in mitosis, 674, 677, 679
spine, flexibility of, 284; of vertebrates, 245, 246, 269
Spirochetes, 487
spleen, 569
splicing, of genes in DNA, 563, 574, 765, 766
sponges, 73, 120, 121, 198; digestion in, 163, 164; life cycle of, 331
spongy bone, 284
spore-bearing plants, 420–1
spore cases, of bread-mould fungus, 458
spores, 109, 420; asexual, 452, 458, 460; motile, 459; of bacteria, 526, 532, 533, 536, 537; of bread mould fungus, 457, 458, 459; of club mosses, 381, 420; of horsetails, 381, 420; of fungi, 451, 458, 462, 466, 468, 473, 474; of mosses, 379, 380; of sac fungi, 460; of slime moulds, 468; of sporozoans, 517; of true ferns, 382, 420–1; of water fungi, 459; of wheat rust, 463; of whisk ferns, 381, 420; sexual, 375, 376, 452, 457, 460, 466
sporophytes, 380, 381, 382, 420, 421; trees as, 422
Sporozoa, 484, 517–18
sports, injuries in, 306, 309
sprains, 306
spruce trees, black, 409; white, 409
squirrels, as agents in seed dispersal, 431
stamen, 423
Stanley, Wendell M., 489
starches, 129, 131, 142; as stored energy, 128, 376, 630; converted from glucose by plants, 130, 656; digestion of 149, 150, 153; stored in parenchyma tissue, 389, 396; stored in rhizomes, 403
starfish, 75, 164; nerve net of, 240; reproduction in, 697
starvation, 138
stems, 391, 397, 399–403, 429, 436, 646; adaptations of, 402–3, 441; and adventitious roots, 397; and photosynthesis, 399, 406; asexual

PHOTO CREDITS

Abbreviations: r-right, l-left, t-top, b-bottom, c-centre
IMS — IMS Creative Communications, University of Toronto
ISTC — Industry, Science & Technology Canada, Ottawa
MTLB — Picture Collection, Metropolitan Toronto Library Board
OMAF — Ontario Ministry of Agriculture and Food, Guelph.
OME — Ontario Ministry of Education, Toronto
OMNR — Ontario Ministry of Natural Resources, Toronto

Cover Photo   The Stock Market

UNIT I The Study of Life

1: Werner Braun/Canapress. 2: The Bettmann Archive. 4: (t) NASA; (b) Thom Henley. 5: (tr) MTLB; (bl) D'Lynn Waldron/The Image Bank Canada; (bc) S. Achernar/The Image Bank Canada; (br) National Library of Medicine. 6: Birgitte Nielsen. 9: (bl) The Science Museum, London. 10: (t) Rudolf Freund/Wellcome Historical Medical Museum. 11: Walter Dawn/Photo Researchers. 12: (t) Bill Ivy; (b) Fox Photos/Canapress. 13,14: MTLB. 15: Wards Natural Science Establishment Inc. 17: (t) V. Wilkinson/Valan Photos; (bl) Larry Miller; (bc) J.R. Page/Valan Photos; (br) Richard Harington/Canapress. 21: Russ Kinne/Educational Images. 22: Canapress. 24: (t) Canapress; (b) E.R. Degginger/Animals, Animals. 32: Birgitte Nielsen. 34:MTLB. 35: (t) Marion Stirrup/Canapress; (b) OMNR. 36: TV Ontario. 37: Art Wolfe/The Image Bank Canada. 39: (l) Lynn M. Stone/The Image Bank Canada; (r) W. Randall/Focus Stock Photo. 40: (tl) Bill Ivy; (tr) J.A. Wilkinson/Valan Photos; (bl & br) Breck P. Kent/Animals, Animals. 45: Dr. Robert Weaver/Hahnemann Medical College and Hospital. 46: (t & bl) Birgitte Nielsen; (br) STEM. 52: MTLB. 60: Dr. Jeremy Burgess/Science Photo Library. 61: Birgitte Nielsen. 63: James Prince/Photo Researchers.
Colour Section   Pond scene: OMNR. Farm scene: OMAF.

UNIT II Animals

67; Stephen Dalton/Photo Researchers. 68: Canapress. 70: Da Rocha Filho Rubens/Image Bank Canada. 71: (l) OMNR; (c) ISTC; (r) Canapress. 72: Bill Ivy. 73: Harold V. Green/Valan Photos. 74: (l) Dr. William C. Marquardt/Educational Images; (r) Mike English/Focus Stock Photo. 75: (t) Birgitte Nielsen; (bl) Ben Cropp/Canapress; (br) W.H. Hodge/Peter Arnold Inc. 76: (both) Bill Ivy. 84: Animals, Animals. 87: Austral/Canapress. 88,89: OME. 90: Bruce Roberts/Photo Researchers. 91: Chris Schwarz/Canapress. 99: (both) IMS. 100: Dr. Peter Hochachka. 102: IMS. 103: Dr. Tony Brain, Science Photo Library/Photo Researchers. 105: (both) IMS. 107: Canapress. 108: World Wildlife Fund. 110: (l) Larry McDougal/Canapress; (r) Canapress. 113: OME. 114: Birgitte Nielsen. 115: (l) Miriam Austerman/Animals, Animals; (r) OMNR. 117: (t) G.I. Bernard/Animals, Animals; (b) OMNR. 119: Ontario Hydro. 120: Dr. Aubrey Crich. 121: Ontario Science Centre. 122: Ontario Ministry of the Environment. 126: Kai Visionworks. 128: OMAF. 131: Birgitte Nielsen. 132: (both) Reproduced with permission. American Heart Association. 134: Birgitte Nielsen. 139: Canapress. 147: Canapress. 148: Birgitte Nielsen. 156: Banting and Best Dept. of Medical Research, University of Toronto. 158: World Wildlife Fund. 160: (b) Bill Ivy. 161: Robert McCaw. 162: Stochl/Canapress. 166: John Skrypnyk/Canapress. 170: Canapress. 173: Canapress. 174: (t) Yoav/Phototake; (b) Grant Heilman/Miller Comstock. 177: Robert Knauft/Photo Researchers. 178: (tl) Biophoto Associates/Photo Researchers; (tr) Nina Lampen/Phototake; (bl) Photo Researchers; (br) Manfred Kage/Peter Arnold Inc. 179: Birgitte Nielsen. 181: IMS. 194: Ed Lettau/Photo Researchers. 196: Canapress. 201: Tony Robertson/University of Toronto Communications. 202: OME. 203: (all) Birgitte Nielsen. 208, 214, 222: IMS. 215: Kidney Foundation of Canada. 226: Hans Dossenbach/Canapress. 228: Immunex Corporation. 229: Photo Researchers. 233, 235: Birgitte Nielsen. 238: Toronto Star/Canapress. 240: Ford Motor Company of Canada. 241: Eric Grave/Photo Researchers. 243: Lewis/Photo Researchers. 250: Canadian Standards Association. 251: IMS. 254: Jim Shea/Canapress. 261: (top three) Bill Ivy; (bl & bc) Bill Ivy; (br) Ralph Reinhold/Animals, Animals. 263: Biophoto Associates/Photo Researchers. 267: UPI/Bettmann Newsphotos. 269: Canapress. 270: IMS. 272: (t) National Archives of Canada, C24981; (b) Canapress. 274: Canapress. 275: Ken Oakes/Canapress. 277: Birgitte Nielsen. 280: Hugh Wesley/Canapress. 282: TV Ontario. 284: (t) Canapress; (b) Harold M. Lambert/Miller Comstock. 285: (both) IMS. 288: Josef Stucker/Canapress. 289: (top two) IMS; (b) Carolina Biological Supply Company. 293: Laurent Rebours/Canapress. 294: NASA. 295: (t) Pat Flatley/Athlete Information Bureau; (b) Hans Pfletschinger/Canapress. 296: Carolina Biological Supply Company. 299: (tl) Canapress; (tr) Dilip Mehta/ISTC; (b) Gordon S. Smith/Photo Researchers. 300: Jacques Nadeau/Canapress. 301: Carolina Biological Supply Company, 302: IMS. 305: John Felstead/Canapress. 311: Birgitte Nielsen. 312: Dr. Aubrey Crich. 313: (t) Carolina Biological Supply Company; (b) OMNR. 316: Hans Pfletschinger/Canapress. 320: Leonardo da Vinci/MTLB. 323: (tl) Carl Roessler/Animals, Animals; (tr) Terence A. Gili/Animals, Animals; (b) Animals, Animals. 324: Don Fawcett/Photo Researchers. 325: (all) Carolina Biological Supply Company. 328: H. Bickle/OMNR. 329: Bates Littlehales/Animals, Animals. 332: Bucky Reeves/Photo Researchers. 333: K.R. Preston-Mafham/Animals. 334: (l) Miriam Austerman/Animals, Animals; (r) OMNR. 336: (t) Bill Ivy; (b) MTLB. 337: World Wildlife Fund. 338: Canapress. 339: Gerard Lacz/Peter Arnold Inc. 344: OMNR. 345: OMAF. 355: Birgitte Nielsen. 363: (l) Julius Schmid/Canapress; (r) IMS/Faculty of Microbiology. 364: Adam Stoltman/Canapress. 365: Cecil H. Fox/Photo Researchers. 366: Canapress.
Colour Section   Walrus: Brian Milne/Animals, Animals. Panda, Tree frog, and Nudibranch: Zig Leszczynski/Animals, Animals. Snake: OMNR. Eagle: Glenn Elison. Whale: Richard Kolar/Animals, Animals. Caterpillar: Patti Murray/Animals, Animals. Moth: Donald Specker/Animals, Animals.

UNIT III Plants and Fungi

371: Derek Bullard. 372: Paul D. Kroeger. 374: (l) Herman H. Giethoorn/Valan Photos; (r) Canapress. 375: (l) OMNR; (r) Agripress/Focus Stock Photo. 376: Trovati/Canapress. 377: (l) Hugh Spencer/Photo Researchers; (r) Bob Mansour. 378: Alan Wilkinson/Valan Photos. 379: (both) Carolina Biological Supply Company. 381: (l) John Allen/Canapress; (r) Dr. Charles R. Belinky/Educational Images. 382: Bill Ivy. 383: OMNR. 386: Davis/The Globe and Mail. 392: (l) Joseph R. Pearce/Valan Photos; (r) Birgitte Nielsen. 393: International Development and Research Canada. 397: (t) Birgitte Nielsen; (b) Grant Heilman Photography. 398: Dave McLaughlin/Ontario Ministry of the Environment. 399: (t) Brian Kent/Canapress; (b) Birgitte Nielsen. 400: (t) Grant Heilman Photography; (b) OMAF. 401: Hugh Spencer/Photo Researchers. 402: (t) Howard Livick/Canapress; (b) Grant Heilman Photography; 403, 405: Grant Heilman Photography. 404: (both) Gary Beechey/Abitibi-Price Inc. 406: (t) V. Wilkinson/Valan Photos; (b) Robert McCaw. 407: (both) Runk & Schoenberger/Grant Heilman Photography. 408: (t) Ed Reschke/Peter Arnold Inc; (b) OMNR. 409: (tl) TV Ontario; (tc) Don McPhee/Valan; (tr) Pam Hickman/Valan Photos; (b) OMNR. 410: Birgitte Nielsen. 415: OMAF. 418: Pierre Charot/Valan Photos. 425: Wayne Lankinen/Valan Photos. 426: (tl & tc) Bill Ivy; (tr) OMNR; (b-all) Carolina Biological